TERRORISM AND COUNTERTERRORISM

UNDERSTANDING THE
NEW SECURITY ENVIRONMENT

READINGS & INTERPRETATIONS

About the Authors

Colonel Russ Howard, a career Special Forces officer, is now a professor and department head at the United States Military Academy. As a Special Forces officer, Colonel Howard served at every level of command, including: A Detachment Commander in the 7th Special Forces Group to Group, B Detachment Commander in the 1st Special Forces Group, Battalion Commander in the Special Warfare Center and School, and Commander of the 1st Special Forces Group. In preparation for his academic position, Colonel Howard earned degrees from San Jose State University, the University of Maryland, the Monterey Institute of International Studies, and Harvard University. Presently, he is finishing a Ph.D. in international security studies at the Fletcher School of Law and Diplomacy. During the course of his career Colonel Howard has had antiterror and counterterror responsibilities, and has taught and published articles on terrorism subjects.

Captain Reid Sawyer, a career Military Intelligence officer, is an instructor of political science at the United States Military Academy. As an Intelligence officer, Captain Sawyer served in counter-narcotics and special operations assignments. Captain Sawyer earned his undergraduate degree from the United States Military Academy and holds a masters degree from Columbia University. Captain Sawyer has lectured on terrorism to various groups and is currently working on a research project for the Institute of National Security Studies on the efficacy of counterterrorism measures. Captain Sawyer is the current director of terrorism studies at West Point.

TERRORISM AND COUNTERTERRORISM

UNDERSTANDING THE NEW SECURITY ENVIRONMENT

READINGS & INTERPRETATIONS

RUSSELL D. HOWARD
COLONEL USA

REID L. SAWYER
CAPTAIN USA

FOREWORD BY
BARRY R. McCAFFREY
GENERAL USA (RET.)

The **McGraw-Hill** Companies

Book Team

Vice President and Publisher   *Jeffrey L. Hahn*
List Manager   *Theodore Knight*
Director of Production   *Brenda S. Filley*
Director of Technology   *Jonathan Stowe*
Developmental Editor   *Ava Suntoke*
Copy Editor   *Robin N. Charney, Cynthia Goss*
Designer   *Charles Vitelli*
Typesetting Supervisor   *Juliana Arbo*
Typesetting   *Cynthia Powers*
Proofreader   *Diane Barker*
Permissions Editor   *Rose Gleich*

McGraw-Hill/Dushkin

A Division of The *McGraw-Hill* Companies

530 Old Whitfield Street, Guilford, Connecticut 06437

Cover Design *Michael Campbell*

The credit section for this book begins on page 625 and is considered an extension of the copyright page.

Library of Congress Control Number 2002106286

ISBN 0-07-283778-0

Printed in the United States of America

10 9 8 7 6 5 4 3 2 1

http://www.mhhe.com

Visit the Online Learning Center With PowerWeb at

http://www.dushkin.com/terrorism/

Contents in Brief

Contents

Chapter 4   *Religion*   *120*

Chapter 5   *Weapons of Mass Destruction*   *156*

Chapter 6   *The Threat of Other Forms of Terrorism*   *204*

Part II
Countering the Terrorist Threat   272

Foreword

On September 11, 2001, the United States was confronted with the stark reality of modern terrorism. The brutal murder of thousands of innocent lives stripped away our ability to ignore the threat posed by the emergence of transnational terrorist organizations. The terrorism we witnessed on September 11, was a giant escalation of an evolving threat. Prior to these tragic attacks, Americans had witnessed a steadily growing series of violent attacks culminating in more than 5,000 casualties in the terrorist bombings of our East African embassies in 1998. Now the question is not *if* further terrorist attacks will occur in the United States, but *when* and what magnitude. One thing is certain, terrorists will continue to try to adapt to the changing counterterror security environment.

Terrorism, at its very roots, centers on fear and targets our liberal democratic values. The fear generated by terrorism speaks to our vulnerabilities and the government's apparent lack of ability to stop further attacks. The current proliferation of lethal technologies, combined with radical ideologies, potentially presents truly horrific scenarios. We will continue to witness new forms of terrorism, be they viruses that selectively attack target populations or suicide bombers attempting to slaughter our children in our nation's schools. It is imperative for all of us to study and learn about these new threats. We will be driven to understand why terrorism occurs and how best to counter terrorism's driving forces. The goal of this superb collection is to heighten the reader's awareness of the critical issues related to the threat of terrorism. Although it is impossible for any single work to address the entire breadth of the terrorism field, this volume captures the most salient pieces on the subject.

There are many terrorism experts in academia. However, there are only a handful of individuals who combine impressive academic credentials with extensive special operations combat and training experience. The editors of this compilation, Colonel Russ Howard and Captain Reid Sawyer, are two distinguished scholars who have also spent careers on the cutting edge of U.S. military special operations. Their combined experience of over 30 years in the front lines of the struggle to prevent terrorism provides them with a distinct and uniquely informed perspective on the current war on terrorism. Together they have gathered and edited the best works of more than 15 of the leading commentators on terrorism at a critical time in our nation's history.

This superbly researched book also reflects their experience in teaching security-related courses in the Department of Social Sciences at West Point. Colonel Howard and Captain Sawyer have refined their thinking on the topic by their experimentation with the curriculum in these national security courses. We suggest that students of national security polity will find this book to be a unique combination of well-known and astute thinkers who have articulated the current and future policy implications of terrorism. The relevant experience of both Howard and Sawyer as editors places them in the best position to "connect the dots" of this wide-ranging material.

There is much uncertainty about the future. However, we are sure that only through diligent and creative study can America effectively address this very real asymmetrical threat to our national security. We are challenged to develop a conceptual framework to reevaluate the security environment. Clearly we must craft flexible and effective counterterrorism strategies. The policy solutions to this complex threat of terrorism do not lie solely with our military, or even our government. Instead, we must create cooperative efforts to find a national solution to manage the terrorist threat that involves a partnership with the international community combined with an integrated and coherent strategy, which unites community, state, and federal authorities supported by business, the health professions, and academia. We also cannot allow ourselves to become trapped in overly simplistic views of the threat. Our challenge is to dramatically embrace our domestic security while carefully preserving our precious freedoms guaranteed in the Bill of Rights, as well as the safety and dignity of foreigners living among us.

Through the thoughtful study of the definitions, issues, and recommendations provided by these accomplished authors and the editors, we can hopefully move toward a better understanding of terrorism and its causes.

Barry R. McCaffrey

Preface

The haunting image of New York's falling Twin Towers defined the reality of the "new terrorism" for the United States. Americans had faced terrorism before September 11; however, in its previous incarnations, it was not as organized, deadly, or personal as the attacks inflicted that day on New York City and Washington, D.C.

In 1984, when I first became involved in antiterrorism and counterterrorism efforts, most international and national terrorism was ideological. It was part of the East versus West, Left versus Right confrontation—a small but dangerous sideshow to the greater, bipolar, Cold War drama. In the past, terrorism was almost always the province of groups of militants that had the backing of political forces and states hostile to American interests. Under the old rules, "terrorists wanted a lot of people watching, not a lot of people dead."[1] They did not want large body counts because they wanted converts; they also wanted a seat at the table. Today's terrorists are not particularly concerned about converts, and rather than wanting a seat at the table, "they want to destroy the table and everyone sitting at it."[2]

What is new to me and my generation, but not to my coeditor Reid Sawyer and his peers, is the emergence of terrorism that is not ideological in a political sense. Instead it is inspired by religious fundamentalist and ethnic-separatist elements, who might be individuals akin to the Unabomber, or like-minded people working in cells, small groups, or larger coalitions.[3] They do not answer completely to any government; they operate across national borders and have access to funding and advanced technology.[4] Such groups are not bound by the same constraints or motivated by the same goals as nation-states. Unlike state-sponsored groups, religious extremists, ethnic separatists, and lone Unabombers are not susceptible to traditional diplomacy or military deterrence; there is no state to negotiate with or to retaliate against. And today's terrorists are not concerned about limiting casualties. In fact, religious terrorists such as al Qaeda, in particular, want casualties—lots of them.[5]

The new terrorism is not an ideological "ism" like communism or capitalism whose value can be debated in the classroom or decided at polls. Rather, it is an ancient tactic and instrument of conflict. The only difference is that the new terrorism has a global reach that it did not have before the advent of globalization and the information revolution. It can ride on the back of the Web and use advanced communications to move immense financial flows from Sudan to the Philippines, or from Australia to banks in Florida.[6] And for $28.50, any Internet surfer, including terrorists, can purchase the book *Bacteriological Warfare: A Major Threat to North America*, which teaches how to grow deadly bacteria.

The United States and its citizens are clearly favored targets of the "new terrorists," and many wonder why. "Why Do They Hate Us?" was the banner headline in *Newsweek* and the *Christian Science Monitor* soon after 9/11. Why is it that Islamic fundamentalists hate us? After all, was it not America that saved those who follow the Islamic faith in Kuwait and continues to protect them in Bosnia and Kosovo? Is it, as some suggest, *jihad*, a war of faiths between Christians and Muslims? Or, is the United States a target because of the resentment that has spread through societies demoralized by their recent history? "A sense of failure and injustice is rising in the throats of millions," because Arab nations have lost three wars against Israel, their arch-foe and America's ally.[7]

At the same time, many feel that globalization, beyond being a technological tool for terrorists, is either separately or in conjunction with religious fundamentalism a root cause of terrorism. Extreme Muslim fundamentalists and others who have missed its rewards worry that unbridled globalization is exploiting workers and replacing ancient cultures with McDonald's and Mickey Mouse.[8] According to some, globalization is based on the American economic system, and because the United States is the dominant world power, it has succeeded in expanding the reach of its version of globalization to more and more areas of the world. Furthermore, the gap between the rich and poor in most countries has grown wider during the last 20 years of U.S.-led globalization. As a result, animosities, which spawn terrorist acts against America, have grown as the poor have watched American wealth and hegemony expand, while they have received scarcely any benefit.[9]

There are other theories about rising terrorism and future targets, many of which will be covered in this book. One thing is certain, however. America is a target. It has been attacked and will be again, unless the attacks can be prevented (or preempted). Rudolph Giuliani, New York City's former mayor, made this very clear to West Point's graduating class of 2002, when he was the guest speaker at their final dinner banquet. He theorizes that America was attacked because it prizes political and economic freedom, elects its political leaders, and has lifted people out of poverty. He also told the cadets that America was attacked because it has religious freedom and respects human rights and the rights of women. America's adversaries do not, and they are threatened by the freedoms we have. "We are right and they are wrong," Giuliani said to thunderous applause. "There is no excuse and no justification for these attacks," he said. The mayor then told the cadets that "We still have a lot of battles to win, but we have actually won the war on terrorism because the terrorists tried, but could not break our spirit."

This book, edited at West Point, will address these "battles to win": how to fight and win them, and why America and the free world are in the dubious position of having to fight the battles in the first place. Why edit the book at West Point? More importantly, why have two career soldiers edit the book? Brigadier General Dan Kaufman, West Point's Dean, answered these questions in a recent *Los Angeles Times* interview. "Suddenly now the world is a much more dangerous place," he said. "The nation is at risk again. The notion that the American homeland is vulnerable is new to all of us. Given where West Point sits—50 miles from ground zero—there is a sense of immediacy here."[10]

Organization

Terrorism and Counterterrorism: Understanding the New Security Environment, Readings and Interpretations, is organized in two parts. Part I analyzes the philosophical, political, and religious roots of terrorist activities around the world and discusses the national, regional, and global effects of historical and recent terrorist acts. In addition to material on the threats from suicide bombers, as well as chemical, biological, radiological, and nuclear weapons, there are also important contributions that examine new and growing threats: narcoterrorism, cyberterrorism, genomic terrorism, and agroterrorism. Part II considers responses to terrorism.

Part I

Part I contains five chapters. Chapter 1, which consists of articles by Bruce Hoffman, Paul Pillar, and Eqbal Ahmad, defines terrorism and addresses several specific questions, in some cases from very different perspectives: What is terrorism? What is counterterrorism? Who is a terrorist? Who are terrorists? And, why do these questions matter? Hoffman's "Defining Terrorism" emphasizes the changing nature of terrorism. He succinctly defines its past and present, explains its evolution, and predicts where it might be headed in the future. His offering is a "Terrorism 101," an important primer that will prepare the reader for the rest of the book. Like Hoffman, Paul Pillar in his article, "The Dimensions of Terrorism and Counterterrorism," considers what terrorism is and why it is worrisome. As the title suggests, however, Pillar goes further by identifying the necessary elements and limitations of any counterterrorism policy. A CIA veteran, Pillar believes counterterrorism policy should not stand alone but be part of a broader effort to maintain national security and that it needs to be integrated into all foreign policy decision-making. Ahmad's "Terrorism: Theirs and Ours" also emphasizes change. "To begin with," he writes, "terrorists change. The terrorist of yesterday is the hero of today, and the hero of yesterday becomes the terrorist of today." His example is Osama bin Laden, who was once an American ally in the fight against the Soviet Union and is now public enemy number one.

What motivates people to turn to terrorism is covered in chapter 2. Articles by professional colleagues Martha Crenshaw and Louise Richardson look at more than the traditional psychological, cultural, and socioeconomic reasons for terrorism. Addressing terrorism in a greater globalization context in "The Logic of Terrorism: Terrorist Behavior as a Product of Strategic Choice," Crenshaw shows that terrorism is a perfectly rational and logical choice for some individuals and groups: "The central problem is to determine when extremist organizations find terrorism useful....Terrorism is not the only method of working toward radical goals, and thus it must be compared to the alternative strategies available to dissidents."

Louise Richardson's "Global Rebels" also helps the reader distinguish between terrorism and other forms of violence, especially political violence. She also articulates the distinctions between the different types of terrorist-sponsored relationships between terrorists and "Axis of Evil" states.

Chapter 3 explores the rise and impact of the new terrorism in greater depth and then looks at some of the technological and control mechanisms that make today's ethnonationalist terrorists more difficult to detect and defeat than the left-wing and right-wing terrorists of earlier eras. In his second article in this volume, Bruce Hoffman begins the dialogue in "The Modern Terrorist Mindset: Tactics, Targets and Technologies." A RAND analyst and a highly respected self-described terrorist "geek," Hoffman expertly discusses the advantages present-day terrorists have over their counterparts from the sixties through the eighties.

A trio of other RAND specialists, John Arquilla, David Ronfeldt, and Michele Zanini, suggest in "Networks, Netwar, and Information-Age Terrorism" that a new type of enemy and warfare will be the product of the information revolution and the rise of new, more complex forms of terrorism. New systems and organizations and modes of conflict used by modern-day terrorists will inevitably affect the nature and styles of warfare. Using "netwar" and "cyberwar" as weapons, terrorists—a new form of enemy—will attack modern societies' vulnerabilities. Writing primarily to the U.S. Air Force, the RAND specialists recommend that new organizations, strategy, technology, and doctrine will be required to defeat those who perpetrate netwar and cyberwar.

An old saying I learned as a child is, More people have been killed in the name of God than for any other reason. Things have not changed. Indeed the articles in Chapter 4 argue that religious terrorism is on the rise and is unprecedented in its militancy and activism. "Between the mid-1960s and the mid-1990s," writes Magnus Ranstorp, "the number of fundamentalist movements of all religious affiliations tripled worldwide." In his article, "Terrorism in the Name of Religion," Ranstorp explores the reasons for the dramatic increase of religious-motivated terrorism and identifies the causes and enemies that promote violence out of religious belief in both established and newly formed terrorist groups. The post–Cold War security environment figures prominently in his analysis. Mark Juergensmeyer's "Logic of Religious Violence" uses the struggle of the Sikhs in India as a case study to suggest why some religions "propel the faithful rather easily into militant confrontation," while others do not. "The pattern of religious violence of the Sikhs could be that of Irish Catholics, or Shi'ite Muslims in Palestine, or fundamentalist Christian bombers of abortion clinics in the United States." He argues that violence associated with religion is not an aberration but arises from the fundamental beliefs of all major religions.

Chapter 5 explains why weapons of mass destruction (WMDs)—chemical, biological, radiological, and nuclear—are becoming the weapons of choice among terrorist organizations and some governments. Jessica Stern's "Getting and Using the Weapons" shows how chemical and biological weapons, along with a simple nuclear device that spews radioactive isotopes, are ideal terrorist tools. She argues, however, that "despite the evidence of such weapons as instruments of terror, terrorists have seldom used them," as the technical obstacles of acquiring the weapons and disseminating or exploding them are considerable.

Most contributors to this chapter agree that lumping all WMDs in one category is probably a mistake. MacArthur Foundation fellow Christopher F. Chyba makes this point in his post–September 11 article, "Toward Biological Security." A former member of the National Security Council in the Clinton administration, Chyba points out that WMDs differ greatly: "Put simply, biological weapons differ from nuclear or chemical weapons, and any biological security strategy should begin by paying attention to these differences." According to him, "An effective strategy for biological security will encompass nonproliferation, deterrence and defense, but the required mix of these components will be very different from those in strategies for nuclear or even chemical weapons."

Chapter 6 identifies nontraditional forms of terrorism and potential terrorist weapons that could be used with deadly results. "Narcotics, Terrorism, and International Crime: The Convergence Phenomenon," by General Barry McCaffrey and Major

John Basso, uses case studies from different world regions to illustrate the insidious and debilitating nature of narcoterror. General McCaffrey, former drug czar in the Clinton administration, is the ideal person to address this issue. He is still passionate about halting the flow of drugs into America and stopping drug production in the less developed world.

Gregory J. Rattray's "The Cyberterrorism Threat" paints a grim "digital" picture of the potential for mayhem should adversaries target America's sophisticated communications networks: "Looking to the future, we can expect cyberterrorism to become a more significant national security concern." According to Rattray, the effectiveness of digital attacks will increase, and so will U.S. vulnerabilities to these attacks.

Jason Pate and Gavin Cameron assess the potential economic impact of a biological weapons attack in an article entitled "Covert Biological Weapons Attacks Against Agricultural Targets: Assessing the Impacts Against U.S. Agriculture." They argue that while U.S. agriculture is too diversified to be catastrophically affected by a single attack, where crop cultivation is localized or is in regions that are economically dependent on a single crop, an attack could potentially devastate a particular crop or area. Furthermore, chokepoints in meat-producing areas could multiply the effects of an attack: "Due to the scale of the industry, such an attack would cause major economic losses and have a national impact."

"Single Issue Terrorism," by G. Davidson Smith identifies several "single-issue" groups that have resorted to terrorism in the past and will do so again in the future. Animal rights activists, abortion rights activists, and environmentalists are the three groups Smith analyzes. In each case he examines the issue, targets, and tactics used by the groups and concludes that single-issue militancy remains dangerous, despite lower levels of activity in recent years.

Part II

Part II of this book deals with past, present, and future, national and international, responses to terrorism and defenses against it. Organized into four chapters, the essays and articles in Part II analyze and debate the practical, political, ethical, and moral questions raised by military and nonmilitary responses, including preemptive actions, outside the context of declared war. In addition, five detailed appendices—"Background Information on Designated Foreign Terrorist Organizations," "Significant Terrorist Incidents, 1961–2001," "Chemical and Biological Weapons: Possession and Programs Past and Present," "Statement by the President in His Address to the Nation, September 11, 2001," and "Terrorist Incidents, 1981–2001"—are provided at the end of Part II.

Chapter 7 examines the challenge to democratic and human rights norms that democracies must contemplate when facing terrorist threats. It also examines the "just war" theory as it might apply to protracted warfare with nonstate actors.

Laura Donohue's "Fear Itself: Counterterrorism, Individual Rights, and U.S. Foreign Relations Post 9-11" argues that the Bush administration must be careful not to impinge too drastically on the individual rights of Americans in the pursuit of security from terrorists. After examining several strong arguments for and against widespread detention and questioning, military courts, capital punishment, and wider surveillance measures, Donohue sides with those against stronger measures. Infringing on individual rights, says Donohue, will breed cynicism and suspicion, which American citizens, allies, and enemies can ill afford, as they face the threat of global terror.

In his final article in this book, "A Nasty Business," Bruce Hoffman notes the difficulty intelligence organizations in democracies have in collecting intelligence against terrorists: "Gathering 'good intelligence' against terrorists is an inherently brutish enterprise, involving methods a civics class might not condone." Hoffman also advances the question asked by many after September 11: What aspects of their civil rights, liberties, and freedoms are Americans willing to give up in order to prosecute the war on terrorism?

In his speech to West Point's 2002 graduates, President George W. Bush spoke of preemption as a means of dealing with terrorists. "Our security," said President Bush, "will require all Americans to be forward-looking and resolute, to be ready for preemptive action when necessary to defend our liberty and to defend our lives." Historically, Americans have been leery of using military force for preemptive purposes, because just war doctrine justifies the use of force only after one is attacked. Three just war articles clarify the doctrine when applied to terrorism, nonstate actors, and weapons of mass destruction. "Terrorism and Just War Doctrine," by Anthony Clark Arend concludes that although "the nature of terrorists and terrorist actions raises a number of critical challenges for just war doctrine, that doctrine offers a great deal of guidance for counterterror operations." At the same time, Arend also seems to support President Bush's "preemptive action" comments, by suggesting that a state has the right to preempt terrorist actions if it can show that an attack is imminent and if its response is proportionate to the threatened attack.

In "NBC-Armed Rogues: Is There a Moral Case for Preemption?" Brad Roberts supports the notion of preemptive action, particularly if it would stop a nuclear, chemical, or biological attack. While agreeing that there is a moral case for preemption, however, Roberts asserts that "it is not quite as tidy as policy-makers might desire."

The selections in Chapter Eight discusses strategies (or the lack thereof) of both terrorists and those who must fight them. In "The Soft Underbelly of American Primacy: Tactical Advantages of Terror," Richard K. Betts explains why America is a target and why its enemies use a strategy of terrorism. "A strategy of terrorism is most likely to flow from the coincidence of two conditions: Intense political grievance and gross imballance of power." "Political and cultural power make the United States a target for those who blame it for their problems," says Betts. However, American economic and military power prevents them from attacking the United States by conventional means. Therefore, explains Betts, America's enemies attack asymmetrically, using "terror tactics as their strategy for coercion."

In an article written specifically for this book titled "Bin Laden's War," James S. Robbins outlines in detail Osama bin Laden's grand strategy and operational plan. In concept they were brilliant, says Robbins. However, they were doomed to failure because bin Laden underestimated the power of the United States and the resolve of the American people. According to Robbins, "Osama bin Laden allowed his capabilities to outpace his strategy. He discovered and exploited seams in American security to conduct a brilliant, innovative and stunning act of violence." However, says Robbins, "by taking terrorism to unprecedented extremes, he mobilized the American national will, and raised the U.S. commitment" to a greater level than his or one that he could imagine. "Furthermore," Robbins explains, "by overestimating his defensive capabilities and underestimating the offensive power of the United States, he [bin Laden] found himself trapped in an indefensible position and unable to prosecute the follow-on attacks of his campaign plan."

"The Real Intelligence Failure on 9/11 and the Case for a Doctrine of Striking First" by Richard Shultz and Andreas Vogt is another original article written for this book. Shultz and Vogt argue—unsurprisingly—that the events of 9/11 were partly the result of intelligence and coordination failures of the CIA and FBI. Information concerning the attacks was in the hands of both agencies before 9/11, say Shultz and Vogt, but the two organizations simply failed to share the information and put "two and two together." However, the authors also maintain that the intelligence failures went well beyond simple analysis and coordination problems. They contend that the FBI, CIA, and the Pentagon did not understand terrorism as a strategy for a new type of "4th generation" warfare. Before 9/11, "terrorism was seen as a secondary national security challenge—not a clear and present danger—even after the deadly 1998 East Africa embassy bombings." Fortunately, the authors believe that President Bush and Secretary of Defense Rumsfeld understand what 4th generation warfare is and have a doctrine to fight it. The new "Bush Doctrine," first articulated by Bush at West Point, emphasizes preemption over deterrence and containment, two key components of cold war doctrine and thinking.

Barry Posen's offering, "The Struggle Against Terrorism: Grand Strategy, Strategy, and Tactics," asserts that the United States should pursue a comprehensive grand strategy of selective engagement to prosecute its campaign against terrorism. Posen introduces the idea that special operations forces are the ideal for executing a selective engagement strategy. "Flexible, fast, and relatively discriminate forces are essential," Posen argues, and "the United States has large special operations forces well suited to the counterterror mission."

"Explaining the United States' Decision to Strike Back at Terrorists" is the only article in Chapter 8 written before September 11. In it, author Michelle Malvesti presents an explanatory model describing when the United States will use military force in response to a terrorist attack. According to Malvesti, when six factors (immediate perpetrator identificaiton, perpetrator repetition, U.S. government officials are targets, flaagrant terrorist behavior, *fait accompli* incident, and a vulnerable perpetrator) are evident in a terrorist attack against the United States, the perpetuator should expect an American military response. The strengths of Malvesti's work are its detailed analysis and predictive value. Had Osama bin Laden read her work prior to September 11, perhaps he would have thought twice about ordering the attack.

Organizational change is the topic of chapter 9, and the question that its four readings address is, How must the organizations charged with American security change to thwart the terrorism threat? Ashton Carter concludes in "The Architecture of Government in the Face of Terrorism" that it is not practical for someone in the federal government to be in charge of a counterterror effort that must "inherently cut across all agencies of the federal government, state and local government, and the private sector....What is required instead is a multiyear, multi-agency program of invention and investment devised in the White House, embedded in the president's budget submissions and defended by him to Congress, and supported by appropriate law and regulation."

I agree, particularly with regard to security in the "homeland" against biological and chemical threats. In my article, "The National Security Act of 1947 and Biological and Chemical Weapons: A Mid-Century Mechanism for New Millennium Threats," I argue that nothing short of a change to America's national security legislation will posture the country for counterterrorism success. I also imply that an American intelligence community created 50 years ago cannot hope to cope with the requirements of the terrorism threat. Dick Betts does not agree. In "Fixing Intelligence," Betts argues that reorganizations usually prove to be three steps forward and two back, because "the intelligence establishment is so vast and complex that the net impact of reshuffling may be indiscernible."

Although written before 9/11, Martha Crenshaw's "Counterterrorism Policy and the Political Process" is descriptive of how difficult it is for any president, including George W. Bush, to implement a coherent counterterrorism policy. "Due to pressures from Congress," says Crenshaw, "the president will not be able to set the agenda for counterterrorism policy with as much freedom as he can in other policy areas." Crenshaw also contends that implementation of counterterrorism policy decisions will "also be affected by controversy, due to rivalries among agencies with operational responsibilities." Thus she predicted—correctly—before 9/11, "it will be difficult for any administration to develop a consistent policy based on an objective appraisal of the threat of terrorism to American national interests."

Chapter 10 discusses different counterterror instruments. Some of these, such as special operations forces, have received a good deal of press; others, such as assassination, are very controversial. Two offerings discuss the role of special operations forces. The first, by former special operator Sam Sarkesian, traces the history of special forces from World War II until their use in Afghanistan. He concludes that special forces is ideal for the type of unconventional warfare practiced in Afghanistan, but warns that special forces must be kept distinct from mainstream military strategy and doctrine. In "The Limits of Military Power," Rob de Wijk agrees with Sarkesian, but laments the fact that the defense organizations of the West do not have enough special operations forces.

Targeting terrorists is discussed by Daniel B. Pickard in "Legalizing Assassination? Terrorism, the Central Intelligence Agency, and International Law." In this article Pickard confirms that assassination is counter to U.S. policy, but he argues that in special circumstances the policy could change because "assassinations of terrorists abroad conducted by intelligence officers are potentially permissible under U.S. law.... The question that remains," Packard says, "is whether a change in policy would be effective in protecting America, its citizens, and its ideals."

"Business Versus Terror," by David J. Rothkopf, explains that an alliance of doctors, venture capitalists, and corporate project managers—the private sector army—is the United States's not-so-secret weapon and best hope. "Its best troops," Rothkopf argues, "will be regiments of geeks rather than the special forces that struck the first blows against the Taliban in Afghanistan."

Almost half of the offerings in this rather eclectic reader on terrorism were written after September 11 and were written because of that terrible event. Rather eerily, almost all of the pre–September 11 articles either predict or discuss the likelihood or possibility of a catastrophic terrorist event occurring on American soil. No one paid attention then. Let's hope that some will now pay attention to both this book and the others like it that are sure to come.

Russell D. Howard

Notes

1. Quote attributed to Brian Jenkins in 1974. See Jessica Stern, "Loose Nukes, Poisons, and Terrorism: The New Threats to International Security," June 19, 1996.
2. James Woolsey, 1994
3. Stephen A. Cambone, *A New Structure for National Security Policy Planning*, Washington D.C.: Government Printing Office, 1996, p. 43.
4. Gideon Rose, "It Could Happen Here—Facing the New Terrorism," *Foreign Affairs*, March-April, 1999, p. 1.
5. Bruce Hoffman, *Inside Terrorism*, New York: Columbia University Press, 1998, p. 205.
6. Paul Mann, "Modern Military Threats: Not All They Might Seem?" *Aviation Week & Space Technology*, April 22, 2002, p. 1 (Gordon Adams quote).
7. Peter Ford, "Why Do They Hates Us," *Christian Science Monitor*, September 27, 2001, p. 1.
8. http://globalization.about.com/library/weekly/aa100101a.htm
9. http://discuss.washingtonpost.com/wp-srv/zforum/02/nation_christison0410.htm
10. John Hendren, "At West Point a New Breed of Cadet," *Los Angeles Times*, May 31, 2002, p. 17.

Part 1

Defining the Threat of Terrorism

Chapter 1

Terrorism Defined

Chapter 1 introduces the problems inherent in defining a topic as complex as terrorism. In the news everywhere, used to describe events from the Philippines to Central America, from the Middle East to the United States, we "think we know what it is when we see it." But is that enough? Bruce Hoffman does not think so. In his reading "Defining Terrorism" he struggles to come up with a definition of the term that avoids the "promiscuous" and imprecise labeling of a range of acts. He provides dictionary definitions but finds them to be "unsatisfying" because ultimately a society's definition is a reflection of the political and social tenor of the times. Hoffman traces the historical use of the term "terrorism" from the reign of terror that followed the French Revolution; to the communist and fascist movements in Russia, Italy, and Germany; to the narco-terrorism of the 1990s. He concludes with a definition that seeks to distinguish terrorists from guerrillas, ordinary criminals, and assassins.

Paul Pillar, because of his years of experience in the U.S. Army and Central Intelligence Agency, approaches terrorism from a practical, problem-solving vantage point. As such, his primary intention is to provide sound counterterrorism policy. Pillar feels that arguing the semantics of a precise definition is "confusing" and "cumbersome" and that it does not ultimately help one to determine good policy. He begins his study of terrorism and counterterrorism from a working definition used by the U.S. government, "as good a definition as any." The reading that follows examines the effects, both direct and indirect, of terrorism and outlines the four elements of good counterterrorism policy. The selection concludes with Pillar's reflections on the evolving nature of the world order, and the need for policy that adapts to change.

Eqbal Ahmad, in contrast to Paul Pillar, finds the official definition of and approach to terrorism to be an extremely limiting one, which stirs up emotion without "exercising our intelligence." Ahmad maintains that we do need to know what terrorism is before we can determine how to stop it. Most important, we must first study the motives of the terrorists. Throughout his reading, Ahmad uses Osama bin Laden and his transformation from U.S. ally to terrorist as a case study. His reading concludes with three recommendations to the United States for dealing with terrorism, which, although written in 1998, are remarkably prophetic in light of the events of September 11, 2001.

Defining Terrorism

Bruce Hoffman is an authoritative analyst of terrorism and a recipient of the U.S. Intelligence Community Seal Medallion, the highest level of commendation given to a nongovernment employee. He is currently the director of the Washington, D.C., office of the RAND Corporation, where he heads the terrorism research unit, and he regularly advises both governments and businesses throughout the world. The following reading is a chapter from his book *Inside Terrorism*.

W hat is terrorism? Few words have so insidiously worked their way into our everyday vocabulary. Like 'Internet'—another grossly over-used term that has similarly become an indispensable part of the argot of the late twentieth century—most people have a vague idea or impression of what terrorism is, but lack a more precise, concrete and truly explanatory definition of the word. This imprecision has been abetted partly by the modern media, whose efforts to communicate an often complex and convoluted message in the briefest amount of air-time or print space possible have led to the promiscuous labelling of a range of violent acts as 'terrorism'. Pick up a newspaper or turn on the television and—even within the same broadcast or on the same page—one can find such disparate acts as the bombing of a building, the assassination of a head of state, the massacre of civilians by a military unit, the poisoning of produce on supermarket shelves or the deliberate contamination of over-the-counter medication in a chemist's shop all described as incidents of terrorism. Indeed, virtually any especially abhorrent act of violence that is perceived as directed against society—whether it involves the activities of anti-government dissidents or governments themselves, organized crime syndicates or common criminals, rioting mobs or persons engaged in militant protest, individual psychotics or lone extortionists—is often labelled 'terrorism'.

Dictionary definitions are of little help. The pre-eminent authority on the English language, the much-venerated *Oxford English Dictionary [OED]*, is disappointingly unobliging when it comes to providing edification on this subject, its interpretation at once too literal and too historical to be of much contemporary use:

> **Terrorism:** A system of terror. 1. Government by intimidation as directed and carried out by the party in power in France during the revolution of 1789–94; the system of 'Terror'. 2. *gen*. A policy intended to strike with terror those against whom it is adopted; the employment of methods of intimidation; the fact of terrorizing or condition of being terrorized.

These definitions are wholly unsatisfying. Rather than learning what terrorism is, one instead finds, in the first instance, a somewhat potted historical—and, in respect of the modern accepted usage of the term, a uselessly anachronistic—description. The second definition offered is only slightly more helpful. While accurately communicating the fear-inducing quality of terrorism, the definition is still so broad as to apply to almost any action that scares ('terrorizes') us. Though an integral part of 'terrorism', this definition is still insufficient for the purpose of accurately defining the phenomenon that is today called 'terrorism'.

A slightly more satisfying elucidation may be found in the *OED*'s definition of the perpetrator of the act than in its efforts to come to grips with the act itself. In this respect, a 'terrorist' is defined thus:

> 1. As a political term: a. Applied to the Jacobins and their agents and partisans in the French Revolution, esp. to those connected with the Revolutionary tribunals during the 'Reign of Terror'. b. Any one who attempts to further his views by a system of coercive intimidation; *spec.* applied to members of one of the extreme revolutionary societies in Russia.

This is appreciably more helpful. First, it immediately introduces the reader to the notion of terrorism as a *political* concept. As will be seen, this key characteristic of terrorism is absolutely paramount to understanding its aims, motivations and purposes and critical in distinguishing it from other types of violence.

Terrorism, in the most widely accepted contemporary usage of the term, is fundamentally and inherently political. It is also ineluctably about power: the pursuit of power, the acquisition of power, and the use of power to achieve political change. Terrorism is thus violence—or, equally important, the threat of violence—used and directed in pursuit of, or in service of, a political aim. With this vital point clearly illuminated, one can appreciate the significance of the additional definition of 'terrorist' provided by the *OED*: 'Any one who attempts to further his views by a system of coercive intimidation'. This definition underscores clearly the other fundamental characteristic of terrorism: that it is a planned, calculated, and indeed systematic act.

Given this relatively straightforward elucidation, why, then, is terrorism so difficult to define? The most compelling reason perhaps is because the meaning of the term has changed so frequently over the past two hundred years.

The Changing Meaning of Terrorism

The word 'terrorism' was first popularized during the French Revolution. In contrast to its contemporary usage, at that time terrorism had a decidedly *positive* connotation. The system or *régime de la terreur* of 1793–4—from which the English word came—was adopted as a means to establish order during the transient anarchical period of turmoil and upheaval that followed the uprisings of 1789, as it has followed in the wake of many other revolutions. Hence, unlike terrorism as it is commonly understood today, to mean a *revolutionary* or anti-government activity undertaken by non-state or subnational entities, the *régime de la terreur* was an instrument of governance wielded by the recently established revolutionary *state*. It was designed to consolidate the new government's power by intimidating counter-revolutionaries, subversives and all other dissidents whom the new regime regarded as 'enemies of the people'. The Committee of General Security and the Revolutionary Tribunal ('People's Court' in the modern vernacular) were thus accorded wide powers of arrest and judgement, publicly putting to death by guillotine persons convicted of treasonous (i.e. reactionary) crimes. In this manner, a powerful lesson was conveyed to any and all who might oppose the revolution or grow nostalgic for the *ancien régime*.

Ironically, perhaps terrorism in its original context was also closely associated with the ideals of virtue and democracy. The revolutionary leader Maximilien Robespierre firmly believed that virtue was the mainspring of a popular government at peace, but that during the time of revolution must be allied with terror in order for democracy to triumph. He appealed famously to 'virtue, without which terror is evil; terror, without which virtue is helpless', and proclaimed; 'Terror is nothing but justice, prompt, severe and inflexible; it is therefore an emanation of virtue.'

Despite this divergence from its subsequent meaning, the French Revolution's 'terrorism' still shared at least two key characteristics in common with its modern-day variant. First, the *régime de la terreur* was neither random nor indiscriminate, as terrorism is often portrayed today, but was organized, deliberate and systematic. Second, its goal and its very justification—like that of contemporary terrorism—was the creation of a 'new and better society' in place of a fundamentally corrupt and undemocratic political system. Indeed, Robespierre's vague and utopian exegeses of the revolution's central goals are remarkably similar in tone and content to the equally turgid, millenarian manifestos issued by many contemporary revolutionary—primarily left-wing, Marxist-oriented—terrorist organizations. For example, in 1794 Robespierre declared, in language eerily presaging the communiqués issued by groups such as Germany's Red Army Faction and Italy's Red Brigades nearly two centuries later:

> We want an order of things… in which the arts are an adornment to the liberty that ennobles them, and commerce the source of wealth for the public and not of monstrous opulence for a few families… In our country we desire morality instead of selfishness, honesty and not mere 'honor', principle and not mere custom, duty and not mere propriety, the sway of reason rather than the tyranny of fashion, a scorn for vice and not a contempt for the unfortunate…

Like many other revolutions, the French Revolution eventually began to consume itself. On 8 Thermidor, year two of the new calendar adopted by the revolutionaries (26 July 1794), Robespierre announced to the National Convention that he had in his possession a new list of traitors. Fearing that their own names might be on that list, extremists joined forces with moderates to repudiate both Robespierre and his *régime de la terreur*. Robespierre and his closest followers themselves met the same fate that had befallen some 40,000 others: execution by guillotine. The Terror was at an end; thereafter terrorism became a term associated with the abuse of office and power—with overt 'criminal' implications. Within a year of Robespierre's demise, the word had been popularized in English by Edmund Burke who, in his famous polemic against the French Revolution, described the 'Thousands of those Hell hounds called Terrorists… let loose on the people'.

One of the French Revolution's more enduring repercussions was the impetus it gave to anti-monarchial sentiment elsewhere in Europe. Popular subservience to rulers who derived their authority from God through 'divine right of rule', not from their subjects, was increasingly questioned by a politically awakened continent. The advent of nationalism, and with its notions of statehood and citizenship based on the common identity of a people rather than the lineage of a royal family, were resulting in the unification and creation of new nation-states such as Germany and Italy. Meanwhile, the massive socio-economic changes engendered by the industrial revolution were creating new 'universalist' ideologies (such as communism/Marxism), born of the alienation and exploitative conditions of nineteenth-century capitalism. From this milieu a new era of terrorism emerged, in which the concept had gained many of the familiar revolutionary, anti-state connotations of today. Its chief progenitor was arguably the Italian republican extremist, Carlo Pisacane, who had forsaken his birthright as duke of San Giovanni only to perish in 1857 during an ill-fated revolt against Bourbon rule. A passionate advocate of federalism and mutualism, Pisacane is remembered less on this account than for the theory of 'propaganda by deed', which he is credited with defining—an idea that has exerted a compelling influence on rebels and terrorists alike ever since. 'The propaganda of the idea is a chimera,' Pisacane wrote. 'Ideas result from deeds, not the latter from the former, and the people will not be free when they are educated, but educated when they are free.' Violence, he argued, was necessary not only to draw attention to, or generate publicity for, a cause, but to inform, educate and ultimately rally the masses behind the revolution. The didactic purpose of violence, Pisacane argued, could never be effectively replaced by pamphlets, wall posters or assemblies.

Perhaps the first organization to put into practice Pisacane's dictum was the Narodnaya Volya, or People's Will (sometimes translated as People's Freedom), a small group of Russian constitutionalists that had been founded in 1878 to challenge tsarist rule. For the Narodnaya Volya, the apathy and alienation of the Russian masses afforded few alternatives to the resort to daring and dramatic acts of violence designed to attract attention to the group and its cause. However, unlike the many late twentieth-century terrorist organizations who have cited the principle of 'propaganda by deed' to justify the wanton targeting of civilians in order to assure them publicity through the shock and horror produced by wholesale bloodshed, the Narodnaya Volya displayed an almost quixotic attitude to the violence they wrought. To them, 'propaganda by deed' meant the selective targeting of specific individuals whom the group considered the embodiment of the autocratic, oppressive state. Hence their victims—the tsar, leading members of the royal family, senior government officials—were deliberately chosen for their 'symbolic' value as the dynastic heads and subservient agents of a corrupt and tyrannical regime. An intrinsic element in the group's collective beliefs was that 'not one drop of superfluous blood' should be shed in pursuit of aims, however noble or utilitarian they might be. Even having selected their targets with great care and the utmost deliberation, group members still harboured profound regrets about taking the life of a fellow human being. Their unswerving adherence to this principle is perhaps best illustrated by the failed attempt on the life of the Grand Duke Serge Alexandrovich made by a successor organization to the Narodnaya Volya in 1905. As the royal carriage came into view, the terrorist tasked with the assassination saw that the duke was unexpectedly accompanied by his children and therefore aborted his mission rather than risk harming the intended victim's family (the duke was killed in a subsequent attack). By comparison, the mid-air explosion caused by a terrorist bomb on Pan Am flight 103 over Lockerbie, Scotland, December 1988 indiscriminately claimed the lives of all 259 persons on board—innocent men, women and children alike—plus eleven inhabitants of the village where the plane crashed.

Ironically, the Narodnaya Volya's most dramatic accomplishment also led directly to its demise. On 1 March 1881 the group assassinated Tsar Alexander II. The failure of eight previous plots had led the conspirators to take extraordinary measures to ensure the success of this attempt. Four volunteers were given four bombs each and deployed along the alternative routes followed by the tsar's cortege. As two of the bomber-assassins stood in wait on the same street, the sleighs carrying the tsar and his Cossack escort approached the first terrorist, who hurled his bomb at the passing sleigh, missing it by inches. The whole entourage came to a halt as soldiers seized the hapless culprit and the tsar descended from his sleigh to check on a bystander wounded by the explosion. 'Thank God, I am safe,' the tsar reportedly declared—just as the second bomber emerged from the crowd and detonated his weapon, killing both himself and his target. The full weight of the tsarist state now fell on the heads of the Narodnaya Volya. Acting on information provided by the arrested member, the secret police swept down on the group's safe houses and hide-outs, rounding up most of the plotters, who were quickly tried, convicted and hanged. Further information from this group led to subsequent arrests, so that within a year of the assassination only one member of the original executive committee was still at large. She too was finally apprehended in 1883, at which point the first generation of Narodnaya Volya terrorists ceased to exist, although various successor organizations subsequently emerged to carry on the struggle.

At the time, the repercussions of the tsar's assassination could not have been known or appreciated by either the condemned or their comrades languishing in prison or exiled to Siberia. But in addition to precipitating the beginning of the end of tsarist rule, the group also deeply influenced individual revolutionaries and subversive organizations elsewhere. To the nascent anarchist movement, the 'propaganda by deed' strategy championed by the Narodnaya Volya provided a model to be emulated. Within four months of the tsar's murder, a group of radicals in London convened an 'anarchist conference' which publicly applauded the assassination and extolled tyrannicide as a means to achieve revolutionary change. In hopes of encouraging and coordinating worldwide anarchist activities, the conferees decided to establish an 'Anarchist International' (or 'Black International'). Although this idea, like most of their ambitious plans, came to nought, the publicity generated by even a putative 'Anarchist International' was sufficient to create a myth of global revolutionary pretensions and thereby stimulate fears and suspicions disproportionate to its actual impact or political achievements. Disparate and uncoordinated though the anarchists' violence was, the movement's emphasis on individual action or operations carried out by small cells of like-minded radicals made detection and prevention by the police particularly difficult, thus further heightening public fears. For example, following the assassination of US President William McKinley in 1901 (by a young Hungarian refugee, Leon Czolgocz, who, while not a regular member of any anarchist organization, was nonetheless influenced by the philosophy), Congress swiftly enacted legislation barring known anarchists or anyone 'who disbelieves in or is opposed to all organized government' from entering the United States. However, while anarchists were responsible for an impressive string of assassinations of heads of state and a number of particularly notorious bombings from about 1878 until the second decade of the twentieth century, in the final analysis, other than stimulating often exaggerated fears, anarchism made little tangible impact on either the domestic or the international politics of the countries affected. It does, however, offer an interesting historical footnote: much as the 'information revolution' of the late twentieth century is alleged to have made the means and methods of bomb-making and other types of terrorist activity more readily available via the Internet, on CD-ROM, and through ordinary libraries and bookstores, one of anarchism's flourishing 'cottage industries' more than a century earlier was the widespread distribution of similar 'how-to' or DIY-type manuals and publications of violence and mayhem.

On the eve of the First World War, terrorism still retained its revolutionary connotations. By this time, growing unrest and irredentist ferment had already welled up within the decaying Ottoman and Habsburg Empires. In the 1880s and 1890s, for example, militant Armenian nationalist movements in eastern Turkey pursued a terrorist strategy against continued Ottoman rule of a kind that would later be adopted by most of the post–Second World War ethno-nationalist/separatist movements. The Armenians' objective was simultaneously to strike a blow against the despotic 'alien' regime through repeated attacks on its colonial administration and security forces, in order to rally indigenous support, as well as to attract international attention, sympathy and support. Around the same time, the Inner Macedonian Revolutionary Organization (IMRO) was active in the region overlapping present-day Greece, Bulgaria and Serbia. Although the Macedonians did not go on to suffer the catastrophic fate that befell the Armenians during the First World War (when an estimated one million persons perished in what is considered to be the first officially implemented genocide of the twentieth century), IMRO never came close to achieving its aim of an independent Macedonia and thereafter degenerated into a mostly criminal organization of hired thugs and political assassins.

The events immediately preceding the First World War in Bosnia are of course more familiar because of their subsequent cataclysmic impact on world affairs. There, similar groups of disaffected nationalists—Bosnian Serb intellectuals, university students and even schoolchildren, collectively known as Mlada Bosnia, or Young Bosnians—arose against continued Habsburg suzerainty. While it is perhaps easy to dismiss the movement, as some historians have, as comprised of 'frustrated, poor, dreary and maladjusted' adolescents—much as many contemporary observers similarly denigrate modern-day terrorists as mindless, obsessive and maladjusted—it was a member of Young Bosnia, Gavrilo Princip, who is widely credited with having set in motion the chain of events that began on 28 June 1914, when he assassinated the Habsburg Archduke Franz Ferdinand in Sarajevo, and culminated in the First World War. Whatever its superficially juvenile characteristics, the group was nonetheless passionately dedicated to the attainment of a federal South Slav political entity—united Slovenes, Croats and Serbs—and resolutely committed to assassination as the vehicle with which to achieve that aim. In this respect, the Young Bosnians perhaps had more in common with the radical republicanism of Giuseppe Mazzini, one of the most ardent exponents of Italian unification in the nineteenth century, than with groups such as the Narodnaya Volya—despite a shared conviction in the efficacy of tyrannicide. An even more significant difference, however, was the degree of involvement in, and external support provided to, Young Bosnian activities by various shadowy Serbian nationalist groups. Principal among these was the pan-Serb secret society, the Narodna Obrana ('The People's Defence' or 'National Defence').

The Narodna Obrana had been established in 1908 originally to promote Serb cultural and national activities. It subsequently assumed a more subversive orientation as the movement became increasingly involved with anti-Austrian activities—including terrorism—mostly in neighbouring Bosnia and Hercegovina. Although the Narodna Obrana's exclusionist pan-Serbian aims clashed with the Young Bosnians' less parochial South Slav ideals, its leadership was quite happy to manipulate and exploit the Bosnians' emotive nationalism and youthful zeal for their own purposes. To this end, the Narodna Obrana actively recruited, trained and armed young Bosnians and Hercegovinians from movements such as the Young Bosnians who were then deployed in various seditious activities against the Habsburgs. As early as four years before the archduke's assassination, a Hercegovinian youth, trained by a Serb army officer with close ties to the Narodna Obrana, had attempted to kill the governor of Bosnia. But, while the Narodna Obrana included among its members senior Serbian government officials, it was not an explicitly government-controlled or directly state-supported entity. Whatever hazy government links it maintained were further and deliberately obscured when a radical faction left the Narodna Obrana in 1911 and established the Ujedinjenje ili Smrt, 'The Union of Death' or 'Death or Unification'—more popularly known as the Crna Ruka, or the 'Black Hand'. This more militant and appreciably more clandestine splinter has been described by one historian as combining

> the more unattractive features of the anarchist cells of earlier years—which had been responsible for quite a number of assassinations in Europe and whose methods had a good deal of influence via the writings of Russian anarchists upon Serbian youth— and of the [American] Ku Klux Klan. There were gory rituals and oaths of loyalty, there were murders of backsliding members, there was identification of members by number, there were distributions of guns and bombs. And there was a steady traffic between Bosnia and Serbia.

This group, which continued to maintain close links with its parent body, was largely composed of serving Serbian military officers. It was led by Lieutenant-Colonel Dragutin Dmitrievich (known by his pseudonym, Apis), himself of the chief of the Intelligence Department of the Serbian general staff. With this key additional advantage of direct access to military armaments, intelligence and training facilities, the Black Hand effectively took charge of all Serb-backed clandestine operations in Bosnia.

Although there were obviously close links between the Serbian military, the Black Hand and the Young Bosnians, it would be a mistake to regard the relationship as one of direct control, much less outright manipulation. Clearly, the Serbian government was well aware of the Black Hand's objectives and the violent means the group employed in pursuit of them; indeed, the Serbian Crown Prince Alexander was one of the group's benefactors. But this does not mean that the Serbian government was necessarily as committed to war with Austria as the Black Hand's leaders were, or that it was prepared to countenance the group's more extreme plans for fomenting cross-border, anti-Habsburg terrorism. There is some evidence to suggest that the Black Hand may have been trying to force Austria's hand against Serbia and thereby plunge both countries into war by actively abetting the Young Bosnians' plot to assassinate the archduke. Indeed, according to one revisionist account of the events leading up to the murder, even though the pistol used by Princip had been supplied by the Black Hand from a Serb military armoury in Kragujevac, and even though Princip had been trained by the Black Hand in Serbia before being smuggled back across the border for the assassination, at the eleventh hour Dmitrievich had apparently bowed to intense government pressure and tried to stop the assassination. According to this version, Princip and his fellow conspirators would hear nothing of it and stubbornly went ahead with their plans. Contrary to popular assumption, therefore, the archduke's assassination may not have been specifically ordered or even directly sanctioned by the Serbian government. However, the obscure links between high government officials and their senior military commanders and ostensibly independent, transnational terrorist movements, and the tangled web of intrigue, plots, clandestine arms provision and training, intelligence agents and cross-border sanctuary these relationships inevitably involved, provide a pertinent historical parallel to the contemporary phenomenon known as 'state-sponsored' terrorism (that is, the active and often clandestine support, encouragement and assistance provided by a foreign government to a terrorist group), which is discussed below.

By the 1930s, the meaning of 'terrorism' had changed again. It was now used less to refer to revolutionary movements and violence directed against governments and their leaders, and more to describe the practices of mass repression employed by totalitarian states and their dictatorial leaders against their own citizens. Thus the term regained its former connotations of abuse of power by governments, and was applied specifically to the authoritarian regimes that had come to power in Fascist Italy, Nazi Germany and Stalinist Russia. In Germany respectively, the accession to office of Hitler and Mussolini had depended in large measure on the 'street'—the mobilization and deployment of gangs of brown- or black-shirted thugs to harass and intimidate political opponents and root out other scapegoats for public vilification and further victimization. 'Terror? Never,' Mussolini insisted, demurely dismissing such intimidation as 'simply… social hygiene, taking those individuals out of circulation like a doctor would take out a bacillus'. The most sinister dimension of this form of 'terror' was that it became an intrinsic component of Fascist and Nazi governance, executed at the behest of, and in complete subservience to, the ruling political party of the land—which had arrogated to itself complete, total control of the country and its people. A system of government-sanctioned fear and coercion was thus created whereby political brawls, street fights and widespread persecution of Jews, communists and other declared 'enemies of the state' became the means through which complete and submissive compliance was ensured. The totality of party control over, and perversion of, government was perhaps most clearly evinced by a speech given by Hermann Goering, the newly appointed Prussian minister of the interior, in 1933. 'Fellow Germans,' he declared,

> My measures will not be crippled by any judicial thinking. My measures will not be crippled by any bureaucracy. Here I don't have to worry about Justice; my mission is only to destroy and exterminate, nothing more. This struggle will be a struggle against chaos, and such a struggle I shall not conduct with the power of the police. A bourgeois State might have done that. Certainly, I shall use the power of the State and the police to the utmost, my dear Communists, so don't draw any false conclusions; but the struggle to the death, in which my fist will grasp your necks, I shall lead with those there—the Brown Shirts.

The 'Great Terror' that Stalin was shortly to unleash in Russia both resembled and differed from that of the Nazis. On the one hand, drawing inspiration from Hitler's ruthless elimination of his own political opponents, the Russian dictator similarly transformed the political party he led into a servile instrument responsive directly to his personal will, and the state's police and security apparatus into slavish organs of coercion, enforcement and repression. But conditions in the Soviet Union of the 1930s bore little resemblance to the turbulent political, social and economic upheaval afflicting Germany and Italy during that decade and the previous one. On the other hand, therefore, unlike either the Nazis or the Fascists, who had emerged from the political free-for-alls in their own countries to seize power and then had to struggle to consolidate their rule and retain their unchallenged authority, the Russian Communist Party had by the mid-1930s been firmly entrenched in power for more than a decade. Stalin's purges, in contrast to those of the French Revolution, and even to Russia's own recent experience, were not 'launched in time of crisis, or revolution and war... [but] in the coldest of cold blood, when Russia had at last reached a comparatively calm and even moderately prosperous condition'. Thus the political purges ordered by Stalin became, in the words of one of his biographers, a 'conspiracy to seize total power by terrorist action', resulting in the death, exile, imprisonment or forcible impressment of millions.

Certainly, similar forms of state-imposed or state-directed violence and terror against a government's own citizens continue today. The use of so-called 'death squads' (often off-duty or plain-clothes security or police officers) in conjunction with blatant intimidation of political opponents, human rights and aid workers, student groups, labour organizers, journalists and others has been a prominent feature of the right-wing military dictatorships that took power in Argentina, Chile and Greece during the 1970s and even of elected governments in El Salvador, Guatemala, Colombia and Peru since the mid-1980s. But these state-sanctioned or explicitly ordered acts of *internal* political violence directed mostly against domestic populations—that is, rule by violence and intimidation by those *already* in power against their own citizenry—are generally termed 'terror' in order to distinguish that phenomenon from 'terrorism', which is understood to be violence committed by non-state entities.

Following the Second World War, in another swing of the pendulum of meaning, 'terrorism' regained the revolutionary connotations with which is it most commonly associated today. At that time, the term was used primarily in reference to the violent revolts then being prosecuted by the various indigenous nationalist/anti-colonialist groups that emerged in Asia, Africa and the Middle East during the late 1940s and 1950s to oppose continued European rule. Countries as diverse as Israel, Kenya, Cyprus and Algeria, for example, owe their independence at least in part to nationalist political movements that employed terrorism against colonial powers. It was also during this period that the 'politically correct' appellation of 'freedom fighters' came into fashion as a result of the political legitimacy that the international community (whose sympathy and support was actively courted by many of these movements) accorded to struggles for national liberation and self-determination. Many newly independent Third World countries and communist bloc states in particular adopted this vernacular, arguing that anyone or any movement that fought against 'colonial' oppression and/or Western domination should not be described as 'terrorists', but were properly deemed to be 'freedom fighters'. This position was perhaps most famously explained by the Palestine Liberation Organization (PLO) chairman Yassir Arafat, when he addressed the United Nations General Assembly in November 1974. 'The difference between the revolutionary and the terrorist,' Arafat stated, 'lies in the reason for which each fights. For whoever stands by a just cause and fights for the freedom and liberation of his land from the invaders, the settlers and the colonialists, cannot possibly be called terrorist... '

During the late 1960s and 1970s, terrorism continued to be viewed within a revolutionary context. However, this usage now expanded to include nationalist and ethnic separatists groups outside a colonial or neo-colonial framework as well as radical, entirely ideologically motivated organizations. Disenfranchised or exiled nationalist minorities—such as the PLO, the Quebecois separatist group FLQ (Front de Libération du Québec), the Basque ETA (Euskadi ta Askatasuna, or Freedom for the Basque Homeland) and even a hitherto unknown South Moluccan irredentist group seeking independence from Indonesia—adopted terrorism as a means to draw attention to themselves and their respective causes, in many instances with the specific aim, like their anti-colonial predecessors, of attracting international sympathy and support. Around the same time, various left-wing political extremists—drawn mostly from the radical student organizations and Marxist/Leninist/Maoist movements in Western Europe, Latin America and the United States—began to form terrorist groups opposing American intervention in Vietnam and what they claimed were the irredeemable social and economic inequalities of the modern capitalist liberal-democratic state.

Although the revolutionary cum ethno-nationalist/separatist and ideological exemplars continue to shape our most basic understanding of the term, in recent years 'terrorism' has been used to denote broader, less distinct phenomena. In the early 1980s, for example, terrorism came to be regarded as a calculated means to destabilize the West as part of a vast global conspiracy. Books like *The Terror Network* by Claire Sterling propagated the notion to a receptive American presidential administration and similarly susceptible governments elsewhere that the seemingly isolated terrorist incidents perpetrated by disparate groups scattered across the globe were in fact linked elements of a massive clandestine plot, orchestrated by the Kremlin and implemented by its Warsaw Pact client states, to destroy the Free World. By the middle of the decade, however, a series of suicide bombings directed mostly against American diplomatic and military targets in the Middle East was focusing attention on the rising threat of state-sponsored terrorism. Consequently, this phenomenon—whereby various renegade foreign governments such as the regimes in Iran, Iraq, Libya and Syria became actively involved in sponsoring or commissioning terrorist acts—replaced communist conspiracy theories as the main context within which terrorism was viewed. Terrorism thus became associated with a type of covert or surrogate warfare whereby weaker states could confront larger, more powerful rivals without the risk of retribution.

In the early 1990s the meaning and usage of the term 'terrorism' were further blurred by the emergence of two new buzzwords: 'narco-terrorism' and the so-called 'gray area phenomenon'. The former term revived the Moscow-orchestrated terrorism conspiracy theories of previous years while introducing the critical new dimension of narcotics trafficking. Thus 'narco-terrorism' was defined by one of the concept's foremost propagators as the 'use of drug trafficking to advance the objectives of certain governments and terrorist organizations'—identified as the 'Marxist-Leninst regimes' of the Soviet Union, Cuba, Bulgaria and Nicaragua, among others. The emphasis of 'narco-terrorism' as the latest manifestation of the communist plot to undermine Western society, however, had the unfortunate effect of diverting official attention away from a bona fide emerging trend. To a greater extent than ever in the past, entirely criminal (that is, violent, *economically* motivated) organizations were now forging strategic alliances with terrorist and guerrilla organizations or themselves employing violence for specifically political ends. The growing power of the Colombian cocaine cartels, their close ties with left-wing terrorist groups in Colombia and Peru, and their repeated attempts to subvert Colombia's electoral process and undermine successive governments constitute perhaps the best-known example of this continuing trend.

Those who drew attention to this 'gray area phenomenon' were concerned less with grand conspiracies than with highlighting the increasingly fluid and variable nature of subnational conflict in the post–Cold War era. Accordingly, in the 1990s terrorism began to be subsumed by some analysts within the 'gray area phenomenon'. Thus the latter term came to be used to denote 'threats to the stability of nation states by non-state actors and non-governmental processes and organizations'; to describe violence affecting 'immense regions or urban areas where control has shifted from legitimate governments to new half-political, half-criminal powers'; or simply to group together in one category the range of conflicts across the world that no longer conformed to traditionally accepted notions of war as fighting between the armed forces of two or more established states, but instead involved irregular forces as one or more of the combatants. Terrorism had shifted its meaning again from an individual phenomenon of subnational violence to one of several elements, or part of a wider pattern, of non-state conflict.

Why Is Terrorism So Difficult to Define?

Not surprisingly, as the meaning and usage of the word have changed over time to accommodate the political vernacular and discourse of each successive era, terrorism has proved increasingly elusive in the face of attempts to construct one consistent definition. At one time, the terrorists themselves were far more cooperative in this endeavour than they are today. The early practitioners didn't mince their words or hide behind the semantic camouflage of more anodyne labels such as 'freedom fighter' or 'urban guerrilla'. The nineteenth-century anarchists, for example, unabashedly proclaimed themselves to be terrorists and frankly proclaimed their tactics to be terrorism. The members of Narodnaya Volya similarly displayed no qualms in using these same words to describe themselves and their deeds. However, such frankness did not last. The Jewish terrorist group of the 1940s known as Lehi (the Hebrew acronym for Lohamei Herut Yisrael, the Freedom Fighters for Israel, more popularly known simply as the Stern Gang after their founder and first leader, Abraham Stern) is thought to be one of the last terrorist groups actually to describe itself publicly as such. It is significant, however, that even Lehi, while it may have been far more candid than its latter-day counterparts, chose as the name of the organization not 'Terrorist Fighters for Israel', but the far less pejorative 'Freedom Fighters for Israel'. Similarly, although more than twenty years later the Brazilian revolutionary Carlos Marighela displayed few compunctions about openly advocating the use of 'terrorist' tactics, he still insisted on depicting himself and his disciples as 'urban guerrillas' rather than 'urban terrorists'. Indeed, it is clear from Marighela's writings that he was well aware of the word's undesirable connotations, and strove to displace them with positive resonances. 'The words "aggressor" and "terrorist"', Marighela wrote in his famous *Handbook of Urban Guerrilla War* (also known as the 'Mini-Manual'), 'no longer mean what they did. Instead of arousing fear or censure, they are a call to action. To be called an aggressor or a terrorist in Brazil is now an honour to any citizen, for it means that he is fighting, with a gun in his hand, against the monstrosity of the present dictatorship and the suffering it causes.'

This trend towards ever more convoluted semantic obfuscations to side-step terrorism's pejorative overtones, has, if anything, become more entrenched in recent decades. Terrorist organizations almost without exception now regularly select names for themselves that consciously eschew the word 'terrorism' in any of its forms. Instead these groups actively seek to evoke images of:

- freedom and liberation (e.g. the National Liberation Front, the Popular Front for the Liberation of Palestine, Freedom for the Basque Homeland, etc.);
- armies or other military organizational structures (e.g. the National Military Organization, the Popular Liberation Army, the Fifth Battalion of the Liberation Army, etc.);
- actual self-defence movements (e.g. the Afrikaner Resistance Movement, the Shankhill Defence Association, the Organization for the Defence of the Free People, the Jewish Defense Organization, etc.);
- righteous vengeance (the Organization for the Oppressed on Earth, the Justice Commandos of the Armenian Genocide, the Palestinian Revenge Organization, etc.);

—or else deliberately choose names that are decidedly neutral and therefore bereft of all but the most innocuous suggestions or associations (e.g. the Shining Path, Front Line, al-Dawa ('The Call'), Alfaro Lives—Damn It!, Kach ('Thus'), al-Gamat al-Islamiya ('The Islamic Organization'), the Lantero Youth Movement, etc.).

What all these examples suggest is that terrorists clearly do not see or regard themselves as others do. 'Above all I am a family man,' the arch-terrorist Carlos, 'The Jackal', described himself to a French newspaper following his capture in 1994. Cast perpetually on the defensive and forced to take up arms to protect themselves and their real or imagined constituents only, terrorists perceive themselves as reluctant warriors, driven by desperation—and lacking any viable alternative—to violence against a repressive state, a predatory rival ethnic or nationalist group, or an unresponsive international order. This perceived characteristic of self-denial also distinguishes the terrorist from other types of political extremists as well as from persons similarly involved in illegal, violent avocations. A communist or a revolutionary, for example, would likely readily accept and admit that he is in fact a communist or a revolutionary. Indeed, many would doubtless take particular pride in claiming either of those appellations for themselves. Similarly, even a person engaged in illegal, wholly disreputable or entirely selfish violence activities, such as robbing banks or carrying out contract killings, would probably admit to being a bank robber or a murderer for hire. The terrorist, by contrast, will *never* acknowledge that he is a terrorist and moreover will go to great lengths to evade and obscure any such inference or connection. Terry Anderson, the American journalist who was held hostage for almost seven years by the Lebanese terrorist organization Hezbollah, relates a telling conversation he had with one of his guards. The guard had objected to a newspaper article that referred to Hezbollah as terrorists. 'We are not terrorists,' he indignantly stated, 'we are fighters.' Anderson replied, 'Hajj, you are a terrorist, look it up in the dictionary. You are a terrorist, you may not like the word and if you do not like the word, do not do it.' The terrorist will always argue that it is society or the government or the socio-economic 'system' and its laws that are the *real* 'terrorists', and moreover that if it were not for this oppression, he would not have felt the need to defend either himself or the population he claims to represent. Another revealing example of this process of obfuscation-projection may be found in the book *Invisible Armies*, written by Sheikh Muhammad Hussein Fadlallah, the spiritual leader of the Lebanese terrorist group responsible for Anderson's kidnapping. 'We don't see ourselves as terrorists,' Fadlallah explains, 'because we don't believe in terrorism. We don't see resisting the occupier as a terrorist action. We see ourselves as *mujihadeen* [holy warriors] who fight a Holy War for the people.'

On one point, at least, everyone agrees: terrorism is a pejorative term. It is a word with intrinsically negative connotations that is generally applied to one's enemies and opponents, or to those with whom one disagrees and would otherwise prefer to ignore. 'What is called terrorism', Brian Jenkins has written, 'thus seems to depend on one's point of view. Use of the term implies a moral judgement; and if one party can successfully attach the label *terrorist* to its opponent, then it has indirectly persuaded others to adopt its moral viewpoint.' Hence the decision to call someone or label some organization 'terrorist' becomes almost unavoidably subjective, depending largely on whether one sympathizes with or opposes the person/group/cause concerned. If one identifies with the victim of the violence, for example, then the act is terrorism. If, however, one identifies with the perpetrator, the violent act is regarded in a more sympathetic, if not positive (or, at the worst, an ambivalent) light; and it is not terrorism.

The implications of this associational logic were perhaps most clearly demonstrated in the exchanges between Western and non-Western member states of the United Nations following the 1972 Munich Olympics massacre, in which eleven Israeli athletes were killed. The debate began with the proposal by the then UN Secretary-General, Kurt Waldheim, that the UN should not remain a 'mute spectator' to the acts of terrorist violence then occurring throughout the world but should take practical steps that might prevent further bloodshed. While a majority of the UN member states supported the Secretary-General, a disputatious minority—including many Arab states and various African and Asian countries—derailed the discussion, arguing (much as Arafat would do two years later in his own address to the General Assembly) that 'people who struggle to liberate themselves from foreign oppression and exploitation have the right to use all methods at their disposal, including force'.

The Third World delegates justified their position with two arguments. First, they claimed that all bona fide liberation movements are invariably decried as 'terrorists' by the regimes against which their struggles for freedom are directed. The Nazis, for example, labelled as terrorists the resistance groups opposing Germany's occupation of their lands, Moulaye el-Hassen, the Mauritanian ambassador, pointed out, just as 'all liberation movements are described as terrorists by those who have reduced them to slavery'. Therefore, by condemning 'terrorism' the UN was endorsing the power of the strong over the weak and of the established entity over its non-established challenger—in effect, acting as the defender of the status quo. According to Chen Chu, the deputy representative of the People's Republic of China, the UN thus was proposing to deprive 'opposed nations and peoples' of the only effective weapon they had with which to oppose 'imperialism, colonialism, neo-colonialism, racism and Israeli Zionism'. Second, the Third World delegates argued forcefully that it is not the violence itself that is germane, but its 'underlying causes': that is, the 'misery, frustration, grievance and despair' that produce the violent acts. As the Mauritanian representative again explained, the term 'terrorist' could 'hardly be held to apply to persons who were denied the most elementary human rights, dignity, freedom and independence, and whose countries objected to foreign occupation'. When the issue was again raised the following year, Syria objected on the grounds that 'the international community is under legal and moral obligation to promote the struggle for liberation and to resist any attempt to depict this struggle as synonymous with terrorism and illegitimate violence'. The resultant definitional paralysis subsequently throttled UN efforts to make any substantive progress on international cooperation against terrorism beyond very specific agreements on individual aspects of the problem (concerning, for example, diplomats and civil aviation).

The opposite approach, where identification with the victim determines the classification of a violent act as terrorism, is evident in the conclusions of a parliamentary working group of NATO (an organization comprised of long-established, status quo Western states). The final report of the 1989 North Atlantic Assembly's Subcommittee on Terrorism states: 'Murder, kidnapping, arson and other felonious acts constitute criminal behavior, but many non-Western nations have proved reluctant to condemn as terrorist acts what they consider to be struggles of natural liberation.' In this reasoning, the defining characteristic of terrorism is the act of violence itself, not the motivations or justification for or reasons behind it. This approach has long been espoused by analysts such as Jenkins who argue that terrorism should be defined 'by the nature of the act, not by the identity of the perpetrators or the nature of their cause'. But this is not an entirely satisfactory solution either, since it fails to differentiate clearly between violence perpetrated by states and by non-state entities, such as terrorists. Accordingly, it plays into the hands of terrorists and their apologists who would argue that there is no difference between the 'low-tech' terrorist pipe-bomb placed in the rubbish bin at a crowded market that wantonly and indiscriminately kills or maims everyone within a radius measured in tens of feet and the 'high-tech' precision-guided ordnance dropped by air force fighter-bombers from a height of 20,000 feet or more that achieves the same wanton and indiscriminate effects on the crowded marketplace far below. This rationale thus equates the random violence inflicted on enemy population centres by military forces— such as the Luftwaffe's raids on Warsaw and Coventry, the Allied firebombings of Dresden and Tokyo, and the atomic bombs dropped by the United States on Hiroshima and Nagasaki during the Second World War, and indeed the countervalue strategy of the post-war superpowers' strategic nuclear policy, which deliberately targeted the enemy's civilian population—with the violence committed by substate entities labelled 'terrorists', since both involve the infliction of death and injury on noncombatants. Indeed, this was precisely the point made during the above-mentioned UN debates by the Cuban representative, who argued that 'the methods of combat used by national liberation movements could not be declared illegal while the policy of terrorism unleashed against certain peoples [by the armed forces of established states] was declared legitimate'.

It is a familiar argument. Terrorists, as we have seen, deliberately cloak themselves in the terminology of military jargon. They consciously portray themselves as bona fide (freedom) fighters, if not soldiers, who—though they wear no identifying uniform or insignia—are entitled to treatment as prisoners of war (POWs) if captured and therefore should not be prosecuted as common criminals in ordinary courts of law. Terrorists further argue that, because of their numerical inferiority, far more limited firepower and paucity of resources compared with an established nation-state's massive defence and national security apparatus, they have no choice but to operate clandestinely, emerging from the shadows to carry out dramatic (in other words, bloody and destructive) acts of hit-and-run violence in order to attract attention to, and ensure publicity for, themselves and their cause. The bomb-in-the-rubbish-bin, in their view, is merely a circumstantially imposed 'poor man's air force': the only means with which the terrorist can challenge—and get the attention of—the more powerful state. 'How else can we bring pressure to bear on the world?' one of Arafat's political aides once enquired. 'The deaths are regrettable, but they are a fact of war in which innocents have become involved. They are no more innocent than the Palestinian women and children killed by the Israelis and we are ready to carry the war all over the world.'

But rationalizations such as these ignore the fact that, even while national armed forces have been responsible for far more death and destruction than terrorists might ever aspire to bring about, there nonetheless is a fundamental qualitative difference between the two types of violence. Even in war there are rules and accepted norms of behaviour that prohibit the use of certain types of weapons (for example, hollow-point or 'dum-dum' bullets, CS 'tear' gas, chemical and biological warfare agents), proscribe various tactics and outlaw attacks on specific categories of targets. Accordingly, in theory, if not always in practice, the rules of war—as observed from the early seventeenth century when they were first proposed by the Dutch jurist Hugo Grotius and subsequently codified in the famous Geneva and Hague Conventions on Warfare of the 1860s, 1899, 1907 and 1949—not only grant civilian non-combatants immunity from attack, but also

- prohibit taking civilians as hostages;
- impose regulations governing the treatment of captured or surrendered soldiers (POWs);
- outlaw reprisals against either civilians or POWs;
- recognize neutral territory and the rights of citizens of neutral states; and
- uphold the inviolability of diplomats and other accredited representatives.

Even the most cursory review of terrorist tactics and targets over the past quarter-century reveals that terrorists have violated all these rules. They not infrequently have

- taken hostage civilians, whom in some instances they have then brutally executed (e.g. the former Italian prime minister Aldo Moro and the German industrialist Hans Martin Schleyer, who were respectively taken captive and later murdered by the Red Brigades and the Red Army Faction);
- similarly abused and murdered kidnapped military officers—even when they were serving on UN-sponsored peacekeeping or truce supervisory missions (e.g. the American Marine Lieutenant-Colonel William Higgins, the commander of a UN truce monitoring detachment, who was abducted by Lebanese Shi'a terrorists in 1989 and subsequently hanged);
- undertaken reprisals against wholly innocent civilians, often in countries far removed from the terrorists' ostensible 'theatre of operation', thus disdaining any concept of neutral states or the rights of citizens of neutral countries (e.g. the brutal 1986 machine-gun and hand-grenade attack on Turkish Jewish worshippers at an Istanbul synagogue carried out by the Palestinian Abu Nidal

Organization in retaliation for a recent Israeli raid on a guerrilla base in southern Lebanon); and

- repeatedly attacked embassies and other diplomatic installations (e.g. the bombings of the US embassies in Beirut and Kuwait City in 1983 and 1984, and the mass hostage-taking at the Japanese ambassador's residence in Lima, Peru, in 1996–7), as well as deliberately targeting diplomats and other accredited representatives (e.g. the British ambassador to Uruguay, Sir Geoffrey Jackson, who was kidnapped by leftist terrorists in that country in 1971, and the fifty-two American diplomats taken hostage at the Tehran legation in 1979).

Admittedly, the armed forces of established states have also been guilty of violating some of the same rules of war. However, when these transgressions do occur—when civilians are deliberately and wantonly attacked on war or taken hostage and killed by military forces—the term 'war crime' is used to describe such acts and, imperfect and flawed as both international and national judicial remedies may be, steps nonetheless are often taken to hold the perpetrators accountable for these crimes. By comparison, one of the fundamental *raisons d'être* of international terrorism is a refusal to be bound by such rules of warfare and codes of conduct. International terrorism disdains any concept of delimited areas of combat or demarcated battlefields, much less respect of neutral territory. Accordingly, terrorists have repeatedly taken their often parochial struggles to other, sometimes geographically distant, third party countries and there deliberately enmeshed persons completely unconnected with the terrorists' cause or grievances in violent incidents designed to generate attention and publicity.

The reporting of terrorism by the news media, which have been drawn into the semantic debates that divided the UN in the 1970s and continue to influence all discourse on terrorism, has further contributed to the obfuscation of the terrorist/'freedom fighter' debate, enshrining imprecision and implication as the lingua franca of political violence in the name of objectivity and neutrality. In striving to avoid appearing either partisan or judgemental, the American media, for example, resorted to describing terrorists—often in the same report—as variously guerrillas, gunmen, raiders, commandos and even soldiers. A random sample of American newspaper reports of Palestinian terrorist activities between June and December 1973, found in the terrorism archives and database maintained at the University of St. Andrews in Scotland, provided striking illustrations of this practice. Out of eight headlines of articles describing the same incident, six used the word 'guerrillas' and only two 'terrorists' to describe the perpetrators. An interesting pattern was also observed whereby those accounts that immediately followed a particularly horrific or tragic incident—that is, involving the death and injury of innocent persons (in this instance, the attack on a Pan Am airliner at Rome airport, in which thirty-two passengers were killed)—tended to describe the perpetrators as 'terrorists' and their act as 'terrorism' (albeit in one case only in the headline, before reverting to the more neutral terminology of 'commando', 'militants', and 'guerrilla attack' in the text) more frequently than did reports of less serious or non-lethal incidents. One *New York Times* leading article, however, was far less restrained than the stories describing the actual incident, describing it as 'bloody' and 'mindless' and using the words 'terrorists' and 'terrorism' interchangeably with 'guerrillas' and 'extremists'. Only six months previously, however, the same newspaper had run a story about another terrorist attack that completely eschewed the terms 'terrorism' and 'terrorist', preferring 'guerrillas' and 'resistance' (as in 'resistance movement') instead. The *Christian Science Monitor*'s reports of the Rome Pan Am attack similarly avoided 'terrorist' and 'terrorism' in favour of 'guerrillas' and 'extremists'; an Associated Press story in the next day's *Los Angeles Times* also stuck with 'guerrillas', while the two *Washington Post* articles on the same incident opted for the terms 'commandos' and 'guerrillas'.

This slavish devotion in terminological neutrality, which David Rapoport first observed over twenty years ago, is still in evidence today. A recent article appearing in the *International Herald Tribune* (a Paris-based newspaper published in conjunction with the *New York Times* and *Washington Post*) reported an incident in Algeria where thirty persons had been killed by perpetrators who were variously described as 'terrorists' in the article's headline, less judgementally as 'extremists' in the lead paragraph and as the still more ambiguous 'Islamic fundamentalists' in the article's third paragraph. In a country that since 1992 has been afflicted with an unrelenting wave of terrorist violence and bloodshed that has claimed the lives of an estimated 75,000 persons, one might think that the distinctions between 'terrorists', mere 'extremists' and ordinary 'fundamentalists' would be clearer. Equally interesting was the article that appeared on the opposite side of the same page of the newspaper that described the 'decades of sporadic *guerrilla* [my emphasis] warfare by the IRA' in Northern Ireland. Yet fifty years ago the same newspaper apparently had fewer qualms about using the word 'terrorists' to describe the two young Jewish men in pre-independence Israel who, while awaiting execution after having been convicted of attacking British military targets, committed suicide. Other press accounts of the same period in *The Times* of London and the *Palestine Post* similarly had no difficulties, for example, in describing the 1946 bombing by Jewish terrorists of the British military headquarters and government secretariat located in Jerusalem's King David Hotel as a 'terrorist' act perpetrated by 'terrorists'. Similarly, in perhaps the most specific application of the term, the communist terrorists against whom the British fought in Malaya throughout the late 1940s and 1950s were routinely referred to as 'CTs'—for 'Communist terrorists'. As Rapoport warned in the 1970s, 'In attempting to correct the abuse of language for political purposes our journalists may succeed in making language altogether worthless.'

The cumulative effect of this proclivity towards equivocation is that today there is no one widely accepted or agreed definition for terrorism. Different departments or agencies of even the same government will themselves often have very different definitions for terrorism. The US State Department, for example, uses the definition of terrorism contained in Title 22 of the United States Code, Section 2656f(d):

> premeditated, politically motivated violence perpetrated against noncombatant targets by subnational groups or clandestine agents, usually intended to influence an audience,

while the US Federal Bureau of Investigation (FBI) defines terrorism as

> the unlawful use of force or violence against persons or property to intimidate or coerce a Government, the civilian population, or any segment thereof, in furtherance of political or social objectives,

and the US Department of Defense defines it as

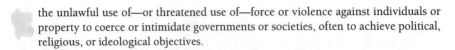

the unlawful use of—or threatened use of—force or violence against individuals or property to coerce or intimidate governments or societies, often to achieve political, religious, or ideological objectives.

Not surprisingly, each of the above definitions reflects the priorities and particular interests of the specific agency involved. The State Department's emphasis is on the premeditated and planned or calculated nature of terrorism in contrast to more spontaneous acts of political violence. Its definition is also the only one of the three to emphasize both the ineluctably political nature of terrorism and the perpetrators' fundamental 'subnational' characteristic. The State Department definition, however, is conspicuously deficient in failing to consider the psychological dimension of terrorism. Terrorism is as much about the threat of violence as the violent act itself and, accordingly, is deliberately conceived to have far-reaching psychological repercussions beyond the actual target of the act among a wider, watching, 'target' audience. As Jenkins succinctly observed two decades ago, 'Terrorism is theatre.'

Given the FBI's mission of investigating and solving crimes—both political (e.g. terrorism) and other—it is not surprising that its definition focuses on different elements. Unlike the State Department, this definition does address the psychological dimensions of the terrorist act described above, laying stress on terrorism's intimidatory and coercive aspects. The FBI definition also identifies a much broader category of terrorist targets than only 'noncombatants', specifying not only governments and their citizens, but also inanimate objects, such as private and public property. The FBI definition further recognizes social alongside political objectives as fundamental terrorist aims—though it offers no clearer elucidation of either.

The Department of Defense definition of terrorism is arguably the most complete of the three. It highlights the terrorist threat as much as the actual act of violence and focuses on terrorism's targeting of whole societies as well as governments. The Defense Department definition further cites the religious and ideological aims of terrorism alongside its fundamental political objectives—but curiously omits the social dimension found in the FBI's definition.

It is not only individual agencies within the same governmental apparatus that cannot agree on a single definition of terrorism. Experts and other long-established scholars in the field are equally incapable of reaching a consensus. In the first edition of his magisterial survey, *Political Terrorism: A Research Guide*, Alex Schmid devoted more than a hundred pages to examining more than a hundred different definitions of terrorism in an effort to discover a broadly acceptable, reasonably comprehensive explication of the word. Four years and a second edition later, Schmid was no closer to the goal of his quest, conceding in the first sentence of the revised volume that the 'search for an adequate definition is still on'. Walter Laqueur despaired of defining terrorism in both editions of his monumental work on the subject, maintaining that it is neither possible to do so nor worthwhile to make the attempt. 'Ten years of debates on typologies and definitions', he responded to a survey of definitions conducted by Schmid, 'have not enhanced our knowledge of the subject to a significant degree.' Laqueur's contention is supported by the twenty-two different word categories occurring in the 109 different definitions that Schmid identified in his survey (see Table 1).

Table 1.1

Frequencies of Definitional Elements in 109 Definitions of 'Terrorism'

	Element	Frequency (%)
1	Violence, force	83.5
2	Political	65
3	Fear, terror emphasized	51
4	Threat	47
5	(Psychological) effects and (anticipated) reactions	41.5
6	Victim–target differentiation	37.5
7	Purposive, planned, systematic, organized action	32
8	Method of combat, strategy, tactic	30.5
9	Extranormality, in breach of accepted rules, without humanitarian constraints	30
10	Coercion, extortion, induction of compliance	28
11	Publicity aspect	21.5
12	Arbitrariness; impersonal, random character; indiscrimination	21
13	Civilians, noncombatants, neutrals, outsiders as victims	17.5
14	Intimidation	17
15	Innocence of victims emphasized	15.5
16	Group, movement, organization as perpetrator	14
17	Symbolic aspect, demonstration to others	13.5
18	Incalculability, unpredictability, unexpectedness of occurrence of violence	9
19	Clandestine, covert nature	9
20	Repetitiveness; serial or campaign character of violence	7
21	Criminal	6
22	Demands made on third parties	4

Source: Alex P. Schmid, Albert J. Jongman et al., *Political Terrorism: A New Guide to Actors, Authors, Concepts, Data Bases, Theories, and Literature.* New Brunswick, Transaction Books, 1988, pp. 5-6.

At the end of this exhaustive exercise, Schmid asks 'whether the above list contains all the elements necessary for a good definition. The answer', he suggests, 'is probably "no".' If it is impossible to define terrorism, as Laqueur argues, and fruitless to attempt to cobble together a truly comprehensive definition, as Schmid admits, are we to conclude that terrorism is impervious to precise, much less accurate definition? Not entirely. If we cannot define terrorism, then we can at least usefully distinguish it from other types of violence and identify the characteristics that make terrorism the distinct phenomenon of political violence that it is.

Distinctions as a Path to Definition

Guerrilla warfare is a good place to start. Terrorism is often confused or equated with, or treated as synonymous with, guerrilla warfare. This is not entirely surprising, since guerrillas often employ the same tactics (assassination, kidnapping, bombings of public gathering-places, hostage-taking, etc.) for the same purposes (to intimidate or coerce, thereby affecting behaviour through the arousal of fear) as terrorists. In addition, both terrorists and guerrillas wear neither uniform nor identifying insignia and thus are often indistinguishable from noncombatants. However, despite the inclination to lump both terrorists and guerrillas into the same catch-all category of 'irregulars', there are none-theless fundamental differences between the two. 'Guerrilla', for example, in its most widely accepted usage, is taken to refer to a numerically larger group of armed individ-uals, who operate as a military unit, attack enemy military forces, and seize and hold ter-ritory (even if only ephemerally during daylight hours), while also exercising some form of sovereignty or control over a defined geographical area and its population. Terrorists, however, do not function in the open as armed units, generally do not attempt to seize or hold territory, deliberately avoid engaging enemy military forces in combat and rarely exercise any direct control or sovereignty either over territory or population.

It is also useful to distinguish terrorists from ordinary criminals. Like terrorists, criminals use violence as a means to attaining a specific end. However, while the violent act itself may be similar—kidnapping, shooting, arson, for example—the purpose or motivation clearly is not. Whether the criminal employs violence as a means to obtain money, to acquire material goods, or to kill or injure a specific victim for pay, he is acting primarily for selfish, personal motivations (usually material gain). Moreover, un-like terrorism, the ordinary criminals' violent act is not designed or intended to have consequences or create psychological repercussions beyond the act itself. The criminal may of course use some short-term act of violence to 'terrorize' his victim, such as waving a gun in the face of a bank clerk during a robbery in order to ensure the clerk's expeditious compliance. In these instances, however, the bank robber is conveying no 'message' (political or otherwise) through his act of violence beyond facilitating the rapid handing over of his 'loot'. The criminal's act therefore is not meant to have any effect reaching beyond either the incident itself or the immediate victim. Further, the violence is neither conceived nor intended to convey any message to anyone other than the bank clerk himself, whose rapid cooperation is the robber's only objective. Perhaps most fundamentally, the criminal is not concerned with influencing or affecting public opinion: he simply wants to abscond with his money or accomplish his mercenary task in the quickest and easiest way possible so that he may reap his reward and enjoy the fruits of his labours. By contrast, the fundamental aim of the terrorist's violence is ulti-mately to change 'the system'—about which the ordinary criminal, of course, couldn't care less.

The terrorist is also very different from the lunatic assassin, who may use identical tactics (e.g. shooting, bombing) and perhaps even seeks the same objective (e.g. the death of a political figure). However, while the tactics and targets of terrorists and lone assassins are often identical, their purpose is not. Whereas the terrorist's goal is again ineluctably *political* (to change or fundamentally alter a political system through his vi-olent act), the lunatic assassin's goal is more often intrinsically idiosyncratic, completely egocentric and deeply personal. John Hinckley, who tried to kill President Reagan in 1981 to impress the actress Jodie Foster, is a case in point. He acted not from political motivation or ideological conviction but to fulfil some profound personal quest (killing the president to impress his screen idol). Such entirely *apolitical* motivations can in no way be compared to the rationalizations used by the Narodnaya Volya to justify its campaign of tyrannicide against the tsar and his minions, nor even to the Irish Republican Army's efforts to assassinate Prime Minister Margaret Thatcher or her successor, John Major, in hopes of dramatically changing British policy towards Northern Ireland. Further, just as one person cannot credibly claim to be a political party, so a lone individual cannot be considered to constitute a terrorist group. In this respect, even though Sirhan Sirhan's assassination of presidential candidate and US Senator Robert Kennedy in 1968 had a political motive (to protest against US support for Israel), it is debatable whether the murder should be defined as a terrorist act since Sirhan belongs to no organized political group and acted entirely on his own, out of deep personal frustration and a profound animus that few others shared. To qualify as terrorism, violence must be perpetrated by some organizational entity with at least some conspiratorial structure and identifiable chain of command beyond a single individual acting on his or her own.

Finally, the point should be emphasized that, unlike the ordinary criminal or the lunatic assassin, the terrorist is not pursuing purely egocentric goals—he is not driven by the wish to line his own pocket or satisfy some personal need or grievance. The terrorist is fundamentally an *altruist*: he believes that he is serving a 'good' cause designed to achieve a greater good for a wider constituency—whether real or imagined—which the terrorist and his organization purport to represent. The criminal, by comparison, serves no cause at all, just his own personal aggrandizement and material satiation. Indeed, a 'terrorist without a cause (at least in his own mind)', Konrad Kellen has argued, 'is not a terrorist'. Yet the possession or identification of a cause is not a sufficient criterion for labelling someone a terrorist. In this key respect, the difference between terrorists and political extremists is clear. Many persons, of course, harbour all sorts of radical and extreme beliefs and opinions, and many of them belong to radical or even illegal or proscribed political organizations. However, if they do not use violence in the pursuance of their beliefs, they cannot be considered terrorists. The terrorist is fundamentally a *violent intellectual*, prepared to use and indeed committed to using force in the attainment of his goals.

By distinguishing terrorists from other types of criminals and terrorism from other forms of crime, we come to appreciate that terrorism is

- ineluctably political in aims and motives;
- violent—or, equally important, threatens violence;
- designed to have far-reaching psychological repercussions beyond the immediate victim or target;
- conducted by an organization with an identifiable chain of command or conspiratorial cell structure (whose members wear no uniform or identifying insignia); and
- perpetrated by a subnational group or non-state entity.

We may therefore now attempt to define terrorism as the deliberate creation and exploitation of fear through violence or the threat of violence in the pursuit of political change. All terrorist acts involve violence or the threat of violence. Terrorism is specifically designed to have far-reaching psychological effects beyond the immediate victim(s) or object of the terrorist attack. It is meant to instil fear within, and thereby intimidate, a wider 'target audience' that might include a rival ethnic or religious group, an entire country, a national government or political party, or public opinion in general. Terrorism is designed to create power where there is none or to consolidate power where there is very little. Through the publicity generated by their violence, terrorists seek to obtain the leverage, influence and power they otherwise lack to effect political change on either a local or an international scale.

1.2   Paul R. Pillar, 2001

The Dimensions of Terrorism and Counterterrorism

A former U.S. Army officer and executive fellow at the Brookings Institute, **Paul R. Pillar** has been a member of the Central Intelligence Agency (CIA) since 1977. In 2000 he was appointed the national intelligence officer for the Near East and South Asia of the National Intelligence Council of the CIA. His particular areas of interest include terrorism, negotiation, and counterterrorist policy. This reading is from his book *Terrorism and U.S. Foreign Policy*.

Delimiting a subject is the first step in dealing with it intelligently, and this is especially true of terrorism and counterterrorism. Terrorism has often been conceived in intractably broad ways, while the costs of terrorism and the ways to combat it tend to be construed too narrowly.

What Terrorism Is

Efforts to define terrorism have consumed much ink. A recent book on terrorism, for example, devotes an entire chapter to definitions; the chapter documents previous definitional attempts by earlier scholars, some of whom gave up the effort.[1] Many students of terrorism clearly consider its definition an important and unresolved issue.[2] The concern about definitions, besides reflecting any scholar's commendable interest in being precise about one's subject matter, stems from the damage done by the countless twisted and polemical uses through the years of the term "terrorism." The one thing on which every user of the term agrees is that terrorism is bad. So it has been a catch-all pejorative, applied mainly to matters involving force or political authority in some way but sometimes applied even more broadly to just about any disliked action associated with someone else's policy agenda.

The semantic quagmire has been deepened not only by indiscriminate application of the term terrorism but also by politically inspired efforts *not* to apply it. This was most in evidence in the 1970s, when multilateral discussion of the subject in the United Nations General Assembly and elsewhere invariably bogged down amid widespread resistance to any condemnation—and hence any labeling as terrorism—of the actions of groups that had favored status as "national liberation movements" or the like. Variations on this pattern have continued to frustrate efforts to arrive at an internationally accepted definition of terrorism.

Another, less frequent, tendentious approach to defining terrorism is to define it in ways that presuppose particular policy responses. For example, define it as a crime if you want to handle it mainly as a law enforcement matter, define it as war if you intend to rely on military means, and so on. Arguing semantics as a surrogate for arguing about policy is a confusing, cumbersome, and ultimately poor way to arrive at a policy.

A reasonable definition of terrorism would capture the key elements of what those leaders and respondents to opinion polls who have expressed concern about terrorism probably have in mind, without being so broad as to include much else that is not in fact the concern of those whose job descriptions mention terrorism. As good a definition as any, given some clarification and minor modification, is the statutory one that the U.S. government uses in keeping statistics on international terrorism: terrorism, for that purpose, means "premeditated, politically motivated violence perpetrated against noncombatant targets by subnational groups or clandestine agents, usually intended to influence an audience."[3] This definition has four main elements.

The first, premeditation, means there must be an intent and prior decision to commit an act that would qualify as terrorism under the other criteria. An operation may not be executed as intended and may fail altogether, but the intent must still be there. The action is the result of someone's policy, or at least someone's decision. Terrorism is not a matter of momentary rage or impulse. It is also not a matter of accident.

The second element, political motivation, excludes criminal violence motivated by monetary gain or personal vengeance. Admittedly, these latter forms of violence often must be dealt with in the same fashion as terrorism for purposes of law enforcement and physical security. Criminal violence can also have political consequences if it is part of a larger erosion of order (as in Russia). And ordinary crime is part of the world of many terrorists, either because they practice it themselves to get money or because they cooperate with criminal organizations.[4] Terrorism is fundamentally different from these other forms of violence, however, in what gives rise to it and in how it must be countered, beyond simple physical security and police techniques. Terrorists' concerns are macroconcerns about changing a larger order; other violent criminals are focused on the microlevel of pecuniary gain and personal relationships. "Political" in this regard encompasses not just traditional left-right politics but also what are frequently described as religious motivations or social issues. What all terrorists have in common and separates them from other violent criminals is that they claim to be serving some greater good.[5]

The third element, that the targets are noncombatants, means that terrorists attack people who cannot defend themselves with violence in return. Terrorism is different from a combat operation against a military force, which can shoot back. In this regard, "noncombatant" means (and has been so interpreted for the government's statistical purposes) not just civilians but also military personnel who at the time of an incident are unarmed or off duty (as at Khubar Towers or at the U.S. Marine barracks in Beirut).

The fourth element, that the perpetrators are either subnational groups or clandestine agents, is another difference between terrorism and normal military operations. An attack by a government's duly uniformed or otherwise identifiable armed forces is not terrorism; it is war. The requirement that nongovernmental perpetrators be "groups" is one point, however, on which the statutory definition could usefully be modified. A lone individual can commit terrorism. Mir Aimal Kansi's shooting spree outside the Central Intelligence Agency was politically motivated, and the four-year manhunt for him was always rightly regarded as a counterterrorist operation. Because there was no indication that he had acted at anyone else's behest, however, his attack never counted in the government's statistics on terrorism. For the present purposes, Kansi and any others like him may be considered one-person terrorist groups.

There is one other respect in which terrorism must be conceived somewhat more broadly than the statutory definition above. Terrorism as an issue is not just a collection of incidents that have already occurred; it is at least as much a matter of what might occur in the future. The threat of a terrorist attack is itself terrorism. Moreover, the mere possibility of terrorist attacks, even without explicit threats, is a counterterrorist problem. Indeed, one of the most vexing parts of that problem concerns groups that have not yet performed terrorist operations (or maybe have not even yet become groups) but might conduct terrorist attacks in the future. There is no good way to record this potential or to quantify it, and it would be pointless to manipulate formal definitions to try to embrace it. But counterterrorist specialists must worry about it. It is part of the subject at hand.

The conception of terrorism given above excludes some things that have occasionally been labeled as "terrorism" and are themselves significant national security issues—in particular, certain possible uses by hostile regimes of their military forces, such as ballistic missiles fired at civilian populations. To be sure, there are some similarities to terrorism, involving the motivations of the perpetrators, the impact on the target populations, and even the identity of some of the governments involved. These other security issues, however, have their own communities to deal with them, both inside and outside government. The relationships between different security issues must be noted and analyzed, but that does mean expanding the concept of an issue beyond workable limits. Counterterrorist specialists have enough on their plates without, say, weighing into debates on ballistic missile defense.

The concept of terrorism delineated here is not just reflected in a U.S. statute. It is also in the mainstream of what most students of terrorism seem to have in mind, despite their collective definitional angst. Moreover, it also is in the mainstream of what modest international consensus has evolved on the subject, at least the farther one gets from large multilateral debating halls and the closer to rooms where practical cooperation takes place. The latter point is important, given the necessarily heavy U.S. dependence on foreign help for counterterrorism. It is also important that whatever concept of terrorism the United States uses not be capable of being twisted to apply to actions the United States itself may take in pursuit of its security interests.

About the latter point, two distinctions are critical. The first is the one between terrorism and the overt use of military force. As the world's preeminent military power, it is in the United States' interest to keep that distinction clear, but this is not just a unilateral U.S. interest. The distinction has a broader moral and legal basis, as reflected in international humanitarian law on armed conflict and its rules requiring combatants to identify themselves openly.[6] The second key distinction is between actions that are the willful result of decisions taken by governmental or group leaders, and actions that result from accidents or impulsive behavior by lower-ranking individuals. The latter are bound to happen, and have happened, in incidents involving the United States, just because of the number of circumstances in which U.S. personnel find themselves in which it could happen. One's concept of terrorism must distinguish clearly—as the definition above does—between, for example, the alleged bombing by Libyan agents of Pan Am 103 and the accidental shooting down of Iran Air 655 in the Persian Gulf by the U.S. cruiser *Vincennes*. Despite the similarities of these incidents (290 people perished in the downing of the Iranian flight in July 1988; 270 people died in the Pan Am incident in December of the same year), and even though Tehran was still calling the Iran Air incident a "crime" more than a decade later, these were fundamentally different events. One was a government's deliberate use of its agents to murder scores of innocent travelers; the other was a tragic case of mistaken identity by a warship's crew that believed itself to be in a military engagement.

The place of clandestine agents and subnational groups in the definition of terrorism requires a bit more reflection, because the United States has used many of both. Not only that, but such use has sometimes involved lethal force, and some of that force has caused civilian casualties. But the real question is whether the intentional (that is, premeditated) infliction of civilian casualties through agents or sponsored groups—say, to undermine a hostile regime—is an option that the United States can safely forswear. It is. For one thing, the irregular use of lethal force against civilians would likely be counterproductive, by enabling the targeted regime to rally popular support in the face of a presumed external threat. Just as important, such methods are contrary to what the American public would support as being consistent with American values (a key test to be applied to any proposed covert action, even ones never likely to become public knowledge). Recent operations such as air strikes against Yugoslavia or Iraq have shown the great emphasis the United States has come to place on *avoiding* civilian casualties, even as collateral damage in a conventional military campaign.[7]

The conceptual lines between terrorism and other forms of politically driven violence are blurry. They would be blurry under any definition. The definition given above is at least as clear as any other, but it still leaves uncertainty as to whether certain specific incidents are acts of terrorism. The U.S. government has an interagency panel that meets monthly to consider such incidents (for the sake only of keeping accurate statistics, not of determining policy). The panel debates such questions as whether a particular target or intended target should be considered a noncombatant. Split votes are not unusual.

Good policy on terrorism does not, however, require hand-wringing about how exactly to define it. For the great majority of counterterrorist activities, the late Justice Potter Stewart's approach toward pornography will suffice: that it is unnecessary to go to great lengths to define it, because one knows it when one sees it.[8] Even though the U.S. government itself has several other definitions of terrorism written for different purposes, definitional discussions are seldom part of intragovernmental deliberations on the subject, beyond the statistic-keeping panel just mentioned. Lawyers do sometimes have to inject precision about whether certain statutory criteria have been met. This usually revolves around not the meaning of terrorism itself, however, but rather, for example, whether certain conditions (such as U.S. citizenship of the victims) are present that would permit a criminal prosecution. In most situations in which a counterterrorist response may be required, government officials simply recognize terrorism when they see it and do what they need to do. Any uncertainty about whether a given incident is terrorism is due not to semantics but rather to incomplete information.

The blurriness of the definitional lines is a salutary reminder that terrorism is but one form of behavior along a continuum of possible political behaviors of those who strongly oppose the status quo. Alternative forms include other types of violence (such as guerrilla warfare), nonviolent but illegal actions, regular partisan or diplomatic activity, or simple expressions of opinion that never even crystallize into something as specific as a political party, resistance movement, or terrorist group. Sound counterterrorist policy does not focus narrowly only on terrorism itself (however defined) but instead takes into account that terrorists have a menu of other tactics and behaviors from which to choose, and that the conflicts underlying terrorism invariably have other dimensions that also affect U.S. interests.

The distinction between terrorism, as defined here, and other forms of violence by subnational groups is apt to be faint in the eyes of some of the people directly involved. The Muslim fight against Indian control of Kashmir, for example, has been a blend of terrorist attacks against civilians and guerrilla warfare against Indian military forces. At least some of the insurgent leaders recognize the distinction publicly and deny attacking civilians. "We are a legitimate freedom movement," said a leader of one of the larger groups, "and we do not want to be stigmatized with the terrorist label."[9] But attacks in Kashmir against cinemas and parliamentary candidates continue, along with ambushes of Indian army patrols. The course of the conflict in Kashmir, and how each side privately views it, will not depend on the exact proportion of attacks against civilian rather than military targets. Both kinds of attack are unjustified in Indian eyes; both kinds are part of an overall struggle for self-determination, in the eyes of the militants. The selection of targets has probably depended in large part on such tactical factors as the physical vulnerabilities of the targets and the local capabilities of the groups.

For most Americans, however—and for many others—the distinction between terrorism against civilians and warfare (including guerrilla warfare) against an army entails an important moral difference. The warrior who dons a uniform is understood to be assuming certain risks that the civilian does not, and the guerrilla who fires at someone who is armed and can fire back is not regarded as embracing the same evil as one who kills the helpless and the unarmed. While the United States must be cognizant of the tendency of many to gloss over such distinctions, it should not let the distinctions be forgotten. Its message should be that terrorist techniques, in any context, are unacceptable.

Which gets to the most important point to remember about definitions: terrorism is a *method*—a particularly heinous and damaging one—rather than a set of adversaries or the causes they pursue. Terrorism is a problem of what people (or groups, or states) *do*, rather than who they are or what they are trying to achieve. (If Usama bin Ladin, for example, did not use or support terrorist methods, he would be of little concern to the United States—probably receiving only minor notice for his criticism of the Saudi government and his role in the Afghan wars.) Terrorism and our attention to it do not depend on the particular political or social values that terrorists promote or attack.[10] And counterterrorism is not a war against some particular foe; it is an effort to civilize the manner in which any political contest is waged.

Why It Matters

Terrorism has many different costs. The direct physical harm inflicted on people and property is the most obvious, but it is by no means the only, or even the most important, cost. It is the most measurable ones, in that deaths and injuries can be counted and property damage can be assessed. The significance of even these direct physical costs can be a matter of debate, however, involving disagreements over exactly what should be measured and against what standard the measurement should be compared.

Start with the question of whose casualties to count. In any discussion of U.S. policy, U.S. citizens are clearly the primary concern. Six hundred and sixty-six American citizens died from international terrorism in the 1980s and 1990s.[11] During the same period 190 Americans died from domestic terrorism within the United States, for a total of 856 American deaths from terrorism during the past two decades.[12] Going beyond U.S. citizens, however, greatly expands the numbers. Deaths of all nationalities from international terrorist incidents during the same twenty years totaled 7,152. (There were also more than 31,000 wounded.) The scale of death and suffering expands yet another order of magnitude if one takes account of terrorism that is not "international" because it takes place within a single nation's borders and directly involves only that country's nationals. There are no statistics on this type of terrorism worldwide, but consider just one of the bloodier examples: Algeria. Most published estimates of the number killed in Algeria by the extremist violence that broke out in 1992 are around 100,000. Many of these deaths were not from terrorism, but many others were, including particularly gruesome mass throat-slittings in villages. Even without U.S. citizens being involved, and even without considering the indirect effects that might be more significant for U.S. interests, this scale of bloodshed warrants attention. The death toll has certainly been at least comparable to that of many natural disasters to which the United States has felt obliged to respond. The deaths in Algeria did, in fact, lead the counterterrorism community in the U.S. government to examine ways in which it might help.

Returning to the more direct U.S. concern with American casualties, what is the right frame of reference for assessing their magnitude? To any contention that the victims of terrorism are many—or few—one is entitled to ask, "compared with what?" Against some possible standards of comparison, such as highway deaths (more than 40,000 annually in the United States), the number of victims of terrorism seems tiny. And the number is less than the bathtub drownings, lightning strikes, and some other standards that critics have used. A more appropriate basis for comparison might be other deaths from foreigners committing political violence—that is, warfare. Even there, American fatalities from terrorism are minuscule compared with such major efforts as World War II (291,557 U.S. battle deaths), Korea (33,651) or Vietnam (47,378).[13]

U.S. military activity since Vietnam, however, provides a different perspective. U.S. deaths from nonterrorist hostile action in military operations during the 1980s and 1990s (including the Iranian hostage rescue attempt, peacekeeping in Lebanon, the bombing of Libya, the escorting of Kuwaiti tankers, and Operations Urgent Fury in Grenada, Just Cause in Panama, Desert Storm in the Persian Gulf, Restore Hope in Somalia, and Uphold Democracy in Haiti) totaled 251. Even adding the 263 deaths from nonhostile causes (most of which were incurred in Desert Shield and Desert Storm) yields a total of 514, less than the number of Americans killed by terrorists during the same period. The biggest single inflictor of casualties on the U.S. military during this period was a terrorist attack: the bombing of the U.S. Marine barracks in Beirut in 1983, which killed 241. Besides, some of the other military deaths (the eight who died in the attempt to rescue hostages in Iran in 1980, and the two who were lost during the air strikes against Libya in 1986) were casualties of U.S. responses to terrorism. The nature of the hazard that Americans face in carrying out official duties overseas has evolved over the past quarter century to the point that a commission studying the U.S. overseas presence could state in 1999 that "since the end of the Vietnam War, more ambassadors have lost their lives to hostile actions than generals and admirals from the same cause."[14]

There has been an underlying evolution in how U.S. policymakers view casualties, and this also affects how the consequences of terrorism are likely to be viewed. Since Vietnam, the United States has expended lives, or put them in harm's way, more reluctantly than before. The casualties that the U.S. military suffered in Somalia in 1993 (and their graphic and wrenching coverage in the media) appear to have accentuated this trend. Survey research suggests that policymakers and other civilian and military elites may be overestimating the American public's aversion to casualties in military operations incurred in performance of missions that have at least the potential to be successful.[15] Whether or not that is true, policies and strategies, including warfighting strategies, now place very high priority on minimizing casualties. The remarkable phenomenon of a major military campaign without any U.S. battle casualties—the air war against Yugoslavia in 1999—was the apotheosis of this trend. The trend can only accentuate the significance that Americans will place on whatever American lives are lost to terrorism in the future.

Two other dimensions of what terrorists have been doing lately, or appear poised to do in the future, bear on how to think about the direct physical costs of terrorism. One is that terrorism in recent years has become increasingly lethal. More terrorist attacks than before are designed to inflict high casualties. Deaths from international terrorism more than doubled from the first half of the 1990s to the latter half of the decade, even though the number of incidents declined 19 percent. This trend is associated... with the nature of some of the terrorist groups that have come to the fore during this time, and there is no reason to expect a reversal of the pattern anytime soon.

The other dimension is the much-ballyhooed danger of chemical, biological, radiological, or nuclear (CBRN) terrorism inflicting mass casualties. There are some legitimate reason for concern about this to be greater now than a few years ago. The just-mentioned increased lethality of international terrorism is one reason; the more that terrorists use conventional means to kill large numbers of people, the less of a conceptual leap it is that they would use unconventional means to try to accomplish the same objective. Related to that is the increased role of small, religiously driven groups like the World Trade Center bombers, who are less likely than many larger groups (or states) to be deterred by the consequences of their own escalating violence—because they have no constituent populations to abhor their methods and no fixed assets to be the target of retaliation. The availability of materials and expertise relevant to CBRN weapons is another basis for concern. The focus has been on what might come out of the former Soviet Union (not just "loose nukes" but also substances related to biological or chemical weapons, as well as the knowledge and skills of displaced Soviet weapons scientists) and on weapons-related information that is now readily available on the Internet. Intelligence that shows some terrorist groups to be interested in CBRN capabilities is another concern. So is the precedent set by Aum Shinrikyo's attempt in 1995 to use sarin in a Tokyo subway to inflict mass casualties. Finally, the enormous public attention given to the danger of CBRN terrorism has itself probably increased the danger by pointing out to terrorists some of the possibilities—not only how such weapons might be used but also how much they frighten people.

Public discussion of CBRN terrorism has tended to stress many of these concerns—and the vulnerabilities of the United States to conceivable mass-casualty CBRN attacks—but given less emphasis to reasons that such attacks may still be unlikely. The General Accounting Office [GAO] has noted this pattern and emphasized the important distinction between conceivable terrorist threats and likely ones. The GAO observes that some of the public statements of U.S. officials about the CBRN threat have omitted important qualifications to the information they have presented.[16] The qualifications can be found not only in the classified material that the GAO reviewed but also in what is now a sizable scholarly literature on CBRN terrorism.[17] Experts who have studied the subject in depth have found numerous reasons to doubt whether CBRN terrorism is as much a wave of the future as is widely perceived.

Some of those reasons involve technical and other difficulties that any terrorist would face in acquiring the capability to inflict mass casualties with CBRN devices or agents. Some of the substances in question (for example, virulent forms of pathogens that would be needed to make biological weapons, as distinct from other forms that might be used in the production of vaccines) are not as easy to obtain as is commonly supposed.[18] Even with raw material in hand, there are formidable challenges in converting it into an effective and deployable device. Some toxic agents are difficult to keep both potent and stable. Dissemination is a major challenge, with both biological and chemical agents. Airborne particles containing anthrax, for example, can easily be either too large or too small to infect people through inhalation. Chemical agents need to be produced in large quantities and dispersed over wide areas to have hope of causing large numbers of casualties. Given such challenges, development of a CBRN capability to cause mass casualties would require a major, sophisticated program that is well beyond the reach of the great majority of terrorist groups. Aum Shinrikyo demonstrated this point. Despite being unusually well endowed in money and technical talent and going to great lengths to develop CBRN capabilities, Aum's biological program failed completely, and its attempt to use sarin to kill hundreds or thousands on the Tokyo subway instead killed only twelve.

Other reasons for doubt involve terrorist intentions. Terrorists have generally been tactically conservative and have favored proven methods. The hazards and uncertain effects of using CBRN materials are not likely to be attractive to many of them, particularly given the proven effectiveness of old-fashioned truck bombs—in places as diverse as Beirut and Oklahoma City—in causing casualties numerous enough to be considered "mass." The fear-inducing aspect of an unseen killer like a biological pathogen may have appeal to some terrorists, but the theatrical aspect of an event that makes a loud explosion is apt to appeal to even more. Moreover, the large and well-organized groups that have the best chance of obtaining a CBRN capability are also the ones that—because they have the most to lose by outraging their constituencies or inviting forceful retaliation—are most likely to be deterred from using such a capability. Aum Shinrikyo was an exception, but what may be most significant (with more than five years having passed since the incident in the Tokyo subway) is that Aum did not start a trend.

The foregoing leads to the following conclusions about CBRN terrorism. First, it is a legitimate cause for concern; it represents one more way in which terrorism can entail major costs, and one more reason to be serious about countering it. Second, the actual threat of CBRN terrorism—which is impossible to gauge with anything approaching precision—has probably risen somewhat over the last few years but is much less than the alarmist treatment of the subject in the United States would lead one to believe. Third, actual CBRN attacks would (as with such attacks in the past) be more likely to cause few, rather than many, casualties. Their impact would be less a matter of the direct physical effects than the indirect psychological effects on the target population. How a government conditions its public to think about such an attack... is thus critical in determining what the impact will be.

A fourth conclusion (bearing in mind the preceding two) is that the specter of CBRN terrorism should not be the main basis for shaping thinking about terrorism overall or for organizing efforts to confront it. It would be a mistake to redefine counterterrorism as a task of dealing with "catastrophic," "grand," or "super" terrorism, when in fact these labels do not represent most of the terrorism that the United States is likely to face or most of the costs that terrorism imposes on U.S. interests. A CBRN incident that causes very many casualties is the sort of high-impact, low-probability event that, because of the high impact, policy must take into account. The potentially high consequences may be reason enough to devote more attention and resources to preparing for such an event. But the low-probability aspect of the scenario should also be remembered, and the scenario should not be allowed to distort or downgrade the attention paid to more probable forms of terrorism.

Similar considerations apply to cyberterrorism, about which high concern is even more recent, and the uncertainties even greater. Some terrorist groups have indeed demonstrated considerable sophistication with computers and computer networks. Presumably some groups that lack the necessary expertise for conducting electronic sabotage could purchase it from venal and adventurous individuals. Electronic attacks to date that have been associated with terrorist groups have been few and simple, such as "spam" attacks in which large numbers of messages overload a government's server. The capability of terrorist groups to conduct electronic attacks more damaging than these incidents, or than the nonterrorist sabotage that has occasionally disabled major web sites, is more questionable. Terrorist intentions regarding cyberterrorism are even more problematic. Linking the objectives of actual terrorist groups to scenarios of electronic sabotage that would serve those objectives is conjecture.

To express such skepticism is not to deny the worth of security measures that would protect against unconventional terrorism, not only because of the potentially high consequences of such terrorism but also because many of those measures would also guard against other dangers. Almost all of the steps being taken to safeguard the nation's electronic infrastructure from terrorist groups, for example, would also help to protect it against attacks from the sources that, based on recent experience, seem to pose the main threat of electronic sabotage: individual hackers, and perhaps others driven by nonterrorist motives. This last point is true as well of some measures to defend against biological terrorism, which might include a strengthening of the public health system (including, perhaps, the additional acquisition of vaccines or antidotes) that would be needed anyway to deal effectively with natural or accidental outbreaks of disease.[19]

Terrorism in general, even when conducted with conventional means, tends to have greater psychological impact relative to the physical harm it causes than do other lethal activities, including warfare. In this regard, the earlier comparisons with casualties from past military operations understate, in a sense, the significance of terrorism. The distinction between the fair fight of an open military engagement and the unfair one of a terrorist attack on helpless victims comes into play. Ask the average American if the life of a soldier who dies in battle is worth the same as the life of a countryman who has died from terrorism, and the answer will be yes. But ask after each type of event how much shock and revulsion that American is feeling, and the reaction will be stronger after the terrorist incident. That the felt impact of terrorism tends to be disproportionate to the material damage has led some to argue that if government (and others who comment on terrorism) would only play down its significance and treat it more like ordinary crime, its actual importance and usefulness to the terrorist would lessen.[20] How government publicly portrays terrorism does indeed matter. But however, much one might try to talk down the subject, some of the special shock of a terrorist attack will always be there; it is in the nature of the event.

The indirect costs of terrorism are, overall, significantly greater than the direct physical ones. The indirect costs are many and varied. They start with the fear instilled in individual citizens, and what it leads those citizens to do. The fear itself—the sheer mental discomfort—is a cost. So is the economic effect of fearful citizens not taking trips or not patronizing certain businesses. And so is the social effect of those citizens arming themselves or ostracizing fellow citizens of particular ethnic backgrounds that are associated with terrorism, or doing any of a number of other dysfunctional things that less fearful citizens would not do.

Countermeasures against terrorism are also a major indirect cost. Price tags can be placed on some of them but capture only part of the expense. What was labeled as the terrorism-related portion of the Clinton administration's budget for fiscal year 2000, for example, amounted to about $10 billion, although that is a malleable figure depending on what one includes under the counterterrorist label. To take a single type of expense as a more tractable example, the panel chaired by retired Admiral William Crowe that studied the bombings in East Africa estimated that $14 billion would be required over ten years to implement its recommendations for improving the security of U.S. diplomatic missions.[21] Federal expenditures are only part of the picture, because many security countermeasures against terrorism are expenses of state or local governments or of the private sector. And the cost of many measures cannot realistically be estimated at all, although they have innumerable second- and third-order effects that, aggregating them over the entire nation, are surely huge. Every time someone empties his pockets and takes a detour through a metal detector to gain access to a public building, there are costs—which may include not only inconvenience to an individual but also the time and thus the expense involved in transacting a piece of business.

The expenditures made in responding to a problem beg the question, of course, of how many of those expenditures have been necessary and effective. Most of the success stories about countermeasures against terrorism are fragmentary and anecdotal, and it is impossible to calculate how much trouble would have occurred in their absence. But the very fact that so many resources are consumed—however necessary or unnecessary, effective or ineffective, any particular countermeasure may be—is itself a reason for the subject to command policy attention.

With some antiterrorist programs—including some big, expensive ones—past effectiveness and the future need to spend substantial resources are easier to see. Aviation security is an example. A major success story over the past quarter century has been a drastic reduction in skyjackings. Although some other factors affecting terrorists' choice of methods have been involved, the chief reason for this welcome development has been a comprehensive security system that has made it much harder to bring on board an aircraft the wherewithal to hijack it. This system is costly, including the visible costs of x-ray machines, metal detectors, and the staff to operate them, as well as less visible costs such as lengthening the time required to make business trips. The Federal Aviation Administration is now endeavoring to reduce the vulnerability of civil aviation in the United States to the other terrorist threat it faces—in-flight bombings—by enhancing procedures for screening checked baggage on domestic flights. The FAA estimates that this single change would cost $2.8 billion over ten years.[22]

Finally, the costs of terrorism embrace a host of other political and policy effects. They include the governmental equivalent of fear among individual citizens—that is, the government does not do certain things (which could be anything from a trip by a VIP to the holding of a New Year's celebration), or does them in a more gingerly or less effective manner, than it otherwise would because of fear of terrorist attacks. Costs also include the shaping of the political environment in unfavorable ways. Any challenge to government's monopoly on the use of force (which terrorism and other politically motivated violence necessarily entails) affects citizens' views toward government itself, including the trust they place in it to meet their needs for order and security.[23]

The costs of terrorism also include major effects on U.S. foreign relations and foreign interests, especially the following.

First, the possibility of terrorist attacks inhibits, or at least complicates, a wide range of U.S. activities overseas and the maintenance of an official U.S. presence abroad. This includes the necessary concern that almost any official American working overseas must have with security (and in some places it is a high concern), which means a distraction from that official's primary job. It also includes major security-driven operational decisions having significant impact on other missions. For example, the United States vacated its embassy in Sudan in February 1996 (without formally breaking diplomatic relations) because of terrorism. The specific concerns were not only with the terrorism-related policies of the Sudanese government but also with whether U.S. officials living and working in Khartoum would be safe, given the presence in Sudan of a rogue's gallery of international terrorist groups.[24] The absence of a resident diplomatic mission in Sudan, which has the largest territory of any African country and touches on numerous conflicts in the unstable northeastern and East Africa regions, unavoidably hinders support for U.S. interests in the area. One of the things it has hindered is collection of intelligence, including intelligence on terrorist threats that could materialize elsewhere. (It is worth remembering that most of those arrested in June 1993 for plotting to bomb the Hudson River tunnels and other landmarks in New York City were Sudanese.)

A similar security-driven redeployment was the move, following the bombing of Khubar Towers in 1996, of nearly 4,000 U.S. troops in Saudi Arabia from the urban areas of Dhahran and Riyadh to the isolated (and hence less vulnerable to terrorism) Prince Sultan Air Base. The move itself cost $200 million (which the U.S. and Saudi governments agreed to split). Perhaps more costly was the impact on morale, training, and readiness of the isolation and accompanying changes in deployment policy, including the withdrawal of command sponsorship for dependents and the cutting in half (from ninety days to forty-five) of the tours of the fighter pilots who overfly Iraq.[25]

Besides the impediments to official U.S. activity, there are also security-related complications for the private sector. If a U.S. business decides to brave the risk of terrorism in making a direct investment in a hazardous area, it will have expenses for security that will be an added cost of doing business. If the risk dissuades it from making the investment, then an opportunity for making and repatriating profits, and for enhancing employment in the local economy, will have been lost.

A second cost of terrorism in terms of foreign policy is the undermining of peace processes, including ones in which the United States has invested heavily and which, absent the disruption of fresh terrorist attacks, might otherwise be ripe for progress. The series of suicide bombings in Israel by Hamas and the Palestine Islamic Jihad in early 1996, for example, caused popular support for the Labor Party's peace policies to crumble, paved the way for Benjamin Netanyahu's upset election victory, and retarded progress toward further Arab-Israeli accords. In Northern Ireland, attacks in August 1998 by the republican splinter group calling itself the "Real IRA" (especially a car bomb in Omagh that killed 29 and injured at least 330) led to an unraveling of the Good Friday peace accord to the point that, later in the year, the agreement seemed close to collapse. More recently, it has been the main IRA's retention of its means of terror (the issue of "decommissioning of arms") that has been the principal reason for setbacks in the Northern Ireland peace process, such as the temporary suspension of the provincial government in February 2000.

Third, terrorism risks enflaming other regional conflicts that are already closer to war than to peace. (The spark that ignited World War I—the assassination of Archduke Francis Ferdinand—was a terrorist act.) The hijacking by Kashmiri militants of an Indian airliner in December 1999, for example, led to a new round of recriminations between India and Pakistan and raised the temperature of their dispute. Neither this incident nor most others like it have led to a war, but they at least temporarily increase the danger of one breaking out.

Fourth, the concern of an otherwise friendly government that it will become a target of terrorism may dissuade it from cooperating with the United States. Sometimes it fears being perceived as doing Washington's bidding. Sometimes what Washington asks it to do is unpopular for other reasons. In either case the specific fear is that extreme opponents of the requested cooperation will strike back with violence. The cooperation in question may range from diplomatic support to the hosting of a military deployment.

And fifth, terrorism can destabilize friendly governments. This is much less common than merely influencing the policies of such governments, and terrorism itself seldom topples regimes. It has sometimes caused major damage to the social or economic fabric of important countries, however, and as a result has called regimes' political stamina into question. This was true of Peru at the height of Sendero Luminoso's campaign of violence, and to a lesser degree of Egypt when terrorist attacks devastated that country's economically vital tourist industry in the early 1990s.

None of these costly consequences for U.S. foreign relations results *only* from terrorism. Numerous other political, economic, military, diplomatic, and cultural dimensions of the global environment (or regional environments) also affect them. Many of these dimensions involve the United States directly or are subject to U.S. influence. This is part of why counterterrorist policy must be considered and formulated as an integral part of U.S. foreign policy. Counterterrorism is one means by which to pursue the objectives implied above—stable and cooperative allies, effective regional peace processes, and so forth—and others as well. The means, including counterterrorism, used to pursue these objectives must be employed as part of a consistent, well-integrated strategy. And in the judgment of history, whether these objectives are achieved is likely to be at least important as the means used to achieve them.

Of course, the basic counterterrorist goal of saving lives and property from terrorist attack is a worthy end in its own right and not just a means. Indeed, some of the objectives posited above, such as effective regional peacemaking, could just as appropriately be viewed as means toward, among other things, the end of reducing violence, especially terrorist violence. The permutations of ends and means relationships between counterterrorism and other foreign policy goals are innumerable. That is the point. Counterterrorism is part of a larger, complicated web of foreign policy endeavors and interests, with numerous trade-offs and unintended consequences that should not be ignored.

The Elements of Counterterrorist Policy

No single approach makes an effective counterterrorist policy. The policy must have several elements. In that respect, counterterrorism is similar to many other policy problems, including other ones that involve the physical well-being of the public.

Consider, for example, highway safety. Highway deaths and injuries are a function of the highways themselves, the vehicles that travel them, the traffic laws, the enforcement of those laws, and the drivers. Government can reduce deaths and injuries somewhat through action on each of these fronts (for example, installing guard rails, raising crash resistance standards for cars, lowering speed limits, putting more police on patrol, tightening licensing requirements for drivers). Each type of measure addresses only part of the problem. Each has diminishing returns. Each entails compromises with other interests, such as competing demands for use of tax dollars, ease and efficiency in getting people where they want go, or environmental concerns. So some measures are taken in all of these areas, rather than concentrating safety efforts in only one of them.

The major fronts on which the problem of terrorism can be addressed are the root conditions and issues that give rise to terrorist groups in the first place and motivate individuals to join them; the ability of such groups to conduct terrorist attacks; the intentions of groups regarding whether to launch terrorist attacks; and the defenses erected against such attacks. Each of these corresponds to a phase in the life cycle of terrorism, from simmering discontent to the conduct of an actual terrorist operation. As with the example of highway safety, important and useful work can be done on each front. But also like that example, efforts on any one front are insufficient to manage the problem and are necessarily limited by competing objectives and equities. Effective counterterrorism requires attention to all four areas.

Roots

Cutting the roots of terrorism is not commonly thought of—or officially expressed as—an element of U.S. counterterrorist policy, for a couple of reasons. One is that it is farther removed than any of the other elements from the here-and-now worries of imminent threats, actual attacks, and what to do about them. It is not as pressing a concern as other counterterrorist work, the links between roots and people actually getting killed or maimed are often tenuous and twisted, and cause-and-effect relationships are difficult to prove. The other reason is that doing something about roots involves the management of numerous foreign policy matters that are not primarily the responsibility of people who call themselves counterterrorist officials. In fact, it embraces a huge swath of U.S. foreign policy on such things as regional and local conflicts, political instability within states, and social and economic conditions in countries in which terrorist groups have arisen or could arise.

Just because a cause-and-effect relationship is difficult to measure, however, does not make it nonexistent. Conditions do matter. Terrorists and terrorist groups do not arise randomly, and they are not distributed evenly around the globe. Scholars who have examined the origins of subnational political violence in general have pointed to the need to consider the perceived deprivation and other grievances that provide motives for violence, as well as the calculations and political opportunities of dissident leaders who mobilize such discontent, to understand better when and where violence breaks out.[26]

Two types of antecedent conditions are germane to the emergence of terrorists. One consists of the issues expressed directly by the terrorists and those who sympathize with their cause: political repression, a lack of self-determination, the depravity of their rulers, or whatever. People who are angry over such issues are more likely to resort to extreme measures, including terrorism and other forms of violence, than ones who are not. Palestinian support for violence against Israeli targets, for example, has to some extent varied inversely with progress in the peace process aimed at realizing Palestinian self-determination. This is true even though most Palestinians realize that Islamist terrorism against Israel has been counter-productive in the sense of retarding the peace process itself, boosting electoral support for harder-line Israeli leaders, undermining the economy of the Occupied Territories, and causing the Palestinian Authority to be preoccupied with security rather than with political development.[27]

The other type of root condition includes the living standards and socioeconomic prospects of populations that are, or may become, the breeding stock for terrorists. Terrorism is a risky, dangerous, and very disagreeable business. Consequently, few people who have a reasonably good life will be inclined to get into that business, regardless of their political viewpoint. Those who have more desolate lives and little hope of improving them will have fewer reservations about getting into it. The majority of terrorists worldwide are young adult males, unemployed or underemployed (except by terrorist groups), with weak social and familial support, and with poor prospects for economic improvement or advancement through legitimate work. To take the Palestinian example, most members of the extremist Palestine Islamic Jihad are of low social origin and live in poverty in the bleak neighborhoods or refugee camps of the Gaza Strip.[28] Hamas also does its most successful recruiting in Gaza.

The connection between lifestyles and proclivity for terrorism has been the basis for a technique that has been used successfully to get low-level members of certain terrorist groups to leave the terrorist business and to stay out of it. Tell the young man that if he cuts all ties with his current organization he will receive assistance in finding a job and a new place to live. Tell him also that the financial assistance he receives will depend partly on his getting married (and, preferably, having children). Settling down into a stable family life with some means of supporting it makes a return to terrorism very unlikely. For such reclamation cases, the principal roots of terrorism have been severed.

Obviously not every terrorist or potential terrorist can be bought off in this way. Policy initiatives on a larger scale do affect the roots of terrorism, however. Peace processes that lead to some measure of self-determination may do so. Political reforms that open up peaceful channels for dissent may do so. And economic development that improves prospects for a better standard of living may do so. The possibilities for snipping away at the roots of terrorism in these and similar ways should be noted and made part of the policy deliberations. But there are three major constraints on what can be done by focusing on roots alone.

The first constraint is the complexity of the relationship between antecedent conditions and the emergence of terrorists. It is not nearly as simple a matter as giving disgruntled people votes or a higher income. No one has produced a good algorithm for the many variables that, in combination, breed terrorists. In the nineteenth century, terrorism frequently emerged in direct response to repression, but the correlation between political grievances and terrorism in more recent times is less obvious.[29] In fact, terrorism today appears more often in free than in unfree societies.[30] Peace processes that realize the aspirations of a majority may, at least in the short term, enflame a minority that opposes a settlement for other reasons. As for economic conditions, one must take account of cases such as the emergence of Islamic terrorist groups in some wealthy Muslim societies like Kuwait but not in some poor ones like Niger.[31] The tearing of traditional social fabrics by economic development may have actually encouraged terrorism in some places.

The second constraint is that counterterrorism can never be the only consideration, or sometimes even the chief one, in determining U.S. policies that affect the economic well-being of certain foreign populations or self-determination for certain ethnic groups. Resource limitations obviously weigh heavily on decisions regarding economic assistance. On the political side, U.S. support for even so long-standing a principle as self-determination has always been limited by a variety of interests and concerns.[32] Some things that an unhappy, potentially terrorist-breeding, population may consider unjust may be viewed by the United States, for politically and ethically sound reasons, as not unjust and in no need of major change. The likely effect on emergent terrorism should be one factor, but only one of many, that is brought to bear on policies that affect these sorts of political and economic conditions overseas.

And third, no matter how much effort is expended on cutting out roots of terrorism, there will always remain a core of incorrigibles—and these will include the terrorists about whom the United States must worry the most. They will remain because for some individuals (even though they are sane and political, not pathological), terrorism also serves personal needs—self-fulfillment, making a big mark, or following some other inner demon—that have little to do with the order of the outside world.[33] They will also remain because the viewpoints of some are simply too extreme to be accommodated. And they will remain because once terrorist groups and terrorist leaders emerge, they develop their own goals and dynamics that go beyond the causes that may have bred them in the first place. The second and third of these factors, and probably the first, apply, for example, to Usama bin Ladin and his inner circle. As former State Department counterterrorism coordinator L. Paul Bremer has put it: "There's no point in addressing the so-called causes of bin Ladin's despair with us. We are the root cause of his terrorism. He doesn't like America. He doesn't like our society. He doesn't like what we stand for. He doesn't like our values. And short of the United States going out of existence, there's no way to deal with the root cause of his terrorism."[34]

Capabilities

Reducing the ability of terrorist groups to conduct attacks—conduct them effectively, or in many different places—is at the heart of U.S. counterterrorist programs (especially in the narrow sense of counterterrorism as offensive efforts against terrorists, as distinct from defensive antiterrorism programs). This work involves a variety of intelligence, legal, and other counterterrorist instruments....

Attacking terrorist capabilities has been an effective way of reducing many brands of terrorism. Most of the successes have been unpublicized, piecemeal acts of disruption—a cell rolled up here, a terrorist operative arrested there. A more visible and dramatic example of how effective even a single blow against a group can be was the Peruvian raid in April 1997 at the Japanese ambassador's residence in Lima, which had been seized four months earlier by the Tupac Amaru Revolutionary Movement (MRTA). The raid not only freed all but one of the seventy-two remaining hostages; it also crippled the MRTA's capability to conduct future terrorism. Several of the group's most able operational leaders died in the raid.

As with the other elements of counterterrorist policy, however, a focus on degrading the capabilities of groups has inherent limitations. One limitation, as the bombing in Oklahoma City demonstrated, is that even the infliction of mass casualties does not always require much capability. That horror was accomplished with two men, a truck, and homemade fertilizer-based explosives. A prior detention (or just investigation) of Timothy McVeigh and Terry Nichols conceivably could have prevented the bombing, but there was nothing else that authorities could have done before the incident to reduce terrorist capabilities to conduct it. Infrastructures and networks of cells—which are critical to the ability of many foreign terrorist groups to conduct attacks—were not present in the case.

Too little capability for U.S. authorities to go after is one limitation; too much capability is yet another one. A major transnational terrorist group such as Lebanese Hizballah is simply too large and widespread an organization to wipe out with a few well-conceived counterterrorist operations. Using such operations to chip away at Hizballah's capabilities is, and should remain, a priority task for U.S. counterterrorism.

Such operations can be effective at least in curtailing the group's ability to strike in certain regions. But such a group is not as vulnerable as a smaller one like the MRTA. It must be assumed that, even in the face of vigorous counterterrorist operations, the group will retain a capability that must be negated through the other elements of counterterrorist policy.

Intentions

There is indeed an enormous amount of terrorist capability around the world, in the hands of groups as well as hostile states, which could inflict major harm on the United States (or others) if those who control that capability decided to do so. This includes not only avowedly anti-American groups such as Lebanese Hizballah (which has not directly carried out a confirmed terrorist attack against a U.S. target since at least 1996) but also highly capable groups (such as Hamas or the Tamil Tigers) that have directed their violence elsewhere. Having less rather than more terrorism is thus a function not only of degrading terrorist capabilities but also of terrorist leaders *choosing*—for whatever reason—not to use what capabilities they have to attack. In short, terrorist intentions matter.

The intentions of terrorist groups (what the leaders of groups that already exist choose to do) raise some of the same motives and issues that are related to terrorism's roots (why terrorist groups arise in the first place and people join them). The status of the Arab-Israeli peace process, for example, affects Palestinian terrorism through its influence on intentions (decisions by Hamas's leadership on whether, when, and against what targets to stage attacks) as well as on roots (the emergence of Hamas and the Palestine Islamic Jihad in the first place and the willingness of young Palestinians to be recruited for suicide missions). Again, the issues involved go well beyond counterterrorism, and policy decisions on them necessarily also reflect other objectives and equities.

Measures that are more commonly regarded as counterterrorism also affect terrorist intentions. Punishing terrorists through prosecution or retaliatory strikes, for example, might have some deterrent effect…. The posture that the United States takes toward the political aspirations of groups it has officially branded as terrorist affects the intentions of those groups. The same could be said of state sponsors of terrorism.

One of the longest standing and most frequently expressed tenets of U.S. counterterrorist policy also has to do with terrorist intentions: that the United States will make no concessions to terrorists. The principle is simple: that not rewarding terrorism will give terrorists less incentive to try using it again. It would be difficult to prove that the principle always works in practice, but some analysis has pointed to past patterns of how terrorists have attempted to coerce different states at different times to suggest it has some validity.[35]

The U.S. part of the record is clouded by the fact that the United States has at times made concessions to terrorism. The most notorious instance was the Iran-Contra affair, in which the United States secretly sold arms to Iran in 1986 as part of an effort to gain release of hostages held by Iranian-backed terrorists in Lebanon. That episode certainly tarnished the U.S. image of steadfastness against terrorism, but in some respects terrorists still have good reason to view the United States as one of their most obdurate opponents. Even Israel—despite being a famously hard-line fighter against terrorism that has refused to make concessions while hostages were held—has struck deals with extremist opponents, including ones in which large numbers of prisoners were released in return for much smaller numbers of Israeli nationals. It is with regard to the classic type of terrorist coercion—holding the target country's citizens hostage to obtain a release of prisoners—that the United States has stood most firm. Even Iran-Contra did not involve opening any U.S. jail cells.

A benefit of that firmness was seen after the MRTA's capture of the Japanese ambassador's residence in Lima. The six U.S. officials who were at the reception when the terrorists struck were among the first to be released. The kidnappers let them go five days after the incident began while keeping 140 other hostages, including many foreign officials as well as Peruvians. The MRTA probably calculated (correctly) that to the extent the United States stayed directly involved, it would counsel a harder line to the Peruvian leadership than would many of the Asian and Latin American governments whose officials the MRTA had also seized.

An obvious limitation to firmness in any hostage incident is the immediate risk to the lives of the hostages. No government, the United States included, can promise itself or anyone else that it would never, under any circumstances, make concessions to save the lives of its citizens. Its management of the incident would have to take into account the magnitude and credibility of the harm being threatened, along with its own longer-term credibility and reputation. Accordingly, the rhetorical emphasis of this aspect of U.S. counterterrorist policy perhaps should be less on "no concessions" and more on the slightly more flexible "terrorism will not be rewarded." A concession made in the face of an immediate threat of great harm need not constitute a reward unless the terrorists were demanding some irreversible act, and there are few of those (even released prisoners can be recaptured).[36] Once the immediate peril is over, the terrorists can be hunted to the ends of the earth and appropriate action taken to ensure that when the books on the incident are closed, it will not count as a reward for terrorism.[37] Certainly no government need feel obliged to observe commitments made under duress. Consider the repatriation of the crew of the USS *Pueblo*, a U.S. Navy ship that North Korea seized in 1968; the United States repudiated the "admission" (of violating territorial waters) demanded by the North Koreans even as it was signing it.

A broader limitation on how much can be expected from this kind of firmness is that the classic hostage-and-specific-demand incident is simply not as big a part of international terrorism as it used to be. Although U.S. citizens have been bit players in a few such incidents in recent years (such as the Lima event and the hijacking of the Air India jet), U.S. crisis managers have not for a long time had to wrestle directly with dramatic, well-publicized, hostage situations in which lives are staked against a need to stay tough on terrorism. The great majority of terrorist attacks today (and most of the best-known recent incidents) involve terrorists going right out and killing people, rather than making specific demands and putting themselves in a position to kill people if the demands are not met. The very U.S. firmness discussed above (and stronger backbones grown by some other governments) probably has had something to do with this, and to that extent it is another endorsement for a policy of firmness....

Terrorists who suddenly detonate a bomb may still be looking for a concession, even though there are no apparent hostages and no explicit negotiations. Hizballah's bombings of the U.S. and French embassies in Beirut in April 1983, for example, and its attacks later that year on the U.S. Marine barracks and a French military base, were aimed largely at expelling from Lebanon the multilateral peacekeeping force of which the U.S. and French contingents were a part. In such circumstances, the United States is in a sort of bargaining relationship with the terrorists, whether or not it wants to be or says it is. It cannot ignore the public demands of the terrorist group, and its own policies regarding the subject matter of those demands are in effect part of the negotiation.[38] So there is yet an opportunity to demonstrate firmness, but one with even more potential problems and complications than in the traditional hostage incident. Refusal to act the way the terrorists want not only risks further attacks along the lines of what has already occurred (which was certainly an implicit threat in Lebanon) but also may mean continuing a policy that is unwise or unsustainable for other reasons. The alternative is to do what the terrorists would wish (which the United States and its allies did in Lebanon, pulling their troops out in early 1984), which—regardless of how the move is billed and the other reasons for it—may be seen as a concession to terrorism.

Other terrorist attacks are conducted without any particular concessions in mind; the destruction is more of an end in itself, motivated by hatred or revenge. With those who would wage this brand of terrorism (exemplified by the bombing of the World Trade Center by Ramzi Yousef's group), there is no way to influence intentions over the long term—whether by being steadfast in not rewarding terrorism, or being forceful in punishing it, or through any other means. The incorrigibility of such people is the main limitation of this element of counterterrorism. An ad hoc terrorist such as Yousef, who was not part of any permanent organization, is particularly unlikely to be deterred for long or to be coaxed on to a less violent path. Yousef was out to kill as many Americans as he could, he and his colleagues did not have fixed assets that could be bombed in retaliation, and he showed no sign of caring about his cohorts being caught and prosecuted.

Defenses

The one way in which the bin Ladins and Yousefs can be deterred is at the short-term, tactical level, by erecting security countermeasures that persuade them that a contemplated attack would fail. Some security measures that the United States has used overseas have had this effect. In at least one recent instance, a plot to attack a U.S. embassy was called off in the planning stage because the terrorists concluded that the security they had observed there could not be overcome. Antiterrorist defenses, therefore, are another way to influence terrorist intentions.

Physical defenses are also an element in their own right in saving lives from terrorism, even where they do not deter. And lives are saved even when attacks are not defeated entirely. The security measures at Khubar Towers, which kept the explosive-laden truck from penetrating the perimeter of the compound, prevented a death toll that would have far exceeded the nineteen U.S. servicemen who were killed. Similarly, in both Nairobi and Dar es Salaam in 1998, physical barriers and the refusal of guards to admit onto embassy grounds the trucks used by the terrorists greatly minimized U.S. casualties. Besides, the bigger the bomb the terrorists have to build, and the larger and more complex their operation has to become to defeat the defenses, the greater the chance that their operation will be compromised and discovered.

Antiterrorist defenses constitute a very large proportion of the U.S. fight against terrorism, certainly in resources but also in leadership attention. At the state and local level and in the private sector defenses are virtually the entire effort. Efforts at the federal level include defensive measures at both home and abroad. The two major overseas defensive programs—protection for U.S. diplomatic and military installations—have each received renewed emphasis in response to attacks in recent years.

On the diplomatic side, the bombings in Nairobi and Dar es Salaam highlighted the failure to meet standards for embassy security that had been established after earlier tragedies in Lebanon (the so-called Inman standards, after Admiral Bobby R. Inman, who chaired an Advisory Panel on Overseas Security in 1985). As of mid-1999, 229 of the 260 U.S. diplomatic posts worldwide still lacked the 100-foot setback (from the compound perimeter) specified in the Inman standards.[39] The funding level that the Crowe panel recommended is unlikely to be reached, but the Clinton administration in its last year budgeted more than $1.1 billion for embassy security in fiscal year 2001 and requested $3.4 billion in advance appropriations for fiscal years 2002 through 2005.[40]

Protection for military forces received a comparable fillip from the attack at Khubar Towers. In September 1996, Secretary of Defense William Perry issued a fresh directive on defending against terrorism (DoD Directive 2000.12) and initiated numerous enhancements to U.S. force protection efforts. A new section, headed by a general officer, within the Joint Staff was given responsibility for coordinating and promoting the military's antiterrorism efforts, promulgating doctrine on the subject, implementing a comprehensive training program, and conducting vulnerability assessments of installations around the world. The annual military antiterrorist budget is now about $3.5 billion.

The cost of defensive measures—particularly in dollars but also in restrictions on freedom of movement—is their main limitation. Comprehensive protection for everything in the terrorists' sights would be prohibitively expensive. As the Crowe panel acknowledged, "We understand that there will never be enough money to do all that should be done. We will have to live with partial solutions and, in turn, a high level of threat and vulnerability for quite some time."[41] A related limitation is that terrorists sometimes respond to security countermeasures by shifting their attention to more vulnerable targets. In some cases this means—given the terrorists' own limitations on where and how they can operate—that no attack occurs. But in others it means that a target with less robust defenses gets hit. The shift can be from one specific target to another (for example, from military bases to private businesses).[42]

Another limitation is that some terrorists are remarkably resourceful in adapting to, and overcoming, antiterrorist defenses. The Irish Republican Army (IRA), for example, has cleverly changed its methods for detonating bombs, using devices ranging from radar guns to photographic flash equipment, to stay ahead of the British use of electronic measures to prevent detonations.[43] Yousef demonstrated comparable operational cleverness with the method he devised for bombing U.S. airliners over the Pacific (and which he successfully tested, with a small amount of explosive, on a Philippine Airlines plane in December 1994). The technique involved bringing on board innocuous-looking items (including a prepared digital watch and a bottle for contact lens solution that really contained a liquid explosive), assembling them in a lavatory, and leaving the assembled device hidden on the aircraft when the terrorist got off at an intermediate stop.

Such ingenuity points to the limitations of using technology to defend against terrorism. It is not as if good minds have not been put on the problem. The federal government has a Technical Support Working Group that oversees a vigorous program of research, development, and rapid prototyping of antiterrorist technologies; the program has grown rapidly in recent years to reach an annual budget of close to $40 million. The Defense Science Board, an advisory body that includes some of the nation's leaders in applying technology to problems of national security, devoted its 1997 summer study to transnational threats, including terrorism, and how to respond to them.[44] The threat itself is not, at bottom, technological. Technology is useful in limited ways in defending against it but is not itself a solution.

All counterterrorist work—regardless of the instruments employed, the particular partners enlisted, or the specific enemies confronted—involves one or more of the elements just described. The limitations of each are patent; the need to address all of them together is strong. But the challenges facing U.S. counterterrorist policy reflect not just the limitations of counterterrorism itself. That policy must be adapted to a real world in which both the terrorist threat and the place of the United States as a terrorist target have evolved in important ways.

Notes

1. Bruce Hoffman, *Inside Terrorism* (Columbia University Press, 1998), chap. 1. Another recent chapter-length discussion of definitions is in David Tucker, *Skirmishes at the Edge of Empire: The United States and International Terrorism* (Praeger, 1997), chap. 2, pp. 51–69.
2. See, for example, the several articles on the subject in the autumn 1996 issue of the journal *Terrorism and Political Violence*, particularly Andrew Silke, "Terrorism and the Blind Men's Elephant," vol. 8 (Autumn 1996), pp. 12–28.
3. 22 U.S.C. 2656f (d).
4. For an argument that terrorism and crime should be kept conceptually distinct, see Phil Williams, "Terrorism and Organized Crime: Convergence, Nexus, or Transformation," in Brad Roberts, ed., *Hype or Reality: The "New Terrorism" and Mass Casualty Attacks* (Alexandria, Va.: Chemical and Biological Arms Control Institute, 2000), pp. 117–45. A contrasting view is in Roger Mead and Frank Goldstein, "International Terrorism on the Eve of a New Millennium," *Studies in Conflict and Terrorism*, vol. 20 (July-September 1997), p. 301.
5. Hoffman, *Inside Terrorism*, p. 43.
6. The discussion in chapter 4 on multilateral diplomacy addresses further what these rules, and recent modifications to them, imply for counterterrorism.
7. Assassination as a possible counterterrorist tactic is discussed in chapter 4.
8. Concurring opinion by Justice Stewart in *Jacobellis v. Ohio*, 378 U.S. 184, 197 (1964).
9. Quoted in Pamela Constable, "Kashmiri Rebels Pressure Pakistan," *Washington Post*, October 20, 1999, p. 23.
10. As Brian Jenkins has pointed out, this conception of terrorism does involve one value judgment: that an end does not justify the means. Brian M. Jenkins, "Terrorism: A Contemporary Problem with Age-old Dillemmas," in Lawrence Howard, ed., *Terrorism: Roots, Impact, Responses* (Praeger, 1992), p. 14.
11. International terrorism includes any incident that is terrorism under the statutory definition given above and that involves two or more nationalities when one considers the perpetrators, the victims, and the location of the incident.
12. Statistics are from unpublished FBI data.
13. Statistice on U.S. military casualties are Department of Defense data (web1.wbs.osd.mil/mmid/m01/sms223r.htm (November 2001).

14. Overseas Presence Advisory Panel, *America's Overseas Presence in the 21st Century* (Washington, November 1999), p. 38.

15. Peter D. Fravet and Christopher Gelpi, "How Many Deaths Are Acceptable? A Surprising Answer," *Washington Post*, November 7, 1999, p. B3.

16. General Accounting Office, *Combating Terrorism: Issues in Managing Counterterrorist Programs*, T-NSIAD-00 145 (April 6, 2000), pp.3–4.

17. The most comprehensive study is Richard A. Falkenrath, Robert D. Newman, and Bradley A. Thayer, *America's Achilles' Heel: Nuclear, Biological, and Chemical Terrorism and Covert Attack* (MIT Press, 1998). Despite the somewhat ominous title, this is a well researched work that lays out arguments both for and against the idea that terrorists are likely to employ unconventional weapons. A useful survey is Roberts, *Hype or Reality*, especially the chapter by Brian Jenkins, which summarizes points on which there appears to be consensus among most specialists. A recent book that touches on diverse aspects of the subject is Jessica Stern, *The Ultimate Terrorists* (Harvard University Press, 1999). Jonathan B. Tucker, ed., *Toxic Terror: Assessing Terrorist Use of Chemical and Biological Weapons* (MIT Press, 2000), examines several past cases of attempted or reported terrorists use of chemical or biological substances. Reasons to be skeptical about the magnitude of an unconventional terrorist threat are discussed in David C. Rapoport, "Terrorism and Weapons of the Apocalypse," *National Security Studies Quarterly*, vol. 5 (Summer 1999), pp. 49–67; Ehud Sprinzak, "The Great Superterrorism Scare," *Foreign Policy*, no. 112 (Fall 1998), pp. 110–24; Jonathan B. Tucker and Amy Sands, "An Unlikely Threat," *Bulletin of the Atomic Scientists*, vol. 55 (July-August 1999), pp. 46–52; Brian M. Jenkins, "The Limits of Terror: Constraints on the Escalation of Violence, " *Harvard International Review*, vol. 17 (Summer 1995), pp. 44–45, 77–78; Henry Sokolski, "Rethinking Bio-Chemical Dangers," *Orbis*, vol. 44 (Spring 2000), pp. 207–19; the exchange on "WMD Terrorism" in *Survival*, vol. 40 (Winter 1998–99), pp. 168–83; and part 1 of the *First Annual Report of the Advisory Panel to Assess Domestic Response Capabilities for Terrorism Involving Weapons of Mass Destruction*, December 15, 1999.

18. This is all the more true of acquiring a usable nuclear device or the fissile material necessary to make one, both of which—despite the breakdown of many of the controls in the former USSR—are still protected by significant safeguards. Partly for this reason, use of a device producing a nuclear yield is the least likely CBRN terrorist event. Use of radioactive material as a containment to be dispersed by a conventional bomb is more probable.

19. W. Seth Carus, "Biohazard," *New Republic*, vol. 221 (August 2, 1999), pp. 14–16.

20. See, for example, John Mueller and Karl Mueller, "Sanctions of Mass Destruction," *Foreign Affairs*, vol. 78 (May-June 1999), p. 44.

21. *Report of the Accountability Review Boards on the Bombings of the US Embassies in Nairobi, Kenya and Dar es Salaam, Tanzania on August 7, 1998* (January 8, 1999), Key Recommendations, sec. 1.A.12 (www.terrorism.com/state/accountability_report.html [November 2000]).

22. FAA Notice 99-05, "Security of Checked Baggage on Flights Within the United States," *Federal Register*, vol. 64 (April 19, 1999), p. 19230. This cost estimate is a maximum, assuming a combination of profiling of passengers and matching passengers with their bags. Greater use of explosives detection machines (which are hardly inexpensive themselves) might reduce the cost.

23. Philip B. Heymann, *Terrorism and America: A Commonsense Strategy for a Democratic Society* (MIT Press, 1998), p. 16.

24. Barbara Crossette, "Fearing Terrorism, U.S. Plans to Press Sudan," *New York Times*, February 2, 1996, p. A6.

25. Steven Lee Myers, "At a Saudi Base, U.S. Digs In, Gingerly, for a Longer Stay," *New York Times*, December 29, 1997, p. A1.

26. See, for example, the research on ethnically based conflict reported in Ted Robert Gurr, *Minorities at Risk: A Global View of Ethnopolitical Conflicts* (Washington: U.S. Institute of Peace Press, 1993).

27. Khalil Shikaki, "The Politics of Paralysis II: Peace Now or Hamas Later," *Foreign Affairs*, vol. 77 (July-August 1998), pp. 35–36.

28. Ziad Abu-Amr, *Islamic Fundamentalism in the West Bank and Gaza: Muslim Brotherhood and Islamic Jihad* (Indiana University Press, 1994), p. 96.

29. Walter Laqueur, "Reflections on Terrorism," Foreign Affairs, vol. 65 (Fall 1986), p. 91.

30. Leonard B. Weinberg and William L. Bubank, "Terrorism and Democracy: What Recent Events Disclose," *Terrorism and Political Violence*, vol. 10 (Spring 1998), pp. 108–18.

31. Daniel Pipes, "It's Not the Economy, Stupid: What the West Needs to Know about the Rise of Radical Islam," *Washington Post*, July 2, 1995, p. C2.

32. Richard N. Haas, *Conflicts Unending: The United States and Regional Disputes* (Yale University Press, 1990), p. 53.

33. See Martha Crenshaw, "How Terrorists Think: What Psychology Can Contribute to Understanding Terrorism," in Howard, *Terrorism: Roots, Impact, Responses*, pp. 71–93; Jerrold M. Post, "Terrorist Psycho-logic: Terrorist Behavior as a Product of Psychological Forces," in Walter Reith, ed., *Origins of Terrorism: Psychologies, Ideologies, Theologies, States of Mind* (Cambridge University Press, 1990), pp. 25–40; Robert S. Robins and Jerrold M. Post, *Political Paranoia: The Psychopolitics of Hatred* (Yale University Press, 1997), chaps. 4 and 6; and Laqueur, *The New Terrorism*, pp. 93–96.

34. *The NewsHour with Jim Lehrer*, Public Broadcasting System, August 25, 1998.

35. See, for example, Richard Clutterbuck, "Negotiating with Terrorists," in Alex P. Schmid and Ronald D. Crelinsten, eds., *Western Responses to Terrorism* (London: Frank Cass, 1993), p. 285.

36. Thomas C. Schelling, "What Purposes Can 'International Terrorism' Serve?" in R. G. Frey and Christopher W. Morris, eds., *Violence, Terrorism, and Justice* (Cambridge University Press, 1991), pp. 31–32.

37. See Heymann, *Terrorism and America*, pp. 40–46; and Tucker, *Skirmishes at the Edge of Empire*, pp. 74–80.

38. Schelling, "What Purposes Can 'International Terrorism' Serve?" p. 25.

39. Fact Sheet on Funding for Embassy Security, Department of State, August 4, 1999 (www.uninfo.state.gov/topical/pol/terror/99080404.htm [October 2000]).

40. White House Fact Sheet on Embassy Security Funding, February 10, 2000 (www.usinfo.state.gov/topical/pol/terror/00021004.htm [November 2000]).

41. *Report of the Accountability Review Boards*, Introduction.

42. Walter Enders and Todd Sandler in "The Effectiveness of Anti-Terrorism Policies: A Vector-Autoregression-Intervention Analysis," *American Political Science Review*, vol. 87 (December 1993), pp. 829–44, analyze statistics on terrorist incidents to conclude that the fortification of diplomatic installations has reduced attacks on those installations but has led terrorists to conduct more assassinations instead. They reach a similar conclusion about the installation of metal detectors in airports.

43. Hoffman, *Inside Terrorism*, pp. 180–82.

44. Defense Science Board 1997 Summer Study Task Force, *DoD Responses to Transnational Threats*, volume 1: Final Report (October 1997).

1.3   Eqbal Ahmad, 1998

Terrorism: Theirs & Ours

Eqbal Ahmad was born in India but moved to the newly created state of Pakistan in 1947. His theories about national liberation and anti-imperialism developed over years of involvement in radical causes worldwide. Ahmad spent the last years of his life addressing the conflict between India and Pakistan regarding Kashmir and speaking out against the rise of Islamic fundamentalism and the influence of the Taliban in Pakistan. The following reading is a transcript of a public talk he gave at the University of Colorado in October 1998. Ahmad died in 1999.

Eqbal Ahmad was one of the major activist scholars of this era. He was born in India probably in 1934. He was never quite sure. He left with his brothers for the newly created state of Pakistan in 1947. In 1996, the BBC did a powerful and moving TV documentary chronicling Ahmad's trek in a refugee caravan from his village in Bihar to Pakistan. The film, not shown on PBS in the U.S., is remarkable not just as an historical document but also for providing insight into the dangers of sectarian nationalism. Ahmad's secular thinking was surely shaped by the wrenching communal and political violence he experienced as a youngster. Even before the subcontinent was engulfed in the homicidal convulsions of 1947, Ahmad witnessed his own father murdered before him.

Ahmad came to the United States in the 1950s to study at Princeton. Later he went to Algeria. It was there that his ideas about national liberation and anti-imperialism crystallized. He worked with Frantz Fanon, author of The Wretched of the Earth, *during the revolt against the French. Returning to the U.S., he became active in the civil rights and anti-Vietnam War movements. It was during his involvement in the latter that I first heard his name. He was accused of plotting to kidnap Henry Kissinger. The trumped-up charges were dismissed.*

I did my first interview with him in the early 1980s in his apartment on New York's Upper West Side. It was memorable. I had just gotten a new tape recorder. I returned home thinking, Wow, I've got a great interview. I hit play and discovered the tape was blank. I had failed to turn the machine on. With considerable embarrassment I explained to him what happened. He said, "No problem." He invited me over the next day and we did another interview. This time, I pressed the right buttons. Whenever I tell that story, his friends would nod and say, "That's Eqbal."

Ahmad's radical politics and outspoken positions made him a pariah in academic circles. After years of being an intellectual migrant worker, Hampshire College in Amherst, Massachusetts, hired him in the early 1980s as a professor. He taught there until his retirement in 1997. He spent most of his final years in Islamabad where he wrote a weekly column for Dawn, *Pakistan's oldest English-language newspaper. His political work consisted chiefly of trying to bridge differences with India on the issues of Kashmir and nuclear weapons. He was also speaking out against the rise of Islamic fundamentalism and was concerned about the possible Talibanization of Pakistan.*

Eqbal Ahmad died in Islamabad, Pakistan, on May 11, 1999. His close friend Edward Said wrote, "He was perhaps the shrewdest and most original anti-imperialist analyst of the postwar world, particularly of the dynamics between the West and postcolonial Asia and Africa; a man of enormous charisma, dazzling eloquence, incorruptible ideals, unfailing generosity and sympathy…. Whether on the conflict between Israelis and Palestinians or India and Pakistan, he was a force for a just struggle but also for a just reconciliation…. Humanity and genuine secularism… had no finer champion."

"Terrorism: Theirs & Ours" was one of Eqbal Ahmad's last public talks in the United States. He spoke at the University of Colorado at Boulder in October 1998. It was broadcast nationally

and internationally on my weekly Alternative Radio *program. Eqbal Ahmad's near pro-phetic sense is stunning. After the September 11 terrorist attacks, I aired the speech again. Listeners called in great numbers requesting copies. They almost all believed that the talk had just been recorded.*

—David Barsamian

U ntil the 1930s and early 1940s, the Jewish underground in Palestine was de-scribed as "terrorist." Then something happened: around 1942, as news of the Holo-caust was spreading, a certain liberal sympathy with the Jewish people began to emerge in the Western world. By 1944, the terrorists of Palestine, who were Zionists, suddenly began being described as "freedom fighters." If you look in history books you can find at least two Israeli prime ministers, including Menachem Begin,[1] appearing in "Wanted" posters saying, TERRORISTS, REWARD [THIS MUCH]. The highest reward I have seen of-fered was 100,000 British pounds for the head of Menachem Begin, the terrorist.

From 1969 to 1990, the Palestine Liberation Organization (PLO) occupied center state as a terrorist organization. Yasir Arafat has been repeatedly described as the "chief of terrorism" by the great sage of American journalism, William Safire of The *New York Times*. On September 29, 1998, I was rather amused to notice a picture of Yasir Arafat and Israeli prime minister Benjamin Netanyahu standing on either side of President Bill Clinton. Clinton was looking toward Arafat, who looked meek as a mouse. Just a few years earlier, Arafat would appear in photos with a very menacing look, a gun holstered to his belt. That's Yasir Arafat. You remember those pictures, and you'll remember the next one.

In 1985, President Ronald Reagan received a group of ferocious-looking, turban-wearing men who looked like they came from another century. I had been writing about the very same men for *The New Yorker*. After receiving them in the White House, Reagan spoke to the press, referring to his foreign guests as "freedom fighters." These were the Afghan mujahideen. They were at the time, guns in hand, battling the "Evil Empire." For Reagan, they were the moral equivalent of our Founding Fathers.

In August 1998, another American President ordered missile strikes to kill Osama bin Laden and his men in Afghanistan-based camps. Mr. bin Laden, at whom fifteen American missiles were fired to hit in Afghanistan, was only a few years earlier the moral equivalent of George Washington and Thomas Jefferson. I'll return to the subject of bin Laden later.

I am recalling these stories to point out that the official approach to terrorism is rather complicated, but not without characteristics. To begin with, terrorists change. The terrorist of yesterday is the hero of today, and the hero of yesterday becomes the terrorist of today. In a constantly changing world of images, we have to keep our heads straight to know what terrorism is and what it is not. Even more importantly, we need to know what causes terrorism and how to stop it.

Secondly, the official approach to terrorism is a posture of inconsistency, one which evades definition. I have examined at least twenty official documents on ter-rorism. Not one offers a definition. All of them explain it polemically in order to arouse our emotions, rather than exercise our intelligence. I'll give you an example which is representative. On October 25, 1984, Secretary of State George Shultz gave a long speech on terrorism at the Park Avenue Synagogue in New York City. In the State Department Bulletin of seven single-spaced pages, there is not a single clear definition of terrorism. What we get instead are the following statements. Number one: "Terrorism is a modern barbarism that we call terrorism." Number two is even more brilliant; "Terrorism is a form of political violence." Number three: "Terrorism is a menace to Western moral values." Do these accomplish anything other than arouse emotions? This is typical.

Officials don't define terrorism because definitions involve a commitment to analysis, comprehension, and adherence to some norms of consistency. That's the second characteristic of the official approach to terrorism. The third characteristic is that the absence of definition does not prevent officials from being globalistic. They may not define terrorism, but they can call it a menace to good order, a menace to the moral values of Western civilization, a menace to humankind. Therefore, they can call for it to be stamped out worldwide. Anti-terrorist policies therefore, must be global. In the same speech he gave in New York City, George Shultz also said: "There is no question about our ability to use force where and when it is needed to counter terrorism." There is no geographical limit. On the same day, U.S. missiles struck Afghanistan and Sudan. Those two countries are 2,300 miles apart, and they were hit by missiles belonging to a country roughly 8,000 miles away. Reach is global.

A fourth characteristic is that the official approach to terrorism claims not only global reach, but also a certain omniscient knowledge. They claim to know where terrorists are, and therefore, where to hit. To quote George Shultz again, "We know the difference between terrorists and freedom fighters and as we look around, we have no trouble telling one from the other." Only Osama bin Laden doesn't know that he was an ally one day and an enemy another. That's very confusing for Osama bin Laden. I'll come back to him toward the end; it's a real story.

Fifth, the official approach eschews causation. They don't look at why people resort to terrorism. Cause? What cause? Another example: on December 18, 1985, *The New York Times* reported that the foreign minister of Yugoslavia—you remember the days when there was a Yugoslavia—requested the secretary of state of the U.S. to consider the causes of Palestinian terrorism. The secretary of state, George Shultz, and I'm quoting from *The New York Times*, "went a bit red in the face. He pounded the table and told the visiting foreign minister, "There is no connection with any cause. Period." Why look for causes?

A sixth characteristic of the official approach to terrorism is the need for the moral revulsion we feel against terror to be selective. We are to denounce the terror of those groups which are officially disapproved. But we are to applaud the terror of those groups of whom officials do approve. Hence, President Reagan's statement, "I am a contra." We know that the contras of Nicaragua were by any definition terrorists, but the media heed the dominant view.

More importantly to me, the dominant approach also excludes from consideration the terrorism of friendly governments. Thus, the United States excused, among others, the terrorism of Pinochet, who killed one of my closest friends, Orlando Letelier, one of Chilean president Salvador Allende's top diplomats, killed in a car bombing in Washington, DC in 1976. And it excused the terror of Zia ul-Haq, the military dictator of Pakistan, who killed many of my friends there. All I want to tell you is that according to my ignorant calculations, the ratio of people killed by the state terror of Zia ul-Haq, Pinochet, Argentinian, Brazilian, Indonesian type, versus the killing of the PLO and other organizations is literally, conservatively 1,000 to 1. That's the ratio.

History unfortunately recognizes and accords visibility to power, not to weakness. Therefore, visibility has been accorded historically to dominant groups. Our time—the time that begins with Columbus—has been one of extraordinary unrecorded holocausts. Great civilizations have been wiped out. The Mayas, the Incas, the Aztecs, the American Indians, the Canadian Indians were all wiped out. Their voices have not been heard, even to this day. They are heard, yes, but only when the dominant power suffers, only when resistance has a semblance of costing, of exacting a price, when a Custer is killed or when a Gordon is besieged. That's when you know that there were Indians or Arabs fighting and dying.

My last point on this subject is that during the Cold War period, the United States sponsored terrorist regimes like Somoza in Nicaragua and Batista in Cuba, one after another. All kinds of tyrants have been America's friends. In Nicaragua it was the contra, in Afghanistan, the mujahideen.

Now, what about the other side? What is terrorism? Our first job should be to define the damn thing, name it, give it a description other than "moral equivalent of founding fathers" or "a moral outrage to Western civilization." This is what *Webster's Collegiate Dictionary* says: "Terror is an intense, overpowering fear." Terrorism is "the use of terrorizing methods of governing or resisting a government." This simple definition has one great virtue: it's fair. It focuses on the use of violence that is used illegally, extra-constitutionally, to coerce. And this definition is correct because it treats terror for what it is, whether a government or private group commits it.

Have you noticed something? Motivation is omitted. We're not talking about whether the cause is just or unjust. We're talking about consensus, consent, absence of consent, legality, absence of legality, constitutionality, absence of constitutionality. Why do we keep motives out? Because motives make no difference. In the course of my work I have identified five types of terrorism; state terrorism, religious terrorism (Catholics killing Protestants, Sunnis killing Shiites, Shiites killing Sunnis), criminal terrorism, political terrorism, and oppositional terrorism. Sometimes these five can converge and overlap. Oppositional protest terrorism can become pathological criminal terrorism. State terror can take the form of private terror. For example, we're all familiar with the death squads in Latin America or in Pakistan where the government has employed private people to kill its opponents. It's not quite official. It's privatized. In Afghanistan, Central America, and Southeast Asia, the CIA employed in its covert operations drug pushers. Drugs and guns often go together. The categories often overlap.

Of the five types of terror, the official approach is to focus on only one form—political terrorism—which claims the least in terms of loss of human lives and property. The form that exacts the highest loss is state terrorism. The second highest loss is created by religious terrorism, although religious terror has, relatively speaking, declined. If you are looking historically, however, religious terrorism has caused massive loss. The next highest loss is caused by criminal terrorism. A Rand Corporation study by Brian Jenkins examining a ten-year period (1978 to 1988) showed fifty percent of terrorism was committed without any political cause. No politics. Simply crime and pathology. So the focus is on only one, the political terrorist, the PLO, the bin Laden, whoever you want to take.

Why do they do it? What makes terrorists tick?

I would like to knock out some quick answers. First, the need to be heard. Remember, we are dealing with a minority group, the political, private terrorist. Normally, and there are exceptions, there is an effort to be heard, to get their grievances recognized and addressed by people. The Palestinians, for example, the superterrorists of our time, were dispossessed in 1948. From 1948 to 1968 they went to every court in the world. They knocked on every door. They had been completely deprived of their land, their country, and nobody was listening. In desperation, they invented a new form of terror: the airplane hijacking. Between 1968 and 1975 they pulled the world up by its ears. That kind of terror is a violent way of expressing long-felt grievances. It makes the world hear. It's normally undertaken by small, helpless groupings that feel powerless. We still haven't done the Palestinians justice, but at least we all know they exist. Now, even the Israelis acknowledge. Remember what Golda Meir, prime minister of Israel, said in 1970: There are no Palestinians. They do not exist.

They damn well exist now.

Secondly, terrorism is an expression of anger, of feeling helpless, angry, alone. You feel like you have to hit back. Wrong has been done to you, so you do it. During the hijacking of the TWA jet in Beirut, Judy Brown of Belmar, New Jersey, said that she kept hearing them yell, "New Jersey, New Jersey." What did they have in mind? She thought that they were going after her. Later on it turned out that the terrorists were referring to the U.S. battleship New Jersey, which had heavily shelled the Lebanese civilian population in 1983.

Another factor is a sense of betrayal, which is connected to that tribal ethic of revenge. It comes into the picture in the case of people like bin Laden. Here is a man who was an ally of the United States, who saw America as a friend; then he sees his country being occupied by the United States and feels betrayal. Whether there is a sense of right and wrong is not what I'm saying. I'm describing what's behind this kind of extreme violence.

Sometimes it's the fact that you have experienced violence at other people's hands. Victims of violent abuse often become violent people. The only time when Jews produced terrorists in organized fashion was during and after the Holocaust. It is rather remarkable that Jewish terrorists hit largely innocent people or U.N. peacemakers like Count Bernadotte of Sweden, whose country had a better record on the Holocaust. The men of Irgun, the Stern Gang, and the Hagannah terrorist groups came in the wake of the Holocaust. The experience of victimhood itself produces a violent reaction.

In modern times, with modern technology and means of communications, the targets have been globalized. Therefore, globalization of violence is an aspect of what we call globalization of the economy and culture in the world as a whole. We can't expect everything else to be globalized and violence not to be. We do have visible targets. Airplane hijacking is something new because international travel is relatively new, too. Everybody now is in your gunsight. Therefore the globe is within the gunsight. That has globalized terror.

Finally, the absence of revolutionary ideology has been central to the spread of terror in our time. One of the points in the big debate between Marxism and anarchism in the nineteenth century was the use of terror. The Marxists argued that the true revolutionary does not assassinate. You do not solve social problems by individual acts of violence. Social problems require social and political mobilization, and thus wars of liberation are to be distinguished from terrorist organizations. The revolutionaries didn't reject violence, but they rejected terror as a viable tactic of revolution. That revolutionary ideology has gone out at the moment. In the 1980s and 1990s, revolutionary ideology receded, giving in to the globalized individual. In general terms, these are among the many forces that are behind modern terrorism.

To this challenge rulers from one country after another have been responding with traditional methods. The traditional method of shooting it out, whether it's with missiles or some other means. The Israelis are very proud of it. The Americans are very proud of it. The French became very proud of it. Now the Pakistanis are very proud of it. The Pakistanis say, Our commandoes are the best. Frankly, it won't work. A central problem of our time: political minds rooted in the past at odds with modern times, producing new realities.

Let's turn back for a moment to Osama bin Laden. *Jihad*, which has been translated a thousand times as "holy war," is not quite that. *Jihad* in Arabic means "to struggle." It could be struggle by violence or struggle by non-violent means. There are two forms, the small *jihad* and the big *jihad*. The small *jihad* involves external violence. The big *jihad* involves a struggle within oneself. Those are the concepts. The reason I mention it is that in Islamic history, *jihad* as an international violent phenomenon had for all practical purposes disappeared in the last four hundred years. It was revived suddenly with American help in the 1980s. When the Soviet Union intervened in Afghanistan, which borders Pakistan, Zia ul-Haq saw an opportunity and launched a *jihad* there against godless communism. The U.S. saw a God-sent opportunity to mobilize one billion Muslims against what Reagan called the Evil Empire. Money started pouring in. CIA agents starting going all over the Muslim world recruiting people to fight in the great *jihad*. Bin Laden was one of the early prize recruits. He was not only an Arab, he was a Saudi multimillionaire willing to put his own money into the matter. Bin Laden went around recruiting people for the *jihad* against communism.

I first met Osama bin Laden in 1986. He was recommended to me by an American official who may have been an agent. I was talking to the American and asked him who were the Arabs there that would be very interesting to talk with. By *there* I meant in Afghanistan and Pakistan. The American official told me, "You must meet Osama." I went to see Osama. There he was, rich, bringing in recruits from Algeria, from Sudan, from Egypt, just like Sheikh Abdul Rahman, an Egyptian cleric who was among those convicted for the 1993 World Trade Center bombing. At that moment, Osama bin Laden was a U.S. ally. He remained an ally. He turned at a particular moment. In 1990 the U.S. went into Saudi Arabia with military forces. Saudi Arabia is the holy place of Muslims, home of Mecca and Medina. There had never been foreign troops there. In 1990, during the build-up to the Gulf War, they went in in the name of helping Saudi Arabia defend itself. Osama bin Laden remained quiet. Saddam was defeated, but the American foreign troops stayed on in the land of the kaba (the sacred site of Islam in Mecca). Bin Laden wrote letter after letter saying, Why are you here? Get out! You came to help but you have stayed on. Finally he started a *jihad* against the other occupiers. His mission is to get American troops out of Saudi Arabia. His earlier mission was to get Russian troops out of Afghanistan.

A second point to be made about him is that he comes from a tribal people. Being a millionaire doesn't matter. His code of ethics is tribal. The tribal code of ethics consists of two words: loyalty and revenge. You are my friend. You keep your word. I am loyal to you. You break your word, I go on my path of revenge. For him, America has broken its word. The loyal friend has betrayed him. Now they're going to go for you. They're going to do a lot more. These are the chickens of the Afghanistan war coming home to roost.

What is my recommendation to America?

First, avoid extremes of double standards. If you're going to practice double standards, you will be paid with double standards. Don't use it. Don't condone Israeli terror, Pakistani terror, Nicaraguan terror, El Salvadoran terror, on the one hand, and then complain about Afghan terror or Palestinian terror. It doesn't work. Try to be even-handed. A superpower cannot promote terror in one place and reasonably expect to discourage terrorism in another place. It won't work in this shrunken world.

Do not condone the terror of your allies. Condemn them. Fight them. Punish them. Avoid covert operations and low-intensity warfare. These are breeding grounds for terrorism and drugs. In the Australian documentary about covert operations, *Dealing with the Demon*, I say that wherever covert operations have been, there is a drug problem. Because the structure of covert operations, Afghanistan, Vietnam, Nicaragua, Central America, etcetera, have been very hospitable to the drug trade. Avoid covert operations. It doesn't help.

Also, focus on causes and help ameliorate them. Try to look at causes and solve problems. Avoid military solutions. Terrorism is a political problem. Seek political solutions. Diplomacy works. Take the example of President Clinton's attack on bin Laden. Did they know what they were attacking? They say they know, but they don't know. At another point, they were trying to kill Qadaffi. Instead, they killed his young daughter. The poor child hadn't done anything. Qadaffi is still alive. They tried to kill Saddam Hussein. Instead they killed Laila bin Attar, a prominent artist, an innocent woman. They tried to kill bin Laden and his men. Twenty-five other people died. They tried to destroy a chemical factory in Sudan. Now they are admitting that they destroyed a pharmaceutical plant that produced half the medicine for Sudan.

Four of the missiles intended for Afghanistan fell in Pakistan. One was slightly damaged, two were totally damaged, one was totally intact. For ten years the American government has kept an embargo on Pakistan because Pakistan was trying, stupidly, to build nuclear weapons and missiles. So the U.S. has a technology embargo on my country. One of the missiles was intact. What do you think the Pakistani official told the *Washington Post*? He said it was a gift from Allah. Pakistan wanted U.S. technology. Now they have the technology, and Pakistan's scientists are examining this missile very carefully. It fell into the wrong hands. Look for political solutions. Military solutions cause more problems than they solve.

Finally, please help reinforce and strengthen the framework of international law. There was a criminal court in Rome. Why didn't the U.S. go there first to get a warrant against bin Laden, if they have some evidence? Enforce the United Nations. Enforce the International Court of Justice. Get a warrant, then go after him internationally.

Note

1. Yitzhak Shamir is the other.

Chapter 2

Why Terrorism?

The psychology behind the motivation and behavior of terrorists has been examined extensively, but the public, as well as many specialists, have often been content to write off terrorists as irrational fanatics. Rather than see terrorism as an unintended outcome or the last resort of pathological individuals, Martha Crenshaw examines the use of terrorism as a deliberate strategy. She describes a framework of rational decision making, examining the calculations of cost versus benefit that go into the choice of terrorism as a weapon. Crenshaw concludes that neither the psychological nor the strategic explanation alone is adequate for examining terrorist behavior, but offers the strategic choice framework as an "antidote" to the persistent psychological stereotypes that she believes are nonproductive and potentially dangerous.

In the second selection, Louise Richardson examines the different levels of state sponsorship of terrorism, ranging from complete state control, such as in the case of Iran, to state financial support with no hope of control, such as Muammar al-Qaddafi's support for the Irish Republican Army. The U.S. government has tended to focus on state-sponsored terrorism as an instrument of foreign policy, reflected in the State Department's required annual list of state sponsors. But Richardson focuses here on terrorist movements as transnational connections among nonstate actors, and she encourages those responsible for directing counterterrorist strategy to examine the many possible levels of interaction between state and nonstate actors.

The Logic of Terrorism: Terrorist Behavior as a Product of Strategic Choice

Martha Crenshaw is the John Andrus professor of government at Wesleyan University, where she has taught international politics since 1974. She is the editor, with John Pimlott, of the *International Encyclopedia of Terrorism* and the author of countless articles and texts on the subject of political terrorism. Crenshaw currently serves on a task force concerning foreign policy toward the Islamic world at the Brookings Institution.

This [selection] examines the ways in which terrorism can be understood as an expression of political strategy. It attempts to show that terrorism may follow logical processes that can be discovered and explained. For the purpose of presenting this source of terrorist behavior, rather than the psychological one, it interprets the resort to violence as a willful choice made by an organization for political and strategic reasons, rather than as the unintended outcome of psychological or social factors.[1]

In the terms of this analytical approach, terrorism is assumed to display a collective rationality. A radical political organization is seen as the central actor in the terrorist drama. The group possesses collective preferences or values and selects terrorism as a course of action from a range of perceived alternatives. Efficacy is the primary standard by which terrorism is compared with other methods of achieving political goals. Reasonably regularized decision-making procedures are employed to make an intentional choice, in conscious anticipation of the consequences of various courses of action or inaction. Organizations arrive at collective judgments about the relative effectiveness of different strategies of opposition on the basis of abstract strategic conceptions derived from ideological assumptions. This approach thus allows for the incorporation of theories of social learning.

Conventional rational-choice theories of individual participation in rebellion, extended to include terrorist activities, have usually been considered inappropriate because of the "free rider" problem. That is, the benefits of a successful terrorist campaign would presumably be shared by all individual supporters of the group's goals, regardless of the extent of their active participation. In this case, why should a rational person become a terrorist, given the high costs associated with violent resistance and the expectation that everyone who supports the cause will benefit, whether he or she participates or not? One answer is that the benefits of participation are psychological....

A different answer, however, supports a strategic analysis. On the basis of surveys conducted in New York and West Germany, political scientists suggest that individuals can be *collectively* rational.[2] People realize that their participation is important because group size and cohesion matter. They are sensitive to the implications of free-riding and perceive their personal influence on the provision of public goods to be high. The authors argue that "average citizens may adopt a collectivist conception of rationality because they recognize that what is individually rational is collectively irrational."[3] Selective incentives are deemed largely irrelevant.

One of the advantages of approaching terrorism as a collectively rational strategic choice is that it permits the construction of a standard from which deviations can be measured. For example, the central question about the rationality of some terrorist organizations, such as the West German groups of the 1970s or the Weather Underground in the United States, is whether or not they had a sufficient grasp of reality—some approximation, to whatever degree imperfect—to calculate the likely consequences of the courses of action they chose. Perfect knowledge of available alternatives and the consequences of each is not possible, and miscalculations are inevitable. The Popular Front for the Liberation of Palestine (PFLP), for example, planned the hijacking of a TWA flight from Rome in August 1969 to coincide with a scheduled address by President Nixon to a meeting of the Zionist Organization of America, but he sent a letter instead.[4]

Yet not all errors of decision are miscalculations. There are varied degrees of limited rationality. Are some organizations so low on the scale of rationality as to be in a different category from more strategically minded groups? To what degree is strategic reasoning modified by psychological and other constraints? The strategic choice framework provides criteria on which to base these distinctions. It also leads one to ask what conditions promote or discourage rationality in violent underground organizations.

The use of this theoretical approach is also advantageous in that it suggests important questions about the preferences or goals of terrorist organizations. For example, is the decision to seize hostages in order to bargain with governments dictated by strategic considerations or by other, less instrumental motives?

The strategic choice approach is also a useful interpretation of reality. Since the French Revolution, a strategy of terrorism has gradually evolved as a means of bringing about political change opposed by established governments. Analysis of the historical development of terrorism reveals similarities in calculation of ends and means. The strategy has changed over time to adapt to new circumstances that offer different possibilities for dissident action—for example, hostage taking. Yet terrorist activity considered in its entirety shows a fundamental unity of purpose and conception. Although this analysis remains largely on an abstract level, the historical evolution of the strategy of terrorism can be sketched in its terms.[5]

A last argument in support of this approach takes the form of a warning. The wide range of terrorist activity cannot be dismissed as "irrational" and thus pathological, unreasonable, or inexplicable. The resort to terrorism need not be an aberration. It may be a reasonable and calculated response to circumstances. To say that the reasoning that leads to the choice of terrorism may be logical is not an argument about moral justifiability. It does suggest, however, that the belief that terrorism is expedient is one means by which moral inhibitions are overcome....

The Conditions for Terrorism

The central problem is to determine when extremist organizations find terrorism useful. Extremists seek either a radical change in the status quo, which would confer a new advantage, or the defense of privileges they perceive to be threatened. Their dissatisfaction with the policies of the government is extreme, and their demands usually involve the displacement of existing political elites.[6] Terrorism is not the only method of working toward radical goals, and thus it must be compared to the alternative strategies available to dissidents. Why is terrorism attractive to some opponents of the state, but unattractive to others?

The practitioners of terrorism often claim that they had no choice but terrorism, and it is indeed true that terrorism often follows the failure of other methods. In nineteenth-century Russia, for example, the failure of nonviolent movements contributed to the rise of terrorism. In Ireland, terrorism followed the failure of Parnell's constitutionalism. In the Palestinian-Israeli struggle, terrorism followed the failure of Arab efforts at conventional warfare against Israel. In general, the "nonstate" or "substate" users of terrorism—that is, groups in opposition to the government, as opposed to government itself—are constrained in their options by the lack of active mass support and by the superior power arrayed against them (an imbalance that has grown with the development of the modern centralized and bureaucratic nation-state). But these constraints have not prevented oppositions from considering and rejecting methods other than terrorism. Perhaps because groups are slow to recognize the extent of the limits to action, terrorism is often the last in a sequence of choices. It represents the outcome of a learning process. Experience in opposition provides radicals with information about the potential consequences of their choices. Terrorism is likely to be a reasonably informed choice among available alternatives, some tried unsuccessfully. Terrorists also learn from the experiences of others, usually communicated to them via the news media. Hence the existence of patterns of contagion in terrorist incidents.[7]

Thus the existence of extremism or rebellious potential is necessary to the resort to terrorism but does not in itself explain it, because many revolutionary and nationalist organizations have explicitly disavowed terrorism. The Russian Marxists argued for years against the use of terrorism.[8] Generally, small organizations resort to violence to compensate for what they lack in numbers.[9] The imbalance between the resources terrorists are able to mobilize and the power of the incumbent regime is a decisive consideration in their decision making.

More important than the observation that terrorism is the weapon of the weak, who lack numbers or conventional military power, is the explanation for weakness. Particularly, why does an organization lack the potential to attract enough followers to change government policy or overthrow it?

One possibility is that the majority of the population does not share the ideological views of the resisters, who occupy a political position so extreme that their appeal is inherently limited. This incompatibility of preferences may be purely political, concerning, for example, whether or not one prefers socialism to capitalism. The majority of West Germans found the Red Army Faction's promises for the future not only excessively vague but distasteful. Nor did most Italians support aims of the neofascist groups that initiated the "strategy of tension" in 1969. Other extremist groups, such as the *Euzkadi ta Akatasuna* (ETA) in Spain or the Provisional Irish Republican Army (PIRA) in Northern Ireland, may appeal exclusively to ethnic, religious, or other minorities. In such cases, a potential constituency or like-minded and dedicated individuals exists, but its boundaries are fixed and limited. Despite the intensity of the preferences of a minority, its numbers will never be sufficient for success.

A second explanation for the weakness of the type of organization likely to turn to terrorism lies in a failure to mobilize support. Its members may be unwilling or unable to expend the time and effort required for mass organizational work. Activists may not possess the requisite skills or patience, or may not expect returns commensurate with their endeavors. No matter how acute or widespread popular dissatisfaction may be, the masses do not rise spontaneously; mobilization is required.[10] The organization's leaders, recognizing the advantages of numbers, may combine mass organization with conspiratorial activities. But resources are limited and organizational work is difficult and slow even under favorable circumstances. Moreover, rewards are not immediate. These difficulties are compounded in an authoritarian state, where the organization of independent opposition is sure to incur high costs. Combining violent provocation with nonviolent organizing efforts may only work to the detriment of the latter.

For example, the debate over whether to use an exclusively violent underground strategy that is isolated from the masses (as terrorism inevitably is) or to work with the people in propaganda and organizational efforts divided the Italian left-wing groups, with the Red Brigades choosing the clandestine path and Prima Linea preferring to maintain contact with the wider protest movement. In prerevolutionary Russia the Socialist-Revolutionary party combined the activities of a legal political party with the terrorist campaign of the secret Combat Organization. The IRA has a legal counterpart in Sinn Fein.

A third reason for the weakness of dissident organizations is specific to repressive states. It is important to remember that terrorism is by no means restricted to liberal democracies, although some authors refuse to define resistance to authoritarianism as terrorism.[11] People may not support a resistance organization because they are afraid of negative sanctions from the regime or because censorship of the press prevents them from learning of the possibility of rebellion. In this situation a radical organization may believe that supporters exist but cannot reveal themselves. The depth of this latent support cannot be measured or activists mobilized until the state is overthrown.

Such conditions are frustrating, because the likelihood of popular dissatisfaction grows as the likelihood of its active expression is diminished. Frustration may also encourage unrealistic expectations among the regime's challengers, who are not able to test their popularity. Rational expectations may be undermined by fantastic assumptions about the role of the masses. Yet such fantasies can also prevail among radical undergrounds in Western democracies. The misperception of conditions can lead to unrealistic expectations.

In addition to small numbers, time constraints contribute to the decision to use terrorism. Terrorists are impatient for action. This impatience may, of course, be due to external factors, such as psychological or organizational pressures. The personalities of leaders, demands from followers, or competition from rivals often constitute impediments to strategic thinking. But it is not necessary to explain the felt urgency of some radical organizations by citing reasons external to an instrumental framework. Impatience and eagerness for action can be rooted in calculations of ends and means. For example, the organization may perceive an immediate opportunity to compensate for its inferiority vis-à-vis the government. A change in the structure of the situation may temporarily alter the balance of resources available to the two sides, thus changing the ratio of strength between government and challenger.

Such a change in the radical organization's outlook—the combination of optimism and urgency—may occur when the regime suddenly appears vulnerable to challenge. This vulnerability may be of two sorts. First, the regime's ability to respond effectively, its capacity for efficient repression of dissent, or its ability to protect its citizens and property may weaken. Its armed forces may be committed elsewhere, for example, as British forces were during World War I when the IRA first rose to challenge British rule, or its coercive resources may be otherwise overextended. Inadequate security at embassies, airports, or military installations may become obvious. The poorly protected U.S. Marine barracks in Beirut were, for example, a tempting target. Government strategy may be ill-adapted to responding to terrorism.

Second, the regime may make itself morally or politically vulnerable by increasing the likelihood that the terrorists will attract popular support. Government repressiveness is thought to have contradictory effects; it both deters dissent and provokes a moral backlash.[12] Perceptions of the regime as unjust motivate opposition. If government actions make average citizens willing to suffer punishment for supporting antigovernment causes, or lend credence to the claims of radical opponents, the extremist organization may be tempted to exploit this temporary upsurge of popular indignation. A groundswell of popular disapproval may make liberal governments less willing (as opposed to less able) to use coercion against violent dissent.

Political discomfort may also be internationally generated. If the climate of international opinion changes so as to reduce the legitimacy of a targeted regime, rebels may feel encouraged to risk a repression that they hope will be limited by outside disapproval. In such circumstances the regime's brutality may be expected to win supporters to the cause of its challengers. The current situation in South Africa furnishes an example. Thus a heightened sensitivity to injustice may be produced either by government actions or by changing public attitudes.

The other fundamental way in which the situation changes to the advantage of challengers is through acquiring new resources. New means of financial support are an obvious asset, which may accrue through a foreign alliance with a sympathetic government or another, richer revolutionary group, or through criminal means such as bank robberies or kidnapping for ransom. Although terrorism is an extremely economical method of violence, funds are essential for the support of full-time activists, weapons purchases, transportation, and logistics.

Technological advances in weapons, explosives, transportation, and communications also may enhance the disruptive potential of terrorism. The invention of dynamite was thought by nineteenth-century revolutionaries and anarchists to equalize the relationship between government and challenger, for example. In 1885, Johann Most published a pamphlet titled *Revolutionary War Science*, which explicitly advocated terrorism. According to Paul Avrich, the anarchists saw dynamite "as a great equalizing force, enabling ordinary workmen to stand up against armies, militias, and police, to say nothing of the hired gunmen of the employers."[13] In providing such a powerful but easily concealed weapon, science was thought to have given a decisive advantage to revolutionary forces.

Strategic innovation is another important way in which a challenging organization acquires new resources. The organization may borrow or adapt a technique in order to exploit a vulnerability ignored by the government. In August 1972, for example, the Provisional IRA introduced the effective tactic of the one-shot sniper. IRA Chief of Staff

Sean MacStiofain claims to have originated the idea: "It seemed to me that prolonged sniping from a static position had no more in common with guerrilla theory than mass confrontations."[14] The best marksmen were trained to fire a single shot and escape before their position could be located. The creation of surprise is naturally one of the key advantages of an offensive strategy. So, too, is the willingness to violate social norms pertaining to restraints on violence. The history of terrorism reveals a series of innovations, as terrorists deliberately selected targets considered taboo and locales where violence was unexpected. These innovations were then rapidly diffused, especially in the modern era of instantaneous and global communications.

It is especially interesting that, in 1968, two of the most important terrorist tactics of the modern era appeared—diplomatic kidnappings in Latin America and hijackings in the Middle East. Both were significant innovations because they involved the use of extortion or blackmail. Although the nineteenth-century Fenians had talked about kidnapping the prince of Wales, the People's Will (Narodnaya Volya) in nineteenth-century Russia had offered to halt its terrorist campaign if a constitution were granted, and American marines were kidnapped by Castro forces in 1959, hostage taking as a systematic and lethal form of coercive bargaining was essentially new....

Terrorism has so far been presented as the response by an opposition movement to an opportunity. This approach is compatible with the findings of Harvey Waterman, who sees collective political action as determined by the calculations of resources and opportunities.[15] Yet other theorists—James Q. Wilson, for example—argue that political organizations originate in response to a threat to a group's values.[16] Terrorism can certainly be defensive as well as opportunistic. It may be a response to a sudden downturn in a dissident organization's fortunes. The fear of appearing weak may provoke an underground organization into acting in order to show its strength. The PIRA used terrorism to offset an impression of weakness, even at the cost of alienating public opinion: in the 1970s periods of negotiations with the British were punctuated by outbursts of terrorism because the PIRA did want people to think that they were negotiating from strength.[17] Right-wing organizations frequently resort to violence in response to what they see as a threat to the status quo from the left. Beginning in 1969, for example, the right in Italy promoted a "strategy of tension," which involved urban bombings with high numbers of civilian casualties, in order to keep the Italian government and electorate from moving to the left.

Calculation of Cost and Benefit

An organization or a faction of an organization may choose terrorism because other methods are not expected to work or are considered too time-consuming, given the urgency of the situation and the government's superior resources. Why would an extremist organization expect that terrorism will be effective? What are the costs and benefits of such a choice, compared with other alternatives? What is the nature of the debate over terrorism? Whether or not to use terrorism is one of the most divisive issues resistance groups confront, and numerous revolutionary movements have split on the question of means even after agreeing on common political ends.[18]

The costs of terrorism. The costs of terrorism are high. As a domestic strategy, it invariably invites a punitive government reaction, although the organization may believe that the government reaction will not be efficient enough to pose a serious threat. This cost can be offset by the advance preparation of building a secure underground. *Sendero Luminoso* (Shining Path) in Peru, for example, spent ten years creating a clandestine organizational structure before launching a campaign of violence in 1980. Furthermore, radicals may look to the future and calculate that present sacrifice will not be in vain if it inspires future resistance. Conceptions of interest are thus long term.

Another potential cost of terrorism is loss of popular support. Unless terrorism is carefully controlled and discriminate, it claims innocent victims. In a liberal state, indiscriminate violence may appear excessive and unjustified and alienate a citizenry predisposed to loyalty to the government. If it provokes generalized government repression, fear may diminish enthusiasm for resistance. This potential cost of popular alienation is probably least in ethnically divided societies, where victims can be clearly identified as the enemy and where the government of the majority appears illegal to the minority. Terrorists try to compensate by justifying their actions as the result of the absence of choice or the need to respond to government violence. In addition, they may make their strategy highly discriminate, attacking only unpopular targets.

Terrorism may be unattractive because it is elitist. Although relying only on terrorism may spare the general population from costly involvement in the struggle for freedom, such isolation may violate the ideological beliefs of revolutionaries who insist that the people must participate in their liberation. The few who choose terrorism are willing to forgo or postpone the participation of the many, but revolutionaries who oppose terrorism insist that it prevents the people from taking responsibility for their own destiny. The possibility of vicarious popular identification with symbolic acts of terrorism may satisfy some revolutionaries, but others will find terrorism a harmful substitute for mass participation.

The advantages of terrorism. Terrorism has an extremely useful agenda-setting function. If the reasons behind violence are skillfully articulated, terrorism can put the issue of political change on the public agenda. By attracting attention it makes the claims of the resistance a salient issue in the public mind. The government can reject but not ignore an opposition's demands. In 1974 the Palestinian Black September organization, for example, was willing to sacrifice a base in Khartoum, alienate the Sudanese government, and create ambivalence in the Arab world be seizing the Saudi Arabian embassy and killing American and Belgian diplomats. These costs were apparently weighed against the message to the world "to take us seriously." Mainstream Fatah leader Salah Khalef (Abu Iyad) explained: "We are planting the seed. Others will harvest it.... It is enough for us now to learn, for example, in reading the *Jerusalem Post*, that Mrs. Meir had to make her will before visiting Paris, or that Mr. Abba Eban had to travel with a false passport."[19] George Habash of the PFLP noted in 1970 that "we force people to ask what is going on."[20] In these statements, contemporary extremists echo the nineteenth-century anarchists, who coined the idea of propaganda of the deed, a term used as early as 1877 to refer to an act of insurrection as "a powerful means of arousing popular conscience" and the materialization of an idea through actions.[21]

Terrorism may be intended to create revolutionary conditions. It can prepare the ground for active mass revolt by undermining the government's authority and demoralizing its administrative cadres—its courts, police, and military. By spreading insecurity—

at the extreme, making the country ungovernable—the organization hopes to pressure the regime into concessions or relaxation of coercive controls. With the rule of law disrupted, the people will be free to join the opposition. Spectacular humiliation of the government demonstrates strength and will and maintains the morale and enthusiasm of adherents and sympathizers. The first wave of Russian revolutionaries claimed that the aims of terrorism were to exhaust the enemy, render the government's position untenable, and wound the government's prestige by delivering a moral, not a physical, blow. Terrorists hoped to paralyze the government by their presence merely by showing signs of life from time to time. The hesitation, irresolution, and tension they would produce would undermine the processes of government and make the Czar a prisoner in his own palace.[22] As Brazilian revolutionary Carlos Marighela explained: "Revolutionary terrorism's great weapon is initiative, which guarantees its survival and continued activity. The more committed terrorists and revolutionaries devoted to anti-dictatorship terrorism and sabotage there are, the more military power will be worn down, the more time it will lose following false trails, and the more fear and tension it will suffer through not knowing where the next attack will be launched and what the next target will be."[23]

These statements illustrate a corollary advantage to terrorism in what might be called its excitational function: it inspires resistance by example. As propaganda of the deed, terrorism demonstrates that the regime can be challenged and that illegal opposition is possible. It acts as a catalyst, not substitute, for mass revolt. All the tedious and time-consuming organizational work of mobilizing the people can be avoided. Terrorism is a shortcut to revolution. As the Russian revolutionary Vera Figner described its purpose, terrorism was "a means of agitation to draw people from their torpor," not a sign of loss of belief in the people.[24]

A more problematic benefit lies in provoking government repression. Terrorists often think that by provoking indiscriminate repression against the population, terrorism will heighten popular disaffection, demonstrate the justice of terrorist claims, and enhance the attractiveness of the political alternative the terrorists represent. Thus, the West German Red Army Faction sought (in vain) to make fascism "visible" in West Germany.[25] In Brazil, Marighela unsuccessfully aimed to "transform the country's political situation into a military one. Then discontent will spread to all social groups and the military will be held exclusively responsible for failures."[26]

But profiting from government repression depends on the lengths to which the government is willing to go in order to contain disorder, and on the population's tolerance for both insecurity and repression. A liberal state may be limited in its capacity for quelling violence, but at the same time it may be difficult to provoke to excess. However, the government's reaction to terrorism may reinforce the symbolic value of violence even if it avoids repression. Extensive security precautions, for example, may only make the terrorists appear powerful.

Summary. To summarize, the choice of terrorism involves considerations of timing and of the popular contribution to revolt, as well as of the relationship between government and opponents. Radicals choose terrorism when they want immediate action, think that only violence can build organizations and mobilize supporters, and accept the risks of challenging the government in particularly provocative way. Challengers who think that organizational infrastructure must precede action, that rebellion without the masses is misguided, and that premature conflict with the regime can only lead to disaster favor gradualist strategies. They prefer methods such as rural guerrilla warfare, because terrorism can jeopardize painfully achieved gains or preclude eventual compromise with the government.

The resistance organization has before it a set of alternatives defined by the situation and by the objectives and resources of the group. The reasoning behind terrorism takes into account the balance of power between challengers and authorities, a balance that depends on the amount of popular support the resistance can mobilize. The proponents of terrorism understand this constraint and possess reasonable expectations about the likely results of action or inaction. They may be wrong about the alternatives that are open to them, or miscalculate the consequences of their actions, but their decisions are based on logical processes. Furthermore, organizations learn from their mistakes and from those of others, resulting in strategic continuity and progress toward the development of more efficient and sophisticated tactics. Future choices are modified by the consequences of present actions.

Hostage Taking as Bargaining

Hostage taking can be analyzed as a form of coercive bargaining. More than twenty years ago, Thomas Schelling wrote that "hostages represent the power to hurt in its purest form."[27] From this perspective, terrorists choose to take hostages because in bargaining situations the government's greater strength and resources are not an advantage. The extensive resort to this form of terrorism after 1968, a year that marks the major advent of diplomatic kidnappings and airline hijackings, was a predictable response to the growth of state power. Kidnappings, hijackings, and barricade-type seizures of embassies or public buildings are attempts to manipulate a government's political decisions.

Strategic analysis of bargaining terrorism is based on the assumption that hostage takers genuinely seek the concessions they demand. It assumes that they prefer government compliance to resistance. This analysis does not allow for deception or for the possibility that seizing hostages may be an end in itself because it yields the benefit of publicity. Because these limiting assumptions may reduce the utility of the theory, it is important to recognize them.

Terrorist bargaining is essentially a form of blackmail or extortion.[28] Terrorists seize hostages in order to affect a government's choices, which are controlled both by expectations of outcome (what the terrorists are likely to do, given the government reaction) and preferences (such as humanitarian values). The outcome threatened by the terrorist—the death of the hostages—must be worse for the government than compliance with terrorist demands. The terrorist has two options, neither of which necessarily excludes the other: to make the threat both more horrible and more credible or to reward compliance, a factor that strategic theorists often ignore.[29] That is, the cost to the government of complying with the terrorists' demands may be lowered or the cost of resisting raised.

The threat to kill the hostages must be believable and painful to the government. Here hostage takers are faced with a paradox. How can the credibility of this threat be assured when hostage takers recognize that governments know that the terrorists' control over the situation depends on live hostages? One way of establishing credibility is to divide the threat, making it sequential by killing one hostage at a time. Such tactics also aid terrorists in the process of incurring and demonstrating a commitment to carrying out their threat. Once the terrorists have murdered, though, their incentive to surrender voluntarily is substantially reduced. The terrorists have increased their own costs of yielding in order to persuade the government that their intention to kill all the hostages is real.

Another important way of binding oneself in a terrorist strategy is to undertake a barricade rather than a kidnapping operation. Terrorists who are trapped with the hostages find it more difficult to back down (because the government controls the escape routes) and, by virtue of this commitment, influence the government's choices. When terrorists join the hostages in a barricade situation, they create the visible and irrevocable commitment that Schelling sees as a necessary bond in bargaining. The government must expect desperate behavior, because the terrorists have increased their potential loss in order to demonstrate the firmness of their intentions. Furthermore, barricades are technically easier than kidnappings.

The terrorists also attempt to force the "last clear chance" of avoiding disaster onto the government, which must accept the responsibility for noncompliance that leads to the deaths of hostages. The seizure of hostages is the first move in the game, leaving the next move—which determines the fate of the hostages—completely up to the government. Uncertain communications may facilitate this strategy.[30] The terrorists can pretend not to receive government messages that might affect their demonstrated commitment. Hostage takers can also bind themselves by insisting that they are merely agents, empowered to ask only for the most extreme demands. Terrorists may deliberately appear irrational, either through inconsistent and erratic behavior or unrealistic expectations and preferences, in order to convince the government that they will carry out a threat that entails self-destruction.

Hostage seizures are a type of iterated game, which explains some aspects of terrorist behavior that otherwise seem to violate strategic principles. In terms of a single episode, terrorists can be expected to find killing hostages painful, because they will not achieve their demands and the government's desire to punish will be intensified. However, from a long-range perspective, killing hostages reinforces the credibility of the threat in the next terrorist incident, even if the killers then cannot escape. Each terrorist episode is actually a round in a series of games between government and terrorists.

Hostage takers may influence the government's decision by promising rewards for compliance. Recalling that terrorism represents an iterative game, the release of hostages unharmed when ransom is paid underwrites a promise in the future. Sequential release of selected hostages makes promises credible. Maintaining secrecy about a government's concessions is an additional reward for compliance. France, for example, can if necessary deny making concessions to Lebanese kidnappers because the details of arrangements have not been publicized.

Terrorists may try to make their demands appear legitimate so that governments may seem to satisfy popular grievances rather than the whims of terrorists. Thus, terrorists may ask that food be distributed to the poor. Such demands were a favored tactic of the *Ejercito Revolucionario del Pueblo* (ERP) in Argentina in the 1970s.

A problem for hostage takers is that rewarding compliance is not easy to reconcile with making threats credible. For example, if terrorists use publicity to emphasize their threat to kill hostages (which they frequently do), they may also increase the costs of compliance for the government because of the attention drawn to the incident.

In any calculation of the payoffs for each side, the costs associated with the bargaining process must be taken into account.[31] Prolonging the hostage crisis increases the costs to both sides. The question is who loses most and thus is more likely to concede. Each party presumably wishes to make the delay more costly to the other. Seizing multiple hostages appears to be advantageous to terrorists, who are thus in a position to make threats credible by killing hostages individually. Conversely, the greater the number of hostages, the greater the cost of holding them. In hijacking or barricade situations, stress and fatigue for the captors increase waiting costs for them as well. Kidnapping poses fewer such costs. Yet the terrorists can reasonably expect that the costs to governments in terms of public or international pressures may be higher when developments are visible. Furthermore, kidnappers can maintain suspense and interest by publishing communications from their victims.

Identifying the obstacles to effective bargaining in hostage seizures is critical. Most important, bargaining depends on the existence of a common interest between two parties. It is unclear whether the lives of hostages are a sufficient common interest to ensure a compromise outcome that is preferable to no agreement for both sides. Furthermore, most theories of bargaining assume that the preferences of each side remain stable during negotiations. In reality, the nature and intensity of preferences may change during a hostage-taking episode. For example, embarrassment over the Iran-*contra* scandal may have reduced the American interest in securing the release of hostages in Lebanon.

Bargaining theory is also predicated on the assumption that the game is two-party. When terrorists seize the nationals of one government in order to influence the choices of a third, the situation is seriously complicated. The hostages themselves may sometimes become intermediaries and participants. In Lebanon, Terry Waite, formerly an intermediary and negotiator, became a hostage. Such developments are not anticipated by bargaining theories based on normal political relationships. Furthermore, bargaining is not possible if a government is willing to accept the maximum cost the terrorists can bring to bear rather than concede. And the government's options are not restricted to resistance or compliance; armed rescue attempts represent an attempt to break the bargaining stalemate. In attempting to make their threats credible—for example, by sequential killing of hostages—terrorists may provoke military intervention. There may be limits, then, to the pain terrorists can inflict and still remain in the game.

Conclusions

This essay has attempted to demonstrate that even the most extreme and unusual forms of political behavior can follow an internal, strategic logic. If there are consistent patterns in terrorist behavior, rather than random idiosyncrasies, a strategic analysis may reveal them. Prediction of future terrorism can only be based on theories that explain past patterns.

Terrorism can be considered a reasonable way of pursuing extreme interests in the political arena. It is one among the many alternatives that radical organizations can choose. Strategic conceptions, based on ideas of how best to take advantage of the possibilities of a given situation, are an important determinant of oppositional terrorism, as they are of the government response. However, no single explanation for terrorist behavior is satisfactory. Strategic calculation is only one factor in the decision-making process leading to terrorism. But it is critical to include strategic reasoning as a possible motivation, at a minimum as an antidote to stereotypes of "terrorists" as irrational fanatics. Such stereotypes are a dangerous underestimation of the capabilities of extremist groups. Nor does stereotyping serve to educate the public—or, indeed, specialists—about the complexities of terrorist motivations and behaviors.

Notes

1. For a similar perspective (based on a different methodology) see James DeNardo, *Power in Numbers: The Political Strategy of Protest and Rebellion* (Princeton, N.J.: Princeton University Press, 1985). See also Harvey Waterman, "Insecure 'Ins' and Opportune 'Outs': Sources of Collective Political Activity," *Journal of Political and Military Sociology* 8 (1980): 107–12, and "Reasons and Reason: Collective Political Activity in Comparative and Historical Perspective," *World Politics* 33 (1981): 554–89. A useful review of rational choice theories is found in James G. March, "Theories of Choice and Making Decisions," *Society* 20 (1982): 29–39.

2. Edward N. Muller and Karl-Dieter Opp, "Rational Choice and Rebellious Collective Action," *American Political Science Review* 80 (1986): 471–87.

3. Ibid., 484. The authors also present another puzzling question that may be answered in terms of either psychology or collective rationality. People who expected their rebellious behavior to be punished were more likely to be potential rebels. This propensity could be explained either by a martyr syndrome (or an expectation of hostility from authority figures) or intensity of preference—the calculation that the regime was highly repressive and thus deserved all the more to be destroyed. See pp. 482 and 484.

4. Leila Khaled, *My People Shall Live: The Autobiography of a Revolutionary* (London: Hodder and Stoughton, 1973), 128–31.

5. See Martha Crenshaw, "The Strategic Development of Terrorism," paper presented to the 1985 Annual Meeting of the American Political Science Association, New Orleans.

6. William A. Gamson, *The Strategy of Social Protest* (Homewood, Illinois: Dorsey Press, 1975).

7. Manus I. Midlarsky, Martha Crenshaw, and Fumihiko Yoshida, "Why Violence Spreads: The Contagion of International Terrorism," *International Studies Quarterly* 24 (1980): 262–98.

8. See the study by David A. Newell, *The Russian Marxist Response to Terrorism: 1878–1917* (Ph.D. dissertation, Stanford University, University Microfilms, 1981).

9. The tension between violence and numbers is a fundamental proposition in DeNardo's analysis; see *Power in Numbers*, chapters 9–11.

10. The work of Charles Tilly emphasizes the political basis of collective violence. See Charles Tilly, Louise Tilly, and Richard Tilly, *The Rebellious Century 1830–1930* (Cambridge: Harvard University Press, 1975), and Charles Tilly, *From Mobilization to Revolution* (Reading, Mass.: Addison-Wesley, 1978).

11. See Conor Cruise O'Brien, "Terrorism under Democratic conditions: The Case of the IRA," in *Terrorism, Legitimacy, and Power: The Consequences of Political Violence,* edited by Martha Crenshaw (Middletown, Conn.: Wesleyan University Press, 1983).

12. For example, DeNardo, in *Power in Numbers*, argues that "the movement derives moral sympathy from the government's excesses" (p. 207).

13. Paul Avrich, *The Haymarket Tragedy* (Princeton: Princeton University Press, 1984), 166.

14. Sean MacStiofain, *Memoirs of a Revolutionary* (N.p.: Gordon Cremonisi, 1975), 301.

15. Waterman, "Insecure 'Ins' and Opportune 'Outs'" and "Reasons and Reason."

16. *Political Organizations* (New York: Basic Books, 1973).

17. Maria McGuire, *To Take Arms: My Year with the IRA Provisionals* (New York: Viking, 1973), 110–11, 118, 129–31, 115, and 161–62.

18. DeNardo concurs; see *Power in Numbers*, chapter 11.

19. See Jim Hoagland, "A Community of Terror," *Washington Post*, 15 March 1973, pp. 1 and 13; also *New York Times*, 4 March 1973, p. 28. Black September is widely regarded as a subsidiary of Fatah, the major Palestinian organization headed by Yasir Arafat.

20. John Amos, *Palestinian Resistance: Organization of a Nationalist Movement* (New York: Pergamon, 1980), 193; quoting George Habash, interviewed in *Life Magazine*, 12 June 1970, 33.

21. Jean Maitron, *Histoire du mouvement anarchiste en France (1880–1914)*, 2d ed. (Paris: Société universitaire d'éditions et de librairie, 1955), 74–5.

22. "Stepniak" (pseud. for Sergei Kravshinsky), *Underground Russia: Revolutionary Profiles and Sketches from Life* (London: Smith, Elder, 1883), 278–80.

23. Carlos Marighela, *For the Liberation of Brazil* (Harmondsworth: Penguin, 1971), 113.

24. Vera Figner, *Mémoires d'une révolutionnaire* (Paris: Gallimard, 1930), 206.

25. *Textes des prisonniers de la "fraction armée rouge" et dernières lettres d'Ulrike Meinhof* (Paris: Maspéro, 1977), 64.

26. Marighela, *For the Liberation of Brazil*, 46.

27. Schelling, *Arms and Influence* (New Haven, Conn.: Yale University Press, 1966), 6.

28. Daniel Ellsburg, *The Theory and Practice of Blackmail* (Santa Monica: Rand Corporation, 1968).

29. David A. Baldwin, "Bargaining with Airline Hijackers," in *The 50% Solution*, edited by William I. Zartman, 404–29 (Garden City, N.Y.: Doubleday, 1976), argues that promises have not been sufficiently stressed. Analysts tend to emphasize threats instead, surely because of the latent violence implicit in hostage taking regardless of outcome.

30. See Roberta Wohlstetter's case study of Castro's seizure of American marines in Cuba: "Kidnapping to Win Friends and Influence People," *Survey* 20 (1974): 1–40.

31. Scott E. Atkinson, Todd Sandler, and John Tschirhart, "Terrorism in a Bargaining Framework," *Journal of Law and Economics* 30 (1987): 1–21.

2.2   Louise Richardson, 1998

Global Rebels: Terrorist Organizations as Trans-National Actors

Political scientist **Louise Richardson** is the Executive Dean of the Radcliffe Institute for Advanced Study. Since 1989 she has taught at Harvard University on international relations, terrorist movements, foreign policy, and international security. Her current research focuses on decision making inside terrorist movements.

The widespread usage of the term terrorism, in many contexts, has rendered the word almost meaningless. Today, its only universally understood connotation is so pejorative that even terrorists don't admit to being terrorists anymore. A glance at current usage reveals child abuse, racism, and gang warfare all incorrectly described as terrorism. Thus, if terrorism is to be analyzed in any meaningful way, it must be readily distinguishable from other forms of violence, especially other forms of political violence. In this article, terrorism is defined as politically motivated violence, directed against non-combatant or symbolic targets and designed to communicate a message to a broader audience. The critical feature of terrorism is the deliberate targeting of innocents in an effort to convey a message to another party. This particular characteristic differentiates terrorism from the most proximate form of political violence: the irregular warfare of the guerrilla. While it could certainly be argued that states engage in terrorism, this article focuses on non-state actors: terrorist movements.

Although terrorism is most often targeted against domestic political structures to effect political change, this article focuses on the international connections between terrorists. Political scientists coined the term trans-nationalism when they realized that the prevailing state-centric paradigm could not adequately explain the extent and impact of international interactions. Trans-nationalism denotes the interplay between non-state actors—international interactions not directed by states. On the other hand, transgovernmentalism refers to relations between sub-units of governments not controlled by the national executives.

US Perceptions of Terrorism

The United States tends to see terrorism less as a trans-national force and more as an international one. More specifically, the United States generally perceives international terrorism as deliberately directed by governments, usually against US targets. In the 1980s, the notion of an extensive, covert Soviet conspiracy to undermine the West prevailed. Today, the prevailing image is that of the radical Islamic fundamentalist following instructions from Middle Eastern capitals. International terrorism, therefore, is seen as state-sponsored terrorism, and state-sponsored terrorism, like terrorism more generally, is something only the bad guys do.

In response to public concern about state-sponsored terrorism, the US State Department is required to report annually to Congress on the patterns of global terrorism and to list the states considered sponsors of terrorism. Congress then imposes trade sanctions on the designated states. Currently, there are seven states on the list: Cuba, Iran, Iraq, Libya, North Korea, Sudan and Syria. This list, of course, is a political instrument and reflects far more than the extent of state-sponsored terrorism. The economies of Cuba and North Korea, for example, ensure that neither government is in any position to promote, much less fund, international terrorism. Indeed, in 1995, the North Korean government repudiated terrorism and any support for it. The two governments remain on the list, ostensibly for providing a safe haven to terrorists, but more likely because domestic pressure from Cuban voters in Florida and alliance relations with South Korea make their removal politically difficult.

A more objective assessment of the evidence suggests that the use of terror as an instrument of foreign policy might not be the exclusive domain of expansionist communists or mad mullahs. Even impeccably liberal democracies might engage in such action. In the 1980s, however, the firmly held belief was that the United States faced a deliberate and dedicated cadre of communists under orders from Moscow to undermine the West. Among the staunch proponents of this view were President Reagan and his Secretary of State, Alexander Haig. There can be little doubt that terrorist movements did receive assistance from the Eastern bloc in the 1980s. Members of the German Red Army Faction clearly found refuge and financial support in East Germany. In 1982, Congressional hearings revealed extensive Soviet-funded training facilities provided for liberation movements operating in Sub-Saharan Africa. However, the hearings failed to establish a definite link between the training facilities and Soviet bloc control over the liberation movements.

Generally speaking, financial support for a group may purchase influence but not control over its activities. The same holds true for relations between allies. The vast sums of money that the United States gives Israel translate into US government influence, not control, over Israeli policy. Similarly, in spite of all the aid given the mujahadeen in their fight against the Russians, the US government has precious little influence on the factious Afghan fighters.

For numerous reasons, a state might decide to sponsor terrorism as an instrument of foreign policy. Until the end of the Cold War, scholars widely maintained that the bipolar structure of the international system lent itself to the sponsorship of terrorism. According to the argument, the nuclear stalemate between the superpowers made direct conflict too costly to contemplate, but competition inevitable. Therefore, the superpowers sought indirect outlets for competition: arms races, proxy wars (as in Ethiopia), or sponsorship of terrorism (as in southern Africa). In light of the continuation of terrorism in the face of the transformation of the international power structure from a bipolar to a unipolar system, it is more difficult to argue that the international distribution of power determines the use of terror. Nevertheless, the attractions of sponsorship remain the same. The costs are low, and if the terrorists succeed, the benefits are high. However, if they fail, sponsors can easily and plausibly disavow the group's actions.

Seen in this light, it is easier to understand how US support for Chilean anti-Allende forces in the 1970s, the Nicaraguan Contras in the 1980s, or for anti-Castro forces throughout that period could be interpreted as the use of terror as an instrument of foreign policy—a more neutral concept than state-sponsored terrorism. The US government had many good reasons to undermine the regimes in Santiago, Managua, and Havana and certainly had the military prowess to do so. However, because overt action would have generated both an international and domestic uproar, the government sought to operate behind the scenes by helping local groups with the same goals. The US rationale was very similar to that offered by Eastern-bloc governments at the time, and it may explain the failure of communication between the right, which saw a Soviet-led, communist backed, terrorist conspiracy, and the left, which feared a US-led, antisocialist, terrorist conspiracy. Terrorism, then, can be sponsored both by strong states reluctant to demonstrate their strength openly and by weak states that believe that they have no other effective weapons in their arsenal.

Five Degrees of Separation

Important distinctions exist between different types of terrorist-sponsor relationships. These ties range from full state direction at one end of the spectrum to simple support at the other end. The case of Iran, the country widely and rightly viewed as the primary state sponsor of terrorism at present, illustrates several of these distinctions.

First, at one end of the continuum—where state control is complete—is the murder of dissidents. The State Department accuses Iran (and Iraq) of state-sponsored terrorism in their killing of dissidents overseas: either leaders of domestic opposition groups or, as in the case of Iran, former officials of the Shah's regime. These individuals are invariably killed by members of Iranian or Iraqi intelligence services operating abroad. Among the more celebrated Iranian cases are the 1991 murder of the former Prime Minister Shahpur Bakhtiar and his aide in Paris and the 1996 discovery in Belgium of a massive mortar in a ship's cargo of pickles. The ship in question belonged to a wholly-owned subsidiary of the Iranian intelligence service, and the mortar was believed to have been intended for a prominent Iranian dissident.

The second stage along the continuum of control is the recruitment and training of operatives specifically for an overseas mission. While accurate information about these cases is extremely difficult to obtain, a good example is the three-year-long German trial of an Iranian and four Lebanese charged with the 1992 murder of Kurdish dissidents in Berlin. The trial revealed the long arm of Iranian intelligence. The four accused were convicted while the prosecutors charged that supreme leader Khamenei and President Rafsanjani approved the operation. The judge indicted the Iranian Minister of Intelligence for the crime.

The murder of dissidents, while reprehensible, does not constitute terrorism per se. It represents a strategy of illegal state repression rather than state-sponsored terrorism. The action is highly discriminating and is carried out against an intended target by what amounts to an arm of the government. Thus, assassinations of dissidents remain quite distinct from the random violence associated with terrorism.

The third step along the continuum is reached when a government closely controls and directs the actions of a terrorist group. Complete control exists in only a few cases and generally involves the use of intelligence services. Nevertheless, some Middle Eastern terrorist movements, albeit not many, appear to have very little independence from their sponsors. Two such examples are the Saiqa Palestinian Group and the Popular Front for the Liberation of Palestine-General Command (PLFP-GC). Both organizations receive directions from their main sponsor, Syria. In the case of the PLFP-GC, its leader—Ahmad Jibril—is a former captain in the Syrian Army. Moreover, the movement has its headquarters in Damascus and is heavily dependent on Syria for financial and logistical support.

The fourth level of control is by far the most common. In this case, a government provides training, funds, and safe haven for an autonomous terrorist group. This relationship is common for most of the Palestinian groups which jealously guard their independence. They accept assistance from several sponsors, in part to avoid exclusive dependence on any one. Most groups, like Hamas, try to supplement their government funding—in this case from Iran—with support from Palestinian expatriates and private benefactors in places like Saudi Arabia. In some cases, groups even accept help from sworn enemies. For example, the Kurdistan Worker's Party (PKK) accepts support from both Iran and Iraq, as well as from Syria.

When one of the these terrorist groups commits an atrocity, one of the sponsoring states is usually blamed. While the state may indeed be pleased by the action, it may not have had any prior-knowledge of it. Thus, the sponsoring state may be responsible for the action in a moral sense, by supporting the perpetrators, but it is not directly responsible.

In its years at the forefront of the Western alliance, the United States has reacted with frustration when its enemies have exaggerated its influence over its allies. The United States can only try to persuade its allies but cannot dictate to them. In the same fashion, the United States tends to exaggerate the influence of other states on the actions of the terrorists they sponsor. Certainly the states have the ability to hurt the movements by denying them support, but they are rarely in a position to dictate. In February 1996, for example, the Iranian vice president met with Hamas leaders in Damascus immediately after several bombings in Israel, and he praised their successful efforts. A week later, Hamas claimed responsibility for two more bombings. There is no reason to believe that Hamas was following explicit Iranian instructions. They did not need to. As both Iran and Hamas share a virulent antipathy to the State of Israel, one does not need to direct the operations of the other. At the final step on the continuum of state control, the actions of a terrorist movement merely serve the ends of a sponsoring state. The state then offers financial support because it identifies its interests with that of the group. The support of the Libyan leader, Muammar al-Qaddafi, for the Irish Republican Army (IRA) can be seen in this light. Qaddafi actually knew very little about the situation in Northern Ireland or about the campaign waged by the IRA. He nevertheless provided the organization with training facilities, financial support, and several ships full of weaponry, simply because he knew that they were operating against Britain. His goal was to punish Britain for its collaboration in the US bombing of Tripoli, and his support of the IRA was a means to that end. IRA acceptance of Qaddafi's support, however, in no way led them to alter their military strategy.

An undifferentiated view of state-sponsorship of terrorism—one which fails to appreciate these different types of relationships—is unlikely to facilitate an understanding of the motivations underlying trans-national terrorism. Hence, an effective counter terrorist strategy would be difficult to develop.

Exporting Revolution

Another aspect of state-sponsored terrorism differentiates Iran from other countries on the US government's list of state sponsors: Iran's efforts since the successful 1979 revolution to export its revolution overseas. Religion has long been a powerful trans-national force in international relations. It does not respect national boundaries and has generated centuries of jurisdictional disputes between secular and clerical leaderships. The Ayatollah Khomeini, a Shiite Muslim cleric who led the Iranian revolution, provided a theological justification for fundamentalist terrorism. He argued that Islam was threatened with destruction and that Shiite believers were obliged to fight in its defense.

It is important to bear in mind, however, that Iranian-sponsored terrorism is not solely or even primarily directed against the West; rather, it is directed against surrounding Gulf states, particularly Bahrain, Kuwait, Saudi Arabia, and Iraq. The Western victims of Iranian-sponsored terrorism have often been incidental. They were either caught in the embassy at the onset of the revolution, were kidnapped by the Iranian-backed Hezbullah group in Lebanon, or were victims of Iranian-backed terror in Israel. The rhetoric denouncing the United States as "the Great Satan" notwithstanding, Iran has not, in fact, led a terrorist war against the West.

Iran's support for terrorism is closely linked to support for Shiite opposition groups in nearby Gulf states. In 1987, when a Kuwaiti Shiite bombed a Kuwaiti oil installation and a Bahraini engineer tried to sabotage Bahrain's oil refinery, Iran sanctioned both incidents. In the late 1980s, there was a wave of terrorist activity in Kuwait backed by Shiite terrorists groups, which in turn, were supported by Iran. At one point, a Kuwaiti airplane was hijacked in an effort to secure the release of seventeen members of an Iranian-backed terrorist group. This type of activity, of course, is precisely the kind to which the West has been exposed for years, but it is clearly a mistake to think that such hostility is directed solely against the West. In 1988, Iran adjusted its sights and began to focus on Saudi Arabia after the death of 257 Iranian pilgrims making the hajj. Iran publicly called for the overthrow of the Saudi ruling family. Shiite Muslims were recruited and trained by Iran, and they carried out a wave of attacks directed against Saudi officials and the Saudi airline. Harsh repression by the Saudi authorities could not eliminate the terrorist incidents.

The widely held view that Middle Eastern terrorism exclusively targets the West is misplaced. Iranian-backed groups have sought to export the Iranian revolution to surrounding states, while radical Islamic groups such as al-Gama'at al-Islamiyya and al-Jihad in Egypt have tried to overthrow the secular leadership of their own government.

Terrorist Networks

The relationships between states and terrorist movements do not correspond directly to the pure form of trans-nationalism because they include a state as part of the equation. These relationships do not correspond to trans-governmentalism either, as they are not connections between subgroups of governments. Rather, they reflect an under-theorized, hybrid type of trans-nationalism between a state and an autonomous movement. The traditional state-centric paradigm sufficed to explain the cases where a sponsoring government directly controls terrorist movements. However, the cases in which movements remain independent or quasi-independent of any particular state suggest yet another level of international interaction.

Terrorist movements demonstrate a purer form of trans-national interaction in the relationships they form with each other. Insofar as terrorist movements coalesce and form linkages to operate together and have an independent impact on state policy, they are indeed trans-national actors. Given the clandestine nature of most terrorist groups, it is difficult to find evidence to demonstrate the extent of these linkages. Nevertheless, the evidence that exists shows that connections between groups occur for a variety of reasons: a shared ideology, a shared enemy, or simply, shared training facilities.

The left-wing social revolutionary movements that operated in Europe in the 1970s and 1980s—the German Red Army Faction (RAF), the Italian Red Brigades, and the French Direct Action—had much in common. Their members came from a similar social strata—the disaffected children of privilege. These men and women were motivated by a desire to destroy the corruption of contemporary capitalism and to replace it with a new, but ill-defined order based on Marxist-Leninist principles. The European revolutionaries formed linkages based on ideological affinity, establishing anti-imperialist fronts facilitated by their geographic proximity.

Other less-likely groups formed trans-national links for the simple reason of a shared enemy, usually the United States. The cooperation between several Palestinian and European groups provide a fitting example. Palestinian groups offered financial support to groups like the Italian Red Brigades if they, in turn, would intensify their attacks on US and NATO targets. These linkages were driven less by ideological affinity and more by the imperatives of the age old political dictum, "the enemy of my enemy is my friend." Members of disparate terrorists groups often made initial contact during sessions in Middle Eastern or North African training camps. Shared operating procedures and training with particular weapons both facilitated the formation of personal contacts and the execution of future joint operations.

A simple examination of the personnel involved in several celebrated terrorist escapades unearths dramatic evidence of trans-national collaboration. Members of the German Red Army Faction and the Popular Front for the Liberation of Palestine have exhibited a particular adroitness at forming international terrorist teams. The RAF participated in the 1975 kidnapping of eleven OPEC oil ministers in Vienna. The following year, the group participated in the Palestinian hijacking of an Air France airliner to Entebbe, Uganda, and in 1977, collaborated again in a hijacking of a Lufthansa plane to Mogadishu. The Lod massacre of 1972 also demonstrated the extent of international connections. The attack in a Tel Aviv airport was executed by members of the Japanese Red Army which had earlier joined with the PFLP in a "Declaration of World War." Members of the JRA subsequently took refuge in North Korea.

Trans-national relations between terrorist movements are not confined to Europe and the Middle East. A 1993 explosion under an auto repair shop in Managua, Nicaragua, revealed what one diplomat at the scene deemed "a one stop shopping center for Latin terrorists." Aside from the extensive arsenal which included tons of explosives, hundreds of assault rifles, and tens of surface to air missiles, the cache revealed an extensive filing system documenting the collaboration of Argentinean, Basque, Canadian, Chilean, Nicaraguan, Salvadoran, and Uruguayan terrorists. Besides the treasure trove of hundreds of passports and identification papers, the files provided detailed documentation of observations on scores of wealthy Latin American businessmen, ten of whom had already been kidnapped. Those convicted in the kidnapping of the Brazilian supermarket chain owner Abilio Diniz included a multinational group of Argentinians, Canadians, Chileans, and a Brazilian.

Historically, shared support from Cuba served to forge international links between terrorist groups in Latin America. The Managua explosion demonstrated that groups also cooperated without Cuban support. Moreover, it is important to note that even with their massive arsenal and documentation, these groups are only known to have succeeded in kidnapping ten wealthy Latin Americans. Like most terrorists, they have not, in fact, posed a vital security threat to the countries in which they operate.

International links between terrorist movements take many forms. Some groups are directed by states, some are independent of states, some have state involvement. The trans-national links between terrorist groups are so varied that any one power cannot possibly orchestrate the entire network even at a regional level, much less a global one. These findings have implications both for policy makers and for academics. For academics, insofar as many of these links reflect a hybrid form of interaction between trans-nationalism and trans-governmentalism, they suggest an under-theorized area of international interaction. For policy makers, the fear of the specter of state sponsored terrorism replacing the global Soviet threat to US interests is clearly misplaced. Policymakers as well as academics would do well to draw critical distinctions between the relationships of movements and those who assist them because the most effective counter-terrorist strategy will be one directed to the source of terrorism.

Chapter 3

The New Terrorism Model

The authors in this chapter examine the new model of terrorism.

Dr. Bruce Hoffman explores the mindset of terrorists and the tactics they use in their quest for power and, ultimately, political change. Although terrorists believe in the efficacy of violence in achieving change, he believes their actions are not random, crazed, or capricious acts: killing for the sake of killing. They are carefully planned and conservatively executed plans. Innocent people do get in the path of their actions, but Hoffman explains that terrorists are performing targeted acts to gain recognition and publicity. Today, however, terrorists are taking on ever more dramatic and destructively lethal deeds to gain the same attention that a less bloody action may have garnered in the past—and violence is ratcheted upward to retain the media's and the public's attention. For example, when Timothy McVeigh, the convicted Oklahoma City bomber, was asked by his attorney if he could have drawn attention to his grievances against the U.S. government without killing anyone, he reportedly answered: "That would not have gotten the point across."

John Arquilla, David Ronfeldt, and Michele Zanini examine changes in terrorism in the information age. The classic motivation and rationales will not change, but conduct and operational characteristics will. The authors explore—often in what they outline as a deliberately speculative manner—organizational changes in a new era that allow for less hierarchical structures and flatter networks of power with dense communications; they look at changes in strategy and technology and how terrorism is evolving in a direction they label *netwar*. Implications for the U.S. military and a look at how recent developments in Middle Eastern terrorism can be seen as early signs of a move toward netwar-type terrorism are covered.

The Modern Terrorist Mindset: Tactics, Targets and Technologies

An international expert on terrorism and political violence, **Dr. Bruce Hoffman** is the RAND Corporation's vice president of external affairs and director of its Washington, D.C. office. He is well known for *Inside Terrorism* (1998), which has been translated into foreign language editions in nine countries and was the founding director of the Center for the Study of Terrorism and Political Violence at the University of St. Andrews in Scotland. In 1998, Hoffman was awarded the Santiago Grisolía Prize and the accompanying chair in violence studies by the Queen Sofia Center for the Study of Violence (Valencia, Spain). Even before the terrorist attacks on September 11, he was consulting with governments and businesses on terrorism and political violence.

The wrath of the terrorist is rarely uncontrolled. Contrary to both popular belief and media depiction, most terrorism is neither crazed nor capricious. Rather, terrorist attacks are generally as carefully planned as they are premeditated.... [T]he terrorist act is specifically designed to communicate a message. But, equally as important, it is also conceived and executed in a manner that simultaneously reflects the terrorist group's particular aims and motivations, fits its resources and capabilities and takes into account the 'target audience' at whom the act is directed. The tactics and targets of various terrorist movements, as well as the weapons they favour, are therefore ineluctably shaped by a group's ideology, its internal organizational dynamics, the personalities of its key members and a variety of internal and external stimuli.

The Nexus of Ideological and Operational Imperatives

All terrorist groups seek targets that are lucrative from their point of view. As such, they also employ tactics that are consonant with their overriding political aims. Whereas left-wing terrorists like the German RAF and Italian Red Brigades (RB) have selectively kidnapped and assassinated persons whom they blamed for economic exploitation or political repression in order to attract publicity and promote a Marxist-Leninist revolution, terrorists motivated by a religious imperative have engaged in more indiscriminate acts of violence, waged against a far wider category of targets: encompassing not merely their declared enemies, but anyone who does not share their religious faith. Ethno-nationalist/separatist arguably fall somewhere in between. On the one hand, the violent campaigns waged by groups like the PLO [Palestine Liberation Organization], IRA [Irish Republican Army], and ETA [Euzkadi ta Akatasuna] have frequently been more destructive and have caused far greater casualties than those of their left-wing counterparts. But, on the other, their violence has largely been restricted to a specifically defined 'target set': namely the members of a specific rival or dominant ethno-nationalist group.[1]

Perhaps the least consequential of all these terrorist group categories (both in terms of frequency of incidents and impact on public and governmental attitudes), has been the disparate collection of recycled Nazis, racist 'political punk rockers' and other extreme right-wing elements who have emerged over the years in various European countries. But even their sporadic and uncoordinated, seemingly mindless violence—fuelled as much by beer and bravado as by a discernible political agenda—is neither completely random nor unthinkingly indiscriminate. Indeed, for all these categories, the point is less their innate differences than the fact that their tactical and targeting choices correspond to, and are determined by, their respective ideologies, attendant mechanisms of legitimization and justification and, perhaps most critically, by their relationship with the intended audience of their violent acts.

The overriding tactical—and, indeed ethical—imperative for left-wing terrorists, for example, has been the deliberate tailoring of their violent acts to appeal to their perceived 'constituencies'. In this manner, terrorist attacks are planned and executed in a way that either reflects or conforms to the ethos and attitudes of the terrorists' particular target audience. For example, in a 1978 interview, the German left-wing terrorist Michael 'Bommi' Baumann denounced the hijacking of a Lufthansa passenger plane the previous year by terrorists seeking the release of imprisoned RAF members as 'madness... you can't take your life and place it above that of children and Majorca holiday-makers and say: My life is valuable! That is elitarian madness, bordering on Fascism'. [2] For Baumann, the deliberate involvement of innocent civilians in that terrorist operation was not only counterproductive, but wrong. It was counterproductive in that it tarnished the left-wing terrorists' image as a true 'revolutionary vanguard'—using violence to draw attention to themselves and their cause and 'educate' the public about what the terrorists perceive as the inequities of the democratic-capitalist state. It was also wrong in itself because innocent persons—no matter what the political justification—should not be the victims of terrorist acts directed against the state.

For this reason, left-wing terrorists' use of violence historically has been heavily proscribed. Their self-styled crusade for social justice is typically directed against governmental or commercial institutions or specific individuals whom they believe represent capitalist exploitation and repression. They are therefore careful not to undertake actions that might alienate potential supporters or their perceived constituency. Accordingly, left-wing violence tends to be highly discriminate, selective and limited. Persons epitomizing the terrorists' main ideological animus—wealthy industrialists like Hans Martin Schleyer (who was kidnapped and later murdered by the RAF in 1977) or leading parliamentarians like Aldo Moro (who similarly was kidnapped and subsequently murdered by the Red Brigades)—are deliberately selected and meticulously targeted for their intrinsic 'symbolic' value. 'You know that we did not kidnap Moro the man, but [rather] his function', Mario Moretti, the leader of the Red Brigade's Rome column who masterminded the operation, explained during his November 1984 trial. For Moretti, Moro was first and foremost a powerful symbol: a former prime minister and reigning Christian Democratic Party chief; a political wheeler-dealer par excellence and architect of the impending historic compromise with the Italian Communist Party that would fundamentally alter the country's political landscape and further marginalize the RB. He was, in the terrorists' eyes, the 'supreme manager of power in Italy' for the past twenty years, who Moretti described as the 'demiurge of bourgeois power'. Hence, by abducting so important a leader and profound a symbol, the RB sought to galvanize the Italian left and thereby decisively transform the political situation in their favour.[3]

Even when such less discriminate tactics as bombing are employed, the violence is meant to be equally 'symbolic'. That is, while the damage caused and destruction inflicted is actually quite real, the terrorists' main purpose is not to destroy property or obliterate tangible assets, but to dramatize or call attention to a political cause. The left-wing terrorist group decision-making process is perhaps depicted most clearly in Baumann's description of the planning of a 1969 terrorist attack by the group known as the 'Tupamaros West Berlin' (a precursor of both the Second of June Movement and the original RAF). Baumann and his colleagues wanted to stage an operation that would simultaneously attract attention to themselves and their cause, publicize the plight of the Palestinian people and demonstrate the West German left's solidarity and sympathy with the Palestinians' struggle. '[W]e sat down and pondered what would be a story that nobody could miss, that everyone would have to talk about and everyone would have to report', Baumann recalled. 'And we came up with the right answer—a bomb in the Jewish Community Centre—and on the anniversary of the "Crystal Night"[4] during the Third Reich.... [T]hough it didn't explode, the story [still] went round the world'.[5] By striking on this particular date, against this specific target, with its deep—and unmistakable—symbolic significance, the group sought to draw a deliberate parallel between Israeli oppression of the Palestinians and Nazi persecution of the Jews.[6]

The left-wing terrorists' use of 'armed propaganda' (e.g., violent acts with clear symbolic content) is thus a critical element in their operational calculus. It is also the principal vehicle through which these organizations both 'educate' the masses through their self-anointed role as 'revolutionary vanguard'. The RB's first official 'strategic resolution', for example, stressed exactly this theme. 'It is not a question of organizing the class movement within the area of armed struggle', the 1975 document stated, 'but of entrenching the organization of the armed struggle and the political realization of its historical necessity within the class movement'.[7] A less turgid explanation of this strategy was later offered by Patrizio Peci, the group's Turin column leader when he reflected how, 'As crazy as it might seem, the plan in a few words was this: First phase, armed propaganda.... Second phase, that of armed support... Third phase, the civil war and victory. In essence, we were the embryo, the skeleton of the future... the ruling class of tomorrow in a communist society'.[8] The RAF drew similar parallels in its exegesis of the relationship between the terrorist vanguard and "the people". 'Our original conception of the organization implied a connection between the urban guerrilla and the work at the base', the document entitled, 'Sur la Conception de la Guerilla Urbaine' explained.

> We would like it if each and all of us could work at the neighborhoods and factories, in socialist groups that already exist, influence discussion, experience and learn. This has proved impossible....
>
> Some say that the possibilities for agitation, propaganda and organization are far from being eradicated and that only when they are, should we pose the question of arms. We say: it will not really be possible to profit from any political actions as long as armed struggle does not appear clearly as the goal of the politicisation.[9]

This approach is not entirely dissimilar from that of many ethno-nationalist/separatist groups. These terrorist movements also see themselves as a revolutionary vanguard—if not in classic Marxist-Leninist terms, at least as a spearhead: similarly using violence to 'educate' their fellow national or ethnic brethren about the inequities imposed upon them by the ruling government and the need for communal resistance and rebellion. As one Basque nationalist bluntly told an interviewer, 'ETA is the vanguard of our revolution'.[10] Accordingly, like all ethno-nationalist/separatist terrorists, ETA uses demonstratively symbolic acts of violence to generate publicity and rally support by underscoring the powerlessness of the government to withstand the nationalist expression they champion and thereby embarrass and coerce it into acceding to the group's irredentist demands. Their 'target audience', however, is not just the local, indigenous population but often the international community as well. These groups, accordingly, recognize the need to tightly control and focus their operations in such a manner as to ensure the continued support of their local 'constituencies' and the sympathy of the international community as well. What this essentially means is that their violence must always be seen or perceived as both purposeful and deliberate; sustained and omnipresent. Gerry Adams himself expressed precisely this point in an article he wrote in 1976 to commemorate the 1916 Easter Uprising's sixtieth anniversary. 'Rightly or wrongly, I am an IRA Volunteer', Adams explained,

> and, rightly or wrongly, I take a course of action as a means to bringing about a situation in which I believe the people of my country will prosper... The course I take involves the use of physical force, but only if I achieve the situation where my people can genuinely prosper can my a course of action be seen, by me, to have been justified.[11]

Indeed, as the veteran Northern Ireland correspondent David McKittrick points out, 'Sinn Féin in its efforts to build a political machine in both parts of Ireland, has [always] been concerned to project IRA violence as the clinical and carefully directed use of force'.[12]

The more successful ethno-nationalist/separatist terrorist organization, therefore, will be able to determine an effective level of violence that is at once 'tolerable' for the local populace, tacitly acceptable to international opinion and sufficiently modulated so as not to provoke massive governmental crackdown and reaction. The IRA has demonstrably mastered this synchronization of tactics to strategy. Since the mid-1980s, according to Patrick Bishop and Eamonn Mallie, the organization's military high command has clearly recognized that, 'Republican strategy required a certain level of violence—but only enough to distort the private and public life of the North, and to make sure that the military arm was properly exercised'.[13] What this has often resulted in is the targeting of members of the security forces (e.g., ordinary policemen and soldiers) in preference to the terrorists' avowed enemies in some rival indigenous community. This is true in Northern Ireland, where fewer than 20 percent of the IRA's victims between 1969 and 1993 were Protestant civilians[14] and in Spain, where more than 60 percent of fatalities inflicted by the Basque ETA have been members of the Spanish security forces.[15]

Certainly, 'traitors', informants, and other collaborators amongst their own brethren are regularly targeted; but here the terrorist group must be careful to strike another balance between salutary, if sporadic, 'lessons' that effectively intimidate and compel compliance from their own communities and more frequent and heavy-handed episodes that alienate popular support, encourage co-operation with the security forces and therefore prove counterproductive. By the same token, highly placed government officials and security force commanders will, when the opportunity presents itself and the political conditions are propitious, also be attacked. But because of a combination of uncertain—and possibly undesirable—political and security repercussions coupled with difficulties of both gaining access to these VIPs and the considerable effort required of such operations; they are generally eschewed in favour of more lucrative, if less spectacular, operations that, moreover, conform to the terrorists' perceptions of what are regarded as 'legitimate' or 'acceptable'—however abhorrent—targets.

The terrorist campaign is thus like a shark in the water: it must keep moving forward—no matter how slowly or incrementally—or die. Hence, when these more 'typical' targets fail to sustain the momentum of a terrorist campaign or when other, perhaps even totally unrelated events overshadow the terrorists and shunt their cause out of the public eye, terrorists often have to resort to more violent acts to dramatically refocus attention back upon themselves. But it would be a mistake to see these acts—which often involve the bombing of public gathering places or the hijacking of airliners—as random or senseless....[F]ollowing the Palestinian terrorists' failure to mount a concerted guerrilla campaign against Israel in the occupied West Bank and Gaza Strip after the 1967 Six Day War, the PFLP [Popular Front for the Liberation of Palestine] began hijacking international airliners. The purpose of these operations was not to wantonly kill or otherwise harm innocent persons (in contrast to many subsequent terrorists' targeting of civil aviation) but to use the passengers as pawns in pursuit of publicity and the extraction of concessions from unsympathetic governments. As one of the group's most famous hijackers, the aforementioned Leila Khaled, once explained, 'Look, I had orders to seize the plane, not to blow it up.... I care about people. If I had wanted to blow up the plane no one could have prevented me'.[16]

Even when terrorists' actions are not as deliberate or discriminate, and when their purpose is in fact to kill innocent civilians, the target is still regarded as 'justified' because it represents the terrorists' defined 'enemy'. Although incidents may be quantitatively different in the volume of death or destruction caused, they are still qualitatively identical in that a widely known 'enemy' is being specifically targeted. This distinction is often accepted by the terrorists' constituents and at times by the international community as well. The recognition that the Palestinians obtained in the wake of the 1972 Munich Olympics massacre is a particularly prominent case in point. The poignant message left behind by the terrorist team thus struck precisely the sympathetic chord they had intended: 'We are neither killers nor bandits', their letter stated. 'We are persecuted people who have no land and no homeland.... We are not against any people, but why should our place here be taken by the flag of the occupiers... why should the whole world be having fun and entertainment while we suffer with all ears deaf to us?'[17] As the PFLP's Bassam Abu Sharif explained, 'For violence to become fruitful, for it to get us to our aims, it should not be undertaken without a proper political base and intention'.[18] While the logic in such a case may well be contrived, there is nonetheless a clear appreciation that violence has it limits and, moreover, if used properly, it can pay vast dividends. In other words, the level of violence must be kept within the bounds of what the terrorists' 'target audience' will accept.

But acts of terrorism, like battles in conventional wars, are difficult to limit and control once they are started, and they often result in tragedy to civilians who are inadvertently caught up in the violence. One well-known example is the tragic bombing that occurred at Enniskillen, Northern Ireland in November 1987, causing the deaths of 11 innocent bystanders and injuries to 63 others attending a memorial ceremony. The IRA was quick to describe the incident as an accident resulting from the 'catastrophic consequences'[19] of an operation against British troops gone awry. In this instance, there was an acceptance of some grievous wrong, even if it was clothed with layers of self-serving justifications of 'catastrophic consequences' and 'accidents' to highlight that distinction. Eamon Collins, a former IRA terrorist, describes the organization's reaction to another botched attack that also accidentally claimed the lives of innocent civilians some years later:

> The IRA—regardless of their public utterances dismissing the condemnations of their behaviour from church and community leaders—tried to act in a way that would avoid severe censure from within the nationalist community; they knew they were operating within a sophisticated set of informal restrictions on their behaviour, no less powerful for being largely unspoken.[20]

The Basque ETA is no different: alternately threatening and remorseful in communiqués that seek to absolve themselves of responsibility for their violent deeds but that nonetheless still reap the rewards of introspection and self-criticism. 'We claim responsibility for the failed action against a member of the Spanish police', reads one, 'following the placing of an explosive charge under his car. We very much deplore the accidental injuries involuntarily caused to his neighbor… and we wish his prompt and complete recovery'.[21]

Right-wing terrorism, on the other hand, has often been characterized as the least discriminate, most senseless type of contemporary political violence. It has earned this reputation mostly as a result of the seemingly mindless 'street' violence and the unsophisticated attacks that in recent years have increasingly targeted immigrants, refugees, guest workers and other foreigners in many European countries, but especially in the former East Germany and other Communist-bloc states;[22] but also from an inchoate bombing campaign that briefly convulsed Western Europe in the early 1980s. If the means of the right-wing terrorists sometimes appear haphazardly planned and often spontaneously generated; their ends are hardly less indistinct. Essentially, their ostensible goal is the destruction of the liberal-democratic state to clear the way for a renascent National Socialist ('Nazi') or fascist one. But the extent to which this is simply an excuse for the ego-centric pleasure derived from brawling and bombing, preening or parading in 1940s-era Nazi regalia is less apparent given that the majority of right-wing groups often do not espouse any specific program of reform, preferring to hide behind vague slogans of strident nationalism, the need for racial purity and the re-assertion of governmental strength. In sum, the democratic state is somewhat reflexively assailed for its manifold weakness—its liberal social welfare policies and tolerance of diverse opinion—alongside its permitting of dark-skinned immigrants in the national labour force and of Jews and other minorities in positions of power or influence. The right-wing terrorists believe that their respective nation's survival is dependent upon the exorcism of these elements from its environs; only by becoming politically, racially, and culturally homogeneous can the state recover its strength and again work for its natural citizens rather than the variegated collection of interlopers and parasites who now sap the nation of its strength and greatness.

It should be noted that, whilst the European groups share many similarities with their American counterparts (e.g., racism, anti-Semitism, xenophobia and a hatred of liberal government), they differ fundamentally in their mechanisms of legitimization and justification. Whereas the U.S. groups may be more accurately categorized as religious—rather than strictly as right-wing—terrorists because of the pivotal roles that liturgy, divine inferences and clerical sanction play in underpinning and motivating their violence; the European right's ideological foundations are avowedly secular with neither theological imperatives nor clerics exerting any significant influence whatsoever. Indeed, the ill-defined, amorphous contours of the contemporary European extreme right's political philosophy can be summed up by either the refrain from a popular song by the British white power band, "White Noise" as: 'Two pints of lager and a packet of crisps. Wogs out! White Power!'[23] or the folk song composed by Gottfried Küssel, an Austrian neo-Nazi organization's Führer, as 'Do you see his nose, no? Do you know his nose? His nose you do not know? It is crooked and ugly? Then hit him in the face. He is a Jew, a damned Jew, bloodsucker of the European race'.[24] By comparison, the lunatic and far-fetched millenarian views of American Christian white supremacists appear as deeply profound theological treatises.

For this reason, perhaps, rarely has European right-wing terrorism transcended the boundaries of either street brawls or the crude Molotov cocktail hurriedly tossed into a refugee shelter or a guest workers' dormitory (even though, of course, such crude acts of violence possess the same tragic potential to kill and maim just as much as more sophisticated terrorist operations do). Nonetheless, it would be a mistake to see right-wing violence as completely indiscriminate or entirely irrational. Indeed, the few times when the neo-Nazis have attempted more ambitious types of operations have sent shock-waves throughout the continent. In August 1980, for instance, a powerful explosion tore through the crowded Bologna, Italy rail station in the midst of the summer holiday crush. At the time, the 84 persons killed (and 180 wounded) was second only to the record 91 who had perished in a single terrorist act in the Irgun's bombing of the King David Hotel 34 years before. The bombing that occurred less than a month later at the popular Munich Oktoberfest celebration, killing 14 persons and injuring another 215 persons, therefore raised fears of a new terrorist onslaught more lethal and indiscriminate than that waged by either the European leftist terrorist organizations or the continent's various ethno-nationalist/separatist groups. In the end, it never materialized. Instead, the pattern of right-wing terrorism in Europe over the past twenty years or so has mostly involved sporadic attacks albeit specifically directed against particular types of targets: primarily refugee shelters and immigrant workers' hostels, anarchist houses and political party offices and Arab and African immigrants walking along the street as well as Jewish-owned property or businesses.

Accordingly, as crude and relatively unsophisticated and indeed intellectually depraved as this terrorist category may appear, like all forms of terrorism even right-wing violence is not based on some pathological obsession to kill or beat up as many people as possible; but on a deliberate policy of intimidating the general public into acceding to specific demands or pressures. The right-wing terrorists, therefore, see themselves if not as a revolutionary vanguard, then as a catalyst of events that will lead to the imposition of an authoritarian form of government. Thus, like other terrorist movements, they too tailor their violence to appeal to their perceived constituency—be it fellow extreme nationalists, intransigent racists and xenophobes, reactionary conservatives, or militant anti-communists—and, with the exception of a handful of noteworthy, but isolated, indiscriminate bombings, they seek to keep the violence they commit within the bounds of what the ruling government will tolerate without undertaking massive repressive actions against the terrorists themselves.

Moreover, the point... of how terrorists consciously learn from one another, is evident with respect to at least some German right-wing terrorist elements. This suggests aspirations toward a more planned and coherent campaign of violence than hitherto has existed and poses with it the possibilities of a more serious future threat. As long ago as 1981, Manfred Roeder, for a time Germany's leading neo-Nazi, advocated the emulation of left-wing terrorist targeting and tactics in hopes of endowing the movement with a clearer purpose and attainable goal. For the rightists, however, there was another factor: envy of the attention, status and occasional tactical victories won by left-wing terrorists in groups such as the RAF, alongside the realization that indiscriminate terrorist attacks will not result in the attainment of the neo-Nazi's goals. 'The RAF had brought terrorism to modern Europe', Ingo Hasselbach, one of Roeder's successors, recently recalled, 'and even though they could not have been more opposed to our ideology, we respected them for their fanaticism and skill'. What Hasselbach thus advocated for his Kameradschaft (e.g., 'Nazi brotherhood'), before his own disillusionment forced him to break completely with the movement he had so enthusiastically once championed, was the same lethally discriminate campaign of terrorism pursued by the RAF. Like the original founders of the 'Baader-Meinhoff' Group twenty years before, Hasselbach also believed that his National Alternative Berlin (NA) neo-Nazi organization could not achieve its political objectives by attempting to operate as a legal political party. Accordingly, he sought to mould the group into a terrorist organization modelled on the RAF and therefore laid plans to assassinate prominent Jews and Communists and leading politicians. 'We wanted to bring neo-Nazi terrorism up to the level of that carried out by the radical Left', Hasselbach later explained,

> striking at targets that would be both better guarded and more significant—targets that would do serious damage to the democratic German state while driving home our racial message. There was, for instance, talk of assassinating Gregor Gusi, the head of the reformed Communist Party, the PDS; he was East Germany's most prominent Jew and leader of the Communists to boot. He was not only a major politician but the political representative of the former GDR system. We also considered hitting Ignatz Bubis, the new head of the Jewish community, as well as a number of politicians in Bonn—including the interior minister and Chancellor Kohl himself.[25]

Like other terrorist organizations, the more sophisticated right-wing groups also seek targets that are likely to advance their aims. In this respect, their terrorist acts are as calculated as those of the left-wing organizations they try to emulate. Publicity and attention are of course paramount aims; but at the same time there is a conscious recognition that only if their violence is properly calculated and in at least in some (however idiosyncratic way) regulated, will they be able to achieve the effect(s) they desire and the political objectives they seek. As an IRA terrorist once said, 'You don't bloody well kill people for the sake of killing them'.[26] This is not, however, the case with many of the religious terrorist movements.... For them, violence still has an instrumental purpose but, unlike secular terrorists, it is often an end in itself—a sacred duty executed in direct response to some theological demand or imperative. For example, a 1990 study of Lebanese Shi'a terrorists revealed that none of the sample were interested in influencing an actual or self-perceived constituency or with swaying popular opinion: their sole preoccupation was serving God through the fulfilment of their divinely-ordained mission(s).[27] Hence, for religious terrorists there are demonstrably fewer constraints on the actual infliction of violence and a more open-ended and indiscriminate category of enemies is clearly evident. The leader of an Egyptian terrorist cell, for instance, professed absolutely no remorse when he was told that an attack he had planned against visiting Israeli Jews had instead killed nine German tourists. His matter-of-fact response was that 'infidels are all the same'.[28] Indeed, how else can one explain the mad plots of the American Christian white supremacists? Or the Aum sect's wanton and repeated attempts to use of chemical warfare nerve agents indiscriminately against populous urban centres? Or the cataclysmic aim of the Jewish Temple Mount bombers in Israel? The contemplation of such wholesale acts of violence is thus a direct reflection of the fact that religious terrorists, unlike their secular counterparts, do not seek to appeal to any constituency or authority other than their own god or religious figures and therefore feel little need to regulate or calibrate their violence.

The Individual and Internal Organizational Dynamics of Terrorist Groups

All terrorists, however, doubtless have one trait in common: they live in the future: that distant—yet imperceptibly close—point in time when they will assuredly triumph over their enemies and attain the ultimate realization of their political destiny. For the religious groups, this future is divinely decreed and the terrorists themselves specifically anointed to achieve it. The inevitability of their victory is taken for granted, as a 1996 communiqué issued by the Egyptian Islamic Group reveals. Citing Koranic verse, the document brusquely dismisses even the possibility that its secular opponents might succeed. 'They plot and plan and God too plans', it declares, 'but the best of planners is God'. Therefore the group must faithfully and resolutely 'pursue its battle... until such time as God would grant victory—just as the Prophet Mohammed did with the Quredish until God granted victory over Mecca'.[29]

For the secular terrorist, their eventual victory is as inexorable as it is predetermined. Indeed, the innate righteousness of their cause itself assures success. 'Our struggle will be long and arduous because the enemy is powerful, well-organised, and well-sustained from abroad', Leila Khaled wrote in her autobiography published 25 years ago. 'We shall win because we represent the wave of the future... because mankind is on our side, and above all because we are determined to achieve victory'.[30] Comparatively small in number, limited in capabilities, isolated from society and dwarfed by both the vast resources of their enemy and the enormity of their task; the secular terrorist, accordingly, necessarily functions in an inverted reality where the sought-after, ardently pursued future defines their existence, rather than the oppressive, angst-driven, and incomplete present. 'You convince yourself that to reach this utopia', the Red Brigades' Adriana Faranda later recalled of the group's collective mindset, 'it is necessary to pass through the destruction of society which prevents your ideas from being realised'.[31] By ignoring the present and literally "soldiering on" despite hardship and adversity, terrorists are able to compensate for their abject weakness and thereby overcome the temporal apathy or hostility of a constituency whom they claim to represent. 'We made calculations', Faranda's comrade-in-arms, Patrizio Peci explained in his memoirs. 'The most pessimistic thought that within twenty years the war would be won, some said within five, ten. All, however, thought that we were living through the most difficult moment, that gradually things would become easier...'.[32] The left-wing terrorists thus console themselves that the travails and isolation of life underground are but a mere transitory stage on the path to final victory.

The longevity of most modern terrorist groups, however, would suggest otherwise. Rapoport, for example, estimates that the life expectancy of at least 90 percent of terrorist organizations is less than a year and that nearly half of those that make it that far have ceased to exist within a decade.[33] Thus the optimistic clarion calls to battle issued by terrorists groups the world over in communiqués, treatises and other propaganda have a distinctly hollow ring given the grim, empirical reality of their organizational life cycles. 'NEVER BE DETERRED BY THE ENORMOUS DIMENSIONS OF YOUR OWN GOALS', a communiqué issued by the left-wing French terrorist group, Direct Action proclaimed in 1985:[34] yet, less than two years later the group had effectively been decapitated by the capture of virtually its entire leadership and shortly afterwards fell into complete lassitude. Similarly, in 1978 the RB's leader, Renato Curio, bragged about a struggle that he envisioned would last 40 years: within a decade, however, even this terrorist organization—for a time one of Europe's most formidable—had collapsed under the weight of arrests and defections.[35]

Some categories of terrorist groups admittedly have better chances of survival—and perhaps success—than others. Historically, although religious movements like the Assassins persisted for nearly two centuries and the Thugs remained active for more than 600 years, in modern times ethno-nationalist/separatist terrorist groups have typically lasted longest and been the most successful. Al-Fatah, the Palestinian terrorist organization led by Yasir Arafat, for example, was founded in 1957. The PLO itself is now 34 years old. The Basque group ETA was established in 1959, while the current iteration of the IRA, formally known as the 'Provisional Irish Republican Army' is nearly thirty years old and is itself the successor of the older 'Official IRA' that was founded nearly a century ago and who can in turn be traced back to the various Fenian revolutionary brotherhoods that had periodically surfaced since Wolfe Tone's rebellion in 1789. However, except the immediate post-war era of massive de-colonialization, success for ethno-nationalist terrorist organizations has rarely involved the actual realization of their stated, long-term goals of either self-determination or nationhood. Rather, it has more often amounted to a string of key tactical victories that have sustained prolonged struggles and breathed new life into faltering—and in some instances, geriatric—terrorist movements.

The resiliency of these groups is doubtless a product of the relative ease with which they are able to draw sustenance and support from an already existent constituency—e.g., their fellow ethno-nationalist brethren. By contrast, both left- and right-wing terrorist organizations must actively proselytize among the politically aware and radical, though often uncommitted, for recruits and support: thus rendering themselves vulnerable to penetration and compromise. The ethno-nationalists derive a further advantage from their historical longevity by being able to appeal to a collective revolutionary tradition and even at a time a pre-disposition to rebellion. This assures successive terrorist generations both a steady stream of recruits from their respective community's youth and a ready pool of sympathizers and supporters among their more nostalgic elders. Hence, these groups' unique ability to replenish their ranks from within already close, tightly-knit communities means that even when an ongoing campaign shows signs of flagging, the mantle can be smoothly passed to a new generation. Abu Iyad, Arafat's intelligence chief, can therefore dismiss as mere ephemeral impediments the cul-de-sacs and round-abouts that have long plagued the Palestinian liberation movement. '[O]ur people will bring forth a new revolution', he wrote some twenty years ago. 'They will engender a movement much more powerful than ours, better armed and thus more dangerous to the Zionists.... And one day, we will have a country'.[36]

The ethno-nationalists' comparative success, however, may have as much to do with the clarity and tangibility of their envisioned future—the establishment (or re-establishment) of a national homeland from within some existing country—as to these other characteristics. The articulation of so concrete and comprehensible a goal is by far the most potent and persuasive rallying cry. It also makes the inevitability of their victory appear both palpable and readily attainable; if of course prolonged and protracted. Few therefore would have doubted Martin McGuinness's 1977 pledge that the IRA would keep 'blattering on until Brits leave'[37] or Danny Morrison's declaration 12 years later that only 'when it is politically costly for the British to remain in Ireland, they'll go... it won't be triggered until a large number of British soldiers are killed and that's what's going to happen'.[38]

Left-wing terrorist movements, by comparison, appear doubly disadvantaged. They not only lack the sizeable, existing pool of potential recruits available to most ethno-nationalist groups, but among all terrorist categories they have formulated the least clear and most ill-defined vision of the future. Prolific and prodigious though their myriad denunciations of the evils of the militarist, capitalist state may be, precious little information is forthcoming about its envisioned successor. 'That is the most difficult question for revolutionaries', Kozo Okamoto, the surviving member of the three-man JRA [Japanese Red Army] team that staged the 1972 Lod Airport massacre replied when asked about the post-revolutionary society that his group sought to create. 'We really do not know what it will be like'.[39] The RAF's Gudrun Ennslin similarly brushed aside all questions about the group's long-term aims. 'As for the state of the future, the time after victory', she once said, 'that is not our concern... we build the revolution, not the socialist model'.[40] This inability to coherently, much less cogently, articulate their future plans possibly explains why the left-wing's terrorist campaigns have historically been the least effectual.

Even when left-wing terrorists have attempted to conceptualize a concrete vision of the future, their efforts have hardly produced anything more lucid or edifying than verbose disquisitions espousing an idiosyncratic interpretation of Marxist doctrine. 'We have applied the Marxist analysis and method to the contemporary scene—not transferred it, but actually applied it', Ennslin wrote in a collection of RAF statements published by the group in 1977 (and subsequently banned by the German government). Yet no further exegesis is offered about the desired result, except the belief that Marxism be rendered obsolete when the revolution triumphs and the 'capitalist system has been abolished'.[41] Slightly more reflective is the exposition offered by the American radical Jane Alpert who, in her memoir explains how she and her comrades-in-arms

> believed that the world could be cleansed of all domination and submission, that perception itself could be purified of the division into subject and object, that power playing between nations, sexes, races, ages, between animals and humans, individuals and groups, could be brought to an end. Our revolution would create a universe in which all consciousness was cosmic, in which everyone would share the bliss we knew from acid, but untainted by fear, possessiveness, sickness, hunger, or the need for a drug to bring happiness.[42]

Nonetheless this vision comes across as so vague and idyllic as to appear almost completely divorced from reality: an effect, perhaps, of its drug-induced influence. That drugs played a part in the formulation of other leftist terrorist's strategies is an interesting, though perhaps over-exaggerated, sidelight. Baumann, for example, also recounts the centrality of drugs to the would-be revolution. 'We said integrate dope into praxis too', he recalled, 'no more separate..., but a total unification around this thing, so that a new person is born out of the struggle'.[43] It should be noted, though, that a study commissioned by the Italian secret services in the 1970s discovered (somewhat counter intuitively) that right-wing terrorists were in fact more prone to abuse[44] and indeed to use drugs more than their left-wing counterparts. Two Italian psychiatrists conducting a related study attributed this to the rightists' innate psychological instability, at least compared to Italian left-wing terrorists. 'In the right-wing terrorism', Drs. Franco Ferracuti and Franceso Bruno wrote, 'the individual terrorists are frequently psychopathological and the ideology is empty; in left-wing terrorism, ideology is outside of reality and terrorists are more normal and fanatical'.[45]

But it would be a grave error to dismiss the left-wing terrorists as either totally feckless and frivolous or completely devoid of introspection or seriousness of purpose. For them, the future was simply too large and abstract a concept to comprehend: instead, action—e.g., terrorist attacks specifically designed to effect the revolution—was embraced as a far more rewarding pursuit. Hence, [Algerian National Front leader and writer, Frantz] Fanon—and not Marx—arguably exerted the greater influence. For example, Susan Stern, a member of the 1970s-era American left-wing terrorist group, The Weathermen, recalled the dynamic tension between thought and action that permeated the group and affected all internal debate. 'Once we tore down capitalism, who would empty the garbage, and teach the children and who would decide that?', she and her comrades would often consider.

> Would the world be Communist? Would the Third World control it? Would all whites die? Would all sex perverts die? Who would run the prisons—would there be prisons? Endless questions like these were raised by the Weathermen, but we didn't

have the answers. And we were tired of trying to wait until we understood everything.[46]

The RAF's seminal treatise, 'Sur la Conception de la Guerilla Urbaine', evidences the same frustration. Quoting fellow revolutionary, Eldridge Cleaver, a leader of the Black Panther Party, an African-American radical political organization active during the 1960s, it states: 'For centuries and generations we have contemplated and examined the shit from all sides. "Me, I'm convinced that most things which happen in this country don't need to be analysed much longer", said Cleaver. The RAF put the words of Cleaver into practice'.[47]

Indeed, all terrorists are driven by this burning impatience coupled with an unswerving belief in the efficacy of violence. The future that they look forward to is neither temporal nor born of the natural progression of mankind: rather, it is contrived and shaped, forged and moulded and ultimately determined and achieved by violence. 'What use was there in writing memoranda?', Begin rhetorically inquired to explain the Irgun's decision to resume its revolt in 1944.

> What value in speeches?... No, there was no other way. If we did not fight we should be destroyed. To fight was the only way to salvation.
> When Descartes said: "I think, therefore, I am," he uttered a very profound thought. But there are times in the history of peoples when thought alone does not prove their existence.... There are times when everything in you cries out: your very self-respect as a human being lies in your resistance to evil.
> We fight, therefore we are![48]

Thirty years later, Leila Khaled similarly invoked the primacy of action over talk and bullets instead of words. 'We must act, not just talk and memorise the arguments against Zionism', she counselled;[49] a view echoed by Yoyes, an ETA terrorist who lost faith in the endless promises that 'independence can be won by peaceful means. It's all a lie.... The only possibility we have of gaining our liberty is through violence.'[50] As the neo-Nazi Ingo Hasselbach recalled of his own experience, 'The time for legal work and patience was through. The only thing to do was to turn our Kameradschaft into a real terrorist organization'.[51]

For some terrorists, however, the desire for action can lead to an obsession with violence itself. Abu Nidal, for example, was once known and admired for his 'fiery and unbending nationalism'; whereas today he is universally disdained as little more than an 'outlaw and killer'.[52] Eamon Collins describes a similar transformation in his IRA-gunman cousin, Mickey, who, Collins realized, had gradually 'lost any sense of the wider perspective, and was just obsessively absorbed by the details of the next killing'.[53] Andreas Baader is perhaps a different type altogether. From the very start of the RAF's campaign, he never wavered from his conviction that the terrorist's only 'language is action'.[54] Baumann, who knew Baader well, remembers the RAF's founder as a 'weapons maniac, [who] later developed an almost sexual relationship with pistols (the Heckler and Koch type in particular)'.[55] Indeed, according to Baader himself, 'Fucking and shooting [were] the same thing'.[56] Unquestionably a man of action and not words, he preferred, in the terrorist vernacular, "direct actions"—bank robberies, vandalism and arson, bombings and armed attacks—to debate and discourse. 'Let's go, then!' was Baader's immediate response, for example, when his lover and group co-leader Ensslin suggested that the group bomb an American military base in retaliation for the U.S. Air Force's mining of North Vietnam's Haiphong harbour in 1972. Despite being the leading figure of an organization dedicated to achieve profound political change, he had absolutely no time for politics, which he derisively dismissed as a load of 'shit'.[57] Baader's whole approach can be summed up in the advice he gave to a wavering RAF recruit. 'Either you come along [and join the revolution and fight]', he said, 'or you stay forever an empty chatterbox'.[58]

Although Baader may perhaps be an extreme example of this phenomenon, the undeniable cynosure for all terrorists is indeed action and, perhaps even more so, the thrill and heady excitement that accompanies it. Peci's 222-page account of his life as a Red Brigadist, for instance, is devoted more to recounting in obsessive detail the types of weapons (and their technical specifications) used on particular RB operations and which group members actually did the shooting than to elucidating the organization's ideological aims and political goals.[59] Baumann is particularly candid about the cathartic relief that an operation brought to a small group of individuals living underground, in close proximity to one another, constantly on the run and fearful of arrest and betrayal. The real stress, he said, came from life in the group—not from the planning and execution of attacks.[60] Others like Stern, Collins, the RAF's Silke Maier-Witt, and the RB's Susana Ronconi are even more explicit about the "rush" and the sense of power and accomplishment that they derived from the violence that they inflicted. 'Nothing in my life had ever been this exciting', Stern enthused as she drifted deeper into terrorism.[61] Collins similarly recalls how he led an 'action-packed existence' during his six years in the IRA: 'living each day with the excitement of feeling I was playing a part in taking on the Orange State'.[62] For Maier-Witt the intoxicating allure of action was sufficient to overcome the misgivings she had about the murder of Schleyer's four bodyguards in order to kidnap the man himself. 'At the time I felt the brutality of that action.... [But it] was a kind of excitement too because something had happened. The real thing', she consoled herself, had 'started now'.[63] Ronconi is the most expansive and incisive in analyzing the terrorist's psychology. 'The main thing was that you felt you were able to influence the world about you, instead of experiencing it passively', thereby combining intrinsic excitement with profound satisfaction. 'It was this ability to make an impact on the reality of everyday life that was important', she explained, 'and obviously still is important'.[64]

For the terrorist, success in having this impact is most often measured in terms of the amount of publicity and attention that they receive. Newsprint and air-time are thus the coin of the realm in the terrorists' mindset: the only tangible or readily empirical means that they have with which to gauge their success and assess their progress. In this respect, little distinction or discrimination is made between good or bad publicity: the satisfaction of simply being noticed is often regarded as sufficient reward. 'The only way to achieve results', the JRA, for example, boasted in its communiqué claiming credit for the aforementioned 1972 Lod Airport massacre, in which 26 people were slain (including 16 Puerto Rican Christians on a pilgrimage to the Holy Land), 'is to shock the world right down to its socks'.[65] The arch-terrorist, Carlos, 'The Jackal', reportedly meticulously clipped and had translated newspaper accounts about him and his deeds.[66]

'[T]he more I'm talked about', Carlos once explained to his terrorist colleague later turned apostate Hans-Joachim Klein, 'the more dangerous I appear. That's all the better for me'.[67] Similarly, when Ramzi Ahmed Yousef, the alleged mastermind behind the 1993 bombing of New York's World Trade Center, was apprehended in Pakistan two years later, police found in his possession two remote-control explosive devices along with a collection of newspaper articles detailing his exploits.[68]

However, for Carlos and Yousef as for many other terrorists, this equation of publicity and attention with success and self-gratification has the effect of locking them onto an unrelenting upward spiral of violence in order to retain the media and public's attention.[69] Yousef, for example, planned to follow the World Trade Center bombing with the assassinations of Pope John II and the then-prime minister of Pakistan, Benazir Bhutto, and the near-simultaneous inflight bombings of 11 U.S. passenger airliners. Klein in fact describes escalation as a 'force of habit' among terrorists; an intrinsic product of their perennial need for validation which in turn is routinely assessed and appraised on the basis of media coverage. The effect is that terrorists today feel driven to undertake ever more dramatic and destructively lethal deeds in order to achieve the same effect that a less ambitious or bloody action may have had in the past. To their minds at least, the media and public have become progressively inured or de-sensitized to the seemingly endless litany of successive terrorist incidents: thus requiring a continuous upward ratcheting of the violence in order to retain the media and public's interest and attention. As Klein once observed, the more violent things get, the more people will respect you. The greater the chance of achieving your demands.[70] Timothy McVeigh, the convicted Oklahoma City bomber, seemingly offered the same explanation when asked by his attorney whether he could not have achieved the same effect of drawing attention to his grievances against the U.S. government without killing anyone. 'That would not have gotten the point across', McVeigh reportedly replied. 'We needed a body count to make our point'.[71] In this respect, although the Murrah Building bombing was doubtless planned well in advance of the portentously symbolic date of 19 April deliberately chosen by McVeigh, he may nonetheless have felt driven to surpass in terms of death and destruction the previous month's dramatic and more exotic nerve-gas attack on the Tokyo underground in order to guarantee that his attack too received the requisite media coverage and public attention.

The terrorists' ability to attract—and, moreover, to continue to attract—attention, however, is most often predicated on the success of their attacks. The most feared terrorists are arguably those that are the most successful in translating thought into action: ruthless and efficient, demonstrating that they are able to make good on their threats and back up their demands with violence. This organizational imperative to succeed, however, in turn imposes on some terrorist groups an ironical operational conservatism. Hence, radical in their politics, terrorists are frequently just as conservative in their operations: adhering to an established modus operandi that, to their minds at least, minimizes failure and maximizes success. 'The main point is to select targets where success is 100% assured', the doyen of modern international terrorism, George Habash, once explained.[72] For the terrorist, therefore, a combination of solid training, sound planning, good intelligence and technological competence are the essential prerequisites for a successful operation. 'I learned how to be an effective IRA member', Collins reminisced about his two-year-long training and induction period: 'how to gather intelligence, how to set up operations, how to avoid mistakes'.[73] Similarly, an unidentified American left-wing radical who specialized in bombings, detailed in a 1970 interview the procedures and extreme care that governed all his group's operations. The 'first decision', he said, is

> political—determining appropriate and possible targets. Once a set of targets is decided on, they must be reconnoitered and information gathered on how to approach the targets, how to place the bomb, how the security of the individuals and the explosives is to be protected. Then the time is chosen and a specific target. Next there was a preliminary run-through—in our case a number of practice sessions.... The discipline during the actual operation is not to alter any of the agreed-upon plans or to discuss the action until everyone's safe within the group again. Our desire is not just for one success but to continue as long as possible.[74]

Good intelligence, therefore, is as critical for the success of an operation as it is for terrorists' own survival. An almost Darwinian principle of natural selection thus seems to affect terrorist organizations, whereby (as previously noted) every new terrorist generation learns from its predecessors, becoming smarter, tougher, and more difficult to capture or eliminate. In this respect, terrorists also analyze the 'lessons' from mistakes made by former comrades who have been either killed or apprehended. Press accounts, judicial indictments, courtroom testimony, and trial transcripts are meticulously culled for information on security force tactics and methods and then absorbed by surviving group members. The third generation of the RAF that emerged in the late 1980s is a classic example of this phenomenon. According to a senior German official, group members routinely study 'every court case against them to discover their weak spots'. Hence, having learned about the techniques used by the authorities against them from testimony presented by law enforcement personnel in open court (in some instances having been deliberately questioned on these matters by sympathetic attorneys), the terrorists consequently are able to undertake the requisite countermeasures to avoid detection. For example, where previously German police could usually obtain fingerprints from the bottom of toilet seats or the inside of refrigerators, surviving RAF members began to apply a special ointment to their fingers that, after drying, prevents fingerprints and thus thwarted their identification and incrimination.[75] As a spokesperson for the Bundeskriminalamt lamented in the months immediately preceding the RAF's unilateral declaration of a cease-fire in April 1992, the '"Third Generation" learnt a lot from the mistakes of its predecessors—and about how the police works... they now know how to operate very carefully'.[76] Indeed, according to a former member of the group, Peter-Juergen Brock, serving a life sentence for murder, the RAF before the cease-fire had 'reached maximum efficiency'.[77]

Similar accolades have also been bestowed on the current generation of IRA fighters. At the end of his tour of duty in 1992 as General Officer Commanding British Forces in Northern Ireland, General Sir John Wilsey, had described the IRA as 'an absolutely formidable enemy. The essential attributes of their leaders are better than ever before. Some of their operations are brilliant in terrorist terms'.[78] By this time, too, even the IRA's once comparatively unsophisticated Loyalist terrorist counterparts had absorbed the lessons from their own past mistakes and had consciously emulated the IRA to become disquietingly more 'professional' as well. One senior RUC [Royal Ulster

Constabulary] officer noted this change in the Loyalists' capabilities, observing that they too were now increasingly 'running their operations from small cells, on a need to know basis. They have cracked down on loose talk. They have learned how to destroy forensic evidence. And if you bring them in for questioning, they say nothing'.[79]

Finally, success for the terrorist is dependent not only on their ability to keep one step ahead of the authorities but of the counter-terrorist technology curve as well. The terrorist group's fundamental organizational imperative to act also drives this persistent search for new ways to overcome, circumvent or defeat governmental security and countermeasures. The IRA's own relentless quest to pierce the armour protecting both the security forces in Northern Ireland and the most senior government officials in England illustrates the professional evolution and increasing operational sophistication of a terrorist group. The first generation of early 1970s IRA devices, for example, were often little more than crude anti-personnel bombs, consisting of a handful of roofing nails, wrapped around a lump of plastic explosive that were detonated simply by lighting a fuse. Time bombs from the same era were hardly more sophisticated. They typically were constructed from a few sticks of dynamite and commercial detonators stolen from construction sites or rock quarries attached to ordinary battery-powered alarm clocks. Neither device was terribly reliable and often put the bomber at considerable risk. The process of placing and actually lighting the first type of device carried with it the inherent potential to attract undesired attention while affording the bomber little time to effect the attack and make good his or her escape. Although the second type of device was designed to mitigate precisely this danger, its timing and detonation mechanism was often so crude that accidental or premature explosions were not infrequent, thus causing some terrorists inadvertently to kill themselves—what is known in Belfast as 'own goals'. About 120 IRA men have been killed this way since 1969.[80]

In hopes of obviating, or at least reducing, these risks, the IRA's bomb makers invented a means of detonating bombs from a safe distance using the radio controls for model aircraft purchased at hobby shops. Scientists and engineers working in the British Ministry of Defence's (MoD) scientific research and development ('R&D') division in turn developed a system of electronic countermeasures and jamming techniques for the Army that effectively thwarted this means of attack. However, rather than abandon this tactic completely, the PIRA began to search for a solution. In contrast to the state-of-the-art laboratories, huge budgets, and academic credentials of their government counterparts, the IRA's own 'R&D' department toiled in cellars beneath cross-border safe houses and the back rooms of urban tenements for five years before devising a network of sophisticated electronic switches for their bombs that would ignore or bypass the Army's electronic countermeasures. Once again, the MoD scientists returned to their laboratories; emerging with a new system of electronic scanners able to detect radio emissions the moment the radio is switched on—and, critically, just tens of seconds before the bomber can actually transmit the detonation signal. The almost infinitesimal window of time provided by this 'early warning' of impending attack is just sufficient to allow Army technicians to activate a series of additional electronic measures to neutralize the transmission signal and render detonation impossible. For a time, this countermeasure proved effective as well. But then the IRA discovered a means to outwit even this countermeasure. Utilizing radar detectors, such as those used by motorists in the United States to evade speed traps, in 1991 the group's bomb makers fabricated a detonating system that can be triggered by the same type of hand-held radar gun used by police throughout the world to catch speeding motorists. Since the radar gun can be aimed at its target before being switched on, and the signal that it transmits is nearly instantaneous, no practical means currently exists that allows the time needed either to detect or intercept the transmission signal. Moreover, shortly afterwards, the IRA's 'R&D' units developed yet another means to detonate bombs using a photo-flash "slave" unit that can be triggered from a distance of up to 800 meters by a flash of light. The device, which sells for between £60 and £70, is used by commercial photographers to produce simultaneous flashes during photo shoots. The IRA bombers attach the unit to the detonating system on a bomb and then simply activate it with a commercially-available, ordinary flash gun.

Not surprisingly, therefore, the IRA bombers have earned a reputation for their innovative expertise, adaptability, and cunning. 'There are some very bright people around', the British Army's Chief Ammunitions Technical Officer (CATO) in Northern Ireland commented. 'I would rate them very highly for improvisation. PIRA bombs are very well made'.[81] A similar accolade was offered by the staff officer of the British Army's 321 Explosives and Ordinance Disposal Company: 'We are dealing with the first division', he said. 'I don't think there is any organization in the world as cunning as the IRA. They have had 20 years at it and they have learned from their experience. We have a great deal of respect for their skills... not as individuals, but their skills'.[82] While not yet nearly as good as the PIRA, the province's Loyalist terrorist groups have themselves also been on a 'learning curve' with regard to bomb-making: reportedly having become increasingly adept in the construction, concealment and surreptitious placement of bombs.

Moreover, in certain circumstances, even attacks that are not successful in conventionally-understood military terms of casualties inflicted or assets destroyed, can still be a success for the terrorists provided that they are technologically daring enough to garner media and public attention.[83] Thus, while the IRA failed to kill then-Prime Minister Margaret Thatcher at the Conservative Party's 1984 conference in Brighton, the technological ingenuity involving the bomb's placement at the conference site weeks before the event and its detonation timing device powered by a computer microchip nonetheless succeeded in capturing the world's headlines and providing the IRA with a platform from which to warn Mrs. Thatcher and all other British leaders: 'Today we were unlucky, but remember we only have to be lucky once—you will have to be lucky always'.[84] Similarly, although the remote-control mortar attack staged by the IRA on No. 10 Downing Street—as Prime Minister John Major and his Cabinet met at the height of the 1991 Gulf War—failed to hit its intended target, the attack nonetheless successfully elbowed the war out of the limelight and shone renewed media attention on the terrorists, their cause and their impressive ability to strike at the nerve-centre of the British government even at a time of heightened security. 'The Provies are always that step ahead of you', a senior RUC officer has commented. 'They are very innovative'.[85] Although the technological mastery employed by the IRA is arguably unique among terrorist organizations, experience has nonetheless demonstrated repeatedly that, when confronted by new security measures, terrorists will seek to identify and exploit new vulnerabilities, adjusting their means of attack accordingly and often carrying on despite the obstacles placed in their path.

Conclusion

'All politics is a struggle for power', wrote C. Wright Mills, and 'the ultimate kind of power is violence'.[86] Terrorism, accordingly, is where politics and violence intersect in hopes of producing power. And, terrorism ineluctably involves the quest for power: power to dominate and coerce, to intimidate and control, and ultimately to effect fundamental political change. Violence (or, the threat of violence) is thus the sine qua non of terrorism; evidencing the terrorists' irreducible conviction that only through violence can their cause triumph and their long-term political aims be attained. Terrorists therefore plan their operations in a manner that will shock, impress and intimidate: ensuring that their acts are sufficiently daring and violent enough to capture the attention of the media and, in turn, of the public and government as well. Thus, rather than being seen as indiscriminate or senseless, terrorism is actually a very deliberate and planned application of violence. In this respect, terrorism can be seen as a concatenation of five individual processes, designed to achieve sequentially, the following key objectives:

1. Attention. Through dramatic, attention-riveting acts of violence, terrorists seek to focus attention on themselves and their causes through the publicity they receive, most often from news media coverage.

2. Acknowledgement. Having attracted this attention, and thrust some otherwise previously ignored or hitherto forgotten cause onto the state's—or, often more desirably, the international community's—agenda, terrorists seek to parlay their new-found notoriety into winning acknowledgement (and perhaps even sympathy and support) of their cause.

3. Recognition. Terrorists attempt to capitalize on the interest and acknowledgement their violent acts have generated by obtaining recognition of both their rights (e.g., acceptance of the justification of their cause) and of their particular organization as the spokesman of the constituency whom the terrorists purport to, or in some cases, actually do, represent.

4. Authority. Armed with this recognition, terrorists seek the authority to effect the changes in government and/or society that is at the heart of their movement's struggle (e.g., change in government or in the entire state structure, or the re-distribution of wealth, re-adjustment of geographical boundaries, assertion of minority rights, etc.).

5. Governance. Having acquired authority, terrorists seek to consolidate their direct and complete control over the state, their homeland and/or their people.

Whilst some terrorist movements have been successful in achieving the first three objectives, rarely in modern times has any group attained the latter two. Nonetheless, all terrorists exist and function in hopes of reaching this ultimate end. For them, the future rather than the present defines their reality. Indeed, they can console themselves that it was only a decade ago that the then-Prime Minister Thatcher said of the African National Congress, 'Anyone who thinks it is going to run the government in South Africa is living in cloud-cuckoo land'.[87] Exactly ten years after Mrs. Thatcher's remark, Queen Elizabeth II, greeted Nelson Mandela on his first official state visit to London.

Notes

1. Peter H. Merkl, 'Prologue', in Peter H. Merkl (ed.), *Political Violence and Terror* (Berkeley: University of California Press, 1986), p. 8.
2. Quoted in Peter Neuhauser, 'The Mind of a German Terrorist', *Encounter*, vol. LI, no. 3 (September 1978), p. 81.
3. Quoted in Richard Drake, *The Aldo Moro Murder Case* (Cambridge and London: Harvard University Press, 1995), pp. 118–119.
4. On the night of 10 November 1938, German storm troopers destroyed virtually every synagogue in Germany and set fire to some 7,000 Jewish businesses. About 30,000 Jews were arrested and thrown into concentration camps. The event takes its name from the broken plate glass windows of the Jewish-owned stores.
5. Neuhauser, 'The Mind of a German Terrorist', pp. 83–84.
6. Moreover, Baumann's vignette, like the previously discussed 1972 Munich Olympics operation, again underscores how even attacks that fail to achieve their ostensible objective (e.g., the successful detonation of a bomb and attendant damage and destruction caused) can nonetheless still fulfil a terrorist group's immediate objectives and therefore just as effectively serve its wider intentions.
7. Quoted in Alison Jamieson, *The Heart Attacked: Terrorism and Conflict in the Italian State* (London and New York: Marion Boyars, 1989), p. 89.
8. Patrizio Peci, *Io, l'infame* (Trans. I, *The Scoundrel*) (Milan: Arnoldo Mondadori, 1983), p. 46.
9. 'RAF Philosophy' in *The German guerrilla: terror, reaction, and resistance*, pp. 98–99.
10. Quoted in McDonald, *Shoot The Women First*, p. 11.
11. Quoted in Peter Taylor, *Provos: The IRA and Sinn Fein* (London: Bloomsbury, 1997), p. 201.
12. David McKittrick, *Despatches from Belfast* (Belfast: Blackstaff Press, 1989), p. 77.
13. Patrick Bishop and Eamonn Mallie, *The Provisional IRA* (London: Corgi, 1989), p. 387.
14. Robert W. White, 'The Irish Republican Army: An Assessment of Sectarianism', *Terrorism and Political Violence*, vol. 9, no. 1 (Spring 1997), p. 44.
15. 'But Basques aren't Irish', *The Economist* (London), 20 July 1996.
16. Quoted in McKnight, *The Mind of the Terrorist*, p. 26.
17. Quoted in Dobson, *Black September*, p. 95.
18. Quoted in McKnight, *The Mind of the Terrorist*, p. 26.
19. Quoted in Howell Raines, 'With Latest Bomb, I.R.A. Injures Its Own Cause', *New York Times*, 15 November 1987.
20. Eamon Collins, with Mick McGovern, *Killing Rage* (London: Granta, 1997), p. 296.
21. Quoted in McDonald, *Shoot The Women First*, p. 5.
22. See, for example, the compelling autobiographical account of the German neo-Nazi, Ingo Hasselbach, with Tom Reiss, *Führer-Ex: Memoirs of a Former Neo-Nazi* (London: Chatto & Windus, 1996).
23. Quoted in Bill Buford, *Among The Thugs* (London: Mandarin, 1992), p. 154.
24. Hasselbach, *Führer-Ex*, p. 119.
25. Ibid., pp. 274–275.
26. Quoted in McKnight, *The Mind of the Terrorist*, p. 179.
27. Ayla H. Schbley, 'Religious Terrorists: What They Aren't Going to Tell Us', *Terrorism*, vol. 13, no. 3 (Summer 1990), p. 240.
28. Quoted in Agence France Press, 'Bomber wanted to kill Jews', *The Times* (London), 15 October 1997.
29. Islamic Group in Egypt, 'Statement on U.S. Sentencing of Shiekh Rahman', 19 January 1996.
30. Leila Khaled, *My People Shall Live: The Autobiography of a Revolutionary* (London: Hodder and Stoughton, 1973), p. 209.
31. Quoted in Jamieson, *The Heart Attacked*, p. 271.
32. Peci, *Io, l'infame*, p. 46.
33. Rapoport, 'Terrorism', p. 1067.
34. Quoted in Bonnie Cordes, 'When Terrorists Do the Talking: Reflections on Terrorist Literature', *The Journal of Strategic Studies*, vol. 10, no. 4 (December 1987), p. 155.

35. Quoted in 'Inside the Red Brigades', *Newsweek* (New York), 15 May 1978.
36. Abu Iyad, *My Home, My Land*, p. 226.
37. Quoted in David Blundy, 'Inside The IRA', *Sunday Times* (London), 3 July 1977.
38. Quoted in M. L. R. Smith, *Fighting For Ireland? The Military Strategy of the Irish Republican Movement* (London and New York: Routledge, 1995), p. 224.
39. Quoted in Patricia G. Steinhoff, 'Portrait of a Terrorist: An Interview with Kozo Okamota', *Asian Survey*, vol. xvi, no. 9 (September 1976), pp. 844–845.
40. Quoted in I. Fetscher and G. Rohrmoser, *Analysen zum Terrorismus (Analyses on the Subject of Terrorism): Ideologien und Strategien (Ideologies and Strategies)*, vol. 1 (Bonn: Westdeutscher Verlag, 1981), p. 327.
41. Gudrun Ensslin, 'Statement of 19 January 1976' in *Red Army Faction*, Texte der RAF (RAF Texts) (Malmö, Sweden: Verlag Bo Cavefors, 1977), p. 345.
42. Jane Alpert, *Growing Up Underground* (New York: William Morrow, 1981), pp. 141 and 175.
43. Baumann, *Terror or Love?* p. 49.
44. Anonymous, 'Notes for the First Analysis of the Phenomenon of Terrorism of The Right' (unpublished study commissioned by the Italian secret services, no date), p. 2.
45. Franco Ferracuti and Franceso Bruno, 'Psychiatric Aspects of Terrorism in Italy' (unpublished study commissioned by the Italian secret services, no date), pp. 18 & 20.
46. Susan Stern, *With the Weathermen: The Personal Journey of a Revolutionary Woman* (Garden City, NY: Doubleday, 1975), p. 90. Alpert, in her memoir, describes similar discussions and frustrations giving way to action. See Alpert, *Growing Up Underground*, pp. 140–141 & 155.
47. 'RAF Philosophy' in *The German guerrilla: terror, reaction, and resistance*, pp. 99–100. Alpert similarly recalls how her lover and fellow terrorist, Sam Melville, quickly passed the point where he was fed up with talk and ready for action. 'Sam, after a few days, dispensed with theorizing and got down to what interested him: hideouts, disguises, dynamite, plastique, secret communiqués'. See Alpert, *Growing Up Underground*, p. 155.
48. Begin, *The Revolt*, p. 46.
49. Khaled, *My People Shall Live*, p. 110.
50. Quoted in Taylor, *States of Terror*, p. 159.
51. Hasselbach, *Führer-Ex*, p. 272.
52. Seale, *Abu Nidal: A Gun for Hire*, p. 57.
53. Collins, *Killing Rage*, p. 177.
54. Quoted in Michael Seufert, 'Dissension Among the Terrorists: Killing People Is Wrong', *Encounter*, vol. 51, no. 3 (September 1978), p. 84.
55. Neuhauser, 'The Mind of a German Terrorist', pp. 82–83. Heckler & Koch is a leading German weapons manufacturer, producing "top of the line" handguns, sub-machine guns and other small arms.
56. Quoted in Aust, *The Baader-Meinhof Group*, p. 97.
57. Quoted in Jillian Becker, *Hitler's Children: The Story of the Baader-Meinhof Gang* (London: Panther Books, 1978), p. 90.
58. Quoted in Ibid, p. 244.
59. Observation of Dr. Sue Ellen Moran, a RAND consultant, in April 1985.
60. Neuhauser, 'The Mind of a German Terrorist', p. 85.
61. Stern, *With the Weathermen*, p. 41.
62. Collins, *Killing Rage*, p. 363.
63. Quoted in Taylor, *States of Terror*, p. 125.
64. Quoted in McDonald, *Shoot the Women First*, p. 198.
65. Quoted in McKnight, *The Mind of the Terrorist*, p. 180.
66. Klein specifically recalls that when the German newsmagazine, *Der Speigel*, serialized a book about Carlos written by an English journalist (presumably Colin Smith's *Carlos: Portrait of a Terrorist* (London: Andre Deutsch, 1976), he 'kept all the articles and had them translated'. Bougereau, 'An Interview with Hans Joachim Klein', in Ibid., p. 38.
67. Quoted in Ibid., p. 36.
68. James Bone and Alan Road, 'Terror By Degree', *The Times Magazine* (London), 18 October 1997.

69. See, for example, David Hearst, 'Publicity key element of strategy', *The Guardian* (London), 31 July 1990; and, David Pallister, 'Provos seek to play havoc with British nerves and life-style', *The Guardian* (London), 31 July 1990.

70. Quoted in Jean Marcel Bougereau, 'An Interview with Hans Joachim Klein', in Ibid., pp. 12 & 39.

71. Quoted in James Brooke, 'Newspaper Says McVeigh Described Role in Bombing', *New York Times*, 1 March 1997.

72. Quoted in Oriana Fallaci, 'Interview with George Habash', *Life Magazine* (New York), 12 June 1970.

73. Collins, *Killing Rage*, pp. 65–66.

74. Quoted in 'Bombs Blast a Message of Hate', *Life Magazine* (New York), 27 March 1970.

75. See Frederick Kempe, 'Deadly Survivors: The Cold War Is Over But Leftist Terrorists in Germany Fight On', *Wall Street Journal*, 27 December 1991.

76. Quoted in Adrian Bridge, 'German police search for Red Army Faction killers', *The Independent* (London), 6 April 1991.

77. Quoted in Kempe, 'Deadly Survivors'.

78. Quoted in Edward Gorman, 'How to stop the IRA', *The Times* (London), 11 January 1992.

79. Quoted in William E. Schmidt, 'Protestant Gunmen Are Stepping Up the Violence in Northern Ireland', *New York Times*, 29 October 1991.

80. 'Terrorists killed by their own devices', *The Independent* (London), 20 February 1996.

81. Quoted in Ian Graham, 'Official: IRA Using "Bigger, Better" Bombs', *London Press Association*, 23 January 1992.

82. Quoted in Edward Gorman, 'Bomb disposers mark 21 years in Ulster', *The Times* (London), 7 November 1992.

83. *See*, for example, Maria McGuire, *To Take Arms: A Year in the Provisional IRA* (London: Macmillan, 1973), p. 62.

84. Quoted in 'Outrage not a reason for inaction', *Manchester Guardian International Edition*, 21 October 1984.

85. Interview, North Armagh, Northern Ireland, August 1992.

86. C. Wright Mills, *The Power Elite* (London and New York: Oxford University Press, 1956), p. 171.

87. Quoted in 'Don't spoil the party', *The Economist* (London), 13 July 1996.

3.2 John Arquilla, David Ronfeldt, and Michele Zanini, 1999

Networks, Netwar, and Information-Age Terrorism

John Arquilla is a RAND Corporation consultant and an associate professor of defense analysis at the United States Naval Postgraduate School in Monterey, California.

David Ronfeldt is a senior social scientist at RAND whose research focuses on issues such as information revolution, netwar, and the rise of transnational networks of nongovernmental organizations.

Michele Zanini is a researcher at RAND. These experts are all contributors to the book *Countering the New Terrorism* (1999).

T he rise of network forms of organization is a key consequence of the ongoing information revolution. Business organizations are being newly energized by networking, and many professional militaries are experimenting with flatter forms of organization. In this [selection], we explore the impact of networks on terrorist capabilities, and consider how this development may be associated with a move away from emphasis on traditional, episodic efforts at coercion to a new view of terror as a form of protracted warfare. Seen in this light, the recent bombings of U.S. embassies in East Africa, along with the retaliatory American missile strikes, may prove to be the opening shots of a war between a leading state and a terror network. We consider both the likely context and the conduct of such a war, and offer some insights that might inform policies aimed at defending against and countering terrorism.

A New Terrorism (With Old Roots)

The age-old phenomenon of terrorism continues to appeal to its perpetrators for three principal reasons. First, it appeals as a weapon of the weak—a shadowy way to wage war by attacking asymmetrically to harm and try to defeat an ostensibly superior force. This has had particular appeal to ethnonationalists, racist militias, religious fundamentalists, and other minorities who cannot match the military formations and firepower of their "oppressors"—the case, for example, with some radical Middle Eastern Islamist groups vis-à-vis Israel, and, until recently, the Provisional Irish Republican Army (PIRA) vis-à-vis Great Britain.

Second, terrorism has appealed as a way to assert identity and command attention—rather like proclaiming, "I bomb, therefore I am." Terrorism enables a perpetrator to publicize his identity, project it explosively, and touch the nerves of powerful distant leaders. This kind of attraction to violence transcends its instrumental utility. Mainstream revolutionary writings may view violence as a means of struggle, but terrorists often regard violence as an end in itself that generates identity or damages the enemy's identity.

Third, terrorism has sometimes appealed as a way to achieve a new future order by willfully wrecking the present. This is manifest in the religious fervor of some radical Islamists, but examples also lie among millenarian and apocalyptic groups, like Aum Shinrikyo in Japan, who aim to wreak havoc and rend a system asunder so that something new may emerge from the cracks. The substance of the future vision may be only vaguely defined, but its moral worth is clear and appealing to the terrorist.

In the first and second of these motivations or rationales, terrorism may involve retaliation and retribution for past wrongs, whereas the third is also about revelation and rebirth, the coming of a new age. The first is largely strategic; it has a practical tone, and the objectives may be limited and specific. In contrast, the third may engage a transcendental, unconstrained view of how to change the world through terrorism.

Such contrasts do not mean the three are necessarily at odds; blends often occur. Presumptions of weakness (the first rationale) and of willfulness (in the second and third) can lead to peculiar synergies. For example, Aum's members may have known it was weak in a conventional sense, but they believed that they had special knowledge, a unique leader, invincible willpower, and secret ways to strike out.

These classic motivations or rationales will endure in the information age. However, terrorism is not a fixed phenomenon; its perpetrators adapt it to suit their times and situations. What changes is the conduct of terrorism—the operational characteristics built around the motivations and rationales.

This [selection] addresses, often in a deliberately speculative manner, changes in organization, doctrine, strategy, and technology that, taken together, speak to the emergence of a "new terrorism" attuned to the information age. Our principal hypotheses are as follows:

- **Organization.** Terrorists will continue moving from hierarchical toward information-age network designs. Within groups, "great man" leaderships will give way to flatter decentralized designs. More effort will go into building arrays of transnationally internetted groups than into building stand-alone groups.
- **Doctrine and strategy.** Terrorists will likely gain new capabilities for lethal acts. Some terrorist groups are likely to move to a "war paradigm" that focuses on attacking U.S. military forces and assets. But where terrorists suppose that "information operations" may be as useful as traditional commando-style operations for achieving their goals, systemic *disruption* may become as much an objective as target *destruction*. Difficulties in coping with the new terrorism will mount if terrorists move beyond isolated acts toward a new approach to doctrine and strategy that emphasizes campaigns based on swarming.
- **Technology.** Terrorists are likely to increasingly use advanced information technologies for offensive and defensive purposes, as well as to support their organizational structures. Despite widespread speculation about terrorists using cyberspace warfare techniques to take "the Net" down, they may often have stronger reasons for wanting to keep it up (e.g., to spread their message and communicate with one another).

In short, terrorism is evolving in a direction we call *netwar*. Thus, after briefly reviewing terrorist trends, we outline the concept of netwar and its relevance for understanding information-age terrorism. In particular, we elaborate on the above points about organization, doctrine, and strategy, and briefly discuss how recent developments in the nature and behavior of Middle Eastern terrorist groups can be interpreted as early signs of a move toward netwar-type terrorism.

Given the prospect of a netwar-oriented shift in which some terrorists pursue a war paradigm, we then focus on the implications such a development may have for the U.S. military. We use these insights to consider defensive antiterrorist measures, as well as proactive counterterrorist strategies. We propose that a key to coping with information-age terrorism will be the creation of interorganizational networks within the U.S. military and government, partly on the grounds that it takes networks to fight networks.

Recent Views About Terrorism

Terrorism remains a distinct phenomenon while reflecting broader trends in irregular warfare. The latter has been on the rise around the world since before the end of the

Cold War. Ethnic and religious conflicts, recently in evidence in areas of Africa, the Balkans, and the Caucasus, for awhile in Central America, and seemingly forever in the Middle East, attest to the brutality that increasingly attends this kind of warfare. These are not conflicts between regular, professional armed forces dedicated to warrior creeds and Geneva Conventions. Instead, even where regular forces play roles, these conflicts often revolve around the strategies and tactics of thuggish paramilitary gangs and local warlords. Some leaders may have some professional training; but the foot soldiers are often people who, for one reason or another, get caught in a fray and learn on the job. Adolescents and children with high-powered weaponry are taking part in growing numbers. In many of these conflicts, savage acts are increasingly committed without anyone taking credit—it may not even be clear which side is responsible. The press releases of the protagonists sound high-minded and self-legitimizing, but the reality at the local level is often about clan rivalries and criminal ventures (e.g., looting, smuggling, or protection rackets).[1]

Thus, irregular warfare has become endemic and vicious around the world. A decade or so ago, terrorism was a rather distinct entry on the spectrum of conflict, with its own unique attributes. Today, it seems increasingly connected with these broader trends in irregular warfare, especially as waged by nonstate actors. As Martin Van Creveld warns:

> In today's world, the main threat to many states, including specifically the U.S., no longer comes from other states. Instead, it comes from small groups and other organizations which are not states. Either we make the necessary changes and face them today, or what is commonly known as the modern world will lose all sense of security and will dwell in perpetual fear.[2]

Meanwhile, for the past several years, terrorism experts have broadly concurred that this phenomenon will persist, if not get worse. General agreement that terrorism may worsen parses into different scenarios. For example, Walter Laqueur warns that religious motivations could lead to "superviolence," with millenarian visions of a coming apocalypse driving "postmodern" terrorism. Fred Iklé worries that increased violence may be used by terrorists to usher in a new totalitarian age based on Leninist ideals. Bruce Hoffman raises the prospect that religiously-motivated terrorists may escalate their violence in order to wreak sufficient havoc to undermine the world political system and replace it with a chaos that is particularly detrimental to the United States—a basically nihilist strategy.[3]

The preponderance of U.S. conventional power may continue to motivate some state and nonstate adversaries to opt for terror as an asymmetric response. Technological advances and underground trafficking may make weapons of mass destruction (WMD—nuclear, chemical, biological weapons) ever easier for terrorists to acquire.[4] Terrorists' shifts toward looser, less hierarchical organizational structures, and their growing use of advanced communications technologies for command, control, and coordination, may further empower small terrorist groups and individuals who want to mount operations from a distance.

There is also agreement about an emergence of two tiers of terror: one characterized by hard-core professionals, the other by amateur cut-outs.[5] The deniability gained by terrorists operating through willing amateurs, coupled with the increasing accessibility of ever more destructive weaponry, has also led many experts to concur that terrorists will be attracted to engaging in more lethal destruction, with increased targeting of information and communications infrastructures.[6]

Some specialists also suggest that "information" will become a key target—both the conduits of information infrastructures and the content of information, particularly the media.[7] While these target-sets may involve little lethal activity, they offer additional theaters of operations for terrorists. Laqueur in particular foresees that, "If the new terrorism directs its energies toward information warfare, its destructive power will be exponentially greater than any it wielded in the past—greater even than it would be with biological and chemical weapons."[8] New planning and scenario-building is needed to help think through how to defend against this form of terrorism.[9]

Such dire predictions have galvanized a variety of responses, which range from urging the creation of international control regimes over the tools of terror (such as WMD materials and advanced encryption capabilities), to the use of coercive diplomacy against state sponsors of terror. Increasingly, the liberal use of military force against terrorists has also been recommended. Caleb Carr in particular espoused this theme, sparking a heated debate.[10] Today, many leading works on combating terrorism blend notions of control mechanisms, international regimes, and the use of force.[11]

Against this background, experts have begun to recognize the growing role of networks—of networked organizational designs and related doctrines, strategies, and technologies—among the practitioners of terrorism. The growth of these networks is related to the spread of advanced information technologies that allow dispersed groups, and individuals, to conspire and coordinate across considerable distances. Recent U.S. efforts to investigate and attack the bin Laden network (named for the central influence of Osama bin Laden) attest to this. The rise of networks is likely to reshape terrorism in the information age, and lead to the adoption of netwar—a kind of information-age conflict that will be waged principally by nonstate actors. Our contribution… is to present the concept of netwar and show how terrorism is being affected by it.

The Advent of Netwar—Analytical Background[12]

The information revolution is altering the nature of conflict across the spectrum. Of the many reasons for this, we call attention to two in particular. First, the information revolution is favoring and strengthening network forms of organization, often giving them an advantage over hierarchical forms. The rise of networks means that power is migrating to nonstate actors, who are able to organize into sprawling multi-organizational networks (especially all-channel networks, in which every node is connected to every other node) more readily than can traditional, hierarchical, state actors. Nonstate-actor networks are thought to be more flexible and responsive than hierarchies in reacting to outside developments, and to be better than hierarchies at using information to improve decisionmaking.[13]

Second, as the information revolution deepens, conflicts will increasingly depend on information and communications matters. More than ever before, conflicts will revolve around "knowledge" and the use of "soft power."[14] Adversaries will emphasize "information operations" and "perception management"—that is, media-oriented measures that aim to attract rather than coerce, and that affect how secure a society, a military, or other actor feels about its knowledge of itself and of its adversaries. Psychological disruption may become as important a goal as physical destruction.

Thus, major transformations are coming in the nature of adversaries, in the type of threats they may pose, and in how conflicts can be waged. Information-age threats are likely to be more diffuse, dispersed, multidimensional, and ambiguous than more traditional threats. Metaphorically, future conflicts may resemble the Oriental game of *Go* more than the Western game of chess. The conflict spectrum will be molded from end to end by these dynamics:

- *Cyberwar*—a concept that refers to information-oriented military warfare—is becoming an important entry at the military end of the spectrum, where the language has normally been about high-intensity conflicts (HICs).
- *Netwar* figures increasingly at the societal end of the spectrum, where the language has normally been about low-intensity conflict (LIC), operations other than war (OOTW), and nonmilitary modes of conflict and crime.[15]

Whereas cyberwar usually pits formal military forces against each other, netwar is more likely to involve nonstate, paramilitary, and irregular forces—as in the case of terrorism. Both concepts are consistent with the views of analysts such as Van Creveld, who believe that a "transformation of war" is under way.[16] Neither concept is just about technology; both refer to comprehensive approaches to conflict—comprehensive in that they mix organizational, doctrinal, strategic, tactical, and technological innovations, for offense and defense.

Definition of Netwar

To be more precise, netwar refers to an emerging mode of conflict and crime at societal levels, involving measures short of traditional war, in which the protagonists use network forms of organization and related doctrines, strategies, and technologies attuned to the information age. These protagonists are likely to consist of dispersed small groups who communicate, coordinate, and conduct their campaigns in an internetted manner, without a precise central command. Thus, information-age netwar differs from modes of conflict and crime in which the protagonists prefer formal, stand-alone, hierarchical organizations, doctrines, and strategies, as in past efforts, for example, to build centralized movements along Marxist lines.

The term is meant to call attention to the prospect that network-based conflict and crime will become major phenomena in the decades ahead. Various actors across the spectrum of conflict and crime are already evolving in this direction. To give a string of examples, netwar is about the Middle East's Hamas more than the Palestine Liberation Organization (PLO), Mexico's Zapatistas more than Cuba's Fidelistas, and the American Christian Patriot movement more than the Ku Klux Klan. It is also about the Asian Triads more than the Sicilian Mafia, and Chicago's Gangsta Disciples more than the Al Capone Gang.

This spectrum includes familiar adversaries who are modifying their structures and strategies to take advantage of networked designs, such as transnational terrorist groups, black-market proliferators of WMD, transnational crime syndicates, fundamentalist and ethno-nationalist movements, intellectual property and high-sea pirates, and smugglers of black-market goods or migrants. Some urban gangs, back-country militias, and militant single-issue groups in the United States are also developing netwar-like attributes. In addition, there is a new generation of radicals and activists who are just beginning to create information-age ideologies, in which identities and loyalties may shift from the nation-state to the transnational level of global civil society. New kinds of actors, such as anarchistic and nihilistic leagues of computer-hacking "cyboteurs," may also partake of netwar.

Many—if not most—netwar actors will be nonstate. Some may be agents of a state, but others may try to turn states into *their* agents. Moreover, a netwar actor may be both subnational and transnational in scope. Odd hybrids and symbioses are likely. Furthermore, some actors (e.g., violent terrorist and criminal organizations) may threaten U.S. and other nations' interests, but other netwar actors (e.g., peaceful social activists) may not. Some may aim at destruction, others at disruption. Again, many variations are possible.

The full spectrum of netwar proponents may thus seem broad and odd at first glance. But there is an underlying pattern that cuts across all variations: the use of network forms of organization, doctrine, strategy, and technology attuned to the information age.

More About Organizational Design

The notion of an organizational structure qualitatively different from traditional hierarchical designs is not recent; for example, in the early 1960s Burns and Stalker referred to the *organic* form as "a network structure of control, authority, and communication," with "lateral rather than vertical direction of communication." In organic structure,[17]

> omniscience [is] no longer imputed to the head of the concern; knowledge about the technical or commercial nature of the here and now task may be located anywhere in the network; [with] this location becoming the ad hoc centre of control authority and communication.

In the business world, virtual or networked organizations are being heralded as effective alternatives to bureaucracies—as in the case of Eastman Chemical Company and the Shell-Sarnia Plant—because of their inherent flexibility, adaptiveness, and ability to capitalize on the talents of all members of the organization.[18]

What has long been emerging in the business world is now becoming apparent in the organizational structures of netwar actors. In an archetypal netwar, the protagonists are likely to amount to a set of diverse, dispersed "nodes" who share a set of ideas and interests and who are arrayed to act in a fully internetted "all-channel" manner. Networks come in basically three types (or topologies) (see Figure 1):[19]

- The *chain* network, as in a smuggling chain where people, goods, or information move along a line of separated contacts, and where end-to-end communication must travel through the intermediate nodes.
- The *star*, hub, or wheel network, as in a franchise or a cartel structure where a set of actors is tied to a central node or actor, and must go through that node to communicate and coordinate.
- The *all-channel* network, as in a collaborative network of militant small groups where every group is connected to every other.

Figure 1

Types of Networks

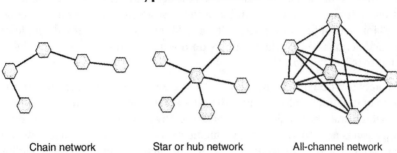

Chain network   Star or hub network   All-channel network

Each node in the diagrams of Figure 1 may be to an individual, a group, an institution, part of a group or institution, or even a state. The nodes may be large or small, tightly or loosely coupled, and inclusive or exclusive in membership. They may be segmentary or specialized—that is, they may look alike and engage in similar activities, or they may undertake a division of labor based on specialization. The boundaries of the network may be well defined, or blurred and porous in relation to the outside environment. All such variations are possible.

Each type may be suited to different conditions and purposes, and all three may be found among netwar-related adversaries—e.g., the chain in smuggling operations, the star at the core of terrorist and criminal syndicates, and the all-channel type among militant groups that are highly internetted and decentralized. There may also be hybrids. For example, a netwar actor may have an all-channel council at its core, but use stars and chains for tactical operations. There may also be hybrids of network and hierarchical forms of organization, and hierarchies may exist inside particular nodes in a network. Some actors may have a hierarchical organization overall, but use networks for tactical operations; other actors may have an all-channel network design, but use hierarchical teams for tactical operations. Again, many configurations are possible, and it may be difficult for an analyst to discern exactly what type of networking characterizes a particular actor.

Of the three network types, the all-channel has been the most difficult to organize and sustain historically, partly because it may require dense communications. However, it gives the network form the most potential for collaborative undertakings, and it is the type that is gaining strength from the information revolution. Pictorially, an all-channel netwar actor resembles a geodesic "Bucky ball" (named for Buckminster Fuller); it does not resemble a pyramid. The design is flat. Ideally, there is no single, central leadership, command, or headquarters—no precise heart or head that can be targeted. The network as a whole (but not necessarily each node) has little to no hierarchy, and there may be multiple leaders. Decision-making and operations are decentralized, allowing for local initiative and autonomy. Thus the design may sometimes appear acephalous (headless), and at other times polycephalous (Hydra-headed).[20]

The capacity of this design for effective performance over time may depend on the presence of shared principles, interests, and goals—at best, an overarching doctrine or ideology—that spans all nodes and to which the members wholeheartedly subscribe. Such a set of principles, shaped through mutual consultation and consensus-building, can enable them to be "all of one mind," even though they are dispersed and devoted to different tasks. It can provide a central ideational, strategic, and operational coherence that allows for tactical decentralization. It can set boundaries and provide guidelines for decisions and actions so that the members do not have to resort to a hierarchy—"they know what they have to do."[21]

The network design may depend on having an infrastructure for the dense communication of functional information. All nodes are not necessarily in constant communication, which may not make sense for a secretive, conspiratorial actor. But when communication is needed, the network's members must be able to disseminate information promptly and as broadly as desired within the network and to outside audiences.

In many respects, then, the archetypal netwar design corresponds to what earlier analysts called a "segmented, polycentric, ideologically integrated network" (SPIN):[22]

> By segmentary I mean that it is cellular, composed of many different groups.... By polycentric I mean that it has many different leaders or centers of direction.... By networked I mean that the segments and the leaders are integrated into reticulated systems or networks through various structural, personal, and ideological ties. Networks are usually unbounded and expanding.... This acronym [SPIN] helps us picture this organization as a fluid, dynamic, expanding one, spinning out into mainstream society.

Caveats About the Role of Technology

To realize its potential, a fully interconnected network requires a capacity for constant, dense information and communications flows, more so than do other forms of organization (e.g., hierarchies). This capacity is afforded by the latest information and communications technologies—cellular telephones, fax machines, electronic mail (e-mail), World Wide Web (WWW) sites, and computer conferencing. Moreover, netwar agents are poised to benefit from future increases in the speed of communication, dramatic reductions in the costs of communication, increases in bandwidth, vastly expanded connectivity, and integration of communication with computing technologies.[23] Such technologies are highly advantageous for a netwar actor whose constituents are geographically dispersed.

However, caveats are in order. First, the new technologies, however enabling for organizational networking, may not be the only crucial technologies for a netwar actor. Old means of communications such as human couriers, and mixes of old and new systems, may suffice. Second, netwar is not simply a function of the Internet; it does not take place only in cyberspace or the infosphere. Some key *battles* may occur there, but a *war's* overall conduct and outcome will normally depend mostly on what happens in the real world. Even in information-age conflicts, what happens in the real world is generally more important than what happens in the virtual worlds of cyberspace or the infosphere.[24] Netwar is not Internet war.

Swarming, and the Blurring of Offense and Defense

This distinctive, often ad-hoc design has unusual strengths, for both offense and defense. On the offense, networks are known for being adaptable, flexible, and versatile vis-à-vis opportunities and challenges. This may be particularly the case where a set of actors can engage in *swarming*. Little analytic attention has been given to swarming, yet it may be a key mode of conflict in the information age. The cutting edge for this possibility is found among netwar protagonists.[25]

Swarming occurs when the dispersed nodes of a network of small (and perhaps some large) forces converge on a target from multiple directions. The overall aim is the *sustainable pulsing* of force or fire. Once in motion, swarm networks must be able to coalesce rapidly and stealthily on a target, then dissever and redisperse, immediately ready to recombine for a new pulse. In other words, information-age attacks may come in "swarms" rather than the more traditional "waves."

In terms of defensive potential, well-constructed networks tend to be redundant and diverse, making them robust and resilient in the face of adversity. Where they have a capacity for interoperability and shun centralized command and control, network designs can be difficult to crack and defeat as a whole. In particular, they may defy counterleadership targeting—attackers can find and confront only portions of the network. Moreover, the deniability built into a network may allow it to simply absorb a number of attacks on distributed nodes, leading the attacker to believe the network has been harmed when, in fact, it remains viable, and is seeking new opportunities for tactical surprise.

The difficulties of dealing with netwar actors deepen when the lines between offense and defense are blurred, or blended. When *blurring* is the case, it may be difficult to distinguish between attacking and defending actions, particularly when an actor goes on the offense in the name of self-defense. The *blending* of offense and defense will often mix the strategic and tactical levels of operations. For example, guerrillas on the defensive strategically may go on the offense tactically; the war of the *mujahideen* in Afghanistan provides a modern example.

The blurring of offense and defense reflects another feature of netwar: it tends to defy and cut across standard boundaries, jurisdictions, and distinctions between state and society, public and private, war and peace, war and crime, civilian and military, police and military, and legal and illegal. A government has difficulty assigning responsibility to a single agency—military, police, or intelligence—to respond.

Thus, the spread of netwar adds to the challenges facing the nation-state in the information age. Nation-state ideals of sovereignty and authority are traditionally linked to a bureaucratic rationality in which issues and problems can be neatly divided, and specific offices can be charged with taking care of specific problems. In netwar, things are rarely so clear. A protagonist is likely to operate in the cracks and gray areas of society, striking where lines of authority crisscross and the operational paradigms of politicians, officials, soldiers, police officers, and related actors get fuzzy and clash.

Networks Versus Hierarchies: Challenges for Counternetwar

Against this background, we are led to a set of four policy-oriented propositions about the information revolution and its implications for netwar and counternetwar.[26]

Hierarchies have a difficult time fighting networks. There are examples across the conflict spectrum. Some of the best are found in the failings of governments to defeat transnational criminal cartels engaged in drug smuggling, as in Colombia. The persistence of religious revivalist movements, as in Algeria, in the face of unremitting state opposition, shows the robustness of the network form. The Zapatista movement in Mexico, with its legions of supporters and sympathizers among local and transnational nongovernmental organizations (NGOs), shows that social netwar can put a democratizing autocracy on the defensive and pressure it to continue adopting reforms.

It takes networks to fight networks. Governments that would defend against netwar may have to adopt organizational designs and strategies like those of their adversaries. This does not mean mirroring the adversary, but rather learning to draw on the same design principles of network forms in the information age. These principles depend to some extent upon technological innovation, but mainly on a willingness to innovate organizationally and doctrinally, and by building new mechanisms for interagency and multijurisdictional cooperation.

Whoever masters the network form first and best will gain major advantages. In these early decades of the information age, adversaries who have adopted networking (be they criminals, terrorists, or peaceful social activists) are enjoying an increase in their power relative to state agencies.

Counternetwar may thus require effective interagency approaches, which by their nature involve networked structures. The challenge will be to blend hierarchies and networks skillfully, while retaining enough core authority to encourage and enforce adherence to networked processes. By creating effective hybrids, governments may better confront the new threats and challenges emerging in the information age, whether generated by terrorists, militias, criminals, or other actors.[27] The U.S. Counterterrorist Center, based at the Central Intelligence Agency (CIA), is a good example of a promising effort to establish a functional interagency network,[28] although its success may depend increasingly on the strength of links with the military services and other institutions that fall outside the realm of the intelligence community.

Middle Eastern Terrorism and Netwar

Terrorism seems to be evolving in the direction of violent netwar. Islamic fundamentalist organizations like Hamas and the bin Laden network consist of groups organized in loosely interconnected, semi-independent cells that have no single commanding hierarchy.[29] Hamas exemplifies the shift away from a hierarchically oriented movement based on a "great leader" (like the PLO and Yasser Arafat).[30]

The netwar concept is consistent with patterns and trends in the Middle East, where the newer and more active terrorist groups appear to be adopting decentralized, flexible network structures. The rise of networked arrangements in terrorist organizations is part of a wider move away from formally organized, state-sponsored groups to privately financed, loose networks of individuals and subgroups that may have strategic guidance but enjoy tactical independence. Related to these shifts is the fact that terrorist groups are taking advantage of information technology to coordinate the activities of dispersed members. Such technology may be employed by terrorists not only to wage information warfare [IW], but also to support their own networked organizations.[31]

While a comprehensive empirical analysis of the relationship between (a) the structure of terrorist organizations and (b) group activity or strength is beyond the scope of this paper,[32] a cursory examination of such a relationship among Middle Eastern groups offers some evidence to support the claim that terrorists are preparing to wage netwar. The Middle East was selected for analysis mainly because terrorist groups based in this region have been active in targeting U.S. government facilities and interests, as in the bombings of the Khobar Towers, and…, the American embassies in Kenya and Tanzania.

Middle Eastern Terrorist Groups: Structure and Actions

Terrorist groups in the Middle East have diverse origins, ideologies, and organizational structures, but can be roughly categorized into traditional and new-generation groups. Traditional groups date back to the late 1960s and early 1970s, and the majority of these were (and some still are) formally or informally linked to the PLO. Typically, they are also relatively bureaucratic and maintain a nationalist or Marxist agenda. In contrast, most new-generation groups arose in the 1980s and 1990s, have more fluid organizational forms, and rely on Islam as a basis for their radical ideology.

The traditional, more-bureaucratic groups have survived to this day partly through support from states such as Syria, Libya, and Iran. The groups retain an ability to train and prepare for terrorist missions; however, their involvement in actual operations has been limited in recent years, partly because of successful counterterrorism campaigns by Israeli and Western agencies. In contrast, the newer and less hierarchical groups, such as Hamas, the Palestinian Islamic Jihad (PIJ), Hizbullah, Algeria's Armed Islamic Group (GIA), the Egyptian Islamic Group (IG), and Osama bin Laden's Arab Afghans, have become the most active organizations in and around the Middle East.

The traditional groups. Traditional terrorist groups in the Middle East include the Abu Nidal Organization (ANO), the Popular Front for the Liberation of Palestine (PFLP), and three PFLP-related splinters—the PFLP-General Command (PFLP-GC), the Palestine Liberation Front (PLF), and the Democratic Front for the Liberation of Palestine (DFLP).

The ANO was an integral part of the PLO until it became independent in 1974. It has a bureaucratic structure composed of various functional committees.[33] The activism it displayed in the 1970s and 1980s has lessened considerably, owing to a lessening of support from state sponsors and to effective counterterrorist campaigns by Israeli and Western intelligence services.[34] The very existence of the organization has recently been put into question, given uncertainty as to the whereabouts and fate of Abu Nidal, the leader of the group.[35]

The PFLP was founded in 1967 by George Habash as a PLO-affiliated organization. It has traditionally embraced a Marxist ideology, and remains an important PLO faction. However, in recent years it has suffered considerable losses from Israeli counterterrorist strikes.[36] The PFLP-General Command split from the PFLP in 1968, and in turn experienced a schism in the mid-1970s. This splinter group, which called itself the PLF, is composed of three subgroups, and has not been involved in high-profile acts since the 1985 hijacking of the Italian cruise ship *Achille Lauro*.[37] The PFLP was sub-jected to another split in 1969, which resulted in the Democratic Front for the Libera-tion of Palestine. The DFLP resembles a small army more than a terrorist group—its operatives are organized in battalions, backed by intelligence and special forces.[38] DFLP strikes have become less frequent since the 1970s, and since the late 1980s it has limited its attacks to Israeli targets near borders.[39]

What seems evident here is that this old generation of traditional, hierarchical, bu-reaucratic groups is on the wane. The reasons are varied, but the point remains—their way of waging terrorism is not likely to make a comeback, and is being superseded by a new way that is more attuned to the organizational, doctrinal, and technological imper-atives of the information age.

The most active groups and their organization. The new generation of Middle Eastern groups has been active both in and outside the region in recent years. In Israel and the occupied territories, Hamas, and to a lesser extent the Palestinian Islamic Jihad, have shown their strength over the last four years with a series of suicide bombings that have killed more than one hundred people and injured several more.[40] Exploiting a strong presence in Lebanon, the Shi'ite Hizbullah organization has also staged a number of at-tacks against Israeli Defense Forces troops and Israeli cities in Galilee.[41]

The al-Gama'a al-Islamiya, or Islamic Group (IG), is the most active Islamic ex-tremist group in Egypt. In November 1997 IG carried out an attack on Hatshepsut's Temple in Luxor, killing 58 tourists and 4 Egyptians. The Group has also claimed re-sponsibility for the bombing of the Egyptian embassy in Islamabad, Pakistan, which left 16 dead and 60 injured.[42] In Algeria, the Armed Islamic Group (GIA) has been behind the most violent, lethal attacks in Algeria's protracted civil war. Approximately 70,000 Algerians have lost their lives since the domestic terrorist campaign began in 1992.[43]

Recently, the loosely organized group of Arab Afghans—radical Islamic fighters from several North African and Middle Eastern countries who forged ties while resisting the Soviet occupation of Afghanistan[44]—has come to the fore as an active terrorist outfit. One of the leaders and founders of the Arab Afghan movement, Osama bin Laden, a Saudi entrepreneur who bases his activities in Afghanistan,[45] is suspected of sending operatives to Yemen to bomb a hotel used by U.S. soldiers on their way to Somalia in 1992, plotting to assassinate President Clinton in the Philippines in 1994 and Egyptian President Hosni Mubarak in 1995, and of having a role in the Riyadh and Khobar blasts in Saudi Arabia that resulted in the deaths of 24 Americans in 1995 and 1996.[46] U.S. officials have pointed to bin Laden as the mastermind behind the U.S. embassy bomb-ings in Kenya and Tanzania, which claimed the lives of more than 260 people, including 12 Americans.[47]

To varying degrees, these groups share the principles of the net-worked organiza-tion—relatively flat hierarchies, decentralization and delegation of decisionmaking au-thority, and loose lateral ties among dispersed groups and individuals.[48] For instance, Hamas is loosely structured, with some elements working openly through mosques and social service institutions to recruit members, raise funds, organize activities, and dis-tribute propaganda. Palestinian security sources indicate that there are ten or more Hamas splinter groups and factions with no centralized operational leadership.[49] The Pales-tine Islamic Jihad is a series of loosely affiliated factions, rather than a cohesive group.[50]

The pro-Iranian Hizbullah acts as an umbrella organization of radical Shiite groups, and in many respects is a hybrid of hierarchical and network arrangements; although the formal structure is highly bureaucratic, interactions among members are volatile and do not follow rigid lines of control.[51] According to the U.S. Department of State, Egypt's Islamic Group is a decentralized organization that operates without a single operational leader,[52] while the GIA is notorious for the lack of centralized authority.[53]

Unlike traditional terrorist organizations, Arab Afghans are part of a complex network of relatively autonomous groups that are financed from private sources forming "a kind of international terrorists' Internet."[54] The most notorious element of the network is Osama bin Laden, who uses his wealth and organizational skills to support and direct a multinational alliance of Islamic extremists. At the heart of this alliance is his own inner core group, known as Al-Qaeda ("The Base"), which sometimes conducts missions on its own, but more often in conjunction with other groups or elements in the alliance. The goal of the alliance is opposition on a global scale to perceived threats to Islam, as indicated by bin Laden's 1996 declaration of a holy war against the United States and the West. In the document, bin Laden specifies that such a holy war will be fought by irregular, light, highly mobile forces using guerrilla tactics.[55]

Even though bin Laden finances Arab Afghan activities and directs some operations, he apparently does not play a direct command and control role over all operatives. Rather, he is a key figure in the coordination and support of several dispersed activities.[56] For instance, bin Laden founded the "World Islamic Front for Jihad Against Jews and Crusaders."[57] And yet most of the groups that participate in this front (including Egypt's Islamic Group) remain independent, although the organizational barriers between them are fluid.[58]

From a netwar perspective, an interesting feature of bin Laden's Arab Afghan movement is its ability to relocate operations swiftly from one geographic area to another in response to changing circumstances and needs. Arab Afghans have participated in operations conducted by Algeria's GIA and Egypt's IG. Reports in 1997 also indicated that Arab Afghans transferred training operations to Somalia, where they joined the Islamic Liberation Party (ILP).[59] The same reports suggest that the Arab Afghan movement has considered sending fighters to Sinkiang Uighur province in western China, to wage a holy war against the Chinese regime.[60] This group's ability to move and act quickly (and, to some extent, to swarm) once opportunities emerge hampers counterterrorist efforts to predict its actions and monitor its activities. The fact that Arab Afghan operatives were able to strike the U.S. embassies in Kenya and Tanzania substantiates the claim that members of this network have the mobility and speed to operate over considerable distances.

Although the organizational arrangements in these groups do not match all the basic features of the network ideal,[61] they stand in contrast to more traditional groups. Another feature that distinguishes the newer generation of terrorist groups is their adoption of information technology.

Middle Eastern Terrorist Groups and the Use of Information Technology

Information technology (IT) is an enabling factor for networked groups; terrorists aiming to wage netwar may adopt it not only as a weapon, but also to help coordinate and support their activities. Before exploring how Middle Eastern terrorist groups have embraced the new technology, we posit three hypotheses that relate the rise of IT to organization for netwar:

- The greater the degree of organizational networking in a terrorist group, the higher the likelihood that IT is used to support the network's decisionmaking.
- Recent advances in IT facilitate networked terrorist organizations because information flows are becoming quicker, cheaper, more secure, and more versatile.
- As terrorist groups learn to use IT for decisionmaking and other organizational purposes, they will be likely to use the same technology as an offensive weapon to destroy or disrupt.

Middle Eastern terrorist groups provide examples of information technology being used for a wide variety of purposes. As discussed below, there is some evidence to support the claim that the most active groups—and therefore the most decentralized groups—have embraced information technology to coordinate activities and disseminate propaganda and ideology.[62] At the same time, the technical assets and know-how gained by terrorist groups as they seek to form into multi-organizational networks can be used for offensive purposes—an Internet connection can be used for both coordination and disruption. The anecdotes provided here are consistent with the rise in the Middle East of what has been termed *techno-terrorism*, or the use by terrorists of satellite communications, e-mail, and the World Wide Web.[63]

Arab Afghans appear to have widely adopted information technology. According to reporters who visited bin Laden's headquarters in a remote mountainous area of Afghanistan, the terrorist financier has computers, communications equipment, and a large number of disks for data storage.[64] Egyptian "Afghan" computer experts are said to have helped devise a communication network that relies on the World Wide Web, e-mail, and electronic bulletin boards so that the extremists can exchange information without running a major risk of being intercepted by counterterrorism officials.[65]

Hamas is another major group that uses the Internet to share operational information. Hamas activists in the United States use chat rooms to plan operations and activities.[66] Operatives use e-mail to coordinate activities across Gaza, the West Bank, and Lebanon. Hamas has realized that information can be passed securely over the Internet because it is next to impossible for counterterrorism intelligence to monitor accurately the flow and content of Internet traffic. Israeli security officials have difficulty in tracing Hamas messages and decoding their content.[67]

During a recent counterterrorist operation, several GIA bases in Italy were uncovered, and each was found to include computers and diskettes with instructions for the construction of bombs.[68] It has been reported that the GIA uses floppy disks and computers to store and process instructions and other information for its members, who are dispersed in Algeria and Europe.[69] Furthermore, the Internet is used as a propaganda tool by Hizbullah, which manages three World Wide Web sites—one for the central press office (at www.hizbollah.org), another to describe its attacks on Israeli targets (at www.moqawama.org), and the last for news and information (at www.almanar. com.lb).[70]

The presence of Middle Eastern terrorist organizations on the Internet is suspected in the case of the Islamic Gateway, a World Wide Web site that contains information on a number of Islamic activist organizations based in the United Kingdom. British Islamic activists use the World Wide Web to broadcast their news and attract funding; they are also turning to the Internet as an organizational and communication tool.[71] While the vast majority of Islamic activist groups represented in the Islamic Gateway are legitimate, one group—the Global Jihad Fund—makes no secret of its militant goals.[72] The appeal of the Islamic Gateway for militant groups may be enhanced by a representative's claim, in an Internet Newsnet article in August 1996, that the Gateway's Internet Service Provider (ISP) can give "CIA-proof" protection against electronic surveillance.[73]

Summary Comment

This review of patterns and trends in the Middle East substantiates our speculations that the new terrorism is evolving in the direction of netwar, along the following lines:[74]

- An increasing number of terrorist groups are adopting networked forms of organization and relying on information technology to support such structures.
- Newer groups (those established in the 1980s and 1990s) are more networked than traditional groups.
- A positive correlation is emerging between the degree of activity of a group and the degree to which it adopts a networked structure.[75]
- Information technology is as likely to be used for organizational support as for offensive warfare.
- The likelihood that young recruits will be familiar with information technology implies that terrorist groups will be increasingly networked and more computer-friendly in the future than they are today.

Terrorist Doctrines—The Rise of a "War Paradigm"

The evolution of terrorism in the direction of netwar will create new difficulties for counterterrorism. The types of challenges, and their severity, will depend on the kinds of doctrines that terrorists develop and employ. Some doctrinal effects will occur at the operational level, as in the relative emphasis placed on disruptive information operations as distinct from destructive combat operations. However, at a deeper level, the direction in which terrorist netwar evolves will depend upon the choices terrorists make as to the overall doctrinal paradigms that shape their goals and strategies.

At least three terrorist paradigms are worth considering: terror as coercive diplomacy, terror as war, and terror as the harbinger of a "new world." These three engage, in varying ways, distinct rationales for terrorism—as a weapon of the weak, as a way to assert identity, and as a way to break through to a new world—discussed earlier in this [selection]. While there has been much debate about the overall success or failure of terrorism,[76] the paradigm under which a terrorist operates may have a great deal to do with the likelihood of success. Coercion, for example, implies distinctive threats or uses of force, whereas norms of "war" often imply maximizing destruction.

The Coercive-Diplomacy Paradigm

The first paradigm is that of coercive diplomacy. From its earliest days, terrorism has often sought to persuade others, by means of symbolic violence, either to do something, stop doing something, or undo what has been done. These are the basic forms of coercive diplomacy,[77] and they appear in terrorism as far back as the Jewish Sicarii Zealots who sought independence from Rome in the first century AD, up through the Palestinians' often violent acts in pursuit of their independence today.

The fact that terrorist coercion includes violent acts does not make it a form of war—the violence is exemplary, designed to encourage what Alexander George calls "forceful persuasion," or "coercive diplomacy as an alternative to war."[78] In this light, terrorism may be viewed as designed to achieve specific goals, and the level of violence is limited, or proportional, to the ends being pursued. Under this paradigm, terrorism was once thought to lack a "demand" for WMD, as such tools would provide means vastly disproportionate to the ends of terror. This view was first elucidated over twenty years ago by Brian Jenkins—though there was some dissent expressed by scholars such as Thomas Schelling—and continued to hold sway until a few years ago.[79]

The War Paradigm

Caleb Carr, surveying the history of the failures of coercive terrorism and the recent trends toward increasing destructiveness and deniability, has elucidated what we call a "war paradigm."[80] This paradigm, which builds on ideas first considered by Jenkins,[81] holds that terrorist acts arise when weaker parties cannot challenge an adversary directly and thus turn to asymmetric methods. A war paradigm implies taking a strategic, campaign-oriented view of violence that makes no specific call for concessions from, or other demands upon, the opponent. Instead, the strategic aim is to inflict damage, in the context of what the terrorists view as an ongoing war. In theory, this paradigm, unlike the coercive diplomacy one, does not seek a proportional relationship between the level of force employed and the aims sought. When the goal is to inflict damage generally, and the terrorist group has no desire or need to claim credit, there is an attenuation of the need for proportionality—the worse the damage, the better. Thus, the use of WMD can be far more easily contemplated than in a frame of reference governed by notions of coercive diplomacy.

A terrorist war paradigm may be undertaken by terrorists acting on their own behalf or in service to a nation-state. In the future, as the information age brings the further empowerment of nonstate and transnational actors, "stateless" versions of the terrorist war paradigm may spread. At the same time, however, states will remain important players in the war paradigm; they may cultivate their own terrorist-style commandos, or seek cut-outs and proxies from among nonstate terrorist groups.

Ambiguity regarding a sponsor's identity may prove a key element of the war paradigm. While the use of proxies provides an insulating layer between a state sponsor and its target, these proxies, if captured, may prove more susceptible to interrogation and investigative techniques designed to winkle out the identity of the sponsor. On the other hand, while home-grown commando-style terrorists may be less forthcoming with information if caught, their own identities, which may be hard to conceal, may provide undeniable evidence of state sponsorship. These risks for states who think about engaging in or supporting terrorism may provide yet more reason for the war paradigm to increasingly become the province of nonstate terrorists—or those with only the most tenuous linkages to particular states.

Exemplars of the war paradigm today are the wealthy Saudi jihadist, Osama bin Laden, and the Arab Afghans that he associates with. As previously mentioned, bin Laden has explicitly called for war-like terrorism against the United States, and especially against U.S. military forces stationed in Saudi Arabia. President Clinton's statement that American retaliation for the U.S. embassy bombings in East Africa represented the first shots in a protracted war on terrorism suggests that the notion of adopting a war paradigm to counter terror has gained currency.

The New-World Paradigm

A third terrorist paradigm aims at achieving the birth of what might be called a "new world." It may be driven by religious mania, a desire for totalitarian control, or an impulse toward ultimate chaos.[82] Aum Shinrikyo would be a recent example. The paradigm harks back to the dynamics of millennialist movements that arose in past epochs of social upheaval, when *prophetae* attracted adherents from the margins of other social movements and led small groups to pursue salvation by seeking a final, violent cataclysm.[83]

This paradigm is likely to seek the vast disruption of political, social, and economic order. Accomplishing this goal may involve lethal destruction, even a heightened willingness to use WMD. Religious terrorists may desire destruction for its own sake, or for some form of "cleansing." But the ultimate aim is not so much the destruction of society as a rebirth after a period of chaotic disruption.

The Paradigms and Netwar

All three paradigms offer room for netwar. Moreover, all three paradigms allow the rise of "cybotage"—acts of disruption and destruction against information infrastructures by terrorists who learn the skills of cyberterror, as well as by disaffected individuals with technical skills who are drawn into the terrorist milieu. However, we note that terrorist netwar may also be a battle of ideas—and to wage this form of conflict some terrorists may want the Net *up*, not down.

Many experts argue that terrorism is moving toward ever more lethal, destructive acts. Our netwar perspective accepts this, but also holds that some terrorist netwars will stress disruption over destruction. Networked terrorists will no doubt continue to destroy things and kill people, but their principal strategy may move toward the nonlethal end of the spectrum, where command and control nodes and vulnerable information infrastructures provide rich sets of targets.

Indeed, terrorism has long been about "information"—from the fact that trainees for suicide bombings are kept from listening to international media, through the ways that terrorists seek to create disasters that will consume the front pages, to the related debates about countermeasures that would limit freedom of the press, increase public surveillance and intelligence gathering, and heighten security over information and communications systems. Terrorist tactics focus attention on the importance of information and communications for the functioning of democratic institutions; debates about how terrorist threats undermine democratic practices may revolve around freedom of information issues.

While netwar may be waged by terrorist groups operating with any of the three paradigms, the rise of networked groups whose objective is to wage war may be the one most relevant to and dangerous from the standpoint of the military. Indeed, if terrorists perceive themselves as warriors, they may be inclined to target enemy military assets or interests....

[Conclusion] Targeting Terrorists in the Information Age

The transition from hierarchical to networked terrorist groups is likely to be uneven and gradual. The netwar perspective suggests that, for the foreseeable future, various networked forms will emerge, coexisting with and influencing traditional organizations. Such organizational diversity implies the need for a counterterrorism strategy that recognizes the differences among organizational designs and seeks to target the weaknesses associated with each.

Counterleadership strategies or retaliation directed at state sponsors may be effective for groups led by a charismatic leader who enjoys the backing of sympathetic governments, but are likely to fail if used against an organization with multiple, dispersed leaders and private sources of funding. Networked organizations rely on information flows to function, and disruption of the flows cripples their ability to coordinate actions. It is no coincidence, for instance, that while the separation between Hamas political and military branches is well documented, this terrorist group jealously guards information on the connections and degree of coordination between the two.[84]

At the same time, the two-way nature of connectivity for information networks such as the Internet implies that the dangers posed by information warfare are often symmetric—the degree to which a terrorist organization uses information infrastructure for offensive purposes may determine its exposure to similar attacks by countering forces. While it is true that terrorist organizations will often enjoy the benefit of surprise, the IW tactics available to them can also be adopted by counterterrorists.

The key task for counterterrorism, then, is the identification of organizational and technological terrorist networks. Once such structures are identified, it may be possible to insert and disseminate false information, overload systems, misdirect message traffic, preclude access, and engage in other destructive and disruptive activities to hamper and prevent terrorist operations.

Notes

1. For an illuminating take on irregular warfare that emphasizes the challenges to the Red Cross, see Michael Ignatieff, "Unarmed Warriors," *The New Yorker*, March 24, 1997, pp. 56–71.
2. Martin Van Creveld, "In Wake of Terrorism, Modern Armies Prove to Be Dinosaurs of Defense," *New Perspectives Quarterly*, Vol. 13, No. 4, Fall 1996, p. 58.

3. See Walter Laqueur, "Postmodern Terrorism," *Foreign Affairs*, Vol. 75, No. 5, September/October 1996, pp. 24–36; Fred Iklé, "The Problem of the Next Lenin," *The National Interest*, Vol. 47, Spring 1997, pp. 9–19; Bruce Hoffman, *Responding to Terrorism Across the Technological Spectrum*, RAND, P-7874, 1994; Bruce Hoffman, *Inside Terrorism*, Columbia University Press, New York, 1998; Robert Kaplan, "The Coming Anarchy," *Atlantic Monthly*, February 1994, pp. 44–76.

4. See J. Kenneth Campbell, "Weapon of Mass Destruction Terrorism," Master's thesis, Naval Postgraduate School, Monterey, California, 1996.

5. Bruce Hoffman and Caleb Carr, "Terrorism: Who Is Fighting Whom?" *World Policy Journal*, Vol. 14, No. 1, Spring 1997, pp. 97–104.

6. For instance, Martin Shubik, "Terrorism, Technology, and the Socioeconomics of Death," *Comparative Strategy*, Vol. 16, No. 4, October–December 1997, pp. 399–414; as well as Hoffman, 1998.

7. See Matthew Littleton, "Information Age Terrorism," MA thesis, U.S. Naval Postgraduate School, 1995, and Brigitte Nacos, *Terrorism and the Media*, Columbia University Press, New York, 1994.

8. Laqueur, 1996, p. 35.

9. For more on this issue, see Roger Molander, Andrew Riddile, and Peter Wilson, *Strategic Information Warfare: A New Face of War*, RAND, MR-661-OSD, 1996; Roger Molander, Peter Wilson, David Mussington, and Richard Mesic, *Strategic Information Warfare Rising*, RAND, 1998.

10. Caleb Carr, "Terrorism as Warfare," *World Policy Journal*, Vol. 13, No. 4, Winter 1996–1997, pp. 1–12. This theme was advocated early by Gayle Rivers, *The War Against the Terrorists: How to Fight and Win*, Stein and Day, New York, 1986. For more on the debate, see Hoffman and Carr, 1997.

11. See, for instance, Benjamin Netanyahu, *Winning the War Against Terrorism*, Simon and Schuster, New York, 1996, and John Kerry (Senator), *The New War*, Simon & Schuster, New York, 1997.

12. This analytical background is drawn from John Arquilla and David Ronfeldt, *The Advent of Netwar*, RAND, MR-678-OSD, 1996, and David Ronfeldt, John Arquilla, Graham Fuller, and Melissa Fuller, *The Zapatista "Social Netwar" in Mexico*, RAND, MR-994-A, forthcoming. Also see John Arquilla and David Ronfeldt (eds.), *In Athena's Camp: Preparing for Conflict in the Information Age*, RAND, MR-880-OSD/RC, 1997.

13. For background on this issue, see Charles Heckscher, "Defining the Post-Bureaucratic Type," in Charles Heckscher and Anne Donnelon (eds.), *The Post-Bureaucratic Organization*, Sage, Thousand Oaks, California, 1995, pp. 50–52.

14. The concept of soft power was introduced by Joseph S. Nye in *Bound to Lead: The Changing Nature of American Power*, Basic Books, New York, 1990, and further elaborated in Joseph S. Nye, and William A. Owens, "America's Information Edge," *Foreign Affairs*, Vol. 75, No. 2, March/April 1996.

15. For more on information-age conflict, netwar, and cyberwar, see John Arquilla and David Ronfeldt, "Cyberwar is Coming!" *Comparative Strategy*, Vol. 12, No. 2, Summer 1993, pp. 141–165, and Arquilla and Ronfeldt, 1996 and 1997.

16. Martin Van Creveld, *The Transformation of War*, Free Press, New York, 1991.

17. T. Burns and G. M. Stalker, *The Management of Innovation*, Tavistock, London, 1961, p. 121.

18. See, for instance, Jessica Lipnack and Jeffrey Stamps, *The Age of the Network*, Wiley & Sons, New York, 1994, pp. 51–78, and Heckscher, "Defining the Post-Bureaucratic Type," p. 45.

19. Adapted from William M. Evan, "An Organization-Set Model of Interorganizational Relations," in Matthew Tuite, Roger Chisholm, and Michael Radnor (eds.), *Interorganizational Decisionmaking*, Aldine Publishing Company, Chicago, 1972.

20. The structure may also be cellular, although the presence of cells does not necessarily mean a network exists. A hierarchy can also be cellular, as is the case with some subversive organizations. A key difference between cells and nodes is that the former are designed to minimize information flows for security reasons (usually only the head of the cell reports to the

leadership), while nodes in principle can easily establish connections with other parts of the network (so that communications and coordination can occur horizontally).

21. The quotation is from a doctrinal statement by Louis Beam about "leaderless resistance," which has strongly influenced right-wing white-power groups in the United States. See *The Seditionist*, Issue 12, February 1992.

22. See Luther P. Gerlach, "Protest Movements and the Construction of Risk," in B. B. Johnson and V. T. Covello (eds.), *The Social and Cultural Construction of Risk*, D. Reidel Publishing Co., Boston, Massachusetts, 1987, p. 115, based on Luther P. Gerlach and Virginia Hine, *People, Power, Change: Movements of Social Transformation*, The Bobbs-Merrill Co., New York, 1970. This SPIN concept, a precursor of the netwar concept, was proposed by Luther Gerlach and Virginia Hine in the 1960s to depict U.S. social movements. It anticipates many points about network forms of organization that are now coming into focus in the analysis not only of social movements but also some terrorist, criminal, ethno-nationalist, and fundamentalist organizations.

23. See Wolf V. Heydenbrand, "New Organizational Forms," *Work and Occupations*, No. 3, Vol. 16, August 1989, pp. 323–357.

24. See Paul Kneisel, "Netwar: The Battle Over Rec.Music.White-Power," *ANTIFA INFOBULLETIN*, Research Supplement, June 12, 1996, unpaginated ASCII text available on the Internet. Kneisel analyzes the largest vote ever taken about the creation of a new Usenet newsgroup—a vote to prevent the creation of a group that was ostensibly about white-power music. He concludes that "The *war* against contemporary fascism will be won in the 'real world' off the net; but *battles* against fascist netwar are fought and won on the Internet." His title is testimony to the spreading usage of the term *netwar*.

25. Swarm networks are discussed by Kevin Kelly, *Out of Control: The Rise of Neo-Biological Civilization*, A William Patrick Book, Addison-Wesley Publishing Company, New York, 1994. Also see Arquilla and Ronfeldt, 1997.

26. Also see Alexander Berger, "Organizational Innovation and Redesign in the Information Age: The Drug War, Netwar, and Other Low-End Conflict," Master's Thesis, Naval Postgraduate School, Monterey, California, 1998, for additional thinking and analysis about such propositions.

27. For elaboration, see Arquilla and Ronfeldt, 1997, Chapter 19.

28. Vernon Loeb, "Where the CIA Wages Its New World War," *Washington Post*, September 9, 1998. For a broader discussion of interagency cooperation in countering terrorism, see Ashton Carter, John Deutch, and Philip Zelikow, "Catastrophic Terrorism," *Foreign Affairs*, Vol. 77, No. 6, November/December 1998, pp. 80–94.

29. Analogously, right-wing militias and extremist groups in the United States also rely on a doctrine of "leaderless resistance" propounded by Aryan nationalist Louis Beam. See Beam, 1992; and Kenneth Stern, *A Force Upon the Plain: The American Militia Movement and the Politics of Hate*, Simon and Schuster, New York, 1996. Meanwhile, as part of a broader trend toward netwar, transnational criminal organizations (TCOs) have been shifting away from centralized "Dons" to more networked structures. See Phil Williams, "Transnational Criminal Organizations and International Security," *Survival*, Vol. 36, No. 1, Spring 1994, pp. 96–113; and Phil Williams, "The Nature of Drug-Trafficking Networks," *Current History*, April 1998, pp. 154–159. As noted earlier, social activist movements long ago began to evolve "segmented, polycephalous, integrated networks." For a discussion of a social netwar in which human-rights and other peaceful activist groups supported an insurgent group in Mexico, see David Ronfeldt and Armando Martinez, "A Comment on the Zapatista 'Netwar'," in John Arquilla and David Ronfeldt, 1997, pp. 369–391.

30. It is important to differentiate our notions of information-age networking from earlier ideas about terror as consisting of a network in which all nodes revolved around a Soviet core (Claire Sterling, *The Terror Network*, Holt, Rinehart & Winston, New York, 1981). This view has generally been regarded as unsupported by available evidence (see Cindy C. Combs, *Terrorism in the Twenty-First Century*, Prentice-Hall, New York, 1997, pp. 99–119). However, there were a few early studies that did give credit to the possibility of the rise of terror networks that were bound more by loose ties to general strategic goals than by Soviet

control (see especially Thomas L. Friedman, "Loose-Linked Network of Terror: Separate Acts, Ideological Bonds," *Terrorism*, Vol. 8, No. 1, Winter 1985, pp. 36–49).

31. For good general background, see Michael Whine, "Islamist Organisations on the Internet," draft circulated on the Internet, April 1998 *(www.ict.org.il/articles)*.

32. We assume that group activity is a proxy for group strength. Group activity can be measured more easily than group strength, and is expected to be significantly correlated with strength. The relationship may not be perfect, but it is deemed to be sufficiently strong for our purposes.

33. Office of the Coordinator for Counterterrorism, *Patterns of Global Terrorism, 1996*, U.S. Department of State, Publication 10433, April 1997.

34. Loeb, 1998; and John Murray and Richard H. Ward (eds.), *Extremist Groups*, Office of International Criminal Justice, University of Illinois, Chicago, 1996.

35. Youssef M. Ibrahim, "Egyptians Hold Terrorist Chief, Official Asserts," *New York Times*, August 26, 1998.

36. Murray and Ward, 1996.

37. *Patterns of Global Terrorism, 1996*, and Murray and Ward, 1996.

38. Murray and Ward, 1996.

39. *Patterns of Global Terrorism, 1995, 1996, 1997*.

40. For instance, in 1997 Hamas operatives set off three suicide bombs in crowded public places in Tel Aviv and Jerusalem. On March 21, a Hamas satchel bomb exploded at a Tel Aviv café, killing three persons and injuring 48; on July 30, two Hamas suicide bombers blew themselves up in a Jerusalem market, killing 16 persons and wounding 178; on September 4, three suicide bombers attacked a Jerusalem pedestrian mall, killing at least five persons (in addition to the suicide bombers), and injuring at least 181. The Palestinian Islamic Jihad has claimed responsibility (along with Hamas) for a bomb that killed 20 and injured 75 others in March 1996, and in 1995 it carried out five bombings that killed 29 persons and wounded 107. See *Patterns of Global Terrorism, 1995, 1996, 1997*.

41. See "Hizbullah," Israeli Foreign Ministry, April 11, 1996. Available on the Internet at *http://www.israel-mfa.gov.il*.

42. See *Patterns of Global Terrorism, 1995, 1996, 1997*.

43. *Patterns of Global Terrorism, 1997*.

44. "Arab Afghans Said to Launch Worldwide Terrorist War," *Paris al-Watan al-'Arabi*, FBIS-TOT-96-010-L, December 1, 1995, pp. 22–24.

45. William Gertz, "Saudi Financier Tied to Attacks," *Washington Times*, October 23, 1996.

46. Tim Weiner, "U.S. Sees bin Laden as Ringleader of Terrorist Network," *New York Times*, August 21, 1998; M. J. Zuckerman, "Bin Laden Indicted for Bid to Kill Clinton," *USA Today*, August 26, 1998.

47. Pamela Constable, "Bin Laden 'Is Our Guest, So We Must Protect Him'," *Washington Post*, August 21, 1998.

48. We distinguish between deliberate and factional decentralization. Factional decentralization—prevalent in older groups—occurs when subgroups separate themselves from the central leadership because of differences in tactics or approach. Deliberate or operational decentralization is what distinguishes netwar agents from others, since delegation of authority in this case occurs because of the distinct advantages this organizational arrangement brings, and not because of lack of consensus. We expect both influences on decentralization to continue, but newer groups will tend to decentralize authority even in the absence of political disagreements.

49. "Gaza Strip, West Bank: Dahlan on Relations with Israel, Terrorism," *Tel Aviv Yedi'ot Aharonot*, FBIS-TOT-97-022-L, February 28, 1997, p. 18.

50. The leader of the PIJ's most powerful faction, Fathi Shaqaqi, was assassinated in October 1995 in Malta, allegedly by the Israeli Mossad. Shaqaqi's killing followed the assassination of Hani Abed, another PIJ leader killed in 1994 in Gaza. Reports that the group has been considerably weakened as a result of Israeli counterleadership operations are balanced by the strength demonstrated by the PIJ in its recent terrorist activity. See "Islamic Group Vows Revenge for Slaying of Its Leader," *New York Times*, October 30, 1995, p. 9.

51. Magnus Ranstorp, "Hizbullah's Command Leadership: Its Structure, Decision-Making and Relationship with Iranian Clergy and Institutions," *Terrorism and Political Violence*, Vol. 6, No. 3, Autumn 1994, p. 304.

52. *Patterns of Global Terrorism, 1996.*

53. "Algeria: Infighting Among Proliferating 'Wings' of Armed Groups," *London al-Sharq al-Aswat*, FBIS-TOT-97-021-L, February 24, 1997, p. 4.

54. David B. Ottaway, "US Considers Slugging It Out With International Terrorism," *Washington Post*, October 17, 1996, p. 25.

55. "Saudi Arabia: Bin-Laden Calls for 'Guerrilla Warfare' Against US Forces," *Beirut Al-Diyar*, FBIS-NES-96-180, September 12, 1996.

56. It is important to avoid equating the bin Laden network solely with bin Laden. He represents a key node in the Arab Afghan terror network, but there should be no illusions about the likely effect on the network of actions taken to neutralize him. The network conducts many operations without his involvement, leadership, or financing—and will continue to be able to do so should he be killed or captured.

57. "Militants Say There Will Be More Attacks Against U.S.," *European Stars and Stripes*, August 20, 1998.

58. For instance, there have been reports of a recent inflow of Arab Afghans into Egypt's Islamic Group to reinforce the latter's operations. See Murray and Ward, 1996, and "The CIA on Bin Laden," *Foreign Report*, No. 2510, August 27, 1998, pp. 2–3.

59. This move was also influenced by the Taliban's decision to curb Arab Afghan activities in the territory under its control as a result of U.S. pressure. See "Arab Afghans Reportedly Transfer Operations to Somalia," *Cairo al-Arabi*, FBIS-TOT-97-073, March 10, 1997, p. 1.

60. "Afghanistan, China: Report on Bin-Laden Possibly Moving to China," *Paris al-Watan al-'Arabi*, FBIS-NES-97-102, May 23, 1997, pp. 19–20.

61. While it is possible to discern a general trend toward an organizational structure that displays several features of a network, we expect to observe substantial differences (and many hierarchy/network hybrids) in how organizations make their specific design choices. Different network designs depend on contingent factors, such as personalities, organizational history, operational requirements, and other influences such as state sponsorship and ideology.

62. Assessing the strength of the relationship between organizational structure and use of information technology is difficult to establish. Alternative explanations may exist as to why newer groups would embrace information technology, such as age of the group (one could speculate that newer terrorist groups have on average younger members, who are more familiar with computers), or the amount of funding (a richer group could afford more electronic gadgetry). While it is empirically impossible to refute these points, much in organization theory supports our hypothesis that there is a direct relationship between a higher need for information technology and the use of network structures.

63. "Saudi Arabia: French Analysis of Islamic Threat," *Paris al-Watan al-'Arabi*, FBIS-NES- 97-082, April 11, 1997, pp. 4–8.

64. "Afghanistan, Saudi Arabia: Editor's Journey to Meet Bin-Laden Described," *London al-Quds al-'Arabi*, FBIS-TOT-97-003-L, November 27, 1996, p. 4.

65. "Arab Afghans Said to Launch Worldwide Terrorist War," 1995.

66. "Israel: U.S. Hamas Activists Use Internet to Send Attack Threats," *Tel Aviv IDF Radio*, FBIS-TOT-97-001-L, 0500 GMT October 13, 1996.

67. "Israel: Hamas Using Internet to Relay Operational Messages," *Tel Aviv Ha'aretz*, FBIS-TOT-98-034, February 3, 1998, p. 1.

68. "Italy: Security Alters Following Algerian Extremists' Arrests," *Milan Il Giornale*, FBIS-TOT-97-002-L, November 12, 1996, p. 10.

69. "Italy, Vatican City: Daily Claims GIA 'Strategist' Based in Milan," *Milan Corriere della Sera*, FBIS-TOT-97-004-L, December 5, 1996, p. 9.

70. "Hizbullah TV Summary 18 February 1998," *Al-Manar Television World Wide Webcast*, FBIS-NES-98-050, February 19, 1998. Also see "Developments in Mideast Media: January–May 1998," Foreign Broadcast Information Service (FBIS), May 11, 1998.

71. "Islamists on Internet," FBIS Foreign Media Note-065EP96, September 9, 1996.
72. "Islamic Activism Online," FBIS Foreign Media Note-02JAN97, January 3, 1997.
73. The Muslim Parliament has recently added an Internet Relay Chat (IRC) link and a "Muslims only" List-Serve (automatic e-mail delivery service). See "Islamic Activism Online," FBIS Foreign Media Note-02JAN97, January 3, 1997.
74. Similar propositions may apply to varieties of netwar other than the new terrorism.
75. We make a qualification here. There appears to be a significant positive association between the degree to which a group is active and the degree to which a group is decentralized and networked. But we cannot be confident about the causality of this relationship or its direction (i.e., whether activity and strength affect networking, or vice-versa). A host of confounding factors may affect both the way groups decide to organize and their relative success at operations. For instance, the age of a group may be an important predictor of a group's success—newer groups are likely to be more popular; popular groups are more likely to enlist new operatives; and groups that have a large number of operatives are likely to be more active, regardless of organizational structure. Another important caveat is related to the fact that it is difficult to rank groups precisely in terms of the degree to which they are networked, because no terrorist organization is thought to represent either a hierarchical or network ideal-type. While the conceptual division between newer-generation and traditional groups is appropriate for our scope here, an analytical "degree of networking" scale would have to be devised for more empirical research.
76. See, for instance, William Gutteridge (ed.), *Contemporary Terrorism*, Facts on File, Oxford, England, 1986; Hoffman and Carr, 1997; and Combs, 1997.
77. See Alexander George and William Simons, *The Limits of Coercive Diplomacy*, Westview Press, Boulder, 1994.
78. Alexander George, *Forceful Persuasion: Coercive Diplomacy as an Alternative to War*, United States Institute of Peace Press, Washington, DC, 1991.
79. Brian Jenkins, *The Potential for Nuclear Terrorism*, RAND, P-5876, 1977; Thomas Schelling, "Thinking about Nuclear Terrorism," *International Security*, Vol. 6, No. 4, Spring 1982, pp. 68–75; and Patrick Garrity and Steven Maaranen, *Nuclear Weapons in a Changing World*, Plenum Press, New York, 1992.
80. Carr, 1996.
81. Brian Jenkins, *International Terrorism: A New Kind of Warfare*, RAND, P-5261, 1974.
82. For a discussion of these motives, see Laqueur, 1996; Iklé, 1997; and Hoffman, 1998, respectively.
83. See, for instance, Michael Barkun, *Disaster and the Millennium*, Yale University Press, New Haven, 1974; and Norman Cohn, *The Pursuit of the Millennium: Revolutionary Messianism in Medieval and Reformation Europe and Its Bearing on Modern Totalitarian Movements*, Harper Torch Books, New York, 1961.
84. Bluma Zuckerbrot-Finkelstein, "A Guide to Hamas," *Internet Jewish Post*, available at *http://www.jewishpost.com/jewishpost/jp0203/jpn0303.htm*.

Chapter 4

Religion

The 1993 bombings of Manhattan's World Trade Center, Aum Shinrikyo's release of sarin nerve gas in the Tokyo underground, and the bombing of a U.S. Federal building in Oklahoma City were acts of terrorism carried out by players with vastly different origins, doctrines, and practices, writes Magnus Ranstorp. Yet Ranstorp recognizes one common thread among these terrorist acts: the perpetrators believed "their actions were divinely sanctioned, even mandated, by God."

Ranstorp charts the rise in terrorism for religious motives and reports that between the mid-1960s and mid-1990s there was a tripling in the number of fundamentalist movements of all religious affiliations. Nearly a quarter of all terrorist groups active in the world today are primarily motivated by religious concerns, yet these groups are also driven by practical political considerations—and it is difficult for observers to distinguish the political from the religious in the terrorist acts these groups commit. Ranstorp explores the motives, the "serious sense of crisis in their environment," which nearly all these groups experience and that fuels an escalation in their activities; the threats of secularization from foreign sources these groups identify and rail against; the hierarchy of power that emanates from a dynamic so-called spiritual leader; the role religious symbolism plays in selecting their targets; and the sense of hope and chance for vengeance these groups offer to followers who suffer under a history of grievances. Contrary to popular opinion, Ranstorp concludes, "Religious terrorism is anything but disorganized or random, but rather driven by an inner logic common among diverse groups and faiths who use political violence to further their sacred causes."

Mark Juergensmeyer looks at the complex relationship between religion and violence, particularly in the context of the militant Sikhs of India and the violence that seized the Punjab region in the 1980s. Juergensmeyer portrays the Sikhs as a group in crisis, "their separate identity within the Indian family is in danger.... Sikhs fear they could be reabsorbed into the amorphous cultural mass that is Hinduism and disappear as a distinct religious community," he writes. The author examines how the words and rhetoric of a charismatic militant leader, Jamail Singh Bhindranwale, can inspire a movement; and at how everyday, political issues can be mingled with a struggle for spiritual survival to create a cosmic struggle that validates violent means for religious and political ends.

Terrorism in the Name of Religion

An internationally recognized expert on terrorism, **Magnus Ranstorp** is a lecturer in international relations at the University of St. Andrews (Scotland) and deputy director of the University's Centre for the Study of Terrorism and Political Violence, where he specialized in the behavior of militant Islamic movements in the Middle East and North Africa. Author of *Hizballah in Lebanon: The Politics of the Western Hostage Crisis* (1996), he gives lectures and briefings on Middle Eastern terrorism to academic, government, and military audiences around the world.

Introduction

On 25 February 1994, the day of the second Muslim sabbath during Islam's holy month of Ramadan, a Zionist settler from the orthodox settlement of Qiryat Arba entered the crowded Ibrahim (Abraham's) Mosque, located in the biblical town of Hebron on the West Bank. He emptied three 30-shot magazines with his automatic Glilon assault-rifle into the congregation of 800 Palestinian Muslim worshippers, killing 29 and wounding 150, before being beaten to death. A longstanding follower of the radical Jewish fundamentalist group, the Kach movement,[1] Baruch Goldstein was motivated by a complex mixture of seemingly inseparable political and religious desiderata, fuelled by zealotry and a grave sense of betrayal as his prime minister was "leading the Jewish state out of its God-given patrimony and into mortal danger."[2] Both the location and the timing of the Hebron massacre were heavily infused with religious symbolism. Hebron was the site of the massacre of 69 Jews in 1929. Also, the fact that it occured during the Jewish festival of Purim symbolically cast Goldstein in the role of Mordechai in the Purim story, meting out awesome revenge against the enemies of the Jews.[3] Israeli Prime Minister Yithzak Rabin, speaking for the great mass of Israelis, expressed revulsion and profound sadness over the act committed by a "deranged fanatic." However, a large segment of militant and orthodox Jewish settlers in West Bank and Gaza settlements portrayed Goldstein as a righteous man and hailed him as a martyr.[4] During his funeral, these orthodox settlers also voiced religious fervor in uncompromising and militant terms directed not only against the Arabs, but also against the Israeli government, which they believed had betrayed the Jewish People and the Jewish state.

Israeli leaders and the Jewish community tried to deny or ignore the danger of Jewish extremism by dismissing Goldstein as belonging, at most, to "the fringe of a fringe"[5] within Israeli society. Sadly, any doubts of the mortal dangers of religious zealotry from within were abruptly silenced with the assassination of prime minister Yitzhak Rabin by a young Jewish student, Yigal Amir, who claimed he had acted on orders of God. He had been influenced by militant rabbis and their *halalic* rulings, which he interpreted to mean that the "pursuer's decree" was to be applied against Israel's leader.[6] Most Israelis may be astonished by the notion of a Jew killing another Jew, but Rabin was ultimately the victim of a broader force which has become one of the most vibrant, dangerous and pervasive trends in the post–Cold War world: religiously motivated terrorism.

Far afield from the traditionally violent Middle East, where religion and terrorism share a long history,[7] a surge of religious fanaticism has manifested itself in spectacular acts of terrorism across the globe. This wave of violence is unprecedented, not only in its scope and the selection of targets, but also in its lethality and indiscriminate character. Examples of these incidents abound: in an effort to hasten in the new millenium, the Japanese religious cult Aum Shinrikyo released sarin nerve gas on the Tokyo underground in June last year;[8] the followers of Sheikh 'Abd al-Rahman's al-Jama'a al-Islamiyya[9] caused mayhem and destruction with the bombing of Manhattan's World Trade Center and had further plans to blow up major landmarks in the New York City area; and two American white supremacists carried out the bombing of a U.S. Federal building in Oklahoma City.[10] All are united in the belief by the perpetrators that their actions were divinely sanctioned, even mandated, by God. Despite having vastly different origins, doctrines, institutions, and practices, these religious extremists are unified in their justification for employing sacred violence, whether in efforts to defend, extend or revenge their own communities, or for millenarian or messianic reasons.[11] This article seeks to explore these reasons for the contemporary rise in terrorism for religious motives and to identify the triggering mechanisms that bring about violence out of religious belief in both established and newly formed terrorist groups.

The Wider Trend of Religious Terrorism

Between the mid-1960s and the mid-1990s, the number of fundamentalist movements of all religious affiliations tripled worldwide. Simultaneously, as observed by Bruce Hoffman, there has been a virtual explosion of identifiable religious terrorist groups from none in 1968 to today's level, where nearly a quarter of all terrorist groups active throughout the world are predominantly motivated by religious concerns.[12] Unlike their secular counterparts, religious terrorists are, by their very nature, largely motivated by religion, but they are also driven by day-to-day practical political considerations within their context-specific environment. This makes it difficult for the general observer to separate and distinguish between the political and the religious sphere of these terrorist groups.

Nowhere is this more clear than in Muslim terrorist groups, as religion and politics cannot be seperated in Islam. For example, Hizb'allah or Hamas operate within the framework of religious ideology, which they combine with practical and precise political action in Lebanon and Palestine. As such, these groups embrace simultaneously short-term objectives, such as the release of imprisoned members, and long-term objectives, such as continuing to resist Israeli occupation of their homelands and liberating all "believers." This is further complicated with the issue of state-sponsorship of terrorism: Religious terrorist groups become cheap and effective tools for specific states in the advancement of their foreign policy political agendas. They may also contain a nationalist-seperatist agenda, in which the religious component is often entangled with a complex mixture of cultural, political, and linguistic factors. The proliferation of religious extremist movements has also been accompanied by a sharp increase in the total number of acts of terrorism since 1988, accounting for over half of the 64,319 recorded incidents between 1970 and July 1995.[13] This escalation by the religious terrorists is hardly surprising given the fact that most of today's active groups worldwide came into existence very recently. They appeared with a distinct and full-fledged organizational apparatus. They range from the Sikh Dal Khalsa and the Dashmesh organizations, formed in 1978 and 1982 respectively[14] and the foundation of the Shi'ite Hizb'allah movement in Lebanon in 1982; to the initial emergence of the militant Sunni organizations, known as Hamas and Islamic Jihad, in conjunction with the 1987 outbreak of the Palestinian Intifada as well as the establishment of the Aum Shinrikyo in the same year.

The growth of religious terrorism is also indicative of the transformation of contemporary terrorism into a method of warfare and the evolution of the tactics and techniques used by various groups, as a reaction to vast changes within the local, regional and global environment over the last three decades. These changes can be seen in numerous incidents, from the spate of hijackings by secular Palestinian terrorists and the mayhem of destruction caused by left- and right-wing domestic terrorists throughout Europe, to today's unprecedented global scope and level of religious extremism.

The evolution of today's religious terrorism neither has occured in a vacuum nor represents a particularly new phenomenon. It has, however, been propelled to the forefront in the post–Cold war world, as it has been exacerbated by the explosion of ethnic-religious conflicts and the rapidly approaching new millenium.[15] The accelerated dissolution of traditional links of social and cultural cohesion within and between societies with the current globalization process, combined with the historical legacy and current conditions of political repression, economic inequality and social upheaval common among disparate religious extremist movements, have all lead to an increased sense of fragility, instability and unpredictability for the present and the future.[16] The current scale and scope of religious terrorism, unprecedented in militancy and activism, is indicative of this perception that their respective faiths and communities stand at a critical historical juncture: Not only do the terrorists feel the need to preserve their religious identity, they also see this time as an opportunity to fundamentally shape the future.[17] There are a number of overlapping factors that have contributed to the revival of religious terrorism in its modern and lethal form at the end of the millennium. At the same time, it is also possible to discern a number of features which are found in all religious terrorist groups across different regions and faiths. These features serve not only to define the cause and the enemy, but also fundamentally shape the means, methods and the timing of the use of the violence itself.

The Causes and the Enemies of Religious Terrorists

A survey of the major religious terrorist groups in existence worldwide in the 1990s would reveal that almost all experience a serious sense of crisis in their environment, which has led to an increase in the number of groups recently formed and caused an escalation in their activities. This crisis mentality in the religious terrorist's milieu is multifaceted, at once in the social, political, economic, cultural, psychological and spiritual sphere. At the same time, it has been greatly exacerbated by the political, economic and social tumult, resulting in a sense of spiritual fragmentation and radicalization of society experienced worldwide in the wake of the end of the Cold War and the extremist's "fear of the forced march toward 'one worldism.'"[18] Yet, this sense of crisis, as a perceived threat to their identity and survival, has been present to varying degrees throughout history. It has led to recurring phases of resurgence in most faiths. In these revivals, the believers use the religion in a variety of ways: they take refuge in the religion, which provides centuries-old ideals by which to determine goals; they find physical or psychological sanctuary against repression; or they may use it as a major instrument for activism or political action. Thus, religious terrorists perceive their actions as defensive and reactive in character and justify them in this way.[19] Islam's *jihad*, for example, is essentially a defensive doctrine, religiously sanctioned by leading Muslim theologians, and fought against perceived aggressors, tyrants, and "wayward Muslims." In its most violent form, it is justified as a means of last resort to prevent the extinction of the distinctive identity of the Islamic community against the forces of secularism and modernism. As outlined by Sheikh Fadlallah, the chief ideologue of Hizb'allah: "When Islam fights a war, it fights like any other power in the world, defending itself in order to preserve its existence and its liberty, forced to undertake preventive operations when it is in danger."[20] This is echoed by Sikh extremists, who advocate that, while violence is not condoned, when all peaceful means are exhausted, "you should put your hand on the sword."[21] The defensive character of protecting one's faith through religious violence is also evident in the Sikh's fear of losing their distinct identity in the sea of Hindus and Muslims.[22] In the United States, the paranoid outlook of white supremacist movements is driven by a mixture of racism and anti-Semitism, as well as mistrust of government and all central authority.[23] This sense of persecution is also visible among the Shi'ites as an historically dominant theme for 13 centuries, manifest in the annual Ashura processions by the Lebanese Hizb'allah, commemorating the martyrdom of Imam Husayn. This event and mourning period have been used as justification and as a driving force behind its own practice of martyrdom through suicide attacks.[24]

Other than a few strictly millenarian or messianic groups (such as Aum Shinrikyo or some Christian white supremacist movements), almost all the contemporary terrorist groups with a distinct religious imperative are either offshoots or on the fringe of broader movements. As such, the militant extremists' decisions to organize, break away or remain on the fringe are, to a large extent, conditioned by the political context within which they operate. Their decisions are shaped by doctrinal differences, tactical and local issues, and the degree of threat that they perceive secularization poses to their cause. This threat of secularization may come either from within the movements themselves and the environment within which they come into contact, or from outside influences. If the threat is external, it may amplify their sense of marginality within, and acute alienation from, society. It may also fuel the need to compensate for personal sufferings through the radical transformation of the ruling order.[25] The internal threat of secularization is often manifest in an vociferous and virulent rejection of the corrupt political parties, the legitimacy of the regime, and also the lackluster and inhibited character of the exisiting religious establishment. Thus, religious terrorism serves as the only effective vechicle for violent political opposition.[26] As explained by Kach's leader, Baruch Marzel, "(w)e feel God gave us in the six-day war, with a miracle, this country. We are taking this present from God and tossing it away. They are breaking every holy thing in this country, the Government, in a very brutal way."[27] Similarily, as voiced by the late Palestinian Islamic Jihad's leader, Fathi al-Shaqaqi, with reference to the Gaza-Jericho agreement between the PLO [Palestine Liberation Organization] and Israel: "Arafat has sold his soul for the sake of his body and is trying to sell the Palestinian people's soul in return for their remaining alive politically."[28] The religious terrorist groups' perception of a threat of secularization from within the same society is also manifest in the symbolism used in the selection of their names, indicating that they have an absolute monopoly of the revealed thruth by God. It is, therefore, not surprising that some of the most violent terrorist groups over the last decade have also adopted names accordingly: Hizb'allah (Party of God), Aum Shinrikyo (The Supreme Truth) and Jund al-Haqq (Soldiers of Truth). These names also endow them with religious legitimacy, historical authenticity, and justification for their actions in the eyes of their followers and potential new recruits. They also provide valuable insight into their unity of purpose, direction and degree of militancy, with names like Jundallah (Soldiers of God), Hamas (Zeal), Eyal (Jewish Fighting Organization) and Le Groupe Islamique du Armé (Armed Islamic Group, GIA) which promises unabated struggle and sacrifice.

The threat of secularization from foreign sources is also the catalyst for springing religious terrorists into action. Intrusion of secular values into the extremist's own environment and the visible presence of secular foreign interference provoke self-defensive aggressiveness and hostility against the sources of these evils. This is especially true against colonalism and neo-colonialism by western civilizations or against other militant religious faiths. These defensive sentiments are often combined with the visible emergence and presence of militant clerical leaders. Such leaders have a more activist and militant ideologies than the mainstream movement from which they have emerged as either clandestine instruments or breakaway groups. It is often the case that these clerical ideologues and personalities act as a centrifugal force in attracting support, strengthening the organizational mechanisms and in redefining the methods and means through terrorism. At the same time, they provide theological justification, which enables their followers to pursue the sacred causes more effectively and rapidly. The so-called spiritual guides, who ultimately overlook most political and military activities while blessing acts of terrorism, can be found in almost all religious terrorist groups: Examples include Hizb'allah's Sheikh Fadlallah and Hamas' Sheikh Yassin, the militant Sikh leader Sant Bhindranwale and Aum Shinrikyo's leader, Shoko Ashara.

Most active terrorist groups with a religious imperative were actually propelled into existence in reaction to key events. These events either served as a catalyst or inspirational model for the organization or gravely escalated the perception of the threat of foreign secularization, or for messianic or millenarian groups, a heightened sense that time was running out. The latter is evident in the growth and increased activism of doomsday cults, awaiting the imminent apocalypse, whose self-prophetic visions about the future have triggered them to hasten the new millennium.[29] This messianic anticipation, for example, was clearly evident in the attack on the Grand Mosque of Mecca in 1979 (the Islamic year 1400) by armed Muslim militants from al-Ikhwan, who expected the return of their Madhi.[30] The formation of Lebanese Hizb'allah can be attributed to the context of the civil war environment and the inspiring example of Ayatollah Khomeini's Islamic revolution in Iran. However, it was Israel's invasion of Lebanon in 1982 and the subsequent foreign intrusion in the form of the western-led Multinational Forces (MNF) that served as a catalyst for Hizb'allah's actual organizational formation and which to this day has continued to fuel its militancy and religious ideology. Similarly, the 1984 desecration by the Indian army of the Golden Temple in Amritsar,

Sikhism's holiest shrine, led not only to the assassination of Prime Minister Indira Gandhi in revenge, but also to a cycle of endless violence between the warring faiths, which hitherto has claimed over 20,000 lives.[31]

In many ways, religious terrorists embrace a total ideological vision of an all-out struggle to resist secularization from within as well as from without. They pursue this vision in totally uncompromising holy terms in literal battles between good and evil. Ironically, there is a great degree of similarity between the stands of the Jewish Kach and Islamic Hamas organizations: Both share a vision of a religious state between the Jordan River and the Mediterrenean Sea; a xenophobia against everything alien or secular which must be removed from the entire land, and a vehement rejection of western culture. This distinction between the faithful and those standing outside the group is reinforced in the daily discourse of the clerics of these terrorist groups. The clerics' language and phraseology shapes the followers' reality, reinforcing the loyalty and social obligation of the members to the group and reminding them of the sacrifices already made, as well as the direction of the struggle.[32] In this task, many religious terrorist groups draw heavily upon religious symbolism and rituals to reinforce the sense of collectiveness. Examples of this emphasis on collectivity include the local reputation of the fighters of the underground military wing of Hamas, famous for never surrendering to arrest,[33] the growth of Hamas martyrology, which lionizes martyrs with songs, poems and shrines,[34] and the frequent symbolic burning and desecration of Israeli and American flags by several Islamic groups across the Middle East. This collectiveness is also reinforced by the fact that any deviation or compromise amounts to treachery and a surrender of the principles of the religious faith is often punishable by death.

The sense of totality of the struggle for these religious warriors is one purely defined in dialectic and cosmic terms as believers against unbelievers, order against chaos, and justice against injustice, which is mirrored in the totality and uncompromising nature of their cause, whether that cause entails the establishment of Eretz Israel, an Islamic state based on *sharia* law or an independent Khalistan ("Land of the Pure"). As such, the religious terrorists perceive their struggle as all-out war against their enemies. This perception, in turn, is often used to justify the level and intensity of the violence. For example, this theme of war is continuously detectable in the writings and statements by the terrorists, as exemplified by Yigal Amir's justification for assassinating Rabin;[35] or by Article 8 of Hamas' manifesto justifying that *jihad* is its path and that "[d]eath for the sake of Allah is its most sublime belief."

This totality of the struggle naturally appeals to its acutely disenfranchized, oppressed, and alienated communities with the promises of change and the provision of constructive alternatives. Unlike their recent historical predecessors, like the fringe al-Jihad organization which assassinated the Egyptian President Anwar Sadat in 1981,[36] many of the existing religious terrorist cells are different in that they can often complement their violence with realistic alternatives to secular submission. This is especially true at the grassroots level, due to the penchant for organization inherent in religion and the backing of a vast network of resources and facilities.[37] This has meant that some religious terrorist groups are not solely relying on violence, but also have gradually built an impressive constituency through a strategy of "re-Islamization or re-Judaization from below."[38] The political dimension is complemented with terrorism in confrontation with the enemy or in defense of the sacred cause. This is a process which began in the early 1970s and culminated in the 1990s with a visible shift in strategy among groups, from relying on terrorism while re-Islamizing their environment to complementing terrorism with the use of the electoral process to advance their sacred causes.

Religious terrorism also offers its increasingly suffering and impatient constituents more hope and a greater chance of vengeance against the sources of their historical grievances than they would otherwise have. This is most effectively illustrated by the 1985 Sikh inflight bombing of an Air India airliner, causing 328 deaths, as well as by Hizb'allah's twin suicide-bombings of the U.S. Marine barracks and the French MNF headquarters in Beirut in 1983, killing 241 and 56 soldiers respectively. Violent acts give these groups a sense of power that is disproportionate to their size. The basis for this feeling of power is enhanced by a strategy of anonymity by the religious terrorist which confuses the enemy. In other words, the covernames are used according to where the religious terrorists have come from and where they are heading. Terrorists of the Muslim faith, particularly Shi'ite groups, employ a wide variety of covernames (in the Shi'ite case rooted in history with the notion of *taqiyyah*, or dissimulation) in efforts to protect their communities against repression or retaliation by the enemy after terrorist acts.[39] Yet, these covernames reveal significantly the currents or directions within movements in alignment with their struggles.[40] As such, the religious terrorists tend to "execute their terrorist acts for no audience but themselves."[41] Although the act of violence in and of itself is executed primarily for the terrorists own community as a sign of strength, it naturally embodies wider elements of fear in their actual or potential enemy targets. The perpetrators adeptly exploit this fear by invoking religious symbolism, such as the release of videotaped images of an endless pool of suicide bombers, ready to be dispatched against new targets.

While the religious extremists uniformly strike at the symbols of tyranny, they are relatively unconstrained in the lethality and the indiscriminate nature of violence used, as it is conducted and justified in defence of the faith and the community. Reflecting the dialectic nature of the struggle itself, various religious terrorist groups also refer to their alien or secular enemies in de-humanizing terms which may loosen the moral constraints for them in their employment of particularly destructive acts of terrorism.[42] As explained by an extremist rabbi in conjunction with the funeral of Baruch Goldstein: "There is a great difference in the punishment becoming a person who hurts a Jew and a person who hurts a gentile.... [t]he life of a Jew is worth much more than the lives of many gentiles." This moral self-purification points to the belief that the perpetrators view themselves as divinely "chosen people," who not only possess religious legitimacy and justification for their propensity for violence, but also often act out of the belief that the violence occurs in a divinely sanctioned juncture in history. For example, the Japanese cult leader Shoko Ashara and his followers believed the world would end in 1997 and launched a sarin nerve gas attack on Tokyo's subway system to hasten the new millennium.[43]

In fact, the lack of any moral constraints in the use of violence cannot only be attributed to the totality of the struggle itself but also to the preponderance of recruits of young, educated and newly-urbanized men (often with very radical, dogmatic, and intolerant worldviews), in contemporary religious terrorist organizations.[44] This increased militancy of a younger generation of religious terrorists can be explained by both the fragmentation of groups into rival splinter factions and also the killing or imprisonment of key founding leaders and ideologues.[45] Apart from removing the older generation of terrorist leadership, the experience of persecution and imprisonment has led to the radicalization of younger recruits into the organizations.[46] Also there seems to be an inverse relationship between size and militancy.[47] The Shi'ite terrorist groups are more prone to martyrdom than their Sunni counterparts, due to their different historical legacies and to the more powerful role of Shi'ite clergymen in directly interceeding between man and God. However, some Sunni groups have recently broken the mold, as evident in the unprecedented series of 13 Hamas suicide-attacks inside Israel (which killed 136 people between 6 April 1994 and 4 March 1996) after the Hebron massacre and, to a lesser extent, the foiled plan by the GIA to explode its hijacked Air France plane over metropolitan Paris in December 1994. However, as explained by Sheikh Fadlallah: "There is no difference between dying with a gun in your hand or exploding yourself. In a situation of struggle or holy war you have to find the best means to achieve your goals."[48]

While the resort to martyrdom by certain groups can be explained by the heightened sense of threat to the groups and their causes within their own environment, it can also be explained by an increasing level of internationalization between groups both in terms of contact, similarity of causes and as examples of strategies. This is particularly evident among Muslim terrorist groups. For example, many Algerian, Egyptian and Palestinian Muslim extremists have participated alongside the Mujahadin fighters in the Afghanistan conflict. They trained with these Afghan fighters and supported them both physically and ideologically in a war "as much about the forging of a new and revolutionary social order as about national liberation."[49] As a significant example of a revolutionary cause within a Sunni context, as opposed to the more narrow Shi'ite example of the Iranian revolution, the Afghan conflict served as a training ground for their own struggles during the 1980s: Following the collapse of communism, these fighters returned to their respective countries to radicalize the Islamic struggle at home, resorting to increasing violence in the process, either within existing movements or as splinter groups.

Yet, the mechanisms of unleashing acts of religious terrorism, in terms of intensity, methods and timing, are tightly controlled by the apex of the clerical hierarchy and most often dependent on their blessing. This was clearly demonstrated in the 1984 Gush Emunim plot to blow up the Temple Mount (or Dome of the Rock), Islam's third holiest site, in part for messianic reasons (to cause a cataclysmic war between Jews and Muslims to hasten the coming of the Messiah) and in part to foil the return of Jewish sacred land to Arabs in return for peace under the Camp David accord. This act of terrorism never materialized due to the lack of rabbinical backing.[50] Similarly, the role of the spiritual leaders within Islamic terrorist organizations is equally pivotal, as displayed by the central role of Sheikh Omar 'Abd al-Rahman of the Egyptian al-Jama'a al-Islamiyya in issuing the directive, or *fatwa*, for both the 1981 assassination of Anwar Sadat and the 1993 bombing of New York's World Trade Center.[51] As such, in most cases the strictly hierarchical nature of religious terrorist groups with a highly disciplined structure and obedient cadres means not only that the main clerical leaders command full control over the political as well as military activities of the organization but also that the strategies of terrorism are unleashed in accordance with general political directives and agendas.[52]

Yet, the use and sanctioning of religious violence requires clearly defined enemies. The newly-formed religious terrorist groups today do not appear in a vacuum nor are their members naturally born into extremism. The identity of the enemy and the decision to use religious violence against them are dependent on, and shaped by, the heightened degree of the sense of crisis threatening their faiths and communities. This, in turn, is influenced by the historical legacy of political repression, economic inequality or social upheaval, and may be exacerbated by ethnic and military disputes. This sense of grievance is uniquely experienced between the faiths and the individual groups, as well as in alignment with the political strategies and tactics adopted to confront them according to local, regional and international contexts. Internally, this militancy may be directed against the corruption or injustices of the polictical system, or against other religious communities; externally, it may be focused against foreign influences, which represent a cultural, economic, or political threat to the respective religious communities. The West, particularly the United States as well as Israel, tends to be the favourite target of this militancy, especially by terrorists of the Muslim faith.[53]

Anti-western sentiments and intense hostility towards Israel for the Muslim terrorist is the result of the historical legacy of political oppression and socio-economic marginalization within the Arab world. These hostilities are combined with the discrediting of secular ideologies and the illegitimacy of current political and economic elites, especially after the 1967 defeat of the Arabs by Israel.[54] This sense of crisis has been exacerbated by the Arab-Israeli conflict which served to reinforce a Muslim inferiority complex due to the inability of either Arab regimes or secular Palestinians to defeat Israel. Simultaneously, the West is perceived to be practising neocolonialism through its Israeli surrogate and its unqualified support for existing "un-Islamic" and "illegitimate" regimes across the Arab world. As such, the Islamist movements and their respective armed "terrorist" wings have gradually propelled themselves to the forefront of politics as the true defender of the oppressed and dispossessed and as the only effective spearhead against Israel's continued existence in the heart of Muslim territory and against the West's presence and interference in the region. Apart from the obvious religious dimensions of the loss of Palestine to Zionism, Muslim militants draw heavily on the symbolism of the historical legacy of the Crusades, pitting Christendom against Islam, to explain their current condition of oppression and disinheritance, and to provide workable solutions and defences against the threat of western encirclement and secularization.[55] The Muslim terrorists rework these historic religious symbols to fit present-day conditions as a vehicle to inspire political action and revolutionary violence against its enemies.

While the identity of the enemy is deeply rooted in both distant and recent history, the turn towards, and the direction of, terrorism by militant Muslim movements against foreign enemies have been following distinct phases according to changes in the political and ideological context in the region. These phases are directly influenced by the Iranian revolution in 1979, the Muslim resistance struggle led by the Mujahadin against the Soviets in Afghanistan, the electoral victory of the Front Islamique du Salut (FIS) in Algeria (1990 to 1991), and the signing of the Israeli-Palestinian Declaration of Principles in September 1993. The Iranian revolution provided a revolutionary model of Islam and inspired Islamic movements to seriously challenge existing regimes at home. Additionally, the internationalization of Muslim terrorist violence against the West and Israel during the 1980s supported Iran's efforts to export the revolution abroad and was a cost-effective instrument to change the foreign policies of western states hostile towards the

Islamic Republic.[56] The Lebanese Hizb'allah movement in particular, was very useful to the Iranian regime in achieving these ends. It also provided Iran with the opportunity to participate, both indirectly and militarily, in the Arab-Israeli conflict.[57] Additionally, Muslim fighters in Afghanistan during the 1980s forged important networks between various groups and individuals which accelerated the activism among Muslim groups on the homefront when these fighters returned home. The FIS electoral victory in Algeria demonstrated to Muslim terrorist groups that they could use the ballotbox rather than relying solely on bullets in efforts to come to power in various Arab states. The election's subsequent nullification by the Algerian military junta led to radicalization of the Islamists and their turn towards terrorism against the state itself and the French government for extending support.

Simultaneously, the gradual resolution of the Israeli-Palestinian conflict threatens the pan-Islamic goal of militant Islamic movements of liberating Jerusalem. This threat has led to accelerated co-ordination between Islamic terrorist groups in efforts to sabotage the peace process and an increased militancy and confrontation against the West, Israel, and supportive Arab regimes. At the same time, the political wings of these terrorist groups seek to continue and extend the process of re-Islamization of society from below. The confluence of these factors over the last two decades has accelerated the militancy of the Muslim terrorist while it clearly demonstrates that they are closely attuned to changes in the local, regional, and international environment, as well as very adept to reformulating their strategies for political and military action accordingly in efforts to protect, extend or avenge their religious communities.

The Means, Methods, and Timing of the Religious Terrorist

In comparison to their secular counterparts, the religious terrorists have not been particularly inventive when it comes to using new types of weaponry in their arsenals, instead relying on the traditional bombs and bullets.[58] Yet the religious terrorists have demonstrated a great deal of ingenuity in terms of the tactics used in the selection of means, methods and timing of violence to cause maximum effect. They have utilized the notion of martyrdom and self-sacrifice through suicide bombings as a means of last resort against their conventionally more powerful enemies. The first time this tactic was employed by the Hizb'allah was against the American, French and later Israeli military contingents present in Lebanon in 1983. It was emulating the actions of the shock troops of the Iranian Revolutionary Guards in their war with Iraq. While the Hizb'allah clerics gradually encountered theological dilemmas in continuing the sanctioning of this method, as suicide is generally forbidden in Islam except for under exceptional circumstances, the Hamas movement felt compelled to adopt suicide bombings in 1994 as a means of last resort in order to sabotage the Israeli-Palestinian peace process.[59] They believed that its actual implementation on the ground would severely threaten Hamas' revolutionary existence. The tactic of suicide bombing was also used to take revenge against its "Zionist enemy" for the Hebron attack. While few terrorist groups adopt large-scale campaigns of suicide missions, the religious terrorist utilizes the traditional methods of assassination, kidnappings, hijackings, and bombings in a skillful combination in alignment with the current political context on the local, regional, and international level. Despite the growth and array of religious terrorist groups with diverse demands and grievances, they are all united not only in the level and intensity of violence used, but also in the role played by religious symbolism in selecting the targets and the timing of the violence itself.

Many of these terrorist groups are compelled to undertake operations with a distinct political agenda for organizational reasons to release imprisoned members or eliminating opponents. Nonetheless, the targets are almost always symbolic and carefully selected to cause maximum psychological trauma to the enemy and to boost the religious credentials of the terrorist group among their own followers. This is clearly evident from the selection by Muslim terrorists of western embassies, airlines, diplomats and tourists abroad as symbolically striking at the heart of their oppressors. This was evident in the selection of major New York City landmarks by Sheikh Rahman's followers or the multiple attacks by the Hizb'allah against U.S. diplomatic and military facilities.[60] In many instances, these groups have adopted a multi-pronged approach of using terrorism. For example, in Algeria the FIS has targeted foreign tourists, businessmen and diplomats, as well as Algerian officials and other Algerians who engage in un-Islamic behaviour (e.g unveiled women or any form of western culture). At the same time, it engages in the re-Islamization of society from below and simultaneously wages a war of attrition on French soil against symbolic civilian and official targets. In other cases, religious terrorists have used powerful symbolism to provoke deliberate reactions by the enemy, such as Dal Khalsa's severing of cows' heads outside two Hindu temples in Amritsar, which provoked massive disturbances between the Sikhs and the Hindus in April 1982.[61] This type of symbolism is also seen in the 1969 arson attack on the al-Aqsa mosque in East Jerusalem by a Jewish extremist and the 1982 plan by Jewish fanatics to blow up Temple Mount in order to spark a cataclysmic war between Muslims and Jews.[62]

Finally, the timing of the violence by religious terrorists is carefully selected to coincide with their own theological requirements or to desecrate their enemies' religious holidays and sacred moments. For example, the 1995 bombing of the Alfred P. Murrah Federal Building in Oklahoma by white supremacists was reportedly scripted after *The Turner Diaries*, but also timed to "commemorate the second anniversary of FBI's assault on the Branch Davidian's Waco, Texas compound; [and] to mark the date 220 years before when the American revolution began at Lexington and Concord."[63] Similarly, the symbolism of the timing of religious violence was also evident in the Algerian GIA's decision to hijacking an Air France plane during Christmas after the killing of two Catholic priests, or the cycle of violence by Hamas' suicide bombings against Israel, occuring in February 1996, on the second commemoration of the Hebron massacre.

Conclusions

This article has sought to demonstrate that, contrary to popular belief, the nature and scope of religious terrorism is anything but disorganised or random but rather driven by an inner logic common among diverse groups and faiths who use political violence to further their sacred causes. The resort to terrorism by religious imperative is also not a new phenomenon, but rather deeply embedded in the history and evolution of the faiths. Religions have gradually served to define the causes and the enemies as well as the means, methods and timing of the violence itself. As such, the virtual explosion of religious terrorism in recent times is part and parcel of a gradual process of what can be likened to neo-colonial liberation struggles. This process has trapped religious faiths within meaningless geographical and political boundaries and constraints, and has been accelerated by grand shifts in the global political, economic, military and socio-cultural setting, compounded by difficult local indigenous conditions for the believers. The uncertainty and unpredictability in the present environment as the world searches for a new world order, amidst an increasingly complex global environment with ethnic and nationalist conflicts, provide many religious terrorist groups with the opportunity and the ammunition to shape history according to their divine duty, cause, and mandate while it indicates for others that the end of time itself is near. As such, it is imperative to move away from treating this new religious force in global politics as a monolithic entity but rather seek to understand the inner logic of these individual groups and the mechanisms that produce terrorism in order to undermine their breeding ground and strength, as they are here to stay. At present it is doubtful that the United States or any western government is adequately prepared to meet this challenge.

Notes

1. The Kach movement was founded in 1971 by the ultra-orthodox American Rabbi Meir Kahane when he emigrated to Israel. The group calls for the establishment of a theocratic state in Eretz (Greater) Israel and the forced expulsion of Arabs. For a useful overview see Raphael Cohen-Almagor, "Vigilant Jewish Fundamentalism: From the JDL to Kach (or 'Shalom Jews, Shalom Dogs'), *Terrorism and Political Violence*, 4, No.1 (Spring 1992): pp.44–66; and Ehud Sprintzak, *The Ascendance of Israel's Radical Right* (New York: Oxford University Press, 1991).
2. "The Impossible Decision," *The Economist*, 11–17 November 1995, p.25.
3. For a discussion of Goldstein's decision to carry out the attack during Purim, see Sue Fiskhoff, "Gentle, Kind and Full of Religious Fervor," *Jerusalem Post*, 27 February 1994; and Chris Hedges and Joel Greenberg, "West Bank Massacre: Before Killing, a Final Prayer and a Final Taunt," *New York Times*, 28 February 1994, p. A1.
4. One of Goldstein's rabbinical mentors, Rabbi Dov Li'or, described him in compassionate terms as a man "who could no longer take the humiliation and the disgrace. Everything he did was in honor of Israel and for the glory of God," in *Yediot Aharanot*, 18 March 1994. Also see: Richard Z. Chesnoff, "It Is a Struggle for Survival," *U.S. News & World Report*, 14 March 1994.
5. Charles Krauthammer, "Deathly Double Standard," *Jerusalem Post*, 6 March 1994.
6. Prior to Rabin's assassination, Yigal Amir had tried two previous times. For a very useful biography of the assassin, see John Kifner, "A Son of Israel: Rabin's Assassin," *New York Times*, 19 November 1995; *idem.*, "Israelis Investigate Far Right; May Crack Down on Speech," *New York Times*, 8 November 1995. One of these traditional exemptions for killing is Din Rodef, or Law of the Pursuer. The rule was first set forth in the 12th century by the great Moses Maimonides, a Spanish Jewish scholar. Going beyond the principle of self-defense, it states that even a witness to the act of someone's trying to kill another is allowed to kill the potential assassin. For Yigal Amir's use of the principle as a defense for killing Rabin, see Raine Marcus, "Amir: I Wanted to Murder Rabin," *Jerusalem Post*, 16 March 1996.
7. As aptly observed by David C. Rapoport in his seminal work, the words "zealot," "assassin" and "thug" all derive from historic fanatic movements within, respectively, Judaism, Islam and Hinduism, respectively. See Bruce Hoffman, *"Holy Terror": The Implications of Terrorism Motivated by a Religious Imperative* (Santa Monica: RAND, 1993) pp. 1–2; and David C.

Rapoport, "Fear and Trembling: Terrorism in Three Religious Traditions," *American Political Science Review*, 78, no. 3 (September 1984) pp. 668–72. For a useful historical overview, see David C. Rapoport, "Why Does Religious Messianism Produce Terror?" in *Contemporary Research on Terrorism*, ed. Paul Wilkinson and A.M. Stewart, (Aberdeen: Aberdeen University Press, 1987) pp. 72–88.

8. The attack on the Tokyo subway was the first recorded instance of a terrorist group committing mass murder with a weapon of mass destruction. The Aum Shinrikyou religious cult was established in 1987 by Shoko Ashara, a nearly blind acupuncturist and yoga master, and is composed of a synthesized mixture of Buddhist and Hindu theology. For a useful brief biographical sketch of Ashara, see James Walsh, "Shoko Asahara: The Making of a Messiah," *Time*, 3 April 1995. The sarin nerve gas attack on Tokyo's subway killed 8 and injured over 5,500. Also see Martin Wollacott, "The Whiff of Terror," *The Guardian*, 21 March 1995.

9. For a useful overview of al-Jama'a al-Islamiyya and its activities in Egypt, see Barry Rubin, *Islamic Fundamentalism in Egyptian Politics* (London: Macmillan 1990).

10. See Stephen Robinson, "The American Fundamentalist," *Daily Telegraph*, 24 April 1995.

11. For a very comprehensive discussion, see Mark Juergensmeyer, ed. "Violence and the Sacred in the Modern World," *Terrorism and Political Violence*, 3, no. 3 (Autumn 1991).

12. Bruce Hoffman (1993), p. 2. The year 1968 is widely recognized as the point of origin for modern international terrorism. It was the beginning of an explosion of hijackings from Cuba to the United States, as well as attacks against Israeli and Western airlines by various Palestinian groups. Also see Barry James, "Religious Fanaticism Fuels Terrorism," *International Herald Tribune*, 31 October 1995, p. 3.

13. See Professor Yonah Alexander, "Algerian Terrorism: Some National, Regional and Global Perspectives," Prepared statement by before the House Committee on International Relations, Subcommittee on Africa, *Federal News Service*, 11 October 1995. This figure should be compared with 8,339 acts of international terrorism during the period 1970 to 1994 with 3,105 incidents occuring after 1988, see RAND-St. Andrews, *Chronology of International Terrorism* (St Andrews: Centre for the Study of Terrorism and Political Violence, University of St. Andrews, March 1996).

14. The Dashmesh (meaning "10th") organization was named after the Sikhs' last guru, Gobind Singh, who, in the eighteenth century, transformed the Sikh community into a warrior class by justifying force when necessary. Both the Dashmesh and the Sikh Dal Khalsa advocate the establishment of an independent Khalistan.

15. The emergence of ethnic-religious conflict over conventional inter-state warfare was illuminated by a 1994 report by the United Nations Development Programme in which only 3 out of a total of 82 conflicts worldwide were between states. See Roger Williamson, "The Contemporary Face of Conflict—Class, Colour, Culture and Confession," in *Jane's Intelligence Review Yearbook—The World in Conflict 94/95* (London: Jane's Information Group, 1995) pp. 8–10. Also see Julia Preston, "Boutros Ghali: 'Ethnic Conflict' Imperils Security," *Washington Post*, 9 November 1993, p. 13. Also see Hans Binnendijk & Patrick Clawson, eds., *Strategic Assessment 1995: U.S. Security Challenges in Transition* (Washington: National Defense University Press, 1995); and Martin Kramer, "Islam & the West (including Manhattan)," *Commentary* (October 1993) pp. 33–37.

16. For the wider debate of the religious resurgence, see Scott Thomas, "The Global Resurgence of Religion and the Study of World Politics," *Millenium*, 24, no. 2 (Summer 1995) and Peter Beyer, *Religion and Globalization* (London: Sage, 1994).

17. As observed: At a time when no one knows precisely what form the future may take, the strength of fundamentalism lies in its ability to promise radical change without having to specify its outlines—since God is claimed as its guarantor," in Mahmoud Hussein, "Behind the Veil of Fundamentalism," *UNESCO Courier*, December 1994, p. 25. Also as stated by an ideologue of Jewish extremist group, Kahane Chai: "We are accountable only to our Creator, to He who chose us for our mission in history," in Amir Taheri, "Comentary: The Ideology of Jewish extremism," *Arab News*, 12 March 1994.

18. Robin Wright, "Global Upheaval Seen as Engine for Radical Groups," *Los Angeles Times*, 6 November 1995.

19. "Fundamentalism Unlimited," *The Economist*, 27 March 1993, p. 67; and Hussein, p. 25.

20. Muhammad Hussein Fadlallah, "To Avoid a World War of Terror," *Washington Post*, 4 June 1986. As reiterated by Sheikh Fadallah: "We are not preachers of violence. Jihad in Islam is a defensive movement against those who impose violence." Laura Marlowe, "A Fiery Cleric's Defense of Jihad," *Time*, 15 January 1996. For further elaboration on this by Sheikh Fadlallah, see *al-Majallah*, 1–7 October 1986.

21. This is often seen in the Sikh slogan: "The Panth [religion] is in danger." See Paul Wallace, "The Siks as a 'Minority' in a Sikh Majority State in India," *Asian Survey*, 26, no. 3 (March 1986) p. 363.

22. Laurent Belsie, "At a Sik Temple, Opinions Reflect Conflicting Religious Traditions," *Christian Science Monitor*, 11 November 1984. For a detailed discussion of the use of violence, see Sohan Singh Sahota, *The Destiny of the Sikhs* (Chandigarh: Modern Publishers, 1970).

23. Bruce Hoffman, "American Right-Wing Terrorism," *Jane's Intelligence Review*, 7, no. 7 (July 1995) pp. 329–30.

24. See John Kifner, "Shiite Radicals: Rising Wrath Jars the Mideast," *New York Times*, 22 March 1987.

25. This theme is developed by David Rapoport, "Comparing Militant Fundamentalist Movements," in *Fundamentalism and the State*, ed. Martin E. Marty and R. Scott Appleby (Chicago: The University of Chicago Press, 1993).

26. See Maha Azzam, "Islamism, the Peace Process and Regional Security," *RUSI Journal* (October 1995) pp. 13–16.

27. Kifner, 19 November 1995.

28. *Al-Hayah*, 4 May 1994. Similarly, according to Hamas' manifesto: "Palestine is a Holy Muslim asset to the end of time, so that no man has the right to negotiate about her or to relinquish [any part of] her," in Amos Oz, "Israel's Far Right Collaborates With Hamas in Thwarting Peace," *The Times*, 11 April 1995.

29. For a useful insight into the dynamics of cults, see Richardo Delgado, "Limits to Proselytizing," *Society* (March/April 1980) pp. 25–33; Margaret Thaler Singer, "Coming of the Cults," *Psychology Today* (January 1979) pp. 73–82.

30. See Robin Wright, "U.S. Struggles to Deal With Global Islamic Resurgence," *Los Angeles Times*, 26 January 1992.

31. For a useful overview, see Pranay Gupte, "The Punjab: Torn by Terror," *New York Times*, 9 August 1985; Vijah Singh, "Les sikhs, une Secte Traditionnelle Saisié par la Terrorisme," *Liberation*, 1 November 1984.

32. For example, this uncompromising position is clearly evident by Hamas' own charter in Article 11: "The land of Palestine is an Islamic trust (*waqf*) to be maintained by succeeding generations of Muslims until the Day of Judgement. In this responsibility, or any part of it, no negligence will be tolerated, and no surrender." *Mithaq Harakat al-Muqawamah al-Islamiyah* (Hamas, 1988).

33. See Michael Kelly, "In Gaza, Peace Meets Pathology," *New York Times*, 29 November 1994, p. 56.

34. See Michael Parks, "Ready to Kill, Ready to Die, Hamas Zealots Thwart Peace," *Los Angeles Times*, 25 October 1994, p. A10. For interesting insight into mentality of suicide bombers, see Joel Greenberg, "Palestinian 'Martyrs,' All Too Willing," *New York Times*, 25 January 1995; and *Ma'ariv*, 30 December 1994, p. 8. For an example of this martyrology with an extensive list of Izzeldin al-Qassem martyrs since 1990, see *Filastin al'Muslimah*, November 1994, p. 14.

35. In a statement in Israeli court, Amir provided the justification: "When you kill in war, it is an act that is allowed," in Russell Watson, "Blame Time," *Newsweek*, 20 November 1995. As explained by Amir, "I did not commit the act to stop the peace process because there is no concept as the peace process, it is a process of war," *Mideast Mirror*, 6 November 1995.

36. For a useful overview of the incident, see Jihad B. Khazen, *The Sadat Assassination: Background and Implications* (Washington: Georgetown University's Center for Contemporary Arab Studies, 1981); and Dilip Hiro, "Faces of Fundamentalism," *The Middle East*, May 1988, pp. 11–12.

37. See Robert Fisk, "'Party of God' develops its own political style," *Irish Times*, 9 February 1995.

38. For a very interesting discussion of this phenomenon, see Gilles Keppel, *The Revenge of God: The Resurgence of Islam, Christianity and Judaism in the Modern World* (London: Polity Press, 1995).

39. For a useful exposition of concealment in Shi'ism, refer to lecture by Prof. Etan Kohlberg, Hebrew University, delivered at the Tel Aviv University (Tel Aviv, Israel: 23 May 1993).

40. See Maskit Burgin, A. Merari, and A Kurz, eds., *Foreign Hostages in Lebanon*, JCSS Memorandum, no. 25, August 1988 (Tel Aviv: Tel Aviv University, 1988).

41. Bruce Hoffman (1993), p. 3.

42. See Bruce Hoffman, "'Holy Terror': The Implications of Terrorism Motivated by a Religious Imperative," in *The First International Workshop on Low Intensity Conflict*, ed. A. Woodcock et al. (Stockholm: Royal Society of Naval Sciences, 1995) p. 43.

43. See Andrew Pollack, "Cult's Prophesy of Disaster Draws Precautions in Tokyo," *New York Times*, 15 April 1995; and Andrew Brown, "Waiting for the End of the World," *The Independent*, 24 March 1995.

44. For example, a survey of imprisoned members of the Egyptian group al-Takfir wal-Hijra (Repentance and Holy Flight) revealed that the average member was in his 20s or early 30s, a university student or recent graduate; had better than average marks in school work; felt intensily about causes but was intolerant of conflicting opinions; and a willingness to employ violence if necessary. See Ray Vicker, "Islam on the March," *Wall Street Journal*, 12 February 1980. For a similar profile of Sikh terrorists, see Carl H. Haeger, "Sikh Terrorism in the Struggle for Khalistan," *Terrorism*, 14 (1991) p. 227. Also see Hala Mustafa, "The Islamic Movements Under Mubarak," in *The Islamist Dilemma: The Political Role of Islamic Movements in the Contemporary Arab World*, ed. Laura Guazzone (Reading: Ithaca Press, 1995) p. 173.

45. For example, see Paul Wilkinson, "Hamas: An Assessment," Jane's Intelligence Review (July 1993) pp. 313–14; and Ziad Abu-Amr, *Islamic Fundamentalism in the West Bank and Gaza* (Indianapolis: Indiana University Press, 1994).

46. As demonstrated in the case of Egypt, "Jihad and other movements were born in [former Presidents] Nasser's and Sadat's prisons," see Robin Wright, "Holy Wars': The Ominous Side of Religion in Politics," *Christian Science Monitor*, 12 November 1987, p. 21. Also see Mustafa, p. 174.

47. Richard Hrair Dekmejian, *Islam in Revolution: Fundamentalism in the Arab World* (Syracuse: Syracuse University Press, 1985) p. 61–62.

48. George Nader, *Middle East Insight* (June-July 1985).

49. See Anthony Davis, "Foreign Combatants in Afghanistan," *Jane's Intelligence Review* (July 1994) p. 327. Also see Raymond Whitaker, "Afghani Veterans Fan Out to Spread the Word—and Terror," *The Independent*, 16 April 1995.

50. For a detailed discussion of this plan, see Ehud Sprinzak, "Three Models of Religious Violence: The Case of Jewish Fundamentalism in Israel," in Marty and Appleby (1993), pp. 475–76. As stated by Sprinzak: "There has been no act by the Jewish underground which did not have a rabbinical backing." *Yediot Aharanot*, 18 March 1994.

51. See Youssef M. Ibrahim, "Muslim Edicts Take on New Force," *New York Times*, 12 February 1995; and Philip Jacobson, "Muhammad's Ally," *The Times Magazine*, 4 December 1993.

52. For example, see *Ma'ariv*, 28 February 1996; Ze'ev Chafets, "Israel's Quiet Anger," *New York Times*, 7 November 1995.

53. As revealed by Hizb'allah manifesto in 1985, "Imam Khomeini, the leader, has repeatedly stressed that America is the reason for all our catastrophes and the source of all malice. By fighting it, we are only exercising our legitimate right to defend our Islam and the dignity of our nation." See Hizb'allah's manifesto reprinted in Augustus Richard Norton, *Amal and the Shi'a: Struggle for the Soul of Lebanon* (Austin: University of Texas Press, 1987) pp. 167–87. See also Martin Kramer, "The Jihad Against the Jews," *Commentary* (October 1994) pp. 38–42.

54. For example, see David Wurmser, "The Rise and Fall of the Arab World," *Strategic Review* (Summer 1993) pp. 33–46.

55. See Fred Halliday, *Islam and the Myth of Confrontation* (London: I.B. Tauris, 1995).

56. For example see Alvin H. Bernstein, "Iran's Low-Intensity War Against the United States," *Orbis*, 30 (Spring 1986) pp. 149–67; and Sean K. Anderson, "Iran: Terrorism and Islamic Fundamentalism," in *Low-Intensity Conflict: Old Threats in a New World*, ed. Edwin G. Corr and Stephen Sloan (Oxford: Westview Press, 1992) pp. 173–95.

57. See Magnus Ranstorp, *Hizballah in Lebanon: The Politics of the Western Hostage-Crisis* (London: Macmillan, 1996).

58. See Bruce Hoffman (1993).

59. See Martin Kramer, "The Moral Logic of Hizbollah," in *Origins of Terrorism: Psychologies, Ideologies, Theologies, States of Mind*, ed. Walter Reich (Cambridge: Cambridge University Press, 1990) pp. 131–57.

60. See Robert M. Jenkins, "The Islamic Connection," *Security Management* (July 1993) pp. 25–30.

61. See Guy Arnold et al, eds., *Revolutionary & Dissident Movements: An International Guide* (Harlow: Longman Group, 1991) p. 141.

62. See Mir Zohair Husain, *Global Islamic Politics* (New York: Harper Collins, 1995) pp. 186–200.

63. Bruce Hoffman, "Intelligence and Terrorism: Emerging Threats and New Security Challenges in the Post–Cold War Era," *Intelligence and National Security*, 11, no. 3 (April 1996) p. 214. For a broader discussion of millenarian terrorism, see Michael Barkun, ed. *Millennialism and Violence* (London: Frank Cass, 1996).

4.2   Mark Juergensmeyer, 1988

The Logic of Religious Violence

Mark Juergensmeyer is a professor at the University of California, Santa Barbara, and also serves as director of the Global & International Studies Program and chair of the Global Peace & Security Program. He was a Fulbright fellow (India), a senior researcher at the American Institute of Indian Studies (India), and a fellow at the Woodrow Wilson International Center for Scholars (Smithsonian Institution). He is author of *The New Cold War? Religious Nationalism Confronts the Secular State* (1993) and *Terror in the Mind of God: The Global Rise of Religious Violence* (2001).

> When the struggle reaches the decisive phase may I die fighting in its midst.
> —Jamail Singh Bhindranwale

In the mid-1970s, when militant young Sikhs first began to attack the Nirankaris—members of a small religious community perceived as being anti-Sikh—few observers could have predicted that that violence would escalate into the savagery that seized the Punjab in the 1980s. The Sikhs as a community were too well off economically, too well educated, it seemed, to be a party to random acts of terror. Yet it is true that militant encounters have often played a part in Sikh history, and in the mid-1960s a radical movement very much like that of the 1980s stormed through the Punjab. The charismatic leader at that time was Sant Fateh Singh, who went on a well-publicized fast and threatened to immolate himself on the roof of the Golden Temple's Akali Takht unless the government made concessions that would lead to the establishment of a Sikh-majority state. The Indian government, captained by Prime Minister Indira Gandhi, conceded, and the old Punjab state was carved in two to produce a Hindu-majority Haryana and a new Punjab. It was smaller than the previous one, and contained enough Sikh-dominated areas to give it a slim Sikh majority.

The violence of this decade, however, seems very different from what one saw in the 1960s.[1] For one thing, the attacks themselves have been more vicious. Often they have involved Sikhs and Hindus indiscriminately, and many innocent bystanders have been targeted along with politically active persons. The new Sikh leader, Jamail Singh Bhindranwale, was stranger—more intense and more strident—than Fateh Singh was, and the goals of Bhindranwale and his allies were more diffuse. Government officials who were trying to negotiate a settlement were never quite certain what their demands were. In fact there was no clear consensus among the activists themselves as to what they wanted, and the items on their lists of demands would shift from time to time. In 1984, shortly before she gave the command for the Indian Army to invade the Golden Temple, an exasperated Indira Gandhi itemized everything she had done to meet the Sikh demands and asked, 'What more can any government do?'[2]

It was a question that frustrated many observers outside the government as well, a good many moderate Sikhs among them. But frustration led to action, and those actions made things worse. The Indian army's brutal assault on the Golden Temple in June 1984, and the heartless massacre of Sikhs by Hindus in Delhi and elsewhere after the assassination of Mrs. Gandhi in November of that year caused the violence to escalate. Still, it is fair to say that quite a bit of bloodshed originated on the Sikh side of the ledger, and within the Sikh community anti-government violence achieved a religious respectability that begs to be explained.

The Rational Explanations

The explanations one hears most frequently place the blame for Sikh violence on political, economic and social factors, and each of these approaches is compelling. The political explanation, for instance, focuses on the weakness of the Sikh political party, the Akali Dal, and its inability to secure a consistent plurality in the Punjab legislature. This is no wonder, since the Sikhs command a bare 51 per cent majority of the post-1966 Punjab. Moreover, the Muslims, who comprised the Punjab's other non-Hindu religious community before 1948, were awarded a nation of their own at the time of India's independence, so it is understandable that many Sikhs would continue to long for greater political power, and even yearn for their own Pakistan.[3]

The economic explanation for Sikh unrest is largely a matter of seeing the achievements of the Sikhs in relation to what they feel their efforts should warrant, rather than to what others in India have received. Compared with almost every other region of India, the Punjab is fairly well-to-do. Yet Sikhs complain, with some justification, that for that very reason they have been deprived of their fair share: resources from the Punjab have been siphoned off to other parts of the nation.[4] Agricultural prices, for example, are held stable in India in part because the government maintains a ceiling on the prices that farmers in rich agricultural areas like the Punjab are permitted to exact. In addition some Sikhs claim that industrial growth has been hampered in the Punjab as the government has encouraged growth in other parts of India, and that the Punjab's agricultural lifeblood—water for irrigation from Punjabi rivers—has been diverted to farming areas in other states.

The social explanation for Sikh discontent is just as straightforward: the Sikhs are a minority community in India, and their separate identity within the Indian family is in danger. Since the religious ideas on which Sikhism is based grew out of the nexus of medieval Hinduism, Sikhs fear they could be reabsorbed into the amorphous cultural mass that is Hinduism and disappear as a distinct religious community.[5] The possibility is real: Sikhism almost vanished in the latter part of the nineteenth century. But in this century secularism is as much a threat as Hinduism, and like fundamentalist movements in many other parts of the world, Sikh traditionalists have seen the secular government as the perpetrator of a dangerous anti-religious ideology that threatens the existence of such traditional religious communities as their own. In the perception of some Sikhs, these two threats—the religious and the secular—have recently combined forces as the Hindu right has exercised increasing political power and Mrs Gandhi's Congress Party has allegedly pandered to its interests.[6]

There is nothing wrong with these political, economic and social explanations of Sikh unrest. Each is persuasive in its own sphere, and together they help us understand why the Sikhs as a community have been unhappy. But they do not help us understand the piety with which a few Sikhs have justified their bloody acts or the passion with which so many of them have condoned them—even the random acts of destruction associated with terrorism. Nor are they the sort of explanations one hears from Sikhs who are most closely involved in the struggle. The socioeconomic and political explanations usually come from observers outside the Sikh community or from those inside it who are least sympathetic to the militant protesters. The point of view of the activists is different. Their frame of reference is more grand: their explanations of the conflict and its causes achieve almost mythical dimensions. To understand this point of view we have to turn to their own words and see what they reveal about the radicals' perception of the world about them.

The Religious Rhetoric of Sikh Violence

To understand the militant Sikh position, I have chosen to focus on the speeches of Jamail Singh Bhindranwale, the man who was without dispute the most visible and charismatic of this generation's militant leaders.[7] He was also the most revered—or despised, depending on one's point of view. During his lifetime he was called a *sant*, a holy man, and a few Sikhs have been bold enough to proclaim him the eleventh *guru*, and thus challenge the traditional Sikh belief that the line of ten gurus ended with Gobind Singh in the early eighteenth century.

Jamail Singh was born in 1947 at the village Rodey near the town of Moga. He was the youngest son in a poor family of farmers from the Jat caste, and when he was 18 years old his father handed him over for religious training to the head of a Sikh center known as the Damdani Taksal. The leader came from the village Bhindran and was therefore known as Bhindranwale, and after his death, when the mantle of leadership fell on young Jamail Singh, he assumed his mentor's name. The young leader took his duties seriously and gained a certain amount of fame as a preacher. He was a stern one at that: Jamail became famous for castigating the easy-living, easy-drinking customs of Sikh villagers, especially those who clipped their beards and adopted modern ways. He carried weapons, and on 13 April 1978, in a bloody confrontation in Amritsar with members of the renegade Nirankaris religious movement, he showed that he was not afraid to use them. This episode was followed by an attack from Nirankaris that killed a number of Bhindranwale's followers, and further counter-attacks ensued.[8] Thus began the bloody career of a man who was trained to live a calm and spiritual life of religious devotion.

Although he was initially at the fringes of Sikh leadership, during the late 1970s Bhindranwale began to be taken seriously within Akali circles because of his growing popularity among the masses.[9] He seemed to have been fixated on the Nirankaris: his fiery sermons condemned them as evil. He regarded them as a demonic force that endangered the very basis of the Sikh community, especially its commitment to the authority of the Sikh gurus. And in time he expanded his characterization of their demonic power to include those who protected them, including the secular government of Indira Gandhi.

Much of what Bhindranwale has to say in sermons of this period, however, might be heard in the sermons of methodist pastors in Iowa or in the homilies of clergies belonging to any religious tradition, anywhere on the globe. He calls for faith—faith in a time of trial—and for the spiritual discipline that accompanies it. In one sermon he rebukes the press and others who call him an extremist, and explains what sort of an extremist he is:

> One who takes the vows of faith and helps others take it; who reads the scriptures and helps others to do the same; who avoids liquor and drugs and helps others do likewise; who urges unity and cooperation; who preaches Hindu-Sikh unity and co-existence... who says: 'respect your scriptures, unite under the flag, stoutly support the community, and be attached to your Lord's throne and home'.[10]

Like many Protestant ministers, Bhindranwale prescribes piety as the answer to every need. 'You can't have courage without reading [the Sikh scriptures]', he admonishes his followers: 'Only the [scripture]-readers can suffer torture and be capable of feats of strength'.[11] He is especially harsh on backsliders in the faith. Those who cut their beards are targets of his wrath: 'Do you think you resemble the image of Guru Gobind Singh?' he asks them.[12] But then he reassures the bulk of his followers. Because of their persistence in the faith, he tells them, 'the Guru will give you strength', adding that 'righteousness is with you'.[13] They will need all the strength and courage they can get, Bhindranwale explains, because their faith is under attack.[14]

Lying only slightly beneath the surface of this language is the notion of a great struggle that Bhindranwale thinks is taking place. On the personal level it is the tension between faith and the lack of faith; on the cosmic level it is the battle between truth and evil. Often his rhetoric is vague about who the enemy really is. 'In order to destroy religion', Bhindranwale informs his congregation, 'on all sides and in many forms mean tactics have been initiated'.[15] But rather than wasting effort in explaining who these forces are and why they would want to destroy religion, Bhindranwale dwells instead on what should be the response: a willingness to fight and defend the faith—if necessary, to the end.

> Unless you are prepared to die, sacrificing your own life, you cannot be a free people.... If you start thinking in terms of service to your community then you will be on the right path and you will readily sacrifice yourself. If you have faith in the Guru no power on earth can enslave you. The Sikh faith is to pray to God, take one's vows before the Guru Granth Sahib [scriptures] and then act careless of consequences to oneself.[16]

At other times Bhindranwale cites what appear to be specific attacks on Sikhism, but again the perpetrators are not sharply defined; they remain a vague, shadowy force of evil. 'The Guru Granth [scripture] has been buried in cowdung and thrown on the roadside', Bhindranwale informs his followers. 'That is your Father, your Guru, that they treat so.'[17] On another occasion he urges his followers to 'seek justice against those who have dishonored our sisters, drunk the blood of innocent persons, and insulted Satguru Granth Sahib'.[18] But the 'they' and the 'those' are not identified.

Occasionally, however, the enemy is more clearly specified: they are 'Hindus', 'the government', 'the press', the Prime Minister—whom he calls that 'lady born to a house of Brahmins'[19]—and perhaps most frequently Sikhs themselves who have fallen from the path. This somewhat rambling passage indicates these diverse enemies and the passionate hatred that Bhindranwale feels towards them:

> I cannot really understand how it is that, in the presence of Sikhs, Hindus are able to insult the [scriptures]. I don't know how these Sikhs were born to mothers and why they were not born to animals: to cats and to bitches.... Whoever insults the Guru Granth Sahib should be killed then and there.... Some youths complain that if they do such deeds then nobody harbours them. Well, no place is holier than this one [the Golden Temple].... I will take care of the man who comes to me after lynching the murderer of the Guru Granth Sahib; I'll fight for his case. What else do you want? That things have come to such a pass is in any event all your own weakness.... The man whose sister is molested and does nothing about it, whose Guru is insulted and who keeps on talking and doing nothing, has he got any right to be known as the son of the Guru? Just think for yourselves![20]

And in a similar vein:

> Talk is not enough against injustice. We have to act. Here you raise your swords but tomorrow you may wipe the dust from the sandals of sister Indira.... We have the right to be Sikhs.... The dearest thing to any Sikh should be the honor of the Guru.... Those foes—the government and Hindus—are not dangerous. Rather one has to be wary of those who profess Sikhism yet do not behave as Sikhs.[21]

As important as Bhindranwale feels the immediate struggle is, he reminds his followers that the Sikh tradition has always been filled with conflict, and that the current battles are simply the most recent chapters in a long ongoing war with the enemies of the faith. The foes of today are connected with those from the legendary past. Indira Gandhi, for instance, is implicitly compared with the Moghul emperors: 'The rulers [the Congress party leaders] should keep in mind that in the past many like them did try in vain to annihilate the Gurus.'[22] In other speeches, Bhindranwale frequently looks to the past for guidance in dealing with current situations. When Sikhs who had sided with government policies come to him for forgiveness, for instance, he refuses. 'I asked that man', explains Bhindranwale, 'had he ever read a page of our history? Was the man who tortured Guru Arjun pardoned?'[23]

Occasionally Bhindranwale refers to some of the specific political, economic and social demands made by more moderate Sikh leaders. He supports these demands, but they are not his primary concern. In fact, the targets of these demands are often characterized simply as 'injustices', illustrations of the fact that the Sikh community is abused and under attack.[24] Since the larger struggle is the more important matter, these specific difficulties are of no great concern to Bhindranwale; they change from time to time. And it is of no use to win on one or two points and fail on others. Compromise is impossible; only complete victory will signal that the tide has turned. For that reason Bhindranwale scolds the Akali leaders for seeking a compromise settlement of the political demands made by Sikh leaders at Anandpur Sahib in 1973. 'Either full implementation of the Anandpur Sahib resolution', Bhindranwale demands, 'or their heads'.[25]

In a sense, then, Bhindranwale feels that individual Sikh demands can never really be met, because the ultimate struggle of which they are a part is much greater than the contestation between political parties and factional points of view. It is a vast cosmic struggle, and only such an awesome encounter is capable of giving profound meaning to the motivations of those who fight for Sikh causes. Such people are not just fighting for water rights and political boundaries, they are fighting for truth itself.

Clearly the religious language of Sikh militants like Bhindranwale is the language of ultimate struggle. But two related matters are not so obvious: why is this language attached to the more mundane issues of human politics and economics? And why is it linked with violent acts?

A Pause for Definitions: Violence and Religion

Before we turn to these questions, however, it might be useful to pause for a moment for definitions. Since I want to look at issues having to do with the general relation between violence and religion, not merely those that affect the Sikhs, it might be useful if I describe what I mean by these terms.

I will restrict my use of the word violence to actions that are aimed at taking human life—that intend to, and do, kill. Moreover, I mean especially abnormal, illegal, shocking acts of destruction. All acts of killing are violent, of course, but warfare and capital punishment have an aura of normalcy and do not violate our sensibilities in the same way as actions that seem deliberately designed to elicit feelings of revulsion and anger from those who witness them.[26] By speaking of violence in this restricted way, I mean to highlight the characteristics that we usually associate with terrorist acts.

The term religion is more difficult to define. I have been impressed with the recent attempts of several sociologists to find a definition that is not specific to any cultural region or historical period, and is appropriate for thinking about the phenomenon in modern as well as traditional societies. Clifford Geertz, for instance, sees religion as the effort to integrate everyday reality into a pattern of coherence that takes shape on a deeper level.[27] Robert Bellah also thinks of religion as the attempt to reach beyond ordinary reality in the 'risk of faith' that allows people to act 'in the face of uncertainty and unpredictability'.[28] Peter Berger specifies that such faith is an affirmation of the sacred, which acts as a doorway to a different kind of reality.[29] Louis Dupré prefers to avoid the term 'sacred', but integrates elements of both Berger's and Bellah's definition in his description of religion as 'a commitment to the transcendent as to *another* reality'.[30]

What all of these definitions have in common is their emphasis on a certain kind of experience that people share with others in particular communities. It is an experience of another reality, or of a deeper stratum of the reality that we know in everyday life. As [Emile] Durkheim, whose thought is fundamental to each of these thinkers, was adamant in observing, religion has a more encompassing force than can be suggested by any dichotomization of the sacred and the profane. To Durkheim, the religious point of view includes both the notion that there is such a dichotomy, and that the sacred aspects of it will always, ultimately, reign supreme.[31] Summarizing Durkheim's and the others' definitions of religion, I think it might be described as the perception that there is a tension between reality as it appears and as it really is (or has been, or will be).

This definition helps us think of religion as the subjective experience of those who use religious language, and in fact it is easier with this definition to speak of religious language, or a religious way of looking at the world, than to speak of religion in a more reified sense.[32] When we talk of the various 'religions', then, we mean the communities that have a tradition of sharing a particular religious point of view, a world view in which there is an essential conflict between appearance and a deeper reality. There is the hint, in this definition, that the deeper reality holds a degree of permanence and order quite unobtainable by ordinary means, as religious people affirm. The conflict between the two is what religion is about: religious language contains images both of grave disorder and tranquil order, and often holds out the hope that despite appearances to the contrary, order eventually will triumph, and disorder will be contained.

Why Does Religion Need Violence?

There is nothing in this definition that requires religion to be violent, but it does lead one to expect religious language to make sense of violence and to incorporate it in some way into the world view it expresses. Violence, after all, shocks one's sense of order and has the potential for causing the ultimate disorder in any person's life: physical destruction and death. Since religious language is about the tension between order and disorder, it is frequently about violence.

The symbols and mythology of Sikhism, for instance, are full of violence. The most common visual symbol of Sikhism is the two-edged sword (*khanda*), supported by two scabbards and surrounded by a circle. Sikhs often interpret the two edges of this sword as symbolizing spiritual and worldly foes,[33] and they say that a battle sword (*kirpan*) is included among the five objects that Sikhs are supposed to wear at all times to symbolize an awareness of these same enemies.[34] Unlike the Bible, the sacred scriptures of the Sikhs—known collectively as the *Guru Granth Sahib*—do not contain accounts of wars and savage acts, but the stories of the Sikhs' historical past are bloody indeed. In fact, these stories have taken on a canonical character within Sikhism, and they more vividly capture the imagination than the devotional and theological sentiments of the scriptures themselves. The calendar art so prominent in most Sikh homes portrays a mystical Guru Nanak, of course, but alongside him there are pictures of Sikh military heroes and scenes from great battles. Bloody images also leap from brightly-colored oil paintings in the Sikh Museum housed in the Golden Temple. There are as many depictions of martyrs in their wretched final moments as of victors radiant in conquest.

Because the violence is so prominent in Sikh art and legend, and because many symbols of the faith are martial, one might think that Sikhs as a people are more violent than their counterparts in other areas of India. But if one leaves aside the unrest of the past several years, I do not think this can be demonstrated. It would be convenient to say that the prestige of violent symbols in the Sikh religion has increased Sikhs' propensity for violent action, or that the Sikh religion is violent because Sikhs as a people are violent, but I do not think either of these arguments can be made very convincingly.

The fact is that the symbols and mythology of most religious traditions are filled with violent images, and their histories leave trails of blood. One wonders that familiarity can prevent Christians from being repulsed by the violent images portrayed by hymns such as 'Onward Christian Soldiers', 'The Old Rugged Cross', 'Washed in the Blood of the Lamb', and 'There is a Fountain Flowing with Blood'. Or perhaps familiarity is not the issue at all. The central symbol of Christianity is an execution device—a cross—from which, at least in the Roman tradition, the dying body still hangs. From a non-Christian point of view, the most sacred of Christian rituals, the eucharist, looks like ritual cannabalism, where the devout eat the flesh and drink the blood of their departed leader. At a certain level, in fact, this interpretation is accurate; yet few would argue that the violent acts perpetrated by Christians over the centuries are the result of their being subjected to such messages.

The ubiquity of violent images in religion and the fact that some of the most ancient religious practices involve the sacrificial slaughter of animals have led to speculation about why religion and violence are so intimately bound together. Some of these speculators are among the best known modern theorists, Karl Marx, for instance, saw religious symbols as the expression of real social oppression, and religious wars as the result of tension among economic classes.[35] Sigmund Freud saw in religious rituals vestiges of a primal oedipal act that when ritually reenacted provide a symbolic resolution of feelings of sexual and physical aggression.[36] More recently, Rene Girard has revived the Freudian thesis but given it a social rather than psychological coloration. Girard sees the violent images of religion as a symbolic displacement of violence from one's own communal fellowship to a scapegoat foe.[37]

What these thinkers have in common is that they see religious violence as a symptom of and symbol for something else: social hostility, in the case of Marx; sexual and physical aggression, in the case of Freud; social competition, in the case of Girard. They may be right: religion and other cultural forms may have been generated out of basic personal and social needs. Yet it seems to me that even without these explanations the internal logic of religion requires that religious symbols and myths express violent meanings.

Religion deals with the ultimate tension between order and disorder, and disorder is inherently violent, so it is understandable that the chaotic, dangerous character of life is represented in religious images. Of course, the religious promise is that order conquers chaos; so it is also understandable that the violence religion portrays is in some way limited or tamed. In Christianity, for example, the very normalcy with which the blood-filled hymns are sung and the eucharist is eaten indicates their domestication. In ritual, violence is symbolically transferred. The blood of the eucharistic wine is ingested by the supplicant and becomes part of living tissue; it brings new life. In song a similarly calming transformation occurs. For, as Christian theology explains, in Christ violence has been corralled. Christ died in order for death to be defeated, and his blood is that of the sacrificial lamb who atones for our sins so that we will not have to undergo a punishment as gruesome as his.

In the Sikh tradition violent images are also domesticated. The symbol of the two-edged sword has become an emblem to be worn on lockets and proudly emblazened on shops and garden gates. It is at the forefront of the worship center in Sikh *gurudwaras* where it is treated as reverently as Christians treat their own emblem of destruction, the cross. And the gory wounds of the martyrs bleed on in calendar art. As I have suggested, Sikh theologians and writers are no more hesitant to allegorize the meaning of such symbols and stories than their Christian counterparts. They point toward the war between good and evil that rages in each person's soul.

The symbols of violence in religion, therefore, are symbols of a violence conquered, or at least put in place, by the larger framework of order that religious language provides. But one must ask how these symbolic presentations of violence are related to real violence. One might think that they should prevent violent acts by allowing violent feelings to be channelled into the harmless dramas of ritual, yet we know that the opposite is sometimes the case. The violence of religion can be savagely real.

Why Does Violence Need Religion?

A reason often given to explain why religious symbols are associated with acts of real violence is that religion is exploited by violent people. This explanation, making religion the pure and innocent victim of the darker forces of human nature, is undoubtedly too easy; yet it contains some truth. Religion in fact is sometimes exploited, and it is important to understand why people who are engaged in potentially violent struggles do at times turn to the language of religion. In the case of the Sikhs, this means asking why the sort of people who were exercised over the economic, political and social issues explored at the beginning of this article turned to preachers like Bhindranwale for leadership.

One answer is that by sacralizing these concerns the political activists gave them an aura of legitimacy that they did not previously possess. The problem with this answer is that most of the concerns we mentioned—the inadequacy of Sikh political representation, for instance, and the inequity of agricultural prices—were perfectly legitimate, and did not need the additional moral weight of religion to give them respectability. And in fact, the people who were primarily occupied with these issues—Sikh businessmen and political leaders—were not early supporters of Bhindranwale. Even when they became drawn into his campaign, their relation with him remained ambivalent at best.

There was one political demand, however, that desperately needed all the legitimization that it could get. This was the demand for Khalistan, a separate Sikh nation. Separatist leaders such as Jagjit Singh Chauhan were greatly buoyed by such words of Bhindranwale as these:

> We are religiously separate. But why do we have to emphasize this? It is only because
> we are losing our identity. Out of selfish interests our Sikh leaders who have only the
> success of their farms and their industries at heart have started saying that there

is no difference between Sikh and Hindu. Hence the danger of assimilation has increased.[38]

When they say the Sikhs are not separate we'll demand separate identity—even if it demands sacrifice.[39]

Bhindranwale himself, interestingly, never came out in support of Khalistan. 'We are not in favor of Khalistan nor are we against it', he said, adding that 'we wish to live in India', but would settle for a separate state if the Sikhs did not receive what he regarded as their just respect.[40] Whatever his own reservations about the Khalistan issue, however, his appeal to sacrifice made his rhetoric attractive to the separatists. It also raised another, potentially more powerful aspect of the sacralization of political demands: the prospect that religion could give moral sanction to violence.

By identifying a temporal social struggle with the cosmic struggle of order and disorder, truth and evil, political actors are able to avail themselves of a way of thinking that justifies the use of violent means. Ordinarily only the state has the moral right to take life—for purposes either of military defense, police protection or punishment—and the codes of ethics established by religious traditions support this position. Virtually every religious tradition, including the Sikhs', applauds non-violence and proscribes the taking of human life.[41] The only exception to this rule is the one we have given: most ethical codes allow the state to kill for reasons of punishment and protection.[42]

Those who want moral sanction for their use of violence, and who do not have the approval of an officially recognized government, find it helpful to have access to a higher source: the meta-morality that religion provides. By elevating a temporal struggle to the level of the cosmic, they can bypass the usual moral restrictions on killing. If a battle of the spirit is thought to exist, then it is not ordinary morality but the rules of war that apply. It is interesting that the best-known incidents of religious violence throughout the contemporary world have occurred in places where there is difficulty in defining the character of a nation state. Palestine and Ireland are the most obvious examples, but the revolution in Iran also concerned itself with what the state should be like, and what elements of society should lead it. Religion provided the basis for a new national consensus and a new kind of leadership.

There are some aspects of social revolution in the Punjab situation as well. It is not the established leaders of the Akali party who have resorted to violence, but a second level of leadership—a younger, more marginal group for whom the use of violence is enormously empowering. The power that comes from the barrel of a gun, as Mao [Tse-tung] is said to have remarked, has a very direct effect. But there is a psychological dimension to this power that may be even more effective. As Frantz Fanon argued in the context of the Algerian revolution some years ago even a small display of violence can have immense symbolic power: the power to jolt the masses into an awareness of their potency.[43]

It can be debated whether or not the masses in the Punjab have been jolted into an awareness of their own capabilities, but the violent actions of the militants among them have certainly made the masses more aware of the militants' powers. They have attained a status of authority rivalling what police and other government officials possess. One of the problems in the Punjab today is the unwillingness of many villagers in the so-called terrorist zones around Batala and Taran Tarn to report terrorist activities to the authorities. The radical youth are even said to have established an alternative government.

By being dangerous the young Sikh radicals have gained a certain notoriety, and by clothing their actions in the moral garb of religion they have given their actions legitimacy. Because their actions are morally sanctioned by religion, they are fundamentally political actions: they break the state's monopoly on morally-sanctioned killing. By putting the right to kill in their own hands, the perpetrators of religious violence are also making a daring claim of political independence.

Even though Bhindranwale was not an outspoken supporter of Khalistan, he often spoke of the Sikhs' separate identity as that of a religious community with national characteristics. The term he used for religious community, *quam*, is an Urdu term that has overtones of nationhood. It is the term the Muslims used earlier in this century in defending their right to have a separate nation, and it is the term that Untouchables used in the Punjab in the 1920s when they attempted to be recognized as a separate social and political entity.[44] Another term that is important to Bhindranwale is *miri-piri*, the notion that spiritual and temporal power are linked.[45] It is this concept that is symbolically represented by the two-edged sword and that justified Sikh support for an independent political party. Young Sikh activists are buttressed in their own aspirations to leadership by the belief that acts that they conceive as being heroic and sacrificial—even those that involve taking the lives of others—have both spiritual and political significance. They are risking their lives for God and the Sikh community.

Not all of the Sikh community appreciates their efforts, however, and the speeches of Bhindranwale make clear that disagreements and rivalries within the community were one of his major concerns. Some of Bhindranwale's harshest words were reserved for Sikhs who he felt showed weakness and a tendency to make easy compromises. In one speech, after quoting a great martyr in Sikh history as having said, 'even if I have to give my head, may I never lose my love for the Sikh Faith', Bhindranwale railed against Sikh bureaucrats and modernized youth who could not make that sacrifice, and ended with a little joke:

> I am sorry to note that many people who hanker after a government position say instead, 'even if I lose my Faith, may I never lose my position'. And our younger generation has started saying this: 'even if I lose my Faith, may a beard never grow on my face'.... If you find the beard too heavy, pray to God saying... 'we do not like this Sikhism and manhood. Have mercy on us. Make us into women....'[46]

But most Sikhs in Bhindranwale's audience, including the youth, were not the sort who would be tempted to cut their hair; and few, especially in the villages where Bhindranwale had been popular, were in a position to 'hanker after a governmental position'. People, such as the Akali leaders whom Bhindranwale castigated for making compromises for the sake of personal gain, were no doubt objects of contempt in the villages long before Bhindranwale came along, and by singling them out, Bhindranwale identified familiar objects of derision—scapegoats—that humbled those who had succeeded in worldly affairs and heightened the sense of unity among those who had not.

Bhindranwale made a great plea for unity. 'Our misfortune is disunity', he told his audiences. 'We try to throw mud at each other. Why don't we give up thinking of mud and in close embrace with each other work with determination to attain our goals.'[47] Those who eventually opposed him, including the more moderate Akali leader, Sant Harchand Singh Longowal, regarded Bhindranwale as a prime obstacle to the very unity he preached.

During the dark days immediately preceding Operation Bluestar in June 1984, the two set up rival camps in the Golden Temple and allegedly killed each other's lieutenants. It is no wonder that many of Bhindranwale's followers, convinced the Indian army had a collaborator inside the Golden Temple, were suspicious when Bhindranwale was murdered in the raid and Longowal was led off safely under arrest. No wonder also that many regarded Longowal's assassination a year later as revenge for Bhindranwale's.

While he was alive, Bhindranwale continued to preach unity, but it was clear that what he wanted was everyone else to unite around him. He and his supporters wished to give the impression that they were at the center, following the norm of Sikh belief and behavior, and that the community should therefore group around them. This message had a particular appeal to those who were socially marginal to the Sikh community, including lower-caste people and Sikhs who had taken up residence abroad. Some of the most fanatical of Bhindranwale's followers, including Beant Singh, the assassin of Indira Gandhi, came from the Untouchable castes (Beant Singh was from the lowest caste of Untouchables, the Sweepers), and a considerable amount of money and moral support for the Punjab militants came from Sikhs living in such faraway places as London, Houston, and Yuba City, California.

These groups gained from their identification with Bhindranwale a sense of belonging, and the large Sikh communities in England, Canada and America were especially sensitive to his message that the Sikhs needed to be strong, united and defensive of their tradition. Many of Bhindranwale's supporters in the Punjab, however, received a more tangible benefit from associating with his cause: politically active village youth and small-time clergy were able to gain support from many who were not politically mobilized before. In that sense Bhindranwale was fomenting something of a political revolution, and the constituency was not unlike the one the Ayatollah Khomeini was able to gather in Iran. In so far as Bhindranwale's message was taken as an endorsement of the killings that some of these fundamentalist youth committed, the instrument of religious violence gave power to those who had little power before.

When Does Cosmic Struggle Lead to Real Violence?

The pattern of religious violence of the Sikhs could be that of Irish Catholics, or Shi'ite Muslims in Palestine, or fundamentalist Christian bombers of abortion clinics in the United States. There are a great many communities in which the language of cosmic struggle justifies acts of violence. But those who are engaged in them, including the Sikhs, would be offended if we concluded from the above discussion that their actions were purely for social or political gain. They argue that they act out of religious conviction, and surely they are to some degree right. Destruction is a part of the logic of religion, and virtually every religious tradition carries with it images of chaos and terror. But symbolic violence does not lead in every instance to real bloodshed, and even the eagerness of political actors to exploit religious symbols is not in all cases sufficient to turn religion towards a violent end. Yet some forms of religion do seem to propel the faithful rather easily into militant confrontation: which ones, and why?

The current resurgence of religious violence around the world has given an urgency to attempts to answer these questions, and to identify which characteristics of religion are conducive to violence. The efforts of social scientists have been directed primarily to the social and political aspects of the problem, but at least a few of them have tried to trace the patterns in religion's own logic. David C. Rapoport, for instance, has identified several features of messianic movements that he believes lead to violence, most of which are characterized by a desire for an antinomian liberation from oppression.[48]

My own list of characteristics comes directly from our discussion of the religious language of cosmic struggle. It is informed by my understanding of what has happened in the Sikh tradition, but it seems to me that the following tenets of religious commitment are found whenever acts of religious violence occur.

1. The Cosmic Struggle Is Played Out in History

To begin with, it seems to me that if religion is to lead to violence it is essential for the devout to believe that the cosmic struggle is realizable in human terms. If the war between good and evil, order and chaos, is conceived as taking place in historical time, in a real geographical location, and among actual social contestants, it is more likely that those who are prone to violent acts will associate religion with their struggles. This may seem to be an obvious point, yet we have some evidence that it is not always true.

In the Hindu tradition, for instance, the mythical battles in the Mahabharata and Ramayana epics are as frequently used as metaphors for present-day struggles as are the actual battles in Sikh and Islamic history and in biblical Judaism and Christianity. Like members of these traditions, Hindus characterize their worldly foes by associating them with the enemies of the good in their legendary battles. The main difference between the Hindus and the others is that their enemies are mythical—that is, they seem mythical to us. To many pious Hindus, however, the stories in the epics are no less real than those recorded in the Bible or in the Sikh legends. A believing Hindu will be able to show you where the great war of the Mahabharata was actually fought, and where the gods actually lived. Moreover, the Hindu cycles of time allow for a cosmic destruction to take place in this world, at the end of the present dark age. So the Hindu tradition is not as devoid of images of divine intervention in worldly struggles as outsiders sometimes assume.[49]

The major tradition that appears to lack the notion that the cosmic struggle is played out on a social plane is Buddhism. But this is an exception that proves the rule, for it is a tradition that is characteristically devoid of religiously sanctioned violence. There are instances in Thai history that provide Buddhist justifications for warfare, but these are rare for the tradition as a whole. In general, Buddhism has no need for actual battles in which the pious can prove their mettle.

2. Believers Identify Personally With the Struggle

The Buddhist tradition does affirm that there is a spiritual conflict, however: it is the clash between the perception that this imperfect and illusory world is real and a higher consciousness that surmounts worldly perception altogether. And in a sense, the struggle takes place in this world, in that it takes place in the minds of worldly persons. This kind of internalization of the cosmic struggle does not in itself lead to violence, and Buddhists are not ordinarily prone to violent deeds. Nor are Sufis, the Islamic mystics who have reconceived the Muslim notion of *jihad*. To many Sufis, the greater *jihad* is not the one involving worldly warfare, but the one within: the conflict between good and evil within one's own soul.[50]

This talk about the cosmic struggle as something inside the self would seem to be easily distinguishable from external violence, but in Sikh theology, including the rhetoric of Bhindranwale, they go hand in hand. 'The weakness is in us', Bhindranwale was fond of telling his followers. 'We are the sinners of this house of our Guru.'[51] Militant Shi'ite Muslims are similarly racked with a sense of personal responsibility for the moral decadence of the world, and once again their tendency toward internalization does not necessarily shield them from acts of external violence. The key to the connection, it seems to me, is that at the same time that the cosmic struggle is understood to impinge about the inner recesses of an individual person, it must be understood as occurring on a worldly, social plane. Neither of these notions is by itself sufficient to motivate a person to religious violence. If one believes that the cosmic struggle is largely a matter of large continuing social forces, one is not likely to become personally identified with the struggle; and if one is convinced that the struggle is solely interior there is not reason to look for it outside. But when the two ideas coexist, they are a volatile concoction.

Thus when Bhindranwale spoke about the warfare in the soul his listeners knew that however burdensome that conflict is, they need not bear it alone. They may band together with their comrades and continue the struggle in the external arena, where the foes are more vulnerable, and victories more tangible. And their own internal struggles impel them to become involved in the worldly conflict: their identification with the overall struggle makes them morally responsible, in part, for its outcome. 'We ourselves are ruining Sikhism', Bhindranwale once told his congregation.[52] On another occasion he told the story of how, when Guru Gobind Singh asked an army of 80,000 to sacrifice their heads for the faith, only five assented. Bhindranwale implied that the opportunity was still at hand to make the choice of whether they were to be one of the five or the 79,995.[53] He reminded them that even though the cosmic war was still being waged, and that the evil within them and outside them had not yet been purged, their choice could still make a difference.

Sikhism is not the only tradition in which this link is forged between the external and internal arenas of the cosmic struggle. Shi'ite Muslims bear a great weight of communal guilt for not having defended one of the founders of their tradition, Husain, when he was attacked and martyred by the vicious Yazid. During the Iranian revolution some of them relived that conflict by identifying specific foes—the Shah and President Jimmy Carter—as Yazids returned. There was no doubt that such people should be attacked. Radical Shi'ites in Iran were not about to compound their guilt and miss an historical opportunity of righting an ancient wrong.

The same sort of logic has propelled many Christians into a vicious anti-Semitism. It is a mark of good Christian piety for individuals to bear the responsibility for the crucifiction of Jesus: the theme of Christians taking part in the denial and betrayal of Jesus is the stuff of many a hymn and sermon. Some Christians believe that the foes to whom they allowed Jesus to be delivered were the Jews. Attacks on the present-day Jewish community, therefore, help to lighten their sense of culpability.

3. The Cosmic Struggle Continues in the Present

What makes these actions of Sikhs, Shi'ites and anti-Semitic Christians spiritually defensible is the conviction that the sacred struggle has not ended in some earlier period, but that it continues in some form today. It is a conviction that also excites the members of the Gush Emunim, a militant movement in present-day Israel, who have taken Israel's victory in the Six Day War as a sign that the age of messianic redemption has finally begun.[54]

Not all Israelis respond to this sign with the same enthusiasm, however, just as not all Christians or Shi'ite Muslims are convinced that the apocalyptic conflict prophesied by their tradition is really at hand. Many of the faithful assent to the notion that the struggle exists within, for what person of faith has not felt the internal tension between belief and disbelief, affirmation and denial, order and chaos? But they often have to be persuaded that the conflict currently rages on a social plane, especially if the social world seems orderly and benign.

Bhindranwale took this challenge as one of the primary tasks of his ministry. He said that one of his main missions was to alert his people that they were oppressed, even if they did not know it. He ended one of his sermons with this fervent plea: 'I implore all of you in this congregation. Go to the villages and make every child, every mother, every Singh realise we are slaves and we have to shake off this slavery in order to survive.'[55]

In Bhindranwale's mind the appearances of normal social order simply illustrated how successful the forces of evil had become in hiding their demonic agenda. His logic compelled him to believe that Punjabi society was racked in a great struggle, even if it showed no indication of it. Long before the Punjab was torn apart by its most recent round of violence, Bhindranwale claimed that an even fiercer form of violence reigned: the appearance of normal order was merely a demonic deception. Bhindranwale hated the veil of calm that seemed to cover his community and recognized that his own followers were often perplexed about what he said: 'Many of our brothers, fresh from the villages, ask, "Sant Ji, we don't know about enslavement." For that reason, I have to tell you why you are slaves.'[56]

The evidence that Bhindranwale gave for the oppression of Sikhs was largely limited to examples of police hostility that arose after the spiral of violence in the Punjab began to grow. Some of his allegations, such as the account he gave of the treatment meted out to followers who hijacked Indian airplanes, have a peculiar ring:

> If a Sikh protests in behalf of his Guru by hijacking a plane, he is put to death....
> None of the Sikhs in these three hijackings attacked any passenger nor did they damage the planes. But the rule is that for a fellow with a turban, there is the bullet....
> For a person who says 'Hare Krishna, Hare Krishna, Hare Rama', there is a government appointment. Sikh brothers, this is a sign of slavery.[57]

Those who attempted to combat Bhindranwale could not win against such logic. If they responded to Sikh violence they would be seen as oppressors. If they did not respond, the violence would escalate. And even if there was neither violence nor repression, the absence of the overt signs of conflict would be an indication to Bhindranwale of a demonical calm.

4. The Struggle Is at a Point of Crisis

On a number of occasions, in referring to the immediacy of the struggle, Bhindranwale seemed to indicate that the outcome was in doubt. His perception of the enormity of the evil he faced and of the torpor of the Sikh response made his prognosis a dismal one.

Sometimes he felt that the best efforts of a few faithful Sikhs were doomed: 'today', he darkly proclaimed, 'the Sikh community is under threat'.[58] But on other occasions he seemed to hold out a measure of hope. Things were coming to a head, he implied, and the struggle was about to enter 'the decisive phase'.[59]

What is interesting about this apocalyptic rhetoric is its uncertainty. If the outcome were less in doubt there would be little reason for violent action. If one knew that the foe would win, there would be no reason to want to fight back. Weston LaBarre describes the terrible circumstances surrounding the advent of the Ghost Dance religion of the Plains Indians: knowing that they faced overwhelming odds and almost certain defeat, the tribe diverted their concerns from worldly conflict to spiritual conflict, and entertained the notion that a ritual dance would conjure up sufficient spiritual force to destroy the alien cavalry.[60]

LaBarre concludes that sheer desperation caused them to turn to religion and away from efforts to defend themselves. But by the same token, if they knew that the battle could be won without a struggle, there also would be little reason for engagement. The passive pacifism of what William James calles 'healthy-souled religion'—mainstream Protestant churches, for example, that regard social progress as inevitable—comes from just such optimism.[61] Other pacifist movements, however, have been directly engaged in conflict. Menno Simons, the Anabaptist for whom the Mennonite church is named, and Mohandas Gandhi are examples of pacifist leaders who at times narrowly skirted the edges of violence, propelled by a conviction that without human effort the outcome they desired could not be won. In that sense Gandhi and Bhindranwale were more alike than one might suspect. Both saw the world in terms of cosmic struggle, both regarded their cause as being poised on a delicate balance between oppression and opportunity, and both believed that human action could tip the scales. The issue that divided them, of course, was violence.

5. Acts of Violence Have a Cosmic Meaning

The human action in the Sikh case is certainly not pacifist, for Bhindranwale held that there would be 'no deliverance without weapons.'[62] He was careful, however, to let the world know that these weapons were not be used indiscriminately: 'It is a sin for a Sikh to keep weapons to hurt an innocent person, to rob anyone's home, to dishonor anyone or to oppress anyone. But there is no greater sin for a Sikh than keeping weapons and not using them to protect his faith.'[63] Contrariwise, there is no greater valor for a Sikh than to use weapons in defense of the faith. Bhindranwale himself was armed to the teeth, and although he never publically admitted to any of the killings that were pinned on him personally, Bhindranwale expressed his desire to 'die fighting', a wish that was fulfilled within months of being uttered.[64]

According to Bhindranwale, those who committed acts of religiously sanctioned violence were to be regarded as heroes and more. Although he usually referred to himself as a 'humble servant, and an 'uneducated fallible person',[65] Bhindranwale would occasionally identify himself with one of the legendary Sikh saints, Baba Deep Singh, who continued to battle with Moghul foes even after his head had been severed from his body. He carried it manfully under his arm.[66] In Bhindranwale's mind, he too seemed destined for martyrdom.

To many Sikhs today, that is precisely what Bhindranwale achieved. Whatever excesses he may have committed during his lifetime are excused, as one would excuse a lethal but heroic soldier in a glorious war. Even Beant Singh, the bodyguard of Indira Gandhi who turned on her, is held to be a saintly hero. Perhaps this has to be: if Indira was such a demonic foe, her assassin must be similarly exalted.

Even those who value the sense of order that religion provides sometimes cheer those who throw themselves into the arena of religious violence. Such people are, after all, struggling for good, and for that reason their actions are seen as ultimately producing order. But until such recognition of their mission can be achieved among the more conservative rank and file, such activists are forced, as prophets and agents of a higher order of truth, to engage in deeds that necessarily startle. Their purpose is to awaken good folk, mobilize their community, insult the evil forces, and perhaps even to demonstrate dramatically to God himself that there are those who are willing to fight and die on his side, and to deliver his judgement of death. The great promise of cosmic struggle is that order will prevail over chaos; the great irony is that many must die in order for certain visions of that victory to prevail and their awful dramas be brought to an end.

Notes

1. For general background on the Punjab crisis in the 1980s and a chronicle of events leading up to it, see Mark Tully and Satish Jacob, *Amritsar: Mrs Gandhi's Last Battle* (London: Cape, 1985), Amarjit Kaur, *et al., The Punjab Story* (New Delhi: Roli Books International, 1984), and Kuldip Nayar and Khushwant Singh, *Tragedy of Punjab: Operation Bluestar and After* (New Delhi: Vision Books, 1984).

2. Indira Gandhi, 'Don't Shed Blood, Shed Hatred', All India Radio, 2 June 1984, reprinted in V. D. Chopra, R. K. Mishra and Nirmal Singh, *Agony of Punjab* (New Delhi: Patriot Publishers, 1984), p. 189. Indian government officials seemed to be genuinely caught off-guard by the Sikh militancy. I remember once in the summer of 1984 when the Indian Consul General in San Francisco turned to me after we had been on a radio talk show and said, 'I haven't a clue; can you tell me why in the devil the Sikhs are behaving like this?'

3. The demand for a Khalistan—a Sikh state similar to Pakistan—was raised by a small number of Sikh militants, including a former cabinet minister of the Punjab, Jagjit Singh Chauhan, who set up a movement in exile in London. It was not, however, a significant or strongly supported demand among Sikhs in the Punjab until after Operation Bluestar in June 1984. The Indian government's account of Chauhan's movement is detailed in a report prepared by the Home Ministry, 'Sikh Agitation for Khalistan', reprinted in Nayar and Singh, *Tragedy of Punjab*, pp. 142–55.

4. The Anandpur Resolution supported by leaders of the Akali Dal focused primarily on economic issues. For an analysis of the Punjab crisis from an economic perspective, see Chopra, Mishra and Singh, *Agony of Punjab*.

5. The fear of the absorption of Sikhism into Hinduism is the frequent refrain of Khushwant Singh; see, for instance, the final chapter of his *History of the Sikhs*, Vol. 2 (Princeton, NJ: Princeton University Press, 1966). He attributes the cause of many of the problems in the Punjab in the mid-1980s to this fear as well; see his *Tragedy of Punjab*, pp. 19–21.

6. For an interesting analysis of the general pattern of religious fundamentalism in South Asia of which the Hindu and Sikh movements are a part, see Robert Eric Frykenberg, 'Revivalism and Fundamentalism: Some Critical Observations with Special Reference to Politics in South Asia', in James W. Bjorkman (ed.), *Fundamentalism, Revivalists and Violence in South Asia* (Riverdale, MD: Riverdale, 1986).

7. I am grateful to Professor Ranbir Singh Sandhu, Department of Civil Engineering, Ohio State University, for providing me with several hours of tape-recorded speeches of Sant Jamail Singh Bhindranwale. Professor Sandhu has translated some of these speeches, and I appreciate his sharing these translations with me. For this article I am relying primarily on the words of Bhindranwale. They are found in the following sources: 'Sant Jamail Bhindranwale's Address to the Sikh Congregation', a transcript of a sermon given in the Golden Temple in November 1983, translated by Ranbir Singh Sandhu, April 1985, and distributed by the Sikh Religious and Educational Trust, Columbus, Ohio; excerpts of Bhindranwale's speeches, translated into English, that appear in Joyce Pettigrew, 'In Search of a New Kingdom of Lahore', *Pacific Affairs*, Vol. 60, No. 1 (Spring 1987) (forthcoming), and interviews with Bhindranwale found in various issues of *India Today* and other publications.

8. The spiritual leader of the Nirankaris, Baba Gurbachan Singh, was assassinated at his home in Delhi on 24 May 1980. Bhindranwale was implicated in the murder, but was never brought to trial. Kuldip Nayar claims that Zail Singh, who became President of India, came to Bhindranwale's defense at that time (Nayar and Singh, *Tragedy of Punjab,* p. 37).

9. It is said that Bhindranwale was first brought into the political arena in 1977 by Mrs Gandhi's son, Sanjay, who hoped that Bhindranwale's popularity would undercut the political support of the Akali party (Nayar and Singh, *Tragedy of Punjab*, p. 31, and Tully, *Amritsar*, p. 57–61).

10. Bhindranwale, 'Address to the Sikh Congregation', pp. 10–11.

11. Bhindranwale, excerpt from a speech, in Pettigrew.

12. Ibid., p. 15.

13. Ibid.

14. Bhindranwale, 'Address to the Sikh Congregation', p. 1.

15. Ibid.

16. Bhindranwale, excerpt from a speech, in Pettigrew.

17. Ibid.

18. Bhindranwale, 'Address to the Sikh Congregation', p. 10.

19. Ibid., p. 2.

20. Bhindranwale, excerpt from a speech, in Pettigrew.

21. Ibid.

22. Ibid.

23. Ibid.

24. Bhindranwale, 'Address to the Sikh Congregation', pp. 1–5, and ibid., p. 14.

25. Bhindranwale, excerpt from a speech, in Pettigrew.

26. For an interesting discussion of the definition of violence and terror in political contexts see Thomas Perry Thornton, 'Terrorism as a Weapon of Political Agitation', in Harry Eckstein (ed.), *Internal War: Problems and Approaches* (New York: The Free Press, 1964); and David C. Rapoport, 'The Politics of Atrocity', in Y. Alexander and S. Finger (eds.), *Terrorism: Interdisciplinary Perspectives* (New York: John Jay, 1977).

27. Clifford Geertz defines religion as 'a system of symbols which acts to establish powerful, pervasive and long-lasting moods and motivations in men by formulating conceptions of a general order of existence and clothing these conceptions with such an aura of factuality that the moods and motivations seem uniquely realistic' ('Religion as a Cultural System', reprinted in William A. Lessa and Evon Z. Vogt, (eds.), *Reader in Comparative Religion: An Anthropological Approach* (New York: Harper & Row, 3rd ed., 1972), p. 168).

28. Robert Bellah, 'Transcendence in Contemporary Piety', in Donald R. Cutler, *The Religious Situation: 1969* (Boston: Beacon Press, 1969), p. 907.

29. Peter Berger, *The Heretical Imperative* (New York: Doubleday, 1980), p. 38. See also his *Sacred Canopy: Elements of a Sociological Theory of Religion* (Garden City, NY: Doubleday, 1967).

30. Louis Dupré, *Transcendent Selfhood: The Loss and Re-discovery of the Inner Life* (New York: Seabury Press, 1976), p. 26. For a discussion of Berger and Dupré's definitions, see Mary Douglas, 'The Effects of Modernization on Religious Change', *Daedalus*, Vol. III, No. 1 (Winter 1982), pp. 1–19.

31. Durkheim describes the dichotomy of sacred and profane in religion in the following way: 'In all the history of human thought there exists no other example of two categories of things so profoundly differentiated or so radically opposed to one another.... The sacred and the profane have always and everywhere been conceived by the human mind as two distinct classes, as two worlds between which there is nothing in common.... In different religions, this opposition has been conceived in different ways'. Emile Durkheim, *The Elementary Forms of the Religious Life*, trans. by Joseph Ward Swain (London: George Allen & Unwin, 1976) (originally published in 1915), pp. 38–9. Durkheim goes on to talk about the sacred things that religions encompass; but the first thing he says about the religious view is the perception that there is this dichotomy. From a theological perspective it seems to me that Paul Tillich is saying something of the same thing in arguing for the necessary connection between faith and doubt (see, for example, the first chapter of his *Dynamics of Faith*).

32. On this point I am in agreement with Wilfred Cantwell Smith who suggested some years ago that the noun 'religion' might well be banished from our vocabulary, and that we restrict ourselves to using the adjective 'religious' (*The Meaning and End of Religion: A New Approach to the Religious Traditions of Mankind* (New York: Macmillan, 1962), pp. 119–53).

33. For the significance of the two-edged sword symbol and its links with the Devi cult revered by people, such as Jats, who have traditionally inhabited the foothills of the Himalayas adjacent to the Punjab, see W. H. McLeod, *The Evolution of the Sikh Community* (Oxford: Clarendon Press, 1976), p. 13.

34. Ibid, pp. 15–17, 51–2. These five objects are known as the five K's, since the name for each of them in Punjabi begins with the letter 'k'. The other four are uncut hair, a wooden comb, a metal bangle and cotton breeches. See also W. Owen Cole and Piara Singh Sambhi, *The Sikhs: Their Religious Beliefs and Practices* (London: Routledge & Kegan Paul, 1978), p. 36.

35. Karl Marx, 'Contribution to the Critique of Hegel's Philosophy of Right', reprinted in Karl Marx and Friedrich Engels, *On Religion* (New York: Schocken Books), p. 42; see also Engels' class analysis of a religious revolt, 'The Peasant War in Germany' in the same volume, pp. 97–118.

36. Sigmund Freud, *Totem and Taboo*, trans. by James Strachey (New York: W. W. Norton, 1950).

37. Rene Girard, *Violence and the Sacred*, trans. by Patrick Gregory (Baltimore and London; Johns Hopkins University Press, 1977); see especially Chapters 7 and 8. What is not clear in this book is how symbolic violence leads to real acts of violence; this link is made in a subsequent study of Girard's, *Scapegoat*, trans. by Patrick Gregory (Baltimore and London: Johns Hopkins University Press, 1986).

38. Bhindranwale, excerpt from a speech, in Pettigrew.

39. Ibid.

40. Bhindranwale, 'Address to the Sikh Congregation', p. 9.

41. See my article, 'Nonviolence', in Mircea Eliade (ed.), *The Encyclopedia of Religion* (New York: Macmillan, 1987). For the ethic of non-violence in Sikhism see Cole and Sambhi, *The Sikhs*, p. 138. For Sikh ethical attitudes in general see Avtar Singh, *Ethics of the Sikhs* (Patiala, India: Punjabi University Press); and S. S. Kohli, *Sikh Ethics* (New Delhi: Munshiram Manoharial, 1975).

42. An excellent anthology of statements of Christian theologians on the ethical justification for war is Albert Marrin (ed.), *War and the Christian Conscience: From Augustine to Martin Luther King, Jr.* (Chicago: Henry Regnery, 1971). On the development of the just war doctrine in Christianity, with its secular parallels, see James Turner Johnson, *Ideology, Reason, and the Limitation of War: Religious and Secular Concepts, 1200–1740* (Princeton: Princeton University Press, 1975).

43. Frantz Fanon, *The Wretched of the Earth* (New York: Grove Press, 1963).

44. For a discussion of the term *qaum* in the Untouchable movements, see my *Religion as Social Vision* (Berkeley and London: University of California Press, 1982), p. 45.

45. Joyce Pettigrew argues that the *miri-piri* concept 'gave legitimacy to the political action organized from within the Golden Temple' (Pettigrew, op. cit.). This 'political action' was the

establishment of an armed camp of which Bhindranwale was the commander; it was to rout this camp that the Indian army entered the Golden Temple on 5 June 1984, in Operation Bluestar.

46. Bhindranwale, 'Address to the Sikh Congregation', p. 13.
47. Ibid., p. 8.
48. David C. Rapoport, 'Why does Messianism Produce Terror?' paper delivered at the 81st Annual Meeting of the American Political Science Association, New Orleans, 27 August–1 September 1985. Although I find Rapoport's conclusions helpful, and in many ways compatible with my own, his emphasis on messianic movements seems unnecessary. The notion of messianism is largely alien to the Asian religious traditions, and much of what he says about it could be said of religion in general. See also his 'Fear and Trembling: Terrorism in Three Religious Traditions', *American Political Science Review* 78:3 (Sept. 1984), pp. 658–77, which includes case studies of the Thugs, Assassins and Zealots and the essays in David C. Rapoport and Y. Alexander (eds.), *The Morality of Terrorism: Religious and Secular Justifications* (New York: Pergamon, 1982).
49. There are also examples in other cultures where mythic battles are thought to have had a historical effect. At a recent presentation at the Wilson Center, for instance, Professor Billie Jean Isbell described the influence of the notion of cosmic cycles of order and chaos in traditional Andean cosmology on the propensity for violence of the Sendero Luminoso tribal people of Peru ('The Faces and Voices of Terrorism', Politics and Religion Seminar, Wilson Center, 8 May 1986).
50. The term *jihad* is derived from the word for striving for something, and implies 'the struggle against one's bad inclinations' as well as what it has come to mean in the popular Western mind, holy war (Rudolph Peters. *Islam and Colonialism: The Doctrine of Jihad in Modern History*, The Hague: Mouton Publishers, 1979, p. 188).
51. Bhindranwale, 'Address to the Sikh Congregation', p. 7.
52. Bhindranwale, excerpt from a speech, in Pettigrew.
53. Bhindranwale, 'Address to the Sikh congregation', p. 13.
54. For an interesting analysis of the Gush Emunim, see Ehud Sprinzak's essay in this volume.
55. Bhindranwale, 'Address to the Sikh congregation', p. 8.
56. Ibid., p. 2.
57. Ibid., p. 3.
58. Bhindranwale, excerpt from a speech, in Pettigrew.
59. Ibid.
60. Weston LaBarre, *The Ghost Dance: Origins of Religion* (London: Allen & Unwin, 1972).
61. William James, *The Varieties of Religious Experience* (Cambridge, MA: Harvard University Press, 1985) (originally published in 1902), pp. 71–108.
62. Bhindranwale, 'Address to the Sikh Congregation', p. 10.
63. Ibid., p. 10.
64. Bhindranwale, excerpt from a speech, in Pettigrew.
65. Bhindranwale, 'Address to the Sikh Congregation', p. 14.
66. Bhindranwale, excerpt from a speech, in Pettigrew.

Chapter 5

Weapons of Mass Destruction

The threat of weapons of mass destruction (WMD) is a complex issue—not just in the discussion of how to detect, deter, and defend against their use, but also in the complicated differences between the devices, technology, and processes needed to obtain and use these weapons. The authors in this chapter look at the likelihood of terrorists and nonstate actors making use of these weapons, and the issues surrounding biological security and the use of chemical weapons.

Nuclear, chemical, and biological weapons are inherently terrorizing—causing moral dread and panic, says Jessica Stern. But despite their appeal, terrorist groups have seldom used them. Stern surveys the likelihood of groups using these agents—including the varying ease or difficulty involved in obtaining the raw materials and having the technical means to disseminate them—and details two successful acts of this type of terrorism: Aum Shinrikyo's attack on the Tokyo subway, and the Rajneesh cult's 1984 act of poisoning salad bars in Oregon with *Salmonella typhimurium*. In the case of Aum Shinrikyo, the author details the massive and long-term organization behind the act: in a November 1995 hearing, the staff of Senator Sam Nunn testified that at the time of the Tokyo attacks, the group had some 50,000 members and assets worth $1.4 billion. However, despite the lack of success by groups attempting to use WMD for terrorist purposes, Stern concludes with a word of caution. Although Aum Shinrikyo's large-scale attacks with biological agents are believed to have failed, Stern warns, "were terrorists to master these technologies they would have the potential to kill not just hundreds but hundreds of thousands of people."

When analysts and policymakers refer to WMD, they group nuclear, biological, chemical, and radiological weapons together, "as if the latter were merely variants on the same type of device," says Christopher F. Chyba. But these weapons "differ greatly in their ease of production, in the challenges they pose for deterrence, and in the effectiveness of defensive measures against them," contends the author. Biological weapons differ from nuclear and chemical, and the United States needs a biological security strategy—both domestic and international—to guard against these unique threats. Chyba details the approaches and the complexities involved in biological security. In some cases, there will be a synergy between guarding against biological weapons and natural disease outbreak; in some case, there will not be a dual-purpose benefit, such as when it is necessary to stockpile an antibiotic supply to guard against a disease that does not occur naturally. Chyba also points to the importance of a strategy that addresses the potential international threat. In the end, says Chyba, it will be vital for scientists to communicate the complexity of the problem to policy makers, and for policy makers to incorporate scientific advice into their decision-making.

According to Michael L. Moodie, the use of chemical weapons is not new. The author traces instances back to 2000 B.C. India, to 400 B.C., and to more modern usage in the nineteenth and twentieth centuries. Despite their long history, says Moodie, chemical weapons pose a new challenge today: the political and technological context has changed, chemical weapons are an attractive option to terrorists and nonstate actors, and the scenarios in which chemical weapons can have a significant impact have increased. Moodie surveys the process of weaponizing these chemical agents and the technical issues surrounding their development, production, and dissemination; he details the CW programs of "rogue" states and the possibility of nonstate actors making use of these weapons. Moodie's discussion illustrates an issue so complex that, as the author says, "No one policy element—intelligence, arms control, export controls, diplomacy, or military capabilities—will provide a complete answer. They must all be made to work together in a genuinely strategic approach."

Getting and Using the Weapons

Jessica Stern is a faculty affiliate of the Belfer Center for Science and International Affairs and a lecturer in public policy at the Kennedy School. She served formerly as the director for Russian, Ukrainian, and Eurasian Affairs at the National Security Council, responsible for national-security policy toward Russia and the former Soviet states and for policies to reduce the threat of nuclear smuggling and terrorism. She is the author of *The Ultimate Terrorists* (1999) as well as many articles on terrorism and weapons of mass destruction.

Humans, regrettably, have used available technologies for destructive as well as for beneficial purposes throughout history.
—*Journal of the American Medical Association*, 1997

Nuclear, chemical, and biological agents, as we have seen, are inherently terrorizing. They evoke moral dread and visceral revulsion out of proportion to their lethality. The government of a country attacked with such weapons would have difficulty controlling panic. Because chemical and biological weapons are silent killers, an attack could occur at any time without warning. The first sign of a biological attack might be "hundreds or thousands of ill or dying patients," a U.S. government scientist warns.[1]

Despite the evident appeal of such weapons as instruments of terror, terrorists have seldom used them. Terrorists have never detonated a nuclear device. They have used chemical agents rarely—most often to poison foods—and biological and radiological agents more rarely still. Except for the chemical attacks carried out by the Aum Shinrikiyo cult in Japan in 1994 and 1995, there have been no cases of large-scale, open-air dissemination. What has held terrorists back? The answer involves both technical constraints, which I discuss [here], and motivational or organizational constraints.... The technical hurdles would be considerable: acquiring the agent or weapon would present one set of difficulties; disseminating or exploding it would present another.

Chemical and Biological Agents

Terrorists might be able to acquire chemical or biological (CB) agents from governments favorable to their cause. CB agents are proliferating. In 1997 Secretary of Defense William Cohen estimated the number of countries with "mature chemical and biological weapons programs" at "about thirty," and the CIA claimed that around twenty nations had developed these weapons.[2] Iran, Iraq, Libya, North Korea, and Syria—all listed by the State Department as supporters of terrorism—are believed to possess chemical weapons and at least some biological weapons. Iraq's CB programs are quite extensive. The small quantities of CB agents required for an attack would make it very difficult to track the flow of the weapons or their component chemicals to terrorist groups.

Terrorists also might be able to steal CB agents from national stockpiles. In Albania in 1997, according to an Albanian military official, antigovernment bandits stole chemical weapons and radioactive materials from four army depots. The stolen materials, the official warned, posed serious health hazards.[3]

Russia's security for chemical weapons is particularly problematic. The storage sites for chemical weapons were revealed in the newspaper *Rossiyskaya Gazeta* in January 1994, and in 1995 the army chief of staff, General Kolesnikov, expressed concern that publication of the locations increased the risk of theft. Kolesnikov also warned that the increases in crime in Russia are worsening the risk of "chemical weapons attacks."[4]

Because chemical and biological agents are relatively easy to produce, a single person with the right expertise could design an entire weapons program. Thus terrorists might acquire CB weapons by taking advantage of the "brain drain"—the prospect that weapons scientists will sell their expertise to the highest bidder. "Because of the deteriorating condition of the military-industrial complex in the former Soviet Union, many specialists in the field of chemical weaponry do not have enough sources of income to support their families and are ready to go anywhere to earn money," Vil Mirzayanov, a Russian chemical weapons scientists, said in 1995. Russian physicists are reportedly providing consulting services to missile and nuclear energy programs in Iran and Pakistan. One physicist reportedly claimed his conscience did not trouble him at all, since, with so many defense specialists now out of work, "If I had not agreed, they would have just found someone else." And Russia is by no means the only country where disaffected or underemployed weapons scientists can be found. Libya has reportedly tried to hire scientists formerly employed in developing biological agents for South Africa.[5]

Terrorist groups that include—or hire—trained chemists would have no difficulty producing chemical agents. A report by the U.S. Office of Technology Assessment claims that "the level of technological sophistication required... may be lower than was the case for some of the sophisticated bombs that have been used against civilian aircraft."[6] Many of the components of these agents are widely sold for industrial purposes. For example, thiodiglycol, an immediate precursor to mustard agent, is used to make ink for ballpoint pens. All that is required to produce mustard from this material is a simple acid that also is easy to obtain.

Pathogens that could be used as crude biological weapons—such as the common food poisons salmonella, shigella, and staphylococcus—are readily available at clinical microbiology laboratories. Terrorists could also produce more deadly agents. Knowledge of microbiology, and of its potential applications to weapons, is increasingly widespread. Kathleen Bailey, after interviewing professors, graduate students, and pharmaceutical manufacturers, concluded that several biologists with only $10,000 worth of equipment could produce a significant quantity of biological agent. The requisite equipment would fit in a small room, she claims, and "the glassware, centrifuges, growth media, etc., can all be manufactured by virtually any country."[7]

Detailed information about how to set up a chemistry laboratory and how to order chemicals without arousing suspicion is published in manuals on poisoning. One manual instructs readers how to disseminate chlorine (a poisonous gas widely used in industry, which was used as a weapon during World War I) in a crowd. In 1982, the year of the first widely reported incident of tampering with pharmaceuticals, the Tylenol case, only a few poisoning manuals were available, and they were relatively hard to find.

Today, how-to manuals on producing chemical and biological agents are advertised in paramilitary journals sold in magazine shops all over the United States, as well as on the Internet.[8] Although criminals are known to have used such manuals in plotting crimes, publishers maintain that publication of murder manuals is protected by the First Amendment.[9]

One of these manuals, *Bacteriological Warfare: A Major Threat to North America,* is described on the Internet as a book for helping readers survive a biological weapons attack. But in fact it also describes the reproduction and growth of biological agents and includes a chapter on "bacteria likely to be used by the terrorist." The book is sold over the Internet for $28.50 and is reportedly advertised on right-wing radio shows. Its author is Larry Wayne Harris, the former member of neo-Nazi organizations who ordered three vials of the bacterium that causes bubonic plague.

Once terrorists managed to acquire chemical and biological agents, they would face the question of how to use them against their targeted populations. Chemical agents are relatively easy to disseminate in enclosed spaces, and they are significantly easier than biological agents to spread over large areas. Key differences for the purposes of dissemination are that chemical agents are volatile (that is, some of the agent will spontaneously form a poisonous gas), while biological agents are not; and most biological agents are susceptible to humidity, desiccation, oxidation, air pollution, heat and shock (such as from explosions), and ultraviolet light, while chemical agents are not. (Anthrax in spore form is less susceptible to these insults than other biological agents.)

The most likely way to spread chemical agents in air would be to disseminate them in enclosed areas. If a suitcase full of nerve agent were opened into the air intake ducts of a building, many of the people inside would probably die. Even less of the agent would be needed to poison passengers on an airplane. Dissemination in open areas would be considerably more difficult. For example, a specially equipped car might be used to spread chemical agent in city streets. Some terrorists might have access to planes or helicopters fitted with crop sprayers, or even (probably only for state-sponsored groups) bombs or missiles.

As for biological agents, the U.S. Army has conducted tests of their dissemination in populated areas using nonlethal microorganisms to simulate biological agents. Six of these tests were conducted in San Francisco in 1950. A ship used an aerosol spray device to release two simulant agents (*Bacillus globigii* and *Serratia marcescens*) at various distances from shore. Air samples were taken at forty-three locations around the Bay Area. The Army's analysts concluded that it was feasible to attack a seaport city by disseminating biological agents from a ship offshore, and that success or failure would largely depend on the meteorological conditions at the time of the attack.[10]

The Army also conducted a test on the New York City subway in June 1966, employing another simulant (*Bacillus subtilis variant niger*). Technicians dropped light bulbs filled with bacteria into the system, either through ventilating grates or onto the roadbeds as the trains entered or left the station. The bulbs broke, releasing the bacteria. Aerosol clouds were momentarily visible after the bulbs were broken, but were ignored by most passengers, some of whom merely brushed off their clothes. Army scientists concluded that a large portion of the working population in downtown New York City would be exposed to disease if pathogenic agents were disseminated in several subway lines during rush hour.[11] New York City authorities were not informed of the test until

1980, when the Army's findings were made available to the general public. The results of this test in particular are quite frightening, but this scenario would require drying and milling or coating of the agent, tasks that might be beyond the capability of terrorist groups.

The Army also tested anti-animal and anti-crop agents, presumably spread with a crop duster. Nonbiological simulants were used in the anti-animal tests, but live agents, including wheat rust and rice blast, were used against crops. The tests were carried out until 1968, principally in Minnesota and Florida.[12]

The three ways of disseminating CB agents tested by the Army—from ships near seaports, on the subway, and with crop dusters—illustrate the kinds of low-technology attacks some terrorists might like to carry out. But it is not clear that they would be able to do so. Agents that kill humans or livestock must be disseminated in the form of aerosols that are respirable: that is, that can be taken into the body through the lungs. To be respirable, particles must be between one and five microns in diameter. Experts disagree about whether terrorists would be able to create such aerosols. Some claim that any college-trained molecular biologist is capable of killing hundreds of thousands of people in a single attack. Others cite Iraq as evidence that even governments have trouble overcoming the technical difficulties of dissemination, implying that terrorists without state sponsors would certainly fail. The Aum Shinrikiyo attacks in Japan lend credence to the latter view, but the truth is probably somewhere between these two viewpoints.[13] Terrorists might not be able to maximize efficiency in designing and building their weapons, but if they used massive amounts of agent it would hardly matter that less than one percent of the agent was effective. It would hardly matter to the victims, at any rate.

Biological agents can be disseminated in liquid or powder form. While producing liquid agent is relatively easy, disseminating it as an infectious aerosol is not. Dry powders can be disseminated far more easily. High-quality powders are complicated to make, however, involving skilled personnel and sophisticated equipment. Milling these powders, according to a U.S. government scientist, "would require a level of sophistication possessed [only] by some state sponsors of terrorism"; this implies that terrorists without state sponsors would have a difficult time indeed.[14]

Terrorists without state sponsors would be unlikely to master the technology required for dispersing liquid agents over broad areas unless they were able to hire skilled scientists trained in government biological weapons programs. But if terrorists used large quantities of liquid agent, then even an off-the-shelf sprayer could pose a significant threat—not to an entire city, but to, for example, passengers on a train.

Besides releasing CB agents into the air, terrorists might try contaminating a water supply or tampering with pharmaceuticals or foods. If the aim was to damage the target country's economy or to injure a particular company, the terrorists would only have to poison a fraction of the target foods in order to create fear. In the United States, cola, milk, and baby food could be particularly vulnerable targets.

Water supplies require collection, treatment, storage, and distribution. The two common sources from which drinking water is collected are ground water (wells) and surface water (rivers and lakes). Wells are more commonly used in rural areas for individual homes, and surface water is more common in big cities. Well systems make easy targets, but they tend to be small. Most surface water systems in the United States are so large that any contamination would probably be diluted too quickly to be harmful. This may not be the case in other countries.

Treatment plants are not very vulnerable, according to an Army study, because an attack would be detected before the contaminated water was widely distributed. But a case of contaminated water in Washington, D.C., in 1994 (not caused by terrorists) suggests that this is not necessarily true. Authorities did not detect high levels of cryptosporidium growing in Washington's water supplies until after the water had been distributed. Residents were instructed to drink only bottled water until authorities could purify the water. A similar outbreak in Milwaukee killed some 100 people. Chemical agents can also be removed from water, although some agents require more elaborate procedures than others.[15]

From treatment plants, water is usually pumped to storage tanks or reservoirs. Attacking a reservoir has been shown to be both costly and ineffective, especially with large reservoirs, in which dilution would soon render contaminants inactive. In the United States water in large reservoirs is routinely treated and tested.[16] But remotely located small reservoirs could nonetheless be vulnerable. There is little security at some of these sites, and the water quality is monitored less often. Attacking distribution networks would require significantly lower quantities of contaminants than attacking an entire reservoir, but the number of people put at risk would decrease commensurately. Distribution networks might be vulnerable, however, to terrorists whose goal was to attack a particular symbolic target or a building of strategic importance.[17]

Radiological Weapons

Detonation of a nuclear device is the least likely form of terrorism involving weapons of mass destruction. But technical challenges would not prevent less dramatic uses of radiological materials, which, although unlikely to kill or injure many people, could impose heavy financial and psychological costs on the targeted government.

Radioactive isotopes can be found at a number of diverse facilities, including hospitals and industrial plants, and in waste from nuclear power plants. While industrial isotopes are found in higher quantities in industrialized countries, nuclear waste is found all over the world. Unlike chemical, biological, or nuclear weapons, radiological weapons (now generally called radiation-dispersal devices or RDDs) are not banned by any international treaty.

The U.S. Department of Energy maintains a database of cases of smuggling of nuclear materials reported in the press, including not only fissile materials but also nonfissile radioisotopes. Most thefts of nuclear materials have occurred in the former Soviet Union, and most have involved nonfissile radioisotopes. But other countries are by no means immune to loss or theft. The U.S. General Accounting Office estimates that, between 1955 and 1977, unaccounted-for special nuclear (that is, fissile) materials totaled in the thousands of kilograms.[18] These losses are almost certainly attributable to accounting errors, but they indicate a distressing lack of care.

Terrorists who obtained radiological materials would next face the technical hurdles of turning them into RDDs. In experiments conducted in the 1940s and 1950s, the U.S. military found that disseminating gamma-emitting radiological agents in air involved enormous difficulties because of the heat generated by the material and the problem of dissipation.[19] Gamma emitters require heavy shielding, and some have to be used immediately because of radioactive decay. The military contemplated dispersing the substances using artillery shells, mortar shells, aircraft, and "fission aerial bombs or fission projectiles." The effects would be highly dependent on weather conditions and terrain. Cities would be very costly to attack. Stafford Warren found that "something approaching 100 times greater concentration" would be required for built-up areas because structures would absorb a large portion of the radiation.[20]

The U.S. government concluded after years of study that RDDs were not militarily useful. Iraq, too, apparently renounced them as impractical. But radiological weapons might meet some terrorists' objectives, especially if the terrorists were more interested in imposing financial costs or creating panic than in killing. Even if the terrorists used a crude dissemination device or a quantity of radioactive material too small to present a serious threat to health, fear of radiation could cause panic. When the United States was considering producing RDDs in the 1940s and 1950s, the demoralizing of personnel was explicitly mentioned as one of the "specific uses" of radiological warfare.[21]

The costs imposed on a targeted facility or government would be immense. In 1966 an American B-52 bomber collided with another plane over Spain. The conventional explosives in two of the B-52's hydrogen bombs detonated and dispersed plutonium over several hundred acres. Workers had to plow up 285 acres and remove soil from 5.5 acres, which was shipped back to the United States. The cost of the cleanup, including finding and recovering the bombs, was $100 million (in 1966 dollars), including $10 million for recovery of a bomb that fell into the sea.[22]

A relatively easy way for terrorists to disperse radioisotopes (or chemical or biological agents) would be through the ventilation system of a building. Terrorists might also use sprayers or blowers to disseminate fine powder, or release the powder from the top of a tall building. The U.S. military also considered placing radioactive material in enemy water supplies, which might work for small-scale operations but would not be very effective where water is kept in large reservoirs.[23]

After police seized a series of small nuclear caches in Germany in the spring and summer of 1994, numerous stories in the press warned that terrorists could use stolen plutonium to poison water supplies. It is possible to make soluble plutonium compounds, but in fact metallic plutonium sinks. Moreover, plutonium is more readily absorbed by the lungs than by the gastrointestinal tract, so it is an inefficient agent for poisoning water or food.

Nuclear facilities such as power plants may be attractive targets for terrorists. People who live near these facilities are highly sensitized to the health risks of radiation. The regulatory procedures that have been devised to deal with reactor accidents are more rigorous than required for public safety but not rigorous enough to reassure the public. For example, if a radiation level five times higher than background were detected outside Rocky Flats in Colorado, officials would be required to evacuate the city even though scientists consider this level harmless.[24] A terrorist whose objective was to create panic and wreak havoc (rather than to kill people) could take advantage of these tight regulations: a relatively small amount of radioactive material disseminated near Rocky Flats would be enough to force the city to evacuate—with significant economic and psychological repercussions for residents.

Power reactors are also vulnerable to sabotage. Spent fuel rods contain cesium-137 and other gamma-emitting isotopes. Sabotage would probably require the complicity of plant employees, but terrorists might also be able to damage a reactor or a tank holding radioactive waste by placing explosives outside the fence or attacking the plant by plane.[25] An explosion would be significantly more dangerous than a fire. Antinuclear terrorists in Germany have already tried to sabotage the transport of spent fuel rods, although there is no evidence that they were trying to steal the rods.[26]

Nuclear Weapons

Only the most sophisticated terrorist groups would be likely to consider manufacturing their own nuclear weapons. For these groups, the binding constraint would probably be the acquisition of fissile materials, which are much more highly protected than nonfissile radioactive isotopes. A spate of thefts of nuclear materials in the former Soviet Union makes it clear that the current system for protecting fissile materials is inadequate.

The former Soviet Union is not the only potential source of fissile materials. In May 1997 security officers at Rocky Flats, a nuclear facility fifteen miles from Denver, Colorado, told federal investigators that security had grown so weak that terrorists would be able to penetrate the facility. Large amounts of weapons-grade material are stored at the plant, which produced plutonium during the Cold War. The plant's director of security and safeguards had quit "in disgust" a month earlier, claiming that he could no longer ensure the safety of Denver's citizens. He also warned that an antigovernment group called the Montana Militia had tried to recruit members from among the plant's guards. Although the recruitment attempts were reportedly unsuccessful, they suggest that antigovernment groups may be interested in nuclear or radiological terrorism. A government inquiry also revealed security lapses at other U.S. nuclear sites.[27]

In the unlikely, but not impossible, event that terrorists managed to buy or steal a sufficient quantity of fissile material, a key question is whether they could make a detonable nuclear device, with or without state sponsorship. A group of designers of nuclear weapons was commissioned in 1987 to consider this possibility. The group concluded that building a crude nuclear device was "within reach of terrorists having sufficient resources to recruit a team of three or four technically qualified specialists," with expertise in "several quite distinct areas [including] the physical, chemical and metallurgical properties of the various materials to be used... technology concerning high explosives... electric circuitry; and others."[28] Terrorists might even be able to detonate plutonium oxide powder without actually making a bomb, the designers said, although such an operation would be extremely dangerous and would require "tens of kilograms" of material. The new availability of nuclear material on the black market is therefore particularly troubling.

South Africa's secret nuclear program, closed down in 1989 and revealed to the world by President de Klerk in 1993, provides some insight into how a sophisticated terrorist group could build a nuclear bomb if it had access to fissile materials. The South African experience makes clear that "virtually anybody can make a bomb," according to Ambassador Thomas Graham: "The number of people required is relatively small, and a wealthy backer of a terrorist organization could provide the funds. We're talking about millions—not billions—of dollars, and hundreds—not thousands—of people (including support staff)."[29]

While enriching the uranium required a large infrastructure and technical expertise, South African officials demonstrated the ease of making nuclear weapons once the highly enriched uranium (HEU) is in hand. Most of the equipment required to make the bombs was easy to procure covertly. By the time de Klerk canceled the program, South Africa had acquired a secret plant for enriching uranium for bombs; a stockpile of weapons-grade uranium; and six gun-assembly fission weapons (the kind of weapon the United States used against Hiroshima).[30]

Waldo Stumpf, the head of South Africa's Nuclear Energy Corporation, estimated in 1994 that the entire project, including enriching the uranium, cost $200 million. "The nuclear deterrent programme was considered to be a far more cost-effective alternative to the development of, for example, a fighter aircraft capability," Stumpf said. It cost "less than 5 percent of the defense budget at the time."[31] Costs would have been significantly lower had South Africa been able to purchase the HEU. Thus, if a terrorist group had access to HEU, the cost of producing the bomb could be significantly less than $200 million.

Whenever possible, the South African technicians used simple machines not controlled for export. For example, they used a two-axis machine tool (designed for making two-dimensional shapes) to create the three-dimensional shape necessary for the gun-assembly device.[32]

In the early 1980s the project employed about 100 people, more than half of them in administrative support and security; 40 people worked in the weapons program, David Albright reports, but only 20 were actually building the weapons. By 1989, when the program ended, the workforce had risen to 300, half of whom worked in the weapons program.[33]

The number of people actually involved in making the weapons is shockingly small, but it is significantly more than the "three or four technically qualified specialists" envisioned by the group of nuclear weapons designers. Nonetheless, South Africa's experience shows that some terrorist groups (for example Hezbollah) have sufficient financial resources, although they apparently lack the requisite expertise and/or the requisite fissile material.

Instead of building their own weapon, terrorists (or a terrorist-supporting regime) might try to steal or buy a nuclear warhead. Stealing a warhead would require overcoming security at a site where weapons are stored or deployed, taking possession of the bomb, and bypassing any locks intended to prevent unauthorized detonation of the weapon. This would clearly be easier if the terrorists were able to obtain the assistance of insiders (whether through persuasion, coercion, or bribery). Reports occasionally surface about former Soviet soldiers who are willing to sell warheads, and about terrorists' alleged interest in purchasing them, but no instance of an actual sale has been confirmed.[34]

Russia's approximately 6,000 long-range strategic weapons are protected by locks, making it impossible—at least in principle—to launch them without high-level authority. But thousands of shorter-range tactical weapons have less sophisticated protections or no locks at all. These short-range weapons would be both easier to steal and easier to detonate.

A leaked CIA report warns of the potential in Russia for "conspiracies within nuclear armed units." The report attributes the increased risk of conspiracy to deteriorating living conditions and morale, "even among elite nuclear submariners, nuclear warhead handlers, and the Strategic Rocket Forces." Submarines are a particular source of concern: Russian naval officers know a lot more about nuclear weapons than their ground force counterparts, since they must be able to operate autonomously at sea.[35]

General Aleksandr Lebed, a former head of President Yeltsin's Security Council, has claimed that most of the atomic demolition munitions or "suitcase bombs" in the former Soviet arsenal are unaccounted for. It is not possible at this point to confirm or deny Lebed's claim, but these bombs, if they exist, would be perfect terrorist devices because they would be small enough to be carried by one man.[36]

The Case of Aum Shinrikiyo

The most successful and most publicized terrorist use of weapons of mass destruction to date was the case of the Japanese cult called Aum Shinrikiyo. In our attempt to understand modern terrorism it is worth taking a detailed look at this cult and its leader.[37]

Shoko Asahara, whose original name was Chizuo Matsumoto, was born on the southern Japanese island of Kyushu. His father wove straw floor mats (tatami) for a living, and was barely able to feed his family. The family of six lived in a small shack with a dirt floor. Asahara was blind in his left eye and only half-sighted in his right. Sighted children taunted him, and he in turn taunted those whose vision was worse than his own. At the boarding school for blind children that he attended, he tortured and tricked his classmates into performing services for him, and duped them in financial scams. From childhood on, Asahara was determined to make money.

After high school Asahara founded a clinic, where he charged high fees, the equivalent of up to $7,000, for a three-month course of treatment, which included yoga, "herbal tonics," and acupuncture. He also peddled his treatments to senior citizens in Tokyo's top hotels, charging them thousands of dollars to "cure" their rheumatism with tonics made of ingredients such as dried orange peel and alcohol. Eventually he was arrested for fraud, but the court-imposed fine of about $1,000 was a tiny fraction of his profits.

In 1984 Asahara formed a company called Aum Inc., which produced health drinks and ran yoga schools. Like many Japanese people in the 1980s, Asahara developed an interest in spirituality. He traveled to India, where he perfected his meditation technique, learning, he claimed, to levitate. He also claimed he could pass through solid walls, intuit people's thoughts, and chart people's past lives.

In 1986 a Japanese New Age journal, *Twilight Zone,* ran pictures of Asahara apparently suspended in midair in the lotus position. Attendance at his yoga schools rose, and with the profits Asahara was able to open schools throughout Japan. Soon afterward he claimed he heard a message from God while meditating, telling him that he had been chosen to lead God's army. At about the same time he met a radical historian who predicted that Armageddon would come by the year 2000. Only a small group would survive, the historian told Asahara, and the leader of that group would emerge in Japan. Asahara immediately cast himself as that leader. He began planning for Armageddon and his leadership role, and changed the name of his company to Aum Shinrikiyo (Aum Supreme Truth).

Asahara chose Shiva the Destroyer as the principal deity for Aum Supreme Truth, though he also emphasized the Judeo-Christian notion of Armageddon. At a seminar in 1987 he made his first prediction: nuclear war would break out between 1999 and 2003. There were fewer than fifteen years to prepare, he warned. Nuclear war could be averted, but only if Aum opened a branch in every country on earth. Those who were spiritually enlightened would survive even a nuclear holocaust.

Asahara found new ways to expand his revenues. He encouraged his students to cut off all ties with the outside world and to hand over all their assets as a way to foster their spiritual development. Asahara sold clippings from his beard for $375 a half-inch and his dirty bath-water (called Miracle Pond) for $800 a quart. He also opened a compound near Mount Fuji, which eventually included a very expensive (and hazardous) hospital, as well as laboratories for research on weapons of mass destruction [WMD].

Many of those attracted to Asahara's promise of spiritual enlightenment were scientists, physicians, and engineers from Japan's top schools. One was Seiichi Endo, who had been trained at Kyoto University and was working at the university's viral research center. Another was Hideo Murai, a brilliant astrophysicist who became Asahara's "engineer of the apocalypse." According to David Kaplan and Andrew Marshall, who have studied Aum Shinrikiyo, "The high-tech children of postindustrial Japan were fascinated by Aum's dramatic claims to supernatural power, its warnings of an apocalyptic future, its esoteric spiritualism."[38]

Asahara was able to attract Russian scientists and engineers to the cause. Russia was like a supermarket for Asahara. He bought weapons and training, and he recruited among Russia's scientific elite, who were now unemployed or unpaid and seeking new missions. During the early 1990s Russia's Minister of Defense Grachev reportedly paved the way for three groups of Aum Shinrikiyo cult members to spend three days with military units in the Taman and Kantemirov divisions, where, for a fee, they were trained to use military equipment. The cult reportedly also received substantial assistance from Oleg Lobov, who was then the head of President Yeltsin's Security Council. The Russian Prosecutor General's office is investigating allegations by a Japanese cult member that Lobov provided assistance to the poison gas program.[39]

Asahara became obsessed with WMD, in part because he was convinced that the CIA planned to use such weapons against Japan. Moreover, he believed his group would need every available weapon to survive Armageddon. He put his scientists to work on developing WMD. He also sent a deputy on several trips to Russia to purchase weapons and scientific assistance.

Soon these efforts began to pay off. Asahara directed a series of attacks using biological agents. Cult members have confessed to carrying out nine such attacks, including at the Japanese Diet, at the Imperial Palace, elsewhere in Tokyo, and at two American naval bases: Yokosuka and Yokohama. In April 1990 members reportedly drove through the city of Tokyo with a convoy of three trucks outfitted to spray botulinum toxin. The convoy drove by the American naval bases, where they attempted to spread the poison, and to Narita airport. No botulinum was reported detected, however, during any of these attacks, and no one was reported ill. Next the cult tried spreading anthrax. In July 1993 members tried to disseminate anthrax at several sites, including near the Imperial Palace and near the Diet. They again fitted a truck with a special sprayer and drove it around the city. These attacks also failed.[40]

The cult tried spreading anthrax from the roof of its headquarters building. Members put a steam generator on the roof and poured anthrax spores into it, then turned on a sprayer and fan and waited to see the results. Small birds died, and the generator emitted a putrid smell that permeated the neighborhood. It smelled like burning flesh, one resident told the press. When inspectors went to the Aum building to ask questions, they were told that the smell was from a mix of soybean oil and perfume—Chanel No. 5—which the cult was burning to purify the building.[41]

The group was more successful with chemical weapons. In June 1994 residents of Matsumoto, a mountain resort a hundred miles west of Tokyo, noticed a strange fog hugging the earth. Soon thereafter some residents experienced nausea, vomiting, pain in their eyes, and difficulty breathing. By the next morning 7 people had died and 200 were ill. A total of 600 eventually became ill. Dogs lay dead in the streets, and dead fish floated in a nearby pond. Doctors investigating the incident noted that victims had markedly reduced levels of acetylocholinesterase (an enzyme necessary for proper functioning of the nervous system), a sign that they had been exposed to toxic organophosphate-based insecticides or nerve agents. But even after traces of sarin, a nerve agent, were found in the pond, authorities did not suspect terrorism. No terrorist group had claimed responsibility, and the idea that terrorists could be responsible for such a heinous crime seemed too far-fetched to be believed. In fact, as subsequently became known, Aum Shinrikiyo had carried out the attack. Asahara's intention was to poison three judges living in the area. The judges survived the attack when the wind changed direction, but the poison spread over the town.[42]

Nine months later, on March 20, 1995, the cult used sarin again, this time in a deadly incident that attracted media attention. By this time the police were closing in on the group, and its scientists had to work fast. The terrorists placed hastily made sarin-filled polyethylene pouches on five Tokyo subway cars, and then punctured the pouches with sharpened umbrella tips. Sarin is sufficiently volatile that no special dissemination devices were necessary. Soon after the pouches were punctured, poisonous fumes filled the cars. Despite the crude technique, 12 people died and more than 5,000 were injured, many seriously enough to require hospitalization. Two subsequent attacks failed, in part because Tokyo police were on the lookout for suspicious packages. On May 5, 1995, cult members left small plastic bags, one containing sodium cyanide and the other sulfuric acid, in Tokyo's Shinjuku train station with the intention of disseminating cyanide gas. And on July 4, 1995, similar improvised chemical devices were found in restrooms in four stations.[43]

The Aum Shinrikiyo cult intended to kill many thousands of people. The 1995 poison-gas attack in the Tokyo subway was carried out in haste and did not represent the cult's full potential. The group had built up a large production capacity for chemical weapons and was working on plans for disseminating chemical and biological agents over some major Japanese city. Cult members had hidden a bottle containing an ounce of VX—reportedly enough to kill about 15,000 people—which was recovered by the Tokyo police in September 1996. They had amassed hundreds of tons of chemicals used in the production of sarin—reportedly to make enough sarin to kill millions. They had bought a Russian Mi-17 combat helicopter and two remotely piloted vehicles to disseminate the agent over populated areas. Police found a large amount of *Clostridium botulinum,* together with 160 barrels of growth media (required for growing the bacteria). The cult was reportedly cooperating with North Korea, with former Soviet Mafia groups, and indirectly with Iran, in smuggling nuclear materials and conventional munitions out of Russia through Ukraine.[44] Members reportedly visited Zaire on the pretext of providing medical assistance to victims of the Ebola virus, with the actual objective of acquiring a sample of the virus to culture as a warfare agent. The group was also actively trying to purchase Russian nuclear warheads, according to the CIA, and may have been plotting a chemical attack in the United States.[45]

In November 1995 Senator Sam Nunn held a hearing on Aum Shinrikiyo. The senator's staff testified that at the time of the Tokyo attack Aum Shinrikiyo had some 50,000 members, 30,000 of whom were Russians. It had assets worth $1.4 billion and offices in Bonn, Sri Lanka, New York, and Moscow as well as in several Japanese cities. U.S. officials admitted that, despite the alarming range of Aum Shinrikiyo's activities, it was not on the "radar screen" of the U.S. intelligence community.[46]

Other Cases

Before the Aum Shinrikiyo incidents, other terrorists had attempted or threatened to use chemical, biological, or radiological agents, but usually on a scale so small that the media hardly noticed. Most of the incidents involved threats that were never carried out, although some of the threats were very costly to the targeted companies or governments. In the rare cases when these agents have been used, they have been used more as weapons of mass impact than as weapons of mass destruction: few people have been killed.

A common use of these agents is to commit economic sabotage either against specific companies or against entire industries. For example, the Animal Liberation Front (ALF) claimed to have spiked Mars chocolate bars with rat poison to protest research on tooth decay conducted on live monkeys. No poison was found, but Mars reported losses of $4.5 million. British police later charged four members of the ALF with injecting toxic mercury into turkeys sold in supermarkets as a protest against their slaughter during the Christmas season. The same group was suspected of poisoning eggs in British supermarkets in 1989. The eggs were punctured and marked with a skull and crossbones. An attached message signed "ALF" warned that the eggs had been poisoned. While the product-tampering crimes committed in the United States in the late 1980s were not committed by terrorists, the costs imposed on industry demonstrate the potential effectiveness of economic terrorism. In 1986 alone, U.S. pharmaceutical manufacturers destroyed over $1 billion worth of pharmaceuticals because of tampering or threats of tampering and spent another $1 billion making their products more resistant to tampering.[47]

Chemical and radiological agents have also been used to meet more traditional terrorist objectives: to attack symbolic targets, to assassinate individuals, or to commit small-scale acts of random violence. Several groups have planned to attack water supplies, although no known attack has been successful. In 1972, a U.S. neo-Nazi group, the Order of the Rising Sun, was found in possession of a large quantity of typhoid bacillus, which it reportedly intended to use to poison water supplies in several midwestern cities. Another incident involved a plot by several right-wing extremist groups to overthrow the U.S. government. One of the groups, The Covenant, the Sword, and the Arm of the Lord, had stockpiled some thirty gallons of cyanide for the purpose of polluting municipal water supplies. The group was apprehended before the plot could be carried out.[48]

While the terrorists involved in these two incidents were plotting alarmingly destructive attacks, it is unlikely that either of the planned attacks would have succeeded. The chlorine in U.S. reservoirs would have killed the typhoid bacillus, and dilution would have rendered the cyanide harmless. Attacking a small, unprotected water supply could be more effective. Ramzi Youssef, the convicted mastermind of the bombing of the World Trade Center, reportedly threatened in a letter to poison water supplies in the Philippines. The letter was found on his person at the time of his arrest. In it he claimed to be able to produce chemical agents for use against "vital institutions and residential populations and the sources of drinking water."[49]

A few attacks have involved radioactive isotopes. In 1995 Shamil Basayev, the leader of the Chechen group that had earlier taken more than 1,000 hospital patients hostage, buried a packet of radioactive cesium in Izmailovski Park in Moscow to demonstrate his capabilities.[50] Izmailovski Park is a popular recreation spot for both Russians and tourists. Had Basayev actually disseminated radioactive cesium, he would have imposed heavy costs on the Russian government. In a bizarre case on Long Island in 1996, three people became convinced that county officials were covering up the crash landing of space aliens in their county. They acquired five canisters of radioactive radium, with which they planned to assassinate county officials by poisoning the officials' toothpaste, air conditioning, and automobiles. Their ultimate objective was to seize control of the county government, but members were apprehended before they were able to poison anyone, much less achieve their ambitious agenda.[51]

The single U.S. case involving the actual use of biological agents occurred in September 1984, when members of the Rajneeshee cult in Oregon poisoned salad bars with *Salmonella typhimurium*. The cult had established a commune on a large ranch, part of which was incorporated as the city of Rajneeshpuram. Local residents objected to the commune and challenged the city's charter in the courts. The cult sought to ensure the victory of its own candidate in the November 1984 elections for country commissioner. Members considered various ideas for accomplishing this goal, including vote fraud, and decided to prevent nonmembers from voting by making them ill. In September, as a trial run, members contaminated salad bars in ten local restaurants; 751 people became ill. The cult then abandoned the plot, however, in part because members judged their candidate would not prevail in the election. The Rajneeshee involvement in the outbreak of illness was not established until a year later, during investigations of cult members for other, unrelated crimes.[52]

These cases are instructive. First, no terrorist group has acquired a nuclear weapon, although Aum Shinrikiyo attempted to do so. Second, the most destructive biological attack involved a crude food poison, rather than air dissemination of a deadly agent. While such poisons are somewhat easier to procure than deadlier agents, the ability of a terrorist group to contaminate a salad bar is alarming, as is the health authorities' difficulty in determining the cause of the outbreak of illness. This case raises the question of whether other outbreaks of disease, assumed to have resulted from natural causes, may actually have been caused by deliberate sabotage or terrorism.

The most destructive incident, Aum Shinrikiyo's attack on the Tokyo subway, involved disseminating a chemical agent in an enclosed space. This method and the contamination of food are probably the easiest ways to use weapons of mass destruction, and are likely to remain the most common forms of terrorism involving these weapons.

All of Aum Shinrikiyo's large-scale attacks with biological agents are believed to have failed. Very little is known about why they were unsuccessful. There are many strains of *Clostridium botulinum* and *Bacillus anthracis*. Experts now believe the cult may have grown weak strains of the microbes, possibly, in the case of the anthrax, a relatively harmless vaccine strain. The cult also had difficulty aerosolizing the agent in respirable particle size. Sprayers used to create anthrax mists became clogged, for example, a problem that other terrorists would be likely to confront as ell.[53] Were terrorists to master these technologies they would have the potential to kill not just hundreds but hundreds of thousands of people.

Notes

1. Prepared statement of Edward Eitzen, U.S. Congress, Senate, Committee on Governmental Affairs, Permanent Subcommittee on Investigations, *Hearings on Global Proliferation of Weapons of Mass Destruction*, 104th Cong., 1st sess., pt. 1, Oct. 31, 1995, 112. More likely, doctors would observe large numbers of cases that resembled the flu. By the time doctors realized their patients had been victims of an attack, it would be too late to save their lives.

2. Cohen, speech to the Conference on Terrorism, Weapons of Mass Destruction, and U.S. Strategy, University of Georgia, April 28, 1997. Prepared statement of George Tenet, U.S. Congress, Senate, Select Committee on Intelligence, *Hearing on Current and Projected National Security Threats to the United States*, 105th Cong., 1st sess., Feb. 5, 1997.

3. "Albania: Army Officer Urges Return of Looted Chemical Weapons," FBIS-EEU-97-096, transcribed text, April 6, 1997. Source: Paris AFP in English 1740 GMT April 6, 1997.

4. Agence France Presse, "Russian Security Inadequate for Chemical Weapons Storage," Aug. 2, 1995.

5. Prepared statement of Vil Mirzayanov, U.S. Senate, *Hearings on Global Proliferation of WMD*, Nov. 1, 1995. A. Cooperman and K. Belianinov, "Moonlighting by Modem in Russia," *U.S. News and World Report*, April 17, 1995. James Adams, "Gadaffi Lures South Africa's Top Germ Warfare Scientists," *Sunday Times*, Feb. 26, 1995.

6. Office of Technology Assessment, *Technology against Terrorism: The Federal Effort* (Washington: GPO, 1991), 51–52.

7. Raymond Zilinskas, "Terrorists and BW: Inevitable Alliance?" *Perspectives in Biology and Medicine* 34 (Autumn 1990). Eitzen, prepared statement. Interview with Dr. Kathleen Bailey, Dec. 1995.

8. It is quite easy to purchase these manuals. I called one such publishing house and told the operator I wanted to buy manuals with instructions on how to poison people. She asked whether I was interested in bombs or silencers as well. I told her no, I only wanted to poison people. She asked for my credit card number and mailing address, and that was the end of our conversation.

9. The most prominent example is a case in which a killer followed instructions provided in a manual entitled *Hit Man*. See *Rice v. Paladin Enterprises, Inc.*, 940 F. Supp. 836 (D. Md. 1996), appeal docketed, no. 96-2412 (4th circuit).

10. Leonard A. Cole, *Clouds of Secrecy: The Army's Germ Warfare Tests over Populated Areas* (Totowa, N.J.: Rowman and Littlefield, 1988), 163. The Army carried out the tests in the belief that the simulants were harmless to human health, but a few people were adversely affected and one hospital patient died. The Army ended such simulated attacks against human beings in the 1960s.

11. Ibid., 68. *U.S. Army Activities in the United States Biological Warfare Programs, 1942–1977* (Washington: Department of the Army, 1977), vol. 1, 6–3; vol. 2, IV-E-1-1.
12. *U.S. Army Activities in Biological Warfare Programs*, vol. 2, IV-E-5-1-5A-1.
13. See Ron Purver, "Chemical and Biological Terrorism: The Threat According to the Open Literature," Canadian Security Intelligence Service, June 1995.
14. William Patrick, "Biological Terrorism and Aerosol Dissemination," *Politics and the Life Sciences*, Sept. 1996, 209; and interviews at Fort Detrick. Eitzen, prepared statement, 112.
15. Stephen C. Reynolds, "The Terrorist Threat to Domestic Water Supplies" (U.S. Army Corps of Engineers, Aug. 1987), unclassified/limited distribution. Seymour S. Block, *Disinfection, Sterilization, and Preservation* (Philadelphia: Lea and Febiger, 1991). U.S. Army Environmental Hygiene Agency, Aberdeen Proving Ground, "Position Paper: Threat of Chemical Agents in Field Drinking Water," March 1982. Cryptosporidium lives in human and animal intestines and is secreted in feces. It can be found in most surface water, particularly after heavy rains. It is often difficult to identify and is not always killed by routine chlorination.
16. B. J. Berkowitz et al., "Superviolence: The Civil Threat of Mass Destruction Weapons" (Washington: Advanced Concept Research, 1972). Zilinskas, "Terrorists and BW."
17. Reynolds, "Terrorist Threat to Water Supplies."
18. General Accounting Office, "Commercial Nuclear Fuel Facilities Need Better Security," May 2, 1977, ii, cited in J. K. Campbell, "The Threat of Non-State Proliferation" (manuscript, Defense Intelligence Agency).
19. Letter from V. Bush to General Groves, Nov. 15, 1943, Bush-Conant Files, RG 227, folder 157, National Archives.
20. "Military Use of Radio-Active Materials and Organization for Defense," S-1 files, and "Report of the Subcommittee of the S-1 Committee on the Use of Radioactive Material as a Military Weapon," 7, in Bush-Conant Files, RG 227, folder 157, National Archives. "Fission aerial bombs or fission projectiles" may refer to atomic weapons wrapped in cobalt or another gamma emitter or, more likely, a conventional bomb containing radioactive material.
21. "Military Use of Radio-Active Materials," Bush-Conant Files.
22. Information provided by Doug Stephens, Lawrence Livermore National Laboratory. W. M. Place, F. C. Cobb, and C. G. Defferding, "Palomares Summary Report," Field Command, Defense Nuclear Agency, Technology and Analysis Directorate, Kirtland Air Force Base (Jan. 1975). Randy Maydew, "Find the Missing H-Bomb," *Air Combat*, Nov.-Dec. 1996.
23. "Military Use of Radio-Active Materials," Bush-Conant Files.
24. David Albright, personal communicaiton, Sept. 24, 1996.
25. Experts became concerned about the possibility of truck bombs at power plants after a car crashed through the gate at Three Mile Island in 1993. Matthew Wald, "US Examining Ways to Protect Nuclear Plants against Terrorists," *New York Times*, April 23, 1993. Sandia National Laboratory concluded in 1984 that "unacceptable damage to vital reactor systems could occur from a relatively small charge at close distances and also from larger but still reasonable size charges at large setback distances." "Weekly Information Report to the NRC Commissioners," April 20, 1984, enclosure E, 3. In 1994 the Nuclear Regulatory Commission demanded security upgrades at commercial reactors that would make a truck bomb attack more difficult.
26. Germany's federal counter-sabotage agency, the BFV, determined that escalating violence accompanying the transport of spent fuel was the "work of terrorists" who might have contacts with the Red Army Faction. "State, GNS Differ over Strategy to Defy Saboteurs at Gorleben," *Nuclear Fuel*, Jan. 13, 1997, 11.
27. Rocky Flats held 11.9 metric tons of weapons-grade plutonium as of Sept. 1994 and 2.8 metric tons of HEU as of Feb. 1996. U.S. Department of Energy, "Storage and Disposition of Weapons-Usable Fissile Materials Final Programmatic Environmental Impact Statement, Summary," DOE/EIS-0229, Dec. 1996, S-5. Jim Carrier, "Flats Security Lax, Ex-Officials Warn," *Denver Post*, May 20, 1997. James Brooke, "Plutonium Stockpile Fosters Fears of a Disaster Waiting to Happen," *New York Times*, Dec. 11, 1996. John J. Fialka, "Energy Department Report Faults Security at Weapons Plants," *Wall Street Journal*, June 16, 1997.

28. Paul Leventhal and Yonah Alexander, *Preventing Nuclear Terrorism* (Lexington, Mass.: Lexington Books, 1987), 9, 58.

29. Interview with Ambassador Thomas Graham, Nov. 25, 1996.

30. David Albright, "South Africa's Secret Nuclear Weapons," ISIS Report (Institute for Science and International Security), May 1994. Graham interview, Waldo Stumpf, "South Africa's Nuclear Weapons Programme," in Kathleen C. Bailey, *Weapons of Mass Destruction: Costs Versus Benefits* (New Delhi: Manohar, 1994), 71. Albright claims there were seven weapons, but Stumpf says only six were completed.

31. Stumpf, "South Africa's Nuclear Weapons Programme," 75, 76. Cost figures assume 1994 exchange rates (presumable in 1994 dollars).

32. Albright, "South Africa's Secret Nuclear Weapons."

33. Ibid. I was able to confirm in general terms these approximate figures in interviews with U.S. government officials who had interviewed South African nuclear specialists.

34. William Arkin of Greenpeace says he came close to buying a nuclear warhead from a Russian soldier working at a storage site in East Germany in the early 1990s. The soldier told Arkin he had found a way to gain access to the warheads during the transition between shifts. "The orientation of security," Arkin explains, "was very heavily weighted toward defending against a NATO attack. It was not heavily weighted toward protesters, or public intervention, or terrorists." Quoted in William Burrows and Robert Windrem, *Critical Mass* (New York: Simon and Schuster, 1994), 249. The CIA has noted Aum Shinrikiyo's apparent interest in buying nuclear warheads from Russia: Statement for the record by John Deutch, U.S. Senate, *Hearings on Global Proliferation of WMD,* pt. 2, S.Hrg 104–422, 104th Cong., 2nd sess., March 20, 1996, 7. And Renssalaer Lee cites a 1991 letter reportedly faxed to the Russian nuclear weapons laboratory Arzamas-16, allegedly from Islamic Jihad, offering to buy a nuclear warhead. The director of Arzamas reportedly also told Lee that Iraqi agents had offered $2 billion for a warhead in 1993. Interview with Lee, Nov. 12, 1996. I have found no other reports of this letter.

35. Bill Gertz, "Russian Renegades Pose Nuke Danger," *Washington Times*, Oct. 22, 1996. Interview with an expert on Russian nuclear weapons, Oct. 16, 1996.

36. Unclassified cable, Moscow 13851, TOR: 0316032, June 1997.

37. This section is based on David E. Kaplan and Andrew Marshall, *The Cult at the End of the World* (New York: Crown, 1996).

38. Ibid., 28.

39. "Prosecutors Investigate Lobov's Links to Religious Sect," FBIS-SOV-97144, May 24, 1997; "Lobov Faces Questions over Investigation of Japanese Sect," FBIS-SV-97-084, April 25, 1997; both trans. from Moscow Interfax.

40. CIA, "The Chemical, Biological and Radiological Terrorist Threat from Non-State Actors," paper presented to Aspen Strategy group conference "The Proliferation Threat of Weapons of Mass Destruction and U.S. Security Interest," Aspen, Colo., Aug. 1996. William Broad, "How Japan Germ Terror Alerted World," *New York Times*, May 26, 1998.

41. Ibid. Another biological attack also failed: on March 15, 1995, cult members planned to release botulinal toxin at Kasumigaseki station, but a member struck by a guilty conscience neglected to arm the devices.

42. John F. Quinn, "Terrorism Comes to Tokyo: The Aum Shinri Kyo Incident," paper presented to the Association of Former Intelligence Officers, 1996 Annual Convention, Falls Church, Va., Oct. 1996. Authorities assumed the sarin had formed spontaneously from pesticide residues. Leonard Cole, *The Eleventh Plague* (New York: Freeman, 1996), citing *Mainichi Daily News*, June 30, July 2, July 9, and July 16, 1994.

43. See Jonathan B. Tucker, "Chemical/Biological Terrorism: Coping with a New Threat," *Politics and the Life Sciences* 15 (Sept. 1996). Ron Purver, "The Threat of Chemical/Biological Terrorism" Commentary 60 (Aug. 1995). Kaplan and Marshall, *Cult at the End of the World.* Interviews with John Sopko. Quinn, "Terrorism Comes to Tokyo." CIA, "Chemical, Biological and Radiological Threat."

44. "Tokyo Police Find Bottle of a Cult's Deadly Gas," Associated Press, *New York Times*, Dec. 12, 1996, 15. Nicholas D. Kristof, "Tokyo Syspect in Gas Attack Erupts in Court," *New York*

Times, Nov. 8, 1996, 14. Cole, *Eleventh Plague*, 155. Ed Evanhoe says that after Asahara was arrested North Korea may have moved its nuclear smuggling base of operations to Tumen, China, making use of a North Korean organized-crime ring to smuggle nuclear-related equipment as well as nuclear materials. Email from Evanhoe, Nov. 5, 1996.

45. Staff Report, U.S. Senate, *Hearings on Global Proliferation of WMD*, Nov. 1, 1995. Statement for the Record by John Deutch, 7. Nicholas D. Kristof, "Japanese Cult Said to Have Planned Nerve-Gas Attacks in U.S.," *New York Times*, March 23, 1997.

46. Staff Report, U.S. Senate, *Hearings on Global Proliferation of WMD*, Nov. 1, 1995.

47. Joseph Pilat, "World Watch: Striking Back at Urban Terrorism," *NBC Defense and Technology International* (June 1986), 18. "Animal Rights Activists Attack Scientists' Homes," Associated Press, *Los Angeles Times*, March 13, 1985. Rand database. *Product Tampering and the Threat to Tamper* (Los Angeles: Foundation for American Communications, undated), 3.

48. James Campbell, "Weapons of Mass Destruction and Terrorism: Proliferation by Non-State Actors" (Master's thesis, Naval Postgraduate School, 1996). Rand database. *Arkansas Gazette*, April 27, 1987, cited in Bruce Hoffman. " 'Holy Terror': The Implications of Terrorism Motivated by Religious Imperative," Rand Paper P-7834, 1993.

49. "New Charges Filed against Alleged Leader of Bombing," *Washington Post*, Oct. 7, 1995, 14.

50. Cesium-137, a radioisotope used in the treatment of cancer, is a waste product of nuclear reactors. It has a relatively long half-life, and areas contaminated with it require extensive cleanup. It can be absorbed into the food chain and is carcinogenic. Mark Hibbs, "Chechen Separatists Take Credit for Moscow Cesium-137." Nuclear Fuel 20, no. 25 (Dec. 4, 1995), 5.

51. John McQuiston, "Plot against L.I. Leaders Is Tied to Fear of UFO's" *New York Times*, June 22, 1996. "Two Charged in Plot to Poison Long Island GOP Officials; Radium, Weapons Cache Found in House," *Washington Post*, June 14, 1996. Larry Sutton, "Bail Denied in Radium Plot," *New York Daily News*, June 25, 1996.

52. Prepared Statement of John O'Neill, U.S. Senate, *Hearings on Global Proliferation of WMD*, Nov. 1, 1995, 241. Thomas J. Torok et al., "A Large Community Outbreak of Salmonellosis Caused by International Contamination of Restaurant Salad Bars," *JAMA* 278, no. 5 (Aug. 6, 1987); Seth Carus, "The Rajneesh in Oregon," paper presented at a workshop on Patterns of Behavior Associated with Chemical and Biological Terrorism, Monterey Institute, Washington, June 1998. The Rajneeshees' true motivations are not clear. If their goal was exclusively to make their victims ill, rather than to affect a target audience (by, for example, frightening the local residents), this incident may not, strictly speaking, fit the definition of terrorism used in this book.

53. Broad, "How Japan Germ Terror Alerted World."

5.2 Christopher F. Chyba, 2002

Toward Biological Security

Christopher F. Chyba is an associate professor and codirector of Stanford University's Center for International Security and Cooperation (CISAC). He holds the endowed Carl Sagan Chair for Study of Life in the Universe at the SETI Institute (Mountain View, Calif.). Chyba served on the staff of the National Security Council in the Clinton administration.

Misplaced Analogies

The anthrax attacks on the United States in the autumn of 2001, and the fear and confusion that followed, made clear that the country lacks a comprehensive strategy for biological security—the protection of people and agriculture against disease threats, whether from biological weapons or natural outbreaks. Too often, thinking about biological security has been distorted by misplaced analogies to nuclear or chemical weapons. An effective strategy must leave these analogies largely behind and address the special challenges posed by biological threats.

A strategy for biological security must confront drug-resistant and emerging diseases—more than 30 of which have entered the human population over the past quarter-century. There is no good analogue to this naturally occurring threat in the realm of nuclear or chemical weapons. Moreover, diseases may be targeted against livestock or crops as well as against human populations. And outbreaks of deadly, contagious, and long-incubating diseases such as smallpox have to be detected and stopped rapidly wherever in the world they occur. Fortunately, once formulated, a sound strategy for biological security will help sustain itself because many of its core provisions will benefit public health even apart from acts of bioterror.

In fact, many of the tools used to address natural disease threats will be needed to respond to an intentional attack. The U.S. response to the anthrax attacks has emphasized the importance of improving domestic defenses. These measures include stockpiling vaccines and antibiotics, as well as improving local and national disease surveillance and other public health tools. To be effective these domestic measures must be sustained for decades and keep pace with the biotechnology revolution. International steps—such as improving surveillance for and response to outbreaks of infectious diseases and securing pathogen stocks worldwide—are also crucial to an effective strategy. Yet most of these international measures have been ignored so far in the current focus on immediate domestic needs.

Part of the problem is the very vocabulary we use. Analysts and policymakers refer casually to "WMD" (weapons of mass destruction) or "NBCR" (nuclear/biological/chemical/radiological) weapons, as if the latter were merely variants on the same type of device. In fact, these weapons differ greatly in their ease of production, in the challenges they pose for deterrence, and in the effectiveness of defensive measures against them. The post–September 11 focus on WMD and whether they are in the hands of enemy states or groups risks overlooking these complexities. Put simply, biological weapons differ from nuclear or chemical weapons, and any biological security strategy should begin by paying attention to these differences.

The WMD Continuum

Imagine a line that begins with nuclear weapons at one extreme, continues through chemical, radiological, and biological weapons, and terminates with cyber-weapons (designed to attack computers or critical infrastructure) at the far end. As one moves along this continuum through the different so-called weapons of mass destruction (to which "cyber-weapons" have been added here for purposes of illustration), the difficulties facing nonproliferation become increasingly apparent. At the nuclear extreme, nonproliferation is comparatively robust, whereas at the cyber end it is enormously difficult.

Nuclear nonproliferation policy seeks to limit the number of nations that have nuclear weapons and keep such weapons out of the hands of subnational groups altogether. Any effective approach must guarantee warhead security and prevent the diversion of nuclear material from civilian programs to military or terrorist uses. Article III of the nuclear Nonproliferation Treaty (NPT) provides the legal basis for a near-global verification regime to detect the diversion of fissile material—verification carried out by the UN's International Atomic Energy Agency (IAEA). The agency uses inspections, audits of nuclear material and records, and surveillance cameras and instrumentation to monitor more than 1,000 facilities worldwide.

The IAEA's verification efforts have worked in part because the facilities needed to produce uranium or plutonium for weapons are big and hard to hide. Of course, inspections are not foolproof. Iraq, for example, made significant progress in enrichment of indigenous uranium despite being a party to the NPT and subject to IAEA inspections. This experience led the IAEA to propose strengthened safeguards to include the right to inspections on short notice of undeclared, suspect locations. Yet there have also been important successes. In 1992, IAEA inspectors in North Korea found discrepancies indicating that a plutonium reprocessing plant at Yongbyon had been used more often than the government had declared. In the face of new challenges, the NPT verification regime must evolve rapidly enough to continue playing an important nonproliferation role.

The United States and the nearly 40 other nations of the Nuclear Suppliers Group further pursue nonproliferation by adhering to consensual guidelines restricting nuclear and nuclear-related "dual-use" exports—i.e., material that can serve both civilian and military purposes. These guidelines are intended to supplement the NPT by controlling the transfer of listed items without hindering the legitimate international nuclear cooperation called for by Article IV of the NPT. Through the Cooperative Threat Reduction (CTR) program with the Soviet Union's successor states, the United States has also acted to impede the theft or sale of nuclear material as well as the movement of nuclear scientists from the former Soviet Union to what the Clinton administration first called "rogue states" and later termed "states of concern." Of course, in addition to these multilateral and bilateral measures, diplomatic pressure and security guarantees have also played their roles, and intelligence has been vital throughout.

For all its difficulties, nuclear nonproliferation has been reasonably successful in part because the production of weapons-grade plutonium or uranium is difficult (requiring reactors or enrichment plants, respectively), and this imposes conspicuous bottleneck on any would-be weapons programs. Few of the necessary facilities exist and they can be monitored if declared, or risk discovery by intelligence-gathering if not. (Of course, intelligence findings do not guarantee an end to proliferation concerns, as Iran's case shows.) Because the theft of weapons-grade nuclear material can allow a state or group to circumvent these bottlenecks, preventing nuclear theft has become a high priority in the post–Cold War world.

As challenging as preventing the spread of nuclear weapons has been, preventing the proliferation of cyber-weapons could be insurmountably difficult. Governments can and should control the export of certain high-end computers and components. But cyber-attacks can be launched from almost any of the more than 100 million computers worldwide that have access to the Internet. Applying standard nonproliferation techniques to these computers would therefore ultimately require unannounced inspections or the monitoring of hundreds of millions of residences and businesses. Cyber-security may benefit from certain nonproliferation measures, but it renders traditional inspection approaches absurd. Moreover, automated monitoring of the source and content of electronic messages to identify illicit activities would face its own enormous obstacles.

Falling between the nuclear and cyber extremes of the WMD continuum are chemical, radiological, and biological weapons. Maintaining an international verification regime for chemical weapons is harder than for nuclear weapons because of the larger number of relevant facilities and dual-use materials. The Organization for the Prohibition of Chemical Weapons, established under the Chemical Weapons Convention (CWC), must contend with an entire industrial sector and more than 6,000 inspectable facilities. Nevertheless, under the CWC, governments have declared chemical weapons stocks and opened them to international verification, three of the four declared possessor states have begun destroying their stocks, and inspectors have examined hundreds of dual-use chemical plants. The declaration of 70,000 metric tons of chemical agents by the United States, Russia, India, and South Korea, along with additional states' declarations of chemical weapons production facilities, old chemical weapons, and abandoned chemical weapons, constitute a valuable achievement. The verified elimination of chemical stockpiles and the destruction or conversion of production facilities will be a clear gain for international security—especially once Russia begins destroying its 40,000 metric tons of chemical weapons, some of which currently remains vulnerable to theft. These achievements are valuable regardless of the disturbing absence of Iraq, North Korea, and other states of concern from the CWC regime. The regime is further supplemented by the Australia Group of 33 nations that, like the Nuclear Suppliers Group, establishes consensual national guidelines restricting the export of chemicals and technology that can be used to make weapons.

Biological weapons also fall between the nuclear and cyber ends of the WMD continuum but are even harder to control than chemical weapons. True, the Biological and Toxin Weapons Convention (BWC) established a norm against the production and stockpiling of biological weapons, and the 1925 Geneva Protocol forbids their use. The Australia Group also works to impede the transfer of biological agents and technology where possible through national export controls. Nevertheless, any biological nonproliferation regime will necessarily be less robust than its nuclear counterpart, because much of the relevant material, technology, and knowledge is already far more widely distributed and will become more so in the coming decades.

Scientists can acquire potentially deadly biological agents in the course of legitimate research: for instance, U.S. and British government institutes previously distributed the Ames anthrax strain used in the autumn 2001 attacks to a dozen or so laboratories. Naturally occurring disease outbreaks are another source of lethal organisms: the Ames strain is common in eastern Texas, for example. Indeed, natural outbreaks are the ultimate origin of the agents historically used in nations' biological weapons programs. Moreover, the fermenters required to produce these biological agents in large quantities are widely used in the pharmaceutical, biotechnology, and even beer industries.

Weaponizing these diseases—going from the organism to a preparation that is particularly suitable for distribution as a powder or liquid aerosol—has proved difficult for terrorists. The Japanese group Aum Shinrikyo failed to weaponize anthrax despite devoting substantial financial and scientific resources to the task. But the group's repeated, unsuccessful attempts to spray liquid anthrax aerosol throughout downtown Tokyo in 1993 demonstrated that attacks designed to cause massive urban casualties were no longer in the realm of the fantastic. Then, last autumn's attacks in the United States, when professional-grade anthrax powder was sent through the mail, made clear that an individual or group has now either successfully crossed the weaponization threshold or succeeded in acquiring such material from a national weapons program.

Genetic modification of biological agents (to make them resistant to vaccines or antimicrobial drugs, for instance) probably remains beyond the capabilities of terrorist groups for the time being—although the illicit Soviet program did carry out such work and scientists have in effect done the same in research contexts. This sort of biotechnical know-how is spreading quickly.

Blocking Biology

The challenges posed by biological nonproliferation—the dual-use character of materials and equipment, the small amounts of agents initially needed and their availability from natural outbreaks, and the dynamic nature of biotechnology—guarantee that an effective strategy for biological security will look very different from the corresponding techniques used to curtail the spread of nuclear or chemical weapons. Biological security requires a different mix of nonproliferation, deterrence, and defense.

The BWC provides the legal basis for preventing the spread of biological weapons. However, the Bush administration in July 2001 rejected the draft compliance protocol to the BWC, arguing that it could jeopardize U.S. companies' proprietary information, did not provide sufficient protection for U.S. biodefense programs, and would not improve verification capabilities. By thus abandoning six years of negotiations, the United States is now not in a strong political position to pursue multilateral nonproliferation initiatives. Nevertheless, Washington should act to improve international control of dangerous pathogens, either within the BWC framework (perhaps by supporting the proposal of a like-minded ally) or in a new forum. Within the United States, the shipment of deadly diseases has been monitored since 1997. A national inventory and consolidation of facilities with dangerous strains and development of a gene library are the obvious next steps. Had these been in place in October 2001, the anthrax investigation could have proceeded more quickly.

Hundreds of culture collections containing dangerous organisms also exist around the world. Although terrorists can acquire pathogens from natural disease outbreaks, existing collections offer the easiest sources. The United States should therefore work with other nations to put into place international standards for the secure storage and transport of biological stocks that could be used for weapons. If it is no longer politically feasible for the United States to pursue such an objective within the BWC framework after having rejected the draft compliance protocol, it should consider, as Michael Barletta, Amy Sands, and Jonathan Tucker of the Monterey Institute of International

Studies have suggested, pursuing a "Biosecurity Convention" to this end, consistent with, but if need be outside of, the BWC.

Certain bilateral steps are also crucial. The CTR and related programs have helped prevent the loss of biological-weapons scientists to states of concern and provided the United States with details of the biological weapons programs in Ukraine, Kazakhstan, and Uzbekistan, as well as Russia's Biopreparat program. But other key Russian facilities under the ministries of defense and health have remained closed to outsiders. Spending for the biological component of CTR has now been increased from three percent to ten percent of the total CTR budget; at a minimum Washington should maintain this level of commitment. The Bush administration should also approach the Russian government at a high level so that the United States can inventory, consolidate, secure, and ultimately acquire samples or gene sequences of Russian bioweapons strains and conduct scientific exchanges with those Russian bioweapons facilities that remain closed. A similar bilateral agreement with Uzbekistan in summer 2001 gave the United States access to Vozrozhdeniye Island in the Aral Sea, where Americans will help dismantle Soviet-era bioweapons facilities and clean up remaining live agents, including those that resulted from open-air testing.

Unstoppable?

Deterrence through the threat of retaliation has been the central strategy for preventing the use of weapons of mass destruction against the United States or its allies. And deterrence may remain effective against a state's use of biological weapons. But biological terrorism by subnational groups poses special challenges in this regard. Deterring any form of terrorism is difficult, since some terrorist groups may be unconcerned about retaliation or may hope to remain unidentified. But the biological case is especially problematic. Because some diseases incubate without symptoms for days or even weeks, tracing an attack back to its perpetrators can prove difficult. Terrorists might even hope that their attack would go unrecognized as such. For instance, when followers of the Bhagwan Shree Rajneesh infected 750 Oregonians with salmonella in 1984, it was more than a year before authorities determined that the infection had been intentionally spread.

The summer 1999 outbreak of the West Nile Virus in New York illustrates how difficult it can be in some circumstances to distinguish an intentional attack from a natural outbreak. Before the disease killed seven people in the New York City area, West Nile had never before occurred in the western hemisphere. Due to bird migration, the virus has now spread to 27 states. Although the outbreak was apparently "natural" in origin, perhaps caused by an infected traveler or mosquito transported from the Middle East, it is remarkable that in April 1999, only a few months before the outbreak, an Iraqi defector had claimed that Saddam Hussein planned to weaponize the virus.

The United States should do what it can to increase the likelihood that an attack will be attributable. An essential resource is a DNA library of as many strains of relevant biological agents as can be assembled. DNA "fingerprinting" of the agent causing an outbreak is an important forensic tool, but it is most useful if the fingerprints are already on file. (DNA fingerprinting does not identify the perpetrator, however—only the weapon used. In this sense it is more like ballistics testing than human fingerprinting.)

The United States needs a DNA library not only of natural and weaponized strains within U.S. collections but also of those located in inventories around the world. Again, cooperation with the states of the former Soviet Union is important.

In addition to the difficulties of attribution, some terrorist groups may also believe themselves to be invulnerable to retaliation, may be unconcerned by it, or may even intend to provoke it. Such groups are obviously poor candidates for deterrence through the threat of retaliation. However, deterrence by denial—deterring enemies by convincing them that biological defenses are credible and that therefore an attack would be unlikely to succeed—may be a more useful tool for biological security than it was for nuclear weapons. Of course, warning and prevention are preferable to coping with the consequences of an attack, so intelligence remains vital. But as the anthrax mail attacks made clear, biological terrorism can occur with little or no warning.

Defense Without Borders

The intrinsic challenges of stopping the spread of biological weapons, and the difficulties posed for deterrence suggest that biological security strategy should lean more heavily toward defense than has been true of nuclear or chemical security strategy. Building biological defenses will of course require appropriate steps by the Defense and Justice Departments. But just as important, and for too long overlooked, biological security means improvements in domestic and international public health.

Prior to September 11, 2001, a number of analysts had in fact argued just this point: that a robust defense against bioterrorism must be based on improved public health. Because disease incubation times for some agents can be as long as weeks, the first responders to a biological attack are likely to be health care workers rather than fire, police, or military personnel. Public health surveillance for signs of unusual disease is therefore critical. Improvements in "sensitivity" and "connectivity" are required. Sensitivity means the recognition by health care workers that an illness is out of the ordinary; connectivity is the reporting of this recognition to local, state, and national authorities, and consequent timely help with diagnosis and treatment. The anthrax mail attacks tragically confirmed the importance of disease surveillance, since the speed with which doctors recognized the signs of anthrax infection determined whether patients were treated immediately or sent home, only to return later to die.

In 1999, the U.S. government initiated the Biological Preparedness and Response Program (BPRP) within the Centers for Disease Control and Prevention. This program put in place many of the crucial steps required for a domestic public health defense against bioterrorism. The BPRP created the National Pharmaceutical Stockpile (NPS) of antibiotics and other drugs that could be rapidly deployed to counter domestic outbreaks. The BPRP also funded pilot projects to bolster disease surveillance, improved capacity at the state and local levels, and sponsored research. In fiscal year 2000, the BPRP budget stood at $155 million, an amount that some experts viewed as only one-tenth the funding needed for the tasks required. But at the time, there was legitimate disagreement—indeed, there still is—over the right balance between spending to prepare for rare but potentially disastrous events such as bioterrorism, and spending to counter naturally occurring infectious diseases that are already killing many individuals every day.

Nonetheless, the October 2001 anthrax crisis would have seemed far more dire had the NPS not existed, and the understandable public tendency to begin self-medicating with antibiotics would have been even more difficult to contain. One of the great hazards of this response is its likely acceleration of antibiotic resistance in bacteria—resistance that can then be swapped between bacteria of different species. For the same reason, it is important that the poultry industry is reducing the quantities of antibiotics fed to healthy chickens, and analogous practices in other livestock industries should be similarly scrutinized. An effective biological security strategy must cast its net far wider than traditional national security issues.

Fortunately, many of the steps that are needed to prepare for bioterrorism will also improve recognition of and responses to natural disease outbreaks. Spending on biological defenses therefore represents a win-win situation in which society benefits even if no further bioterrorist attacks take place. The West Nile outbreak again provides an example: had better communication between veterinarians and public health officials existed in early summer 1999, when crows began to die in New York City, the outbreak could have been recognized months earlier.

After the anthrax mail attacks, attitudes toward domestic public health spending to prepare for bioterrorism rapidly changed. In a discussion of how much annual spending would be required to improve preparedness, a member of Congress remarked last autumn, "One or two billion dollars? That kind of money is easier done than said right now." Indeed, the 2002 emergency supplemental appropriations bill and a separate bioterrorism bill include billions of dollars in new spending for biological defense. These bills include steps to expand the pharmaceutical stockpile, increase stores of the smallpox vaccine, strengthen state and local preparedness, and improve food safety. Domestically, the right steps are being funded. The challenge will be to sustain this commitment as the psychological distance from September 11 grows.

Admittedly, not all measures taken against bioterrorism have dual uses. The NPS antibiotic supply is unlikely to be needed to counter natural outbreaks, and storing the smallpox vaccine prepares for a disease that no longer exists in the natural world. Because antibiotics have a finite shelf life, making the expanded NPS financially sustainable may require the government to create incentives for research into extending antibiotic shelf life (something that market forces themselves may not encourage) and ensuring sufficient extra production capacity in the event of a crisis.

Other forms of research must also continue. Standard antibiotics are effective against all the bacteria that are commonly listed as biological agents, but the Soviet bioweapons program produced strains of anthrax resistant to some antibiotics, and such bioengineering will become more widely available. Vaccines are available for some viral agents, such as smallpox, but there are no effective drugs for others, such as many of the viral hemorrhagic fevers (e.g., Ebola or Marburg, which the Soviets reportedly weaponized). For the foreseeable future, therefore, we are locked into a kind of biological defensive arms race in which researchers will need to develop different or more broadly effective antimicrobial drugs and vaccines against possible new threats.

An effective defense against bioterror also requires the means to distribute vaccines and antimicrobial drugs effectively, perhaps amid the extremely challenging circumstances of public panic. The effects of public fear should not be underestimated, and the lessons from real or potential mass casualty situations involving invisible, lingering threats are sobering. Aum Shinrikyo's 1995 sarin nerve gas attack in the Tokyo subway system injured hundreds of Japanese citizens, but 5,000 sought help at hospital emergency rooms. Similarly, when the governor of Pennsylvania in 1979 suggested the evacuation of pregnant women and preschool children living within a five-mile radius of the Three Mile Island nuclear power plant—in effect recommending that a few thousand people leave the area—between one and two hundred thousand fled. Responses to these sorts of reactions should be planned before crises occur.

Beyond the Water's Edge

The U.S. government's response to last fall's bioterrorist attacks rightly highlighted the importance of domestic public health measures but showed little appreciation for the fact that no response can succeed if it stops at the nation's borders. International measures are crucial to a successful strategy for reasons as simple as arithmetic. Many diseases, such as plague and smallpox, have lengthy incubation times (an average of 2 to 3 days and 12 days, respectively). But the flight time between virtually any two cities in the world is now less than 36 hours. Carriers of smallpox, whether terrorists or unwitting victims, could transport the disease around the world before they ever showed signs of illness. Some 140 million people enter the United States by air every year. Although improvements to border protection are important, neither the United States nor other nations can hope to protect themselves exclusively by guarding their frontiers. For both humanitarian and national security reasons, outbreaks of emerging infectious diseases need to be addressed overseas as well as domestically. When possible they should be prevented, but if that does not happen, such outbreaks need to be detected, diagnosed, and controlled as quickly as possible.

Any outbreak of a highly contagious, lethal, and long-incubating disease such as smallpox poses a grave international threat. In 1972, a single religious pilgrim returned to Yugoslavia from Mecca via several days in Iraq, where he had contracted smallpox. Smallpox had spread to Iraq from Iran, where a family had introduced it after acquiring it while traveling through Afghanistan. The disease in Yugoslavia went undiagnosed while the original infected individual spread the disease to others, one of whom traveled 100 miles by bus. To contain the resulting outbreak, Tito's government vaccinated 18 million people and quarantined some 10,000 in commandeered hotels and apartment buildings ringed with troops and barbed wire. By comparison, on September 11, 2001, the United States had fewer than 15 million doses of smallpox vaccine available to a larger and far more mobile society. Epidemiological models indicate that quarantine can to some extent be traded off against vaccination to control an outbreak. But better preparation with appropriate vaccines or drugs will diminish the curtailment of civil liberties that would otherwise be needed to control contagious outbreaks.

These lessons are not limited to bioterrorist outbreaks. AIDS is a naturally occurring disease that recently emerged in the human population. It has since killed more than 450,000 Americans and 22 million people worldwide. The importance of recognizing such new contagious illnesses early, rather than after they have spread across the globe, is terribly clear. The United States must act to prevent disease outbreaks, detect those (whether natural, artificial, or ambiguous) that do occur, and ensure an effective response. The six laboratories that the Defense Department has overseas to perform research on infectious diseases are an important resource that should be further strengthened, but a broader international response is also required.

Rapid detection of outbreaks requires improvements in international disease surveillance, for which the chronically underfunded World Health Organization (WHO) is central. In the event of a bioweapons attack abroad, reference laboratories (designed to examine environmental and medical samples) must be available overseas, or else U.S. domestic capacity will be swamped with international samples. Cost estimates begin in the tens of millions of dollars annually for minimal improvements in international disease surveillance and reference lab capacity, through the creation of regional WHO centers that build wherever possible on existing facilities. With its vast new spending on bioterrorism defense, the United States should allocate resources to fund these and other such serious, sustainable improvements in global public health. Whether the next threat is smallpox or a new AIDS-like epidemic disease, improving global infectious disease surveillance and response will be good for both humanitarian reasons and national security.

The United States is also creating a smallpox vaccine stockpile sufficient for all Americans. Although one recent epidemiological simulation suggests that a stockpile of 40 million doses would be sufficient to control likely outbreaks, it is difficult to predict whether a real attack would be as limited as that simulation assumes. Moreover, it should be clear from the public response to last autumns' anthrax scare that no White House will want to find itself in a position of having to explain to the American people why only some are eligible to receive vaccinations after an attack. The American people—like most people throughout the world—have for decades not been routinely vaccinated against smallpox, and the vaccine's effectiveness attenuates after ten years. The global population is now more vulnerable to smallpox than any large population has been since the illness devastated Native Americans after European explorers brought it to the Americas.

But even a stockpile for all U.S. citizens is insufficient. In the event of a smallpox outbreak overseas—whether in a NATO ally or in the developing world—humanitarian concern, international opinion, and its own self-interest will pressure the United States to shut down the outbreak and limit its spread. The WHO smallpox vaccine stockpile stands at half a million doses. The United States must either augment its national stockpile so that it can respond internationally without jeopardizing its own citizens or work with the WHO to increase international supplies. Of course, the United States should encourage other nations to do the same, but it should not allow others' inaction to prevent it from acting in its own security interest to improve global public health.

Speaking Truth in Power

An effective strategy for biological security will encompass nonproliferation, deterrence, and defense, but the required mix of these components will be very different from those in strategies for nuclear or even chemical weapons. Perhaps most strikingly, effective biological security demands that the United States act to improve global disease surveillance and response capacity—an element of "defense" that has no good nuclear or chemical analogue. Biological security also requires ongoing research to counter emerging potential threats driven by biotechnology. It is as much about public health, science, and technology as it is about military strategy.

These needs emphasize the vital role that scientific advice will continue to play in national security. Yet the U.S. government is not well equipped to harness such advice. Congress eliminated its Office of Technology Assessment in 1995, and the president's science adviser has played a diminishing White House role over the past few decades. The Office of Science and Technology Policy [OSTP], which is directed by the science adviser, is inherently weak bureaucratically. Few national security decisions naturally flow through it. As a result, the OSTP is only as strong in this arena as is the relationship between the science adviser and the president.

And too often, that relationship is weak. Both sides are to blame: too few scientists are good communicators and effective bureaucrats, and too few presidents recognize science as a priority. Nor does every policymaker appreciate that scientific integrity will at times require an unpopular answer. But as with intelligence, bending technical analysis to a particular policy risks producing deception rather than information.

The scientific and technical challenges of the coming decades will grow only more grave and incessant. Scientific complexity will be increasingly important for policymakers to understand and to communicate competently to the public. Policymakers must better incorporate scientific advice into their decision-making, or they risk falling prey to more, and more dangerous, misplaced analogies.

5.3   Michael L. Moodie, 1999

The Chemical Weapons Threat

Michael L. Moodie is president of the Chemical and Biological Arms Control Institute in Washington, D.C. He is a former assistant director of the U.S. Arms Control and Disarmament Agency where, among other issues, his bureau had the lead responsibility for negotiating the Chemical Weapons Convention and for issues relating to the Biological Weapons Convention.

Chemical weapons (CW) pose a challenge that is both old and new. The challenge is old in two senses. First, the use of gas as a weapon of war dates far back in time. "Toxic fumes" appeared in conflicts in India as far back as 2000 BC. In 400 BC, Sparta reportedly used wood saturated with pitch and sulfur under besieged city walls to choke defenders. In 1591, Germans used combinations of shredded hooves and horns with a fetid gum resin to produce noxious clouds to disrupt enemy forces.[1] Second, even "modern" CW have been around for some time; the science involved is not cutting edge. Sir Humphrey Davy prepared phosgene in 1811. Another English chemist, John Stenhouse, prepared chloropicrin in 1848, and the chemical today known as mustard gas was synthesized in

1854. The most lethal chemical agents, the nerve gases, were initially developed from German research into organophosphorus pesticides in the 1930s.

Despite their long history, however, CW also pose a new challenge. In particular, the context surrounding CW—both politically and technically—has changed, and those changes may influence calculations about their potential utility. The number of possible CW possessors has grown, and some of their arsenals are increasingly sophisticated. CW represent an option of increasing interest to nonstate actors, particularly terrorists. Scenarios in which CW could have a significant impact—on the outcome of military conflict, or on the well-being of civilians—have expanded.

CW remain the least glamorous of the weapons of mass destruction; but they have been the most used. CW must be dealt with on their own terms. They cannot be addressed as lesser-included cases of nuclear or even biological weapons. If we are complacent about our ability to respond effectively to the challenges posed by CW, we are likely only to increase the risks to our military forces and civilian populations alike.

This chapter summarizes the challenges posed by CW. It first examines the technical issues associated with their development, production, and dissemination. It then addresses the proliferation of CW both by states and by nonstate actors. Finally, it discusses some of the novel ways in which CW may be used.

CW: The Technical Dimension

CW capabilities can vary greatly in their sophistication, but each chemical agent uniquely combines a set of characteristics and properties that makes it appropriate for use as a weapon. These include:

- *Lethality:* the extent to which the agent will cause fatalities
- *Mode of action:* the route by which the agent causes its effects (inhalation, dermal exposure, mucous membrane, or oral ingestion)
- *Speed of action:* the time between exposure and effect
- *Stability:* the resistance of the agent to degradation, which is important during storage and dissemination
- *Persistence:* the length of time an agent remains a hazard once it is released into the environment
- *Toxicity:* the quantity of a substance required to achieve a given effect[2]

These characteristics for various categories of CW agents are summarized in table 1-1. Combinations of these different characteristics, of course, mean that different agents have more or less utility for specific situations, depending on the objectives. An advanced CW capability would entail production of several agents with a mix of these different characteristics mated to a variety of delivery systems. In contrast, a crude program would be able to produce only one or two agents and few delivery systems.

Categories of Chemical Agents

CW agents are usually classified on the basis of their impact on the human body. People are the only target of a CW attack. These are perhaps the only weapons in which this is the case. They are usually categorized into choking, blister, blood, incapacitating, and nerve agents.

Table 1

Chemical Agents and Their Characteristics

	Physical state	Persistency	Delivery	Route	Target
Blister agents	Liquid, solid	High	Vapor, aerosol, liquid	Lungs, eyes, skin	Man, animals
Blood agents	Liquid, vapors	Low	Vapor	Lungs	Man, animals
Choking agents	Liquid	Low	Vapor	Lungs, eyes, skin	Man, animals
Incapacitants	Liquid, solid	Low	Aerosol, liquid	Lungs, skin	Man, animals
Nerve agents	Liquid	Low to high	Vapor, aerosol, liquid	Lungs, eyes, skin	Man, animals

Source: Gordon M. Burck, "Biological, Chemical, and Toxin Warfare Agents," in Susan Wright, ed., *Preventing a Biological Arms Race* (Cambridge, MA: MIT Press, 1990), Appendix A.

Choking agents, including chlorine and phosgene, are also called pulmonary agents because they attack lung tissue and cause pulmonary edema (excess fluid in the lungs). They were the first CW used during World War I and are estimated to have accounted for 80 percent of the chemical casualties during that conflict.[3] This CW category also highlights the problems confronting efforts to control CW proliferation in that the simple agents, such as chlorine, also have widespread commercial uses and are produced in the thousands, if not millions, of tons per year all around the world.

Blister agents, also known as vesicants, include mustard gas (both sulfur mustard and nitrogen mustard), and Lewisite. These chemicals burn the skin or other parts of the body; they can act on eyes, mucous membranes, and lungs. Mustard gas was used widely in World War I and in the Iran-Iraq War, and Japan may have used Lewisite against China in the 1930s. Blister agents, particularly mustard gas, were also a major component of both the US and Soviet CW arsenals.

Blood agents, in which cyanide is a critical component, are called such because their impact is carried through the body in the blood. Hydrogen cyanide and cyanogen chloride are the two most important agents in this category; they produce their effect by interfering with oxygen utilization at the cellular level. Although cyanide-based agents were used in World War I, they were largely unsuccessful because of the large amounts needed to saturate a given space and the fact that in vapor form it is difficult to maintain a lethal concentration. Cyanogen chloride was introduced to overcome this problem. As with chlorine, cyanide compounds are produced in vast quantities for commercial purposes, including mineral extraction, printing, photography, and paper, textile, and plastic production.

Incapacitating agents, such as BZ or LSD, produce either stimulant or depressive effects on the central nervous system. The results are disabling conditions that may persist for hours or days. Such agents are not usually lethal, and do not produce permanent injuries. Incapacitating agents have been more the subject of exploration than

Table 2

Toxicity of Nerve Agents on Skin

Agent	LD$_{50}$ amount (mg)
Tabun	1,000
Sarin	1,700
Soman	50
VX	10

Source: Medical Management of Chemical Casualties Handbook, US Army Medical Research Institute of Chemical Defense (Sep. 1995).

of systematic weaponization as agents. Iraq, however, was believed to be working before the Gulf War on a new incapacitant, known as "Agent 15," which is though to be similar to BZ.[4]

Nerve agents, divided into G- and V-agents, are the most feared CW. Essentially, these agents affect the transmission of nerve impulses by inhibiting the functioning of the vital enzyme acetylcholinesterase, which hydrolizes acetylcholine wherever it is released. They are the most toxic of CW (see tables 2 and 3). Some nerve agents, particularly VX, also tend to be highly persistent.

G-series nerve agents were discovered in 1936 by Gerhard Schrader of the German firm IG Farben while he was doing research on new organophosphorous pesticides, although G-agents can be 100 to 1,000 times more poisonous than those pesticides.[5] They are rapid-acting, and generally penetrate the body through inhalation, although they can also be absorbed through the skin. The V-series agents were originally discovered in 1948 by British scientists also involved in new pesticide research. Both the US and USSR conducted military development in the 1960s.[6] The major penetration route for an agent such as VX is through skin absorption rather than inhalation.

Today, nerve agents constitute 80 percent of the CW stockpile declared by Russia as part of its obligations under the Chemical Weapons Convention (CWC). The nerve agent sarin was also the agent used by the Aum Shinrikyo in its March 1995 attack on the Tokyo subway. Prior to the Gulf War, Iraq produced 210 tons of tabun and 790 tons of sarin, some of which was weaponized. It also acknowledges having produced VX but denies loading it in munitions, a claim that is disrupted by the US and other members of the international community.

Pathways to Proliferation

Securing a CW capability is not necessarily an easy task. An advanced program pursued by a state must include several dimensions, each of which involves several steps. These steps are summarized in figure 1 [page 190].

Three important points must be made. First, producing the agent is not the same as developing a weapon. Depending on the purpose of the weapon, many additional steps must be successfully taken before a weapons capability is achieved. Obviously, lesser performance requirements, such as those that terrorists might seek, create less demanding weapons-development processes.

Table 3

Lethal Toxicity Figures for Selected Chemical Agents

Agent	Ct_{50} (mg-min/m3)*
Selected nerve agents	
Tabun	200–400
Sarin	100–200
Soman	50–70
VX	1–50
Selected blister agents	
Pure mustard	1,500 inhalation; 10,000 skin
Lewisite	Greater than 1,500
Selected blood agents	
Phosgene	3,200
Hydrogen cyanide	2,500-5,000
Cyanogen chloride	11,000

*Refers to the lethal concentration time that will kill 50 percent of the exposed population (milligram-minutes/cubic meter).
Source: US Army Handbook on the Field Aspects of NBC Defensive Operations, Field Manual (FM) 8-9, Part III.

Second, when comments are made—as the US government does—that a state is pursuing a CW program of concern, intelligence on which such comments are based is not always sufficient to locate the program's status precisely in this process. A country may be conducting research on various agents, for example, without necessarily having made the decision to go to full-scale production, let alone weaponization. In some cases, however, we just will not know the difference between a dabbler and a committed proliferator.

Third, while there are similarities in various programs, they are not necessarily identical, and it is wrong to assume that the current or future pathways for CW proliferation are the same as those that led to the development of CW capabilities in the past. Nine different production processes for sulfur mustard, for example, have been documented.[7] The US and Soviet Union produced VX through different processes, and methods used by Iraq and the US to develop G-category agents were also quite different.[8]

As the Office of Technology Assessment (OTA) has pointed out, each pathway "involves tradeoffs among simplicity, speed, agent shelf-life, and visibility. The choice of pathway would therefore be affected by the urgency of a country's military requirement for a CW stockpile, its desire to keep the program secret, its level of concern over workers safety and environmental protection, and the existence of embargoes on precursor materials and production equipment."[9]

Weaponizing Chemical Agents

The critical requirements for turning an agent into an effective weapon is that it be toxic enough to produce the desired level of casualties and stable enough to survive dissemination either through explosion of the delivery mechanism or passage through a spray device. Meeting these requirements usually takes three steps:

1. Selecting and using chemical additives, including stabilizers, freezing-point depressants, thickeners, carriers, or antiagglomerants, to stabilize or augment the effects of the agent
2. Designing and producing munitions for dispersal of the agent
3. Filling, storage, and transport of the munitions

Filling operations, in particular, are extremely hazardous. The major technical hurdle is sealing the deadly agent inside the munition or delivery vehicle without leakage or contamination. Not all parties seeking a CW capability, however—whether states or terrorists—are concerned about the safety of either their personnel or the environment. Several members of the Aum Shinrikyo, for example, were injured and perhaps died in the process of the cult's developing its biological and chemical weapons.[10]

Chemical munitions are designed to convert a bulk payload of liquid or powdered agent into an aerosol of microscopic droplets that can be readily absorbed through the skin or inhaled. The optimal size for dermal absorption is about 70 microns and for inhalation 1 to 5 microns. Achieving the correct particle size or putting the particles into aerosol form can both pose problems for the proliferator. The importance of aerosolizing the chemical agent was demonstrated by the Aum Shinrikyo subway attack. The fact that the sarin was allowed to evaporate rather than be delivered as an aerosol was one of the key factors in limiting casualties. Had Aum been able to develop an effective aerosolization mechanism—which they tried to do—the number of casualties would likely have been much higher.

The Iraqi CW program demonstrated that a wide variety of delivery platforms can be used to disseminate chemical agents. They can range from the unsophisticated plastic bags used by the Aum Shinrikyo to ballistic missiles, on which Iraq had loaded chemical warheads. Iraq also had chemical munitions for its rockets, aerial bombs, and artillery, as well as aerial spray tanks.[11] Delivery systems need not be high-tech, however, and can also include such "unconventional" systems as insect foggers, paint sprayers, and crop dusters.

Even if a proliferator can successfully engineer a CW delivery vehicle, the success of a CW attack is not necessarily guaranteed. Meteorological conditions will also play a role in determining the outcome. A number of atmospheric or ground conditions can influence the action of a chemical agent, including the following.

- *Air temperature:* The higher the temperature, the greater the rate of evaporation of particles, thereby decreasing their size; colder weather prevents evaporation, reducing concentrations in the air but lengthening the period of ground contamination.
- *Ground temperature:* This also influences the evaporation rate, thereby increasing or decreasing the duration of contamination.
- *Exposure to sun:* This has a similar effect.
- *Humidity:* High relative humidity leads to enlargement of aerosol particles.
- *Precipitation:* Light rain disperses the agent, while heavy rain dilutes and displaces it; snow increases persistence of contamination by slowing down evaporation.

(Continued on page 191)

Figure 1

Steps to Securing CW Capability

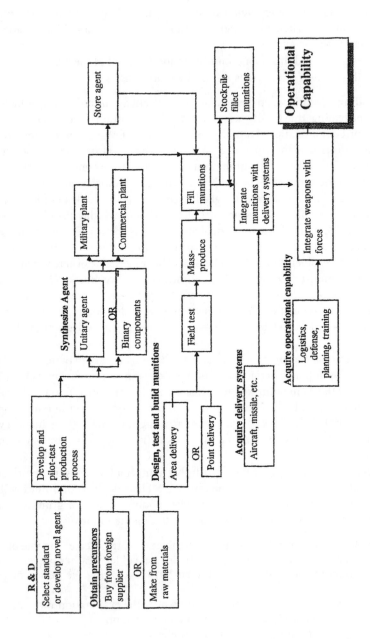

Source: OTA, Technologies Underlying WMD (1993).

- *Wind speed and direction:* High winds disseminate the agent farther, but may dilute lethal concentrations sooner. Chemical clouds are most effective when winds are steady and at less than 4 knots.
- *Soil conditions:* Agent penetration of soil reduces the risk of contamination by contact but increases persistence because factors that could cause evaporation are prevented from acting.

Finally, CW attackers must take terrain into account. Open, flat terrain maximizes the lethal dispersion of the agent, while hilly or urban terrain can create atmospheric turbulence, which impedes even distribution of the agent and increases its vertical dilution, thereby reducing casualties.

Clearly, the use of chemical agents as effective weapons is not necessarily an easy task. The severity of the technical challenge depends on a number of factors, including the nature of the target (e.g., whether combat troops—protected or not—or civilians), the desired level of casualties, meteorological and topographical conditions, and choice of delivery system. This is not to argue that even the most demanding technical challenge is beyond the reach of many or most CW proliferators. Indeed, Iraq demonstrated what a committed proliferator can do. Nor is it to suggest that simpler technical challenges, such as use by terrorists, will not have significant effects. The case of Aum Shinrikyo was one in which luck played a big part in limiting the number of casualties. Rather, it is to argue that those who respond to the CW challenge must be as aware as the proliferators themselves of the full range of factors that influence the use of CW. Without such a comprehensive understanding, responses—at both policy and operational levels—could be off target.

Ongoing Challenges

An argument can be made that few military technologies have evolved as little as CW over the past fifty years.[12] This does not mean, however, that the problems posed by CW remain unchanged. Three developments in particular present ongoing challenges to those responsible for confronting the CW threat. They are the dual-use nature of much chemical material and equipment, the diffusion of chemical production capabilities, and the possibility of the development of new chemical agents.

First, dual use. The fact that many agents and much equipment involved in making CW also have legitimate commercial uses makes it a more difficult problem to control. A sulfur mustard plant using sulfur monochloride and ethylene (as the US and USSR did during World War II), for example, could be hidden at an oil refinery, which is an excellent source of ethylene and could also extract the necessary sulfur from petroleum or natural gas.[13] At the level of chemical agent, an excellent example of the dual-use problem is thiodiglycol, a key precursor for large-scale production of mustard gas, which also happens to be a key component of ballpoint-pen ink. More generally, many of the precursors that could be used in CW production are commercially used in quantities surpassing millions of tons per year.

The problem of dual use also creates alternatives for would-be proliferators. In the case of Iraq, for example, when confronted by a prospective embargo of thiodiglycol that it was importing from foreign sources, Baghdad developed an indigenous capability for mustard production based on reacting ethylene with hydrogen sulfide, both of which are widely available.[14] As an alternative to producing familiar chemical agents with different precursors, a proliferator might also look to develop more obscure CW using readily available precursors.

The international community has recognized the problem inherent in the dual-use nature of chemical material and equipment. It has attempted to regulate critical precursors through the activities of both the Australia Group (AG) and the CWC. The AG is an informal mechanism for the coordination of export controls related to chemical (and biological) materials and equipment. The 31-member AG is currently under attack from radical nonaligned countries, frequently led by Iran, for being discriminatory and as a violation of the spirit of the CWC. In response, members of the AG, frequently led by the US, argue that the AG not only is consistent with the CWC but also provides a mechanism for implementing the commitment of CWC parties not to transfer equipment or material that could facilitate development of another country's CW program. They also argue that the AG remains an important tool in the fight against BCW proliferation based on a continuing role for export controls (even if their focus shifts from denial to other functions),[15] the group's focus on material and equipment of greatest proliferation concern, and its enhancement of individual national efforts through coordination.

The CWC places limits on access to and flow of certain chemicals that are divided into three categories (defined by a combination of their utility in making CW and their commercial use and availability) and imposes on parties different sets of declaration and on-site obligations regarding these categories. The authors of the CWC recognized, however, that for precursors that were widely available and had widespread commercial utility, the ability to verify their nonuse in CW programs would be extremely difficult.

Second, diffusion. CW proliferation has been described as an "unfortunate side effect of a process that is otherwise beneficial and anyway impossible to stop: the diffusion of competence in chemistry and chemical technology from the rich to the poor parts of the world."[16] Trade and investment figures related to the chemical industry underline the extent of diffusion:

- Exports from the developed world to developing nations increased from $33 billion in 1980 to $57 billion in 1991.
- Annual direct investment in development countries by US chemical manufacturers more than doubled from $4.05 billion in 1983 to $9.98 billion in 1993.
- The developing countries' share of US investment in overseas chemical industries remained a steady 21 percent in the decade from 1983 to 1993.[17]

The result of this diffusion of chemical production capability is that today more than 100 countries have the capability—if not the intent—to produce at least simple CW, such as phosgene, hydrogen cyanide, or sulfur mustard. Obviously, a smaller number of countries can produce nerve agents, whose production involves more complex and difficult reaction steps. This diffusion of capability increasingly creates a world of "virtual CW programs" in which the critical factors shaping the proliferation landscape are not technical but political.

The diffusion of chemical production capabilities also increases the sources from which potential proliferators can purchase the necessary precursors. The Australia Group is limited in membership, and will remain so. Many countries do not belong to the AG and will not, and these nonmembers may not maintain export controls with the same tenacity as member countries. Moreover, despite the commitment of CWC parties to put effective export controls into place, global chemical trade is likely only to expand in the years ahead.

Another dimension of the diffusion problem is expertise. This aspect takes two forms. One is the leakage of experts from places (particularly the former Soviet Union) that had major CW programs. The second is the training of foreign nationals in the US and elsewhere in the West in disciplines, such as chemistry and chemical engineering, that might be exploited for CW purposes. This is not to say that all foreign students in the hard sciences or engineering are proliferation risks, but experience—such as that with Iraq—has demonstrated that foreign-trained nationals often take lead roles in a proliferator's WMD programs.

The third ongoing challenge is the prospect that, despite the fact that the number of CW agents has remained virtually static for many years, new chemical agents could be developed. This problem was highlighted by reports of Russia's development of a novel chemical agent called Novichok ("newcomer").

A September 20, 1992 *Moscow News* article coauthored by Vil Mirzayanov and Lev Fedorov alleged that the Russian CW complex was developing a new generation of CW.[18] The program, which began in 1982 and was code-named Foliant, had the apparent goal of developing new binary weapons in response to the Reagan Administration's CW initiatives. According to Mirzayanov, an employee for twenty-six years at the All-Union State Scientific Research Institute for Organic Chemistry and Technology where the program was conducted, by 1987 Soviet scientists had created the new nerve gas, Novichok, which has been alleged to be ten times more lethal than VX.[19] According to Mirzayanov, Novichok was based on chemical compounds developed between 1985 and 1991, dubbed Substance A-230 and A-232, with a toxicity that surpasses any known chemical agent by a factor of five to eight. Mirzayanov also claims that the Soviets developed in 1990 a binary CW code-named Substance 33, of which 15,000 tons were produced in the city of Novocheboksarsk while documentation was altered to give the impression that VX was being produced.[20] Responding to an investigation into Mirzayanov's claims by Russian authorities, the Institute's director wrote a letter to the Russian Security Ministry stating the institute had "synthesized, studied, and tested a number of new chemical combinations of different classes that significantly surpass VX...."[21]

If Mirzayanov's allegations are true, then Russia has covertly developed a new class of CW that it has not declared under the CWC. Moreover, it did so in a way consciously designed to circumvent the treaty by ensuring that the precursors for such an agent do not appear on the CWC schedules. Beyond the development of new agents, technological advances for more effective CW programs may result from current laboratory research on chemical defenses. Researchers are examining the impact of various agents at the molecular level. Although the purpose of such research is development of more effective antidotes, it could also assist in the development of novel compounds. An additional concern has been expressed about countries that are seeking to circumvent the CWC by modifying existing agents to avoid detection or by weaponizing "second string" agents of known but less effective poisons. A further worry is development of penetrant chemicals to defeat chemical defenses, particularly "mask breakers" capable of saturating gas-mask filters.[22] This is an example of the continuing risk that a novel

Table 4

Chemical Weapons Programs: Declared or Suspected

Declared CW production facilities or stockpiles	Suspected CW production facilities or stockpiles
China	Egypt
France	Iran
Japan	Israel
India	Libya
Iraq	Myanmar
Russia	North Korea
South Korea	Syria
UK	Taiwan
US	Vietnam

Sources: Gordon Burck and Charles Flowerree, *International Handbook on Chemical Weapons Proliferation* (Westport, CT: Greenwood Press, 1991); Office of Technology Assessment, *Proliferation of Weapons of Mass Destruction: Assessing the Risks* (Washington: Government Printing Office, 1993).

technology will be developed to reverse the current ascendancy of defense over offense in the chemical field.

CW Proliferation

CW proliferation is a problem at both the state and nonstate actor levels. On the state level, US government spokesmen generally charge that as many as two dozen nations are pursuing CW programs of concern. Unfortunately, most public government discussions of this issue do not specify all of the countries on the list, but make the broad claim and then focus on the same limited number of countries of particular concern.

Table 4 summarizes nonofficial assessments of the CW proliferation problem at the state level. The countries identified as being suspected of pursuing CW programs were listed in a 1993 study by the OTA because they appeared on lists of suspected CW proliferators in more than two-thirds of the nongovernmental studies OTA assessed. Since that study, the CWC has entered into force (in 1997), requiring that all parties declare both existing or former CW production facilities and CW stockpiles. Prior to the CWC's entry into force only the US and the Soviet Union/Russia had declared CW stockpiles, and Iraq was forced to admit its program following the Gulf War. Following entry into force of the CWC, however, five other countries declared existing or former CW production facilities—China, France, the United Kingdom, Japan, and India.[23] The latter two, in particular, were surprising. Furthermore, in addition to the US and Russia, India and South Korea declared possession of a CW stockpile, and again the latter two surprised the international community.

Those declarations, while welcome, leave many questions unanswered about the existence or status of CW programs in other countries. Among suspected proliferators, most of the attention has focused on Iraq, Iran, Syria, Libya, and North Korea. A brief survey of these "rogue" states highlights some of the problems posed by CW proliferation at the same level.

Iraq

Iraq's CW program provides a disturbing example of the capabilities a committed proliferator can achieve. Iraq produced thousands of tons of CW beginning in the early 1980s, and weaponized them on a range of delivery systems, including artillery shells, rockets, gravity bombs, aerial spray tanks, and Scud-type missile warheads. It began to use some of these weapons early in the war with Iran, and by 1987 Iraq had developed the skills to use CW in direct support of ground operations.[24]

At the time of the Gulf War, Iraq had an inventory of about 1,000 metric tons of CW, split evenly between blister agents such as mustard and nerve agents. It was also beginning to weaponize VX. Iraq had made preparations for a CW offensive with chemical defense equipment and extensive written instructions in the Kuwaiti theater of operations.[25] The reason Iraq did not use CW against coalition forces is the subject of considerable debate. Explanations range from the mundane and technical (e.g., that the weather conditions were not appropriate) to the operational (e.g., that coalition forces moved too quickly to be found and present themselves as good CW targets), to the strategic (e.g., that Saddam Hussein was deterred from using CW by US threats of overwhelming retaliation[26]).

Following the Gulf War, UNSCOM destroyed more than 40,000 CW munitions (28,000 filled and 12,000 empty), 480,000 liters of CW agent, 1,800,000 liters of chemical precursors, and eight different types of delivery systems.[27] Following the defection of Hussein Kamal, Iraq also admitted that it had:

- Produced larger amounts of VX than it had previously disclosed
- Researched in-flight mixing of binary CW
- Perfected techniques for the large-scale production of a VX precursor that is well suited to long-term storage

The ongoing dispute over Iraqi VX weaponization reflects continuing concerns over Baghdad's ability to reconstitute its CW program. According to one US estimate, Iraq could restart limited mustard agent production within a few weeks, full-scale production of sarin within a few months, and pre-Gulf War levels of production, including VX, within two to three years. Since the Gulf War, Iraq has also rebuilt two facilities it once used for CW production.[28]

Iran

During the Iran–Iraq War, Iran used CW to retaliate for Iraqi CW use. According to one study, at present, "chemical and biological weapons are seen as potentially important tactical force-multipliers and the core component of Iran's strategic forces."[29] For this reason, Iran has put a high priority on its CW program. According to the US Department of Defense, Iran now manufacturers weapons for blister, blood, and choking agents, and is believed to be conducting research on nerve agents.[30] Its delivery systems include artillery shells and bombs. Despite its priority, the US government does not believe that

Iran has in place yet a totally indigenous program, but remains dependent on foreign source of supply, particularly China, for technology and equipment.[31]

Iran, however, has signed and ratified the CWC. As a consequence, it assumed an obligation to declare its current and past CW production activities as well as any existing stockpiles. That initial declaration was due in January 1998, thirty days after Iran became a party to the treaty; the submission was a year late. Unfortunately, the contents of Iran's declaration are not widely available. Its distribution even in the OPCW is highly restricted. What Iran has declared, therefore, is not possible to determine, although preparations are under way for the conduct of inspections there.

Syria

Syria is alleged to have a long-standing CW program, first begun in the 1970s. By the late 1980s, Syria was reported to have at least two CW facilities in operation, one near Damascus and the second near Homs.[32] The Syrian CW inventory is believed to contain both blister and nerve agents, although one report suggests that the Israelis at least believe that the bulk of the arsenal is made up of sarin.[33] Syrian delivery systems are said to include thousands of aerial bombs as well as some Scud-type warheads.[34]

As with Iran, Syria has relied on extensive external assistance in its CW program. Former CIA Director William Webster stated in testimony that "West European firms were instrumental in supplying the required precursor chemicals and equipment."[35] Other sources of support are alleged to include China, India, North Korea, and Russia.[36]

Syria's primary security concern is its military balance with Israel, and its CW capabilities must be seen in that context. Their operational utility is likely to be considered most seriously in the context of a conflict that involves Syrian efforts to retake the Golan Heights. In this case, CW may be seen as a force-multiplier for Syrian forces on the offensive that would demoralize and disorganize Israeli forces defending the territory and disrupt Israeli plans to mobilize reserves and bring to bear the power of its air force.

Libya

Libya has both produced and used CW. Its program began in earnest in the 1980s with the completion of the CW plant at Rabta, which is alleged to have produced up to 100 tons of blister and nerve agent.[37] The plant was closed down after strong diplomatic efforts were made and media attention gave foreign involvement in its construction high visibility.[38] Analysts generally agree that Libya used some of its limited CW inventory in Chad.

Despite its efforts, however, the Libyan threat remains only marginally credible. Its stocks are low, making it impossible to sustain use. Moreover, its delivery capabilities are poor. In fact, the efforts to use CW in Chad were not all that effective. On one occasion, for example, artillery-delivered gas reportedly blew back across Libyan troops. The Libyan armed forces would also have enormous difficulties bringing its CW-armed artillery into play against any but the most unsophisticated opponent, given their vulnerability to modern counter-battery tactics and the dominance of the air that any Libyan opponent would likely secure.[39]

North Korea

One country whose CW program is far beyond marginally capable is North Korea. North Korea can produce significant quantities of a wide variety of CW—blister, choking, and nerve agents, including VX. According to defectors, North Korea produces twenty different chemical agents for use in weapons at more than a dozen sites.[40] Estimates suggest an annual production potential of 4,500 tons in peacetime and 12,000 tons in wartime with between 1,000 and 5,000 tons already stockpiled.[41]

The North Korean CW program began in the 1950s in the belief that they could provide a deterrent against aggression by South Korea and the US. By the 1990s, however, CW have come to be viewed primarily as "operational-level weapons," and the North Korean military is said to have studied both the Iran–Iraq War and Operation Desert Storm to determine how it can use its CW to best effect. North Korea could use its CW to attack US or allied forces deployed along the demilitarized zone as well as to isolate the peninsula from US strategic reinforcement by closing ports and airfields in the south. Some scenarios even suggest a threat of CW (and possibly BW) use against Japan as a further means of shutting down US military operations. Several US military planners suggest that any conflict on the Korean peninsula is likely to witness North Korean use of CW (and possibly BW) from the outset.

Although the proliferators summarized briefly here are remarkably diverse in their strategic cultures, doctrines, and decision-making processes, a common element is their continued willingness to resort to violence to settle disputes or secure national interests.[42] It may be they believe that it is good to be seen as a bit dangerous. Another common element that surfaces in looking at these countries is their emphasis on self-reliance. This emphasis is most pronounced in the case of North Korea with its philosophy of *juche,* but other countries such as Iran and Libya also stress the importance of not being dependent on others for their security. With peace treaties concluded between Israel and Egypt and Jordan, Syria sees itself as the last remaining Arab state with the will and the requirement to balance Israeli military capabilities—both conventional and unconventional—and appears to define its CW program in that context.

Enhancing freedom of action vis-à-vis developed countries does not appear to be a major motivation in the pursuit of CW thus far. This situation may be changing, however, as open discussion has occurred in some developing countries about the need for a capability to deter intervention by developed states.[43] Only one example is the oft-quoted statement by an Indian general to the effect that a major lesson of the Gulf War is that a developing country should not go to war with the US without nuclear weapons (NW). For states that do not consider NW an option for political, technical, or financial reasons, BCW could become increasingly attractive alternatives as they search for leverage to exploit the weaknesses of stronger states. The use of BCW in such "asymmetric strategies" has become a key issue for US military planners.

Although the CW programs of the five countries briefly described here are usually considered the most serious proliferation problems, CW capabilities are not limited to these few states. Egypt is generally believed to have used CW in Yemen in the early 1960s, and there is no evidence that it has eliminated that now-aging capability. Egypt is not a party to the CWC, arguing that it will not join the treaty until Israel moves toward the Non-Proliferation Treaty. Israel, too, is generally considered to have a significant CW capability.[44] It has signed but not ratified the CWC, and a debate is now under way as to whether it should do so. Israeli military officials are questioning why they should relinquish this option that may have some value as a deterrent in kind in the region. In contrast, Israel's chemical industry worries that the limitations on trade with nonparties that will be introduced three years after the CWC's entry into force could injure their competitive position in the global chemical market. Taiwan is not allowed to sign the CWC, although it has indicated it would like to do so. In the meantime, concerns remain about its possible CW program, which lies well within the country's technical capacity. A number of other countries—Vietnam, Myanmar, and Pakistan—are also considered potential CW proliferators, although the extent of their program does not seem to produce levels of anxiety comparable to those of the "rogues" described earlier.

The Nonstate Actor Challenge

The Aum Shinrikyo's sarin attack in the Tokyo subway in 1995, which killed 12 people and produced more than 5,000 casualties, stunned the world. The attack in Japan had sparked a global debate about whether the taboo against terrorist use of BCW has been broken, the extent to which nations should expect similar attacks in the future, and the steps countries should take to prepare for and respond to this new challenge. For some people, terrorist use of BCW presents the major threat from such weapons in the future.

Is such a concern justified in light of the historical record, which shows limited terrorist interest in BCW? Canadian intelligence analyst Ron Purver, who conducted an extensive survey of the unclassified literature dealing with terrorism,[45] has identified three categories of meaningful explanation for the nonuse of BCW by terrorists. The first category includes factors that relate to the nature and goals of terrorist groups, including fear of alienating public opinion, the perceived lack of control over the weapon itself, and the lack of suitable or commensurate demands that would make the threat of use of such weapons credible. A second category identifies factors that represent continuing constraints on terrorist BCW use, including the difficulty of ensuring group cohesion in the face of a possible controversial action, fear of government retaliation, and technical constraints which, although not insurmountable, add to the complexity and risks of an operation and could increase the prospect of failure. The third category of explanation highlights factors that are not always apposite, and could be losing their cogency. These factors include an alleged disinclination toward mass or indiscriminate killing, the absence of a need to resort to such weapons, alleged satisfaction with existing methods, and the perceived lack of precedent for BCW use.[46]

Have the factors that restrained terrorist use of BCW in the past so lost their cogency that we should expect widespread use of them in the future? Not necessarily. It is the case that technical factors have become less restrictive as a result of proliferation, technology diffusion, and the internet. But technical barriers were never all that high in the past; nor have they completely disappeared.[47] It is also true that trends in terrorist activity show that while the number of terrorist incidents in recent years has declined, the number of persons killed in such incidents has increased.[48] But terrorists always possessed the capacity to kill more people than they actually killed, even using traditional instruments such as guns and bombs. The ultimate impact of the changes in constraints on terrorist use of BCW remains ambiguous.

Has the taboo, then, been broken? Answering the question begins with the appreciation that change in the motivations propelling terrorist groups has fostered a more complex array of groups, some of whom may indeed be attracted to the use of such weapons.

Brad Roberts identifies three types of traditional terrorist actors: those who use terror to demand a seat at the political table and compel respect for a cause, those who resort to violence in the hope of spurring such an overreaction by the state that the people rise up to overthrow it, and state-sponsored terrorists who are used by foreign powers to gain political leverage.[49] For a variety of reasons, none of these groups has been attracted to BCW use in the past, and there is little evidence to indicate that they are likely to find such weapons attractive for their purposes in the future.

The terrorism landscape has become more complicated, however, with the emergence of other groups. Terrorism expert Bruce Hoffman describes these new entrants as

> rather different terrorist "entities" with arguably less comprehensible nationalist or ideological motivations [which] frequently embrace not only far more amorphous religious and millenarian aims but are themselves less cohesive organizational entities, with a more diffuse structure and membership. Even more disturbing is that... their goals embrace mystical, almost transcendental, and divinely-inspired imperatives or a violently anti-government form of "populism reflecting far-fetched conspiracy notions based on a volatile mixture of seditious, racial, and religious dicta."[50]

Such groups hold different conceptions of political power and define their relationship with society in terms far different from those of the traditional terrorist. As a consequence, they also hold distinct views on the place of violence in their cause and the acceptability of inflicting mass casualties on innocent populations.

It is these groups that are likely to feel unrestrained in the use of chemical or biological weapons. Aum Shinrikyo, for example, was a unique combination of millenarian cult, terrorist organization, and criminal enterprise that sought to hasten the collapse of the government of Japan and the conflict between Japan and the US that had been predicted by its charismatic leader, Shoko Asahara.[51] Closer to home, concern exists about the interest being demonstrated in BCW by elements of the so-called "Christian militia," particularly through their exchanges on the internet. One might ask, for example, why such groups are trying to recruit crop dusters from west Texas who used to fly for the former Nicaraguan dictator, Anastasio Somoza.

The more complex pattern of terrorism at the end of the twentieth century does not imply that terrorists will necessarily find it easy to acquire, develop, or effectively utilize CW on a regular basis. Nor does it suggest that such weapons will never be used. Trying to predict how and when CW will appear is a perilous undertaking. Terrorism expert Brian Jenkins, however, has offered the following propositions:

- Terrorists are more likely to threaten BCW use than actually to use them in attacks.
- CW will prove more prevalent than biological weapons because they are seen to be "easier" to produce and control.
- Small-scale attacks are more likely than large ones.

- Readily available chemicals, such as cyanide, are more likely to be used than more exotic agents (although the Aum attack with sarin suggests an interest in some of the more sophisticated substances).
- Crude dispersal in enclosed areas is the most likely form of attack.
- While more instances of BCW attack will occur, they are not likely to become commonplace.[52]

If Jenkins's last point is correct, then policymakers confront one of their most vexing dilemmas: a potential contingency with low probability but high consequences. Such issues are the most difficult for defining appropriate policy responses. The threat must neither be hyped nor ignored. Shaping effective responses must be given some priority, but not always the highest. Financial resources directed to meeting that threat must be neither excessive nor inadequate. Drawing those lines is extremely difficult.

CW Use: A Range of Troubling Options

Current thinking about the threat posed by CW has been shaped in large part by the legacy of the Cold War. In the context of the East–West standoff, CW were a concern to NATO because the Warsaw Pact was viewed as capable of delivering chemical agents in huge quantities and of the proper type with precision delivery systems and to do so for prolonged periods of time so as to sustain lethal concentrations. The view was also that Soviet forces had the mobility and skill to exploit the tactical opportunities created by such action, thereby creating the prospect of dominating the battlefield. This focus on the impact of CW on battlefield outcomes was reinforced by the way CW were used in the Iran–Iraq War, the most significant use of CW since World War I.

Thinking in such terms today is too narrow.[53] Even in major wars, CW have a broader range of uses than has generally been appreciated. Their use may be threatened, for example, to dissuade military action or deter intervention by an outside state or coalition before actual military conflict begins. CW may also be used to cripple the intervention in its early stages to prevent the conflict from progressing to a decisive encounter. Regimes defeated on the battlefield may also resort to CW to prevent the elaboration of a postconflict outcome that represents a strategic defeat and threatens the existence of the regime or severely limits its freedom of action.

Increasing US dependence on force projection and the accompanying military strategy premised on quick deployment of forces makes the US particularly vulnerable to these broader CW attacks. One government study, for example, highlighted this problem, noting on the basis of war games and other analyses that an

> enemy using relatively small quantities of chemical and biological weapons could exploit vulnerabilities... [and] that military operations conducted according to the tenets of power projection were executable only on delayed and disrupted schedules when CONUS deployment facilities, prepositioned materiel, or key reception sites in the area of responsibility were attacked with chemical and biological weapons.[54]

Major theater wars, however, are not likely to be the most frequent conflict situations in which US forces find themselves in the future. Rather, lower scale conflicts, such as peace enforcement operations, humanitarian assistance missions, or noncombatant evacuations are more likely scenarios. Confronting CW use in such scenarios has been given almost no attention by defense planners or policymakers. Threatening use or even using CW to compel the departure of US forces in such situations is one possible contingency. So, too, is CW use to target congregating civilians preparing for evacuation. State-sponsored terrorism in the US in the context of such prewar or nonwar conflicts is perhaps a more likely contingency than an isolated attack by terrorists.

Policymakers and defense planners must pay greater attention to such potential uses of CW. In the context of the drive to eliminate CW as weapons of war, their use in these nonwar but intense conflicts could become the prevalent mode in which CW continue to be exploited by those seeking political and military advantage.

Conclusion

The changing context of post-Cold War security dynamics is creating a new environment that may change the calculations of the costs and benefits associated with developing, acquiring, and exploiting CW. The growing attraction of "asymmetrical strategies" and the emergence of new terrorist entities are only two aspects of this changing environment. Diminished technical barriers deriving from the diffusion of chemical-related materials, equipment, and expertise is another. The growing number of possible contingencies in which CW might be useful resulting from the more diverse forms of conflict the world is witnessing since the end of the Cold War creates additional opportunities.

The context may be new, but the challenge confronting those responsible for dealing with the CW threat remains much the same. In short, they must drive up the costs of pursuing and exploiting a CW capability as high as possible while minimizing the potential benefit that might be derived from doing so. The costs that must be imposed clearly go well beyond the financial to political and security losses as well. Minimizing benefits, particularly through exploiting defense capabilities—both active and passive—represents another means of deterring not just the use of the capability, but the political decisions to go down the CW road in the first place. The critical challenge is to shape the calculations of decisionmakers who might be contemplating the acquisition of CW capabilities in such a way that the only attractive option is one away from CW proliferation. Meeting the challenge will require a multifaceted strategy that relies on a panoply of policy tools. No one-policy element—intelligence, arms control, export controls, diplomacy, or military capabilities—will provide a complete answer. They must all be made to work together in a genuinely strategic approach. Only such an approach will maximize efforts to respond effectively to the threats posed by CW.

Notes

1. Javed Ali, Leslie Rodrigues, and Michael Moodie, *Jane's US Chemical-Biological Defense Guidebook* (Alexandria: Jane's Information Group, 1998), pp. 21–22.
2. Toxicity can be measured by various factors such as LD_{50} (the dose that kills 50 percent of the exposed population), or ID_{50} (the dose that incapacitates 50 percent of the exposed population).
3. *Jane's Defense Guidebook,* p. 50.
4. "Iraq CW Capability During the Gulf War/Agent 15," UK Ministry of Defence Press Release (Feb. 10, 1998).

5. The differences in toxicity derive from the nature of the chemical groups surrounding the phosphorous atom. There are four such groups, one of which is a double-bonded oxygen.

6. Office of Technology Assessment, *Technologies Underlying Weapons of Mass Destruction* (Washington: Government Printing Office, 1993), p. 24.

7. Ibid., p. 21.

8. Ibid., p. 17

9. Ibid., p. 18

10. Testimony of Kyle Olson, Hearings before the Permanent Subcommittee on Investigations of the Committee on Government Affairs, US Senate (Oct. 31, 1995), pp. 107–8.

11. "Iraq Weapons of Mass Destruction Program," US Government White Paper, United States Information Agency (Feb. 13, 1998), p. 11.

12. See, e.g., *Technologies Underlying Weapons of Mass Destruction,* p. 18.

13. Ibid., p. 21.

14. Ibid., p. 23.

15. For a discussion of this shift, see Brad Roberts, "Article III: Non-Transfer," in Graham S. Pearson and Malcolm Dando, eds., *Strengthening the Biological Weapons Convention: Key Points for the Fourth Review Conference,* Department of Peace Studies, University of Bradford (Sep. 1996), p. 37.

16. Julian Perry Robinson, "Chemical Weapons Proliferation: The Problem in Perspective," in Trevor Findlay, ed., *Chemical Weapons and Missile Proliferation* (Boulder, CO: Lynne Rienner, 1991), p. 26.

17. Brad Roberts, "Rethinking Export Controls on Dual-Use Materials and Technologies From Trade Restraints to Trade Enablers," *The Arena,* no. 2, Chemical and Biological Arms Control Institute (Jun. 1995), pp. 2–3.

18. Lev Fedorov and Vil Mirzayanov, "A Poisoned Policy," *Moscow News,* no. 39 (1992).

19. Will Englund, "Ex-Soviet Scientist Says Gorbachev's Regime Created New Nerve Gas in '91," *Baltimore Sun* (Sep. 16, 1992).

20. Vil Mirzayanov, *Wall Street Journal* (May 25, 1994).

21. 263 *Science* (Feb. 25, 1994), p. 1083.

22. *Technologies Underlying Weapons of Mass Destruction,* p. 28.

23. "Declarations of Chemical Weapons Activities," Chemical and Biological Nonproliferation Project, Henry L. Stimson Center, http://www.stimson.org/cwc/declar.htm.

24. Anthony Cordesman, *Case Study 3: Iraq,* Deterrence Series (Alexandria: Chemical and Biological Arms Control Institute, 1998), p. 33.

25. Ibid., p. 34.

26. Iraqi Deputy Prime Minister Tariq Aziz indicated to Ambassador Rolf Ekéus, then Executive Chairman of the UN Special Commission on Iraq (UNSCOM), that Iraq interpreted the US threat to be one of nuclear retaliation. Ambassador Ekéus is reluctant to fully accept this explanation at face value, however, given the Iraqi propensity to tell their listeners what they think they want to hear.

27. "Iraqi Weapons of Mass Destruction Programs," p. 5.

28. Ibid., p. 6.

29. Michael Eisenstadt, *Case Study 4: Iran,* Deterrence Series (Alexandria: Chemical and Biological Arms Control Institute, 1998), p. 25.

30. US Department of Defense, *Proliferation: Threat and Response* (Dec. 1997), p. 5.

31. Ibid.

32. Ahmed Hashim, *Case Study 1: Syria,* Deterrence Series (Alexandria: Chemical and Biological Arms Control Institute, 1998), p. 7.

33. Ibid., p. 8.

34. M. Zuhair Diab, "Syria's Chemical and Biological Weapons: Assessing Capabilities and Motivations," *The Nonproliferation Review* (Fall 1997), p. 105.

35. Ahmed Hashim, p. 8.

36. M. Zuhair Diab, p. 106. The extent of Soviet/Russian support is the subject of some debate. Hashim, for example, suggests that far from supporting Syrian efforts, the Soviet Union sent a military delegation to warn Damascus that it would not support Syrian CW in combat.

(Hashim, p. 8.) In contrast, Diab quotes Israeli Defense Minister Yitzhak Mordechai as saying in 1996 that Russian scientists were helping Syria to manufacture VX, an allegation the Russians denied. (Diab, p. 106).

37. DoD, *Proliferation: Threat and Response*, p. 15.
38. German companies, in particular, took a lead role in the construction of the plant. The German firm Imhausen-Chemie, for example, was the prime contractor. Japanese companies were also involved, particularly in providing a metal-working plant with Japanese-made machine tools. French companies were alleged to have provided chemical reaction cauldrons, and Dutch and Hong Kong firms were used for shipping and distribution. See OTA, *Technologies Underlying Weapons of Mass Destruction*, pp. 42–43.
39. Robert Waller, *Case Study 2: Libya*, Deterrence Series (Alexandria: Chemical and Biological Arms Control Institute, 1998), p. 7.
40. Joseph Bermudez, *Case Study 5: North Korea*, Deterrence Series (Alexandria: Chemical and Biological Arms Control Institute, 1998), p. 5.
41. Ibid., p. 9.
42. The brief discussion that follows is taken from Michael Moodie, *Chemical and Biological Weapons: Will Deterrence Work?* Deterrence Series (Alexandria: Chemical and Biological Arms Control Institute, 1998), pp. 29–31.
43. Former Indian Army Chief of Staff, General K. Sundarji, for example, has endorsed the notion of a "minimum deterrent" to discourage "US bullying" and possible "racist aggression from the West." Cited in Brad Roberts, "Between Panic and Complacency: Calibrating the Chemical and Biological Warfare Threat," in Stuart E. Johnson, *The Niche Threat: Deterring the Use of Chemical and Biological Weapons* (Washington: National Defense University Press, 1997), p. 27.
44. Gordon Burck and Charles Flowerree, *International Handbook on Chemical Weapons Proliferation* (Westport, CT: Greenwood Press, 1991).
45. Ron Purver, *Chemical and Biological Terrorism: The Threat According to the Open Literature* (Jun. 1995).
46. These categories are presented in Ron Purver, "Understanding Past Non-Use of CBW by Terrorists," in Brad Roberts, ed., *Terrorism with Chemical and Biological Weapons: Calibrating Risks and Responses* (Alexandria: Chemical and Biological Arms Control Institute, 1997), pp. 71–72.
47. See Karl Lowe, "Analyzing Technical Constraints on Bio-Terrorism: Are They Still Important?" ibid., pp. 53–64.
48. Bruce Hoffman, "Viewpoint—Terrorism and WMD: Some Preliminary Hypotheses," *The Nonproliferation Review* (Spring-Summer 1997), p. 47.
49. Brad Roberts, "Has the Taboo Been Broken?" in Roberts, *Terrorism with CBW*, pp. 129–30.
50. Bruce Hoffman, "Viewpoint—Terrorism and WMD," p. 47.
51. For an excellent examination of the Aum Shinrikyo, see the testimony of John Sopko and the attached report, "Global Proliferation of Weapons of Mass Destruction: A Case Study of the Aum Shinrikyo," in *Global Proliferation of Weapons of Mass Destruction*, Hearings before the Permanent Subcommittee on Investigations, Committee on Governmental Affairs, US Senate, Part I (Oct. 31 and Nov. 1, 1995), pp. 15–102.
52. Brian M. Jenkins, "Understanding the Link Between Motives and Methods," in Roberts, *Terrorism with CBW*, p. 51.
53. This discussion is based in part on the work of Brad Roberts, who has done extensive analyses of unexpected uses of weapons of mass destruction.
54. "Assessment of the Impact of Chemical and Biological Weapons on Joint Operations in 2010 (The CB 2010 Study)," US Department of Defense, http//www.nbc-med.org/publications/cb2010.htm.

Chapter 6

The Threat of Other Forms of Terrorism

In this chapter, authors explore other threats: ways in which terrorist groups could expand their power and their powers of destruction. A criminal-terrorist connection—where terrorist groups look to crime as a way to generate more operational funds—cyberterrorism, and biological attacks against the agricultural supply are potentially three such areas. Nationalist and religious campaigns do not have a monopoly on terrorist tactics: militant groups involved in animal rights, environmentalism, and abortion are examples of what author G. Davidson Smith terms "single-issue terrorism."

According to Barry R. McCaffrey and John A. Basso, the September 11 attacks demonstrated the power produced by the collision of three explosive trends: the U.S. as a sole superpower in the post–cold war era, and the one clear oppressor left to blame for the woes of underdeveloped peoples; a funding vacuum left after the end of the cold war, which led insurgent and terrorist organizations to turn to criminal activity to gain funds; and terrorists' perceived need for massive loss of life, to gain the attention of the media and the world. "Money is a natural centrifugal force," say McCaffrey and Basso in their exploration of this second trend. "Terrorists are necessarily pulled toward it. Criminals have always sought it. Money, and the means of gaining it, brings these two very different lethal organizations together. This magnetic attraction was born of post–Cold War conditions." The authors present examples where they draw a connection between crime and terrorist groups, using the Revolutionary Armed Forces of Columbia (FARC), the Kurdistan Workers Party (PKK), and al-Qaeda as examples of criminal-based funding; and they offer recommendations for dealing with this lethal pairing.

"A major terrorist campaign waged principally or solely via digital attacks has not occurred," writes Gregory J. Rattray. Yet, cyberterrorism will likely evolve as another tool for groups looking to achieve their objectives, and information systems have become both a weapon and a target of warfare. Rattray admits that it is difficult to define the exact scope of what constitutes cyberterrorism, yet he offers potential examples that would cause destruction and massive disruption: causing train accidents with large death counts by tampering with digital switching systems, causing stock market disruptions by denying service to computer and communications systems, corrupting key information within a system that requires high confidence for its use. Rattray cautions that in the United States—a society so heavily reliant on information systems—policymakers need to understand the constraints in the use of cyberterrorism, the possibilities for its use, and why it has not yet emerged as a prevalent terrorist strategy. The author surveys cyberterrorist potential and briefly reviews what the United States has done to contain the threat, warning that it may just be a matter of time before terrorist groups tap this weapon. Rattray sums up with a quote from the 1991 National Research Council *Computers at Risk* report: "The modern thief can steal more with a computer than a gun. Tomorrow's terrorist may be able to do more damage with a keyboard than a bomb."

Jason Pate and Gavin Cameron explore the likelihood of terrorists mounting a biological attack on the agricultural supply as yet another tool for their political ends. In Fiscal Year 2001, the U.S. Department of Agriculture (USDA) requested $41.3 million for counterterrorism, 96 percent of which ($39.8 million) was devoted to defense against weapons of mass destruction. In FY2000, the USDA's WMD [weapons of mass destruction] defense was $7.3 million. Clearly the USDA has focused significant resources on this problem. There have been instances of agricultural product contamination, yet few could be termed "agricultural terrorism" in the United States. The authors explore the costs and impact when crops or livestock are destroyed, using as one example the 1999 frost decimation of the California orange supply. They cite 21 incidents—based on the Database of WMD Terrorism Incidents at the Monterey Institute Center for Nonproliferation Studies—that might be classified as subnational biological weapons agricultural attacks, the earliest of which occurred in Kenya in 1952. These incidents were generally a means of extortion, intimidation, or economic punishment, but they did not wreak catastrophic damage and destruction. The authors point out that attacking a diverse industry spread throughout a region as vast as the United States would require a sophisticated, multipronged attack, but they warn that there is a gap between what has occurred and this perceived danger. Further research needs to be done to determine "whether there is a genuine danger and whether the terrorist threat has evolved to the point that terrorists now see agriculture as a worthwhile target."

"The term 'Single-Issue Terrorism'," writes G. Davidson (Tim) Smith, "is broadly accepted as extremist militancy on the part of groups or individuals protesting a perceived grievance or wrong usually attributed to governmental action or inaction." Smith surveys the three causes where a militant fringe has resorted to threats, violence, and destruction of property to achieve their ends: animal rights, environmentalism, and abortion. He surveys the militant activities and groups involved with each issue and concludes that single-issue militancy remains dangerous—and it will continue to attract individuals who are willing to resort to militant means for "selfish or believed-to-be altruistic reasons," creating extraordinary problems for the ranks of law enforcement and the criminal justice system.

Narcotics, Terrorism, and International Crime: The Convergence Phenomenon

Barry R. McCaffrey, a U.S. Army General who is now retired from active duty, is the Olin Distinguished Professor of National Security Studies at the United States Military Academy, West Point and president of a consulting firm specializing in international security issues. General McCaffrey stepped down as the Director of the White House Office of National Drug Control Policy in January 2001. He is also a national security and terrorism analyst for NBC News.

John A. Basso is a Major in the U.S. Army and an Instructor in Economics at the U.S. Military Academy, West Point.

Introduction

Past as Prologue

The 9/11 attacks on the World Trade Center and the Pentagon demonstrated the power produced by the collision of three combustible trends; the perverse logic of the terrorist mind put the United States in the middle of this explosion. These three trends changed the nature of terror attacks. First, as NATO won the Cold War, the United States became the terrorist target of choice. The elimination of Soviet superpower status, and with it the end of the USSR's role as the enemy of freedom-loving people, left one clear oppressor to blame for the woes of underdeveloped peoples. It also left a clear global leader to influence regardless of the cause being supported through terror. The second trend is related to the funding vacuum brought about by the end of Cold War superpower competition. Insurgent groups and terrorist organizations turned to narcotics, kidnapping, extortion, bank robbing, and other criminal activities as a relatively easy way to gain funds. While some extremist groups had never relied on these criminal funding sources, the opening of borders that came about with the collapse of the U.S.S.R allowed these groups to take advantage of the same changes that rebel groups exploited. The final trend, the perceived need for massive loss of life to capture global attention, developed as 24-hour news media bombarded consumers with an enormous number of stories each week. To be heard, be loud, was the lesson learned by insurgents and terrorists.

As the unwitting source of each of these trends, America will continue to bear the cruel costs of their confluence. It is vital that we recognize that the evolution of these three trends has not paused. Instead, the recent acceleration of America's unipolar role, when linked to greater interaction between terrorist organizations and transnational criminal organizations (TCOs), increases both the possibility of another attack against the U.S. and the likelihood that terrorist groups will be able to gain the resources necessary for even more devastating attacks. Future terrorist mega-events may well include a fourth reactive element—the availability of chemical, biological, radiological, and nuclear material (CBRN). It is the American government's role to defuse this terrorist explosion before it goes off, and the wire that needs to be snipped can be found in the link between terrorist and criminal organizations.

Significance

The introduction of CBRN material to the terrorist-criminal equation underscores why it is so important to comprehend the links between terrorist organizations and transnational criminal organizations (TCOs). If scholars are correct in the conclusion that criminal organizations are increasingly linked to each other and form a global criminal network, then a terrorist who taps into this network will gain extraordinary reach.[1] For instance, a terrorist group may acquire the capability to access not only drug production revenue in Latin America, but also highly enriched uranium (HEU) or plutonium through the Russian mafia. Additionally, tapping into this network facilitates contact with other terrorist organizations. Understanding the convergence of terrorist organizations and TCOs will be one of the keys to the future security of American citizens. In this chapter we identify what conditions foster connections between terrorist organizations and criminal organizations. We then use representative examples to show how these connections are made, and, importantly, how they may be broken. We conclude by using this understanding to develop policy recommendations on how best to respond to these dangerous trends. To set the stage, the next section provides an elaboration of the three combustive trends that set the conditions for 9/11.

Strategic Environment

U.S. as Target

History has shown that a clear way to gain the support of a constituency is to blame their problems on someone other than themselves. In the post–Cold War era, the U.S., as the only remaining superpower, became the natural target for blame. Osama bin Laden made that clear in a 1997 interview with CNN's Peter Arnett: "The collapse of the Soviet Union made the U.S. more haughty and arrogant and it has started to look at itself as a master of this world and established what it calls the New World Order."[2] Additionally, as Yossef Bodansky (director of the Congressional Task Force on Terrorism and Unconventional Warfare) reported, bin Laden places the blame for the Saudi financial crisis, increased Saudi taxes, and the deteriorating Saudi education system on the U.S.[3]

CIA counterterrorism expert Paul Pillar points out that the proportion of attacks on U.S. interest have risen from 31% in the 1980s to 37% in the 1990s.[4] The role of America as a primary target will continue based on wide-spread perceptions of the U.S. as carrying out unilateral policy and maintaining close ties to Israel, as well as the consistent global poverty coupled with self-evident U.S. massive material wealth. Additionally, those terrorist groups that do not wish to attack the U.S. directly, such as the IRA, may well try to influence their target by gaining U.S. support. Even attacks not carried out directly against American citizens seek to influence U.S. policy.

Changes to Funding Sources

Money is a natural centrifugal force. Terrorists are necessarily pulled toward it. Criminals have always sought it. Money, and the means of gaining it, brings these two very different lethal organizations together. This magnetic attraction was born of post–Cold War conditions. Money has always been a concern for insurgent groups. War requires weapons. However, since the end of Cold War superpower state sponsorship, ideological insurgents have had to look for alternative ways to raise funds. And, these insurgents have had to often turn to terrorism because the states they rebel against have become too strong militarily to allow any reasonable chance at success in conventional civil war. Even some of the modern extremist terrorist groups that never benefited from Cold War funding have moved toward criminal-based funding. The ability to use the chaos wrought by terrorism and insurgency to produce coca or opium and then move narcotics through soft borders is tempting. Likewise, kidnapping of foreign company employees and extortion have grown in prevalence. These groups are drawn together because of their complimentary capabilities. Terrorists can create chaotic circumstances that allow for illicit activities. Criminal organizations have pre-established networks to move and sell narcotics and launder money. The result is that some terrorists and criminal organizations converge and become partners working together to gain revenue. Additionally, some terrorist organizations transform themselves to be able to conduct criminal activities in-house so that they can generate their own revenue. In either case, these terrorist groups become part of a network of criminal organizations, which are considered to be possible sources for CBRN material.

Increased Scope of Attacks

Black September surprised the world with their 1972 attack on the Israeli Olympic team. Twelve innocent people died. Islamic Jihad stunned the world in 1983 with their attack on the Marine Barracks in Beirut. Two hundred and forty-one U.S. Marines died. Aum Shinrikyo raised world terror to new levels with their 1995 Tokyo subway attack—12 Japanese died and over 3,000 were hospitalized from exposure to sarin gas. Al-Qaeda's staggering 1998 East Africa U.S. embassy bombings killed 264 and wounded over 5,000 people. The magnitude of the 9/11 attack was not an aberration. While there are some exceptions, generally terrorists are trying to increase the scope of their carnage in each successive campaign of attacks.[5] This observation holds true not just for extremist terrorist groups, but also for ethno-nationalist groups.[6] Terrorists believe that gaining international attention is vital to their cause. In the mind of a terrorist, to get the world's attention—to win—dramatic bloodshed is necessary.[7] Massive bloodshed, though, is not easy to achieve. As the world wakes up to the threat of terrorism, it will be even more difficult to successfully plan, resource, and execute dramatically successful attacks. Success will require flexibility, particularly in acquiring resources for these terrorist operations. Both single spectacular attacks and sustained operations may require large amounts of cash. Shoestring budgets are unlikely to suffice. And, as the previous section outlined, the financial tactics of terrorist groups like Abu Sayyaf, the FARC, and al-Qaeda have evolved as rapidly as the scope of attacks seen in Munich, Beirut, and Tokyo. It has been widely reported that each of these groups has to some degree pursued criminal activities to fund their ultimate goals. In order to craft effective counterterrorism strategy, we must understand how and why terrorist groups collaborate with criminal organizations.

Hypothesis

Previous Work

Some very impressive scholarly work has been done outlining the factors that influence insurgent group behavior.[8] Insurgent groups differ from terrorist groups. Specifically, we define terrorist groups as those who have crossed a line and chosen to target innocent civilians for psychological impact. Once this line is crossed, they are more willing to expand their range of funding sources and the nature of their attacks. The new breed of extremist terror groups significantly differ in their aims from ethno-nationalist groups and in their use of terror as not just an isolated tactic, but as an all-encompassing strategy to gain the change they seek.[9] Nonetheless, there are enough similarities between typical rebel groups and terrorists to warrant an analysis of the burgeoning literature on the incidence of civil war. Paul Collier, director of the Development Research Group of the World Bank, has examined civil wars since 1965 to determine if evidence exists to support the popular perception that rebels begin civil wars to rid their state of an unjust regime, or if instead rebels simply aspire to criminal wealth. Since asking rebels their rationale would inevitably lead to a narrative focused on issues of grievance, Collier instead measures motivation through causal factors that he broadly groups as consistent with greed or grievance. His results overwhelmingly indicate that economic agendas have a greater role in the incidence and continuation of civil war than does grievance.[10]

Terrorism scholar Chris Dishman superbly extends this type of analysis to the relationship between terrorist groups and organized crime.[11] Based on his conclusion that the costs of collaboration outweigh the benefits, Dishman finds that cooperation between the two groups may occur, but it will be short lived. He further argues that terrorist organizations and criminal organizations will continue to shy away from collaborative arrangements, because their aims and motivations are different than those of their potential collaborators. In general, he believes that these different groups will instead choose to remain on an authentic political or criminal course.[12] Dishman supports this hypothesis by using case studies to outline out how terrorist groups and organized crime have used violence in the past. The terrorist and criminal groups he studies draw and maintain a clear distinction between violence used to advance profit aims and violence used for political reasons. He demonstrates, however, that criminal motives and the lure of profit will transform the aims of some terrorist leaders. This transformation toward profit-making blurs the distinction between violence used to advance political aims and that used to increase revenue. In particular, Dishman warns, "Terrorists and guerrilla groups who view their cause as futile, might turn their formidable assets towards crime—all the while under a bogus political banner." While Dishman's work is excellent, some might suggest that it is far too general and relies too heavily on cases that existed in a world that did not have such open borders and information technologies for coordinating activities on a global basis. By failing to distinguish between insurgent groups and terrorists or between different types of terrorist groups, and by failing to recognize that historical cases miss the complexity of the modern relationship between organized crime and terrorists, we believe that Dishman has missed the meaningful convergence relationships between these dangerous organizations. Instead, Dishman believes that terrorist organizations simply undergo transformation, a conclusion that some experts believe is incorrect.

Typology and Hypothesis

To understand why the terrorist groups most likely to strike the United States are likely to converge into partnerships with criminal organizations, we must analyze their motivations. As the U.S. prosecutes a broad war on terror, we must sort out which terrorist groups will transform themselves to take on the capabilities of a profit-driven criminal group, and which terrorist groups will remain true to their ideological cause. The vital first step in crafting policy options to defeat these groups will be understanding their vulnerabilities. Three general outcomes exist for terrorist organizations in their dealings with criminal organizations. Terrorist organizations may converge, meaning form a partnership with criminal organizations; terrorist groups may transform themselves into quasi-criminal organizations; or they might maintain themselves as pure terrorist organizations.

Terrorist groups will approach the decision of what type of partnership to pursue based on two independent variables. First, terrorist groups must identify whether they intend to seek a future legitimate governance role. While terrorist actions will always have some political aspect to them (or they would not meet RAND terrorism expert Bruce Hoffman's regularly cited definition of terrorism), the political action may have little to do with gaining a governing role in a state.[13] In fact, we suggest that a sea change in terrorism has taken place. Many new groups are extremist in nature instead of ethno-nationalist, and will generally not seek a role in state governance. Second, all terrorist groups must determine whether their followers will continue to support them if they pursue criminal activities to gain revenue or resources for future terror attacks. Wesleyan Professor and terrorism expert Martha Crenshaw has outlined the rational calculations terrorists make in deciding whether to act. We believe they make this same calculation regarding funding. Terrorists must determine if their actions will cause a loss of popular support from their followers.[14] If so, their ability to interact with criminal organizations is constrained. These two variables, desire to govern and support for criminal activity, interact to determine in large part which path terrorist groups take regarding cooperation with criminal organizations.

Clear logic underlies each part of the typology. For instance, Sendero Luminoso (The Shining Path) participated in criminal activities that its followers supported, but only in an effort to fund Abimael Guzman's bizarre Maoist vision. Sendero never lost its desire to govern. On the other hand, we would suggest that the FARC, after determining that it could not play an active role in the Colombian state, fully transformed itself and turned its focus almost exclusively to profit via criminal activity. In doing so, the FARC lost all but the most determined of its ideological followers. While these two cases briefly illustrate the interaction of the key independent variables, a deeper examination of the convergence case is warranted given the clear danger to U.S. citizens.

We suggest that a vital part of the typology is the differentiation between modern extremist terrorist organizations and those that are of the traditional ethno-nationalist type. We need to determine the ultimate motivation of the group. In our judgement, extremist groups do not seek an active role in governing a state. Moreover, the ideal they seek to achieve so overshadows the distortions to that ideal, that their followers see criminal activity as a minor irritant. For example, Shoko Asahara's followers in the millenarian cult Aum Shinrikyo have been accurately described as extremely well educated. Yet, as Walter Laqueur of the Center for Strategic and International Studies perceptively points out, these same followers not only supported the smuggling of weapons from Russia, they also managed to make the cruel and bizarre mental leap that releasing sarin gas on innocent Japanese citizens in the Tokyo subway would aid in preventing an American WMD attack on Japan.[15]

These groups always believe that the ends justify the means. Osama bin Laden implicitly made this point in a 1998 interview with ABC News, during which he altered his previous sentiment that only U.S. military personnel and facilities were targets of his terror campaign and added American civilians to his target list. As experts have pointed out, this escalation was made "despite the fact that the Koran itself is explicit about the protections offered to civilians."[16] We suggest that the ramifications are clear. If the ends justify any means for some terrorist organizations, then collaboration with criminal organizations will be likely. This partnership is particularly probable if those criminal organizations can provide both revenue and a capability that the terrorist organization does not possess. As our typology indicates in the lower right corner of the box in figure 6-1, in the future we can expect to see convergence between criminal groups and so-called extremist terrorist groups like al-Qaeda. Extremist groups generally have no genuine desire to govern and their followers are not averse to these groups' criminal connections.

Given al-Qaeda's alleged business structure, which Peter Bergen expertly outlines in *Holy War, Inc.*, this focus on capabilities should not surprise us. Seeking out a partner to gain a capability that you lack has long been the model in the business world, and now we are seeing terrorist groups sophisticated enough to organize as businesses. The frightening part of these capability-based partnerships is that some criminal organizations may have more to exchange than a narcotics distribution network and the cash to fund terrorist operations and training. Some of these TCOs, particularly those that operate in the former Soviet Union and in Pakistan, may also have the capability to acquire CBRN material. Some observers have questioned whether these criminal groups would have the motivation to pursue such transactions, particularly given the assumption that collaboration with terrorists would naturally lead to greater law enforcement attention.

Observers who make this case about criminal organizations are trapped in the same thinking that led to faulty logic regarding whether terrorists would converge with TCOs. We believe that Transnational Criminal Organizations are businesses. Just as businesses seek partners to gain the capabilities they lack, so too will TCOs seek partners. As we have already seen in Colombia, Afghanistan, and Burma, terrorist groups will bring narcotics production and some distribution capacity to the bargaining table. Terrorist groups are particularly well suited to the task of narcotics production since the chaotic environment they create will lead to lawlessness and the ability to conduct illicit business. Effective monopolies create barriers to entry by other firms through legal restrictions, like patents and copyrights, or through exorbitant start-up costs as seen in the jumbo-jet industry. Terrorist groups involved in drug production gain a monopoly

Figure 6-1

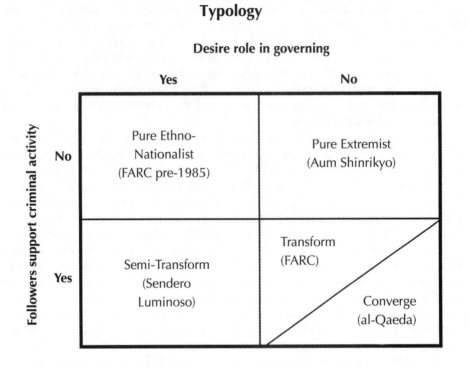

Typology

Desire role in governing

	Yes	No
No	Pure Ethno-Nationalist (FARC pre-1985)	Pure Extremist (Aum Shinrikyo)
Yes	Semi-Transform (Sendero Luminoso)	Transform (FARC) / Converge (al-Qaeda)

Followers support criminal activity

on the control of land for the growing of coca or opium. They maintain a barrier to entry through violence. The behavior and values of both the criminal organizations and their terrorist partners becomes congruent.

A second potential argument that might cause criminal organizations to avoid partnering with terrorist groups is the question of scope of violence. Terrorists, even those seeking a legitimate role in a state, are willing to cross lines that many citizens see as sacrosanct. They will carry out kidnapping and murder for instance, and see these terrible acts as legitimate in order to further their cause. Criminal organizations, or at the very least some of their operatives, will also not be queasy about the mass casualty situations that they would create through the sale of CBRN material to terrorists. Crossing this criminal line would not be difficult since both parties will likely feel that the target—the United States—deserves what it gets. It is no secret that some of the poorly paid Russian, Pakistani, North Korean, or Iranian military who may have access to CBRN material maintain strong feelings of animosity toward America.[17] Valentin Tikhonov frighteningly points out in a Carnegie Endowment for International Peace report that given the lack of accountability of tactical nuclear weapons, not to mention weapons grade nuclear material, as well as biological, chemical, and radiological material, the ability of soldiers and scientists to covertly sell this material seems unquestioned.[18] Both sides of the marriage—extremist terrorist organizations and transnational criminal organizations—will see benefits in converging into such a lethal partnership. Arguments that this relationship will be short lived are moot. It only takes one such criminal-terrorist partnership to realize our greatest fear: Terrorists armed with nuclear, chemical, or biological weapons.

Case Studies—Testing the Hypothesis

To flesh out this argument more thoroughly, we believe it is beneficial to examine representative cases of transformed and converged terrorist groups and to outline the evolution of a criminal organization, in order to see characteristics evident in each case. We do not illustrate a pure terrorist group case; each of the groups we examine began as a pure case and eventually changed with their environment. It is useful to see which independent variables mutated over time, leading these groups from a pure state to a transformed or converged state. Our purpose is to gain predictive capability for future instances and devise strategies to attack the exposed flank of terrorist organizations. We realize that our examination is only an initial overview, and that it ultimately deserves more detailed case study analysis. However, it is clear that the differences in the cases we cite hinge to a certain extent on whether terrorists use terror as a tactic as has been prevalent with traditional ethno-nationalist terrorist groups—or if they use terror as a fundamental strategy as we have witnessed in contemporary terrorist organizations. Additionally, we should note that a comprehensive study should examine a number of factors that help steer a terrorist group's decision on whether to partner with criminal organizations. A vital element included in these factors is having the geography that supports criminal trafficking.

FARC—Transformation

Colombia's vicious rebellion is more than 50 years old.[19] The murderous conflict has cost the country over 200,000 lives. Although insurgent activity has ebbed and flowed over the years, the explosive growth of narco-insurgent financing through cocaine and heroin criminal activity has dramatically strengthened the fighting capacity of Colombia's terrorist groups. They have been ultimately transformed into terrorist organizations that use massive violence against the state to cement their capacity to maintain narcotics profits. This dramatic change from a Marxist revolutionary political organization to a transformed terrorist organization occurred as a response to political failure. Colombia's main rebel group, the Revolutionary Armed Forces of Colombia (FARC), failed in its attempt to gain a voice in Colombian governance via politics.

The FARC attempted to enter mainstream Colombian politics in the mid-1980s by establishing the Patriotic Union party. Threatened by their electoral successes, large landowners used paramilitary units, often with the support of Colombia's armed forces, to carry out a methodical campaign of murder against Patriotic Union officials.[20] These paramilitary units later combined to form the United Self-Defense Forces of Colombia (AUC). The introduction of this other armed force, the paramilitary AUC, now estimated at 4,000 to 5,000 strong, marked a critical intensification in Colombian violence. The FARC responded to this threat by increasing its military capacity. However, it had to seek alternate funding sources, primarily narcotics, to gain this increased capability for violence. While the AUC's use of assassinations hurt the FARC's political ambitions, ultimately, it was its immersion in narcotics activities that eliminated all of the FARC's political legitimacy. Additionally, the FARC's great success in gaining drug money—the State Department's 2002 International Narcotics Control Strategy Report (INCSR) says that Colombia's rebel groups now control much of the country's narcotics production and distribution capacity—has in the eyes of many observers completely transformed it from its Marxist past.[21] With around $500 million in profits from processing and shipping cocaine, "FARC rebels are so involved in the drug business that [a senior Colombian military leader] bluntly calls them 'a cartel'."[22] In other words, the FARC no longer appears to seek any significant role in the governance of Colombia and it has a group of followers who will ruthlessly support all types of criminal activity from narcotics and kidnapping to outright extortion of the oil and gas industry. These narco-insurgents who fight under the guise of political grievance will back any criminal actions by the leaders of the FARC. They recognize that these terrorist attacks maintain the chaotic environment that creates the conditions for continued narcotics profits.

PKK—Ethno-Nationalist Converged

Abdullah Ocalan formed the Kurdistan Workers Party (PKK) in 1978. The PKK professed Marxist ideology at its inception; however, by the 1990s it advocated nationalism over communism. To that nationalist end, the PKK began including Islam in its literature in 1989. In 1984 the PKK made its critical strategic change—the adoption of violent terrorist tactics. Between 1984 and 1994, 128 teachers were killed as the PKK attacked the educational institutions that it saw as representative of the Turkish state. As the PKK enlarged its campaign of violence from May 1993 to October 1994, 1,600 total deaths were attributed to the group. In response to this increased violence, the Turkish military was given free rein to defeat the terrorists, and by the spring of 1994, the PKK's impact in Turkey had dramatically decreased.[23] However, the PKK's level of involvement in criminal activity to generate the resources needed to continue its war against Turkey did not diminish.

The U.S. State Department indicated in 1992 that the PKK was involved in the acquisition, importation, and distribution of drugs in Europe. Presumably this move toward illicit activities was driven by the need for funds required to support its desperate struggle against Turkey's escalated anti-terror offense. Yet, after the Turkish Armed Forces stunningly defeated the PKK, by 1994 few Turkish Kurds supported the terrorist's violent tactics. However, they continued to pursue drug trafficking, even reportedly partnering with the Medellin cartel by 1995. Interestingly, although the PKK did not gain internal legitimacy from its own followers—it did gain external recognition. The wife of French President Mitterand even penned a letter of support to "President Ocalan" in 1998.[24] Nonetheless, when Ocalan was captured in Nairobi, Kenya in 1999, the final end of the PKK seemed near. It's curious to note that some elements of the PKK have maintained a discourse that indicates that even now they want some role in governance. Indeed, by February of 2002, the PKK was again threatening to resume its war as the defenders of Kurd cultural autonomy.[25] Regardless of the outcome of its continued political signals, the PKK seems to have effectively converged with criminal organizations. A political group that began as a pure ethno-nationalist terrorist group now has all of the characteristics of a partner of criminal organizations. The 1998 State Department INCSR alleges that the PKK used narcotics trafficking to finance its terror operations. However, the capture of Ocalan and the inevitable drop in funding from Kurds living abroad makes it more likely that the PKK is now using terrorism to support its bottom line.

Al-Qaeda—Extremist Converged

Afghanistan under Taliban rule became the world's leading opium and processed heroin producer. Despite Mullah Omar's ban on poppy cultivation as a first grudging response to world pressure in July 2000, trafficking of Afghan heroin continued through the use of massive stockpiles. It seems almost certain that al-Qaeda used their controlling link to the Taliban to profit from narcotics trafficking.[26] In 1998, before the Taliban's prohibition on production, the Italian government had established a link between the financing of Islamic fundamentalist groups and drug trafficking.[27] This conclusion certainly matches logic: The Taliban was said to have levied a 20 percent tax on drug runners and it is clear that Taliban ties to al-Qaeda were very close and indeed had elements of a subordinate relationship. Moreover, after bin Laden's international bank accounts were frozen, it was clear that he would have had little problem justifying the use of drug money to finance his operations.[28] Bin Laden's closest followers also would have had few problems with this financing method, particularly when the narcotics were being trafficked to Westerners. In fact, *fatwas* from extremist Islamic leaders allow these highly irregular, seemingly un-Islamic actions because they add to the demolition of Western society.

Finally, there is evidence that bin Laden has spent in excess of $3 million dollars trying to purchase a nuclear device from the former Soviet Union. Given his close relationship with the Chechens, it seems likely that the Chechen Mafia facilitated these efforts. It is also probable that he would have approached the Russian Mafia as evidence indicates that they have the capacity to acquire CBRN.[29]

Russian Mafia

The increase in globalization in the 1990s rewarded businesses that took advantage of trends in deregulation by de-localizing and organizing transnational enterprises. Organized crime followed this lead by discarding its traditional pyramid-shaped structure in favor of less visible criminal networks.[30] Russian organized crime reportedly consists of some 110 transnational criminal groups allegedly operating in 40 different countries. The 70,000 members of this extended crime family are believed to control an estimated 50 percent of the Russian economy. There is some evidence of formal agreements linking the Russian Mafia to Colombian narcotics traffickers.[31] There is very little evidence linking the Russian Mafia to terrorist groups. Nonetheless, given the global nature of their business, and the active role the Russian Mafia takes in narcotics trafficking across the porous borders of the former Soviet Union, it seems likely that connections have been made with terrorist groups who participate in narcotics trafficking. As the State Department reports, heroin in Russia is primarily imported by Afghans, Tajiks, and other Central Asians across the southern border with Kazakstan, and then distributed by Russian criminal organizations.

In other words, nationality matters little. Capabilities determine business partnerships. For example, circumstantial evidence exists that links the Russian Mafia to terrorists in an arms for cash (or narcotics) transaction. Between 1992 and 1994, the Russian Army lost 14,400 assault rifles and machine guns, and the 17 shoulder fired anti-tank weapons.[32] There is little doubt that a profit-driven organization like the Russian Mafia would be willing to take the next step and trade CBRN material for revenue. This transaction is particularly likely in a financial environment in which deregulation has made the control and monitoring of payments virtually impossible. Evidence suggests that $300 to $500 billion of crime proceeds are transferred undetected through the world's financial markets each year.[33] The threat of a nuclear armed al-Qaeda is monumental, and it is unquestionably worth asking: Will a profit driven organization, that will have eventually squeezed every possible corrupt dime out of the Russian state apparatus, then turn to an even more profitable transaction if its chances of being caught are minimal?

Conclusion and Recommendations

Case Findings

We believe there is a broad trend that suggests terrorist groups transformed themselves or converged with criminal organizations when they saw diminished chances of defeating government forces or when their funding apparatus collapsed. From the perspective of criminal organizations, there are clear costs to collaboration: The discovery of a criminal-terrorist link would bring unwanted response from national and international law enforcement agencies. But, if it is possible to conceal the link to terrorist organizations these partnerships could prove to be very valuable. We also suggest that the increasing technical ease of laundering funds in the information age global economy makes discovery unlikely for sophisticated money launderers. In the specific case of al-Qaeda, effective law enforcement against illegal contributions via the money laundering rules put in place post-9/11 might produce the unintended consequence of pushing al-Qaeda away from Saudi contributors and toward more extensive partnerships with criminal organizations.[34] If we do not see this reaction by al-Qaeda, we could certainly see the same outcome by other terrorist organizations that will follow bin Laden's operational lead. As Harvard terrorism expert Jessica Stern points out, terrorist tend to copy each other.[35] This type of convergence from a group with the capabilities of al-Qaeda signals the dangers of the fourth trend—the emergence of CBRN weapons. The possession of CBRN weapons combined with the other three trends would return us to the horror we first saw at the birth of the nuclear weapons in 1945. Our current policy must identify effective and rational strategic alternatives for our long-term campaign against terror.

Recommendations

Many would argue that the past 15 years have been marked by a lack of adequate leadership and sensible policy judgments by our democracy's political, economic, media, and military elites in the struggle against global terror. Our leadership was collectively incompetent in the face of growing mountains of evidence indicating that our nation was increasingly at risk of catastrophic losses from terrorist attacks on our citizens, our armed forces, and our economic and political interests. The U.S. did make multiple calls on the global community to create a new international consensus. Still, we never defined the reward and punishment coefficients that would apply to coerce positive responses in the international community.[36] These failures are not excusable. However, our mind-numbing inactivity occurred during an era when terrorism was not at the forefront of the collective American conscience. To persist in our previous mistakes would be criminal given the clear evidence of convergence between criminal organizations and terrorist groups and the potentially deadly CBRN threat that goes along with this partnership. The global community must use the information gathered through the analysis of this convergence trend to forestall or prevent future attacks by applying the information to the four critical areas outlined below.

1. **Common Conceptual Framework**: Our counterterrorism effort lacks a conceptual framework and the leadership necessary to effectively combat this global problem.[37] We cannot hope to tackle this problem piecemeal. Instead, we must construct a broad strategy that examines our intelligence requirements, includes our foreign policy actions writ large, and imaginatively considers the vulnerabilities and weaknesses of terrorist groups. We must analyze each of the specific weapons we hold for severing the bond between terrorists and criminal organizations—and between separate terrorist groups—in a growing global network. Identifying whether terrorist groups will remain pure, transform themselves, or converge with criminal organizations is a critical part of pinpointing those weaknesses.

2. **Intelligence**: The different relationships that convergence and transformation breed denote distinct weaknesses inherent in terrorist groups. With these weaknesses in mind, convergence and transformation trends point our intelligence community toward making three necessary structural changes. First, the Central Intelligence Agency and the Defense Intelligence Agency need to embark on a 10-year crash program to rebuild a global human intelligence capability adequate to warn the U.S. and our allies of the new national security nexus of threats posed by terrorism, drugs, and international criminal organizations. Additionally, these agencies must pursue an ethnically diverse group of intelligence operatives. America is the melting pot, and we need to take advantage of this national strength. This crash program will not come without costs—Congress must fund this initiative. Second, the administration must construct a common organizational scheme that allows for intelligence sharing between these agencies and the FBI. Most importantly, we must construct a single integrating mechanism focused exclusively on counterterror intelligence analysis. America's intelligence community must allocate assets not only to intelligence collection, but also, more critically, to intelligence analysis. We are suffering from information overload. We need sophisticated analysts to digest this raw data and find the operationally useful insights. The convergence and transformation trends are an excellent place to begin this analysis. These trends underscore the need to bridge the gap between the CIA and the FBI and our other intelligence bodies. Lastly, the U.S. must lead the way in creating international mechanisms to coordinate and link national law-enforcement and

intelligence capabilities in close partnership with global finance and treasury officials.[38]

3. **Legitimacy**: Al-Qaeda and other terrorist groups expose themselves to counterattack by partnering with criminal organizations, particularly when they use narcotics trafficking as a revenue source. Al-Qaeda has survived this weakness because they had a higher calling—a Jihad against the West—on which to focus their constituents. To take advantage of this vulnerability, the international community needs to fashion a Jihad against narcotics trafficking that includes anti-drug education by Muslim clerics in the Muslim world. This psyops [psychological operational] strategy—linking al-Qaeda to the very narcotics that have been ruled as unholy by Islamic clerics—could potentially weaken some of al-Qaeda's legitimacy with the young men who in their most impressionable years are shaped by extremist education. Perceived religious legitimacy acts as a catalyst for the young people who choose to martyr themselves for this cause. Any step taken to reduce it is worthwhile.

The difference between a converged terrorist group that still has legitimacy with a broad array of followers and a transformed terrorist group that no longer has broad legitimacy helps define primary steps against these distinct terrorist organizations. For example, al-Qaeda has a legitimacy anchored by anti-Western feelings, so we must also be careful with our military operations in the Arab world. Each person who dies as part of a Western military campaign may add to al-Qaeda's legitimacy and add to the creation of other martyrs, whereas attacking al-Qaeda's legitimacy would weaken the group without the negative side-effects. On the other hand, a strategy attacking the legitimacy of the FARC would not significantly affect its followers. A transformed terrorist organization like the FARC, which has substituted the power of criminal gain for ideological purity, has followers that are unaffected by the obvious criminal nature of the group. In the case of these transformed groups, we need to focus our campaign on crippling them by attacking their means of producing terror, including their narcotics revenue source and the narco-insurgents who defend their drug production facilities.[39] These attacks will not add to the FARC's supporters as they might if carried out against al-Qaeda.

4. **Tailored Response**: The United States should also develop new operational response packages created from all the tools of international power including diplomacy, economic aid, and preemptive offensive action. There are enough similarities between the types of terrorist organizations represented on one hand by al-Qaeda and on the other by the FARC that will guide the analysis that will allow us to defeat them. Determining whether we expect these terrorist groups to stay pure, to transform themselves to gain criminal capabilities, or to partner with criminal organizations is a good place to start in crafting our mix of responses.

A. **Aid**: The United States must develop the political will to devote significant levels of foreign aid—on the order of $5 billion per year—as a central element of our foreign policy.[40] We cannot continue to prosecute the war on terror as an independent part of our foreign policy, which relies primarily on military action. Counterterrorism operations must be broad in scope. Directed U.S. economic aid can help a fledgling democracy strengthen its institutions of government. Directed aid can also help reduce gross extremes in income disparity and poverty, and aid can create educational opportunities by providing alternative schools to compete with fanatical madrassas.

B. Preemptive Offensive Action: Understanding the differences between terrorist and criminal groups that have remained pure, transformed, or converged will help identify the constraints on preemptive offensive action. We must consider the long-term impact of offensive action based on the strength of each of these group's followings. We must not be paralyzed by the notion of preemption and direct offensive action against the terrorists and their supporters. Terrorist groups that maintain devoted followers can still be aggressively attacked if we more effectively share our proof of terrorist involvement with Arab media outlets and international organizations. And our actions and information sharing would be less constrained when dealing with those terrorist groups that have completely transformed to criminal organizations. In most cases, these criminal-terrorist groups simply seek to make a profit. They use terrorism to maintain a chaotic state that allows for illicit activity. These groups have few supporters outside of their organization. It is not normally necessary to constrain our actions based on the unintended production of more terrorists. As an example, the U.S. may consider expanding its Plan Colombia campaign to directly include the FARC. We may also develop a far more aggressive campaign against the Abu Sayyaf Group, which because of its ties with the Philippines Triad and with Cebu-based smugglers, has lost legitimacy in the eyes of traditional Moro leaders.[41]

In addition to U.S. targeting of terrorists, we must focus on transnational criminal organizations and place them at risk if we have proof that they are linked with terrorists. Foreign nations, even those whose economic, military, and political capabilities we value or fear, must also recognize that we will punish them for any support of terror organizations or the criminal groups partnered with them.[42] We must also be willing to reward those who cooperate. A global campaign requires carrots and sticks. The United States finds itself in the unique position to be able to effectively use both. Our recommendations, which are focused on unraveling the next terrorist plot—not the last one—will sharpen the effectiveness of our counterterrorist policy.

Endnotes

1. Alison Jamieson, "Transnational Organized Crime: A European Perspective," in *Studies in Conflict & Terrorism*, Vol. 24, 2001, p. 379.

2. Peter Bergen, *Holy War, Inc.: Inside the Secret World of Osama Bin Laden*, New York: Free Press, 2001, p. 20.

3. Yossef Bodansky, *Bin Laden: The Man Who Declared War on America*, New York: Random House, 2001, p.190-191.

4. Paul R. Pillar, *Terrorism and U.S. Foreign Policy*, Washington, D.C.: Brookings Institution Press, 2001, p. 57, 233.

5. Jessica Stern, *The Ultimate Terrorists*, Cambridge: Harvard University Press, 1999, p. 6. Stern points out that 4,798 deaths were attributed to terrorists in the 1970s, where as between 1990 and 1996, 51,797 deaths were attributed to terrorists.

6. The FARC admit to firing a homemade mortar on 1 May 2002 that killed 117 Colombians seeking protection in a church in the northwest Colombian village of Bojaya. Palestinian suicide bombers have killed over 400 Israelis in the last 18 months of the second intifada.

7. Stern, p. 35.

8. Among the excellent pieces on insurgent groups and civil wars are: I. William Zartman, "The Unfinished Agenda," in Roy Licklider, ed., *Stopping the Killing: How Civil Wars End*, (NYU, 1993) p. 20-34. Michael E. Brown, ed., *The International Dimensions of Internal Conflict*, (MIT, 1996). Robert Harrison Wagner, "The Causes of Peace," in Roy Licklider, ed., *Stopping the Killing: How Civil Wars End*, (NYU, 1993) p. 235-268. Mats Berdal and David Malone, eds., *Greed and Grievance: Economic Agendas in Civil Wars*, Boulder: Lynn Rienner, 2000.

9. Presentation by Bruce Hoffman, West Point, NY, 16 April 2002.

10. Paul Collier, "Doing Well Out of War: An Economic Perspective," in *Greed and Grievance: Economic Agendas in Civil Wars*, Boulder: Lynn Rienner, 2000, p. 96.

11. Chris Dishman, "Terrorism, Crime, and Transformation," in *Studies in Conflict and Terrorism*, Jan 2001, Vol. 24, p. 43–59.

12. Ibid, p. 44.

13. Bruce Hoffman, *Inside Terrorism*, New York: Columbia University Press, 1998, p. 43. Hoffman's definition—terrorism: it is political in aims and motives; it is violent or threatens; it is designed to have far reaching psychological repercussions; it is conducted by an organization or cell and perpetrated by a non-state entity or sub-national group.

14. Martha Crenshaw, "The Logic of Terrorism: Terrorist Behavior as a Product of Strategic Choice," in Walter Reich, ed., *Origins of Terrorism*, Washington, D.C.: Woodrow Wilson Center Press, 1990, p. 17.

15. Walter Laqueur, *The New Terrorism: Fanaticism and the Arms of Mass Destruction*, Oxford: Oxford University Press, 1999, p. 242.

16. Bergen, p. 20.

17. Bill Keller lays out this argument for both Pakistan and Russia in, "Nuclear Nightmare," in the *New York Times Magazine*, 26 May 2002.

18. Valentin Tikhonov, *Russia's Nuclear and Missile Complex: The Human Factor in Proliferation*, Washington, D.C.: Carnegie Endowment for International Peace, 2001.

19. Most date the guerrilla groups back to *la violencia's* start in 1948. Some, however, date the rebellion's beginning to 1965, the year *la violencia* ended.

20. Michael Shifter, "Colombia on the Brink; There Goes the Neighborhood," *Foreign Affairs*, July-August 1999, p.2.

21. State Department, *2002 Colombia INCSR*.

22. Linda Robinson, "In for a Dime, In for a Dollar?," *US News and World Report*, 4 October 1999, p.32.

23. Cindy Jebb, *"The Fight for Legitimacy: Liberal Democracy versus Terrorism,"* The Center for Naval Warfare Studies, June 2001, Newport: U.S. Naval War College, p. 80-81.

24. Ibid, p. 90.

25. "Europe: A Turn for the Worse; Turkey and its Kurds," *The Economist*, 2 Feb 2002.

26. State Department, *2002 Afghanistan INCSR*.

27. Jamieson, p. 383.

28. Ibid.

29. Bodansky, p. 328.

30. Jamieson, p. 378.

31. Ibid.

32. Chris Smith, "Light Weapons—The Forgotten Dimension of the International Arms Trade," in *Brassey's Defence Yearbook*, 1994 (London: Centre for Defence Studies).

33. Jamieson, p. 379.

34. "Terrorist Finance: Follow the Money," in *The Economist*, 1 June 2002, p. 67.

35. Stern, p. 74.

36. Some of these comments previously printed in the October 2001 issue of *Armed Forces Journal International*. Reprinted with the editor's permission from "Challenges to US National Security—Dealing with Madness," by General Barry R. McCaffrey, USA (Ret).

37. Ibid.

38. Elements of this recommendation previously printed in February 2002 issue of *Armed Forces Journal International*. Reprinted with the editor's permission from "Challenges to US National Security—Afghanistan: Denying a Sanctuary to Terror," by General Barry R. McCaffrey, USA (Ret).

39. The State Department's *2002 Colombia INCSR* reports that JTFS UH-1N helicopters, "were struck 50 times by small arms fire from narcoterrorists attempting to disrupt counternarcotics operations."

40. Elements of this recommendation previously printed in February 2002 issue of *Armed Forces Journal International*. Re-printed with the editor's permission from "Challenges to US National Security—Afghanistan: Denying a Sanctuary to Terror," by General Barry R. McCaffrey, USA (Ret).

41. Military sources in the Philippines confirm open source documents like "Abu Sayyaf Financiers and Couriers Nabbed," in the *Philippine Daily Inquirer*, 3 July 2001, that indicate clear evidence of ties between Abu Sayyaf and criminal organizations and the ramifications of these ties on ASG legitimacy.

42. McCaffrey, "Afghanistan: Denying a Sanctuary to Terror."

6.2   Gregory J. Rattray, 2001

The Cyberterrorism Threat

Gregory J. Rattray is a Lieutenant Colonel in the U.S. Air Force and commander of the 23rd Information Operations Squadron, which is responsible for information warfare tactics development. He has published journal articles and book chapters on information warfare, arms control and proliferation issues and is author of *Strategic Warfare in Cyberspace* (2001).

The last decade of the 20th Century has seen the rising concern over a new form of conflict, usually referred to as information warfare. As the US and other nations race forward into an information age, reliance on advanced information systems and infrastructures has grown significantly. Cyberspace has become a new realm for the exchange of digital information to conduct commerce, provide entertainment, pursue education, and a wide range of other activities. Information systems, in particular computer software and hardware, now serve as both weapons and targets of warfare.[1] The possibility of warfare in cyberspace presents opportunity but also involves significant new security risks. As the world's leading military power and the society most reliant on its information systems and infrastructures, the US may well face adversaries searching to find new weaknesses. These adversaries may include terrorists.

Similar to political assassination and car bombs, cyberterrorism could provide a new set of weapons for the weak to challenge the strong. Rapid technological developments based on the Internet and other information infrastructures through the end of the 20th Century create an attractive environment for groups who can not directly confront the US government, yet are willing to use death, destruction and disruption to achieve their objectives. Increasingly, cyberterrorists can achieve effects in the US from nearly anywhere on the globe. Terrorist groups can access global information infrastructures owned and operated by the governments and corporations they want to target. Digital attackers have a wide variety of means to cause disruption and/or destruction. Response in kind by the US government against sophisticated attackers is near impossible due to the difficulty of pinpointing activity in cyberspace and legal strictures on tracing attackers.

The possibility of cyberterrorism receives much attention. The Director of Central Intelligence, George Tenet, cautions about "a growing cyberthreat, the threat from so-called weapons of mass disruption."[2] Noted terrorism expert Walter Laquer observes "… why assassinate a politician or indiscriminately kill people when an attack on electronic switching will produce far more dramatic and long-lasting results."[3] A RAND study on terrorism produced for the US Air Force outlines the possibilities of "cybotage—acts of disruption and destruction against information infrastructures."[4] Yet, so far the US has suffered very little from cyberterrorism despite continuing conflicts with numerous adversaries, including those who employ terrorist means. Improved understanding of cyberterrorism must address why it has yet to fully emerge as a prevalent terrorist strategy. US policymakers need to understand constraints on its conduct as well as possibilities for its use.

What do we know? Evidence exists that cyberterrorism can occur. Government and commercial web sites are defaced almost daily. Computer systems suffer disruptions from intentional e-mail overloads and eruptions of viruses. Hackers of many stripes continue to prove capable of intruding on and exploiting a wide range of computer networks. These incidents can cause significant disruption and financial costs. However, cyberattacks have so far proved at most a nuisance for the US and its national security.

Looking to the future, we can expect cyberterrorism to become a more significant national security concern. Many assert that the US must expect a growth in the number of adversaries willing to use terrorist means.[5] The effectiveness of digital attack means will increase. So will US vulnerabilities to cyberterrorism. Terrorist organizations that wish to use these means can be expected to become smarter about both technological tools and effective targeting strategies. Limits to hitting back against cyberterrorism will remain a difficult problem.

Yet, cyberterrorists too will face significant challenges. When terrorists will develop requisite capabilities to conduct significant cyberattacks remains highly uncertain. The calculus of how cyberterrorism fits in with other terrorist tools, including conventional weapons, weapons of mass disruption, and other techniques will determine the future significance of cyberterrorism. Cyberterrorism may well become a supplement to other terrorist means similar to how information warfare operations complement conventional military forces.

The US President, Congress and many others have clearly recognized concerns raised by cyberterrorism. The Federal government has initiated planning, assigning responsibility, and begun development of organizations to protect the US from cyberattack. However, these efforts are in early stages and must surmount considerable hurdles. The speculative hype combined with lack of real experience with this emerging phenomenon compounds the difficulty. A sound US policy to combat cyberterrorism and investment decisions must emerge from a balanced understanding of the potential threat and its limits.

Cyberterrorism—What Is It and Who Does It?

In general, terrorism proves a difficult topic to set boundaries around. One common approach to defining cyberterrorism is broad inclusiveness in addressing the actors, means and goals involved. My approach endeavors to delineate the threat in terms of factors relevant to evaluating US policy and organizational responses. Definitions and boundaries prove critical in establishing policy, defining organizational responsibilities and addressing resource allocation. So while arguably an artificial exercise, we will begin by answering two key questions—"What types of acts constitute cyberterrorism?" and "Who conducts cyberterrorism?"

This analysis of cyberterrorism centers on the activities of organized, non-state actors pursuing political or systematic objectives against the US.[6] The activities of states conducting hostile activities in cyberspace against the US fall outside the realm of cyberterrorism into areas which can be labeled information warfare, espionage, or public diplomacy. However, we will consider the possibility that states may be associated with non-state actors in the furtherance of cyberterrorism. I also do not consider activities of individuals in the furtherance of personal objectives. However, because even individuals can cause disruption and destruction in cyberspace, the possibility of cyberterrorists cooperating with individuals must be addressed. Also, while cyberespionage and cybercrime should not be lumped in with cyberterrorism, both types of activity could be used to support cyberterrorism.

Taking a stab at what acts constitute "cyberterrorism" involves addressing even fuzzier boundaries. From the traditional perspective, consideration of terrorism focuses on acts or threats of violence calculated to create an atmosphere of fear or alarm. For example, cyberattacks could cause train accidents with large death counts through tampering with digital signaling systems. Additionally, cyberspace presents myriad opportunities to commit acts that cause significant disruption to society without direct loss of life, injury, or harm to material objects. For example, digital attacks might cause stock market disruptions by denying service to computer and communications systems.[7] This analysis of cyberterrorism includes both acts that involve physical violence and those causing significant social disruption based on attacking information systems and infrastructures.

Additionally, cyberterrorists could conduct attacks with the goal of corrupting key information within a system that requires high confidence for its use. Corrupting information about blood types within a hospital data base or strike prices within the stock trade settlement systems would involve much more recovery time and effort than a simple denial of service attack on the same target. Such an attack would inflict direct economic costs from system downtime, checking and correcting data, and settling disputes. Successful cyberterrorist attacks of this sort may also degrade user confidence in provision of services of fundamental importance to society.

Activities labeled as cyberterrorism must include recognition of both destructive and disruptive components. An open question is whether the potential for "mass disruption" created by reliance on information systems in the US will hold even greater appeal than attacks of "mass destruction" through the use of chemical, biological, and nuclear means.[8] Terrorists may prefer cyberattacks capable of causing widespread, observable impact but not involving death and physical disruption rather than use of WMD [weapons of mass destruction] or even conventional attacks in terms of limiting moral outrage and managing public opinion. Alternatively, "mass disruption" inflicted via cyberterrorism may prove too ephemeral to achieve desired effects. Governments and societies subject to cyber-based "mass disruption" may quickly learn to react and respond to such attacks, potentially even building up psychological resistance to such attacks.

Delineating the scope of activities that constitute cyberterrorism is difficult. The information age may well provide terrorist groups new ways to discredit governments and disrupt society to achieve their objectives. Therefore, cyberterrorism should be analyzed in light of the objectives sought.

Motives and Accountability

The nature of cyberterrorist campaigns, the means used, and the targets attacked will all depend on the motives of those groups considering the use of cyberterror means. Traditional analysis of terrorism has concentrated on groups with well-defined purposes for using violence as a means of political coercion.[9] Many terrorist groups such as the Weathermen within the US or the Red Brigade in Italy have engaged in efforts to overthrow or substantially change a political regime. Attacks are launched to undermine the legitimacy of the targeted government and garner support among a disaffected populace. Secessionist groups seeking the creation of new states or political autonomy for an ethnic/religious group also may use terrorist means to publicize their cause. Groups utilizing terrorist means to achieve such objectives include the Popular Front for the Liberation of Palestine and the Provisional IRA. A key feature of terrorism for political coercion is the willingness of groups to take credit for their attacks. The ability to inflict pain provides the principal source of leverage in negotiating with governments to achieve their objectives. Given the desire to secure the support of the general population and possibly to negotiate with governments, such groups may have self-imposed limits in terms of how vigorously and indiscriminately they choose to employ violence.

Taking a broader perspective on the issue of objectives, the use of terrorism by groups with millennial or anarchical objectives has become a source of increasing concern.[10] Rather than pursuing a specific political agenda, such groups may use indiscriminate violence to create a general environment of fear and chaos prior to a general overthrow of Western political order or may even simply seek anarchy as a goal. The Aum Shinrikyo cult took no credit for the use of sarin gas by the cult in Tokyo subways. Laquer has highlighted the potential for such groups to view "superviolence" as an appropriate means to undermine the world political system in seeking their goals.[11]

A new thread in the analysis of terrorist motivations has received the label "war paradigm."[12] This paradigm holds that certain terrorist groups without the ability to confront opponents directly will take a strategic approach to conducting terrorist acts without making specific demands on the opponent. For example, Ramsey Yousef and others who executed the World Trade Center bombing had no known intent to acknowledge their role. The goal of such groups is to inflict damage and wear down opponents as part of an eventual victory in a long-term struggle. The focus of these analyses has been on groups motivated by Muslim fundamentalism, especially those associated with the Saudi jihadist Osama bin Laden. The attacks seen during the second half of the 1990s on US military forces at Khobar Towers and embassies in Nairobi and Dar-es-Saalam may constitute such a campaign. Terrorists waging such campaigns may also see little constraint on inflicting damage or destruction against opponents.

Organization

Changes in the way terrorist groups organize will also impact their motives and perceptions of accountability. Traditional terrorist groups associated with the PLO and IRA relied heavily on tight central control over acts committed by the organization as part of an orchestrated pressure campaign against adversaries. However, the looser organizational structures of groups such as HAMAS and Afgan Arabs may be enabled by the pursuit of less controlled, more destructive activities conducted by groups with anarchist or religious objectives. The "networked" organization of terrorist groups financially supported by Osama bin Laden has increasingly become the archetype for describing a new form of terrorist organization with no clear center of control. John Arquilla and David Ronfeldt have strongly touted the strengths of such an organizational form for terrorists. Networked terrorist organizations could establish alliances of convenience with state sponsors, criminal organizations (especially those involved in the drug trade), and potentially with hacker groups.[13]

The utility for terrorist groups to employ the services of hackers as surrogates in the conduct of cyberterrorism has also received growing attention.[14] Hacker groups have demonstrated a willingness to sell their services to outsiders. In the most well known instance, hackers in Hannover, Germany during the late 1980s sold information they obtained through access to computer systems in Departments of Energy and Defense, defense contractors and NASA to the Soviet KGB.[15] These intruders first began to obtain access in 1986. After their initial discovery in 1988, the process of identification and apprehension of the Hannover hackers by the US and German intelligence and law enforcement agencies took over 18 months. During the Persian Gulf War, a group of Dutch hackers who had intruded into Department of Defense [DoD] systems attempted to sell their services to the Iraqis but were apprehended by Dutch police.[16]

Most analyses of hackers as cybersurrogates for terrorism generally stress the ease and advantages of such activity.[17] It is presumed that terrorist groups will be able to easily contact hackers for hire while keeping their direct involvement hidden through the use of cut-outs and proxies. These hacker groups could then be employed to reconnoiter adversary information systems to identify targets and means of access. If hacker groups can be employed to actually commit acts of cyberterrorism, terrorist groups may improve their ability to avoid culpability or blame.

However, employing cybersurrogates would also involve important risks and disadvantages. Attempting to employ hackers to commit acts of significant disruption that may involve killing people would likely prove much more difficult than buying information for the purposes of intelligence gathering. Contacting and employing hackers would also involve major operational security risks for a terrorist group.[18] At a minimum, the intelligence activities of hackers could be discovered and undermine planned operations. Terrorists without adequate leverage to control cybersurrogates run the risk of hackers being turned into double agents by hostile governments. The costs to a terrorist group of having an operation blown or providing adversaries information regarding their location or the identity of members would weigh heavily against use of such means. Both the German and Dutch hackers were eventually discovered, albeit after fairly long periods of activity and investigation.

The dearth of evidence means the calculus of terrorists considering use of cybersurrogates remains highly speculative at this point. One area for greater consideration is identifying which potential partners terrorist sponsors would consider more trustworthy. Some candidate surrogates, such as ex-security service members, may be considered more adept at maintaining operational security. Former members of the Soviet intelligence services that possess the requisite computer expertise and experience in the black arts of espionage may pose a real concern.[19] Terrorist groups may already have forged links with such potential allies. The subject deserves dedicated intelligence gathering efforts and analysis rather than simple hype.

Hacker Groups and Terrorism

Additionally, one must consider to what degree organized groups of hackers acting on their own accord pose a terrorist threat. For purposes of this analysis, hacker refers to persons or groups who gain access or break into digital systems, particularly networked computer and telecommunications systems. Hackers have a wide range of motivations including thrill seeking, knowledge, recognition, power, and friendship.[20] These individuals have also developed a sophisticated network to communicate ideas and coordinate activity through magazines such as *Phrack* and *2600*, stolen phone services, e-mail distribution lists, Usenet newsgroups, Internet chat rooms, and even full-blown conferences such as DEFCON. According to one survey of hackers, over half of those asked said they work in teams, and more than a third indicated they belong to a specialized hacker group. Groups have names such as Legion of Doom, Masters of Destruction, and Cult of the Dead Cow. These groups have been known to wage conflicts on each other using the public telecommunications networks as a battleground and touting their degree of illicit access as the source of bragging rights.[21] Many groups analyze software weakness and provide digital tools to exploit mainstream software applications such as Microsoft Windows operating systems. Additionally, hackers are dominantly males between the age of 15 and 25, often disaffected with the prevailing social and governmental order. This profile parallels those involved in terrorism.[22] The combination of technological skills and disaffection could make a sufficiently motivated and organized hacker group into a considerable cyberterrorist threat.

Numerous hacker groups have expressed deep animosity against the US and other governments over attempts to prosecute hackers, regulate activity on the Internet and other political issues. The hacker magazine *2600* has orchestrated a major campaign, including a fundraising campaign, to get the government to release Kevin Mitnick convicted of numerous violations of US computer crime laws.[23] In December, the group known as the Legion of the Underground (LoU) issued a "declaration of war" against the governments of the People's Republic of China and Iraq, citing these regimes' repressive human rights policies. The LoU declared its intention to disrupt and disable the Internet in the two countries.[24] East Asia has also witnessed an exchange of digital intrusions targeted at defacing Taiwanese and People's Republic of China government web sites with nationalist symbols and slogans of the hacker's home state.[25]

Thankfully, however, typical terrorists and hackers also have significant differences. Terrorists are generally conservative regarding use of new technologies to conduct operations.[26] Some groups have even conducted attacks to specifically combat the spread of computer technology. A French group called the Computer Liquidation and Deterrence Committee attacked French and American computer companies during the 1980s because "the computer is the tool of the dominant. It is used to exploit, to put on file, to control, and to repress."[27]

Conversely, the Internet community has seen the rise of white-hat hacker groups with a range of objectives. Some such as the LoPht Heavy Industries group based in Boston simply seek to provide information on latest hacker tricks and security weakness in products. LoPht has also called for hackers to cease attacks against the US government and testified for the Senate on how to improve computer security efforts.[28] The hacker community has also demonstrated a willingness to impose discipline on its own against disruptive hacking when the potential government backlash may prove too severe. A coalition of hacker groups formally condemned the LoU's declaration of war. *2600* magazine declared, "This type of threat, even if made idly, can only serve to further alienate hackers from mainstream society and help spread the misperceptions we're constantly battling."[29] So far, the hacker community has stopped shy of conducting activities constituting a serious cyberterrorist threat.

Means and Targets for Cyberterrorism

The headlong rush of the US and other advanced nations into the information age involves new risks. The information systems central to national security, the conduct of government and commerce have significant weaknesses that can be attacked. Yet, such attacks have achieved only limited impacts as we end the 20th Century. To analyze how cyberterrorists might attack the US, we must consider which groups might employ cyberterrorism and for what reasons.

Means for Digital Attack

Terrorists could attack US information infrastructures using a variety of mechanical, electromagnetic, or digital means. Information systems have long been targets of mechanical methods of disruption. Command and control systems can be bombed, fiber-optic cables cut, microwave antennas broken, and computers smashed or simply turned off. The electronic components and transmissions of information systems and networks are vulnerable to jamming, as well as electromagnetic pulses generated by nuclear explosions and other sorts of directed-energy weapons. The rise of digital means of encoding and transferring information has also created new ways to attack information systems. Impacts of digital attacks can range from total paralysis of networks to intermittent shutdown, random data errors, information theft, and data corruption. The tools and techniques for attacking information systems have received detailed attention as the US government, commercial industry, and outside experts have begun to stress the possibilities of information warfare, digital espionage, and computer crime.[30] The analysis below focuses on digital means as the new dimension of the equation appropriately labeled cyberterrorism. The possibility of synergistically employing all three types of attack also requires additional analysis beyond the scope of this [writing].

Cyberterrorists could cause disruption, damage, and destruction through achieving unauthorized access and control over a targeted information system through a vast array of intrusive tools and techniques, commonly referred to as "hacking." Means for successful intrusion range from compromised passwords to sophisticated software for identifying and exploiting known vulnerabilities in operating systems and application software. The difficulty of attaining access and time required to successfully "hack" a system will also depend on the targeted system's defensive measures including proper password and configuration management, patching of known vulnerabilities, and use of firewalls and intrusion detection systems. If control over a targeted computer or network is achieved, cyberterrorists could inflict a wide range of effects. Possibilities range from changing the graphics on a web page to corrupting the delivery schedules for medical supplies or military equipment to denying access to 911 services or air traffic control data, or disrupting telecommunications backbone networks. A principal advantage of intrusion for cyberterrorism is the potential for tight control over the timing, scope, and effects of an attack. According to former Director of the Central Intelligence, John Deutch, "the electron is the ultimate precision weapon."[31]

Another well-known potential means for cyberterrorist attack would be the employment of malicious software code, more commonly referred to as viruses and worms. Malicious software can be broadly defined as software designed to make computer systems operate differently than intended. The effects of viruses and other malicious software range from benign messages displayed at system start up to code that can cause hardware failures and wide-area network overloads. Concern over malicious software increased rapidly after the unintentional release of the Internet Worm by a Cornell graduate student in 1988 disrupted most Internet services for a period of days.[32] During the early 1990s, reacting to and mitigating the consequences of viruses was a major computer security focus. Development of anti-virus software capable of periodic updating has helped mitigate the virus threat. However, 1999 saw a series of virulent outbreaks, including the Melissa virus and Worm. ExploreZip that proved capable of disrupting government, commercial, and other private information systems. A major feature of these viruses has been traffic overloads that occur when the viruses propagate vast amounts of e-mail through networked systems. Creators of malicious software determine the intended impact of running their code. However, the degree of disruption and damage caused by viruses and other code which replicates and passes quickly across networked systems can be much more difficult to control. Cyberterrorists using malicious code created by others may have much less certainty regarding the effects of their attack.

Combining features of both intrusions and malicious code, cyberterrorists could also intentionally corrupt software programs in targeted information systems and infrastructures to cause desired effects. While access to rewrite software code could be achieved through an intrusion, a terrorist group may endeavor to corrupt software in the process of creation or production by emplacing backdoors for access or insert "trojan horses" to cause desired effects at a predetermined time or upon a given command. Software maintenance and updates also present opportunities for such activities. Software code creation and maintenance for systems employed across the globe occur in places like India, Ireland, and Israel. The possibility for insertion of corrupted code as part of the massive effort to update software to fix Year 2000 problems provided a major concern for all sectors of the US government and society.[33] The main protection against such activity would be rigorous quality control over software products used in key systems, but such a process is time-consuming and expensive. As with intrusions, the degree of control possible through corrupted code can allow precision effects. Cyberterrorists could also achieve widespread effects by corrupting code in systems underpinning key information infrastructures. AT&T suffered nation-wide disruption of its telephone network in January 1990 due to a single line of faulty code in an upgrade to its primary switching software.[34] While this error was unintentional, the ability to attack the digital foundations of advanced information infrastructure presents sophisticated cyberterrorists with a significant means of attack.

Cyberterrorists can also disrupt or disable information systems and networks using techniques generically labeled as denial-of-service (DOS) attacks. Common DOS techniques involve overloading targeted e-mail systems by employing automated software and exploiting features of the Internet communications protocol through "smurf" or "SYN flooding" attacks. In recent years, hackers and politically motivated groups have increasingly turned to DOS attacks as a means of responding to specific events and policies by harassing targeted organizations and to draw attention to their complaints. One well-known instance involves a group known as the Electronic Disturbance Theatre (EDT). In October 1998, the EDT targeted the computers of the US military and the Frankfurt Stock Exchange in an effort to overload servers in these networks with the goal of publicizing the cause of the Zapatista rebels in Mexico. Yet, while cyberterrorists can specifically target denial-of-services attacks against known systems connected to network accessible to the attackers, operators of the targeted systems can also modify their systems either preventively or in reaction to the attacks. The Defense Information Technology Center simply reconfigured the targeted computers to refuse to acknowledge the originating Internet addresses in response to the EDT attacks. The EDT computers were overloaded with return messages as a result of employing the automated FloodNet software and forced to reboot.[35] The cat and mouse game of offensive moves and defensive responses will continue to evolve as information technology advances and presents new vulnerabilities to exploit. Cyberterrorism and other types of warfare, espionage, and crime waged in the digital realm will demonstrate this see-saw dynamic.

Another possible approach open to cyberterrorists would be to conduct hoax attacks, publicizing the possibility of intrusive activity and release of viruses. Virus scares can swamp help desks with requests for information. Users and system operators must ensure anti-virus software is up-to-date, creating an additional burden on the networks and wasting time. The Good Times scare in 1994 caused a massive reaction while only infecting a handful of computers.[36] Similarly, the possibility of intrusive activity requires system administrators and computer incident response teams to assume higher states of readiness with an attendant decline in attention to routine operations and maintenance. The US Department of Defense has instituted an Information Operations Condition (INFOCON) system of progressively higher levels to raise the awareness and preparedness of cyberdefenses similar to the THREATCON system use for responding to increased threat of terrorist attack.[37] Attaining the defensive posture called for by higher INFOCON levels would require substantial efforts for those responsible for the DoD information infrastructure and pose constraints on the use of the Department's information resources. Cyberterrorists focused less on high impact events and more on waging a protracted conflict could use hoaxes designed to cause the targeted adversary to waste significant effort without the terrorist having to run the risks of conducting actual attacks. Defensive efforts may suffer over the long-term if multiple hoaxes create a "cry wolf" syndrome regarding calls for increased protection. The impact of hoaxes will be magnified if terrorist groups develop a credible reputation for being able to conduct digital attacks.

Access and Expertise

To use any of the tools and techniques described above, cyberterrorists must have access to the means and the expertise to employ these tools effectively. The prevailing wisdom is that both are readily available. Well-known information warfare pundit Winn Schwartau states, "Anyone can be an information warrior.... Potentially, a hundred million information warriors are poised, and honing their skills while they wait."[38] Numerous analyses cite the vast number of web sites on which hacker tools and techniques can be found and downloaded, as well as the presence of Internet chat sites, conventions, catalogues, and publications in which hackers exchange information.[39] In a similar vein, most analyses also hold that the means for attacking information systems have become both more sophisticated and easier to use. The following figure [Figure 1] from a 1996 GAO [General Accounting Office] report entitled *Information Security: Computer Attacks at Department of Defense Pose Increasing Risks* depicts the evolution of attack tools and required expertise as time has progressed.[40]

One way terrorists may build their expertise and understanding of the potential for digital attacks is through the use of cyberspace for other activities. Increasingly, terrorist groups including the Provisional IRA, Algerian extremists, HAMAS, and others are using the Internet and cellular phones to orchestrate their activities. Many groups have begun to use encryption technology to protect their digital communications. According to Arquilla,

> Egyptian "Afgan" computer experts have helped devise a communication network that relies on the World Wide Web, e-mail and electronic bulletin boards so that extremists can exchange information without a major risk of being intercepted by counterterrorism officials.[41]

The Provisional IRA uses computer databases to catalogue individuals, installations, and other targets.[42] Terrorists and associated groups have also begun to use the Internet as a mechanism for publicity, fundraising, and recruitment. The Zapatistas have established a major presence through the World-Wide Web supported by activists in the US, Europe, and elsewhere.[43] Drug cartels use the Internet in transactions with banks to launder money, and at least potentially, terrorists could use cybercrime to steal money to support their operations.[44] Terrorists may also use advanced information technology for intelligence gathering. Access to commercial satellite imagery may provide

Figure 1

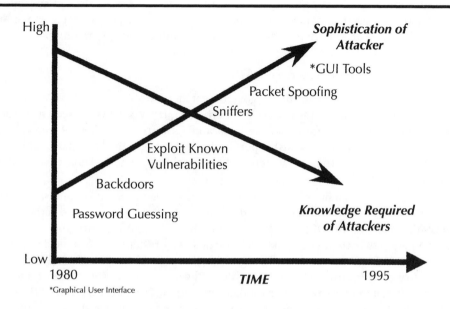

*Graphical User Interface

information for targeting physical attacks. Hacker and information warfare websites may provide conceptual approaches and even lists of targets for cyberterrorism. Evidence is clear that terrorist groups increasingly use advanced information technologies and are building an experiential base that could be used for cyberterrorism.

However, the utility of user-friendly attack technologies and general computer expertise to any terrorist group depends on the nature of the targeted infrastructure and intended effects. Denial of service attacks against Internet connections may require much less sophistication but achieve less controlled effects than attacks based on successful remote access and control of a targeted information system or network. Additionally, a defender's ability to assess vulnerabilities and deny access to known digital attack tools and techniques may also increase the level of technological knowledge required for attacking forces. If key information infrastructures are well protected, achieving surprise and inflicting disruption against significant centers of gravity may require cyberterrorists to employ more technological sophistication, time, and effort. The pool of human capital with the ability to develop sophisticated new attack tools or quietly probe strong, attentive defenses is much more limited than the number of individuals capable of running scripted tools or sending multiple e-mail messages to an Internet address. The Center for Infrastructural Studies stated in early 1998, "According to recent studies, most attacks use standard or well-known script exploits. Our research reveals less than 1,000 hackers in the world who have the professional programming skills to create their own attack scripts."[45]

For cyberterrorists, easily accessible and usable digital attack techniques may equate to more conventional hand grenades and pistols in terms of scale of effects and lack of precision. To develop the digital equivalent of weapons of mass destruction or achieve the precision of sniper rifles may require a much greater degree of technological sophistication and self-reliance on the part of cyberterrorists. Developing collection means and analytical techniques to understand the technological skill and resources of terrorists presents an important challenge for the US intelligence community.

Targets for Cyberterrorist Attacks

Since at least the early 1990s, the US government and outside experts have grown increasingly concerned about the possibility of cyberterrorist attacks as our society has become more reliant on information systems and infrastructure. The 1991 National Research Council *Computers at Risk* report finds, "The modern thief can steal more with a computer than a gun. Tomorrow's terrorist may be able to do more damage with a keyboard than a bomb."[46]

The increasing ability of terrorists and others to attack US critical infrastructures through use of digital attacks has received the most attention.[47] In the wake of the Oklahoma City bombing in 1995, the President set up a Critical Infrastructure Working Group to address both physical and cyber threats. As a result of hacker incidents, Department of Defense exercises, and Congressional prodding, the Presidential Commission on Critical Infrastructure Protection [PCCIP] was set up to analyze the threat to US infrastructures and policy responses for their protection. The PCCIP's October 1997 report, entitled *Critical Foundations*, provides the most comprehensive analysis of the cyberthreat to US infrastructures "essential to minimum operations of the economy and government."[48] The report stresses how the growing reliance on information systems that underpin a whole range of infrastructures including communications, electric power, transportation, and emergency services creates substantial risks for a wide range of digital attacks, including possible cyberterrorism. While a comprehensive discussion is beyond the scope here, possible targets for cyberterrorism include the Supervisory Control and Data Acquisition (SCADA) systems which govern the distribution of telecommunications, electric power, and other infrastructure-based services. The Global Positioning System (GPS) network of satellites, ground control stations, and signaling systems constitutes an infrastructure target whose role in military and civil navigation as well as broadcasting timing signals in cellular communications and other information networks could prove attractive to cyberterrorists. The disruption caused by the failure of a single PanAmSat communications satellite in May 1998 crippled most US paging services as well as a number of data and media communications feeds for hours and, in some cases, a couple days.

While attacking information systems underpinning critical infrastructures presents cyberterrorists with potentially high impact targets, important questions need to be addressed in order to adequately gauge the potential threat. One area of significant uncertainty is how fast infrastructures will be able to recover from digital attacks. Many analysts focus on how many infrastructures have single points of failure that can cause quickly cascading effects, disrupting or disabling effects over a wide area. The Northwest power outage in August 1996 that affected hundreds of thousands of users began by a tree growing into a single power line. Others point to the ability of complex systems to adapt and recover.[49] In the cases of the AT&T switching failure, the Northwest power outage, and the PanAmSat satellite failure, the infrastructure operators were able to recover in a period of hours. What is clearly unknown is how such complex infrastructures would react to orchestrated cyberterrorist attacks instead of unintentional mishaps and accidents.

Another approach would be to attack organizations or institutions with high public visibility. Hackers have proven capable of repeatedly defacing the web pages of corporations such as DuPont and Ford as well as government agencies including the White House, FBI, NASA, and the Air Force. Cyberterrorist attacks may specifically be launched to garner media attention rather than cause physical damage or economic losses. Demonstrated ability to disrupt computerized inventory systems of Wal-Mart or corrupting medical records within a large health management organization would provide prime fodder for media attention. Newspapers have reported that the hacker group, RTMark, has endeavored to depress the stock price of eToys by disrupting the company's web site.[50] Financial institutions have often been listed as a potential target of cyberterrorism. Citigroup admitted in a highly publicized incident that a Russian hacker managed to electronically siphon off $12 million in funds in 1995. While Citigroup actually managed to recover all but $400,000 of this loss, competitors reportedly used the incident to convince commercial clients to switch banks due to the perceived greater insecurity of Citigroup information systems.[51] In 1996, the *London Times* reported that banks, brokerage houses, and investment firms paid hundreds of millions of dollars in blackmail to extortionists to avoid cyberattacks whose capabilities had been demonstrated.[52] The high level of media attention to financial markets and the critical role of public confidence in their activities mark them as prime targets.

Terrorist groups could also conduct digital attacks against media outlets themselves. Indonesian media outlets had their computer systems attacked by hacker groups supporting the Timorese rebels.[53] However, cyberterrorism targeted with an eye towards garnering media attention rather than death and destruction may require more sophisticated targeting and digital attack capabilities than generic attacks against any open targets within the US infrastructure. The disruptive effects of such attacks may prove short-lived, but cyberterrorists could endeavor to shake public confidence in core institutions through such attacks.

Terrorist groups could also use digital attacks to support traditional terrorist operations. As monitoring and sensor systems for protecting people and facilities become increasingly reliant on information technology, digital attacks may prove a useful means of creating opportunities for conventional terrorism. In 1998, the *New York Times* reported a design flaw in a security system widely used in airports, prisons, financial institutions, and the US government allowing digital intruders to access secure areas, unlock doors, and erase evidence of changed access records.[54] Emergency 911 systems have been found vulnerable to computer intrusions and could be targeted by cyberterrorists. Paralyzing communications as a means of slowing emergency responses could plausibly enhance effectiveness of conventional or WMD terrorism. As with any potential tool, terrorist groups could employ cyberattacks synergistically along with other means to achieve their objectives.

Cyberterrorists may also endeavor to make use of "insiders." Reasons for assisting terrorists could include personal gain, revenge, or sheer destructiveness. The assistance of individuals knowledgeable of technical characteristics and operational significance of targeted information and systems would prove of immense value to terrorist groups in launching all types of digital attacks. The threat posed by insiders with authorized access to information resources presents a fundamental information security concern.[55] A network programmer fired by Omega Engineering Corporation in 1996 provides an illustrative case. Upon his departure, the programmer activated a logic bomb that permanently deleted all the company design and production software used to produce high technology measurement and control instruments for the US Navy and NASA. Damage was estimated at $10 million.[56] The 1999 Computer Security Institute/Federal Bureau of Investigation "Computer Crime and Security" survey indicated sixty-five percent of organizations responding had suffered incidents involving insiders.[57] Cyberterrorists intent on causing widespread destruction and damage might use insiders to corrupt SCADA systems or plant viruses. The ability to effectively screen employees, discover attempts at outside recruitment, and identify and mitigate malicious activities quickly will play a role in combating cyberterrorism as part of overall information security efforts.

Thinking About Cyberterrorist Campaigns

With a wide range of available tools and potential targets, cyberterrorist groups may use very different types of campaign strategies to pursue objectives. So far, most attention focuses on the possibility of single events causing catastrophic physical effects such as a plane crash or the failure of control systems in a nuclear power plant. The assumed objective of the attack is widespread publicity for the group's cause and negotiating leverage against governments. A potentially more serious threat that receives less attention would involve cyberterrorist groups adopting a protracted war strategy similar to the ones used by Mao Tse Tung and Ho Chi Minh. Instead of striking the most dramatic target, terrorists waging a protracted guerilla campaign of cyberterror could strike targets of opportunity that also minimized the chance of discovery and retaliation. The objectives of such a campaign may well involve media attention but also target the will of an adversary's government and populace over the long-term.

Developing a strategy for dealing with single cyberterrorist events may focus on improving warning of attacks and the ability to manage the consequences of disasters. Responses to waging a prolonged conflict with cyberterrorists may be quite different. Fighting such adversaries will require improvement in defensive capabilities and recovery capacity of information infrastructures as well as improving means to track down and incapacitate attackers.

Outlining these two broad strategic approaches and their implications simply provides an illustration of the complex situation facing those responsible for dealing with cyberterrorism. The US government must develop a deeper understanding of how different cyberterrorist groups are most likely to operate, potential objectives and capabilities, the risks posed by attacks, and appropriate responses. This analysis must be based on fact, not speculation.

Cyberterrorism—What We Have Observed

Information infrastructures have long served as targets for adversaries in a conflict. Adversaries have always attempted to intercept messengers. The emergence of electronic communications resulted in cutting telegraph lines and underseas cables during wars.

As more communications passed via electromagenetic transmissions, jamming, frequency hopping, and other techniques became a commonplace aspect of military operations known as electronic warfare.

Terrorists have also seen attacks against infrastructures as a means of achieving their traditional objectives. For example, the Provisional IRA in the early and mid-1990s launched major terrorist attacks against transportation and commercial targets in the U.K. with the intent of maximizing societal disruption. In April 1993, a bomb detonated in London caused massive commercial disruption by causing the temporary closure of key financial markets.[58] In the 1970s, the Italian Red Brigades specified destruction of computer systems and installations as a way of striking at the state. They conducted numerous attacks against businesses in the electronics and computer industries.[59] As the functioning of information systems and infrastructures becomes increasingly fundamental to US and other societies, the appeal for terrorists to attack such targets will increase. Lessons learned about what constitutes key features of an adversary's information infrastructure necessary for the conduct of conventional attacks would also prove useful to cyberterrorists considering the use of digital attacks.

Hackers and hacker groups so far have not proven to be significant cyberterrorist actors in terms of conducting digital attacks to create intentional death, destruction, or disruption. While there have been occasional declarations of intent to wage "cyberwar" against the US government, corporations, or other entities, these threats have not resulted in serious campaigns to achieve political or even anarchical objectives. However, the dearth of cyberterrorism by hackers so far does not mean they are not capable of inflicting severe damage via digital attacks. Hackers have intentionally disrupted 911 services, launched viruses degrading the information processing of major corporate and government organizations, and gained access to key computer systems such as domain name servers which underpin information infrastructures in such organizations. A good example of the potential for hackers to become cyberterrorists is provided by an incident in March 1997. In this instance, a teenage hacker penetrated and disabled Bell Atlantic telecommunication switches in the Northeastern US. One of the disabled switches provided phone and data services to the Worchester, Massachusetts airport control tower, and the incident shut down the airport for many hours.[60] If such an attack were purposely targeted and timed when air traffic control was already difficult due to weather or volume of traffic, the difference between what happened in Worchester and a cyberterrorist attack would only be a matter of intent.

An increasingly common phenomena related to cyberterrorism is hacking by technologically literate groups in support of insurgent, environmental, or other political movements. Hacking into and defacing Web pages has proven a most common means to express discontent. However, the rise of purposeful denial-of-service attacks such as the one by the EDT has also caused increased concern. So far, such activities have proven at most temporary nuisances rather than real problems that might coerce targeted governments to change policies. Yet, reacting to such threats already involves increasing resource commitments by organizations such as the Department of Defense and FBI. Such activity clearly falls within the boundaries of terrorist intent discussed earlier. The real question is when does the level of disruption rise to a standard appropriately labeled as terrorism instead of mischief?

In terms of known terrorist groups using digital attacks for cyberterrorism, we have only begun to see such activity occur. The most well-known case has involved the Internet Black Tigers, an offshoot of the Sri Lankan rebel group Liberation Tigers of Tamil Elam. The Internet Black Tigers swamped the e-mail services of numerous Sri Lankan embassies for a period of approximately two weeks.[61] Yet, such attacks comprised a relatively insignificant aspect of the overall terrorist campaign of these rebels and arguably were principally for publicity rather than disruptive objectives.

A major terrorist campaign waged principally or solely via digital attacks has not occurred. As with other forms of conflict, cyberterrorism will likely evolve as another tool for groups to achieve their objectives rather than springing into life in full bloom. That said, successful cyberterrorist attacks could also provoke a rapid rise in activity once such means are a proven way to achieve terrorist goals. The focus for US policy should be to understand the goals of groups who are most likely to employ such a new approach and potential vulnerabilities arising from possible cyberterrorist attacks.

The US Response

The US national government has recognized the growing threat posed by cyberterrorism. A detailed development of US policy and organizational responses to cyberterrorism is beyond the scope here. The section below presents a brief overview of what has been accomplished and what is yet to be done.

Over the past decade, a confluence of concern with information warfare, terrorism against US targets at home and abroad, and the recognition of the increasing reliance on critical infrastructures all have made dealing with cyberterrorism a higher priority on the national security agenda. A spate of books and articles in the mid-1990s focused on the possibility of a digital Pearl Harbor facing the US. The President established a Critical Infrastructure Working Group in 1995 in the wake of the Oklahoma City bombing to address both physical and cyber terrorist threats under the leadership of the Justice Department. Congressional inquires and GAO reports have described the vulnerabilities of our digital infrastructure to hackers and called on the President to detail plans to develop cyber defenses. Such threats have been examined through RAND "Day After in Cyberspace…" wargames and DoD exercises such as Eligible Receiver. These evaluations demonstrated significant national and DoD vulnerabilities that would arise from a structured cyberattack.[62]

Growing demands for a comprehensive response have resulted in the US government putting increasing energy behind its response to possible cyberattacks. In the summer of 1996, the President's Commission of Critical Infrastructure Protection was formed to conduct a comprehensive review and recommend national policy for protecting critical infrastructures against physical and cyber threats. The PCCIP's efforts formed the basis for Presidential Decision Directive [PDD] 63 "Critical Infrastructure Protection" issued in May 1998. In combination with PDD-62 "Protection Against Unconventional Threats to the Homeland and Americans Overseas," the two directives establish a system of organizations, roles, and responsibilities through which the US will respond to terrorism and protect its critical infrastructures during peace and war.

Since the spring of 1998, national efforts against digital attacks have focused on implementing the construct laid out in PDD-63. The Directive created a National

Coordinator for Security, Infrastructure Protection and Counterterrorism on the National Security Council. Departments and agencies within the Federal government have developed sector-specific protection plans across the range of identified critical infrastructures. The Critical Infrastructure Assurance Office (CIAO) in the Commerce Department assists in sectoral planning efforts and their integration into a national plan. The private sector has also started to establish Information Sharing and Analysis Centers (ISACs) as called for in PDD-63. As of late 1999, the first ISAC was established in the banking and finance sector with other ISAC plans under development.[63]

On the operational side, the National Infrastructure Protection Center [NIPC] was established even prior to the issuance of PDD-63 in February 1998.[64] As staffing and resources have increased over the past few years, the NIPC and Federal government agencies have initiated numerous efforts to coordinate activities in response to cyber threats. The NIPC and CIAO are endeavoring to establish linkages with state and local governments as well as the private sector. Yet, the hurdles to improve cyberdefenses are substantial and resources remain limited.

Challenges in Responding to Cyberterrorism

The US intelligence community must play a key role in understanding the threat posed by cyberterrorism. Effective responses require the US both to understand the potential capabilities of cyberterrorist groups and develop advanced warning regarding their intent to use such capabilities. Cyberterrorism presents a very difficult intelligence target. The highly developed imagery and signal intelligence capabilities used to characterize Cold War threats and nation-state military capabilities have limited applicability in providing information to assess whether terrorist groups can effectively employ digital attacks. Also, the skill sets of intelligence analysts required to understand digital communications systems and techniques for exploiting computer weaknesses are not the same as those to characterize capabilities of ballistic missiles and the strength of ground forces. Also, the new skill sets are in high demand in the private sector making them even harder to create and sustain within the US government.[65]

To provide strategic warning of cyberterrorism, the intelligence and defense communities require insight into activities of adversary groups to develop profiles of preparatory steps for digital attacks. In the cyberrealm, distinguishing potential terrorist activity from normal system failures, exploratory hacking, and other threats such as espionage is very difficult. In the spring of 1998, the Department of Defense was initially concerned that hacking activity eventually tracked down to teenagers might have been state-sponsored activity related to US military activities in the Persian Gulf.[66] Conducting counterterrorism involves close coordination between organizations responsible for intelligence, counterintelligence, and combating computer crime. Potential terrorist activity in cyberspace presents particularly acute requirements for such cooperation.

PDD-63 and other policy directives have set in place the organizations and responsibilities. At the national level, the NIPC has primary leadership for detecting and responding to digital attacks. The Defense Department established a Joint Task Force-Computer Network Defense [JTF-CND] to provide centralized capability for the same missions to protect the Defense Information Infrastructure. A program to create a comprehensive Federal Intrusion Detection Network (FIDNet) system under the authority of GSA [General Services Administration] exists.[67] Other organizations in the public and private sectors have established efforts to achieve similar objectives. In addition to the ISACs, a number of computer security associations and consulting firms strive to improve computer and information security in the private sector. These organizations generally work closely with a community of Computer Emergency/Incident Response Teams known as CERTs or CIRTs established by many organizations in both the government and in the private sector.

Yet, despite the presence of such organizations, those responsible for US cyberdefense at all levels have very limited capability to provide tactical warning of impending attacks or assess attacker motivations and objectives. Defensive tools, primarily in the form of various types of intrusion detection systems, have been developed to help identify presence and intent of malicious digital activity. However, current IDS technology relies on identifying known types of exploits and can not easily identify new types of digital attacks, even those based on modifying previous types of exploits.[68] Adequate attack assessment is even tougher. Owners, operators, and defenders of information systems and infrastructures rarely have an adequate picture of what they are protecting. Defenders not only need to understand physical and logical interconnectivity, they also need to understand the operational significance of information and systems which are under attack to properly prioritize their warning, detection, and response efforts.

In specific circumstances, CERT and law enforcement agencies have proven capable of tracking down and punishing attackers. However, the timelines to identify and prosecute responsible individuals in most well-known hacker incidents have been lengthy and the punishments meted out fairly light. The capacity of the NIPC, the JTF-CND, and other organizations to handle big events involving large numbers of sophisticated attackers is unproven. Legal and policy considerations also place constraints on such agencies attempting to precisely identify individuals and organizations responsible for malicious activity in cyberspace. Law enforcement and computer network defense organizations are not allowed to hack back through computer systems to follow the electronic trail of intruders without express permission of system owners or authorized search warrants.[69] Yet, most digital intruders utilize multiple hops through cyberspace before conducting intrusive activity. Also, the CERT and law enforcement communities most closely involved with leading responses to computer intrusions tend to focus on single incidents. Defending against cyberterrorists with long-term objectives and significant attack capabilities will require fighting a campaign, a perspective significantly different than a law enforcement effort focused on building a court case.

Federal government plans also have identified organizations responsible for responding if a cyberterrorist attack caused significant disruption or destruction to mitigate effects and restore capabilities. Under the authority of PDD-63, the Federal Emergency Management Agency (FEMA) would lead consequence management efforts in conjunction with the NIPC, FBI, and state/local authorities. US national-level planning for how to deal with major disruptions to information systems and infrastructures was accelerated due to the requirement to be ready for Year 2000 events. Yet, a continuing consequence management challenge is the lack of detailed knowledge of the network connectivity, information system characteristics, and operational significance of assets that may suffer a cyberterrorist attack. Lack of adequate information infrastructure "mapping" will hamper the prioritization of reconstitution efforts and deployment of available resources. Establishing effective consequence management capabilities also faces difficulties in terms of running operational exercises to simulate large-scale terrorist attacks against complex, interconnected, privately owned and operated information infrastructures. Currently, organizations responsible for responding to cyberterrorism lack understanding of possible modes of system failure and the ability of infrastructures and operating organizations to recover from attacks. Again, those responsible for consequence management efforts should leverage knowledge gleaned from Y2K preparations and experiences with failure and recovery characteristics from Y2K events.[70]

The final step in defending against cyberterrorism is to improve the strength of our information infrastructures against digital attack. The NIPC, in conjunction with sector leads and the ISACs, has the role of identifying critical vulnerabilities and implementing mitigation plans. However, networked information systems and infrastructure at the end of the 20th Century present easy prey for digital intrusion and disruption. The complexity of operating systems such as Windows NT or Linux and applications such as Microsoft Office or SCADA systems combined with the speed of development and new product releases results in foundational pieces of the information infrastructure that have numerous security flaws. These flaws are discovered and disseminated at a rapid pace by the hacker community. As with intrusion detection systems, defensive tools such as firewalls, virus checkers, and network analyzers usually lag development of new attack techniques. Cyberterrorists are among the spectrum of adversaries who can exploit this basic weakness.

The process presently used by many government organizations involves instituting notification and tracking systems to ensure owner/operators of information infrastructures fix known vulnerabilities and update virus defenses to make digital intrusion and disruption more difficult for cyberterrorists and others. For example, the Department of Defense has instituted an Information Assurance Vulnerability Alert system that requires all DoD organizations to patch certain identified vulnerabilities and report compliance within specified timeframes.[71] However, this approach constitutes a rearguard action whose prospects for success are limited. Its success relies heavily on reacting to vulnerabilities after their weakness has already been demonstrated. More fundamentally, the "patching" process means those defending critical US information infrastructures must discover vulnerabilities, notify users, and track the implementation of fixes throughout an extremely diverse infrastructure comprised of and operated by thousands of organizations using thousands of different products implemented and modified by hundreds of thousands of individuals. So far, the procedures and resources employed to reduce infrastructure vulnerabilities to digital attack fall far short of denying access to potential cyberterrorists.

An alternative approach would involve ensuring that key systems and infrastructures were built to make digital attack difficult from the beginning of system concept and design. Such an approach would help mitigate a wide range of threats including cyberterrorism but also address concerns ranging from unintentional problems to cybercrime to information warfare. Yet, US government plans as articulated in PDD-63 and other directives show little desire to pursue such an approach. Huge difficulty faces implementation of a national cyberdefense strategy based on migrating to more stout digital foundations. Fundamentally, the government would have to ensure that owner/operators of key systems and infrastructures employed more secure products. Yet, the forces of technological innovation and competition in the information technology industry have forced commercial producers to move firmly in the direction of deploying products as quickly as possible with a minimum of security and other testing. The booming US economy increasingly relies on this sector as a source of fundamental strength. With the exception of encryption policy, the Clinton Administration avoided any significant moves to interfere with the telecommunications and information technologies industries under the guise of national security.[72] This choice means that the threat from digital attacks will remain significant for the indefinite future.

The US has proactively begun dealing with cyberterrorism as a part of national security. Given that dramatic events have yet to occur to prompt action, such efforts should be lauded. However, while policy directives establish authorities and organizations to provide capabilities to counter cyberterrorism, the US is a long way from having effective defenses against the potential threat. Efforts throughout government and the private sector vary greatly in depth and focus. Human and financial resources are lacking everywhere. Technological and economic considerations limit the government's ability to protect our information systems and infrastructures. The nature of US society and protection of civil liberties also present difficulties for those responsible for protecting US national security in cyberspace.

Policy Options

Improving US capabilities to deal with cyberterrorism will intertwine with a number of other efforts related to information warfare, critical infrastructure protection, and countering computer crime. This section lays out recommendations designed to make cyberterrorism more difficult and dangerous for perpetrators.

US strategy must include efforts to make information systems and infrastructures more robust. The first step in this process is to improve the basic understanding of the technological underpinnings and operational characteristics of our informational centers of gravity. The US government or private sector organizations can not afford to provide robust protection to any and all information resources. Defenders must catalogue key assets and prioritize the deployment of available resources. Such an undertaking will require significant resource investment in organizations such as the NIPC, by government agencies responsible for specific infrastructure sectors, and in the private sector ISACs to create and sustain knowledge of what ought to be protected and how to most effectively accomplish this task. This type of investment would not only serve to counter cyberterrorism but would improve US defensive information warfare and critical infrastructure protection programs at the same time. The US should incorporate lessons from preparing for and responding to Y2K events.

Additionally, identifying key assets and how to effectively protect them must extend beyond the critical infrastructures identified in PDD-63. Most importantly, the US government must find ways to motivate information technology producers to raise the priority of system reliability and security in the production and fielding of new products. Legislative and policy approaches must consider both carrots and sticks. Innovative ideas might include providing the private sector tax breaks for improving protection in key technologies or legislation that establishes liability for losses due to digital intrusions and disruption if companies do not meet proscribed security standards.[73] These efforts would involve economic and social tradeoffs that require thorough evaluation.

Yet, despite obstacles, proactively limiting the opportunities presented to terrorists and other digital attackers by building strong information infrastructures will leverage limited resources much more effectively than trying to patch the holes after systems are in place.

The second set of policy initiatives to address cyberterrorism should focus on steps to make it more dangerous for its perpetrators. Cyberterrorism offers opportunities for attackers to remain anonymous or at least unlocated. The US must improve national security, intelligence, counterintelligence, and law enforcement capabilities to track and identify cyberattackers. To achieve this goal, the US must first improve the exchange of information and cooperation across these communities. The NIPC was created to accomplish this task, but long-standing differences in organizational orientations and cultures must be surmounted. Providing these communities with adequate technological tools, organizational capabilities to fuse information, and skilled people to accomplish the mission will prove costly. While discussions of cyberdefense tend to focus on the technological, more difficult will be justifying the resources necessary to recruit and retain sufficient skilled personnel. The defense, intelligence, and law enforcement communities are losing personnel with computer and information security expertise as fast or faster than they can be trained. Establishing effective analytical methodologies for tracking and hunting down cyberterrorists also requires more attention. Finally, the legal context for US government intelligence and law enforcement efforts intended to combat cyberterrorism and other malicious activity requires examination for possible modification. Initiatives could include enabling the courts to issue a single warrant for law enforcement agencies tracking suspects through multiple locations in cyberspace. Cyberterrorists fearful of rapid identification and response by the US government may well have to modify their tactics and strategies substantially.

Finally, the US government must implement a more proactive education and public awareness strategy. At a minimum, such a strategy must stress awareness of individual and organizational responsibilities and liabilities associated with conducting business, recreation, or other activities in cyberspace. Through the PDD-63 system of organizations, the government needs to establish and promulgate best practices for information system and infrastructure security. Going farther, the Federal government should implement a plan to limit confusion and hype in the event of cyberterrorist attacks. The government can potentially play a key role in identifying and limiting the impact of hoaxes. The most important task of the government at all levels if a cyberterrorist adversary was to wage a sustained campaign of disruption might simply be to provide accurate information about events and responses. In our open society, the US will continue to live with risks from cyberterrorism. The government role must focus on effectively mitigating these risks with the least impact on society as possible.

Conclusion

Much of the current hype about cyberterrorism is built on fear of the unknown. We need to move beyond simple speculation to more structured analysis of the threat and appropriate US responses. We do have sufficient reasons to believe cyberterrorism will become a more significant national security concern. The means are available but employing digital attacks to achieve specific terrorist objectives faces multiple obstacles. Within the US government, the challenge presented by the threat has received increasing attention. Plans have been formulated to address cyberterrorism as a part of the national critical infrastructure protection effort. Yet, these efforts are hampered by the narrow scope of defense efforts and inadequate resources. Developing robust defenses will continue to prove difficult. The most effective approaches to protect against cyberterrorism through establishing secure information systems and infrastructures must contend with technological and economic imperatives at the end of the 20th Century that cut in other directions. Improving the ability to track attackers involves issues of civil liberties and the role of government that require extensive public debate. Most clearly, US efforts to mitigate cyberterrorism will have to advance incrementally on a combination of fronts. We have no silver bullets for combating cyberterrorism. Rather, our nation must remain alert, learn, and invest wisely.

Notes

1. The possibility of digital warfare and terrorism became a widespread concern in the early 1990s largely as a result of reports such as National Research Council, *Computers at Risk: Safe Computing in the Information Age* (Washington, DC: National Academy Press, 1991) and books such as Alvin Toffler and Heidi Toffler, *War and Anti-War: Survival at the Dawn of the 21st Century* (Boston: Little, Brown and Company, 1993).
2. Quoted in Michael Evans, "War Planners Warn of Digital Armageddon" *London Times*, 20 November 1999.
3. Walter Laquer, "Post Modern Terrorism" *Foreign Affairs* Vol. 75, No. 5 (September-October 1996), 35
4. John Arquilla, David Ronfeldt and Michelle Zaninni, "Networks, Netwar and Information Age Terrorism" in *Countering the New Terrorism* (Washington DC: RAND Corporation, 1998), 71.
5. See Bruce Hoffman and Caleb Carr, "Terrorism: Who is Fighting Whom?" *World Policy Journal*, Vol. 14, No.1 (Spring 1997), 97–104.
6. This definition is based on that provided by Ian O. Lesser, "Countering the New Terrorism: Implications for Strategy" in *Countering the New Terrorism* (Washington DC: RAND Corporation, 1998), 85.
7. As of the end of 1999, there are no publicly known examples of purposeful digital attacks disrupting train services or stock markets. However, computer systems failures in Washington DC disrupted early morning Metro service for a period of hours on 20 September 1999. The different US financial markets have shut down at times for short periods due to loss of necessary computer and information services. Reasons for these shut downs vary from backhoes cutting fiber-optic cables in New Jersey to floods in Chicago.
8. On the possibility of use of weapons of mass destruction by terrorists, see Aston Carter, John Deutch and Phillip Zelikow, "Countering Catastrophic Terrorism" *Foreign Affairs* 77, No. 6 (November/December 1998): 80–94; and Richard Falkenrath, Robert D. Neuman and Bradley Thayer, Chapter 3 "The Threat of Nuclear, Biological, or Chemical Attack by Non-State Actors" in *America's Achilles' Heel* (Cambridge MA: MIT Press, 1998), 167–216.
9. This perspective is exemplified by the annual State Department Report, *Patterns of Global Terrorism*.
10. Robert Kaplan, "The Coming Anarchy," *Atlantic Monthly* (February 1994), 44–76; and Martin Van Creveld, "What War is Fought For" *The Transformation of War* (New York: The Free Press, 1991), 124–156.
11. Walter Laquer, *The New Terrorism: Fanaticism and the Arms of Mass Destruction* (Oxford: Oxford University Press, 1999)
12. Caleb Carr, "Terrorism as Warfare" *World Policy Journal* 13, No. 4 (Winter 1996–1997): 1–12.
13. On the general concept of netwar, see John Arquilla and David Ronfeldt, *The Advent of Netwar* (Washington DC: RAND Corporation, 1996). As applied to terrorism, see Arquilla, et al, "Networks, Netwar and Information Age Terrorism."

14. My analysis of the pros and cons of such an approach are fully elaborated in the forthcoming *Strategic Warfare in Cyberspace* (Cambridge MA: MIT Press, 2000).

15. Clifford Stoll, *The Cuckoo's Egg* (New York: Simon & Schuster, Inc., 1989) contains an extensive description of the activities, discovery, and eventually apprehension of the hackers involved in this incident.

16. General Accounting Office, *Computer Security: Hackers Penetrate DOD Computer Systems* (Washington, DC: GAO/T-IMTEC-92-5), 20 November 1991.

17. See for example, Winn Schwartau, *Cyber Terrorism: Protecting Your Personal Security in the Electronic Age* (New York: Thunder Mouth Press, 1996), especially on pp. 543–544.

18. This challenge is discussed in Andrew Rathmell, Richard Overill, Lorenzo Valeri and John Gearson, "The IW Threat from Sub-State Groups" in *Proceedings of the Third International Symposium on Command and Control Research and Technology* (Washington, DC: National Defense University, June 1997), 170.

19. See *Cybercrime, Cyberterrorism and Cyberwarfare: Averting an Electronic Waterloo* (Washington DC: The Center for Strategic and International Studies, December 1998).

20. Bruce Sterling, *The Hacker Crackdown: Law and Order on the Electronic Frontier* (New York: Bantam Books, 1992), 41–145 provides a lucid description of the hacker culture. Also see Dorothy E. Denning, *Information Warfare and Security* (Reading MA: Addison-Wesley, 1999), 46–50, for a concise summary of empirical studies on hacker motivations.

21. See Michelle Satalla and Joshua Quittner, *Masters of Deception: The Gang That Ruled Cyberspace* (New York: Harper Collins Publishing, 1995) for descriptions of such activities.

22. See Nicholas Chantler, "Profile of a Computer Hacker," available at http://www.infowar.com.

23. See information at www.2600.com/home.html.

24. "Call in the Goon Squad" C/NET Dispatches, 18 January 1999, available at hongkong1. cnet.com/Briefs/ Dispatches/China/990118/ss02.html.

25. Associate Press release, "Chinese Cyber Battle: Hackers Put Taiwanese Symbols on Internet Sites" 12 August 1999, available at www.freedomforum.org/international/1999/8/12tapei.asp.

26. See Jessica Stern, *The Ultimate Terrorists* (Cambridge MA: Harvard University Press, 1999), 74–75. Rathmell, et al, 176.

27. Denning, 160.

28. US Congress, Senate, Committee on Governmental Affairs, Testimony of Lopht Heavy Industries on Computer Security, 106th Congress, 2nd Session, 19 May 1998.

29. See previously cited 2600 web site address.

30. As examples of such studies see National Research Council, *Computers at Risk*; Defense Science Board Task Force, *Information Warfare—Defense* (Washington DC: Department of Defense, November 1996); President's Commission on Critical Infrastructure Protection, *Critical Foundations: Protecting America's Infrastructures* (Washington DC: President's Commission on Critical Infrastructure Protection, October 1997); and Statement of Michael A. Vatis, Director, National Infrastructure Protection Center "NIPC Cyber Threat Assessment" to US Senate, Judiciary Committee, Subcommittee on Technology and Terrorism, 6 October 1999.

31. This quote was provided in Captain (USN) Richard P. O'Neill's presentation at an Institute for Foreign Policy Analysis conference on "War in the Information Age," Cambridge, MA, 15 November 1995.

32. Anne W. Branscomb, *Rogue Computer Programs—Viruses, Worms Trojan Horses and Time Bombs: Pranks, Prowess, Protection or Prosecution* (Cambridge MA: Harvard University, Program on Information Resources Policy, I-89–3, September 1989), 1–5.

33. A good analysis is provided by Neil Winton, "Y2K Seen As Possible Cover for Cyberwars" Reuters report on WWW at http://www.zdnet.com/intweek/stories/news/, posted 8 October 1999.

34. Sterling, *The Hacker Crackdown*, 1–39.

35. "Pentagon Beats Back Internet Attack" *Wired News*, 10 September 1998 and George I. Seffers, "Hackers Take Offense at Pentagon Defense," *Defense News*, September 1998, 1.

36. Information on this incident and other virus hoaxes can be found on the Internet at the Department of Energy Computer Incident Advisory Capability (CIAC) web site, ciac.llnl.gov.

37. Chairman of the Joint Chiefs of Staff Memo CM-510–99, "Information Operations Condition," 10 Mar 99 provided the initial directive guidance regarding the establishment of a DoD INFOCON system.

38. Winn Schwartau, "An Introduction to Information Warfare" in Robert L. Pfaltzgraff, Jr. and Richard P. Shultz, Jr., eds. *War in the Information Age: New Challenges for US Security* (London: Brassey's, 1997), 58.

39. This assertion is made in a number of authoritative studies including 1996 Defense Science Board study, *Information Warfare—Defense*, 2–16, and the PCCIP, *Critical Foundations*, 19. This conclusion is also prevalent in the author's discussions with representatives of Software Engineering Institute's Network Survivability and Security Program and CERT Coordinating Center, the Defense Information Systems Agency's Automated Systems Security Incident Support Team (ASSIST), the Air Force Information Warfare Center.

40. General Accounting Office, *Information Security: Computer Attacks at Department of Defense Pose Increasing Risks* (Washington DC: GAO/AMID-96–84, May 1996), 15.

41. Arquilla, et al, " Networks, Netwar and Information Age Terrorism," 65–66.

42. Denning, 68.

43. See Charles Swett, "The Role of the Internet in International Politics" in Robert L. Pfaltzgraff, Jr. and Richard P. Shultz, Jr., eds., *War in the Information Age: New Challenges for US Security* (London: Brassey's, 1997), 292–293; and David Ronfeldt, John Arquilla, Graham Fuller and Melissa Fuller, *The Zapatista Social Netwar in Mexico* (Washington DC: RAND Corporation, 1999).

44. Phil Williams, "Transnational Criminal Organizations and International Security" *Survival*, Vol 36, No. 1 (Spring 1994), 96–113.

45. CIWARS Intelligence Report, 4 January 1998, vol. 2, no. 1 published by the Centre for Infrastructural Warfare, available on the Internet at WWW site at www.iwars.org, accessed 10 February 1998.

46. National Research Council, *Computer at Risk*, 7.

47. History of US efforts to deal with digital warfare and terrorism is discussed in depth in Chapter Five of my *Strategic Warfare in Cyberspace*.

48. *Critical Foundations*, 2.

49. See Office of Science and Technology Policy, *Cybernation: The American Infrastructure in the Information Age* (Washington, DC: The White House, April 1997) for an in-depth analysis of the significance of system complexity related to critical infrastructure protection.

50. "Activist Hackers Target On-Line Toy Company," *Financial Times*, 19 December 1999.

51. Richard Behar, "Who's Reading Your E-Mail," *Fortune* (3 February 1997): 64.

52. Denise Shelton, "Banks Appease On-Line Terrorists" at news.cnet.com, posted 3 June 1996.

53. The Toxyn hacker group published a call for attacks against Indonesian government sites on their web site at toxyn.pt.eu.org beginning in October 1997. The hacker magazine *2600* posted an example of a modified web page at their site at www.2600.com/east_timor/after.html.

54. John Markoff, "Airports Told of Flaw in Security System" *New York Times*, 8 February 1998.

55. See extensive discussion in Fredrick B. Cohen, *Protection and Security on the Information Highway* (New York: John Wiley & Sons, 1995), 33–78.

56. "Fired Programmer Zaps Old Firm," on the Internet at biz.yahoo.com/upi/98/02/17/general _state_and_regional_news/nyzap_1.htm, accessed 10 March 1998.

57. Computer Security Institute/Federal Bureau of Investigation, *Computer Crime and Security Survey* (San Francisco: Computer Security Institute, 1999), 4.

58. Rathmell, 174–5.

59. Denning, 69.

60. Statement of Michael Vatis to Senate Judiciary Committee, 6 October 1999.

61. William Church, *CIWARS Intelligence Report*, 10 May 1998.

62. The history of US efforts to develop a national response to the threat of digital attacks is detailed in Chapter Five of this author's forthcoming *Strategic Warfare in Cyberspace*.

63. This information was provided by the National Coordinator for Security, Infrastructure and Counterterrorism, Richard Clarke, at the "Preparing for Cyberwar" Conference, Arlington VA, 5 October 1999.

64. National Infrastructure Protection Center Fact Sheet, 1999.
65. The problems confronted by the US government in keeping skilled computer security personnel are illuminated by an article by Elizabeth Shogren, "U.S. Tries to Plug Computer Worker Drain," *Los Angeles Times*, 23 November 1999, 1.
66. For descriptions of the incident, see Bradley Graham, "11 US Military Computer Systems Breached This Month," *Washington Post*, 26 February 1998, A01; James Glave, "DOD-Cracking Team Used Common Bug," on *Wired Internet* at www.wired.com, accessed 10 May 1998; and James Glave, "Pentagon Hacker Speaks Out," on *Wired Internet* at www.wired.com, accessed 10 May 1998.
67. See Declan McCullagh, "Surveillance Network Draws Fire" from Wired News Online, 29 July 1999 at www.wired.com/news/news/politics/story/20994.html.
68. Software Engineering Institute, *Detecting Signs of Intrusion* (Pittsburgh PA: Carnegie Mellon University, August 1997).
69. See Office of the Staff Judge Advocate, AF Office of Special Investigations, "Computer Crime Investigator's Handbook" (Andrews AFB MD: AF Office of Special Investigations, May 1999) for detailed explanation of these constraints.
70. This case is strongly stated in the Government Accounting Office study, *Critical Infrastructure Protection: Comprehensive Strategy Can Draw on Year 2000 Experiences* (Washington DC: GAO/AIMD-00-01, 1999). The US Air Force and the National Research Council have instituted a joint effort to conduct a study along these lines.
71. Specifics on the IAVA system are provided by Lt. Beth A. Evans, Technical Analysis Division Chief, DoD CERT, "DoD's IAVA Process" *IAnewsletter 3*, No. 1 (Summer 1999): 8–9.
72. A detailed analysis of this tension is provided in Chapter 5 of *Strategic Warfare in Cyberspace*. The debates within the US over encryption policy are fully addressed in Susan Landau and Whitfield Diffie, *Privacy on the Line: The Politics of Wire Tapping and Encryption*, (Cambridge MA: MIT Press, 1998).
73. An analysis of such approaches in provided in Stephen J. Lusiak, *Public and Private Roles in the Protection of Critical Information-Dependent Infrastructures* (Palo Alto, CA: Stanford University, Center for International Security and Arms Control, March 1997).

6.3   Jason Pate and Gavin Cameron, 2001

Covert Biological Weapons Attacks Against Agricultural Targets
Assessing the Impact Against U.S. Agriculture

Jason Pate is a senior research associate and WMD Terrorism Database Manager at the Center for Nonproliferation Studies (CNS) at the Monterey Institute of International Studies. He is author and coauthor of several publications on WMD terrorism and is a contributor to the book *Toxic Terror: Assessing the Terrorist Use of Chemical and Biological Weapons* (2000).

Gavin Cameron is a lecturer in politics and military history at the University of Salford, England. He has been a research fellow at the Center for Nonproliferaiton Studies and the Belfer Center for Science and International Affairs at Harvard University. He is author of *Nuclear Terrorism: A Threat Assessment for the 21st Century* (1999).

Introduction

Since 1995, analysts, policymakers, and the news media in the United States have focused unprecedented attention on the threat of terrorism involving weapons of mass destruction (WMD), particularly chemical and biological weapons (CBW). The Aum Shinrikyo attack in Tokyo in March 1995 and the Oklahoma City bombing the following month significantly contributed to this phenomenon in two important ways. First, Aum proved that subnational groups could obtain CBW, previously only a theoretical possibility.[1] After the Tokyo incident terrorists using CBW appeared to be an evolving and dangerous threat that required creative new thinking in counter- and antiterrorism policy. Second, the Oklahoma City bombing brought the threat of terrorism to the American heartland. No longer was terrorism a foreign phenomenon characterized by media accounts of masked Islamic fundamentalists taking hostages, hijacking planes, or bombing far-away buildings. The terrorists in this case were Americans targeting Americans: not only had terrorism reached the center of the country, but the terrorist threat originated much closer to home.

In an effort to address this "new" terrorist threat, the United States has tripled spending for CBW counterterrorist programs since 1995. Threat analyses have focused on the vulnerability of American society to attacks involving CBW as well as the spread in the information era of the technologies and know-how associated with such weapons, and many government programs designed to address the CBW terrorist threat reflect this approach. In 1996, Congress passed the Defense Against Weapons of Mass Destruction Act (the Nunn-Lugar-Domenici Domestic Preparedness Program) in an effort to make the United States better prepared to respond to an attack involving CBW. This effort has been characterized by scenario development and training of the first-responder community, under the assumption that an attack would affect primarily civilians in urban areas.

More recently, the threat of a biological attack against an agricultural target, often labeled "agricultural terrorism", has been discussed, although programs to ensure preparedness for such an attack remain largely the purview of a limited part of the U.S. Department of Agriculture (USDA), which has begun to improve its capabilities to respond in the event of disease in animals or crops.[2] In an effort to address the potential threat of attacks against agricultural targets, USDA has developed a six-point strategy to ensure the security of U.S. agriculture, including terrorism prevention and deterrence, international cooperation, domestic consequence management planning, research on counterterrorism capabilities, protection of critical infrastructure, and protection of food supply.[3] This wide-ranging and somewhat vague list resembles many other agencies' counterterrorism plans. Interagency groups have proliferated, also characteristic of U.S. CBW counterterrorism planning in recent years. Several other U.S. agencies besides USDA now have some role in preparedness for agricultural terrorism, including the National Security Council and the Department of Justice.[4] USDA requested a total of $41.3 million for counterterrorism in Fiscal Year (FY) 2001, $39.8 million of which (or 96 percent) is devoted to defense against WMD.[5] In FY 2000, WMD defense accounted for $7.3 million of $12.3 million, or 59 percent of the total.[6] Clearly, USDA has focused significant resources on addressing this problem. For comparison, the Department of Health and Human Services (HHS), the agency responsible for public health, including the Centers for Disease Control and Prevention (CDC), requested $265.4 million for counterterrorism activities for FY 2001, all of which was WMD-related, representing a decrease in funding from $277.6 in FY 2000.[7] The HHS FY 1999 figure, however, was $173.1 million, indicating either that HHS was able to capitalize sooner on the attention given the WMD threat or that the threat was perceived as more pressing in HHS's jurisdiction.[8] The Department of Justice (DOJ) requested $254.7 million in WMD-related funding in FY 2001, an increase of $37.5 million over the previous year.[9] In the U.S. national security community, funding for WMD-related programs has tripled since 1998, but the figures remain a small portion (less than 10 percent) of the total for counterterrorism generally.[10] Other agencies' funding for WMD defense programs has also increased, but in no case has the proportion of WMD funding in the total counterterrorism budget been so great as in the case of USDA. That said, USDA's funding levels, seen as a proportion of the U.S. budget, trail those of other agencies dramatically in WMD-related appropriations, because the Domestic Preparedness Program until very recently has focused on preventing and mitigating attacks targeted directly at humans. The heightened focus on terrorism against agriculture represents a new stage, one with the object of protecting U.S. strategic assets, such as agriculture.

In addition, USDA has requested funding to upgrade a research facility at Plum Island, New York, to Biosafety Level 4, capable of and dedicated to the study of animal and plant pathogens, although local public opinion and congressional representatives have mixed views on the issue.[11] Building on these indicators of growing official attention to the threat of attacks against agricultural targets, including congressional hearings on the issue, news articles have begun to reflect concerns that U.S. agriculture is vulnerable to attack using biological weapons, and arguably this vulnerability, as well as the theoretical ease of carrying out such attacks covertly, makes agricultural targets particularly appealing to terrorists.[12] Terrorists may also find these types of targets appealing because they do not target humans directly and may therefore be more easily justified. Indeed, a recent influential U.S. government report asserted that the "U.S. agricultural sector is especially vulnerable to agroterrorism" and that "a successful attack could result in local or regional economic destabilization" and affect international commerce.[13] The U.S. agricultural sector, including all elements directly or indirectly related to agriculture, represents about 13 percent of the U.S. gross national product and is enormous and diverse; few specific threat assessments of vulnerability exist.[14]

It would be extremely difficult for a terrorist group to perpetrate a significant biological attack against the agricultural economy in the United States, however, for several reasons. First, obtaining and effectively delivering a biological agent against an agricultural target is a task fraught with technical hurdles. Although some agricultural agents can be obtained relatively easily and crudely delivered, to cause a catastrophic incident would require a more sophisticated approach. Second, because crops and livestock in the United States are generally not concentrated, eliminating a segment of the agricultural economy would require a multipronged attack and a sophisticated understanding of the economy. Although not impossible, this type of attack presents significant obstacles. Third, the U.S. agricultural economy has in place networks and plans to respond to an attack once detected, and surveillance of crop and animal disease in the United States is extraordinarily sophisticated. Even if a terrorist group managed to deliver a biological agent effectively against a target, the effects of the attack would likely be severely limited by the U.S. response. Fourth, although a determined group could conceivably carry out a devastating attack, there is no evidence of terrorist groups with the motivation to carry out a catastrophic attack against U.S. agriculture. It is clear however that more research is required before an accurate assessment can be made of the threat terrorism poses to the U.S. agricultural economy.

The purpose of this paper is to assess what economic impact an attack using biological weapons would have on the U.S. agricultural sector. There have been very few instances of what could be deemed "agricultural terrorism" in the United States; the empirical data is therefore quite limited. Although there have been some well-known cases of agricultural product contamination, these cases targeted people more directly rather than the crops or livestock themselves and were thus not examples of subnational actors seeking to eliminate a specific crop or portion of the agricultural base. Without a set of cases to examine, it is extremely difficult to predict accurately what an incident of agricultural terrorism would involve, how it would present itself, how it would be detected, and what its consequences would be.

By looking at natural outbreaks of disease in segments of the agricultural economy in the United States however, it may be possible to identify and quantify the actual impact of an attack against U.S. agriculture. These outbreaks, although they do not carry with them the same level of psychological impact that is normally associated with terrorism, do provide a baseline for economic analysis and estimates of disease impacts on local, regional, and national economies.

The paper discusses definitions of agricultural terrorism and talks about some theoretical reasons why U.S. agriculture may not be particularly vulnerable to an attack. The ideas proposed along these lines are similar to those in theories about the difficulty of perpetrating an effective attack using CBW against any target. After taking a look at the historical record of agricultural terrorism cases and making some observations, the paper reviews a number of naturally occurring outbreaks to provide a basis for determining the impact disease in the agricultural sector might have. To assess the vulnerability of the vast U.S. agricultural economy to terrorist attacks using biological weapons (BW), the paper then analyzes the diversity of U.S. agriculture and comments on the feasibility of attacking regionally focused crops. Finally, the paper draws some conclusions from the data.

Definitions

Before looking to natural outbreaks in an effort to understand what economic impact a subnational BW attack against an agricultural target would have, it is necessary and important to define the term "agricultural terrorism" in the context of the debate surrounding it. One key issue in arriving at such a definition is how to categorize covert BW attacks. Are all such attacks terrorism? In some cases, where there is a terrorist group or individual using BW against agriculture, the term "agricultural terrorism" would obviously apply. In others, the motivations for the attack are criminal in nature with no link to furtherance of an ideological goal. Even in such cases, the attack is likely to have a psychological impact that goes beyond the immediate effects of the attack, a subsequent terrorizing effect. For this reason, these cases are covered in the analysis presented here even though they cannot by any reasonable definition be included as terrorism per se. We are speaking here of subnational attacks against agriculture; to provide as comprehensive analysis as the data allow, we use the term subnational BW attacks against agriculture to include all of these cases. Though cumbersome, this term allows for more accurate analysis. Although attacks using chemical or even conventional weapons against agricultural targets could be considered examples of subnational BW agricultural attacks, for the purposes of this study, subnational BW agricultural attacks refers to the use of disease against agricultural targets, including crops and livestock, in an effort to cause widespread damage to or destruction of the target. This is a separate issue from the use of agents to contaminate specific products; in those cases, the target is actually people, and the incidents look more like consumer product tampering. However, because of the paucity of incidents of actual agricultural terrorism, this paper provides an overview of product contamination cases for context. Because chemical destruction is by nature self-limiting, we have chosen to look specifically in this paper at disease, at attacks using a biological agent.

Although often-cited cases of subnational BW agricultural attacks have involved threats of contamination of specific products, causing significant economic losses through diminished consumer confidence, they did not threaten the loss of an entire segment of the agricultural sector. Although the diffusion, both geographically and typologically, of agricultural production across the United States makes a catastrophic attack on or the total elimination of a significant portion of the national agricultural economy highly unlikely, regional economies could be significantly affected. However, certain segments of the agricultural economy in the United States may be sufficiently concentrated or sufficiently unique that an attack against them could have major regional consequences.

Costs

Although this paper deals overtly with the economics of subnational BW agricultural attacks, a range of costs, in the wider sense, would be associated with such an attack. If crops or livestock are destroyed, then obviously that has a financial impact on the grower or breeder. Depending on the scale of the attack, however, it might have an impact on consumers, both in confidence, in the case of product tampering, and in produce prices. Clearly, if a particular crop is in short supply, or if it has to be imported from a more remote region, then the price of that crop will rise. An example of this phenomenon attributable to natural causes occurred in 1999 when frost decimated the California orange crop, so that oranges had to be shipped from Florida, resulting in a rise in orange prices. Such an occurrence also has a ripple effect: the increase in the price of oranges adversely affected the Florida juice industry even though the frost had hit California. The increased costs were passed to the consumers of orange juice and table oranges. Equally, though, a range of individuals and businesses are likely to suffer as a result of the secondary impact of subnational BW agricultural attacks. For example, if a crop is decimated, agricultural workers are likely to be seriously affected unless they can find alternative employment. In January 1999, for example, unemployment in Tulare County, California, hit 20 percent, largely as a result of the area's spoiled orange crops. A range of industries may depend on certain crops or livestock: a terrorist attack on cattle affects not only the farmer, but also the livestock shippers, stockyards, slaughterhouses, distributors, and so on. The economic impact of an incident depends not only on the scale of an attack, but also on the crop or livestock that is targeted. Where there are substitute goods for those that have been targeted, the economic impact can be reduced. Equally, some livestock or crops have more elastic supply than others, so that output can readily be expanded to fill a gap in the market. For example, because pigs have large litters and reach maturity relatively quickly, the supply of hogs is much more flexible than that of cattle.

Apart from the loss of immediate revenue from a subnational BW agricultural attack, there is also the risk of long-term loss of market share. If distributors, wholesalers, and retailers find acceptable and affordable alternative sources of agricultural produce to replace those affected by the attack, they may not return to their original supplier, even after the crisis has passed. This might be not only a consequence of subnational BW agricultural attacks, but conceivably a motive for them as well. Competitors in a particular market could see these attacks as a means of increasing their market share at the expense of their rivals.

Obviously, a range of other potential costs might also be incurred as a result of a subnational BW agricultural attack. Crops or livestock might need to be replaced. The expense of doing so could be particularly heavy if breeding stocks have to be replaced to replenish supplies of produce. Depending on the agent used to attack agriculture, the affected area will likely need to be decontaminated. Additional costs may include not only "cleaning up" the agent, but also the collection and destruction of infected crops or livestock. If dealing with a virulent and readily transmissible agent such as foot-and-mouth disease (FMD) or certain wind-borne plant pathogens, the need for collection and destruction may extend from those livestock or crops already affected to those in the vicinity, those that *might* be affected, due to the need to establish a *cordon sanitaire* to control the spread of the disease.

Finally, agricultural terrorism may generate political costs. Some of these costs apply to any act of terrorism: the loss of confidence and credibility stemming from a government's inability to protect the country. Specifically, however, terrorism involving BW attacks on agriculture may also result in a heightened need for interagency cooperation, possibly at local, state, and national levels, and calls for increased action against further such attacks.

In summary, subnational BW agricultural attacks may involve a range of costs, both direct and indirect, overtly and hidden. Therefore, when discussing the economic impact of such attacks, it is important to be clear what costs are being incurred and by whom.

Incidents Involving Subnational BW Agricultural Attacks

As of August 2, 2000, the Database of WMD Terrorism Incidents at the Center for Nonproliferation Studies, Monterey Institute, held twenty-one incidents that might be classified as subnational BW agricultural attacks.[15] This represents only a small fraction (2.5 percent) of the total number (853) of incidents contained in the Database. Clearly, in spite of the attention that the threat of agricultural terrorism is now receiving, historically, such attacks have been relatively rare occurrences. Moreover, although high-profile concern over the potential threat is a relatively new phenomenon and has centered in the United States, the historical record suggests that acts of agricultural terrorism have been perpetrated worldwide for decades. Of the twenty-one incidents of subnational CBW agricultural attacks in the Database, five occurred in the United States, but four occurred in Israel, and there have been incidents in Canada, China, Sri Lanka, the Philippines, Australia, Uganda, and Kenya, as well as throughout Europe. The earliest incident in the Database occurred in Kenya in 1952, when members of the Mau-Mau, an anticolonialist group, inserted the latex of the African milk bush plant into cuts made in the skin of thirty-three steers, eight of which died.[16] Even within the United States, members of the Ku Klux Klan supposedly poisoned the water supply of cattle owned by a group of Black Muslims in Ashville, Alabama, in March 1970. A local veterinarian identified the poison as cyanide. The incident may have been part of a sustained campaign of intimidation by the Klan against the owners of the farm. The poison killed thirty cattle and sickened nine others.[17] Clearly, then, the threat of agricultural terrorism is neither new nor limited to the United States.

Agricultural attacks are not primarily a means of targeting people per se: it would be simply illogical to attempt to attack people by targeting agriculture. Subnational agricultural attacks are therefore predominantly a means of extortion, intimidation (as in the example of the alleged Ku Klux Klan attack described above), or economic punishment. Although their impact is primarily financial, agricultural attacks have obvious social consequences as well, that may be used as a tactic for political as well as criminal purposes. In fact, of the twenty-one cases of subnational BW agricultural attacks in the Database, only five were classified as criminally motivated. This is partly a consequence of the Database's inclusion criteria, but it is nevertheless extremely significant that sixteen incidents were classified as politically motivated; agricultural terrorism is a means of political as well as financial extortion. When people have been injured or even killed as a result of agricultural terrorism, it has generally been when the incident closely resembles consumer product tampering. In 1978, the Arab Revolutionary Council used liquid mercury to poison citrus fruit exports from Israel to Europe. Israeli orange exports were reduced by forty percent, and twelve people were injured when they ate contaminated oranges.[18] In this case though, despite the injuries, the primary target of the attack was the Israeli economy. A more serious case was uncovered in May 2000 when inspectors from the Israeli Agricultural Development Authority discovered that Palestinians had been using counterfeit stamps on expired and salmonella-ridden eggs that were then sold throughout Israel. Although they had been operating the scheme for eighteen months, it is unclear how many contaminated eggs were sold or how many people were sickened as a result. In September 1999, two Israelis died of salmonella as a result of eating contaminated eggs. According to Israeli news sources, there may have been "widespread food poisoning in the IDF and among tourists" as a result of the Palestinians' actions.[19] Clearly, in this case, the intended impact was not only economic, but also disruption of the Israeli military and society, a direct and politically motivated attack on people. Palestinian groups, more than other terrorist organizations, appear to have used such attacks as one in a series of strategies. In each case, the actions of such Palestinian groups are examples of the product-tampering type of agricultural terrorism. In 1974 in Genoa, Italy, the "Revolutionary Command" announced that it had "injected toxic substances into Israeli-produced grapefruit."[20] In 1979, the Arab Revolutionary Council threatened to contaminate a range of Israeli agricultural exports to Europe.[21]

In April 1988, again in Italy, the Organization of Metropolitan Proletariat and Oppressed Peoples, acting in support of the Palestinian Intifada, claimed to have injected poison into Israeli grapefruit. Grapefruit contaminated with a non-harmful agent were discovered in Naples and Rome, and the Italian government then withdrew all Israeli grapefruit from sale.[22] Interestingly, Israeli individuals or groups have targeted Palestinian agriculture too, but such attacks have been directed against crops rather than exports. Therefore, they have had a more direct, although possibly less widespread impact than that achieved by Palestinian undermining of consumer confidence in Israeli fruit. In October 1997, settlers from Gosh Etzion sprayed a chemical on grapevines in two Palestinian villages south of Bethlehem. The settlers supposedly destroyed hundreds of vines and up to 17,000 metric tons of grapes.[23] In June 2000, settlers from Efrat released sewer water onto Palestinian fields in Khaddar, near Bethlehem. Farmers estimated their losses at around $5,000.[24] Although the settlers were undoubtedly pursuing a campaign to drive Palestinian farmers from the land, it is unclear whether they sought to do so by poisoning crops with sewage or by simply flooding the fields with the water.

Elsewhere in the world, agriculture has been targeted for a range of political objectives. In 1977, Ugandan dissidents threatened to poison the country's coffee and tea crops in an effort to severely affect Ugandan foreign exchange, thus undermining the economy.[25] The LTTE (Tamil Tigers) threatened to use biological weapons to attack Sri Lankan crops in the mid-1980s.[26] In January 1984, Pater Vivian Wardrop threatened to use FMD to attack livestock in Queensland, Australia, unless prison reforms were undertaken.[27] In none of these cases was there any indication that an attack had actually been perpetrated or that an agent for use against agriculture had been successfully acquired.

Forms of subnational agricultural attacks have been used as a means of settling personal scores. In the mid-1990s, a farmer in China used rat poison to kill twelve of his neighbors' water buffalo, along with four of his neighbors, supposedly because they were better off than he.[28] In 1997, Brian W. "Skip" Lea, of Berlin, Wisconsin, used the fungicide folpet and the illegal pesticide chlordane to contaminate products manufactured by National By-Products, a supplier for Purina Mills animal feed that he regarded as a business competitor.[29]

A number of cases worldwide and the majority of cases in the United States reflect the targeting of exports or products rather than agriculture per se. In the 1980s, Huk terrorists poisoned Dole pineapples in the Philippines that were meant for export. However, the contaminated pineapples were discovered and destroyed, before any harm was done.[30] In September 1997, an ex-Kurdistan Workers Party member claimed that the group planned to target Turkish vegetable exports.[31] In July 1986, threats from the Azanian Peoples Liberation Front, an anti-apartheid group, were published in the Canadian press that South African fruit would be poisoned with a toxic chemical.[32] Although no poisoned fruit was discovered, two Canadian supermarket chains ceased sales of all South African fruit.[33] The South African fruit sales ceased because of the poisoning threat at the time with no clear indication from the two supermarkets when sales would resume.[34] In November 1994, "the David Group" sprayed graffiti on railcars containing grain in Thunder Bay, Canada. Subsequent tests gave no indication, however, that the grain itself had been contaminated.[35] Within the United States, exports have also been a target: in January 2000 an e-mail message spread to internet users that warned, Costa

Rican bananas were contaminated with necrotizing fasciitis, a flesh-eating bacteria.[36] The e-mail message was signed "Manheim Research Institute Center for Disease Control Atlanta Georgia," which is a false organization according to the Centers for Disease Control.[37] No basis was discovered for the threat, and it is doubtful whether it is possible, even theoretically, to contract the disease as a consequence of eating food.[38] Clearly, these cases were targeted at potential consumers of the product.

More interesting was the 1989 case of the Breeders, a previously unknown group that threatened to spread Medfly through California if aerial spraying of pesticides continued in the state. The Medfly infestation in California at that time was unusually large and had a number of characteristics that led investigators to conclude a deliberate infestation was being conducted. No one was ever caught for promoting the spread of the Medfly, however.[39] The case had a number of noteworthy aspects, particularly in that the motivation for the action was environmentalism. Although causing economic damage seems the most likely political reason to perpetrate an act of agricultural terrorism, the Breeders case shows that some single-issue groups might be similarly interested in such a tactic. Protesters concerned with genetically modified foods, as well as environmentalists, seem plausible candidates to consider an act of agricultural terrorism or agro-sabotage. The Breeders used a biological means, Medfly, to attack crops in California. By contrast, most attacks have either been hoaxes or relied on chemical agents to attack agriculture. It is biological, not chemical, weapons however that can potentially have the most widespread effects on agriculture.

Of the agents used or threatened in the incidents of subnational agricultural attacks contained in the Database, eight cases involved threats to poison or contaminate crops or agricultural products with unspecified agents. In none of these cases was an attack actually launched, and all eight were simple hoaxes, threats, or plots. Six incidents in the Database involved a specific chemical agent directed against agriculture and each involved the use of the agent: mercury, cyanide, rat poison, pesticide, fungicide, and an unnamed chemical. None of these incidents could be classified as sophisticated or involving high-end, or warfare, agents. Of the biological incidents in the Database, there were threats to use FMD, necrotizing fasciitis, and an unnamed biological agent. Of these, the threat to use FMD is notable because potential use of the disease on agriculture elicits considerable alarm and concern among U.S. officials and agricultural experts. It is the agricultural equivalent of a threat to use smallpox on a human population, with the difference that FMD is more readily available than is smallpox. Of the biological agents actually used, one was simply sewer water, another was salmonella in eggs, another a plant toxin from the African milk bush, and the last Medfly. Of these, perhaps only the Breeders incident could be considered significant for this study, as it involved the use of a biological agent in a way that could credibly have had widespread impact on agriculture.

It is useful to examine the economic impact of these incidents of agricultural terrorism from the Database. In twelve cases, no costs could be identified beyond the cost of harassment from the threats. In four cases, the perpetrators were able to kill animals, and in two of these four, people were killed as well. In only five cases is it possible to attribute financial costs to the activities. In one case, 17,000 metric tons of grapes were destroyed. In another, 300 pounds of feed were halted from distribution, but it is unclear whether Purina destroyed the feed or simply tested it for contamination. In a third,

Palestinian farmers lost an estimated $5,000. In a fourth case, two supermarket chains in Canada stopped importing South African fruit, but reports gave no estimate of losses in currency. In the most significant case, Israeli orange exports were reduced by 40 percent, but again, reports gave no estimate of costs incurred. In two of the more significant cases, the incident looked more like product tampering than an attack against agriculture. In the other cases, costs were extremely limited and minimal. The historical record therefore suggests that it is difficult to achieve significant damage against agricultural targets, with the possible exception of product tampering.

Naturally Occurring Outbreaks of Disease

One means of determining the costs associated with potential subnational BW agricultural attacks would be to examine the impact of naturally occurring outbreaks of disease, particularly within the United States. Historically, both livestock and crops have been affected by a range of catastrophic diseases. Clearly, though, the impact of a particular outbreak of a disease is dependent on a range of factors: the characteristics of the disease, where it occurs, and the measures taken to deal with it.

At the time of writing, a major outbreak of Foot and Mouth Disease (FMD) is occurring in the United Kingdom and has apparently spread to France, the Netherlands, and Ireland. Affecting ungulates, cloven-hoofed animals such as cattle, pigs, and sheep, the viral infection has resulted in widespread import bans on livestock dairy and meat products from European Union countries. The disease is extremely infectious and can be spread through either direct or indirect (e.g., by dirty straw or on human clothes) contact with an infected animal. The British outbreak originated in a single pig herd in north-east England, where animals ate swill containing infected meat imported illegally from East Asia (FMD is endemic in areas of Africa, the Middle East, and Asia). As the origin of the British outbreak shows, the FMD virus can survive processing, explaining the ban not only of live animals from affected countries, but also of many animal products as well.

Between February 20 and May 14, 2001, 1,595[40] separate cases of FMD were reported in Britain, and a much smaller number of possible cases had been reported in France, the Netherlands, and Ireland. Although the disease has a relatively low mortality rate of around 5 percent of affected animals, mostly those that are young or old, it has a major economic impact. The meat and milk producing capacity of affected animals drastically declines, and there is an increased incidence of miscarriages in animals that have suffered the disease. Within Britain, compensation is available, so it is more economical for a farmer to slaughter the animal than to keep it. More importantly though, recovered animals may still be viral carriers, presenting a continued threat of infection, increasing the incentive to kill such animals.[41]

Although vaccines are available to counter the disease, these should ideally be administered before an animal is exposed to FMD. This is complicated further as there are seven major strains of the disease and several subtypes, limiting the scope of a vaccination to be effective against all varieties of the disease. The "killed" vaccines offer protection for just six to nine months, so animals must be repeated immunized. More important still is the need to sell meat to countries free of FMD. A vaccinated animal cannot be distinguished from one that has had the disease, nor does vaccination prevent an animal from acting as a carrier. Vaccination, therefore, is an expensive option, particularly in countries where the disease is not endemic, and also had implications for trade. Consequently, the more common response has been to destroy every cloven-hoofed animal on affected farms. Britain has already slaughtered 2,657,000 animals and plans to slaughter 75,000 more;[42] European countries have also slaughtered thousands of animals that may have come into contact with British livestock.

As well as incurring import bans, the outbreak of FMD has restricted movement of livestock within Britain. Markets have closed, and only a small number of animals from unaffected herds are being moved to slaughterhouses, under tightly controlled conditions. Since culled animals from affected herds must be burned, rather than sold for meat, the restricted number of animals being slaughtered for food has resulted in a shortage that has had to be satisfied by importing meat from outside the UK, at an increased cost to consumers.

As of May 14, 2001, it was still too early to estimate accurately the economic costs to farmers and the wider agricultural sector, beyond that it will be devastating to both. Even those farms that are unaffected stand to suffer huge losses because the disease compelled all livestock markets to be shut, so most farmers have had no income, only expenses, for the past two months. Moreover, the economic prospects for such farmers are grim: their animals are now mostly past the optimum time to ship them off to slaughter, and when the markets finally do open, the price of meat will plummet because every farmer is in the same situation and will flood the market. Moreover, while there will be compensation for farms where animals are slaughtered as a direct consequence of FMD (either through infection or prevention), the compensation for indirectly affected farms is less certain. Even the money for slaughtered animals is unlikely to be sufficient to return farms to pre-disease levels. The government money is based on stock valuation, rather than being compensation for lost income. Once the outbreak is over, the cost of new animals for replacing herds and flocks is expected to be very high due to the relative scarcity of breeding stock.

The FMD outbreak has had significant political implications: the British government felt obliged to postpone a national election, widely anticipated to be called for May, to June, along with local elections. The government's handling of the crisis has been a source of political debate, and the government department responsible for agriculture, the Ministry of Agriculture, Fisheries and Food (MAFF), is itself under pressure, being accused of bungling the prevention and control of the disease.

However, it is hard to suggest that the outbreak presents a strategic threat to the UK economy: agriculture and even the associated loss of tourism are not significant enough. Farming currently represents 0.9 percent of UK GDP [gross domestic product] and employs 1.5 percent of the UK workforce. The FMD epidemic is likely to reduce the value of the agricultural sector still further, as some farmers decide that their compensation does not permit a return to the occupation that offered economically marginal returns, even before the outbreak. However, the economically more significant impact of the disease will be on tourism. Although FMD only very rarely affects humans (when it presents itself as flu-like symptoms), tourist bookings for holidays in the UK have been severely affected by the disease outbreak. A report by accountants PricewaterhouseCoopers (PWC) on the cost of the outbreak suggested that although the cost to UK agriculture would be between £500m and £1.6 billion, the total cost of the crisis for Britain in

2001 could be between £2.5 billion and £8 billion, or between 0.3 percent and 0.8 percent of GDP.[43] By the end of April, the Centre for Economic and Business Research estimated that the epidemic would cost farmers £3.6 billion, and the British Tourist Authority estimated £2.5 billion of overseas tourist revenue will be lost by the end of the year.[44] Clearly, a major disease outbreak, such as FMD, has the potential to be catastrophic on an individual farm level; be significant to the agricultural sector; but may not be devastating to the economy as a whole. The same distinction could apply in the U.S. In 1999, the sector of the economy directly related to agriculture represented 1.3 percent of U.S. GDP[45] and in 2000 employed 2.6 percent of the U.S. workforce.[46]

In the Netherlands in 1997, five million pigs had to be slaughtered as a result of swine fever. Since the disease, though harmless to humans, is highly lethal to pigs and extremely contagious, entire herds with affected pigs have to be killed to contain its spread. Due to restrictions on transportation and sale of pigs, necessary to control the disease spread, the Dutch government had to impose breeding bans, and 1.5 million piglets had to be slaughtered to relieve the pressure on overcrowded sties. The cost of compensation for the cull and cleanup of affected farms is estimated at $2 billion. Of this sum, the Dutch government contributed $900 million, and the European Union (EU) contributed $1.1 billion from the EU agricultural fund. Moreover, pig breeding usually contributes about $2.25 billion to Dutch exports; the disease knocked a half point off the country's GDP for the year.[47]

A 1999 dioxin (a highly carcinogenic substance) contamination in Belgium cost Belgian food producers and farmers hundreds of millions of dollars. The incident arose from contaminated feed and led to bans of Belgian eggs, poultry, and also beef, pork, and some dairy products across the EU. It is believed that the original contamination was at Verkest, a company providing animal fats to animal feed manufacturers. The impact continued to spread: nine Belgian, one Dutch, and one French feed manufacturer were supplied with contaminated products, leading to bans on all EU chicken and pork in the United States, Japan, and Brazil. By September 1999, estimates of the cost of the incident to Belgian farmers varied at between $750 million and $1.5 billion, and the Belgian government estimated that it had cost the country around $900 million in lost tax revenue, chemical testing, and veterinary bills.[48]

When FMD struck Taiwan in 1997, over four million pigs had to be slaughtered. Before the outbreak, the swine industry represented nearly 60 percent of Taiwan's livestock products. After the outbreak, pork prices collapsed, and it was estimated that damage to the Taiwanese economy might include $3 billion of lost sales, the jeopardizing of 50,000 jobs, and a half point slowdown in the country's economic growth.

Within the United States, the economic consequences of naturally occurring outbreaks have been less catastrophic than overseas. In 1999, the Mexican fruit fly threatened agriculture across California, when it was discovered in San Diego County and Fallbrook County. The fly attacks more than 250 species of fruits, nuts, and vegetables, laying eggs in ripening fruit and thus spoiling it for sale and consumption. The agricultural economy in San Diego County alone is worth $1.2 billion, but it is difficult to determine the effects of subsequent bans on fruit exports from the county by the Australian, New Zealand, Taiwanese, and Japanese governments. Mediterranean fruit flies were discovered in Riverside County, and guava flies were found in Fresno County. According to the California Department of Food and Agriculture, the state's worldwide fruit exports were valued at about $2 billion in 1997, and 1997 combined fruit, nut, and vegetable production was almost 39 million tons, or more than half of total U.S. production.[49] Within the state, 132,000 jobs and $13 billion depend directly or indirectly on fruit farming. However, thanks to a rigorous program of quarantine and eradication, the damage to Californian agriculture was a mere fraction of these figures.

In 1994, late blight, the fungal disease that caused the Irish potato famine in the 1840s, caused $100 million damage in the United States. The costs of attempting to suppress the late blight within the country equaled the direct losses. The majority of seed potatoes come from a single region, Europe, so the late blight developed into a worldwide problem, with outbreaks in the Middle East, South America, Asia, and Africa as well as Europe and North America. In 1997, the International Potato Center in Lima, Peru, estimated losses worldwide from late blight were about $3 billion annually. In 1995, growers in Washington and Oregon alone lost $30 million. In 1994, a single New York grower lost $1 million, despite extensive use of pesticides, as marketable yields fell by 80 percent.

One of the means employed to control the worldwide spread of pathogens is export controls. The World Trade Organization has "phytosanitary" rules that permit even a minor disease outbreak to compel the cessation of a crop's export. This can be seen in the example of the fruit flies in California, or in the case of karnal bunt in Arizona. In the latter example, a relatively mild but highly infectious pathogen was discovered in Arizona wheat. In one day, thirty-two countries banned U.S. wheat imports. It cost the United States hundreds of millions of dollars to eradicate the fungal pest and threatened the country's $5 billion of annual wheat exports.[50]

Differentiating between naturally occurring outbreaks of disease and those caused purposefully by subnational entities is extremely difficult and may be impossible if no group or individual comes forward to claim responsibility for the outbreak. Epidemiological evidence may suggest intentional spread of disease, for example, the appearance of a strain of disease not endemic to the region, or the occurrence of the disease at several nonproximal sites simultaneously. Even this type of information, however, may not be completely reliable. The outbreak of West Nile virus in the northeastern United States that began in September 1999 is such an example, being a naturally occurring outbreak of an exotic, non-indigenous, disease, never previously seen in the United States.[51] In addition, if it were discovered that a particular outbreak had been intentionally caused, would it be in the public's best interests to make that information widely available? Doing so could create panic and incidentally assist the goals of the perpetrator. Naturally occurring outbreaks continue to have economic impacts, but thus far, subnational attacks against agricultural targets have been limited in scope and sophistication. Technical obstacles to effective acquisition, maintenance, and delivery of microorganisms partially explain the limited scope of such attacks, but a more telling explanation is that there is little evidence that subnational groups are interested in this type of attack.

It is widely acknowledged that usable agricultural pathogens are likely to be more easily acquired than are their human equivalents. Dissemination of these agents may also be extremely straightforward, in some cases, such as that of some rusts or FMD, which supposedly require no more than swabbing an infected animal or crop and transferring the sample to a healthy animal or crop elsewhere. The theory holds that these highly infectious diseases would then spread naturally within their new host population. However, rigorous surveillance, quarantine, and eradication programs are likely to help curtail the spread of such diseases, and crop pathogens are generally vulnerable to environmental factors such as light, heat, and wind. Even with frequent transport of agricultural goods across the country, it is reasonable to hope that outbreaks initiated or spread by such methods might be contained within a region. In such circumstances, the attack need not be catastrophic. To achieve widespread effect in all but the most localized crops (such as almonds), multiple attacks would likely be necessary. Discussion of such an approach is beyond the scope of this paper, but it clearly increases the quantities of agent required and the likelihood of being apprehended.

Diversity of U.S. Agriculture

Part of the reason the United States has been able to avoid some of the most catastrophic consequences of agricultural pestilence has been the diversity of the national agricultural economy.[52] In 1997 the market value of agricultural products sold in the United States was more than $208 billion. Although some states clearly had disproportionate shares of the total, it was widely distributed across the states. California was the leading agricultural state, with products valued at $25.2 billion, or 12.1 percent of the U.S. total; Texas was second with $13.4 billion, followed by Iowa ($12.8 billion), Nebraska ($10 billion), and Illinois ($9 billion). The top five states accounted for 34 percent of the U.S. total. However, 27 states, spread across the country, had agricultural products valued at more than $3 billion; 20 states had more than $4 billion of business, and 9 had $6 billion.

A similarly diverse geographical pattern can be seen among individual agricultural products, particularly major crops and livestock. Of the leading states, measured by cash receipts in 1997, Texas produced about 16 percent of U.S. cattle and calves and about 22.5 percent of U.S. cotton; California about 17.2 percent of U.S. dairy products and 14.7 percent of the country's hay; Iowa about 18.5 percent of U.S. corn, 22.4 percent of the country's hogs, and 17.9 percent of its soybeans; Georgia about 16.1 percent of U.S. broilers; and Kansas about 16.8 percent of U.S. wheat. Clearly, although there are some regional concentrations, such as cattle and corn in the Midwest, the scale of production and geographical distances involved offer some level of protection against catastrophic attacks.

Some other crops are far more concentrated and thus potentially substantially more vulnerable to a major attack. Using 1997 cash receipts figures, within the United States, 92.2 percent of grapes, 47 percent of tomatoes, 33.8 percent of oranges, 77.8 percent of lettuce, 100 percent of almonds, and 75.5 percent of strawberries were grown in California; 41.3 percent of tobacco in North Carolina; 53.5 percent of apples in Washington; 38.9 percent of peanuts in Georgia; 43.3 percent of rice in Arkansas; and 65.7 percent of oranges in Florida.

Even within individual states, crops may be further concentrated, making them even more vulnerable to attack. Three adjacent counties in California—Fresno, Madera, and Tulare—produced 55.1 percent of all U.S. grapes in 1997. Another striking example is lettuce. California cultivated 77.8 percent of U.S. lettuce in 1997, and 57 percent of the national acreage for lettuce production was in six bordering counties in that state:

Santa Cruz, Monterey, San Benito, Fresno, San Luis Obispo, and Santa Barbara. Strawberry production provides another impressive illustration. A little over 41 percent of Californian strawberry production, which comprises over 75 percent of total U.S. production, was in two contiguous counties (Santa Cruz and Monterey), and another 33 percent of Californian production was in two nearby counties (Santa Barbara and Ventura).

In addition to these specific concentrations, it is important to note that a few counties spread over many square miles in the relatively compact San Joaquin Valley produce most of these crops. A disease that could affect several crops would have even greater impact on regional economies and aggregate production, thereby increasing the apparent vulnerability of certain sectors of the U.S. agricultural economy.

This geographical diversity of agriculture in the United States can be slightly misleading: although spread over several states, 70 percent of U.S. beef cattle is raised in an area with a 200 mile radius. Moreover, the concentration of animals on individual farms can also magnify the impact of an attack. Large poultry farms may have hundreds of thousands of birds; dairy herds can have thousands of cattle. Some animals, such as pigs and poultry, are often raised intensively and in close quarters. In such cases, even where a disease does not compel that an entire farm be slaughtered, the spread of the disease in such confined conditions may be rapid and extensive. Intensive farming, using large-scale and automated feeding, also increases the scope for attacks that use animal feed as the means of delivery. By contaminating the feed on such a farm, an attacker could legitimately hope to reach a high proportion of the animals.[53]

A similar phenomenon is observable in arable farming in the United States. It is common practice even for large farms to focus on one or two crops, rather than grow a range of different ones. It is therefore entirely possible to threaten thousands of acres of farmland with a single pathogen, because all the fields are planted with the same crop. In such circumstances, even effective surveillance might be a challenge: on large farms, production methods such as spraying and harvesting are highly automated, so it might be weeks before there is an appreciation of the problem. In the meantime, the pathogen may have been widely disseminated by the wind and by insect, bird, or animal vectors.[54] The danger is compounded by the dependence of U.S. agriculture on a few regions for seeds. The Idaho valley provides most of the seed in the country. This greatly increases the opportunities for contaminating seeds and causing a "sleeper" outbreak of disease, capable of blighting crops across the United States.

In summary, the U.S. agricultural sector, as a whole, appears to be sufficiently diverse and vast as to be invulnerable to a catastrophic subnational BW attack with a significant economic impact. That said, certain portions of the agricultural economy might nevertheless be concentrated or organized in such a way that a sophisticated attack could have significant economic consequences at the regional, state, or local level.

Conclusion

Although agriculture throughout the world, including within the United States, is extremely vulnerable to attack, because such an attack would be relatively easy to perpetrate, achieving widespread impact from such an attack would be significantly more difficult. In reality, however, there appear to have been relatively few such attacks worldwide that have even sought catastrophic consequences. Rather than seeking to eradicate a crop or type of animal or poultry from a country's agricultural economy, most attackers have focused on damaging consumer confidence. This has meant that such attacks have been much closer to examples of product tampering than to the devastating strikes that have been the focus of a growing number of government reports, academic articles, and newspaper columns. The economic impact of such attacks is, potentially, enormous: within the United States, agriculture is an industry worth hundreds of billions of dollars and, directly or indirectly, employing millions of people. The willingness and ability of an attacker to jeopardize more than a fraction of that however appears limited. Moreover, the size of the United States and the range of agriculture within the country make it likely that even a major attack would be highly damaging rather than crippling to the country's economy. In addition, although the relative ease of releasing of BW agents against agriculture compared to that of BW agents against human targets implies that BW attacks against agriculture could be quite effective, the potential ease of delivery may be offset by these limiting factors. Effective delivery would at the very least require a sophisticated, multi-pronged attack to achieve major effects, one capable also of overcoming the environmental barriers to effective dissemination.

Historically, most attacks against agriculture worldwide have been directed at consumer confidence and could more legitimately be described as credible threats than as genuine attacks. The number of actions directed against agriculture per se has been limited, and none appears to have occurred on the scale presently being envisaged. However, relatively little is known or understood about the threat of subnational BW agricultural attacks. Although the potential vulnerability to attack could be enormous and could have economically disastrous impacts on individual farms and possibly on specific segments of the agricultural economy, the agricultural economy as a whole, as well as the entire U.S. economy, are unlikely to be significantly affected. However, there is currently a gap between what has actually occurred in previous incidents and this perceived danger. Further research needs to be undertaken to ascertain whether there is a genuine danger and whether the terrorist threat has evolved to the point that terrorists now see agriculture as a worthwhile target. Alternatively, this perceived danger may simply be the latest example of vulnerability-driven, rather than intent-driven, threat assessments. In either case, it is important that more work be undertaken to ascertain the scope of the problem, and determine the best means of minimizing the danger.

Notes

1. Although Aum was not the first subnational group to use a chemical or biological agent, the group's acquisition and use of sarin and VX nerve agents, agents thought to be restricted to state-level CW [chemical weapons] programs, was unprecedented.
2. "The Threat of Biological Terrorism to U.S. Agriculture," U.S. Department of Agriculture, undated.
3. Statement by Floyd P. Horn, Administrator, Agricultural Research Service, U.S. Department of Agriculture, before the U.S. Senate Emerging Threats and Capabilities Subcommittee of the Armed Services Committee, October 27, 1999, p. 5.
4. Ibid.
5. "Federal Funding to Combat Terrorism, Including Defense against Weapons of Mass Destruction FY 1998–2001," available at http://cns.miis.edu/research/cbw/terfund.htm.
6. Ibid.
7. Ibid.

8. Ibid.

9. Ibid.

10. Ibid.

11. David Ruppe, "Battle Over Plum Island," available at *ABCNews.com*, accessed January 20,2000.

12. Steve Goldstein, "'Agroterror' Fears Awake; U.S. Crops Seen as Vulnerable," *The Arizona Republic*, June 26, 2000, p. A12; and "Experts Warn of 'Agroterrorism' Threat," *Associated Press*, December 2, 1999.

13. "First Annual Report to the President and the Congress of the Advisory Panel to Assess Domestic Response Capabilities for Terrorism Involving Weapons of Mass Destruction, 1: Assessing the Threat," December 15, 1999, p. 12, available at http://www.rand.org/organization/nsrd/terrpanel/ and accessed on June 23, 2000.

14. Statement by Floyd P. Horn before the Emerging Threats and Capabilities Subcommittee, October 27, 1999, p. 3.

15. The Monterey Institute WMD Terrorism Database is an open-source collection of incidents involving subnational actors and chemical, biological, radiological, and nuclear materials, 1900 to the present. The Database is available by subscription to qualifying organizations. For more information, contact Jason Pate at jpate@miis.edu.

16. Seth Carus, "Bioterrorism and Biocrimes: The Illicit Use of Biological Agents in the 20th Century," National Defense University, Washington D.C., Working paper, August 1998 (March 1999 revision), p. 73.

17. "Poison Is Suspected in Death of 30 Cows On a Muslim Farm," *New York Times*, March 16, 1970, p. 30. James Wooton, "Black Muslims Would Sell Farm to Klan," *New York Times*, March 17, 1970, p. 32. "Wallace Seeking More Policemen," *New York Times*, December 12, 1971, p. 50.

18. Joseph Douglass Jr. and Neil C. Livingstone, *America the Vulnerable: The Threat of Chemical and Biological Warfare* (Lexington, Mass: Lexington Books, 1987) cited in Ron Purver, "Chemical and Biological Terrorism: The Threat According to the Open Literature," (Canadian Security Intelligence Service, unclassified, June 1995), pp. 87–8. Yonah Alexander, "Will Terrorists Use Chemical Weapons?" *JINSA Security Affairs* (June-July, 1990), p. 10 cited in Purver, "Chemical and Biological Terrorism," pp. 87–8.

19. "Counterfeit stamps put on diseased eggs," *Ha'Aretz*, May 23, 2000, available on http://www3.haaretz.co.it/eng/scripts/print.asp?id=78775, accessed on June 23, 2000. "Warnings of contaminated eggs being sold with official stamp," *Israel Wire*, May 26, 2000, available on http://www.israelwire.com/new/00526/00052626.html, accessed on June 23, 2000. "Woman dies from salmonella", *Israel Wire*, September 13, 1999, available at http://www.israelwire.com/New/990913/99091328.html, accessed on June 23, 2000.

20. The RAND-St. Andrews Terrorism Chronology: Chemical/Biological Incidents, 1968–1995, RAND Corporation, Santa Monica, CA.

21. Ibid.

22. Ibid.

23. Shabatai Zvi, "Israeli Settlers Destroy 17,000 Tons of Grapes," *Al-Ayyam*, October 23, 1997, available at http://www.hebron.com/article04-10-23-97.html, accessed on February 17, 2000.

24. "Settlers pump sewerage water into Palestinian groves," *Palestine Information Network*, June 21, 2000, available at http://www.palestine-info.net/daily_news/index.htm, accessed on June 21, 2000. Also available at *Palestine Times*, http://www.ptimes.com/current/news.html, accessed on July 5, 2000.

25. RAND-St. Andrews Terrorism Chronology.

26. Carus, "Bioterrorism and Biocrimes."

27. Purver, "Chemical and Biological Terrorism," p. 35; Tony Duboudin, "Murderer in court over virus threat," *The Times*, February 22, 1984, p. 5; *Reuters*, December 5, 1984.

28. "The Poisoned World—1998," University Sains Malaysia (1998), available at http://prn.U.S.m.my/diary/test298.html, accessed March 29, 1999.

29. Gretchen Schuldt, "Man indicted on charges of tainting animal feed; Berlin plant contaminated with toxic pesticide in 1996," *Milwaukee Journal Sentinel*, September 15, 1999, p. 1. Richard P. Jones, "Product Recalled in Four States; Animal Feed Tainted in Act of Sabotage," *Milwaukee Journal Sentinel*, January 4, 1997, p. 1. "MDA Investigates Possible Feed Contamination," PR *Newswire*, January 6, 1997.

30. Purver, Ron."Chemical and Biological Terrorism: The Threat According to the Open Literature," June 1995. CSIS/SCRS. www.csis-scrs.gc.ca/eng/miscdocs/biblio_e.html.

31. Shyam Bhatla Naxos and Leonard Dayla, "Poison bomber offers secrets for sanctuary," *The Observer*, September 28, 1997, available at http://www.byegm.gov.tr, accessed on May 21, 1998.

32. Purver, Ron. (1995).

33. "Quebec's largest food distributor removes S. African fruit," *Reuters*, July 11, 1986. Michael Babad, "Threats halt sales of S. African fruit at Canadian stores, "*United Press International*," July 15, 1986. Michael Babad, "Canadian stores stop selling South African fruit," *United Press International*, July 16, 1986.

34. "Canadian Food Distributor Removes South African Fruit." 11 July 1986. Reuters North European.

35. "Rail car graffiti not linked to shadowy group (David Organization)," *Canadian Press Newswire*, November 7, 1994.

36. Emery, David. "The Great Banana Scare of 2000." 23 February 2000. http://urbanlegends. a...gends/library/weekly/aa022300a.htm

37. Emery, David. 23 February 2000.

38. "Banana Fits," Urban Legends Reference Pages: Toxin du jour (Banana Fits), available at http://www.snopes.com/toxins/bananas.htm, accessed on July 27, 2000. "False Internet Report About Bananas," National Center for Infectious Diseases, available at http://www.cdc.gov/ncidod/banana.htm, accessed on May 31, 2000. "E-mail at UC Riverside Helped Spread Hoax About Bananas," *Los Angeles Times*, February 16, 2000, p. A18.

39. John Johnson, "Female Medfly Found in Sun Valley Close to Area Targeted Earlier," *Los Angeles Times* January 4, 1990, p. B3. Ashley Dunn, "Officials Advertise to Contact Mystery Group Claiming Medfly Releases," *Los Angeles Times*, February 10, 1990, p. B3. Stephanie Chavez and Richard Simon, "Mystery Letter Puts a Strange Twist on Latest Medfly Crisis," *Los Angeles Times*, December 3, 1988, p. B1 (Orange County Edition).

40. "Foot and Mouth Outbreak: Special Report," *BBC News Online*, available at http://news.bbc.co.uk/hi/english/in_depth/uk/2001/foot_and_mouth/default.stm, accessed on May 14, 2001.

41. "Foot-and-mouth disease: The cost and cures," Business News Special, *The Economist*, March 31, 2001, available at http://www.economist.com/printedition/displayStory.cfm?Story_ID=549904, accessed on April 2, 2001.

42. "Foot and Mouth Outbreak: Special Report," *BBC News Online*, available at http://news.bbc.co.uk/hi/english/in_depth/uk/2001/foot_and_mouth/default.stm, accessed on May 14, 2001.

43. "Foot-and-mouth disease: The costs and cures," Business News Special, *The Economist*, March 31, 2001, available at http://www.economist.com/printedition/displayStory.cfm?Story_ID=549904, accessed on April 2, 2001.

44. "After foot and mouth," *The Economist*, May 3, 2001, available at http://www.economist.com/printedition/displayStory.cfm?Story_ID=611386, accessed on May 14, 2001.

45. "Gross Domestic Product by Industry data," U.S. Bureau of Economic Analysis, available at http://www.bea.doc.gov/bea/dn2/gposhr.htm#1993-99, accessed on April 9, 2001.

46. "Comparative Civilian Labor Force Statistics, Ten Countries, 1959–2000," U.S. Bureau of Labor Statistics, available at http://www.bls.gov/flsdata.htm, accessed on April 9, 2001.

47. Roel Janssen, "Swine Fever strikes," *Europe*, No. 371, November 1997, p. 43.

48. Dick Leonard, "Scandals damage farmers' influence," *Europe*, No. 388, September 1999, p. 44. "Wrap-Up," *Chemical Week*, September 22, 1999, p. 24.

49. "California Agriculture," California Department of Farms and Agriculture, available at http://www.cdfa.ca.gov/statistics, accessed on April 12, 2001.

50. Deborah Mackenzie, "Run, Radish, Run," *New Scientist*, December 18, 1999, pp. 36–9.

51. Jennifer Steinhauer, "Outbreak of Virus in New York Much Broader Than Suspected," *New York Times*, September 28, 1999, p. A1.
52. The information in this section was obtained from http://www.usda.gov and e-mail exchanges with Jim Tippett, State Statistician for the California Department of Agriculture.
53. Corrie Brown, "Agricultural terrorism: A cause for concern," *The Monitor*, Vol. 5, Nos. 1–2, pp. 6–8.
54. Mackenzie, "Run, Radish, Run," pp. 36–9.

6.4   G. Davidson (Tim) Smith, 1998

Single Issue Terrorism

G. Davidson (Tim) Smith is a counterterrorism specialist with the Canadian Security Intelligence Service.

Definition

The term "Single Issue Terrorism" is broadly accepted as extremist militancy on the part of groups or individuals protesting a perceived grievance or wrong usually attributed to governmental action or inaction.[1] Generally three principal issues are regarded to fall under that definition: animal rights, environmentalism, and abortion. This paper addresses those issues, with the focus on activities in the United States, Canada, and the United Kingdom.

Overview

Legitimate and traditionally moderate organizations such as animal welfare societies have for years achieved notable results on behalf of the causes for which they lobby. But, over the past two decades, some of the more popular issues have attracted radical elements that now form an extremist militant core prepared to resorts to threats, violence and destruction of property to achieve their ends. In the case of the abortion issue, this has included murder.

For the most part, legitimate organizations disown the violent fringe. Some, however—notably in the context of the environmental and abortion issues—actively support the militants, or do so tacitly to condemn extremist activities. At least one "legitimate" activist condoned a sniper's wounding of a prominent Vancouver gynæcologist in November 1994, calling the incident "good shooting" and musing that it would not have happened had the doctor not been performing abortions.[2]

There is no archetypal single issue extremist, but some broad characteristics apply. Animal rights activists, environmentalists and abortionists tend to be on the left, politically. The founder of the Animal Liberation Front (ALF) in the UK, for example, is a self-confessed anarchist, as is a senior member of a similar group in Canada. The pro-life side of the abortion debate is drawn largely from the right. The abortion issue, however, is complicated by a religious dimension foreign to the animal rights and environmental questions and draws adherents on both sides from across the political spectrum. Extremists associated with any of these issues come from all walks of life and social levels. For a time, participation in civil disobedience and militancy in support of animal rights campaigns was regarded by many young Britons as an exciting and trendy diversion. A large number of animal rights supporters and environmental extremists can be found among idealistic and impatient university students who have become frustrated with the seemingly slow progress of moderate groups and who seek to achieve their goals more rapidly by direct action.

Although functioning essentially domestically, single issue groups are international in scope. Animal rights supporters claim to be active in more than 40 countries and militant environmentalists have carried out actions in a number of different regions. Both movements publish newsletters—*Arkangel* is the British-based organ of animal-rights supporters and *Earth First!* is the journal of the radical environment movement. Each contains a range of information that includes descriptions of recent actions, techniques for conducting mischief, vandalism and sabotage, the addresses of targets—doctors, scientists, research laboratories—and news about incarcerated activists. All three movements use the Internet for publicity and communications purposes. *The Militant Vegan*, for example, lists Animal Liberation actions in Canada and the United States, with names and locations of targets attacked and tactics employed—all useful for statistical purposes.

A degree of communication takes place among extremist groups within individual issues—not surprising, given the availability of the Net. There are some similarities in terms of group names and operations, such as the Animal Liberation Fronts in Britain and North America, but close linkages among groups are not obvious. Nevertheless, cooperation, affiliation and interlocking memberships do occur. Animal rights supporters and Earth First! activists are known to have integrated working relationships in Canada and the United States.

A number of animal rights extremists are simultaneously members of several different organizations and movements (e.g. Vegans, Feminists, Ecologists) and often pursue their own ideals under the guise of supporting popular causes or legitimate organizations. On one occasion, the Toronto Humane Society was "captured" by a stacked proxy vote, enabling large amounts of money and other resources subsequently to be funnelled to militants.

The extremist fringe of each movement has published some form of handbook or provides Internet instructions on how to engage in mischief, civil disobedience, vandalism, and sabotage—*ecotage* as it is known in Enviro-speak. Some of the suggestions are extremely dangerous, among them potentially lethal methods of tree-spiking which have caused serious injuries. The instructions, often resembling those found in *The Anarchist's Cookbook*, include bomb-making details.

Though the level and scale of single issue-driven terrorism have moderated somewhat over the past two years, certainly in comparison with the turbulent days of the 1980s and early 1990s, the threat has not lessened. Extremist incidents continue to occur, especially associated with animal rights and environmentalism in England and Canada. Currently, abortion remains a volatile issue in the United States, where the first fatal bombing at an abortion clinic occurred on 29 January 1998 in Birmingham,

Alabama. The USA has already registered five murders tied to the abortion issue. In Canada, abortion activists are using the tenth anniversary of the Supreme Court decision lifting Canada's legal restrictions on the practice to focus popular and legislative attention on what is seen as flagging enthusiasm for abortion within the medical profession, although in fact the number of abortions has increased significantly in the past ten years.

Animal Rights

It is necessary to distinguish *animal rights* groups, who insist animals are on a par with humans and should be at liberty, from the traditional *animal welfarists*, who believe humans can use animals provided they treat them compassionately. Most animal rights activists do not advocate the use of violence but are not hesitant about resorting to civil disobedience as a means of gaining attention. The movement's extremist fringe believes that economic sabotage is a valid means to achieve its goal of protecting animals from any harm by humans. To this end, activists use a variety of tactics to inflict economic loss designed to put targeted "offenders" out of business. They have achieved some success. Prohibitive insurance rates, expensive security infrastructure, damaged buildings and equipment, loss of revenue, negative publicity, and destruction of research records representing years of work have forced the closure of many small businesses as well as scientific and commercial research facilities. Activists have boasted they could cause at least $60,000 damage in one week just by smashing windows.[3]

Probably the best-known extremist group in Europe and North America is the Animal Liberation Front (ALF), founded by Ronnie Lee in England in 1976 and still very active. The ALF appeared in Canada in 1981, with a series of break-ins at several university and medical laboratories involving vandalism, arson, and the release of animals; this was followed by attacks on fur stores and meat-packers. First recognized in the United States in 1982, the ALF made the FBI's domestic terrorism list in 1987 with a multimillion dollar arson at a veterinary lab in California. Similar incidents in Arizona and Texas in 1989 were also classified as domestic terrorism.[4]

Among other notable groups are the Hunt Retribution Squad (HRS), a particularly vicious group in Britain; the Animal Rights Militia (ARM), an offshoot of the British ALF, with namesakes in North America; and the relatively new Justice Department, which surfaced first in Britain and then in Canada. The Justice Department, although small, has been an especially dangerous organization, claiming responsibility for a number of letterbombs. An alleged support element for the ALF in the United States is a powerful Virginia-based lobby group, particularly adept at attracting prominent supporters and raising large sums of money, called People for the Ethical Treatment of Animals (PETA). PETA has frequently announced ALF actions, providing news releases almost immediately after events have occurred, indicating at least foreknowledge if not some complicity. PETA has established branches in Canada and Europe in recent years.[5]

Favoured Targets

Research laboratories associated with medical and veterinary schools and clinics, and those which test cosmetics and food products, are favoured targets—animals have been "liberated", hundreds of thousands of dollars worth of equipment and records destroyed, and researchers besieged by graffiti and hate mail. Activists in the UK have distributed derogatory leaflets at the school attended by children of a scientist. In Canada, the home of a scientist was vandalized to commemorate World Day for Lab Animals. Other targets include butcher shops, fish markets, meat packing plants, chicken and egg producers, dog kennels, mink and fox farms, furriers, and even fast-food outlets.

Tactics

Vandalism is the preferred tactic—graffiti spray-painted on buildings, glue poured in door-locks, windows etched with acid or smashed, frequently using slingshot and ball-bearings. Attacks can frequently go beyond that stage—vehicles have been stolen, damaged or burned, tires slashed and fur-bearing animals set free—several thousand expensive mink were released from farms in Western Canada in 1996.[6]

Another effective tactic with costly results has been the threat of product contamination—targeting meat shops, drugstores, supermarkets or department stores. The ALF in Great Britain initiated the practice in 1984, forcing the closure of a butcher shop because of a threat of contaminated meat. Other costly contamination threats have involved shampoo, candy bars and soft drinks; threats of poisoned turkeys at Christmas time have forced the removal of literally millions of items from stores.[7]

Similar incidents have occurred in Canada in the name of the Animal Rights Militia. Tens of thousands of Cold Buster candy bars were recalled in 1992 after claims they had been contaminated with oven cleaner.[8] Just before Christmas in 1994, over $1 million damage resulted from the threat of poisoned turkeys in Vancouver.[9]

The activists' tactical repertoire also includes incendiary techniques and mail bombs. It was a string of firebombs in department stores in England that lead to the arrest of ALF leaders in 1987.[10] During the Christmas rush of 1993, the ALF placed nine firebombs in four Chicago department stores.[11] A series of letterbombs in Britain in 1994, responsibility for which was claimed by the group known as the Justice Department, injured four persons.[12] The following year, a letterbomb was sent to the British Minister of Agriculture, while in Canada a group known as the Militant Direct Action Task Force (MDATF) directed four letterbombs to two white supremacists, a right-wing think-tank which supports the fur industry, and a genetics laboratory.[13]

In 1989, explosive devices were attached to the automobiles of a British veterinary surgeon and a university researcher. The vet barely escaped from her burning car; the researcher was saved when the bomb fell off his car, but a baby in a nearby carriage was injured.[14]

A recent variation of the mailbomb technique, claimed by Britain's Justice Department, featured razor blades allegedly dipped in rat poison or AIDS-infected blood, one of which was mailed to Prince Charles. Similar letters appeared in British Columbia, claimed by a Canadian group using the same name[15] and incorporating a diabolical feature: the return address was that of another targeted individual, thus ensuring that if the original recipient refused to accept the letter and returned it to the alleged sender, another animal rights target would be put at risk.

Professionalism is a hallmark of many extremist groups such as the ALF. They are often organized on a cell structure and thus difficult to identify and penetrate, and their security is relatively good, if rudimentary—for instance, members are dissuaded from using telephone communications to avoid tracing and toll information. Activists carefully research each target, often spending days or months photographing and conducting surveillance on the target facility and staff members, lying in perimeter bushes overnight to establish the routines of security patrols. If possible, activists will sign up for a tour of a target facility, recruit inside help or obtain employment in an attempt to gain information and bypass security alarms. Their dress and actions during raids are intended to intimidate—hoods and camouflage jackets, coveralls, breaking and entering in a violent manner using pickaxe handles and other hazardous tools. They make efforts to destroy research material and to gather intelligence on suppliers or supporters of a research facility for purposes of follow-on targeting. Attacks have occasionally been video-taped to assist in obtaining media coverage or to use in conjunction with subsequent threats. They emphasize making every attack count in the knowledge that improved security arrangements will likely follow.

Terror itself is the chief tactic of the animal rights activists. They use violence with the expressed intent of coercing government to act in a certain manner—to enact particular legislation. Their terrorist methodology is to engender fear by threats of poisoned candy or other consumer goods, by obnoxious graffiti, by abusive and threatening telephone calls, by the mailing of letter bombs, and by the destruction of property.

The Environmental and Abortion issues are no less significant in terms of threat.

Environmentalists

As many as 2,000 moderate or extremist environmental organizations are estimated to be active in Canada alone. The radical environmental movement comprises a broad spectrum of groups and individuals involved in diverse extremist variations of the environmental issue. While resource exploitation and hydro-electric development are their most frequent targets, activists also oppose the nuclear power industry, chemical manufacturers, industrial polluters, urban sprawl, encroaching (sub)urban development of agricultural lands, and other aspects of the modern industrial state.

Animal rights and anarchist groups have made common cause with environmental extremists and in some cases alliances have been formed with native groups. The latter arrangements have not always been popular, however, especially in regard to fishing and hunting issues. Individuals who support extremist philosophies within the environmental movement, while small in number, have demonstrated the willingness and capability to use violence. The most prominent group is Earth First!, whose followers have consistently advocated and employed sabotage as a tactic to defend the environment.

Formed in 1980, Earth First! began to employ violence in 1984 with the introduction of tree spiking, a dangerous practice hazardous both to loggers using chain-saws and at mills where the spikes can cause saw blades literally to explode, as occurred in 1987 when a millworker was seriously injured. In 1985, one of the founders of Earth First!, Dave Foreman, wrote the *ecotage* manual: *A Field Guide to Monkeywrenching*, which details many of the movement's sabotage techniques including tree-spiking.[16] Another *ecotage* volume, entitled *A Declaration of War*, which appeared in North America in 1994, advocated violence, including homicide, against farms, animal research facilities, logging companies and hunters to stop animal and environmental abuses.

Greenpeace is generally credited with being the first environmental group to employ "direct action" in pursuit of its aims. But, impatient with what he considered the slow pace of progress, one of the organization's founders, Canadian Paul Watson, formed the Sea Shepherd Conservation Society, with its off-shoot, Orcaforce. Watson and his supporters have been involved in a number of militant actions against whale hunting, driftnet fishing, seal hunting and other related issues. Recently he undertook activities against logging operations in Canada.

Extremist activity has been more prevalent in Canada of late than in the USA or the UK, although the latter has been the scene of growing activism since the holding of the Earth First! summer gathering in Wales in 1996. Scotland Yard's Special Branch made eco-terrorists a security priority in 1995, partly because of concern that ecological activists resisting new road-building schemes were turning to the violent tactics of the ALF.[17] Some construction workers have been injured by trip-wired booby traps, while others have been shot at with crossbows or have encountered Viet Cong-style man-traps filled with *pungee* stakes; equipment has been damaged or subjected to arson. One "eco-terror" magazine published detailed plans on how to build mortars, firebombs and grenades, and urged the use of buried explosives against the police.[18]

The FBI attributed an act of domestic terrorism to the ecological movement first in 1987, then again in 1988, in 1989, and in 1990. The 1980s incidents, which involved damage to power poles and ski lift equipment in Arizona and the planned destruction of power lines leading to nuclear facilities in Arizona, Colorado and California, were attributed to the Evan Mecham Eco-Terrorist International Conspiracy (EMETIC), although Dave Foreman of Earth First! was among those arrested. The 1990 incident—the downing of power lines in Santa Cruz county, California—was claimed by the Earth Night Action Group.[19]

Moderate environmentalists are active across Canada, but extremists have tended to congregate on the West Coast where the full spectrum of activism has become increasingly militant. Extremists believe direct action is required to disrupt operations or projects that pose an immediate threat to the environment. Fundamental to the philosophy of direct action as espoused by extremists, particularly those of Earth First!, is the determination to do whatever is necessary to disrupt, not merely oppose, any activity they consider detrimental to the environment.

While the broader objective of the militant environmentalists is to draw attention to and sway legislation on behalf of environmental protection, acts of sabotage have a two-fold purpose: to prevent or delay activities, such as logging, from going ahead by destroying equipment and infrastructure, and, akin to animal rights' tactics, to force companies to reconsider their operations. Repeated repairs to damaged equipment, production delays, higher insurance premiums, increased security requirements, unfavourable publicity, all contribute to a company's cost of doing business. In 1995, a logging bridge worth over $2 million was destroyed by fire in British Columbia,[20] while in November a blast at an Alberta logging facility destroyed equipment valued at $5 million.

There are close links between Earth First! in Canada and the United States. Most of the group's actions have been associated with logging operations and have involved destruction of equipment as well as tree spiking. In cross-over actions with animal rights activity, taxidermy shops and hunting outfitters in Western Canada have been subjected to arson attacks and threatening letters, including the razor-blade variety, claimed variously by the Justice Department and a group calling itself The Earth Liberation Army.[21] On another occasion, in the name of The David Organization, supposedly noxious chemicals were spilled in government offices and the head office of a logging company.[22]

Environmental militancy has declined somewhat, in part due to the success of the lobby's efforts. But logging operations on the West coasts of Canada and the United States, especially clear-cutting, combined with growing fishing and hunting controversies on both Canada's East and West coasts, will provide motivation for continued extremist response by environmental and animal rights activists and could lead to serious confrontation between them and those who believe their livelihood is being adversely affected.

The Abortion Issue

The abortion issue is an emotional one, particularly in relation to the pro-life movement and, as a result, the agenda is sometimes captured by extremists. Currently, the fact that some of the more extreme right-wing groups include pro-life declarations in their rhetoric has raised serious concerns.

Most people who oppose abortion do so lawfully, consistent with their pro-life philosophy. Some, however, test the limits of freedom of expression and commit criminal acts in support of their cause. According to the National Abortion Foundation, material damages associated with 42 incidents of vandalism and arson at abortion clinics in the United States during 1996–97 totalled over $1 million.[23]

The incidence of violence is seen to be largely on the part of the fringe element of the pro-lifers, perhaps a result of frustration with unfavourable legislation. But religious connotations cannot be ignored. A worrisome development is the appearance of a fundamentalist anti-abortion handbook, *The Army of God*, which gives detailed instructions on the sabotage of clinics, silencers for guns and C4 explosive, and states, inter alia, "... we are forced to take aim against you... execution is rarely gentle."[24]

Violence against abortionists has largely been confined to the United States and Canada. An attempt by a North American pro-life group to establish a branch in Britain in 1993 was thwarted when the government had the group's representative deported for being "a threat to the public good." In 1988, the Supreme Court of Canada struck down the law restricting the legal availability of abortions in Canada. Since then, the number of abortions sought by Canadian women has grown significantly and the vehemence of pro-life protestors has increased. Many pro-choice activists say they fear an escalation of violence such as the United States has experienced.

The fears may be well-founded—since 1993, five people have been killed, with 11 more persons wounded. Clinics have been subjected to graffiti, noxious gases, and firebombs and staff has been threatened and harassed. Similar events have begun to occur in Canada: sniper incidents in 1994, 1995 and again in 1997 have wounded three Canadian doctors; a clinic was burned and workers here, as in the USA, have increasingly been subjected to threats and harassment.[25]

Although the pro-life movement in Canada is generally poorly organized, it does include several large groups and some prominent individuals with links to the movement in the United States. US activists have addressed rallies in Canada and encouraged

Canadians to adopt aggressive practices. The author of a pro-life publication, recognized and respected in extremist circles, has participated in demonstrations and picketing of clinics and doctors' homes in Canada.

American sociologist Dallas Blanchard has observed that some members of the Canadian pro-life movement whom he has encountered are as capable of violence as US extremists and that the pattern of activity in Canada is similar to that in the United States. An article in the May 1996 edition of *Chatelaine* magazine depicts the current status of the abortion debate in Canada as a battlefield where the fear of violence rules. The atmosphere in clinics resembles a state of siege, with steel bars, security cameras, intercom systems, bomb threats and workers trained in life-saving techniques as well.

The issue will not go away. The potential for continued violence exists. Indeed, the number of abortions sought by Canadian women has grown significantly since the Supreme Court decision of 1988. The vehemence of pro-life protestors has increased and so may their potential for violence if their level of frustration continues to grow, which it may do in the event of unfavourable legislation or legal judgements or the introduction of abortion drugs. In Canada, changes to government funding of abortions may encourage pro-life activists to indulge in more militant activity.

Conclusion

In conclusion, three observations deserve note:

- single issue militancy remains dangerous, despite lower levels of activity during the past two years; each of the issues discussed remains controversial and will continue to attract individuals ready to use extremist tactics for selfish or believed-to-be-altruistic reasons; many of those individuals are highly competent and capable of making effective use of modern technology to devise extremely dangerous devices;
- there are real concerns about the risks of escalation from vandalism to arson to bombs and ever more spectacular incidents; of copy-cat actions by inept individuals which could seriously endanger lives; and of vigilantism, which could create extraordinary problems for law enforcement and criminal justice systems;
- the challenge is to provide an appropriate, reasoned and reasonable response to the threat of single issue terrorism which avoids overreaction and remains within the rule of law.

Notes

1. G. Davidson Smith, *Combating Terrorism*, London, Routledge, 1990, p. 7.
2. *Chatelaine*, May 1996.
3. G. Davidson Smith, *Militant Activism and the Issue of Animal Rights, Commentary* No. 21, CSIS, April 1992.
4. *Terrorism in the United States*, US Department of Justice, Federal Bureau of Investigation, 1989.
5. Susan E. Paris, *Animal Rights Terrorism Must Be Stopped, Mass High Tech*, August 1995.
6. Robin Brunet, *The Cutting Edge of Animal Rights, Alberta Report*, Vol. 23, No. 8, 5 February 1996.
7. G. Davidson Smith, *Political Violence in Animal Liberation, Contemporary Review*, Vol. 247, No. 1434, July 1985.

8. Smith, *Commentary*, CSIS, April 1992.
9. *The Militant Vegan*, Issue 8, 8 February 1995, Internet.
10. Smith, *Commentary*, April 1992.
11. *Chicago Sun-Times*, 1 December 1983.
12. *Independent*, 2 June 1994. See also: *PinkertonRisk*, 24 August 1995.
13. *Toronto Star*, 14 July 1995.
14. *Chicago Tribune*, 6 August 1991.
15. *Victoria Times Colonist*, 13 January 1996.
16. Egan, *From Spikes…* pp. 6–8.
17. *Independent*, 29 December 1994.
18. *The Times* of London, 11 September 1994.
19. *Terrorism in the United States*, US Department of Justice, FBI, 1990.
20. *The Vancouver Sun*, 21 October 1991.
21. *Globe and Mail*, Toronto, 12 July 1995. See also: *Victoria Times Colonist*, 13 January 1996.
22. *Vancouver Province*, 17 October 1994.
23. Summary of Extreme Violence Against Abortion Providers in 1994, 1995, *National Abortion Federation*, Internet.
24. *Chatelaine*, May 1996. See also: *Washington Post*, 17 January 1995.
25. *Toronto Sun*, 17 January 1995. See also: *The Abortion Rights Activist*, Internet.

Part 2

Countering the Terrorist Threat

Chapter 7

The Challenges of Terrorism

Terrorist actions pose some very dramatic and extraordinary challenges to a state and to its code of conduct.

After the September 11 attacks, writes Laura K. Donohue, "In the public realm, Congress became consumed by terrorist measures." Donohue carefully charts the rapid succession of actions taken by the government after 9-11 and explores what she calls the "counterterrorist spiral," a phenomenon common to liberal, democratic states, that captured the nation in the aftermath of the attacks. Donohue not only presents a detailed diary of measures taken, she explores the theory of why actions were taken and, on a deeper level, what the ramifications are for a liberal, democratic state faced with the challenge of balancing the delicate tension between keeping its citizens and their property secure while also preserving the premise of civil liberties. "The difficulty was that while these provisions sought to ensure greater security for Americans," said Donohue, "many of them made serious inroads into the individual rights of both citizens and noncitizens. The consequences are borne not just in the domestic realm, but in U.S. foreign relations."

At a time when a nation is under threat of terrorist actions, intelligence gathering is key. Bruce Hoffman looks at the nasty, brutish business of gathering intelligence about an enigmatic enemy who operates in unconventional ways. The struggles against Osama bin Laden and his minions will rely on good intelligence, writes Hoffman, "But the experiences of other countries, fighting similar conflicts against similar enemies, suggest that Americans still do not appreciate the enormously difficult—and morally complex—problem that the imperative to gather 'good intelligence' entails." Hoffman cites scenarios—both fictional and real—about those who have been responsible for information gathering in times of crises and the unsavory but perhaps necessary measures they have taken. They act in times when extraordinary circumstances require extraordinary measures and must operate under the premise that the innocent have more rights than the guilty. Hoffman quotes a fictional character who faces such a dilemma: "To succumb to humane considerations," the character concludes, "only leads to hopeless chaos.

In conventional international conflict, there is a code of behavior. But—as international law expert Anthony Clark Arend points out—the activities of terrorist groups muddy the waters dramatically on how this "just war"

273

theory is to be applied. "Today, the vast corpus of just war writings deals with questions about the permissibility of the recourse to force *by states* (the principles of *ius ad bellum*) and the conduct of hostilities *by states* (the principles of *ius in bello*)," writes Arend. Since World War II many nonstate actors have appeared on the international stage; how should these standards apply in conflicts with nonstate actors? For example, an element of the theory of discrimination is that innocent civilians are not to be attacked or targeted. In conventional warfare, military personnel are clearly identifiable: terrorists are not. They are—in fact—civilians (albeit not innocent citizens). States have diplomatic channels to pursue peaceful settlement and nonviolent sanctions before resorting to the actions of war; yet terrorist groups do not have the same formal systems of communication for resolving differences. Arend examines a range of issues in just war theory and offers recommendations to preserve the theory of just war while responding to the challenges of terrorism.

Brad Roberts examines the dilemma states face in dealing with rogue nations that flout agreed norms of state behavior; that threaten to use force against those who resist their ambitions; and who seek to acquire means of mass destruction—nuclear, biological, or chemical (NBC) weapons. In dealing with these rogue states, when is a preemptive strike justified? "Given what is now known about Iraq's pre-war unconventional-weapons programs... it is clear that in just a few additional months of sanctions aimed at pressuring Saddam Hussein to withdraw his army from Kuwait, Iraq's nuclear program would have produced one or two weapons while its biological program could have geared up to a very substantial level of production and weaponization," writes Roberts. The author explains the crucial timing in a preemptive strike situation, yet he explores the act of a strike in the context of the just war tradition and outlines specific conditions that would produce a strong moral case for a U.S. preemption, as well as conditions for a weak case. As Roberts concludes, "there is a moral case for a preemption, but it is not quite as tidy as policy-makers might desire."

Fear Itself
Counterterrorism, Individual Rights, and U.S. Foreign Relations Post 9-11*

Laura K. Donohue is a visiting fellow at Stanford University's Center for International Security and Cooperation and an acting assistant professor in political science. Her
research focuses on terrorism and counterterrorism in the United States, the United
Kingdom, the Republic of Ireland, Israel, South Africa, Turkey, and elsewhere. She
is author of *Regulating Violence: Emergency Powers and Counter-Terrorist Law in the
United Kingdom 1922–2000*.

"The only thing we have to fear is fear itself—nameless, unreasoning, unjustified
terror which paralyzes needed efforts to convert retreat into advance."

—Franklin D. Roosevelt, first inaugural address, 1933

So often has it already been asserted that it is almost cliché to state that September
11th shattered Americans' sense of security within the United States. Despite calls to return to "business as usual," by January 2002 the United States had not. The fear that
choked the nation dominated the public—and for many, the private—discourse.

In the public realm, Congress became consumed by terrorist measures. Between
September 11, 2001, and January 11, 2002, ninety-eight per cent of the official business
conducted by the House of Representatives and 97 per cent of [that in] the Senate related to terrorism.[1] Congress proposed more than 450 counterterrorist resolutions,
bills, and amendments. (This compared with approximately 1,300 total in the course of
U.S. history.) Within four months of the attacks, more than two dozen new measures
became law. President Bush issued 12 Executive Orders and 10 Presidential Proclamations related to the attacks. Only a handful addressed the war in Afghanistan. Most dealt
with the domestic realm, the consequences of September 11, and the United States' preparedness for future terrorist attack. The difficulty with many of these measures was
that, while they sought to ensure greater security for Americans, they made serious inroads into individual rights. The consequences are borne not just in the domestic realm,
but in U.S. foreign relations.

---

*Portions of this chapter were published as part of the review of military tribunals in, "Bias, National Security,
and Military Tribunals," *Criminology and Public Policy* (July 2002).

This chapter does three things. First, it looks at characteristics of liberal, democratic states and terrorist challenge that led to what can be termed a "counterterrorist spiral"—one in which the United States became caught in the aftermath of the attacks. Second, the chapter briefly considers the breadth of measures proposed in Washington. Third, it considers four provisions that directly impact individual rights and threaten the domestic realm and American relations with other states: widespread detention and questioning, military tribunals, and capital punishment. It examines the arguments for and against these provisions. The paper concludes with a brief discussion of trends emerging in the Bush Administration's handling of the current threat and the effect of this on the domestic and international realm. The central argument is this: while the pressures that assaulted the Administration derive from the interplay between terrorism and liberal democracy, the substantive form of the response raises long-term concerns. In its exposition of the arguments, the paper draws on the United States's past use of counterterrorist measures, and lessons gleaned from the United Kingdom and the Republic of Ireland, two other liberal, democratic states, in their battles with terrorism throughout the 20th and early 21st centuries.[2]

I. The Counterterrorist Spiral

The most basic obligation borne by a liberal, democratic state is to protect the life and property of the citizens. Significant acts of political terrorism levied within this context have two effects. First, they attack the root of liberal states' authority: the state's ability to protect the citizens is called into question. Second, they question the current government's ability to uphold its compact to exercise state powers in a manner that upholds its most fundamental responsibility.

As a result, the government must not just respond, but it must be *seen* to respond. And not just to terrorism in general, but to each significant attack. Following the 1974 Birmingham bombings, for example, Westminster introduced the Prevention of Terrorism (Temporary Provisions) Act. After the August 15, 1998 Real IRA [Irish Republican Army] bombing in Omagh, Northern Ireland, the United Kingdom adopted the Criminal Justice (Terrorism and Conspiracy) Act and the Republic of Ireland introduced the 1999 Criminal Justice Act.[3] Following the 1995 attack by Timothy McVeigh on the Murrah Federal Building in Oklahoma City, the United States' Congress adopted the 1996 Antiterrorism and Effective Death Penalty Act. And within weeks of September 11th, America witnessed, amongst other provisions, the adoption of PL 107-56, the "United and Strengthening America by Providing Appropriate Tools Required to Intercept and Obstruct Terrorism (USA PATRIOT) Act of 2001."

Before the September 11th attacks, there was already a heightened state of concern in the United States about the prospect of political violence within American bounds. To some extent this related to previous attacks on United States' embassies and military in Kenya, Tanzania, Yemen, and the Middle East. It reflected prior domestic attacks. And it underscored concern at the activities of groups that no longer wanted, as Brian Jenkins famously remarked in the 1970s, "A lot of people watching, not a lot of people dead"—but both a lot of people dead and a lot of people watching.[4] The concern arose not just from the threats posed, but the increasing capabilities of actors to harness advances in technology for destructive ends.

There were numerous indicators of this already heightened concern: for example, the crash of TWA 800 off of Long Island, New York, on July 17, 1996, was immediately viewed as a terrorist attack. Although an inquiry later determined that it was an accident, in the interim the White House Commission on Aviation Security, formed in response to the crash, proposed thirty recommendations to counter possible terrorist attacks on U.S. aircraft. The money trail was similarly telling: between 1994 and 2000 the U.S. doubled its annual expenditures on terrorism, bringing the total to more than $10 billion, with $11.3 billion proposed for 2001.[5] From nothing earmarked specifically for domestic preparedness in 1995, in 1997 the total grew to $130 million, by 2000 topping $1.5 billion.[6] Between 1998 and 2000 the legislature held over 80 sessions on terrorism, involving a wide range of committees. In the Senate the Appropriations, Armed Services, Commerce, Science and Transportation, Environment and Public Works, Foreign Relations, Health, Education, Labor and Pensions, Judiciary Committee, and Select Committee on Intelligence all held hearings. In the House the Armed Security, Commerce, Government Reform, Intelligence, International Relations, Judiciary, Science, Transportation and Infrastructure, and Joint Economic Committee became engaged in the issue.

The proliferation of interest in and concern about terrorism gets at the nature of the threat: sub-state terrorism is a multi-pronged attack. Individuals, groups, networks, and state proxies can adopt various modes of attack. Moreover, it is not a single threat from one particular individual, group, or state. The entities entrusted with the life and property of the citizens must respond. This results in a burgeoning effect in the breadth of measures introduced in response.

Legislative initiatives that cross the gamut often bear social consequences as they become incorporated into state security functions. In the United Kingdom, for example, between 1920 and 1922 political violence claimed 428 lives in Northern Ireland. The 1922 Civil Authorities (Special Powers) Act, introduced to quell the violence, empowered the Civil Authority to impose curfew, close premises, roads and transportation routes, detain and intern, and proscribe organizations. It gave the government the ability to censor newspapers and radio and to ban meetings, processions and gatherings, and the use of cars. The legislation altered the court system. It granted extensive powers of entry, search and seizure, and, in a Draconian catch-all phrase, empowered the Civil Authority "to take all such steps and issue all such orders as may be necessary for preserving the peace and maintaining order." This clause led to over one hundred new regulations, the substance of which ranged from preventing gatherings and processions to outlawing wearing an Easter Lily. The United States' past measures followed a similar path, with the substance ranging from international diplomatic and coercive measures to domestic criminal and non-criminal initiatives.[7]

In the immediate aftermath of an attack and over time the substance of these initiatives tends to become increasingly extreme. There is a relatively straightforward reason for this: with terrorism, there is a tendency to evoke a worst-case scenario. Such acts are surrounded by incomplete information. They are stealthy operations involving not clearly identifiable enemies. More extreme measures are needed to counter more extreme possible threats. Further, the horror of the event creates outrage. The very use of the word signifies a moral opprobrium, a rejection of the actors, aims, and action itself. Resultantly, there is strong pressure on policy-makers to introduce measures with a message. During President Bush's address to Congress following the September 11th attacks, prior to any inquiry into what had happened that allowed such an attack to take place, there was extended applause for increasing the powers available to law enforcement and enhancing intelligence capabilities. At a state level the pressure increased substantially on those who had previously proposed or drafted counterterrorist measures to introduce further provisions. Often measures previously considered Draconian become easily swept through legislatures caught up in the emotion of the most recent attack. The roving wiretap provisions, for instance, rejected during Congressional consideration of the 1996 Anti-terrorism and Effective Death Penalty bill, quickly became incorporated into the USA PATRIOT bill.

With the tide of public sentiment driving concern in the elected chambers, pressure increases to support whatever measures are introduced. If you are against counterterrorist provisions, you are seen somehow as for terrorism. Between 1972 and 2000 this was a frequent charge in Westminster and preventing parties from actively voting against counterterrorist measures during the final reading. In the United States, following September 11th, President Bush boldly asserted in Congress, "Either you are for us, or you are for the terrorists." (And who could be against the "USA PATRIOT" Act?)

Following a significant terrorist attack, a liberal, democratic government, forced to respond and yet also forced to balance the tension between liberal democracy and the possible security threat faced by the state and the population, will often introduce "temporary" counterterrorist measures. The difficulty with this is that in the face of terrorism, it can be extremely difficult to repeal temporary provisions. To withdraw them in the future may require the conclusion either that a level of violence commensurate with the recent, devastating acts is acceptable, or that terrorism is no longer a threat. The former is politically untenable—and, in light of the massive, September 11th attacks—unfathomable, and the second impossible to prove. Terrorism, in a liberal state, is always possible. As destructive technology develops, it will become increasingly difficult to repeal measures that were introduced to meet the exigencies of a less extreme situation. Moreover, many of the measures work. They are effective. And so security forces become reluctant to relinquish them. Often they seep into ordinary criminal usage, becoming more deeply entrenched in the security forces' response to threats. The measures become a baseline on which future measures become built, leading to a steady ratcheting effect wherein provisions simply expand.

The Bush Administration's handling of the "War on Terrorism" September 11–January 11 follows patterns common to liberal, democratic states. The concern raised is that some of the measures, while there are some strong arguments for them, bear serious consequences for the domestic realm and the United States' relations with other states.

II. Response to September 11, 2001

The United States immediately responded to the attacks on the Pentagon and the World Trade Center and the crash of United Flight 93 in Pennsylvania with a wide range of emergency measures.[8] Within 24 hours of the attacks the President issued a declaration of a major disaster in New York[9] and a state of emergency in Virginia.[10] On Friday, September 14th, the President issued an Executive Order declaring a national emergency, which he extended in the Executive Order regarding Financial Transactions on

September 24.[11] In the following eight weeks, the President issued dozens of Proclamations and Executive Orders and the Executive Branch engaged in a widespread antiterrorist campaign. Congress introduced 323 bills and resolutions and adopted 21 laws and resolutions relating to the attacks and the war against terrorism.[12] This pace of new measures in the second eight weeks dropped by almost half—but almost all of these continued to be focused on terrorism.

From the initial emergency, the country swiftly moved into the heart of the counterterrorist spiral. This section will briefly touch on breadth of measures introduced in the subsequent four months. They fall into eight categories: incident management, emergency powers and war measures, consequence management, public statements, security measures, investigation and prosecution, administrative or bureaucratic reorganization, and international relations.

The United States's first concern in dealing with the incident was to secure the sites of the attacks and to prepare for other, immediate, possible attacks. Every branch entrusted with the life and property of the citizens reacted. For instance, the Executive Branch called the military into action. The Department of Health and Human Services mobilized medical personnel and supplies. First responders in New York began to mount operations around the clock. The FAA grounded flights, closed airports, and diverted international flights. Norm Mineta issued orders limiting the movement of vessels in international waters. Amtrak suspended operations.

Second, the federal government introduced extensive emergency powers and war measures. The President declared states of emergency in New York, New Jersey, Virginia, and the United States.[13] On September 18, 2001, President Bush signed Public Law 107-40, the War Powers Resolution and Senate Joint Resolution 23 ("Authorization for Use of Military Force").[14] Two days after the United States' military campaign commenced in Afghanistan, the President notified Congress. By October 2, the military had deployed 29,000 military personnel in two carrier battle groups as well as an amphibious ready group and several hundred military aircraft. Approximately 17,000 members of the Reserve were called to active duty[15] as well as several thousand National Guard operating under state authority.[16] Despite the existence of what became referred to as the "war" in Afghanistan, the Administration did not technically declare war. Nevertheless, military actions commenced and Congressional members introduced a number of traditional wartime measures. For instance, the Senate amended the Treasury and General Government Appropriations Act of 2002 to include war bonds. Under the name "Unity Bonds," the proceeds would go to recovery operations and the war against terrorism.[17] Other bills dealt with price gouging with respect to motor fuels, providing farm credit assistance for reservists, and providing retirement compensation to individuals engaged in active duty.[18] Still others sought to increase the penalty for air piracy.[19] One of the boldest would have required the United Nations to suspend membership of any country that the U.S. Secretary of State labels a state sponsor of terrorism.[20]

Third, in the area of consequence management, three types of responses emerged: measures dealing with the site of the attacks, compassion measures, and economic recovery. PL 107-38 almost immediately provided for $40 billion to be made available to emergency recovery and response agencies and national security activities.[21] More than 30 bills before Congress sought additional funding.[22] Compassion measures included presidential proclamations, such as "Honoring the Victims of the Incidents on

Tuesday, September 11, 2001" (September 12, 2001), the "National Day of Prayer and Remembrance" (September 13, 2001), the "Flags to Half-Staff" (September 14, 2001), and "Citizenship Day and Constitution Week" (September 19, 2001). Memorial services were held at the Pentagon, in New York, at the National Emergency Training Center in Emmitsburg, Maryland, and in Pennsylvania.[23] Congressional measures rapidly piled up: twelve bills aimed at establishing a national day of remembrance, providing Capitol-flown flags to survivors and families of the deceased, granting citizenship post-humously, building monuments, creating national service projects in honor of the victims, and authorizing prayers in the Capitol and in schools.[24] Nineteen statutes, bills, and resolutions focused on acts of heroism. Others focused on financial support to victims, with PL 107-37 providing for expediting payment to emergency personnel killed or injured as a result of September 11.[25] Measures focused on support to victims' families[26] and alleviating the financial penalties for victims.[27] Others looked at children and the effect of terrorism on them.[28] One of the most creative compassion bills advocated the creation of a lifetime pass for free admission to federally-owned parks, to help in the emotional healing process.[29] More than 45 proposals (in the form of bills and resolutions) focused on economic recovery. Their substance ranged from bail-out for insurance companies, hiring workers who lost jobs as a result of the attacks, and tax relief, to protection of the tourism industry, patronage of businesses in New York, and loans for small businesses.[30] The Bush Administration, the Small Business Administration, and others became active on this front in an effort to jump-start the economy.[31] By early February, however, party lines in Congress prevented the passage of an economic stimulus package.[32]

Fourth, various efforts to respond in the public arena were made. Some were more successful than others. Three main efforts mark this area: compassion and patriotism, gaining the moral high ground, and transmitting information. In the first area, public statements honored acts of heroism and encouraged citizens to rally around the flag.[33] A presidential proclamation required that all government flags fly at half staff. Bills in Congress ranged from attempts to rename September 11 "Patriot Day"[34] to prohibiting any social security or other government payment to individuals or entities that prohibit the flag to be flown. The White House invited Islamic and Sikh leaders to Washington and launched the "Friendship through Education" program. It also ensured that high-level officials appeared on Al Jazeera television.[35] The Bush Administration provided $320 million to Afghan people (up from roughly $170 million in 2000 year).[36] In the moral realm, officials made repeated reference to "the evil one" and "fighting the scourge of terrorism." The Administration and Congress tried to provide information to the public in the form of press briefings.

Not all of these efforts were entirely successful. For instance, the money appropriated to Afghanistan fell ludicrously short of providing enough resources for food and medicine to be delivered to victims of the war. Some of President Bush's statements had a devastating effect. The President almost immediately seized on the United States' response as a "crusade." His determination to "smoke out" the enemy led many in Afghanistan and Pakistan to believe that the United States would use chemical and biological weapons in its hunt for Osama bin Laden. These and other statements were then used as proof that more people must join the *jihad* against the United States. In terms of providing information to the United States' public, it quickly became clear that the Bush

Administration and, indeed, Congress, had difficulty knowing how to handle both the terrorist threat and the psychology of responding to terrorism. *Newsweek* captured this lack of competence at the height of the anthrax scare. A political cartoon depicted a man running around in a biological hazard suit shouting, "The sky is falling, the sky is falling!" As an onlooker responded that someone ought to call the Homeland Security Advisor, from the suit we read, "I AM the Homeland Security Advisor!"

Fifth, population control, transportation security, vital infrastructure protection, credible threat warnings, and immigration and border control constitute the security measures adopted in the four months following the attacks. A debate on the use of identity cards quickly followed widespread efforts to control the movement of people at all airports and, more specifically, in New York and Washington, DC. Transportation security stood second only to economic recovery in the number of initiatives introduced into Congress. Within eight weeks of the attack nearly 30 bills before Congress addressed airline security. On November 19th one of these became PL 107-71.[37] Other initiatives sought to impose strictures on crop dusters, introduce more widespread use of sky marshals and the national guard in airports, and place limits on flight training. Vital infrastructure protection initiatives included water sources and transportation routes, public transportation, agriculture, food supply, information networks,[38] health services—particularly in the event of an attack using weapons of mass destruction—and the transfer of explosives and hazardous material.[39] In an innovative but controversial change from how other liberal, democratic states have responded, the United States federal and state officials began issuing "Credible threat warnings." For instance, on October 11th, Governor Tom Ridge indefinitely extended a general warning. The State Department issued one in relation to travel to the Philippines, and Governor Gray Davis of California issued one in regard to bridges throughout the state. The federal government also considered and adopted numerous immigration and border control initiatives. The INS issued new orders. The Executive Branch initiated discussions with Mexico and Canada to make immigration more compatible. Eleven bills before Congress would have provided for greater military defense of the nation's borders, airports, and seaports.[40]

Sixth, in the area of investigation and prosecution, the federal government engaged in widespread detention and interrogation. It also adopted broader surveillance tools, instituted new financial strictures and rewards, altered the judicial system, and required greater information sharing between agencies. The House passed legislation requiring the CIA director to implement the changes recommended by the June 2000 National Commission on Terrorism.[41] It increased the "Most Wanted Terrorist" list to 30 people and provided about $30 million in reward money for the September 11 attacks, with an additional $1 million for anthrax cases. The investigation quickly became the most comprehensive in FBI history, with 4,000 out of 11,500 agents, and 7,000 out of 25,000 employees exclusively focused on terror.[42] The FBI arrested more than 20 individuals for anthrax hoaxes.[43] In October, six of the twenty-eight groups included on the list of foreign terrorist organizations designated by the Secretary of State were linked to Osama bin Laden.[44] The USA PATRIOT Act prevented citizens from supporting any designated terrorist organization for which all financial assets became blocked. The Administration froze the assets of 47 groups and individuals both in the U.S. and overseas. Operation Green Quest, a multi-agency initiative staffed by the IRS, Secret Service, FBI, DOJ [Department of Justice], and Customs began to focus on counterfeiting, credit card fraud, fraudulent import and export schemes, drug trafficking, and cash smuggling. Modeled after the scheme that implicated the mafia, the operation follows the money sources for suspected terrorist operations. On December 5, 2001, at the request of the Attorney General, the State Department designated 39 entities as terrorist organizations pursuant to the USA PATRIOT Act. An increased emphasis on information sharing led to initiatives such as President Bush's insistence that the directors of the FBI and CIA be present for the other agency's daily briefings with him. Some bills before Congress would have required electronic and other information to be shared between intelligence agencies. The next section of the article will go into more detail on extended detention and interrogation, expanded surveillance powers, and alterations to the judicial system.

Seventh, in an attempt to answer the question "who is in charge?", the Bush Administration and Congress introduced new bureaucratic nodes and reorganized the federal administrative structures handling the prevention, prosecution, and management of actual attacks. It is one of the characteristics of a liberal state's response to terrorism that the immediate assumption is that something was broken, which allowed the act to occur. Answering it with bureaucratic reorganization is one way to demonstrate to the population that the government is doing something to respond. The Intelligence Authorization Act for 2002 included a Commission on National Security Readiness to identify structural impediments to the effective collection, analysis, and sharing of information on national security threats, particularly terrorism. President Bush created a number of special counterterrorist advisory positions. On October 23, the President named Ambassador Craig Senior Director/Special Assistant to the President for Combating Terrorism.[45] Dick Clarke became the President's Special Advisor for Cyber Security. General Wayne Downing assumed the position of National Director and Deputy National Security Advisor for Combating Terrorism. One of the most publicized changes was the establishment of the Office of Homeland Security.[46] Run by Governor Tom Ridge and established at a Cabinet-level position, one of the first recommendations was to create a Foreign Terrorist Tracking Task Force, which was established by Homeland Security Presidential Directive 2 on October 29, 2001.[47] This task force combined information from the INS [Immigration and Naturalization Service], FBI, and State, and became housed in the Attorney General's [AG's] office.

The Attorney General, John Ashcroft, centralized counterterrorist prosecution. He established ninety-three U.S. Attorney Antiterrorism Task Forces, (in every U.S. Attorney office in the United States) with the aim to improve information sharing between federal, state and local law enforcement agencies and, in a capacity unprecedented in law enforcement, "to help craft strategy to prevent terrorism across the country." The Attorney General also created a Terrorism Task Force to head up the investigation into September 11. Assistant AG Michael Chertoff, head of the Criminal Division, will take the case, instead of individual U.S. Attorney's offices. In the Senate a bill was to create a new Deputy AG for Terrorism. Ten bills before Congress dealt with the further creation of new structures.[48] There was also extensive discussion about whether the FBI should be dedicated solely to terrorism.

Eighth, the federal government also introduced a number of international measures aimed at creating economic (dis)incentives and garnering support for a global "war on terrorism." In the first area, the Bush Administration lifted sanctions on Pakistan and India, provided $100 million in funding to Pakistan, designated Indonesia as a beneficiary development country (modification of duty-free treatment), signed a free trade agreement (FTA) with Jordan, only the third ever signed by the U.S.,[49] and continued stringent import and export controls on suspected state sponsors of terrorism. The United States engaged in diplomatic exchanges, pressing for the United Nations' resolutions and public statements from other countries to support the war effort and to introduce more stringent domestic counterterrorist measures within the home country. The U.S. applied pressure to a number of countries to choke the financial flows to al Qaida and other cells and sought to impress on other states both the practical and moral aspect of the attacks on their citizens and the United States' citizens working in the World Trade Center towers.

Many of these measures, such as the war itself, had a significant impact on American relations with other states. I do not here, however, specifically address the war. Instead, I narrow in on the counterterrorist measures most directly impacting individual rights that transcend state boundaries and thus bear both domestic and international consequences. They come from the sixth category: investigation and prosecution. I suggest that while they derive from an understandable dynamic, and that while there are strong arguments for their use, there are stronger arguments against their operation.

III. Measures Impacting Individual Rights

Terrorism itself is antithetical to liberal democracy. It violates the right to life and property and bypasses due process of law. It seeks to accomplish its goal outside the democratic process.[50] It tries to replace reason with emotion, and in so doing assumes a desire to return to rationality.[51] Terrorism takes for granted that a cost-benefit analysis will favor meeting the demands of those engaged in violence. Although it is levied against the population in general, it tries to change the behavior of the leaders, the elite—and its very nature is therefore undemocratic. When an open society has been taken advantage of in this manner the immediate response is to close it.

This reaction gives rise to at least two areas of concern: incursions into the civil liberties of citizens and incursions into non-citizens' individual and human rights. The first results in tension between new measures and constitutional norms. It also may potentially impact domestic tranquility. The second introduces tension in relations with other states. New counterterrorist measures are often justified on the grounds that they apply to "non-citizens" and are therefore acceptable. Such measures are aided by the psychology resulting from an act of terrorism. Following a significant attack, citizens or subjects become deeply suspicious of individuals fitting the political, ethnic, ideological, or religious profile of the perpetrators. The result is random violence against the ethnic group, a tendency to scapegoat, and, frequently, the suspension of ordinary judicial processes.

We generally understand civil rights to arise from the concept of democratic government—the codification of individuals' right to participate in the political realm in order to advance one's own ideas. Often overlapping in common usage, civil liberties arise from the concept of liberalism, or limited government. They protect individuals' abilities to form and express preferences or convictions and to act upon them without limitation from government in the private sphere. Such designations blur together in consideration of freedom of thought, conscience, expression, movement, privacy and autonomy in the management of one's personal affairs, voluntary association, and political participation.

Civil rights or civil liberties incorporate, but can be distinguished from, human rights, which provide a basic standard of treatment for all people, regardless of nationality. The Universal Declaration of Human Rights, agreed by the United Nations in 1948, includes thirty articles.[52] Some of the most important include equality; the right not to be discriminated against based on race, color, sex, religion, property, or birth; the right to life, liberty and security; and the right not to be enslaved. It also includes the right not to be subjected to cruel, inhuman, or degrading treatment or punishment; to be treated as a person before the law and to receive equal protection under the law; to an effective remedy by the competent national tribunals for violations of rights granted by the state; and not to be subjected to arbitrary arrest, detention, or exile. Articles protect the right of individuals to obtain a fair and public hearing by an independent and impartial tribunal and the right to the presumption of innocence in a trial in which the individual is afforded "all the guarantees necessary for his defense."

This paper addresses three measures introduced by the United States in the wake of September 11th that violate civil rights and freedoms and human rights. The next section provides information related to the extended detention of non-citizens, the introduction of military tribunals, and the stated intent of the Bush Administration to seek the death penalty in its response to al Qaida. It evaluates the arguments for and against these provisions.

A. Detention and Questioning

Immediately following the attacks, the Bush Administration compiled a list from Immigration and Naturalization Service (INS) and State Department records, of all males aged 18–33 from twenty Middle Eastern and European countries who had entered the United States after January 2000. Investigators contacted more than 200 universities to get the names of students from Islamic countries. On September 17, 2001, the INS reassigned more than half of its 2,000 investigators to searching for terrorist suspects. Three days later the INS issued an interim order, which expanded INS pre-charge powers, allowing the organization to determine "within a reasonable period of time" whether or not someone should be held or released on their own recognizance pending a trial.

The government subsequently questioned more than 5,000 non-citizens and held more than 1,200 for further interrogation. The Attorney General refused to release the names and location of those held for questioning. The FBI conducted over 500 searches.[53] Legislation passed by Congress expanded the federal government's powers to detain non-citizens. The USA PATRIOT Act not just allowed but required the detention of anyone the AG had reasonable grounds to believe was connected to terrorism or was a threat to national security. The statute did not specify a time period. Detention without trial could continue until the suspect was either deported or determined no longer to be a threat.[54] The legislation expanded the definition of "engage in terrorist activity" to committing, or inciting to commit a terrorist act, preparing or planning a terrorist act, gathering information on potential targets for a terrorist act, or soliciting funds for a terrorist activity or organization. It lifted the previous requirement that the individual knew, or could reasonably know, that the funds were going in furtherance of terrorist ends. Terrorist organizations included any organization so designated by the Secretary of State, a group of two or more individuals, whether organized or not, engaged in terrorist activity, and organizations engaged in charitable service if the military arm attached. This legislation retroactively applied the measures to all aliens or acts by aliens, regardless of when the act took place.

In a little-publicized but nonetheless extremely significant INS order issued a few weeks after the attack, the Attorney General became empowered to ignore immigration judges' rulings and hold non-citizens indefinitely. Additionally, on October 31, 2001, a Bureau of Prisons (BOP) regulation authorized the BOP and the Department of Justice (DOJ) to monitor communications between the individuals being held and their attorneys where the Attorney General determined that the individual was likely to use the communication to further acts of terrorism.[55] Those allowed to be monitored include individuals who have not been convicted of any offence, on certification by the Attorney General "that reasonable suspicion exists to believe that an inmate may use communications with attorneys or their agents to facilitate acts of terrorism." The certification could last up to one year and was not subject to judicial review. As of January 11th, criminal charges had been brought against 60 people in federal custody, with another 563 held on minor immigration violations.

There are many arguments in favor of these measures and using extended detention to respond to the attacks. The most important was the need to interrupt possible ongoing al Qaida operations. Proponents argue that the attacks took the American security establishment by surprise. Extended detention bought time for the INS to scan the pool of non-citizens present in the U.S. and for intelligence agencies to gather more information. Additionally, by increasing the number of individuals fitting the profile of the supposed hijackers under federal control, the odds of finding individuals involved in the planning and execution of September 11th increased. The Attorney General claimed that the names of those incarcerated were withheld to protect the privacy of the innocent and to prevent al Qaida from obtaining accurate information on which operatives might be in U.S. custody.[56] He justified the BOP order on the grounds that communication between prisoners and their attorneys may allow detainees to, at best, communicate with the terrorist organization and, at worst, provide enough contact to conduct further operations. Another argument frequently put forward at the time was that non-citizens did not deserve the same protections as citizens, and so what might not be appropriate for an American protected by the Constitution was perfectly acceptable for an alien. Finally, the Bush Administration offered the al Qaida training manual, recovered during a raid in England, which specified how to take advantage of the openness of American society. The manual taught how to take advantage of due process of law. Extraordinary measures were necessary to counter the special training in how to abuse the American legal and judicial system. They would interrupt al Qaida's strategy and throw the organization off guard.

Some of these arguments, such as interrupting possible ongoing operations and undermining al Qaida's strategy, provide strong arguments for the use of such measures. But there are also strong arguments on the other side. One of the most important is precisely that extended detention and questioning interrupted due process of law, undermining one of the central tenets of the American judicial system. Critics point to the fact that many were held incommunicado, and it was difficult to get information on where they had been taken.[57] In addition to the BOP order, the detainees were questioned without an attorney present, despite client-attorney privilege being seen as essential to effective legal representation and protected by international law. Critics claim that the Department of Justice did not demonstrate the need for new rules to protect against attorneys who may help to facilitate future or ongoing criminal activity. Under existing law, federal authorities could seek appropriate remedies under the well-established "crime-fraud" exception to attorney-client privilege. It was already possible to conduct closed door hearings before a federal judge, and, without the offending attorney present, the court could order monitoring of all communications if necessary. The judge could have removed a suspect attorney from the case. Moreover, the prosecutors were free to initiate criminal proceedings against offending attorneys. Such procedures ensured judicial review, protected legitimate attorney-client communications, and provided the appropriate powers for authorities to investigate and prevent criminal activity without obstruction.

Critics charge that the sweep equated to harassment of an ethnic minority. Of the more than 1,200, some of whom were held for months, only a handful were considered material witnesses, with others held on minor immigration violations. This suggested a violation of equal protection before the law and a discriminatory regime based on religion and ethnicity—violating two rights protected in the Universal Convention of Human Rights. It also sent a message that it was all right to discriminate based on ethnicity. Reports of physical abuse proliferated.[58] Security force members who refused to cooperate in the widespread ethnic profiling became subject to severe criticism.[59]

The concern was not just that the action would cause tension within the United States between the minority, Middle-Eastern Islamic community and others, but that such mistreatment played in to the hands of those levying the attacks, making it possible that individuals previously not involved would become alienated from the American state. Critics pointed to the previous use of widespread detention for ethnic and political minorities, pointing out that they had become an embarrassment in American history.[60] They claim that what might seem reasonable at the time later may prove not to be.

In regard to the immigration measures introduced, one could argue that such widening, as with the suspension of client-attorney privilege, was simply unnecessary. Prior to the new orders the federal government had extensive powers. It could detain without bond any alien with any visa status violation if INS instituted removal proceedings and had reason to believe that the alien posed a threat to national security or was at risk of flight. The alien did not have to be charged specifically with terrorist activity.[61] The INS claimed prior to September 11th that it could detain such aliens on the basis of secret evidence presented in camera and *ex parte* to an immigration judge. The INS previously could deny entry to any alien it had reason to believe may engage in any unlawful activity, including terrorist activity or supporting terrorist activity in the United States, and to any member of a designated terrorist group.[62] Terrorist activity was defined broadly, to include virtually any use or threat to use a firearm with intent to endanger person or property (other than for mere personal monetary gain), and any provision of support for such activity.[63] Additionally, the Secretary of State already had broad, generally unreviewable authority under the 1996 Anti-Terrorism and Effective Death Penalty Act to designate "foreign terrorist organizations," making it illegal to materially support such groups.[64] Al Qaida was already on this list.

It is not just on domestic soil that the United States detained and questioned foreign nationals. At the time of writing, the United States had detained more than 500 people at Camp X-Ray in Guantanamo Bay, Cuba, and hundreds more in Afghanistan.[65] Pictures showing the detainees being shackled and forced on their knees with their eyes and mouths covered spurred a storm of international criticism.[66] On February 8, 2002, the Bush Administration announced that it would extend the Geneva Conventions to the Taliban but not to members of al Qaida, whom the Administration classified as "unlawful combatants." This announcement glossed over the conditions under which the United States questioned Taliban and al Qaida captives over the four previous months. To extend the Geneva Conventions, the Administration argued, would be to consider al Qaida a legitimate organization. The Attorney General stated that al Qaida did not represent soldiers of a legally constituted foreign government.[67] The Bush Administration indicated that, following interrogation, some detainees would be returned to their home countries with the assurance they would be brought to justice.

The detainees derived from over 35 countries. International concern at the treatment of the detainees ranged from formal inquires and public statements from foreign governments to discussion within the United Nations' auspices. U.N. Secretary-General Kofi Annan emphasized that the prisoners "should be treated" in accordance with established norms of law, internationally and otherwise. He added, "The U.S. is a nation of laws. There's been quite a lot of debate about the application of the Geneva Convention.... Whether they are prisoners of war or common prisoners, there are certain rights and certain standards which have to be respected."[68] Pressure began to mount from countries the United States could ill afford to alienate, such as Saudi Arabia, which had more than 100 nationals being held by the United States, and the United Kingdom, with five nationals under American detention. What makes the issue of detainees particularly concerning is that the two options currently on the table are to either hold them indefinitely or to subject them to military tribunal.

B. Military Tribunals

On November 13, 2001, President Bush issued the military order: "Detention, treatment, and trial of certain non-citizens in the war against terrorism." Claiming his authority as Commander in Chief, Bush cited the emergency and potential of terrorist groups to inflict mass casualties, death, and disruption in the United States. This order suspended the use of domestic criminal courts. It applied to non-citizens whom there was reason to believe were members of al Qaida, engaged in or threatening to engage in acts of international terrorism that targeted U.S. citizens, property, national security, economy, or foreign policy, or who had harbored such an individual. The order allowed for the detention and prosecution outside the United States by military tribunal (five uniformed officers), with rules of evidence relaxed to include evidence with "probative value to a reasonable person." The proceedings could be conducted in secret, with the death penalty inflicted by a two-thirds vote. The order eliminated any right of appeal.

An outcry erupted both overseas and within the United States. Charges that the Executive Branch had failed to consult its allies, attorneys in the Defense Department, Congress, and expert legal advisors proliferated. In the domestic realm, an unusual confluence of the right and left on the political spectrum emerged.[69] In Congress, HR 3468, the Lofgren-Harmon bill, sought to create Congressional oversight over the tribunals.[70] After consulting more widely, the Bush Administration "leaked" new rules in late December 2001 that were more in line with the Geneva Conventions. The new guidelines required the presumption of innocence and required that guilt be proven beyond reasonable doubt (instead of preponderance of evidence). The new rules required a two-thirds vote for guilty verdicts, except in the case of the death penalty, where a unanimous verdict became required. They created a three-judge appeals panel, and opened the trials to the public and press except when national security might be at stake. The rules appointed military defense lawyers, but allowed the defendants to choose civilian attorneys. They allowed for hearsay and material gathered without a warrant (such as papers seized during battles, intelligence intercepts concerning bin Laden, and video recordings).

As with detention, there are some strong arguments in favor of military tribunals. I will here briefly outline five. First, military tribunals represent an accepted mode of trial for individuals accused of war crimes. Proponents point to the Defense Department's predecessor, "the War Department, which conducted 2,668 military tribunals in Germany and Japan during and after WWII for foreign soldiers and civilians accused of war crimes."[71] For use of military tribunals in a domestic context, the Administration cited the 1942 *Ex parte Quirin*, when eight German saboteurs were tried and found guilty of offences against the United States. The state executed six.

Second, the claim could be made that ordinary courts are simply insufficient for prosecuting acts of international terrorism. Rules of evidence are cumbersome. Interrogation and searches conducted on the battlefield don't fit the Supreme Court's Miranda decision or the Fourth Amendment search-and-seizure rules. Special rules are necessary to protect sources and information—who collects it, how it is collected, and what the information itself may be. The publicity afforded by a regular trial would simply play into terrorists' hands. Individuals argue that there is the need for a swift result to demonstrate swift justice for the horrific attacks of September 11th. A lengthy trial and appeals process, in this environment, is simply unacceptable.

Third, the Geneva Convention of 1949, relative to the treatment of prisoners of war, doesn't apply to al Qaida—and so al Qaida prisoners do not deserve in the conduct of justice to be protected by it. The convention requires prisoners to be part of a fighting force that adheres to organized structure of command. It demands that they wear a distinctive military uniform or insignia, carry arms openly, and grant reciprocal respect for the laws of war.

Fourth, the recent failure of the Lockerbie trials, brought in response to the downing of Pan Am 103 in 1988, demonstrates that an international court or tribunal would be ineffective. Tried by Scottish judges in a neutral country (the Netherlands), one of the two Libyans charged was found not guilty. The other initiated a lengthy appeals process. In the course of the prosecution the UN lifted its sanctions against Libya and the Libyan government renewed contact with the United States.

Fifth, the claim that it is better to let one guilty person go free than to have one innocent person incarcerated is reversed in the case of the possible mass destruction of human life. This deeply utilitarian argument demands that the protection of society outweighs the protection of individual rights, and it is one that has been codified in the past in the imposition of stricter penalties on crimes that threaten the very fabric of society.

The military tribunals introduce a more lax regime that might be more likely to incarcerate an innocent person. But this risk is justified. Moreover, it is morally repugnant to let a "terrorist," who has engaged in an act both politically and morally offensive to society, go free.

Again, just as there are strong arguments for the use of military tribunals, there are also stronger arguments against them. First, the president did not have the power to introduce the tribunals. The Constitution clearly gives this power to Congress. The difficulty with appeal to the military tribunals in World War II and the 1942 German saboteur case is that Congress had specifically authorized the president, in its Articles of War, to establish military commissions to try spies, those harboring the enemy, and those violating the laws of war. Congress repealed this measure in 1956. Further, in 1942, Congress had declared war. But, in September 2001, Congress simply authorized military force against those "nations, organizations or individuals" responsible for the attacks. Further, the military order collapsed the distinction between the executive and judicial branches—a distinction rigorously protected by the Constitution as long as civilian courts continued to be open for business.

Second, there is nothing wrong with using the ordinary criminal system to try suspected terrorists. In the Southern District of New York, Mary Jo White, the federal prosecutor, obtained a one hundred per cent conviction rate for the twenty-six jihad conspirators accused of complicity in previous attacks both in the United States and against American personnel and property overseas. The trials demonstrated that the criminal system had adequate procedures for dealing with classified information. This was, precisely, the point of the Classified Information Procedures Act: to protect National Security.

Openness marked past terrorism trials. Those addressing the 1993 World Trade Center bombing, the attacks in Kenya and Tanzania, the "Unabomber," and the attack on the Murrah Federal Building in Oklahoma were conducted openly. Judges can order that witness' identities or key documents be held back from the discovery process. In most of the New York cases the jurors were anonymous. The prosecutors, defense attorneys, and even judges didn't know the jurors' names. The courts excused anyone afraid to serve and placed key witnesses in federal protection programs.[72]

The Bush Administration's decision to try Zacarias Moussaoui in a federal district court, rather than military tribunal, further demonstrates the salience of the domestic judicial system. He is charged with conspiring to murder people in the United States "resulting in the death of thousands of persons on September 11, 2001." If this, the most fundamental charge that can be levied against al Qaida, can be tried in a regular court, then so can charges of conspiracy to commit other crimes that have not yet become manifest. Vice President Dick Cheney's defense of the decision not to try Moussaoui by military tribunal was that decision was "primarily based on an assessment of the case against Moussaoui, and that it can be handled through the normal criminal justice system without compromising sources or methods of intelligence.... And there's a good, strong case against him."[73] But this suggests that if there is a strong case against someone, then they can be tried in a federal court. If it is a weak case, then someone becomes subject to the military tribunal.

Opponents to military tribunals note that publicity isn't a problem in the domestic court system. The trials in New York were not televised. Defendants who might try to turn the witness stand into an opportunity to put forward their doctrinal beliefs become subject to difficult cross-examination. Individuals who interrupt the proceedings can be sent to rooms with closed-circuit television. And as for the length of the trial, critics of military tribunals claim that there is actually a benefit to it. The New York trials were long—the longest stretching up to six months. But in that time the state built up a considerable amount of information about al Qaida. Moreover, the institution of trial by military officers stole the opportunity from the ordinary citizens, the primary target of attacks, to participate in the administration of justice.

Third, as with the new INS powers, opponents claim that the new, extraordinary powers are simply not warranted. They encompass unacceptably wide powers of jurisdiction and fail to establish minimum guarantees for human rights. The order allows for indefinite detention. It is far from clear on the right of defendants to know charges and evidence against them. It says nothing about access to families, visitors, or attorney. It includes an overly-broad number of triable offences. It is not limited to just those engaged in war crimes but "any and all offenses triable by military commission." Further, the order authorizes the trial of any non-citizen accused of "acts of international terrorism," without defining it. So the government gets to determine who is a terrorist—a deeply political term that can be used in any number of ways.

Opponents also argue that the principle of it being better to let one innocent person be incarcerated than to let one guilty person capable of mass destruction go free is not sound. In an age where technology allows for the massive infliction of loss of life and destruction of property, this argument could be extended to any number of crimes. It is a fundamental shift in the very basis of the United States' legal system. One could also argue that the introduction of this extraordinary process is simply unacceptable. *Ex parte Milligan* arose out of the Civil War—a war that tore at the very existence of the United States. In its decision the United States Supreme Court overturned the conviction of a man found guilty by military tribunal of plotting insurrection in Indiana on behalf of the confederacy. The court wrote, "The Constitution of the United States is a law for rulers and people, equally in war and in peace, and covers with the shield of its protection all classes of men, at all times, and under all circumstances. No doctrine, involving more pernicious consequences, was ever invented by the wit of man than that any of its provisions can be suspended during any of the great exigencies of government. Such a doctrine leads directly to anarchy or despotism."

Fourth, a court designed to increase convictions undermines justice. The very existence of the tribunals assumes that an individual is guilty until proven innocent. In his testimony before the Senate Judiciary Committee, the Attorney General, John Ashcroft, said, "foreign terrorists who commit war crimes against the United States… are not entitled to, and do not deserve, the protection of the American Constitution." With this in mind, one would be forgiven for asking, if it has already been determined that an individual is a terrorist, why bother with a trial at all? As Laurence Tribe, the noted professor of Constitutional Law at Harvard University, put it, "The more you use ad hoc procedures, the more it looks like you're structuring the procedure to bring about a certain result."[74] Quite apart from issues of internal legitimacy, this approach will simply anger American allies and drive non-allied nations further away.

Fifth, terrorist acts lead to extremely emotional atmospheres. Yet it is precisely when many people are crying out for revenge that particular care must be taken. There are many examples from the United States' history where this was of issue. I will here cite two. The execution of Mary Surratt, who was convicted by a military tribunal on the basis of shaky evidence and hung for President Lincoln's murder. A civil court that operated in a less heated environment later exonerated her son. The trial of General Tomoyuki Yamashita, the commander of Japanese forces in the Philippines, provides a second. Justices Frank Murphy and Wiley Rutledge filed dissents that detailed the tribunal's failure to provide a fair trial. Murphy wrote, "By this flexible method a victorious nation may convict and execute any and all leaders of a vanquished foe, depending on the prevailing degree of vengeance and the absence of any effective judicial review." General MacArthur pushed through the sentence without even waiting to read the decision of the Supreme Court in what was regarded as an effort to stave off calls to hang the Emperor of Japan.[75]

Sixth, opponents could point to the dramatic international impact of the use of the military tribunals. They set a low standard that may be adopted by other nations and used as a basis for repressing people, including American citizens, seeking to exercise basic freedoms. Within weeks of the attacks various world leaders had begun to capitalize on the United States' "war on terrorism." Vladimir Putin, the Russian president, repeatedly used September 11 and U.S. campaign to demand a free hand in response to Chechen rebels. In Guatemala, a new anti-terror commission was staffed by ex-military officials, who intimidated and murdered human rights and Mayan Indian activists. And in Zimbabwe, President Robert Mugabe was even more opportunistic. Anyone who objected to the expropriation of white-owned land was considered a "terrorist." Mugabe's government proposed a new security bill that punishes terrorism and other vague offenses with the death penalty.[76]

The military tribunals violate international law. The Third Geneva Convention requires that no prisoner be tried by a court failing to offer "the essential guarantees of independence and impartiality." But the tribunals give the president final authority to select who is tried, who tries them, who is put to death—and who is on appeals boards. As Tribe has elsewhere commented, "All the rules about proof beyond reasonable doubt and other similar protections can look tremendous but not add up to anything if in the end there is no guarantee of an appeal outside the executive branch."[77] In brief, the tribunals provide the executive branch with too much power.

Just as shifts in foreign policy affect international perception of the United States, the tribunals will harm U.S. past and future credibility abroad. It is simply inconsistent with previous American opposition to similar orders issued by other countries. Throughout the 1990s the U.S. State Department's reports on human rights throughout the world criticized the use of secret arrests and military tribunals in Peru, Egypt, Nigeria, Russia, and elsewhere. More recently the U.S. government registered its discontent with Peru's treatment of Lori Berenson, charged with aiding and abetting Shining Path terrorists. The U.S. government demanded that she be given a second, civilian trial, after she had been found guilty in a military tribunal. If states don't themselves adopt a similar structure, the tribunals may well be seen internationally as illegitimate. In addition to the arguments above, the U.S. military only has a handful of attorneys that have any experience in conducting a capital trial. (The last such case was in 1996).[78] The military expressed concern that American officers who conduct tribunals may be found guilty of war crimes internationally.

Moreover, American soldiers may find themselves subject to similar procedures in other countries. As one military legal expert put it, "If the U.S. government is going to pull the wool out from under the Geneva Conventions, that is going to be serious for our soldiers."[79] It is not clear that designating the Taliban as protected under the Geneva Conventions but removing the suspected al Qaida operatives from its protection will address this concern. Members of al Qaida all have nationalities, and their home states may well decide that the United States, in refusing to treat their nationals under the auspices of the Geneva Conventions, has abrogated from the treaty.

C. Death Penalty

The order governing military courts included capital punishment in its auspices. In the rules leaked in late December the infliction of the penalty would require the unanimous agreement of the panel of military officers presiding over the trial.

I will here outline three central arguments for the use of the death penalty for terrorism. First, capital punishment fits the crime. This argument particularly resonates in the American context, where claims that the supreme crime requires the supreme punishment proliferate. Terrorist acts are not just murder, but a threat to society and the *politas*. Traditionally, the most serious crimes are treason and acts of war—acts that terrorism mimics if not commits. Moreover, the mass killing of innocents or noncombatants is not just a crime against this society or state, but a crime against civilization. Proponents argue that it is a just punishment: an eye for an eye, and a tooth for a tooth.[80] A life sentence, or a lesser punishment, would simply be inadequate. The United States uses the death penalty for "lesser crimes," which would make it inconsistent not to apply to the most heinous of all—mass attack on unarmed civilians.

Proponents claim further that the punishment is appropriate because terrorists can't be reformed.[81] Additionally, where the act of terrorism is irrational and plays strongly on emotion, capital punishment restores rationality.[82] Supporters point to safeguards in the system and say they are ample to prevent the execution of the wrong person.[83] They suggest that the perpetrator actually gets a better end than the victim: the guilty has the opportunity to prepare, whereas the victim, possibly in extended pain, doesn't have the opportunity to make peace.[84] For those who fear death, it is seen as appropriate to counter terror with terror. And the public does not want to see this form of punishment abolished.[85]

Second, supporters see the use of the death penalty as a deterrent. Individuals suggest that if it is not used against the perpetrators of such acts, an increase in them will occur.[86] With a reduced fear of punishment, "lesser" supporters may assume more central roles in terrorist organizations.[87] Eliminating the penalty would place civilians and state security forces at heightened danger.[88] Further, by providing for a life sentence terrorists will harbor hope of reprieve—something that should not be nurtured. And its elimination would provide terrorists an overwhelming advantage over the population and the security forces.[89] It would lead to an increase in public anxiety.[90]

Third, maintaining capital punishment sends important messages. It creates a social stigma against use of violence for political ends.[91] And it plays an important role in retribution as a way of holding individuals responsible.[92] As for those actively seeking death and becoming martyrs through their execution, they would be martyrs anyway.

They have already taken on the state. And neither they nor their supporters accept the legitimacy of the legal order anyway. By eliminating capital punishment the order will not be suddenly more acceptable. Finally, while civilization may be moving toward abolition, it can't be hastened through legislation.[93] To reach this stage, such violence would no longer exist. So as long as there is terrorism, there will be the necessity of having capital punishment.

Again, there are stronger arguments against use of the death penalty for, specifically, terrorism. First, is the claim that it is not a deterrent.[94] Numerous studies have reached this conclusion for ordinary crime. The 1953 Royal Commission on Capital Punishment, Amnesty International report on Canada (Where the murder rate per thousand fell after abolition), and 1988 United Nations Committee on Crime Prevention and Control provide some examples. In the United Kingdom and Ireland, during consideration of whether to eliminate the death penalty, one often-cited source was Albert Pierpoint, Britain's official hangman for more than 25 years. Pierpoint was responsible for more than 400 deaths, many of which related to political crimes regarding Ireland. He later wrote in his autobiography, "I do not now believe that any one of the hundreds of executions I carried out has in any way acted as a deterrent against future murder. Capital punishment, in my view, achieved nothing except revenge."[95]

One could argue that the argument is even more pronounced for terrorism, where most terrorist organizations teach that individuals may well die. If individuals were deterred by death, they would not be engaged in terrorist action. One need only think of groups like the PKK, where the average lifespan of a fighter is eighteen months, or the IRA, where members are told that within two years they either will be dead or in prison. Many activists, such as those in Hammas or Hizb'allah may actually seek death to thereby demonstrate complete commitment to cause. Moreover, the death serves to heighten publicity for the cause and, most importantly, to create martyrs. As Che Guevara lay in final repose in Bolivia and Bobby Sands became memorialized on walls throughout Northern Ireland, the dead heroes assume a mystical, religious quality—a sense magnified when tried in military courts, as warriors, as the weak David taking on Goliath. As one TD [Teachta Dála, member of parliament] in Ireland put it in the Irish Parliament,

> Let us consider for a moment the mind of the terrorist. It is fair to say that in many cases down through the years terrorism has thrived on publicity. On going back over our history and our fight for freedom, one can see the manner in which the death penalty was used by our freedom fighters to build the code of martyrdom, the concept of heroism. The ultimate deterrent of capital punishment was used to highlight the cause of the freedom fighter.[96]

In numerous cultures a great respect develops for martyrs and the families of martyrs, making the death penalty not only not a deterrent, but something to be sought. This is especially true for movements making extensive use of suicide bombers.

Second, with capital punishment there is the danger of miscarriage of justice that cannot be rectified.[97] Evolution in theory governing criminal law suggests that the proper aim of punishment is rehabilitation. Rehabilitation may counter social and economic structures and even psychological tendencies that give rise to violence. But capital punishment, by its very nature, is not reformative. It is hard to be rehabilitated when you are dead. Moreover, no matter how stringent a structure has been created, human judgment remains fallible.[98] And so the wrong people may be sent to the gallows—an occurrence made more likely by the emotive atmosphere that surrounds acts of terror.[99]

The release of the Birmingham Six vividly drew this point. Six Irish men served 16 years for wrongful conviction for the 1974 IRA pub bombing in Birmingham that left 21 people dead.[100] In 1991 the appeal court overturned their convictions, determining that evidence had been suppressed and falsified and incriminating statements extracted by physical force. In the case of the Guildford Four, seven people died in IRA pub bombings in Guildford, Surrey.[101] The British judicial system incarcerated four men for 15 years. They were released in 1989.[102] As he left the Old Bailey, Gerald Conlon, one of the Guildford Four, thanked God that capital punishment had not existed at the time of his arrest; otherwise the Secretary of State would have had to make his apology in a graveyard.[103] Such miscarriages of justice become even more likely when the evidentiary and other rules are softened, as is typical of counterterrorism and present in the introduction of military tribunals.

Civilization writ-large, and particularly, the United States' closest allies, are moving toward abolition.[104] The list of liberal, democratic states that have abolished it steadily expands: Holland (1870), Belgium (1863), Norway (1905), Denmark (1930), Sweden (1921), Italy (1948), Finland (1949), Portugal (1867),[105] the United Kingdom (1957), and Ireland (1990). Abolition is seen as progressive, and revenge has become distinguished as an outmoded concept.[106] The death penalty contradicts right to life, which has been recognized in numerous international and domestic instruments as an inalienable right.

Some argue further that life imprisonment presents a greater punishment than the fear of death.[107] Life imprisonment re-institutes reason, in place of the irrationality of either the act of terror or the further taking of human life.[108]

With the growing international norm against the use of the death penalty, its continued use harms America's relations with other countries. The European Union has refused to extradite suspects to the United States unless it receives assurances that death penalty will not be applied. Within months of his arrest, France condemned the trial of Zacarias Moussaoui, a French citizen accused of being 20th hijacker in the September 11th attacks. Spain, which arrested eight people suspected of complicity in the attacks, refused to extradite them. The Finnish parliament similarly said it would refuse to extradite if threatened by the death penalty. The growing international norm may keep perpetrators from being held responsible for their actions. As one British newspaper, the *Observer*, put it, "The British Government's view, which *The Observer* shares, is that bin Laden, Omar, and their colleagues, if captured, should be tried according to international law and under due process. Those indicted for direct complicity in the attacks of 11 September may be prosecuted in the U.S., since the crimes took place on American soil. But this can happen only if they are seized by the U.S. authorities or extradited by other countries, which may refuse to do this because the U.S. operates the death penalty."[109]

IV. Conclusion

One characteristic of terrorism is that it evokes a wide set of reactions. It challenges a liberal, democratic state's ability to fulfill its most basic obligation: to protect the life and property of the citizens. In some instances terrorism goes further, attacking the legitimacy of the state's monopoly over administrative structures and coercive measures. Reason of state dictates that when such attacks threaten the life of the country, the obligation of the government to respond intensifies. September 11th was seen as more than terrorism—as an act of war levied on the territorial integrity of the United States. With reason of state widely touted in justification, the Bush Administration and Congress introduced extraordinary powers.

The problem with this claim is that national security becomes a broad justification for any number of actions taken on the basis of information not available to the public. In his December 2001 testimony to the Senate Judiciary Committee, the Attorney General stated, "I trust that Congress will respect the proper limits of Executive Branch consultation that I am duty-bound to uphold. I trust, as well, the Congress will respect this President's authority to wage war on terrorism and defend our nation and its citizens with all the power vested in him by the Constitution and entrusted to him by the American people."[110]

The Bush Administration asked the public to trust them. Yet liberal democracy is founded on the concept of limited government. Distrust, with good reason, underlies the constitutional underpinning of the United States. Despite carefully crafted limitations, the United States has, in its history, seen abuse of the powers that are granted to the state. Prior to the attacks, considerable powers were available that already impacted on individual rights. While terrorism demands a response from the state—it has been seen to have failed to perform its most basic obligation: the protection of the lives and property of the citizens—it also drives states to do things they otherwise wouldn't contemplate. As Roosevelt so eloquently stated, the only thing we have to fear is fear itself. People are afraid, and, driven by fear, the government has introduced shortcuts. But these are expensive shortcuts with long-term effects.

Perhaps the most serious risk is that in enacting these measures the government plays into the hands of those engaged in such actions. In a liberal state, the steady incursion into civil rights will increase domestic dissent. At risk is not just the alienation of American citizens, but the marginalization of ethnic minorities. Moreover, such measures risk initiating a backlash against the government from right-wing ideologues committed to less government interference and an increasing number of strictures on the power of the government. This becomes increasingly true as there is seepage into criminal law, and such measures become less and less exceptional while new ones steadily expand the power of the central authority.

Equally important, these measures risk fomenting international dissent, alienating citizens and elites in other countries, and breeding cynicism at American efforts to further the establishment of democratic regimes. Such a unilateral rejection of basic equal rights angers allies. The French Foreign Minister "scoffs at the 'hyperpuissance'; the German Foreign Minister huffs about being treated as 'satellites,'"[111] and the general tone of U.S.-European relations daily gathers an increasing chill. As the United States becomes increasingly ethnically diverse and less Euro-centric, the intangible links between ethnic and religious groups in America and overseas will become weaker. Simultaneously, with a GDP larger than the United States, European power may well increase. In 1998 Steve Walt cogently argued that trans-Atlantic relations will be placed under increasing stress.[112] Measures such as those highlighted in this paper go some way toward accelerating such a process.

The line between security and liberty is, indeed, a difficult one to draw. There are strong arguments for and against widespread detention and questioning, military courts, and capital punishment. But if September 11th was an attack against civilization, and not just against America, the United States should count on civilization to respond. Crimes committed in America could be tried on U.S. soil, where the average citizens, deeply affected by the horrific attacks of September 11th, would have an opportunity to participate in the administration of justice. Those committed overseas could be subjected to UN tribunal or to an International Criminal Court, demonstrating the United States' commitment to universal individual rights. This is not a time for the United States—or the Administration—to be acting unilaterally or under a veil of secrecy. Such actions breed cynicism and suspicion, two conclusions America can ill afford its allies or enemies overseas to reach, as it faces the threat of global terror.

Notes

1. These numbers reflect the percentage of all resolutions, bills, and amendments proposed in each house that related all or in part to terrorism, counterterrorism, or consequence management measures.
2. For purposes of this paper I consider terrorism therefore to be acts that involve the following elements: violence, fear, a broader audience, clear purpose, political power, perpetrated against noncombatants, and instrumental. In this paper I focus on sub-state terrorism perpetrated against the United States, United Kingdom, and Ireland.
3. 29 died in the attack. ("Omagh bomb claims 29th victim," BBC News, 18 March 1999. http://news.bbc.co.uk/hi/english/events/northern_ireland/focus/newsid_165000/165159.stm) The British legislation allowed for individuals suspected of complicity in terrorist operations to be convicted on the word of a senior police officer. Silence in the face of such accusation became seen as corroboration of such police evidence. The British statute also allowed for the government to seize a convicted person's assets and made it illegal to conspire within the UK to commit terrorist acts outside the country. Ireland announced the new measures 19 November 1999.
4. Perhaps the most oft-cited example was the 1996 attack by Aum Shinrikyo on the subway system in Tokyo. For further discussion of this attack see *Toxic Terror*, edited by Jonathan Tucker.
5. Figures provided by the Office of Management and Budget, reprinted in Peter Eisler, "This is only a test, but lives still at stake," *USA Today*, Friday, July 7, 2000, 5A.
6. Figures for fiscal year 1997 from General Accounting Office, *Combating Terrorism: Need for Comprehensive Threat and Risk Assessments of Chemical and Biological Attacks*, GAO/NSIAD-99-163, September 1999. Figures for fiscal years 2000 and 2001 are from Office of Management of Budget, *Annual Report to Congress on Combating Terrorism: Including Defense Against Weapons of Mass Destruction/Domestic Preparedness and Critical Infrastructure Protection*, May 18, 2000, p. 45.
7. See Donohue, 2001.
8. For example, the State Department closed U.S. embassies in Tokyo, Bangkok, New Delhi, Jakarta, and Canberra and placed the other U.S. embassies worldwide on high alert. Employees evacuated the UN building in New York and federal buildings in Washington, D.C. The Secret Service secured the President, Vice President, Speaker of the House, national security team, the Cabinet, and senior staff members. The CIA operations center moved. The National Security Agency sent all but essential personnel home.
9. http://www.whitehouse.gov/news/releases/2001/09/.
10. http://www.whitehouse.gov/news/releases/2001/09/.

11. September 14, 2001 http://www.whitehouse.gov/news/releases/2001/09/20010914-6.html; see also http://www.whitehouse.gov/news/releases/2001/09/20010924-1.html.

12. These numbers include public bills, amendments, and private bills. Of the total, approximately 40 originated in House committees, and approximately 130 in Senate committees.

13. http://www.whitehouse.gov/news/releases/2001/09/. Additional bills before congress, H.R. 3086 and S. 1570, would provide the Secretary of Education with specific waiver authority to respond to conditions in the national emergency. On October 20, 2001 the President also introduced an Executive Order adding HHS to Defense capabilities in time of war (http://www.whitehouse.gov/news/releases/2001/10/).

14. PL 107-40 included two resolutions from each house of Congress: H.J.RES.64 and S.J.RES 23. Two additional declarations of war, H.J.Res 62 and H.J.RES 63, were referred to the House International Relations Committee and received no further action.

15. Executive Order; Ordering the Ready Reserve of the Armed Forces to Active Duty And Delegating Certain Authorities to the Secretary of Defense And the Secretary of Transportation; September 12, 2001 http://www.whitehouse.gov/news/releases/2001/09/20010914-5.html .

16. http://www5.cnn.com/2001/US/10/01/inv.frozen.assets/index.html.

17. S.AMDT.1574 to H.R.2590 (Treasury and General Government Appropriations Act, 2002). See also H.R.2899, H.R.2900, H.R.3021, H.R.3111, S.1430, S.1431, and S.1432.

18. See H.RES.238, S.1519, and S.1531.

19. H.R.3074, H.R.3076.

20. H.Con.Res. 293. H.R.3049 would have provided for the removal of the Taliban in Afghanistan.

21. The Emergency Supplemental Appropriations Act for Recovery from and Response to Terrorist Attacks on the United States, FY 2001 President Authorizes Emergency Response Fund Transfer; Text of a Letter from the President to the Speaker of the House of Representatives; October 22, 2001.

22. H.R.2215, H.R.3129, H.R.3174, H.AMDT.318 to H.R.2586, S.RES.171, S.1546, S.AMDT.1562 to H.R.2500.

23. Defense Department Pentagon memorial—October 11, 2001; New York Memorial Service; National Firefighters Memorial—at the National Emergency Training Center; Emmitsburg, Maryland October 7, 2001, Pennsylvania Memorial Service, http://www.whitehouse.gov/news/releases/2001/09.

24. H.CON.RES.230, H.CON.RES.235, H.J.RES.71, H.R.2897, H.R.2982, H.R.2991, H.R.3036, S.J.RES.25, S.1556, H.CON.RES.223, H.CON.RES.239.

25. H.R.2882 became Public Law No.:107-37.

26. H.CON.RES.228.

27. H.R.3175.

28. See for example H.R.3106, S.1539, and S.1623.

29. H.R.2976.

30. H.RES.241, H.R.2884, H.R.2902, H.R.2930, H.R.2938, H.R.2940, H.R.2945, H.R.2946, H.R.2947, H.R.2955, H.R.2961, H.R.2968, H.R.3007, H.R.3011, H.R.3041, H.R.3045, H.R.3055, H.R.3067, H.R.3073, H.R.3090, H.R.3112, H.R.3137, H.R.3140, H.R.3141, H.R.3143, H.R. 3157, H.R.3210, S.1433, S.1440, S.1446, S.1454, S.1487, S.1493, S.1499, S.1500, S.1505, S.1532, S.1541, S.1544, S.1552, S.1578, S.1583, S.1622, S.1624.

31. Only one bill before Congress (H.R. 2956) addressed rebuilding the actual structures attacked on September 11.

32. *New York Times*, February 7, 2002.

33. H.CON.RES.225.

34. H.J.RES.71 became Public Law No: 107-89.

35. For instance, National Security Advisor Condoleezza Rice announced during an interview on Al Jazeera television: "I would like to say to the Arab and Muslim world the following. I would like to say that America is a country that respects religious difference. America is a country that has many people of different religions within it."

36. Prime Time News Conference; http://www.whitehouse.gov/news/releases/2001/10/20011011-7.html#status-war. See also http://www.whitehouse.gov/news/releases/2001/10/20011004.html announcing $320MM package and intent to distribute through UN agencies.

37. 71.S.1447 became Public Law No: 107-71.

38. H.R.2925, H.R.3035, H.R.3178, H.R.3184, H.R.3198, S.1456, S.1480, S.1528, S.1550, S.1551, S.1593, S.1608.

39. H.R.3091, H.R.3123, S.1557, S.1569.

40. H.R.2960, H.R.3013, H.R.3077, H.AMDT.316 to H.R.2586, S.1214, S.1429, S.1518, S.1559, S.1588, S.1618, S.1627.

41. H.AMDT.365 to H.R.2883, H.R.3108, S.1448, S.1510.

42. Terror attacks bring profound changes in FBI focus October 28, 2001. Posted: 1:46 PM EST (1846 GMT) http://www5.cnn.com/2001/LAW/10/28/inv.attacks.fbifocus.ap/index.html.

43. Radio Address by the President to the Nation, The Oval Office, November 3, 2001; http://www.whitehouse.gov/news/releases/2001/11/2011103.html.

44. These include al Qaeda, Islamic Movement of Uzbekistan, Egyptian Islamic Jihad, Gama'a al-Islamiyya in Egypt, Harakat ul-Mujahidin in Pakistan, and Abu Sayyaf Group in the Philippines. Several Middle East terrorist groups remain on the list, including Hezbollah, Hamas and the Popular Front for the Liberation of Palestine. The Israeli extremist groups Kahane Chai and Kach have been merged into one group, under the name Kahane Chai. Baruch Goldstein, who opened fire on a Hebron mosque in 1994, killing 29 Muslims as they prayed, was linked to the group. The State Department dropped the Japanese Red Army and the Tupac Amaru Revolutionary Movement from the list. Designation lasts two years.

45. http://www.whitehouse.gov/news/releases/2001/10/20011023-26.html.

46. Laid out in an Executive Order of October 8, 2001 (http://www.whitehouse.gov/news/releases/2001/10/20011008-2.html). Organization and Operation of the Homeland Security laid out in Homeland Security Presidential Directive-1, October 29, 2001 (http://www.whitehouse.gov/news/releases/2001/10/20011030-1.html).

47. Foreign Terrorist Tracking Task Force; Homeland Security Presidential Directive-2; October 29, 2001.

48. H.R.3026, S.RES.165, S.1449, S.1462, S.1490, S.1529, S.1534, H.R.3078.

49. H.R.2603, signed into law Sept. 28, 2001 (http://www.whitehouse.gov/news/releases/2001/09/20010928-1.html). See also http://www.whitehouse.gov/news/releases/2001/09/20010928-12.html.

50. Alex P. Schmid and Albert J. Jongman, with the collaboration of Michael Stohl, *Political terrorism: A new guide to actors, authors, concepts, data bases, theories, and literature* (New York: North-Holland Publishing Co.), 1998.

51. Ibid.

52. Universal Declaration of Human Rights, G.A. res. 217A (III), U.N. Doc. A/810 at 71 (1948).

53. Ashcroft's testimony before Congress, http://judiciary.senate.gov/tel20601f-ashcroft.htm.

54. Right of appeal existed to the United States Court of Appeals or District of Columbia Circuit Court.

55. 66 Fed. Reg, 55061-66066 (October 31, 2001), effective October 30, 2001.

56. "Out of respect for their privacy, and concern for saving lives, we will not publicize the names of those detained." (Attorney General John Ashcroft during hearings to Senate Judiciary Committee.)

57. On October 29, twenty organizations filed a FOIA request with the Justice Department, the FBI and the INS to challenge the unprecedented level of secrecy surrounding detentions.

58. For example, Hasnain Javid, a Pakistani student held for three days, claims to have been severely beaten by other inmates. The guards ignored his yells for help. Later he allegedly was stripped naked and again assaulted. Again, the guards ignored it. Mohamed Maddy, an Egyptian arrested October 3, claims to have been assaulted by the guards in the Metropolitan District Center. Osama Awadallah, a 21-year old Jordanian student living in Southern California, says he was taken to the same detention center and beaten and kicked by guards who insulted Islam and forced him against a U.S. flag. Middle Eastern detainees in North Carolina claim to have been stripped naked and subjected to freezing temperatures by the

guards. When they tried to convey this to people outside the prison, any phone calls were cut off (http://www.cnn.com/2001/US/10/24/inv.jail.death).

59. Interview by author of Chief Mark Kroeker of the Portland, Oregon, police department January 2002.

60. For example, during the Red Scare of the early 20th century the U.S. government picked up 6,000 people in 33 cities throughout the United States. Taken into custody because of their political affiliation, they were placed into "bull pens" and beaten into signing confessions. 566 people eventually were deported. These "Palmer Raids" became a blemish on American history. A second, well-known example followed the attack on Pearl Harbor. In 1942 the U.S. government interned more than 100,000 people of Japanese descent, more than two-thirds of whom were U.S. citizens. Deemed to be a threat to U.S. national security, in 1988 the government finally apologized and paid restitution to the Japanese internees. A third example is drawn from the Cold War. The McCarthy era saw the introduction of the McCarran-Walter act, which empowered the government to prevent noncitizens that adhered to proscribed ideas from living in the United States. In 1990 Congress withdrew the McCarran-Walter Act political exclusion and deportation grounds. (Testimony of Professor David Cole on Civil Liberties and Proposed Anti-Terrorism legislation before the Subcommittee on the Constitution, Federalism and Property Rights of the Senate Judiciary Committee, October 3, 2001; http://judiciary.senate.gov/tel00301sc-cole.html.)

61. 8 U.S.C. § 1226, 8 C.F.R. § 241.

62. 8 U.S.C. § 1182(a)(3).

63. 8 U.S.C. § 1227(a)(4). [Pursuant to the Alien Terrorist Removal provisions in the 1996 Antiterrorism Act, the INS may use secret evidence to establish deportability on terrorist activity grounds.

64. 8 U.S.C. § 1189, 18 U.S.C. § 2339B.

65. http://www.cnn.com/2002/US/02/04/ret.detainees.flights/index.html.

66. http://www.cnn.com/2002/WORLD/europe/02/08/ret.cuba.redcross/index.html.

67. http://www.cnn.com/2002/US/02/01/guantanamo.detainees/index.html.

68. http://www.cnn.com/2002/US/02/01/guantanamo.detainees/index.html.

69. Senator Edward Kennedy and conservative columnist William Safire agreed on this point, as did the Executive Directors of Amnesty International USA, Human Rights Watch, the International Human Rights Law Group, the International League for Human Rights, the Lawyers Committee for Human Rights, Minnesota Advocates for Human Rights, Physicians for Human Rights and the Robert F. Kennedy Memorial Center for Human Rights.

70. This legislation would authorize the use of military tribunals in response to the September 11th attacks but would limit their jurisdiction to foreign nationals captured overseas. The bill prohibits the suspension of habeas corpus without congressional authorization and requires further congressional action should the courts continue in operation past 2005.

71. *USA Today*, December 31, 2001, "Proposal would widen defendants' rights," by Toni Locy and Richard Willing.

72. The judge who presided at many of the trials, Kevin T. Duffy, does have 24-hour security that may well last the rest of his life, but this was a choice he made to oversee the trials.

73. January 6, 2002, Senator Joseph L. Lieberman, *The Houston Chronicle*.

74. Quoted in the *New York Times*, December 29, 2001, B7, "A Nation Challenged: Civil liberties; Draft rules for Tribunals Ease Worries, but not all," by Katharine Q. Seelye.

75. Stephen Ives Jr, "Vengeance Did Not Deliver Justice," *The Washington Post*, December 30, 2001.

76. "The Antiterror Bandwagon," December 28, 2001, *The New York Times*, A18, Editorial.

77. *The New York Times*, December 29, 2001, "A Nation Challenged: Civil Liberties; Draft Rules for Tribunals Ease Worries, but Not All" by Katharine Seelye, 7B, col. 5.

78. Since 1961 there have been no federal executions arising from military cases. The last capital case, that of Jessie Quintanilla, convicted of murdering an executive officer and attempting to murder two other Marines at Camp Pendleton, was in 1996. (*Los Angeles Times*, December 29, 2001, "Response to Terror.")

79. Francis A. Boyle, expert on the law of war at the University of Illinois. *The New York Times*, December 26, 2001. "A Nation Challenged: the Justice System; Critics' Attack on Tribunals Turns to Law Among Nations," by William Glaberson.

80. Mr. Derrig, Dail Debates 5 December 1951, Vol. 128, cols. 428–30.

81. See for instance the *Garda News*, quoted in the Dail Debates, 1 June 1990, Vol. 399(a), cols. 1224–1225.

82. Mr. Derrig, Minister for Lands, Dail Debates 30 January 1952, Vol. 129, col. 138.

83. Mr. Derrig, Minister for Lands, Dail Debates 30 January 1952, Vol. 129, col. 138.

84. General MacEoin, Dail Debates, 5 December 1951, Vol. 128, cols. 426–7. See also MacEoin, Dail Debates, 5 December 1963, Vol. 206, col. 769.

85. Mr. Derrig, Dail Debates 5 December 1951, Vol. 128, cols. 429–30.

86. Mr. Derrig, Minister for Lands, Dail Debates 30 January 1952, Vol. 129, col. 137.

87. Mr. Cogan, Dail Debates, 5 December 1951, Vol. 128, col. 413–4.

88. Mr. Derrig, Minister for Lands, Dail Debates 30 January 1952, Vol. 129, col. 137–8; Mr. Cogan, Dail Debates, 5 December 1951, Vol. 128, col. 413–5.

89. Mr. Dogan, Dail Debates, 5 December 1951, Vol. 128, col. 415.

90. Mr. Derrig, Minister for Lands, Dail Debates 30 January 1952, Vol. 129, col. 137; and 5 December 1951, Vol. 128, col. 430.

91. Mr. Charles Haughey, Minister of Justice, Dail Debates, 6 November 1963, Vol. 205, col. 1001.

92. Mr. Derrig, Minister for Lands, Dail Debates 30 January 1952, Vol. 129, col. 139.

93. Mr. Derrig, Minister for Lands, Dail Debates 30 January 1952, Vol. 129, col. 137.

94. Mr. Charles Haughey, Minister of Justice, Dail Debates, 6 November 1963, Vol. 205, col. 1001.

95. Quoted in Dail Debates, 1 June 1990, Vol. 399(a), col. 1222.

96. Mr. Flanagan, Dail Debates, 1 June 1990, Vol. 399(a), col. 1206.

97. Mr. Cogan, Dail Debates, 5 December 1951, Vol. 128, col. 413. See also Mr. Charles Haughey, Minister of Justice, Dail Debates, 6 November 1963, Vol. 205, col. 1001.

98. Mr. MacBridge, Dail Debates, 21 November 1951, Vol. 127, col. 1165.

99. Mr. Flanagan, Dail Debates, 1 June 1990. Vol. 399(a), cols. 1207–1208.

100. In 1991 British authorities released Hugh Callaghan, Paddy Joe Hill, Gerry Hunter, Richard McIlkenny, Billy Power, and Johnny Walker, who had spent over 16 years in jail. See http://www.oireachtas-debates.gov.ie/D.0402.199011010060.html, and http://www.parliament.the-stationery-office.co.uk/pa/cm199091/cmhansrd/1991-01-14/Orals-2.html.

101. "Blair's apology to Guildford Four," *Guardian Unlimited*, 6 June 2000, http://www.innocent.org.uk/cases/guildford4/#the grauniad.

102. Paul Hill, Gerry Conlon, Paddy Armstrong, and Carole Richardson.

103. Paraphrased in Dail Debates, 1 June 1990, Vol. 399(a), col. 1254. Paddy Hill, one of the Birmingham Six, made a similar point, that while his incarceration had been terrible, things could be worse—if capital punishment had been around, he wouldn't be there to complain. Ibid.

104. See for instance Mr. T. F. O'Higgins, Dail Debates, 10 December 1963, Vol. 206, col. 846; and Mr. Flanagan, Dail Debates, 1 June 1990, Vol. 399(a), col. 1212.

105. Mr. MacBride, Dail Debates, 5 December 1951, Vol. 128, col. 409.

106. Mr. O'Donnell, Dail Debates 30 January 1952, col. 141–2; Mr. MacBride, Dail Debates, 30 January 1952, Vol. 129, col. 154; Mr. Dunne, Dail Debates, 5 December 1951, Vol. 128, col. 419.

107. Mr. O. Flanagan, Dail Debates 30 January 1952, Vol. 129, col. 142; General MacEoin, Dail Debates 5 December 1951, Vol. 128, col. 426.

108. See for instance Dr. Browne, Dail Debates, 7 November 1963, Vol. 205, col. 1096.

109. Editorial, *The Observer*, January 6, 2002, "Comment: U.S. justice would be an injustice: the UN must try terrorists."

110. Ashcroft testimony to Senate Judiciary Committee, December 6, 2001.

111. Andrew Rawnsley, "How to deal with the American goliath," *The Observer*, Sunday, February 24, 2002.

112. Stephen Walt, "The Ties That Fray: Why Europe and America Are Approaching a Parting of the Ways," *The National Interest*, Winter 1998/99.

A Nasty Business

An international expert on terrorism and political violence, **Bruce Hoffman** is the RAND Corporation's vice president of external affairs and director of its Washington, D.C., office. He is well known for *Inside Terrorism* (1998), which has been translated into foreign language editions in nine countries, and was the founding director of the Center for the Study of Terrorism and Political Violence at the University of St. Andrews in Scotland. In 1998, Hoffman was awarded the Santiago Grisolía Prize and the accompanying chair in violence studies by the Queen Sofia Center for the Study of Violence (Valencia, Spain). Even before the terrorist attacks on September 11, he was consulting with governments and businesses on terrorism and political violence.

Intelligence is capital," Colonel Yves Godard liked to say. And Godard undeniably knew what he was talking about. He had fought both as a guerrilla in the French Resistance during World War II and against guerrillas in Indochina, as the commander of a covert special operations unit. As the chief of staff of the elite 10th Para Division, Godard was one of the architects of the French counterterrorist strategy that won the Battle of Algiers, in 1957. To him, information was the sine qua non for victory. It had to be zealously collected, meticulously analyzed, rapidly disseminated, and efficaciously acted on. Without it no antiterrorist operation could succeed. As the United States prosecutes its global war against terrorism, Godard's dictum has acquired new relevance. Indeed, as is now constantly said, success in the struggle against Osama bin Laden and his minions will depend on good intelligence. But the experiences of other countries, fighting similar conflicts against similar enemies, suggest that Americans still do not appreciate the enormously difficult—and morally complex—problem that the imperative to gather "good intelligence" entails.

The challenge that security forces and militaries the world over have faced in countering terrorism is how to obtain information about an enigmatic enemy who fights unconventionally and operates in a highly amenable environment where he typically is indistinguishable from the civilian populace. The differences between police officers and soldiers in training and approach, coupled with the fact that most military forces are generally uncomfortable with, and inadequately prepared for, counterterrorist operations, strengthens this challenge. Military forces in such unfamiliar settings must learn to acquire intelligence by methods markedly different from those to which they are accustomed. The most "actionable," and therefore effective, information in this environment is discerned not from orders of battle, visual satellite transmissions of opposing force positions, or intercepted signals but from human intelligence gathered mostly from the indigenous population. The police, specifically trained to interact with the public, typically have better access than the military to what are called human intelligence sources. Indeed, good police work depends on informers, undercover agents, and the apprehension and interrogation of terrorists and suspected terrorists, who provide the additional information critical to destroying terrorist organizations. Many today who argue reflexively and sanctimoniously that the United States should not "over-react" by over-militarizing the "war" against terrorism assert that such a conflict should be largely a police, not a military, endeavor. Although true, this line of argument usually overlooks the uncomfortable fact that, historically, "good" police work against terrorists has of necessity involved nasty and brutish means. Rarely have the importance of intelligence and the unpleasant ways in which it must often be obtained been better or more clearly elucidated than in the 1966 movie *The Battle of Algiers.* In an early scene in the film the main protagonist, the French paratroop commander, Lieutenant Colonel Mathieu (who is actually a composite of Yves Godard and two other senior French army officers who fought in the Battle of Algiers), explains to his men that the "military aspect is secondary." He says, "More immediate is the police work involved. I know you don't like hearing that, but it indicates exactly the kind of job we have to do."

I have long told soldiers, spies, and students to watch *The Battle of Algiers* if they want to understand how to fight terrorism. Indeed, the movie was required viewing for the graduate course I taught for five years on terrorism and the liberal state, which considered the difficulties democracies face in countering terrorism. The seminar at which the movie was shown regularly provoked the most intense and passionate discussions of the semester. To anyone who has seen *The Battle of Algiers,* this is not surprising. The late Pauline Kael, doyenne of American film critics, seemed still enraptured seven years after its original release when she described *The Battle of Algiers* in a 900-word review as "an epic in the form of a 'created documentary'"; "the one great revolutionary 'sell' of modern times"; and the "most impassioned, most astute call to revolution ever." The best reviews, however, have come from terrorists—members of the IRA; the Tamil Tigers, in Sri Lanka; and 1960s African-American revolutionaries—who have assiduously studied it. At a time when the U.S. Army has enlisted Hollywood screenwriters to help plot scenarios of future terrorist attacks, learning about the difficulties of fighting terrorism from a movie that terrorists themselves have studied doesn't seem farfetched.

In fact, the film represents the apotheosis of cinema verite. That it has a verisimilitude unique among onscreen portrayals of terrorism is a tribute to its director, Gillo Pontecorvo, and its cast—many of whose members reprised the real-life roles they had played actually fighting for the liberation of their country, a decade before. Pontecorvo, too, had personal experience with the kinds of situations he filmed: during World War II he had commanded a partisan brigade in Milan. Indeed, the Italian filmmaker was so concerned about not giving audiences a false impression of authenticity that he inserted a clarification in the movie's opening frames: "This dramatic re-enactment of The Battle of Algiers contains NOT ONE FOOT of Newsreel or Documentary Film." The movie accordingly possesses an uncommon gravitas that immediately draws viewers into the story. Like many of the best films, it is about a search—in this case for the intelligence on which French paratroops deployed in Algiers depended to defeat and destroy the terrorists of the National Liberation Front (FLN). "To know them means we can eliminate them," Mathieu explains to his men in the scene referred to above. "For this we need information. The method: interrogation." In Mathieu's universe there is no question of ends not justifying means: the Paras need intelligence, and they will obtain it however they can. "To succumb to humane considerations," he concludes, "only leads to hopeless chaos."

The events depicted on celluloid closely parallel those of history. In 1957 the city of Algiers was the center of a life-and-death struggle between the FLN and the French authorities. On one side were the terrorists, embodied both on screen and in real life in Ali La Pointe, a petty thief turned terrorist cell leader; on the other stood the army, specifically the elite 10th Para Division, under General Jacques Massu, another commander on whom the Mathieu composite was based. Veterans of the war to preserve France's control of Indochina, Massu and his senior officers—Godard included—prided themselves on having acquired a thorough understanding of terrorism and revolutionary warfare, and how to counter both. Victory, they were convinced, would depend on the acquisition of intelligence. Their method was to build a meticulously detailed picture of the FLN's apparatus in Algiers which would help the French home in on the terrorist campaign's masterminds Ali La Pointe and his bin Laden, Saadi Yacef (who played himself in the film). This approach, which is explicated in one of the film's most riveting scenes, resulted in what the Francophile British historian Alistair Horne, in his masterpiece on the conflict, *A Savage War of Peace*, called a "complex organigramme [that] began to take shape on a large blackboard, a kind of skeleton pyramid in which, as each fresh piece of information came from the interrogation centres, another [terrorist] name (and not always necessarily the right name) would be entered." That this system proved tactically effective there is no doubt. The problem was that it thoroughly depended on, and therefore actively encouraged, widespread human-rights abuses, including torture.

Massu and his men—like their celluloid counterparts—were not particularly concerned about this. They justified their means of obtaining intelligence with utilitarian, cost-benefit arguments. Extraordinary measures were legitimized by extraordinary circumstances. The exculpatory philosophy embraced by the French Paras is best summed up by Massu's uncompromising belief that "the innocent [that is, the next victims of terrorist attacks] deserve more protection than the guilty." The approach, however, at least strategically, was counterproductive. Its sheer brutality alienated the native Algerian Muslim community. Hitherto mostly passive or apathetic, that community was now driven into the arms of the FLN, swelling the organization's ranks and increasing its popular support. Public opinion in France was similarly outraged, weakening support for the continuing struggle and creating profound fissures in French civil-military relations. The army's achievement in the city was therefore bought at the cost of eventual political defeat. Five years after victory in Algiers the French withdrew from Algeria and granted the country its independence. But Massu remained forever unrepentant: he insisted that the ends justified the means used to destroy the FLN's urban insurrection. The battle was won, lives were saved, and the indiscriminate bombing campaign that had terrorized the city was ended. To Massu, that was all that mattered. To his mind, respect for the rule of law and the niceties of legal procedure were irrelevant given the crisis situation enveloping Algeria in 1957. As anachronistic as France's attempt to hold on to this last vestige of its colonial past may now appear, its jettisoning of such long-standing and cherished notions as habeas corpus and due process, enshrined in the ethos of the liberal state, underscores how the intelligence requirements of counter-terrorism can suddenly take precedence over democratic ideals.

Although it is tempting to dismiss the French army's resort to torture in Algeria as the desperate excess of a moribund colonial power, the fundamental message that only information can effectively counter terrorism is timeless. Equally disturbing and instructive, however, are the lengths to which security and military forces need often resort to get that information. I learned this some years ago, on a research trip to Sri Lanka. The setting—a swank oceanfront hotel in Colombo, a refreshingly cool breeze coming off the ocean, a magnificent sunset on the horizon—could not have been further removed from the carnage and destruction that have afflicted that island country for the past eighteen years and have claimed the lives of more than 60,000 people. Arrayed against the democratically elected Sri Lankan government and its armed forces is perhaps the most ruthlessly efficient terrorist organization-cum-insurgent force in the world today: the Liberation Tigers of Tamil Eelam, known also by the acronym LTTE or simply as the Tamil Tigers. The Tigers are unique in the annals of terrorism and arguably eclipse even bin Laden's al Qaeda in professionalism, capability, and determination. They are believed to be the first nonstate group in history to stage a chemical-weapons attack when they deployed poison gas in a 1990 assault on a Sri Lankan military base—some five years before the nerve-gas attack on the Tokyo subway by the apocalyptic Japanese religious cult Aum Shinrikyo. Of greater relevance, perhaps, is the fact that at least a decade before the seaborne attack on the U.S.S. Cole, in Aden harbor, the LTTE's special suicide maritime unit, the Sea Tigers, had perfected the same tactics against the Sri Lankan navy. Moreover, the Tamil Tigers are believed to have developed their own embryonic air capability—designed to carry out attacks similar to those of September 11 (though with much smaller, noncommercial aircraft). The most feared Tiger unit, however, is the Black Tigers—the suicide cadre composed of the group's best-trained, most battle-hardened, and most zealous fighters. A partial list of their operations includes the assassination of the former Indian Prime Minister Rajiv Gandhi at a campaign stop in the Indian state of Tamil Nadu, in 1991; the assassination of Sri Lankan President Ranasinghe Premadasa, in 1993; the assassination of the presidential candidate Gamini Dissanayake, which also claimed the lives of fifty-four bystanders and injured about one hundred more, in 1994; the suicide truck bombing of the Central Bank of Sri Lanka, in 1996, which killed eighty-six people and wounded 1,400 others; and the attempt on the life of the current President of Sri Lanka, Chandrika Kumaratunga, in December of 1999. The powerful and much venerated leader of the LTTE is Velupillai Prabhakaran, who, like bin Laden, exercises a charismatic influence over his fighters. *The Battle of Algiers* is said to be one of Prabhakaran's favorite films.

I sat in that swank hotel drinking tea with a much decorated, battle-hardened Sri Lankan army officer charged with fighting the LTTE and protecting the lives of Colombo's citizens. I cannot use his real name, so I will call him Thomas. However, I had been told before our meeting, by the mutual friend—a former Sri Lankan intelligence officer who had also long fought the LTTE—who introduced us (and was present at our meeting), that Thomas had another name, one better known to his friends and enemies alike: Terminator. My friend explained how Thomas had acquired his sobriquet; it actually owed less to Arnold Schwarzenegger than to the merciless way in which he discharged his duties as an intelligence officer. This became clear to me during our conversation. "By going through the process of laws," Thomas patiently explained, as a parent or a teacher might speak to a bright yet uncomprehending child, "you cannot fight terrorism." Terrorism, he believed, could be fought only by thoroughly "terrorizing" the terrorists—that is, inflicting on them the same pain that they inflict on the innocent. Thomas had little confidence that I understood what he was saying. I was an academic, he said, with no actual experience of the life-and-death choices and the immense responsibility borne by those charged with protecting society from attack. Accordingly, he would give me an example of the split-second decisions he was called on to make. At the time, Colombo was on "code red" emergency status, because of intelligence that the LTTE was planning to embark on a campaign of bombing public gathering places and other civilian targets. Thomas's unit had apprehended three terrorists who, it suspected, had recently planted somewhere in the city a bomb that was then ticking away, the minutes counting down to catastrophe. The three men were brought before Thomas. He asked them where the bomb was. The terrorists—highly dedicated and steeled to resist interrogation—remained silent. Thomas asked the question again, advising them that if they did not tell him what he wanted to know, he would kill them. They were unmoved. So Thomas took his pistol from his gun belt, pointed it at the forehead of one of them, and shot him dead. The other two, he said, talked immediately; the bomb, which had been placed in a crowded railway station and set to explode during the evening rush hour, was found and defused, and countless lives were saved. On other occasions, Thomas said, similarly recalcitrant terrorists were brought before him. It was not surprising, he said, that they initially refused to talk; they were schooled to withstand harsh questioning and coercive pressure. No matter: a few drops of gasoline flicked into a plastic bag that is then placed over a terrorist's head and cinched tight around his neck with a web belt very quickly prompts a full explanation of the details of any planned attack.

I was looking pale and feeling a bit shaken as waiters in starched white jackets smartly cleared the china teapot and cups from the table, and Thomas rose to bid us good-bye and return to his work. He hadn't exulted in his explanations or revealed any joy or even a hint of pleasure in what he had to do. He had spoken throughout in a measured, somber, even reverential tone. He did not appear to be a sadist, or even manifestly homicidal. (And not a year has passed since our meeting when Thomas has failed to send me an unusually kind Christmas card.) In his view, as in Massu's, the innocent had more rights than the guilty. He, too, believed that extraordinary circumstances required extraordinary measures. Thomas didn't think I understood—or, more to the point, thought I never could understand. I am not fighting on the front lines of this battle; I don't have the responsibility for protecting society that he does. He was right: I couldn't possibly understand. But since September 11, and especially every morning after I read the "Portraits of Grief" page in *The New York Times*, I am constantly reminded of Thomas—of the difficulties of fighting terrorism and of the challenges of protecting not only the innocent but an entire society and way of life. I am never bidden to condone, much less advocate, torture. But as I look at the snapshots and the lives of the victims recounted each day, and think how it will take almost a year to profile the approximately 5,000 people who perished on September 11, I recall the ruthless enemy that America faces, and I wonder about the lengths to which we may yet have to go to vanquish him.

The moral question of lengths and the broader issue of ends versus means are, of course, neither new nor unique to rearguard colonial conflicts of the 1950s or to the unrelenting carnage that has more recently been inflicted on a beautiful tropical island in the Indian Ocean. They are arguably no different from the stark choices that eventually confront any society threatened by an enveloping violence unlike anything it has seen before. For a brief period in the early and middle 1970s Britain, for example, had something of this experience—which may be why, among other reasons, Prime Minister

Tony Blair and his country today stand as America's staunchest ally. The sectarian terrorist violence in Northern Ireland was at its heights and had for the first time spilled into England in a particularly vicious and indiscriminate way. The views of a British army intelligence officer at the time, quoted by the journalist Desmond Hamill in his book *Pig in the Middle* (1985), reflect those of Thomas and Massu.

> Naturally one worries—after all, one is inflicting pain and discomfort and indignity on other human beings... [but] society has got to find a way of protecting itself... and it can only do so if it has good information. If you have a close-knit society which doesn't give information then you've got to find ways of getting it. Now the softies of the world complain—but there is an awful lot of double talk about it. If there is to be discomfort and horror inflicted on a few, is this not preferred to the danger and horror being inflicted on perhaps a million people?

It is a question that even now, after September 11, many Americans would answer in the negative. But under extreme conditions and in desperate circumstances that, too, could dramatically change—much as everything else has so profoundly changed for us all since that morning. I recently discussed precisely this issue over the telephone with the same Sri Lankan friend who introduced me to Thomas years ago. I have never quite shaken my disquiet over my encounter with Thomas and over the issues he raised—issues that have now acquired an unsettling relevance. My friend sought to lend some perspective from his country's long experience in fighting terrorism. "There are not good people and bad people," he told me, "only good circumstances and bad circumstances. Sometimes in bad circumstances good people have to do bad things. I have done bad things, but these were in bad circumstances. I have no doubt that this was the right thing to do." In the quest for timely, "actionable" intelligence will the United States, too, have to do bad things—by resorting to measures that we would never have contemplated in a less exigent situation?

7.3   **Anthony Clark Arend, 1998**

Terrorism and Just War Doctrine

Anthony Clark Arend is an associate professor of government at Georgetown University and adjunct professor at the Georgetown University Law Center. His main research and teaching interests are in the areas of international law, international organization, and constitutional law of U.S. foreign relations; he is especially interested in international law relating to the use of force and international legal theory. He is author of several books and numerous articles. Among his recent publications is the book, *Legal Rules and International Society* (1999).

W hen classic just war theory developed, the world consisted of a variety of political entities—kingdoms, principalities, empires, and the like. With the passage of time, however, the territorial state emerged as the primary political unit, and writers in this tradition began to apply just war doctrine exclusively to the behavior of states. Today, the vast corpus of just war writings deals with questions about the permissibility of the recourse to force *by states* (the principles of *ius ad bellum*) and the conduct of hostilities *by states* (the principles of *ius in bello*).[1]

Since the Second World War, however, the world has witnessed the emergence of a number of non-state actors on the international stage. Among these actors are terrorist groups. Over the last several decades, the Palestine Liberation Organization [PLO], the Hezbollah, the Irish Republican Army [IRA], the Abu Nidal Group, the Red Brigade, the Red Army, and numerous other groups have used force against a variety of state and non-state targets. Their activities have elicited forcible responses by states—the United States and Israel, in particular.[2] Yet because these groups are not states and operate quite differently from states, it is unclear just how the principles of contemporary just war doctrine would apply to states attempting to counter these terrorist groups.

My purpose here is to attempt to find out—that is, to apply contemporary just war doctrine to state efforts to respond to terrorist actions. Parts one and two will explore the traditional *ius ad bellum* and *ius in bello* principles in relation to terrorism, and part three will offer several recommendations for making just war doctrine more applicable to the terrorist threat.

Ius Ad Bellum and Terrorism

Classic just war doctrine was most concerned about when a political entity could justly undertake the use of force.[3] Plato and Aristotle, Augustine and Aquinas, and others searched for specific criteria that could be used to determine when war was justly entered into, and modern just war theorists have continued to use and refine these criteria. Today, while there is no single set that all just war theorists use, six elements figure in most contemporary discussions of *ius ad bellum;* competent authority, just cause, right intention, last resort, probability of success, and proportionality.

1. Competent Authority

To be justly undertaken, a war or other use of force must be initiated by a legitimate authority. As Aquinas explained, "[a] private individual may not declare war...."[4] Instead, "since responsibility for public affairs is entrusted to the rul[ers], it is they who are charged with the defence of the city, realm, or province."[5] In the world of today, the notion of competent authority has generally been understood to mean that *states* can declare or otherwise initiate hostilities. Whether any entity other than a state has the authority to do so is less clear. Given the historic support within the just war tradition for "just revolution," there seems to be reason to think that certain *revolutionary groups* may constitute competent authority.[6] But just what criteria such a group would need to meet remains unclear.[7] It would also seem logical to conclude that *the United Nations* can be considered a competent authority, given the authority vested in it by states. As states ratified the United Nations Charter, they did so with the understanding that the Charter empowered the Security Council to authorize the use of force when the Council determined that there was a threat to the peace, breach of the peace, or act of aggression.[8]

When the concept of competent authority is applied to the use of force against terrorists, on the surface it seems to provide no particular difficulty. Clearly, states are the entities that respond to terrorists, and states are the competent authorities *par excellence*. On closer examination, however, the situation is a bit murkier. In recent discussions of competent authority, scholars have explored precisely who or what body within a state is empowered to authorize the use of force. Can the American president do so alone? Or must Congress, which under the Constitution has the authority to "declare war," be involved in the decision? Virtually all scholars would argue that when the United States is under direct attack, the president can use force without the consent of Congress. But beyond that, scholars and public officials differ considerably on the circumstances under which the president can use force without congressional approval.

This problem is especially acute with respect to terrorism and its unconventional methods of warfare. Terrorists do not generally wear military uniforms and engage in overt attacks across international borders. It is not to be expected that a terrorist group will march across the U.S.–Mexican border with flags flying. Instead, terrorists will attack military and diplomatic installations abroad, take hostages, and kill civilians. Under American constitutional law, it is not clear whether the president has the authority to respond forcibly without the consent of Congress. The War Powers Resolution provides that the president can introduce troops into hostilities only "pursuant to (1) a declaration of war, (2) specific statutory authorization, or (3) a national emergency created by attack upon the United States, its territories or possessions, or its armed forces."[9] It does not provide for the use of force in response to actions against U.S. nationals abroad. Yet, presidents have certainly asserted such a right. In 1985, for example, Ronald Reagan unilaterally authorized force to bring down an Egyptian aircraft carrying terrorists allegedly involved in the *Achille Lauro* highjacking.[10]

2. Just Cause

The second criterion, just cause, can be divided into (a) the substance of the cause and (b) comparative justice.

a. The Substance of the Cause.   Every just war theorist—from the most ancient to the most recent—has asserted that for war to be properly undertaken, there must be a substantive just cause, some legitimate reason for going to war. A state cannot simply declare war. Underlying this concept is a critical element of just war doctrine: there is always a presumption against the recourse to force. As the National Conference of Catholic Bishops has observed, "just-war teaching has evolved... as an effort to prevent war; only if war cannot be rationally avoided, does the teaching then seek to restrict and reduce its horrors."[11] It does this, they explain, "by establishing a set of rigorous conditions which must be met if the decision to go to war is to be morally permissible."[12] Especially today, they continue, "such decision... requires extraordinarily strong reasons for overriding the presumption *in favor of peace* and *against war*."[13]

But while just war theorists agree that there must be a just cause, they do not agree on exactly what qualifies as a substantive just cause. Augustine wrote in the broadest of terms, explaining that "those wars are generally defined as just which avenge some wrong, when a nation or a state is to be punished for having failed to make amends for the wrong done, or to restore what has been taken unjustly."[14] More recently, James

Childress has refined this concept of substantive just cause by narrowing it to three circumstances: "to protect the innocent from unjust attack," "to restore rights wrongfully denied,"and "to re-establish a just order."[15]

Regarding the first of these circumstances there is universal agreement. All just war theorists would assert that a state can use force in the event of an armed attack. Indeed, Article 51 of the United Nations Charter guarantees states a *legal* right to "individual or collective self-defense if an armed attack occurs."[16] But the precise meaning of "armed attack" is unclear, especially in regard to terrorism. When does a terrorist action constitute an armed attack? Must it occur in the territory of the aggrieved state? Must it be of a particular intensity? Would an isolated terrorist action amount to an armed attack, or would it have to be part of an ongoing effort? Would the *threat* of an armed attack be sufficient? In other words, could a state justly engage in preemptive or anticipatory self-defense?

More problems arise with the second category of Childress's understanding of substantive just cause, the use of force "to restore rights wrongfully denied." In general just war discussions, scholars would probably take this to mean that force can be used in the face of genocide or other massive human-rights violations. With respect to state actions, a government that engages in genocide or other systematic abuses of the rights of its citizens may be liable to forcible intervention. Indeed, a growing body of literature discusses circumstances under which a "humanitarian" intervention can be justly undertaken.[17] But how the concept of humanitarian intervention would translate to terrorist activity is uncertain. If terrorists were killing or torturing innocents on a massive scale or taking large numbers of people hostage, that action would probably be equivalent to genocide by a state. But what if a terrorist group were causing a group of people to live in great fear for their lives, without actually doing physical harm on a large scale—could such a "reign of terror" give rise to a just intervention? Could a state argue that the mere presence of some terrorist groups poses such a threat to the indigenous population that a forcible action would be justified?

Finally, there are also difficulties with Childress's third category, that force can be justly undertaken "to re-establish a just order." What is a "just order," and when would terrorists violate it? Over the past several years, non-state actors of a variety of sorts have caused a tremendous degree of instability in states. In Lebanon, Somalia, the former Yugoslavia, Liberia, and Sierra Leone, for example, such actors have prevented the centralized government from exercising effective control over large portions of the state's territory. Would such a cast justify intervention? Could it be argued that force is necessary "to preserve," in the words of the U.S. Catholic bishops, "conditions necessary for decent human existence"?[18]

b. Comparative Justice. It is not enough that a state have a substantive just cause for force: it must also satisfy the requirement of comparative justice. While scholars differ on its meaning, this requirement seems to acknowledge that while all parties to a dispute may have substantive just causes, not all such causes justify the resort to force. As the American bishops conceive of comparative justice, the issue is two-fold: "which side is sufficiently 'right' in a dispute, and are the values at stake critical enough to override the presumption against war?"[19] In other words, for a state to use force, its "just cause" should be better than its opponent's and must be worth the "violence, destruction, suffering, and death"[20] caused by war.

Here I will take the first aspect of the bishops' definition of comparative justice—which side is sufficiently "right"?—to reflect a proper understanding of that concept. The latter aspect—is the just cause worth the evil to be produced in the war?—can, I believe, be subsumed under the concept of proportionality and will be discussed later.

To apply the requirement of comparative justice to terrorism may seem at first to produce an extremely undesirable result. Typically, terrorist groups are motivated by legitimate causes. The Irish Republican Army has fought against the British for its "unjust occupation" of Northern Ireland. For years, the PLO challenged Israeli possession of the West Bank, the Golan Heights, and other territories. An observer might be inclined to conclude that comparative justice was indeed on the side of these groups. But terrorism introduces another factor into the calculation. What is abhorrent about terrorism is not the cause for which it is acting but the nature of the act. While certain terrorist groups may indeed have legitimate reasons for desiring change in the status quo, the methods of terrorism are in and of themselves impermissible. Targeting innocent civilians and other non-combatants, taking hostages, killing and torturing prisoners of war—these are completely unacceptable violations of the concept of *ius in bello*.

This aspect of terrorism introduces an important challenge to just war doctrine. How can we evaluate the comparative-justice requirement when the methods of one party are clearly unjust from the perspective of *ius in bello?*

3. Right Intention

Aristotle, one of the earliest proponents of the notion of the just war, explained that the ultimate purpose of war must be to establish peace. Just wars are to be fought out of a desire for charity and peace.[21] The purpose is not to obliterate an enemy but to end the aberrant behavior that has breached the peace. As Augustine noted, "the desire to hurt, the cruelty of vendetta, the stern and implacable spirit, arrogance in victory, the thirst for power, and all that is similar, all these are justly condemned in war."[22] Accordingly, revenge, hatred, and the demonization of the enemy have no place in a just war.[23]

This requirement of *ius ad bellum* is one of the most difficult in a conventional war.[24] It is a rare war in which the enemy is not portrayed as evil and the notion of revenge is not present—think of the American propaganda about the Germans and the Japanese during the Second World War. And for terrorist actions, the problem is even greater. Given the tactics of terrorist groups and their often fanatic ideology, it is quite easy to vilify them beyond reason. Moreover, because their deeds engender international outrage, the desire for punishment or revenge sometimes seems to be the main motivation for forcible response.

4. Last Resort

Hostilities should commence only after peaceful alternatives have been explored. There is, however, some disagreement among just war commentators as to how much effort should be expended on exploring these other methods of dispute resolution. The American bishops, for example, state that "all peaceful alternatives must have been exhausted,"[25] while William V. O'Brien notes that "all reasonable efforts to avoid it [war] while protecting the just cause should be tried."[26] The latter approach, requiring all "reasonable" efforts at avoidance, seems to make the most sense. In any conflict, an observer could always argue that there was "one more" alternative that had not been explored.

But even if we understand this criterion as requiring that we exhaust all reasonably peaceful remedies, terrorism raises special difficulties. In conventional international conflict, there are established diplomatic channels and international organizations that have states as parties. Such institutions provide clear methods for pursuing peaceful settlement and non-violent sanctions. Before the Gulf War, for example, the United States and its allies pursued traditional diplomacy and various multilateral methods available through the United Nations. Such methods are not formally available with terrorist groups. They do not have diplomatic missions in the traditional sense and are normally not members of international organizations, and they are not readily susceptible to economic sanctions and other non-violent pressures. As a consequence, it is unclear how a state could reasonably be said to have exhausted peaceful methods of dispute resolution in dealing with terrorists. Furthermore, efforts to establish any form of official contact may be seen as granting a legitimacy to the terrorist group that would help its cause. Israel's reluctance to negotiate with the PLO stemmed in part from this fear.

5. Probability of Success

A state should engage in the use of force only if the action is likely to succeed. As the American bishops note, the purpose of this requirement "is to prevent irrational resort to force or hopeless resistance when the outcome of either will clearly be disproportionate or futile."[27] But, they continue, "the determination includes a recognition that at times defense of key values, even against great odds, may be a 'proportionate' witness."[28]

But how is success defined when this criterion is applied to terrorism? In a standard war, success means the aggression is ended, or the territory is returned, or the status quo ante is reestablished. But does success against terrorism mean the ending of a particular series of terrorist acts? The capture or death of all the terrorists? Because of the tenacity of terrorists, success can often be elusive. How many years should a state fight against a PLO or an IRA?

6. Proportionality

While this criterion is also present in *ius in bello* calculations, as a *ius ad bellum* category proportionality means that "the damage to be inflicted and the costs incurred by war must be proportionate to the good expected by taking up arms."[29] Are the just causes sufficient to outweigh the injustices of war? Needless to say, this can be a perplexing calculation. It is difficult to anticipate the full consequences of a war. The tragedy far outstretches the number of persons killed or injured and the amount of property damage. War can destroy entire cultures and break the spirit of nations.[30]

In regard to terrorist actions, the requirement of proportionality does not seem to pose any more problems that it does in conventional international conflict; it may even present fewer. First, since terrorist groups do not have full authority and control over a territory, it could be contended that force against them would have less significant long-term consequences than force against a state. Second, it also seems logical to assume that the type of force used against terrorists is likely to be less destructive than the force necessary to combat state actions.

Ius In Bello and Terrorism

Once a state has properly undertaken to use force, once it has satisfied the requirements of *ius ad bellum,* the conflict must then meet the *ius in bello* requirements in order to be considered just.[31] Over the years, two *in bello* criteria have emerged: proportionality and discrimination.

1. Proportionality

Here the requirement is that the means used in war be proportionate to the ends to be achieved. This means two things. First, any given use of force must be proportionate to the military end sought in that particular case. For example, if the military objective in a battle can be achieved by destroying the communications center of a particular unit, then only the amount of force necessary to accomplish that task should be used. Anything beyond that would be considered disproportionate and, thus, impermissible. Second, proportionality means that, as William V. O'Brien puts it, a military action "must be proportionate in the context of the grand strategic and moral ends of the war."[32] In his book on Israeli's conflict with the PLO, O'Brien notes that "an action might be justified in purely military terms at the tactical or strategic level, but not justified as part of a total pattern of behavior when viewed from the standpoint of the grand strategic ends of the war."[33] Specific uses of force must be proportionate not only in context but also to the overall goals of the general conflict.

Proportionality seems more difficult to apply at the tactical level of terrorism than at the grand strategic level. This is because at the specific case level, proportionality has frequently been understood to mean that the response to a specific terrorist act must be at roughly the same level of force as the act itself.[34] Oscar Schachter, for example, has observed that from a legal perspective, "the U.N. Security Council in several cases, most involving Israel, has judged proportionality by comparing the response on a quantitative basis to the *single attack* which preceded it."[35] This approach has been called "tit-for-tat proportionality."[36] The difficulty with it is that it could lead to a vicious cycle of terrorist acts and equivalent responses without any real progress toward ending the series of acts.

When the problem of terrorism is viewed through the lens of the broader goals, however, another approach to proportionality becomes plausible. This is what has been called the "eye-for-a-tooth" approach or "deterrent proportionality."[37] As O'Brien has explained, "counter-terror measures should be proportionate to the purposes of counter-terror and defense, viewed in the total context of hostilities as well as the broader political-military strategic context."[38] Accordingly, "the referent of proportionality" is "the overall pattern of past and projected acts."[39] Under this approach, a state responding to a terrorist act would be able to use force not just proportionate to that single act but proportionate to the terrorists' accumulated past acts and anticipated future acts. This approach makes a great deal of sense in light of the peculiar problem of terrorism; yet it is not universally accepted.

2. Discrimination

The principle of discrimination "prohibits direct intentional attacks on noncombatants and nonmilitary targets."[40] Needless to say, all these terms—"direct intentional attack," "noncombatants," and "nonmilitary targets"—have inspired debate.[41] This is especially true with regard to nuclear-weapons use and targeting.[42] Leaving aside these general debates, let us consider difficulties that the principle of discrimination presents for counterterrorism efforts.

A basic element of discrimination is that innocent civilians are not to be attacked or targeted. In a conventional war, military personnel are clearly identifiable. They wear uniforms, use military vehicles, and stay in military installations. Terrorists are not nearly so easy to identify. They do not necessarily wear uniforms or live in military compounds. They are, in fact, civilians. But they are not innocent civilians. Hence, one of the greatest difficulties is figuring out exactly who the guilty parties are. The matter becomes even more complicated because terrorists frequently use innocent civilians and normally immune targets—such as hospitals and churches—as covers. A terrorist group may have its headquarters in the middle of a crowded city, where innocent people go about their daily activities. How can any targeting policy that complies with the requirement of discrimination be established in such conditions?

Terrorism and Just War: Recommendations

Given the particular difficulties that terrorism poses for contemporary just war doctrine, I would like to make some recommendations regarding application of the *ius ad bellum* and *ius in bello* principles. These recommendations seek to preserve the spirit of just war thinking while responding to the specific challenges that terrorism presents.

The Principles of *Ius ad Bellum*

1. Competent Authority. The real question here is whether under domestic constitutional arrangements it should be easier to use force against terrorists than to engage in conventional war. My recommendation is that more freedom should be given to the executive of a state—the president of the United States in particular—to respond to terrorism. Short, quick actions against terrorist targets should be permitted. Without this type of accommodation, it could be very difficult to intervene in a timely fashion to prevent future terrorism.

2. Just Cause. First, regarding *substantive just cause*:

Under traditional just war doctrine, *self-defense* is the most obvious just cause. But how this applies to terrorism is somewhat unclear. I suggest that terrorist actions be regarded as an armed attack, engendering the right of self-defense, under the following circumstances.[43] First, a terrorist attack against targets within a particular state should be considered tantamount to an armed attack. If, for example, terrorists blew up New York's World Trade Center, that would constitute an attack upon the United States. Second, a terrorist attack against state targets abroad—such as embassies and military bases—should be regarded as an armed attack. If terrorist groups attacked an American military base in Germany, the United States could use force in self-defense to respond to that act. Third, significant attacks upon the citizens of a state who are outside that state's territory should be regarded as an attack upon that state. This is harder to specify. Certainly, an isolated action against a few citizens abroad is tragic, but does it amount to an armed attack that would engender the right of forcible response? My own sense is that only when such acts are of significant proportion should they be considered an armed attack. Of course, "significant" is open to varying interpretations; but I believe that this criterion can be a starting point.

Must a state experience an act of terrorism before using force, or can it act preemptively to prevent such an act? Many scholars hold that under contemporary international law, states maintain a right of *anticipatory self-defense*.[44] Traditionally, however, the right can be asserted only if the state (1) can show necessity and (2) responds proportionately. In other words, the state must first demonstrate that if it does not respond immediately an attack will occur, and its response must be proportionate to the threatened attack.

I believe that these same criteria can be applied to anticipatory self-defense to preempt terrorist actions. If a state can show that an armed attack, as defined above, is imminent, and if it responds proportionately, such actions should be considered permissible.

As for *terrorist "genocide"*: Most just war theorists would assert that if a state engages in genocide or similar massive violations of human rights, another state can intervene justly to prevent further human suffering. I strongly suggest that this concept of "humanitarian intervention" be applied to terrorist actions. If a terrorist group is involved in wide-scale killings and terrorizing, an outside state should be able to intervene justly even if it or its citizens are not directly affected. If, for example, a terrorist group in the Sudan is murdering hundreds of innocent civilians, the United States would have a substantive just cause to intervene.

Concerning the second category of just cause, *comparative justice*:

While it is clear that terrorists may indeed have just motivation for their actions, their methods are fundamentally unjust. I recommend that the methods employed by the terrorist be part of the comparative-justice calculation. Even if a group is pursuing a valid cause, if it uses indiscriminate killings, torture, hostage-taking, and other such abhorrent methods, those actions should tip the balance against the terrorists.

3. Right Intention.   Any use of force—even for a just cause—tends to be accompanied with a vilification of the enemy and a desire for revenge. This tendency is especially strong in response to actions by terrorists. I believe, however, that the same strict standard of right intention must also be applied to terrorists. While it is always proper to acknowledge an evil deed as evil, terrorists are human beings who must be dealt with out of charity. The purpose of using force against them must be to end their abhorrent actions, not to exact revenge. While it is of course impossible to change the hearts of decisionmakers who respond to terrorists, at the very least just war theorists should condemn rhetoric that savors of revenge.

4. Last Resort.   This *ius ad bellum* requirement poses a particular problem for counterterrorist actions because the normal diplomatic channels available to states do not exist for terrorist groups. While states understandably wish not to legitimize the terrorist group through negotiations, the presumption against the use of forces requiring a good-faith exploration of peaceful alternatives. I am not suggesting that compromises should be struck with terrorists that would be fundamentally unjust, or that states should engage in negotiations if to do so would enhance the terrorists' status. Rather, I am suggesting that states should not immediate assume that only forcible methods exist. They should make an effort to determine if any other methods would secure a just result. It may very well be that in virtually all cases, the problems of attempting to pursue such alternatives would greatly outweigh the cost of forcible action. Nonetheless, the examination of these non-forcible options should still be undertaken. It is a fundamental tenet of just war thinking that force is not to be chosen without an exploration of other options.

5. Probability of Success. Another difficulty with counterterror actions is how to define success. What would be a successful forcible action against terrorists? I recommend that success be defined as the elimination of the terrorist threat. This may not mean the capture of all members of a particular terrorist group, but rather the effective ending of the terrorist actions.

This goal is unlikely to be achieved by force alone, since force does not deal with the underlying causes of the terrorism—a desire for territory, a desire to participate in the political system, and the like. While states should not accede to terrorist "demands," they must give some consideration to addressing the underlying causes if they are to succeed in eradicating the terrorist threat.

The Principles of *Ius in Bello*

1. Proportionality. Some would argue that each specific forcible response to terrorists must be directly proportionate to the proximate terrorist act. Given the nature of terrorism, however, I recommend adoption of the "deterrent proportionality" approach discussed above, according to which a state may respond in a manner proportionate to the accumulated past acts of the terrorists and their anticipated future acts. While this approach clearly introduces a greater element of subjectivity than the "tit-for-tat" approach, it is more suited to prevention of further terrorist actions.

2. Discrimination. Once a determination has been made that it is permissible to use force to respond to terrorism, against what targets can a state act? This is a very difficult question, given the differences between terrorists and conventional warriors. In keeping with the importance of the principle of discrimination, I offer a couple of recommendations, aware that the precise targets will vary depending upon circumstances.[45] First, a clearly identifiable terrorist camp or training facility would be a legitimate target. Second, if the terrorists are being supported by another state, military assets in that state would be legitimate targets. Thus, if it were clearly established that Libya was providing a great deal of support to a particular terrorist group, Libyan weapons and military installations would be legitimate targets.

To conclude: While the nature of terrorists and terrorist actions raises a number of critical challenges for just war doctrine, that doctrine offers a great deal of guidance for counterterror operations. It is my hope that the observations presented here will help to illuminate this guidance.

Notes

1. Among the most important works on the just war tradition are: Paul Ramsey, *The Just War: Force and Political Responsibility* (1968); James Turner Johnson, *Ideology, Reason, and the Limitation of War* (1975); and *Just War Tradition and the Restraint of War: A Moral and*

Historical Inquiry (1981); Michael Walzer, *Just and Unjust Wars* (1977); William V. O'Brien, *The Conduct of Just and Limited War* (1981) and, earlier, *War and/or Survival* (1969).

2. See Robert J. Beck and Anthony Clark Arend, "Don't Tread on Us: International Law and Forcible State Responses to Terrorism." *Wisconsin International Law Journal* 12 (1994): 153–219, for an examination of recent forcible responses to terrorism.

3. This is a point made by William V. O'Brien in *Law and Morality in Israel's War with the PLO* (1991), 275.

4. St. Thomas Aquinas, *Summa Theologies, Secunda Secundae.* 15 Q. 40 (Art. 1)" cited in O'Brien. *The Conduct of Just and Limited War,* 17.

5. Ibid.

6. See National Conference of Catholic Bishops (NCCB), *The Challenge of Peace: God's Promise and Our Response* (1983), 28–29.

7. O'Brien, *The Conduct of Just and Limited War,* 18–19.

8. U.N. Charter, Arts. 39–51.

9. War Powers Resolution, sec. 2(c).

10. Beck and Arend, "Don't Tread on Us," 175–76.

11. NCCB, *The Challenge of Peace,* 27.

12. Ibid.

13. Ibid.

14. St. Augustine, Book LXLLIII, *Super Josue,* gu. X; cited in O'Brien, *The Conduct of Just and Limited War,* 20.

15. James A. Childress, "Just-War Criteria," in Thomas A. Shannon, ed., *War or Peace: The Search for New Answers,* 46; cited in O'Brien, *The Conduct of Just and Limited War,* 20.

16. U.N. Charter, Art. 51.

17. See, for example, Richard B. Lillich, ed., *Humanitarian Intervention and the United Nations* (1973); Natalino Ronzitti, *Rescuing Nationals Abroad Through Military Coercion and Intervention on the Grounds of Humanity* (1985); Fernando Teson, *Humanitarian Intervention* (1988).

18. NCCB, *The Challenge of Peace,* 28.

19. Ibid., 29.

20. Ibid.

21. As Professor O'Brien observes, "right intention insists that charity and love exist even among enemies." O'Brien, *The Conduct of Just and Limited War,* 34.

22. Augustine, *Contra Faustum* (LXXIV); cited in O'Brien; *The Conduct of Just and Limited War,* 33–34.

23. See John Foster Dulles, *War, Peace and Change* (1939), for a fascinating discussion of this dilemma.

24. See O'Brien, *The Conduct of Just and Limited War,* 34–35.

25. NCCB, *The Challenge of Peace,* 30.

26. O'Brien, *Law and Morality in Israel's War with the PLO,* 280.

27. NCCB, *The Challenge of Peace,* 30.

28. Ibid.

29. Ibid, 31.

30. See Anthony Clark Arend and Robert J. Beck, *International Law and the Use of Force* (London: Routledge, 1993).

31. NCCB, *The Challenge of Peace,* 31.

32. O'Brien, *Law and Morality in Israel's War with the PLO,* 281.

33. Ibid.

34. See Beck and Arend, "Don't Tread on Us," 206–9, for a discussion of different legal interpretations of proportionality.

35. Oscar Schachter, "The Extra-Territorial Use of Force Against Terrorist Bases," *Houston Journal of International Law* 11:215, 315 (emphasis added).

36. Beck and Arend, "Don't Tread on Us," 207.

37. Ibid.

38. William V. O'Brien, "Reprisal, Deterrence and Self-Defense in Counterterror Operations," *Virginia Journal of International Law*, 30: 462, 477.

39. Ibid., 472.

40. O'Brien, *The Conduct of Just and Limited War*, 42.

41. Ibid.

42. See NCCB, *The Challenge of Peace*, 31–34.

43. This draws upon recommendations that Robert Beck and I presented in "Don't Tread on Us," 216–19.

44. See Beck and Arend, *International Law and the Use of Force*, 71–79, for a discussion of anticipatory self-defense under international law.

45. These recommendations also draw upon Beck and Arend, "Don't Tread on Us," 218–19.

7.4   Brad Roberts, 1998

NBC-Armed Rogues: Is There a Moral Case for Preemption?

An expert on the proliferation and control of weapons of mass destruciton, **Brad Roberts** is an analyst at the Institute for Defense Analyses (Alexandria, Virginia) and an adjunct professor at George Washington University. He also acts as chairman of the research advisory council of the Chemical and Biological Arms Control Institute. Roberts is the author of *Weapons Proliferation in the 1990s* (1995).

In May 1996, Secretary of Defense William J. Perry declared that new chemical-weapons facility in the desert of Libya "will not be allowed to begin production," implying that the United States would use military force to secure this promise.[1] Would such an action seem right, not only to Americans but to citizens and opinion-makers in other countries? Would it *be* right, which is to say defensible in moral terms?

The long-running debate over what to do about Libya's chemical-weapons program is symptomatic of a larger problem: what to do—if anything—about the emergence of a number of states that flout agreed norms of state behavior, both domestic and international; that use and threaten to use force to coerce those who resist their ambitions; and that seek to acquire arsenals of nuclear, biological, or chemical (NBC) weapons to abet these purposes. These are the "rogue" or "backlash" states identified in 1994 by then National Security Advisor Anthony Lake.[2] Perry's statement about Libya reflects the view of many, inside and outside the U.S. government, that preemptive military strikes on the mass-destruction weaponry of such states are essential both for the security of their neighbors and for the interests of the international community.

When policy-makers in Washington and other capitals debate whether or not, or how, to strike preemptively, the choices are highly contentious. Both action and inaction set precedents with long-term consequences. Doing what national-interest calculations call for is not always doing what is right by the hearts and minds of the American people or its friends and allies.

What does moral reflection contribute to the policy debate about preemption? In particular, what does the just war tradition instruct about the value of the different choices?[3] Can there be a moral case—indeed, a moral imperative—for preemption, in addition to a national-interest or legalistic case? In what follows I will offer some speculative answers to these questions. I will begin by reviewing the ethical considerations that typically shape the policy debate about preemption: (1) Is the action undertaken as a last resort? (2) Does it have a reasonable chance of success? (3) Will the action be proportional to the threat being removed? Each will be evaluated in light of the specific attributes of NBC threats. [I] will go on to explore two further considerations. First, self-defense: When and how can preemption be justified as an essential act of self-protection? And second, competent authority: What political legitimacy is needed to establish the authority to make preemptive strikes?

This review of criteria illuminates the various ways in which the specific NBC dimension of the targeted threat shapes ethical considerations associated with preemption. Two conclusions stand out from this review. One is that in some important places the just war tradition stops a bit short. Thus some further elaboration of the tradition seems warranted on the basis of the new strategic realities created by proliferators armed with weapons of mass destruction. The other conclusion is that tradition imposes some obligations on policy that are not typically appreciated in the policy world. An act of preemption cannot be deemed just simply if it meets the first three criteria stated above. The requirements posed by the self-defense and competent-authority criteria cannot be overlooked. Meeting those requirements, moreover, proves to be more complicated than might be expected, given certain attributes of the problem under discussion here.

This leads to a third and more general conclusion, one that is hardly surprising: A moral case for preemption is possible—even a moral imperative in some cases—but only under certain specific conditions. This [selection] evaluates a range of scenarios in which preemption may or may not be justified. It concludes with an assessment of the moral obligations that would follow a preemptive strike.

Why is it important for the policy-maker to think more fully through the moral context of preemption? It is not simply a matter of making preemption more palatable to an American public reluctant to use force for reasons of national interest. Rather, the answer has to do with the particular historical moment, defined by two factors. One is the emergence of the United States as "the world's only superpower"—as a state with unparalleled military power leading an international system in which most of the other states of the world participate as willing partners. The other is the ongoing diffusion of technologies and materials that can be used to produce nuclear, biological, and chemical weapons. If the United States fails to use its power in ways that others will accept as just, a terrible backlash could result. Cooperation could weaken, U.S. leadership could be delegitimized, and weapons could proliferate much more broadly. The future stability of international affairs and the moral framework of American action are thus inextricably intertwined.[4]

Three Prudential Considerations

Just war concepts are hardly new to the policy debate about when and how to use military force. The memoirs of public officials along with public statements of the moment reveal a good deal of concern and often debate about whether particular military actions will be just, and will be perceived as just by the American public and the international community. Policy-makers typically focus on three just war criteria: Can the proposed use of force be defended as a *last resort* effort, after all other means to manage the problem have been tried and failed? Is there a *reasonable chance of success?* And will the action have an effect *proportionate* to the problem it is aimed at solving? When the military act in question is a preemptive strike against the NBC arsenals of rogue states, these criteria require especially careful analysis, largely because the risks and possible consequences loom larger than in many other types of military action.

1. Last Resort

The last-resort criterion is generally understood to require that military action shall not be undertaken unless all other means have been tried and have failed; war-making, after all, should not be the first or preferred course of action in dealing with the war-mongering behavior of a potential aggressor. In fact, the moral requirement is a bit more subtle. Just war thinking does not require that every conceivable alternative course of action in dealing with the war-mongering behavior of a potential aggressor. In fact, the moral requirement is a bit more subtle. Just war thinking does not require that every conceivable alternative course of action be exhausted. As Michael Walzer has argued, "taken literally... 'last resort' would make war morally impossible. For we can never reach lastness, or we can never know that we have reached it."[5] The moral obligation requires an assessment of all means available to meet a particular threat—economic, political, and military—and, of those deemed *sufficient* to do so, a preference for means other than war.

In the 1993 debate over preemptive military strikes against the nuclear assets of North Korea, Tokyo and Beijing were unpersuaded that this criterion had been met. Both believed that the United States was looking too readily to military solutions when the problem might still be susceptible to political and economic management. The Libyan chemical facility still fails to meet this criterion in the eyes of many countries; they are more impressed by the history of enmity between Washington and Muammar Qaddafi than by Washington's efforts to use other means at its disposal, such as a trade embargo or legal prosecution, to suppress the Libyan chemical-weapons program.

But the requirement that military action be taken only in last resort does not mean that military action must be forestalled until it cannot be successful (or can succeed only at far higher cost). In Bosnia, for example, the decision of the NATO [North Atlantic Treaty Organization] allies to use force only in last resort contributed to a widening of the war and a substantial increase in human suffering—the just war tradition would arguably have required a narrow interpretation of the "last resort" criterion and an earlier intervention.[6] Particularly when rogue regimes and weapons of mass destruction are a part of the threat calculus, the last-resort criterion should probably be subject to a quite narrow interpretation. Economic sanctions may take months or years to have an effect (and indeed, their likelihood of success is hotly debated). In contrast, weapons programs may quickly reach maturity once a confrontation begins to take shape. Given what is now known about Iraq's pre-war unconventional-weapons programs, for example, it is clear that in just a few additional months of sanctions aimed at pressuring Saddam Hussein to withdraw his army from Kuwait, Iraq's nuclear program would have produced one or two weapons while its biological program could have geared up to a very substantial level of production and weaponization. Moreover, where arsenals already exist, deferring a preemptive strike may induce an aggressor to disperse his weapons and give him the time to do so, greatly reducing the likelihood that preemption will eliminate them. In both scenarios, buying time could cost lives, literally hundreds of thousands of them.

2. Reasonable Chance of Success

This criterion requires that military actions not be undertaken unless they offer a meaningful prospect of eliminating the threat against which they are targeted. The just war tradition dictates that suffering be minimized. Again, the requirement is a bit more subtle than generally conceived. It requires not simply eliminating the threat but restoring a peace that has been disordered by the threat.

If a preemptive strike fails to eliminate an aggressor's nuclear weapons and motivates retaliation, those weapons may be unleashed, causing the loss of a great many lives. The North Korean case, for example, failed to meet the reasonable-chance-of-success criterion because there was little certainty of the number of nuclear weapons produced there, of their location in a massive network of underground storage and transfer facilities, and of North Korea's capacity to use biological and chemical weapons to attack the South even if it were stripped of its nuclear weapons. The Libyan case presents similar considerations.

The difficulty presented by the reasonable-success criterion is magnified by the fact that many NBC assets are located in underground facilities that are very hard to attack successfully. In the case of the Libyan plant, for example, some administration statements have indicated that it might not be possible to destroy the plant without resort to nuclear weapons. This would undoubtedly raise questions of proportionality. Even if the United States acquires some reliable means other than nuclear weapons to destroy hardened underground facilities, gaining high-confidence intelligence about the location of such facilities or other weapons deployment sites may prove extremely difficult.

But "success" in this criterion need not mean perfect success. A preemptive strike that eliminates some but not all of an aggressor's NBC weapons could have a variety of benefits. It might induce greater caution and more conservative behavior by removing any doubt the aggressor might have entertained about the ability or will of the United States to meet his challenges. It might also leave the aggressor with so few weapons and delivery systems that they could readily be defeated by active and passive defensive measures, thus rendering his NBC weapons essentially irrelevant to any direct battlefield confrontation he might initiate.

3. Proportionality

The proportionality criterion is generally understood to require that the minimum necessary force be used. The just war tradition dictates that suffering be minimized, particularly the suffering of noncombatants, and military actions that cause more casualties than they prevent can hardly be deemed just. But once again, the precise requirements of the tradition are a bit more subtle. The proportionality criterion puts two obligations on those who would use force: regarding *ius in bello* (what it is right to do in using force), it requires that only minimum force consistent with the aim be used; and regarding *ius ad bellum* (when it is right to resort to force), it requires that the overall costs of action be less substantial than the costs of inaction. Will the good to be achieved by the resort to violence outweigh the damage to be done, both to individuals and to the community of nations?

With regard to *ius in bello,* it would seem at first glance that virtually any preemption of an aggressor's use of NBC weapons should pass the proportionality test—preventing the use of weapons of mass destruction should by definition save the lives of hundreds of thousands if not millions of people, in exchange for the much smaller number of lives that might be lost in the preemptive strike. The North Korean case failed to meet this test, however, because preemptive military action by the United States was seen as likely to precipitate a broader war on the Korean peninsula, one initiated by Pyongyang in response to U.S. actions. Even if stripped of its nuclear weapons, North Korea would possess a formidable capability to destroy South Korea's military and economic infrastructure and to hold Seoul hostage. In contrast, an attack on the Libyan chemical-weapons facility would be unlikely to pose these difficulties and could more easily met the proportionality requirement.

With regard to *ius ad bellum,* the proportionality of preemption is clouded by a number of factors. Even if preemption successfully prevents the aggressor's use of those weapons, the cost of that thwarted aggression cannot be known—certainly not publicly proven. The United States would find itself in the position of tallying *actual* casualties caused by its actions against casualties that the aggressor *might* have caused had he not been stopped. This would undoubtedly lead to debate about whether the aggressor would indeed have used his weapons as the United States believed he would. It is important to note that most NBC arsenals have been used not militarily but politically, to coerce a potential adversary to make an important concession (either to do or to refrain from doing something). The costs of this "use" of NBC weapons cannot readily be compared with the costs of preemptive military attack upon them. But such comparisons are necessary in the moral world. The potential coercive use of NBC arsenals does provide a moral basis for preemption, insofar at it is necessary to repel injury or to punish evil. From the perspective of the just war tradition, this moral claim is valid whether or not coercion has been openly backed by military threats. Appeasement, after all, has typically emboldened assertive leaders. Sometimes it has fueled acts of aggression that have produced many casualties and have been reversed only at high cost.

These three criteria draw on both *ius ad bellum* and *ius in bello* dimensions of the just war tradition. They present a substantial set of moral requirements for dealing with NBC-armed rogue states. But they are only the beginning of the story. They do not reflect a comprehensive reading of what that tradition requires of military action. They are in fact what one moral philosopher has termed "contingent prudential judgments."[7] Two prior criteria must be satisfied: the requirements that any use of force be in self-defense, and that any use of force be authorized by a competent authority.

Preemption and Self-Defense

Moral philosophy establishes that wars of self-defense are just, whereas wars of aggression are not. But there has long been a healthy debate about precisely what constitutes a war of self-defense. A scholar of just war in the mid-sixteenth century wrote, "There is a single and only just cause for commencing a war... namely, wrong received."[8] In our day Michael Walzer has argued, "Nothing but aggression can justify war.... There must actually have been a wrong, and it must actually have been received (or its receipt must be, as it were, only minutes away). Nothing else warrants the use of force in international society."[9] In the debate about preemption, the crucial issue is in those "minutes away": how proximate must the threat of the use of those weapons be? Does the just war tradition require waiting until the very last minute?

As James Turner Johnson has argued, much contemporary Catholic thought on war echoes this very circumscribed right to self-defense—"a defensive response to an attack still in progress."[10] Johnson attributes this way of thinking primarily to the Church's rejection of war as a viable instrument of order and peace under virtually any circumstances, and especially in the nuclear era.

A survey of other perspectives, both contemporary and historical, suggests that this circumscribed view is not universally held. Hugo Grotius wrote in 1625 that "the first just cause of war... is an injury, which even though not actually committed, threatens our persons or our property."[11] To safeguard against wars of aggression, Grotius emphasized that it was essential to be certain about the enemy's intent to attack. Elihu Root said in 1914 that international law did not require the aggrieved state to wait before using force in self-defense "until it is too late to protect itself."[12] Writing in 1977, Michael Walzer argued that "states can rightfully defend themselves against violence that is imminent but not actual." However, Walzer rejects boastful ranting, arms races, and hostile acts short of war as legitimate bases of preemption, arguing that "injury must be 'offered' in some material sense as well."[13]

The United Nations Charter incorporates competing notions. In its Chapter 7, special rights are reserved for the Security Council to use force in response to threats to international peace and security; those threats are not specifically limited to instances of outright aggression. On the other hand, Article 51 of the Charter, which affirms the right of self-defense "if an armed attack occurs," is generally interpreted to forbid claims of self-defense *except* in cases of armed attack.[14]

International law restricts the right of states to resort to the offensive use of force in preemptive modes. As Johnson notes, "Under the controverted first-use/second-use distinction, aggression is defined as the first use of force regardless of circumstances, while defense becomes second use alone."[15]

This distinction is controverted for the simple reason that aggression does not usually begin, and injury is not usually "offered," when the first weapons are fired. Hot wars are usually but one phase of a competition of interest and power. In relations among states in an anarchic system, competition is inevitable. But it is usually pursued with "soft power," namely political and economic means, rather than the harder forms. War itself is frequently the culmination of a failure of other means to coerce, dissuade, or compel others. As Clausewitz noted, the aggressor is often peace-loving, and it is his resistant victim who causes war to erupt: "A conqueror is always a lover of peace (as Bonaparte always asserted of himself); he would like to make his entry into our state unopposed; in order to prevent this, we must choose war."[16]

War-Making Versus Preemption

Other than the mechanistic and unreliable use of the first-use/second-use distinction, what criteria can be used to distinguish illegitimate acts of war-making from legitimate acts of preemption? Walzer offers some useful commentary on this point:

> The line between between legitimate and illegitimate first strikes is not going to be drawn at the point of imminent attack but at the point of sufficient threat. That phrase is necessarily vague. I mean it to cover three things: a manifest intent to injure, a degree of active preparation that makes that intent a positive danger, and a general situation in which waiting, or doing anything other than fighting, greatly magnifies the risk.... Instead of previous signs of rapacity and ambition, current and particular signs are required; instead of an "augmentation of power," actual preparation for war; instead of the refusal of future securities, the intensification of present dangers.[17]

Walzer and others also emphasize the importance of illegal actions by the prospective aggressor, which is to say actions that abrogate specific legal undertakings of the state or that contravene accepted principles of international law.

The acquisition of weapons of mass destruction might fit many of these criteria quite well—these are actions that can confirm an intent to injure, create a positive danger, and raise the risks of waiting. Their dispersal in time of crisis would certainly signal preparation for war. But to acquire such weapons and to prepare for their use is not the same as what Walzer calls "actual preparation for war" or "the intensification of present dangers"—these are qualities that have to do with the nature of the regime itself. As George Weigel has argued:

> Iraqi and North Korean nuclear-weapons programs do not exist in a historical vacuum. They are the expressions of evil, real-world political intentions whose character has been made plain over many years. Precisely for the same reason that we do not think about preemptive action against Britain and France, we can, without collapsing into the moral vulgarities of Realpolitik, consider proportionate and discriminate preemptive action against Iraq and North Korea.[18]

Rogue regimes have already established their aggressive intent—this is the essence of their characterization as "rogue" or "backlash." Their acquisition of NBC weapons is yet another confirmation of that intent. The moral obligation that falls upon them is to conform to established norms of interstate behavior. The moral obligation that falls on their potential victims is to protect themselves. But, given the particular nature of NBC weapons, such protection may be extremely costly if it must await the first blow with those weapons.

Threats to Peace and Order

Moreover, rogue regimes generally threaten not just the immediate sovereignty of their neighbors but the order that is the foundation of long-term sovereignty. They may pose threats to regional peace. For example, had Saddam Hussein been able to use his weapons of mass destruction to secure aggression with conventional weapons in the Middle East, and thus to emerge as a regional hegemon, there would have been significant repercussions for other states in the region—not only those whom he might seek to coerce to do his bidding, such as Egypt or Turkey, but those whom he might seek to defeat or destroy, such as Iran or Israel. In the Far East, were North Korea to prove successful in using its NBC capabilities to coerce the great powers into taking steps that compromised South Korea's safety and well-being, power relations in the region would undergo a period of deeply unsettling realignment, perhaps leading others in the region to acquire NBC weapons of their own.

Rogue regimes may also pose threats to the global order. If an NBC-armed rogue were able to challenge a major commitment or interest of one of the established nuclear powers, and thereby cause that power to back down and appease, others could draw the conclusion that the security guarantees of the great powers—and especially the United States—and the already limited promise of collective security are paper tigers. Similarly, the acquisition of weapons of mass destruction in contravention of existing legal undertakings, such as the Nuclear Non-Proliferation Treaty or the Biological and Toxin Weapons Convention, could lead to an unraveling of the international effort to control the proliferation of such weapons. That could prove highly damaging to international security. Many states have the capability to build NBC weapons but for the moment are uninterested in doing so. The actions of an NBC-armed rogue could lead to the wildfire-like building of mass destruction arsenals in regions in conflict and in regions now free of such weapons. Such far-reaching changes in the distribution of power and in the credibility of the major powers would be likely to erode sharply the international processes and institutions that for the moment at least are the foundation of international order. These changes could eviscerate the norms and principles of the U.N. Charter, if not lead to their eclipse by new norms antithetical to the interests of justice and peace.

To put it differently: in the international system that exists today, many small and medium-sized states depend upon international norms and collective mechanisms to compensate for their own modest capabilities to provide for their own security. Even the great powers experience a great deal of economic interdependence. Therefore, defending the stability of the system is in the national interest of many states. The world-order argument thus creates an additional moral justification for preemption. Protecting world order is long-term self-defense.

This way of thinking about the just-cause criterion contrasts with the narrow view of self-defense now in vogue. But it is in fact consistent with other elements of the just war traditions, elements that have been eclipsed by the emphasis on defense against aggression. Two other criteria have traditionally been used to define justifiable defensive wars: those aimed at the recovery of something wrongfully taken, and those aimed at the punishment of evil.[19] According to Johnson, in this way of thinking about just cause, just wars were those required to establish a just political and social order among states, "an order that was necessary for the presence of peace."[20] Such a view of war is well ingrained in the balance-of-power school of international politics. In the nineteenth century, for example, Britain viewed war as necessary to maintain a status quo in Europe that made possible the progress of liberty and thus increased the chances for zones of peace built on shared commercial and social interests.

This view of what can justify war predates the Industrial Revolution and the emergence in the twentieth century of total war, i.e., war that mobilizes all the resources of a society to defeat if not annihilate an enemy society similarly mobilized. Of course, wars of complete annihilation are not unknown in history, but technical and scientific sophistication has brought them to a new scale and immediacy. The view of war as a legitimate instrument of peace has lost favor in the Catholic Church not least because of this transformation of war, leading many to conclude that no war could pass the prudential tests cited above.[21]

Two Weaknesses in the Debate

This line of argument helps to expose the two basic weaknesses in the way the moral debate about the use of force draws upon the just war tradition. One relates to collective self-defense. Although the tradition posits the right of states to act in collective self-defense, the moral debate focuses almost exclusively on wars between two states—the aggressor and the aggrieved. In the international system of the late twentieth century, states coexist with multilateral institutions, transnational processes, global norms, and an international community. Aggression threatens interests far larger than those of the sovereignty of a given state. If aggression between states were permitted to return as a common mode of behavior, societies on every continent would pay a price. This suggests that in the moral calculation, the value of defeating an aggressive regime and thereby perhaps deterring similar ones must be added to the values of protecting the national sovereignty of individual states.

The second basic weakness relates to the nuclear revolution in international affairs. The moral debate on nuclear weapons is locked in a time now passed. In the memorable debate on the nuclear bomb in the early 1980s, the U.S. Catholic bishops by and large deemed unjust both the means and the ends of nuclear war, arguing that there is virtually no imaginable real-world circumstance in which the use of nuclear weapons could be satisfied as just *in bello;* the Vatican did accept the possibility of a just nuclear peace, albeit reluctantly.[22] Although arguments will long continue, there is much to suggest that the peace secured in the Cold War and the victory that brought its end have much to do with nuclear weapons. The point here is that most of the moral philosophizing on matters nuclear is held hostage to this era now past—an era when nuclear war was a matter of East-West brinkmanship and global armageddon.

In the post–Cold War era, wars and threats by rogue states armed with nuclear weapons pose new questions. The particular issue from the point of view of this paper is that preemption entails the risk of nuclear confrontation—but not armageddon. If the preemptive strike is not successful in eliminating an aggressor's NBC weapons, and he opts to use them in reply, preemption would have unleashed a terrible chain of events. Wars such as this may or may not prove to be massively destructive, depending on the choices made by the aggressor and the character of the arsenals and delivery systems available to him, as well as the choices made by the United States about how to reply (and its defensive and offensive capabilities). No rogue has the nuclear capacity to annihilate a major power, although each major power has the capacity to annihilate a rogue. Limited nuclear wars of the kind long dismissed in the Cold War are now a matter requiring serious reflection. The United States must consider whether or how to use nuclear weapons in meeting the aggression of such states, not simply in deterrence or for national survival, but for larger purposes of international order. This new agenda permits no easy answers.

Some have seen an escape from the dilemmas of U.S. nuclear use in increased reliance on conventional rather than nuclear means to carry out attacks of strategic significance. The exceptional technical ability of the U.S. military to employ military force discriminately and to use conventional weaponry in precision strikes has fueled a perception that the United States has minimized, to the extent possible, the costs to noncombatants and the risks to anyone other than the soldiers and military infrastructure of the state being struck preemptively. This may make it easier to justify attacks on the NBC arsenals of rogue states.

The overwhelming military power in the hands of the United States does make it easier to threaten attacks. But reliance on overwhelming power and on military actions that impose essentially no cost in American lives raises proportionality questions of its own—questions that troubled senior U.S. policy-makers on the last day of Desert Storm as they considered the reported savagery of the "highway to death." Moreover, conventional preemption may not prevent an aggressor from using his unconventional weapons. The United States may then feel compelled to use its own nuclear weapons, whether for reasons of proportionality (so as not to suffer huge casualties in observing a nuclear taboo already broken by the aggressor) or for punishment (to establish the point that aggression with nuclear weapons is intolerable). In sum, conventional options are unlikely to eliminate nuclear dilemmas.

Preemption and Competent Authority

The second criterion for the just use of force that must be met *before* considerations of last resort, proportionality, and reasonable chance of success is that the decision to go to war must be made by a competent authority. The purpose of this requirement is to limit the right to make war to sovereign entities, thereby denying it to individuals or groups whose use of violence is not constrained by the dictates of international society and international law.

The competent-authority requirement is most easily met in wars between two sovereign nations. It is also met in wars of cooperative self-defense, albeit less directly. Moral philosophy permits states not only to act in self-defense but to make common cause in self-defense with others. Thus, under the rule that an attack on one is an attack on all, even a nation not directly attacked by an aggressor's first acts of war has a just cause to undertake military actions in reply.

But in the scenarios considered here, a particular difficulty emerges. Does the United States have the necessary authority to undertake preemptive strikes against rogue states that have not first made military attacks on it? This is one sense a trite questions: The United States is, after all, sovereign entity. But in another sense it is more profound: if it is not the party immediately threatened by a rogue's NBC weapons, and if it is not in a formal alliance with such a party, by what means is its authority deemed legitimate? The cause may be just, but what makes it America's fight?

The United States faces a real dilemma in establishing its authority in this regard: if it arrogates to itself the right to determine when and how to strike at nations it considers outside the law, it may be judged as having put itself above the law. The United States finds itself, after all, in a peculiar historical moment. As the world's dominant military, economic, and political power, it has been cast in the role of primary defender of the global status quo—of the existing balance of global power and of the institutions it has labored to put in place to promote global stability, prosperity, and liberty. As the defender of the status quo, it has a special stake in turning back the aggressions and deterring the potential aggressions of rogue nations. The concern that the United States not put itself above the law is particularly evident among its closest allies, for their partnership with the United States is based on a belief in its benign use of power and on the legitimacy it enjoys within their societies as a steward of common interests. Both of these qualifications would be eroded by acts outside the law.

As A. J. Bacevich has argued: "Like Great Britain at the end of the nineteenth century, the United States at the end of the twentieth is a dominant world power with an interest above all in perpetuating that dominance. The existing order—the distribution of wealth and influence, the basic rules governing the game of world politics—suits us, and we are committed to its preservation."[23] To be sure, there are some fundamental differences between the system of today, in which the United States *is dominant,* and one *dominated by* the United States. Other nations have joined with it in building the current rules and institutions of order, and they remain free to seek an alternative order. Today, the vast majority of states side with the United States in its commitment to the status quo, so long as this permits them the opportunity to make evolutionary changes in ways that promote justice, peace, and prosperity. The genuine challengers to the status quo are few and far between, though many states aspire to improve their lot, which means not only gains in well-being or political status but also enhanced security. Because the so-called status quo has a certain promise of such goals, it is a status quo of unique and unprecedented character.

But this does not eliminate the moral issue for the United States as the primary beneficiary and defender of this status quo. How does it distinguish morally between preemptive actions with a world-order purpose and those that, though wrapped in world-order rhetoric, are in the service of primarily U.S. interests?

Supports for Authority

One answer might be for the United States to seek endorsement by the U.N. Security Council of a decision to strike preemptively. There could be many practical reasons not to consider such a move, not least the warning to the rogue state likely to be given by such an action, which might induce it to disperse its weapons and perhaps to use them before losing them. But the focus here is on establishing just authority. As Eugene Rostow has observed, it is not obligatory for a state exercising its right to self-defense to seek U.N. approval;[24] moreover, the Security Council has the legal authority to act not merely to uphold the right of self-defense but in reply to threats of whatever kind to international peace and security. But the Security Council lacks the moral authority to act as a sovereign. It lacks competent authority in two ways: absence of public account-ability, and absence of a command-and-control system for the use of force.[25]

An alternative answer to the competent-authority dilemma might be to stimulate creation of a broad international coalition to carry out, and support, preemptive action. The moral benefit of this approach would be to attach American power and actions to a broad base of international sovereignty.

But this too poses problems. From a practical point of view, it is likely to prove very difficult to assemble such a coalition—preemption is a notoriously unpopular mea-sure, and every hint that the United States might be considering a preemptive attack generates strong reactions among allies as well as potential adversaries. Moreover, it is not clear that this would solve the moral dilemma. As Walzer has argued, "when the world divides radically into those who bomb and those who are bombed, it becomes morally problematic even if the bombing in this or that instance is justifiable."[26]

A third approach would be to rely on unilateral action by the United States in the context of a strong moral argument. Such a case might build on its right to self-defense—after all, the United States seems to be a likely target of weapons possessed by leaders who believe the United States to be the primary defender of a corrupt status quo. It might also draw on the moral duty to help others. And the U.S. case would also have to draw on the obligations of a security guarantor that fall on it as a permanent member of the Security Council—after all, the NBC capabilities of the rogue pose a threat to the interests of international peace and stability.

In fact, the United States has begun to make this latter case. Anthony Lake's orig-inal characterization of the rogue-state problem was careful to look beyond the weapons programs of the named states to their flagrant disregard for basic norms of international society, including principally their regular reliance on violence to maintain domestic power and to coerce, if not invade and defeat, their neighbors. Lake thus was careful to frame a normative context for addressing the rogue-state problem that went beyond the national-interest arguments about military capability and power.[27]

This normative framework may provide an international context in which U.S. ac-tions are legitimized. It seems unlikely to establish the United States as a competent au-thority in a moral sense, however, as the expression of this normative framework is a series of multilateral treaties and institutions that by definition distribute rights and au-thority through the international system. Unilateral action by the United States in sup-port of those norms would be inconsistent with its commitment to the mechanisms that embody those norms. Moreover, so long as the United States finds itself isolated in making the case that certain states are rogues, any military actions based on this moral case will be open to the charge that they are merely national-interest actions hidden under the rubric of world-order interests. In fact, the Clinton administration's charac-terization of this set of states as rogues, and its subsequent policies to isolate them and undertake counterproliferation preparations for possible military action against their NBC weapons, are much criticized, not least by U.S. friends and allies abroad who see such actions as an effort to put the United States above or outside the law.[28]

The particular problem with this approach is that the United States sometimes acts in defense of interests that it but not others see as common, or in defense of norms that it asserts but others do not support. For example, in the mid-1980s the United States tried to make a moral case for preemptive attacks on Libya based on the latter's chemical-weapons production activities at Rabta, a case that was politically flawed by the fact that the United States was itself a possessor of chemical weapons and was at the time engaged in the production of such weapons. Even some U.S. allies questioned the moral basis of what appeared to be a punitive if not vengeful act. Similarly, in 1996 the U.S. case for preemption of Libyan chemical plants was weakened by the United States' own continued possession of chemical weapons and its reluctance to ratify the Chemical Weapons Convention. To be sure, there are fundamental differences between the "regimes" in Washington and Tripoli or Baghdad; but the isolation of the United States on these issues underscores how inconsequential those moral differences have proven to be politically.

This review suggests that there is no easy answer to the competent-authority requirement of the just war tradition in the current historical moment. Policy-makers will logically be drawn to the argument that if each approach is inadequate, the best approach is to do all three in combination. Making a clear normative argument, while also building a coalition and seeking a U.N. mandate, would help to satisfy many citizens that preemptive action meets the basic moral requirement of political legitimacy. But whether it would also satisfy moral philosophers is another question. This leads to a conclusion analogous to that in the discussion of self-defense: contemporary moral reasoning based on the just war tradition has not taken into account the moral requirements of a changing world.

Assessing the U.N.'s Authority

But within the tradition there are some touchstones for the path ahead. The emphasis should be on a critique of the moral authority of the Security Council. As noted above, such a critique rests on two key points: the absence of public accountability, and the absence of a command-and-control system for the use of force. Are these in fact the appropriate criteria by which to assess the competent authority of the U.N. to endorse preemptive action?

The Security Council does reflect a certain type of accountability. The Council is accountable to the principles that guide its actions, to the states that are its members, and thus indirectly to the citizens of those states. The indirect nature of its democratic credentials is analogous to that of the U.S. president in the days when he was put into office by the process of indirect election that was the Electoral College, before the electors were bound by the popular vote. The Council's capacity to use power is, moreover, subject to a number of checks and balances. In a global political system of states, what higher moral authority can exist than the collective will of nations?

The U.N. itself does not of course possess full sovereignty. But it does have certain clearly identified, clearly circumscribed, areas of authority. One is the Security Council's right to authorize the use of force to defend peace and security. For this purpose, it does not have the command-and-control system of a state. But it does have such a system appropriate to its particular role—a system that weaves together national command with multilateral institutions and processes. This too is subject to checks and balances. Its capacity to use force is thus limited to ad hoc circumstances, with the use of borrowed forces under charters granted by state members. The command and control flows from those who are directly responsible in the system.

Moreover, the U.N. embodies an agreed set of norms within the international community about behaviors within and among states that are either appropriate or inappropriate. To be sure, some states ignore the U.N. Charter (though ever fewer, as democracy takes hold in many parts of the world). And to be sure, there are fundamental political divisions within the organization. But it does reflect a consensus-based global normative structure. It is the only institution that aspires to represent the interests of the whole community of nations, and thus the only one with strong moral authority in purporting to defend those interests. Its most powerful members assume special obligations in their role as guarantors of international peace and security on the Security Council, though how they fulfill those duties—and how well they do so—is hotly contested.

The point here is not that the U.N. is sufficiently like a state to establish its sovereignty. Rather, it has a certain moral authority sufficient to the competent-authority requirement. The U.N. can provide the normative framework for actions by a state or group of states in defense of world-order interests. The U.N. is essential, not because it is supranational and "above" its member states, but because its normative attributes redress the competent-authority shortfall.

Invoking the U.N.'s Authority

But how is that authority invoked and operationalized? The moral authority of the U.N. would most clearly be engaged if the General Assembly, the Secretary General, and the Security Council unanimously agreed that a particular threat to world order was so egregious as to require preemptive military action. Such unanimity is of course highly unlikely. Political division implies that the U.N. will not reliably be able to act in times of crisis and will find it difficult to cope with questions of preemption. But the absence of unanimity is not necessarily a moral deficiency, as ethical issues are not determined in popularity contests.

On preemption, the Council possesses the authority to authorize such actions, given its special responsibilities, and the Charter legalizes the associated actions. But whether the competent-authority requirement also requires the assent of the Council for each and every act of preemption by a permanent member for world-order purposes is doubtful. In those cases where prior approval is sought from the Council, the moral requirement probably does not even necessitate an affirmative vote from the Council. To veto a just act is not to rob the act of its justness. General and broad reinforcement of this duty could help to bolster the moral case for specific acts of preemption.

Establishing the competent authority of a world-order defense argument would seem to require more than reliance on the Security Council, however. After all, many states see the Council itself as symptomatic of an *unjust* world order. The Council's authority is hotly contested by many who see it as an anachronism of a world war now a half century past, and as a body dominated by "the world's only superpower," whose use of power is unfettered and whose singular ability to mobilize the U.N. deprives the Security Council of a meaningful role beyond one that serves U.S. interests.[29] The moral authority of the Council can be buttressed only by addressing these concerns.

A footnote to this discussion of competent authority is in order. The competent-authority requirement is intended to bolster the role of sovereigns in international affairs. Under international law, sovereignty has become virtually sacrosanct. But while all states may be equal before the law, all sovereigns do not possess the same degree or type of sovereignty. This ambiguity may have been tenable at a time when the purpose of just war thinking was to codify war as a right of states, but it seems ever less acceptable. A dictator who holds power by the ruthless use of repression, torture, extortion, and murder cannot be equated morally with leaders somehow representing the will of the body politic. Why should he have equal legitimacy in waging war, especially if he is also making war on his own people? Sovereignty requires consent for its proper exercise. Such consent should be an increasingly important measure of sovereignty in an age in which widespread industrialization and technical innovation are putting massively destructive weapons and long-range delivery systems into the hands of more and more individuals or regimes whose grip on power derives from force, not popular will.

When Is Preemption Just?

There can, then, be no blanket reply to the question, Is there a moral case for preemption? Some acts of preemption will be deemed just, others unjust. For yet others, some elements of a moral case will be present, others absent.

The strongest moral case for U.S. preemption exists under the following conditions: (1) an aggressor has actually threatened to use his NBC weapons, has taken steps to ready the means to do so, and has specifically threatened the United States (including its territory, citizens, or military forces); (2) those NBC weapons have been built in violation of international law; (3) the aggressor's threatened actions invoke larger questions about the credibility of security guarantees or the balance of power within a region; (4) the president has secured the approval of the U.S. Congress; and (5) the United States has secured the backing of the U.N. Security Council and any relevant regional organization. The prudential tests of last resort, proportionality, and reasonable chance of success must also be met.

The weakest case for preemption exists when: (1) a state has made no NBC threats and has no prior behavior of aggression; (2) those weapons are permitted under international law (because the state is not a party to the relevant treaties); (3) the preemption is the culmination of a worsening bilateral relationship with the United States, driven by a loss of objectivity in Washington; and (4) U.S. actions have been condemned by the U.N. or opposed by the Security Council. Even if the intended strike meets all the prudential tests, it cannot be accepted as just under these conditions.

In the middle are a range of scenarios with mixed ethical configurations, drawing on the following factors: Threatened attacks on U.S. allies establish the same moral case as threatened attacks on the United States. Threats that generate Security Council agreement and action should also establish a credible moral case, even where those threats are to international order and not merely to the sovereignty of a particular state. Threats that call into question U.S. security guarantees, even if not formal alliances, also offer less strong but credible moral cases. Preemptive attacks in response not to explicit threats but to implicit intentions as perceived in NBC weapons programs offer a less strong moral case, unless backed by other signals of aggressive intent.

This is not to argue that all acts of military preemption by the United States require approval by others if they are to be just. Rather, preemptions conceived by the United States as necessary to defend world-order interests, rather than those deemed necessary because of alliance guarantees or more discrete and specific national interests, require a normative framework that the United States alone cannot provide in its "unipolar moment."[30]

Moral Obligations Following Preemption

The just war tradition also imposes obligations in the aftermath of military action. One is the requirement to make a moral case for the action that has been undertaken. As Weigel has argued, "the presumption is always for peace, and the burden of moral reasoning lies with those who argue for the justness of a particular resort to war."[31]

Justice requires a clear explication of the moral reasoning that led to the chosen course of action. Especially in an era when many countries, both adversaries and allies, fear a hegemonic United States that puts itself above the law in defending its perceived national-security interests, it is incumbent upon the United States to establish that its actions are consistent not merely with the letter of the law but also with the spirit of justice and peace that underpins it. Making this case would help to heal the domestic divisions likely to be caused by preemptive military attack. It would also help to reassure those in other countries who might interpret U.S. preemption as signaling a more bellicose America more likely to intervene abroad.

Making the moral case for a world-order act means making the case to the world community, which of course encompass many different cultures and ethical traditions. A moral cast that draws only on the just war tradition of Westerners and Christians may be rejected by others as cultural imperialism. Moral philosophers face a critical challenge in building up a dialogue across cultures, one that gives them common terms of reference even if not common traditions. There are many obvious differences among cultures and ethical traditions, especially on questions of war. But because problems of war, peace, and justice are universal, there is good reason to believe that beneath the apparent cultural differences are some fundamental commonalities.[32]

A second moral obligation after a preemptive strike is to alleviate the suffering caused by U.S. actions. This may not be practical in cases where a regime that is antithetical to U.S. interests remains firmly entrenched, especially if it exploits the public-relations value of U.S.-inflicted casualties. But it may be practical where preemption leads to the collapse of the regime, or at least to the emergence of new political forces within the targeted country that would accept U.S. humanitarian assistance. Especially in those cases where preemption of nuclear attack leads to acts of retribution by the targeted country, perhaps with remaining nuclear or biological weapons, the United States will have a moral obligation beyond what it might normally feel to help minimize and redress human suffering.

A third requirement is to make a just settlement of the issues in dispute. If U.S. action is deemed necessary to recover something wrongfully taken or to punish evil, then its post-strike actions must work toward those ends.

Concluding Observations

In summary, there is a moral case for preemption, but it is not quite as tidy as policy-makers might desire. The just war tradition puts a number of obligations on policy.

Preemption must meet the three basic prudential requirements (last resort, reasonable chance of success, proportionality). But it must first meet the requirements that the action be in self-defense and be authorized by competent authority. Not all contemplated acts of preemption are likely to meet all these criteria. It is not clear that every one must be met for an act to be just.

The latter two requirements (self-defense, competent authority) pose particular difficulties today. The current historical moment is characterized by the simultaneous appearance of two unprecedented factors: (1) broad international diffusion of the technical competence to inflict mass destruction, and (2) a unipolar international order in which the United States finds itself cast as the defender of a status quo. This implies not least that the United States must use its power in ways that others will accept as just; otherwise a terrible backlash could result.

The particular difficulties posed today are as follows. First, the self-defense requirement is too narrow in a world in which the security of so many depends upon the orderliness of the system; defending that order must have a moral quality analogous to that of defending the sovereignty of individual parts, but that quality is not well established in moral theory. Moreover, the self-defense requirement engages nuclear arguments rooted in an era now past. Addressing these problems requires returning to the nuclear debate, but in the light of current strategic realities, and then reconnecting moral debate to that part of the just war tradition that accepts war as an instrument of order under certain conditions.

Second, the competent-authority requirement is rooted in an era long past. Today policy-makers must cope with overlapping national and international institutions and sovereignties, and with world-order problems that transcend the interests of individual states. Addressing this problem requires formulating principles by which just war criteria can be satisfied by international institutions. The logical focal point is the U.N.—especially the Security Council. The potential moral legitimacy of actions endorsed by the U.N. is high, but its own weak legitimacy suggests how difficult this task will be.

Two final observations, the first on the disjunction between moral philosophy and international law on preemption. As noted earlier, international law has had the effect over time of progressively narrowing the legal recourse to war. Moral philosophy has not similarly constrained the just recourse to war. If law exists to serve justice, what is the authority of law that is inconsistent with moral reasoning? The law should permit what justice requires. Moreover, how does a nation that does not want to be above the law act in ways that moral reasoning requires? A world in which the only legal recourse to self-defense is in retaliation for an aggressor's first strike is a world that has legalized the coercive use of weapons arsenals and has made more likely the operational use of those weapons by those not constrained by moral reasoning or even the purposes of state. How tolerable is this when the weapons in question are weapons of mass destruction?

The second observation relates to the contribution of just war thinking to world-order politics. The problem of war has naturally attracted a great deal of ethical debate. But the behavior of states in modes other than warfare has attracted less attention from the moral philosophers. Moreover, the record reflects little or no effort to look beyond the ethical debate about the behavior of states to the normative attributes of world order. We think we know what just wars are, but we are a lot less clear about just statecraft. We think we know that the order the United States seeks to defend and/ or lead is a good one, but we are a lot less clear about the criteria and reasoning sufficient to this claim.

Moral philosophy could make a substantial contribution to the construction of a more just and peaceful world for the next century if it would direct more energy to such questions. At the very least, such a dialogue should help to clarify the moral duties that fall upon the United States in its special historical moment and help it to see more clearly when and how to use its power, and when not to.

Notes

1. Philip Shenon, "Perry, in Egypt, Warns Libya to Halt Chemical Weapons Plant," *New York Times*, April 4, 1996, 4.
2. W. Anthony Lake, "Confronting Backlash States," *Foreign Affairs* 73, no. 2 (1994). The author recognizes that Lake's views are not broadly accepted and that many question the right of the United States to deem others "rogues." But for lack of a better shorthand, the term is used here to refer to the category of states as defined.
3. For a summary discussion of the just war tradition, see chapter 1, "The Catholic Tradition of Moderate Realism," in George Weigel, *Tranquillitas Ordinis: The Present Failure and Future Promise of American Catholic Thought on War and Peace* (Oxford: Oxford University Press, 1987), 25–45. See also Michael Walzer, *Just and Unjust Wars*, 2d ed. (New York: Basic Books, 1992).
4. For a review of these themes, see Brad Roberts, "1995 and the End of the Post–Cold War Era," *Washington Quarterly* 18, no. 1 (Winter 1995).
5. Walzer, *Just and Unjust Wars*, xiv.
6. See Jane M. O. Sharp, "Appeasement, Intervention and the Future of Europe," and Ken Booth, "Military Intervention: Duty and Prudence," in Lawrence Freedman, ed., *Military Intervention in European Conflicts* (Oxford: Blackwell Publishers, 1994).
7. James Turner Johnson, "Just Cause Revisited," this volume, 26.
8. Francisco de Vitoria, *On the Law of War*, sec. 13.
9. Walzer, *Just and Unjust Wars*, 62.
10. Johnson, "Just Cause Revisited," 26.
11. Hugo Grotius, *The Law of War and Peace*, bk. 2, chap. 1, sec. 2.
12. Elihu Root, "The Real Monroe Doctrine," *American Journal of International Law* 35 (1914): 427.
13. Walzer, *Just and Unjust War*, 74, 80.
14. Morton A. Kaplan and Nicholas deB. Katzenbach, "Resort to Force: War and Neutrality," In Richard A. Falk and Saul H. Mendlovitz, eds., *The Strategy of World Order*, vol. 2, *International Law* (New York: World Law Fund, 1966).
15. Johnson, "Just Cause Revisited," 25.
16. Clausewitz, *On War*, trans. Michael Howard and Peter Paret (Princeton, N.J.: Princeton University Press, 1976), 370.
17. Walzer, *Just and Unjust Wars*, 81.
18. George Weigel, "Just War After the Cold War," in *Idealism Without Illusions: U.S. Foreign Policy in the 1990s* (Washington, D.C.: Ethics and Public Policy Center, 1994), 155.
19. Ibid., 153.
20. Johnson, "Just Cause Revisited," 9.
21. Ibid., 19–24.
22. See Weigel, *Tranquillitas Ordinis*, 257–85.
23. A. J. Bacevich, "Just War in a New Era of Military Affairs," this volume, 74.

24. Eugene Rostow, "Competent Authority Revisited," This volume, 55.

25. Johnson, "Just Cause Revisited," 31.

26. Walzer, *Just and Unjust Wars*, xxi.

27. Lake, "Confronting Backlash States."

28. Michael Klare, *Rogue States and Nuclear Outlaws: America's Search for a New Foreign Policy* (New York: Hill and Wang, 1995).

29. See Rosemary Righter, *Utopia Lost: The United Nations and World Order* (New York: Twentieth Century Fund Press, 1995).

30. The term is Charles Krauthammer's, used to describe the United States as the dominant power in a world no longer bipolar, because of the collapse of the Soviet Union, but not yet multipolar. See Krauthammer, "The Unipolar Moment," *Foreign Affairs* 70, no. 1 (1991)' 23–33.

31. Weigel, *Tranquillitas Ordinis*, 37.

32. John Kelsay, *Islam and War: A Study in Comparative Ethics* (Louisville, Ky.: Westminster/John Knox Press, 1993).

Chapter 8

Strategic Approaches to Combating Terrorism

Four authors explore the September 11 tragedies as a cornerstone—on how the events of a single day can focus new light on America's stature in the world, and how the tragedies that occurred in the space of a few hours have caused a deep ripple effect in the nation's government and its policy-making efforts.

Richard K. Betts maps out the landscape, explaining why terror can be an effective means against a nation as powerful as the United States, why such tactics have impact despite a great imbalance of power. "American global primacy is one of the causes of this war," he writes. It is not just the way the nation and its moves are perceived by certain parties around the world: "Remaking the world in the Western image is what Americans assume to be just, natural, and desirable, indeed only a matter of time. But that presumption is precisely what energizes many terrorists' hatred," writes Betts. It is also the perception at home. But a nation's power does not make it invincible: "For many," he says, "primacy was confused with invulnerability." Betts discusses the tactics and countermeasures of this situation, when "intense political grievance and gross imbalance of power" became an explosive equation for terror.

James S. Robbins shows how, in the aftermath of the September 11 attacks, the United States countered the terror that al-Qaeda brought to U.S. shores—and how the goals these terrorists hoped to achieve were never fully realized. Robbins details "Bin Laden's War"—the background and the escalation of events that led to 9-11. The assault on the U.S. was "a tactical masterpiece," says Robbins. But it fell short of Osama bin Laden's ultimate goals, which became clear as the United States plotted its countermeasures and world opinion rang in during the days and weeks that followed the 9-11 tragedies. For one, as Robbins says, bin Laden underestimated his enemy, who he believed had "a reputation for strength but no staying power when it came to a hard fight." Instead, the attacks "aroused the wrath of the American people" who rallied behind the Commander in Chief—and Robbins makes reference to Pearl Harbor, to the waking of the proverbial sleeping giant. Rather than non-Americans around the world feeling indifferent to the attack, the reaction Robbins believes bin Laden expected, the attacks incited global outrage. Bin Laden also did not succeed in getting the Muslim world to rally around his cause, nor did he achieve the damage to the U.S. economy that Robbins feels he intended. "The war that Osama bin Laden planned to wage against the United States is over," write Robbins, "and he has lost."

According to Richard Shultz, the failure of the intelligence community to prevent the September 11 attacks goes much deeper than the missed clues that might have led them to detect an impending threat. The author views the core of the problem as "a near decade-long reluctance to come to terms with the fact that international terrorists—most importantly al Qaeda—were undergoing a systematic transformation in terms of how they organize, deploy, and fight." Shultz details just how al-Qaeda is organized, with new information on the group and how the group operates, and he outlines the shift in thinking in national security policy, as championed by President Bush and Secretary of Defense Donald Rumsfeld, that will be necessary to fight this new war.

Barry R. Posen advocates for a grand strategy to combat terrorism. "The United States faces a long war against a small, elusive, and dangerous foe," he writes. Posen defines the adversary, the al-Qaeda network; he maps out the group's goals and structure and explains the depth of its motives: "It seeks to expel the most powerful state in history from a part of the world that has been central to U.S. foreign policy… and it intends to do so without a standing military…. It will seek to kill Americans so long as the United States does not give in to its demands," says Posen. The author advocates for a long-term, comprehensive strategy in dealing with the group. The effort he outlines will require discipline and determination; it will necessitate significant changes in U.S. national security; it will require tactics to deplete the resources of the group and the willingness to deal harshly with states who harbor them; and it will shape U.S. foreign policy, for "the United States will need friends, and thus must prioritize among its many foreign policy and defense policy initiatives," says Posen, to sustain a coalition for a protracted battle against a ruthless foe.

The chapter concludes with a reading by Michele Malvesti. Written before September 11, it presents a model to explain when the United States will use military force in response to a terrorist attack. According to Malvesti, when six factors (immediate perpetrator identification, perpetrator repetition, U.S. government officials are targets, flagrant terrorist behavior, *fait accompli* incident, and a vulnerable perpetrator) are associated with a terrorist attack against the United States, the perpetrator should expect an American military response. The strength of Malvesti's work is in its predictive value. Had Osama bin Laden read her work prior to September 11, perhaps he would have thought twice about ordering the attack.

The Soft Underbelly of American Primacy: Tactical Advantages of Terror

Richard K. Betts is a specialist on national security policy and military strategy. He is director of the Institute of War and Peace Studies at Columbia University and was a senior fellow and research associate at the Brookings Institution in Washington, D.C. Betts has served on the National Commission on Terrorism and the U.S. Senate Select Committee on Intelligence. He is author, editor, and coauthor of several books on the subject, including *The Irony of Vietnam: The System Worked* (1979), which won the Woodrow Wilson Prize.

In given conditions, action and reaction can be ridiculously out of proportion.... One can obtain results monstrously in excess of the effort.... Let's consider this auto smash-up.... The driver lost control at high speed while swiping at a wasp which had flown in through a window and was buzzing around his face.... The weight of a wasp is under half an ounce. Compared with a human being, the wasp's size is minute, its strength negligible. Its sole armament is a tiny syringe holding a drop of irritant, formic acid.... Nevertheless, that wasp killed four big men and converted a large, powerful car into a heap of scrap.
                                                                     —Eric Frank Russell[1]

To grasp some implications of the new first priority in U.S. foreign policy, it is necessary to understand the connections among three things: the imbalance of power between terrorist groups and counterterrorist governments; the reasons that groups choose terror tactics; and the operational advantage of attack over defense in the interactions of terrorists and their opponents. On September 11, 2001, Americans were reminded that the overweening power that they had taken for granted over the past dozen years is not the same as omnipotence. What is less obvious but equally important is that the power is itself part of the cause of terrorist enmity and even a source of U.S. vulnerability.

There is no consensus on a definition of "terrorism," mainly because the term is so intensely pejorative.[2] When defined in terms of tactics, consistency falters, because most people can think of some "good" political cause that has used the tactics and whose purposes excuse them or at least warrant the group's designation as freedom fighters rather than terrorists. Israelis who call the Khobar Towers bombers of 1996 terrorists might reject that characterization for the Irgun, which did the same thing to the King David Hotel in 1946, or some Irish Americans would bridle at equating IRA bombings in Britain with Tamil Tiger bombings in Sri Lanka. Anticommunists labeled the Vietcong terrorists (because they engaged in combat out of uniform and assassinated local officials), but opponents of the Saigon government did not. Nevertheless, a functional definition is more sensible than one conditioned on the identity of the perpetrators. For this article, terrorism refers to the illegitimate, deliberate killing of civilians for purposes of punishment or coercion. This holds in abeyance the questions of whether deliberate killing of civilians can ever be legitimate or killing soldiers can be terrorism.

In any case, for all but the rare nihilistic psychopath, terror is a means, not an end in itself. Terror tactics are usually meant to serve a strategy of coercion.[3] They are a use of force designed to further some substantive aim. This is not always evident in the heat of rage felt by the victims of terror. Normal people find it hard to see instrumental reasoning behind an atrocity, especially when recognizing the political motives behind terrorism might seem to make its illegitimacy less extreme. Stripped of rhetoric, however, a war against terrorism must mean a war against political groups who choose terror as a tactic.

American global primacy is one of the causes of this war. It animates both the terrorists' purposes and their choice of tactics. To groups like al Qaeda, the United States is the enemy because American military power dominates their world, supports corrupt governments in their countries, and backs Israelis against Muslims; American cultural power insults their religion and pollutes their societies; and American economic power makes all these intrusions and desecrations possible. Japan, in contrast, is not high on al Qaeda's list of targets, because Japan's economic power does not make it a political, military, and cultural behemoth that penetrates their societies.

Political and cultural power makes the United States a target for those who blame it for their problems. At the same time, American economic and military power prevents them from resisting or retaliating against the United States on its own terms. To smite the only superpower requires unconventional modes of force and tactics that make the combat cost exchange ratio favorable to the attacker. This offers hope to the weak that they can work their will despite their overall deficit in power.

Primacy on the Cheap

The United States has enjoyed military and political primacy (or hegemony, unipolarity, or whatever term best connotes international dominance) for barely a dozen years. Those who focus on the economic dimension of international relations spoke of American hegemony much earlier, but observers of the strategic landscape never did. For those who focus on national security, the world before 1945 was multipolar, and the world of the cold war was bipolar. After 1945 the United States had exerted hegemony within the First World and for a while over the international economy. The strategic competition against the Second World, however, was seen as a titanic struggle between equal politicomilitary coalitions and a close-run thing until very near the end. Only the collapse of the Soviet pole, which coincided fortuitously with renewed relative strength of the American economy, marked the real arrival of U.S. global dominance.

The novelty of complete primacy may account for the thoughtless, indeed innocently arrogant way in which many Americans took its benefits for granted. Most who gave any thought to foreign policy came implicitly to regard the entire world after 1989 as they had regarded Western Europe and Japan during the past half-century: partners in principle but vassals in practice. The United States would lead the civilized community of nations in the expansion and consolidation of a liberal world order. Overwhelming military dominance was assumed to be secure and important across most of the domestic political spectrum.

Liberal multilateralists conflated U.S. primacy with political globalization, indeed, conflated ideological American nationalism with internationalist altruism.[4] They assumed that U.S. military power should be used to stabilize benighted countries and police international violence, albeit preferably camouflaged under the banner of institutions such as the United Nations, or at least NATO. They rejected the idea that illiberal impulses or movements represented more than a retreating challenge to the West's mission and its capacity to extend its values worldwide.

Conservative unilateralists assumed that unrivaled power relieved the United States of the need to cater to the demands of others. When America acted strategically abroad, others would have to join on its terms or be left out of the action. The United States should choose battles, avoid entanglements in incompetent polities, and let unfortunates stew in their own juice. For both multilateralists and nationalists, the issue was whether the United States would decide to make an effort for world welfare, not whether a strategic challenge could threaten its truly vital interests. (Colloquial depreciation of the adjective notwithstanding, literally vital U.S. interests are those necessary to life.)

For many, primacy was confused with invulnerability. American experts warned regularly of the danger of catastrophic terrorism—and Osama bin Ladin explicitly declared war on the United States in his *fatwa* of February 1998. But the warnings did not register seriously in the consciousness of most people. Even some national security experts felt stunned when the attacks occurred on September 11. Before then, the American military wanted nothing to do with the mission of "homeland defense," cited the Posse Comitatus act to suggest that military operations within U.S. borders would be improper, and argued that homeland defense should be the responsibility of civilian agencies or the National Guard. The services preferred to define the active forces' mission as fighting and winning the nation's wars—as if wars were naturally something that happened abroad—and homeland defense involved no more than law enforcement, managing relief operations in natural disasters, or intercepting ballistic missiles outside U.S. airspace. Only in America could the nation's armed forces think of direct defense of national territory as a distraction.

Being Number One seemed cheap. The United States could cut the military burden on the economy by half after the cold war (from 6 percent to 3 percent of GNP) yet still spend almost five times more than the combined military budgets of all potential enemy states. And this did not count the contributions of rich U.S. allies.[5] Of course the margin in dollar terms does not translate into a comparable quantitative margin in manpower or equipment, but that does not mean that a purchasing power parity estimate would reduce the implied gap in combat capability. The overwhelming qualitative superiority of U.S. conventional forces cuts in the other direction. Washington was also able to plan, organize, and fight a major war in 1991 at negligible cost in blood or treasure. Financially, nearly 90 percent of the bills for the war against Iraq were paid by allies. With fewer than 200 American battle deaths, the cost in blood was far lower than almost anyone had imagined it could be. Less than a decade later, Washington waged another war, over Kosovo, that cost no U.S. combat casualties at all.

In the one case where costs in casualties exceeded the apparent interests at stake—Somalia in 1993—Washington quickly stood down from the fight. This became the reference point for vulnerability: the failure of an operation that was small, far from home, and elective. Where material interests required strategic engagement, as in the oil-rich Persian Gulf, U.S. strategy could avoid costs by exploiting its huge advantage in conventional capability. Where conventional dominance proved less exploitable, as in Somalia, material interests did not require strategic engagement. Where the United States could not operate militarily with impunity, it could choose not to operate.

Finally, power made it possible to let moral interests override material interests where some Americans felt an intense moral concern, even if in doing so they claimed, dubiously, that the moral and material stakes coincided. To some extent this happened in Kosovo, although the decision to launch that war apparently flowed from overoptimism about how quickly a little bombing would lead Belgrade to capitulate. Most notably, it happened in the Arab-Israeli conflict. For more than three decades after the 1967 Six Day War, the United States supported Israel diplomatically, economically, and militarily against the Arabs, despite the fact that doing so put it on the side of a tiny country of a few million people with no oil, against more than ten times as many Arabs who controlled over a third of the world's oil reserves.

This policy was not just an effect of primacy, since the U.S.–Israel alignment began in the cold war. The salience of the moral motive was indicated by the fact that U.S. policy proceeded despite the fact that it helped give Moscow a purchase in major Arab capitals such as Cairo, Damascus, and Baghdad. Luckily for the United States, however, the largest amounts of oil remained under the control of the conservative Arab states of the Gulf. In this sense the hegemony of the United States within the anticommunist world helped account for the policy. That margin of power also relieved Washington of the need to make hard choices about disciplining its client. For decades the United States opposed Israeli settlement of the West Bank, terming the settlements illegal; yet in all that time the United States never demanded that Israel refrain from colonizing the West Bank as a condition for receiving U.S. economic and military aid.[6] Washington continued to bankroll Israel at a higher per capita rate than any other country in the world, a level that has been indispensable to Israel, providing aid over the years that now totals well over $100 billion in today's dollars.[7] Although this policy enraged some Arabs and irritated the rest, U.S. power was great enough that such international political costs did not outweigh the domestic political costs of insisting on Israeli compliance with U.S. policy.

Of course, far more than subsidizing Israeli occupation of Palestinian land was involved in the enmity of Islamist terrorists toward the United States. Many of the other explanations, however, presuppose U.S. global primacy. When American power becomes the arbiter of conflicts around the world, it makes itself the target for groups who come out on the short end of those conflicts.

Primacy and Asymmetric Warfare

The irrational evil of terrorism seems most obvious to the powerful. They are accustomed to getting their way with conventional applications of force and are not as accustomed as the powerless to thinking of terror as the only form of force that might make their enemies do their will. This is why terrorism is the premier form of "asymmetric warfare," the Pentagon buzzword for the type of threats likely to confront the United

States in the post-cold war world.[8] Murderous tactics may become instrumentally appealing by default—when one party in a conflict lacks other military options.

Resort to terror is not necessarily limited to those facing far more powerful enemies. It can happen in a conventional war between great powers that becomes a total war, when the process of escalation pits whole societies against each other and shears away civilized restraints. That is something seldom seen, and last seen over a half-century ago. One does not need to accept the tendentious position that allied strategic bombing in World War II constituted terrorism to recognize that the British and Americans did systematically assault the urban population centers of Germany and Japan. They did so in large part because precision bombing of industrial facilities proved ineffective.[9] During the early phase of the cold war, in turn, U.S. nuclear strategy relied on plans to counter Soviet conventional attack on Western Europe with a comprehensive nuclear attack on communist countries that would have killed hundreds of millions. In the 1950s, Strategic Air Command targeteers even went out of their way to plan "bonus" damage by moving aim points for military targets so that blasts would destroy adjacent towns as well.[10] In both World War II and planning for World War III, the rationale was less to kill civilians per se than to wreck the enemy economies—although that was also one of Osama bin Laden's rationales for the attacks on the World Trade Center.[11] In short, the instrumental appeal of strategic attacks on noncombatants may be easier to understand when one considers that states with legitimate purposes have sometimes resorted to such a strategy. Such a double standard, relaxing prohibitions against targeting noncombatants for the side with legitimate purposes (one's own side), occurs most readily when the enemy is at least a peer competitor threatening vital interests. When one's own primacy is taken for granted, it is easier to revert to a single standard that puts all deliberate attacks against civilians beyond the pale.

In contrast to World War II, most wars are limited—or at least limited for the stronger side when power is grossly imbalanced. In such cases, using terror to coerce is likely to seem the only potentially effective use of force for the weaker side, which faces a choice between surrender or savagery. Radical Muslim zealots cannot expel American power with conventional military means, so they substitute clandestine means of delivery against military targets (such as the Khobar Towers barracks in Saudi Arabia) or high-profile political targets (embassies in Kenya and Tanzania). More than once the line has been attributed to terrorists, "If you will let us lease one of your B-52s, we will use that instead of a truck bomb." The hijacking and conversion of U.S. airliners into kamikazes was the most dramatic means of asymmetric attack.

Kamikaze hijacking also reflects an impressive capacity for strategic judo, the turning of the West's strength against itself.[12] The flip-side of a primacy that diffuses its power throughout the world is that advanced elements of that power become more accessible to its enemies. Nineteen men from technologically backward societies did not have to rely on home-grown instruments to devastate the Pentagon and World Trade Center. They used computers and modern financial procedures with facility, and they forcibly appropriated the aviation technology of the West and used it as a weapon. They not only rebelled against the "soft power" of the United States, they trumped it by hijacking the country's hard power.[13] They also exploited the characteristics of U.S. society associated with soft power—the liberalism, openness, and respect for privacy that allowed them to go freely about the business of preparing the attacks without observation by the state security apparatus. When soft power met the clash of civilizations, it proved too soft.

Strategic judo is also apparent in the way in which U.S. retaliation may compromise its own purpose. The counter offensive after September 11 was necessary, if only to demonstrate to marginally motivated terrorists that they could not hope to strike the United States for free. The war in Afghanistan, however, does contribute to polarization in the Muslim world and to mobilization of potential terrorist recruits. U.S. leaders can say that they are not waging a war against Islam until they are blue in the face, but this will not convince Muslims who already distrust the United States. Success in deposing the Taliban may help U.S. policy by encouraging a bandwagon effect that rallies governments and moderates among the Muslim populace, but there will probably be as many who see the U.S. retaliation as confirming al Qaeda's diagnosis of American evil. Victory in Afghanistan and follow-up operations to prevent al Qaeda from relocating bases of operation to other countries will hurt that organization's capacity to act. The number of young zealots willing to emulate the "martyrdom operation" of the nineteen on September 11, however, is not likely to decline.

Advantage of Attack

The academic field of security studies has some reason to be embarrassed after September 11. Having focused primarily on great powers and interstate conflict, literature on terrorism was comparatively sparse; most of the good books were by policy analysts rather than theorists.[14] Indeed, science fiction has etched out the operational logic of terrorism as well as political science. Eric Frank Russell's 1957 novel, from which the epigraph to this article comes, vividly illustrates both the strategic aspirations of terrorists and the offense-dominant character of their tactics. It describes the dispatch of a single agent to one of many planets in the Sirian enemy's empire to stir up fear, confusion, and panic through a series of small covert activities with tremendous ripple effects. Matched with deceptions to make the disruptions appear to be part of a campaign by a big phantom rebel organization, the agent's modest actions divert large numbers of enemy policy and military personnel, cause economic dislocations and social unrest, and soften the planet up for invasion. Wasp agents are infiltrated into numerous planets, multiplying the effects. As the agents' handlers tell him, "The pot is coming slowly but surely to the boil. Their fleets are being widely dispersed, there are vast troop movements from their overcrowded home-system to the outer planets of their empire. They're gradually being chivvied into a fix. They can't hold what they've got without spreading all over it. The wider they spread the thinner they get. The thinner they get, the easier it is to bite lumps out of them."[15]

Fortunately al Qaeda and its ilk are not as wildly effective as Russell's wasp. By degree, however, the phenomenon is quite similar. Comparatively limited initiatives prompt tremendous and costly defensive reactions. On September 11 a small number of men killed 3,000 people and destroyed a huge portion of prime commercial real estate, part of the military's national nerve center, and four expensive aircraft. The ripple effects, however, multiplied those costs. A major part of the U.S. economy—air travel—shut down completely for days after September 11. Increased security measures dramatically increased the overall costs of the air travel system thereafter. Normal law enforcement activities of the Federal Bureau of Investigation were radically curtailed as legions of agents were transferred to counterterror tasks. Anxiety about the vulnerability of nuclear power plants, major bridges and tunnels, embassies abroad, and other high-value targets prompted plans for big investments in fortification of a wide array of facilities. A retaliatory war in Afghanistan ran at a cost of a couple billion dollars a month beyond the regular defense budget for months. In one study, the attacks on the World Trade Center and the Pentagon were estimated to cost the U.S. economy 1.8 million jobs.[16]

Or consider the results of a handful of 34-cent letters containing anthrax, probably sent by a single person. Besides killing several people, they contaminated a large portion of the postal system, paralyzed some mail delivery for long periods, provoked plans for huge expenditures on prophylactic irradiation equipment, shut down much of Capitol Hill for weeks, put thousands of people on a sixty-day regimen of strong antibiotics (potentially eroding the medical effectiveness of such antibiotics in future emergencies), and overloaded police and public health inspectors with false alarms. The September 11 attacks and the October anthrax attacks together probably cost the perpetrators less than a million dollars. If the cost of rebuilding and of defensive investments in reaction came to no more than $100 billion, the cost exchange ratio would still be astronomically in favor of the attack over the defense.

Analysts in strategic studies did not fall down on the job completely before September 11. At least two old bodies of work help to illuminate the problem. One is the literature on guerrilla warfare and counterinsurgency, particularly prominent in the 1960s, and the other is the offense-defense theory that burgeoned in the 1980s. Both apply well to understanding patterns of engagement between terrorists and counterterrorists. Some of the axioms derived from the empirical cases in the counterinsurgency literature apply directly, and offense-defense theory applies indirectly.

Apart from the victims of guerrillas, few still identify irregular paramilitary warfare with terrorism (because the latter is illegitimate), but the two activities do overlap a great deal in their operational characteristics. Revolutionary or resistance movements in the preconventional phase of operations usually mix small-unit raids on isolated outposts of the government or occupying force with detonations and assassinations in urban areas to instill fear and discredit government power. The tactical logic of guerilla operations resembles that in terrorist attacks: the weaker rebels use stealth and the cover of civilian society to concentrate their striking power against one among many of the stronger enemy's dispersed assets; they strike quickly and eliminate the target before the defender can move forces from other areas to respond; they melt back into civilian society to avoid detection and reconcentrate against another target. The government or occupier has far superior strength in terms of conventional military power, but cannot counterconcentrate in time because it has to defend all points, while the insurgent attacker can pick its targets at will.[17] The contest between insurgents and counterinsurgents is "tripartite," polarizing political alignments and gaining the support of *attentistes* or those in the middle. In today's principle counterterror campaign, one might say that the yet-unmobilized Muslim elites and masses of the Third World—those who were not already actively committed either to supporting Islamist radicalism or to combating it—are the target group in the middle. As Samuel Huntington noted, "a revolutionary war is a war of attrition."[18] As I believe Stanley Hoffman once said, in rebellions the insurgents win as long as they do not lose, and the government loses as long as it does not win. If al Qaeda-like groups can stay in the field indefinitely, they win.

Offense-defense theory applied nuclear deterrence concepts to assessing the stability of conventional military confrontations and focused on what conditions tended to give the attack or the defense the advantage in war.[19] There were many problems in the specification and application of the theory having to do with unsettled conceptualization of the offense-defense balance, problematic standards for measuring it, and inconsistent applications to different levels of warfare and diplomacy.[20] Offense-defense theory, which flourished when driven by the urge to find ways to stabilize the NATO-Warsaw Pact balance in Europe, has had little to say directly about unconventional war or terrorism. It actually applies more clearly, however, to this lower level of strategic competition (as well as to the higher level of nuclear war) than to the middle level of conventional military power. This is because the exchange ratio between opposing conventional forces of roughly similar size is very difficult to estimate, given the complex composition of modern military forces and uncertainty about their qualitative comparisons; but the exchange ratio in both nuclear and guerrilla combat is quite lopsided in favor of the attacker. Counterinsurgency folklore held that the government defenders need something on the order of a ten-to-one advantage over the guerrillas if they were to drive them from the field.

There has been much confusion about exactly how to define the offense-defense balance, but the essential idea is that some combinations of military technology, organization, and doctrine are proportionally more advantageous to the attack or to the defense when the two clash. "Proportionally" means that available instruments and circumstances of engagement give either the attack or the defense more bang for the buck, more efficient power out of the same level of resources. The notion of an offense-defense balance as something conceptually distinct from the balance of power means, however, that it cannot be identified with which side wins a battle or a war. Indeed, the offense-defense balance can favor the defense, while the attacker still wins, because its overall margin of superiority in power was too great, despite the defense's more efficient use of power. (I am told that the Finns had a saying in the Winter War of 1939–40: "One Finn is worth ten Russians, but what happens when the eleventh Russian comes?") Thus, to say that the offense-defense balance favors the offensive terrorists today against the defensive counterterrorists does not mean that the terrorists will prevail. It does mean that terrorists can fight far above their weight, that in most instances each competent terrorist will have much greater individual impact than each good counterterrorist, that each dollar invested in a terrorist plot will have a bigger payoff than each dollar expended on counterterrorism, and that only small numbers of competent terrorists need survive and operate to keep the threat to American society uncomfortably high.

In the competition between terrorists on the attack and Americans on the defense, the disadvantage of the defense is evident in the number of high-value potential targets that need protection. The United States has "almost 600,000 bridges, 170,000 water systems, more than 2,800 power plants (104 of them nuclear), 190,000 miles of interstate pipelines for natural gas, 463 skyscrapers... nearly 20,000 miles of border, airports, stadiums, train tracks."[21] All these usually represented American strength; after September 11 they also represent vulnerability:

> Suddenly guards were being posted at water reservoirs, outside power plants, and at bridges and tunnels. Maps of oil and gas lines were removed from the Internet. In Boston, a ship carrying liquefied natural gas, an important source of fuel for heating New England homes, was forbidden from entering the harbor because local fire officials feared that if it were targeted by a terrorist the resulting explosion could lay low much of the city's densely populated waterfront. An attack by a knife-wielding lunatic on the driver of a Florida-bound Greyhound bus led to the immediate cessation of that national bus service.... Agricultural crop-dusting planes were grounded out of a concern that they could be used to spread chemical or biological agents.[22]

Truly energetic defense measures do not only cost money in personnel and equipment for fortification, inspection, and enforcement; they may require repealing some of the very underpinnings of civilian economic efficiency associated with globalization. "The competitiveness of the U.S. economy and the quality of life of the American people rest on critical infrastructure that has become increasingly more concentrated, more interconnected, and more sophisticated. Almost entirely privately owned and operated, there is very little redundancy in this system."[23] This concentration increases the potential price of vulnerability to single attacks. Tighter inspection of cargoes coming across the Canadian border, for example, wrecks the "just-in-time" parts supply system of Michigan auto manufacturers. Companies that have invested in technology and infrastructure premised on unimpeded movement "may see their expected savings and efficiencies go up in smoke. Outsourcing contracts will have to be revisited and inventories will have to be rebuilt."[24] How many safety measures will suffice in improving airline security without making flying so inconvenient that the air travel industry never recovers as a profit-making enterprise? A few more shoe-bomb incidents, and Thomas Friedman's proposal to start an airline called "Naked Air—where the only thing you wear is a seat belt" becomes almost as plausible as it is ridiculous.[25]

The offense-dominant character of terrorism is implicit in mass detentions of Arab young men after September 11, and proposals for military tribunals that would compromise normal due process and weaken standard criminal justice presumptions in favor of the accused. The traditional liberal axiom that it is better to let a hundred guilty people go free than to convict one innocent reflects confidence in the strength of society's defenses—confidence that whatever additional crimes may be committed by the guilty who go free will not grossly outweigh the injustice done to innocents convicted, that one criminal who slips through the net will not go on to kill hundreds or thousands of innocents. Fear of terrorists plotting mass murder reversed that presumption and makes unjust incarceration of some innocents appear like unintended but expected collateral damage in wartime combat.

Offense-defense theory helps to visualize the problem. It does not help to provide attractive solutions, as its proponents believed it did during the cold war. Then offense-defense theory was popular because it seemed to offer a way to stabilize the East-West military confrontation. Mutual deterrence from the superpowers' confidence in their counteroffensive capability could substitute for defense at the nuclear level, and both sides' confidence in their conventional defenses could dampen either one's incentives to attack at that level. Little of this applies to counterterrorism. Both deterrence and defense are weaker strategies against terrorists than they were against communists.

Deterrence is still relevant for dealing with state terrorism; Saddam Hussein or Kim Jon-Il may hold back from striking the United States for fear of retaliation. Deterrence offers less confidence for preventing state sponsorship of terrorism; it did not stop the Taliban from hosting Osama bin Laden. It offers even less for holding at bay transnational groups like al Qaeda, which may lack a return address against which retaliation can be visited, or whose millenialist aims and religious convictions make them unafraid of retaliation. Defense, in turn, is better than a losing game only because the inadequacy of deterrence leaves no alternative.[26] Large investments in defense will produce appreciable reductions in vulnerability, but will not minimize vulnerability.

Deterrence and defense overlap in practice. The U.S. counteroffensive in Afghanistan constitutes retaliation, punishing the Taliban for shielding al Qaeda and sending a warning to other potential state sponsors. It is also active defense, whittling down the ranks of potential perpetrators by killing and capturing members of the Islamist international brigades committed to jihad against the United States. At this writing, the retaliatory function has been performed more effectively than the defensive, as the Taliban regime has been destroyed, but significant numbers of Arab Afghans and al Qaeda members appear to have escaped, perhaps to plot another day.

Given the limited efficacy of deterrence for modern counterterrorism, it remains an open question how much of a strategic success we should judge the impressive victory in Afghanistan to be. Major investments in passive defenses (airline security, border inspections, surveillance and searches for better intelligence, fortification of embassies, and so forth) are necessary, but will reduce vulnerability at a cost substantially greater than the costs that competent terrorist organizations will have to bear to probe and occasionally circumvent them. The cost-exchange ratio for direct defense is probably worse than the legendary 10:1 ratio for successful counterinsurgency, and certainly worse than the more than 3:1 ratio that Robert McNamara's analysts calculated for the advantage of offensive missile investments over antiballistic missile systems—an advantage that many then and since have thought warranted accepting a situation of mutual vulnerability to assured destruction.[27]

The less prepared we are to undertake appropriate programs and the more false starts and confusions that are likely, the worse the cost-exchange ratio will be in the short term. The public health system, law enforcement organizations, and state and local bureaucrats are still feeling their way on what, how, and in which sequence to boost efforts. The U.S. military will also have to overcome the natural and powerful effects of inertia and attachments to old self-conceptions and preferred programs and modes of operation. Impulses to repackage old priorities in the rhetoric of new needs will further dilute effectiveness of countermeasures.

Nevertheless, given low confidence that deterrence can prevent terrorist attacks, major improvements in defenses make sense.[28] This is especially true because the resource base from which the United States can draw is vastly larger than that available to transnational terrorists. Al Qaeda may be rich, but it does not have the treasury of a great power. Primacy has a soft underbelly, but it is far better to have primacy than to face it. Even at an unfavorable cost exchange ratio, a number of defensive measures are a sensible investment, but only because our overwhelming advantage in resources means that we are not constrained to focus solely on the most efficient countermeasures.

At the same time, as long as terrorist groups remain potent and active, a serious war plan must exploit efficient strategies as well. Given the offense-dominant nature of terrorist operations, this means emphasis on counter-offensive operations. When terrorists or their support structures can be found and fixed, preemptive and preventive attacks will accomplish more against them, dollar for dollar, than the investment in passive defenses. Which is the more efficient use of resources: to kill or capture a cell of terrorists who might otherwise choose at any time to strike whichever set of targets on our side is unguarded, or to try to guard all potential targets? Here the dangers are that counteroffensive operations could prove counterproductive. This could easily happen if they degenerate into brutalities and breaches of laws of war that make counterterrorism begin to appear morally equivalent to its target, sapping political support and driving the uncommitted to the other side in the process of polarization that war makes inevitable. Whether counteroffensive operations gain more in eliminating perpetrators than they lose in alienating and mobilizing "swing voters" in the world of Muslim opinion depends on how successful the operations are in neutralizing significant numbers of the organizers of terrorist groups, as opposed to foot soldiers, and in doing so with minimal collateral damage.

Primacy and Policy

September 11 reminded those Americans with a rosy view that not all the world sees U.S. primacy as benign, that primacy does not guarantee security, and that security may now entail some retreats from the economic globalization that some had identified with American leadership. Primacy has two edges—dominance and provocation. Americans can enjoy the dominance but must recognize the risks it evokes. For terrorists who want to bring the United States down, U.S. strategic primacy is a formidable challenge, but one that can be overcome. On balance, Americans have overestimated the benefits of primacy, and terrorists have underestimated them.

For those who see a connection between American interventionism, cultural expansiveness, and support of Israel on one hand, and the rage of groups that turn to terrorism on the other, primacy may seem more trouble than it's worth, and the need to revise policies may seem more pressing. But most Americans have so far preferred the complacent and gluttonous form of primacy to the ascetic, blithely accepting steadily growing dependence on Persian Gulf oil that could be limited by compromises in lifestyle and unconventional energy policies. There have been no groundswells to get rid of SUVs, support the Palestinians, or refrain from promoting Western standards of democracy and human rights in societies where some elements see them as aggression.

There is little evidence that any appreciable number of Americans, elite or mass, see our primacy as provoking terrorism. Rather, most see it as a condition we can choose at will to exploit or not. So U.S. foreign policy has exercised primacy in a muscular way in byways of the post-cold war world when intervention seemed cheap, but not when doing good deeds threatened to be costly. Power has allowed Washington to play simultaneously the roles of mediator and partisan supporter in the Arab-Israeli conflict. For a dozen years nothing, with the near exception of the Kosovo War, suggested that primacy could not get us out of whatever problems it generated.

How far the United States goes to adapt to the second edge of primacy probably depends on whether stunning damage is inflicted by terrorists again, or September 11 gradually fades into history. If al Qaeda and its ilk are crippled, and some years pass without more catastrophic attacks on U.S. home territory, scar tissue will harden on the soft underbelly, and the positive view of primacy will be reinforced. If the war against terrorism falters, however, and the exercise of power fails to prevent more big incidents, the consensus will crack. Then more extreme policy options will get more attention. Retrenchment and retreat will look more appealing to some, who may believe the words of Sheik Salman al-Awdah, a dissident Saudi religious scholar, who said, "If America just let well enough alone, and got out of their obligations overseas... no one would bother them."[29]

More likely, however, would be a more violent reaction. There is no reason to assume that terrorist enemies would let America off the hook if it retreated and would not remain as implacable as ever. Facing inability to suppress the threat through normal combat, covert action, and diplomatic pressure, many Americans would consider escalation to more ferocious strategies. In recent decades, the march of liberal legalism has delegitimized tactics and brutalities that once were accepted, but this delegitimation has occurred only in the context of fundamental security and dominance of the Western powers, not in a situation where they felt under supreme threat. In a situation of that sort, it is foolhardy to assume that American strategy would never turn to tactics like those used against Japanese and German civilians, or by the civilized French in the *sale guerre* in Algeria, or by the Russians in Chechnya in hopes of effectively eradicating terrorists despite astronomical damage to the civilian societies within which they lurk.

This possibility would highlight how terrorists have underestimated American primacy. There is much evidence that even in the age of unipolarity, opponents have mistakenly seen the United States as a paper tiger. For some reason—perhaps wishfully selective perception—they tend to see retreats from Vietnam, Beirut, and Somalia as typical weakness of American will, instead of considering decisive exercises of power in Panama, Kuwait, Kosovo, and now, Afghanistan.[30] As Osama bin Laden said in 1997, the United States left Somalia "after claiming that they were the largest power on earth. They left after some resistance from powerless, poor, unarmed people whose only weapon is the belief in Allah.... The Americans ran away."[31]

This apparently common view among those with an interest in pinning America's ears back ignores the difference between elective uses of force and desperate ones. The United States retreated where it ran into trouble helping others, not where it was saving itself. Unlike interventions of the 1990s in Africa, the Balkans, or Haiti, counterterrorism is not charity. With vital material interests involved, primacy unleashed may prove fearsomely potent.

Most likely America will see neither absolute victory nor abject failure in the war against terror. Then how long will a campaign of attrition last and stay popular? If the United States wants a strategy to cut the roots of terrorism, rather than just the branches, will American power be used effectively against the roots? Perhaps, but probably not. This depends of course on which of many possible root causes are at issue. Ironically, one problem is that American primacy itself is one of those roots.

A common assertion is that Third World poverty generates terrorism. While this must certainly be a contributing cause in many cases, there is little evidence that it is either a necessary or sufficient condition. Fundamentalist madrassas might not be full to overflowing if young Muslims had ample opportunities to make money, but the fifteen Saudis who hijacked the flights on September 11 were from one of the most affluent of Muslim countries. No U.S. policy could ever hope to make most incubators of terrorism less poor than Saudi Arabia. Iran, the biggest state sponsor of anti-American terrorism, is also better off than most Muslim countries. Poverty is endemic in the Third World, but terrorism is not.

Even if endemic poverty were the cause, the solution would not be obvious. Globalization generates stratification, creating winners and losers, as efficient societies with capitalist cultures move ahead and others fall behind, or as elite enclaves in some societies prosper while the masses stagnate. Moreover, even vastly increased U.S. development assistance would be spread thin if all poor countries are assumed to be incubators of terrorism. And what are the odds that U.S. intervention with economic aid would significantly reduce poverty? Successes in prompting dramatic economic development by outside assistance in the Third World have occurred, but they are the exception more than the rule.

The most virulent anti-American terrorist threats, however, do not emerge randomly in poor societies. They grow out of a few regions and are concentrated overwhelmingly in a few religiously motivated groups. These reflect political causes—ideological, nationalist, or transnational cultural impulses to militant mobilization—more than economic causes. Economic development in an area where the political and religious impulses remain unresolved could serve to improve the resource base for terrorism rather than undercut it.

A strategy of terrorism is most likely to flow from the coincidence of two conditions: intense political grievance and gross imbalance of power. Either one without the other is likely to produce either peace or conventional war. Peace is probable if power is imbalanced but grievance is modest; the weaker party is likely to live with the grievance. In that situation, conventional use of force appears to offer no hope of victory, while the righteous indignation is not great enough to overcome normal inhibitions against murderous tactics. Conventional war is probable if grievance is intense but power is more evenly balanced, since successful use of respectable forms of force appears possible.[32] Under American primacy, candidates for terrorism suffer from grossly inferior power by definition. This should focus attention on the political causes of their grievance.

How are political root causes addressed? At other times in history we have succeeded in fostering congenial revolutions—especially in the end of the cold war, as the collapse of the Second World heralded an End of History of sorts.[33] The problem now, however, is the rebellion of anti-Western zealots against the secularist end of history. Remaking the world in the Western image is what Americans assume to be just, natural, and desirable, indeed only a matter of time. But that presumption is precisely what energizes many terrorists' hatred. Secular Western liberalism is not their salvation, but their scourge. Primacy could, paradoxically, remain both the solution and the problem for a long time.[*]

---

[*]The author thanks Robert Jervis for comments on the first draft.

Notes

1. William Wolf in Eric Frank Russell, *Wasp* (London: Victor Gollancz, 2000, originally published 1957), 7.
2. "The word has become a political label rather than an analytical concept." Martha Crenshaw, *Terrorism and International Cooperation* (New York: Institute for East-West Security Studies, 1989), 5.
3. For a survey of types, see Christopher C. Harmon, "Five Strategies of Terrorism," *Small Wars and Insurgencies* 12 (Autumn 2001).
4. Rationalization of national power as altruism resembles the thinking about benign Pax Britannica in the Crowe Memorandum: "... the national policy of the insular and naval State is so directed as to harmonize with the general desires and ideals common to all mankind, and more particularly... is closely identified with the primary and vital interests of a majority, or as many as possible, of the other nations.... England, more than any other non-insular Power, has a direct and positive interest in the maintenance of the independence of nations, and therefore must be the natural enemy of any country threatening the independence of others, and the natural protector of the weaker communities." Eyre Crowe, "Memorandum on the Present State of British Relations with France and Germany," 1 January 1907, in G. P. Gooch and Harold Temperley, eds., *British Documents on the Origins of the War, 1898–1914*, vol. 3: *The Testing of the Entente, 1904–6* (London: His Majesty's Stationery Office, 1928), 402–403.
5. At the end of the twentieth century, the combined military budgets of China, Russia, Iraq, Yugoslavia (Serbia), North Korea, Iran, Libya, Cuba, Afghanistan, and Sudan added up to no more than $60 billion. *The Military Balance, 1999–2000* (London: International Institute for Strategic Studies, 1999), 102, 112, 132, 133, 159, 186, 275.
6. Washington certainly did exert pressure on Israel at some times. The administration of Bush the Elder, for example, threatened to withhold loans for housing construction, but this was a marginal portion of total U.S. aid. There was never a threat to cut off the basic annual maintenance payment of several billion dollars to which Israel became accustomed decades ago.
7. The United States has also given aid to friendly Arab governments—huge amounts to Egypt and some to Jordan. This does not counterbalance the aid to Israel, however, in terms of effects on opinions of strongly anti-Israeli Arabs. Islamists see the regimes in Cairo and Amman as American toadies, complicit in betrayal of the Palestinians.
8. Theoretically, this was anticipated by Samuel P. Huntington in his 1962 analysis of the differences between symmetrical intergovernmental war and asymmetrical antigovernmental war. "Patterns of Violence in World Politics" in Huntington, ed., *Changing Patterns of Military Politics* (New York: Free Press of Glencoe, 1962), 19–21). Some of Huntington's analysis of insurrectionary warfare within states applies as well to transnational terrorism.
9. The Royal Air Force gave up on precision bombing early and focused deliberately on night bombing of German cities, while the Americans continued to try precision daylight bombing. Firestorms in Hamburg, Darmstadt, and Dresden, and less incendiary attacks on other cities, killed several hundred thousand German civilians. Over Japan, the United States quickly gave up attempts at precision bombing when weather made it impractical and deliberately resorted to an incendiary campaign that burned most Japanese cities to the ground and killed at least 300,000 civilians (and perhaps more than half a million) well before the nuclear attacks on Hiroshima and Nagasaki, which killed another 200,000. Michael S. Sherry, *The Rise of American Air Power: The Creation of Armageddon* (New Haven: Yale University Press, 1987), 260, 413–43.
10. The threat of deliberate nuclear escalation remained the bedrock of NATO doctrine throughout the cold war, but after the Kennedy administration, the flexible response doctrine made it conditional and included options for nuclear first-use that did not involve deliberate targeting of population centers. In the Eisenhower administration, however, all-out attack on the Soviet bloc's cities was integral to plans for defense of Western Europe against Soviet armored divisions.

11. In a videotape months after the attacks, bin Laden said, "These blessed strikes showed clearly that this arrogant power, America, rests on a powerful but precarious economy, which rapidly crumbled... the global economy based on usury, which America uses along with its military might to impose infidelity and humiliation on oppressed people, can easily crumble.... Hit the economy, which is the basis of military might. If their economy is finished, they will become too busy to enslave oppressed people.... America is in decline; the economic drain is continuing but more strikes are required and the youths must strike the key sectors of the American economy." Videotape excerpts quoted in "Bin Laden's Words: 'America Is in Decline,' the Leader of Al Qaeda Says," *New York Times*, 28 December 2001.

12. This is similar to the concept of political judo discussed in Samuel L. Popkin, "Pacification: Politics and the Village," *Asian Survey* 10 (August 1970); and Popkin, "Internal Conflicts—South Vietnam" in Kenneth N. Waltz and Steven Spiegel, eds., *Conflict in World Politics* (Cambridge, MA: Winthrop, 1971).

13. Soft power is "indirect or cooptive" and "can rest on the attraction of one's ideas or on the ability to set the political agenda in a way that shapes the preferences that others express." It "tends to be associated with intangible power resources such as culture, ideology, and institutions." Joseph S. Nye, Jr., "The Changing Nature of World Power," *Political Science Quarterly*, 105 (Summer 1990): 181. See also Nye, *Bound to Lead: The Changing Nature of American Power* (New York: Basic Books, 1990).

14. For example, Bruce Hoffmann, *Inside Terrorism* (New York: Columbia University Press, 1998); Paul R. Pillar, *Terrorism and American Foreign Policy* (Washington, DC: Brookings Institution Press, 2001); Richard A. Falkenrath, Robert D. Newman, and Bradley S. Thayer, *America's Achilles' Heel: Nuclear, Biological, and Chemical Terrorism and Covert Attack* (Cambridge: MIT Press, 1998).

15. Russell, *Wasp*, 64. The ripple effects include aspects of strategic judo. Creating a phony rebel organization leads the enemy security apparatus to turn on its own people. "If some Sirians could be given the full-time job of hunting down and garroting other Sirians, and if other Sirians could be given the full-time job of dodging or shooting down the garroters, then a distant and different life form would be saved a few unpleasant chores.... Doubtless the military would provide a personal bodyguard for every big wheel on Jaimec; that alone would pin down a regiment." Ibid., 26, 103.

16. Study by the Milken Institute discussed in "The Economics: Attacks May Cost 1.8 Million Jobs," *New York Times*, 13 January 2002.

17. Mao Tse-Tung's classic tracts are canonical background. For example, "Problems of Strategy in China's Revolutionary War" (especially chap. 5) in *Selected Works of Mao Tse-Tung* (Beijing: Foreign Languages Press, 1967), vol. i, and "Problems of Strategy in Guerrilla War Against Japan," in *Selected Works*, vol. ii (1967). Much of the Western analytical literature grew out of British experience in the Malayan Emergency and France's role in Indochina and Algeria. For example, Franklin Mark Osanka, ed., *Modern Guerrilla Warfare* (New York: Free Press, 1962); Gerard Chaliand, ed., *Guerrilla Strategies: An Historical Anthology from the Long March to Afghanistan* (Berkeley: University of California Press, 1982); Roger Trinquier, *Modern Warfare: A French View of Counterinsurgency*, Daniel Lee, trans. (New York: Praeger, 1964); David Galula, *Counterinsurgency Warfare: Theory and Practice* (New York: Praeger, 1964); Sir Robert Thompson, *Defeating Communist Insurgency* (New York: Praeger, 1966); Richard L. Clutterbuck, *The Long Long War: Counterinsurgency in Malaya and Vietnam* (New York: Praeger, 1966); George Armstrong Kelly, *Lost Soldiers: The French Army and Empire in Crisis, 1947–1962* (Cambridge: MIT Press, 1965),chaps. 5–7, 9–10; W. P. Davison, *Some Observations on Viet Cong Operations in the Villages* (Santa Monica, CA: RAND Corporation, 1968). See also Douglas S. Blaufarb, *The Counter-Insurgency Era: U.S. Doctrine and Performance, 1950 to the Present* (New York: Free Press, 1977); D. Michael Shafer, *Deadly Paradigms: The Failure of U.S. Counterinsurgency Policy* (Princeton: Princeton University Press, 1988); Timothy J. Lomperis, *From People's War to People's Rule: Insurgency, Intervention, and the Lessons of Vietnam* (Chapel Hill: University of North Carolina Press, 1996).

18. Huntington, "Patterns of Violence in World Politics," 20–27.

19. George Quester, *Offense and Defense in the International System,* 2nd ed. (New Brunswick, NJ: Transaction Books, 1988); Robert Jervis, "Cooperation Under the Security Dilemma," *World Politics* 30 (January 1978); Jack L. Snyder, *The Ideology of the Offensive: Military Decision Making and the Disasters of 1914* (Ithaca, NY: Cornell University Press, 1984); Stephen Van Evera, *Causes of War: Power and the Roots of Conflict* (Ithaca, NY: Cornell University Press, 1999), chaps. 6–8; Charles L. Glaser and Chaim Kaufmann, "What Is the Offense-Defense Balance and Can We Measure It?" *International Security* 22 (Spring 1998).

20. For critiques, see Jack S. Levy, "The Offensive/Defensive Balance of Military Technology," *International Studies Quarterly* 28 (June 1984); Scott D. Sagan, "1914 Revisited," *International Security* 11 (Fall 1986); Jonathan Shimshoni, "Technology, Military Advantage, and World War I: A Case for Military Entrepreneurship," *International Security* 15 (Winter 1990/91); Richard K. Betts, "Must War Find a Way?" *International Security* 24 (Fall 1999); Betts, "Conventional Deterrence: Predictive Uncertainty and Policy Confidence," *World Politics* 37 (January 1985).

21. Jerry Schwartz, Associated Press dispatch, 6 October 2001, quoted in Brian Reich, "Strength in the Face of Terror: A Comparison of United States and International Efforts to Provide Homeland Security" (unpublished paper, Columbia University, December 2001), 5.

22. Stephen E. Flynn, "The Unguarded Homeland" in James F. Hoge, Jr. and Gideon Rose, eds., *How Did This Happen? Terrorism and the New War* (New York: PublicAffairs, 2001), 185.

23. Ibid., 185–186.

24. Ibid., 193–194.

25. Thomas L. Friedman, "Naked Air," *New York Times,* 26 December 2001.

26. See Steven Simon and Daniel Benjamin, "America and the New Terrorism," *Survival* 42 (Spring 2000); 59, 66–69, 74.

27. Estimates in the 1960s indicated that even combining ABM systems with counterforce strikes and fallout shelters, the United States would have to counter each Soviet dollar spent on ICBMs with three U.S. dollars to protect 70 percent of the industry, assuming highly ABMs (.8 kill probability). To protect up to 80 percent of the population, far higher ratios would be necessary. Fred Kaplan, *The Wizards of Armageddon* (New York: Simon and Schuster, 1983), 321–324.

28. For an appropriate list of recommendation see *Countering the Changing Threat of International Terrorism,* Report of the National Commission on Terrorism, Pursuant to Public Law 277, 105th Congress (Washington, DC, June 2000). This report holds up very well in light of September 11.

29. Quoted in Douglas Jehl, "After Prison, a Saudi Sheik Tempers His Words," *New York Times,* 27 December 2001.

30. See data in the study by Barry M. Blechman and Tamara Cofman Wittes, "Defining Moment: The Threat and Use of Force in American Foreign Policy," *Political Science Quarterly* 114 (Spring 1999).

31. Quoted in Simon and Benjamin, "America and the New Terrorism," 69.

32. On why power imbalance is conducive to peace and parity to war, see Geoffrey Blainey, *The Causes of War,* 3rd. ed. (New York: Free Press, 1988), chap. 8.

33. Francis Fukuyama's thesis was widely misunderstood and caricatured. He noted that the Third World remained mired in history and that some developments could lead to restarting history. For the First World, the defeated Second World, and even some parts of the Third World, however, the triumph of Western liberalism could reasonably be seen by those who believe in its worth (as should Americans) as the final stage of evolution through fundamentally different forms of political and economic organization of societies. See Fukuyama, "The End of History?" *National Interest* no. 16 (Summer 1989); and Fukuyama, *The End of History and the Last Man* (New York: Free Press, 1992).

Bin Laden's War

James S. Robbins is a national security analyst and a frequent contributor to the *National Review Online*. He earned his Ph.D. from the Fletcher School of Law and Diplomacy.

> "Some terrorism is ill-advised."
> —Osama bin Laden

The September 11, 2001 al Qaeda assault on the United States was a tactical masterpiece. The terrorists achieved total surprise, damaged their intended targets greater than they had anticipated, and the attacks will be recorded in history as an epochal event. Yet, for all their tactical brilliance, the terror attacks were poorly suited to achieving al Qaeda's strategic goals. Placed in that context, they represented strategic overreach, a failure to understand the relationship between the techniques of terror and the objectives of warfighting.

Bin Laden's Grand Strategy

The key document for understanding bin Laden's strategic plan is his August 23, 1996 "Declaration of War Against the Americans Occupying the Land of the Two Holy Places."[1] In this lengthy document bin Laden spells out in detail both his objectives and his planned means of achieving them.

Bin Laden pursued four principal strategic goals. The first and most important of these was to expel the United States military from the Arabian peninsula. This was central to all other objectives in the region. Bin Laden states succinctly that "there is no more important duty than pushing the American enemy out of the Holy Land. No other priority, except Belief, could be considered before it."[2] US forces had come to Saudi Arabia in August 1990 in response to Saddam Hussein's invasion of Kuwait. Bin Laden, the son of a wealthy and politically influential construction magnate, fresh from victory over the Soviet Union in Afghanistan, had offered the Saudi state the services of his army of Mujahedin, but King Fahd declined the offer. Bin Laden considered the mere presence of the "infidel armies of the American Crusaders" so close to the holy places of Islam a scandal. However, he was told this was a necessary defensive measure and would only be temporary.[3]

Six years later, US forces remained in Saudi Arabia, which by then had become a base for the prosecution of the post war containment of Iraq; a "launching pad for aggression" according to bin Laden. He argued that the United Nations embargo and continued American military action inside Iraq had led to the deaths of millions of Iraqis.[4] The United States was also causing economic dislocations inside Saudi Arabia, and US troops and civilian contractors brought with them harmful social influences.[5] The Saudi regime had become increasingly corrupted, straying from the dictates of the *Sharia*. Islamicist scholars, holy men and dissidents who questioned these developments were arrested or exiled, and bin Laden's Saudi citizenship was revoked in 1994 (he had fled the country three years earlier). "It is out of date and no longer acceptable to claim that the presence of the crusaders is necessity and only a temporary measure to protect the land of the Two Holy Places," bin Laden declared. "The regime has torn off its legitimacy."[6]

The second strategic goal was the overthrow of the corrupt Muslim (and particularly Arab) regimes, and the restoration of the "pious Caliphate." Bin Laden viewed the 1920 Treaty of Servés as the root of all evil in the region. This treaty had dismantled the Ottoman Empire and established the modern Arab state system.[7] According to bin Laden, the Zionist-Crusader alliance had broken up the region into small, bickering countries in order to control it. A united Arab-Muslim *Ummah* would command power far exceeding any of the modern states. "The existence of such a large country with its huge resources under the leadership of the forthcoming Islamic State, by Allah's Grace, represents a serious danger to the very existence of the Zionist State in Palestine."[8] Furthermore, bin Laden envisaged a pure Islamic state, guided by the *Sharia,* a Muslim utopia of virtue. The first step to creating this pan-Islamic superpower was removing the United States from the region. The rest would be elementary. "If the United States is beheaded," he claimed, "the Arab kingdoms will wither away."[9]

The third major strategic goal was the destruction of the state of Israel and the creation of a Palestinian homeland. Israel, the traditional nemesis of the Islamicists, was seen both as a creature of the United States, and a force that controlled American actions through the international Zionist conspiracy. America's close association with Israel increased the importance of the United States as a target. "Our duty is to fight whomever is in the trench of the Jews," bin Laden stated. "America and the American people are free, they have entered the trench, and they will get what is coming to them.... We swore that America will never dream of safety, until safety becomes a reality for us living in Palestine."[10]

Finally, bin Laden sought to punish the United States for its global acts of aggression against Muslims. Bin Laden believed that the United States had been the main instigator of violence against the Islamic world since the end of the Cold War, and sought thereby to keep Muslims from uniting. Almost every al Qaeda public statement refers to Muslims killed in various parts of the world, particularly in Palestine and Iraq. The United States was also the primary source of cultural contamination, which sought to extinguish Islam as a moral force.[11] This claim of physical and cultural "self-defense" became the primary rallying point and legitimizing factor of the struggle, and every subsequent action was characterized as a response to aggression. Bin Laden stated in 1996, "Terrorizing you, while you are carrying arms on our land, is a legitimate and morally demanded duty. It is a legitimate right well known to all humans and other creatures."[12] Self-defense was also the background of his infamous October 21, 2001 statement, "if killing the ones that kill our sons is terrorism, then let history witness that we are terrorists."[13]

The Need for Violence

Osama bin Laden saw himself and his movement as a revolutionary vanguard, a catalyst that would bring about a global Muslim resurgence. Violence was a fundamental aspect of his struggle. At a June 1998 special session of the World Islamic Alliance held in Kandahar, bin Laden, waving a Koran, stated forcefully, "You cannot defeat heretics with this book alone, you have to show them the fist!"[14] Violence was necessary, he argued, because the corrupted Muslim regimes, under sway of the United States, had closed every peaceful avenue of reform. Nothing remained but armed resistance.

However, violence had to be suited to the existing political and social conditions, and to realities on the ground. Bin Laden did not deceive himself that the United States was a weak adversary; it was powerful, too much so to be attacked frontally. The 1996 Declaration of War explicitly stated the need for asymmetric engagement. The small Arab and Muslim conventional armies could not play a part in expelling the United States from their countries, they were too weak. Their task would come later, when it was time to rebel and overthrow the illegitimate regimes they served. Meanwhile, al Qaeda would begin unconventional warfare against the Crusaders. "Due to the imbalance of power between our armed forces and the enemy forces, a suitable means of fighting must be adopted, i.e., using fast-moving light forces that work under complete secrecy. In other words to initiate a guerrilla warfare, where the sons of the nation, and not the military forces, take part in it."[15] Bin Laden's war would seek to demoralize and exhaust the enemy through persistent, small-scale attacks, avoiding pitched battle and exposure to a massive conventional counter-assault. Al Qaeda would hold the initiative, set the terms of engagement, strike sharply and unexpectedly, then withdraw to safety while the enemy attempted to respond.

Bin Laden implemented this strategy in the years leading up to the 9/11 attacks. The bombings in Riyadh on November 13, 1995, at Khobar Towers, on June 25, 1996, at the American embassies in Kenya and Tanzania on August 7, 1998, and of the U.S.S. Cole on October 12, 2000, were all battles in bin Laden's anti-American campaign. In each of these attacks, bin Laden followed the precepts of guerrilla war. He did not seek a decisive engagement. He struck overseas, attacked government and military targets and avoided direct confrontation. US responses were largely ineffective, at least in disrupting the al Qaeda network as a whole, or harming bin Laden personally. The most noteworthy attempt was the August 20, 1998 cruise missile attack on terrorist bases in Afghanistan and the al-Shifa pharmaceutical plant in Sudan. Less spectacular but more effective were the arrests of senior al Qaeda members in Europe and the United States.[16]

The cruise missile attack in particular helped convert bin Laden into a radical Muslim folk hero. Even before then, Muslims in Pakistan were naming their newborn sons Osama;[17] surviving the fury of the Americans made bin Laden a global celebrity. An analysis in the Egyptian opposition press observed, "What better proof that Bin Laden had hurt the United States and satisfied the desire of the Muslims than for Clinton himself to stand up and repeat the name of Bin Laden three times as he announced the strikes against Sudan and Afghanistan?... Had the United States not responded in this way, Bin Laden might not have become such a legendary hero."[18] Note that in his August 20, 1998 address to the nation the President referred to bin Laden and his network eight times, not three, and called him "perhaps the preeminent organizer and financier of international terrorism in the world today."

Bin Laden consistently denied any involvement with these or other acts of terror, while also acknowledging his admiration and support for those who committed them. For example, of the Riyadh and Khobar Towers bombings he said, "This was an incident on the basis of which Western propaganda masters are trying to prove me a terrorist. But this is a baseless allegation. I have denied this allegation several times and I still deny it." However, he noted that "challenging the authority of the United States will be a good deed in Islam in every respect…. It is the duty of every Muslim to struggle for its annihilation. It is up to you whether you consider it *jihad* or terrorism."[19]

During these years his network was growing, studying the United States, and learning lessons from their attacks. On February 23, 1998, he announced the formation of the World Islamic Front with representatives of extremist groups from Egypt, Pakistan and Bangladesh, in addition to his own. He did so in the form of a *fatwa* which restated briefly the charges leveled against the United States in the 1996 Declaration of War, and widened the scope of the struggle by stating that "the ruling to kill the Americans and their allies—civilians and military—is an individual duty for every Muslim who can do it in any country in which it is possible to do it."[20]

Bin Laden's success, his growing reputation, and the ineffectiveness of US responses fed his desire to escalate the conflict, take the war to the American homeland, and bring about a climactic battle with the infidel enemy. The germ of a plan may already have been present in 1998 when he stated, "In Iran [in 1980], US planes collided with each other and were destroyed. In the future also the Americans will face destruction from collisions among themselves."[21]

Al Qaeda's 9/11 Operational Plan

The September 11, 2001 attacks were intended to accomplish the following:

- Demonstrate that the US homeland can be attacked successfully
- Take revenge for the deaths of Muslims by killing Americans
- Publicize al Qaeda's cause
- Damage US prestige
- Damage the US economy (WTC attack)
- Strike and disrupt the US military headquarters, and demoralize its troops (Pentagon attack)
- Decapitate the US leadership (White House attack)
- Generate a fearful, terrorized, alienated US public
- Create harsh, widespread domestic US crackdown and end freedom in America
- Deter future US action through fear of follow-on attacks

The extent to which al Qaeda accomplished these objectives will be discussed below. The September 11, 2001 attacks were well planned, exploited numerous gaps in American domestic security, and were at least 75% successful (that is, three of four aircraft hit their intended targets—the hijackings *per se* were entirely successful).[22] The attacks were unexpected, visually horrifying, and caused more physical damage than the planners expected. Bin Laden, who said he was the most optimistic of all, had calculated that three or four floors would be hit in each World Trade Center tower, and the sections above might collapse as well. "This is all that we had hoped for," he said.[23] The total destruction of both towers was a grotesque windfall.

Bin Laden assumed that an attack of this magnitude would court a vigorous response, and had accounted for this in his operational plan. The impenetrable sanctuary of Afghanistan was the keystone of bin Laden's defensive strategy. His Declaration of War states "By the Grace of Allah, a safe base is now available in the high Hindukush Mountains in Khurasan; where the largest infidel military force of the world was destroyed. And the myth of the superpower was withered in front of the Mujahedin cries of *Allahu Akbar*."[24] He was familiar with the country, had fought there during the Soviet occupation, had friends, a reputation, and under Taliban rule lived in a radical Muslim state suited to his ideological predisposition. He had returned to Afghanistan May 18, 1996, fleeing possible arrest or extradition from the Sudan, where he had taken refuge in 1992. That same year the Taliban had come to power, and bin Laden quickly developed a close relationship with Taliban leader and former Mujahid Mullah Mohammed Omar.[25] The Taliban became trustworthy allies, and protected bin Laden in the aftermath of the 1998 Embassy attacks. The Taliban rebuffed overtures by the US for bin Laden's extradition, stating that he was their guest and it would be a violation of the rules of hospitality to surrender him. They suggested the US produce evidence for a trial to be held under the auspices of Islamic law, but neither evidence nor trial was forthcoming. The assassination of anti-Taliban Afghan resistance fighter Ahmed Shah Massoud on September 9, 2001 has been credited to bin Laden perhaps as payment in advance to the Taliban for their support during the expected 9/11 response, or a preemptive measure to deny the United States a potential ally inside the country.[26]

Bin Laden and the Taliban also felt they could rely on the continued support of Pakistan. The Pakistani regime was instrumental in creating the Taliban movement, and Pakistani military intelligence (SIS) gave logistics, intelligence and manpower support to the Taliban during their rise to power and afterwards. Furthermore, relations between Washington and Islamabad had soured since the end of the Soviet war in Afghanistan, particularly when the United States imposed sanctions to protest Pakistani nuclear tests in May of 1998, and after the October 1999 military coup which brought to power General Pervez Musharraf. A friendly Pakistan would guarantee Afghanistan's eastern flank and the critical mountain sanctuaries bin Laden had constructed in the 1980s and revisited and strengthened in the late 1990s.

Bin Laden also believed that the Muslim world would rally to his cause. He had stated in his Declaration of War, and again in his 1998 *fatwa,* that resistance to the Crusaders was a duty for all Muslims, a sacred obligation. Should the United States and its allies attempt to take concerted action against him, they would be answered by mass demonstrations. If the corrupt Muslim regimes attempted to crack down on the demonstrators, the people would rise up against them as well. Bin Laden may also have thought that the non-Muslim world would not support the United States, since they had criticized previous US attacks, and might feel threatened by the possibility of sharing in the retribution should they get involved.

Bin Laden felt well prepared for an American military response. After the 1998 cruise missile attack bin Laden secured bombproof bunkers in Tora Bora, sacked most of his bodyguards, and made other improvements to his personal security system.[27] He was confident that he could survive an attack from the air, or US-sponsored covert action.

Ayman al-Zawahiri, bin Laden's chief aid, said, "we aren't afraid of bombardment, threats and acts of aggression. We suffered and survived Soviet bombings for 10 years in Afghanistan and we are ready for more sacrifices."[28] To prevent another spate of arrests outside Afghanistan, he retracted parts of his network to the mountain sanctuary in the weeks before the attacks were to take place.

Bin Laden also felt secure from an American ground offensive. He was a veteran of the 10-year guerrilla struggle with the Soviet Union, and the Soviet defeat in Afghanistan was his major formative experience. He was convinced that the Mujahedin not only defeated the Soviet military but also brought about the collapse of the entire Soviet Empire. "With insignificant capabilities, with a small number of RPG's, with a small number of antitank mines, with a small number of Kalashnikov rifles, they managed to crush the greatest empire known to mankind," he stated. "They crushed the greatest military machine."[29] An important event took place during a 1987 Soviet offensive against Mujahedin training camps in eastern Afghanistan, particularly the al-Ansar "Lion's Den" where bin Laden had taken refuge. He and 35 Arab fighters held off a large force for two weeks until the Soviets withdrew.[30] This story created the legend of "bin Laden the warrior," and fed his self-image and personal mythology as well. After the war, bin Laden consistently downplayed the contributions of others in defeating the Soviets, particularly the United States, which in his view played no consequential role whatsoever.

Not only could the United States be bested on the ground in Afghanistan, it would in fact be easier than defeating the Soviets. Bin Laden believed that the United States was a paper tiger, with a reputation for strength but no staying power when it came to a hard fight. His experience had shown that the United States was intensely casualty averse, and a dramatic body-bag-producing event would be sufficient to drive the Americans from the country. Bin Laden frequently cited the American withdrawals after successful attacks against US forces in Beirut (1983) and Mogadishu (1993). In fact, bin Laden took personal credit for the latter: "It is true that my companions fought with Farah Adid's forces against the US troops in Somalia.... You will be astonished that Farah Adid had only 300 soldiers while I had sent 250 Mujahedin.... In one explosion, one hundred Americans were killed, then 18 more were killed in fighting. One day our men shot down an American helicopter. The pilot got out. We caught him, tied his legs and dragged him through the streets. After that, 28,000 US soldiers fled Somalia. The Americans are cowards."[31]

This then was bin Laden's vision of the course of the conflict. He and his associates in Afghanistan would be safe from diplomatic maneuvers, covert action, missile strikes, or air attacks. Should the United States invade Afghanistan, it would become embroiled in a Soviet-style guerrilla war, an endless, futile hunt in the mountains for the stealthy, experienced *jihadis*. The Muslim world would be in an uproar, and international opinion would be skeptical at best. The Americans would become demoralized after suffering only a few combat losses, and pull out. Meanwhile al Qaeda would pummel the US with follow-on terror attacks inside the American homeland. Its people frantic, its economy in a downward spiral, its forces demoralized, the United States would be compelled to withdraw from the Middle East, bringing about the opportunity for the creation of the Caliphate and the destruction of the Zionist entity. Osama bin Laden would then take his rightful position at the head of the Muslim *Ummah,* and set about constructing his utopia.

Al Qaeda's Operational and Strategic Failure

The 9/11 attacks accomplished some of bin Laden's goals (see Table 1). They proved that the United States could be struck at home.[32] The objective of revenge was also satisfied, at least in part. The total casualties did not seem to satisfy al Qaeda sympathizers, who claim that they still have the right to kill four million Americans.[33] It is also worth noting that Muslims were among those killed on September 11.

Many of bin Laden's objectives had mixed, mainly negative outcomes. For example, al Qaeda did manage to publicize its cause, in a dramatic and unambiguous way that bin Laden praised as beneficial. "Those young men said in deeds, in New York and Washington, speeches that overshadowed all other speeches made everywhere else in the world.... This event made people think (about true Islam) which benefited Islam greatly."[34] Yet, the attention the attacks generated was more negative than positive. Likewise, US prestige was damaged in areas where bin Laden might expect public approbation—spontaneous celebrations broke out in some parts of the world upon news of the attacks. But elsewhere, particularly in the western world, 9/11 brought forth an outpouring of sympathy, and fostered a renewed respect for the United States. Actions that bin Laden thought would be greeted by global indifference, satisfaction, or at least understanding, in fact generated disgust, fear and outrage. Bin Laden had brought perspective to the sometimes argumentative western allies, had shown them why they were allies to begin with. His brutality clarified their shared values. He reminded the civilized nations of the world what it means to be civilized. By early November 2001, the evident lack of global sympathy and support for his own cause led bin Laden to condemn the entire world in the form of the UN.[35]

The US economy was a critical target of the 9/11 attacks. Al Qaeda had (correctly) pinpointed the economy as the US center of gravity, the source of its national power, as well as of the "materialist way of life" for which he had contempt. Bin Laden and his followers had developed a fixation on the World Trade Center, and seemed to believe it was the centerpiece of the US economy. (In fact, it was not even the headquarters of a single major corporation.) In October 2001, bin Laden discussed in detail the blows he had inflicted on the US economy, and claimed that the attack would cost $1 trillion "by the lowest estimate."[36] However, more than half of this was accounted for by losses on Wall Street, which regained its pre-9/11 value by December. Furthermore, it is unclear whether the brief economic contraction of the fall and winter of 2001 was caused by the attacks or was a natural turn of the business cycle that the attacks simply exacerbated. Regardless, the US economy was diverse and robust enough to overcome the impact of 9/11, and it was clear by December that this objective had not been achieved in any lasting sense. In bin Laden's last verifiable statement to date, he appealed for more attacks on the economy.[37]

The Pentagon, "the biggest center of military power in the world," also held symbolic value for al Qaeda.[38] The Pentagon attack did some damage, but hardly enough to achieve the military objectives that bin Laden sought. Yet, striking at the heart of the DOD had a very important psychological impact. In his Declaration of War, bin Laden told the Secretary of Defense, "Your problem will be how to convince your troops to fight." One cannot overstate the motivational effect the blow at the Pentagon had on the men and women of the US military. As an Air Force Lieutenant Colonel said bitterly on

(Continued on page 362)

Table 1	
The Balance Sheet	
What al Qaeda Expected	**What Actually Happened**
Effects of the 9/11 Attacks	
Demonstrate that the US homeland can be attacked successfully	Accomplished
Take revenge for deaths of Muslims	Accomplished, in that Americans died—yet so did American Muslims
Publicize al Qaeda's cause	Mixed result, cause publicized but not in a positive light for the most part
Damage US prestige	Mixed result, attack welcomed by those who already hated the US, generated sympathy elsewhere
Damage US economy (WTC attack)	Mixed result, WTC successfully attacked, economic effects were temporary and did not affect US military power
Strike and disrupt US military HQ, demoralize military (Pentagon attack)	Mixed result, Pentagon successfully attacked, created brief disruption, generated total commitment among members of the military
Decapitate US leadership (White House attack)	Failed, attack on White House not carried out; resulted in very motivated and capable leadership with clear mandate for unlimited action
Generate a fearful, terrorized, alienated US public	Failed, public united behind leadership, motivation to seek retribution far outweighed fear of future attacks
Create harsh, widespread domestic US crackdown and end freedom in America	Failed, limited domestic roundups approved by the public
Deter future US action for fear of follow-on attacks	Failed, US undeterred, in fact highly motivated, united, and eager to join battle immediately
Expected Responses and Their Effects	
Continued support from the Taliban	Taliban continued to support and protect al Qaeda
Continued support from Pakistan	Pakistan aligned with the US
Muslim world united behind their cause, mass demonstrations and uprisings	Radical Muslim world united rhetorically, a few small demonstrations, no uprisings
Non-Muslim world opinion neutral; noting validity of Muslim complaints; mildly supportive	Non-Muslim world opinion rallied to US side against terrorism and in favor of Afghan attack
US air attacks on Afghanistan would be ineffective	Advanced munitions and vastly improved targeting capabilities produced unprecedented results

US ground attacks on Afghanistan would be a graveyard for US forces as it was for the Soviet Union	Innovative US operation succeeded in overthrowing Taliban regime, destroying al Qaeda sanctuary
Casualty-averse US military and public would not accept hard fighting	Motivated US military and public accepts sacrifices in a clear just cause
Planned follow-on terror attacks would reinforce effects of initial strikes	Follow-on attacks disrupted; al Qaeda networks effectively broken up or muted

that day, "they hit the *home office*."[39] After this, there could hardly be a question of the desire of the armed forces of the United States to seek al Qaeda's annihilation.

Many desired outcomes resulted in unequivocal failures. The decapitation strike at the White House failed when the passengers of United Airlines Flight 93, alerted to what was happening over portable phones, acted spontaneously to save their own lives or at least disrupt the plans of the hijackers, and in so doing died heroically. But even had the plan been carried out, President Bush was not present at the White House at the time, and had the structure been destroyed he still would have been able to conduct the affairs of state and direct the US response from several emergency command posts.

The greatest miscalculation, and the most significant shortcoming in the al Qaeda plan, was the belief that the attacks would demoralize the US public, that they would terrorize America to the point where an effective response would be impossible. It is true that the attacks generated fear—bin Laden noted with some enthusiasm that a month afterwards, "70% of the American people even until today still suffer from depression and psychological trauma."[40] Yet, in addition to fear, the attacks produced unprecedented national unity and hatred for bin Laden and his cause. His actions made Americans aware of something he had already known but they perhaps had not—that the United States was at war with an implacable and dangerous foe who was targeting the American way of life and was willing to take any action, no matter how barbaric, to harm this country.

In January 2002, a bin Laden sympathizer compared the 9/11 attacks favorably to the 1941 Japanese surprise attack at Pearl Harbor, and claimed that al Qaeda "has inflicted the biggest psychological defeat of the Americans in their entire history."[41] This statement reveals the terrorists' obsession with technical capabilities over strategic goals. Al Qaeda did achieve surprise on the level of Pearl Harbor, but they also precisely replicated the US national response of unity, anger, and desire for vengeance. Japanese Admiral Isoroku Yamamoto's comment is as aptly applied to 9/11; al Qaeda "awakened a sleeping giant and instilled in him a terrible resolve." Had bin Laden continued to wage his war overseas, hitting only military and government targets, he would not have engaged the American national will, or generated an overwhelming military response. The "Battles of New York and Washington," however, represent a classic case of strategic overreach. Bin Laden aroused the wrath of the American people, who handed their Commander in Chief the power to wage unlimited war on their behalf against al Qaeda. Any question of deterring the United States or other countries for fear of follow-on attacks was overwhelmed by the desire to strike back, to pursue the enemy regardless of cost or sacrifice, and to see justice done. Bin Laden was no longer facing a country distracted by internal political squabbles and lacking the leadership and national will to take the concerted action necessary to respond effectively to his provocations. He changed that himself on 9/11. It was indeed Pearl Harbor.

The magnitude of bin Laden's strategic miscalculation became apparent as the US response developed in the weeks and months following the attacks. One bright note for bin Laden was that the Taliban stood by him, following exactly the same play book as 1998 (saying he was a guest who could not be handed over because of traditions of hospitality, asking for evidence that bin Laden was indeed behind the attacks, offering to have an Islamic trial if evidence was produced, and so forth). This of course did not sway the United States, and it placed the Taliban regime in the position of being accused of "harboring terrorists," thus becoming a legitimate target.

Pakistan surprised both bin Laden and the Taliban by withdrawing support and siding with the United States. Realist theory would have predicted this—there was very little to be gained for Pakistan by taking a stand in favor of overt terrorism and against the most powerful country in the world, especially given the motivation of the United States to carry out the mission. General Musharraf faced potential domestic disturbances and the possibility of a coup, but he was able to maintain control, fire high-ranking pro-Taliban members of his government (particularly in the ISI and the military) and mute potential internal disturbances. Bin Laden pleaded for the Pakistani people to rise up against Musharraf in November, but the response was insignificant.[42]

Likewise, there was no general uprising in the Islamic world to protest US actions, or those of the "corrupt" Muslim governments. There was strong rhetorical support from many Muslim groups, but few demonstrations. The US received valuable cooperation from several Muslim Central Asian states bordering Afghanistan. Most mainstream Islamic groups rushed to announce that bin Laden's strain of radical Islam was not representative of Muslim belief in general. It soon became clear that bin Laden was not the folk hero he thought he was. He had believed that a concerted attack on him and his cause would inflame the passions of the Muslim Street and create chaos. This reflects the same hubris that had primed bin Laden for overreach, the overweening self image that is frequently the fate of the authoritarian, messianic leader who closes himself off from the world and surrounds himself with worshippers. As noted above, the reaction of non-Muslim states was also not what bin Laden expected. US allies rallied to the cause, and many of them sent troops or provided other support to augment US fighting forces.

Bin Laden's trump card was his defensive bastion in Afghanistan, and it too proved not to live up to expectations. The US air campaign became a test for new and improved weapons systems and capabilities, which were used in innovative ways. The Hellfire-armed Predator UAV is an example, as well as JDAMS munitions, ground spotters calling in air support from strategic bombers, even the employment of World War II-era bunker busters that were still in the inventory. Likewise, the ground campaign was not the war bin Laden had anticipated. Using a creative approach based on augmenting indigenous resistance forces with spearhead capabilities of Special Operations Forces, and later reinforced with conventional ground troops, the United States was able to seize the initiative and change the calculus of the battlefield. It is noteworthy that the United States engaged the enemy asymmetrically, while the Taliban relied on heavy forces and static positions instead of resorting to guerrilla war. This was a significantly different conflict from what bin Laden expected, or could even conceive.

Furthermore, bin Laden did not face the timid, casualty averse-enemy he had predicted. This was not Somalia, in which the American people had little understanding of why the United States was involved and what the sacrifice was for. In Afghanistan the public, the leadership, and the military were prepared to accept the casualties that might be necessary to prosecute the struggle. Bin Laden had, through his own actions, created this motivation. As it turned out, the United States and its allies suffered few casualties in the fall and winter of 2001, which is an indication both of Allied warfighting prowess and the inability of al Qaeda or the Taliban to mount a meaningful defense.

Finally, the expected al Qaeda follow-on attacks outside Afghanistan were not executed successfully. On October 10, 2001, an al Qaeda spokesman stated that "the battle will continue to be waged on [US] territory until it leaves our lands." Four days later another spokesman warned that "the aircraft storm will not stop," and advised Muslims living in the United States not to travel by plane or live in tall buildings.[43] Bin Laden had to show his relevance by attacking shortly after the US began to bomb Afghanistan October 7; the logic of violence as a means of communication demanded it. At least one attack was attempted, by shoe-bomber Richard Reid on December 22. However, the United States and its allies had moved effectively to break up the al Qaeda network still operating outside of Afghanistan and short-circuit any other attack plans. When major terror incidents failed to manifest themselves in the days and weeks following the commencement of hostilities in Afghanistan, it was clear that the original al Qaeda campaign plan was in terminal disarray.

Conclusion

Osama bin Laden allowed his capabilities to outpace his strategy. He discovered and exploited seams in American security to conduct a brilliant, innovative and stunning act of violence, but in so doing deviated from the long-term strategy necessary to pursue a successful guerrilla struggle. Two basic asymmetries were involved, one of forces, and the other of perceptions and will. Bin Laden benefited in the years before 9/11 from the fact that the United States was not on a war footing. By taking terrorism to unprecedented extremes, he mobilized the American national will, and raised the US level of commitment to his own or greater. In so doing, he lost his most important advantage. Furthermore, by overestimating his defensive capabilities and underestimating the offensive power of the United States, he found himself trapped in an indefensible position and unable to prosecute the follow-on attacks of his campaign plan.

As of this writing the War on Terrorism is ongoing, and bin Laden's fate unknown. The United States may face future attacks, perhaps even on the scale of 9/11 or greater. However, the critical imbalance in perceptions and commitment has been redressed, and future attackers will not benefit from the same lack of American awareness or resolve. Regardless of events yet to come, the war that Osama bin Laden had planned to wage against the United States is already over, and he has lost. It is no longer bin Laden's war, but America's.

Notes

1. "Declaration of War Against the Americans Occupying the Land of the Two Holy Places (Expel the Infidels from the Arab Peninsula)," *Al Quds Al Arabi*, August 23, 1996. *Al Quds Al Arabi* is a London-based Arabic newspaper with ties to al Qaeda. Hereafter cited as "1996 Declaration of War."
2. "1996 Declaration of War."
3. A good compendium of facts on Osama bin Laden and his intellectual and religious development can be found in John L. Esposito's *Unholy War: Terror in the Name of Islam*, New York: Oxford University Press (2002).
4. When asked about the alleged half-million Iraqi children who had died during the embargo, US Secretary of State Madeline Albright stated, "We think the price is worth it." ("Punishing Saddam," CBS News 60 Minutes, May 12, 1996.) Official statements of this nature were extremely harmful to the image of the United States in the Muslim world.
5. In an article by Abu-Ayman al-Hilali entitled "Highlights on the Political Thinking of Imam Bin Laden in Light of His Latest Speech" (*Al-Ansar* WWW-Text in Arabic 23 Jan 02 pp 22–29) he defines globalization as "the total invasion of the ideological, political, and economic tenets and values of the cultural existence of the Islamic nation."
6. "1996 Declaration of War."
7. The process of the creation of this system is ably chronicled in David Fromkin's *A Peace to End All Peace: The Fall of the Ottoman Empire and the Creation of the Modern Middle East*, New York: Avon Books (1989).
8. "1996 Declaration of War."
9. Interview with Osama bin Laden by Hamid Mir, Jalalabad, Afghanistan. Published in Islamabad *Pakistan* in Urdu, March 18, 1997.
10. Transcript of bin Laden interview, dated October 21, 2001, posted on May 23, 2002 on Qoqaz.net, text in English. Hereafter cited as October 21, 2001 bin Laden interview.
11. When asked if his struggle was a symptom of the "Clash of Civilizations," bin Laden said, "I say that there is no doubt in this." October 21, 2001 interview.
12. "1996 Declaration of War."
13. October 21, 2001 bin Laden interview.
14. Sanobar Shermatova, "Islamic Sword-Bearer," Moscow *Moskovskiye Novosti* in Russian, January 31, 1999, No 4 p 14.
15. "1996 Declaration of War."
16. Among them were Wahdi Al-Haj, an architect of the embassy bombings, arrested in Texas; Mamduh Muhammad Mahmud Salim, a financial and logistics adviser, arrested in Munich; and Khaled Fuaz, apprehended in London.
17. Rahimullah Yusufzai, "In the Way of Allah," Islamabad *The News* (Internet Version) in English June 15, 1998.
18. "Analysis: Why Bin-Laden Gained Popularity Among Ordinary Moslems," Cairo *Al-Sha'b* (Internet Version) in Arabic, September 27, 2001.
19. Interview With Osama bin Laden, Islamabad *Al-Akhbar* in Urdu, March 31, 1998, pp 1, 8.
20. "Jihad Against Jews and Crusaders," World Islamic Front Statement, February 23, 1998.
21. Interview With Osama bin Laden, March 31, 1998 (op. cit.).
22. Note that the claims of tactical brilliance and secrecy of the hijackers has been called into question by recent revelations of security lapses on their part. The factor most assisting them was the lack of awareness by the public of possible threats; thus, behavior that would seem suspicious post-9/11 and be reported was not taken seriously. See for example the bizarre behavior of 9/11 ringleader Mohammed Atta, "Face to Face With a Terrorist," ABC News, June 6, 2002.
23. Text of Osama bin Laden tape released by the Department of Defense, Dec 13, 2001.
24. "1996 Declaration of War."
25. Relations were so close that Mullah Omar took bin Laden's youngest daughter for one of his wives.

26. Massoud was killed by an exploding video camera carried by assassins posing as journalists. Note that bin Laden had never allowed those who interviewed him to bring their own cameras, and in cases where unanticipated cameras appeared bin Laden can be seen to be visibly nervous.

27. See for example, "Usama Bin Laden Moves Into Missile-Proof Bunkers," Karachi *Jasarat* in Urdu 24 Jul 99 pp 8, 7; and Jason Burke, "Bin Laden's Life Down On The Farm; Jason Burke Follows The Trail Through Afghanistan To The Hideaway Of America's Enemy," The London *Observer* (Internet version) July 4, 1999. Bin Laden allegedly had six doubles.

28. Rahimullah Yusufzai, "From the Horse's Mouth," Islamabad *The News* (Internet Version) in English, August 27, 1998. Jalaluddin Haqqani, who ran some of the training camps, said "Two Red Army air and ground attacks, artillery shelling and scores of air raids failed to destroy the Zhavara camps. What can 60 or 70 long-range Tomahawk cruise missiles do to a place as fortified as Zhavara?" Rahimullah Yusufzai, "Exporting Jehad?" Karachi *Newsline* in English, September 1998, pp. 36, 37, 39.

29. "Usamah Bin-Ladin, the Destruction of the Base," Interview with Usamah Bin-Ladin, Presented by Salah Najm, Conducted by Jamal Isma 'il in an unspecified location in Afghanistan, Al-Jazirah Television, June 10, 1999.

30. "Usamah Bin-Ladin, the Destruction of the Base," op. cit.

31. Interview with Osama bin Laden by Hamid Mir; in Jalalabad, Islamabad *Pakistan* in Urdu, March 18, 1997. In the 1996 Declaration of War bin Laden states, "when tens of your solders were killed in minor battles and one American Pilot was dragged in the streets of Mogadishu you left the area carrying disappointment, humilation, defeat and your dead with you.... It was a pleasure for the heart of every Muslim and a remedy to the chests of believing nations to see you defeated in the three Islamic cities of Beirut, Aden and Mogadishu."

32. One of the videotaped wills of a 9/11 hijacker stated that he felt it was "Time to kill Americans on their own turf." "Al-Jazeera shows September 11 suicide bomber reading last will," AFP, Tuesday April 16, 2002.

33. Suleiman Abu Gheith, "In the Shadow of Lances," alneda.com, June 7, 2002. Note that al Qaeda claims it has the right to kill 2 million children and 2 million adults, and to use weapons of mass destruction.

34. Text of Osama bin Laden tape released by the Department of Defense, Dec 13, 2001.

35. Al-Jazirah Television in Arabic November 3, 2001, 1247 GMT.

36. October 21, 2001 bin Laden interview.

37. "It is important to hit the economy, which is the base of [US] military power... If the economy is hit they will become preoccupied." Al-Jazirah Television in Arabic December 27, 2001.

38. October 21, 2001 bin Laden interview.

39. To the author, September 11, 2001.

40. October 21, 2001 bin Laden interview.

41. Abu-Ubayd al-Qurashi: "The Fourth Generation of Wars," *Al-Ansar* WWW-Text in Arabic, January 28, 2002.

42. Al-Jazirah Satellite Channel Television in Arabic November 1, 2001, 1357 GMT. Bin Laden also said "it is a duty on the brothers in Pakistan to make a strong serious move [against the government], for the victory of the religion of Allah, and the victory of the Prophet Muhammad." October 21, 2001 bin Laden interview.

43. Bin Laden stated that... "with the Grace of Allah, the battle has moved inside America. We will strive to keep it going—with Allah's permission—until victory is attained or until we meet Allah through martyrdom." October 21, 2001 bin Laden interview.

The Real Intelligence Failure on 9/11 and the Case for a Doctrine of Striking First

Richard H. Shultz is a professor of International Politics and the director of the International Security Studies Program at the Fletcher School of Law and Diplomacy. He is coeditor and author of *Security Studies for the 21st Century* (1997), as well as author of numerous other publications. He is currently writing a book on military-media relations.

Andreas Vogt is program and research coordinator of the Fletcher School of Law and Diplomacy's International Security Studies Program (ISSP) while pursuing his Ph.D. in international relations as a H. B. Earhart Fellow. He also lectures at Tufts University and organizes and participates in international security-related conferences and simulations. He has served with NATO and with UN peacekeeping forces.

*F*ollowing the 9/11 terrorist attack a number of media revelations asserted that it could have been prevented if only the intelligence community (IC) had acted on information in its possession regarding the impending attack. This article explains why and how the intelligence agencies failed on September 11th and assesses the need for and viability of preemptive military options for striking first to combat terrorism. First, it describes how the IC doggedly refused to regard terrorism as war through the 1990s. Second, the authors explain that an alternative perspective challenged this orthodoxy in the early 1990s, arguing that war was changing and entering its 4th generation. Third, based on new information about al Qaeda, the article addresses how al Qaeda organized for and executed its war, by delineating al Qaeda's organizational structure, ideology, linkages with other terrorist groups and supporting states, use of sanctuary, and financial base, and then detailing its targeting, weapons, and warfighting strategy. This assessment reveals how the al Qaeda network bears an unmistakable resemblance to 4th generation asymmetrical warfare and not to the 1990s profile portrayed by the IC. Finally, the authors demonstrate that President Bush has grasped 4th generation warfare by advocating preemptive strikes against terrorists.*

Introduction

Now that the Senate and House committees' bipartisan panel has opened its investigation of the September 11 surprise attack, the performance of the intelligence community (IC) has moved to center stage. The panel seeks to ascertain what the IC knew about the hijackers before September 11, and what it did with that information.

In the weeks preceding the opening session a number of media revelations pointed to the failure of both the FBI and CIA to put "two and two" together. First came the accounts this past May that the Bureau ignored a July 5, 2001, memo written by a Phoenix field agent warning that several Islamic radicals he had under surveillance were enrolled in aeronautical school and could be seeking to infiltrate our civil aviation system. For two weeks a relentless media wondered why the FBI had failed to act on this warning.

Then in early June the spotlight refocused on the CIA. *Newsweek* led the charge. Its June 4, 2002, cover story read "The 9/11 Terrorists the CIA Should Have Caught." The CIA allegedly possessed information about two of the hijackers dating back to an al Qaeda meeting in Malaysia in January 2000. Here are the particulars:

> A few days after the Kuala Lumpur meeting... the CIA tracked one of the terrorists, Nawaf Alhazmi, as he flew from the meeting to Los Angeles. Agents discovered that another of the men, Khalid Almihdhar, had already obtained a multiple-entry visa that allowed him to enter and leave the United States as he pleased... [D]uring the year and nine months after the CIA identified them as terrorists, Alhazmi and Al-mihdhar lived openly in the United States, using their real names, obtaining driver's licenses, opening bank accounts and enrolling in flight schools—until the morning of September 11, when they walked aboard American Airlines Flight 77 and crashed it into the Pentagon.[1]

Astonishingly, says *Newsweek*, the CIA sat on these intelligence nuggets and "did not notify the FBI, which could have covertly tracked them to find out their mission."[2]

While it is imperative to discover whether a handful of intelligence nuggets could have prevented 9/11, we do not believe what occurred that day can be explained simply by missed warnings. The real intelligence failure has to do with how the IC, and the Clinton administration it served, did not understand and incorrectly assessed the transformation that terrorist organizations like al Qaeda were undergoing in the 1990s.

Indeed, significant differences can be seen between how the IC viewed this transformation before 9/11 and what we now know about al Qaeda, its alliances with other terrorist groups, and linkages with states that support it. These dissimilarities point to an astonishing failure of intelligence analysis. In two critical ways, the IC did not abide by the counsel of the ancient Chinese strategist Sun Tzu. Recall what he advised. First, study war: "War is a matter of vital importance to the state.... It is mandatory that it be thoroughly studied." Second, "Know the enemy."

Moreover, as we will contend later, the lessons from 9/11 necessitate a fundamental reevaluation and overhaul of U.S. policy for facing up to and combating terrorism. This is exactly what the White House has undertaken to do through the molding of a new national security doctrine that adds preemptive military options to the president's quiver. The emerging Bush doctrine radically changes a U.S. government mindset and two-decade-old defensive counterterrorism policy from conceding the initiative to the terrorists to seizing the initiative by striking first through offensive military operations. It is long overdue.

Turning a Blind Eye: Assessing Terrorism in the 1990s

Each year since the early 1980s the intelligence community has produced classified estimates of trends and developments in international terrorism. A declassified summary of these analytic products—*Patterns of Global Terrorism*—is released annually by the

U.S. State Department's Office of the Coordinator for Counterterrorism. It is an instructive source for deducing how the IC assessed the evolution of the terrorist threat through the 1990s.

Other open source materials can likewise help us assemble an informed impression of the IC's pre-9/11 perspective on terrorism. These include IC testimony at congressional hearings, studies and reports by contractors that support the IC like RAND, and publications by serving intelligence officers such as the former deputy chief of CIA's Counterterrorism Center, Paul Pillar.[3] These sources tell us a great deal about how the intelligence community evaluated international terrorism as the 1990s drew to a close. Here are its principal deductions:

First, terrorism was not war. According to Pillar, terrorism "is not accurately represented by the metaphor of war. Unlike most wars, it has neither a fixed enemy nor the prospect of coming to closure, be it through a win or some other denouement."[4] Even after Usama bin Laden issued a declaration of war against America in 1998 when he called on his followers "to abide by Allah's order by killing Americans... anywhere, anytime, and wherever possible," the U.S. continued to abstain from regarding terrorism as war.

If terrorism was not war, then what was it? The U.S. Government defined it as a crime. And those who carried out such attacks—not the leaders who gave the orders to do so nor states who provided sanctuary and succor—were to be brought before American courts through extradition, rendition, or arrest. The U.S. established specific laws for prosecution and made "bring terrorists to justice for their crimes" the keystone of its policy for combating terrorism.

In terms of trends, the IC reported that terrorist incidents were down—though increasingly lethal and indiscriminate—and that the U.S. was the primary target. These developments were attributed to the growing number of radical religious groups—primarily militant Islamists—that wanted to kill as many Americans as possible. Such movements believed they were carrying out divine mandates that justified deadly and wholesale carnage. The IC also detected changes in how terrorist organizations were structured. In the 1980s they were organized hierarchically with a clear command and control structure.

Those who belonged to these groups were also considered professionals with well-defined political objectives. In the 1990s the IC noted that new terrorist organizations were emerging that were less cohesive, more diffuse, amorphous, and populated by amateurs. While fanatically motivated because of their religious and millenarian aims, the rank-in-file were the antithesis of 1980s' skilled practitioners. Those who carried out the 1993 World Trade Center bombing were illustrative. For the IC this was the gang that couldn't shoot straight.

Organizational devolution, in turn, negated the likelihood of an international terrorist network. Also working against global linkages and cooperative arrangements were political, philosophical, and spiritual differences among groups and states. Pillar put it this way:

> The fault lines are numerous. Ethnic, national, and socioeconomic differences have
> impeded efforts at unity, as have differing security perspectives. Sectarian differences
> are also significant—particularly, but not solely, the split between Sunni and Shia...
> The great ethnic, religious, and national divisions of the Muslim world are turning
> out to be stronger than all the calls to Islamic solidarity.[5]

Declining state support for terrorist groups likewise undercut the prospects for an international terrorist network. By the end of the 1990s seven states—Cuba, Libya, Iran, Iraq, North Korea, Sudan, and Syria—remained on the IC's state sponsorship list, but their involvement was said to be shrinking because these states had other more vital interests at stake. While Afghanistan was not officially listed as a state sponsor, late 1990s editions of *Patterns of Global Terrorism* expressed concern over the sanctuary that the Taliban provided to al Qaeda (to be discussed in more detail below).

Finally, the IC did not discern the growing importance of non-state supporters—a phenomenon of the 1990s. New players included religious leaders and their organizations, charities and other NGOs, and wealthy individuals.

As the 1990s drew to a close, this was the U.S. government's appraisal of the challenge of terrorism. To be sure, individual members held different views. Still, terrorism was seen as a secondary national security challenge—not a clear and present danger—even after the deadly 1998 East Africa embassy bombings. It still was not war, although the Clinton administration became somewhat more willing to go beyond the law enforcement approach and use limited cruise missile strikes against targets in Afghanistan and Sudan.

A New Form of Warfare

By the time the *USS Cole* was bombed in October 2000 Washington finally knew it was in a deadly struggle with al Qaeda, but it still shunned a military campaign to destroy it and the states that gave it help. In the words of Pillar, such an effort would be hopeless— "If there is a 'war' against terrorism, it is a war that cannot be won… terrorism cannot be defeated—only reduced, attenuated, and to some degree controlled."[6]

Beyond the refusal of the U.S. intelligence community, and for that matter the military establishment, to classify terrorism as warfare because it was not a serious enough danger, other reasons also contributed to this reluctance. Most important, terrorism was not war because it did not resemble modern war as the spooks and soldiers had known it, studied it, and practiced it. Therefore, *ipso facto*, it could not be war.

In the early 1990s an alternative perspective challenged this orthodoxy, arguing that war was undergoing big changes—transformation—and entering its 4th generation. The 1st generation—classical nation-state war—had been perfected by Napoleon. This was followed by industrial age war of attritions based on massive firepower. It reached its apogee in WWI. Maneuver warfare, introduced by the Germans in WWII and refined by the U.S. in the 1980s, marked the 3rd generation.

Among the first to propose that a new form of war was emerging was Martin van Creveld in his 1991 book *The Transformation of War*. Although considered a master military historian and author of two widely read earlier books—*Supplying War* and *Command in War*—most American strategic analysts and military professionals considered his new work too far out. The following forecast was flatly rejected as the musings of an eccentric intellectual:

> The modern paradigm for warfare, in which nation-states wage war for reasons of state, using formal militaries… [is] being eclipsed by a post-modern approach…. As war between states exits through one side of history's revolving door, low intensity conflict among different organizations will enter through the other…. National

sovereignties are being undermined by organizations [non-state actors] that refuse to recognize the states' monopoly over armed violence.[7]

In 1991 the U.S. had just pulled off one of the most spectacular conventional land battles in modern military history. In 100 hours it rolled around and over an Iraqi army that many expected to put up a serious fight. In the afterglow of that feat, van Creveld's assertion that 3rd generation conventional maneuver warfare was in the final stages of abolishing itself required too great a leap of faith for most specialists to take seriously. A review of *The Transformation of War* prepared for the Office of the Undersecretary of Defense for Policy charged that van Creveld was not "a balanced strategic thinker," had "scant evidence for his view," and made "numerous unsubstantiated assertions."

Those few who embraced van Creveld's line of reasoning sought to understand how non-state actors, particularly terrorist organizations who were in the midst of their own transformation, were adapting to globalization, network-based organization, and information age technologies. How would these developments affect the terrorist's capacity to execute unconventional attacks—asymmetrical operations in the lexicon of the Pentagon—against the nation-states they targeted? How would terrorist groups cooperate among themselves and with state sponsors in order to operate and fight globally?

During the latter 1990s a picture began to emerge. Its architects included Charles Dunlap, an Air Force colonel who in 1996 published a highly provocative essay, "How We Lost the High-Tech War of 2007: A Warning from the Future."[8] It is a tale of how radical Islamic terrorists go to war with and defeat the U.S. using inconceivably barbaric and gruesome terrorist tactics. Few took Dunlap seriously.

Then there was Ralph Peters, yet another outspoken and controversial colonel. His 1990s essays in *Parameters: U.S. Army War College Quarterly* contended that future enemies would include tyrants, warlords, chieftains, ayatollahs, demagogues, gangsters, drug lords, and other thugs who would wage ferocious non-American-style warfare. No one in the Army had much time for Peters' grim and unlikely suppositions. In 1998 he retired but continued to write and speak.[9]

Another outspoken proponent of 4th generation warfare in the 1990s was Franklin "Chuck" Spinney, an analyst in the Pentagon's Office of Program Analysis and Evaluation. His web site is one stop shopping. Spinney is a brusque critic of the American military establishment he serves. He has charged that the Pentagon has lagged woefully behind the curve in developing the right military response for 4th generation warriors who have and will continue to target the U.S. Heavy firepower, attrition tactics, and long-range, high-altitude bombers are simply not the answers, he asserted.[10]

As the 1990s came to an end, the precepts that these eclectic oddball strategists believed terrorist groups would adopt as a part of what van Creveld had first called a "post-modern transformation of war" were as follows:

- Warfare will be highly irregular, unconventional, and decentralized in approach.
- Asymmetrical operations will be employed to bypass the superior military power of nation-states to attack and exploit political, economic, population, and symbolic targets. In doing so, terrorists groups backed by states will seek to demoralize the psyche of both government and its populace.

- Both the organization and operations of 4th generation warriors will be masked by deception, denial, stealth, and related techniques of intelligence tradecraft. They will wear no uniforms and will infiltrate and blend into the populations of the nation-states they seek to attack.
- Terrorist organizations and operations will be profoundly affected by information age technologies. The development of network-based terrorist organizations connected transnationally through cell phones, fax machines, e-mail, web sites, and the Internet will provide these non-state actors with global reach.
- Modern communications and transportation technologies will have a profound effect on this new battlefield. Not only will there be no fronts but the old distinctions between civilian and military targets will become irrelevant.
- Laws and conventions of war that apply to nation-states will not constrain terrorists and their state sponsors as they seek new and innovative means, including weapons of mass destruction, to inflict terrible carnage on civilians and nonmilitary targets.
- 4th generation warriors, frequently in the name of religiously based ideologies, will be remorseless enemies for the states they challenge. Their operations will be marked by unlimited violence, unencumbered by compassion.
- Countering terrorists and other non-state actors will be difficult for the armies of post-modern states. Terrorist organizations will have few, if any, targets that are vulnerable to modern conventional weapons systems. However, these conventional means are relevant against the state sponsors of terrorism.

Prior to the attack of September 11th the notion that a new kind of war based on these emerging principles would have a dramatic effect on how, when, and where terrorists were able to strike. Moreover, that those attacks could take place against targets in the great cities of America was considered nothing more than the unfounded reflections of a handful of strategic iconoclasts. The official U.S. government perspective on the evolution of terrorism in the 1990s was far from simpatico with these propositions.

What We Now Know: Al Qaeda Prepares for War

Since the attack of September 11th we have learned a great deal about al Qaeda. That information is used here to address two fundamental questions—how is al Qaeda organized for war and how does it carry it out? More specifically, we will scrutinize a vast amount of open source materials to: one, delineate al Qaeda's organizational structure, ideology, linkages with other terrorist groups and supporting states, Afghanistan sanctuary, and financial base; and two, detail its targeting, weapons, and warfighting strategy.

This assessment reveals how intimately the al Qaeda network bears an unmistakable resemblance to the template of 4th generation warfare and *not* to the 1990s profile portrayed by the intelligence community. Furthermore, it pinpoints the truest cause of the intelligence failure that took place on September 11th and the need for a new national security doctrine for fighting the war on terrorism.

I. The al Qaeda Organization

Al Qaeda, as a terrorist group, is a child of 1990s globalization. As with international businesses, globalization had a transforming effect on how al Qaeda organized itself. Unlike hierarchically structured terrorist groups of the 1980s, Usama bin Laden (UBL) established a networked organization of small dispersed units that can deploy nimbly, anywhere, anytime. It is characterized by doctrine, configuration, strategy, and technology in sync with the information age.

During the 1990s, al Qaeda created an elaborate set of connections with several like-minded terrorist groups and terrorist-sponsoring states by, among other things, establishing cells across the globe in as many as 60 countries.

Before deconstructing the structural make-up of bin Laden's handiwork, it is essential to consider his message and how it has been exploited to assemble a multinational alliance among several extremist groups that may operate locally as well as transnationally.

A broad politico-religious appeal

Al Qaeda owes its global infrastructure to its broad appeal. Contrary to intelligence assessments of the 1990s that asserted its followers were exclusively Middle Eastern, Arab, and Sunni, post-9/11 evidence reveals otherwise. Its attraction is much wider, cutting across and linking groups that intelligence professionals like Pillar believed were so different that it "impeded efforts at unity." Recall his claim: "The great ethnic, religious, and national divisions of the Muslim world are turning out to be stronger than all the calls to Islamic solidarity."

Al Qaeda's wide-ranging politico-religious viewpoint attracted both militant Middle Eastern Islamic-oriented groups as well as broader pan-Islamic elements.[11] Al Qaeda exploits conditions that breed extremism. These include failing states characterized by excessive political and economic stagnation, rampant corruption, and brutal repression.

These developments are present in several regimes, including Egypt, Algeria, and Saudi Arabia, and each has experienced the rise of extremist Islamic groups who employ terrorist tactics. Al Qaeda calls for the use of force to overthrow these failed governments and to drive out Western influence. It is with terrorist organizations and individuals from these places that bin Laden has forged his most important alliances.

UBL also exploits other internal conflicts to recruit associates. These include arrangements with groups fighting regimes that are charged with repressing Muslim minorities (e.g., Bosnia, Kosovo, and India), as well as with movements fighting to establish independent states (e.g., Palestinians and Chechens). Finally, al Qaeda exploits the U.S. military presence and foreign policy initiatives in the Middle East, American relations with several of the failed Arab states just identified, and U.S. commitment to Israel.

These ideological themes can be found in UBL communiqués and declarations. Illustrative are the *fatwas*—religious decrees—he has issued. Take for example his 1996, "Declaration of War Against the Americans Occupying the Land of the Two Holy Places." The themes noted above saturate that diatribe. The same is true of his 1998 announcement of the formation of the "World Islamic Front for Jihad against the Jews and Crusaders."[12]

Since 9/11 there have been numerous reports that demonstrate how UBL's message resonates with a wide range of ethnic, religious, and national groups throughout the Muslim world. Al Qaeda uses them in the hope of fostering nothing short of an international Islamic jihad.

A globally networked organization

In a 1997 interview bin Laden described al Qaeda as "a product of globalization and a response to it."[13] It could simply not have operated in the 1980s as it did in the 1990s. Information age technologies and cyber networks allowed al Qaeda to recruit, communicate, establish cells and operatives, and attack targets globally.

Networked organizations share several basic features. First, communication and coordination within them are not formally specified but emerge and change according to the task at hand. Relationships are informal and marked by varying degrees of intensity according to the needs of the organization. Second, linkages to individuals and groups outside the main organization usually complement the internal network. Third, internal and external ties are facilitated by shared norms and values. Thus internal self-managing teams plan and execute operations, while external linkages with a complex association of contributing groups provide a constellation of support activities.[14]

Al Qaeda, which emerged in 1988 and expanded through the 1990s, adopted these features. Its basic internal network is organized vertically with bin Laden, the emir-general, at the top, followed by other al Qaeda leaders.[15] Horizontally, it is allied with numerous other terrorist groups.

Below bin Laden is the *shura majlis* or the consultative council. Four committees report to it. A military committee recruits fighters, runs training camps, and launches terrorist operations. It also oversees other clandestine functions including a special office for procuring, forging or altering identity documents such as passports and visas. A finance committee accrues the resources necessary to sustain al Qaeda. Justifying its actions by issuing rulings on shari'a law is the responsibility of the religious/legal committee. Finally, the media committee disseminates information in support of al Qaeda's political and military activities.

The al Qaeda leadership oversees a loosely tied network of cells that cannot be easily traced back to it. Each operates autonomously with its members not knowing the identity of other cells. Thus if one cell is compromised it will not betray others. The pattern that has emerged is of a web of cells around the world that provide the intelligence and manpower to execute terrorist attacks against the U.S. and other targets.

Due to its broad politico-religious dogma, al Qaeda has the capacity to infiltrate and operate out of Muslim communities that exist across the globe. It has established clandestine cells from New Zealand to India to the United States. In the Middle East, it receives the support of Islamic philanthropists and foundations to underwrite its organizational expansion.

Compartmentalization, secrecy, and deception differentiate al Qaeda from other globally networked organizations. These tools of intelligence tradecraft are drawn on to secure its network at all levels, including... cyberspace. Al Qaeda training manuals stress the importance of deception and denial methods. Ahmed Ressam, the al Qaeda operative who failed to bomb Los Angeles International Airport at the end of 1999, highlighted at his trial the extent to which these methods were stressed during training sessions at camps in Afghanistan.[16] It is unknown how al Qaeda became so adept at these professional spy procedures. Perhaps a state's intelligence service provided the instruction? If so, the likely suspects would include Iraq (which learned it from the KGB) or Iran.

To prepare the groundwork for the 1998 East Africa embassy bombings, several al Qaeda operatives were deployed as sleeper agents. For several years they burrowed into Kenyan and Tanzanian society. Then in August 1998 they struck. Western intelligence agencies now know there are other sleeper cells in Europe and North America waiting to be activated.[17]

The Mohammad Atta cells that carried out the attacks on the World Trade Center and Pentagon illustrate how al Qaeda operates. Using public data, Valdis Krebs has mapped a portion of that network centered on the 19 dead hijackers. His diagram discloses how compartmented and dispersed hijackers on the same team were from each other. Cell members were connected through the judicious use of transitory shortcuts in the network. Meetings were held to link up distant parts of the Atta cells to coordinate tasks and report progress. After coordination was accomplished, the crossties went dormant until the need for their synchronization arose again.[18]

The hijack cells were integrated and synchronized for the operation by the Egyptian-born Atta. He came to al Qaeda through Egyptian Islamic Jihad, the group led by Ayman al-Zawahri, bin Laden's top lieutenant. Additionally, Khaled al-Midhar and Nawaq al-Hamzi, two other hijackers, were filmed at a January 2000 meeting in Kuala Lumpur with known al Qaeda operatives. Finally, several of the hijackers were trained at al Qaeda camps in Afghanistan.[19]

Within a week of the attacks, U.S. authorities concluded that the planning of the operation began as early as 1999, when some of the suspected 19 hijackers began to take flight training lessons in the U.S.[20] Furthermore, the 9/11 hijackers did not work alone. Other al Qaeda members and affiliates provided necessary skills and knowledge, and also served as conduits for transferring money.

The 9/11 hijackers were also linked to an underground network of Islamic militants in Europe that had grown over several years around al Qaeda.[21] Starting in 2000, European intelligence agencies began uncovering al Qaeda cells in Germany, Italy, France, the U.K., and Spain who were planning attacks on American targets. This was learned as a result of the arrest by United Arab Emirates police of Djamel Beghal, a French-Algerian Islamist, transiting through Dubai to France. While in French custody, Beghal confessed that he had received instructions from bin Laden's chief of operations, Abu Zubayda, to bomb U.S. targets in Europe.[22]

Training camps and sanctuary in Afghanistan

Landlocked Afghanistan provided al Qaeda with a unique political, security, and geographic shield. In return, al Qaeda forces fought alongside the Taliban, providing it with an important military capability, while bin Laden provided Taliban leaders with millions of dollars.

Hundreds of documents found in Afghanistan reveal an al Qaeda presence of several thousand. It established offices, communications facilities, guesthouses, training centers, and barracks. Training manuals, students' notebooks, ledgers, military records, communications and code books, and IBM desktop computers shed considerable light on al Qaeda's methods, preoccupations, and ambitions. Extensive interviews with Kabul residents present a picture of al Qaeda as a law unto itself.

At the same time, the evidence demonstrates that there was constant liaison between al Qaeda and the Taliban Ministries of Defense, Interior, and Suppression of Vice and Propagation of Virtue. "U.S. intelligence estimates suggest that between 1996 and 2001 some U.S. $100 million was given to the Taliban, effectively ensuring al Qaeda's organizational autonomy within Afghanistan and considerable influence within key ministries."[23]

Al Qaeda training camps, many of them dispersed in the rugged Afghan terrain in Afghanistan, played a vital role in the organization. The Meivand camp in the Rod Para Mountains is illustrative. Before it was destroyed, it could support the training of up to 700 fighters at any given time. Above ground, the camp consisted of more than 50 buildings, including a hospital. Below ground, a large cave complex, equipped with running water and electricity, was used for storage, housing, and security.[24]

This al Qaeda infrastructure also served the organization's global ambitions by drawing tens of thousands of radical Islamic militants to Afghanistan. While in the camps these individuals were assessed, recruited, and deployed for global operations. Others were assigned to the al Qaeda-led Arab and international brigades that fought alongside Taliban forces against the Northern Alliance. How many foreign Islamic militants received training in al Qaeda's camps in Afghanistan since the 1980s? Estimates range between 50,000 and as many as 100,000.

Documents unearthed in early January 2002 in the rubble of the Meivand camp portray an efficient operation that boasted to new terrorist recruits of its involvement in the 9/11 attacks. One of the instructors spoke about the planning of that attack, claiming that the airplanes that crashed in New York and Washington were part of a larger plan to hijack 25 airliners around the world.[25]

Linkages with other terrorist organizations

Al Qaeda has established both formal and informal affiliations—or linkages—with several Middle Eastern and Asian radical Islamist groups that employ terrorism against their own governments. For example, many of its members were drawn from two Egyptian organizations—the Islamic Group and Islamic Jihad. Two Algerian factions, the Armed Islamic Group and the Salafist Group for Preaching and Combat, likewise have strong ties with al Qaeda. In Yemen, where his family originated, bin Laden has formed bonds with Jaish Aden Abin al Islami. Finally, al Qaeda has allied a horde of smaller radical Islamist entities in northern Iraq, Saudi Arabia, Tunisia, Libya, Morocco, and elsewhere.[26]

In Asia, al Qaeda affiliates include three Islamist factions fighting in Kashmir, and the Moro Islamic Liberation Front and the Abu Sayaaf Group in the Philippines. With respect to the latter, evidence presented at the trial of terrorists involved in the first World Trade Center bombing (1993) show that these ties go back to the early 1990s.[27]

The federal trial in New York of those accused of plotting the 1998 bombings of the U.S. embassies in Kenya and Tanzania also revealed evidence of how al Qaeda established linkages with several radical Islamist groups, including the Egyptian Islamic Jihad and the Armed Islamic Group of Algeria. Court documents also describe the intimate relationship between al Qaeda and the Taliban.[28]

Perhaps the most interesting and controversial arrangement established by UBL was the one with Hizballah and its Iran patron. Recall that during the latter 1990s the U.S. intelligence community assumed that Sunni and Shia terrorist groups could never cooperate because of their sharply divergent interpretations of Islam. We now know that this supposition was flawed.

In 1995 and again in 1996, al Qaeda operatives are reported to have contacted Iran's Ministry of Intelligence and Security (MOIS) proposing to join forces against America.[29] "In June 1996, MOIS hosted a meeting of terrorist leaders in Tehran. Among those present were Imad Mugniyah, Hizballah's master terrorist planner, whose operations against the U.S. go back to the 1983 bombing of the Marine Corps barracks in Beirut, and senior aides to bin Laden. Subsequently, high-ranking al Qaeda officials met with Mugniyah on several occasions."[30]

During the trial of al Qaeda operatives, it was reported that a representative of bin Laden met with an official of the Iranian government prior to the bombings of the U.S. embassies in East Africa in order to establish an anti-U.S. alliance.[31] Ali Mohamed, who was convicted of conspiracy in those bombings, testified: "I arranged security for a meeting in the Sudan between Mughniyah, Hizballah's chief, and bin Laden... Hizballah provided explosives training for al Qaeda and al-Jihad," he added.[32]

According to the Director of Central Intelligence, George Tenet, "Iran continues to provide support—including arms transfers—to Palestinian rejectionist groups and Hizballah. Tehran has also failed to move decisively against al Qaeda members who have relocated to Iran from Afghanistan."[33]

Contradicting the intelligence community mantra of the 1990s—Sunni and Shia terrorist groups never cooperate—Tenet added: "while al Qaeda represents a broad-based Sunni worldwide extremist network, it would be a mistake to dismiss possible connections to either other groups or state sponsors—either Sunni or Shia. There is a convergence of common interest in hurting the U.S., its allies, and interests that make traditional thinking in this regard unacceptable."[34]

Evidently, collaboration against hated enemies takes precedence over denominational differences, as can be seen in the al Qaeda-Hizballah-Iran axis. Finally, related to the matter of Sunni-Shia solidarity is the widely reported linkage between Shia Iran and Hizballah and Sunni Palestinian groups to include Hamas and Islamic Jihad, as well as the secular Palestinian Authority.[35]

State support

Recall that during the 1990s the U.S. intelligence community reported that state support for terrorist groups, to include al Qaeda, was on the wane. This contention can be found in issue after issue of *Patterns of Global Terrorism* released by the State Department. As seen above, Afghanistan clearly contradicted that deduction. Al Qaeda had unprecedented and increasing access and support from the Taliban regime.

It likewise had a close association with Sudan, particularly in the first half of the 1990s, establishing a working relationship with the government in Khartoum. However, unlike the Taliban, intense diplomatic efforts on the part of the U.S. pressured the Sudanese to compel bin Laden to move his organization to Afghanistan. Nevertheless, the connection between Khartoum and bin Laden remained active up to 9/11.

Al Qaeda also maintained liaison with elements in the government of Yemen, as well as among different tribes, through the 1990s. And it was there that one of al Qaeda's most spectacular operations, the suicide attack on the *USS Cole*, took place in 2000.

In Pakistan, al Qaeda had strong ties with the notorious Inter-Service Intelligence Agency (ISI) since the 1980s. These linkages go back to the Soviet-Afghan War in which ISI was intimately involved with Mujaheddin factions and the non-Afghan Islamic militants. In the 1990s an ISI-al Qaeda-Taliban axis emerged that is believed to still exist— even after *Operation Enduring Freedom* started.[36] There was also, as was previously noted, a connection between al Qaeda and the regime in Iran. The extent of that linkage remains murky, especially in the aftermath of the September 11th attacks. Finally, there has been considerable speculation about ties between al Qaeda and Iraq. This issue has received a great deal of scrutiny by the Bush Administration since 9/11. Here is what we know.

Attention first focused on an April 2000 meeting in Prague between Mohammad Atta and Ahmed Khalil Ibrahim Samir al Ani, a senior Iraqi intelligence operative working under cover as a diplomat. The Czech government, which apparently videotaped the meeting, provided evidence to Washington confirming this fact and has never wavered on the matter.[37] However, what was discussed, if Prague knows, has not been revealed publicly.

This was followed by the revelations of various Iraqi defectors such as Sabah Khodada, a former army officer who served at a terrorist training camp run by the Mukhabarat, Saddam's intelligence service. According to Khodada, foreign personnel were trained in "assassinations, kidnapping, hijacking of airplanes, hijacking of buses, hijacking of trains and other kinds of operations related to terrorism." He also noted that the camp included a Boeing 707. Aspiring hijackers were "trained on how to get weapons inside the plane," and how to adapt to "situations where security will not allow you to get weapons into the plane."[38]

Next came the disclosure in *The New Yorker* (March 2002) about Ansar al-Islam, a radical Islamist group in Kurdish northern Iraq who has connections both to al Qaeda and Iraq's Mukhabarat.[39]

Finally, the civil/class action lawsuit filed on behalf of those seeking damages arising out of the September 11, 2001, terrorist attacks contains further details of Iraq-al Qaeda collaboration. It dates that linkage "to the early 1990s" when, following "the Gulf War, Iraqi agents traveled to the Sudan" to meet with bin Laden operatives. Over the next five years, "from 1991 to 1996," this led to "extensive interaction between al Qaeda and Iraq's intelligence officers." Then, in 1998, "two of bin Laden's senior military commanders met in Baghdad with Qusay Hussein, chief of Iraqi intelligence and son of Saddam." That meeting further cemented the relationship with "Iraq reportedly agreeing to supply al Qaeda with training, intelligence, weapons, and other support."[40]

The money trail

Bin Laden set up an elaborate financial network to ensure the financial well-being of al Qaeda and to support its operational and logistical requirements. Through this, UBL has invested in the future. For example, he has established an unknown number of "sleeper" cells awaiting orders to launch future attacks.[41]

The financial arm of al Qaeda appears to operate like a foundation. It has "high-ranking members selecting suitable applicants, such as a newly-established al Qaeda cell or a like-minded radical Islamist group, and providing financial assistance for terrorist activities."[42]

However, tracking the money is easier said than done. According to recent reports, al Qaeda's financial network experienced a "paradigm shift" well before 9/11. Knowledgeable of the vulnerability of its European bank accounts, al Qaeda apparently shifted its money into commodities more difficult to trace, like gold, diamonds, tanzanite, and sapphires.[43]

In addition to bin Laden's personal fortune, al Qaeda has turned to both legal and illegal activities to raise funds to underwrite its activities during the last decade.[44]

The former includes small business ventures, such as farms and fisheries, as well as larger construction, electronic appliances, and investment firms.

For example, Darkazanli, a Hamburg-based Import-Export Company, was the first private business to have its assets frozen due to suspected links with the 9/11 attacks. An executive order published in September 2001 describes it as a "front group" for al Qaeda and its CEO, Syrian-born Mamoun Darkazanli, as one of bin Laden's main financial lieutenants.[45] As Steven Emerson, an internationally recognized expert on terrorism and the militant Islamic infrastructure in the U.S., states: "Darkazanli offers a strategic paradigm for the manner in which a small, legitimate business with convenient European locations and inconspicuous business transactions, can be misused to launder money, purchase sensitive technical equipment, and facilitate the establishment—both in Europe and elsewhere—of business 'front' groups for al Qaeda."[46] Also worth noticing is the fact that the company's specialty in electronics was an ideal cover for procuring technical equipment for al Qaeda.

Other al Qaeda front companies started to emerge in the early 1990s. These included a Khartoum-based holding company, as well as construction, agriculture, investment, leather, and transportation companies. These business ventures transferred funds to al Qaeda operatives that carried out the East Africa U.S. embassy bombings.[47]

Funding—both wittingly and unwittingly—also comes from dozens of Islamic charities and mosques. A case in point is the Afghanistan-based Al-Wafa Humanitarian Organization. It is believed to have purchased equipment and weapons for al Qaeda. In 1999 the United Nations, under Resolution 1267, authorized the publication of a list of "persons and entities connected with Usama bin Laden." Al-Wafa was one of three charities included. The other two were the Al Rashid Trust and Makhtab Al-Khidamat/Al Kifah.[48]

Another charity that has come under scrutiny is the International Islamic Relief Organization (IIRO). It purportedly provided funds to al Qaeda's affiliate in the Philippines, Abu Sayyaf.[49] Established in 1978, the IIRO is headquartered in Saudi Arabia and has branches around the world. Canada's Security and Intelligence Service found that an IIRO official working there was assisting al Qaeda and UBL.[50]

Islamic charities linked to bin Laden are also located in the United States. Take the Chicago-based Benevolence International Foundation (BIF). The U.S. recently released evidence revealing that its Syrian-born executive-director, Enaam M. Arnaout, is a close associate and fundraiser for bin Laden. Those ties stretch back more than a decade and include assistance to al Qaeda operatives who were attempting to acquire chemical and nuclear weapons. The evidence is based on documents seized in the group's offices in Chicago and Bosnia and on a series of witnesses, including former al Qaeda members currently in U.S. custody.[51]

Drug money also found its way into al Qaeda coffers through the distribution of opium. Along with the Taliban, it produced thousands of metric tons of opium during the latter 1990s in a majority of the 31 Afghan provinces. It was then smuggled through neighboring Central Asian states. [52]

Al Qaeda also received cash from the well heeled. Western intelligence agencies believe Arab businessmen paid bin Laden extortion money to avoid attacks on their interests throughout the Middle East.[53] Other wealthy individuals in various states such as Saudi Arabia gave willingly because they felt affinity and solidarity with the cause of UBL. These donors are believed to give millions of dollars every year.[54]

Finally, al Qaeda appears to have laundered its legal and illegal funds through long-established centers in the Middle East, Asia, Europe, and elsewhere. Global financial centers, including Frankfurt, London, and New York, have frozen more than $100 million in assets tied to al Qaeda, and investigations are currently under way in Malta, Italy, Panama, Singapore, South Africa, and elsewhere to determine whether al Qaeda laundered illicit capital through their financial institutions.[55]

II. Al Qaeda Targeting, Weapons, and Strategy

Since 9/11 we have learned a great deal about how al Qaeda plans and executes terrorist actions. This information has brought out in the open the organization's operational features and shed light on its intentions.

Selecting targets

In 1999 the Jordanian police arrested Khalil Deek in connection with a plot to bomb Amman's main airport on the eve of the millennium. In his possession they discovered a remarkable document that subsequently came to be referred to by Western intelligence agencies as the *Encyclopedia of Jihad*.[56] Consisting of eleven volumes and approximately 7,000 pages, it is considered a key manual for instructing al Qaeda operatives.

The manual paid particularly close attention to the selection of targets to assail and obliterate. They were categorized as follows. First, there were *symbolic targets* such as the Statue of Liberty in New York or the Eiffel Tower in Paris. In this case, the objective was not to kill large numbers, but to deliver a devastating psychological blow by demolishing a cultural icon. Next were *infrastructure targets*, including nuclear power stations, skyscrapers, ports, and train stations. While also having symbolic meaning, their destruction was intended to kill as many as possible. Finally, there were *human targets*— places where large numbers of people congregate or influential public figures. In the latter two cases the objective was to kill the unsuspecting and innocent.

In selecting targets al Qaeda surfed the Internet, collecting vital information posted on U.S. government websites. For example, terrorism vulnerability studies produced by the *U.S. General Accounting Office* were stored on the hard drive of one of al Qaeda's computers found in Afghanistan. These websites provided a rich menu of poorly secured targets. It is evident from this and other examples that al Qaeda was well aware of how official reports and assessments could be of great assistance in planning attacks on the United States. There is also evidence that it compiled information on U.S. nuclear power plants. All of these facts and figures were only a click away on the World Wide Web.

The debriefing of Abu Zubaydah provided additional confirmation that al Qaeda targetters were concentrating on bringing the group's war inside the borders of the United States. CIA Director Tenet said the same thing to the Senate Select Committee on Intelligence in February: "We know that terrorists have considered attacks in the U.S. against high-profile government or private facilities, famous landmarks, and U.S. infrastructure nodes such as airports, bridges, harbors, and dams. Al Qaeda also planned to strike against U.S. interests in Europe, the Middle East, Africa and Southeast Asia." He added that diplomatic and military facilities "are high-risk targets."[57]

Weapons

Al Qaeda weaponry range from standard issue small arms used by terrorists for decades, to plans for either acquiring or producing weapons of mass destruction. This was spelled out in the *Encyclopedia of Jihad*. It offered guidance on how to rig up a door lock to explode when the handle is turned, how to inject frozen food with biochemical agents to create mass panic, as well as how to bring down a plane with a missile. The latter drew on years of guerrilla fighting against the Soviets in the 1980s.

Among the most chilling pages of the manual were those that dealt with bioterrorism that spell out how to disperse lethal organisms and poisons ranging from botulism and viral infections to ricin and anthrax. It also called for maximizing public panic by poisoning medicine, hence jeopardizing treatment of affected individuals.

Another chapter of the *Encyclopedia of Jihad* concentrated on sabotage techniques. For example, one section illustrated how to turn cameras into a bomb. Ahmed Shah Masood, the leader of the Northern Alliance, the resistance organization fighting the Taliban, was assassinated in this way two days before the 9/11 attacks. In addition to analyzing how C4 and Semtex explosives can be used, the encyclopedia contains instructions on the ingredients needed to make bombs from innocuous substances bought in places like supermarkets and hardware stores.[58]

Since the Cold War ended, the acquisition of weapons of mass destruction (WMD) by non-state actors has received considerable attention. During a few distressing weeks last fall U.S. officials believed that this worst-case scenario was about to come true. In October 2001 intelligence warned that terrorists had obtained a 10-kiloton nuclear weapon from the Russian arsenal and planned to detonate it in New York City. The warning turned out to be a false alarm, but because nuclear weapons proliferation experts have suspected that several portable nuclear devices might be missing from the Russian stockpile since the mid-1990s, it was believable.[59]

Following the 9/11 attacks Taliban and al Qaeda access to Pakistan's nuclear arsenal and expertise also became a major worry. Intense media speculation ensued regarding the likelihood that Pakistani nuclear experts were assisting al Qaeda or, worse, that Pakistan's existing nuclear arsenal might fall into their hands.[60]

Documents found in Afghanistan make clear that bin Laden has made frequent attempts to buy nuclear weapons and to acquire the means to produce chemical and biological ones. But, thus far, U.S. forces in Afghanistan have uncovered none. What they did find were several primitive labs and a plethora of blueprints. The extent of al Qaeda's WMD efforts remains a mystery, and until they are discovered, WMD will loom large as a potential threat of catastrophic magnitude.

Information technology

Networked organizations cannot function without information age technology. At the center of al Qaeda's transformation into a post-modern terrorist organization was the Internet and global cellular communications. These cutting edge tools linked its globally deployed cells, nodes, and constituent groups. Through cyberspace bin Laden and his lieutenants planned, coordinated, and executed operations.

By using the Internet, al Qaeda was able to accelerate mobilization and amplify communication between members. As a result, the organization's flexibility was enhanced as tactics could be adjusted more routinely. Moreover, individuals or groups with common goals or agendas were able to form subgroups or cells, meet at a target location, conduct terrorist operations, and then promptly terminate their relationships and re-deploy.

The al Qaeda network's *modus operandi* functioned through websites, e-mail, and cellular communications. A window into this system was opened with the December 1999 arrest of fifteen terrorists in Jordan who intended to carry out attacks against U.S. and Israeli targets during the millennium celebrations. Found in their "safe house"—in addition to bomb-making materials, automatic weapons, and radio-controlled detonators—were computers, zip disks, and cell phones. From the hard drives of those laptops intelligence analysts extracted information about the intended operations, as well as files on bomb making and terrorist training camps in Afghanistan.[61]

Bin Laden's operatives used CD-ROM disks to store and disseminate information on recruiting, bomb making, weapons, and other operational particulars. The *Encyclopedia of Jihad* found in Jordan was on a CD-ROM. This was once considered the extent of al Qaeda's operational knowledge. However, a new volume discovered in Afghanistan, also on a CD-ROM, contained more precise formulas for chemical and biological weapons that can be made from ingredients readily available to the public. In a chapter called the "Science of Explosives," chemical formulas for biological weapons are laid out step-by-step.

Egyptian computer experts directed al Qaeda's communications system. They established a network that used email, the web, and electronic bulletin boards to maximize information exchange between members. However, heading that effort was a Libyan, Abu Anas al-Liby. A member of al Qaeda for over a decade, his technical know-how meant that he quickly became bin Laden's computer expert. He also played a key role in planning the bombing of the embassies in Nairobi and Dar-es-Salaam by traveling to Kenya to take surveillance pictures.

According to reporters who visited bin Laden's headquarters in the mountains of Afghanistan, he "uses satellite phone terminals to coordinate the activities of the group's dispersed operatives and has even devised countermeasures to ensure his safety while using such communication systems."[62] And even though the overthrow of the Taliban forced him to flee his once secure sanctuary, recent reports reveal he is still attempting to use the Internet. Signs of al Qaeda efforts to communicate and re-group online have also been detected.

Warfighting strategy and operations

The *Encyclopedia of Jihad* as well as other training documents found in Afghanistan point to the fact that al Qaeda has given considerable attention to the issues of warfighting strategy and operations. Several volumes in the *Encyclopedia* focused on these topics. They covered the principals of warfare, including battle organization, reconnaissance, infiltration, and ambushes. Examples of these operations are drawn from the Afghan War against the Soviets. Other topics included: how to spy; military intelligence; communications; secret observation; sabotage; and assassination. Al Qaeda also studied the strategy and operational approaches of the United States. Copies of various U.S. military manuals and documents were found in Afghan safe houses.[63]

In terms of doctrine, al Qaeda has grasped the principles of 4th generation warfare. It takes a nonlinear approach to the battlespace, and plans asymmetrical and unconventional attacks by dispersed small units. The war being waged by al Qaeda began with attempts to kill American troops in Yemen in 1992. This was followed by periodic major operations in 1993, 1995, 1996, 1998, and 2000. Since, there have been a number of other smaller attacks in different locations. Other operations have been prevented by good intelligence.

Bin Laden and his al Qaeda network seem "to have developed a swarm-like doctrine that features a campaign of episodic attacks by various nodes of his network—at locations sprawled across global time and space where he has advantages for seizing the initiative, stealthily."[64] Through this strategy they successfully have conducted 4th generation warfare against America.

It's War

On September 11th America suffered its second Pearl Harbor. But the attack that day was an even greater strategic surprise than the one on December 7, 1941. The strikes against the World Trade Center and Pentagon were, quite literally, bolts out of the blue. The U.S. intelligence community was caught fully off guard.

Without a doubt, September 11th was a colossal intelligence failure. However, the reasons for that debacle cannot be attributed just to a handful of what appear, with hindsight, to have been missed warnings. For example, much has been made of two messages intercepted by the National Security Agency on September 10th but not translated until September 12th. "The match is about to begin," said one, while the other declared, "Tomorrow is zero hour." What match? Zero hour for what and where? These telephone comments are too cryptic to be actionable intelligence.

Nor can 9/11 be attributed to a failure to take seriously threat scenarios spun out in government reports. Much has also been made of a 1999 Congressional Research Service forecast that "Suicide bomber(s) belonging to al Qaeda's Martyrdom Battalion could crash-land an aircraft packed with high explosives into the Pentagon, the Central Intelligence Agency, or the White House." But the authors also speculated that the Liberation Tigers of Tamil Ealam could "become angered by President Clinton" and "react by dispatching a Tamil 'belt-bomb girl' to detonate a powerful semtex bomb after approaching the President in a crowd with a garland of flowers."[65]

These missed signals, correct or not, are emblematic of a deeper impediment. The real intelligence failure on September 11th has to do with a near decade-long reluctance by the intelligence community to come to terms with the fact that international terrorists—al Qaeda above all—were undergoing a systematic transformation in terms of how they organize, deploy, and fight.

Al Qaeda grasped the implications and opportunities globalization offered. However, to benefit from it necessitated the creation of a network-based terrorist organization that exploited the tools of the information age. And to secure its new global apparatus, al Qaeda employed the principles and methods of deception and denial typically found in intelligence tradecraft. In effect, UBL inspired a "revolution in terrorist affairs."

With this apparatus al Qaeda was ready for war. Beginning in 1996 it issued edicts to that effect. Its intentions were made crystal clear on February 22, 1998, when bin Laden endorsed a *fatwa* imploring his minions to "kill Americans—including civilians—anywhere in the world." Major terrorist operations followed and plenty of Americans fell.

But the U.S. intelligence community did not grasp the implications of al Qaeda's declarations and operations. It was in a war it did not understand or perhaps failed to recognize was even taking place. The same was true of the Clinton administration. Of course, there were exceptions like Richard Clark, the head of the National Security Council's Counterterrorism Strategy Group. He advocated a much more aggressive policy, to include the use of military force, against al Qaeda. But the Pentagon and State Department wanted nothing to do with such risky military options and fought bureaucratically to block them.

Even as al Qaeda upped the ante through bombings in East Africa, these actions were still not considered acts of war by the U.S. military services and intelligence agencies. International terrorism was a law enforcement matter; a crime to be solved and prosecuted. So ensconced was this mind-set that not even secret presidential instructions to use lethal means to kill bin Laden and his top al Qaeda lieutenants could foster new courses of action. The bureaucracy would not budge.

To be sure, operations were discussed *ad nauseam* and plans to attack frequently drawn up. But in the end, with the exception of the ineffectual August 20, 1998, cruise missile strikes against Afghanistan and Sudan, lethal measures were always nixed in the interagency process. Political, legal, and operational arguments advanced by the Pentagon, State Department, and CIA always persuaded risk adverse senior decision-makers, including the president, not to act forcefully.

Why? The answer has to do with the perceptions and impressions or, more accurately, misperceptions and misimpressions, that shaped and influenced policy choices. Over the 1990s these fostered the conviction that terrorism was neither a level-one national security challenge nor a form of warfare. In fact, those who saw it as such were demeaned as naive and extreme. There was no political will to use force aggressively and offensively because such actions were deemed unnecessary. The end result was September 11th.

The Bush Doctrine: Going on the Offensive

Over the last nine months, President Bush has chartered a new course for combating terrorism. To begin with, in all of his major speeches, he has labeled the attacks on the World Trade Center and Pentagon "an act of war" and told the American people "our nation is at war." Moreover, that war "must and will be waged on our watch."

In his remarks to the 2002 graduating class at West Point, the president explained that the September 11th horror illustrates a "new kind of war fought by a new kind of enemy."[66] Secretary of Defense Donald Rumsfeld has sounded the same warning in numerous public addresses and comments beginning in late September 2001 when he observed, "this war will be a war like none other our nation has faced… Our opponent is a global network of terrorist organizations and their state sponsors…. Even the vocabulary of this war will be different."[67]

Bush and Rumsfeld grasped 4th generation warfare. The following observations are elucidated in speech after speech. The enemy is a non-state actor—terrorist groups—whose capacity to operate has been greatly enhanced by globalization, organizational networking, and information-based technology. They are aided and abetted by states and also receive assistance from public and private organizations and individuals. Sanctuary provided by states allows terrorists like al Qaeda to secure their organizational and operational capabilities. They employ stealth and deception to attack in unconventional and asymmetrical ways. Operations are directed against political, cultural, and population targets with the goal of killing as many as possible.

Not everyone in the Bush administration sees it this way, a fact that was apparent in the internal debate over whether and how to fight in Afghanistan. It was likewise reflected in the initial limited and cautious approach devised by the senior military leadership and endorsed by the State Department. By late October 2001, the ineffectiveness of that strategy was apparent as the Taliban and al Qaeda dug in for the long haul. It took Rumsfeld and the civilian leadership in the Pentagon to devise a winning formula, and the president to put it in motion. It paid off. In December the Taliban fell and al Qaeda was on the run. Victory came by going on the offensive.

As one Taliban stronghold after another collapsed, Washington fell into another internal debate, this time over phase two of the war on terrorism. On the table was Iraq. A long time supporter of terrorism, it also is maniacal in its efforts to build nuclear, chemical, and biological weapons. Several officials in the Bush administration fear that Saddam Hussein not only wants these weapons of mass destruction for himself, but would also supply them to terrorists to use against the U.S., his primary enemy. Other appointees saw it differently.

Essentially, two camps fought it out. One, headed by Secretary of State Colin Powell and his senior associates, argued for a revised version of the Clinton policy of containment, this time through smart sanctions. Most of the economic controls would be lifted to help the Iraqi people, while Saddam's military would be kept in check. To work, serious diplomatic efforts were needed to shut down illegal trade that passed through Jordan, Turkey, Iran, and the Gulf Cooperation Council states. And WMD inspections had to be resuscitated.

In the Pentagon, much to the chagrin of the senior military chiefs who sided with Powell, Rumsfeld and his deputy, Paul Wolfowitz, wanted Saddam removed from power—regime change—through the use of military force. Vice President Cheney concurred. Containment was a nonstarter. It had not worked for Clinton and would not work for Bush. Moreover, the danger and unpredictability of a nuclear-armed Saddam was just too terrible a peril to allow to come to fruition. By February the interagency clash was over. The policy course for the second phase of the war was regime change.

However, no sooner had this debate ended before another interagency squabble started over how to implement regime change.

These interagency mêlées exposed the need for an overarching strategic design—a *Bush doctrine*—for planning and executing the war on terrorism. Throughout the Cold War presidents attached their names to major foreign policy and national security initiatives. While there were differences among them, all of these doctrines were aligned with a security framework anchored by the defensive concepts of deterrence and containment.

In his West Point speech President Bush laid the foundation for a new national security doctrine, one that included offensive action. To fight the war on terrorism, he declared, the defensive constructs of deterrence and containment, while still necessary, were by no means sufficient for the new form of warfare confronting the United States:

> [N]ew threats also require new thinking. Deterrence—the promise of massive retaliation against nations—means nothing against shadowy terrorist networks with no nation or citizens to defend. Containment is not possible when unbalanced dictators with weapons of mass destruction can deliver those weapons on missiles or secretly provide them to terrorist allies. We cannot defend America and our friends by hoping for the best. We cannot put our faith in the word of tyrants, who solemnly sign nonproliferation treaties, and then systemically break them. If we wait for threats to fully materialize, we will have waited too long.[68]

Then the President transformed America's national security paradigm. He told the cadets that they will be part of a military that "must be ready to strike at a moment's notice in any dark corner of the world through *preemptive action* when necessary." [Emphasis added]

In light of the victory in Afghanistan and the fact that the ways of waging war had dramatically changed, adding preemption to America's quiver made strategic sense. Global terrorist networks and tyrannical regimes that support them cannot be relied upon to follow the same calculus that deterred or contained past adversaries. The "new war" demanded new means for fighting it. By declaring that "the war on terrorism will not be won on the defensive," the president reinterpreted the meaning of self-defense. He rejected armed attack as the basis or requirement for using force. Out of necessity, force must be used to preempt terrorists and those states that harbor and provide them with the means of war and terror.

Morally, the inclusion of preemptive operations in the concept of self-defense—or defensive intervention—is anchored in the *just war doctrine*. That doctrine places great importance on the state as the natural institution essential for man's security and development. So strong is the presumption in favor of self-defense that the *just war doctrine* does not confine itself exclusively to defensive measures and the legacy of the nonintervention rule grounded in the peace of Westphalia. Offensive operations are permitted to protect vital rights and interests unjustly threatened, not only injured by other states but also by non-state actors such as terrorist groups.

Preemption and defensive intervention radically changes a U.S. government mindset and a two-decade-old counterterrorism policy from conceding the initiative to seizing it through the use of offensive military options. In doing so, the president has triggered an intense debate inside the U.S. government and among national security specialists. Many find the very notion of preemption profoundly troubling, even as al Qaeda and its state supporters plot new ways to attack America.

"Striking first" likewise worries American opinion leaders. Witness the apprehension expressed by the editorial staff of *The New York Times*. "We are uncomfortable with the idea of Mr. Bush's giving himself carte blanche to make any military intervention he thinks necessary."[69]

However, it also is the case that bin Laden has gone into hiding and Saddam sleeps in different locations each night because they both feel the same uneasiness, distress, and fear that cause angst for Washington bureaucrats and media glitterati. Implementing the Bush doctrine will not only turn bin Laden's and Saddam's trepidations into reality but more important, should put the U.S. on a course to win the war on terrorism by ridding the world of al Qaeda, the Iraqi regime, and others who remain a part of this network of terror.

Notes

1. Michael Isikoff and Daniel Klaidman, "The 9/11 Terrorists the CIA Should Have Caught," *Newsweek* (4 June 2002); available from http://www.i-dineout.com/pages2002/newsweek6.2.02.html; Internet; accessed 4 May 2002.
2. Ibid.
3. Paul Pillar, *Terrorism and U.S. Foreign Policy* (Washington, D.C.: Brookings, 2001). Pillar served in a number of senior managerial and analytic positions at CIA prior to writing this book as a Federal Executive Fellow in the Foreign Policy Studies program of the Brookings Institution. He is currently National Intelligence Officer for the Near East and South Asia.
4. Ibid., 217.
5. Ibid., 53.
6. Ibid., 217–218.
7. Martin van Creveld, *The Transformation of War* (New York: Free Press 1991), 224.
8. Charles Dunlap, "How We Lost the High-Tech War of 2007: A Warning from the Future," *The Weekly Standard* (29 January 1996), 22–28.
9. Ralph Peters, *Fighting for the Future* (Mechanicsburg, PA: Stackpole Books 1999).
10. Spinney's Website, *Defense and the National Interest*; available from http://www.d-n-i.net/; Internet; accessed 10 June 2002.
11. Phil Hirschkorn, Rohan Gunaratna, Ed Blanche, and Stefan Leader, "Blowback," *Jane's Intelligence Review* 13/8 (1 August 2001); available from http://www.counterterror.net/janes1.html; Internet; accessed 6 May 2002.
12. World Islamic Front Statement, "Jihad Against Jews and Crusaders," 23 February 1998; available from http://www.library.cornell.edu/colldev/mideast/wif.htm; Internet; accessed 12 June 2002.
13. Foreign Policy Association, "In Focus—Al Qaeda"; available from http://www.fpa.org/newsletter_info2478/newsletter_info.htm; Internet; accessed 8 May 2002. See also Peter L. Bergen, *Holy War, Inc.: Inside The Secret World of Osama Bin Laden* (New York: The Free Press 2001), 222.
14. Michele Zanini and Sean J.A. Edwards, Chapter II: "The Networking of Terror in the Information Age," 31; available from http://www.rand.org/publications/MR/MR1382/MR1382.ch2.pdf; Internet; accessed 3 May 2002. This chapter draws on RAND research originally reported in Ian Lesser et al., *Countering the New Terrorism* (RAND, 1999).
15. Key figures include the Egyptian-born *Ayman al-Zawahiri*, the ideologist, and disciple of Palestinian scholar-guerrilla organizer Abdullah Azzam, who recruited thousands of Muslims to fight in Afghanistan. Zawahiri was founder of the Egyptian Islamic Jihad, which opposes the Egyptian Government through violent means. He helped forge the

coalition of al-Jihad, al Qaeda, two Pakistani groups and another from Bangladesh in February 1998 to wage war on the U.S. *Mohammed Atef*, the military commander, was also born in Egypt. He headed al Qaeda's military committee and had primary responsibility for supervising training camps in Afghanistan and planning global operations. Among his first were attacks on U.S. troops by providing training to Somali tribes fighting them in 1993. *Abu Zubaydah*, the operations chief, was born in Saudi Arabia. Following the East African embassy bombings he appears to have replaced Atef as the primary contact for recruits and as the organizer of overseas operations.

16. "Trail of a Terrorist," *PBS-Frontline*, Transcript of Program #2004, Original airdate: 25 October 2001; available from http://www.pbs.org/wgbh/pages/frontline/shows/trail/etc/script.html; Internet; accessed 24 June 2002.

17. Hirschkorn et al (note 11).

18. Valdis E. Krebs, "Mapping Networks of Terrorist Cells," *Connections* 24/3 (2002) pp.43-52; available from http://www.orgnet.com/MappingTerroristNetworks.pdf; Internet; accessed 8 May 2002.

19. "The Investigation and the Evidence," *BBC News*, 5 October 2001; available from http://news.bbc.co.uk/hi/english/world/americas/newsid_1581000/1581063.stm.; Internet; accessed 10 June 2002.

20. Stuart Millar, Nick Hopkins, John Hooper, and Giles Foden, "Two Terrorists Were under Investigation by FBI," *The Guardian*, Monday 17 September 2001; available from http://www.guardian.co.uk/wtccrash/story/0,1300,553122,00.html; Internet; accessed 8 June 2002.

21. Craig Pyes, Patrick J. Mcdonnell, and William C. Rempel, "Hijacker Shuttled In and Out of U.S. on Visas Issued by Consulates," *Los Angeles Times*, 16 September 2001; available from http://www.webcom.com/hrin/magazine/la-atta.html; Internet; accessed 8 May 2002.

22. "Patterns of Global Terrorism—2001," U.S. Department of State, (Washington D.C., Office of the Coordinator for Counterterrorism, 21 May 2002); available from http://www.state.gov/s/ct/rls/pgtrpt/2001/html/10247.htm; Internet; accessed 15 June 2002.

23. Anthony Davis, "The Afghan Files: Al-Qaeda Documents from Kabul," *Jane's Intelligence Review* 14/1 (1 February 2002), 16.

24. In addition to [those in] Afghanistan, Indonesian intelligence claims international terrorists, including al Qaeda, have training camps on Sulawesi Island, Indonesia. Moreover, one of the leaders of the Egyptian Islamic Group has said that he spent several months at one of bin Laden's guerrilla training camps in Sudan. See Preston Mendenhall, "Chilling Lessons at Al-Qaida U.," *MSNBC*, 27 January 2001; available from http://www.msnbc.com/news/695030.asp; Internet; accessed 8 May 2002.

25. Ibid.

26. J. T. Caruso, United States Senate, Statement for the Record of Acting Assistant Director Counter Terrorism Division Federal Bureau of Investigation before the Subcommittee on International Operations and Terrorism Committee on Foreign Relations, *Al-Qaeda International* (Washington, D.C., 18 December 2001); available from http://www.fbi.gov/congress/congress01/caruso121801.htm; Internet; accessed 10 May 2002. See also Hirschkorn et al (note 11).

27. In the early 1990s, Ramzi Yousef was sent by bin Laden's officers to the Philippines to train Abu Sayyaf members. Yousef was convicted in September in New York City of a conspiracy to blow up 12 American jumbo jets in one day and convicted in 1997 as the "mastermind" of the 1993 World Trade Center bombing in. See Dale Watson (Chief International Terrorism Section, National Security Division Federal Bureau of Investigation), United States Senate, Statement before the Senate Judiciary Committee Subcommittee on Technology, Terrorism, and Government Information, *Foreign Terrorists in America: Five Years after the World Trade Center* (Washington, D.C., 24 February 1998); available from http://www.fas.org/irp/congress/1998_hr/s980224w.htm; Internet; accessed 4 June 2002. See also Simon Reeve, *The New Jackals: Ramzi Yousef, Osama bin Laden and the Future of Terrorism* (Boston: Northeastern University Press 1999), 72–85.

28. See daily transcripts of the *USA v. Usama bin Laden et al* trial in the Southern District of New York.; available from http://cryptome.org/usa-v-ubl.zip; Internet; accessed 10 June 2002. See also EXECUTIVE ORDER 13129, *Subject: Blocking Property and Prohibiting Transactions With the Taliban* (Washington D.C., Office of External Relations, 4 July 1999); available from http://nodis.hq.nasa.gov/Library/Directives/NASA-WIDE/nasaeoas/eo13129.html; Internet; accessed 10 June 2002.

29. Yoni Fighel and Yael Shahar, "The Al-Qaida-Hizballah Connection," *The International Policy Institute for Counter-Terrorism*, 26 February 2002; available from http://www.ict.org.il/inter_ter/orgdet.cfm?orgid=74; Internet; accessed 15 May 2002.

30. *September 11 Class Action, 2002*; available from http://www.september11classaction.com/Havlish_ Complaint.pdf; Internet; accessed 4 June 2002. According to FBI's Most Wanted Terrorist list, Mugniyah is the alleged head of the security apparatus for the terrorist organization, Lebanese Hizballah. He is thought to be in Lebanon. The list is available from http://www.fbi.gov/mostwant/terrorists/termugniyah.htm; Internet; accessed 4 June 2002.

31. *USA v. Usama bin Laden et al* (note 28).

32. See *United States of America v. Ali Mohamed*, United States District Court Southern District of New York, S (5) 98CR1023, 4 June 1999. See also *September 11 Class Action*, 2002 (note 30).

33. See testimony by George J. Tenet (Director of Central Intelligence), Senate Armed Services Committee, *Worldwide Threat—Converging Dangers in a Post 9/11 World*, (Washington D.C., 19 March 2002); available from http://www.cia.gov/cia/public_affairs/speeches/senate_select_ hearing_03192002.html; Internet; accessed 15 June 2002.

34. Ibid.

35. Hirschkorn et al (note 11).

36. "Al Qaeda Prepares for War," *Jane's Intelligence Digest* (May 31, 2002).

37. "The Czech Interior Minister Stanislav Gross says that terrorist Mohammed Atta, a suspected pilot in the September attacks on the United States, did meet an Iraqi diplomat in Prague. Mr. Gross says this information comes from intelligence services and he says he cannot comment further on the matter. Mr. Gross was reacting to claims in the latest issue of the US weekly *Newsweek*, which says Atta visited Prague but did not meet an Iraqi agent. See *Radio Prague—Print Version* (22 April 2002); available from http://www.radio.cz/print/en/news/27440.; Internet; accessed 13 June 2002.

38. "Gunning for Saddam: Interview with Sabah Khodada," *PBS-Frontline*, 8 November 2001; available from http://www.pbs.org/wgbh/pages/frontline/shows/gunning/; Internet; accessed 15 May 2002. Also see Chris Hedges, "Iraqi Defectors Detail Secret School for Terrorists," *New York Times Service*, Thursday 8 November 2001; available from http://www.sierratimes.com/cgi-bin/warroom/topic.cgi?forum=11&topic=38; Internet; accessed 10 May 2002.

39. Jeffrey Goldberg, "The Great Terror," *The New Yorker*, 25 March 2002; available from http://newyorker.com/fact/content/?020325fa_FACT1; Internet; accessed 20 April 2002.

40. *September 11 Class Action, 2002* (note 30).

41. Trifin J. Roule, Jeremy Kinsell, and Brian Joyce, "Investigators Seek to Break Up Al-Qaeda's Financial Structure," *Jane's Intelligence Review* 13/11 (1 November 2001), 8–11.

42. Ibid.

43. Karen DeYoung and Douglas Farah, "Infighting Slows Hunt for Hidden Al Qaeda Assets; Funds Put in Untraceable Commodities," *The Washington Post*, 18 June 2002, p.1A.

44. Ibid.

45. See testimony by Steven Emerson, House Committee on Financial Services Subcommittee on Oversight and Investigations, PATRIOT Act Oversight: Investigating Patterns of Terrorist Fundraising, *Fund-Raising Methods and Procedures for International Terrorist Organizations* (Washington D.C., 12 February 2002): 13–14; available from http://financialservices.house.gov/media/pdf/021202se.pdf; Internet; accessed 15 June 2002.

46. Ibid.

47. Roule (note 41).

48. See UNITED NATIONS SANCTIONS ORDINANCE (Chapter 537); available from http://www.hksfc.org.hk/eng/licensing/html/intermediaries/003encl-2.pdf; Internet; accessed 12 June 2002.

49. Li Xueying, "The Asia Connection," *The Straits Times*; available from http://straitstimes.asia1.com.sg/mnt/html/webspecial/WTC/osama_asian.html; Internet; accessed 10 May 2002. See also note 26.

50. Emerson (note 45). For information about the IIRO, see its website, *The International Islamic Relief Organization, Saudi Arabia (IIRO)*; available from http://www.arab.net/iiro; Internet; accessed 10 June 2002.

51. Emerson (note 45).

52. See Ahmed Rashid, *Taliban* (New Haven: Yale University Press: 2001) 117-27. See also Véronique Maurus and Marc Roche, "L'homme le plus redouté des Etats-Unis, longtemps entraîné par la CIA...," *Le Monde*, 24 June 2002; available from http://www.lemonde.fr/article/0,5987,3216--221921-,00.html; Internet; accessed 14 June 2002. See also Roule (note 41).

53. Roule (note 41).

54. For information on the link between wealthy individuals and al Qaeda/bin Laden, see Robert O'Harrow Jr., David S. Hilzenrath, and Karen DeYoung, "Bin Laden's Money Takes Hidden Paths To Agents of Terror—Records Hint at Complex Financial Web," *The Washington Post*, Friday 21 September 2001, A13. See also John Mintz "Bin Laden's Finances Are Moving Target," *The Washington Post*, Friday 28 August 1998, A1. See also "The Money: Drying Up the Funds for Terror," *Council on Foreign Relations*; available from http://www.terrorismanswers.com/responses/money.html; Internet; accessed 10 June 2002.

55. See George W. Bush (President of the United States), "George W. Bush Delivers Remarks at the Treasury Department's Financial Crimes Enforcement Network (FINCEN)," (Washington D.C., FDCH Political Transcripts, 7 November 2001); available from http://financialservices.house.gov/media/pdf/021202se.pdf; Internet; accessed 15 June 2002. See also Roule (note 41).

56. Nick Fielding, "By the Book: ENCYCLOPAEDIA OF TERROR: Revealed: The Bloody Pages of Al-Qaeda's Killing Manual," available from http://www.la.utexas.edu/chenry/usme/aip01/msg00360.html; Internet; accessed 8 May 2002.

57. Kim Burger, "One Step Ahead," *Jane's Defence Weekly* 37/1 (20 February 2002), 21.

58. Fielding (note 56).

59. Massimo Calabresi and Romesh Ratnesar, "Can We Stop the Next Attack?," *Time.com*, Sunday 3 March 2002; available from http://www.time.com/time/nation/printout/0,8816,214064,00.html; Internet; accessed 10 May 2002.

60. "The general and the bomb," *Jane's Intelligence Digest* (2 November 2001), 1–4.

61. Zanini (note 14), 40.

62. Ibid., 36–37.

63. Fielding (note 56).

64. Ibid.

65. *The Sociology and Psychology of Terrorism: Who Becomes a Terrorist and Why?* (Washington, D.C.: Library of Congress Federal Research Division 1999), 13–14.

66. See Remarks by President Bush at 2002 Graduation Exercise of the United States Military Academy; available from http://www.whitehouse.gov/news/releases/2002/06/20020601-3.html; Internet; accessed 20 June 2002.

67. Donald Rumsfeld, "A New Kind of War," *The New York Times*, 27 September 2001, sec. I, p.1.

68. Bush (note 66).

69. "Striking First," *The New York Times*, 23 June 2002, sec. IV, p.12.

The Struggle Against Terrorism: Grand Strategy, Strategy, and Tactics

Barry R.Posen is professor of Political Science in the Security Studies Program at the Massachusetts Institute of Technology. His first book, *Sources of Military Doctrine: France, Britain and Germany Between the World Wars* (1986), won the American Political Science Association's Woodrow Wilson Foundation Book Award and Ohio State University's Edward J. Furniss Jr. Book Award. He has been an international affairs fellow with the Rockefeller Foundation and with the Council on Foreign Relations and is also author of *Inadvertent Escalation: Conventional War and Nuclear Risks* (1992).

Three to four thousand people, nearly all American citizens, perished in the aircraft hijackings and attacks on the World Trade Center and the Pentagon on September 11, 2001.[1] They were murdered for political reasons by a loosely integrated foreign terrorist political organization called al-Qaeda. Below I ask four questions related to these attacks: First, what is the nature of the threat posed by al-Qaeda? Second, what is an appropriate strategy for dealing with it? Third, how might the U.S. defense establishment have to change to fight this adversary? And fourth, what does the struggle against al-Qaeda mean for overall U.S. foreign policy?

The Adversary

Al-Qaeda is a network of like-minded individuals, apparently all Muslim but of many different nationalities, that links together groups in as many as sixty countries. Osama bin Laden, a wealthy Saudi who took part in the Afghan rebellion against the Soviet occupation (1979–89), developed this network. He inspires, finances, organizes, and trains many of its members. He seems to be in direct command of some but not all of them. Bin Laden and his associates share a fundamentalist interpretation of Islam, which they have opportunistically twisted into a political ideology of violent struggle. He and his principles enjoy some popular support in the Islamic world, though it is difficult to gauge its depth and breadth. Al-Qaeda wants the United States, indeed the West more generally, out of the Persian Gulf and the Middle East. In bin Laden's view, the United States helps to keep Muslim peoples in poverty and imposes upon them a Western culture deeply offensive to traditional Islam. He blames the United States for the continued suffering of the people of Iraq and for the Israeli occupation of the West Bank and the Gaza Strip. For him, Israel is a foreign element in the Middle East and should be destroyed. The U.S. military presence in Saudi Arabia is a desecration of the Islamic holy places and must end.[2] Once the United States exits the region, al-Qaeda hopes to overthrow the governments of Saudi Arabia and Egypt and replace them with fundamentalist, Taliban-like regimes. It is no wonder that the Saudi regime considered bin Laden so dangerous that it stripped him of his citizenship in 1994.

Al-Qaeda is an ambitious, ruthless, and technically proficient organization. The stark evidence is at hand. It has attacked the United States before, but not with such striking results.[3] For the September 11 attack, at least nineteen men, supported by perhaps a dozen others, plotted for years an action that at least some of them knew would result in their deaths. Each member of the conspiracy had numerous opportunities to defect. The terrorists piloting the four passenger jets understood the level of destruction they would exact. They carefully studied airport security and found the airports that seemed most vulnerable. Several of these men appear to have trained for years in U.S. flight schools to learn enough to pilot an aircraft into a building. The cockpits of the 757 and 767 are quite similar, which does not seem coincidental; a single experienced pilot could tutor all of the hijackers on the fine points of operating the aircraft. Between the two aircraft types, the conspirators could choose from a wide selection of flights. The 767s, the aircraft with the most fuel and hence the greatest destructive potential, were directed at the biggest target, the World Trade Center. The proximity of the departure airports to the targets permitted tactical "surprise." All four planes had small passenger complements relative to their capacity; this hardly seems coincidental given the hijackers' plan to take the aircraft with box-cutters. The hijackings of all four airliners were carefully synchronized. If this had been a Western commando raid, it would be considered nothing short of brilliant. Given the demonstrated motivation and organizational and technical skills of its members, al-Qaeda will likely attempt further large-scale attacks on the United States or its citizens and soldiers abroad, or both.

Al-Qaeda benefited from the direct support of Afghanistan, which had been governed in recent years by the fundamentalist Taliban religio-political movement. The Taliban ruled Afghanistan as a kind of crude police state. Not only was bin Laden protected by the regime, but his money and his forces were a pillar of its power. The Taliban had been asked before by the United States to expel bin Laden but always demurred. This base proved to be of great utility to bin Laden and to al-Qaeda. Individuals came from around the world to receive training in terrorist techniques and tactics.[4] Afghanistan is a large country, with rugged terrain and long and lawless borders, far from any Western base; it is hard to monitor, let alone attack—in other words, a perfect hideout. Without this bastion, bin Laden would probably have been on the run much of the time. Al-Qaeda also seems to have benefited from the tacit support of some other governments; persistent reports suggest that wealthy individuals in several Gulf states have contributed to the organization, with the knowledge though not the active cooperation of their governments. Saudi Arabia is often mentioned by name.[5]

As has often been pointed out, the United States and most developed, democratic countries are extremely vulnerable to terrorist attacks. These are open societies that have not policed their borders successfully. Drugs and illegal immigrants move into the United States with ease; cash, guns, and stolen cars move out. Dangerous activities occur in modern society every day. Aircraft take off and land; hazardous materials—flammable, explosive, or poisonous—move by truck, train, and ship. And in the United States, those with money and some patience can obtain explosives, firearms, and quantities of ammunition. Prosaic means can be employed against everyday targets to produce catastrophic results. One must nevertheless also be concerned about chemical, biological, or nuclear attacks. The ability to make chemical agents and biological poisons is more widespread than ever, though turning the basic ingredients into useful weapons and delivering them effectively on a large scale has thus far not proven easy for small clandestine groups.[6] Nuclear weapons are more difficult to obtain, but fears remain that some of the very large number manufactured during the Cold War, or some of those built by new nuclear states, could fall into the wrong hands. Alternatively, primitive nuclear weapons designs are widely available; getting the fissionable material to make a nuclear bomb is still difficult, but not all of this material is as secure as it should be. Thus the possibility of a major terrorist attack with biological, chemical, or nuclear weapons cannot be ruled out.

Most terrorists do not exploit the vulnerabilities of advanced industrial societies; law enforcement helps to make it difficult, though obviously not impossible. More important, most terrorist organizations do not wish to make the United States an implacable enemy. Many have limited political objectives, which the United States can hinder or help. Al-Qaeda clearly has more ambitious objectives than most terrorist organizations; it seeks to expel the most powerful state in history from a part of the world that has been central to U.S. foreign policy for more than half a century, and it intends to do so without a large standing military. Hence al-Qaeda has opted for large-scale murder to achieve its objectives, and it will seek to kill Americans so long as the United States does not give in to its demands.

What Is to Be Done?

Like any war, or even any large civil project, the war against al-Qaeda and other terrorist groups bent on mass destruction requires a strategy. A strategy lays out an interlinked chain of problems that must be solved to address the ultimate problem, the defeat of the adversary. Although the United States and its allies may never fully destroy al-Qaeda, or aligned organizations, or new organizations that emulate them, the antiterror coalition that the United States has built can aspire to reduce the terrorists to desperate groups of exhausted stragglers, with few resources and little hope of success. A strategy sets priorities and focuses available resources—money, time, political capital, and military power—on the main effort. Strategies have both a military and a diplomatic dimension. Within the military dimension, states may choose among offensive, defensive, and punitive operations. In this war, diplomacy will loom larger than military operations, and within the military dimension, defensive activities will loom larger than offensive and punitive ones. That said, without a militarily offensive component, this war cannot be won. Finally, this is a war of attrition, not a blitzkrieg. Al-Qaeda cannot be rounded up in a night's work. If the United States wishes to pursue a major effort against al-Qaeda, its supporters, and any future imitators, it must be prepared to accept significant costs and risks over an extended period. There will likely be an exchange of blows, in the United States and abroad. This war is necessary because bin Laden and others like him will continue to attack the United States so long as it asserts its power and influence in other parts of the world.

Sound strategy requires the establishment of priorities because resources are scarce. Resources must be ruthlessly concentrated against the main threat. There are two primary adversaries in this fight against terrorism: the extended al-Qaeda organization and the states that support it. Al-Qaeda is the principal terrorist organization that has attempted to engage in mass destruction attacks on the United States.[7] It has shown itself to be more capable and more politically ambitious than most. It is the imminent threat. Other terrorist organizations, however, must be kept under surveillance and attacked preemptively if they seem ready to strike the United States or its allies in mass attacks, or if they appear intent on aligning themselves with al-Qaeda.

Allies are essential for success in the war on terrorism, which helps to explain the determination of President George W. Bush and his administration to build a broad coalition. Bin Laden had training camps and bases in Afghanistan, but in other countries al-Qaeda's presence has been more shadowy. Wherever this organization takes root, it must be fought. But it will not always be necessary or possible for the United States to do the fighting. Allied military and police forces are more appropriate instruments to apprehend terrorists operating within their national borders than are U.S. forces. They have information that the United States may not have, and they know the territory and people better. The odds of finding the adversary and avoiding collateral damage increase to the extent that the "host" nation-state does the hard work. Moreover, host states can deal better politically with any collateral damage—that is, accidental destruction of civilian life and property. Much of the war will look a lot like conventional law enforcement by the governments of cooperative countries. Efforts must also be made to weaken terrorist organizations by attacking their infrastructure; both cooperative and clandestine methods can be used to deny these groups access to funds and matériel.

As noted earlier, al-Qaeda has found tacit and active support from nation-states. In the case of partial or tacit support, it may be assumed that there is some disagreement within the political leadership of the country in question about the wisdom of such a policy. The objective is to induce these states to change their practices through persuasion, bribery, or nonviolent coercion. Again, diplomacy looms large in this struggle. Nevertheless, the United States must be prepared to bypass national governments should they fail to cooperate. Given the utter ruthlessness of al-Qaeda, the United States cannot afford to allow it a sanctuary anywhere. From time to time, U.S. forces may simply need to attack al-Qaeda cells directly. This may be a job for special operations forces who would try to avoid contact with national armed forces. In any case, to deter national armed forces from getting in the way, or to foil them if they try, the United States must maintain a strong conventional military capability. Occasionally, it may be necessary to engage in conventional wars with such countries.

Some regimes may choose to support bin Laden's cause, like the Taliban did in Afghanistan. Where a regime has close relations with the terrorists, it is reasonable to treat the host nation as an ally of al-Qaeda and an enemy of the United States. The United States must be prepared to wage war against such states to destroy terrorist groups themselves, to prevent their reconstitution by eliminating the regimes that support them, and to deter other nation-states from supporting terrorism. The United States must make it clear that direct support of terrorists who try to kill large numbers of Americans is tantamount to participation in the attack. If a nation-state had directed a conventional weapon of war at the World Trade Center, U.S. forces would have retaliated immediately. Particularly in the age of weapons of mass destruction, the United States cannot allow any state to participate in catastrophic attacks on its homeland with impunity.

More intensive defensive precautions can reduce but not eliminate U.S. vulnerability to mass destruction attacks, so deterrence must be the first line of defense. For these reasons, the Taliban regime in Afghanistan had to be destroyed.

Initially, the Bush administration hesitated to embrace the objective of ousting the Taliban regime.[8] The administration was more interested in bin Laden and al-Qaeda than in their hosts, and in his speech of September 20, President Bush gave the Taliban an opportunity to "hand over the terrorists" *or* "share their fate."[9] Even after the first five days of air strikes, in his press conference of October 11, President Bush gave the Taliban a "second chance" to turn over bin Laden and evict his organization from Afghanistan.[10] Given the difficulty of finding these terrorists, as well as the political complexities of waging war in Afghanistan, this was a reasonable offer, though in my judgment a harmful one from the point of view of deterrence of future attacks. Once the Taliban declined the opportunity to cooperate, the United States had no choice but to wage war on them to the extent that was militarily and politically practical, with the objective of driving them from power.[11]

Tactics: Forces and Methods

Any military campaign has defensive and offensive aspects. Because of its geographical position and great military potential, the United States is accustomed to being on the offensive, but in this campaign the defensive must assume equal or greater importance. Considerable time will be required to develop enough political and military pressure on al-Qaeda to suppress its ability to conduct operations. That organization will probably have the opportunity to attack the United States or its friends again. The United States must thus do all it can defensively to reduce the probability of additional attacks on the U.S. homeland, and to limit the damage should such attacks occur. The United States has been taught a costly but valuable lesson about the vulnerability of modern society to terrorism. Thus, even after al-Qaeda is destroyed, the United States will need to maintain its defenses. This means new vigilance in the most fragile corners of the transportation, energy, power, and communication systems and closer attention to the security of government buildings.

The mobilization of thousands of National Guardsmen and reservists after September 11 had the immediate purpose of enhancing U.S. territorial defenses—including more attentive airspace management, port surveillance, and airport security. This is only the beginning. A new or reoriented joint, multiservice command, staffed by active-duty regulars and reservists and dedicated exclusively to territorial defense, should be created to oversee this enduring mission.[12] Many additional military man-hours will likely be required on a sustained basis for territorial defense. Elements of the active armed forces, the Coast Guard, and the National Guard and Reserves may require redirection or expansion, or possibly both. The United States may need to ask its weekend warriors to serve more weekends, and indeed more weeks, each year.

Enhanced intelligence capabilities are necessary for both defense and offense. Students of terrorism and its close cousin, insurgency, invariably stress the critical importance of intelligence.[13] Intelligence must be gathered on terrorist groups overseas. Such intelligence will come not only from U.S. technical surveillance methods and spies but also from the daily hard work of national police forces abroad. The critical importance of intelligence is one of the main reasons why the United States needs the support of allies. U.S. law enforcement agencies will also have to redouble their efforts. Intelligence provides the data necessary for preventive and preemptive attacks by the national military or police forces of the countries in which the terrorist groups have taken refuge, or by U.S. forces. Even tardy warning of terrorist attacks as they get under way may provide a useful and life-saving margin of time. Intelligence from abroad must also be blended with intelligence gathered at home.

More sustained attention is necessary to the organization of the U.S. counterterrorism intelligence effort. Historically, the following has proven of great utility in all kinds of military endeavors: the staffing of a dedicated intelligence center with full-time, long-serving professionals with a deep knowledge of the adversary; the timely collection of intelligence from multiple sources in that center; the analysis of that data for specific information as well as patterns that reveal the adversary's presence or intentions; and the transmission of that data to those who can best use it for offensive or defensive purposes.[14] Anecdotal information suggests that the United States suffered shortcomings in this regard; data may have been present that could have permitted the early detection of the September 11 plot, but it was not fully exploited.[15] Formally, the Central Intelligence Agency's Counterterrorist Center (CTC) is responsible for "coordinating the counterterrorist efforts of the Intelligence Community," including "exploiting all source intelligence."[16] Nevertheless, this intelligence effort has been the subject of persistent criticism, in particular for weaknesses in interagency cooperation; failure to concentrate all potentially useful information in one place, especially information gathered by law enforcement agencies in the United States; and untimely analysis.[17] The CTC's mandate needs to be strengthened so that all useful information gathered by any intelligence or law enforcement agency is concentrated for analysis. The CTC will also require more money and staff.

Offensive action and offensive military capabilities are necessary components of a successful counterterror strategy. Offensive action is required to destroy regimes that align with terrorists; offensive capabilities allow the United States to threaten credibly other regimes that might consider supporting terrorists. Offensive action against terrorists is needed to eliminate them as threats. But even unsuccessful offensive actions, which force terrorist units or terrorist cells to stay perpetually on the move to avoid destruction, will help to reduce their capability. Constant surveillance makes it difficult for them to plan and organize. Constant pursuit makes it dangerous for them to rest. The threat of offensive action is critical to exhausting the terrorists, whether they are with units in the field in Afghanistan or hiding out in cities and empty quarters across the world. This threat will be credible only if the United States launches an offensive operation from time to time, large or small. Offensive action is also necessary to support U.S. diplomacy. Thus far, U.S. diplomats have stressed the concerns of existing and prospective allies that the United States might overreact with excessive and indiscriminate violence. It is disturbing that they believe that U.S. decisionmakers could be so stupid and brutal, but it is a good thing that they understand the deep emotion that drives U.S. purpose. The United States must threaten offensive war so that these allies understand the seriousness of U.S. intent. The more cooperation the United States gets from allies on the intelligence and policing front, the less necessary it becomes for the United States to behave unilaterally, militarily, and with the attendant risks of collateral damage and escalation. If the United States does not act militarily from time to time, this risk will lose its force as an incentive for U.S. allies. Periodically taking the offensive is also necessary to maintain morale at home. Given that al-Qaeda will continue to try to hit the United States and its friends, the public will probably want to see the United States "bring justice to our enemies."[18]

To take the offensive, the United States will need to exploit perishable intelligence on the existence and location of terrorist cells. Flexible, fast, and relatively discriminate forces are essential. The American people and the leaders of the American military must be prepared to accept the risk of significant U.S. casualties in small, hard-hitting raids. Even when other nations cooperate by providing intelligence, and would be willing to arrest or destroy terrorists in their midst, they may lack the capability and need augmentation from the United States. In any event, political decisionmakers in the United States and abroad who approve strikes on the basis of this information will have to come to terms with the risks to innocent civilians. Occasions will surely arise when there are trade-offs between effectiveness against the adversary and casualties to U.S. and allied forces, or to innocents caught in the crossfire. It will occasionally be necessary to err on the side of effectiveness. This is a tragic fact of war that will stress the persuasive skills of U.S. diplomats, as it did in the first weeks of the air campaign against Afghanistan.

The United States has large special operations forces well suited to the counter-terror mission: small groups of highly trained individual fighters from all the services, supported by an array of specially designed and expertly piloted helicopters, aircraft, and small watercraft. (They also include experts at training and advising foreign soldiers.) These forces may be more effective and cause less collateral damage than cruise missiles or precision guided bombs in certain situations. In the past, U.S. decisionmakers have been reluctant to employ these forces because their missions involve a significant risk to the troops. Given the seriousness of the new war and the apparent commitment of the American people, such concerns are likely to diminish. These forces may require additional mobility assets—planes, helicopters, and other more exotic equipment. It may also be reasonable to expand the special operations forces by reorienting some active units such as the 82d Airborne Division and the 101st Air Assault (Helicopter) Division to this mission. The U.S. Marine Corps also deploys many units that could prove useful to the counterterror mission. Three separate reinforced battalions of marines are generally deployed afloat, on special assault ships loaded with helicopters and hovercraft, around the world at any one time. Though the marines judge these forces to be "special operations capable," it would be sensible to stress even further their special operations mission. Moreover, given that most U.S. Navy carrier air wings do not currently fill the hangar space available on existing carriers, it is reasonable to put a company of army or marine special operations troops and their associated helicopters on each one.[19] To permit speedy action, emergency basing and overflight rights around the world must be obtained in advance—yet another task for diplomacy.

The military will also need to augment its ability to gather tactical intelligence to support operations under way. Often the United States will have only a rough idea of where terrorist training camps, quasi regular units, or clandestine units are hiding. An enhanced ability to focus intelligence assets on key objectives is of great importance. Insofar as the adversary operates in small groups without much heavy equipment, the task will be difficult. For the last decade, the United States has experimented with unmanned aircraft, "intelligence drones." It needs to buy more drones, and soon. These devices have been used profitably to police Bosnia and Kosovo. They also played a role in the Kosovo war. Unlike satellites, intelligence drones are extremely flexible; they can focus on a small piece of terrain and remain overhead for several hours at a time. They are just machines, and by current standards not very expensive ones; the American people will not mind losing one every now and then to obtain critical information.[20]

Above all, the "war" against terrorism will require patience and sustained national will. It will take time for the United States and its allies build up a full intelligence picture of the adversary and enhance existing worldwide intelligence capabilities to better detect these elusive foes. As the United States pursues terrorist groups, they will fight back. They will resist locally when U.S. and other forces try to apprehend or destroy them. More important, the terrorists will try to mount additional attacks against the United States, against U.S. installations abroad, and against U.S. allies. Terrorists will attempt this anyway, but in seeking to destroy them, the United States may cause them to accelerate their attacks. The U.S. security establishment will need to be innovative and adaptive, just as the adversary has proven to be.[21] The American people cannot go into this fight without understanding that they may suffer more pain before the problem recedes.

Finally, American leaders will have to fight political and bureaucratic inertia at home and abroad. Prior to September 11, the United States had a counterterror "administered policy." Administered policies prevail in democracies, where the political leadership regularly trades off initiatives that might be highly effective in one policy area against their costs measured in terms of other agendas, values, and policies. Bureaucracies struggle to maintain their autonomy and often fail to cooperate to achieve stated purposes. Change, when it comes, is incremental. Before September 11 the counterterror effort was like any other administered policy; although it enjoyed higher priority and more resources than it once did, it still competed for political, financial, and human resources on a relatively level playing field with many other policies. That approach was entirely reasonable to me, but has been proven wrong. War is different; in war other policies assume significantly lower priority. Because terrorists are elusive, it will be difficult to sustain the kind of focus that war requires. Failure to sustain that focus will allow al-Qaeda to remain quiet, lick any wounds it sustains in the first flush of U.S. anger and coalition solidarity, rebuild its cadres, and then strike again—harder and more effectively than before. While life must go on, a return to treating counterterrorism as an administered policy must await significant evidence of real success in destroying the al-Qaeda organization.

The Diplomacy of a Counterterror War and the Implications for U.S. Grand Strategy

Both enthusiastic allies and quiet back-channel assistance from around the world will be central to a successful counterterror campaign, but allies are not always easy to find. The United States has been spoiled by its Cold War success. Threatened neighbors of the Soviet Union quickly sought alignment with the United States. During Operation Desert Shield, Arab states in the way of Saddam Hussein's legions did not require much persuading to join the U.S. coalition; those farther away needed subsidies just to show up. The war against terrorism is more difficult. The major al-Qaeda terrorist action has been directed against the United States, though attacks both at home and abroad have caught many foreign nationals in the crossfire. States that have been the victims of tenuously related or unrelated terrorist groups have proven responsive to U.S. requests for help (e.g., Russia, India, and Israel). The United States also needs the assistance of states whose leaders believe that (1) they are not terrorist targets, (2) they can easily redirect terror toward others, or (3) their own citizens may sympathize with al-Qaeda.

The United States needs friends, and thus must prioritize among its many foreign policy and defense policy initiatives, because these initiatives have frequently antagonized other governments and peoples. All the governments whose help is required, whether they are democratic or not, must deal with their own publics. Therefore the United States must find ways to explain to their people why cooperation against these terrorists is in their interest. The United States clearly cannot afford to make every state in the world prosperous and happy. It cannot afford to end every conflict in favor of any ally the United States needs. Sometimes the United States will want the help of both parties to a regional conflict, and cannot reward one party at the expense of another. And it cannot afford to peremptorily abandon long-standing allies in a heartbeat. Such actions have their own costs and risks. But the United States must be much more disciplined in its choices, and much more attuned to the views of others, if it is to sustain this coalition over the long term.[22]

In the years since the Cold War ended, the United States has been immensely powerful, and relatively capricious. It has often acted against the interests of others in pursuit of modest gains, as it did in the case of NATO expansion, the Kosovo war, and the Bush administration's early insistence that national missile defenses would be built with or without Russian cooperation. All these policies had alternatives that could have achieved many of the goals of their U.S. advocates while leaving Russia and others less displeased. Similarly the United States has often failed to act out of fear of incurring modest costs: It has applied insufficient pressure on Israel to suppress its settlement policy in the West Bank and Gaza; has shown little creativity in trying to end the politically damaging low-grade war and leaky economic embargo of Iraq; and made no effort to help others inhibit the course of the Rwanda genocide. The American media have been content to cover international politics episodically and often superficially. The U.S. foreign and security policy record is not one of unalloyed failure.[23] It is, however, a record of indiscipline in which calculations of short-term domestic political gains or losses often dominated decisionmaking.

The post–Cold War world of easy preeminence, controlled low-cost wars, budgetary plenty, and choices avoided is over. In the past I argued that the United States failed to settle on a grand strategy to guide its international behavior after the demise of the Soviet Union.[24] Democrats and Republicans could agree on only one thing: The United States should remain the most powerful state in the world. Beyond that, a good many Democrats wanted to use this power to pursue liberal purposes: improving international organizations and institutions, strengthening international treaties, increasing the power of international law, and spreading democracy. Republicans seem to have wanted to use this power to consolidate U.S. superiority and to create still more power. Russia was viewed as perpetually on the verge of backsliding toward Soviet-style imperialism, and China was feared as a budding peer competitor; both needed containment.

Neither political party energetically discussed its preferred policies with the American people. Neither was willing to ask the American people for serious sacrifices to pursue its preferred objectives, and neither had to do so. Sacrifice is now necessary if the United States is to sustain an activist foreign policy, and thus the reasons to pursue such a policy must be explained to and accepted by the American people. Otherwise, if the war on terrorism proves to be not only long but more costly than Americans hope, the temptation to retreat from the world stage will be strong.

Although the outlines are not clear, advocates of alternative U.S. grand strategies during the last decade now seem inclined to superimpose these strategies on the campaign against terror. Advocates of greater restraint in U.S. foreign policy, often unfairly dubbed "neo-isolationists," argue that the United States must retaliate strongly for the September 11 attacks if it is to deter future attacks. But they are uninterested in what comes after, because they believe that the United States should do less in the world. If the United States is less involved, it will be less of a target. If it is less often a target, it needs less assistance to defend itself and its interests. This approach to terror is internally consistent, but it definitely does not defend an active U.S. world role.

Liberal internationalists seem much more interested in the process by which the campaign against terrorism is conducted. The United Nations must be involved at every step. Resort to law must take precedence over tactical advantage. Terrorists must be treated like criminals, not enemies: Police should apprehend them; courts should try them. Military action should occur seldom if at all, and it should always be precise. A state that sponsors terrorism, such as Afghanistan, should be diplomatically isolated, condemned at the UN, subjected to an arms embargo, and economically sanctioned in any way that does not harm the general populace. The United States should join the international criminal court, and as a token of its good intentions sign most of the treaties it has eschewed. This approach preserves a world role for the United States but, given the determination of the adversary and the foibles of other countries, seems doomed to failure.

Primacists have also tried to direct this campaign. Perhaps the strangest advice is rumored to have come from Paul Wolfowitz, the U.S. deputy secretary of defense. He seems to believe that the time is ripe to deal with all of the United States' enemies and problems in the Middle East and Persian Gulf and further consolidate an already dominant U.S. power position. Wolfowitz is reported to have recommended action against Iraq, Syria, and Hezbollah bases in Lebanon.[25] Violent regimes and movements they are, and no strangers to terrorism, but none of them seems to be connected to al-Qaeda and its maximalist objectives and methods. Were this to change, Wolfowitz's inclinations would make more sense. But going after all of them now looks too much like a script written by al-Qaeda propagandists; such attacks would surely cause states whose cooperation the United States needs to see the campaign as anti-Arab and anti-Islam, and sit this war out. Such a multifront attack might produce the very rebellions in Saudi Arabia, the other Gulf states, and Egypt that the United States hopes to prevent. This proposed four-front war is especially odd given that the Bush administration campaigned on the proposition that the U.S. military was incapable of dealing with two nearly simultaneous major regional wars.

One grand strategy advocated over the last decade is broadly consistent with the requirements of an extended counterterror war. That strategy, termed "selective engagement," argues that the United States has an interest in stable, peaceful, and relatively open political and economic relations in the part of the world that contains important concentrations of economic and military resources: Eurasia. This is an interest that others share. In this strategy, U.S. power is meant to reassure the vulnerable and deter the ambitious. This is a big project that requires a careful setting of priorities. Yet its objectives are limited: The project seeks neither power for its own sake, nor the wholesale reform of other states' domestic constitutions, nor a transformation of international politics. The U.S. position in the Persian Gulf and the Middle East is a central element of this strategy. Al-Qaeda aims to challenge this position. Its leaders believe that if the United States left the region, they could take power in the Gulf and in Egypt. Were this to happen, one can easily imagine several possible dangers: a war between Iraq and Saudi Arabia as Saddam Hussein tries to strangle the fundamentalist Islamic baby in the cradle before its strangles him; war with Iran over security, religious, and nationalist issues; or war with Israel. Given the extreme destructiveness of the 1980–88 Iraq-Iran War (500,000 dead), which saw the use of chemical weapons and rocket attacks on cities—as well as the continued presence of chemical, biological, and nuclear weapons, and rocket delivery systems in the area—any of these possible wars could prove devastating for those in the region and harmful to those farther away. Moreover, any one of them would surely affect the production, distribution, and price of oil—still important to the global economy. Their political, military, and economic ripple effects would likely be felt globally, affecting other political relationships. The grand strategy of selective engagement does necessitate the campaign against al-Qaeda. The requirements of that campaign have already forced the Bush administration to act in ways that are more consistent with the strategy of selective engagement than they are with primacy.

The United States faces a long war against a small, elusive, and dangerous foe. That struggle must be pursued with discipline and determination if it is to be successful. The United States requires a strategy to guide its efforts, including the allocation of resources. That strategy must set priorities, because resources are scarce and this war will prove expensive. Significant changes in the U.S. national security establishment, including intelligence collection and analysis, military organization and equipment, and emergency preparedness, will prove essential. Finally, if the United States is to sustain both public and international support for the war on terrorism, it will need to resolve long-delayed questions about its future foreign and security policy through an extended discussion involving policymakers, policy analysts, and the American people.

Notes

1. It is impossible at this time to offer a more precise figure. See Eric Lipton, "Numbers Vary in Tallies of the Victims," *New York Times*, October 25, 2001, pp. B1, B10.

2. United Kingdom, Foreign and Commonwealth Office (FCO), *Responsibility for the Terrorist Atrocities in the United States, 11 September 2001*, pp. 4–5, http://www/fco.gov.uk/news/keythemepages.asp. See also Kenneth Katzman, *Terrorism: Near Eastern Groups and State Sponsors, 2001*, Congressional Research Service, report for Congress, September 10, 2001, pp. 2, 9.

3. FCO, *Responsibility for the Terrorist Atrocities in the United States*, pp. 6–10, links al-Qaeda to the fight against U.S. special operations forces in Somalia in October 1993, to the bombing of the U.S. embassies in Kenya and Tanzania in August 1998, and to the attack on the USS *Cole* in October 2000, as well as to several thwarted operations. See also Katzman,

Terrorism, pp. 10–11, which also links bin Ladin indirectly to the February 1993 World Trade Center bombing.

4. Ali A. Jalali, "Afghanistan: The Anatomy of an Ongoing Conflict," *Parameters*, Vol. 31, No. 1 (Spring 2001), p. 5, http://carlisle-www.army.mil/usawc/Parameters/o1spring;jalali.htm.

5. "Saudi Arabia: The Double-Act Wears Thin," *Economist*, September 29, 2001, pp. 22–23.

6. As of this writing, the anthrax poisonings in the United States do not contradict this statement. Until we know more, all we can conclude is that small amounts of lethal anthrax can be obtained and, through the mail, can hurt or kill small numbers of people.

7. The February 1993 bombing of the World Trade Center is not directly attributed to al-Qaeda, but Ramzi Yusef, convicted of masterminding that crime, reportedly collaborated with al-Qaeda to organize several unsuccessful terrorist efforts in Asia. Katzman, *Terrorism*, p. 10.

8. Indeed, as of late October 2001, both the U.S. Department of State and the U.K. Foreign and Commonwealth Office used elliptical language to discuss coalition war aims in Afghanistan. Secretary of State Colin Powell could only bring himself to say, "There is, however, no place in a new Afghan government for the current leaders of the Taliban regime." See "Campaign against Terrorism," prepared statement for the House International Relations Committee, U.S. Department of State, October 24, 2001, p. 2, http://www.state.gov/secretary/rm/2001. The United Kingdom's statement of war aims suggests that "we require sufficient change in the leadership to ensure that Afghanistan's links to international terrorism are broken." Foreign and Commonwealth Office, "Defeating International Terrorism: Campaign Objectives," p. 1, http://www.fco.gov.uk/news/keythemehome.asp.

9. See "The President's Address," *Washington Post*, September 21, 2001, p. A24.

10. Patrick E. Tyler and Elisabeth Bumiller, "'Just Bring Him In,' President Hints He Will Halt War If bin Laden Is Handed Over," *New York Times*, October 12, 2001, pp. A1, B5.

11. U.S. leaders wisely exercised some restraint; they did not put large ground forces into the country, who would have provided numerous targets for Afghan riflemen and the appearance of a mission of conquest. Nor did they use firepower indiscriminately, and by large-scale killing of Afghan civilians create the appearance of making war on all Muslims.

12. U.S. Department of Defense, *Quadrennial Defense Review Report*, September 30, 2001, p. 19, states that "DOD will review the establishment of a new unified combatant commander to help address complex inter-agency issues and provide a single military commander to focus military support." This is too tentative.

13. "Nearly all of the threatened or their experts agree that the key to an effective response to terrorism is good intelligence and that such intelligence is difficult to acquire." J. Bowyer Bell, *A Time of Terror: How Democratic Societies Respond to Revolutionary Violence* (New York: Basic Books, 1978), p. 134. Douglas S. Blaufarb draws similar lessons from the U.S. counterinsurgency effort in Vietnam: "Small, lightly armed units, pinpointed operations assisted by 'hunter-killer' squads, imaginative psychological warfare operations—and all of this based upon coordinated collection and exploitation of intelligence—should be the main reliance of the military side of the effort. The police, if they have or can be brought to develop the capability, should play a major role in the intelligence effort and in other programs requiring frequent contact with the public." Blaufarb, *The Counterinsurgency Era: U.S. Doctrine and Performance, 1950 to the Present* (New York: Free Press, 1977), p. 308.

14. The clearest historically grounded exposition of this argument is to be found in Patrick Beesly, *Very Special Intelligence* (New York: Ballantine, 1977), pp. 1–24, which details the formation of the Royal Navy's Operational Intelligence Center, to exploit all source intelligence for the antisubmarine warfare campaign early in World War II.

15. James Risen, "In Hindsight, C.I.A. Sees Flaws That Hindered Efforts on Terror," *New York Times*, October 7, 2001, pp. A1, B2. "In hindsight, it is becoming clear that the C.I.A., F.B.I. and other agencies had significant fragments of information that, under ideal circumstances, could have provided some warning if they had all been pieced together and shared rapidly."

16. "The War on Terrorism," DCI Counterterrorist Center, http://www.cia.gov/terrorism.ctc.html.

17. The National Commission on Terrorism, Ambassador L. Paul Bremer III, Maurice Sonnenberg, Richard K. Betts, Wayne A. Downing, Jane Harman, Fred C. Iklé, Juliette N. Kayyem, John F. Lewis, Jr., Gardner Peckham, and R. James Woolsey, *Countering the Changing Threat of International Terrorism*, report of the National Commission on Terrorism (Washington, D.C., June 5, 2000), http://www.fas.org/irp/threat/commission.htm; and James Kitfield, "CIA, FBI, and Pentagon Team to Fight Terrorism," September 18, 2000, GOVEXEC.com, http://www.govexec.com/dailyfed/0900/091900nt.htm.

18. This sentiment was expressed by President Bush in his address to a joint session of Congress on September 20, 2001: "Whether we bring our enemies to justice or bring justice to our enemies, justice will be done." See "The President's Address."

19. If U.S. Army special operations units are to be permanently deployed at sea, they will need to purchase new "marinized" versions of their current helicopters that are better able to fit below decks, communicate with navy vessels and aircraft, and withstand the corrosive effects of salt air.

20. The U.S. Air Force RQ-1A Predator costs about $8 million apiece. This is the price for a small production run; production on a larger scale would reduce the unit cost. The air force currently has only thirteen Predators. Ted Nicholas and Rita Rossi, *Military Cost Handbook*, 22d ed. (Fountain Valley, Calif.: Data Search Associates, 2001), p. 4–2. See also Craig Hoyle, "US Build-Up Highlights UAV shortage," *Jane's Defence Weekly*, October 10, 2001, p. 5.

21. For example, the Bush administration has appointed Governor Tom Ridge head of the new Office of Homeland Security to coordinate the activities of all the disparate governmental organizations that contribute to territorial defense; he controls nothing. It may instead prove necessary to organize a new Department of Territorial Security, to consolidate control over some or all of the following: air surveillance and defense units; the Coast Guard; the Border Patrol, counterterror elements of the FBI; and federal-level emergency medical response, humanitarian relief, and damage-repair capabilities.

22. Examples of the kinds of diplomatic choices that the United States faces abound. Russia can control its own nuclear materials and weapons and provide intelligence; Russia has been unhappy with NATO expansion and the Bush administration's national missile defense program. Saudi Arabia and the Gulf states have great air bases, all used by the United States during the Gulf War. These bases would prove useful if the counterterror campaign expands to Iraq. These countries find U.S. tolerance of Israeli settlement policies on the West Bank and Gaza to be a significant irritant. Though the UN oil-for-food program has enabled Iraq to feed and care for its people—and Saddam Hussein deserves the blame for their current misery—the continuation of Gulf War sanctions and the regular bombing of Iraq by U.S. and British warplanes help Saddam portray Iraq as the aggrieved party in the Arab world. Pakistan, a former close supporter of the Taliban, was alienated by the United States' cavalier treatment after the end of the Soviet occupation of Afghanistan. Pakistan was also, until recently, under economic sanctions enacted to show U.S. displeasure with its May 1998 nuclear weapons tests. Pakistan may have the most political influence over Pashtun tribes in Afghanistan whose cooperation will be needed to bring a stable government to that country.

23. Russia did not collapse; the nuclear weapons of the Soviet Union were gathered up and consolidated in Russia for safekeeping; the Balkan wars ended; and the great and middle powers of the world have not yet fallen into any new cold wars with one another. U.S. foreign policymakers get much of the credit.

24. Barry R. Posen and Andrew L. Ross, "Competing Visions for U.S. Grand Strategy," *International Security*, Vol. 21, No. 3 (Winter 1996/97), pp. 5–53.

25. Steven Mufson and Thomas E. Ricks, "Debate over Targets Highlights Difficulty of War on Terrorism," *Washington Post*, September 21, 2001, p. A25. The article depicts a policy fight between Secretary of State Colin Powell, the principal advocate of a policy focused on al-Qaeda, and Deputy Secretary of Defense Wolfowitz, "pushing for a broader range of targets, including Iraq."

Explaining the United States' Decision to Strike Back at Terrorists

Michele L. Malvesti is a former terrorism analyst at the U.S. Department of Defense. She has published articles on terrorism in political journals and periodicals, and she recently completed a Ph.D. at Tufts University's Fletcher School of Law and Diplomacy. In the post-September 11 world, she has been widely quoted in media outlets, including National Public Radio (NPR), the *Boston Globe*, and the *New Zealand Herald*.

When an anti-US international terrorism incident occurs, the preferred US counter-terrorism response is law enforcement action. Sometimes, however, US decisionmakers supplement or supplant this approach with a 'power' approach via overt military action. Among the more than 2,400 anti-US incidents over a 16-year period, the US has applied military force in response to only three: the 1986 Libyan bombing of a West German discotheque; the 1993 Iraqi attempt to assassinate former President Bush in Kuwait; and the 1998 bombing of two US embassies in East Africa by bin Laden operatives. What differentiates these incidents from other anti-US attacks? Although the presidents who ordered the strikes offered justifications common to each, this article uncovers five other factors that may have greater explanatory power.

Introduction

Over a 16-year period, from 1983 to 1998, more than 2,400 incidents of international terrorism[1] were directed against the citizens, facilities and interests of the United States throughout the world. Over 600 US citizens lost their lives and nearly 1,900 others sustained injuries in these attacks.[2]

During these 16 years, the four-pronged counter-terrorism policy of the United States has remained virtually unchanged.[3] The first element is to refuse to make concessions or strike deals with terrorists. The second element is to bring terrorists to justice for their actions. The third component is to isolate and apply pressure on state sponsors of international terrorism to force them to cease their terrorist-related activities. Finally, the fourth element of US counter-terrorism policy is to strengthen, via co-operative efforts, the capabilities of other countries to combat terrorism.

Within the context of this policy US decision-makers, when confronted with an anti-US incident of international terrorism, have recourse to five broad instruments of statecraft as methods of response.[4] First, US officials could decide to pursue political and diplomatic measures against the terrorist perpetrators and their state sponsors, ranging from public censure and condemnation to the institution of travel barriers to the severance of diplomatic relations. A second option available to US officials is the enactment of economic measures, such as the institution of trade embargoes, the withdrawal of economic aid, the restriction of US investment in a country or the seizure of US-based assets and prohibition of US-based fundraising. A third counter-terrorist measure is the application of direct, overt military action, including bombings, air strikes or other overt uses of military force designed to facilitate the disruption or destruction of a terrorist organization's network. A fourth option is the initiation of covert operations against the terrorists. Covert operations in general can encompass various political, economic and military methods; in response to international terrorism specifically, covert action could include the deployment of US special operations forces to rescue hostages or the secret training of surrogates to penetrate and attack anti-US terrorist cells. The fifth weapon available in the arsenal to counter anti-US international terrorism is law enforcement action—the investigation, pursuit, apprehension and prosecution of terrorist entities. These five offensive methods of response are not mutually exclusive; they overlap in many areas and US decision-makers often opt for a combination of measures. However, law enforcement action is the standard approach used by the United States government today in response to anti-US acts of international terrorism.[5]

Despite the US preference for the juridical option, sometimes decision-makers will supplement or even supplant this 'criminal justice' approach with a 'power' approach via the application of covert operations or overt military action. This article is interested in the latter. Particularly, this article seeks to develop an explanatory theory of the conditions under which the United States decides to move beyond the standard juridical approach and initiate a use of force via overt military action in response to an incident of anti-US international terrorism. Of the more than 2,400 acts of anti-US international terrorism that occurred from 1983–98, it is noteworthy the United States decided to apply overt military force in response to only three. Specifically, the US conducted military air strikes against facilities in Tripoli and Benghazi after determining Libyan complicity in the April 1986 bombing of a West German discotheque that killed three persons, including two US soldiers, and wounded more than 200 others, including 70 US citizens. Second, the US executed strikes against the Iraqi Intelligence Service Headquarters in June 1993 after agents of Iraq conceived, orchestrated and pursued a plot to assassinate former President George Bush via a car bomb in Kuwait that April; Kuwaiti authorities uncovered and thwarted the attempt. Finally, in August 1998 the US executed a two-pronged missile attack against facilities allegedly[6] related to terrorist financier Usama bin Laden in Sudan and Afghanistan in response to the near-simultaneous destruction of the US embassies in Kenya and Tanzania by bin Laden terrorists earlier that month. The two terrorist explosions killed a total of 224 persons, including 12 US citizens, and injured over 4,000 others.

Given the stark disparity between the overall number of anti-US international terrorist incidents and the number of times the United States has decided to execute overt military strikes in response to an attack, what differentiates Libya's bombing of a discotheque frequented by US soldiers, Iraq's plot to assassinate former President Bush and the destruction of two US embassies in East Africa by bin Laden operatives from the more than 2,400 other anti-US terrorist incidents that occurred in a 16-year period? For illustrative purposes, why did the United States opt to apply military action in response to Iraq's plot to assassinate former President Bush, an act that was thwarted by Kuwaiti authorities and thus never materialized, yet has refrained from applying overt military force against Iran and its primary surrogate, Lebanese Hizballah, the terrorist group known responsible for more US deaths than any other terrorist organization to date?[7] Or why, for example, did the United States decide to strike against terrorist-related facilities in Libya in 1986 in response to Tripoli's complicity in the La Belle discotheque bombing, yet favored law enforcement action against Libyan state agents in response to Tripoli's hand[8] in the 1988 destruction of Pan Am flight 103? What factors are unique to the incidents in response to which the US moved beyond standard law enforcement action and applied overt military force?

Toward the Development of an Explanatory Theory

Following each of the three US military retaliatory strikes, Presidents Ronald Reagan and Bill Clinton addressed the nation, publicly offering justifications for the US strikes against Libya, Iraq and bin Laden-related targets, respectively. An examination of these addresses yields factors common to each anti-US terrorist incident that precipitated the application of US military force, thus constructing the foundation of an explanatory theory.

In the wake of the US air raids against terrorist-related targets in Libya, President Reagan offered the following reasons for the strikes.[9] First, he noted the United States had incontrovertible confirmation that the attack, directed against US servicemen in a West German discotheque, was conceived and discharged under the explicit instructions of the Qadhafi regime in Libya. Second, Reagan conveyed he had previously warned the Libyan leader that his regime, which Reagan noted had had a hand in prior anti-US incidents of international terrorism, would be held accountable for any new operations directed against US citizens. Third, the United States had employed other counter-terrorism instruments in response to Libya's sponsorship of international terrorism such as 'quiet diplomacy, public condemnation, economic sanctions, and demonstrations of military force'[10] but none was effective in curbing Qadhafi's foreign policy of terror. Moreover, President Reagan asserted Qadhafi had been engaging in international terrorism with near impunity, observing that for years the Libyan leader

> … suffered no economic or political or military sanction; and the atrocities mounted in number, as did the innocent dead and wounded. And for us to ignore by inaction the slaughter of American civilians and American soldiers, whether in nightclubs or airline terminals, is simply not in the American tradition. When our citizens are abused or attacked anywhere in the world on the direct orders of a hostile regime, we will respond so long as I'm in this Oval Office.[11]

President Bill Clinton, while addressing the US public after he ordered the strikes against Iraq for Baghdad's complicity in the plot to assassinate former President Bush, offered his justifications for the application of military force.[12] First, the President affirmed the United States had compelling confirmation the Iraqi Intelligence Service directed and facilitated the assassination plot against the former President. Second, he contended the plot was not only an attack against Bush but also an attack against the

United States and all its citizens and thus could not have gone unanswered. He later added that Iraqi leader 'Saddam Hussein has demonstrated repeatedly that he will resort to terrorism or aggression if left unchecked.'[13] Third, President Clinton acknowledged to congressional leaders that other possible avenues of response available to the United States to counter Iraq's terrorist aggression such as 'new diplomatic initiatives or economic measures'[14] would not be effective in altering Saddam's behaviour. Additionally, the President noted the retaliatory strikes served as a warning to all terrorists who would strike not only at US leaders but its citizens as well that the US will respond to protect its people. Specifically, he said, 'There should be no mistake about the message we intend these actions to convey to Saddam Hussein, to the rest of the Iraqi leadership, and to any nation, group, or person who would harm our leaders or our citizens. We will combat terrorism. We will deter aggression. We will protect our people'.[15]

Five years later Clinton again addressed the American people to explain why the United States conducted military strikes against targets in Afghanistan and Sudan related to terrorist financier Usama bin Laden. He specified four reasons.[16] First, President Clinton noted the United States had compelling evidence bin Laden's organization conducted the near-simultaneous bombings of the US embassies in Nairobi, Kenya, and Dar es Salaam, Tanzania, that killed 12 US citizens. Second, he noted these attacks were not the first anti-US operations conducted by bin Laden's terrorists; rather, malcontents operating under the rubric of bin Laden's terrorist network had previously conducted terrorist operations against US citizens. Third, the United States had convincing information the terrorists were preparing to execute additional acts of terrorism specifically targeting US citizens. Finally, Clinton asserted the terrorists were attempting to procure chemical weapons.

An Initial Model

Extrapolating from the publicly professed reasons why the United States resorted to overt military retaliation in response to the discotheque bombing, the Bush assassination plot and the East Africa bombings, four explanatory factors are common to all three incidents. First, the United States maintained it had compelling intelligence information regarding who perpetrated each of the incidents. This factor is termed *positive perpetrator identification* and is a necessary, if obvious, requisite for military targeting.

Second, the respective US President asserted each of these positively identified terrorist perpetrators had conducted previous acts of terrorism against US interests. This factor is termed *perpetrator repetition*. For instance, Reagan noted the US would hold Qadhafi responsible for 'any *new* terrorist attacks launched against American citizens',[17] thus conveying the Libyan regime had perpetrated prior acts of international terrorism against US citizens. Although Clinton does not explicitly refer to previous anti-US terrorist acts perpetrated by Iraq, Saddam Hussein's regime had indeed executed prior terrorist initiatives against the United States, particularly during and in the wake of the Persian Gulf War in 1990–91.[18] Thus when Clinton stated the Iraqi leader 'has demonstrated *repeatedly* that he will resort to terrorism or aggression if left unchecked'[19] he was most likely alluding to these prior anti-US terrorist operations. In his statement addressing the 1998 US strikes in Afghanistan and Sudan against bin Laden's terrorist infrastructure, President Clinton clearly noted Usama bin Laden's organization, which the

US has charged with conducting the US embassy bombings in East Africa, had 'executed terrorist attacks against Americans in the past.'[20] Accordingly, there is, at least from the viewpoint of the United States, an established history of Muammar Qadhafi, Saddam Hussein and Usama bin Laden ordering or sponsoring attacks against US interests. This history of conducting terrorist operations has ramifications for the future. Implicit in this factor of *repetition* is the notion of a continued future threat. This is either explicitly stated or, at the very least, alluded to in each of the presidential statements. Indeed, each US strike was undertaken not simply in retaliation for a particular incident but with the larger objectives of attempting to disrupt the terrorists' ability to conduct future acts of terrorism or to force them to alter their behaviour. While the future threat posed by the terrorists is most explicitly illustrated with bin Laden, whom the US claimed was preparing for additional imminent attacks,[21] by having executed prior acts of terrorism, a repetitive pattern is established and this pattern implies a continued threat of future anti-US terrorism.

A third factor common to each of the attacks is *direct US targeting,* which is intertwined with the factor of perpetrator repetition. Inherent in the notion of having established a pattern of attacks against the United States is the fact that the terrorist operations were designed specifically to target US interests. An attack directed against US interests as the primary target contrasts with terrorist incidents during which US citizens or facilities were injured or sustained damage but were not the ultimate target of the incident. For instance, the La Belle discotheque, although not officially connected with the United States, was bombed because it was frequented by US servicemen, who were the primary target of the attack; the 1993 Iraqi operation was designed to kill a specific US citizen—former President Bush; and the vehicle bombs in Kenya and Tanzania explicitly aimed to destroy two US embassies. In these three operations US interests were the ultimate targets of attack. For illustrative contrast purposes, in June 1985, 329 people, including 19 US citizens, died when a bomb detonated aboard an Air India Flight en route to Ireland from Canada. *Patterns of Global Terrorism: 1988* notes Sikh extremists, who target Indian interests as part of a concerted campaign to establish an independent Sikh state, likely executed the operation. The publication also observes that, despite 19 US citizens being killed in the Air India bombing, Sikh groups have not targeted US interests for attack.[22] Indian interests, not those of the US, were the intended victims. Another example would be the October 1994 abduction and subsequent murder of Israeli Army Corporal Nachson Wachsman, a dual US–Israeli citizen, at the hands of Hamas, the Islamic Resistance Movement. Hamas, an organization that has executed numerous attacks against both Israeli military and civilian targets as part of its effort to establish an Islamic Palestinian state in all of Israel, undoubtedly targeted Wachsman for attack because of his status as an Israeli soldier and not because of his US affiliation.

The fourth explanatory factor is *US citizen involvement.* When both Presidents Reagan and Clinton described the international terrorism incidents in response to which the US retaliated, as well as the previous attacks perpetrated by Libya, Iraq and individuals operating under bin Laden's umbrella, they consistently referred not to attacks against US-related facilities or property, for instance, but rather to attacks against US citizens, against the *people* of the United States. President Reagan specifically stated he would hold Qadhafi liable for additional attacks 'launched against

American citizens' and later noted, 'When *our citizens* are abused or attacked anywhere in the world on the direct orders of a hostile regime, we will respond so long as I'm in this Oval Office.'[23] President Clinton affirmed the retaliation against the Iraqi Intelligence Headquarters was a signal 'to any nation, group, or person who would harm *our leaders or our citizens*.'[24] In addressing the nation after the US strikes against bin Laden-related targets in Afghanistan and Sudan, Clinton noted the operation was designed to 'damage their capacity to *strike at Americans and other innocent people*'; to counter those who had 'executed terrorist attacks against *Americans* in the past'; and to thwart additional terrorist operations planned 'against *our citizens* and others'.[25] The emphasis is on the fact that these anti-US terrorist incidents harmed or intended to harm the people—the citizens—of the United States, not merely cause property damage to an unoccupied US embassy warehouse or a US-owned company overseas, for instance. What these attacks have in common then, and what the Presidents placed emphasis on, is the *citizen target*.

In the larger research project upon which this article is based, a four-factor model comprised of *positive perpetrator identification, perpetrator repetition, direct US targeting* and *US citizen involvement* was initially posited toward explaining the US decision to use overt military force in response to a given act of anti-US international terrorism. This model was then tested against the other anti-US incidents of international terrorism that occurred from 1983–98. If the initial model were accurate and all-encompassing in explaining the conditions under which the US will respond with overt military force to a terrorist incident, the test would spotlight only the three terrorist incidents in response to which the US initiated military force. However, if terrorist incidents other than the 1986 La Belle discotheque bombing, the 1993 plot to assassinate George Bush and the 1998 East Africa bombings also met each of the model's four criteria, then the initial model would be incomplete in its explanatory power.

Initial Model Test

The application of the four-factor model against other anti-US incidents of international terrorism over the 16-year period yielded *sixty-one* other anti-US incidents that meet each of the model's four criteria yet failed to incite the US to conduct military action in response (see Table 1). For instance, on 13 May 1990, assassins from the New People's Army (NPA) shot and killed two US Air Force airmen near Clark Airbase in the Philippines. The killings occurred just before exploratory talks were set to begin between the Philippines and the US regarding the future of US military bases in country.[26] The US Department of State's *Patterns of Global Terrorism: 1990* states the group conducted the operation, indicating *positive perpetrator identification*. Further, the NPA, the guerrilla arm of the Communist Party of the Philippines, was dedicated to ousting the Philippine Government via protracted warfare. To this end, the NPA directed its operations against the country's security apparatus, corrupt Filipino politicians and, until US base closures in 1992, against the US military presence in the Philippines, which it opposed.[27] Accordingly, the incident illustrates *direct US targeting* and, with the deaths of two US airmen, *US citizen involvement*. Moreover, the attack is one of 11 in a series of *repetitive anti-US incidents* conducted by the NPA from 1983–98. If these killings—along with the other incidents detailed in Table 1—meet the four

(Continued on page 413)

Table 1

1983-98 Anti-US Incidents Meeting Initial Four-Factor Criteria[62]

Place/date	Target of Attack	Type of Primary Target	Attack Type	Nos. US dead	Culpability	Prior no. Anti-US Incidents 1983-98[63]
1. Lebanon 1/84	Malcolm Kerr	Private US citizen	Assassination	1	Hizballah	3
2. Lebanon 2/84	Frank Regier	Private US Citizen	Abduction	0	Hizballah	4
3. Lebanon 3/84	Jeremy Levin	Private US citizen	Abduction	0	Hizballah	5
4. Lebanon 3/84	William Buckley	Official personnel	Abduction	1	Hizballah	6
5. Lebanon 5/84	Benjamin Weir	Private US citizen	Abduction	0	Hizballah	7
6. Lebanon 9/84	US embassy annex	Official US mission	Vehicle bombing	2	Hizballah	8
7. Lebanon 11/84	Peter Kilburn	Private US citizen	Abduction	1	Hizbal/ Libya[64]	9
8. Kuwait 12/84	KU flight 221	Private US citizens	Slain in hijacking	2	Hizballah	10
9. Lebanon 1/85	Lawrence Jenco	Private US citizen	Abduction	0	Hizballah	11
10. Lebanon 3/85	Terry Anderson	Private US citizen	Abduction	0	Hizballah	12
11. Lebanon 5/85	David Jacobsen	Private US citizen	Abduction	0	Hizballah	13
12. Lebanon 6/85	Thomas Sutherland	Private US citizen	Abduction	0	Hizballah	14
13. Leb/Algeria 6/85	TWA 847/Navy Diver R. Stethem	US serviceman	Slain in hijacking	1	Hizballah	15
14. W. Germany 8/85	Edward Pimental	US serviceman	Killing	1	RAF	2
15. W. Germany 8/85	Rhein-Main airbase	US military site	Car bombing	2	RAF	3
16. W. Germany 4/86	German disco	US servicemen	Bombing	2	Libyan agents	at least 2 prior

Place/date	Target of Attack	Type of Primary Target	Attack Type	Nos. US dead	Culpability	Prior no. Anti-US Incidents 1983-98[63]
17. Pakistan 9/86	Pan Am flight 73	US commercial plane/US citizens	Slain during failed hijacking	2	ANO	2
18. Lebanon 8/96	Frank Reed	Private US citizen	Abduction	0	Hizballah	16
19. Lebanon 9/86	Joseph Cicippio	Private US citizen	Abduction	0	Hizballah	17
20. Lebanon 10/86	Edward Tracy	Private US citizen	Abduction	0	Hizballah	18
21. Lebaanon 1/87	R. Polhill, A. Steen, J. Turner, M. Singh	Private US citizen, 1 US resident alien	Abduction	0	Hizballah	19
22. Greece 4/87	Transport bus	US servicemen	Bombing	0	17 November	2
23. Lebanon 6/87	Charles Glass	Private US citizen	Abduction	0	Hizballah	20
24. Greece 8/87	Transport bus	US servicemen	Bombing	0	17 November	3
25. Philippines 10/87	3 US, 1 Filipino	US servicemen	Assassinations	3	NPA	2
26. Greece 1/88	US DEA official	Official personnel	Assassination attempt	0	17 November	4
27. Lebanon 2/88	William Higgins	US military officer	Abduction/ murder	1	Hizballah	21
28. Spain 3/88	US Air Force bus stop	US servicemen	Moped bombing	0	RAF	4
29. Italy 4/88	USO club	USG-related site	Car bombing	1	JRA	3
30. Peru 6/88	USAID contractor	USG-related person	Ambush killing	1	Shining Path	4
31. Greece 6/88	William Nordeen	US diplomat	Car bombing	1	17 November	5
32. Spain 6/88	Nightclub	US servicemen	Moped bombing	0	RAF	5
33. Colombia 9/88	US oil company executive	Private US citizen	Assass. attempt	0	ELN	4

Place/date	Target of Attack	Type of Primary Target	Attack Type	Nos. US dead	Culpability	Prior no. Anti-US Incidents 1983-98[63]
34. Scotland 12/88	Pan Am flight 103	US commercial plane	Bombing	189	Libyan agents	4
35. Philippines 4/89	Road used by US troops at Clark Airbase	US military site	Attempted mining	0	NPA	3
36. Philippines 4/89	James Roew	US military officer	Assassination	1	NPA	5
37. Philippines 9/89	2 DoD contractors	USG-related persons	Assassinations	2	NPA	6
38. El Salvador 11/89	Private US citizen	Private US citizen	Armed attack	0	FMLN	2
39. Colombia 2/90	3 US citizens	Private US citizens	Abduction	0	ELN	5
40. Philippines 3/90	US citizen	Private US citizen	Assassination	1	NPA	10
41. Philippines 5/90	2 US airmen	US servicemen	Shooting	2	NPA	11
42. Philippines 6/90	Peace Corps volunteer	USG-related person	Abduction	0	NPA	13
43. Colombia 11/90	3 petroleum engineers	Private US citizens	Abduction	0	ELN	6
44. El Salvador 1/91	US military helicopter	US servicemen/ helicopter	Helicopter downing	3	FMLN	3
45. Greece 3/91	Ronald Odell Stewart	US serviceman	Bombing	1	17 November	7
46. Turkey 3/91	John Gandy	DoD contractor	Assassination	1	Dev Sol	2
47. Colombia 1/92	Jose Lopez	Private US citizen	Abduction/ killing	1	ELN	7
48. Turkey 7/92	US hospital admin	Private US citizen	Assass. attempt	0	Dev Sol	4
49. Panama 1/93	3 US missionaries	Private US citizens	Abduction	0	FARC	3
50. Colombia 2/93	Lewis Manning	Private US citizen	Abduction	0	ELN	8

Place/date	Target of Attack	Type of Primary Target	Attack Type	Nos. US dead	Culpability	Prior no. Anti-US Incidents 1983-98[63]
51. Kuwait 4/93	George Bush	Former US president	Assass. attempt	0	Iraqi agents	at least 2 prior
52. Colombia 1/94	2 US missionaries	Private US citizens	Abduction/ killings	2	FARC	4
53. Colombia 4/94	Raymond Rising	Private US citizen	Abduction	0	FARC	5
54. Colombia 9/94	Thomas Hargrove	Private US citizen	Abduction	0	FARC	6
55. Colombia 5/95	US citizen	Private US citizen	Abduction	0	ELN	9
56. Ecuador 12/95	US missionary	Private US citizen	Abduction	0	FARC	8
57. Turkey 9/96	US tourist	Private US citizen	Abduction	0	PKK	3
58. Colombia 12/96	US geologist	Private US citizen	Abduction/ killing	1	FARC	9
59. Colombia 2/97	US citizen	Private US citizen	Abduction	0	ELN	10
60. Colombia 3/97	US citizen	Private US citizen	Abduction	0	FARC	10
61. Colombia 3/98	US citizen	Private US citizen	Abduction	0	FARC	12
62. Colombia 3/98	4 US citizens	Private US citizens	Abduction	0	FARC	13
63. Kenya/Tanz. 8/98	2 US embassies	Official US missions	Vehicle bombings	12	bin Laden's al-Qaida group	at least 2 prior
64. Ecuador 10/98	2 US citizens	Private US citizens	Abduction	0	ELN	13

criteria laid out by Presidents Reagan and Clinton, why did the US not initiate military action in response to these terrorist challenges? The four-factor model, therefore, is not all-encompassing in its explanatory power. Factors other than, or in addition to, positive perpetrator identification, perpetrator repetition, direct US targeting and US citizen involvement must account for the United States' decision to strike at Libyan, Iraqi and bin Laden-related targets.

Explanatory Expansion

A critical review of the history and events surrounding the US strikes against Libya, Iraq and Usama bin Laden yields five additional common characteristics found in their precipitating incidents as well as in the events leading up to the strikes. The first two additional shared properties relate to the terrorist incidents themselves. First, the three incidents were *faits accomplis*—already accomplished and irreversible in nature; they were not on-going incidents. The La Belle discotheque bombing and the US embassy bombings in Kenya and Tanzania were incidents that had come to fruition and were, in effect, over the moment the explosives detonated. There would be no on-going crisis to manage, only consequences with which to contend. The same applies to the plot to assassinate former President Bush. Once Kuwaiti authorities uncovered the plot and arrested those involved in the murderous conspiracy, the immediate crisis itself had been obviated. Materialized bombings, thwarted plots and, for example, assassinations, arsons and armed attacks represent *faits accomplis*. Other types of terrorist incidents, however, are on-going situations that require or, at the very least, lend themselves to crisis management rather than retaliatory armed action. Abductions, hostage barricade incidents and hijackings fall into this latter category. The execution of overt military action during an on-going incident would necessarily place the US citizens involved in danger, either via the military action itself or, if they are held at a site not targeted, via possible retaliation by the terrorists who have them. This is a risk that tends to be operationally and politically unpalatable. It is hypothesized, therefore, that the US is more inclined to use overt military force in response to *fait accomplis* anti-US terrorist incidents, defined here as materialized bombings, thwarted plots, assassinations, arsons and armed attacks, than in response to on-going hostage-related situations where US lives continue to remain at risk.

The second characteristic each of the three incidents has in common is that the primary targets of attack—US servicemen, a former US President and two US embassies—are *related to the US government*. The two US servicemen who died in the La Belle discotheque bombing were members of the US armed forces, carrying out official US military duties overseas. Former President Bush, who was once the chief of state and head of government, was targeted by Iraqi agents in response to actions he undertook as President of the United States. The near-simultaneous bombings that occurred in August 1998 in Nairobi and Dar es Salaam were directed at US diplomatic missions, sovereign US facilities, and at the US diplomatic and government-related personnel inside their walls. These incidents contrast sharply with terrorist incidents directed against US business-related facilities or private US citizens.

Interestingly, with the exception of 1983 and 1990, the type of US target most frequently attacked during the years under examination in this article has been business-related.[28] For instance, of the 111 anti-US terrorist incidents in 1998, 77, or nearly 70 per cent, were bombings of a single US-related business venture—a multinational oil pipeline in Colombia that Colombian terrorists consider a US target.[29] US business-related facilities are probably attacked most frequently due to their relatively low-security profile compared to the security measures in place at US diplomatic missions or US-related military facilities overseas. Moreover, a terrorist's choice of target, be it business or government-related, is contingent upon the terrorist group's capabilities, objectives and, intertwined with these, whether or not the group desires to maximize casualties. Regardless, US businesses were the most frequently attacked target in anti-US international terrorist incidents from 1983–98, yet the three incidents in response to which the US retaliated with armed action had government-related facilities and personnel as the ultimate targets. US officials responsible for counter-terrorism decision-making were probably influenced by the fact that the primary targets in these three trigger incidents were US government-related. Attacks against US diplomatic missions are attacks on sovereign US territory and thus are direct challenges to US power, authority and jurisdiction. US decision-makers probably perceive terrorist incidents perpetrated against US government-related personnel in a similar light; this is highlighted in the extreme case of the plot to assassinate Bush. Indeed, as the evidence began to mount against Iraq, the United States began to examine various courses of action, including the standard juridical response: requesting the government of Kuwait to extradite the suspects to the US to stand trial. However, Central Intelligence Agency and Department of Defense officials reportedly argued a plot to assassinate a former President of the United States mandated more severe punishment.[30] The US, therefore, is more inclined to use military force in response to incidents where the target is a US diplomatic mission or personnel, military facilities or personnel, or other government-related interests such as civilian employees of the Department of Defense, for example, than in response to incidents that do not involve official US government interests.

The third additional property the three trigger incidents have in common is that there was *relatively immediate positive perpetrator identification*. With the La Belle discotheque bombing, intelligence revealed Libya's hand that same night. The bombing had occurred at 1:49 a.m., Saturday 5 April. Just prior to the attack that evening Britain's General Communications Headquarters intercepted a transmission from the Libyan People's Bureau in East Berlin to Tripoli foretelling an upcoming 'joyous event'.[31] Nearly coinciding with the bomb detonation in the discotheque, the British agency received another intercept from the same parties describing the operation as 'a success' and one that could not be linked to the Libyan People's Bureau.[32] Indeed, within hours the United States had its 'smoking gun'.[33]

The 1998 US embassy bombings did not produce a 'smoking gun' the very day the incident occurred, as the La Belle bombing had, but in a press briefing with Secretary of State Madeleine Albright on the day of the US strikes, National Security Advisor Sandy Berger makes it clear that:

> From quite early on in the investigation, the intelligence community began to receive substantial amounts of credible information from many sources and many methods indicating that the Osama bin Laden group of terrorist organizations was responsible for the bombing. And that information culminated in the last few days in the conclusion reached by the intelligence community that we have high confidence that these bombings were planned, financed and carried out by the organization bin Laden leads.[34]

The US had positively identified the perpetrators of the US embassy bombings within days. Indeed, Berger notes that 'Last Friday, exactly a week after the bombings, Director [of Central Intelligence] Tenet, I think, had reached a judgment about responsibility....'[35]

Positive perpetrator identification of the Iraqi plot to assassinate former President Bush did not occur within days, unlike the identification in the other two incidents. To be sure, the United States initially questioned the veracity of information pointing to a plot actually to assassinate Bush; rather, US officials tended more toward an assessment that the suspects were engaging in sabotage.[36] Following the arrest of the suspects, however, President Clinton ordered an investigation into the April 1993 incident. Attorney-General Janet Reno and Director of Central Intelligence James Woolsey presented their findings to the President on Thursday 24 June 1993, Clinton ordered the strikes that Friday and the strikes were executed on Saturday 26 June.[37] Accordingly, from the time the incident occurred in mid April until the findings were given to the President on 24 June, the US had determined responsibility for the incidents within roughly ten weeks.

These relatively immediate assignations of culpability contrast with other terrorist incidents where positive perpetrator identification takes months, sometimes years, to determine. One of the most illustrative examples of 'non-immediate' perpetrator identification is the December 1988 bombing of Pan Am flight 103. It was not until nearly three years after the bombing, in November 1991, that US and British courts indicted two Libyan agents for the attack.[38] The United States, however, once positive perpetrator identification was established in 1991, did not respond to this incident, which met all four initial criteria in the explanatory model, with military action against Libyan terrorist-related targets as it had done against Libya five years earlier; rather, the Bush administration opted for a juridical response.

Defining *relatively immediate positive perpetrator identification* is problematic in that any time period proffered would necessarily be arbitrary. Conceding this inherent problem, however, *relatively immediate positive perpetrator identification* is defined for the purposes of this article as within one year of the incident. Within the confines of this definition, US decision-makers were probably influenced by the relatively immediate identification of the perpetrators. Overt military retaliation is one of the most aggressive instruments available to counter anti-US terrorism and often is perceived as a tool of hostility rather than one of justice. Furthermore, some may argue that a manifestation of hostility could be brought on by the 'heat of the moment', as it were. Accordingly, if the US identified the perpetrators of a particular incident years after the event took place, such as with Pan Am flight 103, it is possible the US, thus removed from the immediacy and hostility of the moment, may be more inclined to pursue other, less aggressive response options. Indeed, while discussing the Bush administration's decision not to use military force against Libya in response to the downing of Pan Am 103, Brent Scowcroft, President Bush's national security advisor, later conceded that 'you have to strike while the situation is hot'. Libya did not emerge as a prime suspect until more than a year after the bombing.'[39] Conversely, the US had identified the perpetrators of the La Belle bombing, the plot to assassinate Bush and the US embassy bombings relatively quickly, while emotions were still raw. Accordingly, the US is more inclined to initiate overt armed force in response to incidents where positive perpetrator identification occurs within one year of the incident than in response to incidents whose perpetrators are identified later than one year.

The fourth additional characteristic the three incidents have in common is that the individuals ultimately responsible for the attacks, Qadhafi, Saddam and bin Laden, each exhibited a very *public and flagrantly defiant attitude against the United States*. For instance, from late December 1985 until April 1986, Reagan pursued a strategy to coerce Qadhafi to alter his behaviour[40] via political measures, economic sanctions and military displays of power, during which time the Libyan leader grew increasingly inflammatory in his anti-US public statements. He not only publicly mocked Reagan's efforts, he applauded previous anti-US terrorist attacks. In one instance, referring to those terrorist groups operating under his influence, Qadhafi affirmed that his state would train them for suicide missions and provide the necessary weapons to execute attacks.[41] The bellicose statements built to a crescendo in late March 1986, when Qadhafi warned, 'It is time for confrontation, for war. If they [the US] want to expand the struggle, we will carry it all over the world'.[42] Ten days later, on 5 April, Libyan-sponsored terrorists placed a bomb in the bathroom of the La Belle discotheque.

Saddam Hussein had been publicly challenging the United States directly and through the United Nations before, during and in the wake of the Gulf War. President Clinton noted in his address that 'Saddam has repeatedly violated the will and conscience of the international community'.[43] In her June 1993 address to the UN Security Council, then-Ambassador to the UN Madeleine Albright noted the United States' displeasure with the continued Iraqi defiance, admonishing Iraq for refusing to comply with UN Security Council Resolutions regarding its weapons of mass destruction and ballistic missile programs, the acceptance of the Iraq–Kuwait boundary and the repression of the Iraqi peoples. More specifically, she asserted that Iraq, during and immediately following the war, let it be known it would hunt down and exact revenge against George Bush.[44] Saddam's regime would come close to fulfilling its threats two years after the allied victory over Baghdad but the plan would not be brought to fruition.

In August 1996, terrorist patron and private financier Usama bin Laden fired what can most likely be considered his opening salvo in the public verbal war with the US: from his headquarters in Afghanistan he called for attacks against US armed forces, professing that Americans must die.[45] Subsequent to this announcement he gave interviews and issued various pronouncements calling for *jihad* against the US. His inflammatory rhetoric and anti-US threats reached their peak in February 1998 when, in the name of a movement called World Islamic Front for Jihad Against the Jews and Crusaders, bin Laden and his allies issued a religious decree exhorting Muslims the world over to kill US citizens, both military and civilian.[46] In late May 1998, the terrorist financier, speaking at a press conference in Afghanistan, proudly claimed the results of his efforts would be visible to the world 'within weeks'.[47] On 7 August 1998, roughly eleven weeks after his May press conference, near-simultaneous vehicle bombs destroyed the US embassies in Nairobi and Dar es Salaam.

Qadhafi, Saddam and bin Laden were sabre-rattlers. They continually drew attention to themselves, making it difficult for the United States to ignore them. To be sure, other terrorist organizations and state sponsors also publicly speak out against the United States, denouncing US policy, publicly condemning US actions and, at times, increasing this rhetoric to inflammatory excitations to violence. Such actions, however, usually are not on a par with the flagrant anti-US behaviour demonstrated by Qadhafi, bin Laden and especially Saddam Hussein, who expressed a willingness to target Bush directly. The words and actions of these men transcended routine criticism of US policy and occasional vehement anti-US outbursts. They were repeatedly flagrant in their support for terrorism, their defiance of international norms and their specific, publicly stated intentions to strike at US interests. Such posturing is difficult to ignore and US decision-makers may have become increasingly hostile over the perpetrators' continued brazenness. The repeated anti-US threats and defiant actions carried out by the perpetrators most likely influenced the decision of US officials to pursue one of the more aggressive counter-terrorism response options. Thus it is hypothesized the US is more inclined to conduct armed action in response to an incident whose perpetrators have repeatedly and publicly challenged the US, making them difficult to ignore, than in response to those incidents whose perpetrators were relatively more subtle or discreet in their approach.

The fifth additional characteristic the La Belle discotheque bombing, the Bush assassination plot and the two US embassy bombings in East Africa have in common is that their *perpetrators were militarily and politically vulnerable to US military response*. Military planners involved with the US strikes against Libya considered Tripoli to be a 'fourth-rate military power' and no match for the $60 bn worth of equipment and personnel the US allocated against the Libyan regime.[48] Politically, Libya was isolated. Even during the Cold War, when the United States and the Soviet Union earnestly competed for influence with Third World countries, Soviet officials called Qadhafi a 'madman' in conversations with US officials and later even distanced themselves publicly from the Libyan leader; indeed, the Libyan state had no significant allies upon which to rely.[49]

Iraq was in a similar position two years after the US and the Allied coalition expelled Iraqi forces from Kuwait. General Colin Powell, Chairman of the Joint Chiefs of Staff, confirmed Iraq's vulnerable military status in a CNN interview the day after the US strikes, noting the regime's air power was relatively impotent and that the US would be able to counter any Iraqi ground operation; indeed, he defined Iraqi's military prowess as a 'mischief-making capability' rather than a 'war-making capability'.[50] Politically, Saddam engaged in flagrant political transgressions against the US and the UN. At the time of the 1986 and 1993 US strikes, both Qadhafi's Libya and Saddam's Iraq, respectively, were international political pariahs and militarily vulnerable to US strikes.

The same case can be made for Usama bin Laden. Militarily, his terrorist locations in Afghanistan and Sudan were vulnerable to US power. Bin Laden did not have military forces under his command with the equipment necessary to counter effectively the US air strikes. Moreover, Afghanistan and Sudan, on whose territories the strikes impacted, most likely posed no threat to the US strikes in the eyes of US military planners. In Afghanistan, while some elements of the former armed forces, National Guard and Border Guard Forces still existed, a national, unified Afghanistan military did not, and while there were tribal militias in the country, factionalization mitigated their threat.[51] Moreover, striking at bin Laden's facilities in Afghanistan and Sudan was politically feasible, or at least likely was deemed so at the time. Afghanistan does not have a government officially recognized by the United States, thus minimizing political fall-out, and Sudan has been on the US State Department's List of State Sponsors of International Terrorism since 1993. The US deemed at the time it most likely had little to lose politically in its relations with either Afghanistan or Sudan.

This is probably a critical component in the United States' decision to bomb facilities related to a non-state actor. Although the ultimate target may be a sub-national actor, its network and facilities necessarily reside on the territory of a sovereign state. What distinguishes bin Laden from other sub-national terrorist entities is that the territories on which his network was located were militarily and, more importantly, politically vulnerable to a US strike. Compare bin Laden's situation with another non-state actor. The New People's Army (NPA), addressed earlier in the article, is known to be responsible for the deaths of eleven US citizens. The United States knows the group operates in the Philippines' rural Luzon, Visayas and areas of Mindanao and has established cells in Manila.[52] Accordingly, the US could have conducted armed action against NPA-related targets but instead supported less aggressive options in response to the NPA terrorist threat.[53] There are most likely numerous reasons why the United States has never decided to apply military action against the NPA, most prominently the US preference for peaceful law enforcement action as a method of response, but another reason likely lies in the action's political inexpedience.

Accordingly, one could hypothesize the United States is more inclined to conduct military retaliatory strikes in response to incidents whose perpetrators are vulnerable to such strikes both militarily and politically. More specifically, the US is more inclined to strike against countries (or the non-state actors residing in countries) that are militarily unable to thwart or significantly confront the strikes and whose relations with the US are politically tenuous, particularly regarding issues of terrorism, than in response to incidents whose perpetrators present military and political challenges to the US.

Public Opinion

Interestingly, the fifth additional factor of political and military vulnerability is echoed in the public outcry noted in the Middle East following the US strike on Baghdad. Some Arab commentators noted, for instance, that the strike was an attempt to increase Clinton's domestic popularity and strengthen his foreign policy initiatives by 'projecting an air of decisiveness and flexing his hi-tech military muscles *at an easy target*'.[54]

Indeed, overall public opinion throughout the Middle East condemned the US military strikes, all three of which occurred on Arab and/or Muslim soil. Many viewed the strikes as illustrative of a double standard perpetrated by the US. In response to the US strikes in Sudan and Afghanistan, for example, one Middle East publication highlighted Washington's desire to use military force against Muslim Sudan and Afghanistan and its contrasting complacency regarding the killing and oppression of Muslims and Arabs, especially Palestinians.[55] The official responses of governments in the region have varied, from Kuwait's public support for the Iraqi strike to muted resignation to vehement condemnation. Although most denounce terrorism and, at the time of the US strikes, were not necessarily endeared with the perpetrators, a former US ambassador in the region observed, '... there is a nationalist component to opposing intervention by outside powers in the Middle East'.[56]

Public opinion in the US stands in sharp contrast.[57] Polls in the wake of the strikes showed 77 per cent of US citizens supported the raid on Libya and 66 per cent supported the strike against Iraq. One poll following the two-pronged strike in Sudan and Afghanistan indicated 66 per cent supported the operation while a second poll showed support at 80 per cent. Accordingly, US public opinion has strongly favoured the US 'power' approach to countering terrorism. That said, these strikes were relatively surgical operations that did not stretch the public's attention span or its tolerance.[58] Recognizing this fact, in the wake of the Libyan raid George Shultz, who advocated the 'power' approach, reassuringly stated, 'we're not going to get into a kind of automatic pilot on this'[59] and, indeed, the US has not.

Conclusion

This article has shown the justifications Presidents Reagan and Clinton publicly offered for their decisions to initiate counter-terrorist military action in 1986, 1993 and 1998 are not sufficient[60] to explain why the United States conducts overt armed action in response to an anti-US terrorist incident; their decisional reasoning failed to differentiate the three precipitating incidents from 61 other anti-US terrorist events. If the resultant four-factor model were sufficient in its explanatory power the US would have executed armed action in response to the 61 additional anti-US terrorist incidents that also met the four-factor model criteria. Accordingly, the occurrence of *positive perpetrator identification, perpetrator repetition, direct US targeting* and *US citizen involvement* does not imply the occurrence of US retaliatory strikes. Rather, considerations other than, or in addition to, these four factors must account for the US decision to initiate overt military force in response to the La Belle discotheque bombing, the plot to assassinate Bush and the US embassy bombings in East Africa. An in-depth review of the Libyan, Iraqi and bin Laden case histories revealed they had five themes in common in addition to the initial four factors: *fait accompli 'trigger' incidents, US government-related targets, relatively immediate perpetrator identification, flagrantly defiant perpetrator behaviour* and *political and military vulnerability*. These five factors are critical additional explanatory components of the US decision to conduct overt military action in response to these three anti-US international terrorist incidents.[61]

Accordingly, despite the stated reasons given by Reagan and Clinton, nine factors unique to the three terrorist incidents may actually explain the US decision to apply overt military force as a counter-terrorism response mechanism. For the sake of brevity, these nine are combined and simplified into six explanatory factors:

1. relatively immediate perpetrator identification
2. perpetrator repetition
3. direct targeting of a US citizen working in an official US government-related capacity
4. the *fait accompli* nature of the incident
5. flagrant anti-US perpetrator behaviour
6. the political and military vulnerability of the perpetrator

Absent from this explanatory model is one factor many terrorism and counter-terrorism researchers initially may have hypothesized would be critical in a US decision to use overt military force as a method of counter-terrorism response: maximization of casualties in an anti-US terrorist incident. It would not be illogical to hypothesize that the more severe an anti-US attack is, the more severe—meaning an overt use of military force—would be the US response. A definition of severity, however, should not be restricted to the number of US casualties in a given incident. While the deaths of 241 US citizens in the 1983 bombing of the US Marine Corps Barracks in Beirut, for instance, undoubtedly is 'severe', a state-orchestrated plot to assassinate a former US President, although never resulting in a single US death, arguably is equally 'severe' an incident. Although maximization of casualties was not a factor in the US decision to use overt military force in response to an anti-US incident of international terrorism, a measure of 'severity' arguably is built into the explanatory model via the factor of 'direct targeting of a US citizen working in an official government-related capacity'.

Predictive Value

Do the modified six explanatory factors account for the totality of circumstances that influence a US decision to use overt military force as a counter-terrorist measure? Admittedly, the model developed in this article narrowly restricts itself to an analysis of the anti-US terrorist incident and concomitant perpetrators rather than incorporating the broader domestic and international modifying conditions that could influence a decision to use military force. For instance, factors such as public opinion, the presidential election cycle, the degree of priority given to counter-terrorism efforts in a presidential administration, the availability of US military units to execute a response and the level of overall anti-US international terrorist activity, to name a few, may also influence the decision of whether or not to supplant the standard juridical response mechanism with overt military force.

Acknowledging that any future US decision to apply military force in response to a terrorist incident will necessarily be made under the rubric of larger modifying conditions, the explanatory model developed in this article does have a degree of predictive value. While the occurrence of all six (modified) factors in future acts of anti-US international terrorism will not necessarily result in the application of overt military action, should the US respond to a particular incident with military force in the future, that incident likely will exhibit some, if not all, of the six explanatory factors. Any future US decision to use military force as a counter-terrorist measure should be examined in light of these findings. Further analysing and explaining the conditions under which this 'power approach' is taken instead of pursuing the standard juridical approach will contribute more than just new research to the fields of crisis decision-making and counter-terrorism strategy; it will provide practical instructive value for those officials faced with making such an important decision in the future.

Notes

1. A debate exists over the precise nature of terrorism and thus a universally accepted definition remains elusive. Since this research project focuses on the US response to anti-US international terrorism, the United States government's definition of terrorism is employed: 'premeditated, politically motivated violence perpetrated against noncombatant targets by sub-national groups or clandestine state agents, usually intended to influence an audience.' Within the parameters of this definition the United States also makes clear the term 'noncombatant' is not restricted to civilians; rather, noncombatants can include military personnel who are either unarmed or off-duty at the time of the incident. Furthermore, the US also considers acts of terrorism attacks that are directed against military facilities or armed mil-

itary personnel when there is not a state of military hostilities. *International terrorism* is an act thus defined but which involves the territory or citizens of more than one state. United States Department of State, *Patterns of Global Terrorism: 1998* (Washington, DC: Department of State April 1999), pp. vi–vii.

2. Data gathered from United States Department of State, *Patterns of Global Terrorism* series for the years 1983–98.

3. See, for example, United States Department of State, *Patterns of Global Terrorism: 1987* (Washington, DC: Department of State August 1988), p. iii and United States Department of State, *Patterns of Global Terrorism: 1998* (note 1), p. iii.

4. See, for example, Louis J. Freeh, *U.S. Government's Response to International Terrorism*, 3 September 1998. Available http://www.fbi.gov/pressrm/congress/98archives/terror.html.

5. The preference for the law enforcement approach, which most likely emanates from the lawful context in which the instrument is applied as well as from its ability to bring to fruition a tangible success—namely, the apprehension and prosecution of a terrorist—in the war against terrorism, is exemplified in the increasing responsibilities, roles and capabilities the US has extended to the Federal Bureau of Investigation (FBI) with respect to anti-US international terrorism. For example, the FBI not only is the lead agency with respect to terrorism executed on US soil but also has jurisdiction when US interests are attacked overseas: 'The FBI's counter-terrorism responsibilities were further expanded in 1984 and 1986, when Congress passed laws permitting the Bureau to exercise federal jurisdiction overseas when a US National is murdered, assaulted, or taken hostage by terrorists, or when certain US interests are attacked', Freeh (note 4).

6. Controversy surrounds the decision to strike the El Shifa pharmaceutical plant in Khartoum, Sudan. US officials claimed the plant was producing deadly chemical agents and was part of bin Laden's infrastructure to acquire a chemical weapons capability. Information revealed since the strike, however, indicates otherwise. See, among others, Vernon Loeb, 'US Wasn't Sure Plant Had Nerve Gas Role', *Washington Post*, 21 August 1999; and James Risen, 'To Bomb Sudan Plant, or Not: A Year Later, Debates Rankle', *New York Times*, 27 October 1999.

7. Based on information compiled from the United States Department of State's *Patterns of Global Terrorism* series, 1983–98. Hizballah is known to be responsible for the deaths of more than 260 US citizens: the April 1983 suicide vehicle bombing of the US embassy in Beirut, Lebanon (17 US killed); the October 1983 bombing of the US Marine Corps Barracks in Beirut (241 US killed); the January 1984 shooting of Malcolm Kerr, President of the American University of Beirut (1 US killed); the March 1984 abduction in Beirut and subsequent death of CIA station chief William Buckley (1 US dead); the suicide truck bombing of the US embassy annex in east Beirut in September 1984 (2 US dead); the singling out and subsequent murder of two US Agency for International Development employees during the December 1984 hijacking of Kuwaiti Airlines flight 221 (2 US killed); the murder of US navy diver Robert Stethem during the June 1985 hijacking of TWA flight 847 (1 US killed); and the February 1988 abduction and subsequent murder of Lt. Col. William Higgins in Lebanon (1 US killed). Hizballah may also be indirectly responsible for the death of US citizen Peter Kilburn, an American University of Beirut librarian. The group abducted Kilburn in November 1984. His body was discovered on 17 April 1986; Libyan involvement—probable retaliation for the April 1986 US air strikes against Tripoli—is suspected in his death.

8. In April 1999, more than seven years after the US and British governments issued indictments, Tripoli surrendered two Libyans accused of planting the bomb on the aircraft. In January 2001, a Scottish court seated in the Netherlands convicted Libyan intelligence agent Abdel Basset Ali al-Megrahi of 270 counts of murder. He was sentenced to life in prison with the possibility of parole after 20 years. Co-defendant Lamen Khalifa Fhima was acquitted.

9. Ronald Reagan, 'Address to the Nation on the United States Air Strike Against Libya', *Public Papers of the Presidents of the United States: Ronald Reagan, 1986,* Book 1 (Washington, DC: GPO 1988), pp. 468–69.

10. Ibid., p. 469.

11. Ibid.

12. Information regarding Clinton's statements are taken from the following two sources: William J. Clinton, 'Address to the Nation on the Strike on Iraqi Intelligence Headquarters'. *Public Papers of the Presidents of the United States: William J. Clinton, 1993,* Book 1 (Washington, DC: GPO 1994), pp. 938–39 and William J. Clinton, 'Letter to Congressional Leaders on the Strike on Iraqi Intelligence Headquarters', *Public Papers of the Presidents of the United States: William J. Clinton, 1993,* Book 1 (Washington, DC: GPO 1994) pp. 940–41.

13. Clinton, 'Address to the Nation' (note 12), p. 938.

14. Clinton, 'Letter to Congressional Leaders' (note 12), p. 940.

15. Clinton, 'Address to the Nation' (note 12), pp. 938–39.

16. William J. Clinton, 'Statement by the President, Edgartown Elementary School, Martha's Vineyard', 20 August 1998. Available http://www.pub.whitehouse.gov/uri-.../oma.eop.gov. us/1998/8/20/2text.1

17. Reagan (note 9), p. 468 (emphasis added).

18. For examples of prior anti-US terrorism incidents perpetrated by Iraqi agents see United States Department of State, *Patterns of Global Terrorism: 1990* (Washington, DC: Department of State 1991), and United States Department of State, *Patterns of Global Terrorism: 1991* (Washington, DC: Department of State 1992).

19. Clinton, 'Address to the Nation' (note 12), p. 938 (emphasis added).

20. Clinton, 'Statement by the President' (note 16).

21. For use of the word 'imminent' see William J. Clinton, *Text of a Letter from the President to the Speaker of the House of Representatives and the President Pro Tempore of the Senate,* 22 August 1998. Available http://www.fas.org/man/dod-101/ops/docs/980822-wh.3.htm.

22. United States Department of State, *Patterns of Global Terrorism: 1988* (Washington, DC: Department of State 1989), p. 81.

23. Reagan (note 9) (emphasis added).

24. Clinton, 'Address to the Nation' (note 12), p. 938 (emphasis added).

25. Clinton, 'Statement by the President' (note 16) (emphasis added).

26. *Patterns of Global Terrorism: 1990* (note 18), p. 44.

27. *Patterns of Global Terrorism: 1998* (note 1), p. 78.

28. See United States Department of State's *Patterns of Global Terrorism* series for the years 1983–98.

29. *Patterns of Global Terrorism: 1998* (note 1), p. 1.

30. Douglas Jehl, 'U.S. Cited Evidence in a Plot on Bush', *New York Times,* 9 May 1993.

31. David C. Martin and John Walcott, *Best Laid Plans: The Inside Story of America's War Against Terrorism* (New York: Harper & Row 1988), p. 285.

32. Ibid., p. 286.

33. Ibid.

34. Madeleine K. Albright and Sandy Berger, *Press Briefing on U.S. Strikes in Sudan and Afghanistan,* 20 August 1998. Available http://secretary.state.gov/www/statements/1998/980820.html

35. Ibid.

36. Jehl (note 30).

37. Clinton, 'Address to the Nation' (note 12), p. 938.

38. *Patterns of Global Terrorism: 1991* (note 18), p. 32.

39. John Lancaster, 'Compromising Positions', *Washington Post Magazine* (9 July 2000), p. 22.

40. See Tim Zimmerman, 'Coercive Diplomacy and Libya', in Alexander L. George and William E. Simons (eds.), *The Limits of Coercive Diplomacy,* 2nd ed. (Boulder, CO: Westview Press 1994), pp. 201–28.

41. Bernard Gwertzman, 'U.S. Navy Exercises Starts Off Libya', *New York Times,* 15 January 1986.

42. John Kifner, 'Qaddafi Threatens a Wider Struggle', *New York Times,* 26 March 1986.

43. Clinton, 'Address to the Nation' (note 12), p. 938.

44. Madeleine K. Albright, 'Albright Addresses UN Security Council', *Cable News Network* Transcript #432–3, 27 June 1993.

45. Karl Vick, 'Assault on a U.S. Embassy: A Plot Both Wide and Deep', *Washington Post,* 23 November 1998.

46. United States Department of State, *Fact Sheet: Usama bin Ladin,* 21 August 1998. Available http://www.state.gov/www/regions/africa/fs_bin_ladin.html.

47. Ibid.

48. Martin and Walcott (note 31), p. 280.

49. Ibid., p. 289.

50. Colin Powell, 'General Colin Powell Discusses US Air Attack on Baghdad', *Cable News Network* Transcript #430–1, 27 June 1993.

51. Central Intelligence Agency, *World Factbook 1998* (Washington, DC: CIA 1998), p. 3.

52. *Patterns of Global Terrorism: 1998* (note 1), p. 78.

53. In accordance with its preference for law enforcement action, the US government supported the legal efforts of the Philippine government in response to the NPA's anti-US terrorist activity. For instance, the Philippine government convicted two NPA operatives for the 1989 assassination of US Army Colonel James Rowe; both were sentenced to life imprisonment in 1991, *Patterns of Global Terrorism: 1991* (note 18), p. 5. The US is not known to have pursued a 'power approach' against the NPA; rather, the US has worked bilaterally with the Philippine government on counter-terrorism measures, *Patterns of Global Terrorism: 1990* (note 18), p. 6.

54. 'Arab Press Rails Against Clinton', *Mideast Mirror,* 28 June 1993 (emphasis added).

55. 'Why Washington's Arab Allies Won't Support Its Missile Strikes', *Mideast Mirror,* 24 August 1998.

56. George D. Moffett III, 'Tallying Diplomatic Score of US Raid on Libya', *Christian Science Monitor,* 16 April 1986, p. 1.

57. Data regarding US public opinion is taken from the following sources: James Reston, 'Leave it to the People?', *New York Times,* 20 April 1986; Reuters, 'Americans Favor Killing Saddam Hussein', *Los Angeles Times,* 29 June 1993; John Diamond, 'At War With Terror; US Missile Attacks Kill at Least 21', *Buffalo News,* 21 August 1998.

58. Martin and Walcott (note 31), p. 312.

59. Ibid.

60. A sufficient condition is defined as 'X is sufficient for Y if the occurrence of X implies the occurrence of Y'. Douglas Dion, 'Evidence and Inference in the Comparative Case Study', *Comparative Politics* 30/2 (1998), p. 128.

61. A full, in-depth case study of the 61 additional anti-US terrorist incidents that met the initial four-factor model yet failed to incite the US to military action was beyond the scope of this research project but a cursory examination of the 61 incidents reveals that none of these incidents also meets every one of the five additional critical conditions. If the results of this cursory examination hold true under an in-depth study they would add credence to the criticality of the five additional conditions. More research into this area will help improve the decisional model.

62. Table sources: US Department of State's *Patterns of Global Terrorism* annual series, 1983–98; and the US Department of Defense's *Terrorist Group Profiles* (Washington, DC: GPO 1988), an outgrowth of then-Vice President Bush's Task Force on Combating Terrorism. Despite the availability of various databases that record international terrorism statistics, only the *Terrorist Group Profiles* publication and the *Patterns of Global Terrorism* series were used as sources. Employing these US government-published documents gave uniformity to the data, as there is an active debate regarding what is and is not an act of terrorism. Since this article attempts to account for the disparity in the US government's decision to initiate overt military action in response to terrorism crises, it was important to use data the US government considers to be anti-US international terrorist incidents.

63. This author notes that while the data used for this article is restricted to the years 1983–98, some of the terrorist groups under examination came into existence and had conducted terrorist attacks prior to 1983. Accordingly, an incident that may appear to be the first or second executed by a group in the timeframe noted actually may be the fourth or fifth. The author acknowledges this anomaly presented by the restricted scope of the research and concedes it presents a methodological inconsistency but contends it does not negate either the overall methodology or the conclusions of this article.

64. See note 7.

Chapter 9

Organizing to Fight Terrorism

The effort of building the proper organization for fighting terrorism entails potential reform on many fronts: reform of government's structure, of national security capabilities, of intelligence practices, and the policy-making process.

Ashton B. Carter delves into the challenges the threat of catastrophic terrorism impose on the U.S. government, and he explores, as he says, "... the need to reengineer the architecture of governance—security institutions and their modes of operation—when war-scale damage results from terrorism." The author explores the history of approaches different administrations have taken to homeland security and concludes that, "Merely coordinating the existing capabilities of the United States to counter catastrophic terrorism is not adequate to protect the nation or the international order from this major new challenge...." Carter advocates for the invention of a new system: a White House-appointed "architect" who will oversee program coordination amongst different agencies. The author maps out a matrix for a multiyear, multiagency program of invention and investment that would be embedded into the president's budget submissions to Congress and supported by appropriate law and regulation.

According to Russell D. Howard, the National Security Act of 1947 "was adequate for a bipolar, state-centric, balance-of-power world, in which the Soviet Union was the enemy and interstate conflict the main threat." But the 1947 Act was created before such incidents as the Oklahoma City bombing and the bombing of the World Trade Center. Now, Howard says, our principal enemies became "failed, failing, and rogue states and transnational actors" and our principal threats are "ethnic and religious conflict, international and domestic terrorism, drugs, and the proliferation of weapons of mass destruction." Howard reviews the threat of weapons of mass destruction and the current U.S. capabilities for a response; he surveys the capabilities of Israel, the United Kingdom, and Canada as models the United States should explore. Interestingly, though his article was written before 9/11, Howard strongly advocates a Homeland Security Command and the use of preemption as a means to fight terrorism. He concludes that the National Security Act needs to be changed to reflect national security requirements in the post–cold war world and offers recommendations. "Neither complacency nor hysteria is called for," concludes Howard. Our intelligence capabilities, however, must be greatly improved and countermeasures such as prevention and preemption must be stressed if America is to avoid future terrorist attacks.

Richard K. Betts explores prospects for reform in the intelligence community. September 11 brought on an immediate backlash—that the biggest intelligence system in the world could not prevent a group of fanatics from carrying out their devastating attacks, and the nation's intelligence services needed to be fixed. Betts delves into the matter more deeply. As he says, "The awful truth is that even the best intelligence systems will have big failures. The terrorists that intelligence must uncover and track are not inert objects; they are living, conniving strategists." He continues that to have a batting average of less than 1,000 seems terrible indeed, but a less-than-perfect average is the reality. The author looks at areas for change: more spending, stronger human intelligence, intelligence gathering on U.S. soil where the process comes under U.S. laws that protect civil liberties. And he delves into the history of intelligence—touching on the surprise attacks at Pearl Harbor—and uncovers a depressing historical pattern. He does not refute that the right reforms can better the nation's batting average, but he presents the reality and cautions that, "Reform will happen, and, on balance, should help. But for too many policymakers and pundits, reorganization is an alluring but illusory quick fix."

Martha Crenshaw explores how American counterterrorism policy is formed and points out that these policies are not simply a response to the threat of terrorism: they are a reflection of the domestic political process. The author introduces the different actors involved: the executive branch; Congress; and entities outside the government, such as interest groups and communities of "experts," business interests, victims and victims' families, and the media. The history of specific policy decisions is presented as an illustration of the complexity of the policy-forming process among actors with competing interests and diffuse authority. The author concludes that it is unlikely the process will change—and unlikely that counterterrorism policy will be based solely on an objective appraisal of the threat of terrorism without being filtered through the political lens.

The Architecture of Government in the Face of Terrorism

Ashton B. Carter is Ford Foundation Professor of Science and International Affairs and codirector, with former secretary of defense William J. Perry, of the Harvard-Stanford Preventive Defense Project. From 1993 to 1996, he served as assistant secretary of defense for international security policy and was twice awarded the Department of Defense Distinguished Service Medal. Before his government service, Carter was director of the Belfer Center for Science and International Affairs at the Kennedy School.

On September 11, 2001, the post–Cold War security bubble finally burst. In the preceding ten years, the United States and its major allies failed to identify and invest in the prevention of "A-list" security problems that could affect their way of life, position in the world, and very survival. Instead they behaved as if gulled into a belief that the key security problems of the post–Cold War era were ethnic and other internal conflicts in Bosnia, Somalia, Rwanda, Haiti, East Timor, and Kosovo. Peacekeeping and peace-making in these places, although engaging important humanitarian concerns, never addressed the vital security interests of the United States, and none of these conflicts could begin to threaten its survival. As if to confirm this point, the official military strategy of the United States during the last decade centered not on peacekeeping but on the challenge of fighting two Desert Storm reruns, one in Korea and one in the Persian Gulf, at the same time. The two-major-theater-war doctrine at least had the virtue of addressing threats to vital U.S. allies and interests. But as the decade wore on, it was increasingly apparent that although important interests were at stake in both major theaters, in neither was U.S. survival in question. The A-list seemed empty, so policy and strategy focused on B- and C-level problems instead.[1]

A-list threats, such as the threat posed by the Soviet Union for the preceding half-century—were indeed absent, but only if threat is understood as the imminent possibility of attack defined in traditional military terms. If taken instead to denote looming problems that could develop into Cold War–scale dangers, the A-list contained at least four major underattended items in the 1990s: (1) the collapse of Moscow's power, (2) the growth of Beijing's military and economic might, (3) proliferation of weapons of mass destruction, and (4) the prospect of catastrophic terrorism. Upon taking office, George W. Bush and his administration claimed to be formulating their strategy around the first two of these items, in a self-proclaimed return to big power realism. But in the wake of the World Trade Center and Pentagon attacks of September 11, the Bush administration is instead finding its agenda dominated by catastrophic terrorism, for which it appears no more or less prepared than its predecessor Bush, Sr., and Clinton administrations.

The challenge of catastrophic terrorism is destined to be a centerpiece of the field of international security studies, and thus of the readers and writers of the pages of this [selection], for the foreseeable future. Today the focus is a particular nest of Islamic extremists operating freely from the lawless failed state of Afghanistan. But the last time that a building in the United States was destroyed in a terrorist attack, the Alfred P. Murrah Federal Building in Oklahoma City in April 1995, the perpetrator was homegrown, an embittered American nihilist operating in the vast anonymity of modern society. One month earlier, an obscure cult in Japan put sarin nerve gas in a Tokyo subway and attempted an airborne anthrax release. Indeed the varieties of extremism that can spawn catastrophic terrorism seem limitless, and they have not been studied as thoroughly by social scientists as have the dynamics of great power rivalry. What is clear is that war-scale destructive power is becoming increasingly available as technology advances. The same advances heighten the complexity and interconnectedness of civilization, making society more vulnerable at the same time it delivers to small groups destructive powers that were formerly the monopoly of states. Thus if security is understood to be the avoidance and control of mass threat, catastrophic terrorism must occupy a central place in security studies, a status that "ordinary" non-mass terrorism never achieved.[2]

The resulting agenda of analysis and policy development is wide. First, the motivations and root causes of catastrophic terrorism—inscrutable as they may now seem—must eventually yield at least in part to careful study.[3] Second, the potential of catastrophic terrorism to transform traditional international relations should also be studied and its policy consequences propounded, as the great powers—the United States, Europe, Japan, Russia, and China—set aside some of the lesser issues that divide them and acknowledge a great common interest in protecting their homelands.[4] This article concerns a third dimension of policy: the need to reengineer the architecture of governance—security institutions and their modes of operation—when war-scale damage results from terrorism.[5]

The Governance Issue

Post–Cold War complacency was only one reason that the United States found itself so surprised by, and so unprepared for, the onset of catastrophic terrorism and the mission of homeland security. A deeper reason is that the security institutions of the U.S. federal government are particularly ill-suited to deliver homeland security. Greater awareness of the threat since September 11 alone will not rectify this problem. There is a fundamental managerial inadequacy, as basic as that of a corporation with no line manager to oversee the making of its leading product.

Pundits have been debating whether the campaign to prevent catastrophic terrorism is a "war" or not. If one sets aside semantics and asks the practical managerial question, Can U.S. preparations for war be easily adapted to preparation for catastrophic terrorism? the answer is no. Preparations for war in the military, diplomatic, and intelligence senses are the province of institutions—the Departments of Defense and State, and the intelligence community—whose focus and missions have been "over there" in the fields of Flanders, the beaches of Normandy, the jungles of Vietnam, and the desert of Kuwait. Their opponents have been foreign governments, and even against them they have not been asked to defend the U.S. homeland in recent history except through the abstraction of nuclear deterrence.

If catastrophic terrorism cannot really be treated as a war, then perhaps it should be conceived as a crime. But the U.S. law enforcement paradigm is also ill-suited to deal with catastrophic terrorism. This paradigm centers on the post facto attribution of crimes to their perpetrators and to prosecution under the law. So deeply entrenched is this model that four weeks after the September 11 attacks, the attorney general had to prod the Federal Bureau of Investigation publicly to shift its efforts from "solving the case" to preventing another disaster.[6] Additionally, if the focus of the war model is foreign perpetrators, the focus of the law enforcement model is the American citizen. Neither model encompasses the transnational drifter that is characteristic of the al-Qaeda operative.

Early in the Bush administration, the new director of the Federal Emergency Management Agency (FEMA) asserted that catastrophic terrorism was not a war or a crime, but a disaster, and thus the province of his agency, even obtaining a presidential directive to that effect.[7] In so doing, he reversed the previous FEMA management, which regarded catastrophic terrorism as a new mission with no funding and thus to be avoided. But even armed with a presidential directive, FEMA seemed unable to convince anyone that acts of God and acts of terror were similar enough that a managerial solution was to be found in combining them.

Thus the federal government lacked a managerial category for catastrophic terrorism, which is neither war, crime, nor disaster, as conventionally understood. Preparations for mass terrorism therefore proceeded haltingly in the 1990s. Some progress was made when preparedness was tied to specific events, such as the 1996 Atlanta Olympics.[8] But elsewhere the preparations were more the result of these efforts of a few well-placed individuals—in the Departments of Defense, Justice, and Health and Human Services—who had become concerned about the problem, than of any overall managerial scheme. As the decade wore on, money did begin to flow to such programs as training state and local governments in weapons of mass destruction.[9] But these efforts were largely the result of congressional initiative and inevitably reflected constituent interests. They did not lead to the development of a program to build a national capability for combating catastrophic terrorism.

Outside the federal bureaucracy, even less was done. State and local governments, key to both prevention and response to this new threat, generally lacked the resources and specialized knowledge to combat catastrophic terrorism. The role of the private sector—for example, in protecting critical infrastructures such as communications and power networks from disruption or in funding protection through insurance—remained undefined.

Before September 11, 2001, therefore, the U.S. government did not have a managerial approach (i.e., a framework for bringing responsibility, accountability, and resources together in sharp focus) to deliver a key public good—security in the homeland against catastrophic terrorism. This managerial deficiency was not unique to catastrophic terrorism. The post–Cold War world spawned a host of novel security missions for government: peacekeeping and post-peacekeeping civil reconstruction, counterproliferation, threat reduction, information warfare, and conflict prevention (or "preventive defense"). Although it is widely agreed that the United States needs to be able to accomplish these missions (even if debate continues over exactly when and where it should perform them), no fundamental changes have been made in the security architecture to create better institutions and capabilities for them.

Indeed, at least on paper the federal structure has changed little since the first burst of innovation in the aftermath of World War II and the onset of these Cold War. No comparable burst occurred in the 1990s. It is as though corporate America was managing the modern economy with the structures of the Ford Motor Company, the Bell System, and United Fruit. Company managements spend a great deal of thought and energy on organizing their functions to align executive authority with key products. The federal government disperses executive authority so thoroughly that few individuals believe they are accountable for any of the government's key security outputs. People rise to the top of the Washington heap because of their policy expertise, not their managerial expertise. Those senior executives who are managerially inclined find their tenures so short and precarious that there seems to be little reward in making changes in "the system" that will make it possible for their successor's successor to be more effective.[10]

Above all, the federal government in the past few decades has eschewed creating new institutions for new missions such as preparedness for catastrophic terrorism. The political climate in the United States has been hostile to "big government," and existing cabinet departments staunchly defend their heritages and authorities, many of which are enshrined in two hundred years of statute. The sense of departmental entrenchment is mirrored on Capitol Hill, where separate authorization and oversight committees protect each "stovepipe"—national security, law enforcement, disaster relief, public health, and so on—as jealously as the executive agencies themselves.

It is not surprising, therefore, that the specter of catastrophic terrorism occasions deep reflections on the nature and structure of governance in the United States. What needs to be done next cannot be understood without reference to these problems, and to past attempts to overcome them.

Four Failed Approaches

In broad outline, four approaches to managing the mission of homeland security have been proposed: the command and control approach of the Clinton administration, the lead agency approach, the establishment of a Department of Homeland Security, and the appointment of a White House coordinator or "czar." To date, the Bush administration appears to be focusing on the last, which like the other three has inherent deficiencies.

The Clinton administration defined its approach in command and control terms: Which federal agency should be in charge of dealing with catastrophic terrorism? Initially, the administration determined that the Department of Justice would "have the lead" in domestic terrorist incidents, while the Department of State would do so in incidents abroad. This approach both reinforced the false distinction between domestic and foreign terrorism and focused on acts in progress rather than on advance detection, prevention, and protection. Later, the Clinton administration promulgated two presidential directives, PDD-62 and PDD-63, which further apportioned the matter of "who's in charge" among the existing agencies according to their traditional functions.[11] Thus, for example, PDD-63 assigned protection of the financial system to the Treasury Department. The fact that this department had no funds, no technology, and little authority to regulate in the field of cybersecurity did not deter the authors of PDD-63. In fact, by focusing on the question of who is in charge, the command and control approach presumed that the government possessed the capabilities to combat catastrophic terrorism;

all that was required was to marshal them effectively under a clear command system. The result was the creation of a host of unfunded mandates, responsibilities assigned with no plan for providing the means to fulfill them. The administration made no provision to build new capability, which was—and remains—the crux of the matter.

A second approach considered was to designate a single lead agency as having the homeland defense mission. In this approach, the proposed lead was usually the Department of Defense. DoD was presumed to have already much relevant technology, an ample budget, and a reputation for carrying out its mission more effectively than most other government agencies.[12] But this approach failed because too much of the relevant capability—for example, for surveillance of potential terrorists on U.S. territory—fell beyond DoD's traditional purview. The Pentagon shared the disinclination to arrogate such sweeping new authorities to itself and proclaimed itself willing to take a strong, but follower, role if another agency would lead the effort.

A third approach called for the creation of a Department of Homeland Security.[13] This approach sought to escape the problem of interagency coordination by concentrating the catastrophic terrorism mission in a single agency. It recognized that none of the existing cabinet departments was a natural lead agency, and that their ingrained cultures would not easily incline them to adopt the new mission. The fallacy in this approach is that interagency coordination could be thus avoided. Suppose, for example, that the Department of Homeland Security sought to develop a more rapid means of determining whether someone was exposed to anthrax. It would soon discover that this effort was redundant with DoD's efforts to develop the same detector technology for battlefield exposure in accordance with its traditional mission. The problem of interagency coordination would not have been eliminated, but only complicated by the introduction of a new agency. Aggregating functions such as customs, immigration, border patrol, and coast guard into a new agency might be efficient, but it can hardly be said that such an entity should have the lead in homeland defense, or that its creation eliminates the inherently interagency nature of catastrophic terrorism.

A fourth approach to organizing the federal government for catastrophic terrorism is to appoint a White House coordinator or "czar." President Bush named Pennsylvania Governor Tom Ridge to such a post within a month of September 11. This approach is the least problematic, because it recognizes that the essence of the solution is the coordination of a wide range of government functions behind a new priority mission. White House czars, however, have usually been ineffective. With no resources or agencies of their own, they are easily reduced to cajoling cabinet departments into doing what the czar prescribes. The czar's instructions inevitably compete with other needs and tasks of the department, and the final outcome of the competition is determined by the cabinet secretary (invoking legal authorities, usually of long standing)and the relevant committees of Congress, not the czar. After the czar is thus overridden a few times, lower-level bureaucrats conclude that the czar's directives can be ignored. As the Washington saying about czars goes, "The barons ignore them, and eventually the peasants kill them."

The Crux of the Managerial Challenge

A solution to the managerial challenge of catastrophic terrorism should have two features that the approaches outlined above lack. First, it should acknowledge the inherent and ineluctable interagency nature of the problem and abandon any idea of creating a single lead agency.[14] Second, the approach should begin the long process of providing the United States with a stock of essential capabilities—tactics, technology, and institutions—that the federal departments, state and local governments, and private sector currently lack. Interagency coordination implies a White House focus. But this focus should not be a "czar" who tries to assume or direct the daily functions of all the agencies involved but an "architect" who designs the capabilities that these agencies need to address the problem. This approach gives the architect budgetary authority (the key to his influence)and applies that influence where it is needed most: to creating needed capabilities rather than stirring up empty command and control disputes over who is in charge of capabilities that are woefully inadequate or do not exist at all. In short, the important function of the White House architect is *program* coordination, not policy coordination or command and control. The program in question is a multiyear, multiagency effort to develop tactics, technology, and where required new institutions for the ongoing struggle against catastrophic terrorism.

Perhaps the most apt analogy for the job required of the White House is provided not by any war that the United States has fought, but rather by the Cold War. In 1949 Josef Stalin's Soviet Union exploded an atomic bomb over the steppes of Kazakhstan. Although no U.S. citizens died in that distant blast, Americans were suddenly gripped by the prospect of warlike damage being visited upon their homeland by a shadowy enemy with global tentacles. George Kennan warned of a long twilight struggle that would test U.S. patience and resolve. The nation mobilized over time a response that was multifaceted, multiagency, and inventive. Nuclear bombers, missiles, and submarines were built for deterrence and retaliation. Spy satellites were launched for warning. Air defenses were deployed around the nation's periphery, and missile defenses were attempted, to raise the price of attack. Civil defense programs sought to minimize casualties if the worst happened. Special relocation sites and procedures were instituted to ensure continuity of constitutional government if Washington was destroyed. NATO and other alliances were formed to get more friends on the U.S. side, and the Marshall Plan sought to ensure that economic desperation did not become an ally of Stalin. U.S. leaders further recognized that this new reality was so dangerous that they needed a capacity to analyze, reflect, and learn, not merely react. They founded such think tanks as the RAND Corporation to devise innovative methods for coping with the era's new danger. In time, ideas such as the theory of deterrence and the theory of arms control were elaborated that were not obvious in 1949 but that helped navigate the world through fifty years of Cold War. With difficulty and many mistakes, the nation also learned to deal with fear of a threat at home without hunting "reds" in the State Department and Hollywood. The Cold War effort was massive, extended throughout most of the federal government, and was coordinated by the White House.

Designing a similar long-range program to counter catastrophic terrorism is the task of these Bush White House in the aftermath of September 11, 2001. The National Security Council (NSC)cannot do the job for two reasons. First, it does not normally convene the full range of departments, especially Justice and Health and Human Services, required for this effort. The NSC has largely focused on foreign problems. More fundamental, since Dwight Eisenhower's day the NSC has slowly lost the capacity for program coordination and become a policy coordination body only.[15] That is, it brings the national security agencies together to decide upon a common policy but does not oversee or influence their internal capabilities or budgets. Indeed the NSC's staff is renowned for its diplomatic and policy expertise, but few have experience managing programs or agencies.

President Bush was therefore correct not to give the homeland security job to the NSC, but instead to found the Office of Homeland Security with a broader membership, chaired by Governor Ridge. It is up to Governor Ridge to avoid the fate of White House czars who try to "run things" from the White House. Instead of taking a command and control approach, Ridge should adopt the architect's programmatic approach, designing a multiyear, multiagency plan that will materially increase the capabilities of the existing departments and agencies so that they can play their part in the campaign against catastrophic terrorism. Such an approach would have the additional salutary effect of overriding the tendency, prevalent as the fiscal year 2002 budget was finalized in the aftermath of September 11, for individual agencies and their oversight committees to craft their own response to the counterterror challenge. In many cases, these responses amounted to little more than long-standing budgetary requests to which the label "counterterrorism" was conveniently applied. Elsewhere, multiple agencies vied to make redundant subscale investments where a single large investment by only one of them is needed.

The homeland security program might be organized functionally according to a time line extending from before a hypothetical incident of catastrophic terrorism to its aftermath. In the first phase, the United States needs better capabilities for *detection* of catastrophic terrorism. This involves surveillance of persons and motives—a delicate matter—but also surveillance of potential means of destruction such as crop dusters, germ cultures, and pilot instruction. Surveillance of means raises far fewer civil liberties issues than does surveillance of persons, and it might be much more effective. A group that evades surveillance becomes subject to *prevention* by efforts to keep destructive means out of their hands. The Nunn-Lugar program to safeguard Russian nuclear weapons and fissile materials is an example of a prevention program. The next stage is *protection*, making borders, buildings, airplanes, and critical infrastructures more difficult to breach, disrupt, or destroy through technical design and procedures. Protection might also mean making people more resilient to disease through vaccination and other public health measures. *Interdiction* or "crisis management" seeks to disrupt and destroy potential perpetrators of catastrophic terrorism and their base of support before they can mount an attack, as in the current campaign in Afghanistan. *Containment* or "consequence management" means limiting the level of damage and the number of casualties by organizing emergency response, public health measures, and restoration of critical functions in the aftermath of a terrorist attack. *Attribution* refers to the capability to find the perpetrators of an act (e.g., by typing an anthrax culture or performing radiochemical analysis of nuclear bomb debris) and choosing retaliation, prosecution, or other response. Finally, as with the RAND Corporation in the Cold War, the nation will need a capacity for *analysis and invention*: studying terrorist tactics and devising countermeasures, understanding motivations and modes of deterrence, drawing lessons from past attacks, creating new technologies, and developing a systematic plan.

Schematically, the result of such an effort by the Office of Homeland Security would resemble a simple matrix, in which functions are arrayed in columns and the

Figure 1

Dimensions of a Homeland Security Program:
The Architect's Program Plan

	Detection	Prevention	Protection	Interdiction	Containment	Attribution	Analysis and Invention
Justice/FBI							
Defense							
Intelligence							
Health and Human Services							
Border (Coast Guard, Border Patrol, Customs, Immigration, etc.)							
FEMA							
Other (Energy, Transportation, Agriculture, State, etc.)							
New Federal Agencies or Nonprofit Institutions							
State and Local Government (supported by federal grants)							
Private Sector (via regulation, subsidy, and indemnification)							

agencies involved in carrying them out in rows (see Figure 1). In each box would appear the agency's responsibility, if any, for possessing capability in that function, with a plan to develop that capability over a period of years. The president would approve such a matrix for each fiscal year extending five years into the future, and would send it to the Congress with his annual budget submission. Although Congress would of course have the last word on the budget, experience shows that it makes only marginal adjustments where there is a strong and clear presidential program on a subject of great national importance.

Key Ingredients of the Homeland Security Program

The homeland security program will have many key components. Below are a few illustrative examples.

Red Team, Blue Team

Most Americans were probably not shocked to learn on September 12 that the U.S. government did not have advance information about the dozen or so individuals residing in the country who plotted and took part in the airline suicide attacks of September 11. They probably were deeply disturbed to learn, however, that the government was as heedless of the tactic used as it was of the perpetrators. The airline security system inspected for guns and bombs, not knives; aircrews were trained to deal with hijackers who sought hostages or conveyance to Cuba, not kamikaze attack. In retrospect, a huge gap existed in the U.S. air safety system. Terrorists detected it before the security system did—and exploited it.

To avoid tactical surprise of this kind, the homeland security effort needs to adopt a standard mechanism of military organizations: competing red and blue teams. The red team tries to devise attack tactics, and the blue team tries to design countermeasures. When the United States developed the first stealth aircraft, for example, the air force created a red team to try to detect and shoot them down. When the red team identified a weakness in the stealth design, the blue team was charged to fix it, systematically balancing risk of detection against the cost and inconvenience of countermeasures.

A comparable red/blue team mechanism should be the central feature of the program for homeland security. To work, the mechanism must be systematic and institutionalized, not ad hoc. It must be independent of the interests—airlines, for example—that stand to be inconvenienced by its findings. It must have the money to conduct experiments, tests, and inspections, not just paper studies. It must be knowledgeable about the technologies of terrorism and protection. Above all, it must be inventive. These criteria all argue for a new institutional founding outside of, but close to, government. Models include the National Academies of Sciences, the RAND Corporation, the Mitre and Mitretek Systems Corporations, the Institute for Defense Analyses, and other nonprofit research organizations established during the Cold War.

Science and Technology

American society has many weaknesses in the battle against catastrophic terrorism. It is large and open. Its infrastructures are complex and interconnected. It values free movement, free speech, and privacy. Its commanding international position is a lightning rod for many international grievances. The United States must therefore draw on its key strengths in ensuring homeland security, among which inventiveness, deriving from its huge science and technology base, is probably most important. The U.S. military has long sought to use superior technology to offset opponents' favorable geography, superior numbers, and willingness to suffer casualties.[16] The homeland security effort requires a program of contract research and technology development that should be conducted outside of government, in universities and private companies. The contracting methods should permit small and entrepreneurial commercial companies that are the drivers of new technology, and not just large government contractors, to participate in the effort. Biotechnology companies, which unlike the aerospace and information technology industries have never had strong ties to national security, should be induced to participate.[17] Finally, "centers of excellence" in counterterrorism should be established. These centers should set out to develop the same depth of expertise represented by the Los Alamos, Livermore, and Sandia National Laboratories in the field of nuclear weapons design during the Cold War.

Transnational Intelligence

A number of studies have called attention to the problem of combining information derived from foreign intelligence collection with information derived from domestic law enforcement.[18] The rules governing collection in the two categories differ for the important reason that U.S. persons enjoy protections from surveillance that do not apply to the overseas activities of the intelligence community. There is no reason, however, why information of both types collected by the U.S. government in accordance with the respective rules for each cannot be combined and correlated. The barriers to doing so are largely bureaucratic. These barriers need to be surmounted in an era when individuals move easily across borders, and when groups fomenting terrorism are likely to be transnational in their membership.[19]

Intelligence of Means

Surveillance of the *means* that terrorists employ is potentially more important than surveillance of *persons*, and raises far fewer civil liberties issues. Placing all Middle Eastern male noncitizens resident in the United States under surveillance, for example, is both objectionable and impractical. But inquiring after all those persons, of whatever nationality, who take flying lessons but are not interested in learning to take off or land, who rent crop dusters, or who seek information on the antibiotic resistance of anthrax strains or the layout of a nuclear power plant is feasible and might be extremely useful.

Likewise, it is undesirable to restrict access by citizens to the Capitol building and congressional office buildings, but there is no fundamental technical barrier to seeding these buildings with sensors that would promptly, and with a low rate of false alarms, detect the presence of anthrax on surfaces and in ventilation systems. Nuclear weapons are much harder to detect, but the streets in the vicinity of these White House could be laced with sensitive detectors that would stand a good chance of finding a nuclear weapon or radiological weapon. Although these detectors would individually have a high rate of false alarms, when networked so that their outputs are correlated in space and time, they could comprise an effective warning system. Such a system is preferable to registering truck drivers or other methods of surveilling persons in the White House vicinity.

Control of Weapons and Materials

Ten years into the Nunn-Lugar program to safeguard nuclear, chemical, and biological weapons and materials in the former Soviet Union, a job remains to be completed.[20] In addition to continuing to support and greatly expand this program, the effort must be extended to Pakistan, where an arsenal of substantial size might fall prey to growing extremism.

The Costs of Protection

Protective measures for homeland security cover a wide spectrum of possibilities: vaccines, air defenses around the White House and nuclear power plants, electronic firewalls around information networks, to name just a few examples. The investments required could be enormous. Who will pay? Private investment could be mandated by regulation. Government could bear or subsidize the costs. Or apportionment of risk and blame could be left to the insurance marketplace and tort courtrooms. The answer will vary from case to case, but the federal government needs to devise a strategy. Crafting the right regulation and legislation, as well as putting the right subsidies in the federal budget, will be a key responsibility of the homeland security architect.

National Information Assurance Institute

A major ingredient of the protection effort must be safeguarding the information infrastructure that resides overwhelmingly in private hands. Developing protective tools and techniques, sharing information on threats between government and private network operators, and establishing the proper balance between regulation and government spending to strengthen networks will require a public-private partnership. These objectives could be accomplished through a nonprofit institution dedicated to this purpose and funded jointly by government and participating private network operators. Several such institutions have already been proposed.[21]

Interdiction

Soon after September 11, President Bush enunciated a principle of U.S. policy against catastrophic terrorism that, if pursued to its logical conclusion, would establish interdiction as an ongoing effort rather than an episodic response to actual attacks. In his first major public pronouncement following the September attacks, the president said, "Either you are with us, or you are with the terrorists."[22] This would seem to imply the need for a continuing program to preempt attack from groups that profess an intention to carry out mass terrorism and to apply pressure, including attack, against those who actively support or harbor them. Taken literally, such a program of interdiction would have profound consequences for U.S. foreign policy, for alliances such as NATO, and for international organizations such as the United Nations.

Public Health Surveillance and Response

Containment of the damage from an incident of mass terrorism requires that the public health and agricultural systems establish capabilities that go well beyond their accustomed mission of protecting against naturally occurring dangers. The powers of the public health authorities to mandate disease surveillance and impose such remedies as quarantine are broad, a holdover from the nineteenth century. These authorities need to be updated to encompass man-made pandemics. The private health care system overall, which under the doctrine of managed care is designed to have the least possible excess capacity during normal times, will need to provide such surge capability as extra hospital beds and stockpiled medications carefully chosen and sized for possible bioterrorism.

State and Local First Response

The Nunn-Lugar-Domenici legislation, passed in 1996, began providing state and local first responders with the equipment and training needed to enhance their vital role in consequence management.[23] Defining the ongoing federal role in supporting state and local government is a major task of the counterterrorism program.

Forensics for Attribution

Ever since the U.S. Air Force sampled the first residue from the Soviet Union's nuclear weapons testing in the 1950s and deduced their detailed design, radiochemical analysis of bomb materials and debris has developed into a sophisticated science. A corresponding effort to type bioterror agents and their chemical preparations is required to attribute attacks to their perpetrators. At this time the FBI, DoD, and the Centers for Disease Control and Prevention all have forensic programs, but none is adequate for counterterror purposes. The counterterror program architect will need to decide which of these programs will be funded to provide the greatly expanded capability the nation needs.

Mobilization and Sunset

Until the mid-twentieth century, successful prosecution of war depended on the ability to mobilize nations and armies. A similar concept is useful in the war on terrorism. In the face of reasonably credible and specific information about actual or imminent mass terrorism, extraordinary measures might be advisable that are undesirable when there are no such warnings. In an emergency, the government will assume special authorities, restrict movement and other freedoms, and impose economic disruptions as the nation hunkers down. It is important to the quality of civil society in the long run that this mobilized state be clearly distinguished in statute and procedures from "normal" times when catastrophic terrorism is an ever-present, but not specifically anticipated, contingency. Experience in the United Kingdom during its century-long struggle against Irish terrorism suggests that even in liberal democracies, powers granted to the government in the name of imminent terrorism are seldom rescinded when the threat recedes.[24] It is therefore important to write into any statute or regulation conferring extraordinary powers on the government a sunset clause describing the time and method of demobilization, placing the burden for extending the mobilization squarely on the government's ability to produce credible and specific information of imminent threat.

Conclusion

Merely coordinating the existing capabilities of the United States to counter catastrophic terrorism is not adequate to protect the nation or the international order from this major new challenge, because the existing capabilities fall far short of what is needed. Nor is it practical to imagine having someone in the federal government who is truly in charge of a mission that inherently cuts across all agencies of the federal government, state and local government, and the private sector. What is required instead is a multiyear, multiagency program of invention and investment devised in the White House, embedded in the president's budget submissions and defended by him to Congress, and supported by appropriate law and regulation. This program should cover all phases in the war against catastrophic terrorism—detection, prevention, protection, interdiction, containment, attribution, and analysis and invention. If President Bush's director of homeland security assumes the role of architect of such an effort, he will provide future presidents with the tools they will need to cope with this enduring problem.

Notes

1. This argument and the corresponding A-, B-, and C-lists are derived from Ashton B. Carter and William J. Perry, *Preventive Defense: A New Security Strategy for America* (Washington, D.C.: Brookings, 1999).

2. Studies dealing with catastrophic terrorism include: Richard A. Falkenrath, Robert D. Newman, and Bradley A. Thayer, *America's Achilles' Heel: Nuclear, Biological, and Chemical Terrorism and Covert Attack* (Cambridge, Mass.: MIT Press, 1998); "A False Alarm (This Time): Preventive Defense against Catastrophic Terrorism," in Carter and Perry, *Preventive Defense*, pp. 143–174; Ashton B. Carter, John M. Deutch, and Philip D. Zelikow, "Catastrophic Terrorism: Tackling the New Danger," *Foreign Affairs*, Vol. 77, No. 6 (November/December 1998), pp. 80–94; Robert T. Marsh, John R. Powers, Merritt E. Adams, Richard P. Case, Mary J. Culnan, Peter H. Daly, John C. Davis, Thomas J. Falvey, Brenton C. Green, William J. Harris, David A. Jones, William B. Joyce, David V. Keyes, Stevan D. Mitchell, Joseph J. Moorcones, Irwin M. Pikus, William Paul Rodgers, Jr., Susan V. Simens, Frederick M. Struble, and Nancy J. Wong, *Critical Foundations: Protecting America's Infrastructures: The Report of the President's Commission on Critical Infrastructure Protection* (Washington, D.C., October 1997); The Gilmore Commission, James S. Gilmore III, James Clapper, Jr., L. Paul Bremer, Raymond Downey, George Foresman, William Garrison, Ellen M. Gordon, James Greenleaf, William Jenaway, William Dallas Jones, Paul M. Maniscalco, Ronald S. Neubauer, Kathleen O'Brien, M. Patricia Quinlisk, Patrick Ralston, William Reno, Kenneth Shine, and Ellen Embrey, *First Annual Report to the President and the Congress of the Advisory Panel to Assess Domestic Response Capabilities to Terrorism Involving Weapons of Mass Destruction I: Assessing the Threat* (Washington, D.C., December 15, 1999), http://www.rand.org/nsrd/terrpanel/terror.pdf; The Gilmore Commission, James S. Gilmore III, James Clapper, Jr., L. Paul Bremer, Raymond Downey, Richard A. Falkenrath, George Foresman, William Garrison, Ellen M. Gordon, James Greenleaf, William Jenaway, William Dallas Jones, Paul M. Maniscalco, John O. Marsh, Jr., Kathleen O'Brien, M. Patricia Quinlisk, Patrick Ralston, William Reno, Joseph Samuels, Jr., Kenneth Shine, Hubert Williams, and Ellen Embrey, *Second Annual Report to the President and the Congress of the Advisory Panel to Assess Domestic Response Capabilities to Terrorism Involving Weapons of Mass Destruction II: Toward a National Security for Combating Terrorism* (Washington, D.C., December 15, 2000), http://www.rand.org/nsrd/terrpanel/terror2.pdf; and The National Commission on Terrorism, Ambassador L. Paul Bremer III, Maurice Sonnenberg, Richard K. Betts, Wayne A. Downing, Jane Harman, Fred C. Iklé, Juliette N. Kayyem, John F. Lewis, Jr., Gardner Peckham, and R. James Woolsey, *Countering the Changing Threat of International Terrorism*, report of the National Commission on Terrorism (Washington, D.C., June 5, 2000), http://www.fas.org/irp/threat/commission.html.

3. Jessica Stern, *The Ultimate Terrorists* (Cambridge, Mass.: Harvard University Press, 1999); and Philip B. Heymann, *Terrorism and America: A Commonsense Strategy for a Democratic Society* (Cambridge, Mass.: MIT Press, 1998).

4. See Stephen M. Walt, "Beyond bin Laden: Reshaping U.S. Foreign Policy," *International Security*, Vol. 26, No. 3 (Winter 2001/02)..

5. Ashton B. Carter and William J. Perry with David Aidekman, "Countering Asymmetric Threats," in Carter and John P. White, eds., *Keeping the Edge: Managing Defense for the Future* (Cambridge, Mass.: MIT Press, 2001), pp. 119–126; and The Hart-Rudman Commission, Gary Hart, Warren B. Rudman, Anne Armstrong, Norman R. Augustine, John Dany, John R. Galvin, Leslie H. Gelb, Newt Gingrich, Lee H. Hamilton, Lionel H. Olmer, Donald B. Rice, James Schlesinger, Harry D. Train, and Andrew Young, *Road Map for National Security: Imperative for Change: The Phase III Report of the U.S. Commission on National Security/21st Century* (Washington, D.C., February 15, 2001).

6. Philip Shenon and David Johnston, "F.B.I. Shifts Focus to Try to Avert Any More Attacks," *New York Times*, October 9, 2001.

7. Vernon Loeb, "Cheney to Lead Anti-Terrorism Plan Team: New FEMA Office Will Coordinate Response Efforts of More Than 40 Agencies, Officials Say," *Washington Post*, May 9, 2001, p. A29.

8. Kennedy School of Government case authored by John Buntin, Parts A-C: "Security Preparations for the 1996 Centennial Olympic Games (Part A)," Case No. C16-00-1582.0; "Security Preparations for the 1996 Centennial Olympic Games: Seeking a Structural Fix (Part B)," Case No. C-16-00-1589.0; and "Security Preparations for the 1996 Centennial Olympic Games: The Games Begin (Part C)," Case No. C16-00-1590.0.

9. Defense against Weapons of Mass Destruction Act 1996 (Nunn-Lugar-Domenici), Public Law 104-201 (H.R.3230), September 23, 1996, National Defense Authorization Act for Fiscal Year 1997, 104th Cong., 2d sess., http://www.fas.org/spp/starwars/congress/1996/pl104-201-xiv.htm.

10. Ashton B. Carter, "Keeping the Edge: Managing Defense for the Future," in Carter and White, *Keeping the Edge*, pp. 1–26.

11. Address by President Bill Clinton at the U.S. Naval Academy, May 22, 1998; White House fact sheet, Combating Terrorism, PDD/NSC-62, Protection against Unconventional Threats to the Homeland and Americans Overseas, May 22, 1998, http://www.fas.org/irp/offdocs/pdd-62.htm; and White House fact sheet, PDD/NSC-63, Critical Infrastructure Protection, May 22, 1998, http://www.fas.org/irp/offdocs/pdd/pdd-63.htm.

12. See Joseph S. Nye, Jr., Philip D. Zelikow, and David S. King, eds., *Why People Don't Trust Government* (Cambridge, Mass.: Harvard University Press, 1996), p. 9 and references therein.

13. Hart-Rudman Commission, *Road Map for National Security*.

14. This does not rule out the possibility of creating an agency that combines the functions of such border-related agencies as the Coast Guard, Border Patrol, Immigration and Naturalization Service, and Customs. Accomplishing this bureaucratic feat, however useful, would require the full-time attention of a senior manager with presidential and congressional support. If Governor Ridge were to assume this task, he would have no time for anything else.

15. John Deutch, Arnold Kanter, and Brent Scowcroft with Chris Hornbarger, "Strengthening the National Security Interagency Process," in Carter and White, *Keeping the Edge*, pp. 265–284.

16. William J. Perry, "Desert Storm and Deterrence," *Foreign Affairs*, Vol. 70, No 4. (Fall 1991), pp. 64–82; and Ashton B. Carter with Marcel Lettre and Shane Smith, "Keeping the Technological Edge," in Carter and White, *Keeping the Edge*, pp. 129–163.

17. Joshua Lederberg, ed., *Biological Weapons: Limiting the Threat* (Cambridge, Mass.: MIT Press, 1999), chap. 1.

18. Gilmore Commission, *First and Second Annual Reports to the President and the Congress*; Carter, Deutch, and Zelikow, "Catastrophic Terrorism"; Hart-Rudman Commission, *Road Map for National Security*; and Heymann, *Terrorism and America*.

19. A specific proposal for combining CIA and FBI intelligence on transnational terrorism is contained in "A False Alarm (This Time)," pp. 143–174; and Carter, Deutch, and Zelikow, "Catastrophic Terrorism."

20. See Matthew Bunn, *The Next Wave: Urgently Needed New Steps to Control Warheads and Fissile Material* (Washington, D.C., and Cambridge, Mass.: Carnegie Endowment for International Peace and Harvard Project on Managing the Atom, April 2000); and Howard Baker and Lloyd Cutler, cochairs, *A Report Card on the Department of Energy's Nonproliferation Programs with Russia* (Washington, D.C.: U.S. Department of Energy, Secretary of Energy Advisory Board, January 10, 2001).

21. "A False Alarm (This Time)," pp. 164–165.

22. President George W. Bush, Address to a Joint Session of Congress and the American People, U.S. Capitol, September 20, 2001.

23. Falkenrath, Newman, and Thayer, *America's Achilles' Heel*; and Richard A. Falkenrath, "The Problems of Preparedness: Challenges Facing the U.S. Domestic Preparedness Program," BCSIA Discussion Paper 2000-28, ESDP Discussion Paper 2000-05 (Cambridge, Mass.: Belfer Center for Science and International Affairs and Executive Session on Domestic Preparedness, John F. Kennedy School of Government, Harvard University, December 2000).

24. Laura K. Donohue, "Civil Liberties, Terrorism, and Liberal Democracy: Lessons from the United Kingdom," BCSIA Discussion Paper 2000-05, ESDP Discussion Paper 2000-01 (Cambridge, Mass.: Belfer Center for Science and International Affairs and Executive Session on Domestic Preparedness, John F. Kennedy School of Government, Harvard University, August 2000).

9.2   Russell D. Howard, 2000

The National Security Act of 1947 and Biological and Chemical Weapons
A Mid-Century Mechanism for End-of-Millennium Threats

Colonel Russell D. Howard is professor and head of the Department of Social Sciences at the United States Military Academy at West Point. He is a career Special Forces officer, who has served at every level of unit command in Special Forces, including command of the 1st Special Forces Group from 1994 to 1996.

America's current national security structure is based on the National Security Act of 1947. That legislation was enacted to correct coordination and operations deficiencies observed during World War II and to facilitate efforts to address the emerging Soviet threat. For the most part, as noted by President [Bill] Clinton on the fiftieth anniversary of the Act, it has worked: "The success of their efforts and of the historic legislation enacted half a century ago is reflected in an outstanding record of achievement: nuclear war averted, the Cold War won, and the nations of the world turning to democracy and free markets." Now, however, many question whether the Act and the institutions and treaty regimes it created are equal to the challenges of post–Cold War global security. In these critics' opinion, the 1947 document was adequate for a bipolar, state-centric, balance-of-power world, in which the Soviet Union was the enemy and interstate conflict the main threat, but not for the unipolar, less state-centric, post–Cold War world in which our principal enemies are failed, failing, and rogue states and transnational actors and the principal threats are ethnic and religious conflict, international and domestic terrorism, drugs, and the proliferation of weapons of mass destruction (WMD).

This paper contends that the critics of the National Security Act are right, especially regarding the proliferation and use of two types of weapons of mass destruction—chemical and biological—in the United States. It begins by reviewing the debate over the seriousness of the chemical/biological weapons threat to U.S. security. It considers the limitations of the 1947 Act and discusses how the U.S. is presently organized to address threats from such weapons, arguing that a streamlined organizational structure under unitary command would be more efficient and timely. It examines how the United Kingdom, Canada, and Israel are organized to handle chemical and biological threats to their homelands and suggests that the United States has much to learn from these important allies.

The paper also discusses certain intelligence reforms that may be necessary to help curtail the use of biological and chemical weapons by terrorists and looks at the viability of deterrence and preemption as means of preventing the use of such weapons. Finally, it identifies some limitations of the Posse Comitatus Act, which severely curbs the use of U.S. military forces against domestic acts of chemical and biological terrorism.

Chemical and Biological Weapons in History

The problem of chemical and biological weapons is not entirely new. The use of mustard gas during World War I is well known, but other examples go back much further. "Toxic fumes" were used in India as early as 2000 BC. The first known use of biological warfare was in 1346 at Kaffa (now Fedossia, Ukraine), where the bodies of Tartar soldiers who had succumbed to plague were catapulted over the walls of the besieged city.[1] During World War II the Japanese produced biological weapons and used them in 1942 at Congshan, China—the only confirmed air attack with biological weapons in modern history.[2] A recent book, *The United States and Biological Warfare: Secrets from the Early Cold War and Korea*, charges that after World War II the United States used knowledge acquired by the Japanese to develop a lethal biological arsenal, which was tested in Korea and China during the Korean War.[3] Iran used chemical weapons during the Iran-Iraq War, perhaps even on its own citizens.[4] Iraq's chemical weapons stockpile and suspected production facilities have motivated United Nations inspections and U.S. missile and air strikes for years. The United States believed that the Serbian army had stocks of lethal chemical weapons, which might be used against the Kosovars.[5] The Center for Nonproliferation Studies at the Monterey Institute of International Studies has identified thirty-one states that have or had chemical or biological weapons programs and have catalogued at least forty-six instances of their use.

A Serious Post–Cold War Problem

At present there is a debate among analysts and scholars about the severity of the threat posed by weapons of mass destruction (WMD), especially biological and chemical weapons. The Hart-Rudman Commission argues in a 143-page report that the most serious potential threat to the United States may be unannounced attacks on American cities by terrorist groups using germ warfare.[6] The report predicts that "Americans will likely die on American soil, possibly in large numbers."[7] The growing threat of domestic terrorism is one of the leading themes of this study, which Secretary William R. Cohen has called the most comprehensive effort of its kind since the National Security Act of 1947.[8] Cohen agrees that WMD threats are extreme.

> I believe the proliferation of weapons of mass destruction presents the greatest threat that the world has ever known. We are finding more and more countries that are acquiring technology—not only missile technology—and are developing chemical weapons and biological weapons capabilities to be used in theater and also on a long-range basis. So I think that is perhaps the greatest threat that any of us will face in the coming years.[9]

Others disagree. Milton Leitenberg, a senior fellow at the Center for International and Security Studies at the University of Maryland, considers the Secretary's comments exaggerated and alarmist. According to Leitenberg, no agency of the U.S. government has prepared a threat analysis indicating that the use of chemical and biological agents by terrorists is imminent or even likely. Rather, "various analysts have provided vulnerability projections and scenarios, which are always easy to concoct in the abstract."[10] So far, Ehud Sprinzak points out, the world has not witnessed any mass-casualty event resulting from unconventional terrorists using WMD. "Most of the funds allocated to countering this threat have been committed on the basis of dubious conjecture and unsubstantiated worst-case scenarios."[11] Brian Jenkins notes that of the eight thousand terrorist incidents recorded between 1968 and 1986, fewer than sixty offered any indication that terrorists considered using chemical or biological agents.[12] Nicholas Wade of the *New York Times* argues that biological weapons are too difficult to disperse to be technically feasible for other than the most sophisticated users.[13] Like most other people, terrorists fear powerful contaminants and toxins about which they know little and which they are uncertain how to fabricate and handle, much less deploy and disperse.[14] "Few countries," writes Jessica Stern, "and even fewer terrorist groups, if any, are now capable of launching an open-air attack that would create mass casualties."[15] Brian Jenkins's often-repeated observation—"terrorists want a lot of people watching, not a lot of people dead"—seems to imply that terrorists are unlikely to resort to weapons of mass destruction.[16]

Use of chemical and biological weapons by terrorists has indeed been rare. One recent exception was the Aum Shinrikyo sarin gas attack on the Tokyo subway. Those involved in the 1993 World Trade Center bombing were gathering the ingredients for a chemical weapon that could have killed thousands.[17] There were sixty-eight investigations into the threatened use of chemical, biological, or nuclear materials in the U.S. in 1997, and eighty-six in the first nine months of 1998, but all turned out to be hoaxes.[18] The only significant case of bioterrorism in the United States occurred in Oregon in 1984, when followers of Indian guru Bhagwan Shree Rajneesh, hoping to sway a local election, unleashed a salmonella poisoning attack in ten restaurants, sickening 751 people but killing none.[19]

Nevertheless, though WMD attacks have so far been extremely rare, there are several reasons why this threat must be taken seriously. First, such attacks have the potential to be unprecedentedly devastating—the United States simply must be capable of preventing them or responding swiftly and efficiently if prevention fails. Second, advances in information technology and the increasing availability of ex-Soviet WMD specialists have made the fabrication and use of biological and chemical weapons a less intimidating prospect for terrorists. Third, there are now many terrorists who do not adhere to Brian Jenkins's dictum—they do want to "see a lot of people dead."

Chemical and Biological Weapons— One Horrible, the Other Worse

Chemical and biological agents are not always distinguished in popular discourse, but there are important differences between them. Agents used in biological weapons are "living organisms or infective material derived from them, which are intended to cause disease or death in man, animals and plants, and which depend for their effects on their ability to multiply in the person, animal or plant."[20] Agents used in chemical weapons are gaseous, liquid, or solid chemical substances which cause death in humans, animals, or plants and which depend on direct toxicity for their effect.[21]

Biological weapons are strategic. They are "incredibly powerful and dangerous. They can kill huge numbers of people if they are used properly, and their effects are not limited to one place or a small target."[22] Biological agents are micro-organisms— bacteria or viruses—that invade the body, multiply inside it, and destroy it.[23] They can infect non-human populations as well, upsetting the entire ecosystem. For example, wild rodents living outside a factory in Omutinsk, Russia, became chronically infected with the Schu-4 military strain of tularemia being manufactured there, a bacterium that causes one type of pneumonia. "It was a hot, lethal strain that came from the United States: an American biological weapon that the Soviets had managed to obtain during the nineteen-fifties."[24] Even though rodents are not a natural host of tularemia, Schu-4 spread among the rodents of Omutinsk. People catch tularemia easily from rodents, and it can be fatal.[25]

Biological weapons are more difficult to acquire and manufacture than chemical weapons, but many states and non-state actors can now construct them. "Culturing the required microorganisms, or growing and purifying toxins, is inexpensive and could be accomplished by individuals with college-level training in biology and a basic knowledge of laboratory technique. Acquiring the seed stocks for pathogenic microorganisms is not particularly difficult."[26] One expert estimates that more than twenty countries may now have biological weapons capability.[27]

Chemical weapons are poisons that kill after making contact with the skin. They are tactical instead of strategic; they can be used for mass-casualty attacks in confined areas, but it is almost impossible to concentrate enough chemicals in the air to kill a great many people over a large territory. Because chemicals are not alive, they cannot be spread by infection, like biological weapons. But chemical weapons are easier to fabricate than biological weapons:

> Chemical weapons suitable for mass-casualty attacks can be acquired by virtually any state and by non-state actors with moderate technical skills. Certain very deadly chemical warfare agents can quite literally be manufactured in a kitchen or basement in quantities sufficient for mass-casualty attacks.[28]

In fact, chemical agents are so easy to make that several countries have added them to their weapons inventories. According to unclassified military information, there were eleven countries with chemical weapons in 1980—by 1997 there were twenty-five.[29]

Chemical and biological attacks require different responses. "After a chemical attack, there is a 'golden hour' within which to make a difference. After that hour, those who are going to survive, do, and those who are not, do not. Once decontaminated and removed from the incident site, or 'hot zone,' victims can be dispersed to hospitals."[30] Biological attacks are more difficult to manage.

> The victims must be immediately isolated in order to prevent the agent from spreading. Potential victims need to be isolated from the definitely uncontaminated public; they also should be isolated from others afflicted with the illness until each individual's degree of contamination can be established. But this type of quarantine is currently impossible. Given today's detection capabilities and the incubation period of biological agents, we'll never know that we've been contaminated. Hence the diabolical genius of a biological agent attack: we become the "unknowing vector" of our own death.[31]

New Technology and the Russian Connection

The Internet has been a major factor in providing WMD "how-to" information to would-be terrorists. By accessing any of a number of search engines, one can get the data necessary to build both chemical and biological weapons. There are also a number of self-published manuals available with information on how to grow and distribute biological toxins.[32]

> One of these manuals, *Bacteriological Warfare: A Major Threat to North America*, is described on the Internet as a book for helping readers survive a biological weapons attack. But in fact it also describes the reproduction and growth of biological agents and includes a chapter on "bacteria likely to be used by the terrorist." The book is sold over the Internet for $28.50 and is reportedly advertised on right-wing radio shows.[33]

The availability of material and expertise from the former Soviet Union also makes proliferation more likely. Between 1969, when the United States halted its biological weapons program, and 1992, the Soviet Union developed the largest and most sophisticated biological weapons program in the world. In 1992 Boris Yeltsen wisely declared that biological weapons activities were illegal. But unfortunately his actions also put many people out of work.[34] Now hundreds and perhaps thousands of unemployed Russian biological and chemical specialists are available to the highest bidder. Among the bidders are the United States, the United Kingdom, Iran, Iraq, and Libya.[35]

The New Terrorism

The noted author Walter Laqueur views the "new terrorism" as actually many terrorisms. According to Laqueur, "the past few decades have seen the birth of dozens of aggressive movements espousing varieties of nationalism, religious fundamentalism, fascism, and apocalyptic millenarianism."[36]

> Most international and domestic terrorism today is not ideological (in the sense of left or right) but is ethnic-separatist in inspiration…. In the past, terrorism was almost always the province of groups of militants that had the backing of political forces; in the future, terrorists might be individuals on the pattern of the Unabomber or like-minded people working in very small groups.[37]

According to Secretary of State Madeleine K. Albright, "What's new is the emergence of terrorist coalitions that do not answer fully to any government, that operate across national borders, and that have access to advanced technology."[38] Such groups are not bound by the same constraints or motivated by the same goals as nation-states.[39] And unlike state-sponsored groups, religious extremists, ethnic separatists, and lone unabombers are not susceptible to traditional diplomacy or military deterrence. There is no state with which to negotiate or against which to retaliate.[40]

No longer are most terrorists concerned about limiting casualties. Religious terrorists, in particular, often seek to inflict many casualties. As Bruce Hoffman observes, "the growth of religious terrorism and its emergence in recent years as a driving force behind the increasing lethality of international terrorism shatters some of our most basic assumptions about terrorists and the violence they commit."[41] Incidents like the Tokyo subway attack and the World Trade Center and Oklahoma City bombings appear to render Brian Jenkins's dictum about casualties obsolete. Altogether, the availability of Russians for hire and of critical WMD information on the Internet, coupled with the lethal motives of the "new terrorists," could portend a bloody and destructive era for which the United States is ill prepared.[42]

Overreaction Is Not the Answer

Recognizing the problem is essential but the United States must avoid overreaction. Achieving total security would be impossible and it would be tragic for the world's most powerful democracy to abandon any of its freedoms and principles in a quest for absolute security.[43]

Also, attempting to achieve total security would be extraordinarily expensive. And, as the General Accounting Office (GAO) and others have pointed out, throwing money at it is not the answer. New programs addressing the biological and chemical weapons threat have made counterterrorism one of the fastest-growing parts of the federal budget. Total U.S. spending could exceed $10 billion in 2000, up from $5.7 billion in 1996. A report released in October 1999 by the GAO charges that lawmakers have dumped too much money into this area, and a growing number of government and private counterterrorism experts agree. These experts say "federal officials are so spooked by the possibility of a chemical or biological attack that they are deliberately hyping the threat to get Congress to cough up coveted cash for prevention programs. And most lawmakers are buying it wholesale."[44] In 1997, for example, Congress ordered the Department of Defense [DoD] to conduct multi-agency training exercises in the nation's 120 largest cities against WMD attacks. Today there are more than 200 training courses, run not only by Defense but also by the Energy Department [DOE], the Justice Department, the Central Intelligence Agency [CIA], the Environmental Protection Agency [EPA], and the Federal Emergency Management Agency [FEMA]. Many believe that these programs are redundant, including one over-trained fire-battalion chief who quipped: "Just how many different ways are we going to cook the same chicken?"[45]

Limitations of the National Security Act

The National Security Act of 1947, which created the Department of Defense, the United States Air Force, the Central Intelligence Agency, and the National Security Council, was intended to correct coordination and operations deficiencies observed during World War II and to address the emerging Soviet threat. For the most part, it worked. Some may believe that America's military services have yet to coordinate their operations optimally, but no one can deny that joint operations are exponentially better organized today than during the Second World War. As for the Soviet threat, it—like the Soviet Union—no longer exists. What has replaced it is very much diminished; if Russia did not have nuclear weapons it would probably not be considered a major power. Russia today has the same GDP [gross domestic product] as New Jersey—hardly the basis of a superpower.

The global security environment has changed. No longer does ideology dictate superpower confrontation. No longer do the superpowers and their surrogates compete for the world's allegiance and resources. No longer do realist and idealist theories based on sovereign state behavior and state interaction provide satisfactory frameworks for discussing American and international security. Nowadays failed, failing, and rogue states and transnational actors are our chief security concerns. They are the main sources of the proliferation of WMD, drugs, international and domestic terrorism, transnational crime, ethnic and religious conflict, and other new security threats. The National Security Act was not designed and has not been adapted to address these threats, as events like Somalia, Haiti, Kosovo, East Timor and Oklahoma City attest.

The crucial question is whether the Act and the structure it established can be made to fit the changed national security environment without drastic revision. Some have concluded, like the Center for Strategic and International Studies in Washington DC, that the current structure has sufficient flexibility.[46] General Wesley Clarke, the Supreme Allied Commander Europe, agrees; he sees no need for "big changes" in the Act and believes that it can be adapted to the post–Cold War world.[47]

I disagree. I believe there are two fundamental weaknesses and deficiencies in the National Security Act. First, the Department of Defense is not organized correctly. Second, roles and missions within the intelligence community do not support today's requirements.

Department of Defense

The Department of Defense is still organized to respond to major interstate conflict, much as it was during the Cold War. Then DoD was required to maintain forces for "prompt and sustained combat operations" against the Soviet Union. Though there was always debate about the proper balance of nuclear and conventional capabilities and the most efficient division of resources among the various services, the defining context—security against a Soviet threat—was relatively unambiguous.[48]

Since the fall of the Soviet Union, the basis for determining the roles, missions, and capabilities of the forces within DoD has been difficult to articulate. Several attempts at redefinition—Bush's "Base Force," Clinton's "Bottom-Up Review," and the Congressionally-mandated "Quadrennial Defense Review and National Defense Panel" —have recommended maintaining a less robust status quo. In essence, the United States has chosen a smaller but heavier version of its Cold War forces, but organized, modernized, and equipped with systems and doctrine appropriate for two simultaneous regional conflicts. Yet except for the Gulf War, our military forces have taken on entirely new missions, such as peacekeeping, peace-enforcement, humanitarian assistance, demining, and counter-proliferation and counterterrorism.[49]

The Unified Command Plan (UCP)—related to but not specifically included in the National Security Act—needs to be changed. At present the major regional commands are the European, Pacific, Central (including the Middle East, Persian Gulf, and North Africa), and the Southern (including Central and South America) Commands. The former Atlantic Command is now the Joint Forces Command, which has responsibility for the Atlantic region and additional "joint" responsibilities to the other commands, including training, force integration, and providing trained and ready forces from the United States.[50]

Absent from the Unified Command Plan is a Homeland Defense Command. Protecting the territory of the United States and its citizens from "all enemies both foreign and domestic" is the principal task of government.[51] The Unified Command Plan is externally oriented: it protects our borders from foreign enemies. It is not organized to defend the homeland against internal attack by either foreign or domestic enemies. The reason for a Homeland Defense Command is the change, both in type and degree, in the principal threats to the United States. Besides the continuing requirement to deter strategic nuclear attack, the United States must now also defend itself against information warfare, weapons of mass destruction, terrorist attacks, and other transnational threats to the sovereign territory of the nation.[52] Above all, the security environment has been significantly altered by the proliferation of biological and chemical weapons and their increasing ease of delivery.[53] The complexity of the chemical and biological weapons challenge lies in the huge number of potential enemies who have access to this asymmetric means of attacking the U.S. in an effort to offset America's conventional and nuclear strength.[54]

An integrated set of active and passive measures for deterring and defending against chemical and biological weapons use is required. These measures must involve a range of federal departments and agencies, which, in turn, must incorporate state and local governments in their planning.[55] Managing the consequences of biological and chemical attacks will also involve all levels of government.[56] Obviously the Department of Defense has a significant role to play in these efforts. But what that role should be will be the topic of a later section in this paper.

The Intelligence Community: We Have Slain the Bear, but There Are Still a Lot of Serpents Around[57]

The Intelligence Community (IC) is a group of thirteen Executive Branch agencies and organizations whose core was established by the National Security Act of 1947.[58] Its mission—to provide an information advantage to those who formulate and execute national policy—has not changed since then, though the nature of the information it deals in has changed markedly. "During the Cold War era, the intelligence community justified its existence by containing Soviet expansion."[59] Now, however, new missions must be defined if the intelligence community is to maintain legitimacy and focus. Perceived legitimacy has been a problem, at least for the community at large. Likewise focus: some critics describe the IC as an ad hoc structure in which each agency or organization makes sense individually but which does not function as a well-integrated whole.[60] Even Congress often views the intelligence agencies as ten or thirteen separate voices rather than as a community.[61]

These problems have prompted an extensive revaluation of U.S. intelligence by a number of commissions and panels. All these studies, performed by the government or by government-sponsored commissions, have, according to Morton Halperin, "reached the same conclusion, which is that the intelligence structures that we have are just right."[62] "One can only view this as remarkable," quips Halperin; "here we have a world in which an intelligence community created fifty years ago to fight the Cold War against the Soviet Union turns out to [have] exactly the right set of structures and exactly the right set of functions to deal with this new post–Cold War world."[63] But suppose, he goes on to ask, that the world really is different? Suppose the intelligence community created fifty years ago is not exactly suited to it? What changes might one make?[64]

Detailed answers to all these questions are beyond the scope of this paper. But many others have been thinking about them, especially with regard to chemical and biological weapons. Gary Hart, for one, co-chair of the commission charged with trying to define the future national security environment, writes: "U.S. intelligence will face more challenging adversaries in the future, and non-state actors will probably play a larger role in issues of war and peace than they have heretofore."[65] As Gideon Rose observes, "The intelligence community is now challenged, because the groups that cause the greatest concern—religious fanatics, cults, and freelance extremists—are precisely those that usually fly below the radar screen of standard intelligence collection."[66] Collecting intelligence on biological weapons programs—even state-run programs—is especially difficult. For example, the intelligence community did not know of Aum Shinrikyo's efforts to produce and use biological agents until after the sarin attacks in the Tokyo subway.[67]

Aum Shinrikyo's attack illustrates several problems that chemical and biological weapons present for the intelligence community. Not enough attention is paid to open-source material; international cooperation is lacking; and there is not enough information-sharing even among U.S. intelligence community organizations.

Nearly a year before its attack on the Tokyo subway system the Aum Shinrikyo group had used the nerve gas sarin in assaults on civilians. Although the Japanese media had reported the news, the U.S. government remained in the dark. Not only did Washington not hear what the Japanese law-enforcement agencies knew, but the

>   Japanese agencies themselves were not aware of what other local organizations in
>   Japan had uncovered. The parties involved did not share their expertise to prevent
>   another attack.[68]

To this day, as Ashton Carter, John Deutch, and Philip Zelikow argue, the U.S. intelligence community lacks a site and a methodology for conducting comprehensive planning of information collection. These experts contend that yields from such sources as overhead reconnaissance, electronic surveillance, clandestine agents, law enforcement databases and informants, and reports from foreign governments can be sifted and organized for maximum effect.[69]

Open-source collection, or lack of it, concerns Morton Halperin, who believes that most of the information today's security policymakers need is available without cloak-and-dagger work. "It is available from open sources, it is available from experts who know the societies, and it is available by going to the countries and dealing with the people."[70] U.S. policymakers now rely primarily for their information on an intelligence community in thrall to the notion that the best way to obtain information is to gather it secretly, from an unwitting source.[71] But instead of focusing on recruiting agents in foreign governments and intercepting messages from satellites, perhaps paying attention to the open press, as the intelligence community should have been doing in Japan before the Tokyo subway attack, would be less costly and more productive.

Although neither Halperin, nor Carter, Deutch, and Zelikow directly addresses creating a new intelligence community, they do suggest some changes to the current structure. Halperin believes that a new research organization, called the Foreign Policy Research Organization or the Central Research Organization, should be created and moved out of CIA headquarters to downtown Washington. It should be housed in a building with easy access and staffed with analysts who understand that for most subjects that policymakers care about—not all, obviously, since there will always be some for which more traditional methods of collection are appropriate—most relevant information can be gathered from public sources.[72] Carter, Deutch, and Zelikow believe that a new institution to gather intelligence on catastrophic terrorism (which includes chemical and biological terrorism) needs to be established. It would be called the National Terrorism Intelligence Center and would collect and analyze information in an effort to provide advance warning of catastrophic events. Their center would be located at the FBI instead of the CIA and would have access to domestic law-enforcement data. "The director of the center would come alternately from the FBI and the CIA, and all intelligence organizations would provide a specified number of professionals."[73]

Richard Falkenrath agrees that changes are needed in the intelligence community to address the threat of chemical/biological terrorism, but his suggestions are functional rather than structural.[74] He feels it is important that the IC watch for the likely signatures of small-scale, improvised chemical and biological weapons programs both in the U.S. and abroad. He also emphasizes that public health capabilities need to be improved—particularly epidemiological surveillance—in order to detect medical evidence of chemical and biological weapons production or use.[75]

All these recommendations are important. Intelligence is the first and most crucial line of defense against chemical and biological weapons attacks.[76] Acquiring chemical and biological warfare (CBW)-related intelligence is unusually difficult but not impossible. Would-be terrorists have problems as well as advantages; and conspiracies are relatively easy to defeat if law-enforcement authorities learn of their existence with adequate lead time and in sufficient detail.[77]

Who's In Charge? Who Should Be?

Critics argue that current U.S. efforts to prevent or respond to biological and chemical terrorism are spread across a vast number of agencies, at different levels of government, with little real coordination or direction. "Bureaucratic styles and missions clash; information is compartmentalized and left unanalyzed; some tasks are duplicated, while others slip through the cracks."[78] This is especially true of domestic incidents. Detection capabilities are limited, integrated analytical and planning efforts are proclaimed but not fully worked out, and the use of military forces—the most capable of dealing with biological and chemical weapons—is limited by the Posse Comitatus laws [prohibiting the armed forces from enforcing civil or criminal law within the United States]. It is by no means clear how all the moving parts of a response to such an attack within the United States would actually function in relation to one another.[79]

Although not a response to a biological weapons attack, the reaction to the recent outbreak of a mosquito-borne virus in New York is instructive. New York City and parts of the state suffered an outbreak of what appeared to be an encephalitis virus. What was initially identified as St. Louis encephalitis—often found in the southern United States—turned out to be West Nile virus. Fortunately, West Nile virus is less virulent than the St. Louis variety, but the initial failure to identify the virus correctly has many concerned. "The encephalitis outbreak in New York is a powerful lesson for public health authorities," remarks Alan Zelicoff, a senior scientist at the Center for National Security and Arms Control at Sandia National Laboratories in New Mexico. "It is a sobering…demonstration of the inadequacies of the U.S. detection network for emerging diseases," including viruses.[80] A fact not lost on local and federal officials responsible for national defense against biological warfare is that the myriad local, state, and federal agencies involved in the New York encephalitis investigation did not always communicate well.[81] Initial samples from victims were screened only against six viruses common in the United States, and investigators did not test for viruses that have been linked to germ warfare.[82] We may never know how a West Nile-like virus suddenly appeared in New York City. But we do know that the United States has far to go before it is prepared to identify and deal with outbreaks of exotic diseases, whether they are spread by nature or deliberately by man.

Presidential Decision Directive 39 (PDD-39) decrees how the United States should be organized to deal with the use of weapons of mass destruction by terrorists. PDD-39 divides the threat, both at home and abroad, into two categories: crisis response and consequence management.[83] "Crisis response refers to instances where the perpetrators of an assault have been discovered before an actual release."[84] Consequence management refers to ways and means of reducing the short-term and long-term effects of an attack.

The Department of State is the lead agency for crisis response and consequence management overseas. State carries out crisis response through its Office of Counterterrorism and consequence management through its Office of Foreign Disaster Assistance.

The Department of Defense supports overseas counterterror operations, including those involving chemical and biological weapons. Walter Slocombe, Undersecretary of Defense for Policy, recently revealed that there are designated Special Mission Units (SMUs) specifically manned, equipped and "trained to deal with a wide variety of transnational threats." According to *Jane's Defense Weekly*, the tactics, techniques, procedures, equipment and personnel of these SMUs remain classified, though it is understood that they have counterterrorism and counter-proliferation responsibilities.[85]

Domestically, the Department of Justice is the lead agency, with the Federal Bureau of Investigation (FBI) responsible for crisis management and the Federal Emergency Management Agency (FEMA) for consequence management. Although the Department of Defense has the largest capability for chemical and biological defense, the main responsibility for dealing with attacks falls on multiple federal, state, and municipal agencies and on the civilian health community. "Most of these organizations are inadequately prepared to deal effectively with the problem."[86]

The assignment of domestic responsibilities under PDD-39 is a matter of debate among policymakers and academics, in two respects. First, there is disagreement about the separation of crisis and consequence management. Next, there is disagreement about who should be in charge.

Although PDD-39 has been an important catalyst for developing anti-CBW strategies, the categorical distinction it draws between preventing and dealing with the consequences of an attack is dangerously flawed.[87] "Given the varied dimensions and manifestations of chemical and biological terrorism," writes Chris Seiple, "the battle of consequence management has been lost if there has not been consultation and planning well before any threat of an incident emerges."[88]

> We must therefore think of crisis response and consequence management as parallel and overlapping continuums that both federal lead agencies and the first responder must keep constantly in view.... Arbitrary distinctions between activities before and after an attack by WMD cannot be extended into planning and operational activities. Should we allow those two continuous and overlapping processes to be compartmentalized—and thus expressed in a simple linear logic because they are considered mutually exclusive—we will fail in our response and thus invite future attacks.[89]

PDD-39 notwithstanding, there is no fine line during or after an attack that allows for a clean transfer of responsibility between the FBI and FEMA.[90] Almost inevitably there will be a "who's in charge" or unity-of-effort problem. This structural confusion is compounded by the FBI's overriding commitment to collecting criminal evidence. The FBI's philosophy is: if you can't prove who did it, the likelihood of future incidents will increase.[91] This is a useful approach to bank robbery or kidnapping, but not necessarily to chemical or biological weapons. The effectiveness of consequence management depends on the quick collection of samples to determine the nature of the agent used and the level of contamination. Solving a crime also depends on collecting samples, but for evidentiary purposes. There is thus, at least in theory, a potential conflict between casualty reduction and criminal investigation.[92] In practice, in order to ensure that there is one overall Lead Federal Agency (LFA), PDD-39 directs FEMA to support the Department of Justice (i.e., the FBI) until the Attorney General transfers the overall LFA role to FEMA.[93]

Presently, FEMA is the right agency for consequence management. Many of the coordination-and-control procedures that FEMA has developed over the years in the course of disaster relief efforts are appropriate for its WMD role. The same cannot be said for the FBI. As many experts have pointed out, biological and chemical weapons are simply not a specialty of the FBI. And where the potential for catastrophic terrorism is concerned, the FBI's reactive law-enforcement approach needs to be supplemented by—perhaps even subordinated to—a more aggressive national security effort directed by the White House and the Pentagon.[94] Carter, Deutch, and Zelikow propose that if a large-scale attack biological or chemical attack is imminent, the PDD-39 structure be pushed aside. They believe that the White House should immediately take charge. Unity of command would be vital, with an operational command structure able to "direct everything from CIA covert operations to air strikes; set up interdiction on ground, at sea, and in air; mobilize thousands of soldiers; and move thousands of tons of freight."[95]

> None of these actions can happen quickly unless plans have already been drawn up and units designated to carry them out, with repeated training and exercises that create the readiness to bring the plans to life. In this situation, the Defense Department would take the leading role. The FBI neither commands the resources nor plans to command them.[96]

In my opinion, Carter and his colleagues are correct. Because it has long prepared to face the grim possibility of chemical and biological weapons on the battlefield, and because it has experience in commanding and controlling large, multifaceted operations, the military has unique capabilities to offer in the domestic-security arena.[97] Currently, participation by the Department of Defense and the U.S. military as lead agencies in a domestic attack is problematic. For one thing, there are legal constraints preventing the Department of Defense from taking such a role. For another, the Department of Defense does not want the job.

The American military is constrained in conducting domestic military operations by the Posse Comitatus Act, which prohibits the Army and Air Force from enforcing civil or criminal law within the United States.[98]

> This historic law, passed in 1878 to preclude the presence of soldiers from deterring voters during Reconstruction, is generally considered a great bulwark in our democratic society. Its proponents cite Posse Comitatus as a clear demonstrable indicator of the properly circumscribed limits of a civilian-controlled army in a representative democracy.[99]

In discrete instances, when the President of the United States believes public order and domestic tranquility are at risk, the President can order the Secretary of Defense to restore public order. "This presidential authority to use federal troops is plenary and not subject to judicial review."[100]

Even though the President has the authority to use federal troops under certain circumstances, instances of such use have been rare. Posse Comitatus remains a "giant bulwark" against Defense Department participation in domestic operations. This is well understood in the Pentagon, as Secretary Cohen has made clear:

> As in the past, any military support [in the wake of a domestic attack] must be just that—support. Both legal and practical considerations demand it. The Posse

Comitatus Act and the Defense Department's implementing policies are clear—the military is not to conduct domestic law enforcement without explicit statutory authority, and we strongly believe no changes should be made to Posse Comitatus.[101]

The Department of Defense has repeatedly affirmed that all military assistance for either crisis response or consequence management will be in support of the Department of Justice (FBI) or the Federal Emergency Management Agency.[102] DoD has recently established a Joint Task Force-Civil Support (JTF-CS) to coordinate military support to the lead agencies and to other state and local authorities.[103] The emphasis is on support and there are no plans for the JTF-CS to take a leadership role in crisis management or response. Its mission is to support designated LFAs with a standing joint organization providing DoD's consequence management capability in response to domestic biological and chemical incidents.[104] According to some reports, however, differences have surfaced over which agency is best prepared for rapid response.

Less than a year after the U.S. Department of Defense created rapid response units to respond to weapons of mass destruction attacks in the U.S., their role has become the subject of debate between federal agencies. DoD officials, backed by the Clinton administration and Congress, insist that only specialized military teams have the training and resources to adequately respond to a catastrophic... biological or chemical attack in the U.S.[105]

DoD contends that specially trained Army National Guard Rapid Assessment and Initial Detection (RAID) teams and the Marine Chemical/Biological Response Force (CBIRF) are best prepared to respond to large-scale disasters, and it has recently expanded the number of RAID teams. On May 22, 1998, Secretary Cohen announced the initial plan: ten regional RAID teams composed of twenty-two highly skilled full-time National Guard personnel.[106] On June 2, 1999, the Clinton Administration requested five more teams, and the Senate Armed Services Committee has requested an additional seventeen, so that as many as twenty-seven RAID units could be dispersed throughout the country.[107]

FEMA and FBI officials contend that the more than 600 hazardous material (HAZMAT) organizations throughout the nation could handle detection and decontamination better than their RAID counterparts. Since there are more of them, it is argued, they could usually respond quicker, and they have more experience cleaning up hazardous material. DoD and Congressional officials counter that civilian HAZMAT squads usually respond to industrial accidents and have little if any experience with the chemical and biological agents that RAID teams are trained to deal with.[108]

The General Accounting Office agrees with the FBI and FEMA and in a recent report asked Congress to consider abolishing the RAID units. According to the GAO, because RAID teams do not have dedicated airlift they probably could not get to the site fast enough to help local responders.[109] In a chemical incident, for example, the first hour or two are critical, but RAID teams cannot guarantee a response time of less than four hours.[110] In the event of a biological weapons attack, the usefulness of the RAID teams is even more questionable, critics say. "Because germ agents such as anthrax or smallpox can be released inconspicuously, there is little likelihood of knowing an attack has occurred until hours or even days later, when sick people start showing up at hospitals or doctors' offices."[111]

Pentagon officials call the teams the "tip of the military spear" that would help civilian agencies tap into other military assets. "The idea is that the RAID teams would help local and state first responders—primarily firefighters, HAZMAT teams and ambulance crews—identify chemical or biological substances used in a terrorist incident and then, if necessary, plug them into the military's pool of weapons and logistics experts."[112] The GAO replies that state and local officials do not agree that RAID teams are needed but instead believe they represent "an unnecessary duplication of assets."[113] "Officials from larger jurisdictions usually have very robust HAZMAT capabilities. These officials consider themselves very experienced in managing HAZMAT emergencies and did not believe the RAID team could suggest anything they did not already practice every day."[114]

Taking sides in this GAO-Pentagon debate is not the purpose of this paper. It is, however, worth noting that the debate is indicative of problems associated with the "mind-numbing array of government agencies—sixty-one in the federal government alone, according to the Center for Nonproliferation Studies—that play some kind of role in domestic defense."[115] Add to these the hundreds of state, county, and municipal public safety organizations throughout the U.S. that could claim some type of jurisdiction in the event of a terrorist attack, and the extreme complexity of response coordination becomes obvious.

Other nations faced with similar threats have more streamlined response mechanisms. A look at how three of them—Israel, the United Kingdom, and Canada—are organized to address chemical and biological terrorism may be useful.

The Israeli Model

Many Middle Eastern countries are now capable of delivering chemical and biological weapons. Operation Desert Storm demonstrated the threat to Israel in this regard. In 1992, under the leadership of Major General Zeev Livne, the Home Front Command was established with three major responsibilities: to prepare civil defense forces for emergencies; to create a central command for all military and emergency forces; and to serve as the primary military and professional authority for civil defense.[116]

Along with overseeing civil defense, rescue and salvage, and domestic security, the Home Front Command also helps civilian authorities maintain equipment and protective gear at service centers throughout the country, staffs an around-the-clock information center to answer civilian queries, and is responsible for developing means of passive protection. For example, in cooperation with the United States, the Command conducts demolition tests to determine the ability of certain materials and structures to withstand attack. All new homes in Israel must now have a "safety zone" that can withstand all but a direct hit from a missile.[117]

To assist the population in preparing for emergencies, an instructional and information division serves in peacetime as well as wartime. Schools and other institutions receive training from special instructors. The Home Front Command has installed some of the world's most advanced control, communication, and electronic-warning systems throughout Israel, monitored by a national control center capable of broadcasting real-time messages to the entire population. The Command's forces are of four kinds: rescue and salvage troops, medical support personnel, fire-fighting personnel, and anti-nuclear,

-biological, and -chemical (NBC) units. Rescue and salvage units are the Command's primary forces, employing a wide range of equipment to locate victims and deal with casualties. A national rescue and salvage unit is on constant alert for both domestic and international rescue missions, and some of these units have recently served with distinction in Turkey and Greece.[118]

In an emergency, the Home Front Command can merge military and civilian fire-fighting and medical units. Medical services, including ambulances, medical corps personnel, and hospitals, hold frequent exercises. Anti-NBC units, including detection and identification teams, are prepared to handle all aspects of response, from identifying substances to decontaminating affected areas. The National Hazardous Materials Information Center operates within the Home Front Command in cooperation with the Ministry of the Environment, providing updated information and online risk assessment for troops in the field. The Center operates around the clock, in peacetime as well as wartime.[119]

Military guards, drawn partly from the army's combat units, are another level in the Command's hierarchy. They are constantly engaged in maintaining security along Israel's border and shoreline and in protecting vital infrastructure. Ninety-seven percent of those serving in the Home Front Command are in the reserve forces. Nevertheless, the Command has equal stature with the three other Front Commands, which are made up of active and reserve forces and have border area responsibilities.[120]

Israel's volatile geopolitical situation—along with the advances in missile technology available to its neighbors—has rendered the country exceptionally vulnerable and necessitates a non-traditional organization like the Home Front Command. During the state of alert in December 1998, the Command established sixty-seven gas mask distribution centers throughout the country, which remained open twenty-four hours a day and could even have supplied tourists if necessary. Hospitals were prepared to deal with chemical and biological casualties. Decontamination stations were equipped and staffed.[121] A robust exercise program, not limited to military and public-safety organizations, helps the society prepare for contingencies: for example, an exercise last April named "Netanya '99," which put one of Netanya's high schools through a drill mimicking the effects of a chemical attack.[122]

The Home Front Command is in charge of civilian forces in peace and war. This differs from the practice of most other democracies and, according to General Livne, was initially "a very difficult concept for civilians to accept." But Israelis understand unity of command—an unequivocal and unambiguous chain of responsibility, authority and accountability[123]—and so eventually the public has accepted military control via the Home Front Command as the most logical way to prepare for attacks with weapons of mass destruction.[124]

The old military maxim that the best defense is a good offense is official Israeli policy. The Israelis will take preemptive action if policymakers have good intelligence and there is a reasonable chance of success. In 1981 Israel had intelligence that the Osirak nuclear reactor in Iraq would produce weapons-grade fuel as a by-product. On June 7, 1981, Israeli Air Force pilots flying F-16s bombed the Osirak facility.[125]

> The raid was skillfully planned. When the Israeli pilots were in Jordanian airspace they conversed in Saudi-accented Arabic and informed Jordanian air controllers that

they were a Saudi patrol gone astray: over Saudi Arabia they pretended to be Jordanians. The first wave of F-16s punched a hole in the reactor dome, after which a second wave of aircraft dropped "dumb" (that is, not laser-guided) bombs with enough accuracy to destroy the reactor core, its containing walls, and the gantry crane.[126]

The Israelis also use retribution to deter terrorism. Following the 1972 massacre of Israeli athletes at the Munich Olympics and a wave of attacks on Israeli diplomats and other civilian targets, Prime Minister Golda Meir decided on a new tactic.[127] The enemy in this case was the shadowy Palestinian group "Black September," established by Yasir Arafat to carry out non-attributable terrorist attacks while the political wing of the PLO [Palestine Liberation Organization] moved toward international respectability.[128] The Israeli answer to Black September was a group called "Wrath of God." In the months following Munich, Wrath of God relentlessly struck back at Black September, conducting daring raids into Beirut to kill the top leadership and tracking down and assassinating other operatives in Europe and elsewhere. By late 1973 Black September had effectively ceased to exist, its few remaining members demoralized and fearful.[129] Although the activities of Wrath of God did not end Palestinian terrorism, it disrupted its operations and undermined its capabilities.[130]

The United Kingdom Model

Because the United Kingdom is a unitary state and a parliamentary democracy, it has advantages over the United States in preparing for and responding to chemical or biological attacks. In contrast to federal systems like the United States and Canada, where power is shared between the central government and state or regional governments, in Britain no powers are reserved for sub-national units of government. The UK does not have several layers of public security organizations as in the U.S., where federal, state, county, and city police agencies co-exist. Instead the United Kingdom has forty-three police constabularies. Each constabulary is independent and is commanded by a Chief Constable.[131] Major public-safety actions of a multi-constabulary or national character are coordinated through the National Reporting Center at Scotland Yard (London Police Headquarters) and the Home Office.[132] Questions of jurisdiction do not arise. After the Oklahoma City bombing, twenty-six federal, state, county, and city agencies could have plausibly claimed jurisdiction over one or another aspect of the investigation.[133] Had a similar tragedy occurred in the UK—say in York—the Chief Constable responsible for York would have been in charge. No one else. Fire-safety forces are organized similarly within the forty-three constabularies, which improves response time, operational efficiency, and coordination.[134]

The United Kingdom's parliamentary system functions more expeditiously in some respects than presidential systems because Parliament combines executive and legislative functions. It can make or overturn laws and establish policies without recourse by the executive, the judiciary, or the monarch. In the United States, executive policy is subject to checks and balances by the legislature and judiciary. In the UK, once policy is set by Parliament, only Parliament can change it.[135] This fusion of legislative and executive powers is expressed in the cabinet.[136]

> Through its collective decision making, the cabinet...shapes, directs, and takes *collective responsibility* for government. Cabinet government stands in stark contrast to

presidential government and is perhaps the most unique feature—and certainly the pivot—of Britain's whole system of government. For it is the body, where the executive and legislature overlap, that control of government rests.[137]

The Home Office, headed by the Home Secretary, is responsible for internal affairs. In the event of a biological or chemical attack in the United Kingdom, crisis and consequence management would be the responsibility of the Home Office. The Home Secretary, his deputy, or another representative would chair an interdepartmental cabinet-working group assembled to manage the event. At a minimum, the Ministry of Defense, Special Branch (MI 5), the Secret Intelligence Service (MI 6), and the Foreign Office would be represented.

At the tactical level, the Chief Constable of the affected region is in charge of ground operations. The Ministry of Defense plays an advisory role unless police forces cannot accomplish their mission. If Defense takes charge of the operation, a written document establishing responsibility and accountability is passed from the Constable to the on-site military commander. When the situation is again within the capabilities of the police, the document is passed back and the military returns to an advisory capacity. For example, during Operation Nimrod, the 1980 British Special Air Service (SAS) raid to retake the Iranian Embassy in London from terrorists, responsibility did not transfer to the SAS military unit until the final hour of the operation. The crisis began at 11:32 a.m. on April 30. The SAS did not receive operational control until May 5 at 7:07 p.m., when "the senior policeman on the scene handed Mike Rose, the commander of 22nd SAS, a signed piece of paper which effectively handed control of the situation over to the SAS."[138] By 7:40 p.m. the SAS had retaken the embassy and "quickly disappeared from the scene before the press showed up."[139]

A Special Air Service team is stationed permanently in London and is responsible to Scotland Yard and ultimately the Home Secretary. The SAS operates under strict guidelines within the UK, and team members, aware that they are liable to prosecution if they employ excessive force, walk a fine line. To repeat, for the SAS to be used, the operation must be beyond the capabilities of civilian police, and written authority must pass from civilian authorities to the military.[140]

Three threat levels—gold, silver, and bronze—determine the nature of the response and the membership of the interdepartmental cabinet-working group. A "gold" event would be classified as catastrophic in the United States and would entail maximum availability of resources. The Prime Minister would be closely involved, perhaps even chairing the working group instead of the Home Secretary. If foreign involvement were found, the Foreign Minister and Defense Minister would probably have responsibility for out-of-country negotiations and operations.

"Silver" is a serious domestic event with no apparent international involvement. The cabinet-working group would be manned at the Minister or Deputy Minister level, and the military would probably remain in an advisory role. A "bronze" event is one that can be handled at the local constabulary level.[141] Frequent exercises are held at all three levels to allow potential members of the interdepartmental working groups a chance to work together.

As a unitary state with a parliamentary democracy, the United Kingdom has some advantages over the United States in handling domestic terrorism. It also has considerable experience: having conducted a counterterror campaign in Northern Ireland for more than two decades, UK security forces have learned much.[142]

The Canadian Model

Throughout its history, Canada has relied on its military to put down rebellions, ethnic confrontations, election violence, strikes, prison violence, and terrorism.[143] Domestic use of Canada's armed forces continues today. "In the past two years large portions of the Canadian Forces have been involved in support of the civilian authorities. This support has included humanitarian assistance to fight floods, forest fires and ice storms." In the case of the Red River flood of 1997 and the severe ice storm of 1998, the military provided assistance to law enforcement agencies as well as ordinary humanitarian support.[144] The Canadian Forces are often asked to supplement civilian security forces at important domestic events, like the 1976 Montreal Olympics, visits by foreign dignitaries, and the G7 Summits [meetings of heads of state or government of the major industrial democracies] in Montebello and Halifax.[145] Among other duties at such events, the Canadian Forces maintain specially trained rapid-response counterterrorism and bomb-disposal units.[146]

The Canadian military can perform this role because Canadian law allows the timely use of military forces in domestic emergencies. In 1988 the Canadian government restructured and simplified its laws in this area. The Emergencies Act identified four types of emergencies: "public welfare (severe natural disasters); public order (threats to the internal security of Canada); international; and war."[147] The Act specifies the powers the government is allowed in each kind of situation. In a Public Order Emergency, for example, the government is "authorized to prohibit public assembly and travel to and from a specified area, and to designate and secure protected places, assume control of public utilities, and impose summary convictions for up to six months of imprisonment."[148] The new act also addresses threats posed by Canadian groups receiving outside support; officials "would have the option of declaring either a Public Order Emergency or an International Emergency in such a situation."[149]

Companion legislation, called the Emergency Preparedness Act, established an organization known as Emergency Preparedness Canada (EPC) under the jurisdiction of the Department of National Defense. Pursuant to this act, "federal and provincial government departments must create administrative machinery and cooperative contingency plans at the provincial level with the Department of National Defense and Emergency Preparedness Canada to respond to the four types of emergencies described in the Emergencies Act."[150] In times of civil unrest or national crisis, provincial premiers and the Solicitor General may ask the military to act in support of police and civil authorities. The Canadian military has provided crowd-control, policing, counter-terrorist, and other forms of support, withdrawing as soon as civil authorities are able to resume control.[151]

A 1994 Defense White Paper, reflecting the end of the Cold War, further refined the domestic roles and missions of the Canadian military. The White Paper specified seven areas in which forces of the Department of National Defense could be deployed: peacetime surveillance and control (sovereignty protection); securing Canadian borders against illegal activity (counter-narcotics); fisheries protection; environmental surveillance; disaster relief; search-and-rescue; and counterterrorism.[152] It also directed that the national dynamic entry (counterterror-hostage rescue) mission be transferred from the Royal Canadian Mounted Police Special Emergency Response team to the army's JTF-2 counterterror unit.[153]

The Canadian approach to supporting civilian authority is extremely flexible. It relies on a carefully designed legal framework and a professional force structure. "Legislation does not prescribe the exact civil-military relationship at the operational and tactical levels, nor does it hamper commanders by dictating the levels of response which may be required in violent situations."[154] In general, Canadian law avoids overly explicit restrictions on the military.[155] This flexibility points up significant differences between Canadian and American political and legal cultures. The Canadian government places great confidence in military professionalism, doctrine, and training. In the United States, on the other hand, the Posse Comitatus Act limits the involvement of the armed forces much more sharply and places severe restrictions on the scope of their activities, even when the military is clearly more qualified than its civilian counterparts to undertake the mission in question.

Organizing for Success

This brief review of how Israel, the United Kingdom, and Canada organize themselves against domestic threats, including those posed by biological and chemical weapons, prompts several observations. First, all three democracies have specified procedures for the use of active and reserve military forces in domestic security matters. In Israel the military is the lead agency in countering domestic threats, and its Home Front Army actually has authority over some civilian agencies in both war and peace. In the United Kingdom, and to a somewhat lesser extent in Canada, the military normally plays a supporting role, though when circumstances dictate, it can become the lead agency in a domestic crisis. In the UK, transfer of authority to and from the military is accomplished by a written document, much like a contract, and the duration of military control is typically very short. In Canada, the time frame for transition to and from military control is established by the laws and policies described above.

As noted, all three states have parliamentary systems, which make for more streamlined policymaking than our presidential system. Israel and the United Kingdom are unitary states, not hampered by several layers of jurisdiction. Canada, though a federal system, mandates that federal and provincial departments create common plans and administrative procedures for responding to several types of emergencies, including CBW attacks.

The United States can learn much from these three allies. All three, though robust democracies, understand that unity of command is essential for proper response to a catastrophic event and that military organizations are more suited to dealing with some types of domestic threats than are civilian organizations. This is particularly true of CBW threats, because combat troops are trained to survive on a contaminated battlefield. Such training is indispensable in an age in which rogue states, failed and failing states, and non-state actors, lacking the means to confront advanced militaries in conventional conflict, may well choose CBW in order to offset this inferiority.[156] Israel, the UK, and Canada all understand that military organizations intensively plan, organize, equip, and train for complex emergencies and that military commanders understand how to organize and coordinate multiple organizations for a common objective. Why not, they might ask their U.S. counterparts, make use of these distinctive capabilities in domestic emergencies?

There may also be other lessons here. Israel's use of preemption and retribution is instructive. During the Cold War, the United States successfully relied on nuclear deterrence to prevent an attack on its homeland. Preemption and retribution were not plausible options in the highly charged nuclear environment. Some commentators, like columnist John Ellis of the Boston *Globe*, believe that nuclear deterrence is still an option. The U.S. must "develop a plan for massive retaliation in the event of a biowarfare outbreak." That plan should be made public, Ellis writes, and broadcast around the world. "One way for biological agents to 'blow back' on those who launch them is nuclear retaliation."[157] It makes sense, argues Jessica Stern, "for governments to signal their intention to respond to state-sponsored terrorist acts with massive retaliation that may even include the use of nuclear weapons."[158] Others question the practicality of nuclear deterrence in a threat environment populated in large part by non-state actors. Threatening to retaliate with nuclear weapons for acts of chemical or biological warfare would not be proportional, they contend, and might undermine efforts toward nuclear non-proliferation.[159] Moreover, the Tokyo subway and Oklahoma City attacks were perpetrated by local residents. How could we have deterred them with nuclear weapons?

Israel's successful record of preempting terrorist attacks is based on good intelligence and an ability to infiltrate terrorist organizations. The U.S. has lagged in this regard, as illustrated most recently by the targeting of a suspected chemical weapons plant in Sudan in an attempt to preempt Osama bin Laden. Unfortunately, it now appears doubtful that there was a clear link between the Al Shifa plant in Khartoum and Mr. bin Laden or that the plant was making chemical weapons.[160] Interestingly, however, Washington's mistake may still have had the desired effect. "Sudan, which has tried for months to convince Washington that it does not support international terrorism, advised the United States on May 22, 1999, that it will sign several anti-terrorism accords and the 1993 convention banning chemical warfare."[161] Could it be that the continued threat of preventive military action, even if misplaced in this instance, convinced the Sudanese to change their behavior?

The dangers of CBW proliferation and use by terrorists warrant the consideration of special preventive measures. The political risks and operational difficulties are substantial but not prohibitive and may well be outweighed by the benefits. Once a CBW program has been underway for some time, the operational requirements for a successful preemption—from accurate intelligence on facilities and sites to target destruction without unacceptable collateral damage—are likely to be very high,[162] although the political risk will be lower to the extent there is evidence of the adversary's capability and intent. From a military perspective, however, the time to strike is at an early stage, when the operational requirements are more manageable but the political risks are greater.[163] Israel often opts, after a cost-benefit analysis, for early action. The United States should consider the early option too—though only when it has developed a better intelligence capability.

As mentioned earlier, the Israelis are meeting the threat of chemical and biological terrorism with a Home Front Command, ninety-seven percent of whose members are reservists. This notion has advocates in the United States. Deborah Lee, Assistant Secretary of Defense for Reserve Affairs, has observed

> The U.S. military reserve components are the appropriate forces to use in homeland defense and WMD response. They live and work in all communities and they have established links to the fire, police and emergency medical personnel who are always the first to arrive at the scene of any incident. Consequently, the Guard and Reserves represent a unique pool of manpower and expertise that, with the proper training and equipment, can support local, state and federal authorities.[164]

The Reserve and Guard bring different advantages to domestic CBW response. Most of the chemical and medical units are located in the Army Reserve.[165] Those in the Guard are largely at the division level and are dedicated to units programmed for international deployments and other contingencies.[166] The Guard's advantage is that, unless federalized, it is an instrument of the governor of the state and not covered by the Posse Comitatus Act. It may therefore enforce civil laws. Once federalized, the National Guard, like the Active Army and the Army Reserve, comes under the Posse Comitatus Act and no longer may be used to reinforce local law-enforcement agencies.[167]

The United Kingdom model offers American policymakers some interesting organizational insights. The interdepartmental working group process within the UK cabinet is more responsive and less cumbersome than the current interagency process in the United States. In the UK, the Home Secretary is in charge and the others at the cabinet table are from the Foreign Office, the Ministry of Defense, the Police and Intelligence Services, and other ministries as necessary. They plan and exercise together and with the forty-three police constabularies throughout the nation. During an emergency, and depending on the level and type of crisis, the Home Secretary assembles the participants and the Home Office manages the response.[168]

By comparison, the Senior Interagency Coordination Group (SICG) charged with identifying, discussing, and resolving issues regarding the federal response to CBW incidents, is composed of six senior members (from FEMA, FBI, DOE, EPA, the Department of Health and Human Services (DHHS) and DoD), as well as representatives from the Department of Agriculture, the Department of Transportation, the Bureau of Justice Assistance, the General Services Administration (GSA), and the National Communications System.[169] The SICG is a coordinating organization, does not exercise, and has no operational responsibilities; nor does it coordinate the myriad state, county, and city agencies involved in CBW response.

Another aspect of the British system that may be transferable is the "gold, silver, bronze" level of threat assessment and response. In that system, the level of mobilization and the rank of those involved corresponds to the level of threat. Gold, silver, and bronze responders know who they are and plan, train, and exercise together. Carter, Deutch, and Zelikow are among those who have recognized the utility of identifying different threat levels.

> The United States needs a two-tier response structure: one for ordinary terrorist incidents that federal law enforcement can manage with interagency help, and another for truly catastrophic terrorist attacks. The government would require two new

offices, one within the office of the defense secretary, and the other within the existing [Joint Forces Command] which already bears operational responsibility for the defense of the American homeland and the majority of U.S. armed forces. These Catastrophic Terrorism Response Offices (CTROS) would coordinate federal, state, and local authorities as well as the private sector to respond to major terrorist threats once they are activated by the president and the defense secretary.[170]

One aspect of the Canadian model may be readily applicable in the United States. The close contingency-planning relationship between Emergency Preparedness Canada [EMC] and the Department of National Defense [DND] could and should have an American counterpart other than the currently overburdened and often criticized FEMA.[171] The EMC-DND relationship, as the reader may recall, is part of the Emergency Preparedness Act, which stipulates how provincial and federal organizations are to coordinate emergencies.[172]

Recommendations

From the preceding survey of potential threats and other states' preparations for them, a number of recommendations emerge. Chief among them: change the National Security Act to reflect security requirements in the post-Cold War world. Include in the Act the legal framework and the organizational and institutional structures necessary for homeland defense. Establish a civilian-led Homeland Defense Command that capitalizes on the strengths of the Reserve and National Guard, which are "particularly well-suited to an increased role in this area, as their infrastructure exists in all fifty states."[173] The participation of the Guard and the Reserve in disaster-relief operations has prepared them to undertake similar, though much more dangerous, counter-CBW operations. Whenever possible, use non-federalized National Guard units, which will not be hindered by Posse Comitatus restrictions. This is especially important during crisis management, when support for law-enforcement agencies is critical.

Some desirable measures may be more feasible than others. Establishing a Homeland Defense Command is unlikely, given the historical and cultural impediments to such an organization. But it should be possible to create a leadership structure embracing the FBI and FEMA which will insure that both crisis and consequence management are handled simultaneously, harmoniously, and efficiently.

> FEMA is used to dealing with natural disasters and having to coordinate with local officials. But an act of terrorism would create both a crime scene and a disaster—making it necessary for agencies that do not usually work together to coordinate their efforts. "Oklahoma City was a good test case," a FEMA official [said], "in the sense that it revealed the competing priorities of the FBI and FEMA. The FBI's principal objective was to preserve evidence, while FEMA wanted only to save lives."[174]

Moreover, FEMA is used to operating in an interagency and intergovernmental context, while the FBI is not. The FBI has traditionally been reluctant to assign its agents to interagency task forces, much less lead them, because J. Edgar Hoover thought the FBI's reputation might suffer if it had to share responsibility for mistakes caused by the bad judgment of other interagency members.[175]

John Deutch and the Commission to Assess the Organization of the Federal Government to Combat the Proliferation of Weapons of Mass Destruction (better known as the Deutch Panel) have called for a national coordinator with the rank of deputy assistant to the President with sufficient authority to "untangle the Gordian knot of jurisdictions that attempt to fight the spread of weapons of mass destruction and the means to deliver such weapons."[176] In my view this recommendation, while a step in the right direction, does not go far enough. For one thing, the Deutch Panel did not address domestic response to acts of terrorism. For another, even with the rank of deputy assistant to the President, the national coordinator they propose would be just that: an agency coordinator—convening meetings, leading the interagency policy process, allocating resources, making budget decisions, and reviewing technology-acquisition problems—rather than a leader with authority to direct agencies in times of crisis.[177] More appealing are the statements of Frank Cilluffo, director of the terrorism task force at the Center for Strategic and International Studies in Washington D.C., who believes there should be a domestic terrorism "czar." Testifying in October 1998 before a Congressional subcommittee, Cilluffo argued for the creation of a new commander-in-chief to oversee homeland defense, under the Defense Department. "What I'm saying is that you want one individual, you want it to be their single, primary mission."[178]

If the Gordian knot is to be cut and the crisis management/consequence management dilemma resolved, one more coordinator, no matter what his or her rank or access, won't get the job done. What's needed is a national *director* with super-agency powers as well as ready access to the President and Congress. This official should be a deputy assistant to the President and reside at the National Security Council (NSC), which by its charter is responsible for advising the President on both domestic and international security. Currently the national coordinator for security, infrastructure protection, and counterterrorism works at the NSC. Why not elevate this position to national director, with authority to direct agencies in the field? The Kissinger and Brzezinski periods, when the NSC was a "superdepartment" that provided guidance for both Defense and State, offers some idea of what the NSC with an operational mission might be like.[179]

The United States needs to enhance its biological and chemical warfare intelligence capabilities. If the intelligence community did nothing else for the next twenty years but concentrate on biological weapons proliferation, writes John Ellis, "it would be money well spent".[180] Most analysts do not go quite that far, but many argue that changes need to be made. As Ernest May observes, what worked when the major threat came from communists in Moscow with nuclear weapons cannot be counted on to work when different enemies are wielding viruses and other weapons of mass destruction.[181]

It is also worth listening to those analysts and policymakers who believe that too much secrecy limits the effective use of intelligence, that too much emphasis is placed on collection and not enough on analysis, and that not enough use is made of open source material. At present admirals and generals routinely complain of not even knowing what they *can* be told.[182] How then can the ultimate consumers of domestic CBW intelligence—local law-enforcement officials, doctors, or scientists not even in government employ (perhaps not even U.S. nationals)—hope to get timely information? They cannot; and thus effective classification, clearance, and dissemination are going to require new rules and perhaps new statutes.[183]

Jane Holl, principal editor of the Carnegie Corporation's *Preventing Deadly Conflicts*, estimates that ninety percent of the intelligence community's budget goes to collection and ten percent to analysis.[184] That ratio needs to be changed drastically. Raw intelligence is of little use to consumers; timely analysis is essential. It is all too possible at present that data pertaining to a CBW attack might get collected but not analyzed and disseminated to those who are charged with preventing an attack. I have already referred to the need to make better use of open sources. Had these been used, the Tokyo subway incident might have been prevented. Finally, one has to question the necessity for thirteen separate intelligence agencies. Are that many really necessary? And if so, are they coordinated effectively? Probably not; consider that the Director of Central Intelligence—the head of the intelligence community according [to] the National Security Act—only controls fifteen percent of the intelligence budget.

Much can be learned from America's major allies: Israel, the United Kingdom, and Canada. All are mature democracies, with their militaries firmly under civilian control. Yet they have no Posse Comitatus restrictions and make effective use of military forces for homeland defense against many threats, including CBW and terrorism. Canada's Emergency Preparedness Act, which defines how its provincial and federal forces should cooperate during domestic emergencies, is worth emulating. So is the United Kingdom's streamlined interdepartmental cabinet decision-making process, with its multi-tiered response structure.

Israel's CBW threat-response organization and doctrine are particularly instructive. Though it is doubtful that Americans would agree to gas mask distribution offices in every population center—after all, many of our soldiers won't allow themselves to be vaccinated against anthrax—it is likely that they would agree with Israel's doctrine concerning preemption. Absent an effective deterrent, particularly against non-state actors, the United States needs to think hard about the use of military force for preemption. Last year's attack on the Sudanese chemical plant is a case in point: even though the strike was a mistake, there was no public outcry in the United States; and eventually, perhaps concerned about further mistakes, the Sudanese signed the Chemical Weapons Convention.

It is time to review the Posse Comitatus Act. None of our allies imposes such strict prohibitions on its military. It no longer makes sense to prevent America's best-qualified CBW-response assets and counterterror forces, which happen to be in the military, from helping the nation cope with the CBW threat.

A final recommendation: put someone unambiguously in charge. As Israel's General Livne points out, the fight against terrorists armed with CBW is a war, and the first principle in war is unity of command. Achieve unity of command and the rest will fall into place.

Conclusion

We all now recognize the increased danger of chemical and biological weapons. Rogue states, failed states, failing states, transnational actors, or even disloyal Americans could surreptitiously deliver one or several such weapons, at home or abroad. The Tokyo subway incident was not science fiction, and the Oklahoma City and World Trade Center bombings could just as easily have been CBW attacks. Anyone who doubts that terrorists can smuggle chemical or biological weapons into New York City should reflect that they could easily be disguised as a bag of cocaine or a brick of marijuana.[185]

Graham Allison has warned that defending America against CBW attack will require eternal, multi-layered vigilance. "As the most open society in the world, America will remain most vulnerable to attacks, especially weapons delivered surreptitiously. In the real world of the next quarter-century, dreams of an invulnerable America are fantasy."[186] Still, many things can be done. A Homeland Defense organization is one, a refocused intelligence community is another. Simply putting a qualified person in a position to achieve unity of command would be a significant start. And from longtime allies faced with the same threat—Israel, the United Kingdom, and Canada—the United States should learn that the military can support domestic security operations without endangering civilian control.

Neither complacency nor hysteria is called for, but rather a modest and sustained investment in intelligence and other countermeasures, from prevention to preemption to preparedness. "Individuals take out insurance policies all the time to hedge against disasters that will probably never occur. This is one case where the United States government can do the same—and be satisfied if the premiums are ultimately wasted."[187]

Notes

1. Rod Stark, "Looking at the Nature of WMD Terrorism," unpublished paper, Southwest Missouri State University, Internet http://www.inforwar.com/ mil_c4i/st..._the_Nature_of_WMD_Terrorism.html, August 30, 1999, 2.
2. John Ellis van Courtland Moon, "Dubious Allegations," *Bulletin of the Atomic Scientists* (May/June 1999):70.
3. The authors base their conclusion on eight central arguments, each of which can be refuted by archival evidence and reasonable counter-arguments.
4. Federation of American Scientists Web Page, "CW Use in Iran-Iraq War http://www.fas.org/irp/gulf/cia/ 960702/72566_01.htm). See also, Encyclopedia of Bioethics, 2544; Physicians for Human Rights Web Site, "Research and Investigations: Chemical Weapons" (http://www.phrusa.org/research/chemical.html); U.S. Department of State, Office of the Spokesman, Press Statement by James P. Rubin, Spokesman, "Anniversary of the Halabja Massacre" (March 16, 1998) (http://secretary.state.gov/www/briefings/statements/1998/ps980316a.html); Peter Sawchyn, "Scientist Details Effects of Chemical Attack on Iraqi Kurds (Evidence shows long-term genetic damage to Halabja residents)," USIS Washington File, April 27, 1998 (http://www.fas. org/news/iraq/1998/04/ 98042702_npo.html).
5. Judith Miller, "U.S. Officials Suspect Deadly Chemical Weapons In Yugoslav Army Arsenal," *New York Times*, April 16, 1999, 1.
6. Steven Lee Myers, "Federal Commission Predicts Increasing Threat of Terrorism," *New York Times*, September 21, 1999, 1.
7. Christopher J. Castelli, "Homeland Terrorism, More Kosovos Ahead, Security Panel Warns," *Inside the Navy*, August 9, 1999, 1.
8. Ibid.
9. Ibid.
10. Milton Leitenberg, "False Alarm," *Washington Post*, August 14, 1999, 15.
11. Ehud Sprinzak, "Terrorism, Real or Imagined--What is the Real Threat, WMC or Car Bombs?" *Washington Post*, August 19, 1998, A21.
12. Brian Michael Jenkins, *The Likelihood of Nuclear Terrorism* (Santa Monica, CA: RAND Corporation, P-7119, July 1985) 6
13. Nicholas Wade, "Germ Weapons: Deadly, but Hard to Use," *New York Times*, November 21, 1997 Internet, www.mtholyoke.edu/acad/intrel/germ. htm.
14. Bruce Hoffman, *Inside Terrorism*, (New York: Columbia University Press, 1998), 198.

15. Jessica Stern, "Taking the Terror Out of Bioterrorism," *New York Times*, April 8, 1998, Internet www.mtholyoke.edu/acad/intrel/stern.htm

16. Jessica Stern, "Loose Nukes, Poisons, and Terrorism: The New Threats to International Security," Unpublished paper. June 19, 1996, 3.

17. William S. Cohen, "Preparing for a Grave New World," *Washington Post*, July 26, 1999, A 19.

18. Ibid. and Steve Macko, "FBI Says There Is a Marked Increase in Number of Domestic WMD Terrorist Threats," *ERRI Daily Intelligence Report*, vol. 4, October 3, 1998, 276.

19. Chitra Ragavan and David E. Kaplan, "The Boom in Bioterror Funds," *U.S. News & World Report*, October 18, 1999, 24.

20. Jessica Stern, *The Ultimate Terrorists* (London: Harvard University Press, 1999), 21.

21. Ibid.

22. Richard Preston, "Annals of Warfare—the Bio Weaponeers," *The New Yorker*, March 9, 1998, 56.

23. Ibid.

24. Ibid.

25. Ibid., 57.

26. Gideon Rose, "It Could Happen Here—Facing the New Terrorism," *Foreign Affairs*, March-April, 1999, 135.

27. _____, "Expert: Russia Retains Biological Weapons Ability," *Dallas Morning News*, October 21, 1999, 1.

28. Rose, 134.

29. Robert Davis, "Rescuers Train for Prospect of Chemical War," *USA Today*, July 29, 1999, 8D.

30. Chris Seiple, "Consequence Management: Domestic Response to Weapons of Mass Destruction," *Parameters* (Autumn 1997): 120.

31. Ibid.

32. C. L. Staten, "Two Men Arrested With Possession of Anthrax," *Emergency Net News Service*, Online. http://emergency.com/lv-antrx.htm August 30, 1999, 2.

33. Stern, *The Ultimate Terrorists*, 51.

34. _____, "Expert: Russia Retains Biological Weapons Ability," *Dallas Morning News*, October 21, 1999, 1.

35. Ibid.

36. Stephen A. Cambone, *A New Structure for National Security Policy Planning*, (Washington D.C.—The Center for Strategic and International Studies), 1998, 113.

37. Ibid.

38. Rose, 131.

39. _____. *Proliferation: Threat and Response*, (Washington D.C.: Government Printing Office, 1996), 43

40. Stern, "Loose Nukes," 11.

41. Bruce Hoffman, *Inside Terrorism*, (New York: Columbia University Press, 1998), 205.

42. Ibid.

43. Rose, 135.

44. Ragavan and Kaplan, 24.

45. Ibid.

46. Harlan K. Ullman, "Who Will Listen, Who Will Lead," Unpublished manuscript, June 1998, 278.

47. Wesley Clark, interviewed at Mons, Belgium. March 8, 1999.

48. Ullman, 279.

49. Ibid, 280.

50. Bradley Graham, "Teamwork as Military Task," *Washington Post*, October 12, 1999, A17.

51. _____, *Transforming Defense--National Security in the 21st Century*, Report of the National Defense Panel, December 1997, 23.
52. Ibid.
53. Ibid., 25.
54. Ibid.
55. Ibid.
56. Ibid., 26
57. James Woolsey.
58. Al Gore, "Intelligence Community," *National Performance Review*, (Washington D.C.: Government Printing Office, 1993).
59. Angela Rogers, *Changing Threat Environment and U.S. Intelligence Community: Challenges in the New Millennium*, Unpublished paper.
60. _____, "Intelligence Community in the 21st Century," *Summary*, U.S. House of Representatives Permanent Select Committee on Intelligence, Washington D.C. (no date), 2.
61. Gore, 9.
62. Morton H. Halperin, "What Should the National Security Act of 1998 Look Like," *U.S. National Security Beyond the Cold War*, Contemporary Issue Series No. 6, (Carlisle, PA.: The Clarke Center, 1997), 34.
63. Ibid. See also "Richard A. Falkenrath, "Confronting Nuclear, Biological and Chemical Terrorism," *Survival* (Autumn 1998): 59.
64. Ibid.
65. _____, "Hart-Rudman Commission: U.S. Faces Homeland Attacks," *Aerospace Daily*, October 6, 1999, 1.
66. Rose, 135.
67. Seth Carus, "Biohazard, Assessing the Bioterrorism Threat," *New Republic*, August 2, 1999, 14.
68. Ashton Carter, John Deutch, and Philip Zelikow, "Catastrophic Terrorism—Tackling the New Danger," *Foreign Affairs* (November-December 1998): 83.
69. Ibid., 84.
70. Halperin, 40.
71. Ibid.
72. Ibid.
73. Carter, 83-84.
74. Falkenrath, 59.
75. Ibid.
76. Ibid.
77. Carter, 84 and Falkenrath, 59.
78. Rose, 136.
79. Ibid., 119.
80. Jennifer Stinhaure and Judith Miller, "In N.Y. Outbreak, Glimpse of Gaps in Biological Defenses," *New York Times*, October, 11, 1999, 1.
81. Ibid.
82. Steinhauer, 1.
83. Seiple, 120.
84. Ibid.
85. Barbara Starr, "USA's Covert Squads to Counter WMD," March 11, 1998, 12.
86. Russell, p. 205. See also, Fred Bayles, "Anti-Terrorism Plans Falling Short," *USA Today*, October 13, 1998, 15A.
87. Seiple, 122.
88. Ibid.
89. Ibid.

90. Kurt A. McNeely, Assistant for Anti-Terrorism/Consequence Management, Office of the Assistant Secretary of Defense for Special Operations and Low Intensity Conflict, Interview, September 14, 1999.

91. Seiple, 124.

92. Ibid. Seiple explains that the FBI and consequence managers were able to work out an arrangement for sample collection at the Atlanta Olympics. However, it was never used. Interestingly, after the bomb attack at the Atlanta Olympics, the threat of biological contamination was never considered by the authorities.

93. _____, *Response and Recovery Terrorism Response Annex*, Federal Emergency Management Agency. http://www.fema.gov/r-n-r/frp/frpterr.htm

94. Gideon Rose, "It Could Happen Here—Facing the New Terrorism," *Foreign Affairs* (March-April, 1999): 136.

95. Carter, 90.

96. Ibid.

97. Willam S. Cohen, "Preparing for a Grave New World," *Washington Post*, July 26, 1999, A19.

98. Thomas R. Lujan, "Legal Aspects of Domestic Employment of the Army," *Parameters* (Autumn 1997): 83. The Navy is not specifically mentioned in the Posse Comitatus Act but has chosen to adhere to its constraints. The Coast Guard is not precluded from domestic operations by the Posse Comitatus Act.

99. Ibid. Found in Congress, House of Representatives, Panel B, *Inquiry into Federal Law Enforcement Actions at Waco, Texas*, July 20, 1995, testimony of Brigadier General Walter P. Huffman, Assistant Judge Advocate General for Military Law and Operations, 14.

100. Ibid., 89.

101. Cohen, A19.

102. John J. Hamre, "U.S. Military Wants No Domestic Law-Enforcement Role," October 5, 1999, 16.

103. Ibid.

104. Dennis M. McCarthy, "Joint Support for WMD Anti-Terrorism and Force Protection Planning," Briefing presented at the *WMD Response in the New Millennium Symposium*, Kirtland Air Force Base, New Mexico, July 21, 1999.

105. Greg Seigle, "USA Infighting Over Who Should Deal With Domestic WMD Attacks," *Jane's Defence Weekly*, July 7, 1999, 1.

106. _____, "Regional Rapid Assessment Element Stationing Plans Announced," *DoD News Releases*, Office of the Assistant Secretary of Defense (Public Affairs), May 22, 1998, 1.

107. J. D. W. Parker, "USA Prepares to Treble Number of RAID Teams," *Jane's Defence Weekly*, June 2, 1999, 1.

108. Seigle.

109. Ron Laurenzo, "GAO: Time to Reassess Guard Anti-Terror Teams," *Defense Week*, July 6, 1999, 1.

110. Bradley Graham, "Sneak-Attack Detectives Prepare to Prowl," *Washington Post*, August 28, 1999, 3.

111. Ibid.

112. Laurenzo.

113. Ibid.

114. Ibid.

115. Jonathan Pate, Center for Nonproliferation Studies, Monterey Institute of International Studies, Interview, February 12, 1999. See also, "Agency Structure for Terrorism Response—Federal Funding to Combat Terrorism," *Chemical and Biological Resource Page*, Center for Nonproliferation, Internet http://www.cns.miis.edu/research/cbw/response.htm

116. Zeev Livne, Israeli Defense and Armed Forces Attache, Interview, October 8, 1999, Washington D.C.

117. Ibid.

118. Ibid.

119. Ibid.

120. Ibid.

121. _____, "The Home Front is Prepared," *Israel Wire*, December 18, 1998, Internet. http://www.israelwire.com/lra/981218/9812184.html

122. _____, "Enough Gas Masks for Everyone," *Israel Wire*, December 18, 1998, Internet. http://www.israelwire.com/lra/981218/981282.html

123. Livne

124. Ibid.

125. Geoff Simons, *Iraq—From Sumer to Saddam*, second ed., (New York: St. Martin's Press, 1996), 320.

126. Ibid. See also, Julie Flint, "Saddam Killing Shias 'Daily,'" *The Observer*, October 4, 1992.

127. Neil C. Livinstone, "Proactive Responses to Terrorism: Reprisals, Preemption, and Retribution," in Charles W. Kegley, Jr., ed. *International Terrorism—Characteristics*, Causes, and Controls (New York: St. Martin's Press, 1990), 225.

128. Ibid.

129. Ibid.

130. Ibid

131. David C. Veness, Assistant Commissioner Specialist Operations, Metropolitan Police Services, London. Interview, March 5, 1999.

132. Mark Kesselman, Christopher S. Allen, David Ost, Joel Krieger, Stephen Hellman, and George Ross, *European Politics in Transition*, 3rd edition, (Boston: Houghton Mifflin Company, 1997) 95.

133. Harlan Ullman, Interview, November 7, 1999.

134. Veness.

135. Kesselman, 84.

136. Ibid.

137. Ibid., 85.

138. _____, "The SAS Raid on the Iranian Embassy," *Overlord—Special Forces and Counterterrorism*, Internet. http://home.istar.ca/~overlord/welcome.html

139. _____, "Operation Nimrod--The Embassy Seige," *Special Forces of the World*. Internet.

140. http://home.istar.ca/~overlord/raidiran.html and http://www.specialforces.dk/reallife/nimrod.htm.

141. Dr. Ray Raymond, Consular Officer, British Consulate, New York, New York. Interview, September 27, 1999. Rules are not hard and fast with regards to the classification and the classification can change within the life span of the crisis.

142. Raymond.

143. T. J. Grant, "Training on Rules of Engagement in Domestic Operations," unpublished paper. Canadian Defense College. Internet. http://www.cfcsc. dnd.ca/irc/amsc/amscl/014.html 1.

144. Ibid.

145. http://www.dnd.ca/menu/legacy/defend_e.htm

146. http://www.dnd.ca/menu/legacy/defend_e.htm

147. Sean M. Maloney, "Domestic Operations: The Canadian Approach," *Parameters* (Autumn 1997): 143.

148. Ibid.

149. Ibid.

150. Ibid.

151. http://www.dnd.ca/menu/legacy/helping_e.htm

152. Maloney, 144.

153. Ibid.

154. Ibid., 148.

155. Ibid.

156. Seiple, 119

157. John Ellis, "What the U.S. Must Do to Combat Biological Weapons," *Boston Globe*, December 10, 1998, A. 31.

158. Stern, 131.

159. Ibid.

160. James Risen, "To Bomb Sudan Plant or Not: A Year Later, Debates Rankle," *New York Times*, October 27, 1999, A14.

161. John M. Goshko, "Sudan to Sign Anti-Terrorism Accords and Join Chemical Warfare Ban," *Washington Post*, May 22, 1999, 20.

162. Lewis A. Dunn, "Proliferation Prevention: Beyond Traditionalism," in William H. Lewis and Stuart E. Johnson, ed. *Weapons of Mass Destruction: New Perspectives of Counterproliferation*. (Washington, DC: National Defense University Press, 1995), 37.

163. Ibid.

164. Deborah R. Lee, "Protecting Americans at Home," *Defense Link*, March, 19, 1998, 2. Online. http://www.defenselink.mil/other_info/deblee.html

165. Mercier, 108.

166. Ibid.

167. _____, "Operations Other Than War Volume II—Disaster Assistance," *Center for Army Lessons Learned Newsletter*, no. 93-6, October 1993, IX 2.

168. Brian Hawtin, Deputy Policy Director, Assistant Under Secretary of State (Policy), Ministry of Defense. Interview, March 4, 1999.

169. H. Allen Holmes, "Domestic Preparedness: U.S. Responses Need Tuning," *Defense Viewpoint*, vol. 13, no. 33, March 26, 1998, 5. Online. www.defenselink.mil/speeches/1998/s19980326-holmas.html

170. Carter, 91.

171. Maloney, 150.

172. Ibid.

173. Peter Grier, "New Roles For the Guard and Reserve," *Air Force Magazine*, November 1999, 17.

174. Stern, 143.

175. James Q. Wilson, *Bureaucracy—What Government Agencies Do and Why They Do It* (New York: Basic Books, 1989), 190.

176. _____, "U.S. Weapons Fight May be Reorganized," *Philadelphia Inquirer*, July 7, 1999, 1.

177. Ibid.

178. C. Mark Brinkley and Gordon Lubold, "Corps' Bio Force Just Not Enough," *Marine Corps Times*, March 29, 1999, 13.

179. Ernest R. May, "Intelligence: Backing Into the Future," *Foreign Affairs* (Summer 1992): 65.

180. Ellis.

181. May, 72.

182. Ibid.

183. Ibid.

184. Jane Holl, multiple discussions.

185. Graham Allison, "Nuclear Lessons," *Boston Globe*, October 27, 1999, 23. The author hopes Dr. Allison won't object to my substituting chemical and biological for nuclear.

186. Ibid.

187. Rose, 137.

Fixing Intelligence

Richard K. Betts is a specialist on national security policy and military strategy. He is director of the Institute of War and Peace Studies at Columbia University and was a senior fellow and research associate at the Brookings Institution in Washington, D.C. Betts has served on the National Commission on Terrorism and the U.S. Senate Select Committee on Intelligence. He is author, editor, and coauthor of several books on the subject, including *The Irony of Vietnam: The System Worked* (1979), which won the Woodrow Wilson Prize.

The Limits of Prevention

As the dust from the attacks on the World Trade Center and the Pentagon was still settling, the chants began: The CIA was asleep at the switch! The intelligence system is broken! Reorganize top to bottom! The biggest intelligence system in the world, spending upward of $30 billion a year, could not prevent a group of fanatics from carrying out devastating terrorist attacks. Drastic change must be overdue. The new conventional wisdom was typified by Tim Weiner, writing in *The New York Times* on October 7: "What will the nation's intelligence services have to change to fight this war? The short answer is: almost everything."

Yes and no. A lot must, can, and will be done to shore up U.S. intelligence collection and analysis. Reforms that should have been made long ago will now go through. New ideas will get more attention and good ones will be adopted more readily than in normal times. There is no shortage of proposals and initiatives to shake the system up. There is, however, a shortage of perspective on the limitations that we can expect from improved performance. Some of the changes will substitute new problems for old ones. The only thing worse than business as usual would be naive assumptions about what reform can accomplish.

Paradoxically, the news is worse than the angriest critics think, because the intelligence community has worked much better than they assume. Contrary to the image left by the destruction of September 11, U.S. intelligence and associated services have generally done very well at protecting the country. In the aftermath of a catastrophe, great successes in thwarting previous terrorist attacks are too easily forgotten—successes such as the foiling of plots to bomb New York City's Lincoln and Holland tunnels in 1993, to bring down 11 American airliners in Asia in 1995, to mount attacks around the millennium on the West Coast and in Jordan, and to strike U.S. forces in the Middle East in the summer of 2001.

The awful truth is that even the best intelligence systems will have big failures. The terrorists that intelligence must uncover and track are not inert objects; they are living, conniving strategists. They, too, fail frequently and are sometimes caught before they can strike. But once in a while they will inevitably get through. Counterterrorism is a competitive game. Even Barry Bonds could be struck out at times by a minor-league pitcher, but when a strikeout means people die, a batting average of less than 1.000 looks very bad indeed.

It will be some time before the real story of the September 11 intelligence failure is known, and longer still before a reliable public account is available. Rather than recap the rumors and fragmentary evidence of exactly what intelligence did and did not do before September 11, at this point it is more appropriate to focus on the merits of proposals for reform and the larger question about what intelligence agencies can reasonably be expected to accomplish.

Spend a Lot to Get a Little

One way to improve intelligence is to raise the overall level of effort by throwing money at the problem. This means accepting additional waste, but that price is paid more easily in wartime than in peacetime. Unfortunately, although there have certainly been misallocations of effort in the past, there are no silver bullets that were left unused before September 11, no crucial area of intelligence that was neglected altogether and that a few well-targeted investments can conquer. There is no evidence, at least in public, that more spending on any particular program would have averted the September 11 attacks. The group that carried them out had formidable operational security, and the most critical deficiencies making their success possible were in airport security and in legal limitations on domestic surveillance. There are nevertheless several areas in which intelligence can be improved, areas in which previous efforts were extensive but spread too thinly or slowed down too much.

It will take large investments to make even marginal reductions in the probability of future disasters. Marginal improvements, however, can spell the difference between success and failure in some individual cases. If effective intelligence collection increases by only five percent a year, but the critical warning indicator of an attack turns up in that five percent, gaining a little information will yield a lot of protection. Streamlining intelligence operations and collection is a nice idea in principle but risky unless it is clear what is not needed. When threats are numerous and complex, it is easier to know what additional capabilities we want than to know what we can safely cut.

After the Cold War, intelligence resources went down as requirements went up (since the country faced a new set of high-priority issues and regions). At the end of the 1990s there was an uptick in the intelligence budget, but the system was still spread thinner over its targets than it had been when focused on the Soviet Union. Three weeks before September 11, the director of central intelligence (DCI), George Tenet, gave an interview to *Signal* magazine that now seems tragically prescient. He agonized about the prospect of a catastrophic intelligence failure: "Then the country will want to know why we didn't make those investments; why we didn't pay the price; why we didn't develop the capability."

The sluice gates for intelligence spending will open for a while. The challenge is not buying some essential element of capability that was ignored before but helping the system do more of everything and do it better. That will increase the odds that bits and pieces of critical information will be acquired and noticed rather than falling through the sieve.

Another way to improve intelligence is to do better at collecting important information. Here, what can be improved easily will help marginally, whereas what could help more than marginally cannot be improved easily. The National Security Agency (NSA), the National Imagery and Mapping Agency (NIMA), and associated organizations can increase "technical" collection—satellite and aerial reconnaissance, signals intelligence, communications monitoring—by buying more platforms, devices, and personnel to exploit them. But increasing useful human intelligence, which everyone agrees is the most critical ingredient for rooting out secretive terrorist groups, is not done easily or through quick infusions of money.

Technical collection is invaluable and has undoubtedly figured in previous counterterrorist successes in ways that are not publicized. But obtaining this kind of information has been getting harder. For one thing, so much has been revealed over the years about U.S. technical collection capabilities that the targets now understand better what they have to evade. State sponsors of terrorism may know satellite overflight schedules and can schedule accordingly activities that might otherwise be observable. They can use more fiber-optic communications, which are much harder to tap than transmission over the airwaves. Competent terrorists know not to use cell phones for sensitive messages, and even small groups have access to impressive new encryption technologies.

Human intelligence is key because the essence of the terrorist threat is the capacity to conspire. The best way to intercept attacks is to penetrate the organizations, learn their plans, and identify perpetrators so they can be taken out of action. Better human intelligence means bolstering the CIA's Directorate of Operations (DO), the main traditional espionage organization of the U.S. government. The DO has been troubled and periodically disrupted ever since the evaporation of the Cold War consensus in the late stage of the Vietnam War provoked more oversight and criticism than spies find congenial. Personnel turnover, tattered esprit, and a growing culture of risk aversion have constrained the DO's effectiveness.

Some of the constraint was a reasonable price to pay to prevent excesses, especially in a post–Cold War world in which the DO was working for the country's interests rather than its survival. After the recent attacks, however, worries about excesses have receded, and measures will be found to make it easier for the clandestine service to operate. One simple reform, for example, would be to implement a recommendation made by the National Commission on Terrorism a year and a half ago: roll back the additional layer of cumbersome procedures instituted in 1995 for gaining approval to employ agents with "unsavory" records—procedures that have had a chilling effect on recruitment of the thugs appropriate for penetrating terrorist units.

Building up human intelligence networks worldwide is a long-term project. It inevitably spawns concern about waste (many such networks will never produce anything useful), deception (human sources are widely distrusted), and complicity with murderous characters (such as the Guatemalan officer who prompted the 1995 change in recruitment guidelines). These are prices that can be borne politically in the present atmosphere of crisis. If the sense of crisis abates, however, commitment to the long-term project could falter.

More and better spies will help, but no one should expect breakthroughs if we get them. It is close to impossible to penetrate small, disciplined, alien organizations like Osama bin Laden's al Qaeda, and especially hard to find reliable U.S. citizens who have even a remote chance of trying. Thus we usually rely on foreign agents of uncertain reliability. Despite our huge and educated population, the base of Americans on which to draw is small: there are very few genuinely bilingual, bicultural Americans capable of operating like natives in exotic reaches of the Middle East, Central and South Asia, or other places that shelter the bin Ladens of the world.

For similar reasons there have been limitations on our capacity to translate information that does get collected. The need is not just for people who have studied Arabic, Pashto, Urdu, or Farsi, but for those who are truly fluent in those languages, and fluent in obscure dialects of them. Should U.S. intelligence trust recent, poorly educated immigrants for these jobs if they involve highly sensitive intercepts? How much will it matter if there are errors in translation, or willful mistranslations, that cannot be caught because there are no resources to cross-check the translators? Money can certainly help here, by paying more for better translators and, over the long term, promoting educational programs to broaden the base of recruits. For certain critical regions of the world, however, there are simply not enough potential recruits waiting in the wings to respond to a crash program.

Sharpened Analysis

Money can buy additional competent people to analyze collected information more readily than it can buy spies who can pass for members of the Taliban—especially if multiplying job slots are accompanied by enhanced opportunities for career development within intelligence agencies to make long service attractive for analysts. Pumping up the ranks of analysts can make a difference within the relatively short time span of a few years. The U.S. intelligence community has hundreds of analysts, but also hundreds of countries and issues to cover. On many subjects the coverage is now only one analyst deep—and when that one goes on vacation, or quits, the account may be handled out of the back pocket of a specialist on something else. We usually do not know in advance which of the numerous low-priority accounts might turn into the highest priority overnight (for example, Korea before June 1950, or Afghanistan before the Soviet invasion).

Hiring more analysts will be a good use of resources but could turn out to have a low payoff, and perhaps none at all, for much of what they do. Having half a dozen analysts on hand for some small country might be a good thing if that country turns out to be central to the campaign against terrorists, but those analysts need to be in place before we know we need them if they are to hit the ground running in a crisis. In most such cases, moreover, those analysts would serve their whole careers without producing anything that the U.S. government really needs, and no good analyst wants to be buried in an inactive account with peripheral significance.

One option is to make better use of an intelligence analyst reserve corps: people with other jobs who come in to read up on their accounts a couple of days each month to maintain currency, and who can be mobilized if a crisis involving their area erupts. There have been experiments with this system, but apparently without enough satisfaction to institutionalize it more broadly.

Of course, the quantity of analysts is less important than the quality of what they produce. Postmortems of intelligence failures usually reveal that very bright analysts failed to predict the disaster in question, despite their great knowledge of the situation, or that they had warned that an eruption could happen but without any idea of when. In fact, expertise can get in the way of anticipating a radical departure from the norm, because the depth of expert knowledge of why and how things have gone as they have day after day for years naturally inclines the analyst to estimate that developments will continue along the same trajectory. It is always a safer bet to predict that the situation tomorrow will be like it has been for the past dozen years than to say that it will change abruptly. And of course, in the vast majority of cases predictions of continuity are absolutely correct; the trick is to figure out which case will be the exception to a powerful rule.

A standard recommendation for reform—one made regularly by people discovering these problems for the first time—is to encourage "outside the box" analyses that challenge conventional wisdom and consider scenarios that appear low in probability but high in consequence. To some, this sort of intellectual shake-up might well have led the intelligence system, rather than Tom Clancy, to anticipate the kamikaze hijacking tactic of September 11.

All well and good. The problem, however, lies in figuring out what to do with the work this great analysis produces. There are always three dozen equally plausible dangers that are possible but improbable. Why should policymakers focus on any particular one of these hypothetical warnings or pay the costs of taking preventive action against all of them? One answer is to use such analysis to identify potential high-danger scenarios for which low-cost fixes are available. If President Bill Clinton had gotten a paper two years before September 11 that outlined the scenario for what ultimately happened, he probably would not have considered its probability high enough to warrant revolutionizing airport security, given all the obstacles: vested interests, opposition to particular measures, hassles for the traveling public. He might, however, have pushed for measures to allow checking the rosters of flight schools and investigating students who seemed uninterested in takeoffs and landings.

Another problem frequently noted is that the analytical corps has become fully absorbed in current intelligence, leaving no time for long-term research projects that look beyond the horizon. This, too, is something that more resources can solve. But as good a thing as more long-range analysis is, it is uncertain how productive it would be for the war on terrorism. The comparative advantage of the intelligence community over outside analysts is in bringing together secret information with knowledge from open sources. The more far-seeing a project, the less likely secret information is to play a role in the assessment. No one can match the analysts from the CIA, the Defense Intelligence Agency (DIA), or the NSA in estimating bin Laden's next moves, but it is not clear that they have a comparative advantage over Middle East experts in think tanks or universities when it comes to estimating worldwide trends in radical Islamist movements over the next decade. Such long-term research is an area in which better use of outside consultants and improved exploitation of academia could help most.

The War at Home

There is a world of difference between collecting intelligence abroad and doing so at home. Abroad, intelligence operations may break the laws of the countries in which they are undertaken. All domestic intelligence operations, however, must conform to U.S. law. The CIA can bribe foreign officials, burglarize offices of foreign political parties, bug defense ministries, tap the phones of diplomats, and do all sorts of things to gather information that the FBI could not do within the United States without getting a warrant from a court. Collection inside the United States is the area where loosened constraints would have done most to avert the September 11 attacks. But it is also the area in which great changes may make Americans fear that the costs exceed the benefits—indeed, that if civil liberties are compromised, "the terrorists will have won."

A Minnesota flight school reportedly alerted authorities a month before September 11 that one of its students, Zacarias Moussaoui, was learning to fly large jets but did not care about learning to take off or land. Moussaoui was arrested on immigration charges, and French intelligence warned U.S. officials that he was an extremist. FBI headquarters nevertheless decided against seeking a warrant for a wiretap or a search, reportedly because of complaints by the chief judge of the Foreign Intelligence Surveillance Court about other applications for wiretaps. After September 11, a search of Moussaoui's computer revealed that he had collected information about crop-dusting aircraft—a potential delivery system for chemical or biological weapons. U.S. officials came to suspect that Moussaoui was supposed to have been the fifth hijacker on United Airlines flight 93, which went down in Pennsylvania.

In hindsight, the hesitation to mount aggressive surveillance and searches in this case—hesitation linked to a highly developed set of legal safeguards rooted in the traditional American reverence for privacy—is exactly the sort of constraint that should have been loosened. High standards for protecting privacy are like strictures against risking collateral damage in combat operations: those norms take precedence more easily when the security interests at stake are not matters of your country's survival, but they become harder to justify when national security is on the line.

There have already been moves to facilitate more extensive clandestine surveillance, and there have been reactions against going too far. There will be substantial loosening of restraint on domestic intelligence collection, but how far it goes depends on the frequency and intensity of future terror attacks inside the United States. If there are no more than seem as serious as September 11, compromises of privacy will be limited. If there are two or three more dramatic attacks, all constraint may be swept away.

It is important to distinguish between two types of constraints on civil liberties. One is political censorship, like the suppression of dissent during World War I. There is no need or justification for this: counterterrorism does not benefit from suppression of free speech. The other type involves compromises of individual privacy, through secret surveillance, monitoring of communications, and searches. This is where pressing up to the constitutional limits offers the biggest payoff for counterterrorist intelligence. It also need not threaten individuals unnecessarily, so long as careful measures are instituted to keep secret the irrelevant but embarrassing information that may inadvertently be acquired as a by-product of monitoring. Similarly, popular but unpersuasive arguments have been advanced against the sort of national identification card common in other democratic countries. The U.S. Constitution does not confer the right to be unidentified to the government.

Even slightly more intrusive information-gathering will be controversial, but if it helps to avert future attacks, it will avert far more draconian blows against civil liberties. Moreover, Americans should remember that many solid, humane democracies—the United Kingdom, France, and others—have far more permissive rules for gathering information on people than the United States has had, and their citizens seem to live with these rules without great unease.

Red Tape and Reorganization

In a bureaucracy, reform means reorganization; reorganization means changing relationships of authority; and that means altering checks and balances. Five days after September 11, Tenet issued a directive that subsequently was leaked to the press. In it he proclaimed the wartime imperative to end business as usual, to cut through red tape and "give people the authority to do things they might not ordinarily be allowed to do.... If there is some bureaucratic hurdle, leap it.... We don't have time to have meetings about how to fix problems, just fix them." That refreshing activism will help push through needed changes. Some major reorganization of the intelligence community is inevitable. That was the response to Pearl Harbor, and even before the recent attacks many though a major shake-up was overdue.

The current crisis presents the opportunity to override entrenched and outdated interests, to crack heads and force the sorts of consolidation and cooperation that have been inhibited by bureaucratic constipation. On balance, reorganization will help—but at a price: mistakes will increase, too. As Herbert Kaufman revealed in his classic 1997 book *Red Tape,* most administrative obstacles to efficiency do not come from mindless obstructionism. The sluggish procedures that frustrate one set of purposes have usually been instituted to safeguard other valid purposes. Red tape is the warp and woof of checks and balances. More muscular management will help some objectives and hurt others.

The crying need for intelligence reorganization is no recent discovery. It is a perennial lament, amplified every time intelligence stumbles. The community has undergone several major reorganizations and innumerable lesser ones over the past half-century. No one ever stays satisfied with reorganization because it never seems to do the trick—if the trick is to prevent intelligence failure. There is little reason to believe, therefore, that the next reform will do much better than previous ones.

Reorganizations usually prove to be three steps forward and two back, because the intelligence establishment is so vast and complex that the net impact of reshuffling may be indiscernible. After September 11, some observers complained that the intelligence community is too regionally oriented and should be organized more in terms of functional issues. Yet back in the 1980s, when William Casey became President Ronald Reagan's DCI and encountered the functional organization of the CIA's analytical directorate, he experienced the reverse frustration. Rather than deal with functional offices of economic, political, and strategic research, each with regional subunits, he shifted the structure to one of regional units with functional subunits. Perhaps it helped, but there is little evidence that it produced consistent improvement in analytical products. There is just as little evidence that moving back in the other direction will help any more.

What about a better fusion center for intelligence on counterterrorism, now touted by many as a vital reform? For years the DCI has had a Counter-Terrorism Center (CTC) that brings together assets from the CIA's directorates of operations and intelligence, the FBI, the DIA, the State Department, and other parts of the community. It has been widely criticized, but many believe its deficiencies came from insufficient resources—something reorganization alone will not cure. If the CTC's deficiencies were truly organizational, moreover, there is little reason to believe that a new fusion center would not simply replace those problems with different ones.

Some believe, finally, that the problem is the sheer complexity and bulk of the intelligence community; they call for it to be streamlined, turned into a leaner and meaner corps. Few such proposals specify what functions can be dispensed with in order to thin out the ranks, however. In truth, bureaucratization is both the U.S. intelligence community's great weakness and its great strength. The weakness is obvious, as in any large bureaucracy: various forms of sclerosis, inertia, pettiness, and paralysis drive out many vibrant people and deaden many who remain. The strength, however, is taken for granted: a coverage of issues that is impressively broad and sometimes deep. Bureaucratization makes it hard to extract the right information efficiently from the globs of it lying around in the system, but in a leaner and meaner system there will never be much lying around.

Some areas can certainly benefit from reorganization. One is the integration of information technologies, management systems, and information sharing. Much has been done within the intelligence community to exploit the potential of information technology in recent years, but it has been such a fast-developing sector of society and the economy in general that constant adaptation may be necessary for some time.

Another area of potential reorganization involves making the DCI's authority commensurate with his or her responsibility. This is a long-standing source of tension, because roughly 80 percent of the intelligence establishment (in terms of functions and resources) has always been located in the Defense Department, where primary lines of authority and loyalty run to the military services and to the secretary of defense. The latest manifestation of this problem was the increased priority given during the 1990s to the mission of support for military operations (SMO)—a priority levied not only on Pentagon intelligence agencies but on the CIA and others as well. Such a move was odd, given that military threats to the United States after the Cold War were lower than at any other time in the existence of the modern intelligence community, while a raft of new foreign policy involvements in various parts of the world were coming to the fore. But the SMO priority was the legacy of the Persian Gulf War and the problems in intelligence support felt by military commanders, combined with the Clinton administration's unwillingness to override strong military preferences.

Matching authority and responsibility is where the test of the most immediate reform initiative—or evidence of its confusion—will come. Early reports on the formation of the Office of Homeland Security indicated that the new director, Tom Ridge, will be responsible for coordinating all of the agencies in the intelligence community. This is odd, because that was precisely the function for which the office of Director of Central Intelligence was created in the National Security Act of 1947. The position of DCI was meant to centralize oversight of the dispersed intelligence activities of the military services, the State Department, and the new Central Intelligence Agency, and to coordinate planning and resource allocation among them.

As the community burgeoned over the years, adding huge organizations such as the NSA, the DIA, NIMA, and others, the DCI remained the official responsible for knitting their functions together. The DCI's ability to do so increased at times, but it was always limited by the authority of the secretary of defense over the Pentagon's intelligence agencies. Indeed, hardly anyone but professionals within the intelligence community understands that there is such a thing as a DCI. Not only the press, but presidents and government officials as well never refer to the DCI by that title; they always speak instead of the "Director of the CIA," as if that person were simply an agency head, forgetting the importance of the larger coordination responsibility.

Is Ridge to become the central coordinating official in practice that the DCI is supposed to be in principle? If so, why will he be better positioned to do the job than the DCI has been in the past? The DCI has always had an office next to the White House as well as at the CIA, and Ridge will have to spend most of his time on matters other than intelligence. A special review by a group under General Brent Scowcroft, the new head of the President's Foreign Intelligence Advisory Board, has reportedly recommended moving several of the big intelligence agencies out of the Defense Department, putting them under the administrative control of the DCI. That would certainly give the DCI more clout to back up the responsibility for coordination. Such a proposal is so revolutionary, however, that its chances of adoption seem slim.

The real problem of DCIs in doing their jobs has generally been that presidents have not cared enough about intelligence to make the DCI one of their top advisers. Assigning coordination responsibility to Ridge may work if the president pays more attention to him than has been paid to the DCI, but otherwise this is the sort of reform that could easily prove to be ephemeral or unworkable—yet advertised as necessary in the short term to proclaim that something significant is being done.

From Age-Old to New-Age Surprise

The issue for reform is whether any fixes at all can break a depressing historical pattern. After September 11, intelligence officials realized that fragmentary indicators of impending action by bin Laden's network had been recognized by the intelligence system but had not been sufficient to show what or where the action would be. A vague warning was reportedly issued, but not one that was a ringing alarm. This is, sadly, a very common occurrence.

What we know of intelligence in conventional warfare helps explain why powerful intelligence systems are often caught by surprise. The good news from history is that attackers often fail to win the wars that they start with stunning surprises: Germany was defeated after invading the Soviet Union, Japan after Pearl Harbor, North Korea after 1950, Argentina after taking the Falkland Islands, Iraq after swallowing Kuwait. The bad news is that those initial attacks almost always succeed in blindsiding the victims and inflicting terrible losses.

Once a war is underway, it becomes much harder to surprise the victim. The original surprise puts the victim on unambiguous notice. It shears away the many strong reasons that exist in peacetime to estimate that an adversary will not take the risk of attacking. It was easier for Japan to surprise the United States at Pearl Harbor than at Midway. But even in the midst of war, surprise attacks often succeed in doing real damage: recall the Battle of the Bulge or the Tet offensive. For Americans, September 11 was the Pearl Harbor of terrorism. The challenge now is to make the next attacks more like Midway than like Tet.

Surprise attacks often succeed despite the availability of warning indicators. This pattern leads many observers to blame derelict intelligence officials or irresponsible policymakers. The sad truth is that the fault lies more in natural organizational forces, and in the pure intractability of the problem, than in the skills of spies or statesmen.

After surprise attacks, intelligence postmortems usually discover indicators that existed in advance but that were obscured or contradicted by other evidence. Roberta Wohlstetter's classic study of Pearl Harbor identified this as the problem of signals (information hinting at the possibility of enemy attack) getting lost in a crescendo of "noise" (the voluminous clutter of irrelevant information that floods in, or other matters competing for attention). Other causes abound. Some have been partially overcome, such as technical limitations on timely communication, or organizational obstacles to sharing information. Others are deeply rooted in the complexity of threats, the ambiguity of partial warnings, and the ability of plotters to overcome obstacles, manipulate information, and deceive victims.

One reason surprise attacks can succeed is the "boy who cried wolf" problem, in which the very excellence of intelligence collection works against its success. There are often numerous false alarms before an attack, and they dull sensitivity to warnings of the attack that does occur. Sometimes the supposed false alarms were not false at all, but accurate warnings that prompted timely responses by the victim that in turn caused the attacker to cancel and reschedule the assault—thus generating a self-negating prophecy.

Attacks can also come as a surprise because of an overload of incomplete warnings, a particular problem for a superpower with world-spanning involvements. In the spring of 1950, for example, the CIA warned President Harry Truman that the North Koreans could attack at any time, but without indications of whether the attack was certain or when it would happen. "But this did not apply alone to Korea," Truman noted in his memoirs. The same reports also continually warned him of many other places in the world where communist forces had the capability to attack.

Intelligence may correctly warn of an enemy's intention to strike and may even anticipate the timing but still guess wrong about where or how the attack will occur. U.S. intelligence was warning in late November 1941 that a Japanese strike could be imminent but expected it in Southeast Asia. Pearl Harbor seemed an impractical target because it was too shallow for torpedo attacks. That had indeed been true, but shortly before December the Japanese had adjusted their torpedoes so they could run in the shallows. Before September 11, similarly, attacks by al Qaeda were expected, but elsewhere in the world, and not by the technical means of kamikaze hijacking.

The list of common reasons why attacks often come as a surprise goes on and on. The point is that intelligence can rarely be perfect and unambiguous, and there are always good reasons to misinterpret it. Some problems of the past have been fixed by the technically sophisticated system we have now, and some may be reduced by adjustments to the system. But some can never be eliminated, with the result being that future unpleasant surprises are a certainty.

Reorganization may be the proper response to failure, if only because the masters of intelligence do not know how else to improve performance. The underlying cause of mistakes in performance, however, does not lie in the structure and process of the intelligence system. It is intrinsic to the issues and targets with which intelligence has to cope: the crafty opponents who strategize against it, and the alien cultures that are not transparent to American minds.

Reform will happen and, on balance, should help. But for too many policymakers and pundits, reorganization is an alluring but illusory quick fix. Long-term improvements are vaguer and less certain, and they reek of the lamp. But if the United States is going to have markedly better intelligence in parts of the world where few Americans have lived, studied, or understood local mores and aspirations, it is going to have to overcome a cultural disease: thinking that American primacy makes it unnecessary for American education to foster broad and deep expertise on foreign, especially non-Western, societies. The United States is perhaps the only major country in the world where one can be considered well educated yet speak only the native tongue.

The disease has even infected the academic world, which should know better. American political science, for example, has driven area studies out of fashion. Some "good" departments have not a single Middle East specialist on their rosters, and hardly any at all have a specialist on South Asia—a region of more than a billion people, two nuclear-armed countries, and swarms of terrorists. Yet these same departments can afford a plethora of professors who conjure up spare models naively assumed to be of global application.

Reforms that can be undertaken now will make the intelligence community a little better. Making it much better, however, will ultimately require revising educational norms and restoring the prestige of public service. Both are lofty goals and tall orders, involving general changes in society and professions outside government. Even if achieved, moreover, such fundamental reform would not bear fruit until far in the future.

But this is not a counsel of despair. To say that there is a limit to how high the intelligence batting average will get is not to say that it cannot get significantly better. It does mean, however, that no strategy for a war against terror can bank on prevention. Better intelligence may give us several more big successes like those of the 1990s, but even a .900 average will eventually yield another big failure. That means that equal emphasis must go to measures for civil defense, medical readiness, and "consequence management," in order to blunt the effects of the attacks that do manage to get through. Efforts at prevention and preparation for their failure must go hand in hand.

9.4   Martha Crenshaw, 2001

Counterterrorism Policy and the Political Process

Martha Crenshaw is John E. Andrus Professor of Government at Wesleyan University. An expert on political terrorism, Crenshaw is a member of a Brookings Institution Task Force on policy toward the Muslim world and participates in National Academy of Sciences panels and roundtables on terrorism and counterterrorism policy. She is a prolific author on the subject and editor of the book *Terrorism in Context* (1995).

American counterterrorism policy is not just a response to the threat of terrorism, whether at home or abroad, but a reflection of the domestic political process. Perceptions of the threat of terrorism and determination and implementation of policy occur in the context of a policy debate involving government institutions, the media, interest groups, and the elite and mass publics. The issue of terrorism tends to appear prominently on the national policy agenda as a result of highly visible and symbolic attacks on Americans or American property. However, the threat is interpreted through a political lens created by the diffused structure of power within the American government.[1]

In general, focusing events, such as crises or disasters, trigger attention to a problem by attracting the attention of the news media and the public.[2] Such sudden and harmful events, rare by definition, come to the notice of the mass public and policy elites simultaneously. In the case of terrorism, focusing events frequently come in clusters, so that it is often difficult to trace a specific policy response to a single event. The reaction to the Oklahoma City bombing, for example, is linked to perceptions of the 1993 World Trade Center bombing and the 1995 Aum Shinrikyo sarin gas attack on the Tokyo subways. Under the Reagan administration, the 1986 military strike against Libya was a response not just to the La Belle disco bombing in Berlin but to earlier attacks such as the TWA and Achille Lauro hijackings and the shooting attacks at the Rome and Vienna airports in 1985. Thus, sequences of events rather than single disasters typically serve as policy catalysts.

As Robert Johnson has emphasized, in the United States threatening events are filtered through a political process that is characterized by lack of consensus among political elites.[3] The decision-making process is disaggregated and pluralistic, and power is diffused. Because not all issues can be dealt with simultaneously, political elites—the president, different agencies within the executive branch, Congress, the media, interest groups, and "experts" in academia and the consulting world—compete to set the national policy agenda. They compete to select certain problems for attention, interpret their meaning and significance, conceive of solutions, put them into practice, and evaluate their outcomes. Despite the secrecy inherent in formulating and implementing policy toward terrorism, issues are developed, interests formed, and policies legitimized through public debates.[4] Decision makers with different identities and preferences define and represent problems, or frame issues, in order to gain public support for their positions. Furthermore, the selection and implementation of policy depend on the particularistic interests of the actors or coalitions that assume the initiative as much as consistent policy doctrine or strategy based on a broad national consensus about what can and ought to be done. Lack of coordination and fragmentation of effort are often the result.

The Politics of the Executive Branch

The political process within the executive branch is characterized by progressive expansion of the number of agencies involved; overlapping lines of authority among them; expansion of jurisdictions to encompass new issues; parochialism; and competition. No agency in the executive branch of the government wants an issue on the agenda unless it has an efficient and acceptable solution for it. Thus, public policy problems such as terrorism are typically linked to proposed solutions that are in turn linked to specific institutions within the government. How an issue is defined will typically determine which government institution has jurisdiction over it and can thus take charge of policy solutions, often with corresponding budget increases. (Spending on antiterrorism programs jumped from \$61.7 million to \$205.3 million in the fiscal 1999 appropriations.[5] Overall spending on terrorism is generally estimated at \$7 billion per year.)

As the definition of the threat of terrorism changes, so too does jurisdiction. If the image of an issue can be changed, then its institutional venue may change accordingly. Issues can be partitioned among agencies, or different institutions can have more or less authority at various stages or sequences of a decision. For example, if terrorism is defined as a crime, it is a problem for the Department of Justice and the nation's law enforcement agencies such as the Federal Bureau of Investigation (FBI). However, if it is defined as warfare or as a threat to national security, responsibility shifts accordingly. The Central Intelligence Agency (CIA) and the military become central to the process. Nevertheless, the FBI did not lose its role. In 1986, major legislation established extraterritorial jurisdiction for crimes committed against Americans abroad, which has led to prosecutions in the World Trade Center bombing and East Africa bombing cases, along with others. Definition of the threat of terrorism as "bioterrorism" in the 1990s brought a host of new agencies into the jurisdictional competition, including Health and Human Services (HHS) and its Center for Disease Control. Previously, when the threat of "super terrorism" was interpreted as the danger of the acquisition of nuclear materials, the Department of Energy assumed a key role. In the 1990s, as the threat of terrorism came to be seen as a threat to the "homeland," not only did local and state governments enter the picture but the military was called on to provide "homeland defense." The Defense Authorization Act for Fiscal Year 1997 called on the Defense Department (DOD) to train local "first responders" and to establish response teams to assist civilian authorities should there be a terrorist incident involving weapons of mass destruction (WMD).[6] The result was Joint Task Force Civil Support, established in 1999.[7]

Responsibility for dealing with terrorism is widely distributed, and lines of jurisdiction tend to be blurred and overlapping, with no clear institutional monopoly of the issue. The U.S. government tried to deal with this problem by establishing the "lead agency" concept. The Department of State is the lead agency for responding to international terrorism, while the FBI is the lead agency for domestic terrorism.[8] Nevertheless, the White House National Security Council (NSC) and the Department of State have traditionally competed for institutional control of the issue of international terrorism, and the FBI and the State Department sometimes clash. For example, Secretary of State Cyrus Vance resigned after his advice against a hostage rescue mission in Iran was overruled by the president and the NSC under National Security Adviser Zbigniew Brzezinski. Former Director of the Central Intelligence Stansfield Turner described the relationship between the NSC and executive branch agencies as it affected the rescue decision:

> The National Security Adviser and his staff often are frustrated because they have no direct authority to carry out the President's decisions. That's the task of the bureaucracy, which frequently resists outside direction, even from the President. Bureaucrats are even more likely to resist what they suspect are directives from the National Security Council staff. A result of these tensions is that the staff of the NSC often attempts to sidestep the bureaucracy and do as much as possible on its own.[9]

Turner and the CIA also resisted the NSC's proposals for covert operations against Iran, seeing the dispute as a case of "the professionalism of the experts keeping the political leadership from undertaking ventures that would be embarrassingly unsuccessful."[10]

Rivalries between the NSC and other executive branch agencies also emerged under the Clinton administration. In April 1998, as a result of having read the Richard Preston novel, *The Cobra Event*, the president held a meeting with a group of scientists and Cabinet members to discuss the threat of bioterrorism. The briefing impressed Clinton so much that he asked the experts to brief senior officials in DOD and HHS. On May 6 they delivered a follow-up report, calling for the stockpiling of vaccines (an idea that was soon dropped). *The Washington Post* reported with regard to the stockpiling proposal that "Some administration officials outside the White House expressed surprise at how fast the president and his National Security Council staff had moved on the initiative..., noting with some concern that it had not gone through the customary deliberative planning process."[11] Critics noted that not all scientific experts were disinterested; some stood to gain financially if the government invested large sums in developing technology against bioterrorism.

In the investigation of the October 2000 bombing of the destroyer *U.S.S. Cole* the State Department was said to be less than enthusiastic about the FBI's hard-line approach to Yemeni authorities.[12] While the FBI appealed to the president to demand that Yemen accept a central FBI role, the State Department countered by warning that the pressure would likely backfire.

Clinton's move to establish the position of a national coordinator for counterterrorism policy on the NSC staff also provoked opposition from within the executive branch. The *New York Times* reported that Clinton's May 1998 initiative "had provoked a bitter fight within the Administration, with the Departments of Defense and Justice opposing a key provision that critics feared would have created a terrorism czar within the White House."[13] As a result, Clinton created a national coordinator with limited staff and no direct budget authority. The *Washington Post* reported, "It is not clear how much real authority [Richard] Clarke will have.... The Defense Department successfully fought off proposals to give this coordinator a large staff and independent budget similar to those of the drug policy coordinator.... Clarke's appears to be essentially a staff job, reporting to National Security Adviser Samuel R. "Sandy" Berger."[14]

Moreover, agencies may reject jurisdiction and try to exclude issues from the agenda, especially if they think that they do not have a solution or that the new task is not appropriate to their mission or routine. The DOD, for example, appears divided and ambivalent about its new role in homeland defense. As early as July 1995, some Pentagon officials were calling for an expanded military role in counterterrorism, but this view did not appear to reflect an internal consensus. In a speech to the Council on Foreign Relations in New York in September 1998, Secretary of Defense William Cohen prominently mentioned terrorism.[15] His description of the military mission, however, was vague; he said that the administration hoped to consolidate the task of coordination into one lead federal agency, and that DOD would provide "active support" for that agency's operation. Falkenrath et al. argued that the DOD is not "fully committed to this mission."[16] The military see "homeland defense" as law enforcement, which the military supports only if ordered and when possible. Essentially, in their view, it is a diversion and misuse of defense dollars, and they would prefer that the entire domestic preparedness program be shifted to the Federal Emergency Management Agency (FEMA). The military's reluctance is confirmed by John Hillen, who sees DOD as dominated by interservice rivalries rather than leadership from the president or the secretary of defense: "Today the services are interested in neither the White House's new wars (peacekeeping, terrorism, organized crime, and the like) nor the Joint Staff's futuristic technological blueprint...."[17] The military really wants to fight wars that are like those of the past, only with upgraded equipment on all sides. In January 1999, press reports announcing Cohen's decision to seek presidential approval for a permanent DOD task force, with a senior officer, to plan for a chemical or biological attack on the U.S. quoted Deputy Defense Secretary John Hamre as saying "Frankly, we're not seeking this job."[18]

Similarly, FEMA did not want to take charge of the domestic preparedness program.[19] FEMA officials opted out on budgetary grounds, fearing that the program would be inadequately funded, and thus be a drain on already scarce resources, and that the agency would then be criticized for ineffective implementation of the program. Since they could not afford the solution, they did not want to take on the problem.

In 1998, the decision to retaliate against the Sudan and Afghanistan also revealed disarray within the executive branch, a state of confusion and contentiousness that threatened to eclipse terrorism as the issue at the forefront of public debate.[20] The FBI and the CIA were accused of failing to share complete information on threats in East Africa with the State Department.[21] Disagreement surfaced between Washington and bureaucracies in the field. The ambassador in Kenya in December 1997, and again in April and May 1998, asked unsuccessfully for support from the State Department Bureau of Diplomatic Security for the construction of a new and less vulnerable building. The decision to retaliate was controversial. Some analysts in the CIA and the State Department Bureau of Intelligence and Research remained unconvinced of the reliability of the evidence linking Osama bin Ladin's network to the pharmaceuticals plant in Khartoum and informed the news media of their doubts after the cruise missile strikes. The FBI and the Defense Intelligence Agency were excluded from the decision. Apparently Chairman of the Joint Chiefs of Staff General Shelton objected to the original targeting plan and succeeded in reducing the number of targets.

Congressional Politics

Congress frequently plays a critical role in shaping the counterterrorism policy agenda, without the constraint of necessarily having to present an integrated solution to the problem. Although the president typically has the most power to set the agenda, he depends on Congress to appropriate funds for the measures he proposes, and Congress can block issues or push forward others that the president has not chosen. Furthermore, executive branch agencies usually have their own channels of communication and influence with congressional committes. Congressional staffers and career bureaucrats often have extensive back-channel contacts. Individuals move back and forth between positions in Congress and in the executive branch. Thus, even if the president wants to keep an issue off the agenda or to minimize a problem, he may have to confront it because congressional actions have captured media and public attention. Confrontation is especially likely when the government is divided along partisan lines. The president cannot afford to appear to ignore a potential threat of terrorism, even if restraint might be the most appropriate and effective response. In the 1990s, the president and Congress often seemed to be engaged in a highly partisan politics of anticipatory blame avoidance.

Examples of congressional influence on critical policy decisions include President Reagan's decision to withdraw American troops from Lebanon in the aftermath of the 1983 bombing of the Marine barracks. Reagan was apparently disuaded by congressional and military opposition encountered in the context of an upcoming campaign for reelection.[22] Initially Reagan resisted the idea of withdrawal, although the House Committee on Armed Services urged him to reconsider his policy and issued its own report critical of security at the Marine barracks. Reagan withheld the release of the DOD's Long Commission report for several days in order to limit the damage he feared it would create as a rallying point for opposition in Congress. Congressional responses from both Republicans and Democrats to Reagan's press conferences and speeches were lukewarm at best. Although the movement to reassess policy was largely bipartisan, House Speaker O'Neill assumed a prominent role in the debate, organizing the passage of resolutions calling for an end to the military presence in Lebanon, and Democratic presidential candidate Walter Mondale seized on withdrawal as a campaign issue. The State Department and the National Security Adviser opposed withdrawal, but DOD and the Joint Chiefs favored it. In early January, Reagan sent his national security adviser, secretary of defense, and the chairman of the Joint Chiefs of Staff to speak with leading House Republicans. Nevertheless, Minority Whip Trent Lott stated publicly that the Republicans had told them that they wanted the Marines out by March 1985. Still, in his State of the Union address in January 1984, Reagan persisted: "We must have the courage to give peace a chance. And we must not be driven from our objectives for peace in Lebanon by state-sponsored terrorism."[23] Within two weeks of the State of the Union address, Reagan announced the withdrawal.

An earlier instance of congressional influence over policy occurred during the Ford administration. Secretary of State Kissinger ordered the recall of the ambassador to Tanzania, Beverly Carter, when he learned that Carter had played an active role in facilitating negotiations for the release of American students held hostage in Zaire. Kissinger took strong exception to this violation of the official policy of no concessions and reportedly intended to end Carter's State Department career, although Carter had expected to be appointed ambassador to Denmark. However, when the Congressional Black Caucus intervened on Carter's behalf, generating negative publicity for the State Department, Kissinger relented.[24] It was also helpful to Carter's defense that he was a former journalist.

In the 1990s, as Richard Falkenrath points out, one source of the difficulties of the domestic preparedness program was "its origin in a series of discrete, uncoordinated legislative appropriations and administrative actions," the result of ad hoc initiatives rather than strategic concept.[25] In 1996, for example, Congress began "earmarking" specific counterterrorism projects, such as providing $10 million for counterterrorism technologies for the National Institute of Justice in the Fiscal Year 1997 Department of Justice budget. The FBI counterterrorism budget was also dramatically increased, largely as a result of the Oklahoma City bombing. Congress also instructed the Departments of Justice and Defense to prepare long-term plans for counterterrorism, and established an independent National Commission on Terrorism to investigate government policy. Lawmakers are also concerned about lack of congressional oversight of administration efforts.

Outside the Government

Actors outside the government also try to shape the public policy agenda. Interest groups and communities of "experts," sometimes associated with professional consulting firms, or think tanks, seek access to decision makers in order to promote favored issues. They often accumulate the scientific or technical information about the problem that then causes decision makers to recognize it. They can promote a specific conception of an issue, such as the idea of a new, more lethal and irresponsible terrorism in the 1990s.[26] They contribute the "talking heads" who appear regularly on television news programs such as CNN. They may also be influential in shaping policy solutions because of their expertise.

Among interest groups, in the area of terrorism, business interests may oppose economic sanctions against state sponsors. Interest groups devoted to protecting civil liberties are likely to oppose measures that restrict individual freedoms, such as expanding the power of the FBI or the use of passenger profiling at airports. The American Civil Liberties Union, for example, has frequently opposed legislative initiatives such as assigning responsibility for domestic preparedness to the military. Along with conservative Republicans, civil liberties interest groups blocked the wiretapping provisions of the 1996 bill.

The families of victims of terrorism, as well as victims themselves, such as the former hostages in Lebanon, have mobilized to influence policy. They have lobbied the State Department as well as the White House and Congress, and gone to the courts to press their claims against Iran and Libya. For example, the Victims of Flight Pan Am 103 organization established a political action committee, a legal committee, an investigation committee, and a press committee. They lobbied the State Department, published a newsletter, picketed Pan Am offices, and met with the president and Congress.[27] They were instrumental in the creation of a presidential Commission on Aviation Security and Terrorism to investigate the bombing. They played an influential role in the 1996 Iran-Libya Sanctions Act of 1996.[28] Their intervention led to major changes in airline procedures for handling disasters.

During the Iran hostage crisis, the families of the victims formed the Family Liaison Action Group, which, according to Gary Sick, "played a crucial role in public and government perceptions throughout the crisis."[29] Sick adds that President Carter promised the families that he would take no action that would endanger the lives of the hostages, although Brzezinski was pressing for a decisive response that would protect national honor.

The early development of counterterrorism policy was influenced by interactions between individual government agencies and specific interest groups. The debate over the Airport Security Act of 1973 shows how insider–outsider coalitions form.[30] The government players included Congress, the Departments of Transportation, State, and Justice, and the Federal Aviation Administration (FAA). The outside actors were the Air Line Pilots Association (ALPA), the Air Transport Association of America (ATAA), and the Airport Operators Council International (AOCI). In the jurisdictional dispute between Justice and the FAA, the ATAA and AOCI preferred the FAA, while ALPA preferred Justice. In fact, Justice did not want jurisdiction. While the interest groups wanted the federal government to take responsibility for airport security measures, the Department of Transportation and the FAA wished to rely on local law enforcement.

All of these actors use the news media to articulate and disseminate their views not only to the public but to other elites. Government officials (or former officials) are the main source of information for reporters, as well as for Congress, sometimes openly and sometimes through strategic leaks. Leaks to the press can be a way of conducting internal battles as much as informing the public. The media's attraction to drama and spectacular events also makes it hard for the government to ignore an issue when policymakers assume that public opinion will track media attention. But the news media do not set the agenda, according to John Kingdon: "The media's tendency to give prominence to the most newsworthy or dramatic story actually diminishes their impact on governmental policy agendas because such stories tend to come toward the end of a policy-making process, rather than at the beginning."[31] The media tend to be responsive to issues already on the agenda, to accelerate or magnify them, rather than initiate attention. They report on what the government is doing or not doing.

Jeffrey D. Simon agrees.[32] He argues that the media image of crisis is due to the way presidents and their aides handle events; the press depends almost exclusively on authoritative official sources. Government officials set the tone through background briefings and off the record interviews as well as public speeches and press conferences. Presidents, not reporters, make hostage seizures into personal dramas. On the other hand, Brigitte Nacos argues that government policy is exceptionally sensitive to the news media and to public opinion, especially during hostage crises.[33] Yet the tone of general mass media coverage of U.S. counterterrorism policy is positive.[34]

Conclusions

It is unlikely that the politics of the domestic policy process will change. Thus, expectations for the future should be grounded in the assumption that the trends described in this article will continue. Terrorist attacks, especially spectacular incidents causing large numbers of casualties or targeting important national symbols, will contribute to putting the issue on the national policy agenda. They focus public attention on the threat of terrorism. However, policy will be developed within a general framework of diffusion of power. Multiple actors, inside and outside government, will compete to set the agenda and to determine policy through public debate, conducted largely in the news media. Each actor, whether an executive branch agency, Congress, or an interest group, wants to forge a national consensus behind its particular preference. Due to pressures from Congress, the president will not be able to set the agenda for counterterrorism policy with as much freedom as he can in other policy areas. Where the president dominates is in the rare use of military force, but these decisions may also be controversial within the executive branch. Implementation of policy decisions will also be affected by controversy, due to rivalries among agencies with operational responsibilities. Thus it will be difficult for any administration to develop a consistent policy based on an objective appraisal of the threat of terrorism to American national interests.

Notes

1. Despite its significance, little systematic attention has been paid to the politics of the counterterrorism policy process. William Farrell's early book, *The U.S. Government Response to Terrorism: In Search of an Effective Strategy* (Boulder, CO: Westview Press, 1982), analyzed the organizations behind counterterrorism policy. David Tucker, *Skirmished at the Edge of Empire: The United States and International Terrorism* (Westport, CT: Praeger, 1997), is also relevant, particularly Chapter 4 (pp. 109–132). Paul Pillar's *Terrorism and U.S. Foreign Policy* will also help fill this gap (Washington, DC: Brookings, 2001).

2. Thomas A Birkland, *After Disaster: Agenda Setting, Public Policy, and Focusing Events* (Washington, DC: Georgetown University Press, 1997).

3. Robert H. Johnson, *Improbably Dangers: U.S. Conceptions of Threat in the Cold War and After* (New York: St. Martin's, 1997), Chapter 2, "American Politics, Psychology, and the Exaggeration of Threat," pp. 31–48.

4. The classic work is John W. Kingdon, *Agendas, Alternatives, and Public Policies*, 2nd ed. (New York: Harper Collins, 1995). See also Frank R. Baumgartner and Bryan D. Jones, *Agendas and Instability in American Politics* (Chicago: University of Chicago Press, 1993) and Deborah A. Stone, *Policy Paradox: The Art of Political Decision Making* (New York: W. W. Norton, 1997).

5. See Congressional Quarterly *Weekly Report*, 16 January 1999, p. 0151.

6. See Richard A. Falkenrath, "Problems of Preparedness: U.S. Readiness for a Domestic Terrorist Attack," *International Security* 25(4) (Spring 2001), pp. 147–186. See also Martha Crenshaw, "Threat Perception in Democracies: 'WMD' Terrorism in the U.S. Policy Debate," presented to the 22nd Annual Scientific Meeting of the International Society for Political Psychology, Amsterdam, 18–21 July 1999.

7. It has 82 members and an annual budget of $8.7 million, and is expected to increase to 121 people by 2003. It is based in Virginia, as part of the U.S. Joint Forces Command. In the event of a request from local or state government authorities, it would probably take direction from FEMA. See James Dao, "Looking Ahead to the Winter Olympics, a Terrorist Response Team Trains," *The New York Times*, 11 April 2001.

8. However, the Federal Emergency Management Agency (FEMA) has jurisdiction over "consequence management," which is in effect disaster response policy in the event of a domestic attack, especially one involving mass casualties.

9. In *Terrorism & Democracy* (Boston: Houghton Mifflin, 1991), p. 39.

10. Ibid., p. 81. Brzezinski set up an NSC committee to oversee covert actions because the CIA estimated that prospects for success were low. The CIA then vetoed the list of operations the NSC suggested, but Brzezinski was reluctant to take the dispute to the president.

11. 21 May 1998, p. A1.

12. See John F. Burns, "U.S. Aides Say the Yemenis Seem to Hinder Cole Inquiry," *The New York Times*, 1 November 2000.

13. 26 April 1998.

14. 23 May 1998, p. A3.

15. For the text of the speech, see ⟨http://www.defenselink.mil/news/Sep1998⟩.

16. Richard A. Falkenrath, Robert D. Newman, and Bradley A. Thayer, *America's Achilles Heel: Nuclear, Biological, and Chemical Terrorism and Covert Attack* (Cambridge, MA: MIT Press, 1998), p. 263. See also Falkenrath, "Problems of Preparedness," p. 162, who says that the military see this role as a distraction from their core mission.

17. "Defense's Death Spiral," *Foreign Affairs* 78(4) (July-August 1999), p. 4.

18. *The New York Times*, 28 January 1999; also *The Hartford Courant*, with *Washington Post* byline, 1 February 1999.

19. See Falkenrath, "Problems of Preparedness," p. 163.

20. On this subject, see James Risen, "To Bomb Sudan Plant, or Not: A Year Later, Debates Rankle," *The New York Times*, 27 October 1999, and Seymour Hersh, "The Missiles of August," *The New Yorker*, 12 October 1998, pp. 34–41.

21. See Report of the Accountability Review Boards: Bombings of the US Embassies in Nairobi, Kenya and Dar Es Salaam, Tanzania on August 7, 1998, 11 January 1999. Available at ⟨http://www.zgram.net/embassybombing.htm⟩. See further details from the classified report in James Risen and Benjamin Weiser, "Before Bombings, Omens and Fears," *The New York Times*, 9 January 1999. According to this account, the Kenyan authorities arrested a group of suspects but the CIA Station Chief declined to interview them.

22. This section relies on research assistance by Karen Millard. See press reports such as Lou Cannon, "Political Pressure for Marine Pullout Likely to Increase," *The Washington Post*, 29 December 1983; Martin Tolchin, "House Leaders Urge New Study of Beirut Policy," *The New York Times*, 3 January 1984; and John Goshko and Margaret Shapiro, "Shultz Asks for Support on Lebanon; Holds Hill Parleys as Pressure for Withdrawal Grows,": *The Washington Post*, 27 January 1984.

23. See text in *The Washington Post*, 26 January 1984, p. A16.

24. See *The New York Times*, 14, 18, and 20 August 1975. Kate Whitman assisted with the research of this case.

25. Falkenrath, "Problems of Preparedness," p. 149.

26. For example, Ian O. Lesser et al., *Countering the New Terrorism* (Santa Monica, CA: Rand Corporation, 1999). The study was commissioned by the Air Force.

27. See Steven Emerson and Brian Duffy, *The Fall of Pan Am 103: Inside the Lockerbie Investigation* (New York: G. P. Putnams' Sons, 1990), especially pp. 221–225.

28. See Gideon Rose's account of the politics of the legislative process in his chapter on Libya in Richard N. Haass, ed., *Economic Sanctions and American Diplomacy* (New York: Council on Foreign Relations, 1998), pp. 129–156, especially pp. 142–144. See also Patrick Clawson's chapter on Iran, pp. 85–106.

29. See his chapter, "Taking vows: The domestication of policy-making in hostage incidents," in *Origins of Terrorism*, edited by Walter Reich (Washington, DC: Woodrow Wilson Center and Cambridge University Press, 1990), pp. 238–239.

30. Joel Rothman assisted with research on this debate. See U.S. Senate, Committee on Commerce, Subcommittee on Aviation, *The Anti-Hijacking Act of 1971*. Hearing. 92nd Cong., 2d sess., 1972.

31. Kingdon, *Agendas, Alternatives, and Public Policies*, p. 59.

32. *The Terrorist Trap: America's Experience with Terrorism* (Bloomington: Indiana University Press, 1994), especially Chapter 7, "Media Players," pp. 261–308.

33. *Terrorism and the Media* (New York: Columbia University Press, 1994).

34. Measured by references to international terrorism in the *Readers' Guide to Periodical Literature* 1968–1998. Database available upon request.

Chapter 10

The Instruments of Counterterrorism

To combat the threat of terrorism, the United States will need to strengthen and develop its counterterrorist tools. Four authors explore potential tools—of military capabilities, of the practice of assassination, and of utilizing a private-sector "army" of techno-experts to develop our best defenses.

Sam C. Sarkesian looks at special forces, for the war against the Taliban has brought renewed attention to these ranks. "The air campaign captured the initial spotlight," says Sarkesian, "but soon the more intriguing focus was on the U.S. Army Special Operations Forces (SOF), because they functioned on the ground in close conjunction with the Northern Alliance." Although the war in Afghanistan has been dubbed a "a new kind of war," the author argues that the tactics and doctrines used are rooted in the past. Sarkesian surveys the history of special forces groups and determines that these ranks have had a checkered past: the Office of Strategic Services (OSS) of World War II were seen by members of the military establishment as "screwball, or worse"; the American political system and its military have always been uneasy with these groups and their unconventional tactics. Yet Sarkesian explains that this type of profile is integral to how these groups need to operate—and to the culture they need to maintain to be successful. They function in an ambiguous arena; they do not always wear uniforms; indexes of success are not easy to determine; they oppose other military forces in unconventional ways. Sarkesian concludes that the Army Special Forces have evolved into an elite force with the ability to succeed in any mission put before them—and they need to be kept distinct from mainstream military strategy and doctrine to function effectively.

According to military expert Rob de Wijk, the events of September 11 "clarified the urgent need to refocus and restructure the way the United States and its allies think about and plan for a military campaign." This effort will require a new approach and new assets: developing irregular forces that are well-practiced in guerrilla tactics and asymmetrical retaliation; strengthening both special operations forces (SOF) and human intelligence (HUMINT), capabilities the author defines as being now scarce; abandoning some beliefs about traditional warfare; and sharpening the skills of coercive diplomacy, when dealing with states. Finally, de Wijk delves into the cultural aspect of this new war, of which a central component, he writes, "is the campaign to win the support of the populace of the opponent. In other words, the United States and its allies must also wage a battle for the hearts and minds of the people… in the Islamic world."

Daniel B. Pickard explores whether the United States should adopt an official policy to approve assassination of known terrorists who threaten U.S. Security. Pickard examines the legal history, as well as complex questions surrounding the legality of officially sanctioned assassination under today's international and U.S. law. "It may be argued, in light of the severe threats posed by terrorists armed with biological, chemical, and nuclear weapons, that it makes no sense to preserve a special and unique protection for verifiable enemies of the country at the possible expense of the lives and well-being of hundreds or thousands of others," he concludes.

"The calculus of the war on terrorism is different from that of the previous wars," says David J. Rothkopf. Five grams of anthrax in an office tower ventilation system, a briefcase-sized nuclear device, or a dose of smallpox in an airport have the power to kill more people than were lost in a decade of fighting in Vietnam. Rothkopf proposes a resource in our midst to combat the odds: "scientists and doctors, venture capitalists and corporate project managers—the private-sector army that is the United States' not-so-secret weapon and best hope." According to Rothkopf, the marriage of the public-private forces is not new, and he details Tom Ridge's first steps toward the partnership and draws the root of the effort back to the Eisenhower administration's Small Business Act of 1958. But the author advises that the public-private coalition requires a new attitude, outlook, and structure; and the focus should be on efforts that require the federal government's participation, where threats to national security could lead to massive physical or economic devastation. These "regiments of geeks" are the unlikely warriors that can develop the software and analytical resources to track terrorists; the sensing systems to detect biological, chemical, and cyber threats; and the biometric devices that will be the next wave in security tools. As Rothkopf notes of these post–9-11 times, "The opportunity is strikingly clear: The United States can defeat terrorists by drawing on the very attributes that inflame its enemies."

The New Protracted Conflict: The U.S. Army Special Forces Then and Now

Sam C. Sarkesian is professor emeritus of political science at Loyola University Chicago and a retired lieutenant colonel of the U.S. Army. He has authored and edited numerous publications on national security; he was a coauthor of *The U.S. Military Profession into the Twenty-First Century: War, Peace, and Politics* (1999) and one of three authors of *U.S. National Security: Policymakers, Processes, and Politics* (2002).

The war against the Taliban and international terrorism focused global attention on the U.S. military. In the first months of this new war, the United States conducted both air and ground operations in Afghanistan in support of the Northern Alliance and moved politically and militarily closer to Pakistan. As 2001 came to a close, the U.S. military campaign appeared to be successful, although the political outcome remained unclear. The air campaign captured the initial spotlight, but soon the more intriguing focus was on the U.S. Army Special Operations Forces (SOF), because they functioned on the ground in close conjunction with the Northern Alliance.

The war on terrorism may be a new sort of conflict, but the role played in it by the Special Forces is not at all "new." The origins of Special Forces stem from the legacy of unconventional conflicts in the American past, and while their history has been difficult and at times troubling, their place in the American political–military system has become increasingly secure.[1]

Introduction

The strategic dimension of the U.S. effort beginning in September 2001 was termed a "new kind of war." However, many of the tactical elements and doctrinal concepts are rooted in the past. From all indications, this new war has the earmarks of the type of unconventional war that the United States has experienced throughout much of its history. Indeed, Americans have consistently responded to unconventional warfare by fielding *ad hoc* fighting units, from Rogers' Rangers in the French and Indian War to the 1st Special Service Force and Office of Strategic Services (OSS) in World War II. But such organizations were considered, by definition, "unconventional" and thus abandoned after each emergency.

Assessing the U.S. Army's involvement in the Seminole Wars (1810–58), for instance, military historian Russell F. Weigley concluded:

> A historical pattern was beginning to work itself out: occasionally the American Army has had to wage guerrilla war, but guerrilla warfare is so incongruous to the

natural methods and habits of a stable and well-to-do society that the American Army has tended to regard it as abnormal and to forget about it whenever possible. Each new experience with irregular warfare has required then, that appropriate techniques be learned all over.[2]

Only in World War II was a systematic effort made to plan and conduct unconventional war, specifically guerrilla warfare through the OSS, a civilian-led organization known primarily for its intelligence and espionage activities, but which also implemented its own "guerrilla" operations under the guidance of William ("Wild Bill") Donovan. From 1942 to 1945, OSS ran unconventional operations behind enemy lines in Europe and Southeast Asia. But military brass still considered the OSS outside the mainstream of the American political–military system, and especially resented its relative freedom of action and apparent disregard for standard operating procedure. Charles Simpson writes that "to many in the regular establishment, the OSS was a bunch of screwballs, or worse. In retrospect, it is easy to see that the type of man who gravitated to the OSS in 1943 had much in common with those who signed up for Special Forces ten years later."[3] And Alfred Paddock recalls that

> In providing leadership in that area, General Donovan's infant organization incurred the wrath of other governmental agencies, including the military services. Opposition to the intelligence and special operations efforts of the OSS was so intense that [Harvard professor] William Langer, Head of Research and Analysis, later observed that "Perhaps Bill Donovan's greatest single achievement was to survive."[4]

In the aftermath of World War II America demobilized and tried to return to an era of normalcy. But this soon evaporated. The international arena and the efforts at rebuilding Western Europe soon led to the creation of the superpower system and bipolar structure. Combined with the outbreak of the Korean War, the strategic landscape changed dramatically.

In Europe, the imbalance of forces was clear. While the U.S. military performed its postwar occupation duties with a spare one or two divisions, the Red Army maintained the equivalent of 100 divisions poised toward Western Europe. NATO had just been formed and the Europeans were still trying to rebuild after the devastation of World War II. At the same time, many in the United States and Europe were convinced that Josef Stalin meant to conquer all of Europe. The outbreak of the Korean War in 1950 greatly increased the danger of that by drawing off U.S. reserves to a far-flung theater in East Asia. Accordingly, the U.S. Army launched new efforts to develop guerrilla war capabilities, primarily to resist a Soviet conquest of Europe. In addition, North Korean guerrillas also pointed to the effectiveness of such type of warfare against conventionally oriented military forces.

In 1952, the 10th Special Forces Group (Airborne) rose from the ashes of the OSS and 1st Special Service Force of World War II. It was the first formal army organization with a permanent mission of unconventional conflict. Simpson concludes that the Army Special Forces were "born out of fear of the universally expected World War III and Soviet strength in Europe, bitter experience in Korea, interservice rivalry, and the beliefs and determination of a handful of proponents. Next would come growing pains."[5]

The evolution of the Special Forces from 1952 to the present was tortuous and complex. Its troubled history reveals bureaucratic infighting and disputes over doctrine and labels, as well as missions.[6] This was to be expected, since the American political system and its military have always been uneasy with unconventional tactics and organizations. Indeed, until relatively recently, military professionals and elected officials have constantly resisted the establishment of "elite" units. Some would even argue that this remains the case even in the current period, the events of September 11 notwithstanding.

The effort to establish a formal special operations capability was first made in 1951 by Colonels Russ Volkman and Aaron Bank:

> At the instigation of Russ Volkman and Aaron Bank in the army's Office of the Chief of Psychological Warfare the army approved formation of the Special Forces Group (SFG) and a psychological warfare-special forces training center at Fort Bragg in December 1951.... As designed by Volkman and Bank, the Special Forces group would be assigned about 2500 men, approximately half 'Lodge Bill' troops—forces recruited from refugees from Eastern Europe.[7]

The 10th SFG "was formed at a strength of ten men" under the command of Colonel Aaron Bank, the first group commander.

> Bank didn't want raw recruits. He wanted the best troops in the Army, and got them: former OSS officers, airborne troops, ex-Ranger troops and combat veterans of World War II and Korea. They were an unusual lot, a motivated bunch, men who were looking for new challenges to conquer—the more arduous the better. Virtually all spoke at least two languages, had at least a sergeant's rank, and were trained in infantry and parachute skills. They were all volunteers willing to work behind enemy lines, in civilian clothes if necessary.[8]

But applicants for the Special Forces from within the regular ranks of the army were few, probably because of the less-than-enthusiastic army-wide support for Special Forces and the rigorous security classification required for Special Forces personnel.[9] Not until the late 1960s did significant numbers of regular army officers volunteer for the Special Forces. Regular army careers were not made by becoming a Special Forces type.

In late 1953, the 10th SFG was reorganized into the 10th and 77th SFGs, with the 10th SFG moving to Bad Tolz, Germany. In the aftermath of the Korean War experience and regardless of the continuing efforts at Fort Bragg, little was said about Special Forces. Indeed, from the beginning the Special Forces were denied special insignia, and personnel were even cautioned not to do anything or wear insignia distinguishing them from the mainstream military.

The Korean War

The Korean War focused army attention on guerrilla operations. Unconventional warfare units were established, but in an *ad hoc* fashion. Attempts were made to conduct a variety of unconventional operations to support the United Nations effort, but their impact was minimal. The operations of the CIA in Korea, combined with unconventional Army operations, created problems in command as well as missions. The Army's unconventional operations included activities aimed at developing and directing partisan warfare, training indigenous groups and individuals to engage in sabotage behind enemy lines, and supplying partisan groups and agents operating behind enemy lines by means of water and air transportation. CIA operations included placing agents to collect intelligence, assisting downed pilots in escape and evasion, organizing small groups for sabotage, and conducting selected tactical operations along both coasts in Korea. The CIA also conducted some guerrilla operations.

There were attempts to coordinate such activities under an overall command structure: Covert, Clandestine, and Relative Activities in Korea under the Commander-in-Chief, Far East. But the separate missions and organizations of the CIA and the Army remained generally unaffected.

> Although the outbreak of the Korean War led to the reconstitution of some Ranger units, army special operations that did occur—infrequent sabotage, tactical recon-naissance, and the taking of prisoners—were controlled by Covert Clandestine Re-connaissance Activities, Korea (CCRAK). This small Korea-oriented covert organization faded away at the end of the conflict.[10]

In early 1953, a group of Special Forces personnel at Fort Bragg volunteered for duty in Korea. These individuals were assigned to units such as the UN Partisan Infantry Korea (UNPIK) and the 8240 Army Unit. But there were no specific operational Special Forces units as such in Korea.

Among other missions, these units engaged in intelligence and clandestine opera-tions. A small group of Special Forces officers were assigned to conduct operations along the west coast of Korea. These units were organized as the 8007 Army Unit, later as the 8112 Army Crash and Rescue Unit and connected with the 8240 Army Unit, 8242 CCRAK, and 8240 UNPIK.

While efforts were made to conduct operations behind enemy lines and along the coast of Korea, successes were few and far between. On the west coast of Korea, one group operated from the island of Cho-do and later Paengnyong-do. Among other ac-tions, the group organized a training camp for Korean agents. Training included marks-manship, team organization for insertion into enemy territory, organization of escape and evasion networks, and intelligence collection.

Two efforts illustrate the difficulty in completing assigned missions. A fairly large Korean fishing vessel was transformed from a sailing vessel to a motor driven one. On one mission, an attempt was made to insert a team during the hours of darkness in the area around Nampo Harbor on the west coast of North Korea. It was undertaken during a U.S. air attack. During the attempted insertion, an intercept was attempted by a North Korean patrol boat. Upon being discovered, the mission was aborted and the fishing vessel returned to the relative safety of its island base. In another incident in an area along the west coast, north of the enemy lines, under the cover of darkness a team was successfully inserted. Unfortunately, the team was never heard from again. With such experience, one can understand why this organization "faded away at the end of the conflict."

As far as can be determined there is no official history of the experience of the Army Special Forces personnel who volunteered for duty in Korea. For example, there is little of anything written about their missions on the west and east coasts of Korea. The involvement of Special Forces personnel in Korea is usually subsumed within the archives of existing units. This is unfortunate because the deployment of Special Forces personnel in the Korean War is the first time that such forces were involved in combat. It deserves a place in the official history of the Korean War.

The involvement of Special Forces personnel in the Korean War and their mis-sions were semi-officially recognized only in 2000, some years after the fact. A Korean

War Special Operations Memorial Stone was placed at Fort Bragg, N.C., "Dedicated to those Americans and Allied Servicemen Who Served with United Nations Unconventional Warfare Forces During the Korean Conflict 1950–54." In that same year, an Internet source acknowledged the involvement of Special Forces personnel in the Korean War.

> By the end of 1952, the first Special Forces troops to operate behind enemy lines had been deployed to Korea on missions that remain classified for nearly 30 years. Anti-communist guerrillas with homes in North Korea and historical ties to Seoul had joined the United Nations Partisan Forces–Korea.... From the tiny islands off the Korean coast... [these forces] conducted raids, rescued downed airmen and maintained electronic facilities.[11]

This was done "under the guidance of Special Forces and other U.S. cadre." In 2001, public recognition was given to the covert organizations and the Special Forces personnel who were involved in the Korean War.

> On March 26, 2001, veterans of the 8240th U.N. Partisan Infantry Korea (UNPIK) received Partisan Honor Medals on behalf of a veterans group in Korea. The group were Korean members of the 8240th. The 8240th trained partisan forces to conduct raids and rescue missions behind enemy lines by air, land and sea from 1950 to 1954. In 1952, Special Forces graduates of the newly formed Special Forces School, 10th AFG (A), were assigned to the 8240th.[12]

Vietnam and After

The most significant upgrade in the history of the Special Forces occurred during the presidency of John F. Kennedy, who visited Fort Bragg in 1962 and imagined the "Green Berets" to be just the sort of force required to fight communist insurgencies in the Third World.

> Everything about the elite troops impressed John F. Kennedy, including the berets. He returned to Washington and sent a message describing the green beret as the symbol of excellence, the mark of distinction, the badge of courage. Shortly thereafter, Army regulations prescribed the color, shape, angle of droop, authorization to wear, and the insignia.[13]

Not surprisingly, Kennedy gave the Special Forces a leading role in the early years of the Vietnam War, with decidedly mixed results for the organization.[14] Commenting on the conduct of unconventional operations by Special Forces in Vietnam, Kelly concludes that "the conduct of these operations was one of the most significant contributions of the Special Forces to the war effort in Vietnam."[15] But as Stanton observes, "in the wake of South Vietnam's total defeat... the Army and its Special Forces fell in such disfavor that the country's unconventional warfare capability nearly disappeared during the 1970s."[16]

The professionalism and heroics celebrated in the John Wayne film *Green Berets* and Sgt. Barry Sadler's number-one hit song of the same name thus failed to survive Americans' disillusionment over the cause in Vietnam. Far from proving the Army's need for a permanent, elite, unconventional force, therefore, the Vietnam War only revived the historical American resistance to the establishment and conduct of special units. As Colonel Francis J. Kelly recounts:

An elite group has always appeared within the Army during every war in which the United States has been engaged.... As surely as such groups arose, there arose also the grievances of the normally conservative military men who rejected whatever was distinctive or different or special.... If a new military program or unit is being developed in order to meet new needs, new threats, or new tactics, consideration should be given to the use of elite U.S. Army units despite the customary resistance to change or elitism usually found in conservative establishments.[17]

In the aftermath of Vietnam, therefore, Army Special Forces were obliged to struggle in hopes of restoring their legitimacy and credibility in the eyes of the public, Congress, and military brass. Only the accession of Ronald Reagan, like that of Kennedy, revived the prospects for unconventional warfare. In 1982, the activation of the first Special Operations Command gave the Army's effort a more meaningful posture, with the inclusion of Special Forces, Ranger units, and civil affairs and psychological warfare units in the new command. In 1987, the U.S. Special Operations Command was created with special operations forces of all military services under its command. The Office of Assistant Secretary of Defense for Special Operations and Low Intensity Conflict was created in 1988. While all of this was not implemented smoothly, special operations did become an integral part of the military system as well as the Department of Defense.

The payoff was evident in the 1991 Gulf War, when the Army's SOF performed with such effectiveness that few civilian or military leaders questioned the need for such forces. As a result, they were ready and waiting when the September 11 terrorist attacks tossed U.S. military forces into the most unconventional warfare of all in the most rugged and remote theater of war.

In the current era, the missions of the Special Forces have increased to include unconventional warfare, direct action, special reconnaissance, foreign internal defense, counterterrorism, psychological operations, civil affairs, coalition warfare/support, humanitarian and civic action, other individual missions (training, advising and assisting host-nation militaries), and other missions.[18]

As noted earlier, in 1990 the U.S. Army first Special Operations Command was redesignated the U.S. Army Special Forces Command (Airborne). This Command has control over five active component groups and exercises training oversight of two Army National Guard groups. Each Group is regionally oriented to support one of the war fighting commanders-in-chief (Pacific and Eastern Asia, Caribbean and Western Africa, Southwest Asia and North Africa, Central and South America, Europe and Western Asia, and Asia). The area orientation of Special Forces Groups can be enhanced by individuals who have the language skills, cultural linkage, understanding of the political–social system, and even connections with people indigenous to the area. A new Lodge Bill may provide the means to strengthen this area orientation by selecting individuals indigenous to the various areas to which Special Forces may be deployed.

Organization and Training

The original Special Forces Group dating from 1952 consisted of 12 A-Teams (called detachments). B-Teams were organized to control more than one A-Team. An A-Team consisted of twelve personnel, and efforts were made to include one from Eastern Europe. Individuals from behind the Iron Curtain were recruited based on the provisions of the Lodge Bill, the purpose of which was to recruit personnel from Eastern Europe and offer them U.S. citizenship upon completing their training and enlisted service in Special Forces. The effort was to attract personnel who had language skills, experience, and would be able to meld into the political–social system of various countries in Eastern Europe. These individuals could prove invaluable once these teams were committed in a Soviet-occupied Europe.

In general, the field and classroom training was based on historical experience and often provided by veterans of World War II guerrilla operations. The primary focus was on organizing guerrilla units and engaging the adversary on hostile territory. Special Forces were thus taught how to set up clandestine communications, avoid contact with regular enemy units, combine with the local civilian populace, and engage in night parachute operations.

Those selected for the Special Forces, then as now, are carefully trained for extended operations in remote and hostile territory.[19] In the current period, training focuses on individual skills including operations and intelligence, communications, medical aid, engineering, and weapons. Each Special Forces soldier is also taught to train, advise, and assist host-nation military or paramilitary forces.[20]

The current training cycle for those selected for Special Forces (those successful in completing the Special Forces Assessment and Selection course) is more formal and longer than that of the earlier period. For example, the Special Forces Qualification Course and other follow-on courses normally take 12–18 months depending on occupational specialty.[21]

The organizational structure of current Special Forces are as follows: At the battalion level, Special Forces operational detachment (SFOD) C consists of a headquarters detachment, including the commander and his staff, five primary staff sections, and a special staff. The next level is an SF Company consisting of a company headquarters, SFOD B and six SFODs A. The SFOD B consists of eleven personnel commanded by a major, and includes a captain (executive officer), a warrant officer, and eight noncommissioned officers.

> The 12-man "A-Team" is the key SF operating element. A captain is the A-team commander, and a warrant officer is its executive officer. Each A-Team includes ten experienced noncommissioned officers, two of whom are trained in each of the five SF functional areas: operations and intelligence, weapons, bridge-building and demolitions, medicine, and communications.[22]

Special Forces Culture and Mind-Sets

Those who volunteer for Special Forces become part of a distinct organizational culture, maintained not only by the selection and training of personnel, but by the indoctrination, cohesion, and mission of Special Forces. "Clearly Special Forces were designed for unconventional warfare, with emphasis on guerrilla operations. This is significant, because in 1952 little attention was given to counterguerrilla, or counterinsurgency, operations."[23]

The concept of unconventional warfare was and is fundamental to the training of Special Forces. To be successful in such warfare, organizational culture and individual mind-sets have to be "unconventional," based on warfare contrary to conventional concepts. "This unconventional, often indirect warfare has long been unappreciated or even disdained by conventional forces."[24]

Characteristics of such warfare show its uniqueness and the gulf between unconventional and conventional mind-sets. The following are five critical characteristics of unconventional warfare.

Asymmetrical

Asymmetrical doctrine and tactics are an offshoot of Sun Tzu's advice to do everything opposite of the adversary—your strength against the adversary's weakness. It follows that the doctrine and tactics employed by those engaged in unconventional warfare avoids challenging conventional military systems conventionally. This is based on the notion that the center of gravity is the political–social milieu of the adversary.[25]

Ambiguous

The battle arena is not necessarily defined in conventional terms or with regard to a specific territory. As the United States learned in Vietnam, body count and territory held are not necessarily real indicators of winning or losing. In unconventional conflicts, the occupation of territory is not necessarily a key factor in winning the conflict.

Equally important, those instigating unconventional warfare do not wear uniforms and can meld into the civilian population. As the United States also learned in Vietnam, those wearing black pajamas were not necessarily Viet Cong, but South Vietnamese peasants—the VC wore black pajamas to easily blend in with the peasantry. Moreover, who won or lost can be hard to determine. Casualties, prisoners, and territorial control are not necessarily indicators of success in unconventional warfare.

Unconventional

Unconventional conflicts require tactics that aim at disrupting the adversary in its weakest dimensions—again following Sun Tzu's notions. Sabotage, terror, and assassination become major elements of unconventional tactics. Organizational structure and tactics are fluid—flexible and adopted to local conditions in which operations occur.

Protracted

Those implementing unconventional warfare are prepared to engage in it over an extended period of time. This challenges the notion of national will, political resolve, and staying power of those trying to respond to unconventional warfare.

Strategic Cultures

The strategic culture shaping unconventional war differs sharply from the usual "American way of war," fixed as it is on seizing the moral high ground and amassing overwhelming force against clearly defined adversaries in pursuit of clear objectives. By contrast, the strategic culture of those waging unconventional warfare must allow for moral ambiguity, shifting definitions of friend and foe (viz., the many "defectors" in Afghanistan), and objectives that change constantly with the play of politics. In short, unconventional conflicts generally follow the principles of Sun Tzu, whereas American conventional doctrine follows Clausewitz.

Special Forces adopts all these principles and concepts for its operations and culture. It is prepared to counter those engaged in such warfare and, at the same time, to engage in unconventional warfare against an adversary engaged in unconventional warfare. This is translated into individual mind-sets. Individual fortitude, capability of operating in small teams with minimum control from higher headquarters, living "off the land," operating more efficiently than the adversary's forces, and capability of integrating into the political-social milieu of the adversary's society are critical parts of this culture.

> The characteristics that have made SOF organizations culture and history distinctive within the primary American military culture have also been the same characteristics that have frequently placed special operations at odds with their conventional peers.[26]

A Final Word

Veterans of the early Special Forces era cherish their hard-won legacy and culture of the "old" era, a culture many believe must endure if the Special Forces are to be successful in their primary mission of unconventional warfare. The most telling view of "old" Special Forces veterans—those that joined the Special Forces in the 1950s—and their legacy comes from a reunion held in Fayetteville, North Carolina, in early June 1982. Commenting on those at the reunion, Simpson writes

> They are a grizzled, likeable, fantastically experienced bunch of tough old bastards who do not apologize to anyone for the wars they have fought and the things they have had to do. On the contrary, they are proud of themselves, their service, and their country. Above all, they are proud to have worn the green beret.[27]

Some see two challenges to this legacy and culture. First are continuing efforts by some within the political-military bureaucracy to shape the Army Special Forces to be more in tune with conventional military forces. Second is the tendency by some to commit Special Forces to simultaneous multiple missions.

The war on international terrorism—a major aspect of which is unconventional warfare—confirms the concept that Special Forces must be kept distinct from mainstream military strategy and doctrine. As pointed out earlier, the culture and mind-set instilled in Special Forces are separate from the characteristics of the mainstream military system, as are the organization and training. Further, committing a particular Special Forces unit to a variety of missions other than unconventional operations simultaneously, and/or having such units engage in one or more of these missions over any length of time, may undermine the skills and mind-sets necessary for success in unconventional warfare. In this respect, missions other than unconventional war must be clearly subordinate, not within the capability of other military units, international organizations, nongovernment organizations, or private military/police systems. The critical factor in these policy efforts is to insure that Special Forces are not transformed into a light infantry-commando type force, a consistent peacekeeping and humanitarian task force, or a substitute for mainstream military forces.

Some of these concerns surfaced at the beginning of the ground campaign in Afghanistan. But by the end of 2001, it appeared that Army Special Forces in Afghanistan were operating well within the parameters of unconventional warfare. Special Forces teams operating with the Northern Alliance melded into tribal groups as part of the anti-Taliban opposition.[28] And there were reports that some within the Special Forces teams were fluent in the local language and familiar with local customs. The Special Forces motto "De Oppresso Liber—To Liberate the Oppressed" was an operational reality in Afghanistan. The hope was that in a new Afghanistan, not only will there be an effective government, but Army Special Forces would not be involved in various peacekeeping and/or humanitarian tasks.

It is clear that Army Special Forces have evolved over a half century to become an elite force with dedication, resolve, fortitude, and determination to succeed in any mission assigned to them, particularly unconventional warfare. No one can fully understand its role today, its culture and the individuals in these Groups without recognizing the "spirit" of Special Forces and its legacy wedded to Colonel Aaron Bank's original 10th SFG at Fort Bragg in 1952. The green beret is the visible sign of such a spirit and legacy. It is "a symbol of excellence, a badge of courage, a mark of distinction in the fight for freedom."[29]

Notes

1. Other sources of background information for this piece include John Prados, *President's Secret Wars: CIA and Pentagon Covert Operations Since World War II* (New York: William Morrow and Co., Inc., 1986); Aaron Bank, *From OSS to Green Berets: The Birth of Special Forces* (Novato, Calif.: Presidio Press, 1986); and John Collins, *Special Operations Forces: An Assessment* (Washington, D.C.: National Defense University Press, 1994). A recent source is Anna J. Simons, *The Company They Keep: Life Inside the U.S. Army Special Forces* (New York: Free Press, 1997). Several references herein the early years and the Korean War are based on the author's experience and reflections.
2. Russell F. Weigley, *History of the United States Army* (New York: Macmillan, 1967), p. 161.
3. Charles M. Simpson, *Inside the Green Berets: The First Thirty Years* (Novato, Calif.: Presidio Press, 1983), p. 11.
4. Alfred H. Paddock, Jr., *U.S. Army Special Warfare: Its Origins* (Washington, D.C.: National Defense University Press, 1982), p. 31.
5. Simpson, *Inside Green Berets*, p. 17.
6. A full historical account is presented in Paddock, *U.S. Army Special Warfare*.
7. Susan L. Marquis, *Unconventional Warfare: Rebuilding U.S. Special Operations Forces* (Washington D.C.: Brookings Institution Press, 1997), p. 11.
8. U.S. Army Special Forces: The Green Berets, *Special Forces: The Early Years* (http://users.aol.com/armysof1/early_years.html).
9. Paddock, *U.S. Army Special Warfare*, p. 149.
10. Marquis, *Unconventional Warfare*, p. 11.
11. See note 8.
12. Special Forces Association, *The Drop*, Summer 2001, p. 63.
13. Simpson, *Inside the Green Berets*, p. 33.
14. For a detailed historical account see Shelby L. Stanton, *Green Berets at War: U.S. Army Special Forces in Southeast Asia 1956–1975* (Novato, Calif.: Presidio Press, 1985). See also Colonel Francis J. Kelly, *U.S. Army Special Forces 1961–1971* (Washington, D.C.: U.S. GPO, 1973), pp. 160–75.
15. Kelly, *U.S. Army Special Forces 1961–1971*, p. 134.
16. Stanton, *Green Berets at War*, p. 293.

17. Kelly, *U.S. Army Special Forces 1961–1971*, p. 160.
18. See http://users.aol.com/armysof1/USAFC.html
19. Ibid., which provides detailed information on the training for officers and enlisted personnel in Special Forces.
20. Glenn W. Goodman, Jr., "Made to Order: U.S. Special Operations Forces Display Their Strengths in Afghanistan War," *Armed Forces Journal International*, Dec. 2001, pp. 68–9.
21. U.S. Army Special Forces: The Green Berets, *Special Forces Qualification Course (SFQC)* (http://users.aol.com/armysof1/).
22. Goodman, "Made to Order," p. 69.
23. Paddock, *US Army Special Warfare*, pp. 149–50.
24. Marquis, *Unconventional Warfare*, p. 6.
25. On asymmetry see Melissa Applegate, *Studies in Asymmetry: Preparing for Asymmetry as Seen Through the Lens of Joint Vision 2020* (Carlisle Barracks, Pa.: U.S. Army War College, Strategic Studies Institute, Sept. 2001).
26. Marquis, *Unconventional Warfare*, p. 264.
27. Simpson, *Inside the Green Berets*, p. 232.
28. See, e.g., Sean D. Naylor, "Not Victims, But Heroes," *Army Times*, Dec. 24, 2001, pp. 14–5 and 17.
29. The U.S. Army Special Forces: The Green Berets, *The Story Behind the Green Berets*. President Kennedy in a White House memorandum for the U.S. Army, Apr. 11, 1962 (http://users.aol.com/armysof1/Beret.html).

10.2   Rob de Wijk, 2001

The Limits of Military Power

Rob de Wijk is an expert on military aspects of security issues at the Clingendael Institute for International Relations (The Netherlands). He also is a professor of international relations at the Royal Military Academy and professor of strategic studies at Leiden University. A former head of the Defence Concepts Division of the Netherlands Ministry of Defence, he is also co-author of *NATO on the Brink of the New Millennium: The Battle for Consensus* (1998).

Defense planning had only fleetingly dealt with the threat of apocalyptic terrorism prior to September 11. If the hastily revised U.S. quadrennial defense guidelines give any insight, the basis of defense planning will now shift from a threat-based model, analyzing whom the adversary might be, to capability-based planning, which focuses more on how an adversary might fight. Adopting this model is a great step forward, but the review itself offers little insight into the question of how an adversary might actually fight and what forces are needed to fight and win future wars.[1] The events of September 11 clarified the urgent need to refocus and restructure the way the United States and its allies think about and plan for a military campaign.

- The West's armed forces are fundamentally flawed. Conceptually, the focus is still on conventional warfare, but the new wars will be unconventional.

- Contemporary concepts, such as limited collateral damage and proportionality, have little value when preparing for the new wars.
- How concepts such as coercive diplomacy and coercion can be used effectively is unclear.

In sum, the United States and its allies face significant practical as well as conceptual challenges. The September 11 attacks demonstrated that terrorism no longer can be considered a tactical or local challenge, requiring cooperation between the national intelligence services and the police. The new terrorism is a strategic or international challenge, requiring international cooperation between intelligence services and armed forces. Meeting the challenge requires a new approach as well as new assets.

'Savage Warfare'

Western armed forces demonstrated their superiority clearly during the Persian Gulf War in 1991 when, after the extensive use of airpower, U.S. ground forces gained a decisive victory over Iraq within 100 hours. In contrast to conventional warfare, which relies on technological capabilities—manned arms and standoff weaponry—to engage the enemy, terrorists fight unconventionally. Technology plays a supporting role at best, for personal protection, communications, and targeting. In the final analysis, however, successes depend on old-fashioned fighting skills and the use of knives or small-caliber arms in search-and-destroy operations.

In conventional warfare, armies take and hold ground, air forces conduct strategic bombing operations and engage the enemy, and navies support land forces by conducting offshore attacks and cutting off lines of supply. This method of operation is the Western way of waging war. The new wars on terrorism, however, will have to deal with irregular forces that practice guerrilla tactics, instill panic, and retaliate asymmetrically—when, where, and how they choose.

Actually, referring to the military campaign now under way as the "new" war demonstrates little understanding of the history of warfare. In 1898, in *Lockhart's Advance through Tirah*, Capt. L. J. Shadwell wrote about "savage warfare" (that is, non-European warfare) "that differs from that of civilized people." Some areas in the world have not changed much since Shadwell's time.

> A frontier tribesman can live for days on the grain he carries with him, and other savages on a few dates; consequently no necessity exists for them to cover a line of communications. So nimble of foot, too, are they in their grass shoes, and so conversant with every goat-track in their mountains that they can retreat in any direction. This extraordinary mobility enables them to attack from any direction quite unexpectedly, and to disperse and disappear as rapidly as they came. For this reason, the rear of a European force is as much exposed to attack as its front or flanks.[2]

In Afghanistan today, the biggest change is that army boots or Nikes have replaced grass shoes. Furthermore, local fighters possess limited numbers of modern weapons systems, such as Stinger antiaircraft missiles, which were acquired during the 1980s when the United States considered Afghans to be freedom fighters who needed support in their struggle against Soviet occupation. The basic Afghani weapons platform is the pickup truck, which carries fighters armed with guns; in mountainous regions, the mule is still the most important mode of transportation.

In most Western countries, irregular warfare has always been considered "savage warfare," for which there is no preparation. Historically, the British and the Dutch, in particular, fought insurgents quite successfully in their colonies. With the loss of Indonesia in the 1950s, the Dutch lost not only all their experience in waging this kind of war but also their mental preparedness for such action.

The Dutch army is now preparing a new field manual on counterinsurgency and counterterrorism. In drafting the manual, the army's staff utilized the old manuals that General Johannes van Heutsz used during the early twentieth century when he was combating insurgents and terrorists in what is now the Republic of Indonesia. Van Heutsz also reorganized his conventional ground forces to confront the insurgents, creating small units of a dozen armed men to carry out search-and-destroy missions. This military action led to an episode that the Dutch do not want to repeat. Today, that army's counterinsurgency operations could be perceived as war crimes. Because no distinction could be made between combatants and noncombatants, the Dutch burnt down entire villages in order to eliminate fighters' bases. For this reason, U.S. secretary of defense Donald Rumsfeld argued that direct attacks on terrorists are useless; forces are required to "drain the swamp they live in."[3]

In addition to consulting van Heutsz's tactics, the Dutch used the British counterinsurgency manual, which is still considered the most detailed manual for this type of warfare. Of the former colonial powers, only the British have not given up their military skills; at the same time, British forces have maintained the mental preparedness needed to carry out counterinsurgency operations.

The West needs special forces to confront irregular fighters such as terrorists, and these forces are not available in large quantities. A distinction should be made between special operations forces (SOF), which are used for covert or clandestine action, and specialized forces, which carry out specialized overt missions. The most famous of all SOF, Great Britain's Special Air Service (SAS), conceived by Captain David Stirling, has existed since 1941. Most SOF—such as Australia's Special Air Service Regiment; Holland's Bijzondere Bijstands Eenheid (BBE); France's new joint Commandement des Operation Speciale (COS) units; Germany's Grenzschutzgruppe (GSG)-9; Israel's Sayeret Matkal/Unit 269; and the U.S. Army 1st Special Forces Operational Detachment, Delta Force, and Naval Special Warfare Development Group—were established in the 1970s as a direct response to terrorist incidents.

When radical supporters of Iran's revolution captured 53 staff members and guards at the U.S. embassy in Tehran in November 1979, however, the United States still had no standing counterterrorist task force. As a result, a rescue team had to be assembled from scratch, and it took six months of preparation before the rescue operation could be launched. Charged with rescuing the hostages was the newly created Delta Force, with the support of U.S. Navy and Air Force airlifts. The tragic end of this attempt is well known. Technical problems and tactical failures caused the operation's abortion, and it ended in disaster in April 1980. Nevertheless, after this failed rescue operation, U.S. SOF received more funding and better equipment and training. Consequently, SOF became an important foreign policy tool for U.S. policymakers.[4]

SOF specialize in clandestinely rescuing hostages. SOF's military tasks focus on infiltrations into enemy territory to carry out sabotage as well as search-and-destroy and rescue missions and forward air control. Western militaries have extremely limited true SOF capabilities, probably no more than 3,000–5,000 troops for all of NATO.

In addition, Western governments have specialized forces that carry out overt actions. The United States has approximately 45,000 such troops; its NATO allies have 20,000–30,000. The U.S. Army Ranger battalions, which specialize in seizing airfields, are among the better known of these units; another is the 82nd Airborne Division, the world's largest parachute force. These forces seize key targets and prepare the ground for the general-purpose forces that follow.

Nevertheless, new concepts such as swarming, netwar, and counternetwar also need to be developed. Deployed SOF and specialized forces must disperse and form a network that covers large areas. These forces must make use of advanced communications, including uplinks and downlinks with unmanned and manned aircraft and satellites to enable quick-response strikes against high-value targets. For the military, netwar requires a different mindset because, unlike traditional formations, it has less hierarchy and less emphasis on combined arms operations.

Even though NATO countries have more than three million individuals in their collective armed services, only a very small portion of them are SOF or specialized armed forces—too few to engage in sustained combat operations. Clearly, it is too late to increase this capability for the campaign in Afghanistan and other countries hosting terrorists. Even if a decision were made to create more of these units, only a small number of young people would be willing or able to join these forces; according to some estimates, less than 10 percent make it through the grueling selection process.

The status of the West's human intelligence (HUMINT) capabilities is similar. For data collection, the intelligence communities of the United States and its NATO allies focus primarily on satellite imagery, signals intelligence, and electronic intelligence. Satellite imagery guides both SOF and HUMINT to targets. Although satellite imagery obtains important strategic information, SOF and HUMINT are the best way to obtain tactical information on the ground, especially because terrorist groups make only limited use of cellular telephones and satellite communications. Since the U.S. cruise missile attacks on his training camps in August 1998, Osama bin Laden no longer uses his satellite telephone, which had made him easy to detect. Instead, he issues "mission orders," instructing his lieutenants orally, in writing, or on videotape that television stations broadcast widely. Consequently, the United States and its allies have no choice but to infiltrate his network.

Tapping into this network is an enormous task, however, because the al Qaeda organization has bases and cells in 50–60 countries, including the United States and most European nations, where so-called sleeper agents live. The individuals who carried out the attacks on the World Trade Center and the Pentagon had been ordinary residents in the United States and other Western countries. Therefore, agents from Islamic states' intelligence communities must infiltrate networks and cells both inside and outside the Islamic world, while Western governments must at the same time recruit agents in the Islamic communities in their own countries. Consequently, effective use of HUMINT requires intensive cooperation among intelligence services worldwide.

Without sufficient HUMINT capabilities, as well as SOF and specialized forces that can effectively address unexpected threats and unconventional warfare—the only option open to the West's opponents—the United States and its allies will find the campaign on terrorism almost impossible. In its most basic form, asymmetrical warfare utilizes one side's comparative advantage against its enemy's relative weakness. Successful asymmetrical warfare exploits vulnerabilities—which are easy to determine—by using weapons and tactics in ways that are unplanned or unexpected. The weakness of Western societies is perceived as their desire to reduce collateral damage by emphasizing technological solutions, the need to maintain coalitions, and the need to adhere to the international rule of law. Moreover, Western industrialized societies are economically and socially vulnerable. Thus, dealing with these new threats requires groups of well-trained, well-equipped, and highly motivated individuals who can infiltrate and destroy terrorist networks.

At the tactical level, the opponent conducting asymmetrical warfare tries to change the course of action in order to prevent the achievement of political objectives. These tactics—including guerrilla warfare, hit-and-run attacks, sabotage, terrorism, and the capture of soldiers who are then shown on television—will confront allied ground forces in Afghanistan and other places that harbor terrorist training camps and headquarters.

At the strategic level, the opponent using asymmetrical tactics exploits the fears of the civilian population, thereby undermining the government, compromising its alliances, and affecting its economy. The September 11 attacks were only partly successful on this score. The fear of further attacks has led to uncertainty about the future among the populations of most Western nations and as a result their economies have fallen into recession. On the other hand, the attackers very likely miscalculated not only the resolve of the leadership and population of the United States but also most of the world's willingness to form and maintain coalitions to fight terrorism.

Direct military action against insurgents and terrorists requires both SOF and HUMINT gathering. Both assets are scarce, however, and not available in the quantities necessary to fight and win sustained wars. Moreover, deploying SOF is extremely risky, and effective engagement requires skills and techniques that come very close to war crimes. Therefore, the United States and its allies need to develop a new defense-planning concept.

The Limited Value of Contemporary Western Concepts

For historical and cultural reasons, the armed forces of Western countries have been disinclined to prepare for military action that was considered uncivilized. As a consequence, policymakers, the military, and the public are psychologically ill-prepared for this war. They have become used to concepts such as limited collateral damage, proportionality of response, and the absence of body bags. The current situation, however, calls for a willingness to abandon these ideas, at least partially, a sacrifice that may be difficult for some individuals and nations to make.

During his visit to Pakistan on October 5, British prime minister Tony Blair called for "proportionate strikes ... [that should] not be directed against the Afghan people."

These concepts have little value when carrying out military operations against insurgents and terrorists for a number of reasons.

- *Collateral damage*. Because asymmetrical fighters do not usually wear uniforms, combatants are indistinguishable from civilians. These fighters depend on the local civilian population for logistics and shelter in rural areas, and in urban areas the population is used as a shield. Moreover, because the Afghan population is loyal to tribes and clans, differentiating between combatants and noncombatants is almost impossible. Thus, the concept of limited collateral damage is almost useless in unconventional warfare, in which civilian casualties cannot be avoided.

- *Proportionality of response*. Proportionality refers to the size and character of the attack and the interests at stake. On September 11, the terrorists turned airliners into weapons of mass destruction. Indeed, for two conventional bombs to cause the death of more than 5,000 civilians is nearly impossible. Additionally, the United States must now defend its national security, leadership, and credibility. If one takes the concept of proportionality literally, retaliation with a few low-yield nuclear weapons would certainly be justifiable, because only nuclear weapons could cause the same amount of damage as the September 11 attacks. Keeping the fragile coalition with Islamic countries together requires less than a proportional response, however, rendering nuclear weapons a non-option.

- *Absence of body bags*. Because vital interests of the United States and its allies are at stake, the concept of an absence of body bags carries little value either. Both Blair and President George W. Bush have the popular political support to withstand the inevitable heavy human losses. General Joseph Ralston, NATO's supreme allied commander, warned, "We cannot be in the mindset of a zero-casualty operation."[5] Whether most European allies are also willing to pay this high price is doubtful. Initially, the Belgian and Dutch governments saw invoking Article 5 of the NATO treaty as a symbolic measure and a demonstration of transatlantic solidarity. Other governments agreed so that they would be consulted on U.S. decisions and have some influence on U.S. decisionmaking. Except for the United Kingdom, few European NATO allies acknowledged that the decision to invoke Article 5 implies sending their own troops to Southwest Asia.

Thus, combating insurgents and terrorists requires mental firmness, a quality evident in the United States and the United Kingdom today but uncertain in other allies. The traditional concepts of proportionality and limited collateral damage, however, do not have much value under the present circumstances.

Coercion and Coercive Diplomacy

Another obstacle to using military means effectively to combat the new threats that terrorism poses is the limited insight that academics, and therefore policymakers, offer into the theories of coercion and coercive diplomacy, as well as governments' lack of experience using them to achieve the desired outcome. Coercion is defined as the deliberate and purposeful use of economic and military power to influence the choices of one's adversaries; coercive diplomacy focuses on the latent use of the instruments of power to influence those choices. The studies on which these theories are based, however, do not have much relevance for policymakers today. The terrorist attacks on the

United States demonstrate the need for policymakers and the military to reevaluate the concepts that underlie their approaches to balancing political ends and military means.

Most theories of coercion find their origin in the Cold War period, but preoccupation with deterrence has distorted the concept. Deterrence as a concept is useless for today's challenges because the world cannot deter individuals such as bin Laden and his lieutenants. Deterrence also does not work for failed states, many of which provide sanctuaries for insurgents and terrorists. Because negotiating with failed states and terrorists is impossible, both coercive diplomacy and coercion are meaningless. The only solution in those cases is direct action with SOF support, backed up by airpower.

The United States can only use coercive diplomacy and coercion against functioning states that actively support or shelter terrorists. For that reason, Vice President Dick Cheney's warning that the "full wrath" of the United States would be brought down against nations sheltering attackers is an indication of the administration's emerging strategy for combating terrorism.

The problem is the West's lack of experience with this approach. Many cases of coercion and coercive diplomacy have failed. For example, the Gulf War was an unprecedented success, but attempts to coerce Saddam Hussein to comply with United Nations (UN) resolutions during the 1990s failed. The humanitarian intervention in Somalia during the early 1990s resulted in failure. The success of Operation Allied Force in the war in Kosovo was limited because it took 78 days to convince Serbian president Slobodan Milosevic to accept a diplomatic solution based on the Rambouillet agreements signed in early 1999.

Existing theories are based primarily on studies that Thomas Schelling, Alexander George, and Robert Pape conducted,[6] yet even these "classics" do not apply to the circumstances that the West faces today. Schelling distinguishes between "brute force" and "compellence." Brute force is aimed at forcing a military solution; compellence is aimed at using the threat of force to influence an actor's choice.[7] According to Schelling, armed conflict can only be averted when the opponent refrains from taking action. This situation requires a deadline because, without a clear ultimatum, threats are hollow.[8] Accordingly, the United States gave Afghanistan's Taliban regime a deadline, which it rejected, to surrender bin Laden and his lieutenants.

For Schelling, coercive diplomacy involves not only undoing a particular action but also threatening the opponent with the use of force, which can bring about complete surrender. The crux of Schelling's approach is "risk strategy": by threatening the civilian population and presenting the prospect of terror, the actor expects the opponent's behavior to change. This notion made sense during the Cold War, when Schelling's book—in which he sought alternatives to the concept of deterrence—was published in 1966. A risk strategy is meaningless in the war against terrorism, however, because the coercers—the United States and its allies—must clearly indicate that the war is not against the Afghan people, but against terrorists and the regime supporting them. Thus there are no civilian populations (such as the Soviet people in the Cold War) to threaten in the effective use of coercion. Worse, excessive military force could split the fragile Islamic alliance that is cooperating with the United States in the war against terrorism. In other words, coercion might not only be ineffective, it might also backfire. For that reason, humanitarian aid for the civilian population accompanied the initial attacks on Afghanistan in early October 2001.

George's study of coercive diplomacy first appeared in 1971; a new edition was published in 1994, in which George tested his theory on more recent cases. George distinguishes between defensive "coercive diplomacy" and offensive "military strategy." Coercive diplomacy consists of using diplomatic means, reinforced with instruments of power. Coercion, in the form of threats or military interventions, must force an adversary to cease unacceptable activities.

George's main argument is that coercion and diplomacy go hand in hand with rewards for the opponent when complying with demands.[9] In the case of the Taliban, Bush and Blair have stated there is no room for compromise and that no rewards will be given for handing bin Laden over. Consequently, the Taliban had no incentive not to fight for its survival, forcing the United States and its allies to confront the prospect of a prolonged struggle and also undermining the fragile coalition forged between Western and Islamic states.

Schelling's and George's theories focus primarily on the latent use of instruments of power, whereas Pape's theory concerns their actual use. Pape posits that coercion is effective when it aims at the benefit side of the cost-benefit calculation that every actor makes. To be effective, the opposing side must consider the cost of surrendering to the demands of the intervening states to be lower than the cost of resistance. Pape argues that this outcome is possible when the actor withholds military success from the opponent, while offering a reward after the demands have been met. Both the Taliban as well as the U.S. and British governments have vital interests at stake; therefore, the Taliban's will to defend and the West's will to coerce are at maximum levels. Consequently, both sides are willing to pay a high price, and neither will give up easily.

Regarding military strategy, Pape focuses on strategic bombing, which can be decisive only in long wars of attrition. The overall superiority of materiel determines the success of this approach, which was Russia's strategy in Chechnya during the strategic bombing campaign in Grozny, a strategy most Western governments severely condemned as inhuman. Nevertheless, a military coalition may have no option but to use elements of an attrition strategy. Given the unavailability of other assets, the destruction of some training camps and underground facilities may require the use of low-yield tactical nuclear weapons or fuel-air explosives. Moreover, some U.S. strategists are reportedly beginning to consider using the threat of a limited nuclear strike as a method of deterring potential adversaries that support terrorist organizations from using chemical and biological weapons or of destroying the storage site of these weapons.[10] Thus, the use of nuclear weapons might actually be militarily useful in the war against terrorism, but potentially grave consequences—such as fracturing the coalition—prevent policymakers from using them.

Pape argues that deposing political regimes is not feasible "because leaders are hard to kill, governments are harder to overthrow, and even if the target government can be overthrown, the coercer can rarely guarantee that its replacement will be more forthcoming."[11] In other words, Blair's warning to the Taliban "to surrender terrorists or to surrender power"[12] does not have many successful historical precedents. The removal of Panama's President Manuel Noriega from power in 1989 is one of the few successful examples.

Pape concluded that the use of airpower can be successful when it denies the opponent the use of military capabilities. This approach requires a strategy of denial—that is, the destruction of key military targets, including headquarters and command and control centers, logistics, and staging areas. In the case of unconventional warfare, however, the number of high-value targets is extremely limited; therefore, there is little to bomb. Consequently, the only strategy that can be successful is a military strategy of control, which requires search-and-destroy missions using land forces such as SOF reinforced by specialized forces and airpower, but as argued earlier, the United States and its allies have very limited capabilities in these areas.

These studies are useful as a starting point for further academic research, but their work has limited utility for contemporary policymaking. Consequently, the September 11 incidents have prompted both policymakers and the military to rethink their basic concepts and to seek another approach to the old challenge of balancing political objectives and military means. For example, a mechanism of second-order change could be developed, aimed at mobilizing neighboring states against a target state. The Islamic Republic of Iran, which is strongly opposed to the Taliban regime, could play a crucial role by putting pressure on Afghanistan. Pressure from Iran would have the added advantage of involving an Islamic country and thus strengthening the coalition. Thus, reexamining old concepts and traditional approaches are essential to employing military means successfully in the campaign on terrorism.

The Battle for Hearts and Minds

A significant component of the new war—one that has been historically successful for both allies and adversaries of the United States—is the campaign to win the support of the populace of the opponent. In other words, the United States and its allies must also wage a battle for the hearts and minds of the people, in this case, in the Islamic world. This effort—using several approaches, including humanitarian aid and propaganda— must be made along with diplomatic measures and military operations. The humanitarian aid that accompanies the bombs being dropped in Afghanistan in the current fight demonstrates that the United States recognizes the importance of this campaign.

Israel serves as an example of the difficulties that a nation confronts in a war against terrorists and of the way the battle to win the hearts and minds of the population can accompany military measures. Terror persists in Israel, despite the fact that the country has military assets that are important for waging this type of war, including defense forces and intelligence services that are among the best in the world, policymakers and a public who are willing to take risks and to accept casualties, and widespread public support for the military even if mistakes are made. Yet the country cannot prevent or deter terrorist acts or attacks with rockets from southern Lebanon. Israel's experience shows that armed forces—trained, structured, and equipped for conventional war—are incapable of dealing with insurgents. Israel had no choice but to develop new tactics, employ different weapons systems, and use small task forces to carry out small-scale operations; but even this shift in modus operandi has not guaranteed success.

Bin Laden, who is accused of being the force behind the September 11 attacks, fights a battle similar to the Intifada but on a global scale. His objective seems to be to unite the Islamic world under a political-religious figure, or caliph, by removing pro-Western regimes, the state of Israel, and the U.S. presence from the Islamic world.

Israel's experience also shows that, at best, governments can only manage the problem of terrorism. Its solution requires offensive military action, heavy security measures to prevent radical elements from carrying out their attacks, and the building of coalitions with moderate political figures. Israel's experience with gaining the support of the civilian population is important. For example, when the security zone in southern Lebanon still existed, Israel carried out a counterinsurgency campaign within it while providing aid to the Lebanese population therein, including projects to rebuild infrastructure and programs to provide health care. On the other side of the coin, radical movements such as Hamas use nongovernmental organizations extensively for these purposes.

Bin Laden is popular because of his "good works" in the Islamic world, especially in Pakistan and Afghanistan. Indeed, in most Islamic countries, radical groups of fundamentalists have developed a social and cultural infrastructure to build an Islamic civil society and fill a vacuum that their countries' governments have neglected. For example, during the 1990s in Egypt, Jordan, the West Bank and Gaza, Afghanistan, and Pakistan, radical movements provided health care, education, and welfare for those nations' poor. After the 1992 earthquake in Cairo, these organizations were on the streets within hours, whereas the Egyptian government's relief efforts lagged behind. In fact, Qur'an study centers have become the single most important source for recruiting new members for the radical movements.

These types of campaigns waged by radical Islamic movements have very successfully undermined the legitimacy of governments and gained the support of the local civilian population. Consequently, the diplomatic and military actions of the United States and its allies should go hand in hand with a campaign for the hearts and minds in order to win the support of the Islamic world's population. In addition to food rations, U.S. aircraft have dropped leaflets and small transistor radios to enable the Afghans to receive Washington's message. Nevertheless, even a dual strategy of humanitarian aid and military intervention does not guarantee success. Other factors must be taken into account.

Clashing Civilizations

The major obstacle to success in the campaign against terrorism is not military, political, or diplomatic, but cultural. Because of strong anti-Western sentiments in the Islamic world, a coalition to counter terrorism is fragile by nature but critical to the success of military measures. The geostrategic changes that occurred in the 1990s have contributed to anti-Western feelings in large parts of the world. First, the West "won" the Cold War, with the United States remaining the sole superpower; and in international relations the "hegemon" is always met with distrust. Second, in 1998 the differences between the United States and non-Western nations countries became clearer as a result of a new version of interventionism.

The year 1998 seems to be a turning point in recent history. Events that took place in 1998 and 1999 indicated that the U.S. approach had once and for all shifted to a narrower and more selective foreign and national security policy of unilateralism and preservation of the nation's dominant position in the world. A number of events contributed to this image:

- In response to the bombings of the U.S. embassies in Kenya and Tanzania, the United States intervened unilaterally—and without a UN Security Council mandate—in Sudan and Afghanistan in August 1998. The U.S. goal was to strike a blow against bin Laden's alleged terrorist network.

- In December that same year, Operation Desert Fox took place, in which the United States and the United Kingdom carried out bombing raids against Iraq. The military action was meant as retribution for Saddam Hussein's obstruction of the UN Special Commission's inspections of Iraq's development of weapons of mass destruction. In 1999 and 2000, the bombings continued, albeit with limited intensity.
- In 1998, the U.S. government decided to increase its defense budget (which had undergone a period of decline) by 5.6 percent, a development that some nations viewed with apprehension.[13]
- In March 1999, Operation Allied Force—led by the United States and without a mandate by the UN Security Council—intervened in Kosovo to force Milosevic to end his terror against the Albanian Kosovars and to find a solution to the situation in Kosovo.
- In July 1999, the United States presented its national missile defense initiative, designed to protect the country against limited attacks by rogue states using ballistic missiles. This development demanded a review of the 1972 Anti-Ballistic Missile Treaty. With the U.S. Senate's refusal to ratify the Comprehensive Test Ban Treaty, a general prohibition on conducting nuclear tests was dropped.

As a result of these events, many non-Western countries began to perceive the United States as a superpower that wants to change the status quo and create a "new world order" according to its own views. Because of the fundamental difference between Western and non-Western ideas, Russia, China, and Islamic countries distrust interventions that are based on normative principles, such as democracy and humanitarianism. According to Chinese commentators, for example, interventions by the United States indicate that the West can impose its liberal values on the rest of the world without fear of confrontation with Russia.[14]

Only Western governments appeal to normative principles as a reason for intervention. The notion that these principles are universal and that sovereignty is secondary to human interest won ground in the 1990s. The concepts of democracy, respect for human rights, the free-market economy, pluralism, the rule of law, and social modernization are deeply rooted in Western culture and are the product of a civilization that developed over centuries. Universal pretensions and a feeling of superiority are not alien to Western culture.

In 1860 Isaac Taylor wrote about the "ultimate civilization." He dealt with the moral supremacy of Western civilization and considered other civilizations barbaric because they held polygamy, prostitution, slavery, and torture to be legal. After the fall of the Berlin Wall in 1989, many came to the conclusion that Western values, particularly democracy, had triumphed. In 1992 Francis Fukuyama even referred to the end of history, because liberal democracies had prevailed and the collapse of dictatorships was supposedly inevitable.[15] In September 2001, Italian prime minister Silvio Berlusconi praised Western civilization as superior to that of the Islamic world and urged Europe to "reconstitute itself on the basis of its Christian roots." In a briefing to journalists, he talked about the "superiority of our civilization, which consists of a value system that has given people widespread prosperity in those countries that embrace it and [that] guarantees respect and religion."[16] Other Western politicians and the Islamic world did not appreciate Berlusconi's frankness.

Beginning in 1990, Western countries believed that they had the evidence for their claim to universal acceptance of their principles because a steadily growing group of countries, including Russia, claimed that they had embraced Western values. Similar declarations by non-Western governments ultimately mean little. First, these governments can pay lip service for purely opportunistic reasons that may relate to other issues of importance to them, such as trade policy. Second, declarations of acceptance of these principles do not necessarily indicate that governments actually embrace them. Their unwillingness to accept the consequences of noncompliance with these principles at times or, in certain situations, their willingness to set aside sovereignty—for example, in the event of a humanitarian disaster—belie these claims. This notion is particularly true for countries, such as Russia and China, that have rebellious minorities, leading to internal unrest, and aspirations to remain great powers.

The British-Canadian scholar and journalist Michael Ignatieff appropriately posed the following question: Whose universal values are actually involved? He pointed out that the outlooks of Western countries, Islamic countries, and authoritarian regimes in East Asia have fundamental differences.[17] In Asia, authoritarian state and family structures dominate for the most part, and democracy and individual rights are secondary. In general, Islamic countries reject the Western concept of the separation of church and state. Apart from Ignatieff's observation, however, the claim of universal acceptance of Western values constitutes a threat in the eyes of many non-Western countries, if acceptance is accompanied by dismissal of the cornerstones of international law, such as sovereignty and noninterference in domestic affairs. These countries perceive even humanitarian interventions as a new form of imperialism that should not be endorsed without question.

The war against terrorism is a golden opportunity for Western nations to enter a new era of cooperation with Russia and China, which are equally concerned about terrorism. Indeed, bin Laden and the Islamic insurgents in Chechnya are linked. Furthermore, the Islamic insurgency in Xinjiang in eastern China has a connection with the Taliban regime and, most probably, bin Laden as well.

The biggest challenge, however, is the resurgence of Islam, which is a mainstream movement and not at all extremist. This resurgence is a product of modernity and of Muslims' attempt to deal with it by rejecting Western culture and influence, committing to Islam as the guide to life in the modern world. Fundamentalism, commonly misperceived as political Islam, is only one aspect of this resurgence, which began in the 1970s when Islamic symbols, beliefs, practices, and institutions won more support throughout the Islamic world. As a product of modernity, the core constituency of Islamic resurgence consists of middle-class students and intellectuals. Even the fundamentalists who carried out the September 11 attacks were well-educated, middle-class men.

Because the resurgence of Islam is fundamentally an anti-Western movement, building coalitions incorporating Islamic nations in the battle against terrorism is not easy. The coalition that was built in the aftermath of the September 11 attacks was primarily based on attitudes against bin Laden, who seeks to establish an undivided *umma* (community of believers) under a political-religious leader—thereby presenting a challenge to most regimes in the Islamic world. Nevertheless, most regimes and large parts of their populations share some of bin Laden's anti-Western sentiments. Consequently, the coalition is fragile and, at best, willing to give only passive support. Thus, many Islamic people will consider a military campaign that is carried out by Western forces as, to use bin Laden's words, "a Zionist Crusade." Unfortunately, a controversial 1996 assertion that conflicts between cultures will dominate future international relations remains germane in the new millennium.[18]

The war on terrorism could improve the West's relations with China and Russia, but, if handled unwisely, it could also lead to a confrontation with the Islamic world. The United States' nightmare scenario is that friendly regimes in the Islamic world will fall and anti-Western regimes willing to play the oil card and support terrorists will emerge. Thus, the immediate consequence of the war on terrorism could be both ineffectiveness and a struggle for energy resources so vital to the Western world.

Limiting Expectations

As the war against terrorism shifts into full gear, the United States and its allies must meet significant practical and conceptual challenges if the campaign is to be successful. A war against terrorists or insurgents can be manageable, at best, if certain approaches are adopted. In principle, the following options, which are not all mutually exclusive, are available to the United States and its allies, depending on the target of the campaign:

- Pursue a military strategy of control in failed states that terrorists use as sanctuaries. Control involves search-and-destroy missions by SOF, supported by specialized forces and airpower. This option requires the United States and its allies to expand the number of SOF and specialized forces significantly.
- Adopt a strategy of coercive diplomacy or coercion against unfriendly regimes to pressure these regimes to end their support of terrorist movements. If they do not comply with these demands, these regimes should be removed from power, which is easier said than done. This strategy requires new thinking about the optimum way to coerce regimes.
- Use HUMINT gathering methods extensively to infiltrate the terrorists' networks in friendly countries and then destroy the terrorist bases from within. This option also requires the United States and its allies to expand their HUMINT capabilities substantially and to embark on even closer cooperation with intelligence services in other countries.
- Wage a campaign to win the hearts and minds of the Islamic people. This option would enable the United States and its allies to gain the support of the populace and thereby drive a wedge between the population and the terrorists or insurgents.

Nevertheless, even if these options are adopted and prove successful at least in the short term, an overriding issue must be addressed in order to achieve long-term success. The primary obstacle to success in the war against terrorism is a cultural one. To some degree, the battle is a clash of civilizations. Political Islam is fundamentally anti-Western, thus the prospect for success is limited. Using military means may exacerbate the potential that this campaign will be cast as a clash of civilizations, ultimately making the problem of terrorism even worse.

Notes

1. U.S. Department of Defense, *Quadrennial Defense Review Report*, September 30, 2001.
2. L. J. Shadwell, *Lockhart's Advance through Tirah* (London: W. Thacker & Co., 1898), pp. 100–105.
3. "Rumsfeld," *International Herald Tribune*, September 19, 2001, p. 6.

4. S. L. Marquis, *Unconventional Warfare: Rebuilding U.S. Special Operations Forces* (Washington, D.C.: Brookings Institution, 1997), p. 2.

5. "Rumsfeld," p. 6.

6. See Thomas A. Schelling, *Arms and Influence* (New Haven: Yale University Press, 1966); Alexander L. George and W. E. Simons, eds., *The Limits of Coercive Diplomacy* (Boulder, Colo.: Westview Press, 1994); Robert A. Pape, *Bombing to Win: Air Power and Coercion in War* (Ithaca, N.Y.: Cornell University Press, 1996). See also Lawrence Freedman, *Strategic Coercion* (Oxford: Oxford University Press, 1998); Colin S. Gray, *Modern Strategy* (Oxford: Oxford University Press, 1999); Richard N. Haass, *Intervention: The Use of American Military Force in the Post–Cold War World* (Washington, D.C.: Carnegie Endowment for International Peace, 1994); Michael O'Hanlon, *Saving Lives with Force: Military Criteria for Humanitarian Intervention* (Washington, D.C: Brookings Institution, 1997); and B. R. Pirnie and W. E. Simons, *Soldiers for Peace* (Santa Monica, Calif.: RAND, 1996).

7. Schelling, *Arms and Influence*, pp. 2–3.

8. Ibid., pp. 69–91; see also Thomas Schelling, *The Strategy of Conflict* (New York and London: Oxford University Press, 1965).

9. George and Simons, *Limits of Coercive Diplomacy*, p. 7.

10. "U.S. Strategists Begin to Favor Threat to Use Nuclear Weapons," *International Herald Tribune*, October 6–7, 2001, p. 4.

11. Pape, *Bombing to Win*, p. 316.

12. Prime Minister Tony Blair, speech to the Labor Party Conference, London, October 2, 2001.

13. International Institute for Strategic Studies, "U.S. Military Spending," *Strategic Comments* 6, no. 4 (May 2000).

14. J. Teufel Dreyer, *The PLA and the Kosovo Conflict* (Carlisle, Penn.: U.S. Army War College, May 2000), p. 3.

15. F. Fukuyama, *The End of History and the Last Man* (New York: Free Press, 1992).

16. "Berlusconi Vaunts West's Superiority," *International Herald Tribune*, September 27, 2001.

17. M. Ignatieff, *Whose Universal Values? The Crisis in Human Rights* (The Hague: Paemium Erasmianum, 1999).

18. Samuel P. Huntington, *The Clash of Civilizations and the Remaking of World Order* (New York: Simon & Schuster, 1996).

10.3   Daniel B. Pickard, 2001

Legalizing Assassination?
Terrorism, the Central Intelligence Agency, and International Law

Daniel B. Pickard is an associate at the law firm of Wiley Rein and Fielding (Washington, D. C.), in International Trade practice. He was formerly an attorney in the Office of General Counsel, the U.S. International Trade Commission.

I. Introduction

Should the United States government adopt an official policy to approve of the assassination, by its intelligence agencies, of known terrorists who are a threat to U.S. national interests? This is the central question that this work will address.

Although recently this question would for many have triggered an instinctive negative response, the question has become a legitimate area of debate and consideration. This debate, however has been clouded by a lack of clarity in the terms and ideas explored. There is significant disagreement as to what "terrorism" actually means. Accordingly, this work will address two definitional questions. First, what exactly is terrorism? This article provides a brief common-sense definition as well as an overview of the dangers that acts of terrorism pose to the United States and the international community. Second, this article will explore the term "assassination." As this word is likely to trigger a visceral response, it is crucial to establish a precise and consistent definition of the term "assassination" before substantive analysis is performed.[1]

Addressing the legality of officially sanctioned assassination under both international law and United States law will be a major focus of this work. Although assassination has traditionally been considered a violation of international law, the author will highlight recent changes and theories which suggest a possible evolution in this regard. Specifically, the author addresses the question whether the traditional jurisprudence of the 18th and 19th centuries, which banned the assassination of heads of state, is applicable to the dangers faced by modern nations in the guise of terrorism. Next, the author will address the fact that United States intelligence agencies are prohibited from conducting assassinations. Surprisingly, U.S. intelligence agencies are not prohibited by law from conducting assassinations; rather, they are prohibited by a revocable order of the president. Attempts by the United States Congress, including the work of the Church Committee, to state an official governmental policy regarding assassination will be examined in detail.

The current inquiry will also require a special focus on the Central Intelligence Agency (CIA) and, specifically, its covert action arm—the Directorate of Operations (DO).

Lastly, this work will discuss public policy considerations regarding forcible responses to terrorists who target U.S. citizens and national interests.

II. Terms Used and Defined in This Work

A. Defining "Terrorism" and its Unique Threat to the United States

What is terrorism?

Terrorism is prohibited under both U.S. and international law. The U.N. General Assembly and a majority of nations have unequivocally condemned as criminal all acts of terrorism, wherever and by whomever committed.[2] Oddly enough, there has been very little agreement on the definition of "terrorism"; academics, governments, and international bodies have struggled with a definition that incorporates all of the various forms of terrorism. For the purposes of this paper, a terrorist attack will be distinguished by three specific qualities:

1. violence, whether actual or threatened;
2. a "political" objective, however conceived; and
3. an intended audience—typically, although not necessarily, a wide one.[3]

Political motivation for purposes of this argument will also include religious or ethnic motivations. The legal scholars, Professors Arend and Beck, define terrorism as "the threat or use of violence with the intent of causing fear in a target group in order to achieve political objectives." The author will adopt this definition for the purposes of the current inquiry.[4]

Under U.S. domestic law, an act of terrorism is defined as an activity that:

(a) involves a violent act or an act dangerous to human life that is a violation of the criminal laws of the United States or of any State, or that would be a criminal violation if committed within the jurisdiction of the United States or of any State; and;

(b) appears to be intended (i) to intimidate or coerce a civilian population; (ii) to influence the policy of a government by intimidation or coercion; or (iii) to affect the conduct of a government by assassination or kidnapping.[5]

The State Department defines terrorism as the "threat or use of violence for political purposes by individuals or groups, whether acting for, or in opposition to, established governmental authority, when such actions are intended to shock, stun, or intimidate a target from wider than the immediate victims." It is readily apparent that in the realms of academics, law enforcement, and diplomacy, the definitions of terrorism are similar, yet they vary.

Connected with definitional issues are concepts of state support. Iraq, Iran, and Libya have been considered "rogue states," due to part to their alleged support of international terrorism. However, there are obviously differing levels of support by sovereign states for "terrorists," and it would be helpful for purposes of the current inquiry to gain a better understanding of the degree to which a state can be considered to actively support international terrorism.

According to some international legal scholars, there are six degrees of association between terrorists and supporting nations, namely (from most supportive to least):

1. terrorist acts performed by actual state officials;
2. state employment of unofficial agents for terrorist acts;
3. state supply of financial aid or weapons;
4. state supply of logistical support;
5. state acquiescence to the presence of terrorists bases within its territory; and
6. state provision of neither active nor passive help.[7]

For the purpose of the current analysis, it is not necessary to find one "correct" definition of terrorism. However, it is appropriate to use one common meaning consistently and which reflects the essence of the various definitions. For the present purposes, terrorism will be used to describe violence, whether actual or threatened, used for a political/religious objective, in order to affect an intended audience, and thereby to alter an issue of public policy.

The issue of state involvement is somewhat more difficult, but no less important. The fundamental question at issue is whether the U.S. government should be allowed to use deadly force against a known terrorist who is a threat to the lives of United States citizens. If a head of state is actively supporting terrorists, the question becomes more confused and troubling. As this article will discuss, the concept of the legality of assassination has been handled differently depending on whether the country is at peace or during times of war. Furthermore, under specific international treaties, heads of states and other diplomatic personnel are provided specific and strong protections from this contemplated form of violence. Therefore, in an attempt to maintain the purity of the analysis, the term "terrorists" will not be used herein to refer to heads of state or other scenarios where the level of state support is sufficiently high to equate the terrorist with an official state actor.

B. The Threat of Terrorism the Modern World

The threat of terrorism in the modern world is difficult to overstate. However, the frequency with which terrorist acts occur appeared to have created a callousness or insensitivity among many. Much has been written in regard to the end of the Cold War model and its related stability, and the beginning of the "new age" of terrorism.[8] There is nothing new about terrorism, however, the threat has been increased exponentially due to the potential use of weapons of mass destruction (WMD). Today, terrorists are feared not only because of their sniper's rifle or car bomb, but also due to their access to biological, chemical, and nuclear weapons.

America, which has long felt protected on its own shores, has begun to experience the pain of international terrorism. The attack on the World Trade Center in New York in 1993 was, to many, an uncomfortable awakening. The destruction of United States embassies in Africa in 1998 further elucidates the threat to American interests due to terrorists. The tragic events of Sept. 11, 2001, have shattered any remaining illusions as to U.S. vulnerability.

The State Department issues regular reports regarding international terrorism. In the 2000 report on the Patterns of Global Terrorism, the State Department indicated that:

> There were 423 international terrorist attacks in 2000, an increase of 8 percent from the 392 attacks recorded during 1999. The main reason for the increase was an upsurge in the number of bombings of a multinational oil pipeline in Colombia by two terrorist groups there. The pipeline was bombed 152 times, producing in the Latin American region the largest increase in terrorist attacks from the previous year, from 121 to 193. Western Europe saw the largest decrease—from 85 to 30—owing to fewer attacks in Germany, Greece, and Italy as well as to the absence of any attacks in Turkey.
>
> The number of casualties caused by terrorists also increased in 2000. During the year, 405 persons were killed and 791 were wounded, up from the 1999 totals of 233 dead and 706 wounded.
>
> The number of anti-U.S. attacks rose from 169 in 1999 to 200 in 2000, a result of the increase in bombing attacks against the oil pipeline in Colombia, which is viewed by the terrorists as a U.S. target.
>
> Nineteen U.S. citizens were killed in acts of international terrorism in 2000. Seventeen were sailors who died in the attack against the USS Cole on 12 October in the Yemeni port of Aden.[9]

As previously stated, the United States has traditionally felt more secure from terrorist threats than many of our allies. The facts described above clearly demonstrate that terrorism poses a very serious threat to American interests and lives. The recent vicious attacks on U.S. soil have removed all doubt. Furthermore, acts of transnational terrorism trigger responses which, themselves, may further destabilize international peace and security. State reactions to international acts of terrorism have involved abductions of suspected terrorists, assassinations of particular terrorists, military strikes against terrorist bases, and military strikes against states allegedly involved in terrorism.[10] Just as importantly, there is little evidence that the threat of terrorist action will decline in the future. It is due to this truly frightening situation of significant international violence, mixed with new access to WMD, that the U.S. position on appropriate responses to terrorism must be continually re-evaluated.

The United Nations' various constitutional organs have clearly stated the dangers to international peace and security posed by terrorist actions. The U.N. Security Council has addressed the question of national sovereignty, the prohibition on the use of force under the Charter and the issue of state sponsored terrorism after the Lockerbie, Scotland bombing.[11] In the preamble to U.N. Security Council Resolution 748, which imposed economic sanctions on Libya, it was set forth that:

> In accordance with the principle of Article 2, paragraph 4 of the Charter of the United Nations, every state has the duty to refrain from organizing, instigating, assisting or participating in terrorist acts in another state or acquiescing in organized activities within its territory directed toward the commission of such acts, when such acts involve a threat or use of force.[12]

There is no reasonable doubt that transnational terrorism is prohibited under both U.S. and international law, and that it is one of the most significant threats to international peace and security.

C. Assassination Defined

If assassination is defined as a form of murder, a per se criminal act, then assassination itself must be unlawful and there is little need for further legal analysis.[13] Furthermore, much of the recent debate concerning assassination has focused on a contextual definition turning on the question of whether the country is in a state of war. If this is the case, and assuming that it is impossible to be in a state of war with private terrorists (as opposed to another nation), then any analysis will be abbreviated. Again, if the traditional notion of assassination under international law is used, then the term will be understood to apply primarily to a head of state, and an in-depth legal and policy analysis will become unnecessary due to recent international treaties which extend protections to heads of state from use of force by other nations when not in a state of war. Furthermore, as noted, "heads of state" have been excluded from the definition of "terrorists" for the purpose of the present analysis. That is to say, if we define assassination as a crime, then it is not necessary to investigate whether it may be a legal foreign policy tool. Further, as per much of the current literature available, assassination viewed in the context of the Laws of War is not terribly helpful as, by almost complete consensus, a nation may not be in a state of war with non-state actors (and such non-state actors are the focus of the current inquiry).[14]

For the present purposes, the term "assassination" will be used to signify the targeted[15] killing of an individual, by an official agent of a nation, regardless of whether a state of war exists.[16] An "official agent" for the current analysis will generally either apply to a member of the military or of the intelligence community (generally in the latter sense an employee or contract agent of the Central Intelligence Agency, as will be explored further below).

Conclusion

As stated above, for the purposes of the current discussion, terrorism will be defined as acts of violence, whether actual or threatened, used for a political/religious objective, in order to affect an intended audience, to alter an issue of public policy. There should be no question as to the severity of the threat of terrorist action to the United States and to international peace and security.

The definition of the word assassination is almost as controversial as the concept. For the present purposes, the term "assassination" will be used to signify the targeted killing by an official agent of a nation of another individual, regardless of whether a state of war exists, and will specifically exclude heads of state as potential targets. The focus of this article will specifically address whether it is permissible for the United States government to authorize the assassination of a foreign terrorist outside of the territorial United States by a member of its intelligence community (or a member of the armed forces acting at the direction of the intelligence community) under both U.S. law and international law.

III. The Traditional Prohibition of Assassination Under International Law

A. Doctrine of Positivism

Legal scholars have argued that assassination is absolutely prohibited under international law, including acts of counter-terrorism.[17] This may not be an accurate statement.

The best understand the traditional prohibition against assassination, it is proper to restate a fundamental doctrine of international law. That is, "the doctrine of positivism... teaches that international law is the sum of the rules by which states have consented to be bound, and that nothing can be law to which they have not consented...."[18] "In the absence of a legal norm restricting a particular state behavior, sovereign states may act as they choose."[19] In other words, unless the existence of a rule prohibiting a specific action can be established, states are permitted to engage in that action. "For example, a state's use of armed force against alleged 'terrorists' bases in response to a prior armed attack would be permissible unless it could be proven that states had earlier consented to a rule prohibiting such a forcible action."[20]

Thus under the generally accepted theory of positivism, unless there is an accepted prohibition against assassination of terrorists under international law, states are permitted to engage in this behavior. A substantive body of international law regulating the use of force within the sovereign territory of another nation exists and is addressed in the next section of this article.

B. Prohibitions on the State Use of Force Under Current International Law and Authorization by the U.N. Security Council

For the purposes of the current analyses, it would be appropriate to briefly discuss the general prohibitions on the use of force under current international law.[21] It is first observed that the United Nations Charter has been established as to dominant international legal paradigm concerning the "use of force." Article 103 of the United Nations Charter ("The Charter" or "The U.N. Charter") states that it supersedes all other international obligations. It reads, "In the event of a conflict between the obligations of the Members of the United Nations under the present Charter and their obligations under any other international agreement, their obligations under the present charter shall prevail."[22] Consequently, questions of the legality of the use of force under international law must be examined as provided for under the framework of the U.N. Charter.

The U.N. Charter establishes a general prohibition on the use of force in Article 2 (4): "All Members shall refrain in their international relations from the threat or use of force against the territorial integrity or political independence of any state, or in any other matter inconsistent with the Purposes of the United Nations."[23] The first "purpose" listed for the United Nations is "to maintain international peace and security and, to that end, to take effective collective measures for the prevention and removal of threats to the peace, and for the suppression of acts of aggression or other breaches of the peace."[24]

The U.N. Charter contains four explicit exceptions to the Article 2 (4) prohibition on the use of force, namely force that is: (1) used in self-defense; (2) authorized by the Security Council; (3) undertaken by the five major powers before the Security Council is functional; and (4) undertaken against the 'enemy' states of the Second World War.[25]

Under Article 39, the Security Council is empowered to "determine the existence of any threat to the peace, breach of the peace or act of aggression."[26] If the Security Council determines that there has been such a threat to, or a breach of, the peace, it may under Article 42 authorize members of the United Nations to use force.[27]

Under the Charter framework, it is conceivable that an international terrorist organization could be identified by the Security Council as a threat to international peace and security. Accordingly, under the powers of Chapter VII of the U.N. Charter, member nations could subsequently be authorized to use military force to remove such a threat. This topic although timely and intriguing, is beyond the scope of the current analysis. If the U.N. Security Council authorized the extra-territorial use of force, then it may be argued that such use of force was per se lawful. Because this contributes little to the analysis, the current inquiry must focus instead on the question of whether the targeted killing of a foreign terrorist may be legally justified outside of express authorization of the U.N. Security Council.

It may be argued that the contemplated actions may be legally justified through the concept of self-defense under international law. The U.N. Charter allows for the use of force by a nation for the purposes of self-defense.[28] Codification of the customary law right of self-defense is found in both Articles 2 (4) and 51. The question of the right to self-defense as a basis for responding to terrorism will be addressed in further detail below.

C. The Evolution of Thought on Assassination Under International Law

1. Early Thought—Seventeenth and Eighteenth Century Jurisprudence

Under traditional concepts of international law, assassination was generally considered as prohibited tactic of war. One legal scholar has recently argued that there has been a considerable evolution in thought in regard to the use of assassination as a tactic in time of war.[29] A summary of her observations follows:

> "Assassination as a tactic of war was a subject frequently discussed by [legal scholars] in the seventeenth and eighteenth centuries."[30] The traditional view of the law of war asserted that a leader or a particular member of an opposing army did not enjoy absolute protection, or that he was not a legitimate target of attack. The primary focus was on the "manner and circumstances in which these individuals could be killed, [concluding] that they [may] not be subject to a treacherous attack. The writings of most reflect concern that the honor of arms be preserved, and that public order and the safety of sovereigns and generals not be unduly threatened."[31]

Alberico Gentili writing in the seventeenth century considered three possibilities in regard to assassination: "(1) the incitement of subjects to kill a sovereign; (2) a secret or treacherous attack upon an individual enemy; and (3) an open attack on an unarmed enemy not on the field of battle. Gentili concluded that each of these actions was to be condemned."[32] The predominant rationale was:

> the danger to individuals and general disorder that would result if opposing sides plotted the deaths of each other's leaders. Just as important, however was the absence of valor [and honor].... Gentili expressly rejected the suggestion that by killing a single leader many other lives might be saved, believing that such an argument ignored considerations of justice and honor.[33]

Hugo Grotius specifically considered the question of "whether, according to the law of nations, it is permissible to kill an enemy by sending an assassin against him."[34] Grotius:

> distinguished between assassins who violated an express or tacit obligation of good faith (such as subjects against their king) and assassins who have no such obligation. Grotius considered it permissible under the law of nature and nations to kill an enemy in any place whatsoever, though he condemned killing by treachery or through the use of the treachery of another.... [Grotius' reasoning against] the use of treachery in regard to assassination was (that) the (rule) prevented dangers to persons of particular eminence from becoming excessive."

Grotius believed that one attribute of sovereignty was the right to wage war, and that the prohibition of treacherous assassination applied only in the context of a 'public war' against a sovereign enemy. Treachery used in fighting enemies who were not sovereign, such as 'robbers and pirates,' while not morally blameless, Grotius said, "goes unpunished among nations by reason of hatred of those against whom it is practiced."[35]

This author will continue to pose the question throughout this work: What are terrorists, if not the pirates of the twenty-first century?

Additionally, although an examination of writings by the early scholars of international law are helpful in casting light on the evolution of thought in this regard, it is suggested that concepts relevant to a discussion of assassination have progressed beyond what these commentators could have envisaged.[36]

The eighteenth century legal scholar Vattel defined assassination as "treacherous murder," which was described as "infamous and execrable, both in him who executes it and in him who commands it."[37] This is in contrast to Bynkershoek who argued that every force in war was lawful, and that the use of poison, assassination or incendiary bombs was lawful in the destruction of an unarmed enemy.[38] The position that everything is legitimate against an enemy in time of war has been universally condemned in modern times.[39]

Vattel agreed with philosopher Jean-Jacques Rosseau that assassination and the use of poison in war were contrary to both customary law and the law of nature.[40] Christian Wolff, another international legal scholar, stood somewhere between Vattel and Bynkershoek in his view of what was unlawful in war. While the law of nature dictated that a prince fighting a just war neither should kill, nor should injure the noncombatant subjects of his enemy, Wolff noted that the customs of certain nations gave a general license to kill all enemy subjects. Unlike Vattel, Wolff regarded assassination, the use of poison, the plundering of private property and the destruction of flour, food, and drink permissible under the law of nature.[41]

Zengel concludes that:

> The consensus of these early commentators that an attack directed at an enemy, including an enemy leader, with the intent of killing him was generally permissible, but not if the attack was a treacherous one. Treachery was defined as betrayal by one owing an obligation of good faith to the intended victim. Grotius and Vattel also objected to making use of another's treachery. Bynkershoek, however, did not.... Gentili dissented, in effect declaring any secret attack to be treacherous, and limiting permissible attacks upon enemy leaders to those on, or in close proximity to, the battlefield. The reasons given for restricting the manner in which an enemy might be attacked personally generally involved perceptions of what constituted honorable warfare, together with a desire to protect kings and generals. Implicit in the latter [argument] is the premise that making war was a proper activity of sovereigns for which they ought not be required to sacrifice their personal safety.[42]

Early jurisprudence on assassination can be said to focus on the legality of targeting a head of state. It bears repeating that this is outside of the current analysis because there is a consensus that such action during peaceful times is prohibited under international law. Furthermore, the targeting of a head of state during a time of war has generally been satisfactorily resolved under *Jus Belli*, the Laws of War analysis. Although these early writers shed light on the present issue, they are obviously not directly responsive to questions concerning modern day terrorists.

2. Evolution of the International Laws of War in the Nineteenth and Twentieth Centuries

The first efforts to codify the customary international law of war, including concepts effecting assassination, appeared in the nineteenth century.[43] The official view of the U.S. Army (as demonstrated in the Leiber Code) in 1863 held that "the law of war does not allow proclaiming either an individual belonging to a hostile army, or a citizen, or a subject of the hostile government, an outlaw, who may be slain without trial by any captor...."[44] The Leiber Code declared that "civilized nations would look with horror upon offers or rewards for the assassination of enemies as a relapse into barbarism."[45] However, it was generally held "that in time of war every enemy combatant was subject to attack anywhere and at anytime, so long as the method of attack was consistent with the law of war."[46] "It was immaterial whether a given combatant was a private soldier, an officer, or even a monarch or a member of [the monarch's] family."[47] Enemy heads of state and important governmental officials who did not belong to the armed forces were protected from attack in the same way as private enemy persons.[48] The Hague Regulations of 1907 codified the ban on assassinations in the context of war under international law.[49]

It can therefore be argued that assassination under customary international law has been understood to mean the selected killing of an individual by treacherous means. "'Treacherous means' include the procurement of another to act treacherously and treachery itself is understood as a breach of duty of good faith toward the victim."[50] Although assassination under international law was originally prohibited, changes over time began to permit selective targeting of individuals. Consistent with the above interpretation, it could therefore be argued that without an obligation of good faith to the individual, such targeting is not treacherous, and accordingly the traditional prohibitions on assassination would not be applicable.

Obviously, issues directly connected with the taking of human life are of the utmost importance of civilized societies. Traditional legal theories prohibited the assassination of a head of state during war. These theories were premised on both the right of a sovereign to wage aggressive war, and on the belief that assassination was treacherous and immoral. Concepts on the law of war evolved during the twentieth century in regard to "lawful targets." Enemy military leaders in times of war are now generally considered appropriate targets whenever and wherever they are.

3. The Modern Concept of Assassination as Anticipatory Self-Defense

Assassination may be a potentially valid legal exercise of a state's right of self-defense under international law.[51] As has been established above, there have existed, and currently are, specific and accepted prohibitions on the use of force under international law. The U.N. Charter, the dominant legal obligation, generally prohibits nations from using force or threatening to use force within the boundaries of another sovereign nation. The Charter explicitly creates an exception to this binding rule in matters of self-defense.[52] This self-defense exception is widely accepted as a rule of customary international law.

Historically, assassination was prohibited against individuals in times of war due to theories connected with the rights of a monarchy and ideals of chivalry. As modern times have progressed, rules of war have been further detailed and codified. There are now understandings in regard to when an individual is a "lawful target" in times of war, regardless of the question of whether he is present on the battlefield.

Professor Beres has advanced significant arguments regarding a nation's right to resort to assassination as a form of anticipatory self-defense.[53] His writings are particularly relevant to the present discussion. Professor Beres acknowledges that generally the use of armed force within the territorial boundaries of another state is prohibited under the U.N. Charter, and that this peremptory norm of nonintervention "would ordinarily be violated by transnational assassination."[54] It is further recognized that in the absence of a state of war, the assassination of an individual in one state upon the orders of another state might also be considered terrorism.[55]

The current analysis focuses on the legality of transnational assassination as a form of anticipatory self-defense when no state of war exists. Professor Beres highlights the fact that as the Convention on the Prevention and Punishment of Crimes Against Internationally Protected Persons, Including Diplomatic Agents, is normally taken as a convention on terrorism, its particular prohibitions on assassination are also relevant.[56] However, it has been argued that the assassination of an individual in another state may be a lawful instance of anticipatory self-defense when it fulfills the general criteria for self-defense under international law.[57] The author notes that Professor Beres' arguments in favor of the legality of assassination are by no means universally accepted.[58]

There is also a significant controversy as to whether Article 51 of the U.N. Charter requires an armed attack to actually occur before the right to self-defense arises or if this is too restrictive an interpretation. Beres has argued that:

> this interpretation ignores the fact that international law cannot reasonably compel a state to wait until it absorbs a devastating or even lethal first strike before acting to protect itself. Moreover, in the nuclear age—when waiting to be struck first may be equivalent to accepting annihilation—the right of anticipatory self-defense is especially apparent.[59]

In light of the potential for devastating terrorist attacks involving WMD, the right of self-defense has been argued to include the option of assassination. Beres accurately points out that:

> [a]lthough the idea of assassination as a remedy is normally dismissed as an oxymoron under international law, there are circumstances wherein it would be decidedly rational and humane. If, for example, the perceived alternative to assassination as anticipatory self-defense is large-scale uses of force—activities taking the form of defensive military strikes—a utilitarian or balance of harms criterion could surely favor assassination.[60]

The author suggests that, under international law, modern day terrorists are hostes humani generis—common enemies of humankind. In the fashion of pirates, who were said by Vattel, "to be hanged by the first person into whose hands they fell." Equally, terrorists are international outlaws and must fall within the scope of this universal jurisdiction.

D. Conclusion

It is safe to conclude that assassination has traditionally been prohibited under international law. However, the early fathers of international law primarily focused their discussions on assassination in times of war and in regard to heads of state. However, compelling arguments can be made that the timely and proportionate use of force directed at specific individual terrorists by a government may meet the legal threshold for justifiable self-defense under international law.[61] There is a global consensus that nations that suffer a terrorist attack are entitled to defend themselves in a timely and proportionate manner.[62] Unfortunately, most analyses dealing with the individual targeting of terrorists have generally applied a traditional laws of war analytical approach.[63]

The concept of terrorists as modern day pirates, in effect hosti humani generis, are evolving with potentially considerable legal consequences. Scholars have maintained that "acts of terrorism like acts of piracy should be declared 'crimes against humanity.'"[64] The similarity between acts of terrorism and piracy, under international law, are compelling, namely: (1) they fail to recognize or act within the law of nations; (2) they use violence against innocents to intimidate and to coerce governments; and

(3) their actions undermine the legal rules that civilized peoples have developed to guide the conduct of nations.[65]

IV. Assassination Under U.S. Law

A. International Law as Law of the United States

The primary focus of this section is to examine how United States domestic law treats the question of assassination of terrorists on foreign lands by employees of the U.S. intelligence community. This section will primarily examine legislation considered by the U.S. Congress and one very important Executive Order issued by the president. It is worth noting, however, that there is not necessarily an artificial wall between international law and U.S. law. The United States Constitution recognizes that international law and federal statutes are supreme to the laws of the various states.[66] This establishes international law as a co-equal as the highest law of the land under the Constitution. Regardless, the following analysis will focus solely on acts of the Congress and the president in regard to the question of whether U.S. intelligence agencies should be permitted to conduct assassinations of terrorists.

B. The Church Committee

Perhaps surprising to many is the fact that the contemplated assassination is not prohibited under U.S. law. As will be discussed below, the CIA is prevented from conducting assassinations by order of the president. This was not always so.

Approximately twenty years ago, CIA assassination attempts caused considerable concern with the American public and on Capitol Hill. Accordingly, the Church Committee was formed to investigate these issues. The Church Committee, chaired by Senator Frank Church, conducted a congressional investigation during the mid-1970s.[67] The Committee thoroughly investigated various allegations regarding U.S. involvement in assassination attempts and recommended a statutory prohibition on such conduct.[68] However, no such law was passed.[69]

The Church Committee issued an internal report on alleged assassination attempts in which it found that the United States Government was implicated in five assassinations or attempted assassinations against foreign government leaders since 1960.[70] "Four of those instances involved plots to overthrow governments dominated by the leaders targeted for assassination, the fifth was an attempt to prevent a new government from assuming power. The interim report noted varying degrees of U.S. involvement."[71]

One case investigated by the Church Committee was that of General Renee Schneider of Chile, who died of injuries sustained during a kidnapping attempt in 1970. "[The] Committee found that the CIA had been actively involved in efforts to prevent Salvadore Allende from taking office as Chile's president, and that General Schneider was thought to be an obstacle to that goal."[72]

Another investigation was conducted regarding the death of President Diem of South Vietnam. Although the United States encouraged and assisted a coup d'etat by South Vietnamese military officers in 1963, it appears that Diem's death, which occurred in the course of the coup, was unplanned and occurred without prior U.S. knowledge.[73]

In yet another investigation, this one relating to the Dominican Republic, "the United States had supported and provided small numbers of weapons to local dissidents with knowledge on the part of some U.S. officials that the dissidents intended to kill President Trujillo."[74] However, it was unclear whether these were the weapons used in the assassination.

In two other cases, the Committee concluded that the CIA had actively and deliberately planned to kill foreign leaders and, in both cases, it was unsuccessful. The Congo's Premier Patrice Lumumba was ultimately killed by individuals with no connection to the United States, and Fidel Castro has survived to this day.[75]

The Committee concluded that outside of war, assassination should be rejected as a foreign policy option. As the primary reason, the Committee cited the belief that assassination is "incompatible with American principle, international order, and morality."[76] The committee also correctly noted the difficulty in predicting the ultimate effect of killing a foreign leader. The report pointed to some of these potential effects, such as:

> the danger that political instability following the leader's death might prove to be an even greater problem for the United States than the actual leader; the demonstrated inability of a democratic government to ensure that covert activities remain secret; and the possibility that the use of assassination by the United States would invite reciprocal or retaliatory action against American leaders.[77]

Although it may be argued that the report asserts that planned assassinations which are instigated by the United States should be prohibited, the Committee did state that U.S. assistance may sometimes be appropriate.[78]

In addition to questioning the propriety of U.S. involvement in assassination, the interim report expressed concern regarding efforts to maintain "plausible deniability," the deliberate use of ambiguous language, and breakdowns in accountability by government officials.[79]

Based on its findings, the Committee recommended legislation that would have made it a criminal offense for anyone subject to the jurisdiction of the United States to assassinate, attempt to assassinate, or conspire to assassinate a leader of a foreign country with which the U.S. was not at war pursuant to a declaration of war, or engaged in hostilities pursuant to the War Powers Resolution.

No such statute was created. Some scholars have suggested that the failure of Congress to enact legislation forbidding assassination might be interpreted as implicit authority for the president to retain this action as a policy option.[80]

It is worth noting that the focus of the congressional investigations appear to concern the propriety of assassinations in regard to heads of state, and not, as per the current investigation, in regard to terrorists. However, due in no small part to the lessons learned from the inquiries made by Congress, this author will emphasize that if assassination of targeted foreign terrorists is to be adopted as a public policy of the U.S. government, extensive oversight by both the executive and legislative bodies must be ensured. The policy section below addresses these concerns.

C. Executive Order 12333

The authority which prohibits assassination is not a "law" but rather a presidential executive order.[81] Although this Executive Order stands as an important public statement of U.S. policy against assassination, it has been argued that the president could countermand on his own authority.[82] It has been argued that the lack of a statutory prohibition might indicate congressional approval to retain assassination as a policy option.[83]

In 1976, President Ford issued an executive order that barred U.S. Government employees or agents from engaging in, or conspiring to engage in, assassination.[84] That prohibition was reissued without significant change by Presidents Carter and Reagan, and is now embodied in Executive Order 12333 pertaining to United States intelligence activities.[85]

Executive Order 12333 specifically states "[n]o person employed by or acting on behalf of the United States Government shall engage in, or conspire to engage in, assassination. No agency of the Intelligence community shall participate in or request any person to undertake activities forbidden by this order."[86] Interestingly, the Order does not define assassination. It has been argued that this prohibition is targeted against peacetime efforts by the U.S. intelligence agency officials to cause the deaths of certain foreign persons whose political activities were judged detrimental to U.S. security and foreign policy objectives.[87]

"The Executive Order prohibiting assassination, in particular has created general uncertainty about the legality of using lethal force."[88] It has been argued that to the extent that these limitations are not in fact mandated by the U.N. Charter, customary principles of international law, or the U.S. Constitution, they are indefensible.[89] Accordingly, if terrorism poses a threat to national security to which the United States must respond effectively, then, to succeed in this effort, policy planners and military strategies must be entitled "to as much flexibility as possible in combating an enemy that accepts no limits based on law, but only those imposed by an effective defense."[90]

D. Conclusion

Assassination, as traditionally viewed, was prohibited under international law, although there is no consensus as to an express and specific current prohibition. Executive Order 12333 prevents members of the United States Intelligence Community from participating in assassination attempts. However, this Executive Order is not law and can be unilaterally revoked by the president.[91] Furthermore, under the current international law paradigm, as created by the U.N. Charter, it is possible to make a good faith argument that, under certain circumstances, assassination of terrorists may be permissible as a form of self-defense. Moreover, the failure of the U.S. Congress to criminalize such assassinations may be seen as passive consent to such operations if needed. Accordingly, it may be argued that assassinations, as currently viewed, are permissible under both international and U.S. domestic law.

Therefore, the next area of inquiry must be whether the adoption of this option would be a sound foreign policy choice—if it is indeed permissible.

V. The Central Intelligence Agency

The question of the legality of assassination of foreign terrorists by U.S. intelligence personnel is quite a different matter than whether it is sound policy. As has been demonstrated above, such use of force may be permissible under international law, and yet not criminalized under U.S. law. An examination of the policy options involved should, at a minimum, include an overview of the agency or agencies that would be expected to conduct the activities required.

A. The CIA—An Overview

The United States Intelligence Community consists of 13 separate agencies, both civilian and military.[92] This article will focus on the Central Intelligence Agency (CIA). The CIA, established by the National Security Act of 1947, is led by the Director of Central Intelligence (DCI), who manages the CIA in addition to serving as head of the Intelligence Community.[93] The CIA is an independent agency, responsible to the president through the DCI, and is accountable to the American people through the intelligence oversight committees of the U.S. Congress.[94]

The CIA's mission is to provide foreign intelligence on national security topics, and to conduct counterintelligence activities, special activities, and other functions related to foreign intelligence and national security, as directed by the president.[95] The CIA collects foreign intelligence information through a variety of clandestine and overt means. The CIA, its "special activities" that are directed by the president, and specifically the case officer (or operations officer), are of central concern to the present question.

B. The Directorate of Operations and "Special Activities"

The CIA is composed of four sections—the Directorate of Administration, the Directorate of Science and Technology, the Directorate of Intelligence, and the Directorate of Operations (also known as the "Clandestine Service"). Of these, the Directorate of Operations (DO) has the task of covertly executing foreign policy, and is the section that would most likely be responsible for conducting assassinations of foreign terrorists. In fact, the DO and the military are the two primary organizations designated to take covert action under Executive Order 12333.[96] It is the DO, therefore, that would most likely be ordered to carry out such clandestine operations.

The president has the authority through the National Security Council to direct the CIA to perform "other functions and duties related to intelligence affecting the national security."[97]

This has been interpreted to include authority to order covert activities that sometimes violate the laws of the country in which they take place and some which involve the use of force or violence. The President's freedom to act in this area has been somewhat restricted by measures designed to increase congressional oversight of covert activities, but those restrictions are more procedural than substantive. If the President made the required finding that a given course of action was important to national security and assuming the required reports were provided to Congress, a covert operation that involved the killing of a specific foreign terrorist leader or other person would not likely be illegal under United States law.[98]

Furthermore, Executive Order 12333 is subject to modification or rescission by the president at any time.[99] Accordingly, a finding by the president, with direction to an intelligence agency to assassinate a foreign terrorist, arguably would result in the constructive rescission of any conflicting provision of Executive Order 12333.[100]

The 1980 Intelligence Oversight Act increased reporting requirements to Congress, and specifically to the Senate and House Select Committees on Intelligence. These reported requirements included current and anticipated intelligence activities.[101] Significantly, the 1980 Intelligence Oversight Act does not require approval of the intelligence committees as a condition precedent to the initiation of any such anticipated intelligence activity.[102] This failure to reserve the power to authorize covert operations has been equated by some as a disclaimer by Congress of any responsibility for deciding whether to authorize specific covert operations.[103]

The Intelligence Authorization Act of 1991 changed the definition of "Covert action" as an activity of the United States Government to influence political, economic, or military conditions abroad, where it is intended that the role of the United States Government will not be apparent or acknowledged publicly, but it does not include activities the primary purpose of which is to acquire intelligence, or traditional counterintelligence activities.[104]

C. Conclusion

The United States Intelligence Community is a diverse system consisting of 13 organizations, both civilian and military. The Central Intelligence Agency, specifically its Directorate of Operations, is the organization that has been ordered to conduct "special activities," which may include the covert use of force in foreign countries. Furthermore, there are now established congressional oversight mechanisms for review of covert actions. Lastly, Executive Order 12333 may either be repealed by the president or otherwise countermanded, if there was a presidential finding that the assassination of a foreign terrorist was in the interest of national security.

VI. Policy Considerations

The assassination of known terrorists (who are not state leaders) in a foreign nation by CIA personnel arguably is not prohibited under U.S. or international law. As this action is not necessarily illegal, it is important to discuss the costs and benefits of adopting this option as an instrument of official U.S. governmental policy.

A. Policy Considerations in Any Covert Action

The author contends that covert operations in general, and any contemplated assassination operations, should be examined on a case-by-case basis by a bipartisan group of executive-legislative overseers.[105] The establishment of such a panel could be composed of members of the National Security Council, and the House and Senate Intelligence Committees, and could lead to some accepted standards that provide general guidance to the deliberations.

Current available scholarly literature provides certain guidelines to be considered when evaluating a proposed covert operation. These considerations include investigation of diplomatic options, compatibility with publicly stated policy options, and weighing the severity of the operation.[106]

B. Assassination as a Permissible Covert Intelligence Operation?

There are tremendously strong arguments on both sides of the debate as to whether the United States should authorize members of its intelligence agencies to commit assassinations of foreign terrorists. The most common arguments in favor of assassination of terrorists can be described as follows:

1. Assassination may preclude greater evil;
2. Assassination produces fewer casualties than retaliation with conventional weapons;
3. Assassination would be aimed at the persons directly responsible for terrorist attacks;
4. Assassination of terrorist leaders would disrupt terrorist groups more than any other form of attack; and
5. Assassination leaves no prisoners to become causes for further terrorist attacks.[107]

The first point, that assassination may preclude greater evil, may be illustrated using the example that it would have been better to kill Hitler before World War II and the holocaust. The flaw noted with this premise is that hindsight is 20-20 vision, and it is difficult to determine when and if this action is appropriate before the actual harm occurs. Further, it can be noted that an environment in which Hitler could rise to power would be just as conducive to his underlings who would be motivated to promote the same agenda.[108] However, there is a definite appeal to the argument that it is a lesser evil to kill one individual terrorist, than to have innocent civilians harmed—potentially from the use of weapons of mass destruction.

The argument that assassination may result in fewer casualties compared to a military operation, and that it is a more precise weapon, is also difficult to refute.[109] Furthermore, even opponents of assassination as a national security option agree that the assassination of a known terrorist leader can have a significant impact on the disruption of a criminal organization.[110] The confusion and great potential for infighting when a leader of a terrorist group is eliminated is also a strong argument for association as an effective weapon in defending national security interests. Less convincing is the argument that having terrorists in jail serves as a motivation for further acts of violence, and that assassination of the terrorist therefore removes this motivation for potential future attacks.

Perhaps one of the most frequently made counterpoints to assassination is the fact that it could lead to the justification for further acts of violence against America.[111] Closely combined with this consideration is the fact that proponents of terrorism, who may hide, have an advantage over democratically elected officials who must be available to the public.[112] Therefore, reasoning is that the assassination of terrorists would bring reprisals against U.S. leaders, and that such leaders are inherently more vulnerable due to the nature of our democracy.[113] This may be a compelling argument, however, it certainly has flaws. To suggest that terrorist leaders would only be motivated to attack a U.S. leader if assassination was ordered is obviously false.

Furthermore, it is a questionable argument that terrorists may be able to provide better security for themselves than that provided by the combined forces of the federal government. It may also be said that a successful operation, in effect one which stopped the leaders of a terrorist group, would by definition prevent retaliation against the

United States. It is also worth noting that this factor of potential retaliation already exists for any action, including overt operations, by the government. The potential for attempted revenge by terrorists may also be a valid factor for our elected officials to consider. This would most assuredly prevent our leaders from making crucial foreign policy decisions too lightly—specifically including the authorization of the assassination of an individual. Lastly, perhaps it should be noted that we expect certain sacrifices from our officials, which may include possibly placing themselves in danger due to decisions that need to be made in order to protect the nation. Another factor to be considered is that nations that declare a policy against assassination are more likely to be the subject of assassination attempts by other nations.[114]

The most compelling argument against assassination, from the author's perspective, is that the targeted killing of an individual, not in time of war and with no due process protections, is morally wrong. A position, which is similar to the one which argues that assassination is morally wrong, is the principle that, in combating terrorism, we ought not to employ actions indistinguishable from those of the terrorists themselves. That is to say that by resorting to this clandestine use of force we become no better than our opponents. It may be fairly said that the United States does not necessarily oppose the causes of certain terrorist groups but that we find their practices, e.g. car bombs, to be repugnant; and that this is the difference between our nation and such criminal groups. However, this does not appear to recognize that the victims of terrorist acts are often innocents, while no such claim can be made concerning eliminations of such terrorist leaders.

C. Possible Implementation

A central concern must be that if the assassination of known dangerous terrorists were officially part of the U.S. policy who then would issue the orders? As briefly discussed above, the author suggests that, at a minimum, the president would have to make an official finding similar to that necessary to launch a covert operation. Although notification to the leaders of Congress is not necessary before a covert operation is initiated, in a matter this grave, it certainly would be prudent. In these most serious of matters, communication and agreement between the executive and legislative leaders becomes more than reasonable. The framework and scenario are fairly easy to comprehend. If the U.S. Intelligence Community became aware of a known terrorist abroad and his imminent plans to attack crucial American interests or U.S. citizens, then the president would be so advised. There would have to be a finding that the individual was not in a position to be arrested, detained, or otherwise prevented from carrying out the attack. It is assumed that arrest and/or extradition from the host state is not an available option. Although the possibility does not exist of arresting the terrorist, an assassination can feasibly be performed. The president would need to make a specific finding regarding the applicable facts and would be obligated under the law to consult with, for example, the senior members of the National Security Council and the majority and minority leaders of both houses of Congress, as well as the two Intelligence Committees, would appear prudent. Upon congressional approval, the CIA could implement the order based on the president's finding.

The creation of such a mechanism would be an undeniably dramatic change in U.S. policy. Such a significant change in public policy must only be implemented after vigorous, informed, and public debate by our elected representatives.

VII. Conclusion

In summary, it is traditionally argued that assassination is prohibited under international law. However, as has been discussed above, although generally treated as prohibited conduct, arguments may be made that under certain conditions the assassination of known terrorists is not a violation of international law. As to domestic law, it has been clearly demonstrated that assassinations of terrorists abroad conducted by intelligence officers are potentially permissible under U.S. law. An executive order exists which currently prohibits such covert operations. However, despite extensive hearings by Congress, no law has been created which prohibits this foreign policy option.

It may be argued, in light of the severe threats posed by terrorists armed with biological, chemical, or nuclear weapons, that it makes no sense to preserve a special and unique protection for verifiable enemies of the country at the possible expense of the lives and well-being of hundreds or thousands of others. Similarly, in the contexts of domestic law and the U.S. policy, it serves little purpose to rule out any particular action as a future option when the issues and circumstances that may then be present are as yet unknown. There are varying degrees of justification for the use of force when a nation's vital interests are threatened, and current Executive Order 12333 has been described as unnecessarily limiting the flexibility of U.S. foreign policy options.[115]

The question that remains is whether this potential change in policy would be effective in protecting America, its citizens, and its ideals.

Notes

1. Assassination has generally been defined as murder, usually of a political, royal, or public person. The origins of the word come from the order of the Assassins, a Muslim sect of the eleventh and twelfth centuries, whose members furthered their own political interests by murdering high officials. The word is derived from assassiyun, Arabic for fundamentalists, from the word assass, foundation. See Linda Laucella, *Assassination: The Politics of Murder* (1998) at ix. To quote one legal scholar, "The greatest obstacle to clarity of thought and expression in distinguishing assassination from tyrannicide is the lack of an agreed-upon definition of assassination.... A review of the literature in the field reveals a stunning imprecision in the use of the term 'assassination.'" Thomas C. Wingfield, *Taking Aim at Regime Estates: Assassination, Tyrannicide, and the Clancy Doctrine*, 22 *Md. J. Int'l L. & Trade* 287, 295 (1998–99).
2. See *International Law*, Pugh (ed.) at 368, citing U.N.G.A. Res. 40/61, 9 December 1985. See also Convention to Prevent and Punish the Acts of Terrorism Taking the Form of Crimes Against Persons and Related Extortion That Are of International Significance, Feb. 2, 1971, 27 U.S.T. 3939, 10 I.L.M. 255.
3. See Anthony Arend & Robert Beck, "Don't Tread on Us: International Law and Forcible State Response to Terrorism," 12 *Wis. Int'l L.J. 153*, 162 (1994).
4. Id. at 163.
5. 18 U.S.C. § 3077 (2000).
6. Arend & Beck, supra note 3, at 163 n. 45 (citing Office of Combating Terrorism, U.S. Dept. of State, Patterns of International Terrorism (1982)).
7. Arend & Beck, supra note 3, at 163 (citing Professor Antonio Cassese).

8. See, e.g., Louis Rene Beres, "On International Law & Nuclear Terrorism," 24 ga. *J. Int'l & Comp. L.* 1 (1994).

9. The United States Department of State, "The Year in Review: Patterns of Global Terrorism 2000" (Aug. 8, 2001), at http://www.state.gov/s/ct/rls/pgtrpt/2000/index.cfm?docid= 2420.

10. See Arend & Beck, supra note 3, at 174.

11. See Arend & Beck, supra note 3, at 171, 172.

12. U.N. SCOR, 47th Sess., U.N. Doc 7 (1992).

13. See Webster's II, *New Riverside University Dictionary*, (1994) (defining assassinate as "1. To murder (a prominent person). 2. To destroy or injure (e.g. an opponent's character) treacherously.").

14. Cf. Daniel Pickard, "When Does Crime Become a Threat to International Peace and Security," 12 *Fla. J. Int'l L.* 1 (1998) (exploring this issue).

15. See Michael N. Schmitt, "State Sponsored Assassination in International and Domestic Law," 17 *Yale J. Int'l L.* 609, at n.1 (1992) ("In military parlance a 'target' is a specific object of attack, and 'targeting' involves directing operations toward the attack of a target.").

16. This definition involves the political element essential to the concept by incorporating state involvement in the definition but does not needlessly include concepts of perfidy and treachery which are more applicable to the laws of war and earlier thoughts on this matter. See Chris Anderson, Comment, 13 Hamline *J. Pub. L. & Pol'y* 291, 294 (1992) (stating that a general definition of assassination is the murder of a targeted individual for political purposes and that another definition is any unlawful killing of a particular person for political purposes); Although none of the domestic or international instruments proscribing assassination actually defines the prohibited conduct, scholars and practitioners have struggled to craft a working definition to serve as a guide to states in fashioning their behavior, and also as a prescriptive norm against which other states could judge and possibly sanction that behavior. Some scholars focus on the killing of internationally protected persons or high-level political figures. Others ignore the victim's status and instead focus on the purpose of the act and presence of any political motivations. Still others tend to analogize assassination to the classic law-of-war prohibition of treacherously killing one's enemy. (citations omitted) Michael N. Schmitt, State-Sponsored Assassination in International and Domestic Law, 17 *Yale J. Int'l L.* 609, 611–12 (1992).

17. See Bert Brandenburg, "Legality of Assassination," 27 Va. *J. Int'l L.* 655 (1987).

18. Arend & Beck, supra note 3, at 158 (citing Brierly, at 51).

19. Id.

20. Id. at 159. The authors state that "they accept the positivist distinction between "legal" and "moral." Hence, while state actions may be morally reprehensible, they may not be legally prohibited. Naturalist legal scholars, of course, reject this view." Id. at n.24.

21. 21. See generally Daniel Pickard, "When Does Crime Become a Threat to International Peace and Security," 12 *Fla. J. Int'l L.* 1 (1998).

22. U.N. Charter art. 103, para. 2.

23. Id. art. 2, para. 4.

24. Id. art. 1, para. 1.

25. See Anthony clark Arend & Robert J. Beck, *International Law & the Use of Force: Beyond the UN Charter Paradigm* 31 (1993).

26. Id. at 31–32. A determination of a threat to international peace and security is solely within the province of the Security Council. The members of the Security Council have issued statements explicitly stating that acts of terrorism may rise to the level of threats to international peace and security. This determination is crucial in that it may result in the use of military might by one or more nations. Once the Security Council has identified a threat to international peace and security, the Charter lays out a framework for the authorization of force. Article 41 provides that: The Security Council may decide what measures not involving the use of armed force are to be employed to give effect to its decisions, and it may call upon the Members of the United Nations to apply such measures. These may include complete or partial interruption of economic relations and of rail, sea, air, postal, telegraphic,

radio, and other means of communication, and the severance of diplomatic relations. U.N. Charter art. 41. This Article authorizes the Security Council to impose non-military sanctions to include, but are not limited to those mentioned. Id. at 48.

27. See U.N. Charter art. 39 ("The Security Council shall determine the existence of any threat to the peace, breach of the peace, or act of aggression and shall make recommendations, or decide what measures shall be taken in accordance with Articles 41 and 42, to maintain or restore international peace and security."). If measures under Article 41 are deemed insufficient by the Security Council, military sanctions can be authorized in accordance with Article 42: Should the Security Council consider that the measures provided for in Article 41 would be inadequate or have proved to be inadequate, it may take such action by air, sea, or land forces as many be necessary to maintain or restore international peace and security. Such action may include demonstrations, blockade, and other operations by air, sea, or land forces of Members of the United Nations. U.N. Charter art. 42.

28. See Schmitt, supra note 15, at 649–50, who states as to self-defense: In summary, a state generally may target those reasonably believed to represent a violent threat to it. If the attack has not occurred, the right to anticipate the attack arises at the point at which the threat can last be thwarted effectively. On the other hand, if the attack is continuing, the timing of the defensive action is irrelevant. It must be emphasized, however, that the previous discussion bears on the issue of assassination only with regard to the likelihood that a killing might indicate political motivation in nonarmed-conflict circumstances. To the extent an action does not meet the standards of self-defense, it might be politically motivated, and therefore might be considered assassination. If the action is a valid exercise of self-defense, it is not (legally) politically motivated. Additionally, if an act in self-defense rises to the level of armed conflict, the only issue as to assassination is treachery. Schmitt involves concepts of political motivation and/or treachery in the definition of assassination. It is questionable if these definitional requirements help to clarify the legal analysis. However, Schmitt indicates that states should not be prevented from acting in self-defense by targeting individual terrorists. Id.

29. See Patricia Zengel, *Assassination and the Law of Armed Conflict*, 134 Mil. L. Rev. 123, at 125 (1991).

30. Id. at 125.

31. Id.

32. Id. at 126 (citing A. Gentili, *De Jure Belli Lilori Tres* (1612) reprinted in 16(2) *The Classics of International Law* 166 (J. Rolfe trans. 1933)) [hereinafter Gentili].

33. Id. at 126 (citing Gentili at 170–72).

34. Zengel, supra note 29, at 127 (citing H. Grotius, *De Jure Belli Ac Pacis Libri Tres* (rev. ed. 1646), reprinted in 3(2) *The Classics of International Law* 653 (F. Kelsey trans. 1925)).

35. Id. at 127 (citing Grotius at 653–56) (emphasis added).

36. See Schmitt, supra note 15, at 617 N. 32 (stating that "the nature of war has changed so much in recent years that the views of the European scholars arguably have only nominal bearing on contemporary norms. The initiation of war, for instance, was legal under customary law at the time of these historical writings.").

37. Zengel, supra note 29, at 128.

38. See Burrus M. Carnahan, "Reason, Retaliation and Rhetoric; Jefferson & the Quest for Humanity in War," 139 Mil. L. Rev. 83, 85 (1993).

39. See Zengel, supra note 29, at 128. The atrocities of the Nazi's and the subsequent legal standards expounded upon by the International Military Tribunals following World War II have clearly demonstrated that not all tactics of war conform with international law. The Geneva Conventions of 1949, which have generally been accepted as binding international law, establish that not all means of injuring an enemy are acceptable.

40. See Carnahan, supra note 38, at 83–84.

41. Christian Wolff, *The Law of Nations Treated According to a Scientific Method* 409–50 (F. Helmelt, trans., Oceana 1984) (1764).

42. Zengel, supra note 29, at 130.

43. See Zengel, supra note 29, at 130.
44. Id. at 130.
45. Id. at 131.
46. Id.
47. Id.
48. See id.
49. See Jami Melissa Jackson, "The Legality of Assassination of Independent Terrorist Leaders: An Examination of National and International Implications," 24 *N.C. J. Int'l L. & Com. Reg.* 5669, 671.
50. Zengel, supra note 29, at 131.
51. See Schmitt, supra note 15, at 648 (stating that states should not be prevented from acting in self-defense by targeting individual terrorists simply because the mode of conflict exists on a different level).
52. See Arend & Beck, supra note 25.
53. See Louis Rene Beres, "On International Law and Nuclear Terrorism," 24 *Ga. J. Int'l & Comp. L.* 1 (1994). See also Louis Rene Beres, *On Assassination as Anticipatory Self-defense: The Case of Israel*, 20 *Hofstra L. Rev.* 321 (1991).
54. Id. at 29 n. 59.
55. See id.
56. But see Michael N. Schmitt, "State Sponsored Assassination in International and Domestic Law," 17 Yale *J. Int'l L.* 609 (Summer 1992). Schmitt states that there are only two treaties which specifically address the topic of assassination, the Charter of the Organization of African Unity and the Convention on the Prevention and Punishment of Crimes Against Internationally Protected Persons, Including Diplomatic Agents. While the first treaty is of questionable value as to universal international law evolution, the latter (often referred to as the New York Convention) "falls short of prescribing an international norm against assassination." Id. at 619. Schmitt argues that the "major failing of the New York Convention is that it accords a target protected status only when the target of the assassination is abroad. Thus, the murder of protected individuals in their home territory do not trigger the treaty provisions." Id. Schmitt argues further that "outside of the law of armed conflict, for instance, no universal prescription outlaws assassination. The one document that addressed the topic, the New York Convention, is limited in scope, and it fails even to mention the word assassination. Indeed it relies on domestic law to criminalize the act." Id. at 678.
57. See Louis Rene Beres, "On International Law and Nuclear Terrorism," 24 *Ga. J. Int'l & Comp. L.* 29–33 (1994). Professor Beres relies upon Vattel for support of his arguments in regard to the legality of assassination as a form of anticipatory self-defense. Beres cites Vattel who argued that: The safest plan is to prevent evil, where that it possible. A Nation has the right to resist the injury another seeks to inflict upon it, and to use force and every other just means of resistance against the aggressor. It may even anticipate the other's design, being careful, however, not to act upon vague and doubtful suspicions, lest it should run the risk of becoming itself the aggressor. Id. at 31.
58. In support of these very controversial propositions, Professor Beres convincingly cites Cicero's defense of Milo: But is there any occasion on which it is proper to slay a man—and there are many such—surely that occasion is not only a just one, but even a necessary one, when violence is offered, and can only be repelled by violence… What is the meaning of our retinues, what of our swords? Surely it would never be permitted to have them if we might never use them. This, therefore, is a law, O judges, not written, but born with us—which we have not learned, or received by tradition, or read, but which we have taken and sucked in and imbibed from nature herself; a law which… is ingrained in us—namely, that if our life be in danger from plots, or from open violence, or from the weapons of robbers or enemies, every means of securing our safety is honorable. For laws are silent when arms are raised, and do not expect themselves to be waited for, when he who waits will have to suffer an undeserved penalty before he can exact a merited punishment. Id. at 31 n. 60.

59. Id. at 32.

60. Id. at 33.

61. See Schmitt, supra note 15, at 645 (concluding that "[w]hen targeting a specific individual is based on a valid exercise of self-defense, killing that individual will rarely be considered assassination, regardless of the applicable law governing assassination." This comment reflects again the definitional problems related to this inquiry. Schmitt states that in the law of armed conflict that assassination is the treacherous killing of a targeted individual) (emphasis added).

62. See Arend & Beck, supra note 3, at 213, which summarizes scholarly opinion as: Legal scholars who have examined the jus ad bellum dimension of the terrorism question would appear to agree on at least four basic principles: Virtually all recognize that (1) if it has suffered an armed attack by terrorist actors, a state is entitled to defend itself forcibly; (2) a victim state's forcible self-defense measures should be timely; (3) a victim state's forcible self-defense measures should be proportionate; and (4) a victim state's forcible self-defense measures should be discriminate and taken against targets responsible in some way for the armed attack. Id. at 213.

63. See Zengel, supra note 29, at 225 (arguing that what is commonly called assassination is best treated as one of many means by which one nation may utilize force against another, and should be considered permissible under the same circumstances and subject to the same constraints that govern the use of force generally).

64. Arend & Beck, supra note 3, at 167, 168 (citing Franz Paasache).

65. Id. (citing Paasache).

66. The US Constitution mandates at Article VI that US treaties are part of the supreme Law of the Land. U.S. Const. art. VI, cl. 2. Furthermore at Article I, Section 8, Congress has the power to "define and punish... Offenses against the Law of Nations." (Using Law of Nations as the 18th century terminology for International Law). Further, the US Supreme Court has held that "International Law is part of our law, and must be ascertained and administered by the courts of justice of appropriate jurisdiction as often as questions of right depending on it are duly presented for their determination." The Paquete Habana 175 U.S. 677, 700 (1900).

67. See Schmitt, supra note 15, at 653.

68. See Schmitt, supra note 15, at 651–61 (arguing that an analysis of the Committee's report provides the following 6 conclusions: 1. Assassination is politically motivated; 2. Clandestine or covert operations are more likely than overt actions to constitute assassination; 3. A ban on assassination does not preclude support for coups in which an official may possibly be killed or assassinated. Instead each operation must be evaluated contextually to determine the likelihood of assassination; 4. A killing justified by imminent physical danger to the United States would be unlikely to amount to assassination; 5. Assassination prohibitions are not limited to heads of state, but cover a range of officials representing states and non-governmental organizations; 6. The term assassination is not meant to cover operations during periods of armed conflict).

69. Lori Damrosch, "The US Constitution in Its Third Century: Foreign Affairs Distribution of Constitutional Authority: Covert Operations," 83 *Am. J. Int'l L.* 795, 800 (1989) (citing Church Comm. Report, at 160, 448).

70. See Zengel, supra note 29, at 141 (citing S. Rep. No. 465, 94th Cong. 2d Sees. (1975)) [hereinafter Interim report].

71. Id. at 142.

72. Id. The Committee further found that the CIA had provided money and weapons to a number of anti-Allende military officers, including the group that attempted to kidnap General Scheider. However, support was withdrawn from that particular group before the attempt was made, although the CIA had continued to support other Chilean dissident groups. Id.

73. See id.

74. Id.

75. See id.

76. See id. at 142.

77. Id. at 142, 143.

78. See id. (the report stated that "[c]oups involve varying degrees of risk of assassination. The possibility of assassination.... is one of the issues to be considered in determining the propriety of US involvement... This country was created by violent revolt against a regime believed to tyrannous, and our founding fathers (the local dissidents of that era) received aid from foreign countries.... we should not today rule out support for dissident groups seeking to overthrow tyrants."). Zengel, supra note 29, at 143 (citing the Interim Report at 258).

79. See Zengel, supra note 29, at 144 (citing Interim Report at 6–7, 260–79).

80. Id.

81. Exec. Order No. 12333 Sec. 2.11, 3 C.F.R. 213 (1981) ("No person employed by or acting on behalf of the United States Government shall engage in, or conspire to engage in, assassination.").

82. See Damrosch, supra note 69, at 800 n. 36 that "as a matter of constitutional power, the president may countermand any constraints embodied in executive orders that he or his predecessors may have issued. Whether an executive order should be rescinded in accordance with the same procedures use to promulgate it, e.g. through publication in the Federal Register, is an issue of procedural nicety rather than constitutional power."

83. Damrosch, supra note 69, at 800.

84. Exec. Order No. 12333 Sec. 2.11, 3 C.F.R. 213 (1981).

85. See Zengel, supra note 29, at 144 (citing Exec. Order 12333).

86. Id. (citing Exec. Order No. 12333, 3 C.F.R. 213 (1982), reprinted in 50 U.S.C. Sec. 401 at 44–51 (1982)). Executive Order 12333 is a comprehensive document addressing the conduct of intelligence operations with the prohibition on assassination as only one issue which is briefly addressed.

87. See Zengel, supra note 29, at 145.

88. Abraham Sofaer, The Sixth Annual Waldemar A. Solf Lecture in International Law: "Terrorism, the Law, and the National Defense," 126 *Mil. L. Rev.* 89, 91 (1989).

89. See id.

90. Sofaer, supra note 88, at 91. See also W. Hays Parks, Memorandum of Law: Executive Order 12333 and Assassination, 1989-DEC Army Law. 4, which concluded that: clandestine, low visibility or overt use of military force against legitimate targets in time of war, or against similar targets in time of peace where such individuals or groups pose an immediate threat to United States citizens or the national security of the United States, as determined by competent authority, does not constitute assassination or conspiracy to engage in assassination, and would not be prohibited by the proscription in [Executive Order] 12333 or by international law. Id. at 1.

91. It has been argued that a U.S. president could legally carry out the assassination of a foreign leader in 4 ways: (1) Ask Congress to declare war, in which case a foreign leader exercising command responsibility would become a legitimate target; (2) Construe Article 51 of the United Nations Charter to permit the assassination based on either a right to self-defense or a right to respond to criminal activities; (3) Narrowly interpret the order as not restricting the president as long as he does not approve specific plans for the killing of individuals; or (4) Overrule the order, create an exception to it, or permit the Congress to do the same. Boyd M. Johnson, Executive Order 12333: The Permissibility of an American Assassination of a Foreign Leader, 25 *Cornell Int'l L. J.* 401, 403 (1992).

92. See United States Intelligence Community, at http://www.cia.gov/ic/icagen2.htm.

93. See id.

94. Id.

95. See id.

96. Specifically, the Order states at 1.8 (3), concerning the CIA, that CIA may conduct "special activities" approved by the president. No agency except the CIA (or the Armed Forces of

the United States in time of war declared by Congress or during any period covered by a report from the president to the Congress under the War Powers Resolution) may conduct any special activity unless the president determines that another agency is more likely to achieve a particular objective. Exec. Order. No. 12333, supra note 81.

97. Zengel, supra note 29, at 146 n. 78.

98. Id.

99. See Zengel, supra note 29, at 146, n. 7.

100. See id.

101. Damrosch, supra note 69, at 798 (citing 50 U.S.C. Sec. 413(a) (1)).

102. See id.

103. See Zengel, supra note 29, at 147.

104. 50 U.S.C.A. § 413b(e) (1996).

105. See L. K. Johnson, "On Drawing a Bright Line for Covert Operations," 86 *Am. J. Int'l L.* 284, 299 (1992).

106. See id. at 306. The author suggests eleven specific guidelines, namely: 1. Whenever possible, shun covert operations in favor of diplomatic resolution of international disputes. 2. Keep covert operations in harmony with publicly stated policy objectives. 3. Conduct only those covert operations which, if exposed, would not unduly embarrass the United States. 4. Consult with intelligence analysts and other experts not just covert action specialists before proceeding. 5. Never bypass established decisionmaking procedures, including reporting requirements (which, except in times of acute emergency ought to be prospective, not merely retrospective). 6. Never violate the laws of the United States (short of the rare Lincolnesque need to save the nation in a time of desperation). 7. Against fellow democracies eschew all but the most routine of covert operations. 8. Even against nondemocratic regimes, remain at the lower, less intrusive, end of the escalation ladder, applying the just war rule of proportionality and rising upward only in despair. 9. Reject arrangements for information sharing or other intelligence activities with any nation practicing, or allowing within its territory a consistent pattern of gross violations of internationally recognized human rights. 10. In almost all cases, reject secret wars, coups d'etat and other extreme measures, for if America's interests are so jeopardized as to require major forceful intervention, properly authorized overt warfare—ideally, multinational in nature and at the invitation of a legitimate government or faction is a more appropriate and honorable option. 11. In considering covert operations, always remember above all the importance to the United States of its longstanding tradition of fair play. Id. at 306.

107. Brian Michael Jenkins, RAND Corp., *Should Our Arsenal Against Terrorism Include Assassination* (1987). Although Jenkins plainly states his position against assassination, he did note that a public opinion poll conducted just before the US air raid on Libya showed that 61 percent of the respondents agreed that the United States should "covertly assassinate known terrorist leaders."

108. See Johnson, supra note 105, at 308.

109. See Jenkins, supra note 107, at 3.

110. See id. The death of Wadi Haddad is cited as evidence that one leader's death can result in a long period of inaction by a terrorist group.

111. Id. at 7.

112. Id.

113. Id. at 7, 8.

114. See Zengel, supra note 29, at 144 (citing David Newman & Tyll van Geel, "Executive Order 12333: The Risks of a Clear Declaration of Intent," 12 *Harv. J. L. & Pub. Pol'y* 433, 443–47 (1989) (stating that the authors' use of game theory analysis disregards the fact that a nation with a policy against assassination can retaliate by other means)).

115. See Zengel, supra note 20, at 155.

Business Versus Terror

David J. Rothkopf is CEO of Intellibridge Corporation, which offers knowledge management and intelligence services to global corporations and organizations, and a former deputy under secretary of commerce for International Trade Policy (1993–1996). He also currently serves as adjunct professor of International and Public Affairs at Columbia University.

(O)nly a new kind of alliance can win the war on terrorism. This alliance will not be one between nations nor will it be bound by a treaty. Instead, it will be unconventional, involve millions of disparate actors, and be guided by rules that will be constantly rewritten. It will be an alliance of a motley army of horizontal partnerships, with a non-traditional leadership structure. Its best troops will be regiments of geeks rather than the special forces that struck the first blows against the Taliban in Afghanistan. These pocket-protector brigades live on rations of cold pizza and coffee, not MREs (the military's "Meal, Ready-to-Eat"). They take orders not from generals or admirals but from markets and stockholders.

The members of this fighting force are scientists and doctors, venture capitalists and corporate project managers—the private-sector army that is the United States' not-so-secret weapon and best hope. These unlikely warriors will provide the software, systems, and analytical resources that will enable the United States to track terrorists. It is they who will develop the sensing systems to detect biological, chemical, and cyber threats. And it is they who will perfect the biometric devices, such as retinal scanners or thumb-print readers or facial-recognition technologies, that will be critical components of next-generation security systems and that will close the gaps Mohammed Atta and his associates revealed.

The Bush administration and terrorism experts know this group is critical. The enormous Pentagon acquisition apparatus has already begun to direct funds to new private-sector ventures that can satisfy immediate and longer-term tactical and strategic needs. Governor Tom Ridge, director of the Office of Homeland Security, has taken the first steps toward institutionalizing the public-private partnership that is absolutely critical to achieving U.S. domestic defense goals. Even smaller operations—such as the Central Intelligence Agency's venture fund In-Q-Tel, Inc. (a private nonprofit created in 1999 to invest in information technology deemed critical to the intelligence community)—have begun directing their comparatively limited resources to addressing the burgeoning, boggling array of threats that Americans now must contemplate.

Nonetheless, many in the Bush Administration acknowledge that these initial steps toward a more effective public-private sector cooperation are inadequate at best. As a result, a vital resource in defending the nation remains underutilized. According to

Fortune magazine, the private sector will spend over $150 billion on homeland security–related expenses such as insurance, workplace security, logistics, and information technology—approximately four times the federal government's announced homeland security budget. And private-sector organizations operate America's transportation networks, power facilities, telecommunications and data networks, healthcare infrastructure, pharmaceutical companies, and most of the security services upon which U.S. critical infrastructures depend. But to date, these companies have been involved in very little of the coordinated planning, drilling exercises, threat evaluation, intelligence sharing, cooperative research, or any of the other steps a national defense strategy requires.

Most of the critical questions about how to achieve this public-private sector cooperation have yet to be asked. And even if we find the right answers, a cultural divide between government and business threatens this partnership. Bridging this divide is crucial because an important shift has taken place in U.S. national security. Once, it was almost entirely the province of the federal government to provide for that security by protecting the nation through overseas alliances, the five branches of the American military, intelligence assets, and other tools of U.S. policy. The war on terrorism, however, has changed all that. With an almost infinite number of threats and targets across the United States and in U.S.-owned facilities around the world, Washington cannot be solely responsible for homeland security. Just as winning this war requires international coalitions, intelligence sharing, and law-enforcement cooperation, so too does it require finding a new division of labor between the public and private sectors.

Soldiers of Fortune 500

The seeds of victory in the war against terrorism were planted long before the emergence of al Qaeda. During the Cold War, the Eisenhower administration—worried that traditional military-industrial partnerships were not producing the technologies essential to defeating the Soviets—created the Small Business Act of 1958, which allowed the predecessors of today's venture capitalists (VCs) to leverage their private capital on a three-to-one basis with funds borrowed from the government at below-market rates. (This leverage was increased to four-to-one in the late 1970s). Essentially, the government said, "If you're willing to put some money behind risky but promising ventures, we'll lend you three bucks for every one you put in. And we'll lend it to you for less than any bank would, because we think this investment is good for the country." This pledge mitigated the risk for investors and thus increased a pool of risk capital that could flow to entrepreneurial ventures.

The verdict is in: This government program has worked big time.

The subsequently growing pool of venture capital produced a number of success stories even before the tech boom of the late 1990s. Companies such as Minute Maid, Digital Equipment Corporation, Eastern Airlines, Federal Express, Apple Computer, and Genentech, Inc. provided the kinds of returns on investment that drew ever greater amounts of capital to the higher returns of venture investments. The connection to the government and, in particular, to the security establishment has been apparent in a number of instances since the very first days of this industry. Even Minute Maid was born from efforts during the Second World War to produce concentrated fruit juice for troops overseas.

The venture-capital boom of the 1990s provided yet more proof that the partner-ship between the security and venture-capital communities has had a circular, self-rein-forcing quality. The Internet and many fundamental breakthroughs in computer and software development emerged from research-and-development (R&D) organizations within the defense establishment, such as the Defense Advanced Research and Projects Agency. Entrepreneurs, in turn, used funds from VCs to develop the companies that en-hanced those technologies, which in turn enabled the creation of the commercial World Wide Web. Today, the military is upgrading its systems by using many of the software, switching and routing technologies, and content innovations developed by the private sector in its process of reinventing and spurring the worldwide growth of the Internet.

The success of this technological development cycle has produced not only an ex-plosion in new technologies but also spectacular growth in the amount of money that is now available to entrepreneurs via VCs. During the last half of the 1990s, U.S. venture investment increased 20-fold, reaching a peak of $102.3 billion in 2000. By that year, over 5,000 companies had tapped this pool. Though the amounts fell dramatically in 2001 to approximately $38 billion, this sum of money is still vastly greater than many of the federal budget's most significant new technology development programs. For example, efforts to counter terrorism involving weapons of mass destruction only garnered $1.7 billion in the fiscal year 2002 budget. Furthermore, government R&D ef-forts are built to serve existing plans and are slowed and guided by ubiquitous, lum-bering bureaucracies. These megaprojects are not the source of much of the out-of-the-box thinking that can come from smaller, less constrained operations. Consequently, it is not surprising that while the defense budget will continue to drive important new technologies, VC financing is still going to be a vital player in the R&D world for some time to come.

And it will be a very agile player. Since the boom of the late 1990s, the United States has moved away from the R&D model that drove most of its growth in the second half of the 20th century, wherein funds flowed from corporate budgets into owned-and-operated corporate laboratories like Bell Labs (where researchers developed telecommu-nications and information processing technologies such as the transistor that helped trigger the Information Revolution) or Xerox's Palo Alto Research Center (famous for developing technologies that led to the icon-driven operating systems common in today's Windows systems). Instead, the new model has entrepreneurial-minded tech-nologists leaving the corporate nest, raising venture capital, test flying their ideas, and then, if they are successful, cashing out by selling those ideas back to large corporations. What has happened, in effect, is that the corporate world has outsourced many of its R&D functions by letting others take the risks.

Today, given the enormous demands for new technologies linked to fighting the war on terrorism and preserving homeland security, VCs are beginning to sense an op-portunity. Once the nearly $38 billion earmarked for homeland security in Bush's fiscal year 2003 budget is divided among the 40 federal agencies involved in combating ter-rorism (not to mention the 50 states and thousands of localities lining up for cash), the amounts for technological development will be comparatively minuscule. Furthermore, the private sector is quickly realizing that impossibly huge demands are being placed on federal, state, and local authorities who must manage their existing "homeland security–related tasks"—such as patrolling borders, processing immigrants, policing streets, and administering the law in an environment where the number of credible and increasingly complex threats has grown in a very short period.

Consequently, the private sector has begun to take care of matters on its own. One example of how the invisible hand of the marketplace is more agile than the heavy hand of bureaucracy comes from the financial sector. Despite the destruction of 17 acres of lower Manhattan last September—including much of the critical infrastructure on that part of the island and the offices of many major players in the financial community— the markets themselves reopened within four days. The reason for this quick recovery was that in the wake of the first bombing of the World Trade Center in 1993, many institutions developed redundant back-office systems and emergency-response plans that were then implemented within hours of last year's attacks on the Twin Towers. Now, of course, many industries are seeing the merits of such an approach and are developing their own standards and systems for coping with such catastrophes.

Companies are not only concerned about physical security but also cybersecurity, and with good reason. According to the CERT Coordination Center (formerly known as the Computer Emergency Response Team) at Carnegie Mellon University's Software Engineering Institute, the number of security incidents on the Internet has increased at an alarming rate. Over 20,000 incidents were reported to CERT in 2000. That number increased to more than 52,000 in 2001. As such, corporations and the U.S. government find themselves sharing the same foxhole as they seek to defend the critical functions of the national infrastructure. One important initiative that has already emerged is the Critical Infrastructure Protection Board chaired by Richard Clarke, the nation's cybersecurity czar. Clarke has been among the government's most effective architects of public-private partnerships in part because he was the driving force behind the government's Y2K efforts. This precedent-setting project was based on the idea that the Y2K bug—which many feared could cause critical computer systems to fail when the calendar hit the year 2000—was a national threat that could not be addressed by the government acting alone.

This ongoing cooperation was easily translated into a response to the war on terrorism after September 11. At that time, business leaders with whom Clarke worked closely—such as Microsoft's Bill Gates and Oracle's Larry Ellison, not generally seen as highly cooperative with one another—announced plans to make security a higher priority at their companies. Gates even circulated a memo to Microsoft staff mandating the establishment of security-related issues as the company's top priority.

The Creative Edge

The culture of innovation that is prevalent in the United States has produced an overwhelming response from the private sector in the aftermath of last year's terrorist attacks. One Pentagon office, the Technical Support Working Group (created to help coordinate interaction with private-sector technology developers), received 12,405 proposals for new technologies in the war on terrorism between October 2001 and January 2002. Similar requests for proposals have in the past garnered 900 to 1,000 responses. At In-Q-Tel, Inc., applications for funding have gone from approximately 700 during the first 30 months of the organization's existence to over 1,000 during the last six. But the Technical Support Working Group funds only about $70 million in such projects a year. And In-Q-Tel, Inc., which is interested in a broad range of technologies—such as Internet search engines, analytical software, and security and privacy technologies—has only funded more than 20 ventures in its short lifetime and allocates only about $30 million a year for investment purposes. Clearly, more such programs are needed if the United States is to tap its rich technological resources. And in addition to providing more financing, the government must be willing to get over the "not-invented-here syndrome" and to share new technologies broadly across agencies.

Again, market forces come to the rescue. In this security-minded environment, demand for these new products is engendering enormous sales potential for innovators even if the government cannot or will not fund them. International Data Corporation, an industry consultant, projects that the global market for information security services will triple from today's levels to over $21 billion by 2005. Similarly, even where relatively new technologies such as biometrics are concerned, growing demand will produce money for new R&D. It is estimated that between 500,000 and 700,000 identity thefts—one of the fastest growing modern crimes—occurred in the United States in 2000. Consequently, the International Biometric Group expects biometric sales to grow from some $500 million this year to almost four times that by the end of 2005. Homeland-security experts have shown particular interest in advanced ID cards with biometric identifiers stored on smart chips. The debate at the federal level about the appropriateness of creating a U.S. national ID card continues. But a market-driven alliance between state motor vehicle administrators (through the American Association of Motor Vehicle Administrators), biometric companies, and manufacturers of sophisticated databases is likely to produce a de facto national ID card by adopting common information standards for driver's licenses.

Given that many bioterrorism experts consider the U.S. food supply to be especially vulnerable to terrorist attacks, there is also a high premium on new bioanalytical devices that can determine whether pathogens reside in food. Taking 30 minutes rather than hours to determine whether a food product has been spiked with a bacterium or some poisonous chemical can mean the difference between life and death for potentially large groups of consumers. To speed the process along, the Washington, D.C., law firm Buchanan Ingersoll has proposed creating an antibioterrorism technology development venture capital fund that would put government dollars in the hands of venture professionals to help locate the most promising technologies for identifying and containing potential biological attacks. The objective would be to accelerate the development of a competitive antibioterrorism industry so that the government could use the technologies while the companies could benefit from other sales of the products developed—much as what happened with the computer, biotech, and Internet development efforts that took place within and in partnership with the government.

Unleashing the Market

Just as it is impossible for government to win this war alone, so too is it impossible for businesses to do the same. Businesses can protect, to some degree, their own assets. They can develop useful new technologies. They can finance innovation and dissemination of cost-effective tools for identifying, reducing, or containing threats. But they cannot wage war overseas, cannot conduct international diplomacy, and most importantly, cannot create a national strategy where one is lacking. Finally, if their willingness to work with the federal government is not reciprocated (right now many companies that have called the federal government with homeland-security ideas have been met with "We're not ready yet" or "We're too overwhelmed") or the potential impact of their ideas is limited (because one government agency grabs them and puts a lid on them), all they can do is wait until another cataclysm drives home the message that the public-private coalition requires a new attitude, outlook, and structure.

The U.S. government can take a range of new approaches that will allow it to further harness the power of this army of gray flannel allies. For starters, lawmakers and regulators need to precisely codify the extent to which privacy rights should be modified to enhance security. Otherwise, corporations will be extremely reluctant to share their databases with the appropriate government agencies. For example, had there been a more effective system in place for sharing data among car rental companies, flight schools, airlines, credit card companies, and federal visa and state driver's license records, U.S. authorities could have had a much easier time identifying and perhaps stopping the terrorist activities of September 2001. However, if the wrong individual ends up being harassed by the government because of a record a private company handed over, how long will it be before lawyers file suit against that company?

By the same token, corporations that cooperate with the government will require indemnification against potential lawsuits by individuals who suffer damages as a consequence of a terrorist attack that succeeds despite the company's best efforts, or worse, because of a failure of their systems and services. Imagine what would happen if it could be proved that 250 people on a plane died because a new piece of expensive technology did not sniff out a bomb on board. Again, instant lawsuits would follow.

Moreover, the U.S. government must be the insurer of last resort in the event of catastrophic attacks, unless we want to see a major rollback in the high-profile, economically important development efforts that also produce high-risk potential targets. Urban areas in major U.S. cities would suffer the greatest losses, as is evidenced by this year's decline in construction of high-rise buildings and megaprojects. Insurance companies would also be forced to raise rates to stratospheric levels in the absence of such protection, thereby undermining the ability of the market to play an optimal role in the partnership.

Another vital step is to clarify exactly what the federal government means by "homeland defense." Is it defense of borders? Defense of the population? Defense against all threats? The answers to these questions will be crucial to developing a clear federal strategy for homeland security. There will be pitfalls if the government offers too broad a definition or too ambitious a set of objectives. The government cannot possibly hope to defend every potential target in the United States from every potential threat. Consequently, the definition and strategy must focus on areas that absolutely require the federal government's participation—specifically, those areas in which threats to national security portend massive physical or economic devastation. Thus, the focus should be on weapons of mass destruction (nuclear, biological, and chemical), weapons of mass disruption (cyberattack and coordinated conventional attacks), and organizations with the inclination either to undertake such attacks or to wage extended war on U.S. citizens or assets. Further clarification in other areas that guide federal action is also necessary: The definition of "first responders" needs to be broadened to include certain public and private healthcare workers. The definition of intelligence must be broadened so that it includes open-source and other unclassified forms of information sharing.

Such information sharing won't work, however, unless all participants have access to the best intelligence available. Only a comparative few will have access to classified components of this information, but tens or hundreds of thousands will need unclassified versions of this data. Even that unclassified information will require the latest encryption technologies to prevent it from falling into the wrong hands. Rather than relying on the traditional, stove-piped approaches in which agencies communicate up and down their organizational charts but not with others in the government who have similar missions, the system needs to have a more decentralized architecture and should offer end-users raw data for their own interpretation. The key will be to harness the more than 1 million pages of new data that appear on the Internet each day. The failure to deliver that intelligence to those who need it will only produce insecurity, doubt, and failure.

In addition to disseminating intelligence, it is vital to foster the dissemination of innovation. While the term "incubator" (in which a company offers space, resources, back-office services, and sometimes management expertise to multiple start-ups simultaneously) lost its former appeal among the tech crowd following the industry's shake-out, the idea of offering government facilities, technology, and potential markets to would-be entrepreneurs will give the U.S. government more mileage for its money and will bring in clusters of talented, market-trained innovators that it might not otherwise be able to attract. Similarly, groups of scientists and technology specialists might donate a week or two a year to participate to simulations of crises that are designed to reassess capabilities and stimulate new strategic or technical thinking about solutions.

Finally, as September 11 recedes into memory, complacency might emerge in the private-sector and among local agencies. To preempt this possibility, private-sector firms with requisite expertise should publish objective evaluations of readiness. Such ratings would be controversial, but they would also motivate states, localities, and companies to optimize their efforts. No city would want to be ranked at the bottom of a "National Homeland Security Readiness Index" lest it deter investment and growth. Nor would political or business leaders want to be seen as falling behind their peers in terms of this critical measure. Creating information products that promote innovation and vigilance is essential to maintaining readiness.

Balance Sheets of Power

The calculus of the war on terrorism is different from that of previous wars. In an instant, the United States can lose more people than died in over a decade in Vietnam. Five grams of anthrax in the heating and ventilation system of an office tower or a mall can kill thousands. A single successful attack using a briefcase-sized nuclear device or a dose of smallpox in an airport could kill tens of thousands or many more. A single vial of hoof-and-mouth disease or bovine spongiform encephalopathy ("mad cow disease") spread around a feedlot in Texas could shut down U.S. beef exports to the world.

But the guards at the feedlot and the mall are rent-a-cops and have neither the training nor the intelligence support to identify or respond to terrorist threats. The sensors that could contain such attacks have yet to be deployed, due to liability issues and cost factors. To stop an attack from a weapon of mass destruction will require a marriage of good intelligence and solid police work, sensing technologies and effective drills, and public and private resources. The government cannot do it alone, and the private sector is not only ready to help but has already made great strides in that direction. The opportunity is strikingly clear: The United States can defeat terrorists by drawing on the very attributes that inflame its enemies. The World Trade Center was a monument to American enterprise, American capital, American technology, the hard work of the American people, U.S. reliance on the marketplace, and the role of the individual. The towers may be gone, but the forces they embodied remain and stand ready to wage war on those who brought the towers down—if only the American people and the U.S. government will let them.

Appendices

Appendix A

Background Information on Designated Foreign Terrorist Organizations

The following descriptive list constitutes the 33 terrorist groups that currently are designated by the Secretary of State as Foreign Terrorist Organizations (FTOs), pursuant to section 219 of the Immigration and Nationality Act, as amended by the Antiterrorism and Effective Death Penalty Act of 1996. The designations carry legal consequences:

- It is unlawful to provide funds or other material support to a designated FTO.
- Representatives and certain members of a designated FTO can be denied visas or excluded from the United States.
- US financial institutions must block funds of designated FTOs and their agents and must report the blockage to the US Department of the Treasury.

Abu Nidal organization (ANO)

a.k.a. Fatah Revolutionary Council, Arab Revolutionary Brigades, Black September, and Revolutionary Organization of Socialist Muslims

Description

International terrorist organization led by Sabri al-Banna. Split from PLO in 1974. Made up of various functional committees, including political, military, and financial.

Activities

Has carried out terrorist attacks in 20 countries, killing or injuring almost 900 persons. Targets include the United States, the United Kingdom, France, Israel, moderate Palestinians, the PLO [Palestine Liberation Organization], and various Arab countries. Major attacks included the Rome and Vienna airports in December 1985, the Neve Shalom synagogue in Istanbul and the Pan Am Flight 73 hijacking in Karachi in September 1986, and the City of Poros day-excursion ship attack in Greece in July 1988. Suspected of assassinating PLO deputy chief Abu Iyad and PLO security chief Abu Hul in Tunis in January 1991. ANO assassinated a Jordanian diplomat in Lebanon in January 1994 and has been linked to the killing of the PLO representative there. Has not attacked Western targets since the late 1980s.

Strength

Few hundred plus limited overseas support structure.

Location/Area of Operation

Al-Banna relocated to Iraq in December 1998, where the group maintains a presence. Has an operational presence in Lebanon including in several Palestinian refugee camps. Financial problems and internal disorganization have reduced the group's activities and capabilities. Authorities shut down the ANO's operations in Libya and Egypt in 1999. Has demonstrated ability to operate over wide area, including the Middle East, Asia, and Europe.

External Aid

Has received considerable support, including safe haven, training, logistic assistance, and financial aid from Iraq, Libya, and Syria (until 1987), in addition to close support for selected operations.

Abu Sayyaf Group (ASG)

Description

The ASG is the most violent of the Islamic separatist groups operating in the southern Philippines. Some ASG leaders have studied or worked in the Middle East and allegedly fought in Afghanistan during the Soviet war. The group split from the Moro National Liberation Front in the early 1990s under the leadership of Abdurajak Abubakar Janjalani, who was killed in a clash with Philippine police on 18 December 1998. His younger brother, Khadaffy Janjalani, has replaced him as the nominal leader of the group, which is composed of several semi-autonomous factions.

Activities

Engages in kidnappings for ransom, bombings, assassinations, and extortion. Although from time to time it claims that its motivation is to promote an independent Islamic state in western Mindanao and the Sulu Archipelago, areas in the southern Philippines heavily populated by Muslims, the ASG now appears to use terror mainly for financial profit. The group's first large-scale action was a raid on the town of Ipil in Mindanao in April 1995. In April of 2000, an ASG faction kidnapped 21 persons, including 10 foreign tourists, from a resort in Malaysia. Separately in 2000, the group abducted several foreign journalists, 3 Malaysians, and a US citizen. On 27 May 2001, the ASG kidnapped three US citizens and 17 Filipinos from a tourist resort in Palawan, Philippines. Several of the hostages, including one US citizen, were murdered.

Strength

Believed to have a few hundred core fighters, but at least 1,000 individuals motivated by the prospect of receiving ransom payments for foreign hostages allegedly joined the group in 2000–2001.

Location/Area of Operation

The ASG was founded in Basilan Province, and mainly operates there and in the neighboring provinces of Sulu and Tawi-Tawi in the Sulu Archipelago. It also operates in the Zamboanga peninsula, and members occasionally travel to Manila and other parts of the country. The group expanded its operations in Malaysia in 2000 when it abducted foreigners from a tourist resort.

External Aid

Largely self-financing through ransom and extortion; may receive support from Islamic extremists in the Middle East and South Asia. Libya publicly paid millions of dollars for the release of the foreign hostages seized from Malaysia in 2000.

Al-Aqsa Martyrs Brigade

Description

The al-Aqsa Martyrs Brigade comprises an unknown number of small cells of Fatah-affiliated activists that emerged at the outset of the current *intifadah* to attack Israeli targets. It aims to drive the Israeli military and settlers from the West Bank, Gaza Strip, and Jerusalem and to establish a Palestinian state.

Activities

Al-Aqsa Martyrs Brigade has carried out shootings and suicide operations against Israeli military personnel and civilians and has killed Palestinians who it believed were collaborating with Israel. At least five US citizens, four of them dual Israeli-US citizens, were killed in these attacks. The group probably did not attack them because of their US citizenship. In January 2002, the group claimed responsibility for the first suicide bombing carried out by a female.

Strength

Unknown.

Location/Area of Operation

Al-Aqsa operates mainly in the West Bank and has claimed attacks inside Israel and the Gaza Strip.

External Aid

Unknown.

Armed Islamic Group (GIA)

Description

An Islamic extremist group, the GIA aims to overthrow the secular Algerian regime and replace it with an Islamic state. The GIA began its violent activity in 1992 after Algiers voided the victory of the Islamic Salvation Front (FIS)—the largest Islamic opposition party—in the first round of legislative elections in December 1991.

Activities

Frequent attacks against civilians and government workers. Between 1992 and 1998 the GIA conducted a terrorist campaign of civilian massacres, sometimes wiping out entire villages in its area of operation. Since announcing its campaign against foreigners living in Algeria in 1993, the GIA has killed more than 100 expatriate men and women—mostly Europeans—in the country. The group uses assassinations and bombings, including car bombs, and it is known to favor kidnapping victims and slitting their throats. The GIA hijacked an Air France flight to Algiers in December 1994. In late 1999 a French court convicted several GIA members for conducting a series of bombings in France in 1995.

Strength

Precise numbers unknown; probably around 200.

Location/Area of Operation

Algeria

External Aid

Algerian expatriates, some of whom reside in Western Europe, provide some financial and logistic support. In addition, the Algerian Government has accused Iran and Sudan of supporting Algerian extremists.

'Asbat al-Ansar

Description

'Asbat al-Ansar—the Partisans' League—is a Lebanon-based, Sunni extremist group, composed primarily of Palestinians, which is associated with Usama bin Laden. The group follows an extremist interpretation of Islam that justifies violence against civilian targets to achieve political ends. Some of those goals include overthrowing the Lebanese Government and thwarting perceived anti-Islamic influences in the country.

Activities

'Asbat al-ansar has carried out several terrorist attacks in Lebanon since it first emerged in the early 1990s. The group carried out assassinations of Lebanese religious leaders and bombed several nightclubs, theaters, and liquor stores in the mid-1990s. The group raised its operational profile in 2000 with two dramatic attacks against Lebanese and international targets. The group was involved in clashes in northern Lebanon in late December 1999 and carried out a rocket-propelled grenade attack on the Russian Embassy in Beirut in January 2000.

Strength

The group commands about 300 hundred fighters in Lebanon.

Location/Area of Operation

The group's primary base of operations is the 'Ayn al-Hilwah Palestinian refugee camp near Sidon in southern Lebanon.

External Aid

Probably receives money through international Sunni extremist networks and Bin Laden's al-Qaida network.

Aum Supreme Truth (Aum)

a.k.a. Aum Shinrikyo, Aleph

Description

A cult established in 1987 by Shoko Asahara, the Aum aimed to take over Japan and then the world. Approved as a religious entity in 1989 under Japanese law, the group ran candidates in a Japanese parliamentary election in 1990. Over time the cult began to emphasize the imminence of the end of the world and stated that the United States would initiate Armageddon by starting World War III with Japan. The Japanese Government revoked its recognition of the Aum as a religious organization in October 1995, but in 1997 a government panel decided not to invoke the Anti-Subversive Law against the group, which would have outlawed the cult. A 1999 law gave the Japanese Government authorization to continue police surveillance of the group due to concerns that Aum might launch future terrorist attacks. Under the leadership of Fumihiro Joyu the Aum changed its name to Aleph in January 2000 and claimed to have rejected the violent and apocalyptic teachings of its founder. (Joyu took formal control of the organization early in 2002 and remains its leader).

Activities

On 20 March 1995, Aum members simultaneously released the chemical nerve agent sarin on several Tokyo subway trains, killing 12 persons and injuring up to 6,000. The group was responsible for other mysterious chemical accidents in Japan in 1994. Its efforts to conduct attacks using biological agents have been unsuccessful. Japanese police arrested Asahara in May 1995, and he remained on trial facing charges in 13 crimes, including 7 counts of murder, at the end of 2001. Legal analysts say it will take several more years to conclude the trial. Since 1997 the cult [has] continued to recruit new members, engage in commercial enterprise, and acquire property, although it scaled back these activities significantly in 2001 in response to public outcry. The cult maintains an Internet home page. In July 2001, Russian authorities arrested a group of Russian Aum followers who had planned to set off bombs near the Imperial Palace in Tokyo as part of an operation to free Asahara from jail and then smuggle him to Russia.

Strength

The Aum's current membership is estimated at 1,500 to 2,000 persons. At the time of the Tokyo subway attack, the group claimed to have 9,000 members in Japan and up to 40,000 worldwide.

Location/Area of Operation

The Aum's principal membership is located only in Japan, but a residual branch comprising an unknown number of followers has surfaced in Russia.

External Aid

None.

Basque Fatherland and Liberty (ETA)

a.k.a. Euzkadi Ta Askatasuna

Description

Founded in 1959 with the aim of establishing an independent homeland based on Marxist principles in the northern Spanish Provinces of Vizcaya, Guipuzcoa, Alava, and Navarra, and the southwestern French Departments of Labourd, Basse-Navarra, and Soule.

Activities

Primarily involved in bombings and assassinations of Spanish Government officials, security and military forces, politicians, and judicial figures. ETA finances its activities through kidnappings, robberies, and extortion. The group has killed more than 800 persons and injured hundreds of others since it began lethal attacks in the early 1960s. In November 1999, ETA broke its "unilateral and indefinite" cease-fire and began an assassination and bombing campaign that has killed 38 individuals and wounded scores more by the end of 2001.

Strength

Unknown; may have hundreds of members, plus supporters.

Location/Area of Operation

Operates primarily in the Basque autonomous regions of northern Spain and southwestern France, but also has bombed Spanish and French interests elsewhere.

External Aid

Has received training at various times in the past in Libya, Lebanon, and Nicaragua. Some ETA members allegedly have received sanctuary in Cuba while others reside in South America.

Al-Gama'a al-Islamiyya (Islamic Group, IG)

Description

Egypt's largest militant group, active since the late 1970s, appears to be loosely organized. Has an external wing with supporters in several countries worldwide. The group issued a cease-fire in March 1999, but its spiritual leader, Shaykh Umar Abd al-Rahman, sentenced to life in prison in January 1996 for his involvement in the 1993 World Trade Center bombing and incarcerated in the United States, rescinded his support for the cease-fire in June 2000. The Gama'a has not conducted an attack inside Egypt since August 1998. Senior member signed Usama Bin Laden's *fatwa* in February 1998 calling for attacks against US. Unofficially split in two factions; one that supports the cease-fire led by Mustafa Hamza, and one led by Rifa'i Taha Musa, calling for a return to armed operations. Taha Musa in early 2001 published a book in which he attempted to justify terrorist attacks that would cause mass casualties. Musa disappeared several months thereafter, and there are conflicting reports as to his current whereabouts. Primary goal is to overthrow the Egyptian Government and replace it with an Islamic state, but disaffected IG members, such as those potentially inspired by Taha Musa or Abd al-Rahman, may be interested in carrying out attacks against US and Israeli interests.

Activities

Group conducted armed attacks against Egyptian security and other government officials, Coptic Christians, and Egyptian opponents of Islamic extremism before the cease-fire. From 1993 until the cease-fire, al-Gama'a launched attacks on tourists in Egypt, most notably the attack in November 1997 at Luxor that killed 58 foreign tourists. Also claimed responsibility for the attempt in June 1995 to assassinate Egyptian President Hosni Mubarak in Addis Ababa, Ethiopia. The Gama'a has never specifically attacked a US citizen or facility but has threatened US interests.

Strength

Unknown. At its peak the IG probably commanded several thousand hard-core members and a like number of sympathizers. The 1999 cease-fire and security crackdowns following the attack in Luxor in 1997, and more recently security efforts following September 11, probably have resulted in a substantial decrease in the group's numbers.

Location/Area of Operation

Operates mainly in the al-Minya, Asyu't, Qina, and Sohaj Governorates of southern Egypt. Also appears to have support in Cairo, Alexandria, and other urban locations, particularly among unemployed graduates and students. Has a worldwide presence, including the United Kingdom, Afghanistan, Yemen, and Austria.

External Aid

Unknown. The Egyptian Government believes that Iran, Bin Laden, and Afghan militant groups support the organization. Also may obtain some funding through various Islamic nongovernmental organizations.

HAMAS (Islamic Resistance Movement)

Description

Formed in late 1987 as an outgrowth of the Palestinian branch of the Muslim Brotherhood. Various HAMAS elements have used both political and violent means, including terrorism, to pursue the goal of establishing an Islamic Palestinian state in place of Israel. Loosely structured, with some elements working clandestinely and others working openly through mosques and social service institutions to recruit members, raise money, organize activities, and distribute propaganda. HAMAS's strength is concentrated in the Gaza Strip and a few areas of the West Bank. Also has engaged in political activity, such as running candidates in West Bank Chamber of Commerce elections.

Activities

HAMAS activists, especially those in the Izz el-Din al-Qassam Brigades, have conducted many attacks—including large-scale suicide bombings—against Israeli civilian and military targets. In the early 1990s, they also targeted Fatah rivals and began a practice of targeting suspected Palestinian collaborators, which continues. Increased operational activity in 2001 during the *intifadah*, claiming numerous attacks against Israeli interests. Group has not targeted US interests and continues to confine its attacks to Israelis inside Israel and the territories.

Strength

Unknown number of hard-core members; tens of thousands of supporters and sympathizers.

Location/Area of Operation

Primarily the West Bank, Gaza Strip, and Israel. In August 1999, Jordanian authorities closed the group's Political Bureau offices in Amman, arrested its leaders, and prohibited the group from operating on Jordanian territory. HAMAS leaders also present in other parts of the Middle East, including Syria, Lebanon, and Iran.

External Aid

Receives funding from Palestinian expatriates, Iran, and private benefactors in Saudi Arabia and other moderate Arab states. Some fund-raising and propaganda activity takes place in Western Europe and North America.

Harakat ul-Mujahidin (HUM) (Movement of Holy Warriors)

Description

The HUM is an Islamic militant group based in Pakistan that operates primarily in Kashmir. It is politically aligned with the radical political party, Jamiat-i Ulema-i Islam Fazlur Rehman faction (JUI-F). Long-time leader of the group, Fazlur Rehman Khalil, in mid-February 2000 stepped down as HUM emir, turning the reins over to the popular Kashmiri commander and his second-in-command, Farooq Kashmiri. Khalil, who has been linked to Bin Laden and signed his *fatwa* in February 1998 calling for attacks on US and Western interests, assumed the position of HUM Secretary General. HUM operated terrorist training camps in eastern Afghanistan until Coalition airstrikes destroyed them during fall 2001.

Activities

Has conducted a number of operations against Indian troops and civilian targets in Kashmir. Linked to the Kashmiri militant group al-Faran that kidnapped five Western tourists in Kashmir in July 1995; one was killed in August 1995 and the other four reportedly were killed in December of the same year. The HUM is responsible for the hijacking of an Indian airliner on 24 December 1999, which resulted in the release of Masood Azhar—an important leader in the former Harakat ul-Ansar imprisoned by the Indians in 1994—and Ahmad Omar Sheikh, who was arrested for the abduction/murder in January–February 2002 of US journalist Daniel Pearl.

Strength

Has several thousand armed supporters located in Azad Kashmir, Pakistan, and India's southern Kashmir and Doda regions. Supporters are mostly Pakistanis and Kashmiris and also include Afghans and Arab veterans of the Afghan war. Uses light and heavy machine-guns, assault rifles, mortars, explosives, and rockets. HUM lost a significant share of its membership in defections to the Jaish-e-Mohammed (JEM) in 2000.

Location/Area of Operation

Based in Muzaffarabad, Rawalpindi, and several other towns in Pakistan, but members conduct insurgent and terrorist activities primarily in Kashmir. The HUM trained its militants in Afghanistan and Pakistan.

External Aid

Collects donations from Saudi Arabia and other Gulf and Islamic states and from Pakistanis and Kashmiris. The HUM's financial collection methods also include soliciting donations from magazine ads and pamphlets. The sources and amount of HUM's military funding are unknown. In anticipation of asset seizures by the Pakistani Government, the HUM withdrew funds from bank accounts and invested in legal businesses, such as commodity trading, real estate, and production of consumer goods. Its fundraising in Pakistan has been constrained since the government clampdown on extremist groups and freezing of terrorist assets.

Hizballah (Party of God)

a.k.a. Islamic Jihad, Revolutionary Justice Organization, Organization of the Oppressed on Earth, and Islamic Jihad for the Liberation of Palestine

Description

Formed in 1982 in response to the Israeli invasion of Lebanon, this Lebanon-based radical Shi'a group takes its ideological inspiration from the Iranian revolution and the teachings of the Ayatollah Khomeini. The Majlis al-Shura, or Consultative Council, is the group's highest governing body and is led by Secretary General Hassan Nasrallah. Hizballah formally advocates ultimate establishment of Islamic rule in Lebanon and liberating all occupied Arab lands, including Jerusalem. It has expressed as a goal the elimination of Israel. Has expressed its unwillingness to work within the confines of Lebanon's established political system; however, this stance changed with the party's decision in 1992 to participate in parliamentary elections. Although closely allied with and often directed by Iran, the group may have conducted operations that were not approved by Tehran. While Hizballah does not share the Syrian regime's secular orientation, the group has been a strong tactical ally in helping Syria advance its political objectives in the region.

Activities

Known or suspected to have been involved in numerous anti-US terrorist attacks, including the suicide truck bombings of the US Embassy in Beirut April 1983 and US Marine barracks in Beirut in October 1983 and the US Embassy annex in Beirut in

September 1984. Three members of Hizballah, 'Imad Mughniyah, Hasan Izz-al-Din, and Ali Atwa, are on the FBI's list of 22 Most Wanted Terrorists for the hijacking in 1985 of TWA Flight 847 during which a US Navy diver was murdered. Elements of the group were responsible for the kidnapping and detention of US and other Western hostages in Lebanon. The group also attacked the Israeli Embassy in Argentina in 1992 and is a suspect in the 1994 bombing of the Israeli cultural center in Buenos Aires. In fall 2000, it captured three Israeli soldiers in the Shabaa Farms and kidnapped an Israeli noncombatant whom it may have lured to Lebanon under false pretenses.

Strength
Several thousand supporters and a few hundred terrorist operatives.

Location/Area of Operation
Operates in the Bekaa Valley, Hermil, the southern suburbs of Beirut, and southern Lebanon. Has established cells in Europe, Africa, South America, North America, and Asia.

External Aid
Receives substantial amounts of financial, training, weapons, explosives, political, diplomatic, and organizational aid from Iran and received diplomatic, political, and logistical support from Syria.

Islamic Movement of Uzbekistan (IMU)

Description
Coalition of Islamic militants from Uzbekistan and other Central Asian states opposed to Uzbekistani President Islom Karimov's secular regime. Before the counterterrorism coalition began operations in Afghanistan in October, the IMU's primary goal was the establishment of an Islamic state in Uzbekistan. If IMU political and ideological leader Tohir Yoldashev survives the counterterrorism campaign and can regroup the organization, however, he might widen the IMU's targets to include all those he perceives as fighting Islam. The group's propaganda has always included anti-Western and anti-Israeli rhetoric.

Activities
The IMU primarily targeted Uzbekistani interests before October 2001 and is believed to have been responsible for five car bombs in Tashkent in February 1999. Militants also took foreigners hostage in 1999 and 2000, including four US citizens who were mountain climbing in August 2000, and four Japanese geologists and eight Krygyzstani soldiers in August 1999. Since October, the Coalition has captured, killed, and dispersed many of the militants who remained in Afghanistan to fight with the Taliban and al-Qaida, severely degrading the IMU's ability to attack Uzbekistani or Coalition interests in the near term. IMU military leader Juma Namangani apparently was killed during an air strike in November. At year's end, Yoldashev remained at large.

Strength
Militants probably number under 2,000.

Location/Area of Operation
Militants are scattered throughout South Asia and Tajikistan. Area of operations includes Afghanistan, Iran, Kyrgyzstan, Pakistan, Tajikistan, and Uzbekistan.

External Aid
Support from other Islamic extremist groups and patrons in the Middle East and Central and South Asia. IMU leadership broadcasts statements over Iranian radio.

Jaish-e-Mohammed (JEM) (Army of Mohammed)

Description
The Jaish-e-Mohammed (JEM) is an Islamic extremist group based in Pakistan that was formed by Masood Azhar upon his release from prison in India in early 2000. The group's aim is to unite Kashmir with Pakistan. It is politically aligned with the radical political party, Jamiat-i Ulema-i Islam Fazlur Rehman faction (JUI-F). The United States announced the addition of JEM to the US Treasury Department's Office of Foreign Asset Control's (OFAC) list—which includes organizations that are believed to support terrorist groups and have assets in US jurisdiction that can be frozen or controlled—in October and the Foreign Terrorist Organization list in December. The group was banned and its assets were frozen by the Pakistani Government in January 2002.

Activities
The JEM's leader, Masood Azhar, was released from Indian imprisonment in December 1999 in exchange for 155 hijacked Indian Airline hostages. The 1994 HUA kidnappings by Omar Sheikh of US and British nationals in New Delhi and the July 1995 HUA/AI Faran kidnappings of Westerners in Kashmir were two of several previous HUA efforts to free Azhar. The JEM on 1 October 2001 claimed responsibility for a suicide attack on the Jammu and Kashmir legislative assembly building in Srinagar that killed at least 31 persons, but later denied the claim. The Indian Government has publicly implicated the JEM, along with Lashkar-e-Tayyiba for the 13 December attack on the Indian Parliament that killed 9 and injured 18.

Strength
Has several hundred armed supporters located in Azad Kashmir, Pakistan, and in India's southern Kashmir and Doda regions, including a large cadre of former HUM members. Supporters are mostly Pakistanis and Kashmiris and also include Afghans and Arab veterans of the Afghan war. Uses light and heavy machine-guns, assault rifles, mortars, improvised explosive devices, and rocket grenades.

Location/Area of Operation
Based in Peshawar and Muzaffarabad, but members conduct terrorist activities primarily in Kashmir. The JEM maintained training camps in Afghanistan until the fall of 2001.

External Aid
Most the the JEM's cadre and material resources have been drawn from the militant groups Harakat ul-Jihad al-Islami (HUJI) and the Harakat ul-Mujahedin (HUM). The

JEM had close ties to Afghan Arabs and the Taliban. Usama Bin Laden is suspected of giving funding to the JEM. The JEM also collects funds through donation requests in magazines and pamphlets. In anticipation of asset seizures by the Pakistani Government, the JEM withdrew funds from bank accounts and invested in legal businesses, such as commodity trading, real estate, and production of consumer goods.

Al-Jihad

a.k.a. Egyptian Islamic Jihad, Jihad Group, Islamic Jihad

Description

Egyptian Islamic extremist group active since the late 1970s. Merged with Bin Laden's al-Qaida organization in June 2001, but may retain some capability to conduct independent operations. Continues to suffer setbacks worldwide, especially after 11 September attacks. Primary goals are to overthrow the Egyptian Government and replace it with an Islamic state and attack US and Israeli interests in Egypt and abroad.

Activities

Specializes in armed attacks against high-level Egyptian Government personnel, including cabinet ministers, and car-bombings against official US and Egyptian facilities. The original Jihad was responsible for the assassination in 1981 of Egyptian President Anwar Sadat. Claimed responsibility for the attempted assassinations of Interior Minister Hassan al-Alfi in August 1993 and Prime Minister Atef Sedky in November 1993. Has not conducted an attack inside Egypt since 1993 and has never targeted foreign tourists there. Responsible for Egyptian Embassy bombing in Islamabad in 1995; in 1998 attack against US Embassy in Albania was thwarted.

Strength

Unknown, but probably has several hundred hard-core members.

Location/Area of Operation

Operates in the Cairo areas, but most of its network is outside Egypt, including Yemen, Afghanistan, Pakistan, Lebanon, and the United Kingdom, and its activities have been centered outside Egypt for several years.

External Aid

Unknown. The Egyptian Government claims that Iran supports the Jihad. Its merger with al-Qaida also boosts Bin Laden's support for the group. Also may obtain some funding through various Islamic nongovernmental organizations, cover businesses, and criminal acts.

Kahane Chai (Kach)

Description

Stated goal is to restore the biblical state of Israel. Kach (founded by radical Israeli-American rabbi Meir Kahane) and its offshoot Kahane Chai, which means "Kahane

Lives," (founded by Meir Kahane's son Binyamin following his father's assassination in the United States) were declared to be terrorist organizations in March 1994 by the Israeli Cabinet under the 1948 Terrorism Law. This followed the groups' statements in support of Dr. Baruch Goldstein's attack in February 1994 on the al-lbrahimi Mosque—Goldstein was affiliated with Kach—and their verbal attacks on the Israeli Government. Palestinian gunmen killed Binyamin Kahane and his wife in a drive-by shooting in December 2000 in the West Bank.

Activities
Organizes protests against the Israeli Government. Harasses and threatens Palestinians in Hebron and the West Bank. Has threatened to attack Arabs, Palestinians, and Israeli Government officials. Has vowed revenge for the death of Binyamin Kahane and his wife.

Strength
Unknown.

Location/Area of Operation
Israel and West Bank settlements, particularly Qiryat Arba' in Hebron.

External Aid
Receives support from sympathizers in the United States and Europe.

Kurdistan Workers' Party (PKK)

Description
Founded in 1974 as a Marxist-Leninist insurgent group primarily composed of Turkish Kurds. The group's goal has been to establish an independent Kurdish state in southeastern Turkey, where the population is predominantly Kurdish. In the early 1990s, the PKK moved beyond rural-based insurgent activities to include urban terrorism. Turkish authorities captured Chairman Abdullah Ocalan in Kenya in early 1999; the Turkish State Security Court subsequently sentenced him to death. In August 1999, Ocalan announced a "peace initiative," ordering members to refrain from violence and requesting dialogue with Ankara on Kurdish issues. At a PKK Congress in January 2000, members supported Ocalan's initiative and claimed the group now would use only political means to achieve its new goal, improved rights for Kurds in Turkey.

Activities
Primary targets have been Turkish Government security forces in Turkey. Conducted attacks on Turkish diplomatic and commercial facilities in dozens of West European cities in 1993 and again in spring 1995. In an attempt to damage Turkey's tourist industry, the PKK bombed tourist sites and hotels and kidnapped foreign tourists in the early to mid-1990s.

Strength
Approximately 4,000 to 5,000, most of whom currently are located in northern Iraq. Has thousands of sympathizers in Turkey and Europe.

Location/Area of Operation

Operates in Turkey, Europe, and the Middle East.

External Aid

Has received safe haven and modest aid from Syria, Iraq, and Iran. Damascus generally upheld its September 2000 antiterror agreement with Ankara, pledging not to support the PKK.

Lashkar-e-Tayyiba (LT) (Army of the Righteous)

Description

The LT is the armed wing of the Pakistan-based religious organization, Markaz-ud-Dawa-wal-Irshad (MDI)—a Sunni anti-US missionary organization formed in 1989. The LT is led by Abdul Wahid Kashmiri and is one of the three largest and best-trained groups fighting in Kashmir against India; it is not connected to a political party. The United States in October announced the addition of the LT to the US Treasury Department's Office of Foreign Asset Control's (OFAC) list—which includes organizations that are believed to support terrorist groups and have assets in US jurisdiction that can be frozen or controlled. The group was banned and its assets were frozen by the Pakistani Government in January 2002.

Activities

The LT has conducted a number of operations against Indian troops and civilian targets in Kashmir since 1993. The LT claimed responsibility for numerous attacks in 2001, including a January attack on Srinagar airport that killed five Indians along with six militants; an attack on a police station in Srinagar that killed at least eight officers and wounded several others; and an attack in April against Indian border security forces that left at least four dead. The Indian Government publicly implicated the LT along with JEM for the 13 December attack on the Indian Parliament building.

Strength

Has several members in Azad Kashmir, Pakistan, and in India's southern Kashmir and Doda regions. Almost all LT cadres are non-Kashmiris, mostly Pakistanis from madrassas across the country and Afghan veterans of the Afghan wars. Uses assault rifles, light and heavy machine-guns, mortars, explosives, and rocket propelled grenades.

Location/Area of Operation

Has been based in Muridke (near Lahore) and Muzaffarabad. The LT trains its militants in mobile training camps across Pakistan-administered Kashmir and had trained in Afghanistan until fall of 2001.

External Aid

Collects donations from the Pakistani community in the Persian Gulf and United Kingdom, Islamic NGOs [nongovernmental organizations], and Pakistani and Kashmiri businessmen. The LT also maintains a website (under the name of its parent organization Jamaat ud-Daawa), through which it solicits funds and provides information on the group's activities. The amount of LT funding is unknown. The LT maintains ties to religious/military groups around the world, ranging from the Philippines to the Middle East and Chechnya through the MDI fraternal network. In anticipation of asset seizures by the Pakistani Government, the LT withdrew funds from bank accounts and invested in legal businesses, such as commodity trading, real estate, and production of consumer goods.

Liberation Tigers of Tamil Eelam (LTTE)

Other known front organizations: World Tamil Association (WTA), World Tamil Movement (WTM), the Federation of Associations of Canadian Tamils (FACT), the Ellalan Force, and the Sangilian Force.

Description

Founded in 1976, the LTTE is the most powerful Tamil group in Sri Lanka and uses overt and illegal methods to raise funds, acquire weapons, and publicize its cause of establishing an independent Tamil state. The LTTE began its armed conflict with the Sri Lankan Government in 1983 and relies on a guerrilla strategy that includes the use of terrorist tactics.

Activities

The Tigers have integrated a battlefield insurgent strategy with a terrorist program that targets not only key personnel in the countryside but also senior Sri Lankan political and military leaders in Colombo and other urban centers. The Tigers are most notorious for their cadre of suicide bombers, the Black Tigers. Political assassinations and bombings are commonplace. The LTTE has refrained from targeting foreign diplomatic and commercial establishments.

Strength

Exact strength is unknown, but the LTTE is estimated to have 8,000 to 10,000 armed combatants in Sri Lanka, with a core of trained fighters of approximately 3,000 to 6,000. The LTTE also has a significant overseas support structure for fund-raising, weapons procurement, and propaganda activities.

Location/Area of Operations

The Tigers control most of the northern and eastern coastal areas of Sri Lanka but have conducted operations throughout the island. Headquartered in northern Sri Lanka, LTTE leader Velupillai Prabhakaran has established an extensive network of checkpoints and informants to keep track of any outsiders who enter the group's area of control.

External Aid

The LTTE's overt organizations support Tamil separatism by lobbying foreign governments and the United Nations. The LTTE also uses its international contacts to procure weapons, communications, and any other equipment and supplies it needs. The LTTE exploits large Tamil communities in North America, Europe, and Asia to obtain funds and supplies for its fighters in Sri Lanka often through false claims or even extortion.

Mujahedin-e Khalq Organization (MEK or MKO)

a.k.a. The National Liberation Army of Iran (NLA, the militant wing of the MEK), the People's Mujahidin of Iran (PMOI), National Council of Resistance (NCR), Muslim Iranian Student's Society (front organization used to garner financial support)

Description

The MEK philosophy mixes Marxism and Islam. Formed in the 1960s, the organization was expelled from Iran after the Islamic Revolution in 1979, and its primary support now comes from the Iraqi regime of Saddam Hussein. Its history is studded with anti-Western attacks as well as terrorist attacks on the interests of the clerical regime in Iran and abroad. The MEK now advocates a secular Iranian regime.

Activities

Worldwide campaign against the Iranian Government stresses propaganda and occasionally uses terrorist violence. During the 1970s the MEK killed several US military personnel and US civilians working on defense projects in Tehran. It supported the takeover in 1979 of the US Embassy in Tehran. In 1981 the MEK planted bombs in the head office of the Islamic Republic Party and the Premier's office, killing some 70 high-ranking Iranian officials, including chief Justice Ayatollah Mohammad Beheshti, President Mohammad-Ali Rajaei, and Premier Mohammad-Javad Bahonar. In 1991, it assisted the government of Iraq in suppressing the Shia and Kurdish uprisings in northern and southern Iraq. In April 1992, it conducted attacks on Iranian Embassies in 13 different countries, demonstrating the group's ability to mount large-scale operations overseas. In recent years the MEK has targeted key military officers and assassinated the deputy chief of the Armed Forces General Staff in April 1999. In April 2000, the MEK attempted to assassinate the commander of the Nasr Headquarters—the interagency board responsible for coordinating policies on Iraq. The normal pace of anti-Iranian operations increased during the "Operation Great Bahman" in February 2000, when the group launched a dozen attacks against Iran. In 2000 and 2001, the MEK was involved regularly in mortar attacks and hit-and-run raids on Iranian military and law enforcement units and government buildings near the Iran-Iraq border. Since the end of the Iran-Iraq War the tactics along the border have garnered few military gains and have become commonplace. MEK insurgent activities in Tehran constitute the biggest security concern for the Iranian leadership. In February 2000, for example, the MEK attacked the leadership complex in Tehran that houses the offices of the Supreme Leader and President.

Strength

Several thousand fighters located on bases scattered throughout Iraq and armed with tanks, infantry fighting vehicles, and artillery. The MEK also has an overseas support structure. Most of the fighters are organized in the MEK's National Liberation Army (NLA).

Location/Area of Operation

In the 1980s the MEK's leaders were forced by Iranian security forces to flee to France. Since resettling in Iraq in 1987, the group has conducted internal security operations in support of the Government of Iraq. In the mid-1980s the group did not mount terrorist operations in Iran at a level similar to its activities in the 1970s, but by the 1990s the MED had claimed credit for an increasing number of operations in Iran.

External Aid

Beyond support from Iraq, the MEK uses front organizations to solicit contributions from expatriate Iranian communities.

National Liberation Army (ELN)—Colombia

Description

Marxist insurgent group formed in 1965 by urban intellectuals inspired by Fidel Castro and Che Guevara. Began a dialogue with Colombian officials in 1999 following a campaign of mass kidnappings—each involving at least one U.S. citizen—to demonstrate its strength and continuing viability, and force the Pastrana administration to negotiate. Peace talks between Bogotá and the ELN, started in 1999, continued sporadically through 2001 until Bogotá broke them off in August, but resumed in Havana, Cuba, by year's end.

Activities

Kidnapping, hijacking, bombing, extortion, and guerrilla war. Modest conventional military capability. Annually conducts hundreds of kidnappings for ransom, often targeting foreign employees of large corporations, especially in the petroleum industry. Frequently assaults energy infrastructure and has inflicted major damage on pipelines and the electric distribution network.

Strength

Approximately 3,000–5,000 armed combatants and an unknown number of active supporters.

Location/Area of Operation

Mostly in rural and mountainous areas of north, northeast, and southwest Colombia, and Venezuela border regions.

External Aid

Cuba provides some medical care and political consultation.

The Palestine Islamic Jihad (PIJ)

Description

Originated among militant Palestinians in the Gaza Strip during the 1970s. PIJ-Shiqaqi faction, currently led by Ramadan Shallah in Damascus, is most active. Committed to the creation of an Islamic Palestinian state and the destruction of Israel through holy war. Also opposes moderate Arab governments that it believes have been tainted by Western secularism.

Activities

PIJ activists have conducted many attacks, including large-scale suicide bombings against Israeli civilian and military targets. The group increased its operational activity in 2001 during the *Intifadah* [Palestinian uprising], claiming numerous attacks against Israeli interests. The group has not targeted US interests and continues to confine its attacks to Israelis inside Israel and the territories.

Strength

Unknown.

Location/Area of Operation

Primarily Israel, the West Bank, and Gaza Strip, and other parts of the Middle East, including Lebanon and Syria, where the leadership is based.

External Aid

Receives financial assistance from Iran and limited logistic support assistance from Syria.

Palestine Liberation Front (PLF)

Description

Broke away from the PFLP-GC in mid-1970s. Later split again into pro-PLO, pro-Syrian, and pro-Libyan factions. Pro-PLO faction led by Muhammad Abbas (Abu Abbas), who became member of PLO Executive Committee in 1984 but left it in 1991.

Activities

The Abu Abbas–led faction is known for aerial attacks against Israel. Abbas's group also was responsible for the attack in 1985 on the cruise ship Achille Lauro and the murder of US citizen Leon Klinghoffer. A warrant for Abu Abbas's arrest is outstanding in Italy.

Strength

Unknown.

Location/Area of Operation

PLO faction based in Tunisia until *Achille Lauro* attack. Now based in Iraq.

External Aid

Receives support mainly from Iran. Has received support from Libya in the past.

Popular Front for the Liberation of Palestine (PFLP)

Description

Marxist-Leninist group founded in 1967 by George Habash as a member of the PLO. Joined the Alliance of Palestinian Forces (APF) to oppose the Declaration of Principles signed in 1993 and suspended participation in the PLO. Broke away from the APF, along with the DFLP, in 1996 over ideological differences. Took part in meetings with Arafat's

Fatah party and PLO representatives in 1999 to discuss national unity and the reinvigoration of the PLO but continues to oppose current negotiations with Israel.

Activities

Committed numerous international terrorist attacks during the 1970s. Since 1978 has conducted attacks against Israeli or moderate Arab targets, including killing a settler and her son in December 1996. Stepped up operational activity in 2001, highlighted by the shooting death of Israeli Tourism Minister in October to retaliation for Israel's killing of PFLP leader in August.

Strength

Some 800.

Location/Area of Operation

Syria, Lebanon, Israel, West Bank, and Gaza.

External Aid

Receives safe haven and some logistical assistance from Syria.

Popular Front for the Liberation of Palestine—General Command (PFLP-GC)

Description

Split from the PFLP in 1968, claiming it wanted to focus more on fighting and less on politics. Opposed to Arafat's PLO. Led by Ahmad Jabril, a former captain in the Syrian Army. Closely tied to both Syria and Iran.

Activities

Carried out dozens of attacks in Europe and the Middle East during 1970s–80s. Known for cross-border terrorist attacks into Israel using unusual means, such as hot-air balloons and motorized hang gliders. Primary focus now on guerrilla operations in southern Lebanon, small-scale attacks in Israel, West Bank, and Gaza.

Strength

Several hundred.

Location/Area of Operation

Headquarters in Damascus with bases in Lebanon.

External Aid

Receives support from Syria and financial support from Iran.

Al-Qaida

Description

Established by Usama Bin Laden in the late 1980s to bring together Arabs who fought in Afghanistan against the Soviet Union. Helped finance, recruit, transport, and train Sunni Islamic extremists for the Afghan resistance. Current goal is to establish a pan-Islamic Caliphate throughout the world by working with allied Islamic extremist groups to overthrow regimes it deems "non-Islamic" and expelling Westerners and non-Muslims from Muslim countries. Issued statement under banner of "The World Islamic Front for Jihad Against the Jews and Crusaders" in February 1998, saying it was the duty of all Muslims to kill US citizens—civilian or military—and their allies everywhere. Merged with Egyptian Islamic Jihad (Al-Jihad) in June 2001.

Activities

On 11 September, 19 al-Qaida suicide attackers hijacked and crashed four US commercial jets, two into the World Trade Center in New York City, one into the Pentagon near Washington, DC, and a fourth into a field in Shanksville, Pennsylvania, leaving about 3,000 individuals dead or missing. Directed the 12 October 2000 attack on the USS Cole in the port of Aden, Yemen, killing 17 US Navy members, and injuring another 39. Conducted the bombings in August 1998 of the US Embassies in Nairobi, Kenya, and Dar es Salaam, Tanzania, that killed at least 301 individuals and injured more than 5,000 others. Claims to have shot down US helicopters and killed US servicemen in Somalia in 1993 and to have conducted three bombings that targeted US troops in Aden, Yemen, in December 1992.

Al-Qaida is linked to the following plans that were not carried out: to assassinate Pope John Paul II during his visit to Manila in late 1994, to kill President Clinton during a visit to the Philippines in early 1995, the midair bombing of a dozen US trans-Pacific flights in 1995, and to set off a bomb at Los Angeles International Airport in 1999. Also plotted to carry out terrorist operations against US and Israeli tourists visiting Jordan for millennial celebrations in late 1999. (Jordanian authorities thwarted the planned attacks and put 28 suspects on trial.) In December 2001, suspected al-Qaida associate Richard Colvin Reid attempted to ignite a shoe bomb on a transatlantic flight from Paris to Miami.

Strength

Al-Qaida may have several thousand members and associates. Also serves as a focal point or umbrella organization for a worldwide network that includes many Sunni Islamic extremist groups, some members of al-Gama'a al-Islamiyya, the Islamic Movement of Uzbekistan, and the Harakat ul-Mujahidin.

Location/Area of Operation

Al-Qaida has cells worldwide and is reinforced by its ties to Sunni extremist networks. Coalition attacks on Afghanistan since October 2001 have dismantled the Taliban—al-Qaida's protectors—and led to the capture, death, or dispersal of al-Qaida operatives. Some al-Qaida members at large probably will attempt to carry out future attacks against US interests.

External Aid

Bin Laden, member of a billionaire family that owns the Bin Laden Group construction empire, is said to have inherited tens of millions of dollars that he uses to help finance the group. Al-Qaida also maintains moneymaking front businesses, solicits donations from like-minded supporters, and illicitly siphons funds from donations to Muslim charitable organizations. US efforts to block al-Qaida funding has hampered al-Qaida's ability to obtain money.

Real IRA (RIRA)

a.k.a. True IRA

Description

Formed in early 1998 as clandestine armed wing of the 32-County Sovereignty Movement, a "political pressure group" dedicated to removing British forces from Northern Ireland and unifying Ireland. The 32-County Sovereignty Movement opposed Sinn Fein's adoption in September 1997 of the Mitchell principles of democracy and nonviolence and opposed the amendment in December 1999 of Articles 2 and 3 of the Irish Constitution, which laid claim to Northern Ireland. Michael "Mickey" McKevitt, who left the IRA to protest its cease-fire, leads the group; Bernadette Sands-McKevitt, his wife, is a founder-member of the 32-County Sovereignty Movement, the political wing of the RIRA.

Activities

Bombings, assassinations, and robberies. Many Real IRA members are former IRA members who left that organization following the IRA cease-fire and bring to RIRA a wealth or experience in terrorist tactics and bombmaking. Targets include British military and police in Northern Ireland and Northern Ireland Protestant communities. RIRA is linked to and understood to be responsible for the car bomb attack in Omagh, Northern Ireland, on 15 August, 1998 that killed 29 and injured 220 persons. The group began to observe a cease-fire following Omagh but in 2000 and 2001 resumed attacks in Northern Ireland and on the UK mainland against targets such as M16 headquarters and the BBC.

Strength

100–200 activists plus possible limited support from IRA hard-liners dissatisfied with IRA cease-fire and other republican sympathizers. British and Irish authorities arrested at least 40 members in the spring and summer of 2001, including leader McKevitt, who is currently in prison in the Irish Republic awaiting trial for being a member of a terrorist organization and directing terrorist attacks.

Location/Area of Operation

Northern Ireland, Irish Republic, Great Britain.

External Aid

Suspected of receiving funds from sympathizers in the United States and of attempting to buy weapons from US gun dealers. RIRA also is reported to have purchased sophisticated weapons from the Balkans. Three Irish nationals associated with RIRA were extradited from Slovenia to the UK and are awaiting trial on weapons procurement charges.

Revolutionary Armed Forces of Colombia (FARC)

Description

Established in 1964 as the military wing of the Colombian Communist Party, the FARC is a Colombia's oldest, largest, most capable, and best-equipped Marxist insurgency. The FARC is governed by a secretariat, led by septuagenarian Manuel Marulanda, a.k.a. "Tirofijo," and six others, including senior military commander Jorge Briceno, a.k.a. "Mono Jojoy." Organized along military lines and includes several urban fronts. In 2001, the group continued a slow-moving peace negotiation process with the Pastrana Administration that has gained the group several concessions, including a demilitarized zone used as a venue for negotiations.

Activities

Bombings, murder, kidnapping, extortion, hijacking, as well as guerilla and conventional military action against Colombian political, military, and economic targets. In March 1999 the FARC executed three US Indian rights activists on Venezuelan territory after it kidnapped them in Colombia. Foreign citizens often are targets of FARC kidnapping for ransom. Has well-documented ties to narcotics traffickers, principally through the provision of armed protection.

Strength

Approximately 9,000–12,000 armed combatants and an unknown number of supporters, mostly in rural areas.

Location/Area of Operation

Colombia with some activities—extortion, kidnapping, logistics, and R&R—in Venezuela, Panama, and Ecuador.

External Aid

Cuba provides some medical care and political consultation.

Revolutionary Nuclei

a.k.a. Revolutionary Cells

Description

Revolutionary Nuclei (RN) emerged from a broad range of antiestablishment and anti-US/NATO/EU leftist groups active in Greece between 1995 and 1998. The group is believed to be the successor to or offshoot of Greece's most prolific terrorist group, Revolutionary People's Struggle (ELA), which has not claimed an attack since January 1995.

Indeed, RN appeared to fill the void left by ELA, particularly as lesser groups faded from the scene. RN's few communiqués show strong similarities in rhetoric, tone, and theme to ELA proclamations. RN has not claimed an attack since November 2000.

Activities

Beginning operations in January 1995, the group has claimed responsibility for some two dozen arson attacks and explosive low-level bombings targeting a range of US, Greek, and other European targets in Greece. In its most infamous and lethal attack to date, the group claimed responsibility for a bomb it detonated at the Intercontinental Hotel in April 1999 that resulted in the death of a Greek woman and injured a Greek man. Its modus operandi includes warning calls of impending attacks, attacks targeting property [and] individuals; use of rudimentary timing devices; and strikes during the late evening-early morning hours. RN last attacked US interests in Greece in November 2000 with two separate bombings against the Athens offices of Citigroup and the studio of a Greek/American sculptor. The groups also detonated an explosive device outside the Athens offices of Texaco in December 1999. Greek targets have included court and other government office buildings, private vehicles, and the offices of Greek firms involved in NATO-related defense contracts in Greece. Similarly, the group has attacked European interests in Athens, including Barclays Bank in December 1998 and November 2000.

Strength

Group membership is believed to be small, probably drawing from the Greek militant leftist or anarchist milieu.

Location/Area of Operation

Primary area of operation is in the Athens metropolitan area.

External Aid

Unknown, but believed to be self-sustaining.

Revolutionary Organization 17 November (17 November)

Description

Radical leftist group established in 1975 and named for the student uprising in Greece in November 1973 that protested the military regime. Anti-Greek establishment, anti-US, anti-Turkey, anti-NATO, and committed to the ouster of US bases, removal of Turkish military presence from Cyprus, and severing of Greece's ties to NATO and the European Union (EU).

Activities

Initial attacks were assassinations of senior US officials and Greek public figures. Added bombings in 1980s. Since 1990 has expanded targets to include EU facilities and foreign firms investing in Greece and has added improvised rocket attacks to its methods. Most recent attack claimed was the murder in June 2000 of British Defense Attaché Stephen Saunders.

Strength
Unknown, but presumed to be small.

Location/Area of Operation
Athens, Greece.

Revolutionary People's Liberation Party/Front (DHKP/C)
a.k.a. Devrimci So, Revolutionary Left, Dev Sol

Description
Originally formed in 1978 as Devrimci Sol, or Dev Sol, a splinter faction of the Turkish People's Liberation Party/Front. Renamed in 1994 after factional infighting, it espouses a Marxist ideology and is virulently anti-US and anti-NATO [North Atlantic Treaty Organization]. Finances its activities chiefly through armed robberies and extortion.

Activities
Since the late 1980s has concentrated attacks against current and retired Turkish security and military officials. Began a new campaign against foreign interests in 1990. Assassinated two US military contractors and wounded a US Air Force officer to protest the Gulf War. Launched rockets at US Consulate in Istanbul in 1992. Assassinated prominent Turkish businessman and two others in early 1996, its first significant terrorist act as DHKP/C. Turkish authorities thwarted DHKP/C attempt in June 1999 to fire light antitank weapon at US Consulate in Istanbul. Conducted its first suicide bombings, targeting Turkish police, in January and September 2001. Series of safehouse raids and arrests by Turkish police over last three years have weakened group significantly.

Strength
Unknown.

Location/Area of Operation
Conducts attacks in Turkey, primarily in Istanbul. Raises funds in Western Europe.

External Aid
Unknown.

The Salafist Group for Call and Combat (GSPC)

Description
The Salafist Group for Call and Combat (GSPC) splinter faction that began in 1996 has eclipsed the GIA since approximately 1998, and currently is assessed to be the most effective remaining armed group inside Algeria. In contrast to the GIA, the GSPC has gained popular support through its pledge to avoid civilian attacks inside Algeria (although, in fact, civilians have been attacked). Its adherents abroad appear to have largely co-opted the external networks of the GIA, active particularly throughout Europe, Africa, and the Middle East.

Activities

The GSPC continues to conduct operations aimed at government and military targets, primarily in rural areas. Such operations include false roadblocks and attacks against convoys transporting military, police, or other government personnel. According to press reporting, some GSPC members in Europe maintain contacts with other North African extremists sympathetic to al-Qaida, a number of whom were implicated in terrorist plots during 2001.

Strength

Unknown; probably several hundred to several thousand inside Algeria.

Location/Area of Operation

Algeria.

External Aid

Algerian expatriates and GSPC members abroad, many residing in Western Europe, provide financial and logistics support. In addition, the Algerian Government has accused Iran and Sudan of supporting Algerian extremists in years past.

Sendero Luminoso (Shining Path, or SL)

Description

Former university professor Abimael Guzman formed Sendero Luminoso in the late 1960s, and his teachings created the foundation of SL's militant Maoist doctrine. In the 1980s SL became one of the most ruthless terrorist groups in the Western Hemisphere; approximately 30,000 persons have died since Shining Path took up arms in 1980. Its stated goal is to destroy existing Peruvian institutions and replace them with a communist peasant revolutionary regime. It also opposes any influence by foreign governments, as well as by other Latin American guerrilla groups, especially the Tupac Amaru Revolutionary Movement (MRTA).

In 2001, the Peruvian National Police thwarted an SL attack against "an American objective," possibly the US Embassy, when they arrested two Lima SL cell members. Additionally, Government authorities continued to arrest and prosecute active SL members, including, Ruller Mazombite, a.k.a. "Camarada Cayo," chief of the protection team of SL leader Macario Ala, a.k.a. "Artemio," and Evorcio Ascencios, a.k.a. "Camarada Canale," logistics chief of the Huallaga Regional Committee. Counterterrorist operations targeted pockets of terrorist activity in the Upper Huallaga River Valley and the Apurimac/Ene River Valley, where SL columns continued to conduct periodic attacks.

Activities

Conducted indiscriminate bombing campaigns and selective assassinations. Detonated explosives at diplomatic missions of several countries in Peru in 1990, including an attempt to car bomb the US Embassy in December. Peruvian authorities continued operations against the SL in 2001 in the countryside, where the SL conducted periodic raids on villages.

Strength

Membership is unknown but estimated to be 200 armed militants. SL's strength has been vastly diminished by arrests and desertions.

Location/Area of Operation

Peru, with most activity in rural areas.

External Aid

None.

United Self-Defense Forces/Group of Colombia (AUC—Autodefensas Unidas de Colombia)

Description

The AUC—commonly referred to as the paramilitaries—is an umbrella organization formed in April 1997 to consolidate most local and regional paramilitary groups each with the mission to protect economic interests and combat insurgents locally. The AUC—supported by economic elites, drug traffickers, and local communities lacking effective government security—claims its primary objective is to protect its sponsors from insurgents. The AUC now asserts itself as a regional and national counterinsurgent force. It is adequately equipped and armed and reportedly pays its members a monthly salary. AUC political leader Carlos Castaño has claimed 70 percent of the AUC's operational costs are financed with drug-related earnings, the rest from "donations" from its sponsors.

Activities

AUC operations vary from assassinating suspected insurgent supporters to engaging guerrilla combat units. Colombian National Combat operations generally consist of raids and ambushes directed against suspected insurgents. The AUC generally avoids engagements with government security forces and actions against US personnel or interests.

Strength

Estimated 6,000 to 8,150, including former military and insurgent personnel.

Location/Area of Operation

AUC forces are strongest in the northwest in Antioquia, Córdoba, Sucre, and Bolivar Departments. Since 1999, the group demonstrated a growing presence in other northern and southwestern departments. Clashes between the AUC and the FARC insurgents in Putumayo in 2000 demonstrated the range of the AUC to contest insurgents throughout Colombia.

External Aid

None.

Appendix B

Significant Terrorist Incidents, 1961–2001

1961–1982

First U.S. Aircraft Hijacked, May 1, 1961: Puerto Rican–born Antuilo Ramierez Ortiz forced at gunpoint a National Airlines plane to fly to Havana Cuba, where he was given asylum.

Ambassador to Guatemala Assassinated, August 28, 1968: U.S. Ambassador to Guatemala John Gordon Mein was murdered by a rebel faction when gunmen forced his official car off the road in Guatemala City and raked the vehicle with gunfire.

Ambassador to Japan Attacked, July 30, 1969: U.S. Ambassador to Japan A. H. Meyer was attacked by a knife-wielding Japanese citizen.

Ambassador to Brazil Kidnapped, September 3, 1969: U.S. Ambassador to Brazil Charles Burke Elbrick was kidnapped by the Marxist revolutionary group MR-8.

U.S. Agency for International Development Adviser Kidnapped, July 31, 1970: In Montevideo, Uruguay, the Tupamaros terrorist group kidnapped USAID police adviser Dan Mitrione; his body was found on August 10.

"Bloody Friday," July 21, 1972: An Irish Republican Army (IRA) bomb attacks killed 11 people and injured 130 in Belfast, Northern Ireland. Ten days later, three IRA car bomb attacks in the village of Claudy left six dead.

Munich Olympic Massacre, September 5, 1972: Eight Palestinian "Black September" terrorists seized 11 Israeli athletes in the Olympic Village in Munich, West Germany. In a bungled rescue attempt by West German authorities, nine of the hostages and five terrorists were killed.

Ambassador to Sudan Assassinated, March 2, 1973: U.S. Ambassador to Sudan Cleo A. Noel and other diplomats were assassinated at the Saudi Arabian Embassy in Khartoum by members of the Black September organization.

Consul General in Mexico Kidnapped, May 4, 1973: U.S. Consul General in Guadalajara Terrence Leonhardy was kidnapped by members of the People's Revolutionary Armed Forces.

Domestic Terrorism, January 27–29, 1975: Puerto Rican nationalists bombed a Wall Street bar, killing four and injuring 60; 2 days later, the Weather Underground claims responsibility for an explosion in a bathroom at the U.S. Department of State in Washington.

Entebbe Hostage Crisis, June 27, 1976: Members of the Baader-Meinhof Group and the Popular Front for the Liberation of Palestine (PFLP) seized an Air France airliner and its 258 passengers. They forced the plane to land in Uganda, where on July 3 Israeli commandos successfully rescued the passengers.

Assassination of Former Chilean Diplomat, September 21, 1976: In Washington, exiled Chilean Foreign Minister Orlando Letelier was killed by a car bomb.

Kidnapping of Italian Prime Minister, March 16, 1978: Premier Aldo Moro was seized by the Red Brigade and assassinated 55 days later.

Iran Hostage Crisis, November 4, 1979: After President Carter agreed to admit the Shah of Iran into the U.S., Iranian radicals seized the U.S. embassy in Tehran and took 66 American diplomats hostage. Thirteen hostages were soon released, but the remaining 53 were held until their release on January 20, 1981.

Grand Mosque Seizure, November 20, 1979: 200 Islamic terrorists seized the Grand Mosque in Mecca, Saudi Arabia, taking hundreds of pilgrims hostage. Saudi and French security forces retook the shrine after an intense battle in which some 250 people were killed and 600 wounded.

U.S. Installation Bombing, August 31, 1981: The Red Army exploded a bomb at the U.S. Air Force Base at Ramstein, West Germany.

Assassination of Egyptian President, October 6, 1981: Soldiers who were secretly members of the Takfir Wal-Hajira sect attacked and killed Egyptian President Anwar Sadat during a troop review.

Murder of Missionaries, December 4, 1981: Three American nuns and one lay missionary were found murdered outside San Salvador, El Salvador. They were believed to have been assassinated by a right-wing death squad.

Assassination of Lebanese Prime Minister, September 14, 1982: Premier Bashir Gemayel was assassinated by a car bomb parked outside his party's Beirut headquarters.

1983

Colombian Hostage-Taking, April 8, 1983: A U.S. citizen was seized by the Revolutionary Armed Forces of Colombia (FARC) and held for ransom.

Bombing of U.S. Embassy in Beirut, April 18, 1983: Sixty-three people, including the CIA's Middle East director, were killed, and 120 were injured in a 400-pound suicide truck-bomb attack on the U.S. Embassy in Beirut, Lebanon. The Islamic Jihad claimed responsibility.

Naval Officer Assassinated in El Salvador, May 25, 1983: A U.S. Navy officer was assassinated by the Farabundo Marti National Liberation Front.

North Korean Hit Squad, October 9, 1983: North Korean agents blew up a delegation from South Korea in Rangoon, Burma, killing 21 persons and injuring 48.

Bombing of Marine Barracks, Beirut, October 23, 1983: Simultaneous suicide truck-bomb attacks were made on American and French compounds in Beirut, Lebanon. A 12,000-pound bomb destroyed the U.S. compound, killing 242 Americans, while 58 French troops were killed when a 400-pound device destroyed a French base. Islamic Jihad claimed responsibility.

Naval Officer Assassinated in Greece, November 15, 1983: A U.S. Navy officer was shot by the November 17 terrorist group in Athens, Greece, while his car was stopped at a traffic light.

1984

Kidnapping of Embassy Official, March 16, 1984: The Islamic Jihad kidnapped and later murdered Political Officer William Buckley in Beirut, Lebanon. Other U.S. citizens not connected to the U.S. Government were seized over a succeeding 2-year period.

Hizballah Restaurant Bombing, April 12, 1984: Eighteen U.S. servicemen were killed, and 83 people were injured in a bomb attack on a restaurant near a U.S. Air Force Base in Torrejon, Spain. Responsibility was claimed by Hizballah.

Golden Temple Seizure, June 5, 1984: Sikh terrorists seized the Golden Temple in Amritsar, India. One hundred people died when Indian security forces retook the Sikh holy shrine.

Assassination of Prime Minister Gandhi, October 31, 1984: The Indian premier was shot to death by members of her security force.

1985

Kidnapping of U.S. Officials in Mexico, February 7, 1985: Under the orders of narcotrafficker Rafael Cero Quintero, Drug Enforcement Administration agent Enrique Camarena Salazar and his pilot were kidnapped, tortured, and executed.

TWA Hijacking, June 14, 1985: A Trans-World Airlines flight was hijacked en route to Rome from Athens by two Lebanese Hizballah terrorists and forced to fly to Beirut. The eight crew members and 145 passengers were held for 17 days, during which one American hostage, a U.S. Navy sailor, was murdered. After being flown twice to Algiers, the aircraft was returned to Beirut after Israel released 435 Lebanese and Palestinian prisoners.

Air India Bombing, June 23, 1985: A bomb destroyed an Air India Boeing 747 over the Atlantic, killing all 329 people aboard. Both Sikh and Kashmiri terrorists were blamed for the attack. Two cargo handlers were killed at Tokyo airport, Japan, when another Sikh bomb exploded in an Air Canada aircraft enroute to India.

Soviet Diplomats Kidnapped, September 30, 1985: In Beirut, Lebanon, Sunni terrorists kidnapped four Soviet diplomats. One was killed, but three were later released.

Achille Lauro **Hijacking, October 7, 1985:** Four Palestinian Liberation Front terrorists seized the Italian cruise liner in the eastern Mediterranean Sea, taking more than 700 hostages. One U.S. passenger was murdered before the Egyptian Government offered the terrorists safe haven in return for the hostages' freedom.

Egyptian Airliner Hijacking, November 23, 1985: An EgyptAir airplane bound from Athens to Malta and carrying several U.S. citizens was hijacked by the Abu Nidal Group.

1986

Aircraft Bombing in Greece, March 30, 1986: A Palestinian splinter group detonated a bomb as TWA Flight 840 approached Athens Airport, killing four U.S. citizens.

Berlin Discotheque Bombing, April 5, 1986: Two U.S. soldiers were killed, and 79 American servicemen were injured in a Libyan bomb attack on a nightclub in West Berlin, West Germany. In retaliation, U.S military jets bombed targets in and around Tripoli and Benghazi.

Kimpo Airport Bombing, September 14, 1986: North Korean agents detonated an explosive device at Seoul's Kimpo Airport, killing five persons and injuring 29 others.

1987

Bus Attack, April 24, 1987: Sixteen U.S. servicemen riding in a Greek Air Force bus near Athens were injured in an apparent bombing attack, carried out by the revolutionary organization known as 17 November.

Downing of Airliner, November 29, 1987: North Korean agents planted a bomb aboard Korean Air Lines Flight 858, which subsequently crashed into the Indian Ocean.

Servicemen's Bar Attack, December 26, 1987: Catalan separatists bombed a Barcelona bar frequented by U.S. servicemen, resulting in the death of one U.S. citizen.

1988

Kidnapping of William Higgins, February 17, 1988: U.S. Marine Corps Lt. Col. W. Higgins was kidnapped and murdered by the Iranian-backed Hizballah group while serving with the United Nations Truce Supervisory Organization (UNTSO) in southern Lebanon.

Naples USO Attack, April 14, 1988: The Organization of Jihad Brigades exploded a car bomb outside a USO Club in Naples, Italy, killing one U.S. sailor.

Attack on U.S. Diplomat in Greece, June 28, 1988: The Defense Attache of the U.S. Embassy in Greece was killed when a car bomb was detonated outside his home in Athens.

Pan Am 103 Bombing, December 21, 1988: Pan American Airlines Flight 103 was blown up over Lockerbie, Scotland, by a bomb believed to have been placed on the aircraft in Frankfurt, West Germany, by Libyan terrorists. All 259 people on board were killed.

1989

Assassination of U.S. Army Officer, April 21, 1989: The New People's Army (NPA) assassinated Col. James Rowe in Manila. The NPA also assassinated two U.S. government defense contractors in September.

Assassination of German Bank Chairman, November 30, 1989: The Red Army assassinated Deutsche Bank Chairman Alfred Herrhausen in Frankfurt.

1990

U.S. Embassy Bombed in Peru, January 15, 1990: The Tupac Amaru Revolutionary Movement bombed the U.S. Embassy in Lima, Peru.

U.S. Soldiers Assassinated in the Philippines, May 13, 1990: The New People's Army (NPA) killed two U.S. Air Force personnel near Clark Air Force Base in the Philippines.

1991

Attempted Iraqi Attacks on U.S. Posts, January 18–19, 1991: Iraqi agents planted bombs at the U.S. Ambassador to Indonesia's home residence and at the USIS [U.S. Information Service] library in Manila.

1992

Kidnapping of U.S. Businessmen in the Philippines, January 17–21, 1992: A senior official of the corporation Philippine Geothermal was kidnapped in Manila by the Red Scorpion Group, and two U.S. businessmen were seized independently by the National Liberation Army and by Revolutionary Armed Forces of Colombia (FARC).

Bombing of the Israeli Embassy in Argentina, March 17, 1992: Hizballah claimed responsibility for a blast that leveled the Israeli Embassy in Buenos Aires, Argentina, causing the deaths of 29 and wounding 242.

1993

Kidnappings of U.S. Citizens in Colombia, January 31, 1993: Revolutionary Armed Forces of Colombia (FARC) terrorists kidnapped three U.S. missionaries.

World Trade Center Bombing, February 26, 1993: The World Trade Center in New York City was badly damaged when a car bomb planted by Islamic terrorists exploded in an underground garage. The bomb left six people dead and 1,000 injured. The men carrying out the attack were followers of Umar Abd al-Rahman, an Egyptian cleric who preached in the New York City area.

Attempted Assassination of President Bush by Iraqi Agents, April 14, 1993: The Iraqi intelligence service attempted to assassinate former U.S. President George Bush during a visit to Kuwait. In retaliation, the U.S. launched a cruise missile attack 2 months later on the Iraqi capital, Baghdad.

1994

Hebron Massacre, February 25, 1994: Jewish right-wing extremist and U.S. citizen Baruch Goldstein machine-gunned Moslem worshippers at a mosque in West Bank town of Hebron, killing 29 and wounding about 150.

FARC Hostage-Taking, September 23, 1994: FARC rebels kidnapped U.S. citizen Thomas Hargrove in Colombia.

Air France Hijacking, December 24, 1994: Members of the Armed Islamic Group seized an Air France Flight to Algeria. The four terrorists were killed during a rescue effort.

1995

Attack on U.S. Diplomats in Pakistan, March 8, 1995: Two unidentified gunmen killed two U.S. diplomats and wounded a third in Karachi, Pakistan.

Tokyo Subway Station Attack, March 20, 1995: Twelve persons were killed, and 5,700 were injured in a sarin nerve gas attack on a crowded subway station in the center of Tokyo, Japan. A similar attack occurred nearly simultaneously in the Yokohama subway system. The Aum Shinrikyo cult was blamed for the attacks.

Bombing of the Federal Building in Oklahoma City, April 19, 1995: Right-wing extremists Timothy McVeigh and Terry Nichols destroyed the Federal Building in Oklahoma City with a massive truck bomb that killed 166 and injured hundreds more in what was up to then the largest terrorist attack on American soil.

Kashmiri Hostage-Taking, July 4, 1995: In India, six foreigners, including two U.S. citizens, were taken hostage by Al-Faran, a Kashmiri separatist group. One non-U.S. hostage was later found beheaded.

Jerusalem Bus Attack, August 21, 1995: Hamas claimed responsibility for the detonation of a bomb that killed six and injured over 100 persons, including several U.S. citizens.

Attack on U.S. Embassy in Moscow, September 13, 1995: A rocket-propelled grenade was fired through the window of the U.S. Embassy in Moscow, ostensibly in retaliation for U.S. strikes on Serb positions in Bosnia.

Saudi Military Installation Attack, November 13, 1995: The Islamic Movement of Change planted a bomb in a Riyadh military compound that killed one U.S. citizen, several foreign national employees of the U.S. Government, and more than 40 others.

Egyptian Embassy Attack, November 19, 1995: A suicide bomber drove a vehicle into the Egyptian Embassy compound in Islamabad, Pakistan, killing at least 16 and injuring 60 persons. Three militant Islamic groups claimed responsibility.

1996

Papuan Hostage Abduction, January 8, 1996: In Indonesia, 200 Free Papua Movement (OPM) guerrillas abducted 26 individuals in the Lorenta nature preserve, Irian Jaya Province. Indonesian Special Forces members rescued the remaining nine hostages on May 15.

Kidnapping in Colombia, January 19, 1996: Revolutionary Armed Forces of Colombia (FARC) guerrillas kidnapped a U.S. citizen and demanded a $1 million ransom. The hostage was released on May 22.

Tamil Tigers Attack, January 31, 1996: Members of the Liberation Tigers of Tamil Eelam (LTTE) rammed an explosives-laden truck into the Central Bank in the heart of downtown Colombo, Sri Lanka, killing 90 civilians and injuring more than 1,400 others, including two citizens.

IRA Bombing, February 9, 1996: An Irish Republican Army (IRA) bomb detonated in London, killing two persons and wounding more than 100 others, including two U.S. citizens.

Athens Embassy Attack, February 15, 1996: Unidentified assailants fired a rocket at the U.S. embassy compound in Athens, causing minor damage to three diplomatic vehicles and some surrounding buildings. Circumstances of the attack suggested it was an operation carried out by the 17 November group.

ELN Kidnapping, February 16, 1996: Six alleged National Liberation Army (ELN) guerrillas kidnapped a U.S. citizen in Colombia. After 9 months, the hostage was released.

Hamas Bus Attack, February 26, 1996: In Jerusalem, a suicide bomber blew up a bus, killing 26 persons, including three U.S. citizens, and injuring some 80 persons, including three other U.S. citizens.

Dizengoff Center Bombing, March 4, 1996: Hamas and the Palestine Islamic Jihad (PIJ) both claimed responsibility for a bombing outside of Tel Aviv's largest shopping mall that killed 20 persons and injured 75 others, including two U.S. citizens.

West Bank Attack, May 13, 1996: Arab gunmen opened fire on a bus and a group of Yeshiva students near the Bet El settlement, killing a dual U.S.-Israeli citizen and wounding three Israelis. No one claimed responsibility for the attack, but Hamas was suspected.

USAID Worker Abduction, May 31, 1996: A gang of former Contra guerrillas kidnapped a U.S. employee of the Agency for International Development (USAID) who was assisting with election preparations in rural northern Nicaragua. She was released unharmed the next day after members of the international commission overseeing the preparations intervened.

Zekharya Attack, June 9, 1996: Unidentified gunmen opened fire on a car near Zekharya, killing a dual U.S./Israeli citizen and an Israeli. The Popular Front for the Liberation of Palestine (PFLP) is suspected.

Manchester Truck Bombing, June 15, 1996: An IRA truck bomb detonated at a Manchester shopping center, wounding 206 persons, including two German tourists, and caused extensive property damage.

Khobar Towers Bombing, June 25, 1996: A fuel truck carrying a bomb exploded outside the U.S. military's Khobar Towers housing facility in Dhahran, killing 19 U.S. military personnel and wounding 515 persons, including 240 U.S. personnel. Several groups claimed responsibility for the attack.

ETA Bombing, July 20, 1996: A bomb exploded at Tarragona International Airport in Reus, Spain, wounding 35 persons, including British and Irish tourists. The Basque Fatherland and Liberty (ETA) organization was suspected.

Bombing of Archbishop of Oran, August 1, 1996: A bomb exploded at the home of the French Archbishop of Oran, killing him and his chauffeur. The attack occurred after the Archbishop's meeting with the French Foreign Minister. The Algerian Armed Islamic Group (GIA) is suspected.

Sudanese Rebel Kidnapping, August 17, 1996: Sudan People's Liberation Army (SPLA) rebels kidnapped six missionaries in Mapourdit, including a U.S. citizen, an Italian, three Australians, and a Sudanese. The SPLA released the hostages 11 days later.

PUK Kidnapping, September 13, 1996: In Iraq, Patriotic Union of Kurdistan (PUK) militants kidnapped four French workers for Pharmaciens Sans Frontieres, a Canadian United Nations High Commissioner for Refugees (UNHCR) official, and two Iraqis.

Assassination of South Korean Consul, October 1, 1996: In Vladivostok, Russia, assailants attacked and killed a South Korean consul near his home. No one claimed responsibility, but South Korean authorities believed that the attack was carried out by professionals and that the assailants were North Koreans. North Korean officials denied the country's involvement in the attack.

Red Cross Worker Kidnappings, November 1, 1996: In Sudan, a breakaway group from the Sudanese People's Liberation Army (SPLA) kidnapped three International Committee of the Red Cross (ICRC) workers, including a U.S. citizen, an Australian, and a Kenyan. On December 9, the rebels released the hostages in exchange for ICRC supplies and a health survey for their camp.

Paris Subway Explosion, December 3, 1996: A bomb exploded aboard a Paris subway train as it arrived at the Port Royal station, killing two French nationals, a Moroccan, and a Canadian, and injuring 86 persons. Among those injured were one U.S. citizen and a Canadian. No one claimed responsibility for the attack, but Algerian extremists are suspected.

Abduction of U.S. Citizen by FARC, December 11, 1996: Five armed men claiming to be members of the Revolutionary Armed Forces of Colombia (FARC) kidnapped and later killed a U.S. geologist at a methane gas exploration site in La Guajira Department.

Tupac Amaru Seizure of Diplomats, December 17, 1996: Twenty-three members of the Tupac Amaru Revolutionary Movement (MRTA) took several hundred people hostage at a party given at the Japanese Ambassador's residence in Lima, Peru. Among the hostages were several U.S. officials, foreign ambassadors and other diplomats, Peruvian

Government officials, and Japanese businessmen. The group demanded the release of all MRTA members in prison and safe passage for them and the hostage takers. The terrorists released most of the hostages in December but held 81 Peruvians and Japanese citizens for several months.

1997

Egyptian Letter Bombs, January 2–13, 1997: A series of letter bombs with Alexandria, Egypt, postmarks were discovered at Al-Hayat newspaper bureaus in Washington, New York City, London, and Riyadh, Saudi Arabia. Three similar devices, also postmarked in Egypt, were found at a prison facility in Leavenworth, Kansas. Bomb disposal experts defused all the devices, but one detonated at the Al-Hayat office in London, injuring two security guards and causing minor damage.

Tajik Hostage Abductions, February 4–17, 1997: Near Komsomolabad, Tajikistan, a paramilitary group led by Bakhrom Sodirov abducted four United Nations military observers. The victims included two Swiss, one Austrian, one Ukrainian, and their Tajik interpreter. The kidnappers demanded safe passage for their supporters from Afghanistan to Tajikistan. In four separate incidents occurring between Dushanbe and Garm, Bakhrom Sodirov and his group kidnapped two International Committee for the Red Cross members, four Russian journalists and their Tajik driver, four UNHCR [UN High Commission for Refugees] members, and the Tajik Security Minister, Saidamir Zukhurov.

Venezuelan Abduction, February 14, 1997: Six armed Colombian guerrillas kidnapped a U.S. oil engineer and his Venezuelan pilot in Apure, Venezuela. The kidnappers released the Venezuelan pilot on February 22. According to authorities, the FARC is responsible for the kidnapping.

Empire State Building Sniper Attack, February 23, 1997: A Palestinian gunman opened fire on tourists at an observation deck atop the Empire State Building in New York City, killing a Danish national and wounding visitors from the United States, Argentina, Switzerland, and France before turning the gun on himself. A handwritten note carried by the gunman claimed this was a punishment attack against the "enemies of Palestine."

ELN Kidnapping, February 24, 1997: National Liberation Army (ELN) guerrillas kidnapped a U.S. citizen employed by a Las Vegas gold corporation who was scouting a gold mining operation in Colombia. The ELN demanded a ransom of $2.5 million.

FARC Kidnapping, March 7, 1997: FARC guerrillas kidnapped a U.S. mining employee and his Colombian colleague who were searching for gold in Colombia. On November 16, the rebels released the two hostages after receiving a $50,000 ransom.

Hotel Nacional Bombing, July 12, 1997: A bomb exploded at the Hotel Nacional in Havana, injuring three persons and causing minor damage. A previously unknown group calling itself the Military Liberation Union claimed responsibility.

Israeli Shopping Mall Bombing, September 4, 1997: Three suicide bombers of Hamas detonated bombs in the Ben Yehuda shopping mall in Jerusalem, killing eight persons, including the bombers, and wounding nearly 200 others. A dual U.S./Israeli citizen was among the dead, and seven U.S. citizens were wounded.

OAS Abductions, October 23, 1997: In Colombia, ELN rebels kidnapped two foreign members of the Organization of American States (OAS) and a Colombian human rights official at a roadblock. The ELN claimed that the kidnapping was intended "to show the international community that the elections in Colombia are a farce."

Yemeni Kidnappings, October 30, 1997: Al-Sha'if tribesmen kidnapped a U.S. businessman near Sanaa. The tribesmen sought the release of two fellow tribesmen who were arrested on smuggling charges and several public works projects they claim the government promised them. They released the hostage on November 27.

Murder of U.S. Businessmen in Pakistan, November 12, 1997: Two unidentified gunmen shot to death four U.S. auditors from Union Texas Petroleum Corporation and their Pakistani driver after they drove away from the Sheraton Hotel in Karachi. The Islami Inqilabi Council, or Islamic Revolutionary Council, claimed responsibility in a call to the U.S. Consulate in Karachi. In a letter to Pakistani newspapers, the Aimal Khufia Action Committee also claimed responsibility.

Tourist Killings in Egypt, November 17, 1997: Al-Gama'at al-Islamiyya (IG) gunmen shot and killed 58 tourists and four Egyptians and wounded 26 others at the Hatshepsut Temple in the Valley of the Kings near Luxor. Thirty-four Swiss, eight Japanese, five Germans, four Britons, one French, one Colombian, a dual Bulgarian/British citizen, and four unidentified persons were among the dead. Twelve Swiss, two Japanese, two Germans, one French, and nine Egyptians were among the wounded.

1988

UN Observer Abductions, February 19, 1998: Armed supporters of late Georgian President Zviad Gamsakhurdia abducted four UN military observers from Sweden, Uruguay, and the Czech Republic.

FARC Abduction, March 21–23, 1998: FARC rebels kidnapped a U.S. citizen in Sabaneta, Colombia. FARC members also killed three persons, wounded 14, and kidnapped at least 27 others at a roadblock near Bogota. Four U.S. citizens and one Italian were among those kidnapped, as well as the acting president of the National Electoral Council (CNE) and his wife.

Somali Hostage-Takings, April 15, 1998: Somali militiamen abducted nine Red Cross and Red Crescent workers at an airstrip north of Mogadishu. The hostages included a U.S. citizen, a German, a Belgian, a French, a Norwegian, two Swiss, and one Somali. The gunmen were members of a subclan loyal to Ali Mahdi Mohammed, who controlled the northern section of the capital.

IRA Bombing, Banbridge, August 1, 1998: A 500-pound car bomb planted by the Real IRA exploded outside a shoe store in Banbridge, North Ireland, injuring 35 persons and damaging at least 200 homes.

U.S. Embassy Bombings in East Africa, August 7, 1998: A bomb exploded at the rear entrance of the U.S. embassy in Nairobi, Kenya, killing 12 U.S. citizens, 32 Foreign

Service Nationals (FSNs), and 247 Kenyan citizens. About 5,000 Kenyans, six U.S. citizens, and 13 FSNs were injured. The U.S. embassy building sustained extensive structural damage. Almost simultaneously, a bomb detonated outside the U.S. embassy in Dar es Salaam, Tanzania, killing seven FSNs and three Tanzanian citizens, and injuring one U.S. citizen and 76 Tanzanians. The explosion caused major structural damage to the U.S. embassy facility. The U.S. Government held Usama Bin Laden responsible.

IRA Bombing, Omagh, August 15, 1998: A 500-pound car bomb planted by the Real IRA exploded outside a local courthouse in the central shopping district of Omagh, Northern Ireland, killing 29 persons and injuring over 330.

Colombian Pipeline Bombing, October 18, 1998: A National Liberation Army (ELN) planted bomb exploded on the Ocensa pipeline in Antioquia Department, killing approximately 71 persons and injuring at least 100 others. The pipeline is jointly owned by the Colombia State Oil Company Ecopetrol and a consortium, including U.S., French, British, and Canadian companies.

Armed Kidnapping in Colombia, November 15, 1998: Armed assailants followed a U.S. businessman and his family home in Cundinamarca Department and kidnapped his 11-year-old son after stealing money, jewelry, one automobile, and two cell phones. The kidnappers demanded $1 million in ransom. On January 21, 1999, the kidnappers released the boy.

1999

Angolan Aircraft Downing, January 2, 1999: A UN plane carrying one U.S. citizen, four Angolans, two Philippine nationals, and one Namibian was shot down, according to a UN official. No deaths or injuries were reported. Angolan authorities blamed the attack on National Union for the Total Independence of Angola (UNITA) rebels. UNITA officials denied shooting down the plane.

Ugandan Rebel Attack, February 14, 1999: A pipe bomb exploded inside a bar, killing five persons and injuring 35 others. One Ethiopian and four Ugandan nationals died in the blast, and one U.S. citizen working for USAID, two Swiss nationals, one Pakistani, one Ethiopian, and 27 Ugandans were injured. Ugandan authorities blamed the attack on the Allied Democratic Forces (ADF).

Greek Embassy Seizure, February 16, 1999: Kurdish protesters stormed and occupied the Greek Embassy in Vienna, taking the Greek Ambassador and six other persons hostage. Several hours later the protesters released the hostages and left the embassy. The attack followed the Turkish Government's announcement of the successful capture of the Kurdistan Workers' Party (PKK) leader Abdullah Ocalan. Kurds also occupied Kenyan, Israeli, and other Greek diplomatic facilities in France, Holland, Switzerland, Britain, and Germany over the following days.

FARC Kidnappings, February 25, 1999: FARC kidnapped three U.S. citizens working for the Hawaii-based Pacific Cultural Conservancy International. On March 4, the bodies of the three victims were found in Venezuela.

Hutu Abductions, March 1, 1999: 150 armed Hutu rebels attacked three tourist camps in Uganda, killed four Ugandans, and abducted three U.S. citizens, six Britons, three New Zealanders, two Danish citizens, one Australian, and one Canadian national. Two of the U.S. citizens and six of the other hostages were subsequently killed by their abductors.

ELN Hostage-Taking, March 23, 1999: Armed guerrillas kidnapped a U.S. citizen in Boyaca, Colombia. The National Liberation Army (ELN) claimed responsibility and demanded $400,000 ransom. On July 20, ELN rebels released the hostage unharmed following a ransom payment of $48,000.

ELN Hostage-Taking, May 30, 1999: In Cali, Colombia, armed ELN militants attacked a church in the neighborhood of Ciudad Jardin, kidnapping 160 persons, including six U.S. citizens and one French national. The rebels released approximately 80 persons, including three U.S. citizens, later that day.

Shell Platform Bombing, June 27, 1999: In Port Harcourt, Nigeria, armed youths stormed a Shell oil platform, kidnapping one U.S. citizen, one Nigerian national, and one Australian citizen, and causing undetermined damage. A group calling itself "Enough is Enough in the Niger River" claimed responsibility. Further seizures of oil facilities followed.

AFRC Kidnappings, August 4, 1999: An Armed Forces Revolutionary Council (AFRC) faction kidnapped 33 UN representatives near Occra Hills, Sierra Leone. The hostages included one U.S. citizen, five British soldiers, one Canadian citizen, one representative from Ghana, one military officer from Russia, one officer from Kyrgyzstan, one officer from Zambia, one officer from Malaysia, a local Bishop, two UN officials, two local journalists, and 16 Sierra Leonean nationals.

Burmese Embassy Seizure, October 1, 1999: Burmese dissidents seized the Burmese Embassy in Bangkok, Thailand, taking 89 persons hostage, including one U.S. citizen.

PLA Kidnapping, December 23, 1999: Colombian People's Liberation Army (PLA) forces kidnapped a U.S. citizen in an unsuccessful ransoming effort.

Indian Airlines Airbus Hijacking, December 24, 1999: Five militants hijacked a flight bound from Kathmandu to New Delhi carrying 189 people. The plane and its passengers were released unharmed on December 31.

2000

Car Bombing in Spain, January 27, 2000: Police officials reported unidentified individuals set fire to a Citroen car dealership in Iturreta, causing damage to the building and destroying 12 vehicles. The attack bore the hallmark of the Basque Fatherland and Liberty (ETA).

RUF Attacks on UN Mission Personnel, May 1, 2000: On May 1 in Makeni, Sierra Leone, Revolutionary United Front (RUF) militants kidnapped at least 20 members of the United Nations Assistance Mission in Sierra Leone (UNAMSIL) and surrounded and opened fire on a UNAMSIL facility, according to press reports. The militants killed five UN soldiers in the attack. RUF militants kidnapped 300 UNAMSIL peacekeepers throughout the country, according to press reports. On May 15 in Foya, Liberia, the kidnappers released 139 hostages. On May 28, on the Liberia and Sierra Leone border, armed militants released unharmed the last of the UN peacekeepers. In Freetown, according to press reports, armed militants ambushed two military vehicles carrying four journalists. A Spaniard and one U.S. citizen were killed in a May 25 car bombing in Freetown for which the RUF was probably responsible. Suspected RUF rebels also kidnapped 21 Indian UN peacekeepers in Freetown on June 6. Additional attacks by RUF on foreign personnel followed.

Diplomatic Assassination in Greece, June 8, 2000: In Athens, Greece, two unidentified gunmen killed British Defense Attache Stephen Saunders in an ambush. The Revolutionary Organization 17 November claimed responsibility.

ELN Kidnapping, June 27, 2000: In Bogota, Colombia, ELN militants kidnapped a 5-year-old U.S. citizen and his Colombian mother, demanding an undisclosed ransom.

Kidnappings in Kyrgyzstan, August 12, 2000: In the Kara-Su Valley, the Islamic Movement of Uzbekistan took four U.S. citizens hostage. The Americans escaped on August 12.

Church Bombing in Tajikistan, October 1, 2000: Unidentified militants detonated two bombs in a Christian church in Dushanbe, killing seven persons and injuring 70 others. The church was founded by a Korean-born U.S. citizen, and most of those killed and wounded were Korean. No one claimed responsibility.

Helicopter Hijacking, October 12, 2000: In Sucumbios Province, Ecuador, a group of armed kidnappers led by former members of defunct Colombian terrorist organization the Popular Liberation Army (EPL) took hostage 10 employees of Spanish energy consortium REPSOL. Those kidnapped included five U.S. citizens, one Argentine, one Chilean, one New Zealander, and two French pilots who escaped 4 days later. On January 30, 2001, the kidnappers murdered American hostage Ronald Sander. The remaining hostages were released on February 23 following the payment of $13 million in ransom by the oil companies.

Attack on U.S.S. *Cole*, October 12, 2000: In Aden, Yemen, a small dingy carrying explosives rammed the destroyer U.S.S. *Cole*, killing 17 sailors and injuring 39 others. Supporters of Usama Bin Laden were suspected.

Manila Bombing, December 30, 2000: A bomb exploded in a plaza across the street from the U.S. embassy in Manila, injuring nine persons. The Moro Islamic Liberation Front was likely responsible.

2001

Srinager Airport Attack, January 17, 2001: In India, six members of the Lashkar-e-Tayyba militant group were killed when they attempted to seize a local airport.

BBC Studios Bombing, March 4, 2001: A car bomb exploded at midnight outside of the British Broadcasting Corporation's main production studios in London.

ETA Bombing, March 9, 2001: Two policemen were killed by the explosion of a car bomb in Hernani, Spain.

Bus Stop Bombing, April 22, 2001: A member of Hamas detonated a bomb he was carrying near a bus stop in Kfar Siva, Israel, killing one person and injuring 60.

Tel-Aviv Nightclub Bombing, June 1, 2001: Hamas claimed responsibility for the bombing of a popular Israeli nightclub that caused over 140 casualties.

Hamas Restaurant Bombing, August 9, 2001: A Hamas-planted bomb detonated in a Jerusalem pizza restaurant, killing 15 people and wounding more than 90.

Terrorist Attacks on U.S. Homeland, September 11, 2001: Two hijacked airliners crashed into the twin towers of the World Trade Center. Soon thereafter, the Pentagon was struck by a third hijacked plane. A fourth hijacked plane, suspected to be bound for a high-profile target in Washington, crashed into a field in southern Pennsylvania. More than 5,000 U.S. citizens and other nationals were killed as a result of these acts. President Bush and Cabinet officials indicated that Usama Bin Laden was the prime suspect and that they considered the United States in a state of war with international terrorism. In the aftermath of the attacks, the United States formed the Global Coalition Against Terrorism.

Source: Office of the Historian, Bureau of Public Affairs, U.S. Department of State, September 28, 2001.

Appendix C

Chemical and Biological Weapons: Possession and Programs Past and Present

This chart summarizes data available from open sources. Precise assessment of a state's capabilities is difficult because most weapons of mass destruction (WMD) programs were, and/or are, secret and cannot be independently assessed. States have been placed in the following categories:

- **Known**: where states have either declared their programs or there is clear evidence of chemical or biological weapons possession.

- **Probable**: where states have been publicly named by government or military officials as "probable" chemical or biological weapons possessors or as producing chemical or biological weapons.

- **Possible**: where states have been widely identified as possibly having chemical or biological weapons or a CBW program by sources other than government officials.

- **Former**: where states have acknowledged having a chemical or biological weapons stockpile and/or CBW program in the past.

- **Weaponized Agents**: where agents are produced in quantity, and/or filled into munitions in specialized formulation with enhanced shelflife or dissemination properties. The chart distinguishes between past and current activities.

- **Research**: possible agents studied; no evidence of weaponization.

Only when countries are known to have weaponized agents is a distinction made between weapons and non-weapons research. In all other cases, the agents are classified as "possible" agents because not enough information is available to determine whether or not weaponization has occurred.

	Chemical				Biological			
Country	Program Status	Possible Agents	Signed CWC[1]	Ratified CWC[1]	Program Status	Possible Agents	Signed BWC[2]	Ratified BWC[2]
Algeria	Possible[3]	Unknown	01/13/93	08/14/95	Research effort, but no evidence of production[4]	Unknown	No	No
Canada	Former program[5]	•mustard •phosgene •lewisite[6]	01/13/93	09/26/95	Former program Started: 1941 Ended: 1945[7]	**Past Weaponized Agents** •anthrax **Research** •brucellosis •rocky mountain spotted fever •plague •tularemia •typhoid •yellow fever •dysentery •rinderpest •botulinum toxin •ricin[8]	04/10/72	09/18/72
China	Probable[9]	Unknown	01/13/93	04/25/97	Likely maintains an offensive program[10]	Unknown	–	11/15/84*
Cuba	Possible[11]	Unknown	01/13/93	04/29/97	Probable research program[87]	Unknown	04/10/72	04/21/76
Egypt	Probable[12]	•mustard •phosgene •sarin •VX[13]	No	No	Likely maintains an offensive program[14]	Unknown[15]	No	No
Ethiopia	Probable[16]	Unknown	01/14/93	05/13/96	–	–	04/10/72	05/26/75
France	Former program[17]	•mustard •phosgene[18]	01/13/93	03/02/95	Former program Started: 1921 Ended: 1926 1927–34 (dormant) Started: 1935 Ended 1940 1940–1945 (German occupa-tion)[19]	**Past Weaponized Agents** •potato beetle **Research** •anthrax •salmonella •cholera •rinderpest •botulinum toxin •ricin[20]	–	09/27/84*

	Chemical				**Biological**			
Country	**Program Status**	**Possible Agents**	**Signed CWC[1]**	**Ratified CWC[1]**	**Program Status**	**Possible Agents**	**Signed BWC[2]**	**Ratified BWC[2]**
Germany	Former program[21]	• phosgene • cyanide • mustard • tabun • sarin • soman[22]	01/13/96	08/12/94	Former program Started: 1915 Ended: 1918 1919–1939 (dormant) Started: 1940 Ended: 1945[23]	**Past Weaponized Agents** • glanders (WWI) • anthrax (WWI) **Research** • foot and mouth disease • plague • rinderpest • typhus • yellow fever • potato beetle • potato blight[24]	04/10/72	11/28/72
India	Former program[25]	Unknown	01/14/93	09/03/96	Research program, but no evidence of production[26]	Unknown	01/15/73	07/15/74
Iran	Known[27]	• mustard • sarin • hydrogen cyanide • cyanogen chloride • phosgene[28]	01/13/93	11/03/97	Likely maintains an offensive program[29]	• anthrax • foot and mouth disease • botulinum toxin • mycotoxins[30]	04/10/72	08/22/73
Iraq	Known; probable reconstitution of program in absence of UN inspections and monitoring[31]	• mustard • sarin • tabun • VX • Agent 15[32]	No	No	Previously active research and production program; probable reconstitution of program in absence of UN inspections and monitoring[33]	**Past Weaponized Agents** • anthrax • botulinum toxin • ricin • aflatoxin • wheat cover smut **Research** • brucellosis • hemorrhagic conjuctivitis virus (enterovirus 70) • rotavirus • camel pox • plague (?) • gas gangrene toxin[34] **Current Research** Unknown	05/11/72	06/19/91**

	Chemical				Biological			
Country	Program Status	Possible Agents	Signed CWC[1]	Ratified CWC[1]	Program Status	Possible Agents	Signed BWC[2]	Ratified BWC[2]
Israel	Probable[35]	Unknown [36]	01/13/93	No	Research, with possible production of agents[37]	Unknown	No	No
Italy	Former program[38]	•mustard •phosgene [39]	01/13/93	12/08/95	–	–	04/10/72	05/30/75
Japan	Former program[40]	•phosgene •hydrogen cyanide •mustard •lewisite •chloropi-crin[41]	01/13/93	09/15/95	Former program Started: 1931 Ended: 1945[42]	**Past Weaponized Agents** •anthrax •plague •glanders •typhoid •cholera •dysentery •paratyphoid **Research** •gas gangrene •influenza •tetanus •tuberculosis •tularemia •salmonella •typhus •glanders tetrodotoxin [43]	04/10/72	06/08/82
Libya	Known[44]	•mustard •sarin •tabun •lewisite •phosgene [45]	No	No[86]	Research, with possible production of agents[46]	Unknown	–	01/19/82*
Myanmar (Burma)	Probable[47]	Unknown	01/14/93	No	–	–	No	No
N. Korea	Known[48]	•adamsite •mustard •hydrogen cyanide •cyanogen chloride •phosgene •sarin •soman •tabun •VX[49]	No	No	Research, with possible production of agents[50]	•anthrax •plague •yellow fever •typhoid •cholera •tuberculosis •typhus •smallpox •botulinum toxin[51]	–	03/13/87*
Pakistan	Probable[52]	Unknown	01/13/93	10/28/97	Possible[53]	Unknown	04/10/72	09/25/74

	Chemical				**Biological**			
Country	**Program Status**	**Possible Agents**	**Signed CWC[1]**	**Ratified CWC[1]**	**Program Status**	**Possible Agents**	**Signed BWC[2]**	**Ratified BWC[2]**
Russia	Known[54]	• Novichok binary nerve agents[55]	01/13/93	11/05/97	Research, some work beyond legitimate defense activities likely[56]	Unknown	04/10/72	03/26/75
Soviet Union	Former program[57]	• sarin • soman • mustard • lewisite • phosgene • VX analogue[58]	01/13/93	11/05/97	Former program Started: 1926 Ended: 1992[59]	**Past Weaponized Agents** • smallpox • plague • tularemia • glanders • Venezuelan equine encephalitis • anthrax • Q fever • Marburg **Research** • Ebola • Bolivian hemorrhagic fever • Argentinian hemorrhagic fever • Lassa fever • Japanese encephalitis • Russian spring-summer encephalitis • brucellosis • Machupo virus • yellow fever • typhus • melioidosis • psittacosis • rinderpest • African swine fever virus • wheat stem rust • rice blast[60]	04/10/72	03/26/75
S. Africa	Former program[61]	• thallium • CR • paraoxon • mustard (WWII)[62]	01/14/93	09/13/95	Former program Started: 1981 Ended: 1993[63]	• anthrax • cholera • plague • salmonella • gas gangrene • ricin • botulinum toxin[64]	04/10/72	11/03/75

	Chemical				Biological			
Country	Program Status	Possible Agents	Signed CWC[1]	Ratified CWC[1]	Program Status	Possible Agents	Signed BWC[2]	Ratified BWC[2]
S. Korea	Former program[65]	Unknown	01/14/93	04/28/97	–	–	04/10/72	06/25/87
Sudan	Possible[66]	Unknown	No	05/24/99*	Possible research program[67]	Unknown	No	No
Syria	Known[68]	•mustard •sarin •VX[69]	No	No	Research, with possible production of agents[70]	•anthrax •botulinum toxin •ricin[71]	04/14/72	No
Taiwan	Probable[72]	Unknown	No	No	Possible research program[73]	Unknown	04/10/72	02/09/73
U.K.	Former program[74]	•phosgene •mustard •lewisite[75]	01/13/93	05/13/96	Former program Started: 1936 Ended:1956[76]	**Past Weaponized Agents** •anthrax **Research** •plague •typhoid •botulinum toxin[77]	04/10/72	03/26/75
U.S.A.	Former program[78]	•mustard •sarin •soman •VX •lewisite •binary nerve agents[79]	01/13/93	04/25/97	Former Program Started: 1943 Ended: 1969[80]	**Past Weaponized Agents** •Venezuelean equine encephalitis •Q Fever •tularemia •anthrax •wheat rust •rice blast **Research** •brucellosis •smallpox •Eastern and Western equine encephalitis •Argentinian hemorrhagic fever •Korean hemorrhagic fever •Bolivian hemorrhagic fever •Lassa fever •glanders •melioidodis •plague	04/10/72	03/26/75

Country	Chemical				Biological			
	Program Status	Possible Agents	Signed CWC[1]	Ratified CWC[1]	Program Status	Possible Agents	Signed BWC[2]	Ratified BWC[2]
U.S.A. (continuted)						•yellow fever •psittacosis •typhus •dengue fever •Rift Valley fever •Chikungunya virus •late blight of potato •rinderpest •Newcastle disease •fowl plague •staph enterotoxin B •botulinum toxin •ricin[81]		
Viet Nam	Possible[82]	Unknown	01/13/93	No	–	–	–	06/20/80*
Yugo- slavia, Federal Republic of (FRY)	Former program[83]	•sarin •mustard •tabun •soman •VX •lewisite •BZ[84]	No	04/20/00*	None/ Unknown[85]	None/ Unknown	04/10/72	10/25/73

*Denotes countries which acceded to the treaty.

**Iraq ratified the BWC following the adoption of the U.N. Security Council Resolution 687, which in addition to establishing UNSCOM [United Nations Special Commission], also "invited" Iraq to ratify the 1972 Convention (Paragraph 7), 04/08/91, gopher://gopher.undp.org/00/undocs/scd/scouncil/s91/4, S/RES/687.

Copyright © 2002 by The Monterey Institute of International Studies. Reprinted by permission.

Notes

1. Organization for the Prohibition of Chemical Weapons, "Signatory States to the Chemical Weapons Convention," http://www.opcw.nl/memsta/namelist.htm.

2. Stockholm International Peace Research Institute, "Ratifications to the BTWC," http://projects.sipri.se/cbw/docs/bw-btwc-rat.html.

   See also U.S. Arms Control and Disarmament Agency, "Parties and Signatories of the Biological Weapons Convention," http://www.state.gov/www.global/arms/treaties/00919_fs_bwcsig.html.

3. Anthony Cordesman, "Weapons of Mass Destruction in the Middle East: Regional Trends, National Forces, Warfighting Capabilities, Delivery Options, and Weapons Effects," http://www.csis.org/mideast/reports WMDinMETrends.pdf, October 4, 1999, p. 14.

4. Algeria is reportedly conducting research into biological weapons, but there is no evidence of a production effort. Cordesman, "Weapons of Mass Destruction in the Middle East," 1999, p. 14.

5. During World War II, Canada manufactured chemical munitions and purchased both lewisite and phosgene from the U.S. Army. In 1946, following the war, Canada destroyed its chemical weapons stockpile. Stockholm International Peace Research Institute, *The Problem of Chemical and Biological Warfare, Volume II: CB Weapons Today*, (New York: Humanities Press, 1971), p. 187.

   See also: John Bryden, *Deadly Allies: Canada's Secret War 1937–1947*, (Toronto, ON: McClelland & Stewart Inc., 1989).

6. As part of its World War II chemical weapons program, Canada produced mustard gas and phosgene and procured quantities of mustard gas, lewisite, and phosgene from the United States. Stockholm International Peace Research Institute, *The Problem of Chemical and Biological Warfare, Volume II: CB Weapons Today*, p. 187.

7. Milton Leitenberg, *Biological Weapons in the Twentieth Century: A Review and Analysis*, http://www.fas.org/bwc/papers/bw20th.htm, 2001.

   Donald Avery, "Canadian biological and toxin warfare research, development and planning, 1925–45," in *Biological and Toxin Weapons: Research, Development and Use from the Middle Ages to 1945*, Erhard Geissler and John Ellis van Courtland Mood, eds., (New York: NY: Stockholm International Peace Research Institute, 1999), pp. 197–214.

   The Office of Technology Assessment includes Canada in a list of countries that have admitted to having had "offensive [biological] weapon munition supplies or development programs in the past." U.S. Congress, Office of Technology Assessment, *Proliferation of Weapons of Mass Destruction: Assessing the Risks*, (Washington, DC: U.S. Government Printing Office, August, 1993), p. 63.

   In 1942, the Canadians began collaborating with the United Kingdom's biological weapons effort. Stockholm International Peace Research Institute, *The Problem of Chemical and Biological Warfare, Volume I: The Rise of CB Weapons* (New York, NY: Humanities Press, 1971), pp. 118–119.

   See also Bryden, *Deadly Allies: Canada's Secret War 1937–1947*.

8. Donald Avery, "Canadian biological and toxin warfare research, development and planning, 1925–45," in *Biological and Toxin Weapons: Research, Development and Use from the Middle Ages to 1945*, Erhard Geissler and John Ellis van Courtland Mood, eds., (New York: NY: Stockholm International Peace Research Institute, 1999), pp. 203–213. Stockholm International Peace Research Institute, *The Problem of Chemical and Biological Warfare, Volume I: The Rise of CB Weapons*, pp. 118–119.

   In its work with the United States and the United Kingdom, Canada conducted research on several biological agents, including botulinum toxin, ricin, rinderpest virus, Rocky Mountain spotted fever, plague, and tularemia. The anthrax that Canada weaponized was done in partnership with both the United Kingdom and the United States. However, most of the research was done outside of Canada. John Fryden, *Deadly Allies: Canada's Secret War 1937–1947*, pp. 108, 120, 210, 218, 223, 243.

9. On March 19, 2002, in Testimony before the Senate Committee on Foreign Relations, Assistant Secretary of State for Intelligence and Research, Carl W. Ford, Jr., stated that "I believe

that the Chinese have an advanced chemical warfare program, including research and development, production, and weaponization capabilities." Ford also stated that "In the near future, China is likely to achieve the necessary expertise and delivery capability to integrate chemical weapons successfully into overall military operations." Carl W. Ford, Jr., Assistant Secretary of State for Intelligence and Research, "Hearing on Reducing the Threat of Chemical and Biological Weapons Before the Senate Committee on Foreign Relations," (Washington, DC), March 19, 2002.

Rear Admiral Thomas Brooks, Director of Naval Intelligence, identified China as a "probable" chemical weapons possessor in testimony before Congress. Rear Admiral Thomas Brooks, Director of Naval Intelligence, statement before the Subcommittee on Seapower, Strategic and Critical Materials, U.S. Congress, House of Representatives, Committee on Armed Services, "Hearings on National Defense Authorization Act for Fiscal years 1992 and 1993 before the Committee on Armed Services," 102nd Congress, Second Session, March 7, 1991, (Washington, DC: Government Printing Office, 1993), p. 107.

China was referred to by the U.S. Department of Defense [DOD] as having "the ability to quickly mobilize the chemical industry to produce a wide variety of chemical agents and delivery means." U.S. Department of Defense, *Proliferation: Threat and Response 2001*, http://www.defenselink.mil/pubs/ptr20010110.pdf, p. 14.

An article in *The Economist* suggests that China might "have destroyed [its] chemical weapons before signing the CWC." "Chemical Weapons. Just Checking," *The Economist* 347 (May 2, 1997), p. 42.

10. "It is possible that China has maintained the offensive biological warfare program it is believed to have had before acceding to the BWC." Carl W. Ford, Jr., Assistant Secretary of State for Intelligence and Research, "Hearing on Reducing the Threat of Chemical and Biological Weapons Before the Senate Committee on Foreign Relations," (Washington, DC), March 19, 2002.

"The United States believes that China had an offensive BW program prior to 1984 when it became a Party to the BWC, and maintained an offensive BW program throughout most of the 1980s. The offensive BW program included the development, production, stockpiling or other acquisition or maintenance of BW agents. China's CBM [Confidence Building Measures]-mandated declarations have not resolved U.S. concerns about this program, and there are strong indications that China probably maintains its offensive program. The United States, therefore, believes that in the years after its accession to the BWC, China was not in compliance with its BWC obligations and that it is highly probable that it remains noncompliant with these obligations." U.S. Department of State, "Adherence to and Compliance with Arms Control Agreements," 1998 Report submitted to the Congress, Washington, DC, http://www.state.gov/www/global/arms/reports/annual/comp98.html.

The DOD states that it is likely China possesses infrastructure adequate to develop and produce biological warfare agents. China has reaffirmed its commitment not to develop biological weapons, but China likely retains some elements of an offensive program. China has acceded to the BWC. U.S. Department of Defense, *Proliferation: Threat and Response 2001*, http://www.defenselink.mil/pubs/ptr20010110.pdf, p. 14.

ACDA reported that "there are strong indications that China probably maintains its offensive [biological] program." Arms Control and Disarmament Agency (ACDA), *Adherence to and Compliance with Arms Control Agreements: 1997 Annual Report to Congress*, (Washington, DC: U.S. Arms Control and Disarmament Agency, 1997), http://www.state.gov/www/global/arms/reports/annual/comp97.html.

11. The following are as cited in a chart in Gordon M. Burck and Charles C. Flowerree, *International Handbook on Chemical Weapons Proliferation*, (New York, NY: Greenwood Press, 1991), pp. 168–171.

   • Thom Shanker, "West underwrites Third World's chemical arms," *Chicago Tribune*, 3 Apr. 1989, pp. 1, 6; and "Lack of candor blocks chemical arms treaty," 4 Apr. 1989, pp. 1, 6 (source given as U.S. government official). Shanker identifies Cuba as probably having chemical weapons.
   • Harvey J. McGeorge, "Chemical addiction," *Defense & Foreign Affairs*, Apr. 1989, pp. 16–19, 32–33. McGeorge lists Cuba as a possible chemical possessor.
   • Senator John S. McCain, "Proliferation in the 1990s: implications for U.S. policy and force planning," Table 1, *Congressional Record*, 2 Nov. 1989, p. S14605; "Estimates are based on a variety of sources, including unclassified testimony by CIA Director William H. Webster, Seth Carus, David Goldberg, Elisa D. Harris and others and do not reflect the estimates of the U.S. Government." The report identifies Cuba as a suspected possessor state.

12. Avner Cohen, "Israel and Chemical/Biological Weapons: History, Deterrence, and Arms Control," The Nonproliferation Review, Vol. 8, No. 3 (Fall-Winter), pp. 41–42.

   Rear Admiral Thomas Brooks identified Egypt as a "probable" chemical weapons possessor in testimony before Congress. Brooks, statement before the Subcommittee on Seapower, Strategic and Critical Materials, 1991, p. 107.

   A summary chart included in an article by Anthony H. Cordesman indicates that Egypt has a stockpile of chemical weapons. Anthony H. Cordesman, "Creeping Proliferation Could Mean a Paradigm Shift in the Cost of War and Terrorism," *Stability and Instability in the Middle East, Volume III*, (Washington, DC: Center for Strategic and International Studies), http://www.csis.org/mideast/stable3h.html.

   See also Dany Shoham, Chemical and Biological Weapons in Egypt." *The Nonproliferation Reivew*, 5 (Spring-Summer 1998), pp. 48–58. For further information on Egypt's weapons of mass destruction programs and capabilities, see the CNS [Center for Nonproliferation Studies] country profile on the "Weapons of Mass Destruction in the Middle East" web page at http://www.cns.miis.edu/research/wmdme/egypt.htm.

13. Egypt likely possesses sarin, VX, mustard, and phosgene. Shoham, "Chemical and Biological Weapons in Egypt," p. 49.

   Russian intelligence reports that Egypt has assimilated "techniques for the production of nerve and blister agents." Russian Federation Foreign Intelligence Service, "A New Challenge After the Cold War: Proliferation of Weapons of Mass Destruction," in *Proliferation Threats of the 1990's*, Hearing Before the Committee on Governmental Affairs, United States Senate, 103rd Congress, First Session, February 24, 1993 (Washington, DC: Government Printing Office, 1993), p. 92.

14. "The United States believes that Egypt had developed biological warfare agents by 1972. There is no evidence to indicate that Egypt has eliminated this capability and it remains likely that the Egyptian capability to conduct biological warfare continues to exist." Arms Control and Disarament Agency, *Adherence to and Compliance with Arms Control Agreements: 1998 Annual Report to Congress*, http://www.state.gov/www/global/arms/reports/annual/comp98.html.

   A Russian intelligence report cites Egypt as having "a program of military-applied research in the area of biological weapons." It also states that there is no evidence that weapons for military use have been developed. Russian Federation Foreign Intelligence Service, *A New Challenge After the Cold War: Proliferation of Weapons of Mass Destruction*, p. 93.

"Egypt appears to have developed several natural pathogens and toxins as warfare agents and has recently taken the first steps to acquire a capability for the genetic engineering of microbial pathogens." Shoham, "Chemical and Biological Weapons in Egypt," p. 56.

Cordesman cites Egypt as researching biological weapons. Cordesman, "Creeping Proliferation Could Mean a Paradigm Shift in the Cost of War and Terrorism," http://www.csis.org/mideast/stable/3h.html.

15. Shoham, in "Chemical and Biological Weapons in Egypt," writes that Egypt has conducted research on anthrax, botulinum toxin, plague, cholera, tularemia, glanders, brucellosis, meliodosis, japanese B. encephalitis, Eastern Equine encephalitis, influenza, smallpox, and mycotoxins. This list has been disputed and there is no other open source information available to verify the agents listed in the Shoham article.

16. Rear Admiral Thomas Brooks identified Ethiopia as a "probable" chemical weapons possessor in testimony before Congress. Brooks, statement before the Subcommittee on Seapower, Strategic and Critical Materials, p. 107.

17. In a 1988 speech to the United Nations, French President Mitterrand claimed that France had no chemical weapons, and would produce none. Victor A. Utgoff, *The Challenge of Chemical Weapons: An American Perspective* (New York, NY: St. Martin's Press, 1991), pp. 123–124.

An article in *The Economist* suggests that France might "have destroyed [its] chemical weapons before signing the CWC." "Chemical Weapons. Just Checking," *The Economist*, p. 42.

18. At the start of World War II, the French had a stockpile of mustard gas and phosgene. Stockholm International Peace Research Institute, *The Problem of Chemical and Biological Warfare, Volume I: The Rise of CB Weapons*, p. 117.

Testing of chemical weapons occurred at a site called B2-Namous in Algeria. Vincent Jauvert, "Quand la France Teste des armes chimiques en Algerie," *Le Nouvel Observateur*, (Oct. 23–29, 1997), pp. 10–22.

19. Olivier Lepick, "French activities related to biological warfare, 1919–45," in *Biological and Toxin Weapons: Research, Development and Use from the Middle Ages to 1945*, Erhard Geissler and John Ellis van Courtland Mood, eds., (New York: NY: Stockholm International Peace Research Institute, 1999), p. 70.

20. Olivier Lepick, "French activities related to biological warfare, 1919–45," in *Biological and Toxin Weapons: Research, Development and Use from the Middle Ages to 1945*, Erhard Geissler and John Ellis van Courtland Mood, eds., (New York: NY: Stockholm International Peace Research Institute, 1999), pp. 78, 82–90.

21. Following World War II, "West Germany unilaterally renounced the manufacture of nuclear, biological and chemical weapons." With the signing of the revised Brussels Treaty in 1954 and the establishment of the Western European Union, West Germany's pledge not to manufacture NBC weapons became an international commitment subject to verification. Utgoff, *The Challenge of Chemical Weapons: An American Perspective*, pp. 90–91.

22. Germany's World War II stockpile of chemical weapons included phosgene, cyanide, mustard gas, sarin, and tabun. Stockholm International Peace Research Institute, *The Problem of Chemical and Biological Warfare, Volume II: CB Weapons Today*, p. 127.

The Germans also reportedly produced soman. Bryden, *Deadly Allies: Canada's Secret War 1937–1947*, p. 181.

23. Milton Leitenberg, *Biological Weapons in the Twentieth Century: A Review and Analysis*, http://www.fas.org/bwc/papers/bw20th.htm, 2001.

Mark Wheelis, "Biological sabotage in World War I," in *Biological and Toxin Weapons: Research, Development and Use from the Middle Ages to 1945*, Erhard Geissler and John Ellis van Courtland Mood, eds., (New York: NY: Stockholm International Peace Research Institute, 1999), p. 35.

Erhard Geissler, "Biological warfare activities in Germany, 1923–45," in *Biological and Toxin Weapons: Research, Development and Use from the Middle Ages to 1945*, Erhard Geissler and John Ellis van Courtland Mood, eds., (New York: NY: Stockholm International Peace Research Institute, 1999), p. 91.

Germany's World War II biological weapons program was not institutionalized until the establishment of a research station at Posen in 1943. As Soviet forces moved toward the Posen facility in March 1945, work at the station ended—"without having accomplished anything very startling." Stockholm International Peace Research Institute, *The Problem of Chemical and Biological Warfare, Volume I: The Rise of CB Weapons*, p. 117.

24. Milton Leitenberg, *Biological Weapons in the Twentieth Century: A Review and Analysis*, http://www.fas.org/bwc/papers/bw20th.htm, 2001.

Erhard Geissler, "Biological warfare activities in Germany, 1923–45," in *Biological and Toxin Weapons: Research, Development and Use from the Middle Ages to 1945*, Erhard Geissler and John Ellis van Courtland Mood, eds., (New York: NY: Stockholm International Peace Research Institute, 1999), pp. 106, 117, 120–121.

Plague, cholera, typhus, and yellow fever were among the agents studied by Germany's biological weapons program. Stockholm International Peace Research Institute, *The Problem of Chemical and Biological Warfare, Volume I: The Rise of CB Weapons*, p. 117.

Anthrax and glanders were used offensively by Germany during World War I in a veterinary sabotage programe. Mark Wheelis, "Biological Sabotage in World War I," in *Biological and Toxin Weapons: Research, Development and Use from the Middle ages to 1945*, Erhard Geissler and John Ellis van Courtland Modd, eds., (New York: NY: Stockholm International Peace Research Institute, 1999), p. 40–57.

25. India acknowledged its chemical warfare program in 1997 and stated that related facilities would be open for inspection. India has a sizable chemical industry which could be source of dual-use chemicals for countries of proliferation concern. U.S. Department of Defense, *Proliferation: Threat and Response 2001*, http://www.defenselink.mil/pubs/ptr20010110.pdf, p. 14.

Under the CWC [Chemical Weapons Convention] India has declared possession of a chemical weapons program. U.S. Department of Defense, *Proliferation: Threat and Response 1997*, http://www.defenselink.mil/pubs/prolif97/so_asia.html#india.

India has declared Category 1, 2, and 3 chemical weapons to the OPCW [United Nations Organization for the Prohibition of Chemical Weapons].

26. India has substantial biotechnical infrastructure and expertise, some of which is being used for biological warfare defense research. U.S. Department of Defense, *Proliferation: Threat and Response 2001*, http://www.defenselink.mil/pubs/ptr20010110.pdf, p. 14.

27. "Iran, a Chemical Weapons Convention (CWC) States party, already has manufactured and stockpiled chemical weapons—including blister, blood, choking, and probably nerve agents, and the bombs and artillery shells to deliver them. During the first half of 2001, Tehran

continued to seek production technology, training, expertise, equipment, and chemicals from entities in Russia and China that could be used to help Iran reach its goal of having an indigenous nerve agent production capability." Central Intelligence Agency, "Unclassified Report to Congress on the Acquisition of Technology Relating to Weapons of Mass Destruction and Advanced Conventional Munitions, 1 January Through 30 June 2001," (Washington, DC: U.S. Central Intelligence Agency, 2001, http://www.cia.gov/cia/publications/bian/bian_jan_2002.htm.

Cordesman, "Weapons of Mass Destruction in the Middle East," http://www.csis.org/mideast/reports/WMDinMETrends.pdf, 1999, pp. 38–40.

Russian Federation Foreign Intelligence Service, *A New Challenge After the Cold War: Proliferation of Weapons of Mass Destruction*, 1993, p. 98.

"Iran's chemical weapons (CW) program is one of the largest in the developing world… we believe Iran's CW program continues and that it possesses a substantial stockpile of weaponized and bulk agent." Robert J. Einhorn, Testimony Before the Senate Foreign Relations Committee, Washington, DC, October 5, 2000, http://www.state.gov/www/policy_remarks/2000/001005_einhorn_sfrc.html.

"In the past Tehran has manufactured and stockpiled blister, blood and choking chemical agents, and weaponized some of these agents into artillery shells, mortars, rockets, and aerial bombs. It is also believed to be conducting research on nerve agents." U.S. Department of Defense, *Proliferation: Threat and Response 2001*, http://www.defenselink.mil/pubs/ptr20010110.pdf, p. 36.

For further information on Iran's weapons of mass destruction programs and capabilities, see the CNS country profile on the "Weapons of Mass Destruction in the Middle East" web page at http://www.cns.miis.edu/research/wmdme/iran.htm.

28. Iran reportedly stockpiled cyanide, phosgene, and mustard gas after 1985. Cordesman, "Creeping Proliferation Could Mean a Paradigm Shift in the Cost of War and Terrorism," http://www.csis.org/mideast/stable/3h.html.

   "At present the industrial production of mustard gas and sarin has been established in Iran." Russian Federation Foreign Intelligence Service, *A New Challenge After the Cold War: Proliferation of Weapons of Mass Destruction*, p. 98.

   Iran "has manufactured and stockpiled chemical weapons, including blister, blood, and choking agents." Central Intelligence Agency, "Report of Proliferation-Related Acquisition in 2001," (Washington, DC: U.S. Central Intelligence Agency, 2001), http://www.odci.gov/cia/publications/bian/bian_feb_2001.htm.

29. "Iran probably began its offensive BW program during the Iran-Iraq war, and it may have some limited capability for BW deployment." Central Intelligence Agency, "Unclassified Report to Congress on the Acquisition of Technology Relating to Weapons of Mass Destruction and Advanced Conventional Munitions, 1 January Through 30 June 2001," (Washington, DC: U.S. Central Intelligence Agency, 2001), http://www.cia.gov/cia/publications/bian/bian_jan_2002.htm.

   Anthony Cordesman, *Weapons of Mass Destruction in Iran: Delivery Systems, and Chemical, Biological, and Nuclear Programs*, (Center for Strategic and International Studies, April 28, 1998), http://www.csis.org/mideast/reports/WMDinIran4-28-98.html, pp. 13–14.

   In a speech to the Fifth Review Conference on the Biological Weapons Convention in Geneva on November 19, 2001, John Bolton, the Undersecretary of State for Arms Control and

International Security, accused Iran of operating a clandestine biological weapons program. Jenni Rissanen, *Acrimonious Opening for BWC Review Conference*, BWC Review Conference Bulletin, (Acronym Institute, November 19, 2001), http://www.acronym.org.uk/bwc/revcon1.htm.

"Iran possesses overall infrastructure and expertise to support a biological warfare program. It pursues contacts with Russian entities and other sources to acquire dual-use equipment and technology and is believed to be actively pursuing offensive biological warfare capabilities. It may have small quantities of usable agent now." U.S. Department of Defense, *Proliferation: Threat and Response 2001*, http://www.defenselink.mil/pubs/ptr20010110.pdf, p. 35.

"Iran probably has produced biological warfare agents and apparently has weaponized a small quantity of those agents." U.S. State Department, *Adherence to and Compliance with Arms Control Agreements:" 1997 Annual Report to Congress*, http://www.state.gov/www/global/arms/reports/annual/comp97.html.

"Western countries have noted attempts by Iranian representatives to buy, unofficially, technology and biological materials used specifically for the production of biological weapons, in particular, mycotoxins." Graham S. Pearson, "The Threat of Deliberate Disease in the 21st Century," *Biological Weapons Proliferation: Reasons for Concern, Courses of Action*, (Washington, DC: The Henry L. Stimson Center, January 1998), p. 31.

30. Anthony Cordesmann, *Weapons of Mass Destruction in Iran: Delivery Systems, and Chemical Biological, and Nuclear Programs*, (Center for Strategic and Internaitonal Studies, April 28, 1998), http://www.csis.org/mideast/reports/WMDinIran4-28-98.html.

31. United Nations, United Nations Special Commission (UNSCOM), "Latest Six-Monthly Report," (April 16, 1998), http://www.un.org/Depts/unscom/sres98-332.htm.

"Since the Gulf War, Iraq has rebuilt key portions of its chemical production infrastructure. Some of Iraq's facilities could be converted fairly quickly to production of chemical warfare agents. Following Operation Desert Fox, Iraq again instituted a rapid reconstruction effort on those facilities to include former dual-use chemical warfare-associated production facilities, destroyed by U.S. bombing. Iraq retains the expertise to resume chemical agent production within a few weeks or months, depending on the type of agent." U.S. Department of Defense, *Proliferation: Threat and Response 2001*, http://www.defenselink.mil/pubs/ptr20010110.pdf, pp. 41–42.

"Iraq retains the technology it acquired before the war and evidence clearly indicates an ongoing research and development effort, in spite of the UN sanctions regime." Cordesman, "Creeping Proliferation Could Mean a Paradigm Shift in the Cost of War and Terrorism," http://www.csis.org/mideast/stable/3h.html.

See also E. J. Hogendoorn, "A Chemical Weapons Atlas," *The Bulletin of the Atomic Scientists*, (September/October, 1997), p. 38.

For further information on Iraq's weapons of mass destruction programs and capabilities, see the CNS country profile on the "Weapons of Mass Destruction in the Middle East" web page at http://www.cns.miis.edu/research/wmdme/iraq.htm and CNS's "Special Collection on the Iraq Crisis" web page at http://www.cns.miis.edu/research/iraq/index.htm.

32. Cordesman, "Creeping Proliferation Could Mean a Paradigm Shift in the Cost of War and Terrorism," http://www.csis.org/mideast/stable/3h.html.

United Nations, United Nations Special Commission (UNSCOM), "Fourth Report under Resolution 1951," (June 10, 1997), http://www.un.org/Depts/unscom/sres97-774.htm.

In the past Iraq produced mustard gas, sarin, tabun, and VX. U.S. Department of Defense, *Proliferation: Threat and Response 2001*, http://www.defenselink.mil/pubs/ptr20010110.pdf, p. 50.

Steve Bowman, in an April 1998 CRS Issue Brief, includes Agent 15 in the list of Iraqi chemical weapons. Steve Bowman, *Iraqi Chemical & Biological Weapons (CBW) Capabilities*, CRS Issue Brief, (Congressional Research Service, April 1998), http://www.fas.org/spp/starwars/crs/98042705_npo._html.

"Agent-15 belongs to the glycollates, a large group of chemicals which also includes the chemical warfare agent BZ. The chemicals block cholinergic nerve transmission in the central and peripheral nervous system... little information is publicly known about Agent-15, except that it is closely related to BZ. The understanding of its physiological effects is based on studies with the latter agent." Stockholm International Peace Research Institute, *Agent-15*, http://projects.sipri.se/cbw/cbw-agents/Agent-15.html.

33. United Nations, United Nations Special Commission (UNSCOM), "Latest Six-Monthly Report" (April 16, 1998), http://www.un.org/Depts/unscom/sres98-332.htm.

Cordesman, "Creeping Proliferation Could Mean a Paradigm Shift in the Cost of War and Terrorism," http://www.csis.org/mideast/stable/3h.html.

"Iraq produced and weaponized significant quantities of biological warfare agents prior to Desert Storm. It admitted biological warfare effort in 1995, after four years of denial, and subsequently claimed to have destroyed all agents. No credible proof, however, has been offered. The UN believes that Baghdad has the ability to reconstitute its biological warfare capabilities within a few weeks or months, and, in the absence of UNSCOM inspections and monitoring during 1999 and 2000, may have produced some biological warfare agents." U.S. Department of Defense, *Proliferation: Threat and Response 2001,* http://www.defenselink.mil/pubs/ptr20010110.pdf, pp. 39–40.

"The United States believes that Iraq is capable of producing biological warfare agents and is probably intent on continuing its offensive BW efforts if the threat of UNSCOM inspections and long-term monitoring are removed." Arms Control and Disarmament Agency (ACDA), *Adherence to and Compliance with Arms Control Agreements: 1995 Annual Report to Congress,* (Washington, DC: U.S. Arms Control and Disarmament Agency), http://dosfan.lib.uic.edu/acda/reports/complian.htm.

In a speech to the Fifth Review Conference on the Biological Weapons Convention in Geneva on November 19, 2001, John Bolton, the Undersecretary of State for Arms Control and International Security, accused Iraq of operating a clandestine biological weapons program. Jenni Rissanen, *Acrimonious Opening for BWC Review Conference,* BWC Review Conference Bulletin, (Acronym Institute, November 19, 2001), http://http://www.acronym.org.uk/bwc/revcon1.htm.

34. Cordesman, "Creeping Proliferation Could Mean a Paradigm Shift in the Cost of War and Terrorism," http://www.csis.org/mideast/stable/3h.html.

Milton Leitenberg, *Biological Weapons in the Twentieth Century: A Review and Analysis,* http://www.fas.org/bwc/papers/bw20th.htm, 2001.

United Nations, United Nations Special Commission (UNSCOM), "Fourth Report under Resolution 1051: (June 10, 1997), http://www.un.org/Depts/unscom/sres97-774.htm.

According to ACDA, Iraq produced anthrax, botulinum toxin, aflatoxin, ricin, wheat cover smut, and researched *Clostridium perfringens* (gas gangrene), hemorrhagic conjuctivitis virus, rotavirus, and camel pox. Arms Control and Disarmament Agency, *Adherence to and Compliance with Arms Control Agreements: 1995 Annual Report to Congress,* http://dosfan.lib.uic.edu/acda/reports/complian.htm.

Iraq's biological weapons program worked with anthrax, botulinum toxin, gas gangrene, aflatoxin, trichothecene mycotoxins, wheat cover smut, and ricin. Graham S. Pearson, "The Threat of Deliberate Disease in the 21st Century," *Biological Weapons Proliferation: Reasons for Concern, Courses of Action,* (Washington, DC: The Henry L. Stimson Center, January 1998), p. 27.

35. Avner Cohen, "Israel and Chemical/Biological Weapons: History, Deterrence, and Arms Control," *The Nonproliferation Review,* Vol. 8, No. 3 (Fall-Winter), pp. 27–53.
Israel has completed extensive research into gas warfare and defense and may have some production facilities. Additionally, Israel may have stocks of bombs, rockets, and artillery. Cordesman, "Creeping Proliferation Could Mean a Paradigm Shift in the Cost of War and Terrorism," http://www.csis.org/mideast/stable/3h.htm.

The *London Sunday Times* reports that Israeli F-16 fighters have been equipped to carry chemical weapons and that their crews have been trained on the use of such weapons. Uzi Mahnaimi, "Israeli Jets Equipped For Chemical Warfare," *London Sunday Times,* October 4, 1998.

"Israel has a store of chemical weapons of its own manufacture... Israel is capable of producing toxic substances of all types, including nerve-paralyzing, blister-producing and temporarily incapacitating substances and so forth. The country has for this a highly developed chemical and petrochemical industry and skilled specialists and also stocks of source material." Russian Federation Foreign Intelligence Service, *A New Challenge After the Cold War: Proliferation of Weapons of Mass Destruction,* 1993.

In a 1974 hearing before the Senate Armed Services Committee, General Almquist stated that Israel had an offensive chemical weapons capability. Senate Armed Services Committee, FY 1975 Authorization Hearing, Part 5, March 7, 1974.

For further information on Israel's weapons of mass destruction programs and capabilities, see the CNS country profile on the "Weapons of Mass Destruction in the Middle East" web page at http://www.cns.miis.edu/research/wmdme/israel.htm.

36. Avner Cohen, "Israel and Chemical/Biological Weapons: History, Deterrence, and Arms Control," *The Nonproliferation Review,* Vol. 8, No. 3 (Fall-Winter), pp. 27–53.

While it is unclear exactly what chemical agents Israel may produce, Dutch officials have identified that an EL Al 747 that crashed in Amsterdam in 1992 was carrying a shipment of DMMP destined for Israel. DMMP is a nerve gas precursor used in the manufacture of sarin gas. Uzi Mahnaimi, "Israel Jets Equipped for Chemical Warfare," *London Sunday Times,* October 4, 1998.

37. Avner Cohen, "Israel and Chemical/Biological Weapons: History, Deterrence, and Arms Control," *The Nonproliferation Review,* Vol. 8, No. 3 (Fall-Winter), pp. 27–53.

Israel has conducted research into weapons and defense and has the ability to produce biological weapons; however, there is no indication of a production effort. Cordesman, "Creeping Proliferation Could Mean a Paradigm Shift in the Cost of War and Terrorism," http://www.csis.org/mideast/stable/3h.html.

A Russian intelligence report indicates that Israel has a biological research program of a general nature "in which elements of a military-applied purpose are present." Russian

Federation Foreign Intelligence Service, *A New Challenge After the Cold War: Proliferation of Weapons of Mass Destruction*, p. 94.

The *London Sunday Times* reports that Israeli F-16 fighters have been equipped to carry biological weapons and that their crews have been trained on the use of such weapons. Uzi Mahnaimi, "Israeli Jets Equipped for Chemical Warfare," *London Sunday Times*, October 4, 1998.

38. As part of the 1947 Peace Treaty, Italy is forbidden from possessing chemical weapons, even for deterrent purposes. Stockholm International Peace Research Institute, *The Problem of Chemical and Biological Warfare, Volume II: CB Weapons Today*, p. 187.

39. The Italian chemical weapons inventory during World War II included mustard gas and phosgene. Stockholm International Peace Research Institute, *The Problem of Chemical and Biological Warfare, Volume I: The Rise of CB Weapons*, p. 292.

40. *The Economist* reports that Japan ended its chemical weapons program "years ago," placing it together with Britain, which ended its program in the 1950s. "Chemical Weapons. Just Checking," *The Economist*, p. 42.

   While Japan might have ended its CW program years ago, it remains legally responsible for hundreds of thousands of chemical munitions it abandoned in China during World War II. In an article discussing the problems involved in disposing of the weapons left behind in China, a Japanese newspaper reports that "[s]ince Japan's postwar defense forces do not have chemical weapons, there is no section in the Japanese government that is completely familiar with neutralization of chemical weapons." Masato Ishizawa, "Chemical Weapons Return to Haunt Japan: Bombs Left in China Pose Dangerous Task of Removal, Disposal," *The Nikkei Weekly*, January 20, 1997, p. 1.

   Chinese officials claim that the Japanese left over two million chemical munitions in China, while Japanese officials insist the number is closer to 700,000. "Chemical weapons," *Mainichi Daily News*, July 28, 1998, p. 2.

   For further information on Japan's abandoned chemical weapons in China, see Hongmei Deng and Peter O'Meara Evans, "Social and Environmental Aspects of Abandoned Chemical Weapons in China," *The Nonproliferation Review*, 4, (Spring-Summer 1997), pp. 101–108.

   See also "Abandoned and Old Japanese Chemical Weapons," http://www.tcp-ip.or.jp/~e-ogawa/CWMENU.HTM.

   George Wehrfritz, Hideko Takayama, and Lijia MacLeod, "In Search of Buried Poison," *Newsweek* 132, (July 20, 1998).

41. Japan's World War II stockpile of chemical weapons included phosgene, chloropicrin (a lung irritant), cyanide, mustard gas, and lewisite. Stockholm International Peace Research Institute, *The Problem of Chemical and Biological Warfare, Volume II: CB Weapons Today*, p. 127.

42. Milton Leitenberg, *Biological Weapons in the Twentieth Century: A Review and Analysis*, http://www.fas.org/bwc/papers/bw20th.htm, 2001.

   Sheldon Harris, "The Japanese biological warfare programme: an overview," in *Biological and Toxin Weapons: Research, Development and Use from the Middle Ages to 1945*, Erhard Geissler and John Ellis van Courtland Mood, eds., (New York: NY: Stockholm International Peace Research Institute, 1999), p. 127.

Between 1937 and 1945, Japan operated a biological weapons program in occupied Manchuria. United States Army, Medical Research Institute of Infectious Diseases (USAMRIID), "Medical Defense Against Biological Warfare Agents Course: History of Biological Warfare," http://www.au.af.mil/au/awc/awcgate/usamriid/bw-hist.htm.

43. Sheldon Harris, "The Japanese biological warfare programme: an overview," in *Biological and Toxin Weapons: Research, Development and Use from the Middle Ages to 1945,* Erhard Geissler and John Ellis van Courtland Mood, eds., (New York: NY: Stockholm International Peace Research Institute, 1999), pp. 138, 140, 142–3, 149.

44. Russian Federation Foreign Intelligence Service, *A New Challenge After the Cold War: Proliferation of Weapons of Mass Destruction,* 1993, p. 100.

Cordesman, "Weapons of Mass Destruction in the Middle East," http://www.csis.org/mideast/reports/WMDinMETrends.pdf, 1999, p. 17.

The U.S. Department of Defense has stated that Libya produced blister and nerve agents in the 1980's at Rabta; employed chemical agents against Chadian troops in 1987; and attempted to construct underground chemical agent production facility at Tarhunah. Both the Rabta and Tarhunah facilities are believed to be inactive, although chemical program not completely abandoned. U.S. Department of Defense, *Proliferation: Threat and Response 2001,* http://www.defenselink.mil/pubs/ptr20010110.pdf, p. 46.

According to the CIA, following the suspension of UN sanctions in April 1999, Tripoli reestablished contacts with sources of expertise, parts, and precursor chemicals abroad, primarily in Western Europe. Libya still appears to have a goal of establishing an offensive CW capability and an indigenous production capability for weapons. CIA, *Unclassified Report to Congress on the Acquisition of Technology Relating to Weapons of Mass Destruction and Advanced Conventional Munitions, 1 January Through 30 June 2000,* http://www.odci.gov/cia/publications/bian/bian_feb 2001.htm.

Libya produced blister and nerve agents in the 1980s and is currently constructing an underground chemical agent production facility at Tarhunah. U.S. Department of Defense, *Proliferation: Threat and Response 1997,* http://www.defenselink.mil/pubs/prolif97/meafrica.html#libya.

"Libya remains heavily dependent on foreign suppliers for precursor chemicals and other key CW-related equipment. Following the suspension of UN sanctions in April 1999, Tripoli reestablished contacts with sources of expertise, parts, and precursor chemicals abroad… Libya still appears to have a goal of establishing an offensive CW capability and an indigenous production capability for weapons." Central Intelligence Agency, "Unclassified Report to Congress on the Acquisition of Technology Relating to Weapons of Mass Destruction and Advanced Conventional Munitions, 1 January Through 30 June 2001," (Washington, DC: U.S. Central Intelligence Agency, 2001), http://www.cia.gov/cia/publications/bian/bian jan 2002.htm.

For further information on Libya's weapons of mass destruction programs and capabilities, see the CNS country profile on the "Weapons of Mass Destruction in the Middle East" web page at http://www.cns.miis.edu/research/wmdme/libya.htm.

45. "In the early 1990s, Rabta was reportedly capable of producing the blister agent sulphurmustard and the deadly nerve agents sarin and tabun… In March 1990, American and German intelligence sources claimed that Libya had produced approximately 30 tons of mustard gas at Rabta." Another plant was also reported to produce lewisite. Joshua Sinai, "Libya's Pursuit of Weapons of Mass Destruction," *The Nonproliferation Review,* 4, (Spring-Summer 1997), p. 94.

According to a Russian source, Libya has produced mustard gas, sarin, and phosgene. Russian Federation Foreign Intelligence Service, *A New Challenge After the Cold War: Proliferation of Weapons of Mass Destruction,* p. 100.

46. In a speech to the Fifth Review Conference on the Biological Weapons Convention in Geneva on November 19, 2001, John Bolton, the Undersecretary of State for Arms Control and International Security, accused Libya of operating a clandestine biological weapons program. Jenni Rissanen, *Acrimonious Opening for BWC Review Conference,* BWC Review Conference Bulletin, (Acronym Institute, November 19, 2001), http://www.acronym.org.uk/bwc/revcon1.htm.

    "Evidence suggests Libya is seeking to acquire the capability to develop and produce BW agents. Such development or production would violate key provisions of the BWC. Libya has also failed to submit the data declarations stipulated in the CBMs. Evidence indicates that Libya has the expertise to produce small quantities of biological equipment for its BW program and that the Libyan Government is seeking to move its research program into a program of weaponized BW agents." Robert J. Einhorn, Testimony Before the Senate Foreign Relations Committee, Washington, DC, October 5, 2000. http://www.state.gov/www/policy remarks/2000/001005 einhorn sfrc.html.

    The CIA reports that Libya may also be seeking to acquire the capability to develop and produce BW agents. CIA, "Unclassified Report to Congress on the Acquisition of Technology Relating to Weapons of Mass Destruction and Advanced Conventional Munitions, 1 January Through 30 June 2000," http://www.odci.gov/cia/publications/bian/bian_feb_2001.htm.

    The Department of State reports that evidence exists to indicate that Libya has the expertise to produce small quantities of biological equipment for its BW program and that the Libyan Government is seeking to move its research program into a program of weaponized BW agents. Arms Control and Disarmament Agency, *Adherence to and Compliance with Arms Control Agreements: 1998 Annual Report to Congress,* http://www.state.gov/www/global/arms/reports/annual/comp98.html.

    "There is information indicating that Libya is engaged in initial testing in the area of biological weapons." Russian Federation Foreign Intelligence Service, *A New Challenge After the Cold War: Proliferation of Weapons of Mass Destruction,* p. 100.

47. Rear Admiral Thomas Brooks identified Myanmar as a "probable" chemical weapons possessor in testimony before Congress. Brooks, statement before the Subcommittee on Seapower, Strategic and Critical Materials, p. 107.

48. "North Korea has a long-standing chemical weapons program. North Korea's domestic chemical industry can produce bulk quantities of nerve, blister, choking, and blood agents. We believe it has a sizeable stockpile of agents and weapons." Carl W. Ford, Jr., Assistant Secretary of State for Intelligence and Research, "Hearing on Reducing the Threat of Chemical and Biological Weapons Before the Senate Committee on Foreign Relations," (Washington, DC), March 19, 2002.

    Joseph S. Bermudez, Jr., *The Deterrence Series, Case Study 5: North Korea,* (Alexandria, VA: Chemical and Biological Arms Control Institute, 1998), p. 5.

    The Department of Defense reports that North Korea's chemical warfare capabilities include the ability to produce bulk quantities of nerve, blister, choking, and blood agents, using its sizeable, although aging, chemical industry. U.S. Department of Defense, *Proliferation: Threat and Response 2001,* http://www.defenselink.mil/pubs/ptr20010110.pdf, p. 11.

Rear Admiral Thomas Brooks identified North Korea as a "probable" chemical weapons possessor in testimony before Congress. Brooks, statement before the Subcommittee on Seapower, Strategic and Critical Materials, p. 107.

The DOD reports that North Korea "[p]roduces and is capable of using a wide variety of [chemical] agents." U.S. Department of Defense, *Proliferation: Threat and Response 1997,* http://www.defenselink.mil/pubs/prolif97/ne asia.html#north.

49. Joseph S. Bermudez, Jr., *The Deterrence Series, Case Study 5: North Korea,* (Alexandria, VA: Chemical and Biological Arms Control Institute, 1998), p. 5.

"North Korea has a chemical weapons program that, according to the CIA, includes mustard and blister agents." Institute for National Strategic Studies, *Strategic Assessment 1997, Flashpoints and Force Structure,* (Washington, DC: National Defense University Press, 1997), http://www.ndu.edu/ndu/inss/sa97/sa97ch11.html.

50. Joseph S. Bermudez, Jr., *The Deterrence Series, Case Study 5: North Korea,* p. 11–12.

In a speech to the Fifth Review Conference on the Biological Weapons Convention in Geneva on November 19, 2001, John Bolton, the Undersecretary of State for Arms Control and International Security, accused North Korea of operating a clandestine biological weapons program. Jenni Rissanen, *Acrimonious Opening for BWC Review Conference,* BWC Review Conference Bulletin, (Acronym Institute, November 19, 2001), http://http://www.acronym. org.uk/bwc/revcon1.htm.

North Korea has pursued biological warfare capability since the 1960's. Furthermore, North Korea possesses infrastructure that can be used to produce biological warfare agents. North Korea may have biological weapons available for use. U.S. Department of Defense, *Proliferation: Threat and Response 2001,* http://www.defenselink.mil/pubs/ptr20010110.pdf, p. 10.

North Korea "[p]ursued biological warfare research and development for many years. Possesses biotechnical infrastructure capable of supporting limited biological warfare effort." U.S. Department of Defense, *Proliferation: Threat and Response 1997,* http://www.defenselink.mil/ pubs/prolif97/ne asia.html#north.

"North Korea is performing applied military-biological research in a whole number of universities, medical institutes, and specialized research institutes. Work is being performed in these research centers with inducers of malignant anthrax, cholera, bubonic plague and smallpox. Biological weapons are being tested on the island territories belonging to the DPRK [Democratic People's Republic of Korea]." Russian Federation Foreign Intelligence Service, *A New Challenge After the Cold War: Proliferation of Weapons of Mass Destruction,* 1993.

51. *The Actual Situation of North Korea's Biological and Chemical Weapons,* Foresight, February 17, 2001, pp. 24–25, translated in FBIS.

South Korea Says North Has Biological, Chemical Weapons, Kyodo News Service, October 23, 1992.

North Korea Advisory Group, Report to the Speaker, U.S. House of Representatives, November 1999.

Bill Gertz, *Hwang Says N. Korea Has Atomic Weapons; Pyongyang Called Off Planned Nuclear Test,* The Washington Times, June 5, 1997, p. A12.

Republic of Korea, Ministry of National Defence, White Paper, 2000, http://www.mnd.go.kr/ mnden/emainindex.html.

"Pyongyang's resources include a rudimentary (by Western standards) biotechnical infrastructure that could support the production of infectious biological warfare agents and toxins such as anthrax, cholera, and plague." U.S. Department of Defense, *Proliferation: Threat and Response 2001*, http://www.defenselink.mil/pubs/ptr20010110.pdf, p. 10.

Joseph S. Bermudez, Jr., *The Deterrence Series, Case Study 5: North Korea*, p. 12.

Russian intelligence reports that North Korea is conducting military applied research on anthrax, cholera, bubonic plague and smallpox. Russian Federation Foreign Intelligence Service, *A New Challenge After the Cold War: Proliferation of Weapons of Mass Destruction*, p. 99.

52. Pakistan has imported a number of dual-use chemicals that can be used to make chemical agents. U.S. Department of Defense, *Proliferation: Threat and Response 2001*, http://www.defenselink.mil/pubs/ptr20010110.pdf, p. 28.
    Rear Admiral Thomas Brooks identified Pakistan as a "probable" chemical weapons possessor in testimony before Congress. Brooks, statement before the Subcommittee on Seapower, Strategic and Critical Materials, p. 107.

    "Pakistan has the ability to transition from research and development to chemical agent production." U.S. Department of Defense, *Proliferation: Threat and Response 1997*, http://www.defenselink.mil/pubs/prolif97/so asia.html#india.

    "[R]esearch of an applied military nature is being conducted" by Pakistan in the area of chemical weapons. Russian Federation Foreign Intelligence Service, *A New Challenge After the Cold War: Proliferation of Weapons of Mass Destruction*, p. 101.

53. Pakistan is believed to have the resources and capabilities to support a limited biological warfare research and development effort. U.S. Department of Defense, *Proliferation: Threat and Response 2001*, http://www.defenselink.mil/pubs/ptr20010110.pdf, p. 28.

54. The Department of Defense reports that Russia has acknowledged the world's largest stockpile of chemical agents of 40,000 metric tons, and has developed a new generation of chemical agents. The DOD believes that Russia still has not divulged the full extent of their chemical agent and weapon inventory. U.S. Department of Defense, *Proliferation: Threat and Response 2001*, http://www.defenselink.mil/pubs/ptr20010110.pdf, p. 57.

    "Russian officials do not deny research has continued but assert that it aims to develop defenses against chemical weapons... Many of the components for new binary agents developed by the former Soviet Union are not on the CWC's schedule of chemicals and have legitimate civil applications, clouding their association with chemical weapons use." Carl W. Ford, Jr., Assistant Secretary of State for Intelligence and Research, "Hearing on Reducing the Threat of Chemical and Biological Weapons Before the Senate Committee on Foreign Relations," (Washington, DC), March 19, 2002.

    The Department of Defense reports that research into chemical weapons continues in Russia, with Russian officials asserting that it is for defensive purposes only. U.S. Department of Defense, *Proliferation: Threat and Response 1997*, http://www.defenselink.mil/pubs/prolif97/fsu.html.#russia.

55. Clifford Krauss, "U.S. Urges Russia to End Production of Nerve Gas," *The New York Times*, February 6, 1997.

    Frank Von Hippel, "Russian whistleblower faces jail," *The Bulletin of Atomic Scientists*, 49, (March, 1993), http://www.bullatomsci.org/issues/1993/m93/m93vonhippel.html.

Russia's chemical weapons program has reportedly developed a new class of advanced binary chemical weapons, referred to as the Novichok series. A-232 is both a unitary agent and a Novichok precursor. Dr. Vil S. Mirzayanov, "Dismantling the Soviet/Russian Chemical Weapons Complex: An Insider's View," *Chemical Weapons Disarmament in Russia: Problems and Prospects,* (Washington, DC: The Henry L. Stimson Center, 1995), pp. 24–25.

56. "Key components of the former Soviet program remain largely intact and may support a possible future mobilization capability for the production of biological agents and delivery systems. Moreover, work outside the scope of legitimate biological defense activity may be occurring now at selected facilities within Russia." Carl W. Ford, Jr., Assistant Secretary of State for Intelligence and Research, "Hearing on Reducing the Threat of Chemical and Biological Weapons Before the Senate Committee on Foreign Relations," (Washington, DC), March 19, 2002.

Milton Leitenberg, *Biological Weapons in the Twentieth Century: A Review and Analysis,* http://www.fas.org/bwc/papers/bw20th.htm, 2001.

The Department of Defense reports that some elements of large FSU [former Soviet Union] biological warfare program may remain intact and could support future agent production, and that some offensive biological warfare activities may be ongoing (p. 54), with the United States continuing to receive unconfirmed reports of offensive biological warfare efforts (p. 57). U.S. Department of Defense, *Proliferation: Threat and Response 2001,* http://www.defenselink.mil/pubs/ptr20010110.pdf.

According to the DOD, some work "outside the scope of legitimate biological defense activity may be occurring" in Russia. U.S. Department of Defense, *Proliferation: Threat and Response 1997,* http://www.defenselink.mil/pubs/prolif97/index.html.

"[S]ome facilities, in addition to being engaged in legitimate activity, may be maintaining the capability to produce BW agents." U.S. Department of State, *1998 Adherence to and Compliance with Arms Control Agreements,* http://www.state.gov/www/global/arms/reports/annual/comp98.html.

57. The Department of Defense reports that Russia has acknowledged the world's largest stockpile of chemical agents of 40,000 metric tons, and has developed a new generation of chemical agents. The DOD believes that Russia still has not divulged the full extent of their chemical agent and weapon inventory. U.S. Department of Defense, *Proliferation: Threat and Response 2001,* http://www.defenselink.mil/pubs/ptr20010110.pdf, p. 57.

58. Stockholm International Peace Research Institute, "Chemical weapons distribution at the Russian Storage sites," http://projects.sipri.se/cbw/research/sipri-bicc-cw-map.html.

59. Milton Leitenberg, *Biological Weapons in the Twentieth Century: A Review and Analysis,* http://www.fas.org/bwc/papers/bw20th.htm, 2001.

60. Milton Leitenberg, *Biological Weapons in the Twentieth Century: A Review and Analysis,* http://www.fas.org/bwc/papers/bw20th.htm, 2001.

"According to its declaration, Russia maintained an offensive research and development program until March 1992 that worked with anthrax, tularemia, brucellosis, plague, Venezuelan equine encephalitis, typhus, and Q-fever. With respect to toxins, Russia claimed that the only natural toxin studied in its program was botulinum toxin." Richard Boucher, U.S. Department of State, "Joint US/UK/Russian Statement on Biological Weapons," Press Release, Office of Public Affairs (Washington, DC: U.S. Department of State, September 14, 1992), cited in Graham S. Pearson, "The Threat of Deliberate Disease in the 21st Century,"

Biological Weapons Proliferation: Reasons for Concern, Courses of Action, (Washington, DC: The Henry L. Stimson Center, January 1998), p. 29.

Russian defector Kanatjan Alibekov (Kenneth Alibek), a former deputy director of the Soviet/Russian biological warfare development program, lists the following agents as either weaponized or researched by the Soviet/Russian program: smallpox, plague, anthrax, Venezuelan equine encephalomyelitis, glanders, brucellosis, Marburg virus, Ebola virus, Argentinian hemorrhagic fever, Machupo virus, yellow fever, Lassa fever, Japanese encephalitis, Russian spring-summer encephalitis, tularemia, typhus, Q-fever, psittacosis, ornithosis, rinderpest virus, African swine fever virus, wheat stem rust, and rice blast. Dr. Kenneth Alibek, statement before the Joint Economic Committee, U.S. Congress, Joint Economic Committee, "Terrorism and Intelligence Operations: Hearing before the Joint Economic Committee", 105th Congress, Second Session, May 20, 1998, http://www.house.gov/jec/hearings/intell/alibek.htm.

61. Lynne Duke, "Doubts Arise on Junking of Chemical Arms; S. African Panel Told Some Drugs, Formulas May Have Been Secretly Held Back," *Washington Post,* July 9, 1998, A24.

    A government spokesman stated that South Africa's chemical weapons program has been "terminated, and that the material for offensive purposes in government storage has been destroyed." The program was shut down in 1993 and its products dumped at sea. Buchizya Mseteka, "S. Africa Says it Terminated Chemical Weapons Scheme," *Reuters,* June 15, 1998.

62. Stephen Burgess and Helen Purkitt, *The Rollback of South Africa's Biological Warfare Program,* INSS Occasional Paper 37, (USAF Institute for National Security Studies, February, 2001), http://www.usafa.af.mil/inss/ocp37.htm.

    David Beresford, "Mandela on apartheid's poison list," *The Age,* June 11, 1998, http://www.theage.com.au/daily/980611/news/news18.html.

    Chris Opperman, "Prosecutors Ecstatic as Basson's Buddy Talks," *Weekly Mail and Guardian* (Johannesburg), June 27, 1997.

    "SADF 'made Ecstasy for riot control,'" *Business Day,* June 10, 1998.

    Lynne Duke, "Doubts Arise on Junking of Chemical Arms; S. African Panel Told Some Drugs, Formulas May Have Been Secretly Held Back," *Washington Post,* July 9, 1998, A24. "Apartheid-Era Scientist: Mandela Was Target for Poisoning," *Edmonton Journal Extra,* June 10, 1998.

    David Beresford, "Apartheid's Lab Rats," *Weekly Mail and Guardian* (Johannesburg), June 12, 1998.

    Andrew Maykuth, "Mandela's Government Becomes Ally of Ex-Foe," *Philadelphia Inquirer,* June 20, 1998.

63. Milton Leitenberg, *Biological Weapons in the Twentieth Century: A Review and Analysis,* http://www.fas.org/bwc/papers/bw20th.htm, 2001.

    Stephen Burgess and Helen Purkitt, *The Rollback of South Africa's Biological Warfare Program,* INSS Occasional Paper 37, (USAF Institute for National Security Studies, February, 2001, http://www.usafa.af.mil/inss/ocp37.htm.

    A government spokesman stated that South Africa's biological weapons program has been "terminated, and that the material for offensive purposes in government storage has been destroyed." The program was shut down in 1993 and its products dumped at sea. Buchizya Mseteka, "S. Africa Says it Terminated Chemical Weapons Scheme," *Reuters,* June 15, 1998.

64. Milton Leitenberg, *Biological Weapons in the Twentieth Century: A Review and Analysis,* http://www.fas.org/bwc/papers/bw20th.htm, 2001.

    Stephen Burgess and Helen Purkitt, *The Rollback of South Africa's Biological Warfare Program,* INSS Occasional Paper 37, (USAF Institute for National Security Studies, February, 2001), http://www.usafa.af.mil/inss/ocp37.htm.

    In his testimony before the Reconciliation and Truth Commission, Dr. Schalk van Rensburg indicated that South Africa's biological weapons program used cholera, anthrax, botulinum toxin, and salmonella in its activities. Beresford, "Mandela on apartheid's poison list," http://www.theage.com.au/daily/980611/news/news18.html.

65. Rear Admiral Thomas Brooks identified South Korea as a "probable" chemical weapons possessor in testimony before Congress. Brooks, statement before the Subcommittee on Seapower, Strategic and Critical Materials, p. 107.
    Citing U.S. government sources, a 1997 article in the *Bulletin of Atomic Scientists* counts South Korea among those states suspected of having chemical weapons. E. J. Hogendoom, "A Chemical Weapons Atlas," p. 38.

    The Economist reports that South Korea is among those countries that, under the Chemical Weapons Convention, have declared possessing chemical weapons. "Chemical Weapons. Just Checking," *The Economist,* p. 42.

    See footnote #13. Shanker, "West underwrites Third World's chemical arms"; McCain, "Proliferation in the 1990s: implications for U.S. policy and force planning," in Burck and Flowerree, *International Handbook on Chemical Weapons Proliferation,* pp. 168–171. Also cited in Burck and Flowerree chart: Elisa Harris, "Chemical weapons proliferation: current capabilities and prospects for control," *New Threats: Responding to the Proliferation of Nuclear, Chemical, and Delivery Capabilities in the Third World,* (Landham, Md: Aspen Strategy Group, 1990), pp. 70–72. Harris classifies South Korea as "seeking to acquire CW weapons or a production capability, or as suspected of possessing CW weapons."

66. There is considerable uncertainty as to Sudan's chemical weapons status. For a well-documented discussion of the debate please refer to the CNS Fact Sheet on Sudan, "Weapons of Mass Destruction Capabilities and Programs," http://www.cns.miis.edu/research/wmdme/sudan.htm.

67. In a speech to the Fifth Review Conference on the Biological Weapons Convention in Geneva on November 19, 2001, John Bolton, the Undersecretary of State for Arms Control and International Security, accused Sudan of operating a clandestine biological weapons program. Jenni Rissanen, *Acrimonious Opening for BWC Review Conference,* BWC Review Conference Bulletin, (Acronym Institute, November 19, 2001), http://http://www.acronym.org.uk/bwc/revcon1.htm.

68. "Syria has a long-standing chemical warfare program, first developed in the 1970s… it has a stockpile of the nerve agent sarin and may be trying to develop advanced nerve agents as well." Carl W. Ford, Jr., Assistant Secretary of State for Intelligence and Research, "Hearing on Reducing the Threat of Chemical and Biological Weapons Before the Senate Committee on Foreign Relations," (Washington, DC), March 19, 2002.

    The DOD reports that Syria "already has a stockpile of the nerve agent sarin that can be delivered by aircraft or ballistic missiles. Additionally, Syria is trying to develop the more toxic and persistent nerve agent VX. In the future, Syria can be expected to continue to improve its chemical production and storage infrastructure." U.S. Department of Defense, *Proliferation: Threat and Response 2001,* http://www.defenselink.mil/pubs/ptr20010110.pdf, p. 43.

Syria has production facilities for nerve gas and possibly other chemical agents. Cordesman, "Creeping Proliferation Could Mean a Paradigm Shift in the Cost of War and Terrorism," http://www.csis.org/mideast/stable/3h.html.

See also M. Zuhair Diab, "Syria's Chemical and Biological Weapons: Assessing Capabilities and Motivations," *The Nonproliferation Review,* 5, (Fall, 1997), pp. 104–111.

For further information on Syria's weapons of mass destruction programs and capabilities, see the CNS country profile on the "Weapons of Mass Destruction in the Middle East" web page at http://www.cns.miis.edu/research/wmdme/syria.htm.

69. CDISS reports that Syria's chemical arsenal contains mustard gas, sarin, and VX. "Devil's Brews Briefing: Syria," Centre for Defence and International Security Studies, Lancaster University, 1996.
    "Syria has reportedly developed the capability to produce both mustard gas and nerve agents." Institute for National Strategic Studies, *Strategic Assessment 1997, Flashpoints and Force Structure,* http://www.ndu.edu/ndu/inss/sa97/sa97ch11.html.

    The CIA reports that Syria has a stockpile of sarin. CIA, *Report of Proliferation-Related Acquisition in 1997,* http://www.cia.gov/cia/publications/acq1997.html#Syria.

70. "Syria is pursuing biological weapons. It has an adequate biotechnical infrastructure to support a small biological warfare program. Without significant foreign assistance, it is unlikely that Syria could advance to the manufacture of significant amounts of biological weapons for several years." Carl W. Ford, Jr., Assistant Secretary of State for Intelligence and Research, "Hearing on Reducing the Threat of Chemical and Biological Weapons Before the Senate Committee on Foreign Relations," (Washington, DC), March 19, 2002.

    In a speech to the Fifth Review Conference on the Biological Weapons Convention in Geneva on November 19, 2001, John Bolton, the Undersecretary of State for Arms Control and International Security, accused Syria of operating a clandestine biological weapons program. Jenni Rissanen, *Acrimonious Opening for BWC Review Conference,* BWC Review Conference Bulletin, (Acronym Institute, November 19, 2001), http://http://www.acronym.org.uk/bwc/revcon1.htm.

    Testifying before Congress in 1991, Rear Admiral Thomas Brooks indicated that Syria had "developed an offensive BW capability." Brooks, statement before the Subcommittee on Seapower, Strategic and Critical Materials, p. 107.

    "Syria's biotechnical infrastructure is capable of supporting limited agent development. However, the Syrians are not believed to have begun any major effort to put biological agents into weapons. Without significant foreign assistance, it is unlikely that Syria could manufacture significant amounts of biological weapons for several years." U.S. Department of Defense, *Proliferation: Threat and Response 2001,* http://www.defenselink.mil/pubs/ptr20010110.pdf, p. 43.

    In its annual report to Congress, ACDA states that "it is highly probable that Syria is developing an offensive biological warfare capability." Arms Control and Disarmament Agency, *Adherence to and Compliance with Arms Control Agreements: 1997 Annual Report to Congress,* http://www.state.gov/www/global/arms/reports/annual/comp97.html.

71. Cordesman, "Weapons of Mass Destruction in the Middle East," http://www.csis.org/mideast/reports/WMDinMETrends.pdf.

72. Rear Admiral Thomas Brooks identified Taiwan as a "probable" chemical weapons possessor in testimony before Congress. Brooks, statement before the Subcommittee on Seapower, Strategic and Critical Materials, p. 107.

73. According to a Russian intelligence report, "Taiwan does not have biological weapons... [however], it has shown signs of conducting biological research of an applied military nature." Russian Federation Foreign Intelligence Service, *A New Challenge After the Cold War: Proliferation of Weapons of Mass Destruction,* p. 104.

   ACDA reports that Taiwan has been upgrading its biotechnology capabilities, but states that the "evidence indicating a BW program is not sufficient to determine if Taiwan is engaged in activities prohibited by the BWC." Arms Control and Disarmament Agency, *Adherence to and Compliance with Arms Control Agreements: 1997 Annual Report to Congress,* http://www.state.gov/www/global/arms/reports/annual/comp97.html.

74. The United Kingdom renounced its chemical weapons option in 1957 and subsequently destroyed its CW capabilities. Edward M. Spiers, *Chemical and Biological Weapons: A Study of Proliferation,* (New York, NY: St. Martin's Press, 1994), pp. 11, 162.

   "Britain decided against building her own nerve-gas factory in the mid-1950s and, having taken that decision, discarded her residual World War II chemical weapons and closed down her chemical weapons research and development program." Julian Perry Robinson, "Appendix C: United States and NATO Chemical Weapons," in *Chemical Weapons and Chemical Arms Control,* Matthew Meselson, ed., (New York, NY: Carnegie Endowment for International Peace, 1978) p. 113.

75. The United Kingdom's World War II stockpile of chemical weapons included phosgene, mustard gas, and lewisite. Stockholm International Peace Research Institute, *The Problem of Chemical and Biological Warfare, Volume II: CB Weapons Today,* p. 127.

76. Milton Leitenberg, *Biological Weapons in the Twentieth Century: A Review and Analysis,* http://www.fas.org/bwc/papers/bw20th.htm, 2001.

   Gradon B. Carter and Graham Pearson, "British biological warfare and biological defence, 1925–45, in *Biological and Toxin Weapons: Research, Development and Use from the Middle Ages to 1945,* Erhard Geissler and John Ellis van Courtland Mood, eds., (New York: NY: Stockholm International Peace Research Institute, 1999), p. 168.

   The Office of Technology Assessment includes the United Kingdom in a list of countries that have admitted to having had "offensive [biological] weapon munition suppliers or development programs in the past." U.S. Congress, Office of Technology Assessment, *Proliferation of Weapons of Mass Destruction,* p. 63.

77. Gradon B. Carter and Graham Pearson, "British biological warfare and biological defence, 1925–45, *Biological and Toxin Weapons: Research, Development and Use from the Middle Ages to 1945,* Erhard Geissler and John Ellis van Courtland Mood, eds., (New York: NY: Stockholm International Peace Research Institute, 1999), pp. 182–4.

   The British biological weapons program involved research on anthrax. Stockholm International Peace Research Institute. *The Problem of Chemical and Biological Warfare, Volume I: The Rise of CB Weapons,* p. 118.

78. The United States stopped production of unitary chemical munitions in 1969. "Chemical and Biological Warfare," *The Military Balance 1988–1989,* (London, UK: IISS, 1988), p. 244.

In November 1985, Congress passed legislation calling for the destruction of 90 percent of the total U.S. stockpile of unitary chemical agents. On May 13, 1991, the Bush administration announced that U.S. stockpiles of both binary and unitary weapons would be destroyed when the CWC entered into force. Amy E. Smithson, *The U.S. Chemical Weapons Destruction Program: Views, Analysis, and Recommendations,* (Washington, DC: The Henry L. Stimson Center, 1994), pp. 96, 99.

79. U.S. Army Soldier and Biological Chemical Command, http://www.sbccom.army.mil/ FactSheets/index.html. The Department of Defense is in the process of reviewing defense information made available on the web. As such, this site may not be accessible at this time.

Included in the U.S. chemical weapons stockpile are 680.19 tons of binary weapons components. Office of Assistant Secretary of Defense, *U.S. Chemical Weapons Stockpile Information Declassified,* (Washington, DC: Department of Defense, January 22, 1996), http:// www.defenselink.mil/news/Jan1996/b012496 bt024-96.html.

80. Milton Leitenberg, *Biological Weapons in the Twentieth Century: A Review and Analysis,* http://www.fas.org/bwc/papers/bw20th.htm, 2001.

"In 1969, President Nixon disestablished offensive studies including the destruction of all stockpiles of agents and munitions." Destruction of biological weapon agent stocks and munitions was accomplished between May 1971 and May 1972. The study of biological weapons continued after 1969, but for defensive purposes only. USAMRIID [U.S. Army Medical Research Institute of Infectious Diseases], "A History of Biological Warfare," http:// www.au.af.mil/au/awc/awcgate/usamriid/bw-hist.htm.

81. National Security Archive, "National Security Decision Memoranda 35 and 44," *The September 11th Source Books: National Security Archive Online Readers on Terrorism, Intelligence and the Next War. Volume III: BIOWAR: The Nixon Administration's Decision to End U.S. Biological Warfare Programs,* http://www.gwu.edu/~nsarchiv/NSAEBB/NSAEBB58/RNCBW22.pdf, July 6, 1970.

Anthrax, brucellosis, Eastern and Western equine encephalitis, Venezuelan equine encephalomyelitis, Argentinian hemorrhagic fever, Korean hemorrhagic fever, Bolivian hemorrhagic fever, Lassa fever, tularemia, and Q-fever are among the biological agents researched by the U.S. program for offensive and/or defense purposes. All research since 1969 has been for defensive purposes. USAMRIID, "A History of Biological Warfare," http:// www.au.af.mil/au/awc/awcgate/usamriid/bw-hist.htm.

According to SIPRI, the U.S. biological program studied the following agents: anthrax, glanders, brucellosis, melioidosis, tularemia, plague, yellow fever, psittacosis, typhus, dengue fever, Rift Valley fever, Chikungunya disease virus, ricin, rice blast, rice brown spot disease, late blight of potato, stem rust of cereal, rinderpest virus, Newcastle disease virus, fowl plague virus. Stockholm International Peace Research Institute, *The Problem of Chemical and Biological Warfare, Volume I: The Rise of CB Weapons,* pp. 122–123.

See also Bryden, *Deadly Allies: Canada's Secret War 1937–1947,* (Toronto, ONT: McClelland & Stewart Inc., 1989).

82. Rear Admiral Thomas Brooks identified Vietnam as a "probable" chemical weapons possessor in testimony before Congress. Brooks, statement before the Subcommittee on Seapower, Strategic and Critical Materials, p. 107.

83. The Pentagon has reported the existence of chemical weapons in the FRY. Judith Miller, "U.S. Officials Suspect Deadly Chemical Weapons in Yugoslav Army Arsenal," *New York Times,* April 16, 1999.

    The Federation of American Scientists has confirmed the existence of four chemical weapons facilities in the former Yugoslavia, three in Serbia and one in Bosnia. The three facilities in Serbia are Prva Iskra, in Baric, Serbia; Miloje Blagojevic in Lucani, Serbia; and Milojie Zakic and Merima in Krusevic, Serbia. The fourth facility is the Military Technical Institute in Potoci near Mostar, Bosnia and Herzegovina. The Federation of American Scientists, "Chemical Agents in the Former Yugoslavia," *Nuclear Forces Guide,* http://www.fas.org/nuke/guide/serbia/cw/index.html, April 23, 2000.

84. "Chemical Agents in the Former Yugoslavia," *Nuclear Forces Guide,* http://www.fas.org/nuke/guide/serbia/cw/index.html, April 23, 2000.

    Pentagon officials believe the FRY possesses sarin, mustard gas, BZ, and CS. Judith Miller, "U.S. Officials Suspect Deadly Chemical Weapons in Yugoslav Army Arsenal," *New York Times,* April 16, 1999.
    Human Rights Watch reports FRY possession of sarin, sulfur mustard, BZ, CS, CN, LSD-25, chloropicrin, cyanogen chloride, soman, tabun, and VX. Human Rights Watch, "Chemical Warfare in Bosnia?", *Human Rights Watch Report,* Vol. 10, No. 9 (D), November 1998.

85. Pentagon officials report that they have no evidence of biological weapons production in the FRY. Judith Miller, "U.S. Officials Suspect Deadly Chemical Weapons in Yugoslav Army Arsenal," *New York Times,* April 16, 1999.

    However, a former Yugoslav army officer claimed in a letter to the UN Secretary General, the UNSC, the Council of Europe, the OSCE, NATO, SFOR, and the governments of ten nations that the FRY is in fact producing biological weapons, although he did not indicate which agents were being produced. Televizija Bosne I Hercegovine, "Bosnian TV Probes Chemical Weapons Production in FRY," *Televizija Bosne I Hercegovine (Sarajevo),* February 6, 1999, FBIS, FTS19990207000460.

86. On December 20, 2001, the New York Times published an article stating that "Libyan leader Col Muammar el-Qadaffi notifies diplomats in Netherlands that he is ready to sign international treaty banning chemical weapons, after spending last two decades building one of largest stockpiles in Middle East." Patrick E. Tyler, "A Nation Challenged: Libya; In Changed World, Qadaffi Is Changing, Too," *New York Times,* December 20, 2001.

87. "The United States believes that Cuba has at least a limited, developmental offensive biological warfare research and development effort." Carl W. Ford, Jr., Assistant Secretary of State for Intelligence and Research, "Hearing on Reducing the Threat of Chemical and Biological Weapons Before the Senate Committee on Foreign Relations," (Washington, DC), March 19, 2002.

Appendix D

Statement by the President in His Address to the Nation

September 11, 2001

Good evening. Today, our fellow citizens, our way of life, our very freedom came under attack in a series of deliberate and deadly terrorist acts. The victims were in airplanes, or in their offices; secretaries, businessmen and women, military and federal workers; moms and dads, friends and neighbors. Thousands of lives were suddenly ended by evil, despicable acts of terror.

The pictures of airplanes flying into buildings, fires burning, huge structures collapsing, have filled us with disbelief, terrible sadness, and a quiet, unyielding anger. These acts of mass murder were intended to frighten our nation into chaos and retreat. But they have failed; our country is strong.

A great people has been moved to defend a great nation. Terrorist attacks can shake the foundations of our biggest buildings, but they cannot touch the foundation of America. These acts shattered steel, but they cannot dent the steel of American resolve.

America was targeted for attack because we're the brightest beacon for freedom and opportunity in the world. And no one will keep that light from shining.

Today, our nation saw evil, the very worst of human nature. And we responded with the best of America—with the daring of our rescue workers, with the caring for strangers and neighbors who came to give blood and help in any way they could.

Immediately following the first attack, I implemented our government's emergency response plans. Our military is powerful, and it's prepared. Our emergency teams are working in New York City and Washington, D.C., to help with local rescue efforts.

Our first priority is to get help to those who have been injured, and to take every precaution to protect our citizens at home and around the world from further attacks.

The functions of our government continue without interruption. Federal agencies in Washington which had to be evacuated today are reopening for essential personnel tonight, and will be open for business tomorrow. Our financial institutions remain strong, and the American economy will be open for business, as well.

The search is under way for those who are behind these evil acts. I've directed the full resources of our intelligence and law enforcement communities to find those responsible and bring them to justice. We will make no distinction between the terrorists who committed these acts and those who harbor them.

I appreciate so very much the members of Congress who have joined me in strongly condemning these attacks. And on behalf of the American people, I thank the many world leaders who have called to offer their condolences and assistance.

America and our friends and allies join with all those who want peace and security in the world, and we stand together to win the war against terrorism. Tonight, I ask for your prayers for all those who grieve, for the children whose worlds have been shattered, for all whose sense of safety and security has been threatened. And I pray they will be comforted by a power greater than any of us, spoken through the ages in Psalm 23: "Even though I walk through the valley of the shadow of death, I fear no evil, for You are with me."

This is a day when all Americans from every walk of life unite in our resolve for justice and peace. America has stood down enemies before, and we will do so this time. None of us will ever forget this day. Yet, we go forward to defend freedom and all that is good and just in our world.

Thank you. Good night, and God bless America.

Appendix E

Terrorist Incidents
1981–2001

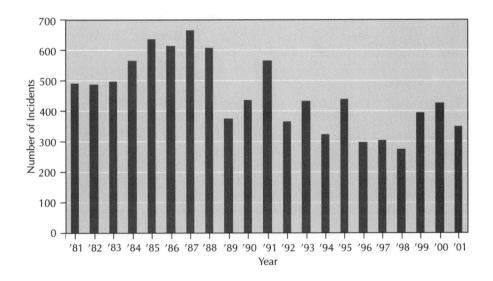

Acknowledgments

Foreword   Copyright © 2002 by Barry R. McCaffrey.

Part 1 Defining the Threat

Chapter 1

1.1   Bruce Hoffman, "Defining Terrorism," *Inside Terrorism* (Columbia University Press, 1998). Copyright © 1998 by Bruce Hoffman. Reprinted by permission of Columbia University Press.

1.2   Paul R. Pillar, "The Dimensions of Terrorism and Counterterrorism," *Terrorism and U.S. Foreign Policy* (Brookings Institution Press, 2001). Copyright © 2001 by The Brookings Institution. Reprinted by permission.

1.3   Eqbal Ahmad and David Barsamian, *Terrorism: Theirs and Ours*, foreword and interview by David Barsamian (Seven Stories Press, 2001). Copyright © 2001 by David Barsamian. Reprinted by permission of Seven Stories Press and Open Media Books.

Chapter 2

2.1   Martha Crenshaw, "The Logic of Terrorism: Terrorist Behavior as a Product of Strategic Choice," in Walter Reich, ed., *Origins of Terrorism: Psychologies, Ideologies, Theologies, States of Mind* (Woodrow Wilson Center Press, 1998). Copyright © 1990, 1998 by The Woodrow Wilson International Center for Scholars. Reprinted by permission of The Johns Hopkins University Press.

2.2   Louise Richardson, "Global Rebels: Terrorist Organizations as Trans-National Actors," *Harvard International Review*, vol. 20, no. 4 (Fall 1998). Copyright © 1998 by *Harvard International Review*. Reprinted by permission.

Chapter 3

3.1   Bruce Hoffman, "The Modern Terrorist Mindset: Tactics, Targets and Technologies," *Columbia International Affairs Online Working Paper* (October 1997). Copyright © 1997 by Columbia University Press. Reprinted by permission.

3.2   John Arquilla, David Ronfeldt, and Michele Zanini, "Networks, Netwar, and Information-Age Terrorism," in Ian O. Lesser, John Arquilla, Bruce Hoffman, David Ronfeldt, Michele Zanini and Brian Jenkins, *Countering the New Terrorism* (RAND Corporation, 1999), pp. 39–72, 80–81.

Chapter 4

Chapter 5

Chapter 6

Part 2. Countering the Terrorist Threat

Chapter 7

7.1   Laura K. Donohue, adapted from "Fear Itself: Counterterrorism, Individual Rights, and U.S. Foreign Relations Post 9-11," Paper Presented at the International Studies Association Convention, New Orleans (March 25, 2002). Copyright © 2003 by Laura K. Donohue. Reprinted by permission of the author.

7.2   Bruce Hoffman, "A Nasty Business," *The Atlantic Monthly* (January 2002). Copyright © 2002 by Bruce Hoffman. Reprinted by permission of the author.

7.3   Anthony Clark Arend, "Terrorism and Just War Doctrine," in Elliott Abrams, ed., *Close Calls: Intervention, Terrorism, Missile Defense, and 'Just War' Today* (Ethics and Public Policy Center, 1998). Copyright © 1998 by Ethics and Public Policy Center. Reprinted by permission of Ethics and Public Policy Center, Washington, D.C.

7.4   Brad Roberts, "NBC-Armed Rogues: Is There a Moral Case for Preemption?" in Elliott Abrams, ed., *Close Calls: Intervention, Terrorism, Missile Defense, and 'Just War' Today* (Ethics and Public Policy Center, 1998). Copyright © 1998 by Ethics and Public Policy Center. Reprinted by permission of Ethics and Public Policy Center, Washington, D.C.

Chapter 8

8.1   Richard K. Betts, "The Soft Underbelly of American Primacy: Tactical Advantages of Terror," *Political Science Quarterly*, vol. 117, no. 1 (2002). Copyright © 2002 by The Academy of Political Science. Reprinted by permission of *Political Science Quarterly*.

8.2   Copyright © 2003 by James S. Robbins.

8.3   Copyright © 2003 by Richard H. Shultz and Andreas Vogt.

8.4   Barry R. Posen, "The Struggle Against Terrorism: Grand Strategy, Strategy, and Tactics," *International Security*, vol. 26, no. 3 (Winter 2001/02). Copyright © 2001 by The President and Fellows of Harvard College and The Massachusetts Institute of Technology. Reprinted by permission of MIT Press Journals.

8.5   Michele L. Malvesti, "Explaining the United States' Decision to Strike Back at Terrorists," *Terrorism and Political Violence*, vol. 13, no. 2 (Summer 2001). Copyright © 2001 by Frank Cass & Company, Ltd.

Chapter 9

9.1   Ashton B. Carter, "The Architecture of Government in the Face of Terrorism," *International Security*, vol. 26, no. 3 (Winter 2001/02). Copyright © 2001 by The President and Fellows of Harvard College and The Massachusetts Institute of Technology. Reprinted by permission of MIT Press Journals.

9.2 Copyright © 2003 by Russell D. Howard.

9.3 Richard K. Betts, "Fixing Intelligence," *Foreign Affairs*, vol. 81, no. 1 (January/February 2002). Copyright © 2002 by The Council on Foreign Relations, Inc. Reprinted by permission.

9.4 Martha Crenshaw, "Counterterrorism Policy and the Political Process," *Studies in Conflict & Terrorism*, vol. 24 (2001). Copyright © 2001 by Taylor and Francis, Inc. Reprinted by permission of Taylor and Francis, Inc., www.routledge-ny.com.

Chapter 10

10.1 Sam C. Sarkesian, "The New Protracted Conflict: The U.S. Army Special Forces Then and Now," *Orbis* (Spring 2002). Copyright © 2002 by Foreign Policy Research Institute. Reprinted by permission of Elsevier Science.

10.2 Rob de Wijk, "The Limits of Military Power," *The Washington Quarterly*, vol. 25, no. 1 (Winter 2002). Copyright © 2001 by The Center for Strategic and International Studies and The Massachusetts Institute of Technology. Reprinted by permission of MIT Press Journals.

10.3 Daniel B. Pickard, "Legalizing Assassination? Terrorism, the Central Intelligence Agency, and International Law," *The Georgia Journal of International and Comparative Law*, vol. 30, no. 1 (Fall 2001). Copyright © 2001 by The Georgia Journal of International and Comparative Law, Inc. Reprinted by permission.

10.4 David J. Rothkopf, "Business Versus Terror," *Foreign Policy* (May/June 2002). Copyright © 2002 by The Carnegie Endowment for International Peace. Reprinted by permission of *Foreign Policy*; permission conveyed through Copyright Clearance Center, Inc.